Westfield Memorial Library
Westfield, New Jersey

DEPRESSION
Handbook & Resource Guide

FIRST EDITION

DEPRESSION

Handbook & Resource Guide

GREY HOUSE PUBLISHING

Grey House Health & Wellness Guides

PUBLISHER: Leslie Mackenzie
EDITORIAL DIRECTOR: Stuart Paterson
MARKETING DIRECTOR: Jessica Moody
EDITORIAL ASSISTANT: Kadie MacDougal

Grey House Publishing, Inc.
4919 Route 22
Amenia, NY 12501
518.789.8700
Fax: 845.373.6390
www.greyhouse.com
books@greyhouse.com

While every effort has been made to ensure the reliability of the information presented in this publication, Grey House Publishing neither guarantees the accuracy of the data contained herein nor assumes any responsibility for errors, omissions or discrepancies. Grey House accepts no payment for listing; inclusion in the publication of any organization, agency, institution, publication, service or individual does not imply endorsement of the editors or publisher.

Errors brought to the attention of the publisher and verified to the satisfaction of the publisher will be corrected in future editions.

Except by express prior written permission of the Copyright Proprietor no part of this work may be copied by any means of publication or communication now known or developed hereafter including, but not limited to, use in any directory or compilation or other print publication, in any information storage and retrieval system, in any other electronic device, or in any visual or audio-visual device or product.

This publication is an original and creative work, copyrighted by Grey House Publishing, Inc. and is fully protected by all applicable copyright laws, as well as by laws covering misappropriation, trade secrets and unfair competition.

Grey House has added value to the underlying factual material through one or more of the following efforts: unique and original selection; expression; arrangement; coordination; and classification.

Grey House Publishing, Inc. will defend its rights in this publication.

Copyright © 2024 Grey House Publishing, Inc.
All rights reserved.

First edition published 2024.
Printed in the United States.

Publisher's Cataloging-In-Publication Data
(Prepared by Parlew Associates)

Title: Depression handbook & resource guide.
Other Titles: Depression handbook and resource guide.
Description: First edition. | Amenia, NY : Grey House Publishing, 2024. | Series: [Grey House health & wellness guides ; 8] | Includes index. | Includes color illustrations. Identifiers: ISBN 9781637005644 (hardback) | ISBN 9781637005651 (ebook)
Subjects: LCSH: Depression, Mental — Handbooks, manuals, etc. | Comorbidity — Handbooks, manuals, etc. | Psychology, Pathological — Handbooks, manuals, etc. | LCGFT: Reference works. | Handbooks and manuals. | BISAC: MEDICAL / Mental Health. | PSYCHOLOGY / Psychopathology / Depression. | PSYCHOLOGY / Reference.
Classification: LCC RC537.D47 2024 (print) | RC537 (ebook) | DDC 616.85—dc23

Table of Contents

Publisher's Note xi
Introduction xiii

Section One: Studies & Statistics

Table of Contents 1
    Contains specific article titles and descriptions

Depressive Disorders 5

Common Comorbidities of Depression
Adjustment Disorders 109
Aging 121
Alzheimer's Disease/Dementia 133
Anxiety Disorders 147
Arthritis 155
Asthma 159
Attention-Deficit/Hyperactivity Disorder (ADHD) 165
Bipolar & Related Disorders 181
Diabetes Mellitus 189
Disruptive, Impulse-Control & Conduct Disorders 197
Dissociative Disorders (DD) 209
Feeding & Eating Disorders 223
Heart Disease 231
Hypertension 235
Impotence 239
Infertility 243
Multiple Sclerosis (MS) 247
Obesity 257
Obsessive-Compulsive Disorder (OCD) 277
Osteoporosis 285
Schizophrenia Spectrum & Other Psychotic Disorders 287
Sexual Disorders 295
Sleep-Wake Disorders 311
Somatic Symptom & Related Disorders 321
Stroke 325
Substance-Related & Addictive Disorders 333
Suicide 371
Trauma & Stressor-Related Disorders 379

Section Two: Depression Resources

Depressive Disorders 391
    Agencies & Associations 393
    Foundations 395
    Libraries & Resource Centers 395

Table of Contents

    Research Centers 396
    Support Groups & Hotlines 396
    Print Resources 397
    Web Sites 398

Section Three: Common Comorbidities of Depression

Adjustment Disorders 403
    Agencies & Associations 404
    Foundations 405
    Support Groups & Hotlines 405
    Print Resources 405
    Web Sites 406

Aging 409
    Agencies & Associations 410
    Foundations 416
    Research Centers 416
    Support Groups & Hotlines 418
    Print Resources 419
    Digital Resources 419
    Web Sites 419

Alzheimer's Disease/Dementia 421
    Agencies & Associations 422
    Foundations 428
    Libraries & Resource Centers 428
    Research Centers 428
    Support Groups & Hotlines 430
    Print Resources 431
    Web Sites 431

Anxiety Disorders 433
    Agencies & Associations 434
    Foundations 436
    Libraries & Resource Centers 436
    Research Centers 436
    Support Groups & Hotlines 436
    Print Resources 436
    Web Sites 436

Arthritis 439
    Agencies & Associations 440
    Foundations 440
    Research Centers 440
    Support Groups & Hotlines 441
    Print Resources 441
    Web Sites 441

Asthma 443
    Agencies & Associations 444
    Foundations 445

Table of Contents

    Research Centers 445
    Support Groups & Hotlines 446
    Print Resources 446
    Web Sites. 446

Attention-Deficit Hyperactivity Disorder (ADHD) 449
    Agencies & Associations. 450
    Foundations 451
    Libraries & Resource Centers 451
    Research Centers 451
    Support Groups & Hotlines 452
    Print Resources 452
    Digital Resources. 452
    Web Sites. 452

Bipolar & Related Disorders 455
    Agencies & Associations. 456
    Foundations 457
    Libraries & Resource Centers 457
    Research Centers 457
    Print Resources 458
    Web Sites. 458

Diabetes Mellitus 461
    Agencies & Associations. 462
    Foundations 464
    Libraries & Resource Centers 469
    Research Centers 469
    Support Groups & Hotlines 472
    Print Resources 472
    Web Sites. 472

Disruptive, Impulse Control & Conduct Disorders 475
    Agencies & Associations. 476
    Foundations 477
    Libraries & Resource Centers 477
    Research Centers 477
    Support Groups & Hotlines 477
    Print Resources 477
    Web Sites. 477

Dissociative Disorders (DD) 479
    Agencies & Associations. 480
    Libraries & Resource Centers 481
    Research Centers 481
    Support Groups & Hotlines 481
    Print Resources 481
    Web Sites. 481

Feeding & Eating Disorders 483
    Agencies & Associations. 484
    Foundations 487

vii

Table of Contents

    Libraries & Resource Centers 487
    Research Centers 487
    Support Groups & Hotlines 488
    Print Resources 489
    Web Sites 489

Heart Disease 491
    Agencies & Associations 492
    Research Centers 492
    Support Groups & Hotlines 495
    Print Resources 495
    Web Sites 495

Hypertension 497
    Agencies & Associations 498
    Research Centers 498
    Support Groups & Hotlines 498
    Print Resources 498
    Web Sites 498

Impotence 501
    Agencies & Associations 502
    Foundations 502
    Research Centers 502
    Support Groups & Hotlines 502
    Print Resources 502
    Web Sites 503

Infertility 505
    Agencies & Associations 506
    Foundations 506
    Research Centers 507
    Support Groups & Hotlines 507
    Print Resources 507
    Web Sites 508

Multiple Sclerosis (MS) 509
    Agencies & Associations 510
    Foundations 510
    Libraries & Resource Centers 510
    Research Centers 510
    Support Groups & Hotlines 511
    Print Resources 511
    Web Sites 511

Obesity 513
    Agencies & Associations 514
    Libraries & Resource Centers 514
    Research Centers 514
    Support Groups & Hotlines 514
    Print Resources 514
    Web Sites 515

Table of Contents

Obsessive-Compulsive Disorder (OCD) 517
    Agencies & Associations................................. 518
    Foundations 519
    Libraries & Resource Centers 519
    Research Centers 519
    Support Groups & Hotlines 519
    Print Resources 519
    Web Sites.. 520

Osteoporosis 521
    Agencies & Associations................................. 522
    Foundations 522
    Libraries & Resource Centers 522
    Research Centers 522
    Support Groups & Hotlines 522
    Web Sites.. 523

Schizophrenia Spectrum & Other Psychotic Disorders 525
    Agencies & Associations................................. 526
    Foundations 527
    Libraries & Resource Centers 527
    Research Centers 527
    Support Groups & Hotlines 527
    Print Resources 528
    Web Sites.. 528

Sexual Disorders 531
    Agencies & Associations................................. 532
    Foundations 533
    Support Groups & Hotlines 533
    Print Resources 533
    Web Sites.. 533

Sleep-Wake Disorders 535
    Agencies & Associations................................. 536
    Foundations 536
    Libraries & Resource Centers 536
    Research Centers 536
    Support Groups & Hotlines 539
    Print Resources 539
    Web Sites.. 539

Somatic Symptom & Related Disorders 541
    Agencies & Associations................................. 542
    Print Resources 542
    Web Sites.. 543

Stroke 545
    Agencies & Associations................................. 546
    Foundations 546
    Research Centers 546
    Support Groups & Hotlines 547

Table of Contents

    Print Resources 547
    Web Sites 547

Substance-Related & Addictive Disorders 549
    Agencies & Associations 550
    Foundations 554
    Libraries & Resource Centers 554
    Research Centers 555
    Support Groups & Hotlines 557
    Print Resources 559
    Web Sites 559

Suicide 563
    Agencies & Associations 564
    Foundations 565
    Libraries & Resource Centers 565
    Support Groups & Hotlines 565
    Print Resources 566
    Web Sites 566

Trauma & Stressor-Related Disorders 569
    Agencies & Associations 570
    Foundations 573
    Libraries & Resource Centers 574
    Research Centers 575
    Support Groups & Hotlines 587
    Print Resources 588
    Web Sites 589

Section Four: Appendixes & Indexes
Glossary of Terms 593
Entry Index 601
Geographic Index 611

Publisher's Note

Grey House Publishing is pleased to announce the *Depression Handbook & Resource Guide*—the eighth volume in a health series that supports our long-standing consumer health titles on such topics as mental health, older Americans, chronic illness, pediatric disorders, and people with disabilities. This title follows the *Dementia Handbook & Resource Guide*, *Cardiovascular Disease Handbook & Resource Guide*, *Autoimmune Diseases Handbook & Resource Guide*, *Nutrition, Obesity & Eating Disorders Handbook & Resource Guide*, *Diabetes Handbook & Resource Guide*, *Autism Spectrum Handbook & Resource Guide*, and *Addiction Handbook & Resource Guide*.

This work covers addiction and related mental health conditions, and 28 common comorbidities, from adjustment disorders to trauma and stressor-related disorders.

The *Depression Handbook & Resource Guide* combines valuable, easy-to-understand educational information for consumers, patients, and their families, with official reports and releases about the different types of depression, mental health in the workforce, anxiety and depression in college-age students, and treatments and further resources for co-occurring conditions. This new volume is arranged in the following sections:

Introduction
This detailed introduction to the book and to depression specifically, written by health specialist Patricia S. Edens, PhD, RN, LFACHE, provides an overview of depression, and includes information on diagnosis, signs and symptoms, treatments, prevention, and seeking help.

Section One: Studies & Statistics
This robust, colorful section of over 380 pages includes detailed reports, journal articles, fact sheets, infographics, and useable materials such as checklists and a healthy eating calendar, from a number of sources including the National Institutes of Health, the Surgeon General's Office, the Substance Abuse and Mental Health Services Administration, the U.S. Department of Health and Human Services, the Centers for Disease Control and Prevention, and more. It begins with an annotated table of contents, followed by a series of booklets on the different primary types of depression, and substantial reports on workplace mental health and anxiety and depression in college-age students.

Following this are helpful backgrounders, facts, and treatment plans about the specific conditions related to depression that are covered in Section Three, including adjustment disorders, aging, Alzheimer's disease and dementia, anxiety disorders, arthritis, asthma, attention-deficit/hyperactivity disorder (ADHD), bipolar and related disorders, diabetes mellitus, disruptive, impulse-control and conduct disorders, dissociative disorders (DD), feeding and eating disorders, heart disease, hypertension, impotence, infertility, multiple sclerosis (MS), obesity, obsessive-compulsive disorder (OCD), osteoporosis, schizophrenia spectrum and other psychotic disorders, sexual disorders, sleep-wake disorders, somatic symptom and related disorders, stroke, substance-related and addictive disorders, suicide, and trauma and stressor-related disorders.

Section Two: Depression Resources
This section details a variety of resources for individuals experiencing depression, their families, and caregivers, including agencies and associations, foundations, libraries and resource centers, research centers, support groups and hotlines, print resources, digital resources, and web sites.

Section Three: Common Comorbidities of Depression
This section includes 28 conditions that are considered to commonly co-occur with depression. Overviews written by Patricia S. Edens detail the conditions themselves, how they relate to

Publisher's Note

depression, and both common and cutting-edge treatment options. Patient, family and caregiver resources follow.

Following that, users will find the following pieces of backmatter:
- **Glossary of Terms** lists major terms and concepts related to depression.
- **Entry Index** lists all directory entries alphabetically.
- **Geographic Index** organizes listings alphabetically by state.

The *Depression Handbook & Resource Guide* is a necessary reference for public and academic libraries, as well as education and health care collections, providing information crucial to individuals suffering from depression, their broader support network, caseworkers, social workers, and other education and health care providers.

Introduction

At some point in life, everyone feels sad or maybe even depressed. Usually, these feelings pass and life returns to normal. When feelings of sadness persist longer than two weeks, it may be depression, which may also be called major depressive disorder. Symptoms of depression may include persistent sadness, feelings of hopelessness or pessimism, irritability, losing interest in things that once brought pleasure like hobbies, difficulty thinking or making decisions, and changes in sleep and appetite. Sometimes depression may be accompanied by vague physical symptoms such as headaches, gastric upset, and pain in muscles and joints that have no identifiable cause. An additional difficulty in recognizing that symptoms are caused by depression is that some symptoms such as aches or pains, digestive disorders or headaches that do not get better with treatment may lead to aggressive attempts to diagnose a physiological reason rather than a psychological reason and may delay appropriate care. Depressive disorders may also be referred to as Major or Persistent Depressive Disorder or Clinical Depression.

Thoughts of death or suicide require immediate help! Call the National Suicide Prevention Lifeline toll-free at 1-800-273-TALK (8255), or consider going to a local hospital or calling 911.

Depression is one of the most common mental health disorders in the United States and may be caused by a variety of factors. Depression can happen at any age, may co-occur with serious illnesses, and may be caused from medication side effects. It is important that the individual understands that depression is treatable. It is also important to understand that transient sadness, such as with loss of a family member or pet, a job loss or major life event such as divorce or moving lasting two weeks or less is probably not depression. If this sadness lasts longer than two weeks or gets progressively worse, a physician visit should be scheduled.

Depressive disorders are considered a mental health issue. There are many other diagnoses including medical conditions, or comorbid conditions, such as arthritis, diabetes mellitus, heart disease and stroke, multiple sclerosis, and sexual disorders that may include a component of depression. Other mental health specific issues with a component of depression may include bipolar disorder, postpartum depression, post-traumatic stress disorder, eating disorders and others.

There are societal, environmental, medical, and economic issues that impact mental health. Homelessness, race and ethnicity, aging, sexual orientation, civil and political unrest, immigration and other factors may all impact the mental health of individuals. Excessive social media use and too much exposure to outside media may also have a negative effect on mental health. Family history of depression, major trauma and stress may increase the risk of depression. Having a chronic disease such as cancer, diabetes or heart disease may lead to depression that requires treatment. Grief and despair may also evolve into depression.

Diagnosis
The signs and symptoms of depression vary person to person, making a definitive diagnosis somewhat difficult to make. Some individuals withdraw while others may be irritable or agitated. Behaviors such as sleeping patterns and eating patterns may change with depression. Insomnia, or a constant desire to sleep, and weight gain or loss may be signs of depression. Fatigue, feeling of hopelessness, problems with concentration and poor work performance, sadness and loss of enjoyment of activities, guilt, and recurring thoughts of death or suicide are all considered in the diagnosis of depression.

Signs and Symptoms of Depression
Recognizing the signs of depression in others is important to seeking treatment in a timely manner. Physical signs of depression may aid in the diagnosis of depression. When talking with the individual, he or she may seem preoccupied and will not make eye contact. Asking questions may

Introduction

demonstrate memory loss or poor concentration. Poor abstract reasoning may occur when asked to state how they would solve a problem. Other signs may include slow speech, sighs, pauses in conversation and slowed body movements. Slowed body movements may be even to the extent of motionless or catatonic, defined as an immobile or unresponsive stupor. Pacing, wringing of hands and tics such as pulling on hair, and tearfulness or sad appearance may also be signs. In individuals who suspect they may be suffering from depression, these same signs may exhibit as memory loss, difficulty with daily tasks, withdrawal from friends and family, work problems from poor concentration and loss of interest in life.

Symptoms occurring daily and lasting longer than two weeks should be reported to the physician. Symptoms may last for weeks, months or indefinitely and interfere with an individual's life to the point that others both notice and become aggravated over time. Symptoms may become so disabling that the person may be unable to eat, maintain self-care and hygiene, or even leave the house.

Admitting You Might Be Depressed

The most important treatment for mental health issues is admitting there is a problem. Seeking out information can be helpful. Sometimes managing the stress of daily life, developing self-care skills and reaching out to others for support is enough, but if feelings or symptoms increase, seek professional help. Recognizing symptoms in self and others is a proactive way to manage mental health conditions before they spiral out of control.

Making the Diagnosis

Once symptoms present and the individual realizes the need for help, a diagnosis needs to be made by a medical professional. While mild cases of depression may be treated with medication from the primary care provider with or without psychotherapy (talk therapy), a referral to a mental health professional may be needed. Knowing what to tell your provider will help to determine your diagnosis.

Making an appointment with a physician is the first step in the diagnostic process. The individual must recognize that he or she needs intervention for a depressive mood. Almost half of people with depression are never diagnosed or treated. Without treatment, more than 10% of people with depression take their own lives. When depression is causing difficulties in life, including relationships, work, and family issues, it is time for action. Listen to what others say to you. If they are saying an individual seems different or seems sad, self-examination is important.

The initial appointment is generally with the primary care doctor or an OB-GYN if female. Before the appointment, it is important for the patient to write a list of concerns, including physical and emotional symptoms, unusual changes in lifestyle or behavior, past illness, family history of depression and all medications, supplements, alcohol, tobacco and recreational drugs used. Often the physician will ask about lifestyle habits such as exercise and diet. The more information provided, the more accurate the diagnosis will be.

During the initial visit, the physician observes and interviews the patient to learn patient and family history, conducts a physical examination and may order laboratory tests to rule out any physical conditions that could be causing symptoms. Viruses, hormonal deficiencies, vitamin deficiencies and some medications may cause depression-type symptoms. The doctor will also ask about alcohol and recreational drug use.

Once the physician reviews patient responses to questioning, observations during the visit including presence of signs and symptoms, any laboratory values and results of the physical examination, a diagnosis of depression can be made. The physician may order medications, psychotherapy or both depending on the individual's assessed needs. Referral to a psychiatrist or psychologist or other healthcare professional for ongoing care may be made. All treatment plans

Introduction

must be individualized so a trial-and-error approach may be needed to determine the best treatment to alleviate or make manageable the individual's depression.

Antidepressants are often ordered to improve brain chemicals that control mood or stress. A medication that has helped the individual or perhaps a family member with depression may be considered. Several different medications may be tried to determine which one best relieves symptoms. Medications require two to four weeks to work and physical symptoms such as sleep, appetite and ability to concentrate may resolve before mood improvements are noted. Antidepressants should never be stopped suddenly; doses should be slowly tapered down, usually after six months to a year after starting.

No supplements should be added after starting medication for depression unless the physician approves. All doctors need to know what the patient is taking so drug interactions can be avoided. For example, St. John's Wart, a botanical product, should never be combined with an antidepressant. The FDA has not approved most supplements, but studies are continuing.

Choosing the right treatment plan is individualized and may need to be adjusted to achieve the best possible outcome. Support groups, complementary therapies, family counseling, inpatient care and other interventions may also be included in the plan of care. Working with mental health professionals is important.

Prevention and Seeking Help

Maintaining a healthy lifestyle may prevent or mitigate some types of depression. Social interactions are important as isolationism increases the risk of depression. Talking about problems may actually make things worse if not seeing a professional for counseling. Discussing problems is often seen as a way to give and receive support, but conversations may make the individual more depressed. Distraction through meditation or prayer, making realistic goals, and developing self-esteem may help. Eating a healthy diet and avoiding alcohol, especially to excess, are useful. Exercise and activities are also effective and cost-effective treatments for sadness and may aid in preventing depression. Exercise is good for the body, may prevent other co-morbid diseases, and may be good for mental health. Exercise as both prevention and treatment of depression has been shown through clinical studies to be beneficial. Maintaining good sleep hygiene, such as a regular bedtime and wake-up time is helpful. Before beginning any new activities, the individual should consult with the physician. Avoid using nicotine, recreational drugs including medications not prescribed to you, and other forms of substance abuse may help in preventing depression.

Seeking help for ongoing feelings of sadness that are interfering with life is healthy. Being proactive to prevent sadness evolving into depression is important. Never be afraid to talk about mental health with your medical providers, family and friends. You may not need help, but someone you love might.

—Patricia S. Edens, PhD, RN, LFACHE

SECTION ONE: STUDIES & STATISTICS

This first section of the *Depression Handbook & Resource Guide* includes the most current research on how depression relates to the featured health conditions, with data, fact sheets, reports, and studies from the National Institutes of Health, the Surgeon General's Office, the Substance Abuse and Mental Health Services Administration, the U.S. Department of Health and Human Services, the Centers for Disease Control and Prevention, and more. Totaling over 380 pages, Studies & Statistics comprises over 30 detailed reports, summaries, journal articles, and fact sheets, with easy to understand graphics. Colorful photos, graphs, charts, and maps help to visualize the data.

DEPRESSIVE DISORDERS

1. **Depression Booklets** 5
   A series of booklets released by the National Institute of Mental Health, covering depression generally, chronic illness and mental health, depression in women, and perinatal depression.

2. **Seasonal Affective Disorder** 37
   A four-page release from the National Institute of Mental Health covering seasonal affective disorder specifically, including signs and symptoms, diagnosis, causes, and treatments.

3. **Children and Mental Health: Is This Just a Stage?** 41
   A four-page release from the National Institute of Mental Health discussing mental health in childhood, when to seek help, first steps for parents, assessing children's behavior, and treatment options. Also includes a one-page supplement on teenage depression.

4. **Workplace Mental Health & Well-Being** 47
   From the Office of the Surgeon General, this report examines the current workplace landscape in the U.S. through the lens of how work can influence mental health, for better or worse. One particular focus is how the COVID-19 pandemic changed the working life of many Americans, and the ramifications of those changes.

5. **Prevention and Treatment of Anxiety, Depression, and Suicidal Thoughts and Behaviors Among College Students** 75
   This report from the Substance Abuse and Mental Health Services Administration looks at the ways that anxiety, depression, and suicidal thoughts can be mitigated, including on-campus and public health-wide interventions.

COMMON COMORBIDITIES OF DEPRESSION

6. **Adjustment Disorder: Current Developments and Future Directions** 109
   An article from the *International Journal of Environmental Research and Public Health* looking at current scientific thoughts on adjustment disorder.

7. **Older Americans Key Indicators of Well-Being** 121
   Excerpts from a report by the Federal Interagency Forum on Aging Related Statistics dealing specifically with health status indicators such as life expectancy, mortality, chronic health conditions, dementia, depressive symptoms, and more.

8. **The Dementias: Hope Through Research** 133
   This release from the National Institutes of Health discusses types of dementia, risk factors, diagnosis and treatment, and current research.

9. **Generalized Anxiety Disorder: When Worry Gets Out of Control** 147
   A National Institute of Mental Health booklet examining generalized anxiety disorder (GAD).

1

Studies & Statistics / Table of Contents

10. **Arthritis in America** 155
    A short info-sheet from the U.S. Department of Health and Human Services looking at how arthritis affects the lives of Americans.

11. **Asthma in Children** 159
    This release from the Centers for Disease Control and Prevention looks at the prevalence of asthma is American children, and what can be done. Also includes a supplement with 10 steps to making your home more asthma-friendly.

12. **Attention-Deficit/Hyperactivity Disorder Booklets** 165
    Two booklets by the National Institute of Mental Health on Attention-Deficit/Hyperactivity Disorder (ADHD), the first looking at ADHD in adults and the second in children and teens.

13. **Bipolar Disorder** 181
    A booklet from the National Institute of Mental Health on bipolar disorder, including types, symptoms, causes, diagnosis, and treatments.

14. **How to Help a Loved One with Diabetes When You Live Far Apart** 189
    A release from the Centers for Disease Control and Prevention discussing how family and friends of people affected by diabetes can help their loved ones from a distance.

15. **Treating Disruptive Behavior Disorders in Children and Teens** 197
    From the Agency for Healthcare Research and Quality, this report is aimed at parents and caregivers of children and teens with disruptive behavior disorders, including causes and treatments.

16. **Separating Fact from Fiction: An Empirical Examination of Six Myths About Dissociative Identity Disorder** 209
    A journal article from *Perspectives* looking in detail at six common myths about dissociative identity disorder (DID).

17. **Eating Disorders: About More Than Food** 223
    A booklet from the National Institute of Mental Health about eating disorders, who is at risk, common types, and treatments.

18. **ABCs of Heart Health** 231
    A short info-sheet from Million Hearts discussing ways to reduce the risk of heart attack and stroke, including a healthy eating calendar.

19. **Hypertension and Blood Pressure** 235
    Includes the Executive Summary from The Surgeon General's Call to Action to Control Hypertension, a checklist for managing blood pressure, and a blood pressure log.

20. **Erectile Dysfunction** 239
    A collaborative Whole Health tool examining erectile dysfunction (ED), causes, and preventions.

21. **A History of Developments to Improve *in vitro* Fertilization** 243
    An examination of recent advancements in the field of *in vitro* fertilization, including safety measures.

22. **Multiple Sclerosis: Hope Through Research** 247
    A release from the National Institute of Neurological Disorders and Stroke on multiple sclerosis (MS), including signs and symptoms, and causes.

Studies & Statistics / Table of Contents

23. **Maintaining a Healthy Weight on the Go: A Pocket Guide** 257
    A colorful and useful guide to developing and maintaining a healthy eating plan for people on the go, including dining out/take-out and fast-food.

24. **Obsessive-Compulsive Disorder: When Unwanted Thoughts or Repetitive Behaviors Take Over** 277
    A booklet from the National Institute of Mental Health examining obsessive-compulsive disorder (OCD), including signs and symptoms, causes, and treatments.

25. **Osteoporosis** 285
    A Q&A-style fact sheet from the Office on Women's Health on osteoporosis.

26. **Schizophrenia** 287
    A booklet from the National Institute of Mental Health covering schizophrenia, including symptoms, causes, and treatments.

27. **The Voice of the Patient: Female Sexual Dysfunction** 295
    Part of a series of reports from the U.S. Food and Drug Administration's Patient-Focused Drug Development Initiative, in this case devoted to perspectives from women with female sexual dysfunction (FSD) on their condition and on currently available therapies.

28. **Understanding Sleep** 311
    A colorful and accessible look at how humans sleep, including anatomy, sleep cycles, sleep mechanisms, how much sleep we need, and more.

29. **Somatic Symptom Disorder: A Diagnostic Dilemma** 321
    A journal article from *BMJ Case Report* on the dilemma faced by doctors presented with a possible diagnosis of somatic symptom disorder, which involves a patient's concern with physical symptoms for which no biological cause is found.

30. **Know Stroke** 325
    A straightforward pamphlet from the National Institute of Neurological Disorders and Stroke helping readers to recognize the signs of stroke, so that victims may be treated immediately and receive the best possible outcome.

31. **Results from the 2020 National Survey on Drug Use and Health** 333
    A series of graphs from the Center for Behavioral Health Statistics and Quality, Substance Abuse and Mental Health Services Administration, and U.S. Department of Health and Human Services, with key findings from the 2020 National Survey on Drug Use and Health, including how substance use intersects with depression.

32. **Suicide Prevention: Resource for Action** 371
    A report from the Centers for Disease Control and Prevention on the importance of establishing suicide-prevention measures, including a list of strategies, and a discussion of the impacts of the COVID-19 pandemic on suicide prevention efforts.

33. **Post-Traumatic Stress Disorder** 379
    A booklet from the National Institute of Mental Health on post-traumatic stress disorder (PTSD), including symptoms, treatments, and why some people develop the disorder while others do not. Also includes a supplement on helping children and adolescents cope with traumatic events.

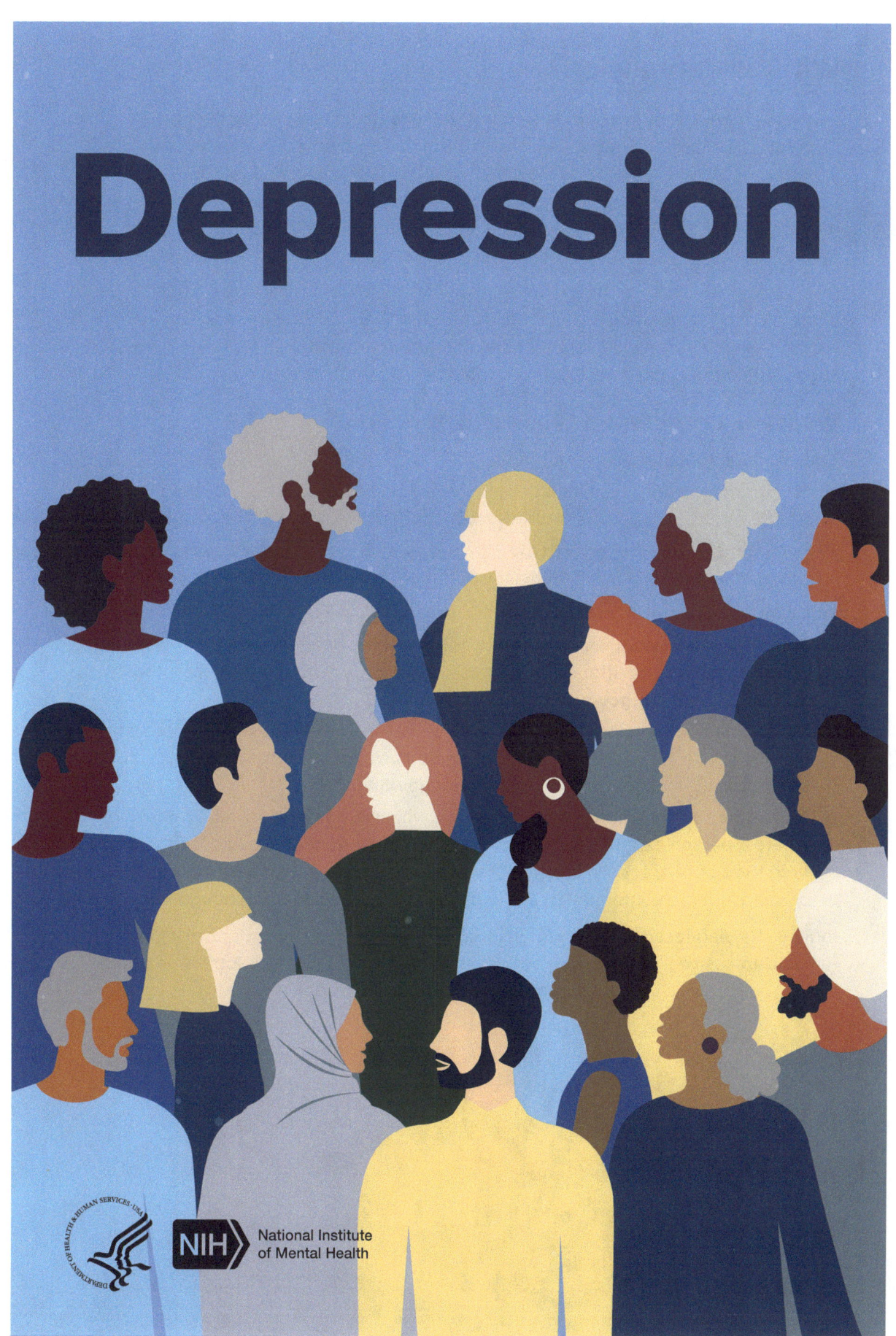

What is depression?

Everyone feels sad or low sometimes, but these feelings usually pass with a little time. Depression (also called major depressive disorder or clinical depression) is different. It can cause severe symptoms that affect how you feel, think, and handle daily activities, such as sleeping, eating, or working. It is an illness that can affect anyone—regardless of age, race, income, culture, or education. Research suggests that genetic, biological, environmental, and psychological factors play a role in depression.

Depression may occur with other mental disorders and other illnesses, such as diabetes, cancer, heart disease, and chronic pain. Depression can make these conditions worse, and vice versa. Sometimes medications taken for these illnesses cause side effects that contribute to depression symptoms.

What are the different types of depression?

Two common forms of depression are:

- **Major depression,** which includes symptoms of depression most of the time for at least 2 weeks that typically interfere with one's ability to work, sleep, study, and eat.
- **Persistent depressive disorder** (dysthymia), which often includes less severe symptoms of depression that last much longer, typically for at least 2 years.

Other forms of depression include:

- **Perinatal depression,** which occurs when a woman experiences major depression during pregnancy or after delivery (postpartum depression). For more information, visit **www.nimh.nih.gov/perinataldepression**.
- **Seasonal affective disorder,** which comes and goes with the seasons, typically starting in late fall and early winter and going away during spring and summer. For more information, visit **www.nimh.nih.gov/SAD**.
- **Depression with symptoms of psychosis,** which is a severe form of depression where a person experiences psychosis symptoms, such as delusions (disturbing, false fixed beliefs) or hallucinations (hearing or seeing things that others do not see or hear). For more information about psychosis, visit **www.nimh.nih.gov/psychosis**.

Individuals diagnosed with bipolar disorder (formerly called manic depression or manic-depressive illness) also experience depression. For more information about this mood disorder, visit **www.nimh.nih.gov/bipolardisorder**.

What are the signs and symptoms of depression?

Common symptoms of depression include:
- Persistent sad, anxious, or "empty" mood
- Feelings of hopelessness or pessimism
- Feelings of irritability, frustration, or restlessness
- Feelings of guilt, worthlessness, or helplessness
- Loss of interest or pleasure in hobbies or activities
- Decreased energy, fatigue, or being "slowed down"
- Difficulty concentrating, remembering, or making decisions
- Difficulty sleeping, early morning awakening, or oversleeping
- Changes in appetite or unplanned weight changes
- Aches or pains, headaches, cramps, or digestive problems without a clear physical cause and that do not ease even with treatment
- **Suicide attempts or thoughts of death or suicide**

> **If you or someone you know is in immediate distress or is thinking about hurting themselves,** call the National Suicide Prevention Lifeline toll-free at 1-800-273-TALK (8255) or the toll-free TTY number at 1-800-799-4TTY (4889). You also can text the Crisis Text Line (HELLO to 741741) or go to the National Suicide Prevention Lifeline website at **https://suicidepreventionlifeline.org**.

How is depression diagnosed?

To be diagnosed with depression, an individual must have five depression symptoms every day, nearly all day, for at least 2 weeks. One of the symptoms must be a depressed mood or a loss of interest or pleasure in almost all activities. Children and adolescents may be irritable rather than sad.

If you think you may have depression, talk to your health care provider. Primary care providers routinely diagnose and treat depression and refer individuals to mental health professionals, such as psychologists or psychiatrists.

During the visit, your provider may ask when your symptoms began, how long they last, how often they occur, and if they keep you from going out or doing your usual activities. It may help to make some notes about your symptoms before your visit. Certain medications and some medical conditions, such as viruses or a thyroid disorder, can cause the same depression symptoms. Your provider can rule out these possibilities by doing a physical exam, interview, and lab tests.

Find tips to help prepare for and get the most out of your visit at **www.nimh.nih.gov/talkingtips**. For additional resources, visit the Agency for Healthcare Research and Quality website at **www.ahrq.gov/questions**.

Does depression look the same in everyone?

Depression can affect people differently, depending on their age.

Children with depression may be anxious, cranky, pretend to be sick, refuse to go to school, cling to a parent, or worry that a parent may die.

Older children and teens with depression may get into trouble at school, sulk, be easily frustrated, feel restless, or have low self-esteem. They also may have other disorders, such as anxiety and eating disorders, attention-deficit hyperactivity disorder, or substance use disorder. Older children and teens are more likely to experience excessive sleepiness (called hypersomnia) and increased appetite (called hyperphagia). In adolescence, females begin to experience depression more often than males, likely due to the biological, life cycle, and hormonal factors unique to women.

Younger adults with depression are more likely to be irritable, complain of weight gain and hypersomnia, and have a negative view of life and the future. They often have other disorders, such as generalized anxiety disorder, social phobia, panic disorder, and substance use disorders.

Middle-aged adults with depression may have more depressive episodes, decreased libido, middle-of-the-night insomnia, or early morning awakening. They also may more frequently report having gastrointestinal symptoms such as diarrhea or constipation.

Older adults with depression commonly experience sadness or grief or may have other less obvious symptoms. They may report a lack of emotions rather than a depressed mood. Older adults also are more likely to have other medical conditions or pain that may cause or contribute to depression. In severe cases, memory and thinking problems (called pseudodementia) may be prominent.

How is depression treated?

Depression treatment typically involves medication, psychotherapy, or both. If these treatments do not reduce symptoms, brain stimulation therapy may be another treatment option. In milder cases of depression, treatment might begin with psychotherapy alone, and medication added if the individual continues to experience symptoms. For moderate or severe depression, many mental health professionals recommend a combination of medication and therapy at the start of treatment.

Choosing the right treatment plan should be based on a person's individual needs and medical situation under a provider's care. It may take some trial and error to find the treatment that works best for you. You can learn more about the different types of treatment, including psychotherapy, medication, and brain stimulation therapies, at **www.nimh.nih.gov/depression**. For information on finding a mental health professional and questions to ask when considering therapy, visit **www.nimh.nih.gov/psychotherapies**.

Medications

Antidepressants are medications commonly used to treat depression. They take time to work—usually 4 to 8 weeks—and symptoms such as problems with sleep, appetite, or concentration often improve before mood lifts. It is important to give medication a chance before deciding whether or not it works.

> **Please Note:** Some individuals—especially children, teenagers, and young adults—may experience an increase in suicidal thoughts or behavior when taking antidepressants, particularly in the first few weeks after starting or when the dose is changed. All patients taking antidepressants should be watched closely, especially during the first few weeks of treatment.
>
> Information about medications changes frequently. Visit the U.S. Food and Drug Administration (FDA) website at **www.fda.gov/drugsatfda** for the latest warnings, patient medication guides, and newly approved medications.

Treatment-resistant depression occurs when a person doesn't get better after trying at least two antidepressants. Esketamine is a newer FDA-approved medication for treatment-resistant depression delivered as a nasal spray in a doctor's office, clinic, or hospital. It often acts rapidly—typically within a couple of hours—to relieve depression symptoms. Individuals usually continue to take an oral antidepressant to maintain the improvement in depression.

Another option for treatment-resistant depression is to add a different type of medication that may make an antidepressant more effective, such as an antipsychotic or anticonvulsant medication or bupropion, an antidepressant that works differently from most.

Medications prescribed by your health care provider for depression can have side effects, but these may lessen over time. Talk to your provider about any side effects that you have. Do not stop taking medications without the help of a health care provider. If you abruptly stop taking your medicine, you may experience severe withdrawal symptoms.

FDA has not approved any natural products for depression. While research is ongoing, some people find natural products, including vitamin D and the herbal dietary supplement St. John's wort, to help depression. Do not use St. John's wort or other dietary supplements for depression before talking to your provider. For more information, visit the National Center for Complementary and Integrative Health website at **www.nccih.nih.gov**.

Psychotherapy

Psychotherapy (also called "talk therapy" or "counseling") teaches individuals with depression new ways of thinking and behaving and helps with changing habits that contribute to depression. Most psychotherapy occurs with a licensed, trained mental health professional in one-on-one sessions or with other individuals in a group setting. Two effective psychotherapies to treat depression include cognitive behavioral therapy (CBT) and interpersonal therapy (IPT). The use of older forms of psychotherapy, such as dynamic therapy, for a limited time also may help some people with depression.

With CBT, people learn to challenge and change unhelpful thinking patterns and behavior to improve their depressive and anxious feelings. Recent advances in CBT include introducing mindfulness principles and the development of specialized forms of therapy targeting particular symptoms, such as insomnia.

IPT focuses on interpersonal and life events that impact mood and vice versa. The goal of IPT is to help people improve their communication skills within relationships, establish social support networks, and develop realistic expectations to help them deal with crises or other issues that may be contributing to or worsening their depression.

Brain Stimulation Therapy

Brain stimulation therapy, which involves activating or inhibiting the brain directly with electricity or magnetic waves, is another option for some people when other depression treatments have not been effective.

The most common forms of brain stimulation therapy include electroconvulsive therapy and repetitive transcranial magnetic stimulation. Other brain stimulation therapies are newer and, in some cases, still experimental. You can learn more about these therapies at **www.nimh.nih.gov/braintherapies**.

How can I find help?

The Substance Abuse and Mental Health Services Administration provides the Behavioral Health Treatment Services Locator, an online tool for finding mental health treatment and support groups in your area, available at **https://findtreatment. samhsa.gov**. For additional resources, visit **www.nimh.nih.gov/findhelp**.

How can I take care of myself?

Once you begin treatment, you should gradually start to feel better. Go easy on yourself during this time. Try to do things you used to enjoy. Even if you don't feel like doing them, they can improve your mood. Other things that may help:

- Try to get some physical activity. Just 30 minutes a day of walking can boost mood.
- Try to maintain a regular bedtime and wake-up time.
- Eat regular, healthy meals.
- Do what you can as you can. Decide what must get done and what can wait.
- Try to connect with other people, and talk with people you trust about how you are feeling.
- Postpone important life decisions until you feel better.
- Avoid using alcohol, nicotine, or drugs, including medications not prescribed for you.

How can I help a loved one who is depressed?

If someone you know has depression, help them see a health care provider or mental health professional. You also can:

- Offer support, understanding, patience, and encouragement.
- Invite them out for walks, outings, and other activities.
- Help them stick to their treatment plan, such as setting reminders to take prescribed medications.
- Make sure they have transportation to therapy appointments.
- Remind them that, with time and treatment, the depression will lift.

> Take comments about suicide seriously, and report them to your loved one's health care provider or therapist. **If they are in immediate distress or thinking about hurting themselves, call 911 for emergency services or go to the nearest hospital emergency room.**

Where can I find clinical trials for depression?

Clinical trials are research studies that look at new ways to prevent, detect, or treat diseases and conditions. Although individuals may benefit from being part of a clinical trial, participants should be aware that the primary purpose of a clinical trial is to gain new scientific knowledge so others may receive better help in the future.

Researchers at the National Institute of Mental Health (NIMH) and around the country conduct many studies with patients and healthy volunteers. Talk to your health care provider about clinical trials, their benefits and risks, and whether one is right for you. For more information, visit **www.nimh.nih.gov/clinicaltrials**.

Chronic Illness and Mental Health
Recognizing and Treating Depression

Studies & Statistics / Chronic Illness and Mental Health: Recognizing and Treating Depression

Chronic illnesses such as cancer, heart disease, or diabetes may make you more likely to have or develop a mental health condition.

It is common to feel sad or discouraged after having a heart attack, receiving a cancer diagnosis, or when trying to manage a chronic condition such as pain. You may be facing new limits on what you can do and may feel stressed or concerned about treatment outcomes and the future. It may be hard to adapt to a new reality and to cope with the changes and ongoing treatment that come with the diagnosis. Favorite activities, such as hiking or gardening, may be harder to do.

Temporary feelings of sadness are expected, but if these and other symptoms last longer than a couple of weeks, you may have depression. Depression affects your ability to carry on with daily life and to enjoy family, friends, work, and leisure. The health effects of depression go beyond mood: Depression is a serious medical illness with many symptoms, including physical ones. Some symptoms of depression include:

- Persistent sad, anxious, or "empty" mood
- Feeling hopeless or pessimistic
- Feeling irritable, easily frustrated, or restless
- Feeling guilty, worthless, or helpless
- Loss of interest or pleasure in hobbies and activities
- Decreased energy, fatigue, or feeling "slowed down"
- Difficulty concentrating, remembering, or making decisions
- Difficulty sleeping, early-morning awakening, or oversleeping
- Changes in appetite or weight
- Aches or pains, headaches, cramps, or digestive problems without a clear physical cause that do not ease even with treatment
- Suicide attempts or thoughts of death or suicide

Remember: Depression is treatable—even if you have another medical illness or condition. For more information, visit the National Institute of Mental Health (NIMH) website to learn more about depression at www.nimh.nih.gov/depression. If you need help starting the conversation, check out the Tips for Talking With Your Health Care Provider fact sheet at www.nimh.nih.gov/talkingtips.

Studies & Statistics / Chronic Illness and Mental Health: Recognizing and Treating Depression

People with other chronic medical conditions are at higher risk of depression.

The same factors that increase the risk of depression in otherwise healthy people also raise the risk in people with other medical illnesses, particularly if those illnesses are chronic (long-lasting or persistent). These risk factors include a personal or family history of depression or family members who have died by suicide.

However, some risk factors for depression are directly related to having another illness. For example, conditions such as Parkinson's disease and stroke cause changes in the brain. In some cases, these changes may have a direct role in depression. Illness-related anxiety and stress also can trigger symptoms of depression.

Depression is common among people who have chronic illnesses such as:

- Alzheimer's disease
- Autoimmune diseases, including systemic lupus erythematosus, rheumatoid arthritis, and psoriasis
- Cancer
- Coronary heart disease
- Diabetes
- Epilepsy
- HIV/AIDS
- Hypothyroidism
- Multiple sclerosis
- Parkinson's disease
- Stroke

Some people may experience symptoms of depression after being diagnosed with a medical illness. Those symptoms may decrease as they adjust to or treat the other condition. Certain medications used to treat the illness also can trigger depression.

Research suggests that people who have depression and another medical illness tend to have more severe symptoms of both illnesses. They may have more difficulty adapting to their medical condition, and they may have higher medical costs than those who do not have both depression and a medical illness. Symptoms of depression may continue even as a person's physical health improves.

A collaborative care approach that includes both mental and physical health care can improve overall health. Research has shown that treating depression and chronic illness together can help people better manage both their depression and their chronic disease.

Children and Adolescents With Chronic Illnesses

Children and adolescents with chronic illnesses often face more challenges than their healthy peers in navigating adolescence. Chronic illnesses can affect physical, cognitive, social, and emotional development, and they can take a toll on parents and siblings. These limitations put children and adolescents at higher risk than their healthy peers of developing a mental illness.

Children and adolescents with chronic illnesses experience many forms of stress. Parents and health care providers should be on the lookout for signs of depression, anxiety, and adjustment disorders (a group of conditions that can occur when someone has difficulty coping with a stressful life event) in young people and their families.

Learn more about mental health in children and adolescents at **www.nimh.nih.gov/children**.

People with depression are at higher risk for other medical conditions.

It may come as no surprise that adults with a medical illness are more likely to experience depression. The reverse is also true: People of all ages with depression are at higher risk of developing certain physical illnesses.

People with depression have an increased risk of cardiovascular disease, diabetes, stroke, pain, and Alzheimer's disease, for example. Research also suggests that people with depression may be at higher risk for osteoporosis. The reasons are not yet clear. One factor with some of these illnesses is that many people with depression may have less access to good medical care. They may have a more challenging time caring for their health—for example, seeking care, taking prescribed medication, eating well, and exercising.

Scientists also are exploring whether physiological changes seen in depression may play a role in increasing the risk of physical illness. In people with depression, scientists have found changes in the way several different systems in the body function that could have an impact on physical health, including:

- Increased inflammation
- Changes in the control of heart rate and blood circulation
- Abnormalities in stress hormones
- Metabolic changes such as those seen in people at risk for diabetes

> There is some evidence that these changes, seen in depression, may raise the risk of other medical illnesses. It also is clear that depression has a negative effect on mental health and everyday life.

Depression is treatable even when another illness is present.

Depression is a common complication of chronic illness, but it does not have to be a normal part of having a chronic illness. Effective treatment for depression is available and can help even if you have another medical illness or condition.

If you or a loved one think you have depression, it is important to tell your health care provider and explore treatment options. You also should inform your health care provider about all your current treatments or medications for your chronic illness or depression (including prescribed medications and dietary supplements). Sharing information can help avoid problems with multiple medicines interfering with each other. It also helps your health care provider stay informed about your overall health and treatment issues.

> Recovery from depression takes time, but treatment can improve your quality of life even if you have a medical illness.

Treating depression with medication, psychotherapy (also called "talk therapy"), or a combination of the two also may help improve the physical symptoms of a chronic illness or reduce the risk of future problems. Likewise, treating the chronic illness and getting symptoms under control can help improve symptoms of depression.

Depression affects each individual differently. There is no "one-size-fits-all" for treatment. It may take some trial and error to find the treatment that works best. You can learn more about the different types of depression treatment—including psychotherapy, medication, and brain stimulation therapies—on NIMH's webpage about depression at www.nimh.nih.gov/depression. Visit the Food and Drug Administration (FDA) website (www.fda.gov/drugsatfda) for the latest information on medication approvals, warnings, and patient information guides.

Participating in Clinical Research

Clinical trials are research studies that look at new ways to prevent, detect, or treat diseases and conditions. Although individuals may benefit from being part of a clinical trial, participants should be aware that the primary purpose of a clinical trial is to gain new scientific knowledge so others may receive better help in the future.

Researchers at NIMH and around the country conduct many studies with patients and healthy volunteers. Talk to your health care provider about clinical trials, their benefits and risks, and whether one is right for you. For more information, visit www.nimh.nih.gov/clinicaltrials.

Studies & Statistics / Chronic Illness and Mental Health: Recognizing and Treating Depression

Finding Help

Behavioral Health Treatment Services Locator

The Substance Abuse and Mental Health Services Administration (SAMHSA) provides this online resource for locating mental health treatment facilities and programs. Find a facility in your state at **https://findtreatment.samhsa.gov**. For additional resources, visit **www.nimh.nih.gov/findhelp**.

Talking to Your Health Care Provider About Your Mental Health

Communicating well with your doctor or health care provider can improve your care and help you both make good choices about your health. Find tips to help prepare for and get the most out of your visit at **www.nimh.nih.gov/talkingtips**. For additional resources, including questions to ask your doctor, visit the Agency for Healthcare Research and Quality website at **www.ahrq.gov/questions**.

> If you or someone you know is in immediate distress or is thinking about hurting themselves, call the **National Suicide Prevention Lifeline** toll-free at 1-800-273-TALK (8255). You also can text the **Crisis Text Line** (HELLO to 741741) or use the Lifeline Chat on the National Suicide Prevention Lifeline website at **https://suicidepreventionlifeline.org**.

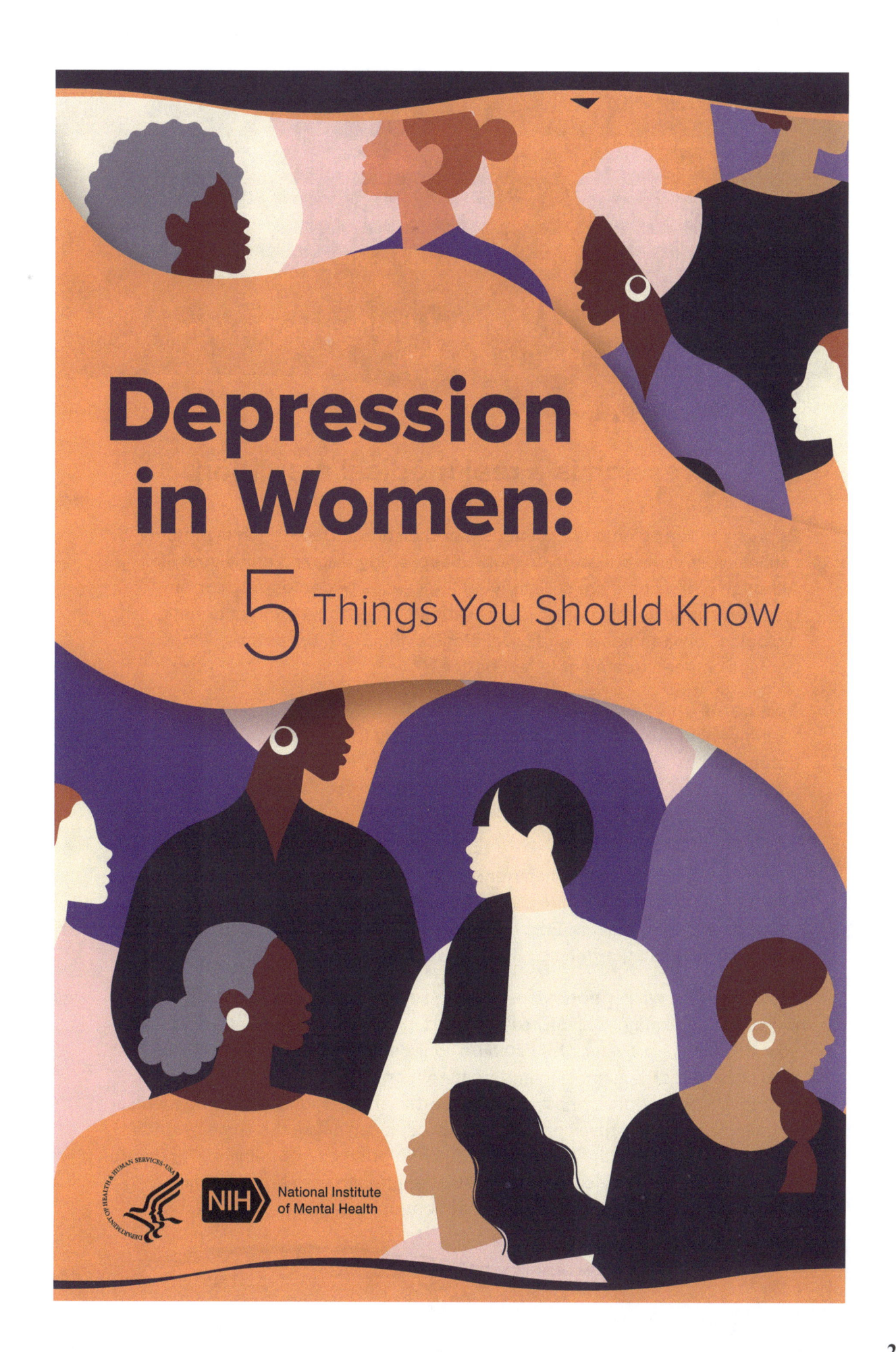

Depression in Women:
5 Things You Should Know

National Institute of Mental Health

Studies & Statistics / Depression in Women: 5 Things You Should Know

Being sad is a normal reaction to difficult times in life. But usually, the sadness goes away with a little time. Depression is different—it is a mood disorder that may cause severe symptoms that can affect how you feel, think, and handle daily activities such as sleeping, eating, or working. Depression is more common among women than men, likely due to certain biological, hormonal, and social factors that are unique to women.

This brochure contains an overview of five things that everyone should know about depression in women.

1. Depression is a real medical condition.

Depression is a common but serious mood disorder. Depression symptoms can interfere with your ability to work, sleep, study, eat, and enjoy your life. Although researchers are still studying the causes of depression, current research suggests that depression is caused by a combination of genetic, biological, environmental, and psychological factors. Most people with depression need treatment to feel better.

You can't just "snap out" of depression.
Well-meaning friends or family members may try to tell someone with depression to "snap out of it," "just be positive," or "you can be happier if you just try harder." But depression is not a sign of a person's weakness or a character flaw. The truth is that most people who experience depression need treatment to get better.

If you are a friend or family member of a woman with depression, you can offer emotional support, understanding, patience, and encouragement. But never dismiss her feelings. Encourage her to talk to her health care provider, and remind her that, with time and treatment, she can feel better.

Most people with depression need treatment to feel better.
If you think you may have depression, start by making an appointment to see your health care provider. This could be your primary doctor or a health provider who specializes in diagnosing and treating mental health conditions (for example, a psychologist or psychiatrist). Certain medications, and some medical conditions, such as viruses or a thyroid disorder, can cause the same symptoms as depression. A health care provider can rule out these possibilities by doing a physical exam, interview, and lab tests. Your health care provider will examine you and talk to you about treatment options and next steps.

Talking to Your Health Care Provider About Your Mental Health

Communicating well with your health care provider can improve your care and help you both make good choices about your health. Find tips to help prepare and get the most out of your visit at **www.nimh.nih.gov/talkingtips**. For additional resources, including questions to ask your health care provider, visit the Agency for Healthcare Research and Quality website at **www.ahrq.gov/questions**.

2. Depression can hurt—literally.

Sadness is only a small part of depression. Some people with depression do not feel sadness at all. A person with depression also may experience many physical symptoms, such as aches or pains, headaches, cramps, or digestive problems. Someone with depression also may have trouble sleeping, waking up in the morning, and feeling tired.

If you have been experiencing any of the following signs and symptoms for at least two weeks, you may be suffering from depression:

- Persistent sad, anxious, or "empty" mood
- Feelings of hopelessness or pessimism
- Irritability
- Feelings of guilt, worthlessness, or helplessness
- Decreased energy or fatigue
- Difficulty sleeping, early-morning awakening, or oversleeping
- Loss of interest or pleasure in hobbies and activities
- Moving or talking more slowly
- Feeling restless or having trouble sitting still
- Difficulty concentrating, remembering, or making decisions
- Changes in appetite or weight
- Thoughts of death or suicide, or suicide attempts
- Aches or pains, headaches, cramps, or digestive problems without a clear physical cause that do not ease even with treatment

Talk to your health care provider about these symptoms. Be honest, clear, and concise—your provider needs to know how you feel. Your health care provider may ask when your symptoms started, what time of day they happen, how long they last, how often they occur, if they seem to be getting worse or better, and if they keep you from going out or doing your usual activities. It may help to take the time to make some notes about your symptoms before you visit your provider.

Studies & Statistics / Depression in Women: 5 Things You Should Know

3. Certain types of depression are unique to women.

Pregnancy, the postpartum period, perimenopause, and the menstrual cycle are all associated with dramatic physical and hormonal changes. Certain types of depression can occur at different stages of a woman's life.

Premenstrual Dysphoric Disorder (PMDD)

Premenstrual syndrome, or PMS, refers to moodiness and irritability in the weeks before menstruation. It is quite common, and the symptoms are usually mild. But there is a less common, more severe form of PMS called premenstrual dysphoric disorder (PMDD). PMDD is a serious condition with disabling symptoms such as irritability, anger, depressed mood, sadness, suicidal thoughts, appetite changes, bloating, breast tenderness, and joint or muscle pain.

Perinatal Depression

Being pregnant isn't easy. Pregnant women commonly deal with morning sickness, weight gain, and mood swings. Caring for a newborn is challenging, too. Many new moms experience the "baby blues"—a term used to describe mild mood changes and feelings of worry, unhappiness, and exhaustion that many women sometimes experience in the first two weeks after having a baby. These feelings usually last a week or two and then go away as a new mom adjusts to having a newborn.

Perinatal depression is a mood disorder that can affect women during pregnancy and after childbirth, and is much more serious than the "baby blues." The word "perinatal" refers to the time before and after the birth of a child. Perinatal depression includes depression that begins during pregnancy (called prenatal depression) and depression that begins after the baby is born (called postpartum depression). Mothers with perinatal depression experience feelings of extreme sadness, anxiety, and fatigue that may make it difficult for them to carry out daily tasks, including caring for themselves, their new child, or others.

If you think you have perinatal depression, you should talk to your health care provider or trained mental health care professional. If you see any signs of depression in a loved one during her pregnancy or after the child is born, encourage her to see a health care provider or visit a clinic.

To learn more about perinatal depression, see the National Institute of Mental Health's (NIMH) Perinatal Depression brochure at **www.nimh.nih.gov/perinataldepression**.

Perimenopausal Depression

Perimenopause (the transition into menopause) is a normal phase in a woman's life that can sometimes be challenging. If you are going through perimenopause, you might be experiencing abnormal periods, problems sleeping, mood swings, and hot flashes. Although these symptoms are common, feeling depressed is not. If you are struggling with irritability, anxiety, sadness, or loss of enjoyment at the time of the menopause transition, you may be experiencing perimenopausal depression.

Depression affects each woman differently.

Not every woman who is depressed experiences every symptom. Some women experience only a few symptoms. Others have many. The severity and frequency of symptoms, and how long they last, will vary depending on the individual and the severity of the illness.

Where Can I Learn More About Depression in Women?

The following agencies have additional information on depression in women.

U.S. Department of Health and Human Services, Office on Women's Health: Depression
www.womenshealth.gov/mental-health/mental-health-conditions/depression

U.S. Food and Drug Administration: Women and Depression
www.fda.gov/consumers/women/women-and-depression

Centers for Disease Control and Prevention: Depression Among Women
www.cdc.gov/reproductivehealth/depression

---

4. Depression can be treated.

Even the most severe cases of depression can be treated. Depression is commonly treated with medication, psychotherapy (also called "talk therapy"), or a combination of the two.

Antidepressants are medications commonly used to treat depression. People respond differently to antidepressants, and you may need to try different medicines to find the one that works best. Researchers also are studying and developing other medications for depression, such as brexanolone for postpartum depression, and esketamine. You can learn about recent developments on these and other medications at **www.nimh.nih.gov/news/science-news** under the topic "Treatments."

Studies & Statistics / Depression in Women: 5 Things You Should Know

There are many different types of psychotherapy, such as cognitive behavioral therapy or interpersonal therapy. The particular approach a therapist uses depends on the condition being treated and the training and experience of the therapist. Therapists also may combine and adapt elements of different approaches.

Depression affects each individual differently. There is no "one-size-fits-all" for treatment. It may take some trial and error to find the treatment that works best. You can learn more about the different types of depression treatment, including psychotherapy, medication, and brain stimulation therapies, on the NIMH website at **www.nimh.nih.gov/depression**. Visit the Food and Drug Administration website at **www.fda.gov/drugsatfda** for the latest information on medication approvals, warnings, and patient information guides.

What to Consider When Looking for a Therapist

Therapists and patients work together, and finding a good match is important. The following tips can help you find the right therapist.

Ask about their areas of expertise. Therapists have different professional backgrounds and specialties. You want to find a therapist who has experience working with your specific condition.

Find out what kinds of treatments they use. Ask if those treatments are effective for dealing with your particular mental health problem or issue.

Find out how you'll evaluate progress. Determine how long treatment is expected to last, and when you should expect to gain relief from symptoms and improve your quality of life.

Don't be afraid to keep looking. Rapport and trust are essential. Discussions in therapy are deeply personal, and it's important that you feel comfortable with the therapist you pick.

5. Researchers at the National Institute of Mental Health (NIMH) and across the country are dedicated to women's mental health research.

Researchers continue to study depression to improve the way this medical condition is diagnosed and treated. For example, NIMH researchers are currently working to understand how and why changes in reproductive hormones trigger mood disorders, including postpartum depression, premenstrual dysphoric disorder, and perimenopausal depression.

NIMH scientists are conducting a large number of research studies with patients and healthy volunteers to better understand why some women are at higher risk than others, and how they can translate these findings into new treatments or new uses of existing treatments.

You can play a role in research by joining a clinical trial.

Clinical trials are research studies that look at new ways to prevent, detect, or treat diseases and conditions. The goal of clinical trials is to determine if a new test or treatment works and is safe. Although individuals may benefit from being part of a clinical trial, participants should be aware that the primary purpose of a clinical trial is to gain new scientific knowledge so that others may be better helped in the future.

In addition to volunteer research opportunities for the patient groups listed above, research opportunities for healthy volunteers are also available. Healthy volunteers play a critical role in our studies.

For more information about clinical research and how to find clinical trials being conducted around the country, visit **www.nimh.nih.gov/clinicaltrials**.

Perinatal Depression

National Institute of Mental Health

Perinatal depression is depression that occurs during or after pregnancy. The symptoms can range from mild to severe. In rare cases, the symptoms are severe enough that the health of the mother and baby may be at risk. Perinatal depression can be treated. This brochure describes the signs and symptoms of perinatal depression and how you or a loved one can get help.

Overview

What is perinatal depression?

Perinatal depression is a mood disorder that can affect women during pregnancy and after childbirth. The word "perinatal" refers to the time before and after the birth of a child. Perinatal depression includes depression that begins during pregnancy (called prenatal depression) and depression that begins after the baby is born (called postpartum depression). Mothers with perinatal depression experience feelings of extreme sadness, anxiety, and fatigue that may make it difficult for them to carry out daily tasks, including caring for themselves or others.

What causes perinatal depression?

Perinatal depression is a real medical illness and can affect any mother—regardless of age, race, income, culture, or education. Women are not to blame or at fault for having perinatal depression: it is not brought on by anything a mother has or has not done. Perinatal depression does not have a single cause. Research suggests that perinatal depression is caused by a combination of genetic and environmental factors. Life stress (for example, demands at work or experiences of past trauma), the physical and emotional demands of childbearing and

How is postpartum depression different from the "baby blues"?

The "baby blues" is a term used to describe mild mood changes and feelings of worry, unhappiness, and exhaustion that many women sometimes experience in the first 2 weeks after having a baby. Babies require around-the-clock care, so it's normal for mothers to feel tired or overwhelmed sometimes. If mood changes and feelings of anxiety or unhappiness are severe, or if they last longer than 2 weeks, a woman may have postpartum depression. Women with postpartum depression generally will not feel better unless they receive treatment.

Postpartum Psychosis

Postpartum psychosis (PP) is a severe mental illness that occurs after childbirth. PP is a medical emergency, and it is important to seek help immediately by calling 911 or going to the nearest emergency room. Women who have PP can have delusions (thoughts or beliefs that are not true), hallucinations (seeing, hearing, or smelling things that are not there), mania (a high, elated mood that often seems out of touch with reality), paranoia, and confusion. Women who have PP also may be at risk for harming themselves or their child and should receive help as soon as possible. Recovery is possible with professional help.

caring for a new baby, and changes in hormones that occur during and after pregnancy can contribute to the development of perinatal depression. In addition, women are at greater risk for developing perinatal depression if they have a personal or family history of depression or bipolar disorder or if they have experienced perinatal depression with a previous pregnancy.

Signs and Symptoms

Some women may experience a few symptoms of perinatal depression; others may experience several symptoms. Some of the more common symptoms of perinatal depression include:

- Persistent sad, anxious, or "empty" mood
- Irritability
- Feelings of guilt, worthlessness, hopelessness, or helplessness
- Loss of interest or pleasure in hobbies and activities
- Fatigue or abnormal decrease in energy
- Feeling restless or having trouble sitting still
- Difficulty concentrating, remembering, or making decisions
- Difficulty sleeping (even when the baby is sleeping), awakening early in the morning, or oversleeping
- Abnormal appetite, weight changes, or both
- Aches or pains, headaches, cramps, or digestive problems that do not have a clear physical cause or do not ease even with treatment
- Trouble bonding or forming an emotional attachment with the new baby
- Persistent doubts about the ability to care for the new baby
- **Thoughts about death, suicide, or harming oneself or the baby**

Only a health care provider can help a woman determine whether the symptoms she is feeling are due to perinatal depression or something else. It is important for women who experience any of these symptoms to see a health care provider.

> **If You Know Someone in Crisis:**
> - Dial 911 in an emergency.
> - Call the toll-free **National Suicide Prevention Lifeline** at 1-800-273-TALK (8255), 24 hours a day, 7 days a week. All calls are confidential. To use the Lifeline Chat, visit **https://suicidepreventionlifeline.org**.
> - Contact the **Crisis Text Line** 24 hours a day, 7 days a week, by texting HELLO to 741741.

Treatment

Treatment for perinatal depression is important for the health of both the mother and the baby, as perinatal depression can have serious health effects on both. With proper treatment, most women feel better and their symptoms improve.

Treatment for perinatal depression often includes therapy, medications, or a combination of the two. If these treatments do not reduce symptoms, brain stimulation therapies, such as electroconvulsive therapy, may be an option to explore. Learn more about these therapies by visiting the National Institute of Mental Health's (NIMH) Brain Stimulation Therapies webpage at **www.nimh.nih.gov/braintherapies**. A health care provider can help women choose the best treatment based on their symptoms.

Psychotherapy

Several types of psychotherapy (sometimes called "talk therapy" or "counseling") can help women with perinatal depression. Two examples of evidence-based approaches that have been used to treat perinatal depression include cognitive behavioral therapy and interpersonal therapy.

Cognitive Behavioral Therapy (CBT)
CBT is a type of psychotherapy that can help people with depression and anxiety. It teaches people different ways of thinking, behaving, and reacting to situations. People learn to challenge and change unhelpful patterns of thinking and behavior as a way of improving their depressive and anxious feelings and emotions. CBT can be conducted individually or with a group of people who have similar concerns.

Interpersonal Therapy (IPT)
IPT is an evidence-based therapy that has been used to treat depression, including perinatal depression. It is based on the idea that interpersonal and life events impact mood and vice versa. The goal of IPT is to help people to improve their communication skills within relationships, to develop social support networks, and to develop realistic expectations that allow them to deal with crises or other issues that may be contributing to their depression.

For information on how to identify a mental health professional and questions to ask when considering therapy, visit the NIMH Psychotherapies webpage at **www.nimh.nih.gov/psychotherapies**.

Medication

Women with perinatal depression are most commonly treated with antidepressants, which are medications used to treat depression. They may help improve the way the brain uses certain chemicals that control mood or stress. Women who are pregnant or breastfeeding should notify their health care provider before starting antidepressants so their health care provider can work to minimize the baby's exposure to the medication during pregnancy or breastfeeding. The risk of birth defects and other problems for babies of mothers who take antidepressants during pregnancy is very low; however, women should work with their health care provider to weigh the risks and benefits of treatment and to find the best solution for their situation. Women may need to try several different medications before finding the one that improves their symptoms and has manageable side effects.

Antidepressants take time—usually 6 to 8 weeks—to work, and symptoms such as sleep, appetite, and concentration problems often improve before mood lifts. It is important to give medication a chance before deciding whether or not it works.

Do not stop taking antidepressants without the help of a health care provider. Sometimes people taking antidepressants feel better and then stop taking the medication on their own, and the depression returns. Stopping medications abruptly can cause withdrawal symptoms. When a woman and her health care provider have decided it is time to stop the medication, the health care provider will help her to decrease the dose slowly and safely. To find the latest information about antidepressants, talk to a health care provider and visit this U.S. Food and Drug Administration (FDA) webpage on the use of medications during and after pregnancy: **www.fda.gov/pregnancy**.

Please Note: In some cases, children, teenagers, and young adults under the age of 25 may experience an increase in suicidal thoughts or behavior when taking antidepressants, especially in the first few weeks after starting or when the dose is changed. Patients of all ages taking antidepressants should be watched closely, especially during the first few weeks of treatment.

If suicidal behaviors are observed, notify a health care provider right away. If you or a loved one is in crisis, call 911 for emergency services or contact the National Suicide Prevention Lifeline (Lifeline) at 1-800-273-TALK (8255). To learn more about the Lifeline, visit **https://suicidepreventionlifeline.org**.

After the birth of a child, many women experience a drop in certain hormones, which can lead to feelings of depression. FDA has approved one medication, called brexanolone, specifically to treat severe postpartum depression. Administered in a hospital, this drug works to relieve depression by restoring the levels of these hormones. To learn more, visit **www.fda.gov/news-events/press-announcements/fda-approves-first-treatment-post-partum-depression**.

Researchers continue to study treatment options for perinatal depression. A health care provider can explain the different treatment options and help women choose the treatment that is right for them.

Studies & Statistics / Perinatal Depression

How can family and friends help?

It is important to understand that depression is a medical condition that impacts the mother, the child, and the family. Spouses, partners, family members, and friends may be the first to recognize symptoms of perinatal depression in a new mother. Treatment is central to recovery. Family members can encourage the mother to talk with a health care provider, offer emotional support, and assist with daily tasks such as caring for the baby or the home.

Support or advocacy groups can offer a good source of support and information. One example of this type of group is Postpartum Support International (**www.postpartum.net**); others can be found through online searches.

Learn More About Perinatal Depression

Federal Resources

- Moms' Mental Health Matters
  (*Eunice Kennedy Shriver* National Institute of Child Health and Human Development, National Child & Maternal Health Education Program)
  www.nichd.nih.gov/MaternalMentalHealth
- Postpartum Depression
  (Office on Women's Health, U.S. Department of Health and Human Services)
  www.womenshealth.gov/mental-health/mental-health-conditions/postpartum-depression
- Medicine and Pregnancy
  (U.S. Food and Drug Administration)
  www.fda.gov/pregnancy
- Postpartum Depression
  (MedlinePlus, National Library of Medicine)
  https://medlineplus.gov/postpartumdepression.html
- "Baby Blues"—or Postpartum Depression? video
  (NIMH)
  www.youtube.com/watch?v=6kaCdrvNGZw
- NIMH research studies on postpartum depression
  www.nimh.nih.gov/labs-at-nimh/join-a-study/adults/adults-postpartum-depression.shtml

Participating in Clinical Research

Clinical trials are research studies that look at new ways to prevent, detect, or treat diseases and conditions. Although individuals may benefit from being part of a clinical trial, participants should be aware that the primary purpose of a clinical trial is to gain new scientific knowledge so that others may be better helped in the future.

Researchers at NIMH and around the country conduct many studies with patients and healthy volunteers. Talk to your health care provider about clinical trials, their benefits and risks, and whether one is right for you.

For more information, visit **www.nimh.nih.gov/clinicaltrials**.

Finding Help

Behavioral Health Treatment Services Locator

The Substance Abuse and Mental Health Services Administration (SAMHSA) provides this online resource for locating mental health treatment facilities and programs. Find a facility in your state at **https://findtreatment.samhsa.gov**. For additional resources, visit **www.nimh.nih.gov/findhelp**.

Talking to Your Health Care Provider About Your Mental Health

Communicating well with a health care provider can improve your care and help you both make good choices about your health. Find tips to help prepare for and get the most out of your visit at **www.nimh.nih.gov/talkingtips**. For additional resources, including questions to ask a provider, visit the Agency for Healthcare Research and Quality website at **www.ahrq.gov/questions**.

Seasonal Affective Disorder

From the **NATIONAL INSTITUTE** *of* **MENTAL HEALTH**

What is seasonal affective disorder?

Many people go through short periods of time where they feel sad or not like their usual selves. Sometimes, these mood changes begin and end when the seasons change. People may start to feel "down" when the days get shorter in the fall and winter (also called "winter blues") and begin to feel better in the spring, with longer daylight hours.

In some cases, these mood changes are more serious and can affect how a person feels, thinks, and handles daily activities. If you have noticed significant changes in your mood and behavior whenever the seasons change, you may be suffering from seasonal affective disorder (SAD), a type of depression.

In most cases, SAD symptoms start in the late fall or early winter and go away during the spring and summer; this is known as winter-pattern SAD or winter depression. Some people may experience depressive episodes during the spring and summer months; this is called summer-pattern SAD or summer depression and is less common.

Get Immediate Help

If you or someone you know is in immediate distress or is thinking about hurting themselves, call the **National Suicide Prevention Lifeline** toll-free at 1-800-273-TALK (8255) or the toll-free TTY number at 1-800-799-4TTY (4889). You also can text the Crisis Text Line (HELLO to 741741) or go to the **National Suicide Prevention Lifeline** website at https://suicidepreventionlifeline.org.

What are the signs and symptoms of SAD?

SAD is not considered a separate disorder but is a type of depression characterized by its recurrent seasonal pattern, with symptoms lasting about 4 to 5 months per year. Therefore, the signs and symptoms of SAD include those associated with major depression, and some specific symptoms that differ for winter-pattern and summer-pattern SAD. Not every person with SAD will experience all of the symptoms listed below.

Symptoms of major depression may include:
- Feeling depressed most of the day, nearly every day
- Losing interest in activities you once enjoyed
- Experiencing changes in appetite or weight
- Having problems with sleep
- Feeling sluggish or agitated
- Having low energy
- Feeling hopeless or worthless
- Having difficulty concentrating
- Having frequent thoughts of death or suicide

For winter-pattern SAD, additional specific symptoms may include:
- Oversleeping (hypersomnia)
- Overeating, particularly with a craving for carbohydrates
- Weight gain
- Social withdrawal (feeling like "hibernating")

Specific symptoms for summer-pattern SAD may include:
- Trouble sleeping (insomnia)
- Poor appetite, leading to weight loss
- Restlessness and agitation
- Anxiety
- Episodes of violent behavior

How is SAD diagnosed?

If you think you may be suffering from SAD, talk to your health care provider or a mental health specialist about your concerns. They may have you fill out specific questionnaires to determine if your symptoms meet the criteria for SAD.

To be diagnosed with SAD, a person must meet the following criteria:
- They must have symptoms of major depression or the more specific symptoms listed above.
- The depressive episodes must occur during specific seasons (i.e., only during the winter months or the summer months) for at least 2 consecutive years. However, not all people with SAD do experience symptoms every year.
- The episodes must be much more frequent than other depressive episodes that the person may have had at other times of the year during their lifetime.

Who develops SAD?

Millions of American adults may suffer from SAD, although many may not know they have the condition. SAD occurs much more often in women than in men, and it is more common in those living farther north, where there are shorter daylight hours in the winter. For example, people living in Alaska or New England may be more likely to develop SAD than people living in Florida. In most cases, SAD begins in young adulthood.

SAD is more common in people with major depressive disorder or bipolar disorder, especially bipolar II disorder, which is associated with recurrent depressive and hypomanic episodes (less severe than the full-blown manic episodes typical of bipolar I disorder). Additionally, people with SAD tend to have other mental disorders, such as attention-deficit/hyperactivity disorder, an eating disorder, an anxiety disorder, or panic disorder. Learn more about these disorders by visiting the NIMH website at www.nimh.nih.gov/health.

SAD sometimes runs in families. SAD is more common in people who have relatives with other mental illnesses, such as major depression or schizophrenia.

What causes SAD?

Scientists do not fully understand what causes SAD. Research indicates that people with SAD may have reduced activity of the brain chemical (neurotransmitter) serotonin, which helps regulate mood. Research also suggests that sunlight controls the levels of molecules that help maintain normal serotonin levels, but in people with SAD, this regulation does not function properly, resulting in decreased serotonin levels in the winter.

Other findings suggest that people with SAD produce too much melatonin—a hormone that is central for maintaining the normal sleep-wake cycle. Overproduction of melatonin can increase sleepiness.

Both serotonin and melatonin help maintain the body's daily rhythm that is tied to the seasonal night-day cycle. In people with SAD, the changes in serotonin and melatonin levels disrupt the normal daily rhythms. As a result, they can no longer adjust to the seasonal changes in day length, leading to sleep, mood, and behavior changes.

Deficits in vitamin D may exacerbate these problems because vitamin D is believed to promote serotonin activity. In addition to vitamin D consumed with diet, the body produces vitamin D when exposed to sunlight on the skin. With less daylight in the winter, people with SAD may have lower vitamin D levels, which may further hinder serotonin activity.

Negative thoughts and feelings about the winter and its associated limitations and stresses are common among people with SAD (as well as others). It is unclear whether these are "causes" or "effects" of the mood disorder, but they can be a useful focus of treatment.

Studies & Statistics / Seasonal Affective Disorder

How is SAD treated?

Treatments are available that can help many people with SAD. They fall into four main categories that may be used alone or in combination:

- Light therapy
- Psychotherapy
- Antidepressant medications
- Vitamin D

Talk to your health care provider about which treatment, or combination of treatments, is best for you. For tips for talking with your health care provider, refer to the NIMH fact sheet, Taking Control of Your Mental Health: Tips for Talking With Your Health Care Provider, at **www.nimh.nih.gov/talkingtips**.

Light Therapy

Since the 1980s, light therapy has been a mainstay for the treatment of SAD. It aims to expose people with SAD to a bright light every day to make up for the diminished natural sunshine in the darker months.

For this treatment, the person sits in front of a very bright light box (10,000 lux) every day for about 30 to 45 minutes, usually first thing in the morning, from fall to spring. The light boxes, which are about 20 times brighter than ordinary indoor light, filter out the potentially damaging UV light, making this a safe treatment for most. However, people with certain eye diseases or people taking certain medications that increase sensitivity to sunlight may need to use alternative treatments or use light therapy under medical supervision.

Psychotherapy or "Talk Therapy"

Cognitive behavioral therapy (CBT) is a type of talk therapy aimed at helping people learn how to cope with difficult situations; CBT also has been adapted for people with SAD (CBT-SAD). It is typically conducted in two weekly group sessions for 6 weeks and focuses on replacing negative thoughts related to the winter season (e.g., about the darkness of winter) with more positive thoughts. CBT-SAD also uses a process called behavioral activation, which helps individuals identify and schedule pleasant, engaging indoor or outdoor activities to combat the loss of interest they typically experience in the winter.

When researchers directly compared CBT with light therapy, both treatments were equally effective in improving SAD symptoms. Some symptoms seemed to get better a little faster with light therapy than with CBT. However, a long-term study that followed SAD patients for two winters found that the positive effects of CBT seemed to last longer over time. For more information on psychotherapies, visit **www.nimh.nih.gov/psychotherapies**.

Medications

Because SAD, like other types of depression, is associated with disturbances in serotonin activity, antidepressant medications called selective serotonin reuptake inhibitors (SSRIs) are also used to treat SAD when symptoms occur. These agents can significantly enhance patients' moods. Commonly used SSRIs include fluoxetine, citalopram, sertraline, paroxetine, and escitalopram.

The U.S. Food and Drug Administration (FDA) also has approved another type of antidepressant, bupropion, in an extended-release form, that can prevent recurrence of seasonal major depressive episodes when taken daily from the fall until the following early spring.

All medications can have side effects. Talk to your doctor about the possible risk of using these medications for your condition. You may need to try several different antidepressant medications before finding one that improves your symptoms without causing problematic side effects. For basic information about SSRIs, bupropion, and other mental health medications, visit **www.nimh.nih.gov/medications**. Also, visit the FDA website at **www.fda.gov/drugsatfda** for the most up-to-date information on medications, side effects, and warnings.

Vitamin D

Because many people with SAD often have vitamin D deficiency, nutritional supplements of vitamin D may help improve their symptoms. However, studies testing whether vitamin D is effective in SAD treatment have produced mixed findings, with some results indicating that it is as effective as light therapy but others detecting no effect.

Studies & Statistics / Seasonal Affective Disorder

Can SAD be prevented?

Because the timing of the onset of winter pattern-SAD is so predictable, people with a history of SAD might benefit from starting the treatments mentioned above before the fall to help prevent or reduce the depression. To date, very few studies have investigated this question, and existing studies have found no convincing evidence that starting light therapy or psychotherapy ahead of time could prevent the onset of depression. Only preventive treatment with the antidepressant bupropion prevented SAD in study participants, but it also had a higher risk of side effects. Therefore, people with SAD should discuss with their health care providers if they want to initiate treatment early to prevent depressive episodes.

Are there clinical trials studying SAD?

NIMH supports a wide range of research, including clinical trials that look at new ways to prevent, detect, or treat diseases and conditions—including SAD. Although individuals may benefit from being part of a clinical trial, participants should be aware that the primary purpose of a clinical trial is to gain new scientific knowledge so that others may be better helped in the future.

Researchers at NIMH and around the country conduct clinical trials with patients and healthy volunteers. Talk to your health care provider about clinical trials, their benefits and risks, and whether one is right for you. For more information about clinical research and how to find clinical trials being conducted around the country, visit **www.nimh.nih.gov/clinicaltrials**.

For More Information

MedlinePlus (National Library of Medicine)
https://medlineplus.gov
(En español: https://medlineplus.gov/spanish)

ClinicalTrials.gov
www.clinicaltrials.gov
(En español: https://salud.nih.gov/investigacion-clinica)

National Institute of Mental Health
Office of Science Policy, Planning, and Communications
Science Writing, Press, and Dissemination Branch
Phone: 1-866-615-6464
Email: nimhinfo@nih.gov
www.nimh.nih.gov

Reprints

This publication is in the public domain and may be reproduced or copied without permission from NIMH. Citation of NIMH as a source is appreciated. To learn more about using NIMH publications, visit **www.nimh.nih.gov/reprints**.

NIH Publication No. 20-MH-8138

Follow NIMH on Social Media @NIMHgov

Children and Mental Health
Is This Just a Stage?

From the **NATIONAL INSTITUTE** *of* **MENTAL HEALTH**

Mental Health in Childhood

Raising a child can be challenging. Even under the best circumstances, their behaviors and emotions can change frequently and rapidly. All children are sad, anxious, irritable, or aggressive at times, or they occasionally find it challenging to sit still, pay attention, or interact with others. In most cases, these are just typical developmental phases. However, such behaviors may indicate a more serious problem in some children.

Mental disorders can begin in childhood. Examples include anxiety disorders, attention-deficit/hyperactivity disorder (ADHD), autism spectrum disorder, depression and other mood disorders, eating disorders, and post-traumatic stress disorder (PTSD). Without treatment, these mental health conditions can prevent children from reaching their full potential. Many adults who seek mental health treatment reflect on the impact of mental disorders on their childhood and wish they had received help sooner.

When to Seek Help

How can you tell the difference between challenging behaviors and emotions that are a normal part of growing up and those that are cause for concern? In general, consider seeking help if your child's behavior persists for a few weeks or longer; causes distress for your child or your family; or interferes with your child's functioning at school, at home, or with friends. **If your child's behavior is unsafe, or if your child talks about wanting to hurt themselves or someone else, seek help immediately.**

Young children may benefit from an evaluation and treatment if they:

- Have frequent tantrums or are intensely irritable much of the time
- Often talk about fears or worries
- Complain about frequent stomachaches or headaches with no known medical cause
- Are in constant motion and cannot sit quietly (*except* when they are watching videos or playing video games)
- Sleep too much or too little, have frequent nightmares, or seem sleepy during the day
- Are not interested in playing with other children or have difficulty making friends
- Struggle academically or have experienced a recent decline in grades
- Repeat actions or check things many times out of fear that something bad may happen

Older children and adolescents may benefit from an evaluation and treatment if they:

- Have lost interest in things that they used to enjoy
- Have low energy
- Sleep too much or too little or seem sleepy throughout the day
- Are spending more and more time alone and avoid social activities with friends or family
- Diet or exercise excessively, or fear gaining weight
- Engage in self-harm behaviors (such as cutting or burning their skin)
- Smoke, drink, or use drugs
- Engage in risky or destructive behavior alone or with friends
- Have thoughts of suicide
- Have periods of highly elevated energy and activity and require much less sleep than usual
- Say that they think someone is trying to control their mind or that they hear things that other people cannot hear

Learn more about warning signs at **www.nimh.nih.gov/children.**

Get Immediate Help

If you, your child, or someone you know is in immediate distress or is thinking about hurting themselves, call the **National Suicide Prevention Lifeline** toll-free at 1-800-273-TALK (8255) or the toll-free TTY number at 1-800-799-4TTY (4889). You also can text the Crisis Text Line (HELLO to 741741) or go to the **National Suicide Prevention Lifeline** website at https://suicidepreventionlifeline.org.

Studies & Statistics / Children and Mental Health: Is This Just a Stage?

First Steps for Parents

If you are concerned about your child's mental health, you can start by talking with others who frequently interact with your child. For example, ask their teacher about your child's behavior in school, at daycare, or on the playground.

You can talk with your child's pediatrician or health care provider and describe the child's behavior, as well as what you have observed and learned from talking with others. You also can ask the health care provider for a referral to a mental health professional who has experience and expertise in treating children. (See the section, Choosing a Mental Health Professional, for additional information.)

Choosing a Mental Health Professional

When looking for a mental health professional for your child, you may want to begin by asking your child's pediatrician for a referral. If you need help identifying a provider in your area, you can call the Substance Abuse and Mental Health Services Administration (SAMHSA) Treatment Referral Helpline at 1-800-662-HELP (4357). You also can search SAMHSA's online Behavioral Health Treatment Services Locator (**https://findtreatment.samhsa.gov**), which lists facilities and programs that provide mental health services. It's especially important to look for a mental health professional with training and experience treating children, particularly your child's specific problems.

Asking questions and providing information to your child's health care provider can improve your child's care. Talking with the health care provider builds trust and leads to better results, quality, safety, and satisfaction. Here are some questions you can ask when meeting with prospective treatment providers:

- Do you use treatment approaches that are supported by research?
- Do you involve parents in the treatment? If so, how are parents involved?
- Will there be "homework" between sessions?
- How will progress be evaluated?
- How soon can we expect to see progress?
- How long should treatment last?

To find ideas for starting the conversation with your health care provider, visit the Agency for Healthcare Research and Quality website (**www.ahrq.gov/questions**) and the National Institute of Mental Health (NIMH) website (**www.nimh.nih.gov/talkingtips**). Additional information about finding a qualified mental health professional is available at **www.nimh.nih.gov/findhelp** and through other organizations listed in the More Information and Resources section of this fact sheet.

Assessing Your Child's Behavior

An evaluation by a mental health professional can help clarify problems underlying your child's behavior and provide reassurance or recommendations for the next steps. An evaluation offers an opportunity to learn about your child's strengths and weaknesses and to determine which interventions might be most helpful.

A comprehensive evaluation of a child's mental health includes the following:

- An interview with the parents to discuss the child's developmental history, temperament, relationships with friends and family, medical history, interests, abilities, and any prior treatment. It is important for the mental health professional to get a picture of the child's current situation—for example, a recent change in schools, an illness in the family, or another change that affects the child's daily life.
- Information gathering from the child's school, such as standardized tests and reports on behavior, capabilities, and difficulties.
- If needed, an interview with the child and the mental health professional's testing and behavioral observations.

Treatment Options

The mental health professional will review the evaluation results to help determine if a child's behavior is related to changes or stresses at home or school or if it's the result of a disorder for which they would recommend treatment. Treatment recommendations may include:

- **Psychotherapy ("talk therapy")**. There are many different approaches to psychotherapy, including structured psychotherapies directed at specific conditions. For more information about types of psychotherapies, visit the NIMH website at **www.nimh.nih.gov/psychotherapies**. Effective psychotherapy for children always includes:

- Parent involvement in the treatment
- Teaching the child skills to practice at home or school (between-session "homework assignments")
- Measures of progress (such as rating scales and improvements on "homework assignments") that are tracked over time.

- **Medications.** As with adults, the type of medicines used for children depends on the diagnosis and may include antidepressants, stimulants, mood stabilizers, or other medications. For general information on specific classes of medications, visit **www.nimh.nih.gov/medications**. Medications are often used in combination with psychotherapy. If multiple health care providers or specialists are involved, treatment information should be shared and coordinated to achieve the best results.
- **Family counseling.** Including family members in treatment can help them to understand how a child's challenges may affect relationships with parents and siblings.
- **Support for parents.** Individual or group sessions for parents that include training and the opportunity to talk with other parents can provide new strategies for supporting a child and managing difficult behavior in a positive way. The therapist also can coach parents on how to communicate and work with schools on accommodations.

To find information about treatment options for specific disorders, visit the NIMH website at **www.nimh.nih.gov/health**. Researchers continue to explore new treatment options for childhood mental disorders; the Participating in a Research Study for Children section in this fact sheet provides information on participating in clinical research.

Working With the School

Children who have behavioral or emotional challenges that interfere with success in school may benefit from plans or accommodations provided under laws that prevent discrimination against children with disabilities. Your child's health care providers can help you communicate with the school.

A first step may be to ask the school whether accommodations such as an individualized education program may be appropriate for your child. Accommodations might include measures such as providing a child with a tape recorder for taking notes, allowing more time for tests, or adjusting seating in the classroom to reduce distraction. There are many sources of information on what schools can and, in some cases, must provide for children who would benefit from accommodations and how parents can request evaluation and services for their child:

- There are Parent Training and Information Centers and Community Parent Resource Centers located throughout the United States. The Center for Parent Information and Resources website (**www.parentcenterhub.org/find-your-center**) lists centers in each state.
- The U.S. Department of Education website (**www.ed.gov**) has detailed information on laws that establish mechanisms for providing children with accommodations tailored to their individual needs and aimed at helping them succeed in school. The Department also has a website on the Individuals with Disabilities Education Act (**https://sites.ed.gov/idea**), and its Office for Civil Rights (**www.ed.gov/about/offices/list/ocr/frontpage/pro-students/disability-pr.html**) has information on other federal laws that prohibit discrimination based on disability in public programs, such as schools.
- Many of the organizations listed in the section, More Information and Resources, also offer information on working with schools as well as more general information on disorders affecting children.

Studies & Statistics / Children and Mental Health: Is This Just a Stage?

More Information and Resources

Information on specific disorders is available on the NIMH website (www.nimh.nih.gov/health).

The following organizations and agencies have information on symptoms, treatments, and support for childhood mental disorders. Some offer guidance for working with schools and finding mental health professionals. Participating in voluntary groups can provide an avenue for connecting with other parents dealing with similar issues.

Please Note: This resource list is provided for informational purposes only. It is not comprehensive and does not constitute an endorsement by NIMH, the National Institutes of Health (NIH), the U.S. Department of Health and Human Services, or the U.S. government.

- American Academy of Child and Adolescent Psychiatry, Facts For Families Guide (www.aacap.org/FFF)
- Association for Behavioral and Cognitive Therapies (www.abct.org)
- Centers for Disease Control and Prevention, Children's Mental Health (www.cdc.gov/childrensmentalhealth)
- Child Mind Institute (https://childmind.org/topics-a-z)
- Mental Health America (www.mhanational.org)
- National Alliance on Mental Illness (www.nami.org)
- National Association of School Psychologists (www.nasponline.org/resources-and-publications/families-and-educators)
- National Federation of Families (www.ffcmh.org)
- Society of Clinical Child and Adolescent Psychology, Effective Child Therapy (https://effectivechildtherapy.org)
- StopBullying.gov (www.stopbullying.gov)

Research on Disorders Affecting Children

NIMH conducts and supports research to help find new and improved ways to diagnose and treat mental disorders that occur in childhood. This research includes studies of risk factors—including those related to genetics, experience, and the environment—which may provide clues to how these disorders develop and how to identify them early.

NIMH also supports efforts to develop and test new interventions, including behavioral, psychotherapeutic, and medication treatments. Researchers are also seeking to determine whether the beneficial effects of treatment in childhood continue into adolescence and adulthood.

Participating in a Research Study for Children

Children are not little adults, yet they are often given medications and treatments that have been tested only in adults. Research shows that, compared to adults, children respond differently to medications and treatments, both physically and mentally. The way to get the best treatments for children is through research designed specifically for them.

Researchers at NIMH and around the country conduct clinical trials with patients and healthy volunteers. Talk to your health care provider about clinical trials, their benefits and risks, and whether one is right for your child. For more information about clinical research and how to find clinical trials being conducted around the country, visit www.nimh.nih.gov/clinicaltrials.

For More Information

MedlinePlus (National Library of Medicine)

https://medlineplus.gov
(En español: https://medlineplus.gov/spanish)

ClinicalTrials.gov

www.clinicaltrials.gov
(En español: https://salud.nih.gov/investigacion-clinica)

National Institute of Mental Health
Office of Science Policy, Planning, and Communications
Science Writing, Press, and Dissemination Branch
Phone: 1-866-615-6464
Email: nimhinfo@nih.gov
www.nimh.nih.gov

Reprints

This publication is in the public domain and may be reproduced or copied without permission from NIMH. Citation of NIMH as a source is appreciated. To learn more about using NIMH publications, visit www.nimh.nih.gov/reprints.

Follow NIMH on Social Media @NIMHgov

NIH Publication No. 21-MH-8085
Revised 2021

Studies & Statistics / Children and Mental Health: Is This Just a Stage?

Teen Depression: More than just moodiness

Being a teenager can be tough, but it shouldn't feel hopeless. If you have been feeling sad most of the time for a few weeks or longer and you're not able to concentrate or do the things you used to enjoy, talk to a trusted adult about depression.

Do I have depression?

- Do you often feel sad, anxious, worthless, or even "empty"?
- Have you lost interest in activities you used to enjoy?
- Do you get easily frustrated, irritable, or angry?
- Do you find yourself withdrawing from friends and family?
- Are your grades dropping?
- Have your eating or sleeping habits changed?
- Have you experienced any fatigue or memory loss?
- Have you thought about suicide or harming yourself?

Depression looks different for everyone. You might have many of the symptoms listed above or just a few.

How do I get help for depression?

- **Talk to a trusted adult** (such as your parent or guardian, teacher, or school counselor) about how you've been feeling.
- **Ask your doctor** about options for professional help. Depression can be treated with psychotherapy (also called "talk therapy"), medication, or a combination of medication and talk therapy.
- **Try to spend time with friends or family,** even if you don't feel like you want to.
- **Stay active and exercise,** even if it's just going for a walk. Physical activity releases chemicals, such as endorphins, in your brain that can help you feel better.
- **Try to keep a regular sleep schedule.**
- **Eat healthy foods.**

You're not alone, and help is available. You can feel better.
To get help, call or text the 988 Suicide & Crisis Lifeline at 988 or chat at 988lifeline.org.

NIH National Institute of Mental Health

nimh.nih.gov/depression
NIMH Identifier No. OM 22-4321

The U.S. Surgeon General's Framework for

Workplace Mental Health & Well-Being

2022

Workplaces Can Be Engines of Mental Health and Well-Being

There are more than 160 million people who are a part of the U.S. workforce today.[1] Work is one of the most vital parts of life, powerfully shaping our health, wealth, and well-being.[2] At its best, work provides us the ability to support ourselves and our loved ones, and can also provide us with a sense of meaning, opportunities for growth, and a community. When people thrive at work, they are more likely to feel physically and mentally healthy overall, and to contribute positively to their workplace.[3] This creates both a responsibility and unique opportunity for leaders to create workplace environments that support the health and well-being of workers.

Although the COVID-19 pandemic may have accelerated the evolution of work and the conversation around workplace mental health and well-being, broad recognition and appreciation for the relationship between the work environment, culture, community, and our health preceded the pandemic.[4,5,6,7] While many challenges outside the workplace may impact well-being—from economic inequality, food insecurity, and housing insecurity to household, educational, and medical debt—there are still many ways that organizations can function as engines for mental health and well-being.[8,9] Organizational leaders, managers, supervisors, and workers alike have an unprecedented opportunity to examine the role of work in our lives and explore ways to better enable all workers to thrive within the workplace and beyond.

The Case for Workplace Mental Health and Well-Being

"Mental health in the workplace: It's not a nice-to-have, it's a must-have."

Human Resources Leader and Business Consultant

Workplace mental health and well-being is a critical priority for public health. It has numerous and cascading impacts for the health of individual workers and their families, organizational productivity, the bottom-line for businesses, and the U.S. economy. The U.S. has a long history of labor organizing that has, over the years, established protections for workers through federal and state laws. The U.S. Department of Labor (DOL) was established "to foster, promote and develop the welfare of working people, to improve their working conditions, and to enhance their opportunities for profitable employment."[10] Since then, laws including the Fair Labor Standards Act, the Civil Rights Act, and the Americans with Disabilities Act have all established crucial worker protections including the minimum wage, overtime regulations, standards for youth employment, and protections from discrimination, across government and private organizations.[11,12,13,14] While Federal and state laws represent a minimum floor of protections for workers, organizations and employers can do more.[15] Consensus scientific bodies and professional societies like the National Academy of Medicine and the American Psychological Association, along with U.S. government agencies such as the Department of Veterans Affairs, the Occupational Safety and Health Administration (OSHA) at DOL, the Substance Abuse and Mental Health Services Administration (SAMHSA), and the Centers for Disease Control and Prevention (CDC) National Institutes of Occupational Safety and Health (NIOSH), have called national attention to the effects of the workplace on health.[7,16,17,18,19,20,21]

Workers manage daily stress that affects their health and organizational performance. These stressors arise from heavy workloads, long commutes, unpredictable schedules, limited autonomy, long work hours, multiple jobs, low wages, and a variety of other work-related challenges on top of responsibilities outside of the workplace.[22,23] Some workers may face other challenges in the workplace, such as hostile or dangerous working conditions, harassment, and discrimination.[24] Research suggests that five workplace attributes are most predictive of whether workers refer to their organization's culture as "toxic": disrespectful, non-inclusive, unethical, cutthroat, and abusive.[24]

Chronic stress leads to overactivation of the "fight or flight" response, among other responses, and can have negative effects on numerous organ systems in the body.[25] Elevated stress hormones disrupt sleep, increase muscle tension, and impair metabolic function.[26] Stress can increase one's vulnerability to infection, the risk for diabetes, and the risk for other chronic health conditions.[27] In fact, chronic stress has also been linked to a higher risk of developing diseases such as high blood

49

Studies & Statistics / Workplace Mental Health & Well-Being

pressure, high cholesterol, heart disease, obesity, cancer, and autoimmune diseases.[25] Such stress can also contribute to mental and behavioral health challenges, including depression, anxiety, suicidal ideation, and substance misuse, and can have negative impacts on the mental health of the children and families of workers.[27, 28, 29, 30, 31]

Competing work and personal demands can also negatively impact the health and well-being of workers in a variety of ways. These role conflicts can magnify psychological stress, increase the risk for health behaviors such as smoking, unhealthy dietary habits, alcohol and substance use, and medication overuse, and cause disruptions to relationships both at work and at home.[32, 33]

The COVID-19 pandemic brought the relationship between work and well-being into clearer focus.[5] Workers across the world reported feeling more stressed in 2021 than they were in 2020.[34] In a separate 2021 survey of 1,500 U.S. adult workers across for-profit, nonprofit and government sectors, 76% of respondents reported at least one symptom of a mental health condition, an increase of 17 percentage points in just two years.[35] Furthermore, 84% of respondents reported at least one workplace factor (e.g., emotionally draining work, challenges with work-life balance, or lack of recognition) that had a negative impact on their mental health. In a survey of more than 2,000 workers conducted by the American Psychological Association by 2022, low salaries, long hours, and the lack of opportunity for advancement were commonly reported as key workplace stressors.[36] Among these same workers, however, **seven in ten reported that their employer is more concerned about the mental health of workers than before.**

> *76% of respondents reported at least one symptom of a mental health condition, an increase of 17 percentage points in just two years.*

While the pandemic did not create these work conditions, it worsened many of them. Rates of anxiety, depression, social isolation, job burnout, and insecurity related to food, housing, and income rose between March 2020 and mid-2022.[5, 37, 38] The Kaiser Family Foundation found that 62% of health workers surveyed reported that pandemic-related worry and stress negatively affected their mental health, while 49% of health workers reported the pandemic negatively impacted their physical health, including sleep issues and frequent headaches.[39] In a 2022 survey, the CDC found that nearly half of the 26,069 U.S. public health workers they surveyed experienced at least one symptom of a mental health condition during the COVID-19 pandemic, including anxiety, PTSD, and depression, and one in twelve experienced suicidal thoughts.[40] *Addressing Health Worker Burnout: The U.S. Surgeon General's Advisory on Building a Thriving Health Workforce*, released in May 2022, further highlights this crisis that has been exacerbated in the setting of the COVID-19 pandemic.[38]

Workers are still finding it challenging to address these burgeoning negative impacts on their mental health and well-being. Mental Health America assessed the perceptions of over 11,000 workers across 17 industries in the United States in 2021.[33] They found that nearly 80% of workers surveyed report that their workplace stress affects their relationships with friends, family, and coworkers, and only 38% of those who know about their organization's mental health services would feel comfortable using them. Organizational leaders must prioritize mental health in the workplace by addressing structural barriers to seeking help and decreasing stigma around accessing mental health support in the workplace.

It is important to note that workers face different challenges based on their occupation, setting, organizational structures, and personal characteristics such as race, sex (including pregnancy, gender identity, and sexual orientation), immigration status, national origin, age, disability, or genetic information. Workforce demographics in the U.S. are shifting, with increases in racial and ethnic minority workers, including foreign-born workers.[41] This population is highly concentrated in non-standard work arrangements (including day-labor, seasonal workers, etc.) which pose unique occupational health safety risks. As the workforce changes, it is imperative that workplaces be intentional in preventing institutionalized bias due to organizational design, work arrangements, technologies, or global climate change.

In addition to the many impacts on the health and well-being of workers themselves, **workplace well-being can affect productivity and organizational performance.** When people feel anxious or depressed, the quality, pace, and performance of their work tends to decline.[42] Workforce shortages are also exacerbated due to early exit from the workforce or missed workdays due to health concerns, work-life conflicts, or burnout.[38,43] All of these challenges have been magnified by many factors over the years, including the rise in chronic diseases, growing mental health concerns, and more recently Long COVID, a post-COVID-19 infection syndrome that can affect multiple organ systems, leading to persistent shortness of breath, fatigue, and impaired concentration.[44,45,46,47]

In addition to the many impacts on the health and well-being of workers themselves, workplace well-being can affect productivity and organizational performance.

All workers are part of larger communities, and their well-being is also impacted by external socio-economic, political, and cultural factors that may be outside of an organization's control. These include what is known as the "U.S. health disadvantage": poorer health, shorter lifespans, higher health care costs, and less access to health care compared with other wealthy countries.[48,49]

Studies & Statistics / Workplace Mental Health & Well-Being

Even so, organizational efforts to invest in workplace well-being, as well as in local organizations and community development, can in turn support the development of a happier, healthier, more productive workforce and contribute to the success and economic well-being of an organization.[37, 50, 51, 52, 53, 54]

Chronic diseases and injuries in the U.S. workforce costs employers more than half a trillion dollars in lost productivity each year.[55] Decades of research have also shown that prioritizing and investing in efforts that address workplace well-being can have significant returns impacting the bottom line. Workplace well-being efforts have notable effects on organizational costs—for example, those associated with reductions in absenteeism and annual health care claims. Organizations that focused on worker well-being have also reported higher productivity and retention rates.

Work is an important social determinant of worker health. Improving the work environment to support workplace mental health and well-being calls for workers at the table. The U.S. labor movement has improved worker well-being by advocating for health care and occupational health and safety regulations and protections, especially in eliminating workplace hazards and preventing accidents.[56] Many components in this Framework have been successfully fought for and won in workplaces across the U.S. by workers themselves, including paid sick and family leave, living wages, and social support at work.[57, 58] Creating an environment where workers' voices are supported without fear of job loss or retaliation is an essential component of healthy organizations.[59, 60]

> *Creating an environment where workers' voices are supported without fear of job loss or retaliation is an essential component of healthy organizations.*

The Surgeon General's Framework for Workplace Mental Health & Well-Being is intended to spark organizational dialogue and change in the workplace. It can also catalyze areas for further research, strategic investment, and broader policy advancement. Centered around the foundational principles of equity and the voices of all workers, it includes five Essentials and necessary components for addressing workplace mental health and well-being based on human needs (see Figure on following page). Organizations can use this Framework to support their workplaces as engines of mental health and well-being.

Studies & Statistics / Workplace Mental Health & Well-Being

Five Essentials for Workplace Mental Health & Well-Being

Centered on the worker voice and equity, these five Essentials support workplaces as engines of well-being. Each Essential is grounded in two human needs, shared across industries and roles.

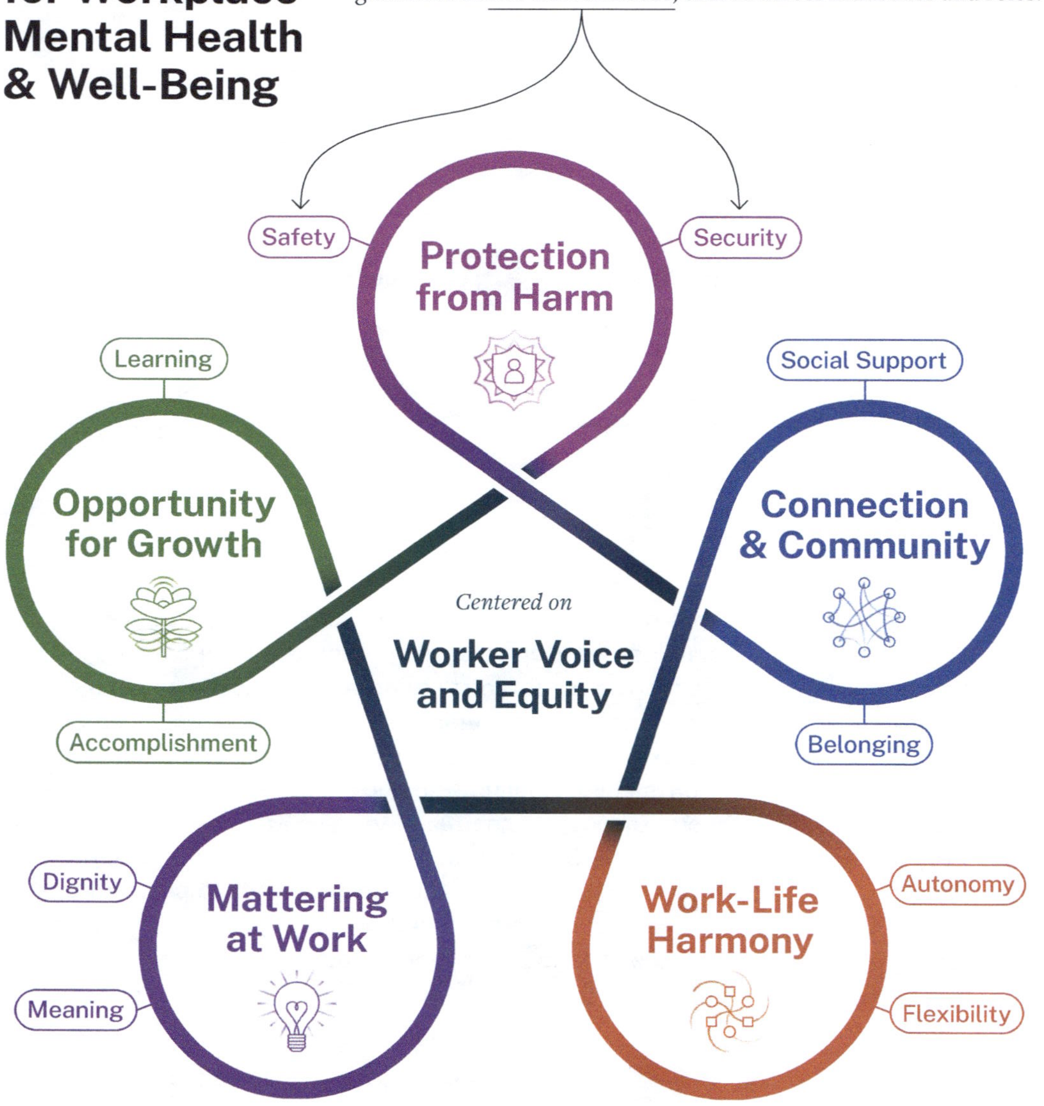

Protection from Harm
- Safety
- Security

Connection & Community
- Social Support
- Belonging

Work-Life Harmony
- Autonomy
- Flexibility

Mattering at Work
- Dignity
- Meaning

Opportunity for Growth
- Learning
- Accomplishment

Centered on *Worker Voice and Equity*

Components

Creating a plan with all workers to enact these components can help reimagine workplaces as engines of well-being.

Protection from Harm
- Prioritize workplace physical and psychological safety
- Enable adequate rest
- Normalize and support mental health
- Operationalize DEIA* norms, policies, and programs

Connection & Community
- Create cultures of inclusion and belonging
- Cultivate trusted relationships
- Foster collaboration and teamwork

Work-Life Harmony
- Provide more autonomy over how work is done
- Make schedules as flexible and predictable as possible
- Increase access to paid leave
- Respect boundaries between work and non-work time

Mattering at Work
- Provide a living wage
- Engage workers in workplace decisions
- Build a culture of gratitude and recognition
- Connect individual work with organizational mission

Opportunity for Growth
- Offer quality training, education, and mentoring
- Foster clear, equitable pathways for career advancement
- Ensure relevant, reciprocal feedback

*Diversity, Equity, Inclusion & Accessibility

Office of the U.S. Surgeon General

53

Studies & Statistics / Workplace Mental Health & Well-Being

Framework Development and Application

This Framework contributes to decades of public health, economic, sociological, and organizational psychology research. It is informed by the voices of many workers and unions based in a variety of occupations and sectors, including retail, childcare, education, hospitality and travel, agriculture, construction, manufacturing, grocery, technology, finance, utilities, government, and health care. It is also informed by conversations with workplace leaders, as well as academic and industry experts. While not an exhaustive literature review of the evidence base, the Framework was developed based on desk research as well as numerous conversations and expert roundtables. The framework includes Five Essentials for Workplace Mental Health & Well-Being:

The Framework can be viewed as a starting point for organizations in updating and institutionalizing policies, processes, and practices to best support the mental health and well-being of workers. Ensuring workplace well-being requires an intentional, ongoing effort by employers and leaders across all levels, with the voices of workers and equity (i.e., a more equitable policy and practice environment) at the center.[61] The Five Essentials can guide leaders, managers, and supervisors, as well as empower workers, to identify and communicate about priority organizational changes needed. Workplace leaders and supervisors across all industries can have a powerful impact on worker well-being by setting organizational culture, shaping the day-to-day experiences of workers, and prioritizing workforce engagement. The most effective leaders express compassion, empathy, and generosity; communicate openly, often, and clearly; and practice human- and wellness-centered leadership by recognizing the connection between individual strengths, growth, and organizational change.[62, 63, 64]

The Five Essentials can be adapted across different workplaces with the recognition that some components may be adapted more extensively for organizations with access to greater resources. Organizations should build in systems for accountability, review existing worker engagement survey data to better understand the needs among disproportionately impacted groups, utilize validated tools for measuring worker well-being, and ensure processes for continuous quality improvement.[65, 66, 67] These systems are critical to sustain workplace structures and practices that advance rather than harm the health and well-being of all workers long-term.[68, 69, 70, 71]

Protection from Harm

Mattering at Work

Connection & Community

Opportunity for Growth

Work-Life Harmony

Studies & Statistics / Workplace Mental Health & Well-Being

Essential 1:
Protection from Harm

> *"The leaders of a company set the tone, and if they're willing to talk about mental health, that trickles all the way down."*
>
> — Workplace Wellness Leader, Technology Sector

The first Essential of this Framework is **Protection from Harm**. This Essential rests on two human needs: **safety** and **security**. More than two-in-five workers surveyed by the American Psychological Association in 2022 reported that health and safety concerns negatively affect their stress level at work.[72]

Workplace safety means all workers are in a safe and healthful work environment, protected from physical harm, injury, illness, and death.[73] This is done through continued efforts to minimize occupational hazards and physical workplace violence, as well as psychological harm such as bias, discrimination, emotional hostility, bullying, and harassment.[74,75] Security builds on safety to include financial, and job security, given the negative effects that layoffs and job loss can have on the workers and their families.[76] (Discussed further in Essential 4).

55

Studies & Statistics / **Workplace Mental Health & Well-Being**

Protection from Harm
Components

- Prioritize workplace physical and psychological safety
- Enable adequate rest
- Normalize and support mental health
- Operationalize Diversity, Equity, Inclusion, and Accessibility (DEIA) norms, policies, and programs

Prioritize workplace physical and psychological safety

The first component of this Essential is to *prioritize workplace physical and psychological health and safety*. People cannot perform well at work if they feel physically or psychologically unsafe.[77,78,79] When workers feel psychologically safe, they speak up without the risk of being punished, retaliated against or humiliated, and without fear of these risks. Racial and ethnic minority workers are at higher risk for workplace injuries, which has led to an increased frequency and prevalence of work-related disabilities for non-Hispanic Black and foreign-born Hispanic workers.[80] Workers such as migrant and seasonal agricultural workers, who are often foreign-born Hispanic workers, may also be disproportionately affected by climate change and subjected to extreme heat stress.[81] They may also face discriminatory practices such as living in fear of potential deportation or losing their job if they report injuries.

To fully address workplace violence, organizations must take all steps to comply with regulations and regularly improve related policies and programs.[79,82,83] Workplace violence is disproportionately experienced by women, whether it comes from a customer, a coworker, or partner who threatens or harms them at work.[84] Between fiscal years 2018 and 2021, the U.S. Equal Employment Opportunity Commission received a total of 98,411 charges alleging harassment (e.g., race, national origin) under any basis and 27,291 charges alleging sexual harassment.[85] Of these, 43% were concurrently filed with a retaliation charge. 62% of all harassment charges were filed by women, and 78% of the sexual harassment charges were filed by women. Of the 1,945 sexual harassment charges filed concurrently with a race charge, 71% were filed by Black/African women. Importantly, the majority of individuals who say they experience harassment never take formal action. Organizational leaders can do more to encourage reporting by protecting workers from harassment and potential retaliation.[85] Certain industries are also at greater risk for workplace violence, including health care, law enforcement and correctional officers, education, and service providers, with taxi drivers being more than 20 times more likely to be murdered on the job than other workers.[86,87,88]

Mitigating harmful impacts in the work environment begins with a review by employers of all existing occupational health and safety legal requirements, and their own workplace policies and conditions to ensure standards and regular compliance.[89] There are numerous resources and validated tools from the CDC and OSHA that organizations can use to guide these efforts (see resources on page 16). Organizations can request technical

56

Studies & Statistics / Workplace Mental Health & Well-Being

assistance, education, and training from OSHA for information on legal requirements, and periodic guidance on and monitoring of implementation of policies and measures to protect worker health and well-being.

Leaders at all organizational levels can collaborate with workers to examine and eliminate workplace hazards, then design, implement, and regularly evaluate programs for workplace safety.[62] Efforts can include, but are not limited to, workstation redesign to prevent injury, including work-related access to lethal means (a risk factor for suicide among workers); ensuring policies for infection prevention and control, and prevention of heat-related illnesses. In addition to specific efforts to prevent physical injury, leaders can collaborate with workers to promote total worker safety. Efforts can include, but are not limited to, increasing access to workplace training and job tools in multiple languages, examining workload and adequacy of resources to meet job demands (e.g. staffing, coverage), reducing long working hours, and eliminating policies and productivity metrics that cause harm (e.g. limiting worker rest or bathroom breaks).[8,90,91,92,93]

Enable adequate rest

The second component is to enable adequate rest. Insufficient rest, whether lack of sleep or lack of quality rest, or from long work hours, night shift work, stress, anxiety, pain, health conditions, medications, caffeine, alcohol, or possibly from lack of refresh breaks or working multiple jobs, can impair the physical, emotional, and mental health of workers.[94] One meta-analysis found that workers who did not get adequate sleep were 1.62 times as likely to have a workplace injury than those who did.[95] Long work hours have been shown to raise workers' risk for exhaustion, anxiety, and depression.[96] Fatigue diminishes productivity as the risk of burnout soars.[97,98] When workers have adequate rest at work, they are less vulnerable to workplace mistakes and injuries.[96,99] Workplace leaders can consider the length of working hours, overtime shifts, and opportunities for offline rest and refresh time.

Normalize and support mental health

Third, organizations can further *normalize and support mental health* while decreasing stigma at work by validating challenges, communicating mental health and well-being as priorities, and offering both support and prevention services. Leaders and managers throughout an organization must be supported to create a culture of inclusivity and to normalize mental health care. This culture includes modeling, communicating, regularly promoting, and supporting workers' access to services throughout all channels of worker engagement. This should also include training and support for supervisors at all levels with resources, including on-call services such as workplace Employee Assistance Programs (EAP) which remain significantly underutilized.[100,101] Organizations can regularly evaluate EAP utilization, and strive to promote, improve, and supplement them based on worker needs. Employers should review benefits packages and provide comprehensive health care coverage that includes access to mental health and substance use care and treatment. Organizations can further make mental health care more easily accessible while ensuring confidentiality by facilitating access disabilities face discrimination and steep employment disparities. As of 2021 U.S. data, only 19% of persons with a disability were employed, compared to 63% of persons without a disability.[109] Employers are required to provide reasonable accommodations to qualified individuals with disabilities. Job Accommodation Network (JAN) and Administration for Community Living's Americans with Disabilities Act National Network provide free training and resources for employees, employers, and job applicants.[110] The White House Executive Order 14035 on DEIA, the U.S. Equal Employment Opportunity Commission, and the U.S. Department of Labor Office of Disability Employment Policy also offer additional resources in these areas.[111, 112, 113]

to both on-site and off-site after-hours care, encouraging time off for mental health care, and supporting access to quality and affordable mental health care services, including telehealth. Workplace leaders can further normalize mental health by supporting organizational and local efforts to address stigma, such as by signing on to the National Alliance for Mental Illness StigmaFree Company Pledge.[102]

Operationalize Diversity, Equity, Inclusion, and Accessibility (DEIA) norms, policies, and programs

The fourth and final component is to *operationalize DEIA norms, policies, and programs*. Prioritizing DEIA norms means operationalizing relevant policies and programs in ways that ensure safety. This includes confronting structural racism, microaggressions, ableism, and implicit bias.[103, 104] In inclusive workplace cultures, all workers, including those with disabilities and from diverse racial and socioeconomic backgrounds, feel safe to be authentic and express their feelings because they trust that their coworkers welcome and value their unique perspectives.[33, 105] When diversity is celebrated as a source of strength, workers experience less stress and anxiety as bias and prejudice is not tolerated.[106, 107] Inclusive leadership is vital for fostering diversity among teams and is required to support a work environment where all team members feel valued and represented.[33, 108]

DEIA also includes considerations for people with disabilities to ensure equitable access to employment, as well as workplace participation, accommodations, and modifications. People with

Studies & Statistics / Workplace Mental Health & Well-Being

Box 1

Protection from Harm
Resources

Manuals, Guidebooks, Training

- Americans with Disabilities Act National Network
- Fundamentals of Total Worker Health® Approaches Centers for Disease Control and Prevention (CDC) / National Institute for Occupational Safety and Health (NIOSH)
- "What is a Safety Climate?" CDC/NIOSH Webinar
- Sleep: An Important Health and Safety Concern at Work CDC Workplace Health Resource Center
- Workforce GPS Guide: Beyond the Record, a Justice-oriented Approach to Background Checks John Jay College Institute for Justice and Opportunity
- Resources and Technical Assistance DOL Office of Disability Employment Policy (ODEP)
- Workplace Violence Program Resources DOL
- Training Resources for Employers to Protect Workers DOL / Occupational Safety and Health Administration (OSHA)
- Spanish-Language Compliance Assistance Resources DOL/OSHA
- Safety & Health Improvement Program Oregon Healthy Workforce Center
- Mental Health Toolkit Employer Assistance and Resource Network on Disability Inclusion (EARN)

Mental Health and Substance Use Recovery Support

- Workplace Supported Recovery CDC/NIOSH
- CDC Mental Health Resources
- Recovery for Every Worker, Every Employer DOL
- What can YOU do?: The "Mental Health at Work: What Can I Do" PSA Campaign DOL
- Drug-Free Workplace Resources Substance Abuse and Mental Health Services Administration (SAMHSA)

Suicide Prevention

If you or someone you know is experiencing emotional distress or thoughts of suicide, help is available. Call the Suicide Prevention Lifeline 24/7 at 988. Or in a crisis, text 741741 for 24/7, confidential, free crisis counseling. Or call the National Alliance for Mental Illness (NAMI) Helpline at 1-800-950-6264, Monday-Friday, 10 a.m. to 10 p.m., ET.

- Preventing Suicide: A Technical Package of Policy, Programs, and Practices CDC
- Comprehensive Blueprint for Workplace Suicide Prevention National Action Alliance for Suicide Prevention
- National Suicide Prevention Lifeline: 988

Other

- Helping Small Businesses DOL/OSHA
- On-Site Consultation DOL/OSHA
- Stigma-Free Company National Alliance for Mental Illness (NAMI)
- Resources for Prioritizing Staff Wellness Office of Head Start
- Wellbeing In The Workplace Guidebook U.S. Chamber of Commerce
- Advancing Health Equity The Community Guide
- Guidelines on Mental Health at Work World Health Organization (WHO)

59

Essential 2:
Connection and Community

> "I don't want to just feel like I know how to perform to belong. I want to feel like I can be exactly who I am and still belong... that's very different."
>
> Mid-career Mental Health Worker

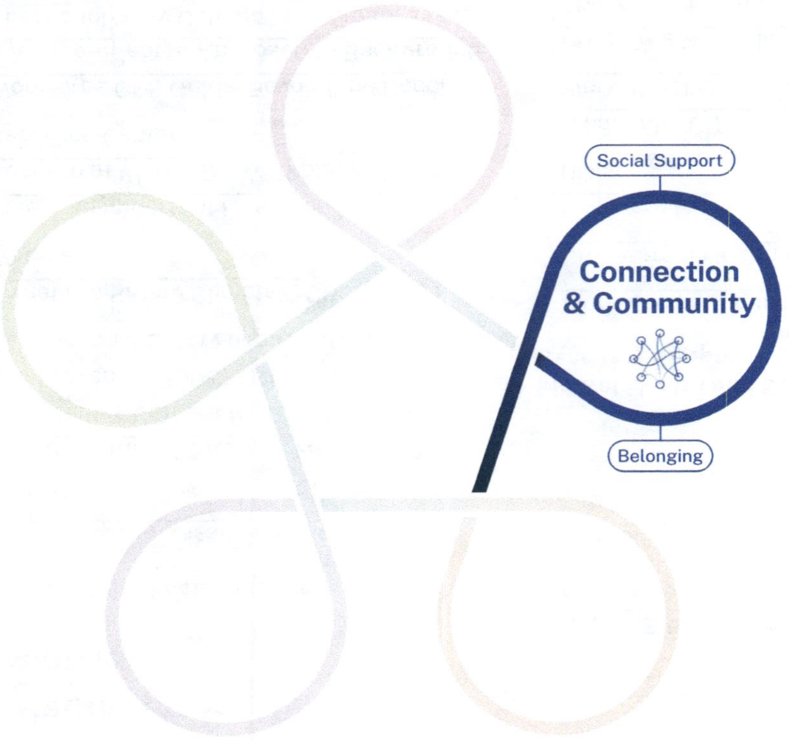

The second Essential is **Connection and Community**. Organizations that create opportunities for social connection and community can also help improve health and well-being.[8, 114] This Essential rests on two human needs: **social support** and **belonging**.

Human beings have an innate need for social connection and the COVID-19 pandemic exacerbated the health and well-being impacts of isolation.[115, 116] The need for social connection extends to the workplace, as supportive relationships are not limited to intimate networks of close family or friends.[114, 117] Given the amount of time people spend in the workplace, the relationships and connections we build there can have a variety of impacts. Having social support, or relationships and networks that can offer physical and psychological help, such as emotional support, informational support, and advice, can mitigate feelings of loneliness and isolation.[118] Belonging is the feeling of being an accepted member of a group, or of connectedness given one's interpersonal relationships.[48] Fostering a sense of belonging and connection within the broader communities they are a part of has the potential to improve the health and well-being of workers and communities, and the prosperity of organizations themselves.[48]

Connection and Community
Components

- Create cultures of inclusion and belonging
- Cultivate trusted relationships
- Foster collaboration and teamwork

Create cultures of inclusion and belonging

The first component of Connection and Community is to *create cultures of inclusion and belonging*. Organizations can begin to build social connections and community at work by encouraging what scientists call prosocial behavior, while guarding against practices, policies, or behaviors that may be barriers to social connection.[119] Prosocial behavior promotes positive social relationships through welcoming, helping, and reassuring others. Organizational cultures that promote belonging can also foster a powerful protective force against bias, discrimination, and exclusion in the workplace.[8,120,121,122] Organizational leaders should cultivate environments and cultures where connection is encouraged, and workers of all backgrounds are included. This may also include support, without fear of retaliation, for workers to have their voices and concerns heard for local policy and program change, such as through associations, cooperatives, and unions.

Cultivate trusted relationships

The second component of this Essential is *cultivating trusted relationships*.[119] Leaders can create structure and opportunities for workers to build trust and better understand one another as whole people and not just as skill sets.[123,124] This mitigates loneliness and helps workers across all levels value and empathize with each other, while helping each other cope with stress and uncertainty.[122,125] Having supportive work relationships can improve performance and is associated with worker engagement and innovation.[115] Many workplace relationships can positively affect worker health and well-being, including those between leaders and workers, among workers collaborating on teams, and between workers and their consumers and customers.[8, 126]

Having clear and consistent communication between workers and leaders is foundational in building trust.[127] Trust can be difficult to foster if workers feel disconnected from their leaders and organizations.[123] Promoting trust among leaders and workers begins with listening to worker concerns and explaining why key decisions are made within an organization.[128] Leaders can build trust through small, everyday interactions such as modeling and inviting others to share important moments of their daily lives with each other.

Foster collaboration and teamwork

The third component is to *foster collaboration and teamwork.* The future of work includes both remote and hybrid work, in a variety of full-time and part-time arrangements, so there is even more need to be intentional about how to build teams, communicate, and collaborate.[129,130,131] Organizational leaders, supervisors, and project managers can communicate the importance of teamwork, encourage regular communication, model authenticity, provide teams with effective collaboration tools, and include time for non-work connection such as community service.[132] Across organizations and within their communities, leaders can also consider community liaisons or Asset-Based Community Development to address issues like racial injustice, LGBTQ+ inequities, and other social determinants of health to support worker well-being and foster connection in the broader community, while improving the bottom line of businesses.[48,133,134]

Box 2

Connection and Community
Resources

- Worker Resource and Organizing Center U.S. Department of Labor (DOL)
- Disability Inclusion in the Workplace: Why It Matters Employer Assistance and Resource Network (EARN)
- Empower Work Text Line
- Work Design Principle #3: Improve Social Relationships in the Workplace The Work and Well-Being Initiative (Harvard T.H. Chan School of Public Health / MIT Sloan School of Management)
- A to Z of Disabilities and Accommodations Job Accommodation Network
- Center for Peer Support Mental Health America
- Find Local Assistance and Network of Partners U.S. Small Business Administration (SBA)

Essential 3: Work-Life Harmony

"I felt powerless in the position. I felt like there was never any freedom to choose things or make decisions [for myself]."

Mid-career worker, currently unemployed, with numerous prior low-wage service sector jobs

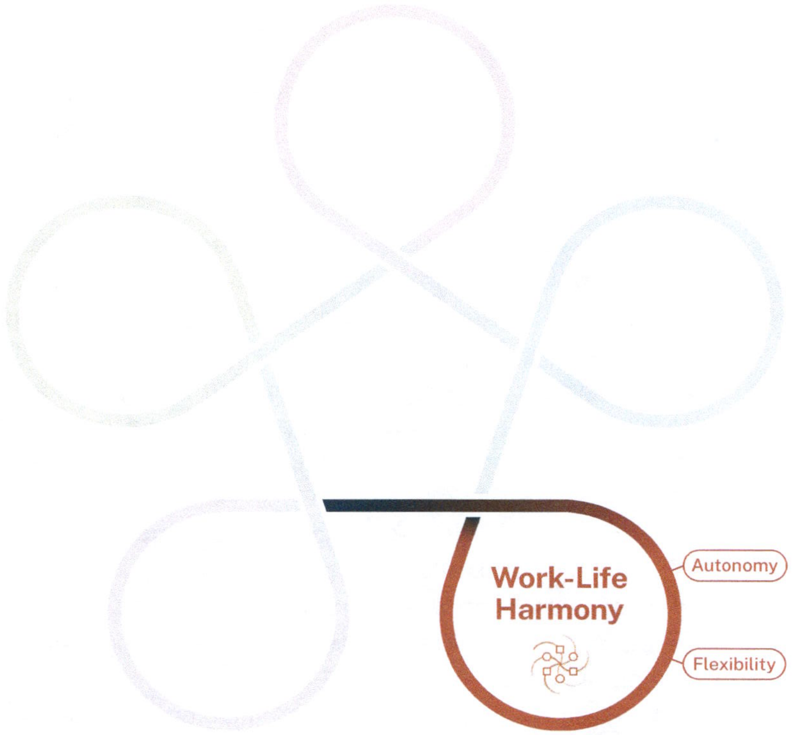

The third Essential is **Work-Life Harmony**. Professional and personal roles and responsibilities can together create work and non-work conflicts.[8,135] The ability to integrate work and non-work demands rests on the human needs of **autonomy** and **flexibility**.[136] Organizations that increase worker autonomy, or how much control one has over how they do their work, and whose workplaces provide greater flexibility, or the ability to work when and where is best for them, see workers who are more likely to succeed and retain staff for longer.[8] The expansion of remote and hybrid work opportunities, driven by the needs of the COVID-19 pandemic and enabled by advances in technology, has a number of impacts on worker mental health and well-being that merit additional research. While some reporting has shown the positive impacts of remote and hybrid work on flexibility, others have indicated negative impacts of blurred work-life boundaries.[137,138]

Organizations must see workers not only for their work roles, but as whole people. They may have many needs, roles, and responsibilities outside of work, whether it is time needed for routine physical and mental health care, an unexpected family issue that requires urgent attention, or for regular time and space for rest, exercise, educational pursuits, and hobbies. Workers who are experiencing, or who care for family members who are experiencing, acute or chronic illness, mental health challenges,

Studies & Statistics / Workplace Mental Health & Well-Being

or a disability may also need additional time to manage their conditions, responsibilities as a caregiver, and care for themselves. This may include having the flexibility to attend multiple regular or unplanned appointments. Many workers may also have caregiving responsibilities for children, older parents, or other dependents.[139,140,141,142] Notably, these responsibilities disproportionately fall on women.[143]

The overload and interference that can arise between work and life roles have been linked to negative health outcomes, including an increased risk of cardiovascular disease, digestive issues, poor sleep quality, and substance use.[144,145,146] On the other hand, workers who feel they can better harmonize their professional and personal needs report greater satisfaction with their work and life and experience fewer symptoms of depression and anxiety.[147,148] In a recent survey by the Society for Human Resource Management, many human resource professionals reported that they recognize the importance of workplace mental health and well-being, but some feel they lack the resources to meet the needs of workers, and others are unsure of which benefits to provide.[149]

Young workers today represent more than one-third of the U.S. workforce and play an important role in shifting societal attitudes and perceptions around work-life harmony.[150] According to a 2022 Deloitte survey among 23,220 Gen Z and Millennial workers (born between 1996-2010 and 1980-1995, respectively) across 46 countries globally, low compensation was the number one cited reason for leaving their jobs in the last two years, and 44% of Gen Zs and 43% of Millennials say many people have recently left their organization due to workload pressure.[151,152] When asked about their priorities in choosing an employer, workers ranked "good work-life balance and learning and development opportunities" highest; workers also wanted more flexibility in where they worked, with 75% preferring hybrid or remote work options.[152] Another group to consider are older adults (aged 65 years and up), for whom organizations can examine work environments and policies to enable them to remain in the workforce longer, while promoting their healthy longevity and well-being.[153]

Work-Life Harmony
Components

- Provide more autonomy over how work is done
- Make schedules as flexible and predictable as possible
- Increase access to paid leave
- Respect boundaries between work and non-work time

Provide more autonomy over how work is done

The first component of work-life harmony is to *provide more autonomy over how work is done*. Organizations that increase opportunities for worker control over how, when, and where work is done can mitigate work and life conflicts, engender more trust in workplaces and coworkers, and improve health.[8,154,155,156]

When possible, increased worker control over scope of work, process for accomplishing projects, and scheduling and location (e.g. condensed hours or work weeks and remote or hybrid work arrangements), can help reduce turnover as workers report greater productivity and increased satisfaction with work.[8, 157, 158, 159] Employers must clearly and frequently communicate with workers to address tensions between the flexibility that staff may want and need, alongside organizational needs.

Make schedules as flexible and predictable as possible

The second component of Work-Life Harmony is to make schedules as flexible and predictable as possible. Many workers are subject to variable and unpredictable work hours and scheduling demands.[160] A Brookings Institute analysis found that, in the leisure and hospitality industry, three-quarters of all workers receive their schedules less than one-month in advance, with most receiving notice less than two weeks in advance.[161] In the construction industry, nearly 40% of workers report receiving their schedules less than one week in advance. Unstable and unpredictable scheduling is linked to increased income volatility and an increased risk of economic hardship, which can degrade physical and mental health.[162] For example, while it may not always be possible to predict job needs and schedules, unstable schedules can make it difficult to obtain accommodations for transportation or personal care at the workplace may not have access to those accommodations on demand, and this instability fuels psychological distress and burnout.[163, 164, 165]

Workers subject to irregular schedules are more likely to report a higher likelihood of psychological distress and poor sleep quality, which is linked to a host of negative health outcomes.[166] Schedule irregularity among workers can also lead to work-life conflicts that adversely affect relationships both in and out of the workplace, including behavioral and mental health challenges in children of working parents.[163, 164, 167, 168] Employers can implement family-friendly policies such as flexible start and end times to work days, and not penalizing workers with lost wages when personal, family needs, or emergencies arise.

Increase access to paid leave

Third, organizations should *increase access to paid leave*—paid sick leave; paid family and medical leave, including paid parental leave for pregnancy and post-partum care; and paid time off for vacation.[169, 170] The U.S. remains the only advanced economy in the Organization for Economic Co-Operation and Development that does not require paid medical and family leave be provided to its workforce.[171] While paid sick leave was available to 79% of U.S. civilian workers in March 2021, there are significant disparities among wage categories. 95% of workers whose average hourly wage placed them in the top 10% of civilian workers had access to paid sick leave, compared to only 35% of those in the bottom 10% of all civilian workers, disproportionately impacting Black and Hispanic workers. Paid family leave remains the least accessible paid leave benefit, available to 23% of civilian workers overall but only 7% of workers in the bottom 10% wage category.[156, 172] Unequal and limited access to paid sick, family, and medical leave, can contribute to a higher percentage of individuals working while

65

sick (or "presenteeism") and the spread of infection at work, as well as decreased productivity, burnout, and labor shortages.[173,174,175,176,177,178] Increasing access to paid sick and other types of leave (e.g., family, medical, school) can reduce the likelihood of lost wages by 30%, positively affect the physical and mental health of workers and their children, improve retention, and reduce the costs associated with turnover.[135,156,179,180]

Respect boundaries between work and non-work time

The fourth component of work-life harmony is to *respect boundaries between work and non-work time*. When leaders and supervisors set, respect, and model clear boundaries between time on and off the job, without penalizing workers for this flexibility needed, workers report a greater sense of well-being.[181] This also helps workers have the critical time needed for rest to optimize their health, productivity, and creativity, while alleviating anxiety or fears of missing work demands. One study among 2,000 faculty and staff across 40 public universities in Australia from June to November 2020 found that staff who had supervisors that expected them to respond to messages after work reported higher levels of psychological distress and emotional exhaustion, including headaches and back pain, than groups whose supervisors did not.[182] Workplace leaders and supervisors across all organizational units can establish policies to limit digital communication outside of work hours, such as after a specific evening hour and on weekends.[183]

Box 3

Work-Life Harmony
Resources

- Work Design Principle #1: Give Employees More Control Over Their Work The Work and Well-Being Initiative (Harvard T.H. Chan School of Public Health / MIT Sloan School of Management)
- Work and Life: A Behavioral Approach to Solving Work-Life Conflict Ideas42
- How Can We Grant Employees More Flexibility in Their Job Positions Mental Health America
- Five Ways Leaders Can Support Remote Work MIT Sloan Management Review
- National Business Group on Health
- Paid Leave National Partnership for Women & Families

Studies & Statistics / Workplace Mental Health & Well-Being

Essential 4: Mattering at Work

> "We are real people. We go home, we have real issues... workers need to know that their employers don't see them as robots."
>
> — Mid-career Emergency Medical Technician

People want to know that they matter to those around them, and that their work makes a difference in the lives of others. Knowing you matter has been shown to lower stress, while feeling like you do not can raise the risk for depression.[184,185]

The fourth Essential is **Mattering at Work**. It rests on the human needs of **dignity** and **meaning**. Dignity is the sense of being respected and valued.[186] When the dignity of workers is affirmed and supported in the workplace, it enhances well-being. Conversely, being made to feel disrespected or not valued may lead to an increase in stress and feelings of anger, cynicism, hostility, and withdrawal.[187] Meaning in the workplace can refer to the sense of broader purpose and significance of one's work. Studies have shown that having meaning and purpose reduces the risk for health complications such as heart attacks and stroke, and when connected to work, can lead to improved productivity and innovation.[186,188,189,190]

Mattering at Work
- Dignity
- Meaning

Studies & Statistics / Workplace Mental Health & Well-Being

Mattering at Work
Components

- Provide a living wage
- Engage workers in workplace decisions
- Build a culture of gratitude and recognition
- Connect individual work with organizational mission

Provide a living wage

The first component of this Essential is to *provide a living wage*. Nearly one-third of U.S. workers earn less than $15 an hour, which is broadly recognized as insufficient to meet the cost of living in many parts of the country.[191] Work and income are critical social determinants of health and well-being.[192] The American Psychological Association's 2022 Work and Well-Being Survey found that workers who worried about their compensation not keeping pace with inflation were more likely to report work as having negative impacts on their mental health.[36] Another recent survey conducted by PricewaterhouseCoopers of 3,000 workers across several industries found that more than half of respondents (56%) reported feeling stressed about their finances, and among "financially-stressed" workers, 49% said that money worries had a severe or major impact on their mental health in the past year.[193] Organizations should review all work resources to meet job demands, including compensation, to offer workers a living wage as well as access to benefits that further promote and protect their health and well-being. This should include mental health supports and, where feasible, retirement plans, workers' compensation, financial and legal services, and caregiving supports (e.g., childcare).

A recent study funded by the National Institute on Minority Health and Health Disparities found that every $1 increase in the minimum wage of U.S. states could reduce the suicide rate among people with a high school education or less by nearly 6%.[194] Increases in the minimum wage across a range of sectors in the U.S. have been shown to improve parent-reported health among young children and reduce racial and ethnic disparities in income.[195,196] Performing uncompensated work, unpaid overtime, or routinely making self-sacrifices for organizations may affect worker health and well-being.[197] Aligned with the Good Jobs Principles outlined by DOL and the U.S. Department of Commerce, organizations must ensure that all workers are paid an equitable, stable, and predictable living wage before overtime, tips, and commission, and that these wages increase as worker skills increase.[93]

Engage workers in workplace decisions

The second component of Mattering at Work is to *engage workers in workplace decisions*. Employers must ensure that they are equitably engaging and empowering all workers to improve workplaces.[198] Employee or worker engagement is the extent to which organizational leaders and supervisors involve workers in developing organizational mission statements, values, goals, and objectives, as well as the level of enthusiasm and commitment that workers have in their work and workplace.[65] A 2022 Gallup State of the Global Workforce Survey found that worker engagement in the U.S. and Canada is low at 33%, yet it is among the highest globally.[34] To identify and respond to their workers' priority well-being needs, leaders can utilize existing engagement surveys, add measures to executive dashboards, and use other validated tools to regularly measure well-being.

Build a culture of gratitude and recognition

Third, in addition to recognizing workers through compensation, workplace leaders can build a culture of gratitude and recognition where workers feel seen, respected, needed, and valued. Supervisors hold a powerful role in shaping organizational culture and worker well-being. Regardless of their position, when people feel appreciated, recognized, and engaged by their supervisors and coworkers, their sense of value and meaning increases, as well as their capacity to manage stress.[199, 200] Researchers have also found that staff who received frequent appreciation at work from colleagues and supervisors were more likely to recognize and appreciate others, and that this culture had positive effects on their sense of feeling valued, as well as on team performance.

Connect individual work with organizational mission

The fourth component is to connect *individual work with organizational mission* and the impact of their work. Shared purpose, or a collective sense of working toward a common goal, assigns further meaning to work, generates pride, and fuels motivation, all while reducing stress.[186] Organizations can help workers see the connection between their day-to-day work and the organizational purpose and mission. Leaders can also reinforce these connections by acknowledging the different roles of individuals, teams, and departments in achieving organizational goals.[201]

Box 4

Mattering at Work
Resources

Manuals, Guidebooks, Toolkits

- Job Quality Toolkit U.S. Department of Commerce
- Tool for Conducting a Pay Analysis to Understand Whether Full-time Hourly Employees Earn Enough Money to Support Their Household Good Jobs Institute
- The Power of Four Words: "What Matters to You?" Institute for Healthcare Improvement
- Addressing Burnout in the Behavioral Health Workforce through Organizational Strategies, Chapter 3- Planning Processes Substance Abuse and Mental Health Services Administration (SAMHSA)
- Healthy Workplace Participatory Program Toolkit University of Massachusetts Lowell
- "Who is Engaged at Work?" Article (2019), American College of Occupational and Environmental Medicine
- "6 Job Quality Metrics Every Company Should Know" Article (2021), Brookings

Measurement Tools

- NIOSH Worker Well-Being Questionnaire Centers for Disease Control and Prevention (CDC) / National Institute for Occupational Safety and Health (NIOSH)
- Workplace Health Promotion CDC
- Valid and Reliable Survey Instruments to Measure Burnout, Well-Being, and Other Work-Related Dimensions National Academy of Medicine (NAM)

Essential 5:
Opportunity for Growth

> *"What makes work hard is when I don't see or sense that the people who are right directly above me, like my boss, advocate for my growth. They don't even have a sense of what's next for me."*
>
> Entry-level Worker, Non-profit Sector

The fifth and final Essential is **Opportunity for Growth**. This Essential rests on the human needs of **learning** and **accomplishment**. Learning is the process of acquiring new knowledge and skills in the workplace, which provides opportunities for individual intellectual, social, professional, and emotional growth.[202] Learning helps workers meet deadlines and reach goals at work, while promoting healthy social interactions.[203,204] Without learning or working towards shared goals, workers can start to feel stagnant, frustrated, and ineffective.[202] While learning is the process of growth, accomplishment is the outcome of meeting goals and having an impact.[205] Accomplishment confers a sense of competence that reduces stress, anxiety, and self-doubt.[206] When organizations create more opportunities for learning, accomplishment, and growth, workers become more optimistic about their abilities and more enthusiastic about contributing to the organization.[207]

Opportunity for Growth
Components

- Offer quality training, education, and mentoring
- Foster clear, equitable pathways for career advancement
- Ensure relevant, reciprocal feedback

Offer quality training, education, and mentoring

The first component of Opportunity for Growth is to *offer quality training, education, and mentoring*. A recent survey of executives at 129 large and midsize U.S. companies found that only 59% of companies surveyed have prioritized worker learning and growth over the past three years.[208] Training to increase skills may also be coupled with opportunities for education outside of work to build knowledge in their own work, or in other areas of interest. Employers can informally promote growth opportunities by showing genuine interest in workers through personal encouragement, coaching, and mentorship.[209, 210]

Foster clear, equitable pathways for career advancement

The second component is to *foster clear, equitable pathways for career advancement*. When organizations provide transparent career pathways and advancement opportunities for all workers, this also fosters inclusion and diversity in the workplace. This should include resources and tools that can better support workers over time and address systematic barriers in the workplace. Opportunities might include accessible professional training programs, career navigation support, tuition reimbursement for classes outside of the workplace, English language courses, and promotion opportunities. For other workers this may take the form of rotations through other departments or organizations, sabbaticals, or being offered new types of responsibilities or assignments that give them an opportunity to stretch their skills or learn new ones. It is critical to ensure an equitable and fair distribution of opportunities and eliminate barriers for advancement among workers of color. With more remote and hybrid work, organizations must also ensure that these work arrangements do not limit access to growth or other career advancement opportunities.[211]

Ensure relevant, reciprocal feedback

The final component is to ensure relevant, reciprocal feedback. Leaders and managers can provide an appropriate level of guidance to help workers by considering their strengths and growth opportunities.[33] Organizations can create more opportunities for genuinely engaging with their workers, especially in a way that is positive, collaborative, and outcome-oriented. This should include equipping all leaders, especially new or mid-level supervisors and managers, with the supportive training, tools, and resources they need to engage, manage, lead, and coach others.[65]

Box 5

Opportunity for Growth
Resources

- Resource Leveraging & Service Coordination to Increase Competitive Integrated Employment for Individuals with Disabilities Federal Joint Communication to State and Local Governments
- Toolkits to Achieve Workplace Change Harvard University Work, Family & Health Network
- Bridging the Advancement Gap: What Frontline Employees Want—and What Employees Think They Want McKinsey & Company
- What Professional Development Opportunities Can We Offer? Mental Health America
- 4 Tools to Help Managers Connect With Remote Teams MIT Sloan School of Management
- President's Executive Order on Diversity Equity Inclusion and Accessibility in the Federal Workforce
- 7 Tips for Making the Most of Your Check-Ins The Management Center
- Learning at Work and Wellbeing What Works Centre for Wellbeing

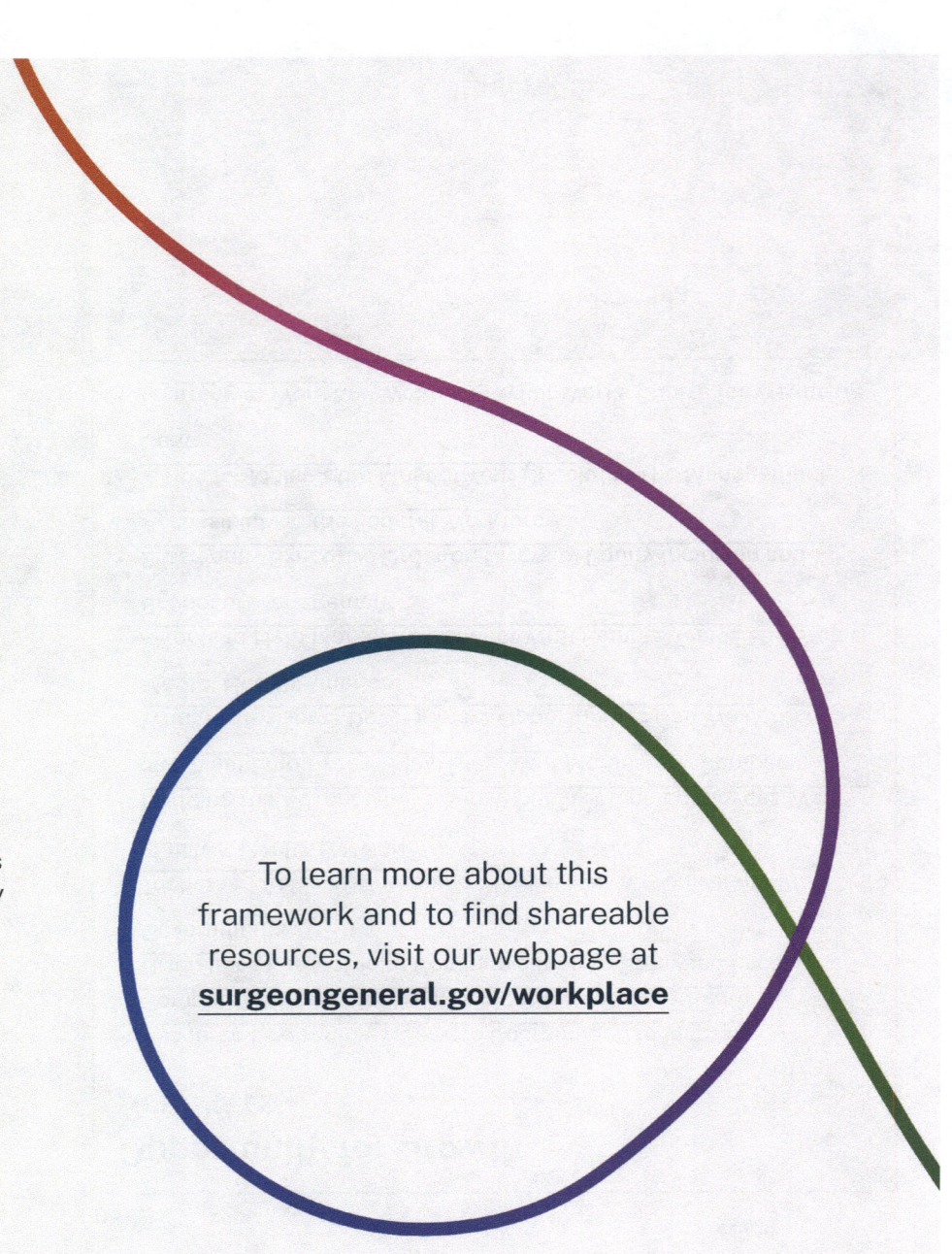

Studies & Statistics / Workplace Mental Health & Well-Being

To learn more about this framework and to find shareable resources, visit our webpage at **surgeongeneral.gov/workplace**

Conclusion

As we recover from the pandemic and rebuild our economy, leaders across organizations, together with workers, have an opportunity to reinvest in the mental health and well-being of our nation's workforce. We can build workplaces that are engines of well-being—showing workers that they matter, that their work matters, and that they have the support necessary to flourish. In doing so, we will foster more resilient, productive, and successful organizations and communities.

This Surgeon General's Framework for Workplace Mental Health & Well-Being underscores the inextricable connection between the well-being of workers and the health of organizations. It offers a foundation and resources that can be used by workplaces of any size, across any industry.

Ultimately, sustainable change must be driven by committed leaders in continuous collaboration with the valued workers who power each workplace. The most important asset in any organization is its people. By choosing to center their voices, we can ensure that everyone has a platform to thrive.

EVIDENCE-BASED RESOURCE GUIDE SERIES

Prevention and Treatment of Anxiety, Depression, and Suicidal Thoughts and Behaviors Among College Students

SAMHSA
Substance Abuse and Mental Health Services Administration

Studies & Statistics / **Prevention and Treatment Among College Students**

CHAPTER 1

Issue Brief

This chapter presents an overview of some of the most common mental health concerns among college students, such as anxiety and depression, focusing on their prevalence, consequences, and related factors.

Transitioning to adulthood is a time of significant change, particularly for college students. While many young adults take on more responsibilities and navigate new relationships, those residing on college campuses must also adapt to living away from home while facing greater academic demands. Surrounded by roommates and peers, college students experience social pressures constantly. They may also have increased access to alcohol and drugs, which can lead to substance misuse. These circumstances may adversely affect a college student's emotional and mental well-being.

Mental health concerns, such as anxiety and depression, are common among college students.[3] While 50 percent of mental illnesses first occur by adolescence, another 25 percent emerge by the mid-20s, overlapping with typical college years.[5] Some students start college with existing mental health conditions. Regardless of when mental health symptoms first appear, college students must navigate these challenges while being away from their network of relationships and support systems. They also have to receive care in an adult-serving behavioral health system, possibly for the first time in their lives.

Student mental health concerns are associated with decreased academic performance, and higher dropout rates in college.[6] Studies have shown that depression and suicidal thoughts and behaviors are associated with lower grade point average.[7-9]

Studies & Statistics / Prevention and Treatment Among College Students

Anxiety refers to anticipation of a future real or perceived threat and is often associated with "muscle tension and vigilance in preparation for future danger and cautious or avoidant behaviors."[10] Symptoms, which are typically persistent, lasting 6 months or more, may also include excessive worry, palpitations, restlessness, being easily fatigued, trembling, feelings of choking, sweating, chest pain, nausea, dizziness, paresthesias (numbness or tingling sensations), problems concentrating, irritability, and sleep disturbances. Anxiety disorders differ from normal feelings of fear or anxiety, in being excessive or persistent. Anxiety disorders include generalized anxiety disorder, panic disorder, specific phobias, agoraphobia, social anxiety disorder (social phobia), selective mutism, substance/medication-induced anxiety disorder, and separation anxiety disorder. Many of the anxiety disorders develop in childhood and tend to persist if not treated.

Depression or depressive disorders, with the classic condition being major depressive disorder, is a mood disorder characterized by the presence of "sad, empty or irritable mood, accompanied by somatic and cognitive changes that significantly affect the individual's capacity to function."[10] A major depressive episode is different from normal sadness and grief, including bereavement, Major depressive disorder symptoms can vary from mild to moderate to severe and can include:

- Depressed mood (e.g., feeling sad, empty, or hopeless) most of the day, nearly every day
- Markedly diminished interest or pleasure in activities once enjoyed (anhedonia)
- Changes in appetite; significant weight loss or gain unrelated to dieting
- Trouble sleeping (insomnia) or sleeping too much (hypersomnia)
- Loss of energy or increased fatigue, nearly every day
- Increase in purposeless physical activity (e.g., inability to sit still, pacing, handwringing) or slowed movements or speech (these actions must be severe enough to be observable by others)
- Feeling worthless or guilty, nearly every day
- Difficulty thinking, concentrating, or making decisions, nearly every day
- Recurrent thoughts of death, recurrent suicidal ideation, or suicide attempt

Suicide is death caused by an intentional self-directed injurious act, carried out with the intent of causing one's own death. Common warning signs of suicidal behavior include:[11]

- Talking about wanting to die, great guilt or shame, and being a burden to others
- Feeling empty, hopeless, trapped or having no reason to live, extremely sad, more anxious, agitated or full of rage, and unbearable emotional or physical pain
- Behaviors such as making a plan or researching ways to die, withdrawing from friends, saying goodbye, giving away important possessions or making a will, taking dangerous risks like driving extremely fast, displaying extreme mood swings, eating or sleeping more or less, and increasing drug or alcohol use.

A **suicide attempt** is a non-fatal, self-directed, and potentially injurious behavior with intent to die. **Suicidal ideation** refers to thinking about or planning suicide. The thoughts lie on a continuum of severity from a wish to die with no method, plan, intent, or behavior, to active suicidal ideation with intent and a specific plan. **Self-harm**, also known as self-directed violence, is behavior that is deliberately self-directed and results in injury or the potential for injury. The term encompasses both suicidal and non-suicidal self-injury (NSSI), and self-harm with unclear intent.

Sources: American Psychiatric Association and Centers for Disease Control and Prevention, National Center for Injury Prevention and Control

Studies & Statistics / Prevention and Treatment Among College Students

Prevalence of Mental Health Concerns in College Students

In 2018, about 69 percent of individuals aged 16 to 24 who graduated from high school or completed a GED or other high school equivalency credential were engaged in post-high school education. Of those seeking further education, 25 percent were enrolled in a 2-year college and 44 percent in a 4-year college.[12]

In recent years, there has been an increase in reported symptoms of mental illness in this population.[2] Mental health diagnoses rose from 22 to 36 percent among college student respondents between 2007 and 2017, with particular increases in the prevalence of depression and suicidal ideation.[13] According to the National College Health Assessment, about 60 percent of respondents felt overwhelming anxiety, while 40 percent experienced depression so severe that they had difficulty functioning.[14]

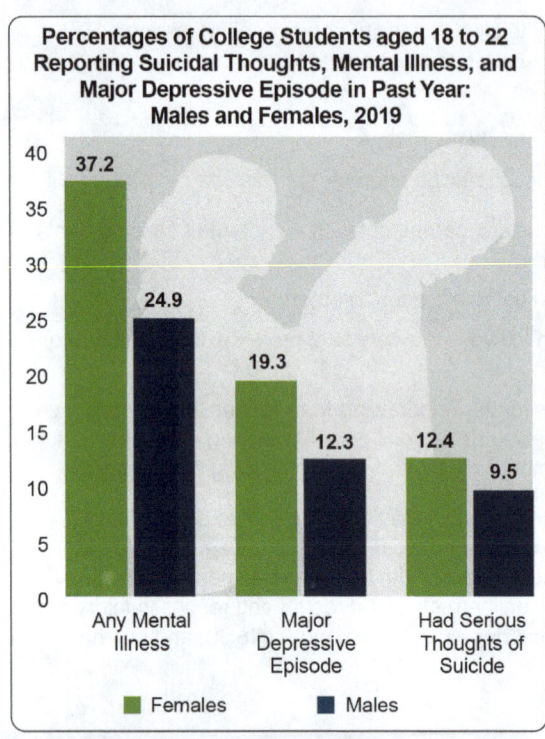

Percentages of College Students aged 18 to 22 Reporting Suicidal Thoughts, Mental Illness, and Major Depressive Episode in Past Year: Males and Females, 2019

Category	Females	Males
Any Mental Illness	37.2	24.9
Major Depressive Episode	19.3	12.3
Had Serious Thoughts of Suicide	12.4	9.5

Source: Center for Behavioral Health Statistics and Quality. (2020). *Results from the 2019 National Survey on Drug Use and Health: Detailed tables.* Rockville, MD: Substance Abuse and Mental Health Services Administration. Retrieved from https://www.samhsa.gov/data

Note that no significance testing was conducted. Differences in prevalence between males and females may not be statistically significant

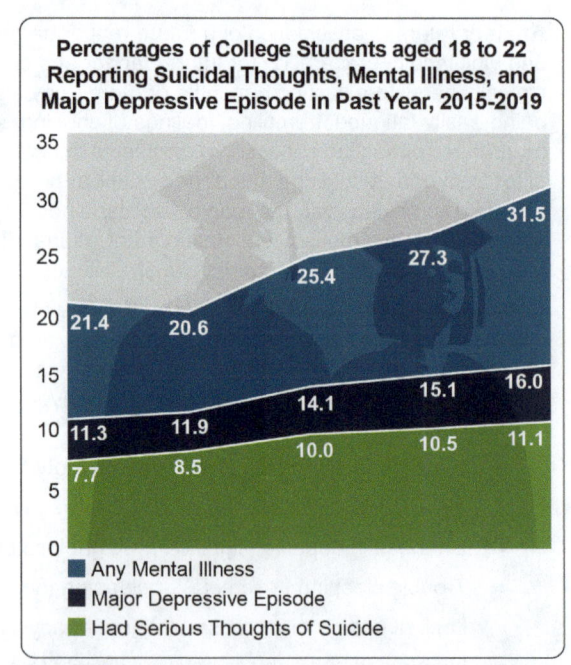

Percentages of College Students aged 18 to 22 Reporting Suicidal Thoughts, Mental Illness, and Major Depressive Episode in Past Year, 2015-2019

Year	Any Mental Illness	Major Depressive Episode	Had Serious Thoughts of Suicide
2015	21.4	11.3	7.7
2016	20.6	11.9	8.5
2017	25.4	14.1	10.0
2018	27.3	15.1	10.5
2019	31.5	16.0	11.1

Source: Center for Behavioral Health Statistics and Quality. (2020). *Results from the 2019 National Survey on Drug Use and Health: Detailed tables.* Rockville, MD: Substance Abuse and Mental Health Services Administration. Retrieved from https://www.samhsa.gov/data

Note that formal trend analyses for the presented period were not conducted.

National Institute of Mental Health (NIMH) defines any mental illness (AMI) as a mental, behavioral, or emotional disorder. AMI can vary in impact, ranging from no impairment to mild, moderate, and even severe impairment (e.g., individuals with serious mental illness). Serious mental illness (SMI) is defined as a mental, behavioral, or emotional disorder resulting in serious functional impairment, which substantially interferes with or limits one or more major life activities.

Additionally, in a 2019 study of over 400 college presidents, 8 out of 10 presidents reported the mental health of their students as a rising priority when compared to the three previous years.[15]

The 2019 National Survey on Drug Use and Health (NSDUH) found that 31.5 percent of full-time college students aged 18 to 22 reported any mental illness in the past year, and 7.5 percent reported serious mental illness (SMI) in the past year. In addition, 16.0 percent of full-time college students reported at least one major depressive episode (MDE) in the past year, and 11.1 percent of students had serious thoughts of suicide in the past year.[16] These rates have been increasing steadily over the past decade.[2]

Gender Differences in Prevalence

Research has found gender differences in the prevalence of mental health concerns among college students. Female students typically exhibit more depressive symptoms and also report higher levels of stress than their male counterparts.[17-20] Additionally, females have reported more self-cutting behaviors than males.[21] Studies have also noted that men often find acknowledging mental health concerns stigmatizing, which, in turn, deters them from disclosing those concerns and seeking help.[22-24]

Sexual Orientation and Gender Identity Differences in Prevalence

Multiple studies have been conducted to explore the differences in college student mental health experiences based on sexual orientation. Compared with their heterosexual counterparts, individuals who identify as gay, lesbian, and bisexual report receiving more counseling or mental health services on college campus.[25] Also, bisexual students are more likely to report mental health diagnoses and suicidal thoughts and behaviors compared to heterosexual and gay/lesbian students.[26]

Gender minority students (individuals who have a gender identity or expression that differs from their assigned sex at birth or does not fit within the male-female classification) are found to experience increased risk of depression, suicidal thoughts, and suicidal attempts, when compared with their cisgender (people whose gender identity matches their sex assigned at birth), lesbian, gay, bisexual, queer, and questioning counterparts.[27-28] Additionally, young people who report undergoing sexual orientation or gender identity conversion also report higher rates of suicide attempts than those who do not.[29] A study using a national dataset of college students found that transgender students are twice as likely to experience anxiety, depression, and panic attacks as cisgender female students.[30]

Race Differences in Prevalence

Studies show that a higher proportion of students who identify as multiracial or Asian/Pacific Islander report feelings of hopelessness, depression, and anger, when compared to their White counterparts.[33] On the annual Healthy Minds web-based survey of 2015, Latino/a, Asian, and multiracial students exhibited more severe depressive symptoms than White students, as measured by scores on the Patient Health Questionnaire-9 (PHQ-9).[34] Research also suggests that Black, Latino/a, and Asian students are individually more likely to consider or attempt suicide, compared to White students.[35] However, other studies find no racial difference in rates of lifetime suicide attempts.[36]

Racial differences also exist regarding access to mental health services for college students. For example, Asian American students are less likely than their Black, Latino/a, or White counterparts to have previously sought mental health services. They are also less likely to know anyone close to them who has used such services.[37]

Potential Sources for Increase in Mental Health Concerns Among College Students in Recent Years[3, 31]

1. Dramatic transition that can bring about adjustment difficulty
2. Intense pressure to succeed academically
3. Increased levels of anxiety and depression in society
4. Rapid evolution of technology and information overload, including social media
5. Economic and financial pressure
6. Food insecurity
7. Stigma against mental illness inhibiting help-seeking; lack of adequate mental health education
8. College counseling centers experiencing overload of demand and dearth of skilled staff

The COVID-19 pandemic, beginning in March 2020, has added to the stress experienced by college students. Among other concerns, students associated the pandemic with fear and worry about their own health and that of their loved ones, difficulty in concentrating, disruptions to sleeping patterns, decreased social interactions due to physical distancing, and increased concerns about academic performance.[32]

Studies & Statistics / Prevention and Treatment Among College Students

Studies have shown that BIPOC students (black, indigenous, and other people of color) utilize mental health services less frequently than White students and are more likely to have unmet mental health needs.[38] One reason for this disparity appears to be related to self-perception; studies have shown that youth of color are less likely to perceive a need for mental health services.[39] This difference in perception may be due to the perceived social stigma associated with seeking mental health treatment.

Similarly, differences exist in barriers that students face in accessing mental health services. Finances are greater barriers for Black and Latina/o students, while White students report a lack of time; all racial/ethnic minority students report cultural sensitivity issues (e.g., sensitivity of the mental health provider) as significant barriers.[40]

Socioeconomic Differences in Prevalence

Research has demonstrated association between adolescents' and young adults' socioeconomic status (SES) and mental illness.[45-47] Studies have particularly indicated a close relationship between low SES and high levels of stress, anxiety, and depression in college students.[48]

Intersectionality

The college population is incredibly diverse, composed of students from a number of backgrounds and identities. A framework of intersectionality asserts that those who belong to more than one historically disenfranchised group, such as those defined by sex, race, religion, gender identity, socioeconomic status, (dis)ability, or sexual orientation, may experience mutually reinforcing effects of disparity and/or systemic inequality.[41] College students with multiple marginalized identities may face particular challenges that may cause or exacerbate mental health symptoms and make seeking and receiving treatment more difficult. Previous studies provide evidence that individuals experiencing discrimination are more likely to use alcohol and other substances as a coping strategy.[42-44] As practitioners and decision-makers on campus address mental health concerns on campus, they should take issues of campus climate and identity into consideration throughout the continuum of care.

Data from the annual Healthy Minds web-based survey of 2015 showed that college students experiencing financial distress and a lack of student medical insurance had higher levels of anxiety, depression, and suicidal ideation.[49] A national study of college students' mental health found that 7 out of 10 students in the sample were stressed because of their personal finances, with 60 percent worrying about having adequate funds to pay for college tuition.[50] The financial burden of student loans is also associated with college students' experience of stress, anxiety, and depression.[51] Additionally, the rising cost of college increases students' anxiety and the pressures on them to succeed academically.[52]

International Student Status Differences in Prevalence

There were more than 1 million international students enrolled at U.S. colleges during the 2019-20 academic year, representing 5.5 percent of all college students.[53] Research suggests that international students seek help for their mental health concerns at rates significantly lower than their domestic student counterparts (32.0 percent vs. 49.8 percent for any formal treatment; 14.9 percent vs. 32.9 percent for pharmaceutical treatment).[54] International students also are more likely to report perceived public stigma and personal stigma towards formal help-seeking.[54] These students may face unique stressors such as language barriers, lack of familiarity with the U.S. education system, cultural misunderstandings or miscommunication, and cultural isolation.[55]

Co-Occurring and Related Conditions

This guide focuses primarily on depression, anxiety, and suicidal thoughts and behaviors, the most common mental disorders among college students. However, there is a wide array of other individual and environmental factors which may be related to or co-occurring with depression, anxiety, and/or suicidal ideation. Practitioners must consider these factors when engaging and treating the college student population.

Regardless of the specific intervention, understanding the potential clinical challenges patients could present and the environmental context producing such challenges will help practitioners to select and implement the most appropriate treatment practices to meet the needs of their patients. This guide presents some of these related issues, including how they may be intertwined with or exacerbate the symptoms of depression, anxiety, and suicidal thoughts and behaviors that college students experience.

Studies & Statistics / Prevention and Treatment Among College Students

Eating Disorders

Eating disorders, such as anorexia nervosa, bulimia nervosa, and binge-eating disorder, are serious and often fatal illnesses. These illnesses are characterized by severe disturbances in people's eating behaviors and related thoughts and emotions. Preoccupation with food, body weight, and shape are common symptoms of eating disorders.

Eating disorders are a significant problem among college students, with an increase in prevalence in the last couple of decades.[56] These disorders in college students increase the risk of negative physical health and psychological consequences, including substance use and depression.[57] Studies have shown that eating disorders often co-occur with anxiety disorders and depression.[58-59]

Alcohol and Substance Use

Alcohol misuse and substance use disorders (SUD) are prevalent on college campuses. According to 2019 NSDUH data, one in eight college students aged 18-22 met the criteria for SUD in the previous year and 8.2 percent of full-time college students met criteria for heavy alcohol use (defined as binge drinking on 5 or more days in the past 30 days).[16] SUD may co-occur with mental illness; adults 18 or older who reported past-year any mental illness (AMI) were more likely than those without mental illness to have used illicit drugs in the past year (38.8 percent versus 16.6 percent). Among adults 18 years of age or older in 2019 3.8 percent (or 9.5 million people) had both AMI and SUD.[60]

The prevalence rates of heavy alcohol use differ by race and ethnicity. Prevalence was highest among Whites (11.8 percent), followed by Asian (4 percent), Hispanics (3.9 percent), and Blacks (2.1 percent).[61] Heavy alcohol use is also less prevalent among those who identify as lesbian, gay, and bisexual (LGB) compared to those who do not (7.6 percent vs. 8.2 percent).[61]

Studies & Statistics / Prevention and Treatment Among College Students

The prevalence rates of SUDs also differ by race and ethnicity. Prevalence was highest among Whites (14.0 percent), followed by Hispanics (12.1 percent), Blacks (11.3 percent), and Asians (8.2 percent).[61] SUD is more prevalent among those who identify as LGB compared to those who do not (18.3 percent vs. 11.9 percent).[61]

Studies have shown that major depressive disorder is a significant predictor of heavy episodic drinking, and substance use is a risk factor for self-injurious behavior and suicidal ideation.[62-64] A review of studies on suicide completion in the general population found that those with opioid use disorder, intravenous drug use, and polydrug use were 14 to 17 times more likely to die of suicide.[65]

Non-suicidal Self-injury

Non-suicidal self-injury (NSSI) is defined as behaviors in which an individual intentionally harms their body without explicit suicidal intent and for reasons that are not socially sanctioned. NSSI typically involves behaviors such as cutting, burning, scratching, and self-battery.[66] Although there is no single clear set of risk factors for NSSI, research has shown that it is often related to depressive and anxiety symptoms in college students.[67] NSSI also increases the chances of suicidal ideation, plans, and attempts.[68] Gender differences have been found in the reasons male and female college students report for their NSSI behaviors: females were more likely to self-injure in hopes that their distress would be recognized, while males report anger and intoxication as contributing factors.[69]

Other Serious Mental Illness

While depression, anxiety, and suicidal thoughts and behaviors are of great concern and common among college students, the college years are also the developmental period when symptoms of SMI first appear. Approximately 75 percent of people with SMI, such as schizophrenia and bipolar disorder, experience symptoms by the age of 25.[70]

According to recent data the prevalence of SMI appears to be highest for young adults aged 18 to 25. However, compared to other adults, this age group appears to be the least likely to receive treatment for their SMI.[16] Early detection and treatment of these disorders are particularly important.

> **Mental Health and Social Support**
>
> One factor that has been shown to promote mental health of college students and act as a buffer against stress and anxiety is social support.[71] Social support, the physical and emotional assistance provided by family and friends, is associated with emotional well-being.[72-73] Both the quantity of social relationships (structural support) and quality of social relationships (functional support) are considered important aspects in determining the positive effects of social support on student mental health.[74]

Yet college students with SMI may face challenges receiving treatment in college. Thirty-four percent of campus counseling centers do not have psychiatrists on staff to assess and treat SMI that requires medication, and only 15 percent of centers have full-time, in-house psychiatric services available.[4] Remaining in college may also be difficult for these students; studies show that adults living with schizophrenia or bipolar disorder are much more likely to have dropped out of college than the general population.[75]

Sexual Assault and Violence

Sexual assault—any nonconsensual sexual act proscribed by federal, tribal, or state law, including when the victim lacks capacity to consent—is a common occurrence on college campuses. More than one in five college women will experience at least one incident of sexual assault during their time at college, and 6.8 percent of undergraduate men have experienced nonconsensual sexual contact.[76] Also, lesbian, gay, bisexual, transgender, and queer/questioning (LGBTQ) students experience higher rates of sexual assault while in college, as compared to their heterosexual, cisgender peers.[76]

Survivors of sexual assault may experience mental health crises or ongoing mental health symptoms as a result. Research has shown that sexual assault is a significant predictor of anxiety, depression, and suicidal thoughts and behaviors.[77-78] In addition, those with mental illnesses may also be at greater risk for sexual assault. A study found that people with post-traumatic stress disorder (PTSD)[a] and depression had a greater risk for sexual assault.[79]

---

[a] According to the American Psychiatric Association, *PTSD* is a psychiatric disorder that may occur in people who have experienced or witnessed a traumatic event, such as a natural disaster, serious accident, terrorist act, war/combat, or rape or who have been threatened with death, sexual violence, or serious injury.

Treatment of Mental Health Concerns on College Campuses

The transition from mental health services for children and adolescents to those for adults is rarely seamless, and transition-aged individuals (individuals who are between 18-24 years) often fall through the cracks during this period. These individuals may not be provided with appropriate support or referrals or may be referred to adult systems with which they are unfamiliar and that are ill-equipped to meet their current needs.[80] Continuity of care can be even more compromised when a student moves to a new location during the transition from youth to adult, as often happens when starting college.

Higher education institutions have the responsibility to provide students with access to mental health services, but they may find it difficult to keep up with the growing demand. The Center for Collegiate Mental Health reported that between Fall 2009 and Spring 2015, counseling center utilization increased by an average of 30 to 40 percent, while college enrollment increased by only 5 percent.[4] In a 2019 survey, 87.3 percent of counseling center directors reported an increased need for services compared to the previous year.[81]

For students who seek counseling, wait times for an appointment can span multiple days, if not weeks.[81] While evidence suggests that as many as 35 percent of college students screen positive for a mental illness, only about 13 percent, on average, actually utilize their campus counseling centers.[4, 81, b] Although some students may choose to forego treatment due to social stigma or personal reasons, others may face difficulty in accessing services.

Counseling centers working at capacity are not always able to serve every student who seeks treatment, may provide shorter or less frequent sessions than desired, or may not offer the types of services needed (e.g., pharmacological services). More than half of counseling centers manage patient demand by referring students off-campus or by triaging them based on perceived urgency.[81] Moreover, higher caseloads per counselor are associated with lower rates of improvement for patients experiencing common mental health concerns.[4] Thus, an overwhelmed counseling center may be less effective in helping students.

Among college students who reported receiving mental health services in the past 12 months (multiple responses possible):[14]

- 55% received services on campus at the health center or counseling center
- 22% received services from a local provider near campus
- 48% received services from a provider in their hometown

Among providers/clinicians at on-campus counseling centers:[4]

- 71% are professional staff members
- 10% are pre-doctoral interns
- 5% are trainees at the doctoral level
- 5% are trainees at the master's level
- 5% are at the post-doctoral level

Among clinicians at on-campus counseling centers (highest degree reported):[4]

- 34% have a degree in counseling psychology
- 33% have a degree in clinical psychology
- 13% have a degree in social work
- 6% have a degree in counselor education
- 3% have a degree in psychiatry

In light of these challenges, higher education institutions need to create a network of supports beyond the typical counseling center. Colleges can leverage their unique environment to identify, prevent, and treat mental health concerns. A multi-pronged holistic approach that includes all levels of the care continuum is required to address student mental health by the college leadership.[88]

Some colleges train members in their community to become "gatekeepers," which are people equipped to respond when they recognize early warning signs of suicide.[89] Gatekeepers interact with students daily and can include anyone with a campus presence, faculty, staff, or even other students.

---

[b] The Center for Collegiate Mental Health (CCMH) data include a sample of counseling centers across the country. Other studies have indicated that the percentage using campus counseling services varies widely.[66]

Studies & Statistics / Prevention and Treatment Among College Students

Administrative Policies of Higher Education Institutions

Various mental health and education-focused organizations have position statements and resources related to administrative policies of higher education institutions to support students' mental health. Some of these statements are summarized below.

Mental Health America's position statement, *College and University Response to Mental Health Crises*,[82] recommends:

- Colleges and universities provide a variety of mental health resources to proactively reach students where they are.
- College and university policies prevent students with mental health conditions from experiencing stigma and discrimination.
- Colleges and universities develop protocols to respond fairly and effectively to students in crisis.
- Policies limit liability for colleges and universities to encourage proper protocols.[82]

Active Minds' *position statement* promotes leave of absence and return from absence policies for mental health concerns at higher education institutions that are in keeping with the provisions of the Americans with Disabilities Act of 1990 (ADA), Section 504 of the Rehabilitation Act of 1973, and best practices recommended by the Judge David L. Bazelon Center for Mental Health Law, a national legal-advocacy organization that advocates for the civil rights, full inclusion and equality of adults and children with mental disabilities.[83]

The American Psychiatric Association's resource on *College Mental Health and Confidentiality* prepares practitioners to provide clinical care within the framework of relevant law.[84]

Campus Pride, a national nonprofit organization for student leaders and campus groups working to create a safer college environment for LGBTQ students, has developed *Best Practices to Support Transgender and Other Gender-Nonconforming Students*, which include gender-inclusive bathrooms and housing policies and preferred name change policies.[85]

The National Association of Student Personnel Administrators' (NASPA) resource *Strategies for Addressing Mental Health Support on Campus* includes ways to effectively support the mental health needs of today's students, such as a robust infrastructure, equity centered policies and procedures, and strong mechanisms for communication, assessment, and improvement.[86]

The Jed Foundation's resource *Student Mental Health and the Law* provides campus professionals with a summary of laws and professional guidelines, as well as related good practice recommendations, to support well-informed decision making around students at risk.[87]

Economic Benefits for Institutions

Colleges' investments in student mental health can not only improve students' individual outcomes (overall health and well-being, academics, etc.), but also produce a number of economic benefits from an institutional perspective. Improving students' mental health is likely to reduce dropout, and this increased retention should result in increased tuition revenues for institutions, as well as higher earnings for students who otherwise would not have graduated.[90] These outcomes may further an institution's academic standing and/or improve its reputation, producing further economic benefits.

Beyond specific academic institutions, the economic benefits of improved campus mental health services could be enormous; one study by the RAND Corporation found that each dollar spent on prevention and early intervention programs by the California Mental Health Services Administration (CalMHSA) produced $6.49 in net societal benefits.[91]

Institutions interested in learning more about the potential economic benefits of student mental health investments may wish to explore the Healthy Minds Network's Return on Investment (ROI) tool.

Another strategy that has become more common in recent years is the use of embedded counselors.[92] This model increases access to mental health services by placing counselors in specific locations across the university, such as residence halls, athletic offices, and professional schools.

Whatever the method of expanding their mental health care system, colleges need to continue to identify opportunities to support the mental well-being of their students. Intervening early, when symptoms are identified, makes for better long-term outcomes for the student over their lifetime, and not just during their college years.[93] Additionally, healthy college students not only gain positive college experiences, but these positive outcomes are also associated with long-term individual, interpersonal, institutional, and community benefits, as depicted in the graphic below.

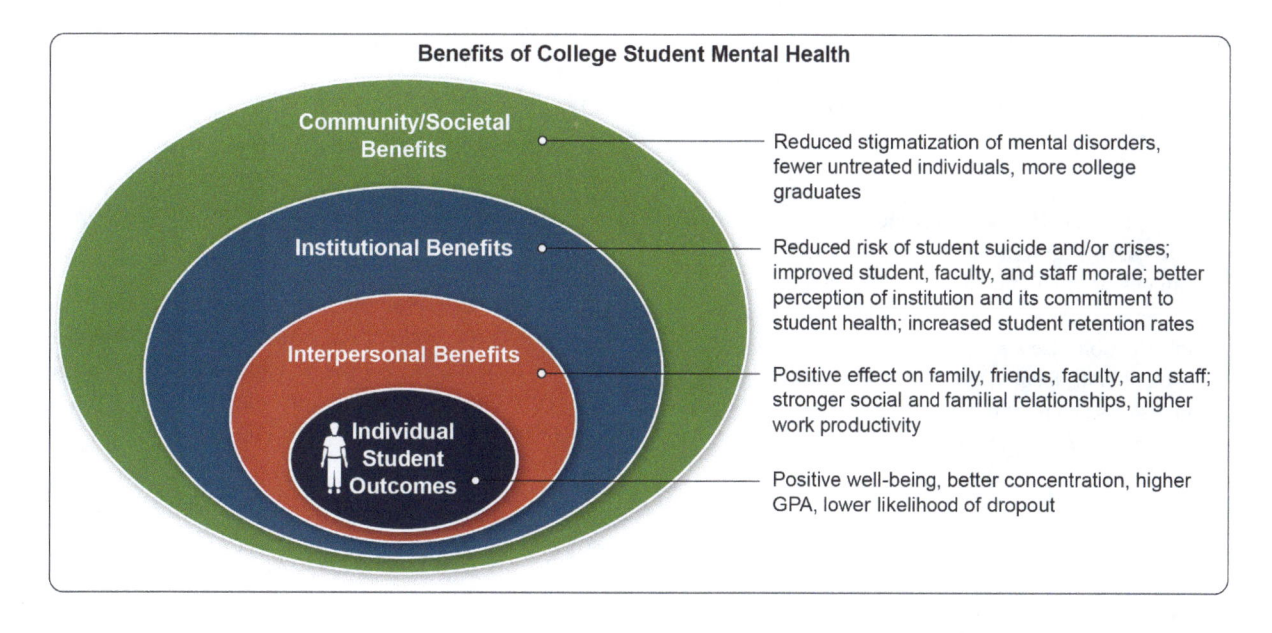

Benefits of College Student Mental Health

- **Community/Societal Benefits**: Reduced stigmatization of mental disorders, fewer untreated individuals, more college graduates
- **Institutional Benefits**: Reduced risk of student suicide and/or crises; improved student, faculty, and staff morale; better perception of institution and its commitment to student health; increased student retention rates
- **Interpersonal Benefits**: Positive effect on family, friends, faculty, and staff; stronger social and familial relationships, higher work productivity
- **Individual Student Outcomes**: Positive well-being, better concentration, higher GPA, lower likelihood of dropout

Studies & Statistics / Prevention and Treatment Among College Students

CHAPTER 2

What Research Tells Us

Effectiveness of Mental Health Interventions in Colleges

Mental disorders frequently begin during young adulthood (ages 18–25 years), when young people are typically in college.[1] Concerns about mental health among college students are exacerbated by factors such as lack of screening for and diagnosis of mental disorders, symptom denial, and inaccessible, inadequate, and/or inappropriate treatment. Evidence-based interventions for prevention, early identification and diagnosis, and treatment programs on college campuses can help reduce these concerns. The campus-based mental health programs presented in this chapter are grouped into two categories:

1. **Campus-wide interventions focused on prevention and early intervention**: The primary purpose of campus-wide interventions is to facilitate and/or increase access to mental health services. These interventions use a public health approach, and help campus staff, faculty, and students recognize students in distress and refer them to individual interventions and therapy available on campus.

   Campus-wide practices include, but are not limited to, universal screenings, self-help apps, gatekeeper trainings, peer-to-peer interventions[a], bystander interventions, and stigma-reduction campaigns.[b] These practices are designed to facilitate access to or improve attitudes toward help-seeking behavior and/or referrals. The practices are intended to be preventative and are typically appropriate for use by all adults who interact with students on a college campus. In addition, universal screenings can capture the mental health needs of all students on campus and help identify those who are at risk for behavioral health challenges.

2. **Clinical interventions**: Clinical interventions are administered by licensed mental health professionals (or graduate interns), typically through the college counseling center. They focus on treatment of specific mental health diagnoses and can be administered in a group or individual format. In the past, these interventions were entirely in-person, but in recent years, colleges have expanded the scope of these practices to include additional clinical services through telehealth, sometimes using external partnerships.

---

[a] Peer-based interventions are defined as a method of teaching or facilitating health promotion that asks people to share specific health messages with members of their own community.

[b] Stigma-reduction campaigns aim to create awareness around and help remove stereotypes associated with mental health issues.

This chapter highlights one campus-wide and four clinical interventions to prevent or treat mental health problems among college students:

Campus-wide/public health interventions

1. Gatekeeper trainings

Clinical interventions

1. Mindfulness-Based Stress Reduction (MBSR)
2. Acceptance and Commitment Therapy (A&CT)
3. Cognitive Behavioral Therapy (CBT)
4. Dialectical Behavior Therapy (DBT)

The chapter also provides an overview of the interventions, including a discussion of the typical settings, demographic groups, intensity and duration, and outcomes attributed to receipt of the intervention. Each program or practice description includes a rating based on its evidence of impact on mental health outcomes, which include:

- Increased understanding and recognition of mental health concerns, especially suicide-related behaviors, and improved understanding of and access to services (campus-wide interventions)
- Improvements in mental health or reductions in severity of symptoms associated with anxiety and depression and in suicidal thoughts and ideation (clinical interventions)

Intervention Selection

Interventions had to meet the following criteria to be considered for inclusion in this guide:

- Be clearly defined and replicable
- Address mental health concerns of college students
- Be currently in use
- Demonstrate evidence of effectiveness
- Have accessible implementation resources and fidelity (the degree to which a program delivers a practice as intended) supports

Evidence Review and Rating

Authors completed a comprehensive review of published research for each selected intervention, to determine its strength as an evidence-based practice. Eligible research studies were required to:

- Employ a randomized or quasi-experimental design, or
- Be a single sample pre-post design or an epidemiological study with a strong counterfactual (i.e., a study that analyzes what would have happened in the absence of the intervention), and
- Have been conducted in the United States since 2000

Descriptive studies, implementation studies, and meta-analyses were not included in the review, but were documented, to understand the interventions better and identify implementation supports for the practices.

Each eligible study was reviewed for evidence of measurable impact on mental health outcomes. In addition, trained reviewers checked each study to ensure rigorous methodology, asking questions such as:

- Are experimental and comparison groups statistically equivalent, with the only difference being that participants in the experimental group received the intervention and those in the comparison group received treatment as usual or no or minimal intervention?
- Was baseline equivalence established between the treatment and comparison groups?
- Were missing data addressed appropriately?
- Were outcome measures reliable, valid, and collected consistently from all participants?

Using these criteria, each study was assessed and given a rating of low, moderate, or high. Only randomized controlled trials, quasi-experimental designs, and epidemiological studies with a strong comparison were eligible to receive a high or moderate rating.

After all studies for a practice were assessed and rated, the practice was placed into one of the three categories (strong evidence, moderate evidence, and emerging evidence) based on its causal evidence level. See Appendix 2 for more information about the evidence review process.

Studies & Statistics / Prevention and Treatment Among College Students

CAUSAL EVIDENCE LEVELS

Strong Evidence

Causal impact demonstrated by at least *two* randomized controlled trials, quasi-experimental designs, or epidemiological studies with a high or moderate rating.

Moderate Evidence

Causal impact demonstrated by at least *one* randomized controlled trial, quasi-experimental design, or epidemiological study with a high or moderate rating.

Emerging Evidence

No study received a high or a moderate rating. The practice may have been evaluated with less rigorous studies (e.g., pre-post designs) that demonstrate an association between the practice and positive outcomes, but additional studies are needed to establish causal impact.

Research Opportunity

This evidence review identified research studies for five prevention/treatment practices. Although the body of research is growing, practitioners continue to face the challenge of limited evidence, particularly from well-designed randomized controlled trials (RCTs), when selecting programs to address mental health concerns of college students. There are other interventions for mental health, but they have not been studied specifically for college students. The field would benefit from more research on impact of these interventions on college students.

Campus-Wide/Public Health Interventions Associated With Mental Health of College Students

Gatekeeper Trainings

Strong Evidence

Overview

Gatekeeper trainings are suicide prevention programs that train participants to recognize warning signs of suicide risk in individuals they interact with and to help them get access to trained mental health services they need in the moment of crisis. Students on college campuses at risk for suicide do not always consult healthcare professionals in the critical period before they harm themselves. During that time period, friends, family, fellow students, and staff can help vulnerable students if they are trained to recognize and respond to suicide risk.[3]

Although various gatekeeper trainings are available for use with college populations, they all have similar foundational principles and objectives, with the common aim of helping adults:

1. Recognize warning signs of psychological distress and suicide exhibited by at-risk students
2. Communicate effectively with these students and encourage them to seek further help

The trainings may differ in their format and delivery methods.

Twenty-one studies of gatekeeper training were considered eligible for this evidence review. Of these studies, one was rated high and four were rated moderate. Sixteen were rated low because they were pre-post design studies or the reviewers identified weaknesses in their study designs. The five high and moderate studies led to an overall rating of "strong support for causal evidence," and included all the gatekeeper trainings mentioned on the next page.

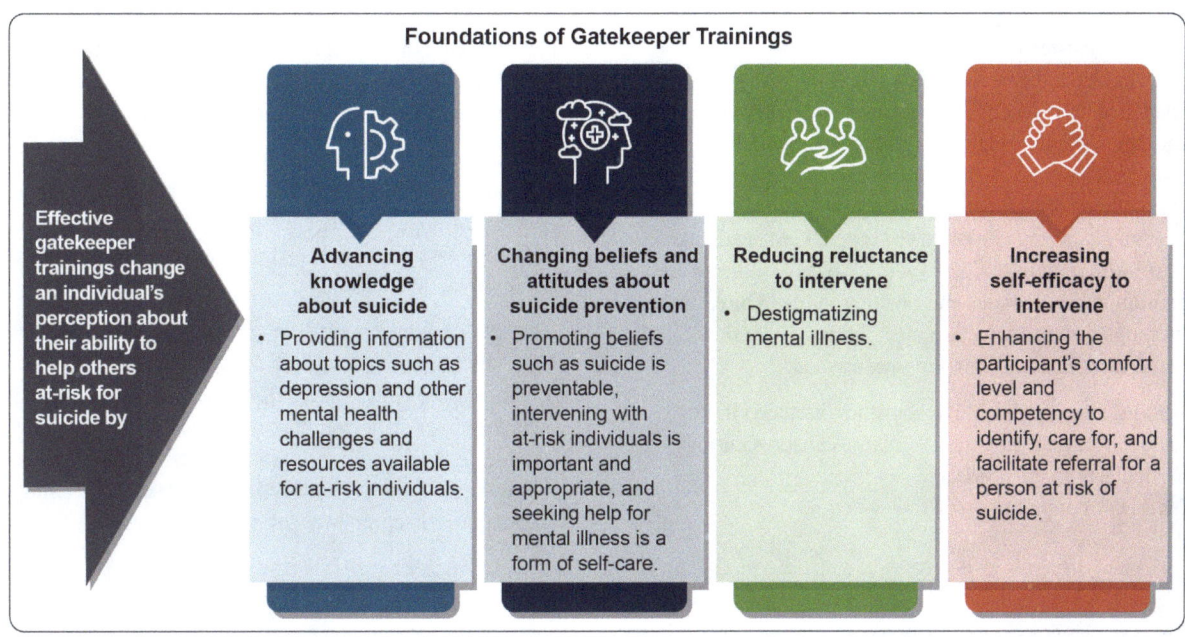

Foundations of Gatekeeper Trainings

Effective gatekeeper trainings change an individual's perception about their ability to help others at-risk for suicide by:

Advancing knowledge about suicide
- Providing information about topics such as depression and other mental health challenges and resources available for at-risk individuals.

Changing beliefs and attitudes about suicide prevention
- Promoting beliefs such as suicide is preventable, intervening with at-risk individuals is important and appropriate, and seeking help for mental illness is a form of self-care.

Reducing reluctance to intervene
- Destigmatizing mental illness.

Increasing self-efficacy to intervene
- Enhancing the participant's comfort level and competency to identify, care for, and facilitate referral for a person at risk of suicide.

Source: Burnetter, C., Ramchand, R., & Ayer, L. (2015). Gatekeeper Training for Suicide Prevention. *Rand Health Quarterly, 5,* 1-16.

Studies & Statistics / Prevention and Treatment Among College Students

Type of Gatekeeper Training	Training Description
Question. Persuade. Refer. (QPR)	Developed by Paul Quinnett, QPR is a specialized training for individuals (students), organizations (large number of college students or staff), and professionals (counselors/therapists on college campuses). The intervention is delivered through online or in-person sessions, each one to two hours long.
Applied Suicide Intervention Skills Training (ASIST)	Developed by LivingWorks, ASIST offers multiple programs focused on crisis resolution with varying time commitments from a one-hour training to a more in-depth, half-day training, to an intensive two-day, 16-hour training.
Campus Connect	Developed by the Syracuse University Counseling Center especially for college campuses, Campus Connect is a two and a half hour, experientially based training that involves participants in multiple interactive exercises.
Kognito	Developed by health simulation company Kognito, this training consists of two online training sessions involving interactive roleplay simulations specifically for college populations; one 45-minute training is designed for faculty, staff, and administrators and another 40-minute training is intended for college students and student leaders.
Mental Health First Aid (MHFA)	Developed by Betty Kitchener and Anthony Jorm from Australia, MHFA USA offers separate courses for adults and youth, each single day sessions running from five to seven hours.

Population of Focus

Although studies of gatekeeper trainings often include students, staff, and faculty on college campuses, the typical participant group included in the studies in this review consisted of resident assistants (RAs).[4-7] RAs, often students themselves, live and work within the residence halls on college and university campuses and, thus, share living space with college students. This proximity gives the RAs more opportunity than most other campus staff to identify stress and anxiety in students.[8] Only one review study included campus staff.[4] Although participants across all five studies were predominantly females and predominantly White, these trainings can be adapted to meet the needs of ethnic/racial communities, wherein they are used.[9]

Although not applicable to any study included in this review, Kognito trainings do offer a version catering particularly to the needs and experiences of the LGBTQ+ community on a college campus.

Practitioner Types

Although staff in health and behavioral healthcare settings particularly benefit from gatekeeper trainings, any campus community member can get trained and certified in implementing these programs. Most gatekeeper trainings included in this review (QPR, ASIST, Campus Connect, and MHFA) offer train-the-trainer models.

The gatekeeper trainings included in this review were delivered by professionals, trained and certified in those specific trainings.[4,6] Since the Kognito trainings include self-administered, web-based modules, live trainers were not involved in that study.

Intensity and Duration of Treatment

Most gatekeeper trainings are delivered in a single training event, which varies from one to five hours and includes either in-person or online sessions.[4,6-7] Kognito trainings are delivered via 40-45-minute pre-recorded, online sessions or simulations. Some gatekeeper trainings require periodical renewals or recertifications.

Outcomes

Studies that contributed to the strong evidence rating of this intervention demonstrated gatekeeper trainings with college students and staff had the following outcomes:

- Decrease in gatekeeper reluctance to intervene[6]
- Increase in participant's likelihood to intervene[6]
- Increase in participant's general self-efficacy[5-7]
- Increase in gatekeeper preparedness[5]
- Increase in participant's knowledge about mental health[7]
- Increase in participant's confidence,[4,7] comfort, and competence[4] in helping at-risk students

Clinical Mental Health Interventions for College Students

Mindfulness-Based Stress Reduction

Strong Evidence

Overview
Mindfulness-Based Stress Reduction (MBSR) is a program that uses mindfulness meditation to reduce stress and anxiety and manage emotions.

Through the three MBSR activities, individuals become attentive to bodily sensations while practicing nonjudgmental awareness of their thoughts.[10] By incorporating MBSR principles into their daily lives, individuals can manage physical and mental symptoms of illness and difficult emotional situations. This process can reduce anxiety and stress and improve mental health.[10-11]

Five studies of MBSR were eligible for review. Of these studies, one rated high and four rated moderate, giving the intervention an overall rating of "strong support for causal evidence."

Components of Mindfulness-Based Stress Reduction

- **Sitting Meditation:** mindful breathing, nonjudgmental awareness of present thoughts
- **Body Scan:** mindful attention to bodily sensations in sequence from feet to head
- **Hatha Yoga:** mindful movement through yoga postures, body awareness

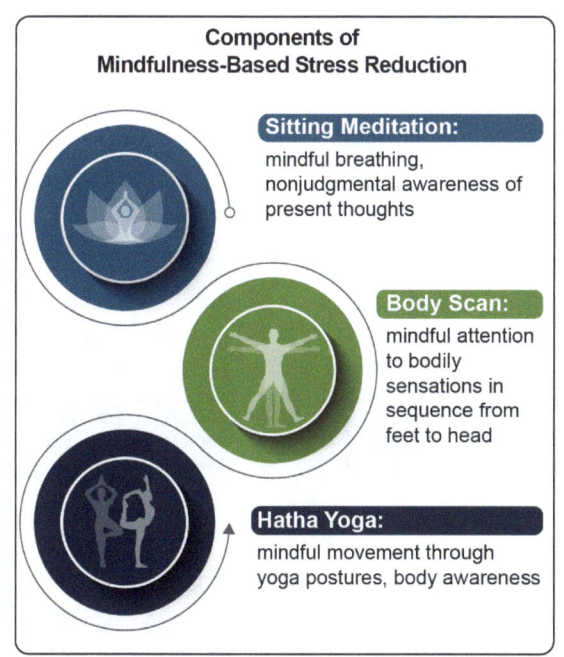

Source: Sharma, M., & Rush, S. E. (2014). Mindfulness-based stress reduction as a stress management intervention for healthy individuals: A systematic review. *Journal of Evidence-Based Complementary & Alternative Medicine, 19(4),* 271-286.

Population of Focus
MBSR was originally designed to relieve suffering in patients with stress and pain.[12] It has since been used with a variety of populations in clinical and non-clinical settings, including cancer patients[13] and employees in the workplace.[14]

Studies included in this evidence review focused on the general college student population, as well as students with depressive symptoms[15] or seeking stress reduction.[16]

Participants across the five studies were predominantly female and predominantly White.[15-19]

Practitioner Types
Online and in-person trainings for certification in MBSR, ranging from 8 to 10 weeks, are available at https://www.mindfulleader.org/. Several studies included in this review utilized certified facilitators to deliver the intervention;[17] at least one other study included doctoral-level graduate student therapists.[15] In another study, the professor of a health course delivered MBSR as part of the class curriculum.[18] In yet another study, students practiced MBSR individually via self-help "bibliotherapy," which involves reading through an MBSR workbook on their own and engaging in digital mindfulness exercises.[16]

Intensity and Duration of Treatment
The standard MBSR program consists of interactive online learning environment, eight weeks of live instructor-led sessions, and a daylong retreat after the sixth week. Participants may also complete at-home exercises for individual practice.

Two studies included in this review utilized a brief version of MBSR, comprising only four weekly sessions.[15, 19] Another study allotted 10 weeks for students to complete the bibliotherapy.[1]

Outcomes
Studies that contributed to the strong rating of this intervention demonstrated that MBSR with college students had the following outcomes:
- Decrease in depressive symptoms[15-16]
- Decrease in symptoms of anxiety[16]

Acceptance and Commitment Therapy

Strong Evidence

Overview
Acceptance and Commitment Therapy (A&CT) aims to increase psychological flexibility. Psychological flexibility is the ability to comprehend current thoughts and emotions and continue or change one's behavior, depending on the situation and one's values.

Eight A&CT studies were eligible for inclusion in this review. Five studies rated high for study design, of which two had statistically significant positive outcomes, and three rated low for study design, giving the intervention an overall rating of "strong support for causal evidence."

Population of Focus
A&CT can be used with a wide variety of populations and age groups to reduce negative behaviors and improve mental health. Populations of focus often include individuals with substance use disorders (SUDs)[20] and people experiencing chronic pain.[21]

Studies included in this evidence review focused on the general college student population, as well as students seeking services from their college counseling centers.[22-23]

Of the studies reviewed, one did not report demographic information of participants.[24] Of the seven studies that did, at least two-thirds of the participants were female in six,[22-23, 25-28] and about half of participants were female in the other.[29] Participants across all seven studies reporting demographics were predominantly White and in four of these studies 10-16 percent of participants were Hispanic or Latino/a.[23, 25, 27-28]

Practitioner Types
Typically, a provider trained in individual or group A&CT implements the treatment. Recent adaptations include using an online, self-guided format, either as standalone or in conjunction with provider-led, in-person sessions.[30-32]

Some studies included in this review delivered A&CT through a self-guided, web-based platform.[27] One study used an in-person, group format led by a facilitator.[23]

Intensity and Duration of Treatment
The duration of A&CT can vary widely, but it is desirable to hold enough sessions to cover the six core principles. One study instructed participants to complete six web-based sessions over four weeks,[27] while another study delivered A&CT more frequently but with briefer sessions (12 biweekly, web-based sessions, each taking 15–30 minutes to complete).[28]

Core Processes of Acceptance and Commitment Therapy (A&CT)

1. **ACCEPTANCE:** Embracing of one's own experiences, thoughts, and feelings rather than avoidance

2. **SELF AS CONTEXT:** Being aware of what one is thinking, feeling, doing, and sensing in any moment

3. **COGNITIVE DEFUSION:** Diminishing the strength of negative thoughts by separating or distancing oneself from these thoughts or memories

4. **VALUES:** Knowing what matters and is important; choosing behaviors aligned with those values

5. **BEING PRESENT:** Consciously paying attention, engaging, and connecting with what is happening in the moment

6. **COMMITTED ACTION:** Taking action and achieving concrete goals consistent with personal values

Source: Hayes, S. C., Luoma, J. B., Bond, F. W., Masuda, A., & Lillis, J. (2006). Acceptance and Commitment Therapy: Model, processes and outcomes. *Behaviour Research and Therapy, 44*, 1-25.

Outcomes
Studies that contributed to the strong rating of this intervention demonstrated that A&CT with college students had the following outcomes:

- Decrease in distress[27, 28]
- Decrease in social anxiety[27]

Cognitive Behavioral Therapy (CBT)

Strong Evidence

Overview

Cognitive behavioral therapy (CBT) is a short-term, goal-oriented psychotherapy treatment enabling individuals to understand their current problems, challenges, and experiences and change patterns of thinking or behaviors. It is commonly used to address depressive and distortive thoughts associated with depression, generalized anxiety disorders, suicidal ideation, eating disorders, and SUD.

CBT helps clients develop accurate assessments of circumstances and their feelings so they can develop realistic strategies to address them. With the CBT approach, clients are trained to evaluate inaccurate thoughts, actions, and negative feelings that may contribute to their depression, anxiety, suicidal ideation, and/or other mental distress.[33]

CBT treatment usually draws on a variety of strategies to try to change clients' thinking and behavioral patterns. These strategies might include building awareness of one's thoughts, identifying negative or inaccurate thoughts, developing a greater sense of confidence, facing one's fears, positive self-talk, and stress management techniques, among others.[34-37]

CBT is available in a variety of forms, including individual therapy, group therapy, and computerized or Internet-guided delivery. These modalities all draw on the foundational principles and goals of CBT described above. However, they can vary widely on several characteristics, including format, duration, and delivery. For each modality, there are also different manuals and implementation protocols.

Twenty-five studies of CBT met the criteria for evidence review. Of these, seven were rated high and four were rated moderate. Fourteen were rated low because they were pre-post design studies or reviewers identified weaknesses in their study designs.

The 11 high and moderate studies gave CBT an overall rating of "strong support for causal evidence." All 11 studies included either group CBT or computerized CBT for the population of focus. Evidence reviewers did not find any studies for individual CBT for this population (i.e., college students) that were rated moderate or high. However, individual CBT is known to be evidence-based, with a solid research base for diverse populations and, hence, is included in this guide.

Population of Focus

The populations of focus were different for the three modalities of CBT. For the studies included in this review:

- **Individual CBT** was used with students who had body image concerns and/or eating disorders,[34-35] attention deficit hyperactivity disorder (ADHD),[36] and depressive symptoms.[37-38] Of the five individual CBT studies reviewed, participants in four studies were more than three-fourths female.[38-42] In three studies, more than 60 percent of participants were White.[39-40, 42] In one study, 40 percent of participants were Black[38], while one study included a sample that was one-third Hispanic[42], and another had a sample that was about one-third Asian.[41]

- **Group CBT** was used with students with ADHD,[43-44] with or at-risk for depression,[34, 36-37, 45-47] with social anxiety disorder (SAD),[31] with public speaking anxiety,[24] and with maladaptive perfectionism.[48] Most of the studies reviewed had predominantly female samples.[24, 34, 36-37, 43, 45-47] Two studies had samples that were one-half female.[35, 48] In six studies, more than 60 percent of participants were White.[35, 43, 45-47] In one study, more than 90 percent of participants were racial/ethnic minorities.[36] Three studies did not present racial/ethnic demographics for their samples.[24, 34, 36]

- **Computerized CBT** interventions were used with general student populations,[49-51] students at-risk for or diagnosed with an eating disorder,[52-53] and students with symptoms of anxiety and depression.[54] All six studies of computerized CBT interventions had samples that were predominantly female.[49-54] In five of these studies samples were also predominantly White[49-51, 53-54]. In the other study half of particants were White, about 20 percent were Asian, and the remaining 30 percent were other racial/ethnic minorities.[52]

Practitioner Types

Individual CBT is implemented in different ways and various manuals for this intervention exist. Consequently, the particular training and/or certification required to deliver this therapy also varies. In the reviewed studies, individual CBT was typically delivered by trained psychologists and/or therapists.[41-42] In one study, doctoral students in clinical psychology delivered individual CBT to students.[39]

There is also a myriad of manuals for variants of group CBT, and training and/or certification for each variant may differ. In the reviewed studies, trained psychologists and/or therapists typically delivered group CBT.[37, 44-45, 47] However, several studies also relied on trained graduate or doctoral students to facilitate or co-facilitate group CBT sessions.[24, 35, 43, 46, 48]

As the name suggests, computerized CBT is delivered to students via computer or mobile app-based platforms. Typically, these platforms present CBT content through video modules or other tools and are therefore self-guided. However, in two of the studies included in this review, online materials were supplemented with limited personal contact; in one study, this comprised scripted support messages sent by program staff, while the other study included weekly motivational messages and up to two phone calls with coaches, who were trained post-secondary students.[50, 53]

Intensity and Duration of Treatment

There is no standard length or prescribed number of sessions for individual CBT.[55] The overall intensity and duration of treatment depends on the kind and severity of problems experienced by the student. However, individual CBT is generally considered to be a shorter-term therapeutic approach.[56] In the reviewed studies, individual CBT was typically delivered once a week, with overall duration varying from 3 to 12 weeks.[38-39, 41]

Group CBT is typically more structured than individual therapy. However, treatment intensity and length may still vary depending on the specific protocol practitioners use and the kinds of problems they treat. In the reviewed studies, group CBT was typically delivered once a week for one to two hours, with overall duration varying from four[24, 47] to eight or more sessions.[35-36, 43-44] One study used a single, multi-hour group workshop approach,[48] though this is not typical for group CBT delivery.

The intensity, duration, and structure of computerized CBT treatments vary, depending on the specific program. In the reviewed studies, some programs set weekly schedules for the content they wanted users to cover, while others provided full access to the platform and allowed users to work at their own pace. For more structured platforms, the overall length of treatment ranged from 2 to 10 weeks.[52, 54]

Outcomes

Studies of individual CBT with a college student sample did not contribute to the high rating of this intervention, so the outcomes from those studies are not included. However, in general population studies, individual CBT is associated with reduction in anxiety[54] and depression.[55]

Studies that contributed to the high rating of this intervention demonstrated that use of group CBT with college students had the following outcomes:

- Decreases in overall depressive symptoms[36-37, 45, 59]
- Decreases in overall anxiety symptoms[36-37]
- Reduction in negative thinking[59]
- Reduction in levels of worry[37]
- Improvements in self-esteem[59]
- Improvements in life satisfaction and happiness ratings[36]

Studies that contributed to the high rating in this evidence review demonstrated that use of computerized CBT interventions with college students had the following outcomes:

- Decreases in overall depressive symptoms[53-54]
- Decreases in eating disorder symptomology,[53] binge eating frequency,[53] and compensatory behaviors (e.g., excessive exercise)[53]

Dialectical Behavior Therapy (DBT)

Moderate Evidence

Overview

Dialectical behavior therapy (DBT) is a psychotherapy treatment originally developed by Dr. Marsha Linehan to treat individuals at-risk for suicide[60] and/or those with borderline personality disorder (BPD).[61] DBT is commonly used to address depressive symptoms, SUDs, post-traumatic stress disorders, and a wide range of other disorders. It focuses on dialectical or opposing strategies of acceptance and change.[61]

DBT has been primarily studied with BPD populations, for which it has been effective at reducing suicidal behaviors and non-suicidal self-injury (NSSI).[62-64] It also has proven efficacy at treating NSSI and depression in adolescents.[64]

Research is limited on DBT's specific effects on college-aged populations. Of the 10 studies eligible for this review, 3 were rated high. Seven were rated low because they were pre-post design studies or reviewers identified weaknesses in their study designs. Of the three highly rated studies, one showed statistically significant positive outcomes. These findings give the DBT intervention an overall rating of "moderate support for causal evidence."

Components of Dialectical Behavior Therapy (DBT)

DBT Skills Training, which teaches clients skills in mindfulness, distress tolerance, interpersonal effectiveness, and emotion regulation.

Individual Psychotherapy, designed to enhance client motivation and apply skills to manage their lives and confront specific challenges.

In-the-Moment Phone Coaching, in which therapists provide coaching to clients on how to apply the skills learned and cope with everyday challenges.

DBT Consultation Teams for Therapists, through which therapists are supported and treatment fidelity is monitored.

Source: Behavioral Tech (n.d.) What is Dialectical Behavior Therapy (DBT)?. https://behavioraltech.org/resources/faqs/dialectical-behavior-therapy-dbt/

Studies & Statistics / Prevention and Treatment Among College Students

Population of Focus
While DBT was originally designed for use with BPD populations, it has since been used with a wide variety of populations to treat an array of mental health concerns. In the studies included in this review, DBT was used for students with test anxiety, with attention-deficit/hyperactivity disorder (ADHD), who reported serious problems with emotion regulation, with symptoms of mood disorders, and those seeking other treatment recommended by college counseling centers.[65-70]

Of the ten studies reviewed, six included samples that were predominantly female.[68, 70-75] Two studies had samples that were slightly more than half female,[65-66] one study was slightly more than half male,[67] and one study did not report any demographic data.[69] Participants in four studies were predominantly White[68, 70-71, 74] while two studies had samples that were about half White,[67, 72] and one study was predominantly composed of racial/ethnic minority students.[72-73] Three studies did not report on the racial/ethnic backgrounds of participants.[65-66, 69] In one study, about 30 percent of students identified as LGBTQ+.[75]

Practitioner Types
DBT practitioners typically undergo intensive training to obtain certification. Certification is offered through the DBT-Linehan Board of Certification (DBT-LBC) to licensed mental health professionals. It requires practitioners to complete 40 hours of didactic training and complete a written exam.[76] In the reviewed studies, DBT was usually delivered by teams including at least one therapist who had undergone certification training, as well as other facilitators, such as counseling center staff, clinical psychology graduate students, and/or nurse practitioners who participated in shorter training modules.[70-72]

Intensity and Duration of Treatment
DBT typically has a duration of about 24 weeks, consisting of weekly skills training groups in addition to hour-long weekly individual therapy sessions. DBT's phone coaching component permits clients to call their therapist between sessions to receive in-the-moment coaching and care. However, of the studies included in this review, several used adapted DBT models, which consisted predominantly of the DBT skills training group component.[65-68, 70, 72-74] These skills group-based therapies varied in duration from 4 to 13 weeks.

Outcomes

Studies that contributed to the moderate rating in this evidence review demonstrated that DBT with college students had the following outcomes:

- Reductions in suicidal ideation[75]
- Reductions in overall depressive symptoms[75]
- Decreased number of non-suicidal self-injury events[75]
- Improvements in social adjustment[75]

Summary of Evidence Review

The guide's evidence review provides support for five practices for prevention and treatment of anxiety, depression, and suicidal thoughts and behaviors among college students, which are summarized below.

Intervention	Gatekeeper training	MBSR	A&CT	CBT	DBT
Review rating for use with college students	Strong evidence	Strong evidence	Strong evidence	Strong evidence	Moderate evidence
Scope	Non-clinical	Clinical	Clinical	Clinical	Clinical
Care continuum	Prevention	Treatment	Treatment	Treatment	Treatment
Intensity and duration of treatment	A single training event	Eight weekly group sessions, lasting 2.5 hours each, and a daylong retreat after the sixth week	As many sessions as required to cover the six core principles	No standard length or prescribed number of CBT sessions	Typical duration is 24 weeks, consisting of weekly individual and group sessions
Specific training available	✓	✓	✓	✓	✓
Web-based version available	✓	✓	✓	✓	✓
Can be practiced by peers	✓	–	–	–	–

97

Studies & Statistics / Prevention and Treatment Among College Students

CHAPTER 3

Guidance for Selecting and Implementing Practices

This chapter provides information for clinicians, counselors, program or college administrators, and other stakeholders interested in implementing an evidence-based intervention to address college students' mental health needs.

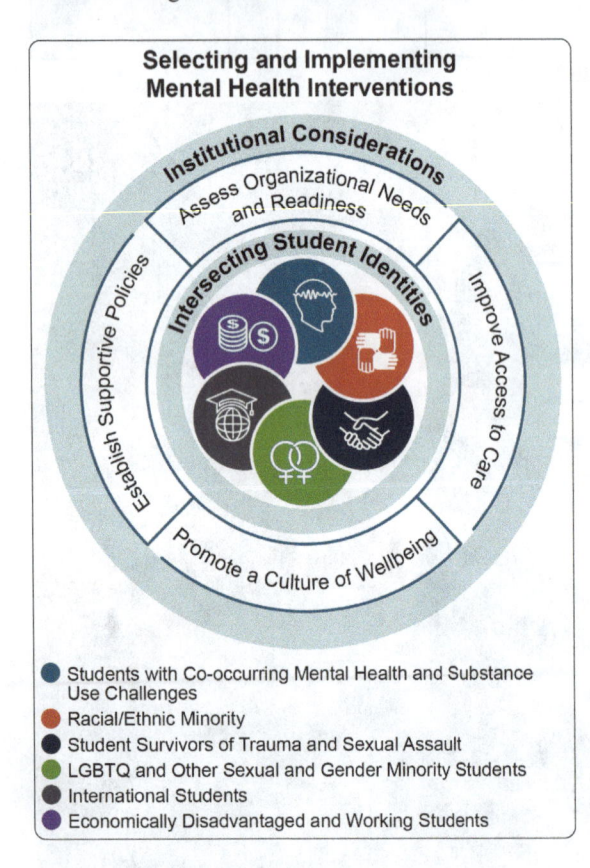

Selecting and Implementing Mental Health Interventions

- Institutional Considerations
- Assess Organizational Needs and Readiness
- Intersecting Student Identities
- Improve Access to Care
- Promote a Culture of Wellbeing
- Establish Supportive Policies

- Students with Co-occurring Mental Health and Substance Use Challenges
- Racial/Ethnic Minority
- Student Survivors of Trauma and Sexual Assault
- LGBTQ and Other Sexual and Gender Minority Students
- International Students
- Economically Disadvantaged and Working Students

The chapter first discusses student-level considerations for practitioners to consider when developing strategies to engage and treat students. Understanding the potential challenges particular student groups have or may experience in their lives allows practitioners and administrators to select and implement the most appropriate practices to meet students' needs.

This chapter also identifies specific strategies colleges can employ at the institutional level to promote student well-being and mitigate implementation challenges.

Considerations When Implementing Mental Health Services for Students

Each student seeking help at a counseling center and/or initiating treatment will present with a unique set of symptoms, experiences, and identities. However, certain groups may exhibit particular characteristics related to their mental health, including common stressors, factors influencing service utilization, and treatment preferences.[1] Special issues and considerations for diverse student populations are presented below, along with strategies for management or implementation of mental health treatment services.

While diversity topics are presented separately, it is important to note that they are intertwined and intersecting. Further, this is not an exhaustive list of diversity parameters or student identities. Finally, while making therapy decisions, practitioners should consider each student the expert on themselves and their identities.[2]

Campus counseling professionals should use a trauma-informed approach while working with students. This approach includes integrating principles of safety, trustworthiness, transparency, peer support, collaboration, mutuality, empowerment, language access, and cultural competency.[3] Practitioners may refer to the Substance Abuse and Mental Health Services Administration's (SAMHSA's) Treatment Improvement Protocol (TIP) on Trauma-Informed Care in Behavioral Health Services for more guidance on implementing a trauma-informed lens when delivering treatment services.

Additionally, colleges should consider using a trauma-informed design when creating the physical space for a counseling center. These designs create spaces that are welcoming and safe, while respecting privacy, identity, and dignity and promoting empowerment.[4]

Students With Co-occurring Mental Health and/or Substance Use Concerns

Consideration:
Students exhibiting common mental health symptoms, such as anxiety or depression, may also have or show symptoms of co-occurring conditions, such as eating disorders, substance use disorders (SUD), and/or serious mental illness (SMI).

Strategies:
- Practitioners treating students with co-occurring conditions should consider the full range of services available on campus and work with the student to plan comprehensive treatment. They can provide students with wraparound care by coordinating across multiple entities (e.g., counseling centers, academic departments, housing, and residential life offices). Students with alcohol misuse and/or substance use disorders, for example, may benefit from campus-based 12-step programs, substance-free housing, or sober social events.[5] Practitioners can help students gain access to available services on campus.

- In addition to care on campus or through college treatment centers, practitioners might consider referring students with co-occurring disorders to off-campus providers. Off-campus treatment providers may offer advantages like more advanced training, familiarity with specific conditions, anonymity for the student, or more in-depth and/or diverse treatment options. These advantages must be balanced with the potential cost, insurance availability, and transportation barriers before making service decisions.

Student Survivors of Trauma and Sexual Assault

Consideration:
Students experiencing mental health challenges may also have experienced previous trauma, including sexual assault. Survivors may avoid treatment because of fear of stigma, concerns about confidentiality, or a desire to avoid traumatic memories.

Strategies:
- Students who display symptoms of anxiety and depression may also have needs related to trauma. These students may need referral to and treatment from a specialist who is trained in treating young adults who have experienced trauma. Counseling centers should establish protocols and workflows to ensure practitioners screen each student for potential specialized services with partnering agencies on- or off-campus. It is best practice to establish memorandums of understanding (MOUs) and/or strong consultative relationships with area specialists in trauma to facilitate continuity of care and continued academic success.

- In addition to referrals to off-campus specialists, all college counseling clinical staff should be trained in appropriate interventions. College counseling centers should also consider supporting professional development and training opportunities for at least two onsite specialists.

- Practitioners and other stakeholders should carefully anticipate and avoid clinical procedures or unintended triggering events that might re-traumatize students. These could undermine trust and slow treatment progress. Campus awareness-raising and advocacy events should be vetted by counseling staff for triggers and/or appropriate trigger warnings.

Studies & Statistics / Prevention and Treatment Among College Students

LGBTQ and Other Sexual and Gender Minority Students

Consideration:
Students belonging to a sexual or gender minority may believe that available services will not support their sexual or gender identity and may avoid seeking help as a result.[6]

Strategies:
- Practitioners should take steps to make services inclusive of all students, including sexual and gender minorities. For example, practitioners should address students using their preferred names and pronouns to affirm their identities (even if legal name and sex assigned at birth are required for administrative purposes).[1] The Association for Lesbian, Gay, Bisexual, and Transgender Issues in Counseling's (ALGBTIC) [Competencies for Counseling LGBQIQA](#) and [Competencies for Counseling Transgender Clients](#) present a number of steps practitioners can take to improve their counseling approach and produce a safe, supportive, and caring environment for individuals.

- Practitioners should take particular care to ensure confidentiality and assure students that their personal information, including sexual orientation and gender identity, will never be disclosed.[1]

- Practitioners should inquire about microaggressions when treating students to gain a clearer picture of their stressors. They should also examine their own potential microaggressions and seek education opportunities for themselves and other counseling staff to address these issues.[7] Practitioners should be well-versed in policies and procedures necessary to file bias complaints should a student report issues related to discrimination in the classroom. They should also be trained in offering supportive resources without forcing or coercing a student into reporting.

Racial/Ethnic Minority Students

Consideration:
Because of stigma, cultural mistrust, and lack of racial/ethnic representation in counseling centers, students who are Black, Indigenous, and people of color (BIPOC) may underutilize mental health services compared to their White peers.[8]

Strategies:
- Colleges should consider diversifying staff who provide mental health services. The racial and ethnic composition of counseling center staff predicts the likelihood of help-seeking for some student populations. For example, the greater the percentage of African American therapists at a counseling center, the more African American students will seek help.[9] There should be organizational processes in place that allow students to select practitioners with shared identity, whenever available.
- Colleges and practitioners should provide culturally sensitive settings for students. This includes acknowledging minority students' experiences of racism and oppression,[10] encouraging students to become active in cultural groups and opportunities,[11] asking students whether they observe any religious or traditional customs that may be helpful in their treatment, and creating safe spaces for student discussion or race-related issues.[10] The Steve Fund and JED Foundation's Equity in Mental Health Framework provides guidance to colleges aiming to better support the mental health needs of minority students.
- When a practitioner identifies their own privileges and biases, both internally in their own clinical training and as appropriate to their clients, it can improve the therapeutic relationship and affirm their clients' identities and experiences.[2] Colleges should consider implementing staff trainings to develop skills, knowledge, and attitudes related to providing care for and understanding the challenges faced by students of color.

International Students
Consideration:
International students may experience challenges related to their cultural concepts of well-being and mental health.[12] Additionally, they are likely to be farther away from their support network of family and friends back home compared to their peers.

Strategies:
- International students may not be aware of mental health support services available on campus, based on experiences in their home country. Focused outreach efforts to international students will help increase awareness of these services.
- Practitioners should consider referring students whose native language is not English and who are not fluent in English to an outside provider who speaks their language. International students may also prefer working with a provider of the same cultural background as themselves. Further, if these services are not available, they should arrange for a professional interpreter (not a family member) when there is a language barrier.

Economically Disadvantaged and Working Students
Consideration:
Students from lower socioeconomic backgrounds and working students may face challenges in seeking and receiving treatment while in college, such as concerns about paying for services and scheduling difficulties.[13]

Strategies:
- Colleges should educate students on services that are already fully or partially covered by tuition and fees.
- Counseling centers should publicize their hours of operation and offer extended and/or flexible hours for treatment when possible.[14-15] Virtual services may also be useful for students with scheduling constraints.[1] Special efforts should be made to accommodate students who have urgent care needs.
- When relevant, practitioners may also provide or refer students to case management or other services to assist them with financial, housing, relational, or other issues.[14]

Institutional Considerations for Implementing Mental Health Services

Implementing mental health practices on campus requires institutional support. There is tremendous variation across institutions of higher education, and each institution will face a unique set of challenges. Colleges need to explore ways in which they can adapt programs/strategies to meet their needs and constraints while still implementing the core components of the intervention.

Before a college implements a new intervention or service, it is important to consider a range of factors. Institutions must ensure that there is appropriate space, technology, training, support, and financial and human resources to implement and sustain new mental health services. The following section provides strategies colleges might consider using when establishing a new mental health program.

Strategies to Assess Organizational Needs and Readiness

Prior to implementing new or expanding upon existing college mental health programs, institutions and counseling centers should conduct a needs assessment to explore the following factors:

- **Identifying available internal resources and local factors:** Colleges need to begin by identifying internal resources (e.g., staffing, technology, space) and local factors (e.g., geography, type of college, availability of transportation and services in the community for referrals) that could affect service delivery and/or be leveraged for implementation. They should use available data to determine whether counseling centers and other campus health services can sufficiently handle caseloads and to identify program gaps. Finally, colleges should assess the "readiness" of the institution to implement a new program successfully.[16]

- **Reviewing existing protocols:** Colleges should review existing protocols related to mental health services provision, such as those for crisis management, confidentiality, and medical leave, and determine if any revisions are needed for the new program(s) (e.g., additional cybersecurity protocols for implementation of an online cognitive behavioral therapy intervention).

- **Exploring financial implications:** Colleges should determine the costs of implementing and sustaining new mental health programs. Administrators should make decisions about whether current resources are sufficient or whether additional funds need to be raised, for example through increasing student health fees, charging fees for use of specific services, reallocating funds from other campus priorities, or working with insurance companies to seek reimbursement.[1,17] It is important to note that program investments may pay dividends in the future through improved academic performance, retention, and graduation rates.[18]

- **Considering characteristics of the student population:** Colleges would benefit from identifying the characteristics of student populations for whom new programs would be implemented, such as unique risk factors, cultures and identities, and barriers to care and making adaptations to facilitate program implementation. Practitioners should use a trauma-informed care approach for therapy with students. Whenever possible, students should be involved in making decisions about their own mental health support services.

Based on results of the needs assessment, institutional leaders should work with their student health teams, administrators, student representatives, and other stakeholders to create an implementation plan that includes the following:

1. Institutional priorities, staffing and/or technology needs, necessary changes to existing policies or systems, and training needs
2. Plans to address equity in delivery of the program
3. Quality improvement plans and expected short- and long-term outcomes with a strategy for measuring them
4. Logic model illustrating the required inputs, planned program activities, and how they will produce desired outcomes (W.K. Kellogg Foundation's logic model development guide can help teams create their logic models)

Strategies to Improve Access to Care

When considering new interventions to support students' well-being, institutions should decide how students will access those interventions. Potential strategies to improve access include:

- **Integrating care where possible:** Integrated care (creating a unified healthcare model) enhances access to services, facilitates timeliness and follow-through on referrals, improves service quality, utilization, and efficiency, and, ultimately, improves student outcomes.[19-21] Schools can integrate care by:

  – *Promoting a "No Wrong Door" approach:* Colleges may have multiple campus organizations, such as the campus counseling center or the healthcare center, that provide mental health screening and counseling services. Regardless of where they enter the campus mental health system, students should be assured that they will receive thoughtful care and be directed to the most appropriate services.[22]

  – *Considering use of electronic medical records (EMRs) or electronic health records:* EMRs and EHRs improve coordination of services and facilitate communication between different providers on campus.

  – *Integrating off-campus providers:* At times, staff may lack the expertise or capacity to appropriately serve students, such as those with chronic mental health needs.[22] In such cases, it may be appropriate to integrate on-campus care with off-campus healthcare providers. Investing in case management and resource navigation staff can help students access appropriate services within an integrated care system.

- **Mitigating structural barriers to care:** Students may face barriers such as a lack of time, financial constraints, or transportation issues when seeking care.[1,13] Strategies to mitigate these barriers include:

  – *Using technology to overcome scheduling or transportation barriers*: Providing online resources, virtual self-guided programs, or telehealth options can reduce these barriers and increase access to care for all students. The Higher Education Mental Health Alliance (HEMHA) developed a guide for implementing telemental services in college settings.

  – *Considering the academic calendar and planning accordingly:* School breaks may result in problems related to continuity of care. If possible, counseling centers should establish services during break periods for students remaining on campus and identify strategies for continuing care with students who will be away from campus. With the student's consent, counselors can work with parents to help students continue care if going home. At a minimum, counseling centers should provide information on their websites about what to do when centers are closed. Practitioners may also be able to make use of the previously discussed strategies around integrating with off-campus providers and telehealth.

- *Educating students on available services and their costs:* Many campuses offer no or low-cost mental health treatment services on campus, but students are not always aware of the actual costs involved (or lack thereof).[23] Counseling and administrative staff should inform the students via center websites about services that are already covered by student health fees and/or insurance or are free.

- *Increasing staff:* Limited capacity to serve help-seeking students continues to be a significant barrier to care. Hiring additional counselors, clinicians, case managers, or other staff is a direct way to increase institutional capacity to meet students' help-seeking needs and can serve as a long-term investment in mental health service capacity.

- *Creating a behavioral intervention team (BIT) to detect risk factors in student behaviors:* Colleges should consider creating a BIT to collect data and collaborate in identifying and mitigating risk factors in student behaviors across the campus. Colleges should ensure that varied partners across the campus, beyond student health agencies, are invited to be a part of these teams.

Strategies to Promote a Culture of Well-Being

Stigma continues to be a major barrier to students seeking help for mental health needs.[13, 24] Colleges should develop and maintain a culture of inclusivity and support to reduce stigma and normalize help-seeking. Potential strategies include:

- **Integrating the importance of health and well-being into all policies, practices, and discussions on campus across both administrative and academic operations:** Colleges can refer to existing guides, such as the Okanagan Charter and others listed at the end of this chapter to implement this strategy.

- **Increasing visibility about the importance of mental health by engaging department chairs, faculty, staff, mentors, and students in discussions of mental health issues:** Colleges may want to create a high-level task force of staff that typically have contact with students, such as resident advisors and academic counselors, or establish a "campus team" to improve coordination and communication across campus departments about mental health issues and potential crises.

- **Promoting active and supportive social relationships:** Colleges can develop smaller "living and learning communities" to foster social groups formed on academic majors or other interests, or otherwise encourage students to join or form campus organizations.[16] Mental health information should also be disseminated to parents to help them recognize stress in their children and foster strong familial relationships.

- **Promoting campus wide mental health:** Colleges can implement trainings and offer support to reduce stress and promote well-being across the campus. All staff interacting directly with students should also understand the role of campus counseling centers and when and how to refer students for care. They should help normalize help-seeking behaviors, promote the de-stigmatization of mental health treatment, and promote self-care and counseling as sustaining measures for well-being.

- **Educating campus community members:** Colleges can help staff, faculty, and students on campus identify and respond to mental health warning signs, both for themselves and others. This preventive measure can be implemented by providing periodic training on mental health issues and responding to individuals in distress. In a recent survey, most faculty members indicated that they feel responsible to help students dealing with mental health concerns and that they would appreciate receiving training on how to support them.[25]

Legal Considerations

At the federal level, three main pieces of legislation are pertinent to colleges' delivery of mental health services:

The Family Educational Rights and Privacy Act (FERPA): FERPA is a federal law that protects students' educational records, including treatment records for care provided on campus at student health or counseling centers. Under FERPA, students' treatment records are only available to professionals providing treatment to the student or other professionals of the student's choice.

The Health Insurance Portability and Accountability Act (HIPAA): HIPAA is a federal law that creates national standards for the protection of personal health information. Typically, FERPA supersedes HIPAA for care provided on campus. However, HIPAA regulations will apply to information kept by community healthcare providers to whom students may be referred or who may provide integrated care.

Title IX: Title IX is a federal law protecting individuals in education programs/activities from discrimination based on sex and applies to any institution receiving federal funding from the U.S. Department of Education. With respect to student mental health services, Title IX has important implications when it comes to sexual assault disclosures. This legislation grants protections to those reporting sex discrimination, including sexual violence. It also obligates some employees to report incidents and trigger an investigation. Colleges should clearly explain the reporting obligations of all employees, and make sure students know where they can find confidential support services.

Colleges should always consult with their general counsel offices regarding their approach to the above legislation. In addition, colleges should be aware that state/local regulations may also apply and need to be considered.

Policies to Support Students' Mental Health and Education

Poorly designed mental health policies, particularly those for medical leave, can create barriers to students seeking help.[26] Institutions can shape their campuses by establishing policies that support students' mental health decisions by:

- **Standardizing and implementing fair policies:** Colleges should develop transparent and standardized medical leave policies that are flexible, focused on student wellness, and developed with student participation. Additionally, the policies should be easy to access, no more rigorous or punitive than those for other medical absences, and explicit in terms of financial and academic consequences.[27]

- **Designing specific protocols:** Colleges should design crisis protocols specifically for acutely distressed or suicidal students, including risk assessments, safety plans, emergency contact notification procedures, and policies guiding involuntary and voluntary leave and/or hospitalization.

- **Establishing clear privacy guidelines:** If necessary, colleges should develop institutional release of information forms with off-campus providers to set up communication protocols and policies for sharing student health information.

- **Establishing and enforcing policies for co-occurring conditions:** Colleges should take measures to reduce alcohol and substance use, such as eliminating alcohol sponsorship of athletic events or other campus activities and alcohol advertising in college publications.[28] Colleges should also consider implementing medical amnesty policies (laws or acts protecting those who seek medical attention from liability as a result of illegal actions), as they address issues like underage drinking or possession of alcohol.

Resources

Numerous resources are available to help health practitioners and administrators implement new mental health programs in a college setting.

Overall Frameworks and Guides for Campus Health

- The Okanagan Charter provides colleges with a common language and set of principles to become a "health and well-being promoting campus."

- The Steve Fund and the JED Foundation's Equity in Mental Health Framework provides institutions with action-oriented recommendations and strategies to strengthen mental health supports for students of color.

- The JED Foundation's Comprehensive Approach to Mental Health Promotion and Suicide Prevention describes strategic areas that should be addressed in community efforts to support mental health and address substance misuse.

- The JED Foundation's Campus Mental Health Action Planning Guide provides readers with a set of principles and recommendations to guide development of a comprehensive plan for mental health promotion on campus.

- The American College Health Association's Trauma Informed Care on College Campus provides a framework for implementing the approach specifically on college campuses.

Tools and Guidance for Implementation

Overall Implementation Guidance

- HEMHA published College Counseling From a Distance: Deciding Whether and When to Engage in Telemental Health Services, a guide focusing on topics for campuses considering implementing telehealth options for students.

- HEMHA's Balancing Safety and Support on Campus guide summarizes literature on "campus teams" and helps colleges make decisions about how these teams should be structured, what they should be tasked with, and how they should operate.

- The JED Foundation's Framework for Institutional Protocols for Acutely Distressed or Suicidal College Students guides administrators seeking to develop or revise protocols for crisis management.

- Center for Collegiate Mental Health's (CCMH) Clinical Load Index provides a distribution of staffing levels that can be used to inform decisions about the resourcing of mental health services in colleges and universities.

Screening Tools

- California Community College Mental Health Screening Tools and an article published by California Community Colleges' Health and Wellness Center provide an overview of screening tools that can be implemented on college campuses.

Treating Particular Populations

- SAMHSA's TIP 57 on Trauma-Informed Care in Behavioral Health Services helps practitioners understand the impact of trauma and develop models of trauma-informed care to support recovery.

- SAMHSA's TIP 59 on Improving Cultural Competence helps practitioners understand the role of culture in service delivery and discusses racial, ethnic, and cultural considerations.

- The Council of National Psychological Associations for the Advancement of Ethnic Minority Interests published a brochure on Psychological Treatment of Ethnic Minority Populations containing guidance for practitioners working with minority patients.

- The Steve Fund's report provides strategies to promote mental health and emotional well-being of young people of color.

- ALGBTIC's Competencies for Counseling LGBQIQA and Competencies for Counseling Transgender Clients present steps practitioners can take to improve their counseling approach and produce a safe, supportive, and caring environment for sexual and gender minority individuals.

Implementation Tools

- The American Foundation for Suicide Prevention's Interactive Screening Program is an online program for campuses that connects students to brief mental health screening and allows them to communicate with counselors and learn about available services.

Studies & Statistics / Prevention and Treatment Among College Students

- The Community Toolbox is a free online resource providing hundreds of training videos on topics related to building healthier communities.
- Campus leaders can use the Healthy Minds Return-on-Investment (ROI) tool to estimate the potential returns on new investments in student mental health.
- The W.K. Kellogg Foundation's logic model development guide helps teams create logic models for their programs.
- The Jed Foundation and the Clinton Foundation's Help a Friend in Need guide can help students identify signs of emotional distress in social media posts and content.
- The Association of College and University Educators' Creating a Culture of Caring provides practical approaches for college and university faculty to support student well-being and mental health.

Substance Use Prevention
- The National Institute on Alcohol Abuse and Alcoholism's College AIM tool can help college leaders identify effective alcohol and drug misuse prevention strategies.
- The Drug Enforcement Administration's Strategic Planning Guide for Preventing Drug Misuse Among College Students provides colleges with a robust framework to implement drug misuse interventions.

Background Literature
- SAMHSA's Behavioral Health Among College Students Information and Resource Kit discusses the prevalence and consequences of substance misuse among college students and provides readers with summaries of current knowledge, links, and directions that make it easier to locate prevention materials.
- The National Academies of Sciences, Engineering, and Medicine published Mental Health, Substance Use, and Well-Being in Higher Education, a consensus study report outlining a variety of possible approaches and recommendations to support delivery of mental health and substance use services and meet students' needs.
- The SAMHSA white paper Promoting Mental Health and Preventing Suicide in College and University Settings describes literature on suicide and suicide prevention on campuses and some prevention efforts.
- The American College Health Association developed a module for colleges to review FERPA and HIPAA legislation.
- The Bringing Theory to Practice's volume Well-Being and Higher Education: A Strategy for Change and the Realization of Education's Greater Purposes is a collection of essays exploring the connections between higher education and mental health and calling on institutions to take an active role in promoting well-being.

Review

Adjustment Disorder: Current Developments and Future Directions

Meaghan L. O'Donnell [1,2,*], James A. Agathos [1,2], Olivia Metcalf [1,2], Kari Gibson [1,2] and Winnie Lau [1,2]

1. Phoenix Australia Centre for Posttraumatic Mental Health, 161 Barry Street, Carlton VIC, Melbourne 3053, Australia
2. Department of Psychiatry, University of Melbourne, Melbourne 3053, Australia
* Correspondence: mod@unimelb.edu.au

Received: 26 June 2019; Accepted: 10 July 2019; Published: 16 July 2019

Abstract: Despite its high prevalence in clinical and consultant liaison psychiatry populations, adjustment disorder research has traditionally been hindered by its lack of clear diagnostic criteria. However, with the greater diagnostic clarity provided in the Diagnostic and Statistical Manual of Mental Disorders – fifth edition (DSM-5) and the International Statistical Classification of Diseases and Related Health Problems, 11th edition (ICD-11), adjustment disorder has been increasingly recognised as an area of research interest. This paper evaluates the commonalities and differences between the ICD-11 and DSM-5 concepts of adjustment disorder and reviews the current state of knowledge regarding its symptom profile, course, assessment, and treatment. In doing so, it identifies the gaps in our understanding of adjustment disorder and discusses future directions for research.

Keywords: adjustment disorder; review; diagnosis; symptoms; nosology; DSM-5; ICD-11; course; trajectory; treatment

1. Introduction

Adjustment disorder describes a maladaptive emotional and/or behavioural response to an identifiable psychosocial stressor, capturing those who experience difficulties adjusting after a stressful event at a level disproportionate to the severity or intensity of the stressor [1]. The symptoms are characterised by stress responses that are out of step with socially or culturally expected reactions to the stressor and/or which cause marked distress and impairment in daily functioning. Unlike posttraumatic stress disorder (PTSD) or acute stress disorder (ASD), which have clear criteria for what constitutes a traumatic event, adjustment disorder criteria does not specify any requirements for what can be regarded as a stressor. Research has identified, however, that stressor events may include both traumatic events, such as exposure to actual or threatened death, as well as non-traumatic stressful events such as interpersonal conflict, death of a loved one, unemployment, financial difficulties, or illness of a loved one or oneself [2].

Prevalence estimates of adjustment disorder vary markedly due to various factors including sampling process, population, and the diversity of measures used for assessment and diagnosis. Population-based studies have found prevalence rates of less than 1%, which may be due to limitations of the diagnostic tools used [3]. Conversely, more recent studies using newer diagnostic tools have found prevalence rates of 2% in general population research [4]. Rates are much higher in specific high-risk samples such as recently unemployed (27%; [5]) and bereaved individuals (18%; [6]).

Adjustment disorder is particularly prevalent in consultation liaison settings [7]. A multisite study in consultation psychiatry services in the United States, Canada, and Australia found that adjustment disorder was diagnosed in 12% of psychiatric consultations, with a further 11% identified as possible cases [8]. In Irish general hospital patients, adjustment disorder represented 18.5% of consultation liaison referrals [7]. At least one psychosocial stressor was noted in 93% of all patients, which included medical illness in 59% of patients. In this setting, the diagnosis was used especially in patients with serious medical conditions, self-harm, injury and poisoning, and in cases presenting with a mixture of somatic and psychic symptoms. Other consultant liaison psychiatry samples have reported a prevalence rate as high as 30% [9]. In emergency department settings when routine psychiatric assessments have been conducted in individuals primarily presenting with self-harm, adjustment disorder was the most common diagnosis (32%; [10]). Among other medical populations, adjustment disorder is also extremely common. A 2011 meta-analysis of oncology-related palliative and non-palliative settings indicated a prevalence rate of 15–19%, comparable to major depressive disorder and higher than anxiety disorders [11]. Research from Japan shows the prevalence of adjustment disorder to be 35% among individuals with recurrent breast cancer [12]. In an acutely ill medical inpatient unit, adjustment disorder was found to be the most common diagnosis (14%), more than double the rates of depressive and anxious disorders [13].

Despite research indicating significant prevalence rates that are often greater than depressive and anxiety disorders in some populations, adjustment disorder has historically attracted little empirical research. Consequently, relatively little is known regarding the phenomenology of the disorder, its neural correlates, prevalence, risk factors, course, or treatment [14–16]. A key contributor to this lack of research has been the absence of clearly defined diagnostic criteria [15], which means operationalising the disorder in an empirical research context has proven difficult [17]. The adjustment disorder concept has attracted significant criticism due to issues related to its diagnostic vagueness. Research has struggled to neatly establish the extent to which adjustment disorder differs from other psychiatric disorders, or from normal adaptive stress responses [18].

Conceptualisation of adjustment disorder, however, is currently in a state of transition. With the most recent revisions of the two main diagnostic manuals used in clinical and research practice, the Diagnostic and Statistical Manual of Mental Disorders (DSM-5) [1] and International Statistical Classification of Diseases and Related Health Problems, 11th edition (ICD-11) [19], adjustment disorder has been increasingly recognised as an important target for research. The aim of this paper is to (i) compare and contrast the DSM-5 and ICD-11 diagnostic criteria for adjustment disorder; (ii) examine the course and trajectory of adjustment disorder; (iii) examine measurement of adjustment disorder; and (iv) discuss adjustment disorder treatment research. In doing so, this paper aims to identify gaps in our current knowledge of adjustment disorder and present directions for future research.

2. Diagnostic Criteria

The historical narrative for adjustment disorder in DSM and ICD has been described elsewhere [20,21] and provides a useful background to the current criteria. In DSM-5, adjustment disorder was reclassified to sit alongside PTSD and ASD in the *Trauma- and Stressor-Related Disorders* chapter [1]. Despite this, the diagnostic criteria remained effectively unchanged from the DSM-IV, as the committee decided that any proposed changes would be atheoretical given the lack of research that had been conducted into the disorder [14,17]. The focus of the DSM-5 approach to adjustment disorder has remained on distress or impairment associated with a stressor that is judged to be excessive (relative to cultural norms). On the other hand, the ICD-11 introduced changes that marked a significant paradigm shift. In line with DSM, ICD recognised adjustment disorder as a stressor related disorder by categorising it within the chapter *Disorders Specifically Associated with Stress*. It diverges from DSM by conceptualising adjustment disorder as a failure to adapt to a stressor as evidenced by preoccupation with the stressor and its consequences. Table 1 provides a summary of both DSM-5 and ICD-11's diagnostic criteria for adjustment disorder.

Table 1. Summary of corresponding DSM-5 [1] and ICD-11 [19] diagnostic criteria for adjustment disorder.

DSM-5	ICD-11
A. Onset of emotional or behavioural symptoms must occur in response to identifiable stressor, and within 3 months of the stressor.	1. Presence of an identifiable psychosocial stressor(s). Symptoms emerge within 1 month of the stressor.
B. These symptoms are clinically significant, marked by: - Distress that is disproportionate to the severity or intensity of the stressor, taking into account contextual and cultural factors. or - Significant impairments in social, occupational or other domains of functioning.	2. Preoccupation related to the stressor or its consequences in the form of at least one of the following: (a) excessive worry about the stressor (b) recurrent and distressing thoughts about the stressor (c) constant rumination about the implications of the stressor. 3. Failure to adapt to the stressor that causes significant impairment in personal, family, social, educational, occupational or other important areas of functioning
C. The disturbance does not meet the diagnostic criteria for another mental disorder, and is not an exacerbation of a pre-existing disorder.	4. Symptoms are not of a sufficient specificity or severity to justify diagnosis of another mental or behavioural disorder.
D. The symptoms do not represent normal bereavement.	
E. Symptoms do not last for more than six additional months after the stressor or its consequences have been resolved.	5. Symptoms typically resolve within 6 months, unless the stressor persists for a longer duration

2.1. Commonalities between DSM-5 and ICD-11

In their current iterations, the DSM-5 and ICD-11 diagnoses of adjustment disorder have many commonalities. Under both sets of criteria, a diagnosis of adjustment disorder must occur in the wake of an identifiable life stressor, and can only be diagnosed in the absence of another clinical diagnosis. Both systems recognise adjustment disorder as a transient condition, with DSM-5 stating that symptoms must not persist longer than six months after the stressor (and its consequences) are resolved, and ICD-11 recognising that symptoms tend to resolve within six months unless the stressor persists for a longer duration. Both additionally outline that emotional distress and functional impairments are key components of the disorder.

2.2. Differences between DSM-5 and ICD-11

The two sets of diagnostic criteria differ in key areas. The ICD-11 definition necessitates the identification of significant impairments in personal, occupational, and/or social functioning. Conversely, DSM-5 does not specifically require functional impairment—it is sufficient to have either impairments in functioning or distress that is disproportionate to the severity of the stressor. The ICD-11 also mandates that symptoms must emerge within one month of the stressor, while the DSM-5 allows a more liberal onset window of three months. Further, the DSM-5 specifies that symptoms cannot represent normal and culturally appropriate bereavement, whereas this is not mentioned by the ICD-11. However, the most significant difference between the diagnostic definitions is that ICD-11 requires symptoms of preoccupation with the stressor and its consequences in the form of rumination, excessive worry and/or recurrent distressing thoughts. DSM-5 gives no guidance as to what symptoms might constitute distress.

Overall, there is growing empirical support for the ICD-11 redefinition. Multiple studies investigating the diagnostic architecture of the disorder have identified items relating to stressor preoccupation and failure to adapt [4,22,23] which relate strongly to the core adjustment disorder concept. One longitudinal study over twelve months showed that intrusive memories was one of the symptoms that predicted adjustment disorder [17], supporting the ICD-11 idea that adjustment disorder is characterised by the mental intrusion of (and preoccupation with) the stressor.

'Failure to adapt' is thought to constitute a stress-response (e.g., sleep disturbances or concentration problems) that results in significant impairment in social, interpersonal, occupational, educational, or other areas of functioning [22]. Confirmatory factory analyses have shown that the two core symptoms of ICD-11 adjustment disorder (i.e., failure to adapt and preoccupations) comprise an accurate model of adjustment disorder symptom architecture, with high levels of model fit [23]. Four accessory symptoms (avoidance, depression, impulsivity, and anxiety) in addition to the core symptoms have also been found [4,23]. This suggests that in addition to the two core ICD-11 symptoms, there is evidence that additional symptoms may inform consideration of the diagnostic criteria.

2.2.1. Subtypes

Another key point of difference between the two systems is that the ICD-11 has removed any reference to adjustment disorder subtypes, preferencing a unifaceted concept of adjustment disorder. Conversely, the DSM-5 delineates the disorder into a series of six subtypes, each signifying the presence of specific symptoms. DSM-5 differentiates between adjustment disorder with (1) depressed mood, (2) anxiety, (3) mixed anxiety and depressed mood, (4) disturbance of conduct, (5) mixed disturbance of emotions and conduct, and (6) unspecified [1]. Yet since the publication of DSM-5, there has been little evidence to support the idea of distinct subtypes of adjustment disorder [17]. In Glaesmer et al.'s [4] six-factor model of adjustment disorder—comprising factors related to preoccupations, failure to adapt, avoidance, depression, anxiety, and impulsivity—inter-correlations between each of the factors were extremely high (between 0.75 and 0.96), suggesting that these were not adequately distinguishable from each other. Given that many of these factors map directly onto the subtypes listed in the DSM-5 (where the 'disturbance of conduct' subtype is mirrored by the 'avoidance' and 'impulsivity' factors), the finding that these are so highly inter-correlated undermines the plausibility of distinct adjustment disorder subtypes. Indeed, this finding has been mirrored in more recent studies using both confirmatory factor analysis and bifactor modelling, which all found that group factors mapping onto DSM adjustment disorder subtypes were highly inter-correlated [23–25]. These findings collectively suggest that there is insufficient evidence at present to substantiate the existence of adjustment disorder subtypes, instead lending support to the unidimensional conception of adjustment disorder outlined in the ICD-11.

2.2.2. Adjustment Disorder as a Subsyndromal Disorder

Both DSM-5 and ICD-11 adhere to the idea that adjustment disorder can only be diagnosed in the absence of another disorder. While most other disorders have the requirement that the symptoms cannot be better explained by another disorder, the adjustment disorder criteria are much more restrictive. As such, it is often conceived of as a subclinical or mild disorder. There is some evidence to suggest that this is indeed the case. In a longitudinal study of serious injury survivors, O'Donnell and colleagues found that across measures of disability, quality of life, anxiety and depression, those with adjustment disorder reported significantly worse outcomes than those with no disorder, but significantly better outcomes than those with another psychiatric diagnosis [17]. Consistent with this, DSM-5 explicitly instructs those presenting with subsyndromal PTSD to be diagnosed with adjustment disorder [1].

The fact that ICD-11 and DSM-5 have taken different approaches to a given diagnosis is not specific to adjustment disorder. Indeed, this issue has been raised in the PTSD literature, given the ICD and DSM nomenclature for PTSD are remarkably different [26]. The issue of whether treatments developed to treat the DSM-5 version of the disorder will be as effective in the treatment of its ICD-11 counterpart remains a challenge to optimising treatment for PTSD as it does for adjustment disorder [27]. Ultimately, while the differences between DSM-5 and ICD-11 adjustment disorder are significant, the divergence of ICD-11 in creating established clear, specific criteria for adjustment disorder has created a significant opportunity. The ICD-11 provides a description of the diagnosis that is much easier to operationalise than DSM-5, and consequently far more research has been conducted into ICD-11 adjustment disorder than DSM-5 adjustment disorder despite DSM-5 diagnosis being in situ since 2013. Since the introduction of the new ICD-11 diagnostic criteria in 2013, a scoping review conducted just three years later in 2016 found 10 new studies on international samples analysing the factor structure, measurement validity, risk factors, and outcomes from treatment intervention studies [28]. By establishing diagnostic criteria, the ICD-11 has given researchers the capacity to explore the research more clearly in a way that the vaguer structure in the DSM-5 does not permit. The ICD-11 proposal has allowed the adjustment disorder field to move ahead significantly.

3. Course and Trajectory

Research into the course of adjustment disorder is largely in its infancy. However, preliminary studies have identified that in some subpopulations, symptoms may increase over time, marking a trajectory toward a more severe disorder. In a study by O'Donnell et al. (2016), trauma survivors who had adjustment disorder 3 months after exposure were 2.67 times more likely to meet criteria for a more severe psychiatric disorder (including PTSD, major depressive disorder, and generalised anxiety disorder) at 12 months, relative to those who had no disorder at 3 months [17]. This finding runs counter to the proposal that adjustment disorder is a short-term diagnosis, with evidence suggesting that the disorder will progress to a more serious disorder in a subset of those diagnosed with adjustment disorder. Further, in this same study, 34.6% of those with adjustment disorder at three months still met the diagnostic criteria at twelve months suggesting a persistence of symptomatology.

Research into the course of PTSD may hold some answers to the trajectory of adjustment disorder over time. There have been a number of studies that have examined the trajectory of PTSD symptoms over time [29–35]. Generally, these studies show that the majority of those who are exposed to trauma typically fall into one of four to five prototypical trajectories (see Figure 1). It is reasonable to posit that those in the circled trajectories represent adjustment disorder given their initial response to the stressor is about 20 on the Clinician Administered PTSD Scale (CAPS; [36]) measure. A normal recovery is experienced by the majority of trauma survivors and is represented by the resilient group (whose initial CAPS score is approximately 10). The trajectories that start with a CAPS score of above 50 represent those with a probable PTSD diagnosis. It is interesting to note that both adjustment disorder trajectories accumulate symptoms over time, again suggesting that adjustment disorder is an early marker for a more severe disorder.

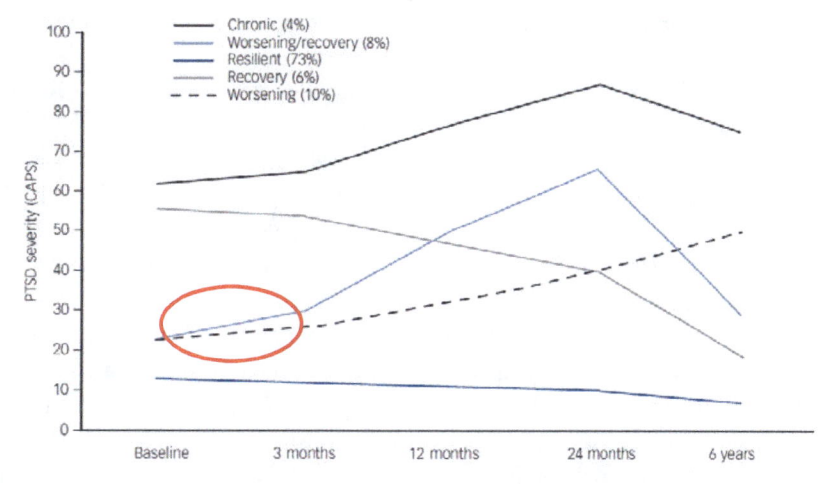

Figure 1. Posttraumatic stress disorder (PTSD) symptom trajectories over time. From Bryant et al. [37]. The red circle indicates the two trajectories of PTSD symptoms that may represent adjustment disorder trajectories.

It is important to recognise that these trajectory analyses are within trauma samples (rather than a stressful events sample) so these adjustment disorder trajectories may represent the more severe end of the spectrum. It is also recognised that these trajectory analyses are more relevant to the DSM-5 construct of adjustment disorder rather than the ICD-11, because they do not include symptoms of rumination or worry. They do, however, provide a useful idea as to the course of adjustment disorder over time, suggesting that adjustment disorder in some populations may have an enduring course.

Although emerging evidence indicates that adjustment disorder is a gateway to more severe psychiatric disorders, it is important to highlight that adjustment disorder is associated with significant negative outcomes in and of itself. Consultant liaison psychiatry research indicates adjustment disorder is significantly associated with suicidality and self-harm, at similar proportions to depressive disorders [38]. Other studies in inpatient populations have likewise found rates of self-harm and suicidality are significantly higher in adjustment disorder compared to other diagnoses [39,40].

4. Assessment

As with most aspects of adjustment disorder, the development of adequate assessment tools historically has been hindered by the fact that diagnostic criteria for the disorder were not clearly specified. However, even now that the ICD-11 has somewhat remedied this shortcoming, there is a clear dearth of measures available for its assessment and diagnosis. Most general structured clinical interviews do not provide any level of assessment of adjustment disorder, with no diagnostic module in either of the Clinical Interview Schedule (CIS; [41]) or the Composite International Diagnostic Interview (CIDI; [42]). Those that do include one, such as the Scheduled Clinical Interview for DSM-5 (SCID; [43]) and the Mini International Neuropsychiatric Interview (MINI; [44]) administer only a few items relating to adjustment disorder, and only as an addendum if none of the diagnostic criteria for any other disorders are met. Naturally, this is in line with the ICD-11 and DSM-5 portrayals of adjustment disorder as a subthreshold disorder—however, these modules are typically too cursory to provide a methodologically adequate measure of adjustment disorder [16,45].

Recently, however, specific measures for adjustment disorder have begun to emerge. One such option is the Diagnostic Interview for Adjustment Disorder (DIAD; [46]), which is a structured clinical interview for adjustment disorder based on the DSM-5 criteria. The DIAD includes 29 items that aim to identify symptoms associated with a stressor, and evaluate the levels of distress and functional impairment associated with these symptoms. Preliminary attempts at validating the measure by the original authors suggested "moderate to good" concept and construct validity [46]. However, as yet there are no external attempts by other authors to validate the DIAD in any clinical trials or studies—it is therefore unclear to what extent the measure actually provides a valid index of adjustment disorder in a clinical context.

The Adjustment Disorder—New Module (ADNM) has been developed for the ICD-11 diagnosis of adjustment disorder, and is available as a structured clinical interview [47] or self-report questionnaire [2]. The first section asks participants to select from a list of stressors (acute and chronic life events) that have been present over the past year, and to identify which was the most prominent or distressing. The second section comprises 20 items, which form six subscales in accordance with ICD-11 criteria relating to pre-occupation, failure to adapt, avoidance, depressive mood, anxiety, and impulse disturbance. A longer-form version with 29 items also exists, but the ADNM-20 seems to be used more commonly [48]. Participants rate on a 4-point Likert scale how often they have experienced particular symptoms during the past two weeks, and overall symptom severity is calculated as a sum of all item scores. Attempts at validating the ADNM have yielded positive results, with studies suggesting good levels of diagnostic specificity and sensitivity [23,48,49]. Condensed forms of the ADNM, such as the ADNM-8 and ADNM-4, have also shown high levels of convergent and construct validity, suggesting these offer an alternative screening tool for assessing adjustment disorder symptoms which is equally valid, but briefer [50,51]. Ultimately, the ADNM and DIAD seem to provide the most comprehensive measures of the ICD-11 and DSM-5 concepts of adjustment disorder respectively, though further research is needed to validate the latter.

5. Treatment and Intervention

To date, there is only one published systematic review of treatments available for adjustment disorder. A 2018 review examined 29 treatment trials investigating current options for psychological and pharmacological intervention [52]. They found that the quality of evidence in these studies was "low" to "very low" according to Grading of Recommendations Assessment, Development and Evaluation (GRADE; [53]) guidelines. A key limitation to most of these studies was the lack of a measure of adjustment disorder, small sample sizes, and lack of follow-up assessments. The authors also raised the issue of the divergence of the ICD-11 and DSM-5 diagnostic classification. For example, the recent trial on self-help intervention was based on the beta version of ICD-11 and they found this intervention had its most useful impact on preoccupation about the event including rumination, worry and intrusive thoughts [54]. While this is very relevant for the ICD-11 diagnosis of adjustment disorder, as discussed earlier, the degree to which this would be useful for those meeting criteria for DSM-5 adjustment disorder is unknown.

Since the publication of the systematic review in 2018, two further randomised controlled trials (RCTs) have been published. One investigated an internet-based self-help intervention known as Brief Adjustment Disorder Intervention (BADI) for the treatment of ICD-11 adjustment disorder [55]. In the self-help trial, completer analysis revealed that BADI reduced ICD-11 adjustment disorder symptoms and increased psychological well-being for those participants who used the intervention at least once in 30 days. The high drop-out rates from this trial (86%) prevent firm conclusions from being drawn. A second study targeted ICD-10 and DSM-IV adjustment disorder, and compared a face-to-face and virtual reality delivered cognitive behavioural therapy (CBT) to the waitlist [56]. Both the face-to-face and virtual reality CBT resulted in significantly greater improvements to adjustment disorder relative to the wait-list controls at pre/post treatment. The virtual reality group had significantly greater longer-term improvements than the standard and wait-list groups. Despite very small sample sizes in this study, as well as the high drop-out rates from the Eimontas et al. study [55], there is early support that technology assisted interventions for adjustment disorder may be useful, though further methodologically rigorous studies are needed.

As adjustment disorder is characterised as a subclinical disorder, it is reasonable to consider that it may be responsive to lower intensity, brief intervention. This is consistent with intervention findings that show adjustment disorder to be responsive to self-help bibliotherapy [54], and other online self-directed interventions [55]. Adjustment disorder interventions might also be amenable to 'task shifting', that is, interventions designed to be delivered by non-specialists in order to increase their accessibility. Recent meta-analyses indicate that use of non-specialists can lead to significant improvements in mental health [57]. A recently developed program, Skills for Life Adjustment and Resilience (SOLAR), aims to address adjustment difficulties and sub-clinical presentations using a brief, non-specialist delivered format. The SOLAR program is currently being tested in Australia, Japan, and the South Pacific. So far, preliminary data drawn from these projects suggest that SOLAR is not only an acceptable and feasible intervention that can be implemented by trained lay workers, it is also effective in reducing adjustment difficulties [58,59].

In summary, the emergence of clear diagnostic criteria with ICD-11 has finally presented the opportunity for new treatment options to be developed and tested. Several emerging treatment options have utilised the internet to complement the therapeutic approach, which is likely to be appealing to individuals with sub-clinical problems such as adjustment disorder [56]. Additionally, treatments that are brief and scalable may be appropriate for the treatment of adjustment disorder. Despite this emerging evidence base, however, the lack of high quality trials that test interventions for adjustment disorder is still a serious concern, and there are no clear recommendations on how to best treat the disorder. As such, there is a clear need for higher quality, methodologically sound treatment trials to aid in both the development of new treatment options and in the validation of current ones.

6. Conclusions

After decades of uncertainty surrounding adjustment disorder, despite research indicating it is a prevalent problem in populations such as consultant liaison psychiatry, it is now a critical time for advancing our knowledge of the disorder. The establishment of clear diagnostic criteria in ICD-11 has produced a number of new studies, yet important questions remain about adjustment disorder—particularly around its phenomenology, course and treatment. Future endeavors might include a focus on emotional and behavioural correlates of adjustment disorder and mechanisms that underpin differences in symptom trajectory (e.g., how adjustment disorder may persist over time or develop into other psychiatric conditions), and how to build the evidence base for treatments designed or adapted for adjustment disorder. As adjustment disorder becomes increasingly legitimised and more clearly defined in the DSM and ICD, researchers in the psychiatric field have the ability to shed new light on a poorly understood disorder. In doing so, we can ensure that adjustment disorder patients have access to appropriate treatment and that clinical judgment is empirically informed.

Author Contributions: Conceptualization, M.L.O. writing—draft preparation, J.A.A.; writing—review and editing, M.L.O., J.A.A., O.M., W.L., and K.G.

Funding: This research was supported through a National Health and Medical Research Council (NHMRC) Program Grant (No. 1073041).

Conflicts of Interest: The authors declare no conflict of interest.

References

1. American Psychiatric Association. Trauma- and stressor-related disorders. In *Diagnostic and Statistical Manual of Mental Disorders (DSM-5®)*, 5th ed.; American Psychiatric Association Publishing: Washington, DC, USA, 2013.
2. Einsle, F.; Köllner, V.; Dannemann, S.; Maercker, A. Development and validation of a self-report for the assessment of adjustment disorders. *Psychol. Health Med.* **2010**, *15*, 584–595. [CrossRef] [PubMed]
3. Gradus, J.L. Prevalence and prognosis of stress disorders: A review of the epidemiologic literature. *Clin. Epidemiol.* **2017**, *9*, 251. [CrossRef] [PubMed]
4. Glaesmer, H.; Romppel, M.; Brähler, E.; Hinz, A.; Maercker, A. Adjustment disorder as proposed for ICD-11: Dimensionality and symptom differentiation. *Psychiatry Res.* **2015**, *229*, 940–948. [CrossRef] [PubMed]
5. Perkonigg, A.; Lorenz, L.; Maercker, A. Prevalence and correlates of ICD-11 adjustment disorder: Findings from the Zurich Adjustment Disorder Study. *Int. J. Clin. Health Psychol.* **2018**, *18*, 209–217. [CrossRef] [PubMed]
6. Killikelly, C.; Lorenz, L.; Bauer, S.; Mahat-Shamir, M.; Ben-Ezra, M.; Maercker, A. Prolonged grief disorder: Its co-occurrence with adjustment disorder and post-traumatic stress disorder in a bereaved Israeli general-population sample. *J. Affect. Disord.* **2019**, *249*, 307–314. [CrossRef]
7. Foster, P.; Oxman, T. A descriptive study of adjustment disorder diagnoses in general hospital patients. *Ir. J. Psychol. Med.* **1994**, *11*, 153–157. [CrossRef]
8. Strain, J.J.; Smith, G.C.; Hammer, J.S.; McKenzie, D.P.; Blumenfield, M.; Muskin, P.; Newstadt, G.; Wallack, J.; Wilner, A.; Schleifer, S.S. Adjustment disorder: A multisite study of its utilization and interventions in the consultation-liaison psychiatry setting. *Gen. Hosp. Psychiatry* **1998**, *20*, 139–149. [CrossRef]
9. Sadock, B.J.; Sadock, V.A. *Kaplan and Sadock's Synopsis of Psychiatry: Behavioral Sciences/Clinical Psychiatry*; Lippincott Williams & Wilkins: Philadelphia, PA, USA, 2015.
10. Taggart, C.; O'Grady, J.; Stevenson, M.; Hand, E.; Mc Clelland, R.; Kelly, C. Accuracy of diagnosis at routine psychiatric assessment in patients presenting to an accident and emergency department. *Gen. Hosp. Psychiatry* **2006**, *28*, 330–335. [CrossRef]

11. Mitchell, A.J.; Chan, M.; Bhatti, H.; Halton, M.; Grassi, L.; Johansen, C.; Meader, N. Prevalence of depression, anxiety, and adjustment disorder in oncological, haematological, and palliative-care settings: A meta-analysis of 94 interview-based studies. *Lancet Oncol.* **2011**, *12*, 160–174. [CrossRef]
12. Okamura, H.; Watanabe, T.; Narabayashi, M.; Katsumata, N.; Ando, M.; Adachi, I.; Akechi, T.; Uchitomi, Y. Psychological distress following first recurrence of disease in patients with breast cancer: Prevalence and risk factors. *Breast Cancer Res. Treat.* **2000**, *61*, 131–137. [CrossRef]
13. Silverstone, P.H. Prevalence of psychiatric disorders in medical inpatients. *J. Nerv. Ment. Dis.* **1996**, *184*, 43–51. [CrossRef] [PubMed]
14. Strain, J.J.; Friedman, M.J. Considering adjustment disorders as stress response syndromes for DSM-5. *Depress. Anxiety* **2011**, *28*, 818–823. [CrossRef] [PubMed]
15. Bachem, R.; Casey, P. Adjustment disorder: A diagnosis whose time has come. *J. Affect. Disord.* **2017**, *227*, 243–253. [CrossRef] [PubMed]
16. Casey, P. Adjustment disorder: New developments. *Curr. Psychiatry Rep.* **2014**, *16*, 451. [CrossRef] [PubMed]
17. O'Donnell, M.L.; Alkemade, N.; Creamer, M.; McFarlane, A.C.; Silove, D.; Bryant, R.A.; Felmingham, K.; Steel, Z.; Forbes, D. A longitudinal study of adjustment disorder after trauma exposure. *Am. J. Psychiatry* **2016**, *173*, 1231–1238. [CrossRef] [PubMed]
18. Baumeister, H.; Maercker, A.; Casey, P. Adjustment disorder with depressed mood. *Psychopathology* **2009**, *42*, 139–147. [CrossRef] [PubMed]
19. World Health Organization. *World Health Organisation International Statistical Classification of Diseases and Related Health Problems*, 11th ed.; World Health Organization: Geneva, Switzerland, 2004.
20. Carta, M.G.; Balestrieri, M.; Murru, A.; Hardoy, M.C. Adjustment Disorder: Epidemiology, diagnosis and treatment. *Clin. Prac. Epidemiol. Ment. Health* **2009**, *5*, 15. [CrossRef]
21. Casey, P.; Bailey, S. Adjustment disorders: The state of the art. *World Psychiatry* **2011**, *10*, 11–18. [CrossRef]
22. Maercker, A.; Brewin, C.R.; Bryant, R.A.; Cloitre, M.; van Ommeren, M.; Jones, L.M.; Humayan, A.; Kagee, A.; Llosa, A.E.; Rousseau, C.; et al. Diagnosis and classification of disorders specifically associated with stress: Proposals for ICD-11. *World Psychiatry* **2013**, *12*, 198–206. [CrossRef]
23. Zelviene, P.; Kazlauskas, E.; Eimontas, J.; Maercker, A. Adjustment disorder: Empirical study of a new diagnostic concept for ICD-11 in the general population in Lithuania. *Eur. Psychiatry* **2017**, *40*, 20–25. [CrossRef]
24. Lorenz, L.; Hyland, P.; Maercker, A.; Ben-Ezra, M. An empirical assessment of adjustment disorder as proposed for ICD-11 in a general population sample of Israel. *J. Anxiety Disord.* **2018**, *54*, 65–70. [CrossRef] [PubMed]
25. Lorenz, L.; Hyland, P.; Perkonigg, A.; Maercker, A. Is adjustment disorder unidimensional or multidimensional? Implications for ICD-11. *Int. J. Methods Psychiatr. Res.* **2018**, *27*, e1591. [CrossRef] [PubMed]
26. O'Donnell, M.L.; Alkemade, N.; Nickerson, A.; Creamer, M.; McFarlane, A.C.; Silove, D.; Bryant, R.A.; Forbes, D. Impact of the diagnostic changes to post-traumatic stress disorder for DSM-5 and the proposed changes to ICD-11. *Br. J. Psychiatry* **2014**, *205*, 230–235. [CrossRef] [PubMed]
27. O'Donnell, M.L.; Alkamade, N.; Forbes, D. Is Australia in the post-traumatic stress disorder petri dish? *Aust. N. Z. J. Psychiatry* **2015**, *49*, 315–316. [CrossRef] [PubMed]
28. Kazlauskas, E.; Zelviene, P.; Lorenz, L.; Quero, S.; Maercker, A. A scoping review of ICD-11 adjustment disorder research. *Eur. J. Psychotraumtol.* **2017**, *8*, 1421819. [CrossRef] [PubMed]
29. Bonanno, G.A.; Galea, S.; Bucciarelli, A.; Vlahov, D. Psychological resilience after disaster: New York City in the aftermath of the September 11th terrorist attack. *Psychol. Sci.* **2006**, *17*, 181–186. [CrossRef] [PubMed]
30. Bonanno, G.A.; Mancini, A.D.; Horton, J.L.; Powell, T.M.; LeardMann, C.A.; Boyko, E.J.; Wells, T.S.; Hooper, T.I.; Gackstetter, G.D.; Smith, T.C. Trajectories of trauma symptoms and resilience in deployed US military service members: Prospective cohort study. *Br. J. Psychiatry* **2012**, *200*, 317–323. [CrossRef]
31. Bryant, R.A.; Nickerson, A.; Creamer, M.; O'Donnell, M.; Forbes, D.; Galatzer-Levy, I.; McFarlane, A.C.; Silove, D. Trajectory of post-traumatic stress following traumatic injury: 6-year follow-up. *Br. J. Psychiatry* **2015**, *206*, 417–423. [CrossRef]
32. deRoon-Cassini, T.A.; Mancini, A.D.; Rusch, M.D.; Bonanno, G.A. Psychopathology and resilience following traumatic injury: A latent growth mixture model analysis. *Rehabil. Psychol.* **2010**, *55*, 1. [CrossRef]

33. Fink, D.S.; Lowe, S.; Cohen, G.H.; Sampson, L.A.; Ursano, R.J.; Gifford, R.K.; Fullerton, C.S.; Galea, S. Trajectories of posttraumatic stress symptoms after civilian or deployment traumatic event experiences. *Psychol. Trauma* **2017**, *9*, 138. [CrossRef]
34. Lam, W.W.; Bonanno, G.A.; Mancini, A.D.; Ho, S.; Chan, M.; Hung, W.K.; Or, A.; Fielding, R. Trajectories of psychological distress among Chinese women diagnosed with breast cancer. *Psychooncology* **2010**, *19*, 1044–1051. [CrossRef] [PubMed]
35. Santiago, P.N.; Ursano, R.J.; Gray, C.L.; Pynoos, R.S.; Spiegel, D.; Lewis-Fernandez, R.; Friedman, M.J.; Fullerton, C.S. A systematic review of PTSD prevalence and trajectories in DSM-5 defined trauma exposed populations: Intentional and non-intentional traumatic events. *PLoS ONE* **2013**, *8*, e59236. [CrossRef] [PubMed]
36. Weathers, F.W.; Bovin, M.J.; Lee, D.J.; Sloan, D.M.; Schnurr, P.P.; Kaloupek, D.G.; Keane, T.M.; Marx, B.P. The Clinician-Administered PTSD Scale for DSM-5 (CAPS-5): Development and initial psychometric evaluation in military veterans. *Psychol. Assess* **2018**, *30*, 383–395. [CrossRef] [PubMed]
37. Bryant, R.A.; O'Donnell, M.L.; Creamer, M.; McFarlane, A.C.; Silove, D. A multisite analysis of the fluctuating course of posttraumatic stress disorder. *JAMA Psychiatry* **2013**, *70*, 839–846. [CrossRef] [PubMed]
38. Casey, P.; Jabbar, F.; O'Leary, E.; Doherty, A.M. Suicidal behaviours in adjustment disorder and depressive episode. *J. Affect. Disord.* **2015**, *174*, 441–446. [CrossRef]
39. Greenberg, W.M.; Rosenfeld, D.N.; Ortega, E.A. Adjustment disorder as an admission diagnosis. *Am. J. Psychiatry* **1995**, *152*, 459. [CrossRef]
40. Kryzhanovskaya, L.; Canterbury, R. Suicidal behaviour in patients with adjustment disorders. *Crisis* **2001**, *22*, 125–131. [CrossRef]
41. Lewis, G.; Pelosi, A.J.; Araya, R.; Dunn, G. Measuring psychiatric disorder in the community: A standardized assessment for use by lay interviewers. *Psychol. Med.* **1992**, *22*, 465–486. [CrossRef]
42. Kessler, R.C.; Üstün, T.B. The world mental health (WMH) survey initiative version of the world health organization (WHO) composite international diagnostic interview (CIDI). *Int. J. Methods Psychiatr. Res.* **2004**, *13*, 93–121. [CrossRef]
43. First, M.B. Structured Clinical Interview for the DSM (SCID). In *The Encyclopedia of Clinical Psychology*; Cautin, R.L., Lilienfeld, S.O., Eds.; American Psychiatric Association Publishing: Philadelphia, PA, USA, 2015; pp. 1–6. [CrossRef]
44. Sheehan, D.V.; Lecrubier, Y.; Sheehan, K.H.; Amorim, P.; Janavs, J.; Weiller, E.; Hergueta, T.; Baker, R.; Dunbar, G.C. The Mini-International Neuropsychiatric Interview (MINI): The development and validation of a structured diagnostic psychiatric interview for DSM-IV and ICD-10. *J. Clin. Psychiatry* **1998**, *59*, 22–23.
45. Maercker, A.; Lorenz, L. Adjustment disorder diagnosis: Improving clinical utility. *World J. Biol. Psychiatry* **2018**, *19*, S3–S13. [CrossRef] [PubMed]
46. Cornelius, L.R.; Brouwer, S.; de Boer, M.R.; Groothoff, J.W.; van der Klink, J.J. Development and validation of the Diagnostic Interview Adjustment Disorder (DIAD). *Int. J. Methods Psychiatr. Res.* **2014**, *23*, 192–207. [CrossRef] [PubMed]
47. Maercker, A.; Einsle, F.; Köllner, V. Adjustment disorders as stress response syndromes: A new diagnostic concept and its exploration in a medical sample. *Psychopathology* **2007**, *40*, 135–146. [CrossRef] [PubMed]
48. Lorenz, L.; Bachem, R.; Maercker, A. The adjustment disorder–new module 20 as a screening instrument: Cluster analysis and cut-off values. *Int. J. Occup. Environ. Med.* **2016**, *7*, 215–220. [CrossRef] [PubMed]
49. Bachem, R.; Perkonigg, A.; Stein, D.J.; Maercker, A. Measuring the ICD-11 adjustment disorder concept: Validity and sensitivity to change of the Adjustment Disorder–New Module questionnaire in a clinical intervention study. *Int. J. Methods Psychiatr. Res.* **2017**, *26*, e1545. [CrossRef] [PubMed]
50. Ben-Ezra, M.; Mahat-Shamir, M.; Lorenz, L.; Lavenda, O.; Maercker, A. Screening of adjustment disorder: Scale based on the ICD-11 and the Adjustment Disorder New Module. *J. Psychiatr. Res.* **2018**, *103*, 91–96. [CrossRef] [PubMed]
51. Kazlauskas, E.; Gegieckaite, G.; Maercker, A.; Eimontas, J.; Zelviene, P. A brief measure of the International Classification of Diseases-11 adjustment disorder: Investigation of psychometric properties in an adult help-seeking sample. *Psychopathology* **2018**, 1–6. [CrossRef]
52. O'Donnell, M.L.; Metcalf, O.; Watson, L.; Phelps, A.; Varker, T. A Systematic Review of Psychological and Pharmacological Treatments for Adjustment Disorder in Adults. *J. Trauma. Stress* **2018**, *31*, 321–331. [CrossRef]

53. GRADE Working Group. Grading quality of evidence and strength of recommendations. *BMJ* **2004**, *328*, 1490. [CrossRef]
54. Bachem, R.; Maercker, A. Self-help interventions for adjustment disorder problems: A randomized waiting-list controlled study in a sample of burglary victims. *Cogn. Behav. Ther.* **2016**, *45*, 397–413. [CrossRef]
55. Eimontas, J.; Rimsaite, Z.; Gegieckaite, G.; Zelviene, P.; Kazlauskas, E. Internet-based self-help intervention for ICD-11 adjustment disorder: Preliminary findings. *Psychiatr. Q.* **2018**, *89*, 451–460. [CrossRef] [PubMed]
56. Quero, S.; Molés, M.; Campos, D.; Andreu-Mateu, S.; Baños, R.M.; Botella, C. An adaptive virtual reality system for the treatment of adjustment disorder and complicated grief: 1-year follow-up efficacy data. *Clin. Psychol. Psychother.* **2019**, *26*, 204–217. [CrossRef] [PubMed]
57. Singla, D.R.; Kohrt, B.A.; Murray, L.K.; Anand, A.; Chorpita, B.F.; Patel, V. Psychological treatments for the world: Lessons from low-and middle-income countries. *Annu. Rev. Clin. Psychol.* **2017**, *13*, 149–181. [CrossRef] [PubMed]
58. Gibson, K.; Forbes, D.; O'Donnell, M.L. Skills for Life Adjustment and Resilience (SOLAR)–A pilot study in Tuvalu. In Proceedings of the 7th World Congress of Asian Psychiatry, Sydney, Australia, 22 February 2019.
59. O'Donnell, M.L.; Lau, W.; Fredrickson, J.; Bryant, R.A.; Bisson, J.; Burke, S.; Busuttil, W.; Coghlan, A.; Creamer, M.; Gray, D.; et al. SOLAR: The Skills fOr Life Adjustment and Resilience Program: A brief intervention to promote adjustment following disaster. In Proceedings of the 34th meeting of the International Society for Traumatic Stress Studies, Washington DC, USA, 9 November 2018.

© 2019 by the authors. Licensee MDPI, Basel, Switzerland. This article is an open access article distributed under the terms and conditions of the Creative Commons Attribution (CC BY) license (http://creativecommons.org/licenses/by/4.0/).

2020 Older Americans
Key Indicators of Well-Being

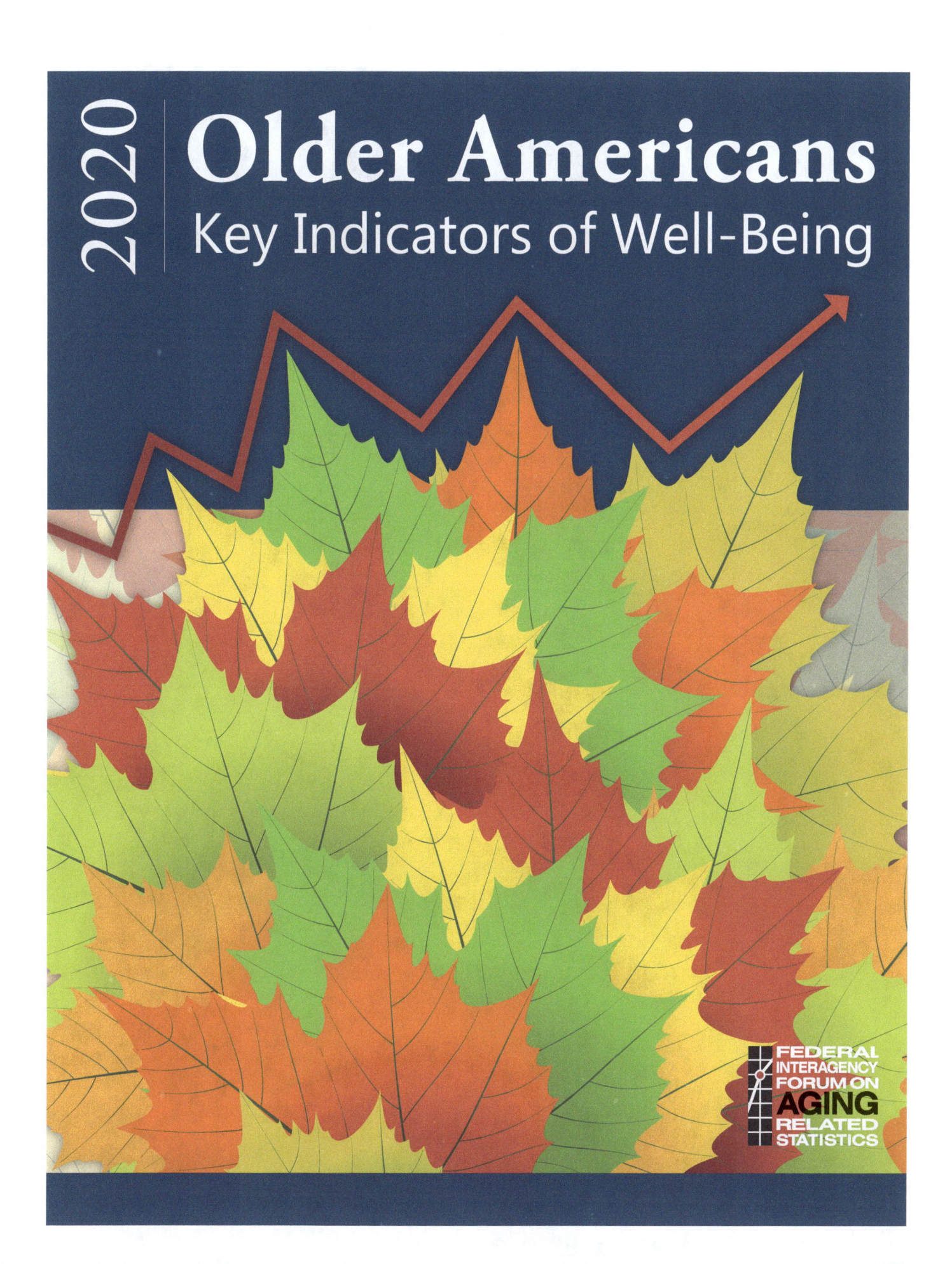

FEDERAL INTERAGENCY FORUM ON AGING RELATED STATISTICS

Studies & Statistics / Older Americans Key Indicators of Well-Being

Health Status

INDICATOR 14: Life Expectancy

Life expectancy is a summary measure of the overall health of a population. It represents the average number of years of life remaining to a person at a given age if death rates remain constant. Improvements in health have resulted in increased life expectancy. However, there are differences in life expectancy by socioeconomic status, and these differences have been increasing over time.[9] Life expectancy in the United States is lower than in many other industrialized countries.[10]

Life expectancy at ages 65 and 85, by race and Hispanic origin and sex, 2006–2018

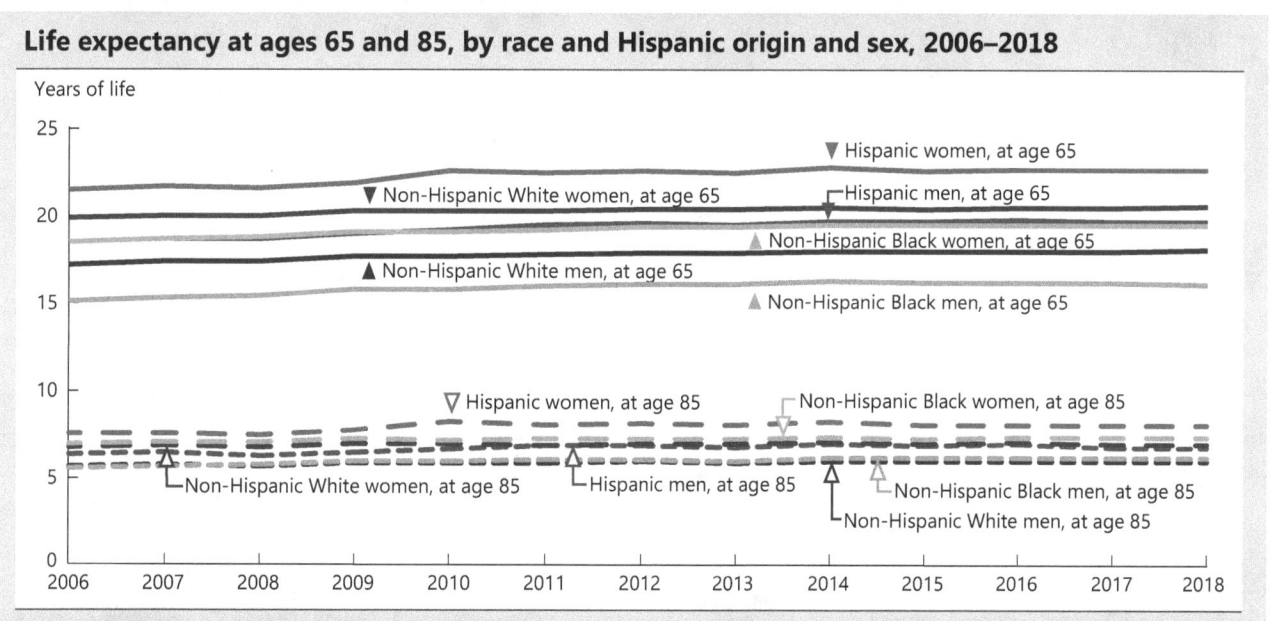

NOTE: Starting with 2018 data, race-specific estimates are tabulated according to the 1997 Revisions to the Standards for the Classification of Federal Data on Race and Ethnicity and are not completely comparable with estimates for earlier years. Persons of Hispanic origin may be of any race.
Reference population: These data refer to the resident population.
SOURCE: National Center for Health Statistics, National Vital Statistics System.

- Under current mortality conditions, people who survive to age 65 can expect to live an average of 19.5 more years overall, 18.1 years for men and 20.7 years for women. In 2018, the life expectancy of people who survive to age 85 was 7.0 years for women and 6.0 years for men.

- Older Americans are living longer. Life expectancies at both age 65 and age 85 have increased for both sexes and for Hispanics, non-Hispanic Whites, and non-Hispanic Blacks. Overall for men, life expectancy at age 65 increased from 17.2 years to 18.1 years from 2006 to 2018, while the increase for women overall was from 19.9 years to 20.7 years. During the same period, life expectancy at age 85 increased from 5.6 years to 6.0 years for men and from 6.7 years to 7.0 years for women.

- In 2018, life expectancy at age 65 was higher among Hispanics than among non-Hispanic Whites and non-Hispanic Blacks for both men and women (19.7, 18.1, and 16.1 years, respectively, for men and 22.7, 20.6, and 19.5 years, respectively, for women). Life expectancy at age 85 was highest among Hispanics (6.7 years for men and 8.0 years for women), but non-Hispanic Blacks had higher life expectancy than non-Hispanic Whites (6.1 years versus 5.9 years for men and 7.3 years versus 6.9 years for women).

Data for this indicator's charts and bullets can be found in Table 14 on page 98.

INDICATOR 15: Mortality

Overall, death rates for the population age 65 and over have declined in recent decades. However, for some causes of death, rates among older Americans have increased in recent years. There are differences in death rates by sex and race and Hispanic origin for many causes of death.[11]

Death rates among people age 65 and over, by selected leading causes of death, 2000–2018

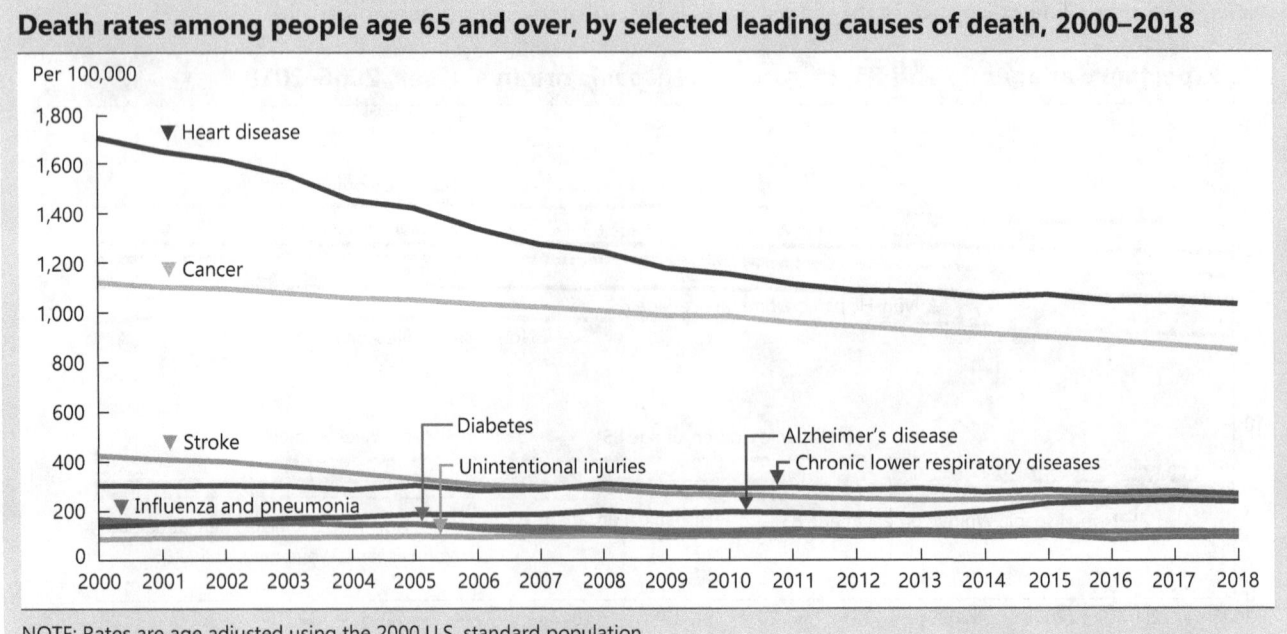

NOTE: Rates are age adjusted using the 2000 U.S. standard population.
Reference population: These data refer to the resident population.
SOURCE: National Center for Health Statistics, National Vital Statistics System.

- In 2018, the leading cause of death among people age 65 and over was heart disease (1,035 deaths per 100,000 U.S. standard population), followed by cancer (849), chronic lower respiratory diseases (270), stroke (252), Alzheimer's disease (239), diabetes (118), unintentional injuries (112), and influenza and pneumonia (96).

- Between 2000 and 2018, the age-adjusted death rate for people age 65 and over declined by 20 percent. Death rates declined for heart disease, cancer, chronic lower respiratory diseases, stroke, diabetes, and influenza and pneumonia. Death rates for Alzheimer's disease and unintentional injuries increased during the same period.

- Heart disease and cancer were the top two leading causes of death in 2018 among all people age 65 and over. They were also the top two leading causes of death for both men and women with men having higher rates of both causes (1,273 per 100,000 U.S. standard population compared with 856 for heart disease and 1,052 versus 702 for cancer).

- Other causes of death also varied among older Americans by sex. For example, in 2018, women had higher age-adjusted death rates from Alzheimer's disease than men (268 per 100,000 U.S. standard population compared with 192), while men had higher age-adjusted rates of death from unintentional injuries (141 per 100,000 U.S. standard population compared with 90).

Data for this indicator's charts and bullets can be found in Tables 15a and 15b on pages 99–100.

INDICATOR 16: Chronic Health Conditions

The risk of chronic diseases increases with age.[12] Chronic conditions usually require ongoing medical care and are major contributors to health care costs.[13] The majority of older adults have multiple chronic conditions, which contribute to frailty and disability.[14] Many of the negative effects of chronic conditions are caused by health risk behaviors that can be changed.[13] The six leading causes of death among older Americans in 2018 were chronic diseases (see Indicator 15: Mortality).

Percentage of people age 65 and over who reported having selected chronic health conditions, by sex, 2018

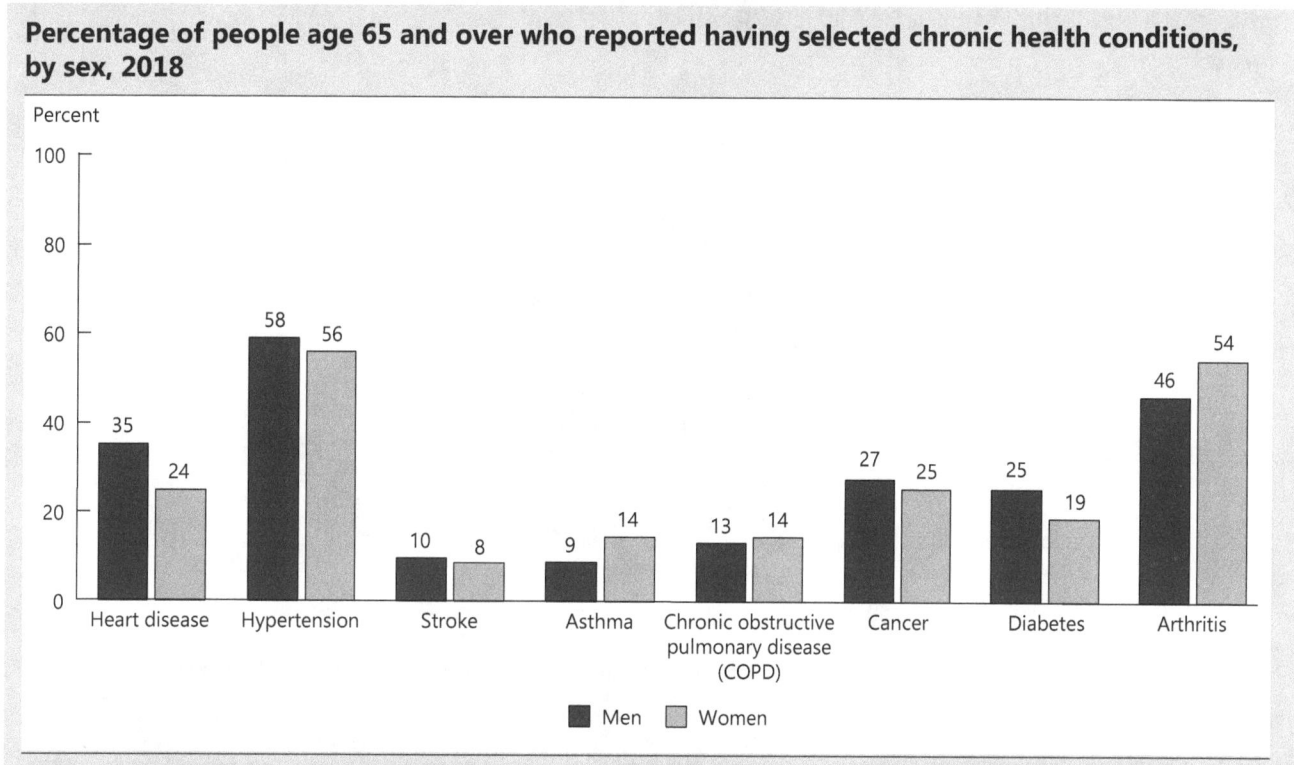

Condition	Men	Women
Heart disease	35	24
Hypertension	58	56
Stroke	10	8
Asthma	9	14
Chronic obstructive pulmonary disease (COPD)	13	14
Cancer	27	25
Diabetes	25	19
Arthritis	46	54

NOTE: Chronic obstructive pulmonary disease (COPD) is defined as responding yes to questions on ever having emphysema, COPD, or having chronic bronchitis in the past 12 months. This definition has changed from previous editions of *Older Americans*.
Reference population: These data refer to the civilian noninstitutionalized population.
SOURCE: National Center for Health Statistics, National Health Interview Survey.

- In 2018, the prevalence of certain chronic health conditions differed by sex. Women reported higher levels of asthma and arthritis than men (14 percent and 54 percent versus 9 percent and 46 percent, respectively). Men reported higher levels of heart disease (35 percent), hypertension (58 percent), cancer (27 percent), and diabetes (25 percent) than women (24 percent, 56 percent, 25 percent, and 19 percent, respectively).

- There were differences by race and ethnicity in the prevalence of certain chronic health conditions. In 2018, among people age 65 and over, non-Hispanic Blacks reported higher levels of hypertension and diabetes than non-Hispanic Whites (68 percent versus 55 percent for hypertension, and 34 percent versus 18 percent for diabetes). Hispanics also reported higher levels of diabetes (33 percent) than non-Hispanic Whites, but lower levels of arthritis than non-Hispanic Whites (44 percent versus 52 percent).

- The prevalence of some chronic health conditions among people age 65 and over has increased over time. The percentage of people who reported hypertension, asthma, chronic obstructive pulmonary disease (COPD), cancer, and diabetes was higher in 2018 compared with 1997. Also, the prevalence of arthritis was higher in 2018 compared with 2002.

Data for this indicator's charts and bullets can be found in Tables 16a and 16b on page 101.

INDICATOR 17: Oral Health

Oral health is an important component of an older person's general health and well-being. Oral health reflects overall health status and is related to the risk and treatment of various chronic conditions.[15] Regular dental care is not covered under Medicare.

Percentage of people age 65 and over who had dental insurance, had a dental visit in the past year, or had no natural teeth, by age group, 2018

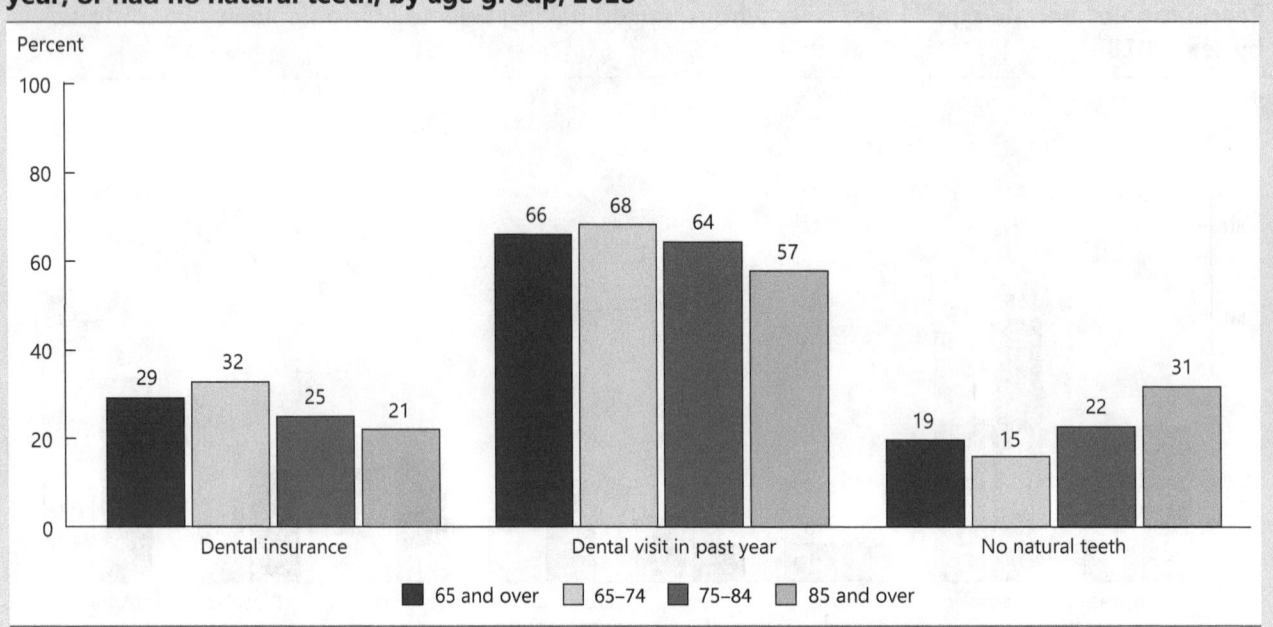

Category	65 and over	65–74	75–84	85 and over
Dental insurance	29	32	25	21
Dental visit in past year	66	68	64	57
No natural teeth	19	15	22	31

NOTE: Dental insurance is estimated from questions on whether the respondent's private health insurance plan covers dental care and whether the respondent has a single service plan covering dental care. Dental visits in the past year were estimated from responses to the question, "About how long has it been since you last saw or talked to a dentist?" The percentage with no natural teeth was estimated from responses to the question, "Have you lost all of your upper and lower natural (permanent) teeth?" All estimates were calculated from the sample adult component of the National Health Interview Survey.
Reference population: These data refer to the civilian noninstitutionalized population.
SOURCE: National Center for Health Statistics, National Health Interview Survey.

- About 29 percent of people age 65 and over reported having dental insurance in 2018. The percentage with dental insurance declines with age, from 32 percent among people ages 65–74 to 21 percent among people age 85 and over.

- In 2018, about 66 percent of people age 65 and over had a dental visit in the past year. The percentage visiting a dentist was higher among people ages 65–74 than among people age 85 and over (68 percent versus 57 percent).

- The prevalence of edentulism, having no natural teeth, was about twice as high among people age 85 and over (31 percent) as among people ages 65–74 (15 percent).

- Similar percentages of men and women age 65 and over in 2018 had dental insurance, had a dental visit in the past year, and had no natural teeth.

- Non-Hispanic White people age 65 and over had lower levels of edentulism than non-Hispanic Blacks and Hispanics (18 percent versus 28 percent and 23 percent, respectively) and higher levels of dental visits than non-Hispanic Blacks and Hispanics.

Data for this indicator's charts and bullets can be found in Tables 17a and 17b on page 102.

INDICATOR 18: Respondent-Assessed Health Status

Asking people to rate their health as excellent, very good, good, fair, or poor provides an indicator of health status easily measured in surveys. It represents physical, emotional, and social aspects of health and well-being. Self-rated health has been shown to predict mortality and health care expenditures.[16,17]

Percentage of people age 65 and over with respondent-assessed good to excellent health status, by age group and race and Hispanic origin, 2018

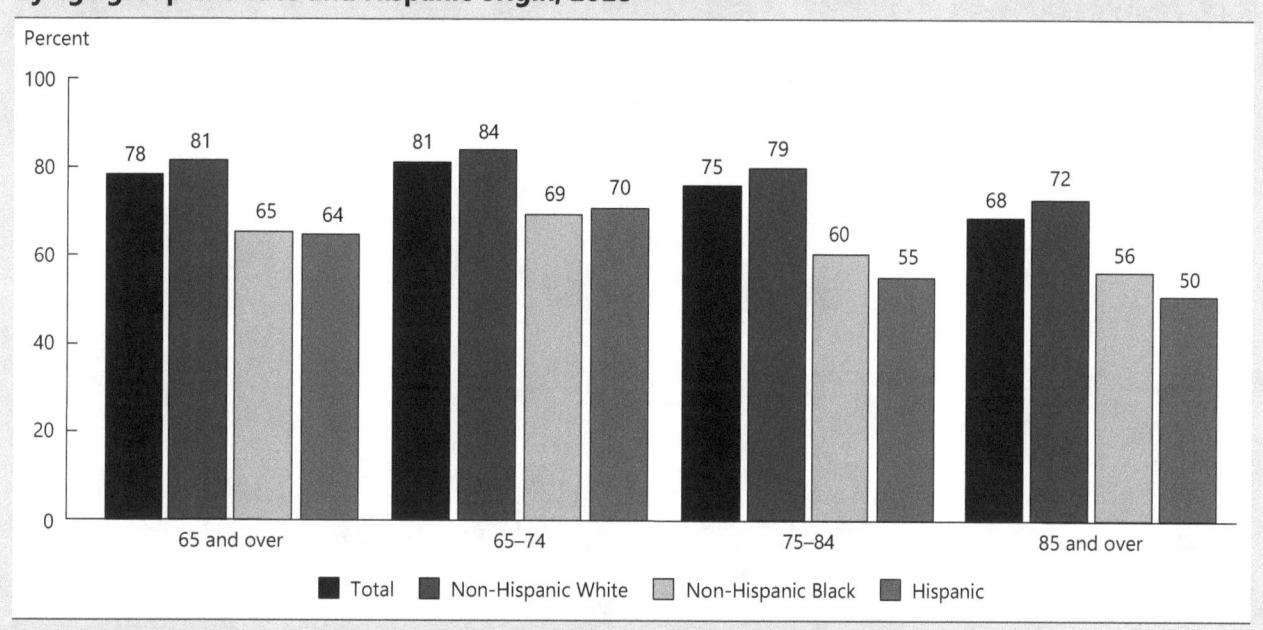

Age group	Total	Non-Hispanic White	Non-Hispanic Black	Hispanic
65 and over	78	81	65	64
65–74	81	84	69	70
75–84	75	79	60	55
85 and over	68	72	56	50

NOTE: Total includes all other races not shown separately. See data sources for the definition of race and Hispanic origin in the National Health Interview Survey.
Reference population: These data refer to the civilian noninstitutionalized population.
SOURCE: National Center for Health Statistics, National Health Interview Survey.

- In 2018, 78 percent of people age 65 and over rated their health as good, very good, or excellent. The levels of health reported by older men and older women were similar.

- The proportion of people reporting good to excellent health was lower among the oldest age groups. Eighty-one percent of those ages 65–74 reported good or better health. At age 85 and over, 68 percent of people reported good or better health. This pattern was also evident within racial and ethnic groups.

- Regardless of age, older non-Hispanic White men and women were more likely to report good to excellent health than their non-Hispanic Black and Hispanic counterparts. Eighty-two percent of non-Hispanic White women age 65 and over reported good to excellent health compared with 65 percent of non-Hispanic Blacks and 61 percent of Hispanics. Among men, the percentages were 80 percent for non-Hispanic White men and 66 percent and 68 percent for non-Hispanic Black and Hispanic men, respectively.

Data for this indicator's charts and bullets can be found in Table 18 on page 103.

Studies & Statistics / Older Americans Key Indicators of Well-Being

INDICATOR 19: Dementia

Dementias, including Alzheimer's disease and other related disorders that cause memory impairment and cognitive decline, affect the health and well-being of the U.S. population (see Indicator 15: Mortality). Dementia is a condition overwhelmingly faced by older adults, although it sometimes affects people under age 65. Increasing age is one of the strongest risk factors for dementia.

Percentage of the non-nursing home population age 65 and over with dementia, by age group and sex, 2011 and 2015

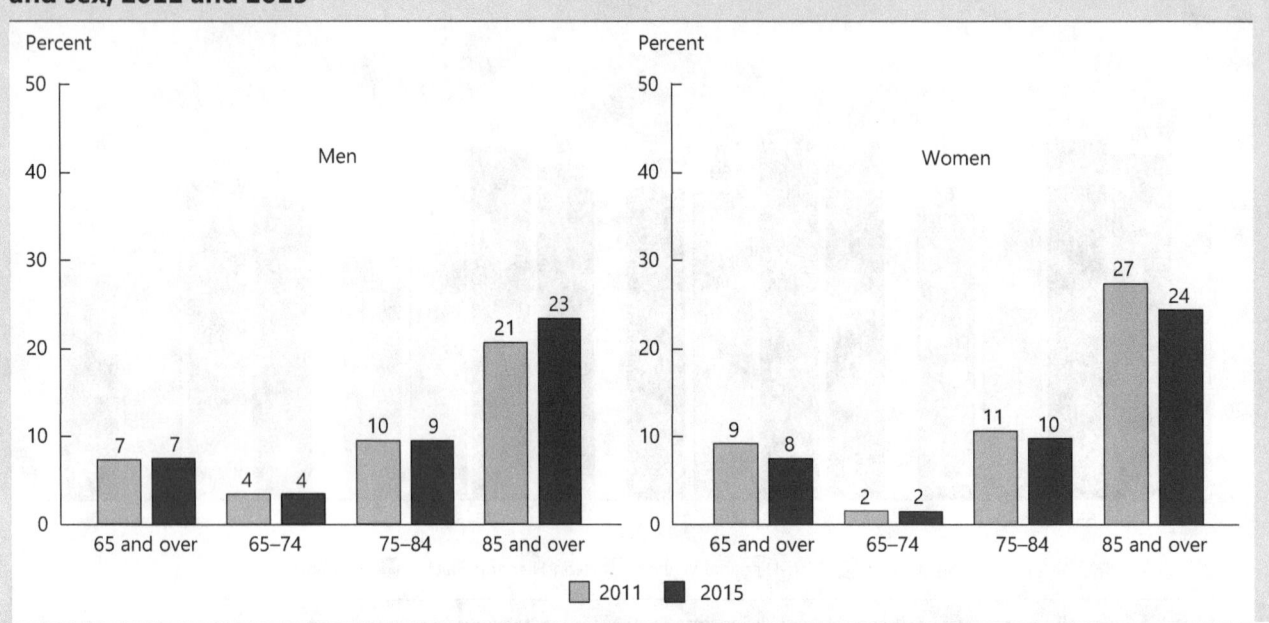

Men:
- 65 and over: 7 (2011), 7 (2015)
- 65–74: 4 (2011), 4 (2015)
- 75–84: 10 (2011), 9 (2015)
- 85 and over: 21 (2011), 23 (2015)

Women:
- 65 and over: 9 (2011), 8 (2015)
- 65–74: 2 (2011), 2 (2015)
- 75–84: 11 (2011), 10 (2015)
- 85 and over: 27 (2011), 24 (2015)

NOTE: The estimate of dementia includes Alzheimer's disease and other related dementias such as frontotemporal, Lewy body, mixed, and vascular dementia. Dementia status in the National Health and Aging Trends Study (NHATS) was determined using three types of information: (1) a report (by the respondent or proxy) that a doctor told the sample person that he or she had dementia or Alzheimer's disease; (2) a score indicating probable dementia on a screening instrument administered to proxy respondents during the interview; and (3) cognitive tests that evaluate memory, orientation, and executive function administered to the respondent during the interview. To minimize potential learning bias and to be classified as having dementia, participants must meet criteria for dementia in two subsequent NHATS rounds, or meet dementia criteria in one round followed by death or loss to follow up in the next round, as described in Freedman, Kaspar, Spillman, and Plassman (2018).[18] Data from 2011 have been revised with the two-round dementia criteria and differ from Indicator 20: Dementia in *Older Americans 2016*.
Reference population: These data refer to Medicare beneficiaries not living in nursing homes.
SOURCE: Office of the Assistant Secretary for Planning and Evaluation, National Health and Aging Trends Study.

- In 2015, 7.4 percent of men (1.4 million) and 7.5 percent of women (1.7 million) age 65 and over not living in nursing homes had dementia. Despite similar overall percentages with dementia in 2015 among women and men, the size of the population of women in these age groups was larger than that of men. As a result, far more women than men had dementia at older ages. Among those age 85 and over, 24.4 percent of women (830,000) and 23.4 percent of men (440,000) had dementia.

- The prevalence of dementia among people age 65 and over remained largely unchanged for men between 2011 and 2015 but declined for women from 9.2 percent to 7.5 percent. Declines in prevalence were observed for women in all age groups, while prevalence among men was unchanged at younger ages and rose slightly in those age 85 and over (from 20.8 percent in 2011 to 23.4 percent in 2015).

- The prevalence of dementia decreases with educational level. In both 2011 and 2015, among people age 65 and over, approximately 16 percent with less than a high school education had dementia compared with 4 percent of people who had a bachelor's degree or more. These differences by educational level were similar for both men and women and across age groups.

Data for this indicator's charts and bullets can be found in Tables 19a through 19e on pages 104–105.

INDICATOR 20: Depressive Symptoms

Depressive symptoms are an important indicator of general well-being and mental health among older adults. People who report many depressive symptoms often experience higher rates of physical illness, greater functional disability, higher health care resource utilization,[19] and dementia.[20]

Percentage of people age 55 and over with clinically relevant depressive symptoms, by sex and age group, selected years, 1998–2018

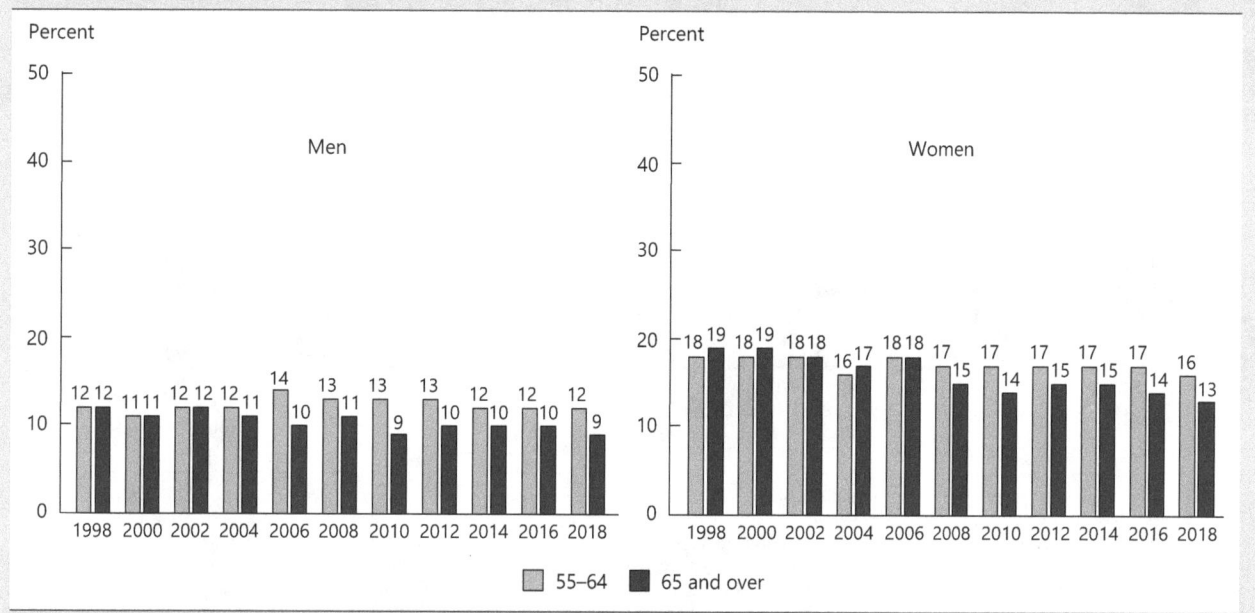

Year	Men 55–64	Men 65+	Women 55–64	Women 65+
1998	12	12	18	19
2000	11	11	18	19
2002	12	12	18	18
2004	12	11	16	17
2006	14	10	18	18
2008	13	11	17	15
2010	13	9	17	14
2012	13	10	17	15
2014	12	10	17	15
2016	12	10	17	14
2018	12	9	16	13

NOTE: The definition of "clinically relevant depressive symptoms" is four or more symptoms out of a list of eight depressive symptoms from an abbreviated version of the Center of Epidemiological Studies Depression Scale (CES-D), adapted by the Health and Retirement Study (HRS). The CES-D scale is a measure of depressive symptoms and is not to be used as a diagnosis of clinical depression. A detailed explanation concerning the "four or more symptoms" cutoff can be found at https://hrs.isr.umich.edu/publications/biblio/5411. Percentages are based on weighted data using the respondent weights from the HRS Tracker file. Age ranges used in previous versions of *Older Americans* were updated.
Reference population: These data refer to the civilian noninstitutionalized population.
SOURCE: National Institute on Aging, Health and Retirement Study.

- Older women were more likely to report clinically relevant depressive symptoms than older men. In 2018, 13 percent of women age 65 and over reported clinically relevant depressive symptoms compared with 9 percent of men. There was no significant change between the sexes in this difference from 1998 to 2018. A slight downward trend is apparent for women in this age group, going from 19 percent in 1998 to 13 percent in 2018.

- The percentage of people ages 55–64 reporting clinically relevant symptoms remained relatively stable during the period. Between 1998 and 2018, the percentage of men in this age group who reported clinically relevant depressive symptoms ranged between 11 percent and 14 percent. For women in this age group, the percentage reporting these symptoms ranged between 16 percent and 18 percent.

Studies & Statistics / Older Americans Key Indicators of Well-Being

Percentage of people age 55 and over with clinically relevant depressive symptoms, by age group and sex, 2018

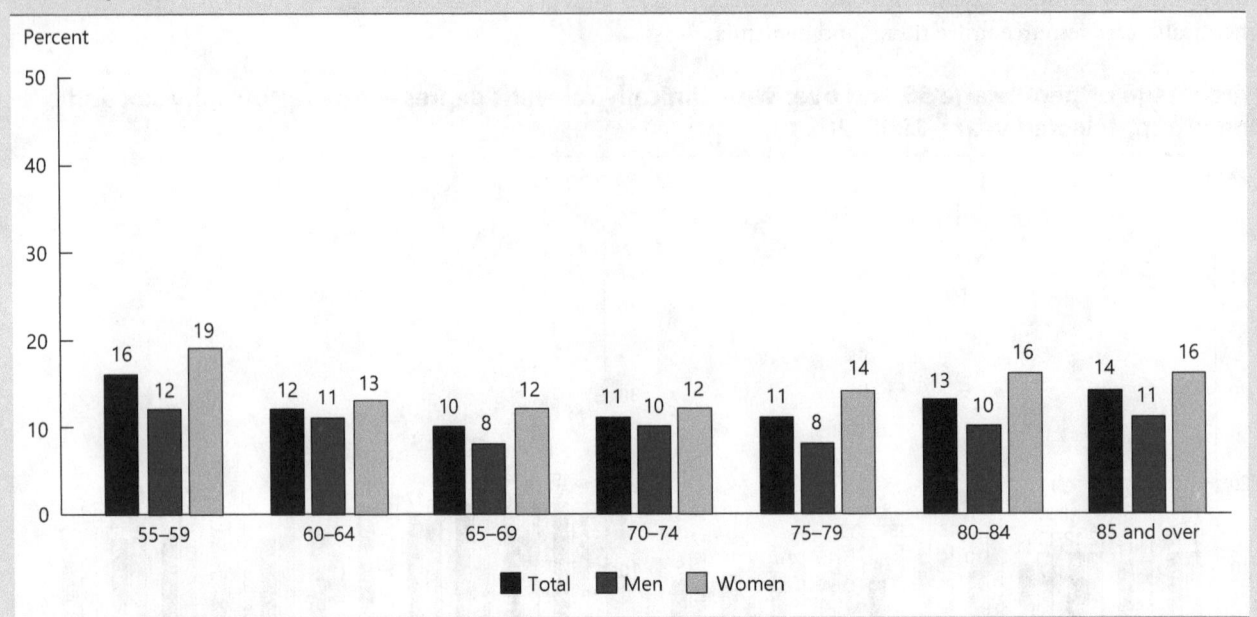

Age group	Total	Men	Women
55–59	16	12	19
60–64	12	11	13
65–69	10	8	12
70–74	11	10	12
75–79	11	8	14
80–84	13	10	16
85 and over	14	11	16

NOTE: The definition of "clinically relevant depressive symptoms" is four or more symptoms out of a list of eight depressive symptoms from an abbreviated version of the Center of Epidemiological Studies Depression Scale (CES-D), adapted by the Health and Retirement Study (HRS). The CES-D scale is a measure of depressive symptoms and is not to be used as a diagnosis of clinical depression. A detailed explanation concerning the "four or more symptoms" cutoff can be found at https://hrs.isr.umich.edu/publications/biblio/5411. Percentages are based on weighted data using the respondent weights from the HRS Tracker file. Age ranges used in previous versions of *Older Americans* were updated.
Reference population: These data refer to the civilian noninstitutionalized population.
SOURCE: National Institute on Aging, Health and Retirement Study.

- The prevalence of depressive symptoms varies by age. In 2018, the percentage of people with clinically relevant depressive symptoms was higher for the youngest age group (16 percent among those ages 55–59) and the oldest age group (14 percent for those age 85 and over) than for people ages 65–69 (14 percent).

- In 2018, for both sexes, a U-shaped pattern is apparent in the prevalence of clinically relevant depressive symptoms. It is especially pronounced for women, with the highest prevalence for those ages 55–59 (19 percent) and those ages 80–84 and 85 and over (both 16 percent) and lowest for women in their late 60s and early 70s (both 12 percent).

Data for this indicator's charts and bullets can be found in Tables 20a and 20b on page 106.

INDICATOR 21: **Functional Limitations**

As people age, illness or injury may result in disability, including limitations in vision, hearing, mobility, communication, cognition, or self-care. These changes may have important implications for work and retirement policies, health and long-term care needs, and policies affecting the built environment, all of which affect the well-being of the older population and the ability to fully and independently participate in society.

Percentage of people age 65 and over with a disability, by functional domain, 2010–2018

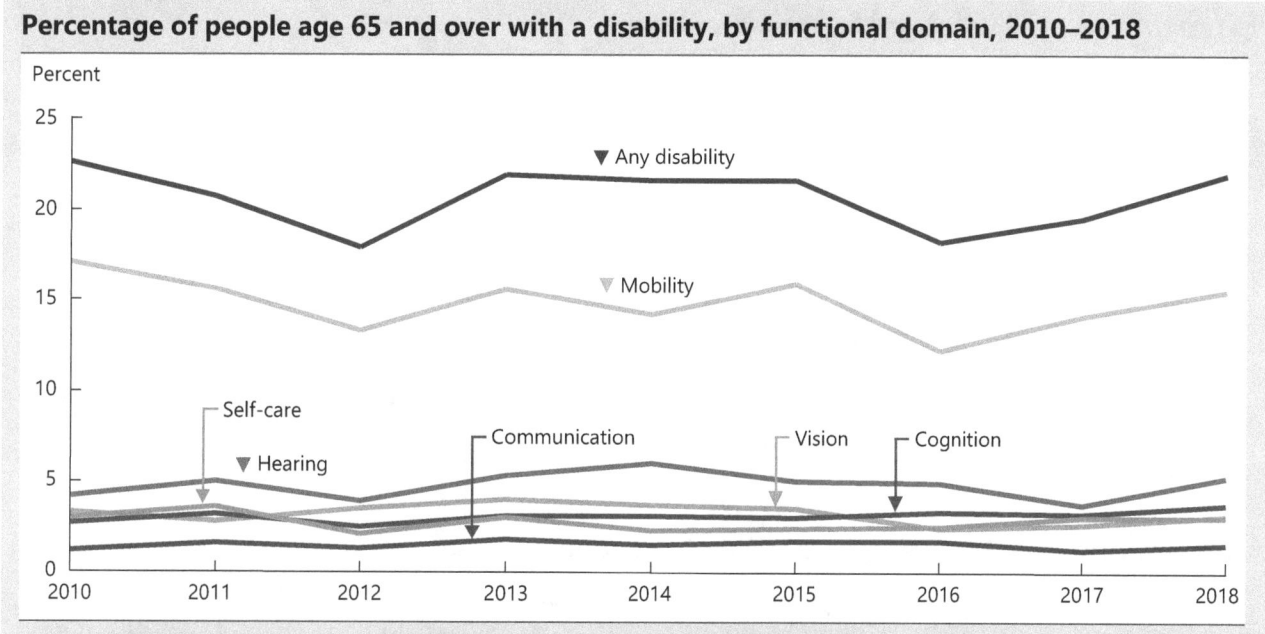

NOTE: Disability is defined as "a lot" or "cannot do/unable to do" when asked about difficulty with seeing, even if wearing glasses (vision); hearing, even if wearing hearing aids (hearing); walking or climbing steps (mobility); communicating, for example, understanding or being understood by others (communication); remembering or concentrating (cognition); and self-care, such as washing all over or dressing (self-care). Any disability is defined as having a lot of difficulty or being unable to do at least one of these activities.
Reference population: These data refer to the civilian noninstitutionalized population.
SOURCE: National Center for Health Statistics, National Health Interview Survey.

- In 2018, 22 percent of the population age 65 and over reported having a disability as defined by having a lot of difficulty or being unable to do at least one of the following functioning domains: vision, hearing, mobility, communication, cognition, or self-care.

- Between 2010 and 2018, the percentage of people age 65 and over who had any disability was stable.

- Difficulties with mobility (walking or climbing stairs) were the most commonly reported disability for those age 65 and over in 2018 (16 percent), followed by hearing (5 percent), cognition (4 percent), and vision and self-care (3 percent each).

- Women were more likely to report any disability than men (24 percent versus 20 percent). Levels of disability in vision and mobility were also higher for women than men (4 percent and 18 percent versus 3 percent and 13 percent, respectively). Men reported higher levels of hearing disability than women (7 percent versus 4 percent).

- Disability increases with age. In 2018, 46 percent of people age 85 and over reported any disability, compared with 16 percent of people ages 65–74. People age 85 and over also had higher levels of disability than people ages 65–74 in all the individual domains of functioning.

- Non-Hispanic Whites age 65 and over were less likely to report having any disability than non-Hispanic Blacks or Hispanics (21 percent versus 29 percent and 27 percent, respectively).

Studies & Statistics / Older Americans Key Indicators of Well-Being

Difficulties performing activities of daily living (ADLs), such as bathing, dressing, and toileting, and instrumental activities of daily living (IADLs), such as housework, shopping, and managing money, affect the ability to live independently. Tracking these changes over time is helpful for planning the care needs of the older population.

Percentage of Medicare beneficiaries age 65 and over who have limitations in performing activities of daily living (ADLs) or instrumental activities of daily living (IADLs), or who are in a long-term care facility, selected years 1992–2017

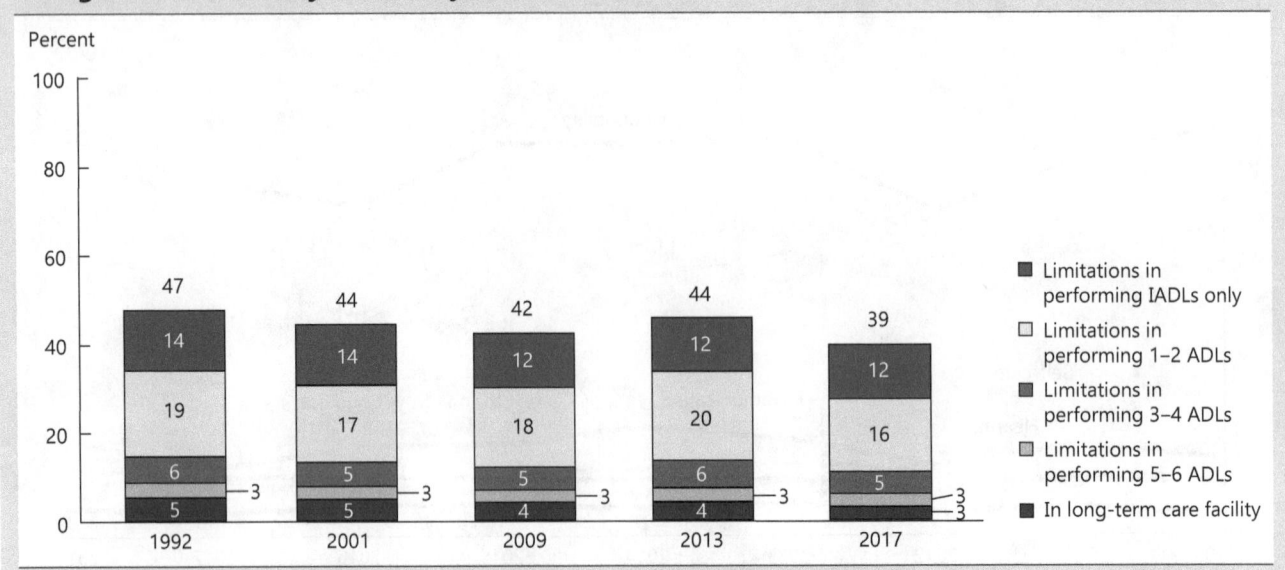

Year	Limitations in performing IADLs only	Limitations in performing 1–2 ADLs	Limitations in performing 3–4 ADLs	Limitations in performing 5–6 ADLs	In long-term care facility	Total
1992	14	19	6	3	5	47
2001	14	17	5	3	5	44
2009	12	18	5	3	4	42
2013	12	20	6	3	4	44
2017	12	16	5	3	3	39

NOTE: A residence is considered a long-term care facility if it is certified by Medicare or Medicaid; has 3 or more beds, is licensed as a nursing home or other long-term care facility, and provides at least one personal care service; or provides 24-hour, 7-day-a-week supervision by a caregiver. Limitations in performing activities of daily living (ADL) refer to difficulty performing (or inability to perform for a health reason) one or more of the following tasks: bathing, dressing, eating, getting in/out of chairs, walking, or using the toilet. Limitations in performing instrumental activities of daily living (IADL) refer to difficulty performing (or inability to perform for a health reason) one or more of the following tasks: using the telephone, light housework, heavy housework, meal preparation, shopping, or managing money. Some estimates have been revised and differ from previous editions of *Older Americans*. Estimates may not sum to the totals because of rounding.
Reference population: These data refer to Medicare beneficiaries who were continuously enrolled during the year.
SOURCE: Centers for Medicare & Medicaid Services, Medicare Current Beneficiary Survey, Access to Care (1992–2013) and Survey File (2015–2017).

- In 2017, 39 percent of people age 65 and over enrolled in Medicare reported limitations in ADLs, IADLs, or were living in a long-term care facility. Roughly 12 percent had difficulty performing one or more IADLs but had no ADL limitations. Approximately 24 percent had difficulty performing at least one ADL, and 3 percent were in a facility.

- The proportion of people age 65 and over with limitations in ADLs, IADLs, or who were living in a long-term care facility, was lower in 2017 than in 1992 (39 percent versus 47 percent).

- Women reported higher levels of limitations than men. In 2017, about 46 percent of female Medicare beneficiaries age 65 and over had difficulty performing ADLs or IADLs, or were in a long-term care facility compared with 31 percent of male Medicare beneficiaries in this age group.

- Levels of limitation varied by age. Among Medicare beneficiaries age 85 and over, 70 percent had difficulty performing ADLs or IADLs or were in a long-term care facility compared with 44 percent of people ages 75–84 and 30 percent of people ages 65–74.

Data for this indicator's charts and bullets can be found in Tables 21a through 21e on pages 107–109.

THE DEMENTIAS
Hope Through Research

LEARN ABOUT:
- Types of dementia
- Risk factors
- Diagnosis and treatment
- Current research

NIH National Institutes of Health

National Institute of Neurological Disorders and Stroke
National Institute on Aging

Diagnosis

To diagnose dementia, a doctor may complete a series of tests and assessments. In many cases, the specific type of dementia may not be confirmed until after the person has died and the brain is examined. Some forms of dementia have similar symptoms and some people may have more than one form of dementia.

Diagnosing a dementia disorder in a living person may include:

- recording the person's current symptoms, vital signs, and current medications
- compiling the person's medical and family history of illness or disease
- a physical exam and laboratory tests of the person's blood, other fluids, and various chemical and hormone levels, to help identify or rule out conditions that may contribute to dementia
- neurological evaluations to assess balance, sensory response, reflexes and other functions, and recordings of electrical activity in the brain
- brain scans to look for structural abnormalities, amyloid plaques and tau tangles, and patterns of altered brain activity that are common in dementia
- cognitive and neuropsychological tests to assess memory, language skills, math skills, problem-solving, and other abilities related to mental functioning
- genetic testing to identify risk for a dementia from gene mutations associated with dementia
- a psychiatric evaluation to help determine if depression or another mental health condition is causing or contributing to a person's symptoms

Treatment and Management

There are currently no treatments to stop dementia in neurodegenerative diseases. Some diseases that can occur at the same time as dementia (such as diabetes and depression) can be treated. Other symptoms that may occur in dementia-like conditions can also be treated, although some symptoms may only respond to treatment for a period of time. A team of specialists familiar with these disorders can help guide patient care. Specialists can include doctors, nurses, and therapists, such as speech and physical therapists.

Medications are available to treat certain behavioral symptoms, as well as delusions, depression, and muscle stiffness. Always consult with a doctor, as some medications may make symptoms worse. Some risk factors for dementia and cognitive impairment such as high blood pressure, can also be treated through a combination of medications and lifestyle changes.

Alzheimer's disease (AD). Most drugs for dementia are used to treat symptoms in AD. One class of drugs, called cholinesterase inhibitors, can temporarily improve or stabilize memory and thinking skills in some people by increasing the activity of the cholinergic brain network—a subsystem in the brain that is highly involved with memory and learning. These drugs include donepezil, rivastigmine, and galantamine. A medication known as memantine, an N-methyl D-aspartate (NMDA) antagonist, is prescribed to treat moderate to severe AD. This drug's main effect is to decrease symptoms, which could enable some people to maintain certain daily functions a little longer than they would without the medication. Memantine may be combined with a cholinesterase inhibitor for added benefits. These drugs are sometimes used to treat other dementias in which AD is believed to co-occur.

The U.S. Food and Drug Administration (FDA) has also approved aducanumab, a disease-modifying therapy, to treat AD. This medication is a human antibody, or immunotherapy, that helps to reduce amyloid plaques in the brain and may help slow the progression of AD, although it has not yet been shown to affect clinical outcomes, such as progression of cognitive decline or dementia.

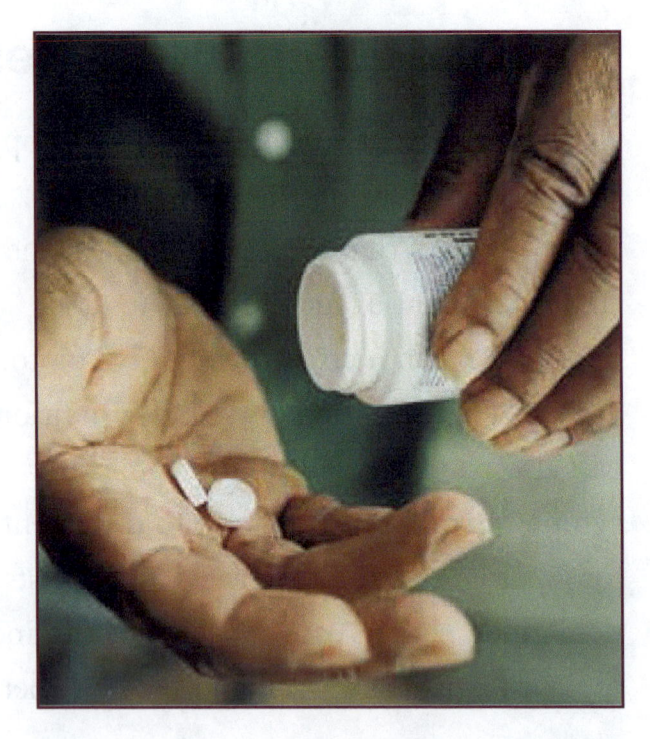

Frontotemporal disorders (FTD). There are no medications approved to treat or prevent FTD and most other types of progressive dementia. Sedatives, antidepressants, and other drugs used to treat Parkinson's and AD symptoms may help manage certain symptoms and behavioral problems associated with the disorders.

Dementia with Lewy bodies (DLB). Medicines available for managing DLB are aimed at relieving symptoms such as gait and balance disturbances, stiffness, hallucinations, and delusions. Studies suggest that the cholinesterase inhibitor drugs used for AD offer some benefit to people with DLB.

Parkinson's disease dementia (PDD). Some studies suggest that the cholinesterase inhibitors used to treat people with AD might improve cognitive, behavioral, and psychotic symptoms in people with PDD. Unfortunately, many of the medications used to treat the motor symptoms of Parkinson's disease worsen the cognitive problems. The FDA has approved rivastigmine (an AD drug) to treat cognitive symptoms in PDD.

Vascular contributions to cognitive impairment and dementia. Dementia caused by vascular conditions is often managed with drugs to prevent strokes or reduce the risk of additional brain damage. Some studies suggest drugs used to treat AD might benefit some people with early vascular dementia. Treating the modifiable risk factors can help prevent additional stroke.

Physical and occupational therapists can help with maintaining physical movement, addressing speech and swallowing issues, and helping people learn new ways to handle loss of skills with everyday tasks such as feeding oneself.

It is important to educate family, friends, and caregivers about a loved one's medical issues. Also, in-person and online support groups available through many disease awareness and caregiver advocacy organizations can give families and other caregivers additional resources, as well as opportunities to share experiences and express concerns. (See the **Resources** section on page 32).

Caring for a Person with Dementia

Caring for someone with dementia can be very hard, both physically and emotionally. Caregivers may face challenges with managing the medical and day-to-day care of people with dementia, as well as changing family and social relationships, loss of work, poor health, stress, decisions about long-term care, and end-of-life concerns.

To stay healthy, caregivers can do the following:

- get regular health care
- ask family and friends for help with errands and other tasks
- arrange for respite care—short-term help to give the regular caregiver a break—or take the person to an adult day care center, a safe, supervised environment for adults with dementia or other disabilities

- spend time doing enjoyable activities, away from the demands of caregiving

- join a support group for caregivers of people with dementia, as these groups allow caregivers to learn coping strategies and share feelings with others in the same position

- see an attorney for issues involving work, employee benefits, family leave, and disability if needed for someone who may have lost their job due to dementia

The organizations listed in the **Resources** section can help with information about caregiver services and support.

For many caregivers, there comes a point when they can no longer take care of the person with dementia without help. Caregivers may want to plan in advance to get home health care services or look for a residential care facility, such as a group home, assisted living facility, or nursing home. The decision to move the person with dementia to a care facility can be difficult, but necessary, and can give caregivers peace of mind to know that the person is safe and getting good care. Contacting a home care agency can be helpful for all caregivers, especially those with ethnic or cultural concerns involving providing care.

End-of-Life Concerns

It is difficult, but important, to plan for the end of life. Legal documents, such as a will, living will, and durable powers of attorney for health care and finances, should be created or updated as soon as possible after a diagnosis of dementia. Early on, many people can understand and participate in legal decisions. But as their illness progresses, it becomes harder to make such decisions. An attorney who specializes in elder law, disabilities, or estate planning can provide legal advice, prepare documents, and make financial arrangements for the caregiving spouse or partner and dependent children. If necessary, the person's access to finances can be reduced or eliminated.

Research

The National Institute of Neurological Disorders and Stroke (NINDS) and the National Institute on Aging (NIA), both parts of the National Institutes of Health (NIH), are the leading federal funders of research on Alzheimer's disease (AD) and related dementias, including Lewy body dementia (LBD), frontotemporal disorders (FTD), and vascular contributions to cognitive impairment and dementia (VCID).

Jointly sponsored clinical trials, research, and research partnerships have improved our understanding of dementia in several areas.

Research Areas

NIA and NINDS, along with other NIH Institutes, Centers, and Offices, support research spanning from basic biology to drug development to clinical studies to evaluating public health outcomes. Within the past several decades, researchers have made great strides toward better understanding of what causes AD and related dementias, and discovering approaches that may prevent, diagnose, and treat them. Research areas of focus include:

- **Biomarkers.** Several research projects are underway to identify dementia biomarkers—biological signs that could indicate disease risk or confirm diagnosis. The course of disease for people with AD or a related dementia varies greatly, and biomarkers may help predict and monitor its progression. These biomarkers could be detected through imaging or even blood tests. Biomarker measures may help researchers improve dementia diagnosis and identify specific changes in the brain.

- **Care and caregiver support.** To support people living with dementia, caregivers, and health providers, NIH has made large investments in research to improve the quality of care and care coordination. Already, research efforts have contributed to improvements in the quality of care—as well as in the resulting health, well-being, and quality of life—for those living with dementia. In addition, NIH support has enabled the development of resources designed to help ease burdens on care providers.

- **Drugs and compounds.** Several drugs and compounds that might slow the progression of AD and other dementias are in various stages of testing. Researchers are testing new drugs as well as exploring whether drugs approved for other conditions might be repurposed to treat dementias.

- **Lifestyle interventions.** Researchers are investigating interventions around exercise, healthy eating, cognitive training, preventive health care, and management of chronic conditions that—if made early in life—may be able to prevent or delay disease symptoms.

- **Genetics.** Scientists continue to look for new genes that may be responsible for the development of AD and other forms of dementia. Identifying more gene mutations and how they may be associated could lead to better strategies for detection, treatment, and prevention.

- **Imaging.** Clinical imaging may help researchers better understand changes in the brains of people with dementia, as well as help diagnose these disorders. NIH funds projects to develop neuroimaging as a core research tool to better understand and treat neurological disorders and conditions, including AD, Parkinson's disease, and stroke.

- **Population studies.** Studying groups of people over time helps scientists identify those at risk of developing dementia or cognitive impairment, better understand the progression of dementia both before and after symptom onset, identify potential genetic causes, and discover biomarkers to help detect and track diseases.

This information also could be used to establish a large network of clinical sites to support therapy development. For these kinds of studies, scientists aim to involve a large group of people who represent the diversity of the U.S. population.

- **Proteins.** NIH-funded research projects seek to better understand how certain proteins misfold and become harmful, as well as the toxic effects of protein buildup and how they are related to the development of dementia.

- **Stem cells.** Scientists can transform stem cells into different cell types and hopefully use them to discover nerve-cell mechanisms and biological changes that lead to the onset and progression of dementias.

Research Partnerships

The National Plan to Address Alzheimer's Disease was created in response to the 2011 National Alzheimer's Project Act (NAPA) and is designed to expand research in AD and related dementias and better meet the needs of families living with these diseases. For more information, see *http://aspe.hhs.gov/national-alzheimers-project-act*.

In support of the National Plan, NIA and NINDS support many research partnerships on dementia, including:

- The **Longitudinal Early-onset Alzheimer's Disease Study (LEADS)** addresses several major gaps in AD and related dementias research. Its primary goal is to develop sensitive clinical and biomarker measures for future clinical and research use. This observational study will enroll and follow 500 cognitively impaired participants and 100 cognitively normal participants ages 40-64 years at approximately 15 sites in the United States. Clinical, cognitive, imaging, biomarker, and genetic characteristics will be assessed.

- The **Accelerating Medicines Partnership**® (AMP®) program is a public-private partnership between the NIH, FDA, multiple biopharmaceutical and life science companies, nonprofit and other organizations to transform the current model for developing new diagnostics and treatments. Current AMP projects include:

  - **AMP PD** (Accelerating Medicines Partnership Parkinson's Disease) will identify and validate the most promising biological targets for therapeutics for Parkinson's disease. For more information, see *https://amp-pd.org*.

  - **AMP AD** (Accelerating Medicines Partnership Alzheimer's Disease) will transform the current model for developing new diagnostics and treatments for AD. For more information, see *www.nia.nih.gov/research/amp-ad*.

Accelerating Medicines Partnership and AMP are registered service marks of the U.S. Department of Health and Human Services.

- **M²OVE-AD** (Molecular Mechanisms of the Vascular Etiology of Alzheimer's Disease) allows scientists from diverse fields to work collaboratively to understand the complex molecular mechanisms by which vascular risk factors influence AD. For more information, see *www.nih.gov/m2ove-ad*.

- The **Dementia with Lewy Bodies Consortium** expands the collection of clinical data and biological specimens in the NINDS **Parkinson's Disease Biomarkers Program** to include data from people with LBD. For more information, see *https://pdbp.ninds.nih.gov/Dementia-with-Lewy-Bodies-Consortium*.

- The **Tau Center Without Walls** increases collaboration and data- and resource-sharing among researchers to better understand the protein tau and its involvement in such disorders as FTD. For more information, see *http://tau-center-without-walls.org/east-cwow*.

- **DetectCID** (Consortium for Detecting Cognitive Impairment, Including Dementia) is establishing, testing, and validating tools for detecting cognitive impairment, including dementia, in primary care and other everyday clinical settings. For more information, see *www.detectcid.org*.

- **MarkVCID** is a research consortium developing new and existing biomarkers for small vessel VCID. This could help improve the efficiency and outcomes of trials designed to test drug effectiveness and safety in humans and speed the development of therapies for the dementias. For more information, see *https://markvcid.partners.org*.

- **DISCOVERY** (Determinants of Incident Stroke Cognitive Outcomes and Vascular Effects on RecoverY) is a study to unravel the mechanisms of post-stroke cognitive disability, early stroke recovery, and potential targets for personalized prevention, intervention, and rehabilitation. For more information, see *www.resilientbrain.org/discovery.html*.

Additional NIH-funded research projects on dementia can be found using NIH RePORTER (*https://reporter.nih.gov*), a searchable database of current and past research projects supported by NIH and other federal agencies. RePORTER also includes links to publications and resources from these projects.

To learn more about research progress and scientific advances, visit *www.alzheimers.gov/taking-action/research-activities*.

What Can You Do?

Call Your Doctor

If you are concerned about memory problems or other symptoms of dementia, call your doctor. If you or someone you know has recently been diagnosed, contact the organizations in the **Resources** section to find out more about dementia care, support, and research. It is important to educate family, friends, and caregivers about a loved one's diagnosis. In-person and online support groups offered by nonprofit organizations can give families and caregivers additional resources and opportunities to share experiences and learn about strategies for care and support.

Participate in a Clinical Trial or Study

Clinical studies offer an opportunity to help researchers find better ways to safely detect, treat, or prevent dementia disorders. All types of volunteers are needed—people with dementia or memory problems, caregivers, at-risk individuals, and healthy volunteers— of all different ages, sexes, races, and ethnicities to ensure that study results apply to as many people as possible, and that treatments will be safe and effective for everyone who will use them. For information about how you can contribute to the goal of finding a treatment or cure for AD or a related dementia, visit the webpage "NIH Clinical Research Trials and You" at *www.nih.gov/health/clinicaltrials*. To search for trials and studies, go to *www.alzheimers.gov/clinical-trials* or *www.clinicaltrials.gov*.

Consider Brain Donation

Donating one's brain after death provides an opportunity to better understand dementia and can lead to improved treatments for future generations. To volunteer, people can register ahead of time through a brain donation program or research study. Learn more at *www.nia.nih.gov/braindonation* and the **NIH NeuroBioBank** at *https://neurobiobank.nih.gov*.

Conclusion

Currently, there are no cures for the common dementias caused by progressive neurodegeneration, including Alzheimer's disease, frontotemporal disorders, and Lewy body dementia. Controlling vascular risk factors such as high blood pressure may reduce the risk of developing dementia decades later.

Learning more about dementia and dementia disorders and how they affect the brain will lead to new and better ways to treat them. Advance care planning and a healthy lifestyle for people living with dementia and their caregivers will allow them to live their lives more fully and meet daily challenges.

NIH and the federal government's AD and related dementias research strategy is training new generations of researchers and clinician-scientists and engaging in innovative partnerships with private industry, nonprofit groups, and more to increase collaboration and broaden access to research resources and data. Through research activities funded by NIA and NINDS, scientists hope that new knowledge about dementia will one day lead to improved diagnosis, new tools and resources, ways to slow disease progression, prevent disease, improve care and caregiver support, and enhance quality of life for people living with dementia.

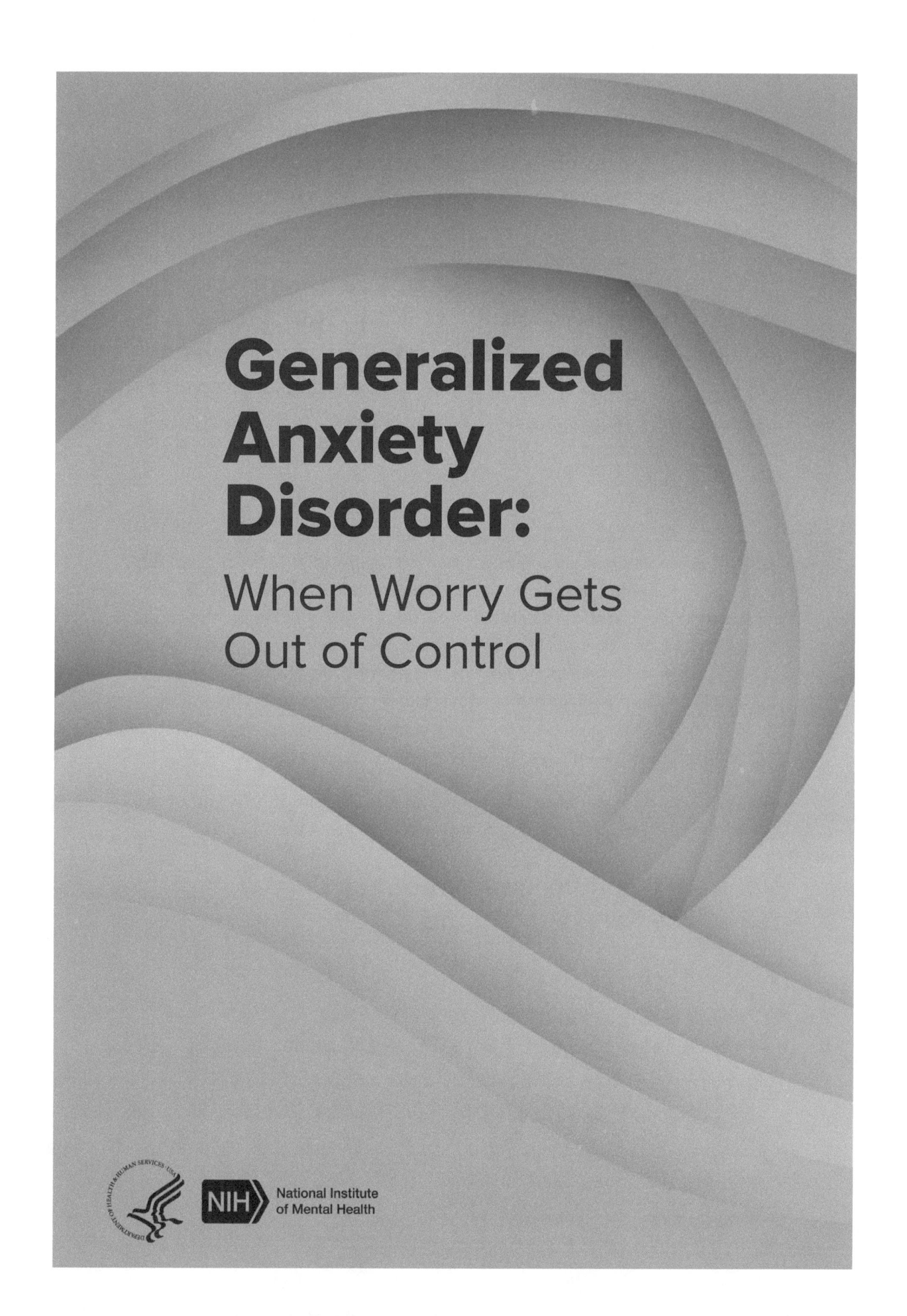

Generalized Anxiety Disorder:

When Worry Gets Out of Control

National Institute of Mental Health

Studies & Statistics / Generalized Anxiety Disorder: When Worry Gets Out of Control

Do you often find yourself worrying about everyday issues for no obvious reason? Are you always waiting for disaster to strike or excessively worried about things such as health, money, family, work, or school?

If so, you may have a type of anxiety disorder called generalized anxiety disorder (GAD). GAD can make daily life feel like a constant state of worry, fear, and dread. The good news is GAD is treatable. Learn more about the symptoms of GAD and how to find help.

What is generalized anxiety disorder?

Occasional anxiety is a normal part of life. Many people may worry about things such as health, money, or family problems. But people with GAD feel extremely worried or nervous more frequently about these and other things—even when there is little or no reason to worry about them. GAD usually involves a persistent feeling of anxiety or dread that interferes with how you live your life. It is not the same as occasionally worrying about things or experiencing anxiety due to stressful life events. People living with GAD experience frequent anxiety for months, if not years.

GAD develops slowly. It often starts around age 30, although it can occur in childhood. The disorder is more common in women than in men.

What are the signs and symptoms of generalized anxiety disorder?

People with GAD may:
- Worry excessively about everyday things
- Have trouble controlling their worries or feelings of nervousness
- Know that they worry much more than they should
- Feel restless and have trouble relaxing
- Have a hard time concentrating
- Startle easily
- Have trouble falling asleep or staying asleep

- Tire easily or feel tired all the time
- Have headaches, muscle aches, stomachaches, or unexplained pains
- Have a hard time swallowing
- Tremble or twitch
- Feel irritable or "on edge"
- Sweat a lot, feel lightheaded, or feel out of breath
- Have to go to the bathroom frequently

Children and teens with GAD often worry excessively about:

- Their performance in activities such as school or sports
- Catastrophes, such as earthquakes or war
- The health of others, such as family members

Adults with GAD are often highly nervous about everyday circumstances, such as:

- Job security or performance
- Health
- Finances
- The health and well-being of their children or other family members
- Being late
- Completing household chores and other responsibilities

Both children and adults with GAD may experience physical symptoms such as pain, fatigue, or shortness of breath that make it hard to function and that interfere with daily life.

Symptoms may fluctuate over time and are often worse during times of stress—for example—with a physical illness, during school exams, or during a family or relationship conflict.

What causes generalized anxiety disorder?

Risk for GAD can run in families. Several parts of the brain and biological processes play a key role in fear and anxiety. By learning more about how the brain and body function in people with anxiety disorders, researchers may be able to develop better treatments. Researchers have also found that external causes, such as experiencing a traumatic event or being in a stressful environment, may put you at higher risk for developing GAD.

How is generalized anxiety disorder treated?

If you think you're experiencing symptoms of GAD, talk to a health care provider. After discussing your history, a health care provider may conduct a physical exam to ensure that an unrelated physical problem is not causing your symptoms. A health care provider may refer you to a mental health professional, such as a psychiatrist, psychologist, or clinical social worker. The first step to effective treatment is to get a diagnosis, usually from a mental health professional.

GAD is generally treated with psychotherapy (sometimes called "talk therapy"), medication, or both. Speak with a health care provider about the best treatment for you.

Psychotherapy

Cognitive behavioral therapy (CBT), a research-supported type of psychotherapy, is commonly used to treat GAD. CBT teaches you different ways of thinking, behaving, and reacting to situations that help you feel less anxious and worried. CBT has been well studied and is the gold standard for psychotherapy.

Another treatment option for GAD is acceptance and commitment therapy (ACT). ACT takes a different approach than CBT to negative thoughts and uses strategies such as mindfulness and goal setting to reduce your discomfort and anxiety. Compared to CBT, ACT is a newer form of psychotherapy treatment, so less data are available on its effectiveness. However, different therapies work for different types of people, so it can be helpful to discuss what form of therapy may be right for you with a mental health professional.

For more information on psychotherapy, visit www.nimh.nih.gov/psychotherapies.

Medication

Health care providers may prescribe medication to treat GAD. Different types of medication can be effective, including:

- Antidepressants, such as selective serotonin reuptake inhibitors (SSRIs) and serotonin-norepinephrine reuptake inhibitors (SNRIs)
- Anti-anxiety medications, such as benzodiazepines

SSRI and SNRI antidepressants are commonly used to treat depression, but they also can help treat the symptoms of GAD. They may take several weeks to start working. These medications also may cause side effects, such as headaches, nausea, or difficulty sleeping. These side effects are usually not severe for most people, especially if the dose starts off low and is increased slowly over time. Talk to your health care provider about any side effects that you may experience.

Benzodiazepines, which are anti-anxiety sedative medications, also can be used to manage severe forms of GAD. These medications can be very effective in rapidly decreasing anxiety, but some people build up a tolerance to them and need higher and higher doses to get the same effect. Some people even become dependent on them. Therefore, a health care provider may prescribe them only for brief periods of time if you need them.

Buspirone is another anti-anxiety medication that can be helpful in treating GAD. Unlike benzodiazepines, buspirone is not a sedative and has less potential to be addictive. Buspirone needs to be taken for 3–4 weeks for it to be fully effective.

Both psychotherapy and medication can take some time to work. Many people try more than one medication before finding the best one for them. A health care provider can work with you to find the best medication, dose, and duration of treatment for you.

For basic information about these and other mental health medications, visit **www.nimh.nih.gov/medications**. Visit the Food and Drug Administration's website (**www.fda.gov/drugsatfda**) for the latest warnings, patient medication guides, and information on newly approved medications.

Support Groups

Some people with anxiety disorders might benefit from joining a self-help or support group and sharing their problems and achievements with others. Support groups are available both in person and online. However, any advice you receive from a support group member should be used cautiously and does not replace treatment recommendations from a health care provider.

Healthy Habits

Practicing a healthy lifestyle also can help combat anxiety, although this alone cannot replace treatment. Researchers have found that implementing certain healthy choices in daily life—such as reducing caffeine intake and getting enough sleep—can reduce anxiety symptoms when paired with standard care—such as psychotherapy and medication.

Stress management techniques, such as exercise, mindfulness, and meditation, also can reduce anxiety symptoms and enhance the effects of psychotherapy. You can learn more about how these techniques benefit your treatment by talking with a health care provider.

To learn more ways to take care of your mental health, visit **www.nimh.nih.gov/mymentalhealth**.

How can I support myself and others with generalized anxiety disorder?

Educate Yourself

A good way to help yourself or a loved one who may be struggling with GAD is to seek information. Research the warning signs, learn about treatment options, and keep up to date with current research.

Communicate

If you are experiencing GAD symptoms, have an honest conversation about how you're feeling with someone you trust. If you think that a friend or family member may be struggling with GAD, set aside a time to talk with them to express your concern and reassure them of your support.

Know When to Seek Help

If your anxiety, or the anxiety of a loved one, starts to cause problems in everyday life—such as at school, at work, or with friends and family—it's time to seek professional help. Talk to a health care provider about your mental health.

Are there clinical trials studying generalized anxiety disorder?

NIMH supports a wide range of research, including clinical trials that look at new ways to prevent, detect, or treat diseases and conditions—including GAD. Although individuals may benefit from being part of a clinical trial, participants should be aware that the primary purpose of a clinical trial is to gain new scientific knowledge so that others may be better helped in the future.

Researchers at NIMH and around the country conduct clinical trials with patients and healthy volunteers. Talk to a health care provider about clinical trials, their benefits and risks, and whether one is right for you. For more information, visit **www.nimh.nih.gov/clinicaltrials**.

Finding Help

Behavioral Health Treatment Services Locator

This online resource, provided by the Substance Abuse and Mental Health Services Administration, helps you locate mental health treatment facilities and programs. Find a facility in your state at **https://findtreatment.samhsa.gov**. For additional resources, visit **www.nimh.nih.gov/findhelp**.

Talking to a Health Care Provider About Your Mental Health

Communicating well with a health care provider can improve your care and help you both make good choices about your health. Find tips to help prepare for and get the most out of your visit at **www.nimh.nih.gov/talkingtips**. For additional resources, including questions to ask a provider, visit the Agency for Healthcare Research and Quality website at **www.ahrq.gov/questions**.

> If you or someone you know is in immediate distress or is thinking about hurting themselves, call the **National Suicide Prevention Lifeline** toll-free at 1-800-273-TALK (8255). You also can text the **Crisis Text Line** (HELLO to 741741) or use the Lifeline Chat on the National Suicide Prevention Lifeline website at **https://suicidepreventionlifeline.org**.

MARCH 2017

CDC Vitalsigns™

Arthritis in America
Time to Take Action!

Everyone knows someone with arthritis. It is a leading cause of disability, and causes pain, aching, stiffness, and swelling of the joints, but is not a normal part of aging. The most common types are osteoarthritis, rheumatoid arthritis, gout, lupus, and fibromyalgia. Arthritis costs at least $81 billion in direct medical costs annually. Many adults with arthritis are prescribed opioid medicines, yet other options for pain are safer. Physical activity can decrease pain and improve physical function by about 40% and may reduce healthcare costs. Still, 1 in 3 adults with arthritis are inactive. Adults with arthritis also can reduce their symptoms by participating in disease management education programs. Only 1 in 10 have taken part in these programs. Adults with arthritis are significantly more likely to attend an education program when recommended by a provider.

Healthcare providers can:

- Urge patients with arthritis to be physically active and to strive for a healthier weight to ease joint pain.
- Recommend patients attend proven educational programs about managing their condition.
- Ask patients about any depression or anxiety, and offer care, treatment, and links to services.
- Consult the guidelines of the American College of Rheumatology or other professional organizations for treatment options, including medicines. http://bit.ly/2m8Ocfb

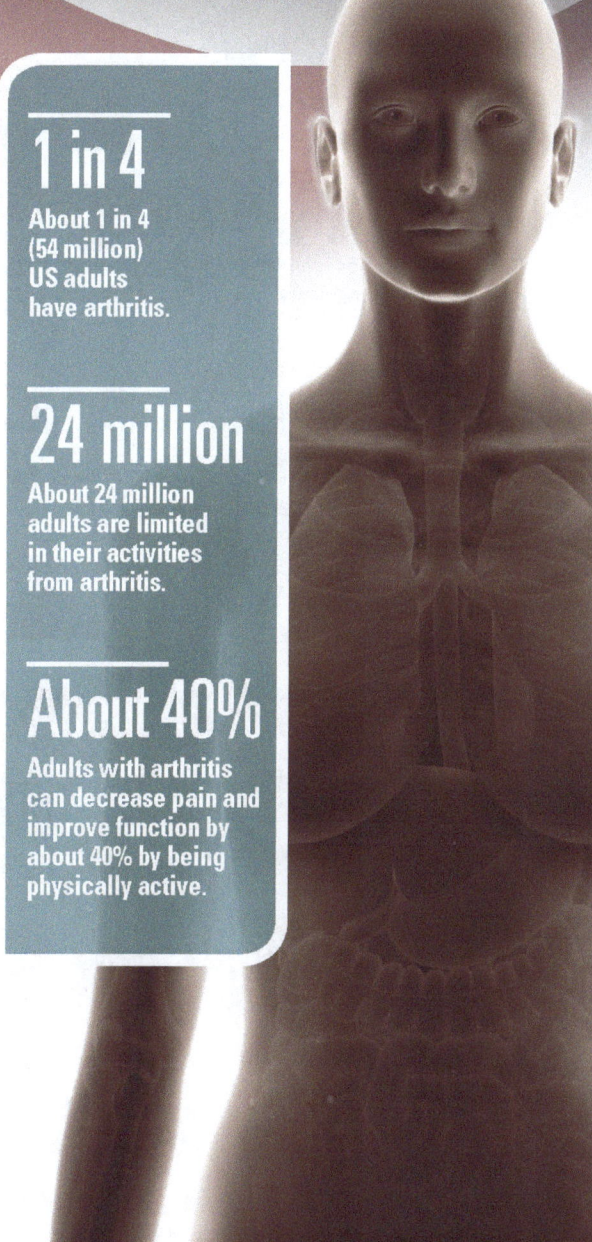

Want to learn more? www.cdc.gov/vitalsigns/arthritis

1 in 4
About 1 in 4 (54 million) US adults have arthritis.

24 million
About 24 million adults are limited in their activities from arthritis.

About 40%
Adults with arthritis can decrease pain and improve function by about 40% by being physically active.

U.S. Department of Health and Human Services
Centers for Disease Control and Prevention

Studies & Statistics / Arthritis in America

Problem:

Arthritis is common and a growing health threat.

Arthritis is common in adults.

- About 1 in 4 (54 million) adults have arthritis.
- More than half of adults with arthritis (32 million) are of working age (18-64 years).

Arthritis is disabling.

- The percent of adults limited by arthritis has increased by about 20% since 2002. The everyday activities of 24 million adults are limited by it, such as holding a cup, lifting a grocery bag, or walking to a car.
- More than 1 in 4 adults with arthritis report severe joint pain.
- Adults with arthritis are more than twice as likely as adults without arthritis to report an injury related to a fall.
- Working-age adults with arthritis have lower employment than those without arthritis.

Arthritis makes it harder to manage heart disease, diabetes or obesity.

- About half of adults with heart disease (49%) or diabetes (47%) have arthritis, as do one-third (31%) of those who are obese.
- About half the adults with arthritis who also have heart disease, diabetes or obesity, have some limitation of their normal activities because of their arthritis.
- Physical activity helps manage all these conditions.
- Increased pain, fear of pain, and lack of knowledge of safe forms of physical activity can make it harder for people with arthritis to be physically active.

Physical activity programs can reduce yearly healthcare costs by about $1,000 per person.

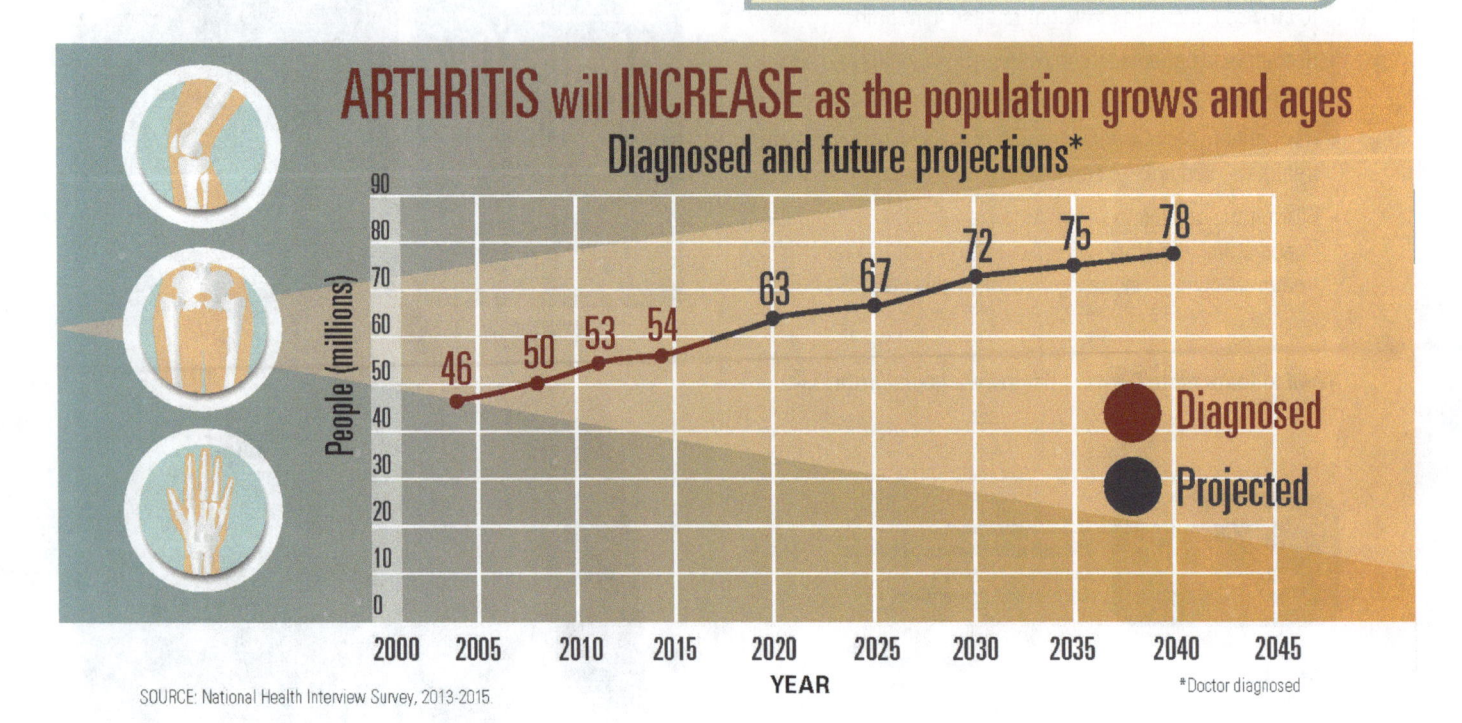

ARTHRITIS will INCREASE as the population grows and ages
Diagnosed and future projections*

People (millions) by Year:
- 2005: 46
- 2010: 50
- 2012: 53
- 2015: 54
- 2020: 63
- 2025: 67
- 2030: 72
- 2035: 75
- 2040: 78

Legend: Diagnosed / Projected

SOURCE: National Health Interview Survey, 2013-2015.

*Doctor diagnosed

156

Studies & Statistics / Arthritis in America

Arthritis effects can be reduced with physical activity.

Arthritis in daily life

- One-third of adults over age 45 with arthritis report anxiety or depression. About 3 in 10 find stooping, bending, or kneeling very difficult.
- More than 20% of adults with arthritis find it very difficult or cannot walk 3 blocks, such as from a parking deck or subway to work.
- African Americans and Hispanics with arthritis are more limited in their activities due to their arthritis.

Managing arthritis

- Arthritis aches and pains are not a normal part of aging.
- Physical activity—walking, swimming, biking—is good for arthritis.
- Physical activity can reduce pain and improve function.

Who has arthritis?

- About 23% of adults have arthritis.
- Nearly 60% of adults with arthritis are women.
- Nearly 60% of people with arthritis are working age.

SOURCE: CDC Vital Signs, March 2017

Studies & Statistics / Arthritis in America

What Can Be Done?

The Federal government is

- Supporting national organizations and programs at local parks and recreation areas, community and senior centers, healthcare facilities, and YMCAs to help adults better manage their arthritis.

- Supporting proven physical activity and educational programs through state health departments, health and human service agencies, and community organizations.

- Funding home and community-based services that help people with arthritis and other chronic diseases maintain and improve their health and independence.

- Providing toolkits and resource materials for organizations delivering community-based physical activity and educational programs for those with chronic diseases.

- Providing courses, guidance, and decision-making tools to primary care physicians to support patients' ability to manage their own condition.

- Collecting data on arthritis in the US and conducting prevention and biomedical research to guide public health activities related to arthritis.

Healthcare providers can

- Urge patients with arthritis to be physically active and to strive for a healthier weight to ease joint pain.

- Recommend patients attend proven educational programs about managing their condition.

- Ask patients about any depression or anxiety, and offer care, treatment, and links to services.

- Consult the guidelines of the American College of Rheumatology or other professional organizations for treatment options, including medicines.
http://bit.ly/2m8Ocfb

Adults with arthritis can

- Learn proven actions to deal with pain, fatigue, anxiety and depression.

- Be physically active (like walking, swimming, or biking) to help maintain and improve strength, flexibility, and endurance.

- Adopt healthy eating habits and lose weight, if necessary.

- Attend educational programs to gain confidence and skills on managing arthritis.

- Use medications correctly under a healthcare provider's care.

State officials and community leaders can

- Promote physical activity and disease management educational programs to adults with arthritis through public health departments, parks and recreation agencies, and community and senior centers.

- Support improvements for more walkable community areas to increase opportunities for physical activity.

- Create a system for healthcare providers and adults with arthritis to locate community-based programs.

- Conduct communications campaigns to promote physical activity or educational programs.

1-800-CDC-INFO (232-4636)
TTY: 1-888-232-6348
www.cdc.gov

Centers for Disease Control and Prevention
1600 Clifton Road NE, Atlanta, GA 30329
Publication date: 03/07/2017

CDC Vitalsigns™

#vitalsigns
FEB. 2018

1 in 12 — About 6 million children in the US ages 0-17 years have asthma.

50% — Asthma hospitalizations for children declined from 10% in 2003 to about 5% in 2013.

1 in 2 — More than half of all children with asthma had 1 or more attacks in 2016.

Asthma in children
Working together to get it under control

Asthma is a serious disease causing wheezing, difficulty breathing, and coughing. Over a lifetime, it can cause permanent lung damage. About 16% of black children and 7% of white children have asthma. While we don't know what causes asthma, we do know how to prevent asthma attacks or at least make them less severe. Today, children with asthma and their caregivers report fewer attacks, missed school days, and hospital visits. More children with asthma are learning to control their asthma using an asthma action plan.* Still, more than half of children with asthma had one or more attacks in 2016. Every year, 1 in 6 children with asthma visits the Emergency Department with about 1 in 20 children with asthma hospitalized for asthma.

Doctors, nurses, and other healthcare providers are:

- Teaching children and parents to manage asthma by using a personalized action plan shared with school staff and other caregivers. Such a plan helps children use medicine properly and avoid asthma triggers like tobacco smoke, pet dander, and air pollution.

- Working with community health workers, pharmacists, and others to ensure that children with asthma receive needed services.

- Working with children and parents to assess each child's asthma, prescribe appropriate medicines, and determine whether home health visits would help prevent attacks.

* Asthma Action Plan, http://bit.ly/2scBt1W

Want to learn more? Visit: www.cdc.gov/vitalsigns

Centers for Disease Control and Prevention
National Center for Environmental Health

Studies & Statistics / Asthma in Children

PROBLEM:
Half of children with asthma had 1 or more attacks in 2016.

Asthma attacks: going down (but still too many).

- Attacks have gone down in children of all races and ethnicities from 2001 through 2016.

- About 50% of children with asthma had an attack in 2016.

- Asthma attacks occurred most frequently among children younger than age 5 in 2016.

- Emergency Department and urgent care center visits related to asthma attacks were highest among children ages 0-4 years and Non-Hispanic black children.

Using medicine as prescribed can prevent asthma attacks.

- Inhaled corticosteroids and other control medicines can prevent asthma attacks.

- Rescue inhalers or nebulizers can give quick relief of symptoms

- But . . . about half of children who are prescribed asthma control medicines do not use them regularly.

Your asthma is well controlled if:

- You have symptoms no more than 2 days a week, and these symptoms don't wake you from sleep more than 1 or 2 nights a month.

- You can do all of your normal activities.

- You have no more than 1 asthma attack a year that requires you to take a pill or liquid for several days to treat the attack.

- Your peak flow, a measurement of how well air moves in and out of your lungs, doesn't drop below 80% of your personal best number.

- You need to take quick-relief medicines no more than 2 days a week.

Asthma medication use among children with asthma in 2013.

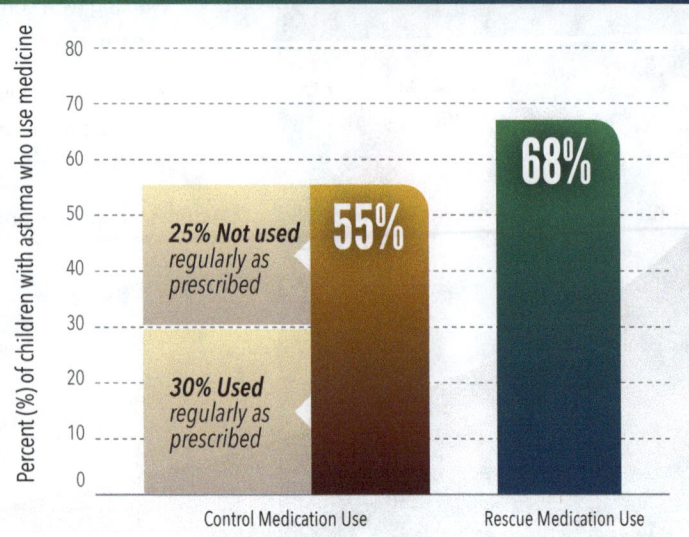

Control Medication Use: 55% (25% Not used regularly as prescribed; 30% Used regularly as prescribed)

Rescue Medication Use: 68%

SOURCE: National Health Interview Survey, 2013. http://bit.ly/2xkU0GA

160

Studies & Statistics / Asthma in Children

Asthma-related hospitalizations and missed school days were fewer in 2013 than in 2003.

Children who were hospitalized for asthma
- 2003: 10%
- 2013: 5%

(Percent (%) hospitalized, ages 0-17 years)

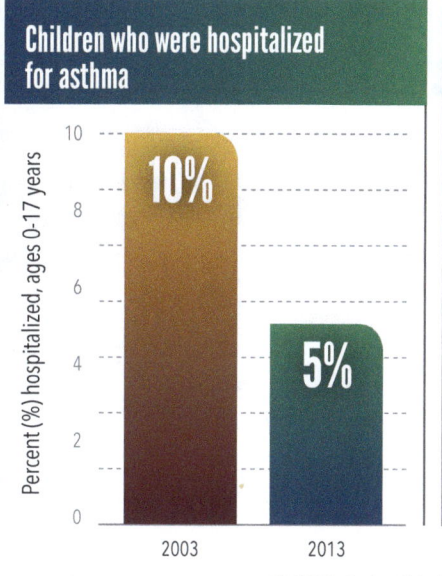

Children with asthma who missed school days
- 2003: 61%
- 2013: 49%

(Percent (%) missing school, ages 5-17 years)

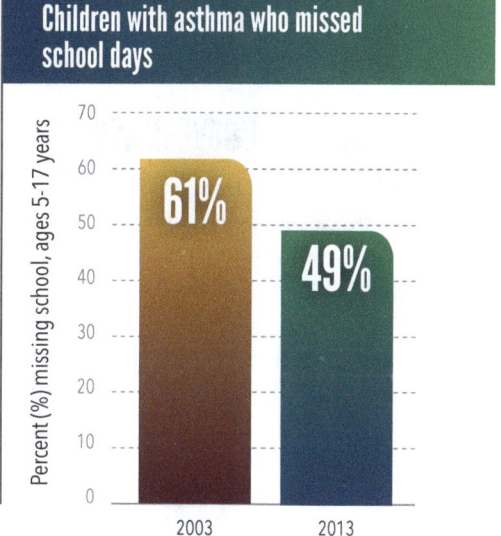

SOURCE: National Health Interview Survey, 2003 and 2013. http://bit.ly/2xkU0GA

> **Average annual medical costs of asthma were nearly $1,000 per child in 2012.**

SOURCE: http://bit.ly/2rtljBe

Healthcare provider asthma education of children in 2013.

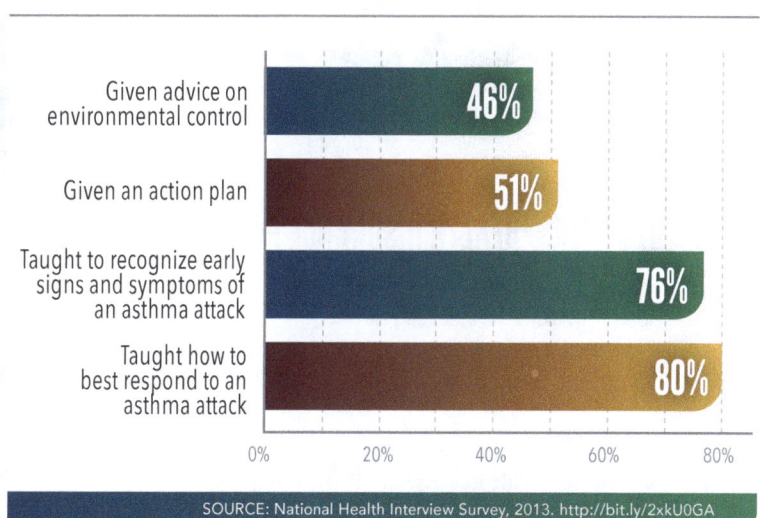

- Given advice on environmental control: 46%
- Given an action plan: 51%
- Taught to recognize early signs and symptoms of an asthma attack: 76%
- Taught how to best respond to an asthma attack: 80%

SOURCE: National Health Interview Survey, 2013. http://bit.ly/2xkU0GA

Studies & Statistics / Asthma in Children

WHAT CAN BE DONE

THE FEDERAL GOVERNMENT IS

- Working with state, territorial, private and non-government partners to support medical management, asthma-self management education, and, for people at high risk, home visits to reduce triggers and help with asthma management. http://bit.ly/2y2XBgs, http://bit.ly/2hPeZ1l

- Providing guidelines, tools such as asthma action plans, and educational messages to help children, their caregivers, and healthcare professionals better manage asthma. http://bit.ly/2scBt1W

- Promoting policies and best practices to reduce exposure to indoor and outdoor asthma triggers such as tobacco smoke and air pollution.

- Tracking asthma rates and assuring efficient and effective use of resources invested in asthma services.

DOCTORS, NURSES, AND OTHER HEALTHCARE PROVIDERS ARE

- Teaching children and parents to manage asthma by using a personalized action plan shared with school staff and other caregivers. Such a plan helps children use medicine properly and avoid asthma triggers like tobacco smoke, pet dander, and air pollution.

- Working with community health workers, pharmacists, and others to ensure that children with asthma receive needed services.

- Working with children and parents to assess each child's asthma, prescribe appropriate medicines, and determine whether home health visits would help prevent attacks.

SOME PAYERS/HEALTH INSURANCE PLANS ARE

- Reimbursing healthcare providers for education of children with asthma, including development of their personalized asthma action plans.

- Providing training and incentives for health care providers to practice guidelines-based medical management.

- Taking actions to improve access to and proper use of asthma medications and devices.

- Providing each child with asthma with the medical and community-based services needed to control his or her asthma.

PARENTS AND CHILDREN ARE

- Learning about asthma, how to manage it, and how to recognize the warning signs of an asthma attack.

- Taking steps to reduce asthma triggers such as tobacco smoke, mold, and pet dander in the home. If caregivers smoke, they should try to quit or at least never smoke around children.

- Making sure children use their asthma controller medicine as prescribed.

- Communicating with schools, other family members, caregivers and healthcare providers about the child's asthma action plan and about asthma symptoms.

SCHOOLS ARE

- Educating school nurses and other school staff about asthma and how to help children control it.

- Carrying out asthma-friendly policies to help children follow their action plans, including stocking quick relief medications, letting older children carry controller and rescue medicines, and helping children take part in school activities, such as exercising indoors when air quality is poor.

- Using CDC's Strategies for Addressing Asthma in Schools. http://bit.ly/2wAtGcj

www.cdc.gov/vitalsigns/childhood-asthma
www.cdc.gov/mmwr

For more information, please contact
Telephone: 1-800-CDC-INFO (232-4636)
TTY: 1-888-232-6348 | Web: www.cdc.gov
Centers for Disease Control and Prevention
1600 Clifton Road NE, Atlanta, GA 30333
Publication date: February 6, 2018

Clearing the Air of Asthma Triggers
10 Steps to Making Your Home Asthma-Friendly

1. **Take it outside.** One of the most common asthma triggers in the home is **secondhand smoke**. Until you can quit, smoke outside, not in your home or car.

2. **Good night, little mite! Dust mites** are also triggers for asthma. For mite population control, cover mattresses and pillows with dust-proof (allergen impermeable) zippered covers. Wash sheets and blankets once a week in hot water.

3. **Play it Safe.** Ozone and particle pollution can cause asthma attacks. Watch for the Air Quality Index (AQI) during your local weather report. When AQI reports unhealthy levels, limit outdoor activities.

4. **A little goes a long way.** Reduce everyday dust build-up, by regularly dusting with a damp cloth and vacuuming carpet and fabric-covered furniture.

5. **Stake your claim. Household pets** can trigger asthma with skin flakes, urine, and saliva. Keep pets outdoors, if possible.

6. **Uninvite unwelcome guests. Cockroaches** can trigger asthma. Don't invite them into your home by leaving food or garbage out. Always clean up messes and spills and store food in airtight containers.

7. **Think before you spray.** Instead of pesticide sprays, control pests by using baits or traps. If sprays are necessary, always circulate fresh air into the room being treated and keep asthma sufferers out of that room for several hours after any spraying.

8. **Break the mold. Mold** is another asthma trigger. The key to controlling mold is controlling moisture. Wash and dry hard surfaces to prevent and remove mold. Replace moldy ceiling tiles and carpet.

9. **Air it out.** Reducing the moisture will control asthma triggers like **mold, cockroaches,** and **dust mites**. Use exhaust fans or open windows when cooking and showering. Fix leaky plumbing or other unwanted sources of water.

10. **Plan *before* the attack.** Work with your doctor or health care provider to develop a written asthma management plan for your child that includes information on your child's triggers and how to manage them.

Post a note. Post this plan on your refrigerator to help *control asthma triggers and reduce asthma attacks in your home*. Share it with those who spend time with your child like teachers, babysitters, and coaches.

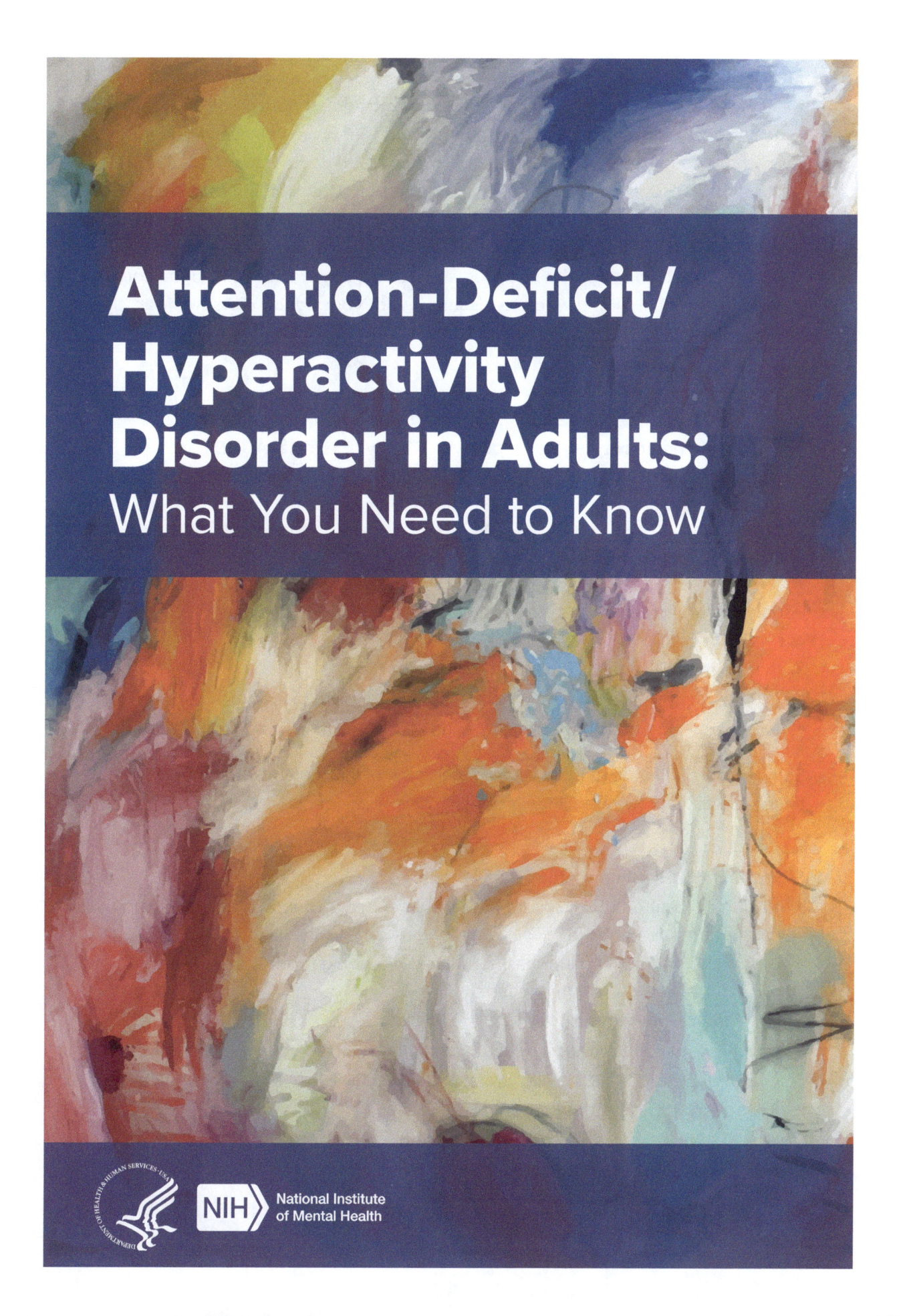

Attention-Deficit/Hyperactivity Disorder in Adults:
What You Need to Know

National Institute of Mental Health

Studies & Statistics / Attention-Deficit/Hyperactivity Disorder in Adults

> **Have you experienced challenges with concentration, impulsivity, restlessness, and organization throughout your life? Have you ever wondered whether you might have attention-deficit/hyperactivity disorder (ADHD)? Although ADHD is well known as a condition that affects children, many adults also experience it. ADHD can be harmful to an individual's social relationships and work and school performance, but effective treatments are available to manage the symptoms of ADHD. Learn about the signs and symptoms of ADHD and when to discuss it with your health care provider.**

What is ADHD?

ADHD is a developmental disorder associated with an ongoing pattern of inattention, hyperactivity, and/or impulsivity. The symptoms of ADHD can interfere significantly with an individual's daily activities and relationships. ADHD begins in childhood and can continue into the teen years and adulthood.

What are the symptoms of ADHD?

People with ADHD experience an ongoing pattern of the following types of symptoms:

- Inattention—having difficulty paying attention
- Hyperactivity—having too much energy or moving and talking too much
- Impulsivity—acting without thinking or having difficulty with self-control

Some people with ADHD mainly have symptoms of inattention. Others mostly have symptoms of hyperactivity-impulsivity. Some people have both types of symptoms.

Signs of inattention may include challenges with:

- Paying close attention to details or making seemingly careless mistakes at work or during other activities
- Sustaining attention for long tasks, such as preparing reports, completing forms, or reviewing lengthy papers
- Listening closely when spoken to directly
- Following instructions and finishing duties in the workplace
- Organizing tasks and activities and managing time
- Engaging in tasks that require sustained attention
- Losing things such as keys, wallets, and phones
- Being easily distracted by unrelated thoughts or stimuli
- Being forgetful in daily activities, such as paying bills, keeping appointments, or returning calls

Signs of hyperactivity and impulsivity may include:
- Experiencing extreme restlessness, difficulty sitting still for extended periods, and/or wearing others out with one's activity
- Fidgeting with or tapping hands or feet or squirming in seat
- Being unable to engage quietly in leisure activities
- Talking excessively
- Answering questions before they are asked completely
- Having difficulty waiting one's turn, such as when waiting in line
- Interrupting or intruding on others

Other mental disorders may occur with ADHD, including anxiety, mood, and substance use disorders. You can learn about other mental disorders at www.nimh.nih.gov/health/topics/.

How is ADHD diagnosed in adults?

ADHD is a disorder that begins in childhood and continues into adulthood. Adults who are diagnosed with ADHD experienced several symptoms of ADHD before the age of 12. As adults, they currently experience at least five persistent symptoms of inattention and/or five persistent symptoms of hyperactivity-impulsivity. These symptoms must be present in two or more settings (for example, home, work, or school; with friends or relatives; in other activities) and interfere with, or reduce the quality of, social, school, or work functioning.

Adults who think they may have ADHD should talk to their health care provider. Primary care providers routinely diagnose and treat ADHD and may refer individuals to mental health professionals. If you need help starting the conversation, check out NIMH's Tips for Talking With Your Health Care Provider fact sheet at www.nimh.nih.gov/talkingtips.

Stress, other mental health conditions, and physical conditions or illnesses can cause similar symptoms to those of ADHD. Therefore, a thorough evaluation by a health care provider or mental health professional is necessary to determine the cause of the symptoms and identify effective treatments. During this evaluation, the health care provider or mental health professional will examine factors including the person's mood, medical history, and whether they struggle with other issues, such as alcohol or substance misuse.

A thorough evaluation also includes looking at the person's history of childhood behavior and school experiences. To obtain this information, an individual's health care provider may ask for permission to talk with partners, family members, close friends, and others who know the individual well. A health care provider or mental health professional may use standardized behavior rating scales or ADHD symptom checklists to determine whether an adult meets the criteria for a diagnosis of ADHD. An individual may complete psychological tests that look at working memory, executive functioning (abilities such as planning and decision-making), visual and spatial (related to space), or reasoning (thinking) skills. Such tests can help identify psychological or cognitive (thinking-related) strengths and challenges and can be used to identify or rule out possible learning disabilities.

How does ADHD affect adults?

Some adults who have ADHD don't know they have it. These adults may feel it is impossible to get organized, stick to a job, or remember to keep appointments. Daily tasks such as getting up in the morning, preparing to leave the house for work, arriving at work on time, and being productive on the job can be especially challenging for adults with undiagnosed ADHD. These adults may have a history of problems with school, work, and relationships. Adults with ADHD may seem restless and may try to do several things at the same time—most of them unsuccessfully. They sometimes prefer quick fixes rather than taking the steps needed to gain greater rewards.

A person may not be diagnosed with ADHD until adulthood because teachers or family did not recognize the condition at a younger age, they had a mild form of ADHD, or they managed fairly well until they experienced the demands of adulthood, especially at work. Sometimes, young adults with undiagnosed ADHD have academic problems in college because of the intense concentration needed for college courses.

It is never too late to seek a diagnosis and treatment for ADHD and any other mental health condition that may occur with it. Effective treatment can make day-to-day life easier for many adults and their families.

What causes ADHD?

Researchers are not sure what causes ADHD, although many studies suggest that genes play a large role. Like many other disorders, ADHD probably results from a combination of factors. In addition to genetics, researchers are looking at possible environmental factors that might raise the risk of developing ADHD and are studying how brain injuries, nutrition, and social environments might play a role in ADHD.

What are the treatments for ADHD?

Treatment for ADHD includes medication, therapy and other behavioral treatments, or a combination of methods.

Medication

Stimulants are the most common type of medication used to treat ADHD. Research shows these medications can be highly effective. Like all medications, they can have side effects and require an individual's health care provider to monitor how they may be reacting to the medication. Nonstimulant medications are also available. Health care providers may sometimes prescribe antidepressants to treat adults with ADHD, although the Food and Drug Administration (FDA) has not approved these medications specifically for treating ADHD.

As with all prescriptions, individuals should disclose other medications they take when discussing potential ADHD medications with a health care provider. Medications for common adult health problems, such as diabetes, high blood pressure, anxiety, and depression, may interact with stimulants. In this case, a health care provider can suggest other medication options.

For general information about stimulants and other medications used for treating mental disorders, see NIMH's Mental Health Medications webpage (**www.nimh.nih.gov/medications**). The FDA website (**www.fda.gov/drugsatfda**) has the latest information on medication approvals, warnings, and patient information guides.

Psychotherapy and Support

Research shows that therapy may not be effective in treating the core symptoms of ADHD. However, adding therapy to an ADHD treatment plan may help individuals better cope with daily challenges. Therapy is especially helpful if ADHD co-occurs with other mental disorders, such as anxiety or depression.

Psychotherapy, including cognitive behavioral therapy, might help an adult with ADHD become more aware of attention and concentration challenges and work on skills to improve organization and use of time in completing daily tasks. For example, they might help individuals break down large tasks into smaller, more manageable steps. Psychotherapy also can help adults with ADHD gain confidence and control impulsive and risky behaviors. Some adults also may find it helpful to get support from a professional life coach or ADHD coach who can help with different skills to improve daily functioning.

For general information about psychotherapies used for treating mental disorders, see NIMH's Psychotherapies webpage (**www.nimh.nih.gov/psychotherapies**).

Complementary Health Approaches

Some people may explore complementary health approaches, such as natural products, to manage symptoms of ADHD. Unlike specific psychotherapy and medication treatments that are scientifically proven to improve ADHD symptoms and impairments, complementary health approaches for ADHD generally have not been found to improve ADHD symptoms and do not qualify as evidence-supported interventions. For more information, visit the National Center for Complementary and Integrative Health at **www.nccih.nih.gov/health/attention-deficit-hyperactivity-disorder-at-a-glance**.

How can I find help?

The Substance Abuse and Mental Health Services Administration (SAMHSA) provides the Behavioral Health Treatment Services Locator (**https://findtreatment.samhsa.gov**), an online tool for finding mental health services and treatment programs in your state. For additional resources, visit **www.nimh.nih.gov/findhelp**.

> If you or someone you know is in immediate distress or is thinking about hurting themselves, call the **National Suicide Prevention Lifeline** toll-free at 1-800-273-TALK (8255) or the toll-free TTY number at 1-800-799-4TTY (4889). You also can text the **Crisis Text Line** (HELLO to 741741) or go to the National Suicide Prevention Lifeline website at **https://suicidepreventionlifeline.org**.

How can I help myself?

Therapy and medication are the most effective treatments for ADHD. In addition to these treatments, other strategies may help manage symptoms:

- Exercise regularly, especially when you're feeling hyperactive or restless.
- Eat regular, healthy meals.
- Get plenty of sleep. Try to turn off screens at least 1 hour before bedtime and get between 7 and 9 hours of sleep every night.
- Work on time management and organization. Prioritize time-sensitive tasks and write down assignments, messages, appointments, and important thoughts.
- Connect with people and maintain relationships. Schedule activities with friends, particularly supportive people who understand your challenges with ADHD.
- Take medications as directed, and avoid use of alcohol, tobacco, and drugs.

Where can I turn if I feel alone in my diagnosis of ADHD?

Adults with ADHD may gain social support and better coping skills by talking with family, friends, and colleagues about their diagnosis. If the people in your life are aware of your diagnosis, they will better understand your behavior. Psychotherapy for families and couples can help relationship problems and teach everyone involved about ADHD. There are also support groups for adults with ADHD.

What should I know about participating in clinical research?

Clinical trials are research studies that look at new ways to prevent, detect, or treat diseases and conditions. Although individuals may benefit from being part of a clinical trial, participants should be aware that the primary purpose of a clinical trial is to gain new scientific knowledge so that others may be better helped in the future.

Researchers at NIMH and around the country conduct many studies with patients and healthy volunteers. Talk to your health care provider about clinical trials, their benefits and risks, and whether one is right for you. For more information, visit NIMH's Clinical Trials webpage at www.nimh.nih.gov/clinicaltrials.

Where can I find more information on ADHD?

The Centers for Disease Control and Prevention (CDC) within the U.S. Department of Health and Human Services (HHS) is the nation's leading health promotion, prevention, and preparedness agency. You can find information about ADHD symptoms, diagnosis, and treatment options, as well as additional resources for families and providers, at www.cdc.gov/adhd.

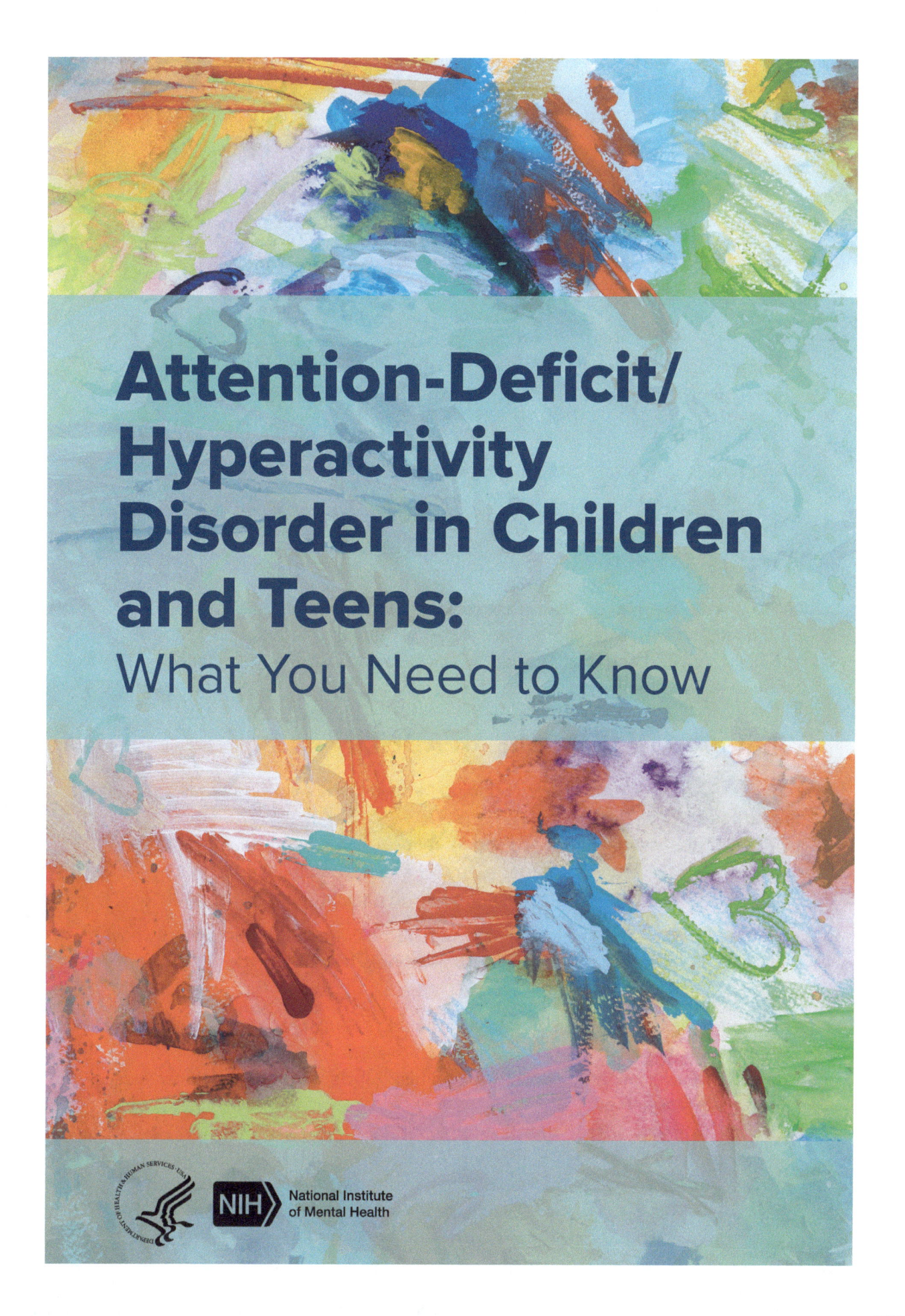

Attention-Deficit/ Hyperactivity Disorder in Children and Teens:
What You Need to Know

Studies & Statistics / Attention-Deficit/Hyperactivity Disorder in Children and Teens

> Have you noticed that your child or teen finds it hard to pay attention? Do they often move around during times when they shouldn't, act impulsively, or interrupt others? If such issues are ongoing and seem to be impacting your child's daily life, they may have attention-deficit/hyperactivity disorder (ADHD).
>
> ADHD can impact the social relationships and school performance of children and teens, but effective treatments are available to manage the symptoms of ADHD. Learn about ADHD, how it's diagnosed, and how to find support.

What is ADHD?

ADHD is a developmental disorder associated with an ongoing pattern of inattention, hyperactivity, and/or impulsivity. Symptoms of ADHD can interfere with daily activities and relationships. ADHD begins in childhood and can continue into the teen years and adulthood.

What are the symptoms of ADHD?

People with ADHD experience an ongoing pattern of the following types of symptoms:
- Inattention—having difficulty paying attention
- Hyperactivity—having too much energy or moving and talking too much
- Impulsivity—acting without thinking or having difficulty with self-control

Some people with ADHD mainly have symptoms of inattention. Others mostly have symptoms of hyperactivity-impulsivity. Some people have both types of symptoms.

Signs of inattention may include:
- Not paying close attention to details or making seemingly careless mistakes in schoolwork or during other activities
- Difficulty sustaining attention in play and tasks, including conversations, tests, or lengthy assignments
- Trouble listening closely when spoken to directly
- Finding it hard to follow through on instructions or to finish schoolwork or chores, or starting tasks but losing focus and getting easily sidetracked

- Difficulty organizing tasks and activities, such as doing tasks in sequence, keeping materials and belongings in order, managing time, and meeting deadlines
- Avoiding tasks that require sustained mental effort, such as homework
- Losing things necessary for tasks or activities, such as school supplies, books, eyeglasses, and cell phones
- Being easily distracted by unrelated thoughts or stimuli
- Being forgetful during daily activities, such as chores, errands, and keeping appointments

Signs of hyperactivity and impulsivity may include:
- Fidgeting and squirming while seated
- Getting up and moving around when expected to stay seated, such as in a classroom
- Running, dashing around, or climbing at inappropriate times or, in teens, often feeling restless
- Being unable to play or engage in hobbies quietly
- Being constantly in motion or on the go and/or acting as if driven by a motor
- Talking excessively
- Answering questions before they are fully asked or finishing other people's sentences
- Having difficulty waiting one's turn, such as when standing in line
- Interrupting or intruding on others, for example, in conversations, games, or activities

How is ADHD diagnosed in children and teens?

To be diagnosed with ADHD, symptoms must have been present before the age of 12. Children up to age 16 are diagnosed with ADHD if they have had at least six persistent symptoms of inattention and/or six persistent symptoms of hyperactivity-impulsivity present for at least 6 months. Symptoms must be present in two or more settings (for example, at home or school or with friends or relatives) and interfere with the quality of social or school functioning.

Parents who think their child may have ADHD should talk to their health care provider. Primary care providers sometimes diagnose and treat ADHD. They may also refer individuals to a mental health professional, such as a psychiatrist or clinical psychologist, who can do a thorough evaluation and make an ADHD diagnosis. Stress, sleep disorders, anxiety, depression, and other physical conditions or illnesses can cause similar symptoms to those of ADHD. Therefore, a thorough evaluation is necessary to determine the cause of the symptoms.

During an evaluation, the health care provider or mental health professional may:
- Examine the child's mental health and medical history.
- Ask permission to talk with family members, teachers, and other adults who know the child well and see them in different settings to learn about the child's behavior and experiences at home and school.
- Use standardized behavior rating scales or ADHD symptom checklists to determine whether a child or teen meets the criteria for a diagnosis of ADHD.
- Administer psychological tests that look at working memory, executive functioning (abilities such as planning and decision-making), visual and spatial skills, or reasoning skills. Such tests can help detect psychological or cognitive strengths and challenges as well as identify or rule out possible learning disabilities.

Does ADHD look the same in all children and teens?

ADHD symptoms can change over time as a child grows and moves into the preteen and teenage years. In young children with ADHD, hyperactivity and impulsivity are the most common symptoms. As academic and social demands increase, symptoms of inattention become more prominent and begin to interfere with academic performance and peer relationships. In adolescence, hyperactivity often becomes less severe and may appear as restlessness or fidgeting. Symptoms of inattention and impulsivity typically continue and may cause worsening academic, organizational, and relationship challenges. Teens with ADHD also are more likely to engage in impulsive, risky behaviors, including substance use and unsafe sexual activity.

Inattention, restlessness, and impulsivity continue into adulthood for many individuals with ADHD, but in some cases, they may become less severe and less impairing over time.

What causes ADHD?

Researchers are not sure what causes ADHD, although many studies suggest that genes play a large role. Like many other disorders, ADHD probably results from a combination of factors. In addition to genetics, researchers are looking at possible environmental factors that might raise the risk of developing ADHD and are studying how brain injuries, nutrition, and social environments might play a role in ADHD.

What are the treatments for ADHD in children and teens?

Although there is no cure for ADHD, currently available treatments may help reduce symptoms and improve functioning. ADHD is commonly treated with medication, education or training, therapy, or a combination of treatments.

Medication

Stimulants are the most common type of medication used to treat ADHD. Research shows these medications can be highly effective. Like all medications, they can have side effects and require an individual's health care provider to monitor how they may be reacting to the medication. Nonstimulant medications are also available. Health care providers may sometimes prescribe antidepressants to treat children with ADHD, although the Food and Drug Administration (FDA) has not approved these medications specifically for treating ADHD. Sometimes an individual must try several different medications or dosages before finding what works for them.

For general information about stimulants and other medications used to treat mental disorders, see NIMH's Mental Health Medications webpage (**www.nimh.nih.gov/medications**). The FDA website (**www.fda.gov/drugsatfda**) has the latest medication approvals, warnings, and patient information guides.

Psychotherapy and Psychosocial Interventions

Several psychosocial interventions have been shown to help children and their families manage symptoms and improve everyday functioning.

- **Behavioral therapy** aims to help a person change their behavior. It might involve practical assistance, such as help organizing tasks or completing schoolwork, learning social skills, or monitoring one's own behavior and receiving praise or rewards for acting in a desired way.
- **Cognitive behavioral therapy** helps a person to become more aware of attention and concentration challenges and to work on skills to improve focus.
- **Family and marital therapy** can help family members learn how to handle disruptive behaviors, encourage behavior changes, and improve interactions with children.

All types of therapy for children and teens with ADHD require parents to play an active role. Psychotherapy that includes only individual treatment sessions with the child (without parent involvement) is not effective for managing ADHD symptoms and behavior. This type of treatment is more likely to be effective for treating symptoms of anxiety or depression that may occur along with ADHD.

For general information about psychotherapies used for treating mental disorders, see NIMH's Psychotherapies webpage (**www.nimh.nih.gov/psychotherapies**).

Parent Education and Support

Mental health professionals can educate the parents of a child with ADHD about the disorder and how it affects a family. They also can help parents and children develop new skills, attitudes, and ways of relating to each other. Examples include parenting skills training, stress management techniques for parents, and support groups that help parents and families connect with others who have similar concerns.

School-Based Programs

Children and adolescents with ADHD typically benefit from classroom-based behavioral interventions and/or academic accommodations. Interventions may include behavior management plans or teaching organizational or study skills. Accommodations may include preferential seating in the classroom, reduced classwork load, or extended time on tests and exams. The school may provide accommodations through what is called a 504 Plan or, for children who qualify for special education services, an Individualized Education Plan (IEP).

To learn more about special education services and the Individuals with Disabilities Education Act (IDEA), visit **https://idea.ed.gov**.

Complementary Health Approaches

Unlike specific psychotherapy and medication treatments that are scientifically proven to improve ADHD symptoms, complementary health approaches for ADHD, such as natural products, do not qualify as evidence-supported interventions. For more information, visit the National Center for Complementary and Integrative Health at **www.nccih.nih.gov/health/attention-deficit-hyperactivity-disorder-at-a-glance**.

How can I find help for my child?

The Substance Abuse and Mental Health Services Administration (SAMHSA) provides the Behavioral Health Treatment Services Locator (**https://findtreatment.samhsa.gov**), an online tool for finding mental health services and treatment programs in your state. For additional resources, visit **www.nimh.nih.gov/findhelp** or see the NIMH Children and Mental Health fact sheet (**www.nimh.nih.gov/health/publications/children-and-mental-health**).

> If you or someone you know is in immediate distress or is thinking about hurting themselves, call the **National Suicide Prevention Lifeline** toll-free at 1-800-273-TALK (8255). You also can text the **Crisis Text Line** (HELLO to 741741) or use the Lifeline Chat on the National Suicide Prevention Lifeline website at **https://suicidepreventionlifeline.org**.

How can I help my child at home?

Therapy and medication are the most effective treatments for ADHD. In addition to these treatments, other strategies may help manage symptoms. Encourage your child to:

- Get regular exercise, especially when they seem hyperactive or restless.
- Eat regular, healthy meals.
- Get plenty of sleep.
- Stick to a routine.
- Use homework and notebook organizers to write down assignments and reminders.
- Take medications as directed.

In addition, you can help your child or teen by being clear and consistent, providing rules they can understand and follow. Also, keep in mind that children with ADHD often receive and expect criticism. You can look for good behavior and praise it and provide rewards when rules are followed.

What should I know about my child participating in clinical research?

Clinical trials are research studies that look at new ways to prevent, detect, or treat diseases and conditions. Although individuals may benefit from being part of a clinical trial, participants should be aware that the primary purpose of a clinical trial is to gain new scientific knowledge so others may receive better help in the future.

Researchers at NIMH and around the country conduct many studies with patients and healthy volunteers. Clinical trials for children are designed with the understanding that children and adults respond differently, both physically and mentally, to medications and treatments. Talk to your health care provider about clinical trials, their benefits and risks, and whether one is right for your child. For more information, visit **www.nimh.nih.gov/clinicaltrials**.

Where can I find more information on ADHD?

The Centers for Disease Control and Prevention (CDC) is the nation's leading health promotion, prevention, and preparedness agency. You can find information about ADHD symptoms, diagnosis, and treatment options, as well as additional resources for families and providers, at **www.cdc.gov/adhd**.

Bipolar Disorder

National Institute of Mental Health

Studies & Statistics / Bipolar Disorder

> Do you have periods of time when you feel unusually "up" (happy and outgoing, or irritable), but other periods when you feel "down" (unusually sad or anxious)? During the "up" periods, do you have increased energy or activity and feel a decreased need for sleep, while during the "down" times you have low energy, hopelessness, and sometimes suicidal thoughts? Do these symptoms of fluctuating mood and energy levels cause you distress or affect your daily functioning? Some people with these symptoms have a lifelong but treatable mental illness called bipolar disorder.

What is bipolar disorder?

Bipolar disorder is a mental illness that can be chronic (persistent or constantly reoccurring) or episodic (occurring occasionally and at irregular intervals). People sometimes refer to bipolar disorder with the older terms "manic-depressive disorder" or "manic depression."

Everyone experiences normal ups and downs, but with bipolar disorder, the range of mood changes can be extreme. People with the disorder have manic episodes, or unusually elevated moods in which the individual might feel very happy, irritable, or "up," with a marked increase in activity level. They might also have depressive episodes, in which they feel sad, indifferent, or hopeless, combined with a very low activity level. Some people have hypomanic episodes, which are like manic episodes, but not severe enough to cause marked impairment in social or occupational functioning or require hospitalization.

Most of the time, bipolar disorder symptoms start during late adolescence or early adulthood. Occasionally, children may experience bipolar disorder symptoms. Although symptoms may come and go, bipolar disorder usually requires lifelong treatment and does not go away on its own. Bipolar disorder can be an important factor in suicide, job loss, ability to function, and family discord. However, proper treatment can lead to better functioning and improved quality of life.

What are the symptoms of bipolar disorder?

Symptoms of bipolar disorder can vary. An individual with the disorder may have manic episodes, depressive episodes, or "mixed" episodes. A mixed episode has both manic and depressive symptoms. These mood episodes cause symptoms that last a week or two, or sometimes longer. During an episode, the symptoms last every day for most of the day. Feelings are intense and happen with changes in behavior, energy levels, or activity levels that are noticeable to others. In between episodes, mood usually returns to a healthy baseline. But in many cases, without adequate treatment, episodes occur more frequently as time goes on.

Studies & Statistics / Bipolar Disorder

Symptoms of a Manic Episode	Symptoms of a Depressive Episode
Feeling very up, high, elated, extremely irritable, or touchy	Feeling very down or sad, or anxious
Feeling jumpy or wired, or being more active than usual	Feeling slowed down or restless
Racing thoughts	Trouble concentrating or making decisions
Decreased need for sleep	Trouble falling asleep, waking up too early, or sleeping too much
Talking fast about a lot of different things ("flight of ideas")	Talking very slowly, feeling unable to find anything to say, or forgetting a lot
Excessive appetite for food, drinking, sex, or other pleasurable activities	Lack of interest in almost all activities
Feeling able to do many things at once without getting tired	Unable to do even simple things
Feeling unusually important, talented, or powerful	Feeling hopeless or worthless, or thinking about death or suicide

Some people with bipolar disorder may have milder symptoms than others. For example, hypomanic episodes may make an individual feel very good and productive; they may not feel like anything is wrong. However, family and friends may notice the mood swings and changes in activity levels as unusual behavior, and depressive episodes may follow hypomanic episodes.

Types of Bipolar Disorder

People are diagnosed with three basic types of bipolar disorder that involve clear changes in mood, energy, and activity levels. These moods range from manic episodes to depressive episodes.

- **Bipolar I disorder** is defined by manic episodes that last at least 7 days (most of the day, nearly every day) or when manic symptoms are so severe that hospital care is needed. Usually, separate depressive episodes occur as well, typically lasting at least 2 weeks. Episodes of mood disturbance with mixed features are also possible. The experience of four or more episodes of mania or depression within a year is termed "rapid cycling."
- **Bipolar II disorder** is defined by a pattern of depressive and hypomanic episodes, but the episodes are less severe than the manic episodes in bipolar I disorder.
- **Cyclothymic disorder** (also called cyclothymia) is defined by recurrent hypomanic and depressive symptoms that are not intense enough or do not last long enough to qualify as hypomanic or depressive episodes.

"Other specified and unspecified bipolar and related disorders" is a diagnosis that refers to bipolar disorder symptoms that do not match the three major types of bipolar disorder.

What causes bipolar disorder?

The exact cause of bipolar disorder is unknown. However, research suggests that a combination of factors may contribute to the illness.

Genes

Bipolar disorder often runs in families, and research suggests this is mostly explained by heredity—people with certain genes are more likely to develop bipolar disorder than others. Many genes are involved, and no one gene can cause the disorder.

But genes are not the only factor. Studies of identical twins have shown that one twin can develop bipolar disorder while the other does not. Though people with a parent or sibling with bipolar disorder are more likely to develop it, most people with a family history of bipolar disorder will not develop it.

Brain Structure and Function

Research shows that the brain structure and function of people with bipolar disorder may differ from those of people who do not have bipolar disorder or other mental disorders. Learning about the nature of these brain changes helps researchers better understand bipolar disorder and, in the future, may help predict which types of treatment will work best for a person with bipolar disorder.

How is bipolar disorder diagnosed?

To diagnose bipolar disorder, a health care provider may complete a physical exam, order medical testing to rule out other illnesses, and refer the person for an evaluation by a mental health professional.

Bipolar disorder is diagnosed based on the severity, length, and frequency of an individual's symptoms and experiences over their lifetime.

Some people have bipolar disorder for years before it's diagnosed for several reasons. People with bipolar II disorder may seek help only for depressive episodes and hypomanic episodes may go unnoticed.

Misdiagnosis may happen because some bipolar disorder symptoms are like those of other illnesses. For example, people with bipolar disorder who also have psychotic symptoms can be misdiagnosed with schizophrenia. Some health conditions, such as thyroid disease, can cause symptoms like those of bipolar disorder. The effects of recreational and illicit drugs can sometimes mimic or worsen mood symptoms.

Conditions That Can Co-Occur With Bipolar Disorder

Many people with bipolar disorder also have other mental disorders or conditions such as anxiety disorders, attention-deficit/hyperactivity disorder (ADHD), misuse of drugs or alcohol, or eating disorders. Sometimes people who have severe manic or depressive episodes also have symptoms of psychosis, such as hallucinations or delusions. The psychotic symptoms tend to match the person's extreme mood. For example, someone having psychotic symptoms during a depressive episode may falsely believe they are financially ruined, while someone having psychotic symptoms during a manic episode may falsely believe they are famous or have special powers.

Looking at symptoms over the course of the illness and the person's family history can help determine whether a person has bipolar disorder along with another disorder.

How is bipolar disorder treated?

Treatment helps many people, even those with the most severe forms of bipolar disorder. Mental health professionals treat bipolar disorder with medications, psychotherapy, or a combination of treatments.

Medications

Certain medications can help control the symptoms of bipolar disorder. Some people may need to try several different medications before finding the ones that work best. The most common types of medications that doctors prescribe include mood stabilizers and atypical antipsychotics. Mood stabilizers such as lithium or valproate can help prevent mood episodes or reduce their severity. Lithium also can decrease the risk of suicide. While bipolar depression is often treated with antidepressant medication, a mood stabilizer must be taken as well, as an antidepressant alone can trigger a manic episode or rapid cycling in a person with bipolar disorder. Medications that target sleep or anxiety are sometimes added to mood stabilizers as part of a treatment plan.

Talk with your health care provider to understand the risks and benefits of each medication. Report any concerns about side effects to your health care provider right away. Avoid stopping medication without talking to your health care provider first. Read the latest medication warnings, patient medication guides, and information on newly approved medications on the Food and Drug Administration (FDA) website at **www.fda.gov/drugsatfda**.

Psychotherapy

Psychotherapy (sometimes called "talk therapy") is a term for various treatment techniques that aim to help a person identify and change troubling emotions, thoughts, and behaviors. Psychotherapy can offer support, education, skills, and strategies to people with bipolar disorder and their families.

Some types of psychotherapy can be effective treatments for bipolar disorder when used with medications, including interpersonal and social rhythm therapy, which aims to understand and work with an individual's biological and social rhythms. Cognitive behavioral therapy (CBT) is an important treatment for depression, and CBT adapted for the treatment of insomnia can be especially helpful as a component of the treatment of bipolar depression. Learn more about psychotherapy at www.nimh.nih.gov/psychotherapies.

Other Treatments

Some people may find other treatments helpful in managing their bipolar disorder symptoms.

- **Electroconvulsive therapy (ECT)** is a brain stimulation procedure that can help relieve severe symptoms of bipolar disorder. ECT is usually only considered if an individual's illness has not improved after other treatments such as medication or psychotherapy, or in cases that require rapid response, such as with suicide risk or catatonia (a state of unresponsiveness).
- **Transcranial Magnetic Stimulation (TMS)** is a type of brain stimulation that uses magnetic waves, rather than the electrical stimulus of ECT, to relieve depression over a series of treatment sessions. Although not as powerful as ECT, TMS does not require general anesthesia and presents little risk of memory or adverse cognitive effects.
- **Light Therapy** is the best evidence-based treatment for seasonal affective disorder (SAD), and many people with bipolar disorder experience seasonal worsening of depression in the winter, in some cases to the point of SAD. Light therapy could also be considered for lesser forms of seasonal worsening of bipolar depression.

Complementary Health Approaches

Unlike specific psychotherapy and medication treatments that are scientifically proven to improve bipolar disorder symptoms, complementary health approaches for bipolar disorder, such as natural products, are not based on current knowledge or evidence. For more information, visit the National Center for Complementary and Integrative Health website at www.nccih.nih.gov.

Coping With Bipolar Disorder

Living with bipolar disorder can be challenging, but there are ways to help yourself, as well as your friends and loved ones.

- Get treatment and stick with it. Treatment is the best way to start feeling better.
- Keep medical and therapy appointments and talk with your health care provider about treatment options.
- Take medication as directed.
- Structure activities. Keep a routine for eating, sleeping, and exercising.

- Try regular, vigorous exercise like jogging, swimming, or bicycling, which can help with depression and anxiety, promote better sleep, and is healthy for your heart and brain.
- Keep a life chart to help recognize your mood swings.
- Ask for help when trying to stick with your treatment.
- Be patient. Improvement takes time. Social support helps.

Remember, bipolar disorder is a lifelong illness, but long-term, ongoing treatment can help manage symptoms and enable you to live a healthy life.

Are there clinical trials studying bipolar disorder?

NIMH supports a wide range of research, including clinical trials that look at new ways to prevent, detect, or treat diseases and conditions—including bipolar disorder. Although individuals may benefit from being part of a clinical trial, participants should be aware that the primary purpose of a clinical trial is to gain new scientific knowledge to help others in the future. Researchers at NIMH and around the country conduct clinical trials with patients and healthy volunteers. Talk to a health care provider about clinical trials, their benefits and risks, and whether one is right for you. For more information, visit **www.nimh.nih.gov/clinicaltrials**.

Finding Help

Behavioral Health Treatment Services Locator

This online resource, provided by the Substance Abuse and Mental Health Services Administration, can help you locate mental health treatment facilities and programs. Find a facility in your state at **https://findtreatment.samhsa.gov**. For additional resources, visit **www.nimh.nih.gov/findhelp**.

Talking to a Health Care Provider About Your Mental Health

Communicating well with a health care provider can improve your care and help you both make good choices about your health. Find tips to help prepare for and get the most out of your visit at **www.nimh.nih.gov/talkingtips**. For additional resources, including questions to ask a provider, visit the Agency for Healthcare Research and Quality website at **www.ahrq.gov/questions**.

> If you or someone you know is in immediate distress or is thinking about hurting themselves, call the National Suicide Prevention Lifeline toll-free at 1-800-273-TALK (8255). You also can text the Crisis Text Line (HELLO to 741741) or use the Lifeline Chat on the National Suicide Prevention Lifeline website at **https://suicidepreventionlifeline.org**. If you suspect a medical emergency, seek medical attention or call 911 immediately.

MANAGING DIABETES

How to Help a Loved One
With Diabetes When You Live Far Apart

Offer your support.

Managing diabetes is not easy, whether a person has just been diagnosed or has been living with diabetes for many years. Family support can help a person with diabetes manage everyday tasks and deal with changes in care over time.

But if you live far away from your loved one with diabetes, you may worry about how you can help. Being prepared with the right information can help you provide support, even from a distance. This short guide offers tips that can help.

Learn about diabetes.

Learning about diabetes can help you understand what your family member is going through and find ways to help them prevent emergencies and manage their health care. It can also make talking with your family member's doctor easier. Here are some tips:

- Learn as much as you can about your loved one's diabetes medicines, supplies, and equipment, including their blood sugar monitor and test strips.
- Go to CDC's Living with Diabetes website to learn more about managing diabetes. See the **Resources for Everyone** section on page 4 of this guide for other ideas.
- Ask your loved one to teach you about how they are managing their diabetes and what kinds of support they may need. For example:
  - ▶ Do they just need someone to check on them now and then?
  - ▶ Do they need someone to take them to appointments or help make medical and financial decisions?
  - ▶ Remember—it's their health, so it's up to them how much they want to share with you. Let them know that you're there to support them if they need you.

Centers for Disease Control and Prevention
National Center for Chronic Disease Prevention and Health Promotion

189

Studies & Statistics / How to Help a Loved One With Diabetes When You Live Far Apart

Gather information and keep in one place.

Gather important information about your loved one's health care, and keep it up to date. Put it in a place that is easy for your loved one or a caregiver to find. Keep copies for yourself. Here are the kinds of information you should collect:

- With your loved one's consent, make sure that at least one family member or close friend gets written permission to receive medical and financial information from the doctor or hospital. Choose one person to talk with all health care providers, if possible.

- Write down the following medical information:
  - Names and phone numbers of your loved one's care team.
  - Names and doses of your loved one's medicines.
  - Names and phone numbers of emergency contacts.

> You can use the **Important Contacts and Medical Information** form on pages 5–6 of this guide to collect this information.

- Make sure your loved one or a caregiver knows how to contact you (or an emergency contact) in an emergency—but tell them to call 911 first.

- Create a list of resources in your loved one's community (see the **Resources for Everyone** section on page 4 for ideas). This list can include information about:
  - **Social support:** Check with your loved one's health care provider for support groups, social services, and other resources in the community.
  - **Financial support:** Look for community discount programs for medicines, blood sugar monitors, diabetes education, nutrition assessment, and counseling.
  - **Practical support:** Ask your loved one's health care providers or diabetes care and education specialist if there is someone who can help them get supplies and learn to use equipment, if needed. Caregivers can also learn to use equipment.

Find resources.

Different kinds of organizations can help with different kinds of resources—like meal planning, diabetes care, diabetes camps for children, housekeeping, or emotional support. Here are some places to go for help:

- **Local diabetes groups, senior centers, faith communities, and other community groups that provide support services.** Your loved one's health care provider may have a list of local services. You can also check the **Resources for Everyone** section on page 4 for ideas.

- **Local pharmacies.** Many pharmacies offer individual and group counseling.

- **Your loved one's health insurance company or Medicare.** Ask what diabetes education and support services are covered. For example, Medicare Part B covers a wide range of diabetes education and training.

- **State health and social services.** Look for information on the state government website where your loved one lives. Ask about community programs for children, seniors, and people with disabilities.

- **Your loved one may need a referral from a health care provider to get services from some organizations.** You can help them work with their doctors to get what they need. Remind your loved one that asking for a referral to a diabetes self-management education and support (DSMES) program might be helpful.

- **To find a DSMES program** recognized by the American Diabetes Association or accredited by the Association of Diabetes Care & Education Specialists, go to the Find a Diabetes Education Program in Your Area website.

Studies & Statistics / How to Help a Loved One With Diabetes When You Live Far Apart

Plan your visits.

- When you visit your loved one, you may worry that you don't have enough time to do everything you want to. Talk with your loved one ahead of time about the kind of help they may need. You may feel less stressed if you can focus on a few important errands or chores during your visit.

- Research your company's leave policies. Some companies allow sick leave to be used to care for a relative.

- Remember that your loved one may need help with things like home cleaning and repairs, shopping, or other tasks that are not directly related to their health.

- Check with your loved one or a caregiver to learn what medical care they may need. This information will help you set clear, realistic goals for your visit. For example:

  - Do they need to see specialists, such as a foot doctor (podiatrist) or eye doctor (optometrist or ophthalmologist)?

  - Do they need more testing supplies?

- Try to make time to do things that are fun and relaxing with your loved one. Suggest taking a walk together. Offer to play a game of cards or a board game.

Stay in touch.

From time to time, ask your loved one how they are coping with their diabetes and how you can help. With your loved one's permission, try to find people in the community—like other family members, friends, or neighbors—who can visit and provide support if needed.

Check in regularly with the people who are providing care to your loved one. Find out how they are coping and how you can help them.

Information in this guide is adapted from Long-Distance Caregiving: Twenty Questions and Answers, published by the National Institute on Aging in 2016.

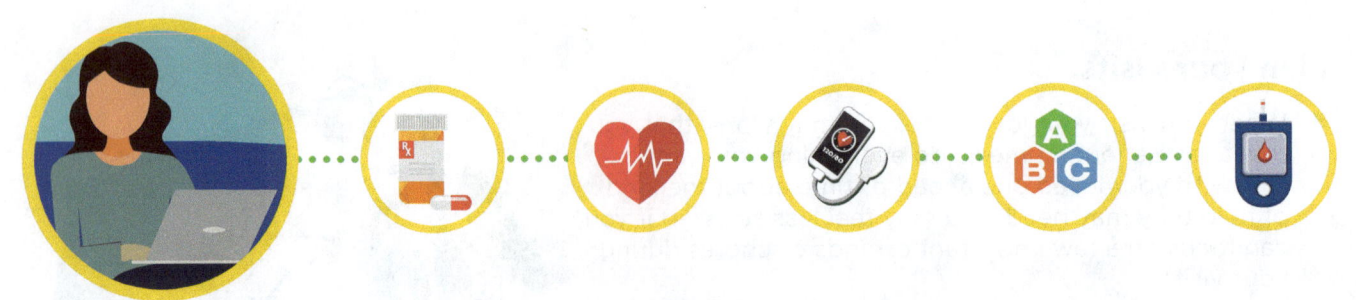

Studies & Statistics / How to Help a Loved One With Diabetes When You Live Far Apart

Resources for Everyone

Association of Diabetes Care & Education Specialists
www.diabeteseducator.org
Links to diabetes care and education specialists and educational resources.

American Diabetes Association
www.diabetes.org
Information about diabetes prevention and treatment, nutrition, and weight loss.

CDC Diabetes Management
www.cdc.gov/diabetes/managing/index.html
General information about healthy living and diabetes care.

CDC Emergency Resources
www.cdc.gov/diabetes/managing/preparedness.html
Resources for people with diabetes who are affected by natural disasters, emergencies, and hazards.

Diabetes Action Network, National Federation of the Blind
https://nfb.org/diabetics
Information about companies and organizations that offer products and information for people with diabetes and vision problems.

Joslin Diabetes Center
www.joslin.org/diabetes-information.html
An online library with information about diabetes care, nutrition, medicines, and exercise.

Learn, Connect, Engage With the Diabetes Online Community
https://beyondtype1.org/the-diabetes-online-community-doc
Information on diabetes online communities.

National Family Caregivers Association
https://www.caringcommunity.org
Tips and guides for caregivers, a bulletin board for peer support, and lists of resources.

FOR MORE INFORMATION ABOUT LIVING WITH DIABETES,
VISIT CDC'S DIABETES WEBSITE.

Note: Website addresses of nonfederal organizations are provided solely as a service to our readers. Provision of an address does not constitute an endorsement by the Centers for Disease Control and Prevention (CDC) or the federal government, and none should be inferred. CDC is not responsible for the content of other organizations' web pages.

Studies & Statistics / How to Help a Loved One With Diabetes When You Live Far Apart

Important Contacts and Medical Information

Use this form to keep important information in one place. Make sure you, your loved one, and your loved one's caregivers all have copies.

Patient Name: _____

Caregiver Name: _____

Emergency Contact: _____

DIABETES CARE TEAM CONTACT INFORMATION

PRIMARY CARE PROVIDER
Name
Phone   E-mail
Notes

DRUGSTORE AND PHARMACIST
Name
Phone   E-mail
Notes

DIABETES SPECIALIST (endocrinologist)
Name
Phone   E-mail
Notes

DENTIST
Name
Phone   E-mail
Notes

NURSE PRACTITIONER
Name
Phone   E-mail
Notes

EYE DOCTOR (optometrist or ophthalmologist)
Name
Phone   E-mail
Notes

PHYSICIAN ASSISTANT
Name
Phone   E-mail
Notes

FOOT DOCTOR (podiatrist)
Name
Phone   E-mail
Notes

COMMUNITY HEALTH WORKER
Name
Phone   E-mail
Notes

MENTAL HEALTH PROVIDER
Name
Phone   E-mail
Notes

DIABETES CARE & EDUCATION SPECIALIST OR DIABETES SELF-MANAGEMENT EDUCATION AND SUPPORT PROGRAM INSTRUCTOR
Name
Phone   E-mail
Notes

OTHER HEALTH CARE PROVIDERS
(such as a dietician or nephrologist)

Studies & Statistics / How to Help a Loved One With Diabetes When You Live Far Apart

MEDICINES

Be sure to list all of the medicines your loved one takes—not just the ones for diabetes. Write down vitamins and other nonprescription (over-the-counter) medicines too.

Pharmacy: _____

Phone Number: _____

PRESCRIPTION DRUGS: DOSE, HOW OFTEN TAKEN	NONPRESCRIPTION DRUGS: DOSE, HOW OFTEN TAKEN

IMPORTANT CONTACTS
(such as neighbors, relatives, or clergy members)

NAME	ROLE	PHONE NUMBER	E-MAIL
In case of emergency, contact:			

NOTE: CALL 911 IN AN EMERGENCY.

Studies & Statistics / How to Help a Loved One With Diabetes When You Live Far Apart

A Research Brief
Screening for Depression and Diabetes Distress in Adults with Type 2 Diabetes

Depression and diabetes distress* often go unrecognized and unaddressed in patients with type 2 diabetes, resulting in poor health outcomes. Early identification and intervention for these mental health conditions can improve diabetes self-care. Health care providers can help close the gap by conducting regular mental health screenings and referring patients for additional care, if needed.

1 in 5 adults with type 2 diabetes has depression.

1 in 3 adults with type 2 diabetes experiences diabetes distress.

Both depression and diabetes distress can increase risk for serious health complications and early death.

ROUTINE MENTAL HEALTH SCREENING AND TREATMENT CAN IMPROVE DIABETES MANAGEMENT, DIABETES OUTCOMES, AND QUALITY OF LIFE

Depression and diabetes distress are common, but screening rates remain low. The American Diabetes Association and the U.S. Preventive Services Task Force strongly recommend routine screenings for depression and diabetes distress in adults with type 2 diabetes. **The strategies below can help address and remove barriers to screening and treatment, and improve patient outcomes.**

BARRIERS TO SCREENING AND TREATMENT		STRATEGIES TO OVERCOME BARRIERS
• Patients lack knowledge about depression symptoms and diabetes distress. • Health care providers lack mental health training.	**INFORM** →	Patients: • Educate them about depression and diabetes distress. • Provide information resources and let them know about available mental health services. Health care providers: • Identify and participate in mental health trainings.
• Health care practices lack access to mental health assessment tools. • Health care practices don't have reminder systems in place for screening. • Health care providers may believe that mental health issues are outside of their scope.	**SCREEN** →	• Use publicly available screening tools such as Patient Health Questionnaire-9, Problem Areas in Diabetes Scale, and Diabetes Distress Scale. • Include alerts in electronic health records to trigger screening. • Identify ways to address mental health issues during routine visits.
• Health care practices have little or no access to mental health specialists.	**REFER** →	• Coordinate care with a health care team that includes mental health professionals to create a treatment plan and problem solve. • Refer patients to diabetes self-management education and support services.

*Diabetes distress: Feelings of worry, stress, frustration, and burnout that come from coping with diabetes.

To Learn More About Diabetes Distress and Depression
Read the peer-reviewed article: Owens-Gary MD, Zhang X, Jawanda S, et al. The importance of addressing depression and diabetes distress in adults with type 2 diabetes. *J Gen Intern Med.* 2019;34(2):320-324. https://doi.org/10.1007/s11606-018-4705-2

Listen to this CDC podcast: Diabetes, Distress, and Depression. Updated January 2017.
https://tools.cdc.gov/medialibrary/index.aspx#/media/id/302814

Centers for Disease Control and Prevention
National Center for Chronic Disease Prevention and Health Promotion
Division of Diabetes Translation

Treating Disruptive Behavior Disorders in Children and Teens

A Review of the Research for Parents and Caregivers

Studies & Statistics / Treating Disruptive Behavior Disorders in Children and Teens

Understanding Your Child's or Teen's Condition

What are disruptive behavior disorders (DBDs)?

DBDs are disorders in which children or teens have trouble controlling their emotions and behavior. Their behavior may be very defiant, and they may strongly conflict with authority figures. Their actions may be aggressive and destructive. All children have mild behavior problems now and then, but DBDs are more severe and continue over time.

DBDs can start when a child is young. Children or teens with a DBD who do not receive treatment often have serious behavior problems at home, at school, or both. They are also more likely to have problems with alcohol or drug use and violent or criminal behavior as they get older.

Examples of DBDs include oppositional defiant disorder, conduct disorder, and intermittent explosive disorder.

Oppositional Defiant Disorder

Children or teens with this disorder may have an angry or irritable mood much of the time. They may argue often and refuse to obey parents, caregivers, teachers, or others. They may also want to hurt someone they think has harmed them.

Conduct Disorder

Children or teens with this disorder may act aggressively toward people, animals, or both. They may bully or threaten someone, start physical fights, use weapons, hurt animals, or force sexual activity on others. They may also destroy property by fire or other means, lie often, or steal. They may stay out late at night, skip school, or run away from home. They may also lack compassion and not feel guilty about harming others.

Intermittent Explosive Disorder

Children or teens with this disorder may have outbursts of aggressive, violent behavior or shouting. They may have extreme temper tantrums and may start physical fights. They often overreact to situations in extreme ways and do not think about consequences. Outbursts happen with little or no warning. They usually last for 30 minutes or less. After the outburst, the child or teen may feel sorry or embarrassed.

How common are DBDs? What causes them?

DBDs are one of the most common types of behavioral disorders in children and teens.

- Out of every 100 children in the United States, about 3 of them have a DBD.
- More boys than girls have a DBD.
- DBDs are more common among children aged 12 years and older.

The cause of DBDs is not known. Things that increase the risk for a DBD include:

- Child abuse or neglect
- A traumatic life experience, such as sexual abuse or violence
- A family history of DBDs

Having a child or teen with a DBD can be very stressful for parents, caregivers, and the whole family. But, there are treatments that may help.

Studies & Statistics / **Treating Disruptive Behavior Disorders in Children and Teens**

Understanding Your Options

How are DBDs treated?

To treat your child's or teen's DBD, your health care professional may recommend psychosocial treatment (treatment with a trained therapist). If needed, your child's or teen's health care professional may also suggest taking a medicine with the psychosocial treatment.

Each child or teen responds differently to different treatments. You may need to try several treatments before finding one that is right for your child or teen.

Studies & Statistics / Treating Disruptive Behavior Disorders in Children and Teens

Psychosocial Treatment

Psychosocial treatment can help improve interactions between you and your child or teen. This is done through programs in which parents and their child or teen meet with a trained therapist. It is important for parents and caregivers to be involved in the treatment.

Some programs focus only on parent training. Other programs also work with the child or teen, the whole family together, or with the child's or teen's teachers.

Parent and child training programs are sometimes done in groups. Sessions usually last 1 to 2 hours and are held each week for 8 to 18 weeks. The programs usually charge a fee. Your insurance may cover some of the costs.

Parent Programs

These programs can help you:

- Respond in a positive way when your child asks for help or wants attention
- Choose realistic goals for your child
- Better monitor your child's behavior
- Learn more effective parenting skills
- Have more confidence in being able to handle situations
- Reduce your stress

The programs help support you and can teach you specific ways to help change your child's behavior without shouting, threatening, or using physical punishment. You can learn to:

- Set clear rules
- Stay calm when asking your child to do something
- Make sure your instructions are clear and right for your child's age
- Explain the consequences of disruptive behavior to your child
- Respond to disruptive behavior with things such as quiet time or a time-out

Studies & Statistics / Treating Disruptive Behavior Disorders in Children and Teens

You can also learn ways to help support your child and:
- Improve your child's social skills
- Help your child build friendships
- Help your child learn how to control his or her emotions
- Teach your child problem-solving skills
- Help your child learn to be independent

Child Programs

These programs can help children:
- Feel more positive about themselves and their family
- Strengthen their social, communication, and problem-solving skills
- Better communicate feelings and manage anger
- Practice good behaviors

Teen Programs

For teens, a trained therapist may meet with parents and also with the whole family together. The therapist may look for patterns in the way family members interact that could cause tension and problems. The therapist can then help your family learn new ways to communicate to avoid conflict.

The therapist can help you learn how to:
- Be more involved with your teen
- Set clear rules and consequences for breaking the rules
- Improve your leadership, communication, and problem-solving skills
- Support your teen

Teacher Programs

These programs can help teachers learn how to:
- Manage behavior in the classroom
- Improve students' social and emotional skills
- Work with parents and keep them involved

Studies & Statistics / Treating Disruptive Behavior Disorders in Children and Teens

What have researchers found about psychosocial treatment for DBDs?

Programs that work with:	Do the programs improve disruptive behavior in:		
	Preschool-age children?	School-age children?	Teens?
Parents only	Yes	Yes	Not reported
Parents and their child or teen	Yes	Yes, it may*	Yes
Parents and the whole family	Yes	Yes, it may*	Yes
Parents and their child's or teen's teachers	Not reported	Yes, it may*	Yes

*More research is needed to know this for sure.

Studies & Statistics / Treating Disruptive Behavior Disorders in Children and Teens

Medicines

Medicines are usually given to children or teens with a DBD only if psychosocial treatment alone does not help enough. Medicines are usually taken together with psychosocial treatment.

Several types of medicines have been used to treat DBDs (see the chart on the next page). These medicines cannot cure DBDs. They are used to reduce symptoms and improve quality of life. The medicines work by changing the way certain chemicals act in the brain.

Medicines work differently in different children or teens. You may have to try several medicines to find one that works for your child or teen.

Note: The U.S. Food and Drug Administration (FDA) approves medicines for certain uses. Health care professionals often prescribe medicines for conditions other than their FDA-approved uses.

Studies & Statistics / Treating Disruptive Behavior Disorders in Children and Teens

What have researchers found about medicines to treat DBDs?

Medicine	About the Medicine	FDA Approval in Children	Researchers found that in children and teens:
Stimulants Examples include: <ul><li>Mixed amphetamine salts (Adderall®, Adderall XR®)</li><li>Methylphenidate (Concerta®, Focalin®, Focalin XR®, Metadate CD®, Metadate ER®, Methylin®, Methylin ER®, Ritalin®, Ritalin LA®, Ritalin SR®)</li></ul>	<ul><li>Stimulants are approved by the FDA to treat ADHD.</li><li>Some health care professionals also use them to treat DBDs.</li><li>Stimulants can be short acting (work for 4 to 6 hours) or long acting (work for 8 to 12 hours).</li></ul>	Approved for children aged 6 and older	Stimulants may improve disruptive behavior.*
Nonstimulant ADHD medicines <ul><li>Atomoxetine (Strattera®)</li><li>Guanfacine ER (Intuniv®)</li></ul>	<ul><li>Atomoxetine (Strattera®) and guanfacine ER (Intuniv®) are approved by the FDA to treat ADHD.</li><li>Some health care professionals also use them to treat DBDs.</li></ul>	Approved for children aged 6 and older	Atomoxetine and guanfacine ER improve disruptive behavior.
Anticonvulsant medicine <ul><li>Divalproex (Depakene®, Depakote®, Depakote ER®)</li></ul>	<ul><li>The anticonvulsant medicine divalproex (Depakene®, Depakote®, Depakote ER®) is approved by the FDA to treat seizures.</li><li>Some health care professionals also use it to treat DBDs.</li></ul>	Approved for use in children, but should be used with extreme caution in children under the age of 2	Divalproex may improve aggression.*
Antipsychotics Examples include: <ul><li>Aripiprazole (Abilify®)</li><li>Risperidone (Risperdal®)</li><li>Ziprasidone (Geodon®)</li></ul>	<ul><li>Antipsychotics are approved by the FDA to treat people with psychosis (a type of mental illness).</li><li>Some health care professionals also use antipsychotics to treat DBDs. Taking these medicines does not mean your child or teen has a psychosis.</li></ul>	Approved for children aged 6 and older	Antipsychotics improve disruptive behavior in the short term.†

ADHD = attention deficit hyperactivity disorder; FDA = U.S. Food and Drug Administration

* More research is needed to know this for sure.

† More research is needed to know how well antipsychotics work in the long term (for longer than 6 months).

Studies & Statistics / Treating Disruptive Behavior Disorders in Children and Teens

What are possible side effects of medicines to treat DBDs?

The FDA lists these possible side effects for medicines to treat DBDs. Just because side effects are possible does not mean your child or teen will have them.

Medicine	Possible Side Effects	Warnings
STIMULANTS		
Mixed amphetamine salts (Adderall®, Adderall XR®) **Methylphenidate** (Concerta®, Focalin®, Focalin XR®, Metadate CD®, Metadate ER®, Methylin®, Methylin ER®, Ritalin®, Ritalin LA®, Ritalin SR®)	■ Stomach ache ■ Decreased appetite ■ Weight loss ■ Trouble falling asleep ■ Headache ■ Nausea and vomiting ■ Increased heart rate ■ Nervousness ■ Worsened tic (uncontrollable movement) ■ Blurred vision and other vision problems	■ Stimulants may cause serious side effects that affect the heart. These medicines may not be safe in children or teens with a history of severe heart problems. Children or teens who have heart problems and take a stimulant should be monitored closely by their doctor. ■ Stimulants can be habit forming. Your child or teen should never take more of the medicine than your doctor has prescribed. ■ Stimulants may cause growth problems in children. The height and weight of children taking a stimulant should be monitored by their doctor.
NONSTIMULANT ADHD MEDICINES		
Atomoxetine (Strattera®)	■ Nausea and vomiting ■ Decreased appetite ■ Feeling tired or sleepy ■ Stomach ache	■ Atomoxetine may increase the risk of suicidal thoughts and behaviors in children and teens. ■ Atomoxetine may cause growth problems in children. The height and weight of children taking this medicine should be monitored by their doctor.
Guanfacine ER (Intuniv®)	■ Low blood pressure ■ Slow heart rate ■ Feeling tired or sleepy ■ Nausea and vomiting ■ Stomach ache ■ Trouble falling asleep ■ Irritability ■ Dizziness ■ Dry mouth	■ Guanfacine ER should not be stopped suddenly, because this can increase blood pressure. ■ Atomoxetine and guanfacine ER may cause serious side effects that affect the heart. These medicines may not be safe in children or teens with a history of severe heart problems. Children or teens who have heart problems and take atomoxetine or guanfacine ER should be monitored closely by their doctor.

Studies & Statistics / Treating Disruptive Behavior Disorders in Children and Teens

Medicine	Possible Side Effects	Warnings
ANTICONVULSANT MEDICINE		
Divalproex (Depakene®, Depakote®, Depakote ER®)	■ Nausea ■ Feeling sleepy ■ Dizziness ■ Vomiting ■ Feeling weak ■ Stomach ache ■ Upset stomach ■ Rash	■ Divalproex may increase the risk of suicidal thoughts or behaviors. ■ Divalproex can cause life-threatening liver and pancreas problems. Children under the age of 2 years are at higher risk for these problems.
ANTIPSYCHOTICS		
Aripiprazole (Abilify®) **Risperidone** (Risperdal®) **Ziprasidone** (Geodon®)	■ Uncontrollable movements, such as tics and tremors ■ Feeling tired or sleepy ■ Nausea and vomiting ■ Blurred vision or other vision problems ■ Changes in appetite (increase or decrease) ■ Weight gain ■ Extra saliva or drooling ■ Cold symptoms (stuffy nose and sore throat)	■ Aripiprazole may increase the risk of suicidal thoughts in children and teens taking antidepressant medicines. ■ Antipsychotics can cause a possibly life-threatening reaction called "neuroleptic malignant syndrome," although this is rare. Symptoms include a high fever, sweating, changes in blood pressure, and muscle stiffness.

Studies & Statistics / Treating Disruptive Behavior Disorders in Children and Teens

Making a Decision

What should I think about when deciding about treatment?

There are several things to think about when deciding which treatment may help your child or teen. As your child or teen grows and develops, his or her treatment may need to be changed. You will need to continue to work with your child's or teen's health care professional over time.

You may want to talk with your child's or teen's health care professional about:

- Psychosocial treatment programs
- Whether a medicine may help your child or teen
- The possible risks of the medicine

Ask your child's or teen's health care professional

- How might psychosocial treatment help my child or teen?
- How do I sign up for a psychosocial treatment program? Which program do you recommend? Why?
- How often would I meet with a therapist and for how long? Would my child or teen meet with the therapist as well? Would the therapist interact with our whole family or with my child's or teen's teachers?
- How will we know if my child or teen may need medicine?
- If my child or teen needs medicine, which medicine might be best?
- How long would my child or teen need to take the medicine?
- What are the risks of taking the medicine?
- How will I know if my child or teen is having a serious side effect? What should I watch for, and when should I call you?
- How long might it take for my child's or teen's treatment to start helping?
- Are there local support groups that could help me?

Perspectives

OPEN

Separating Fact from Fiction: An Empirical Examination of Six Myths About Dissociative Identity Disorder

Bethany L. Brand, PhD, Vedat Sar, MD, Pam Stavropoulos, PhD,
Christa Krüger, MB BCh, MMed (Psych), MD, Marilyn Korzekwa, MD,
Alfonso Martínez-Taboas, PhD, and Warwick Middleton, MB BS, FRANZCP, MD

> **Abstract:** Dissociative identity disorder (DID) is a complex, posttraumatic, developmental disorder for which we now, after four decades of research, have an authoritative research base, but a number of misconceptualizations and myths about the disorder remain, compromising both patient care and research. This article examines the empirical literature pertaining to recurrently expressed beliefs regarding DID: (1) belief that DID is a fad, (2) belief that DID is primarily diagnosed in North America by DID experts who overdiagnose the disorder, (3) belief that DID is rare, (4) belief that DID is an iatrogenic, rather than trauma-based, disorder, (5) belief that DID is the same entity as borderline personality disorder, and (6) belief that DID treatment is harmful to patients. The absence of research to substantiate these beliefs, as well as the existence of a body of research that refutes them, confirms their mythical status. Clinicians who accept these myths as facts are unlikely to carefully assess for dissociation. Accurate diagnoses are critical for appropriate treatment planning. If DID is not targeted in treatment, it does not appear to resolve. The myths we have highlighted may also impede research about DID. The cost of ignorance about DID is high not only for individual patients but for the whole support system in which they reside. Empirically derived knowledge about DID has replaced outdated myths. Vigorous dissemination of the knowledge base about this complex disorder is warranted.
>
> **Keywords:** borderline personality disorder, dissociation, dissociative disorders, iatrogenic, trauma, treatment

Dissociative identity disorder (DID) is defined in the fifth edition of the *Diagnostic and Statistical Manual of Mental Disorders* (DSM-5) as an identity disruption indicated by the presence of two or more distinct personality states (experienced as possession in some cultures), with discontinuity in sense of self and agency, and with variations in affect, behavior, consciousness, memory, perception, cognition, or sensory-motor functioning.[1] Individuals with DID experience recurrent gaps in autobiographical memory. The signs and symptoms of DID may be observed by others or reported by the individual. DSM-5 stipulates that symptoms cause significant distress and are not attributable to accepted cultural or religious practices. Conditions similar to DID but with less-than-marked symptoms (e.g., subthreshold DID) are classified among "other specified dissociative disorders."

DID is a complex, posttraumatic developmental disorder.[2,3] DSM-5 specifically locates the dissociative disorders chapter after the chapter on trauma- and stressor-related disorders, thereby acknowledging the relationship of the dissociative disorders to psychological trauma. The core features of DID are usually accompanied by a mixture of psychiatric symptoms that, rather than dissociative symptoms, are typically the patient's presenting complaint.[3,4] As is common among individuals with complex, posttraumatic developmental disorders, DID patients may suffer from symptoms associated with mood, anxiety, personality, eating, functional somatic, and substance use disorders, as well as psychosis, among others.[3–8] DID can be overlooked due to both this polysymptomatic profile and patients' tendency to be ashamed and avoidant about revealing their dissociative symptoms and history of childhood trauma (the latter of which is strongly implicated in the etiology of DID).[9–14]

From Towson University (Dr. Brand); Koç University School of Medicine (Istanbul) (Dr. Sar); Blue Knot Foundation, Sydney, Australia (Dr. Stavropoulos); University of Pretoria (Dr. Krüger); McMaster University (Dr. Korzekwa); Carlos Albizu University (San Juan) (Dr. Martínez-Taboas); Latrobe University, University of New England, University of Canterbury (New Zealand), and University of Queensland (Australia) (Dr. Middleton).

Original manuscript received 29 October 2014; revised manuscript received 27 January 2015, accepted for publication subject to revision 22 May 2015; revised manuscript received 8 June 2015.

Correspondence: Bethany L. Brand, PhD, Psychology Department, Towson University, 8000 York Rd., Towson, MD 21252. Email: bbrand@towson.edu

© 2016 President and Fellows of Harvard College. This is an open-access article distributed under the terms of the Creative Commons Attribution-Non Commercial-No Derivatives License 4.0 (CCBY-NC-ND), where it is permissible to download and share the work provided it is properly cited. The work cannot be changed in any way or used commercially.

DOI: 10.1097/HRP.0000000000000100

Multiple personality states* have been described by renowned theorists, including Pierre Janet, Sigmund Freud, Alfred Binet, William James, Benjamin Rush, Morton Prince, Boris Sidis, Enrico Morselli, and Sandor Ferenczi.[15–20] The first published cases are those of Jeanne Fery,[20] reported in 1586, and a case of "exchanged personality" that dates to Eberhardt Gmelin's account of 1791.[21] Many of the individuals considered hysterics in the nineteenth century would today be diagnosed with dissociative disorders. Early debates focused upon whether hysteria should be conceptualized as a somatoform condition, a condition of altered states of consciousness, or a condition rooted entirely in suggestion.[16,22]

Current debates about the validity and etiology of DID echo early debates about hysteria and also other trauma-based phenomena such as dissociative amnesia. Historically, trauma has stirred debate within and outside the mental health field; periods of interest in trauma have been followed by disinterest and disavowal of its prevalence and impact.[6,23,24] The previous lack of systematic evidence about the relationship between trauma and clinical symptomatology contributed to misconceptions about trauma-related problems (such as attributing these symptoms to psychosis). The absence of systematic documentation of the extent of child abuse further inhibited efforts to identify and define the complex syndromes that were closely associated with it.[6]

Additionally, a broadening of the range of conditions subsumed by a diagnosis of schizophrenia moved the etiological focus from trauma and dissociation to a variant of genetic illness/brain pathology. Rosenbaum[25] documented that as the concept of schizophrenia began to gain ascendency among clinicians, the concept of DID markedly decreased— a change that likely occurred because schizophrenia and DID have some similar symptoms.[8,26] Yet, early writers on psychoses/schizophrenia (e.g., Kahlbaum, Kraepelin, Bleuler, Meyer, Jung, Schneider, and Bateson) reference cases of "psychosis" that closely resemble, or are seemingly typical of, DID.[27] Bleuler references many such cases, including some in which "the 'other' personality is marked by the use of different speech and voice ... Thus we have here two different personalities operating side by side, each one fully attentive. However, they are probably never completely separated from each other since one may communicate with both."[28(p 147)]

Social, scientific, and political influences have since converged to facilitate increased awareness of dissociation. These diverse influences include the resurgence of recognition of the impact of traumatic experiences, feminist documentation of the effects of incest and of violence toward women and children, continued scientific interest in the effects of combat, and the increasing adoption of psychotherapy into medicine and psychiatry.[18,29] The increased awareness of trauma and dissociation led to the inclusion in DSM-III of posttraumatic stress disorder (PTSD), dissociative disorders (with DID referred to as multiple personality disorder), and somatoform disorders, and to the discarding of hysteria.[30] Concurrently, traumatized and dissociative patients with severe symptoms (e.g., suicidality, impulsivity, self-mutilation) gained greater attention as psychiatry began to treat more severe psychiatric conditions with psychotherapy, and as some acutely destabilized DID patients required psychiatric hospitalization.[31] These developments facilitated a climate in which researchers and clinicians could consider how a traumatized child or adult might psychologically defend himself or herself against abuse, betrayal, and violence. Additionally, the concepts of identity, alongside identity crisis, identity confusion, and identity disorder, were introduced to psychiatry and psychology, thereby emphasizing the links between childhood, society, and epigenetic development.[32,33]

In this climate of renewed receptivity to the study of trauma and its impact, research in dissociation and DID has expanded rapidly in the 40 years spanning 1975 to 2015.[14,34] Researchers have found dissociation and dissociative disorders around the world.[3,12,35–45] For example, in a sample of 25,018 individuals from 16 countries, 14.4% of the individuals with PTSD showed high levels of dissociative symptoms.[35] This research led to the inclusion of a dissociative subtype of PTSD in DSM-5.[1] Recent reviews indicate an expanding and important evidence base for this subtype.[14,36,46]

Notwithstanding the upsurge in authoritative research on DID, several notions have been repeatedly circulated about this disorder that are inconsistent with the accumulated findings on it. We argue here that these notions are misconceptions or myths. We have chosen to limit our focus to examining myths about DID, rather than dissociative disorders or dissociation in general. Careful reviews about broader issues related to dissociation and DID have recently been published.[47–49] The purpose of this article is to examine some misconceptions about DID in the context of the considerable empirical literature that has developed about this disorder. We will examine the following notions, which we will show are myths:

1. belief that DID is a "fad"
2. belief that DID is primarily diagnosed in North America by DID experts who overdiagnose the disorder
3. belief that DID is rare
4. belief that DID is an iatrogenic disorder rather than a trauma-based disorder
5. belief that DID is the same entity as borderline personality disorder
6. belief that DID treatment is harmful to patients

MYTH 1: *DID* IS A FAD

Some authors opine that DID is a "fad that has died."[50–52] A "fad" is widely understood to describe "something (such as an interest or fashion) that is very popular for a short time."[53]

---

*Prior to being renamed dissociative identity disorder, DID was referred to as "multiple personality disorder." Dissociated personality states are referred to by various names, including identities, dissociated self-states, parts, and alters.

As we noted above, DID cases have been described in the literature for hundreds of years. Since the 1980 publication of DSM-III,[30] DID has been described, accepted, and included in four different editions of the DSM. Formal recognition as a disorder for over three decades contradicts the notion of DID as a fad.

To determine whether research about DID has declined (which would possibly support the suggestion that the diagnosis is a dying fad), we searched PsycInfo and MEDLINE using the terms "multiple personality disorder" or "dissociative identity disorder" in the title for the period 2000–14. Our search yielded 1339 hits for the 15-year period. This high number of publications speaks to the level of professional interest that DID continues to attract.

Recent reviews attest that a solid and growing evidence base for DID exists across a range of research areas:

1. DID patients can be reliably and validly diagnosed with structured and semistructured interviews, including the Structured Clinical Interview for Dissociative Disorders–Revised (SCID-D-R)[54] and Dissociative Disorders Interview Schedule (DDIS)[55,56] (reviewed in Dorahy et al. [2014]).[14] DID can also be diagnosed in clinical settings, where structured interviews may not be available or practical to use.[57]
2. DID patients are consistently identified in outpatient, inpatient, and community samples around the world.[12,37–45]
3. DID patients can be differentiated from other psychiatric patients, healthy controls, and DID simulators in neurophysiological and psychological research.[58–63]
4. DID patients usually benefit from psychotherapy that addresses trauma and dissociation in accordance with expert consensus guidelines.[64–66]

An expanding body of research examines the neurobiology, phenomenology, prevalence, assessment, personality structure, cognitive patterns, and treatment of DID. This research provides evidence of DID's content, criterion, and construct validity.[14,55] The claim that DID is a "fad that has died" is not supported by an examination of the body of research about this disorder.

MYTH 2: *DID* IS PRIMARILY DIAGNOSED IN NORTH AMERICA BY *DID* EXPERTS WHO OVERDIAGNOSE THE DISORDER

Some authors contend that DID is primarily a North American phenomenon, that it is diagnosed almost entirely by DID experts, and that it is overdiagnosed.[50,67–69] Paris[50(p 1076)] opines that "most clinical and research reports about this clinical picture [i.e., DID] have come from a small number of centers, mostly in the United States that specialize in dissociative disorders." As we show below, the empirical literature indicates not only that DID is diagnosed around the world and by clinicians with varying degrees of experience with the disorder, but that DID is actually *under*diagnosed rather than overdiagnosed.

Belief That DID Is Primarily Diagnosed in North America
According to some authors, DID is primarily diagnosed in North America.[50,52,70] We investigated this notion in three ways: by examining the countries in which prevalence studies of DID have been conducted; by inspecting the countries from which DID participants were recruited in an international treatment-outcome study of DID; and by conducting a systematic search of published research to determine the countries where DID has been most studied.

First, our results show that DID is found in prevalence studies around the world whenever researchers conduct systematic assessments using validated interviews. Table 1 lists the 14 studies that have utilized structured or semistructured diagnostic interviews for dissociative disorders to assess the prevalence of DID.[80] These studies have been conducted in seven countries: Canada, Germany, Israel, the Netherlands, Switzerland, Turkey, and the United States.[37–39,44,45,71–79]

Second, in addition to the prevalence studies, a recent prospective study assessed the treatment outcome of 232 DID patients from around the world. The participants lived in Argentina, Australia, Belgium, Brazil, Canada, Germany, Israel, the Netherlands, New Zealand, Norway, Singapore, Slovakia, South Africa, Sweden, Taiwan, and the United States.[81] That is, the participants came from every continent except Antarctica.

Third, we conducted a systematic search of published, peer-reviewed DID studies. Using the search terms "dissociative identity disorder" and "multiple personality disorder," we conducted a literature review for the period 2005–13 via MEDLINE, PsycInfo, and the *Journal of Trauma and Dissociation*. This search yielded 340 articles. We selected empirical research studies in which DID or multiple personality disorder had been diagnosed in patients. We recorded authors' countries and institutions, and whether structured interviews were used to diagnose DID. Over this nine-year period, 70 studies included DID patients. Significantly, these studies were conducted by authors from 48 institutions in 16 countries. In 28 (40%) of studies, structured interviews (SCID-D or DDIS) were administered to diagnose DID.

In summary, all three methods contradicted the claim that DID is diagnosed primarily in North America.

Belief That *DID* Is Primarily Diagnosed by *DID* experts
Lynn and colleagues[69(p 50)] argue that "most DID diagnoses derive from a small number of therapy specialists in DID." Other critics voice similar concerns.[50,82,83] Research does not substantiate this claim. For example, 292 therapists participated in the prospective treatment-outcome study of DID conducted by Brand and colleagues.[81] The majority of therapists were not DID experts. Similarly, a national random sample of experienced U.S. clinicians found that 11% of patients treated in the community for borderline personality disorder (BPD) also met criteria for comorbid DID.[84] None of the therapists were DID experts. In an Australian study of 250 clinicians from several mental health disciplines, 52% had diagnosed a

Table 1				
Dissociative Disorder Prevalence Studies				
Study	Country	Number of participants	Diagnostic instrument	Prevalence of DID
Psychiatric inpatient unit				
Ross et al. (1991)[44]	United States	484	DDIS	5.40%
Saxe et al. (1993)[45]	United States	172	DDIS	4.00%
Modestin et al. (1996)[71]	Switzerland	207	DDIS	0.40%
Tutkun et al. (1998)[72]	Turkey	166	DDIS	5.4%[a]
Friedl & Draijer (2000)[38]	Netherlands	122	SCID-D	2.00%
Gast et al. (2001)[39]	Germany	115	SCID-D	0.90%
Ginzburg et al. (2010)[73]	Israel	120	SCID-D	0.80%
Psychiatric outpatient unit				
Şar et al. (2000)[74]	Turkey	150	DDIS	2.0%[a]
Şar et al. (2003)[75]	Turkey	240	SCID-D	2.50%
Foote et al. (2006)[37]	United States	82	DDIS	6.00%
General Population				
Ross et al. (1991)[76]	Canada	454	DDIS	1.30%
Johnson et al. (2006)[77]	United States	658	SCID-D	1.50%
Şar et al. (2007)[78]	Turkey	628	DDIS	1.10%
Substance-dependent inpatients				
Tamar-Gürol et al. (2008)[79]	Turkey	104	SCID-D	5.80%

[a] Clinically confirmed diagnosis.
DDIS, Dissociative Disorders Interview Schedule; SCID-D, Structured Clinical Interview for Dissociative Disorders.

patient with DID.[85] These studies show that DID is diagnosed by clinicians around the world with varying degrees of expertise in DID.

Belief That DID Is Overdiagnosed

A related myth is that DID is overdiagnosed. Studies show, however, that most individuals who meet criteria for DID have been treated in the mental health system for 6–12 years before they are correctly diagnosed with DID.[4,86–89] Studies conducted in Australia, China, and Turkey have found that DID patients are commonly misdiagnosed.[78,89,90] For example, in a study of consecutive admissions to an outpatient university clinic in Turkey, 2.0% of 150 patients were diagnosed with DID using structured interviews confirmed by clinical interview.[74] Although 12.0% were assessed to have one of the dissociative disorders, only 5% of the dissociative patients had been diagnosed previously with any dissociative disorder. Likewise, although 29% of the patients from an urban U.S. hospital-based, outpatient psychiatric clinic were diagnosed via structured interviews with dissociative disorders, only 5% had a diagnoses of dissociative disorders in their medical records.[37] Similar results have been found in consecutive admissions to a Swiss university outpatient clinic[91] and consecutive admissions to a state psychiatric hospital in the United States[45] when patients were systematically assessed with structured diagnostic interviews for dissociative disorders. This pattern is also found in nonclinical samples. Although 18.3% of women in a representative community sample in Turkey met criteria for having a dissociative disorder at some point in their lives, only one-third of the dissociative disorders group had received any type of psychiatric treatment.[78] The authors concluded, "The majority of dissociative disorders cases in the community remain unrecognized and unserved."[78(p 175)]

Studies that examine dissociative disorders in general, rather than focusing on DID, find that this group of patients are often not treated despite high symptomatology and poor functioning. A random sample of adolescents and young adults in the Netherlands showed that youth with dissociative disorders had the highest level of functional impairment of any disorder studied but the lowest rates (2.3%) of referral for mental health treatment.[92] Those with dissociative disorders in a nationally representative sample of German adolescents and young adults were highly impaired, yet only 16% had sought psychiatric treatment.[93] These findings point to the conclusion that dissociative disorder patients are underrecognized and undertreated, rather than being overdiagnosed.

Why is DID so often underdiagnosed and undertreated? Lack of training, coupled with skepticism, about dissociative disorders seems to contribute to the underrecognition and delayed diagnosis. Only 5% of Puerto Rican psychologists surveyed reported being knowledgeable about DID, and the majority (73%) had received little or no training about DID.[94] Clinicians' skepticism, about DID increased as their knowledge about it decreased. Among U.S. clinicians who reviewed a vignette of an individual presenting with the symptoms of DID, only 60.4% of the clinicians accurately diagnosed DID.[95] Clinicians misdiagnosed the patient as most frequently suffering from PTSD (14.3%), followed by schizophrenia (9.9%) and major depression (6.6%). Significantly, the age, professional degree, and years of experience of the clinician were not associated with accurate diagnosis. Accurate diagnoses were most often made by clinicians who had previously treated a DID patient and who were not skeptical about the disorder. It is concerning that clinicians were equally confident in their diagnoses, regardless of their accuracy. A study in Northern Ireland found a similar link between a lack of training about DID and misdiagnosis by clinicians.[96] Psychologists more accurately detected DID than did psychiatrists (41% vs. 7%, respectively). Australian researchers found that misdiagnosis was often associated with lack of training about DID and with skepticism regarding the diagnosis.[85] They concluded, "Clinician skepticism may be a major factor in under-diagnosis as diagnosis requires [dissociative disorders] first being considered in the differential. Displays of skepticism by clinicians, by discouraging openness in patients, already embarrassed by their symptoms, may also contribute to the problem."[85(p 944)]

In short, far from being overdiagnosed, studies consistently document that DID is underrecognized. When systematic research is conducted, DID is found around the world by both experts and nonexperts. Ignorance and skepticism about the disorder seem to contribute to DID being an underrecognized disorder.

MYTH 3: *DID* IS RARE

Many authors, including those of psychology textbooks, argue that DID is rare.[70,97-99] The prevalence rates found in psychiatric inpatients, psychiatric outpatients, the general population, and a specialized inpatient unit for substance dependence suggest otherwise (see Table 1). DID is found in approximately 1.1%–1.5% of representative community samples. Specifically, in a representative sample of 658 individuals from New York State, 1.5% met criteria for DID when assessed with SCID-D questions.[77] Similarly, a large study of community women in Turkey (n = 628) found 1.1% of the women had DID.[78]

Studies using rigorous methodology, including consecutive clinical admissions and structured clinical interviews, find DID in 0.4%–6.0% of clinical samples (see Table 1). Studies assessing groups with particularly high exposure to trauma or cultural oppression show the highest rates. For example, 6% of consecutive admissions in a highly traumatized, U.S. inner city sample were diagnosed with DID using the DDIS.[37] By contrast, only 2.0% of consecutive psychiatric inpatients received a diagnosis of DID via the SCID-D in the Netherlands.[38] The difference in prevalence may partially stem from the very high rates of trauma exposure and oppression in the U.S. inner-city, primarily minority sample.

Possession states are a cultural variation of DID that has been found in Asian countries, including China, India, Iran, Singapore, and Turkey, and also elsewhere, including Puerto Rico and Uganda.[46,100-102] For example, in a general population sample of Turkish women, 2.1% of the participants reported an experience of possession.[102] Two of the 13 women who reported an experience of possession had DID when assessed with the DDIS. Western fundamentalist groups have also characterized DID individuals as possessed.[102] Such findings are inconsistent with the claim that DID is rare.

MYTH 4: *DID* IS AN IATROGENIC DISORDER RATHER THAN A TRAUMA-BASED DISORDER

One of the most frequently repeated myths is that DID is iatrogenically created. Proponents of this view argue that various influences—including suggestibility, a tendency to fantasize, therapists who use leading questions and procedures, and media portrayals of DID—lead some vulnerable individuals to believe they have the disorder.[52,69,83,103-107] Trauma researchers have repeatedly challenged this myth.[48,49,108-111] Space limitations require that we provide only a brief overview of this claim.

A recent and thorough challenge to this myth comes from Dalenberg and colleagues.[48,49] They conducted a review of almost 1500 studies to determine whether there was more empirical support for the trauma model of dissociation—that is, that antecedent trauma causes dissociation, including dissociative disorders—or for the fantasy model of dissociation. According to the latter (also known as the iatrogenic or sociocognitive model), highly suggestible individuals enact DID following exposure to social influences that cause them to believe that they have the disorder. Thus, according to the fantasy model proponents, DID is not a valid disorder; rather, it is iatrogenically induced in fantasy-prone individuals by therapists and other sources of influence.

Dalenberg and colleagues[48,49] concluded from their review and a series of meta-analyses that little evidence supports the fantasy model of dissociation. Specifically, the effect sizes of the trauma-dissociation relationship were strong among individuals with dissociative disorders, and especially DID (i.e., .54 between child sexual abuse and dissociation, and .52 between physical abuse and dissociation). The correlations between trauma and dissociation were as strong in studies that used objectively verified abuse as in those relying on self-reported abuse. These findings strongly contradict the fantasy model hypothesis that DID individuals fantasize their abuse.

Dissociation predicted only 1%–3% of the variance in suggestibility, thereby disproving the fantasy model's notion that dissociative individuals are highly suggestible.

Despite the concerns of fantasy model theorists that DID is iatrogenically created, *no study in any clinical population supports the fantasy model of dissociation*. A single study conducted in a "normal" sample of college students showed that students could simulate DID.[112] That study, by Spanos and colleagues, documents that students can engage in identity enactments when asked to behave as if they had DID. Nevertheless, the students did not actually begin to believe that they had DID, and they did not develop the wide range of severe, chronic, and disabling symptoms displayed by DID patients.[3]

The study by Spanos and colleagues[112] was limited by the lack of a DID control group. Several recent controlled studies have found that DID simulators can be reliably distinguished from DID patients on a variety of well-validated and frequently used psychological personality tests (e.g., Minnesota Multiphasic Personality Inventory-2),[113,114] forensic measures (e.g., Structured Interview of Reported Symptoms),[61,115,116] and neurophysiological measures, including brain imaging, blood pressure, and heart rate.

Two additional lines of research challenge the iatrogenesis theory of DID: first, prevalence research conducted in cultures where DID is not well known, and second, evidence of chronic childhood abuse and dissociation in childhood among adults diagnosed with DID. Three classic studies have been conducted in cultures where DID was virtually unknown when the research was conducted. Researchers using structured interviews found DID in patients in China, despite the absence of DID in the Chinese psychiatric diagnostic manual.[117] The Chinese study and also two conducted in central-eastern Turkey in the 1990s[78,118]—where public information about DID was absent—contradict the iatrogenesis thesis. In one of the Turkish studies,[118] a representative sample of women from the general population (n = 994) was evaluated in three stages: participants completed a self-report measure of dissociation; two groups of participants, with high versus low scores, were administered the DDIS by a researcher blind to scores; and the two groups were then given clinical examinations (also blind to scores). The researchers were able to identify four cases of DID, all of whom reported childhood abuse or neglect.

The second line of research challenging the iatrogenesis theory of DID documents the existence of dissociation and severe trauma in childhood records of adults with DID. Researchers have found documented evidence of dissociative symptoms in childhood and adolescence in individuals who were not assessed or treated for DID until later in life (thus reducing the risk that these symptoms could have been suggested).[11,13,119] Numerous studies have also found documentation of severe child abuse in adult patients diagnosed with DID.[10,13,120,121] For example, in their review of the clinical records of 12 convicted murderers diagnosed with DID, Lewis and colleagues[11] found objective documentation of child abuse (e.g., child protection agency reports, police reports) in 11 of the 12, and long-standing, marked dissociation in all of them. Further, Lewis and colleagues[11(p 1709)] noted that "contrary to the popular belief that probing questions will either instill false memories or encourage lying, especially in dissociative patients, of our 12 subjects, not one produced false memories or lied after inquiries regarding maltreatment. On the contrary, our subjects either denied or minimized their early experiences. We had to rely for the most part on objective records and on interviews with family and friends to discover that major abuse had occurred." Notably, these inmates had already been sentenced; they were all unaware of having met diagnostic criteria for DID; and they made no effort to use the diagnosis or their trauma histories to benefit their legal cases.

Similarly, Swica and colleagues[13] found documentation of early signs of dissociation in childhood records in all of the six men imprisoned for murder who were assessed and diagnosed with DID during participation in a research study. During their trials, the men were all unaware of having DID. And since their sentencing had already occurred, they had nothing to gain from DID being diagnosed while participating in the study. Their signs and symptoms of early dissociation included hearing voices (100%), having vivid imaginary companions (100%), amnesia (50%), and trance states (34%). Furthermore, evidence of severe childhood abuse has been found in medical, school, police, and child welfare records in 58%–100% of DID cases.[11,13,121] These studies indicate that dissociative symptoms and a history of severe childhood trauma are present long before DID is suspected or diagnosed.

Perhaps the "iatrogenesis myth" exists because inappropriate therapeutic interventions can exacerbate symptoms if used with DID patients. The expert consensus DID treatment guidelines warn that inappropriate interventions may worsen DID symptoms, although few clinicians report using such interventions.[66,122] No research evidence suggests that inappropriate treatment *creates* DID. The only study to date examining deterioration of symptoms among DID patients found that only a small minority (1.1%) worsened over more than one time-point in treatment and that deterioration was associated with revictimization or stressors in the patients' lives rather than with the therapy they received.[123] This rate of deterioration of symptoms compares favorably with those for other psychiatric disorders.

MYTH 5: *DID* IS THE SAME ENTITY AS BORDERLINE PERSONALITY DISORDER

Some authors suggest that the symptoms of DID represent a severe or overly imaginative presentation of BPD.[124] The research described below, however, indicates that while DID and BPD can frequently be diagnosed in the same individual, they appear to be discrete disorders.[125,126]

One of the difficulties in differentiating BPD from DID has been the poor definition of the dissociation criterion of BPD in the DSM's various editions. In DSM-5 this ninth criterion of BPD is "transient, stress-related paranoid ideation or severe dissociative symptoms."[1] The narrative text in DSM-5 defines dissociative symptoms in BPD ("e.g., depersonalization") as "generally of insufficient severity or duration to warrant an additional diagnosis." DSM-5 does not clarify that when *additional types* of dissociation are found in patients who meet the criteria for BPD—especially amnesia or identity alteration that are severe and *not transient* (i.e., amnesia or identity alteration that form an enduring feature of the patient's presentation)—the additional diagnosis of a dissociative disorder should be considered, and that additional diagnostic assessment is recommended.

On the surface, BPD and DID appear to have similar psychological profiles and symptoms.[124,127] Abrupt mood swings, identity disturbance, impulsive risk-taking behaviors, self-harm, and suicide attempts are common in both disorders. Indeed, early comparative studies found few differences on clinical comorbidity, history, or psychometric testing using the Minnesota Multiphasic Personality Inventory and the Millon Clinical Multiaxial Inventory.[124,127] However, recent clinical observational studies, as well as systematic studies using structured interview data, have distinguished DID from BPD.[59,128] Brand and Loewenstein[59] review the clinical symptoms and psychosocial variables that distinguish DID from BPD: clinically, individuals with BPD show vacillating, less modulated emotions that shift according to external precipitants.[59] In addition, individuals with BPD can generally recall their actions across different emotions and do not feel that those actions are alien or so uncharacteristic as to be disavowed.[59,128] By contrast, individuals with DID have amnesia for some of their experiences while they are in dissociated personality states, and they also experience a marked discontinuity in their sense of self or sense of agency.[1] Thus, the dissociated activity and intrusion of personality states into the individual's consciousness may be experienced as separate or different from the self that they identify with or feel they can control. Accordingly, using SCID-D structured interview data, Boon and Draijer[128] demonstrated that amnesia, identity confusion, and identity alteration were significantly more severe in individuals with DID than in cluster B personality disorder patients, most of whom had BPD. However, DID and BPD patients did not differ on the severity of depersonalization and derealization. Both groups had experienced trauma, although the DID group had much more severe and earlier trauma exposure.

BPD and DID can also be differentiated on the Rorschach inkblot test. Sixty-seven DID patients, compared to 40 BPD patients, showed greater self-reflective capacity, introspection, ability to modulate emotion, social interest, accurate perception, logical thinking, and ability to see others as potentially collaborative.[58] A pilot Rorschach study found that compared to BPD patients, DID patients had more traumatic intrusions, greater internalization, and a tendency to engage in complex contemplation about the significance of events.[129] The DID group consistently used a thinking-based problem-solving approach, rather than the vacillating approach characterized by shifting back and forth between emotion-based and thinking-based coping that has been documented among the BPD patients.[129] These personality differences likely enable DID patients to develop a therapeutic relationship more easily than many BPD patients.

With regard to the frequent comorbidity between DID and BPD, studies assessing for both disorders have found that approximately 25% of BPD patients endorse symptoms suggesting possible dissociated personality states (e.g., disremembered actions, finding objects that they do not remember acquiring)[126] and that 10%–24% of patients who meet criteria for BPD also meet criteria for DID.[75,126,130,131] Likewise, a national random sample of experienced U.S. clinicians found that 11% of patients treated in the community for BPD met criteria for comorbid DID,[84] and structured interview studies have found that 31%–73% of DID subjects meet criteria for comorbid BPD.[12,72,132] Thus, about 30% or more of patients with DID do *not* meet full diagnostic criteria for BPD. In blind comparisons between non-BPD controls and college students who were interviewed for all dissociative disorders after screening positive for BPD, BPD comorbid with dissociative disorder was more common than was BPD alone (n = 58 vs. n = 22, respectively).[130] It is important to note that despite its prevalence in patients with DID, BPD is *not* the most common personality disorder that is comorbid with DID. More common among individuals with DID are avoidant (76%–96%) and self-defeating (a proposed category in the appendix of DSM-III-R; 68%–94%) personality disorders, followed by BPD (53%–89%).[132,133]

When the comorbidity between BPD and DID is evaluated specifically, the patients with comorbid BPD and DID appear to be *more severely impaired* than individuals with either disorder alone. For example, the participants who had both disorders reported the highest level of amnesia and had the most severe overall dissociation scores.[130] Similarly, individuals who meet criteria for both disorders have more psychiatric comorbidity and trauma exposure than individuals who meet criteria for only one,[134] and they also report higher scores of dissociative amnesia.[135]

In the future, the neurobiology of BPD and DID might assist in their comparison. Preliminary imaging research in BPD suggests the prefrontal cortex may fail to inhibit excessive amygdala activation.[136] By contrast, two patterns of activation that correspond to different personality states have been found in DID patients: *neutral states* are associated with overmodulation of affect and show corticolimbic inhibition, whereas *trauma-related states* are associated with undermodulation of affect and activation of the amygdala on positron emission tomography.[62] Similarly, recent fMRI studies in DID found that the neutral states demonstrate emotional underactivation and that the trauma-related states demonstrate emotional overactivation.[137,138] Perhaps BPD might be thought of as resembling the trauma-related state of DID with amygdala activation, whereas the dissociative pattern found in the neutral state in DID appears to be different from what is found in BPD.[139] Additional research comparing these disorders is needed to further explore the early findings of neurobiological similarities and differences.

What remains open for debate is whether a personality disorder diagnosis may be given to DID patients, because attribution of a clinical phenomenon to a personality disorder is not indicated if it is related to another disorder—in this instance, DID. Hence, the DSM-5 criteria for BPD may be insufficient to diagnose a personality disorder because DID is not excluded. In this regard, some DID researchers have concluded that unmanaged trauma symptoms—including dissociation—may account for the high comorbidity of BPD in DID patients.[75,131] For example, one study found that only a small group of DID patients still met BPD criteria after their trauma symptoms were stabilized.[140] Resolution of this debate may hinge on whether patients diagnosed with BPD are conceptualized as having a severe personality disorder rather than a trauma-based disorder that involves dissociation as a central symptom.

Yet to be studied is the possibility that several overlapping etiological pathways—including trauma,[4,141] attachment disruption,[142–144] and genetics[145–149]—may contribute to the overlap in symptomatology between BPD and DID. In order to clarify which variables increase risk for one or both developmental outcomes, research that carefully screens for both DID and BPD is needed. The apparent phenomenological overlap between the two psychopathologies does not create an insurmountable obstacle for research, because distinct influences may be parsed out via statistical analysis.[135,150] Screening for both disorders would prevent BPD and DID from constituting mutually confounding factors in research specifically about one or the other.[150]

The benefit of accurately diagnosing (1) BPD without DID, (2) DID without BPD, and (3) comorbid DID BPD is that treatment can be individualized to meet patients' needs. A diagnosis of BPD without DID can lead clinicians to use empirically supported treatment for BPD. By contrast, the treatment of DID is different from the treatment of BPD and comprises three phases: stabilization, trauma processing, and integration (discussed below).[66] Given the severity of illness found in individuals with comorbid BPD/DID, clinicians should emphasize skills acquisition and stabilization of trauma-related symptoms in an extended stabilization phase. Early detection of comorbid DID and BPD alerts the therapist to avoid trauma-processing work until the stabilization phase is complete. The trauma-processing phase should be approached cautiously in highly dissociative individuals, and only after they have developed the capacity both to contain intrusive trauma material and to use grounding techniques to manage dissociation.

In summary, DID and BPD appear to be separate, albeit frequently comorbid and overlapping, disorders that can be differentiated on validated structured and semistructured interviews, as well as on the Rorschach test. While the symptoms of DID and BPD overlap, preliminary indications are that the neurobiology of each is different. It is also possible that differences between DID and BPD may emerge regarding the respective etiological roles of trauma, attachment disruption, and genetics.

MYTH 6: *DID* TREATMENT IS HARMFUL TO PATIENTS
Some critics claim that DID treatment is harmful.[52,69,151–153] This claim is inconsistent with empirical literature that documents improvements in the symptoms and functioning of DID patients when trauma treatment consistent with the expert consensus guidelines is provided.[65,66]

Before reviewing the empirical literature, we will present an overview of the DID treatment model. The first DID treatment guidelines were developed in 1994, with revisions in 1997, 2005, and 2011. The current standard of care for DID treatment is described in the International Society for the Study of Trauma and Dissociation's Treatment Guidelines for Dissociative Identity Disorder in Adults.[66] The DID experts who wrote the guidelines recommend a tri-phasic, trauma-focused psychotherapy. In the first stage, clinicians focus on safety issues, symptom stabilization, and establishment of a therapeutic alliance. Failure to stabilize the patient or a premature focus on detailed exploration of traumatic memories usually results in deterioration in functioning and a diminished sense of safety. In the second stage of treatment, following the ability to regulate affect and manage their symptoms, patients begin processing, grieving, and resolving trauma. In the third and final stage of treatment, patients integrate dissociated self-states and become more socially engaged.

Early case series and inpatient treatment studies demonstrate that treatment for DID is helpful, rather than harmful, across a wide range of clinical outcome measures.[64,140,154–158] A meta-analysis of eight treatment outcome studies for any dissociative disorder yielded moderate to strong within-patient effect sizes for dissociative disorder treatment.[64] While the authors noted methodological weaknesses, current treatment studies show improved methodology over the earlier studies. One of the largest prospective treatment studies is the Treatment of Patients with Dissociative Disorders (TOP DD) study, conducted by Brand and colleagues.[159] The TOP DD study used a naturalistic design to collect data from 230 DID patients (as well as 50 patients with dissociative disorder not otherwise specified) and their treating clinicians. Patient and clinician reports indicate that, over 30 months of treatment, patients showed decreases in dissociative, posttraumatic, and depressive symptomatology, as well as decreases in hospitalizations, self-harm, drug use, and physical pain. Clinicians reported that patient functioning increased significantly over time, as did their social, volunteer, and academic involvement. Secondary analyses also demonstrated that patients with a stronger therapeutic alliance evidenced significantly greater decreases in dissociative, PTSD, and general distress symptoms.[160]

Crucial to discussion of whether DID treatment is harmful is the importance of dissociation-focused therapy. A study of consecutive admissions to a Norwegian inpatient trauma program found that dissociation does not substantially improve if amnesia and dissociated self-states are not directly addressed.[161] The study, by Jepsen and colleagues, compared two groups of women who had experienced childhood sexual abuse—one without, and one with, a dissociative disorder (DID or dissociative disorder not otherwise specified). None of the dissociative disorder patients had been diagnosed or treated for a dissociative disorder, and dissociative disorder was not the focus of the inpatient treatment. Thus, the methods of this study reduce the possibility of therapist suggestion. Although both groups had some dissociative symptoms, the dissociative disorder group was more severely symptomatic. Both groups showed improvements in symptoms, although the effect sizes for change in dissociation were smaller for the dissociative disorder group than for the non-dissociative disorder group (d = .25 and .69, respectively). As a result of these findings, the hospital developed a specialized treatment program, currently being evaluated, for dissociative disorder patients (Jepsen E, personal communication, June 2013).

Large, diverse samples, standardized assessments, and longitudinal designs with lengthy follow-ups were utilized in the studies by Brand and colleagues[159] and Jepsen and colleagues.[161] However, neither study used untreated control groups or randomization. Additionally, Brand and colleagues' TOP DD study[159] had a high attrition rate over 30 months (approximately 50%), whereas Jepsen and colleagues[161] had an impressive 3% patient attrition rate during a 12-month follow-up.

DID experts uniformly support the importance of recognizing and working with dissociated self-states.[65] Clinicians in the TOP DD study reported frequently working with self-states.[122] While it is not possible to conclude that working with self-states *caused* the decline in symptoms, these improvements occurred during treatment that involved specific work with dissociated self-states. This finding of consistent improvement is another line of research that challenges the conjecture that working with self-states harms DID patients.[69,152]

Brand and colleagues[47] reviewed the evidence used to support claims of the alleged harmfulness of DID treatment. *They did not find a single peer-reviewed study showing that treatment consistent with DID expert consensus guidelines harms patients.* In fact, those who argue that DID treatment is harmful cite little of the actual DID treatment literature; instead, they cite theoretical and opinion pieces.[52,69,151–153] In their review—from 2014—Brand and colleagues[47] concluded that claims about the alleged harmfulness of DID treatment are based on non-peer-reviewed publications, misrepresentations of the data, autobiographical accounts written by patients, and misunderstandings about DID treatment and the phenomenology of DID.

In short, claims about the harmfulness of DID treatment lack empirical support. Rather, the evidence that treatment results in remediation of dissociation is sufficiently strong that critics have recently conceded that increases in dissociative symptoms do not result from DID psychotherapy.[104] To the same effect, in a 2014 article in *Psychological Bulletin*, Dalenberg and colleagues[49] responded to critics, noting that treatment consistent with the expert consensus guidelines benefits and stabilizes patients.

THE COST OF MYTHS AND IGNORANCE ABOUT *DID*

As we have shown, current research indicates that while approximately 1% of the general population suffers from DID, the disorder remains undertreated and underrecognized. The average DID patient spends years in the mental health system before being correctly diagnosed.[4,71,72,76,79] These patients have high rates of suicidal and self-destructive behavior, experience significant disability, and often require expensive and restrictive treatments such as inpatient and partial hospitalization.[64,162,163] Studies of treatment costs for DID show dramatic reductions in overall cost of treatment, along with reductions in utilization of more restrictive levels of care, after the correct diagnosis of DID is made and appropriate treatment is initiated.[164–166]

Delay in recognition and adequate treatment of DID likely prolongs the suffering and disability of DID patients. Younger DID patients appear to respond more rapidly to treatment than do older adults,[167] which suggests that years of misdirected treatment exact a high personal cost from patients.[166] Needless to say, if clinicians do not recognize the disorder, they cannot provide treatment consistent with expert guidelines for DID.

The myths we have dispelled also have substantial economic costs for the health care system and, more broadly, for society. For example, the myths may deter clinicians and researchers from seeking training in the assessment and treatment of DID, thereby compounding the problems of misunderstanding, lack of recognition, and inappropriate treatment, as we have discussed. The misconception that DID is a rare or iatrogenic disorder may lead to the conclusion that this disorder is one on which resources should not be expended (whereas we have shown the opposite to be the case). In combination, these myths may discourage scholars from pursuing research about DID and also inhibit funding for such research, which exacerbates, in turn, the lack of understanding about, and the currently inadequate clinical services for, DID.

CONCLUSION

An enduring interest in DID is apparent in the solid and expanding research base about the disorder. DID is a legitimate and distinct psychiatric disorder that is recognizable worldwide and can be reliably identified in multiple settings by appropriately trained researchers and clinicians. The research shows that DID is a trauma-based disorder that generally responds well to treatment consistent with DID treatment guidelines.

Our findings have a number of clinical and research implications. Clinicians who accept as facts the myths explored above are unlikely to carefully assess for dissociation. Accurate diagnoses are critical for appropriate treatment planning. *If DID is not targeted in treatment, it does not appear to resolve.*[161,168] The myths we have highlighted may also impede research about DID. The cost of ignorance about DID is high not only for individual patients, but for the whole support system in which they live (e.g., loved ones, health systems, and society). Empirically derived knowledge about DID has replaced outdated myths, and for this reason vigorous dissemination of the knowledge base about this complex disorder is warranted.

Declaration of interest: The authors report no conflicts of interest. The authors alone are responsible for the content and writing of the article.

REFERENCES

1. American Psychiatric Association. Diagnostic and statistical manual of mental disorders. 5th ed. Arlington, VA: APA, 2013.
2. Putnam FW. Dissociation in children and adolescents: a developmental perspective. New York: Guilford, 1997.
3. Simeon D, Loewenstein RJ. Dissociative disorders. In: Sadock BJ, Sadock VA, Ruiz P, eds. Kaplan and Sadock's comprehensive textbook of psychiatry. 9th ed. Philadelphia: Lippincott Williams & Wilkens, 2009;1965–2026.
4. Putnam FW, Guroff JJ, Silberman EK, Barban L, Post RM. The clinical phenomenology of multiple personality disorder: review of 100 recent cases. J Clin Psychiatry 1986;47:285–93.
5. Sar V. The many faces of dissociation: opportunities for innovative research in psychiatry. Clin Psychopharmacol Neurosci 2014;12:171–9.
6. Herman JL. Trauma and recovery. New York: Basic, 1992.
7. Rodewald F, Wilhelm-Gößling C, Emrich HM, Reddemann L, Gast U. Axis-I comorbidity in female patients with dissociative identity disorder and dissociative identity disorder not otherwise specified. J Nerv Ment Dis 2011;199:122–31.
8. Ross CA, Miller SD, Reagor P, Bjornson L, Fraser GA, Anderson G. Schneiderian symptoms in multiple personality disorder and schizophrenia. Compr Psychiatry 1990;31:111–8.
9. Ellason JW, Ross CA, Fuchs DL. Lifetime Axis I and II comorbidity and childhood trauma history in dissociative identity disorder. Psychiatry 1996;59:255–66.
10. Kluft RP. The confirmation and disconfirmation of memories of abuse in DID patients: a naturalistic clinical study. Dissociation 1995;8:253–8.
11. Lewis DO, Yeager CA, Swica Y, Pincus JH, Lewis M. Objective documentation of child abuse and dissociation in 12 murderers with dissociative identity disorder. Am J Psychiatry 1997;154:1703–10.
12. Middleton W, Butler J. Dissociative identity disorder: an Australian series. Aust N Z J Psychiatry 1998;32:794–804.
13. Swica Y, Lewis DO, Lewis M. Child abuse and dissociative identity disorder/multiple personality disorder: the documentation of childhood maltreatment and the corroboration of symptoms. Child Adolesc Psychiatr Clin N Am 1996;5:431–47.
14. Dorahy MJ, Brand BL, Şar V, et al. Dissociative identity disorder: an empirical overview. Aust N Z J Psychiatry 2014;48:402–17.
15. Carlson ET. The history of multiple personality in the United States: I. The beginnings. Am J Psychiatry 1981;138:666–8.
16. Ellenberger HF. The discovery of the unconscious: the history and evolution of dynamic psychiatry. New York: Basic, 1970.
17. Loewenstein RJ. Anna O: reformulation as a case of multiple personality disorder. In: Goodwin JM, ed. Rediscovering childhood trauma: historical casebook and clinical applications. Washington, DC: American Psychiatric Press, 1993;139–67.
18. van der Hart O, Dorahy MJ. History of the concept of dissociation. In: Dell PF, O'Neil JA, eds. Dissociation and the dissociative disorders: DSM-V and beyond. New York: Routledge, 2009:3–26.
19. Sidis B, Goodhart SP. Multiple personality: an experimental investigation into the nature of human individuality. New York: D. Appleton, 1905.
20. van der Hart O, Lierens R, Goodwin J. Jeanne Fery. A sixteenth-century case of dissociative identity disorder. J Psychohist 1996;24:18–35.
21. Gmelin E. Materialen für die Anthropologie. Tübingen, Germany: Cotta, 1791.
22. Guillain G. J.-M. Charcot, 1825–1893: his life—his work. New York: Hoeber, 1959.
23. Herman JL. Complex PTSD: a syndrome in survivors of prolonged and repeated trauma. In: Everly GS Jr, Lating JM, eds. Psychotraumatology: key papers and core concepts in post-traumatic stress. New York: Plenum, 1995;87–100.
24. Chu JA. Rebuilding shattered lives: treating complex PTSD and dissociative disorders 2nd ed. Hoboken, NJ: Wiley, 2011.
25. Rosenbaum M. The role of the term schizophrenia in the decline of diagnoses of multiple personality. Arch Gen Psychiatry 1980;37:1383–5.
26. Kluft RP. First-rank symptoms as a diagnostic clue to multiple personality disorder. Am J Psychiatry 1987;144:293–8.
27. Ross C. Dissociation in classical texts on schizophrenia. Psychosis 2014;6:342–54.
28. Bleuler E. Dementia praecox or the group of schizophrenias. Oxford: International Universities, 1950.
29. Dorahy MJ, van der Hart O, Middleton W. The history of early life trauma and abuse from the 1850s to the current time: how the past influences the present. In: Lanius R, Vermetten E, Pain C, eds. The hidden epidemic: the impact of early life trauma on health and disease. New York: Cambridge University Press, 2010;3–12.
30. American Psychiatric Association. Diagnostic and statistical manual of mental disorders. 3rd ed. Washington, DC: APA, 1980.
31. Tutkun H, Yargic LI, Sar V. Dissociative identity disorder presenting as hysterical psychosis. Dissociation 1996;9:244–52.
32. Erikson EH. Childhood and society. New York: Norton, 1964.
33. Sar V. The scope of dissociative disorders: an international perspective. Psychiatr Clin North Am 2006;29:227–44.
34. Dalenberg C, Loewenstein R, Spiegel D, et al. Scientific study of the dissociative disorders. Psychother Psychosom 2007;76:400–1.
35. Stein DJ, Koenen KC, Friedman MJ, et al. Dissociation in post-traumatic stress disorder: evidence from the World Mental Health Surveys. Biol Psychiatry 2013;73:302–12.
36. Brand BL, Lanius R, Vermetten E, Loewenstein RJ, Spiegel D. Where are we going? An update on assessment, treatment, and neurobiological research in dissociative disorders as

we move toward the DSM-5. J Trauma Dissociation 2012; 13:9–31.
37. Foote B, Smolin Y, Kaplan M, Legatt ME, Lipschitz D. Prevalence of dissociative disorders in psychiatric outpatients. Am J Psychiatry 2006;163:623–9.
38. Friedl MC, Draijer N. Dissociative disorders in Dutch psychiatric inpatients. Am J Psychiatry 2000;157:1012–3.
39. Gast U, Rodewald F, Nickel V, Emrich HM. Prevalence of dissociative disorders among psychiatric inpatients in a German university clinic. J Nerv Ment Dis 2001;189:249–57.
40. Horen SA, Leichner PP, Lawson JS. Prevalence of dissociative symptoms and disorders in an adult psychiatric inpatient population in Canada. Can J Psychiatry 1995;40:185–91.
41. Latz TT, Kramer SI, Hughes DL. Multiple personality disorder among female inpatients in a state hospital. Am J Psychiatry 1995;152:1343–8.
42. Lewis-Fernández R, Martínez-Taboas A, Sar V, Patel S, Boatin A. The cross-cultural assessment of dissociation. In: Wilson JP, So-Kum Tang CC, eds. Cross-cultural assessment of psychological trauma and PTSD. New York: Springer, 2007; 279–317.
43. Lussier RG, Steiner J, Grey A, Hansen C. Prevalence of dissociative disorders in an acute care day hospital population. Psychiatr Serv 1997;48:244–6.
44. Ross CA, Anderson G, Fleisher WP, Norton GR. The frequency of multiple personality disorder among psychiatric inpatients. Am J Psychiatry 1991;148:1717–20.
45. Saxe GN, Van der Kolk BA, Berkowitz R, et al. Dissociative disorders in psychiatric inpatients. Am J Psychiatry 1993;150: 1037–42.
46. Spiegel D, Loewenstein RJ, Lewis-Fernández R, et al. Dissociative disorders in DSM-5. Depress Anxiety 2011;28:E17–45.
47. Brand BL, Loewenstein RJ, Spiegel D. Dispelling myths about dissociative identity disorder treatment: an empirically based approach. Psychiatry 2014;77:169–89.
48. Dalenberg CJ, Brand BL, Gleaves DH, et al. Evaluation of the evidence for the trauma and fantasy models of dissociation. Psychol Bull 2012;138:550–88.
49. Dalenberg CJ, Brand BL, Loewenstein RJ, et al. Reality versus fantasy: reply to Lynn et al. (2014). Psychol Bull 2014;140: 911–20.
50. Paris J. The rise and fall of dissociative identity disorder. J Nerv Ment Dis 2012;200:1076–9.
51. Pope HG Jr, Barry S, Bodkin A, Hudson JI. Tracking scientific interest in the dissociative disorders: a study of scientific publication output 1984–2003. Psychother Psychosom 2006;75: 19–24.
52. McHugh P. Do fads ever die? J Nerv Ment Dis 2013;201: 357–8.
53. http://www.merriam-webster.com/dictionary/fad
54. Steinberg M. Structured Clinical Interview for DSM-IV Dissociative Disorders (SCID-D). Rev. ed. Washington, DC: American Psychiatric Press, 1994.
55. Gleaves DH, May MC, Cardeña E. An examination of the diagnostic validity of dissociative identity disorder. Clin Psychol Rev 2001;21:577–608.
56. Ross CA, Heber S, Norton GR, Anderson D. The Dissociative Disorders Interview Schedule: a structured interview. Dissociation 1989;2:169–89.
57. Loewenstein RJ. An office mental status examination for complex chronic dissociative symptoms and multiple personality disorder. Psychiatr Clin North Am 1991;14:567–604.
58. Brand BL, Armstrong JG, Loewenstein RJ, McNary SW. Personality differences on the Rorschach of dissociative identity disorder, borderline personality disorder, and psychotic inpatients. Psychol Trauma 2009;1:188–205.
59. Brand B, Loewenstein RJ. Dissociative disorders: an overview of assessment, phenomenology and treatment. Psychiatr Times 2010 (Oct);27:62–9.
60. Brand BL, Chasson GS. Distinguishing simulated from genuine dissociative identity disorder on the MMPI-2. Psychol Trauma 2015;7:93–101.
61. Brand BL, Tursich M, Tzall D, Loewenstein RJ. Utility of the SIRS-2 in distinguishing genuine from simulated dissociative identity disorder. Psychol Trauma 2014;6:308–17.
62. Reinders AA, Nijenhuis ER, Quak J, et al. Psychobiological characteristics of dissociative identity disorder: a symptom provocation study. Biol Psychiatry 2006;60:730–40.
63. Reinders AATS, Willemsen ATM, Vos HPJ, den Boer JA, Nijenhuis ERS. Fact or factitious? A psychobiological study of authentic and simulated dissociative identity states. PLoS One 2012;7:e39279.
64. Brand BL, Classen CC, McNary SW, Zaveri P. A review of dissociative disorders treatment studies. J Nerv Ment Dis 2009; 197:646–54.
65. Brand BL, Myrick AC, Loewenstein RJ, et al. A survey of practices and recommended treatment interventions among expert therapists treating patients with dissociative identity disorder and dissociative disorder not otherwise specified. Psychol Trauma 2012;4:490–500.
66. International Society for the Study of Trauma and Dissociation. Guidelines for treating dissociative identity disorder in adults, third revision: summary version. J Trauma Dissociation 2011;12:188–212.
67. Adityanjee Raju GS, Khandelwal SK. Current status of multiple personality disorder in India. Am J Psychiatry 1989;146: 1607–10.
68. Lynn SJ, Fassler O, Knox JA, Lilienfeld SO. Dissociation and dissociative identity disorder: treatment guidelines and cautions. In: Fisher JE, O'Donohue WT, eds. Practitioner's guide to evidence-based psychotherapy. New York: Springer, 2006.
69. Lynn SJ, Lilienfeld SO, Merckelbach H, Giesbrecht T, van der Kloet D. Dissociation and dissociative disorders: challenging conventional wisdom. Curr Dir Psychol Sci 2012;21:48–53.
70. Spanos NP. Multiple identity enactments and multiple personality disorder: a sociocognitive perspective. Psychol Bull 1994; 116:143–65.
71. Modestin J, Ebner G, Junghan M, Erni T. Dissociative experiences and dissociative disorders in acute psychiatric inpatients. Compr Psychiatry 1996;37:355–61.
72. Tutkun H, Sar V, Yargiç LI, Ozpulat T, Yanik M, Kiziltan E. Frequency of dissociative disorders among psychiatric inpatients in a Turkish university clinic. Am J Psychiatry 1998;155: 800–5.
73. Ginzburg K, Somer E, Tamarkin G, Kramer L. Clandestine psychopathology: unrecognized dissociative disorders in inpatient psychiatry. J Nerv Ment Dis 2010;198:378–81.
74. Sar V, Tutkun H, Alyanak B, Bakim B, Baral I. Frequency of dissociative disorders among psychiatric outpatients in Turkey. Compr Psychiatry 2000;41:216–22.
75. Sar V, Kundakci T, Kiziltan E, et al. The Axis-I dissociative disorder comorbidity of borderline personality disorder among psychiatric outpatients. J Trauma Dissociation 2003;4: 119–36.
76. Ross CA. Epidemiology of multiple personality disorder and dissociation. Psychiatr Clin North Am 1991;14:503–17.
77. Johnson JG, Cohen P, Kasen S, Brook JS. Dissociative disorders among adults in the community, impaired functioning, and Axis I and II comorbidity. J Psychiatr Res 2006;40:131–40.
78. Şar V, Akyüz G, Doğan O. Prevalence of dissociative disorders among women in the general population. Psychiatry Res 2007; 149:169–76.

79. Tamar-Gurol D, Sar V, Karadag F, Evren C, Karagoz M. Childhood emotional abuse, dissociation, and suicidality among patients with drug dependency in Turkey. Psychiatry Clin Neurosci 2008;62:540–7.
80. Şar V. Epidemiology of dissociative disorders: an overview. Epidemiol Res Int 2011;2011:404538.
81. Brand B, Classen C, Lanins R, et al. A naturalistic study of dissociative identity disorder and dissociative disorder not otherwise specified patients treated by community clinicians. Psychol Trauma 2009;1:153–71.
82. Boysen GA, VanBergen A. A review of published research on adult dissociative identity disorder: 2000–2010. J Nerv Ment Dis 2013;201:5–11.
83. Lilienfeld SO, Kirsch I, Sarbin TR, et al. Dissociative identity disorder and the sociocognitive model: recalling the lessons of the past. Psychol Bull 1999;125:507–23.
84. Conklin CZ, Westen D. Borderline personality disorder in clinical practice. Am J Psychiatry 2005;162:867–75.
85. Leonard D, Brann S, Tiller J. Dissociative disorders: pathways to diagnosis, clinician attitudes and their impact. Aust N Z J Psychiatry 2005;39:940–6.
86. Loewenstein RJ, Putnam FW. The clinical phenomenology of males with MPD: a report of 21 cases. Dissociation 1990;3:135–43.
87. Martínez-Taboas A. Multiple personality in Puerto Rico: analysis of fifteen cases. Dissociation 1991;4:189–92.
88. Ross CA, Miller SD, Reagor P, Bjornson L, Fraser GA, Anderson G. Structured interview data on 102 cases of multiple personality disorder from four centers. Am J Psychiatry 1990;147:596–601.
89. Middleton W. Dissociative disorders: a personal 'work in progress.' Australas Psychiatry 2004;12:245–52.
90. Xiao Z, Yan H, Wang Z, et al. Trauma and dissociation in China. Am J Psychiatry 2006;163:1388–91.
91. Mueller C, Moergeli H, Assaloni H, Schneider R, Rufer M. Dissociative disorders among chronic and severely impaired psychiatric outpatients. Psychopathology 2007;40:470–1.
92. Ferdinand RF, van der Reijden M, Verhulst FC, Nienhuis FJ, Giel R. Assessment of the prevalence of psychiatric disorder in young adults. Br J Psychiatry 1995;166:480–8.
93. Lieb R, Pfister H, Mastaler M, Wittchen H-U. Somatoform syndromes and disorders in a representative population sample of adolescents and young adults: prevalence, comorbidity and impairments. Acta Psychiatr Scand 2000;101:194–208.
94. Mendez N, Martinez-Taboas A, Pedrosa O. Experiences, beliefs and attitudes of Puerto Rican psychologists toward dissociative identity disorder. Cienc Conducta 2000;15:69–84.
95. Perniciaro LA. The influence of skepticism and clinical experience on the detection of dissociative identity disorder by mental health clinicians. Newton, MA: Massachusetts School of Professional Psychology, 2014.
96. Dorahy MJ, Lewis CA, Mulholland C. The detection of dissociative identity disorder by Northern Irish clinical psychologists and psychiatrists: a clinical vignettes study. J Trauma Dissociation 2005;6:39–50.
97. Beidel D, Bulik C, Stanley M. Abnormal psychology. 3rd ed. Upper Saddle River, NJ: Pearson Education, 2014.
98. Butcher J, Mineka S, Hooley J. Abnormal psychology. 15th ed. Upper Saddle River, NJ: Pearson Education, 2013.
99. Oltmanns T, Emery R. Abnormal psychology. 7th ed. Upper Saddle River, NJ: Pearson Education, 2012.
100. Cardeña E, van Duijl M, Weiner LA, Terhune DB. Possession/trance phenomena. In: Dell PF, O'Neil JA, eds. Dissociation and the dissociative disorders: DSM-V and beyond. New York: Routledge, 2009;171–81.
101. Ross CA. Possession experiences in dissociative identity disorder: a preliminary study. J Trauma Dissociation 2011;12:393–400.
102. Sar V, Alioğlu F, Akyüz G. Experiences of possession and paranormal phenomena among women in the general population: are they related to traumatic stress and dissociation? J Trauma Dissociation 2014;15:303–18.
103. Kihlstrom JR. Dissociative disorders. Annu Rev Clin Psychol 2005;1:227–53.
104. Lynn SJ, Lilienfeld SO, Merckelbach H, et al. The trauma model of dissociation: inconvenient truths and stubborn fictions. Comment on Dalenberg et al. (2012). Psychol Bull 2014;140:896–910.
105. McHugh P. Resolved: multiple personality disorder is an individually and socially created artifact: affirmative. J Am Acad Child Adolesc Psychiatry 1995;34:957–9.
106. Piper A, Merskey H. The persistence of folly: a critical examination of dissociative identity disorder. Part I. The excesses of an improbable concept. Can J Psychiatry 2004;49:592–600.
107. Spanos NP, Burgess C. Hypnosis and multiple personality disorder: a sociocognitive perspective. In: Lynn SJ, Rhue JW, eds. Dissociation: clinical and theoretical perspectives. New York: Guilford, 1994;136–55.
108. Brown D, Frischholz EJ, Scheflin AW. Iatrogenic dissociative identity disorder—an evaluation of the scientific evidence. J Psychiatry Law 1999;27:549–637.
109. Gleaves DH. The sociocognitive model of dissociative identity disorder: a reexamination of the evidence. Psychol Bull 1996;120:42–59.
110. Gleaves DH, Hernandez E, Warner MS. The etiology of dissociative identity disorder: reply to Gee, Allen and Powell (2003). Prof Psychol Res Pr 2003;34:116–8.
111. Kihlstrom JF, Glisky ML, Angiulo MJ. Dissociative tendencies and dissociative disorders. J Abnorm Psychol 1994;103:117–24.
112. Spanos NP, Weekes JR, Menary E, Bertrand LD. Hypnotic interview and age regression procedures in the elicitation of multiple personality symptoms: a simulation study. Psychiatry 1986;49:298–311.
113. Butcher JN, Graham JR, Ben-Porath YS, Tellegen A, Dahlstrom WG. Manual for the administration and scoring of the MMPI-2. Minneapolis: Minnesota University Press, 2001.
114. Brand BL, Chasson GS, Polermo CA, Donato FM, Rhodes KP, Voorhees EF. Truth is in the details: a comparison of MMPI-2 item endorsements by patients with dissociative identity disorder patients versus simulators. J Am Acad Psychiatry Law (forthcoming) .
115. Rogers R, Sewell KW, Gillard ND. Structured Interview of Reported Symptoms-2 (SIRS-2) and professional manual. Lutz, FL: Psychological Assessment Resources, 2010.
116. Brand BL, McNary SW, Loewenstein RJ, Kolos AC, Barr SR. Assessment of genuine and simulated dissociative identity disorder on the structured interview of reported symptoms. J Trauma Dissociation 2006;7:63–85.
117. Yu J, Ross CA, Keyes BB, et al. Dissociative disorders among Chinese inpatients diagnosed with schizophrenia. J Trauma Dissociation 2010;11:358–72.
118. Akyüz G, Doğan O, Sar V, Yargiç LI, Tutkun H. Frequency of dissociative identity disorder in the general population in Turkey. Compr Psychiatry 1999;40:151–9.
119. Gleaves DH, Hernandez E, Warner MS. Corroborating premorbid dissociative symptomatology in dissociative identity disorder. Prof Psychol Res Pr 1999;30:341–5.
120. Chu JA, Frey LM, Ganzel BL, Matthews JA. Memories of childhood abuse: dissociation, amnesia, and corroboration. Am J Psychiatry 1999;156:749–55.

121. Coons PM. Confirmation of childhood abuse in child and adolescent cases of multiple personality disorder and dissociative disorder not otherwise specified. J Nerv Ment Dis 1994;182: 461–4.
122. Myrick AC, Chasson GS, Lanius R, Leventhal B, Brand BL. Treatment of complex dissociative disorders: a comparison of interventions reported by community therapists versus those recommended by experts. J Trauma Dissociation 2015;16: 51–67.
123. Myrick AC, Brand BL, Putnam FW. For better or worse: the role of revictimization and stress in the course of treatment for dissociative disorders. J Trauma Dissociation 2013;14: 375–89.
124. Lauer J, Black DW, Keen P. Multiple personality disorder and borderline personality disorder: distinct entities of variations on a common theme? Ann Clin Psychiatry 1993;5: 129–34.
125. Dell P, Laddis A. Is borderline personality disorder a dissociative disorder? Paper presented at the European Society for Trauma and Dissociation conference, Belfast, April 2010.
126. Korzekwa MI, Dell PF, Links PS, Thabane L, Fougere P. Dissociation in borderline personality disorder: a detailed look. J Trauma Dissociation 2009;10:346–67.
127. Kemp K, Gilbertson AD, Torem MS. The differential diagnosis of multiple personality disorder from borderline personality disorder. Dissociation 1988;1:41–6.
128. Boon S, Draijer N. The differentiation of patients with MPD or DDNOS from patients with a cluster B personality disorder. Dissociation 1993;6:126–35.
129. Hall TJ. Rorschach indices of dissociation across multiple diagnostic groups. Ann Arbor, MI: ProQuest Dissertations, 2002.
130. Sar V, Akyuz G, Kugu N, Ozturk E, Ertem-Vehid H. Axis I dissociative disorder comorbidity in borderline personality disorder and reports of childhood trauma. J Clin Psychiatry 2006; 67:1583–90.
131. Ross CA. Borderline. personality disorder and dissociation. J Trauma Dissociation 2007;8:71–80.
132. Dell PF. Axis II pathology in outpatients with dissociative identity disorder. J Nerv Ment Dis 1998;186:352–6.
133. Ellason JW, Ross CA, Fuchs DL. Assessment of dissociative identity disorder with the Millon Clinical Multiaxial Inventory–II. Psychol Rep 1995;76:895–905.
134. Ross CA, Ferrell L, Schroeder E. Co-occurrence of dissociative identity disorder and borderline personality disorder. J Trauma Dissociation 2014;15:79–90.
135. Sar V, Alioğlu F, Akyuz G, Karabulut S. Dissociative amnesia in dissociative disorders and borderline personality disorder: self-rating assessment in a college population. J Trauma Dissociation 2014;15:477–93.
136. Schmahl C, Bremner JD. Neuroimaging in borderline personality disorder. J Psychiatr Res 2006;40:419–27.
137. Schlumpf YR, Nijenhuis ERS, Chalavi S, et al. Dissociative part-dependent biopsychosocial reactions to backward masked angry and neutral faces: an fMRI study of dissociative identity disorder. Neuroimage Clin 2013;3:54–64.
138. Schlumpf YR, Reinders AA, Nijenhuis ER, Luechinger R, van Osch MJ, Jancke L. Dissociative part-dependent resting-state activity in dissociative identity disorder: a controlled fMRI perfusion study. PLoS One 2014;9:e98795.
139. Sar V, Unal SN, Ozturk E. Frontal and occipital perfusion changes in dissociative identity disorder. Psychiatry Res 2007; 156:217–23.
140. Ellason JW, Ross CA. Two-year follow-up of inpatients with dissociative identity disorder. Am J Psychiatry 1997;154: 832–9.
141. Battle CL, Shea MT, Johnson DM, et al. Childhood maltreatment associated with adult personality disorders: findings from the collaborative longitudinal personality disorders study. J Pers Disord 2004;18:193–211.
142. Classen CC, Pain C, Field NP, Woods P. Posttraumatic personality disorder: a reformulation of complex posttraumatic stress disorder and borderline personality disorder. Psychiatr Clin North Am 2006;29:87–112.
143. Harari D, Bakermans-Kranenburg MJ, van Ijzendoorn MJ. Attachment, disorganization, and dissociation. In: Vermetten E, Dorahy M, Spiegel D, eds. Traumatic dissociation: neurobiology and treatment. Washington, DC: American Psychiatric Publishing, 2007;31–54.
144. Levy KN. The implications of attachment theory and research for understanding borderline personality disorder. Dev Psychopathol 2005;17:959–86.
145. Becker-Blease KA, Deater-Deckard K, Eley T, Freyd JJ, Stevenson J, Plomin R. A genetic analysis of individual differences in dissociative behaviors in childhood and adolescence. J Child Psychol Psychiatry 2004;45:522–32.
146. Jang KL, Paris J, Zweig-Frank H, Livesley WJ. Twin study of dissociative experience. J Nerv Ment Dis 1998;186: 345–51.
147. Torgersen S, Lygren S, Øien PA, et al. A twin study of personality disorders. Compr Psychiatry 2000;41:416–25.
148. Waller NG, Ross CA. The prevalence and biometric structure of pathological dissociation in the general population: taxometric and behavior genetic findings. J Abnorm Psychol 1997;106:499–510.
149. Zanarini MC, Frankenburg FR, Yong L, et al. Borderline psychopathology in the first-degree relatives of borderline and Axis II comparison probands. J Pers Disord 2004;18: 449–7.
150. Sar V, Ross C. Dissociative disorders as a confounding factor in psychiatric research. Psychiatr Clin North Am 2006; 29:129.
151. Gee T, Allen K, Powell RA. Questioning premorbid dissociative symptomatology in dissociative identity disorder: comment on Gleaves, Hernandez and Warner (1999). Prof Psychol Res Pr 2003;34:114–6.
152. Lilienfeld SO. Psychological treatments that cause harm. Perspect Psychol Sci 2007;2:53–70.
153. Lambert K, Lilienfeld SO. Brain stains. Sci Am Mind 2007;18:46.
154. Ellason JW, Ross CA. Millon Clinical Multiaxial Inventory–II. Follow-up of patients with dissociative identity disorder. Psychol Rep 1996;78:707–16.
155. Kluft RP. Treatment of multiple personality disorder. A study of 33 cases. Psychiatr Clin North Am 1984;7:9–29.
156. Ross CA, Haley C. Acute stabilization and three-month follow-up in a trauma program. J Trauma Dissociation 2004; 5:103–12.
157. Coons PM, Bowman ES. Ten-year follow-up study of patients with dissociative identity disorder. J Trauma Dissociation 2001;2:73–89.
158. Coons PM. Treatment progress in 20 patients with multiple personality disorder. J Nerv Ment Dis 1986;174:715–21.
159. Brand BL, McNary SW, Myrick AC, et al. A longitudinal naturalistic study of patients with dissociative disorders treated by community clinicians. Psychol Trauma 2013;5: 301–8.
160. Cronin E, Brand BL, Mattanah JF. The impact of the therapeutic alliance on treatment outcome in patients with dissociative disorders. Eur J Psychotraumatology 2014;5:1–9.
161. Jepsen EKK, Langeland W, Sexton H, Heir T. Inpatient treatment for early sexually abused adults: a naturalistic 12-month follow-up study. Psychol Trauma 2014;6:142–51.

162. Foote B, Smolin Y, Neft DI, Lipschitz D. Dissociative disorders and suicidality in psychiatric outpatients. J Nerv Ment Dis 2008;196:29–36.
163. Mueller-Pfeiffer C, Rufibach K, Perron N, et al. Global functioning and disability in dissociative disorders. Psychiatry Res 2012;200:475–81.
164. Loewenstein RJ. Diagnosis, epidemiology, clinical course, treatment, and cost effectiveness of treatment for dissociative disorders and MPD: report submitted to the Clinton Administration Task Force on Health Care Financing Reform. Dissociation 1994;7:3–11.
165. Ross CA, Dua V. Psychiatric health care costs of multiple personality disorder. Am J Psychother 1993;47:103–12.
166. Lloyd M. How investing in therapeutic services provides a clinical cost saving in the long term. 2011. At http://www.hsj.co.uk/1-september-2011/1200418.issue
167. Myrick AC, Brand BL, McNary SW, et al. An exploration of young adults' progress in treatment for dissociative disorder. J Trauma Dissociation 2012;13:582–95.
168. Kluft RP. The older female patient with a complex chronic dissociative disorder. J Women Aging 2007;19:119–37.

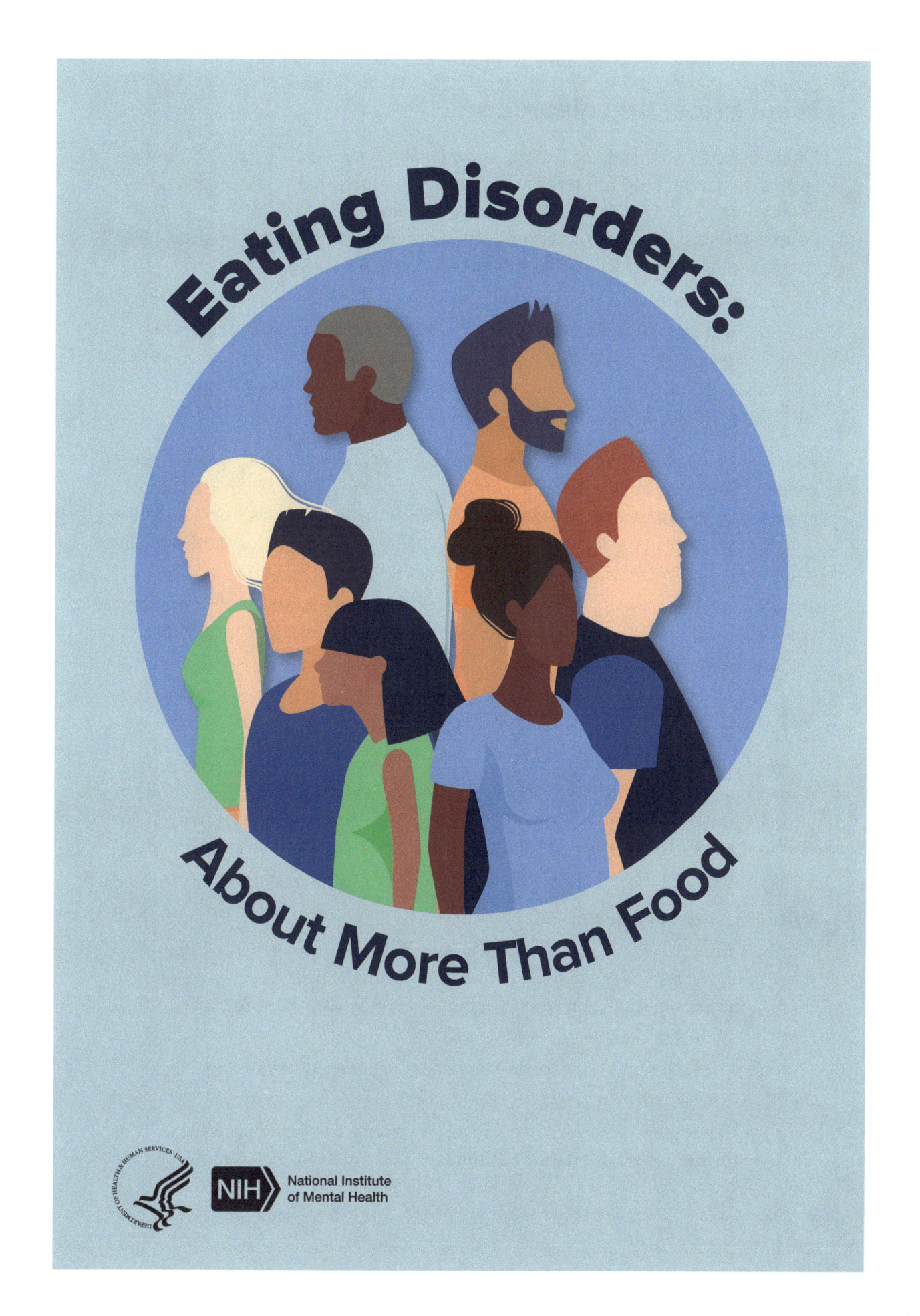

Eating Disorders: About More Than Food

National Institute of Mental Health

What are eating disorders?

Eating disorders are serious, biologically influenced medical illnesses marked by severe disturbances to one's eating behaviors. Although many people may be concerned about their health, weight, or appearance from time to time, some people become fixated or obsessed with weight loss, body weight or shape, and controlling their food intake. These may be signs of an eating disorder.

Eating disorders are not a choice. These disorders can affect a person's physical and mental health. In some cases, they can be life-threatening. With treatment, however, people can recover completely from eating disorders.

Who is at risk for eating disorders?

Eating disorders can affect people of all ages, racial and ethnic backgrounds, body weights, and genders. Even people who appear healthy, such as athletes, can have eating disorders and be extremely ill. People with eating disorders can be underweight, normal weight, or overweight. In other words, you can't tell if someone has an eating disorder by looking at them.

The exact cause of eating disorders is not fully understood. Research suggests a combination of genetic, biological, behavioral, psychological, and social factors can raise a person's risk.

What are the common types of eating disorders?

Common eating disorders include anorexia nervosa, bulimia nervosa, binge-eating disorder, and avoidant restrictive food intake disorder. Each of these disorders is associated with different but sometimes overlapping symptoms. People exhibiting any combination of these symptoms may have an eating disorder and should be evaluated by a health care provider.

What is anorexia nervosa?

Anorexia nervosa is a condition where people avoid food, severely restrict food, or eat very small quantities of only certain foods. They also may weigh themselves repeatedly. Even when dangerously underweight, they may see themselves as overweight.

There are two subtypes of anorexia nervosa: a *restrictive* subtype and a *binge-purge* subtype.

Restrictive: People with the restrictive subtype of anorexia nervosa severely limit the amount and type of food they consume.

Binge-Purge: People with the binge-purge subtype of anorexia nervosa also greatly restrict the amount and type of food they consume. In addition, they may have binge-eating and purging episodes—eating large amounts of food in a short time followed by vomiting or using laxatives or diuretics to get rid of what was consumed.

Symptoms of anorexia nervosa include:

- Extremely restricted eating and/or intensive and excessive exercise
- Extreme thinness (emaciation)
- A relentless pursuit of thinness and unwillingness to maintain a normal or healthy weight
- Intense fear of gaining weight
- Distorted body or self-image that is heavily influenced by perceptions of body weight and shape
- Denial of the seriousness of low body weight

Over time, anorexia nervosa can lead to numerous serious health consequences, including:

- Thinning of the bones (osteopenia or osteoporosis)
- Mild anemia
- Muscle wasting and weakness
- Brittle hair and nails
- Dry and yellowish skin
- Growth of fine hair all over the body (lanugo)
- Severe constipation
- Low blood pressure
- Slowed breathing and pulse
- Damage to the structure and function of the heart
- Drop in internal body temperature, causing a person to feel cold all the time
- Lethargy, sluggishness, or feeling tired all the time
- Infertility
- Brain damage
- Multiple organ failure

Anorexia nervosa can be fatal. It has an extremely high death (mortality) rate compared with other mental disorders. People with anorexia are at risk of dying from medical complications associated with starvation. Suicide is the second leading cause of death for people diagnosed with anorexia nervosa.

Studies & Statistics / Eating Disorders: About More Than Food

> If you or someone you know is in immediate distress or is thinking about hurting themselves, call the **National Suicide Prevention Lifeline** toll-free at 1-800-273-TALK (8255). You also can text the **Crisis Text Line** (HELLO to 741741) or use the Lifeline Chat at the **National Suicide Prevention Lifeline** website at **https://suicidepreventionlifeline.org**. If you suspect a medical emergency, seek medical attention or call 911 immediately.

What is bulimia nervosa?

Bulimia nervosa is a condition where people have recurrent episodes of eating unusually large amounts of food and feeling a lack of control over their eating. This binge eating is followed by behaviors that compensate for the overeating to prevent weight gain, such as forced vomiting, excessive use of laxatives or diuretics, fasting, excessive exercise, or a combination of these behaviors. Unlike those with anorexia nervosa, people with bulimia nervosa may maintain a normal weight or be overweight.

Symptoms and health consequences of bulimia nervosa include:

- Chronically inflamed and sore throat
- Swollen salivary glands in the neck and jaw area
- Worn tooth enamel and increasingly sensitive and decaying teeth from exposure to stomach acid when vomiting
- Acid reflux disorder and other gastrointestinal problems
- Intestinal distress and irritation from laxative abuse
- Severe dehydration from purging
- Electrolyte imbalance (too low or too high levels of sodium, calcium, potassium, and other minerals), which can lead to stroke or heart attack

What is binge-eating disorder?

Binge-eating disorder is a condition where people lose control of their eating and have reoccurring episodes of eating unusually large amounts of food. Unlike bulimia nervosa, periods of binge eating are not followed by purging, excessive exercise, or fasting. As a result, people with binge-eating disorder are often overweight or obese.

Symptoms of binge-eating disorder include:

- Eating unusually large amounts of food in a short amount of time, for example, within two hours
- Eating rapidly during binge episodes
- Eating even when full or not hungry
- Eating until uncomfortably full
- Eating alone or in secret to avoid embarrassment
- Feeling distressed, ashamed, or guilty about eating
- Frequent dieting, possibly without weight loss

What is avoidant restrictive food intake disorder?

Avoidant restrictive food intake disorder (ARFID), previously known as selective eating disorder, is a condition where people limit the amount or type of food eaten. Unlike anorexia nervosa, people with ARFID do not have a distorted body image or extreme fear of gaining weight. ARFID is most common in middle childhood and usually has an earlier onset than other eating disorders. Many children go through phases of picky eating, but a child with ARFID does not eat enough calories to grow and develop properly, and an adult with ARFID does not eat enough calories to maintain basic body function.

Symptoms of ARFID include:

- Dramatic restriction of types or amount of food eaten
- Lack of appetite or interest in food
- Dramatic weight loss
- Upset stomach, abdominal pain, or other gastrointestinal issues with no other known cause
- Limited range of preferred foods that becomes even more limited ("picky eating" that gets progressively worse)

How are eating disorders treated?

Eating disorders can be treated successfully. Early detection and treatment are important for a full recovery. People with eating disorders are at higher risk for suicide and medical complications.

A person's family can play a crucial role in treatment. Family members can encourage the person with eating or body image issues to seek help. They also can provide support during treatment and can be a great ally to both the individual and the health care provider. Research suggests that incorporating the family into treatment for eating disorders can improve treatment outcomes, particularly for adolescents.

Treatment plans for eating disorders include psychotherapy, medical care and monitoring, nutritional counseling, medications, or a combination of these approaches. Typical treatment goals include:

- Restoring adequate nutrition
- Bringing weight to a healthy level
- Reducing excessive exercise
- Stopping binge-purge and binge-eating behaviors

People with eating disorders also may have other mental disorders (such as depression or anxiety) or problems with substance use. It's critical to treat any co-occurring conditions as part of the treatment plan.

Specific forms of psychotherapy ("talk therapy") and cognitive-behavioral approaches can treat certain eating disorders effectively. For general information about psychotherapies, visit **www.nimh.nih.gov/psychotherapies**.

Research also suggests that medications may help treat some eating disorders and co-occurring anxiety or depression related to eating disorders. Information about medications changes frequently, so talk to your health care provider. Visit the U.S. Food and Drug Administration (FDA) website at **www.fda.gov/drugsatfda** for the latest warnings, patient medication guides, and FDA-approved medications.

Where can I find help?

If you're unsure where to get help, your health care provider is a good place to start. Your health care provider can refer you to a qualified mental health professional, such as a psychiatrist or psychologist, who has experience treating eating disorders.

You can learn more about getting help and finding a health care provider on the National Institute of Mental Health (NIMH) webpage, Help for Mental Illnesses, at **www.nimh.nih.gov/findhelp**. If you need help identifying a provider in your area, call the Substance Abuse and Mental Health Services Administration (SAMHSA) Treatment Referral Helpline at 1-800-662-HELP (4357). You also can search SAMHSA's online Behavioral Health Treatment Services Locator (**https://findtreatment.samhsa.gov**), which lists facilities and programs that provide mental health services.

For tips on talking with your health care provider about your mental health, read NIMH's fact sheet, Taking Control of Your Mental Health: Tips for Talking With Your Health Care Provider, at **www.nimh.nih.gov/talkingtips**.

For additional resources, visit the Agency for Healthcare Research and Quality website at **www.ahrq.gov/questions**.

Are there clinical trials studying eating disorders?

NIMH supports a wide range of research, including clinical trials that look at new ways to prevent, detect, or treat diseases and conditions, including eating disorders. Although individuals may benefit from being part of a clinical trial, participants should be aware that the primary purpose of a clinical trial is to gain new scientific knowledge so that others may be better helped in the future.

Researchers at NIMH and around the country conduct clinical trials with patients and healthy volunteers. Talk to your health care provider about clinical trials, their benefits and risks, and whether one is right for you. For more information about clinical research and how to find clinical trials being conducted around the country, visit **www.nimh.nih.gov/clinicaltrials**.

ABCS of Heart Health
To reduce the risk of heart attack or stroke

Every year, Americans suffer more than **1.5 million heart attacks and strokes.** But following the ABCS can help reduce your risk and improve your heart health.

A: Take **a**spirin as directed by your health care professional.

B: Control your **b**lood pressure.

C: Manage your **c**holesterol.

S: Don't **s**moke.

A Take aspirin as directed by your health care professional.

Ask your health care professional if aspirin can reduce your risk of having a heart attack or stroke. Be sure to tell your health care professional if you have a family history of heart disease or stroke, and mention your own medical history.

B Control your blood pressure.

Blood pressure measures the force of blood pushing against the walls of the arteries. If your blood pressure stays high for a long time, you may suffer from high blood pressure (also called hypertension). High blood pressure increases your risk for heart attack or stroke more than any other risk factor. Find out what your blood pressure numbers are, and ask your health care professional what those numbers mean for your health. If you have high blood pressure, work with your health care professional to lower it.

C Manage your cholesterol.

Cholesterol is a waxy substance produced by the liver and found in certain foods. Your body needs cholesterol, but when you have too much, it can build up in your arteries and cause heart disease. There are different types of cholesterol: One type is "good" and can protect you from heart disease, but another type is "bad" and can increase your risk. Talk to your health care professional about cholesterol and how to lower your bad cholesterol if it's too high.

S Don't smoke.

Smoking raises your blood pressure, which increases your risk for heart attack and stroke. If you smoke, quit. Talk with your health care professional about ways to help you stick with your decision. It's never too late to quit smoking. Call 1-800-QUIT-NOW today.

Million Hearts® is a national initiative to prevent 1 million heart attacks and strokes by 2017. It is led by the Centers for Disease Control and Prevention and the Centers for Medicare & Medicaid Services, two agencies of the Department of Health and Human Services.

The Million Hearts® word and logo marks and associated trade dress are owned by the U.S. Department of Health and Human Services (HHS). Use of these marks does not imply endorsement by HHS.

Heart disease and stroke are the first and fourth leading causes of death in the United States. Together, these diseases cause 1 in 3 deaths. **The good news is that you can reduce your risk by following the ABCS!**

Studies & Statistics / ABCs of Heart Health

Rosa was caring for her granddaughter when she felt a sharp pain in her chest that didn't go away. At the hospital, the health care professional told her that she had high blood pressure and that it had caused a heart attack. Rosa was surprised—she didn't feel bad most of the time and didn't know she had high blood pressure. The health care professional gave Rosa medicine to help control her blood pressure and prevent another heart attack. Rosa takes her medicine every day so she can keep her blood pressure under control. It's important to Rosa to stay healthy. She wants to see her granddaughter grow up and get married one day.

What do I need to know about high blood pressure?

High blood pressure is the leading cause of heart attack and stroke in the United States. It can also damage your eyes and kidneys. **One in three American adults has high blood pressure, and only about half of them have it under control.**

How is blood pressure measured? Two numbers (for example, 140/90) help determine blood pressure. The first number measures systolic pressure, which is the pressure in the blood vessels when the heart beats. The second number measures diastolic pressure, which is the pressure in the blood vessels when the heart rests between beats.

When and how should I take my blood pressure? Take your blood pressure regularly, even if you feel fine. Generally, people with high blood pressure have no symptoms. You can take your blood pressure at home, at many pharmacies, and at your doctor's office.

The doctor is not the only health care professional who can help you follow the ABCS. Nurses, pharmacists, community health workers, health coaches, and other professionals can work with you and your doctor to help you achieve your health goals.

Need confidential health information? Call the Su Familia Helpline at 1-866-783-2645 today.

Su Familia: The National Hispanic Family Health Helpline offers free, reliable information on a wide range of health issues in Spanish and English. The health promotion advisors can help Hispanic clients find affordable health care services in their community.

How can I control my blood pressure? Work with your health care professional to make a plan for controlling your blood pressure. Be sure to follow these guidelines:

- **Eat a healthy diet.** Choose foods low in trans fat and sodium (salt). Most people in the United States consume more sodium than recommended. Everyone age 2 and up should consume less than 2,300 milligrams (mg) of sodium per day. Adults age 51 and older; African Americans of all ages; and people with high blood pressure, diabetes, or chronic kidney disease should consume even less than that: only 1,500 mg of sodium per day.

- **Get moving.** Staying physically active will help you control your weight and strengthen your heart. Try walking for 10 minutes, 3 times a day, 5 days a week.

- **Take your medications.** If you have high blood pressure, your health care professional may give you medicine to help control it. It's important to follow your health care professional's instructions when taking the medication and to keep taking it even if you feel well. Tell your health care professional if the medicine makes you feel bad. Your health care team can suggest different ways to reduce side effects or recommend another medicine that may have fewer side effects.

Stay Connected

facebook.com/MillionHearts

twitter.com/@MillionHeartsUS

Visit millionhearts.hhs.gov and pledge to live a longer, healthier life today.

Studies & Statistics / ABCs of Heart Health

Eat Smart, Move More!

Building healthy habits doesn't happen overnight, but **making small changes every day can make a big difference for your heart and brain health**. Eating a healthy diet, maintaining a healthy weight, and getting enough physical activity can help you lower your risk for heart disease and stroke.

This calendar can help you reach your healthy eating and physical activity goals one step at a time. Here are some ideas to get you started and some space for you to fill in your own goals. Don't forget to celebrate the big AND small wins—you got this!

Sunday	Monday	Tuesday	Wednesday	Thursday	Friday	Saturday
	Experiment with a new heart-healthy recipe, like these oven-baked sweet potatoes. https://bit.ly/2JioEwG		Find small ways to get active throughout the day. Take the stairs, or power walk during your lunch break! http://bit.ly/2mOagPK			Headed to the grocery store? Check food labels for the amount of sodium per serving, and see if there are low/no sodium options available. http://bit.ly/2GcPqDw
Try mapping out your meals for the week. Planning ahead can help you stick to a healthy eating lifestyle! http://bit.ly/2sXykUo		Instead of dining out, cook meals at home and pack leftovers to help cut back on sodium. These Brussels sprouts would make the perfect side! http://bit.ly/2memcbY		Simple swaps can make your meals and snacks healthier. Go for veggies with hummus instead of chips and dip. http://bit.ly/3t0TF9u		
	Power through your day with smart snacking. Bring sliced apples or bell peppers to satisfy your cravings. http://bit.ly/2iPRnGM		Some of the saltiest foods may not even taste salty. Watch out for the top sources of sodium in your diet. http://bit.ly/2ccVH3a			Move a little more every day. Track your physical activities for the week—even vacuuming and gardening could count! http://bit.ly/2HVe8dg
		Add flavor without the salt. Try a new spice or herb, like paprika or thyme. https://bit.ly/3eE20Mz		Rethink your drink. Instead of soda or sweetened juices, try flavoring your water with cucumbers or lemons. http://bit.ly/2k5Wun0	Ordering from a restaurant? Split your meal with a friend or family member to lower your sodium intake. http://bit.ly/2aXvxfR	

Additional resources

- Recipes for a Heart-Healthy Lifestyle (Million Hearts®)
- Sodium Reduction (CDC)
- Healthy Eating for a Healthy Weight (CDC)
- DASH Eating Plan (NHLBI)
- Healthy Eating Tools (MyPlate)
- Move Your Way (HHS)

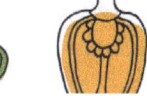

233

The Surgeon General's Call to Action to Control Hypertension

Executive Summary

Nearly half of U.S. adults have hypertension, or high blood pressure, and only about one in four of those individuals has their hypertension under control. Hypertension is a major preventable risk factor for heart disease and stroke, which are the first and fifth leading causes of death in the United States, respectively. People of all ages are impacted by hypertension, but certain groups have disproportionately high rates of hypertension and its related health consequences.

The Surgeon General's Call to Action to Control Hypertension (*Call to Action*) seeks to avert the negative health effects of hypertension by identifying evidence-based interventions that can be implemented, adapted, and expanded in diverse settings across the United States. Although many of the interventions described in this *Call to Action* can help prevent hypertension, the focus of the publication is on improving control among the millions of U.S. adults who already have hypertension. This *Call to Action* outlines three goals to improve hypertension control across the United States, and each goal is supported by strategies intended to accelerate actions to achieve success:

- **Goal 1.** Make hypertension control a national priority.
- **Goal 2.** Ensure that the places where people live, learn, work, and play support hypertension control.
- **Goal 3.** Optimize patient care for hypertension control.

The *Call to Action* recognizes the conditions in which people are born, live, learn, work, play, worship and age directly impact opportunities for success and drive health equality. Broadly achieving health equity in the U.S. will require dynamic societal shifts.

Goals and Strategies to Improve Hypertension Control

Prioritize Control Nationally
- ☑ Increase Awareness of Health Risks
- ☑ Recognize Economic Burden
- ☑ Eliminate Disparities

Cultivate Community Supports
- ☑ Promote Physical Activity Opportunities
- ☑ Promote Healthy Food Opportunities
- ☑ Connect to Lifestyle Change Resources

Optimize Patient Care
- ☑ Use Standardized Treatment Approaches
- ☑ Promote Team-Based Care
- ☑ Empower and Equip Patients
- ☑ Recognize and Reward Clinicians

Promoting Health Equity

Source: Adapted from the U.S. Department of Health and Human Services. *The Surgeon General's Call to Action to Control Hypertension.* Washington, DC: U.S. Dept. of Health and Human Services, Office of the Surgeon General; 2020.

In support of advancements in health equity, this *Call to Action* focuses on specific and tangible interventions that can be tailored, replicated and scaled to impact one of the highest burden health conditions in the U.S. This *Call to Action* provides targeted strategies that different sectors can take to collectively improve hypertension control across the United States.

In many areas, we know what works, but we need to replicate and expand these efforts and continue to explore new interventions to achieve control across all population groups. We must act to preserve the nation's cardiovascular health now and into the future. **Together, we've got this!**

Additional Resources

Surgeon General's Call to Action to Control Hypertension
- **Sectors and Strategies**
- **Partner Toolkit**

CDC High Blood Pressure

Hypertension Control Change Package

We've Got This!

High blood pressure control is possible.

For more information, visit **surgeongeneral.gov** or **cdc.gov/bloodpressure**.

Studies & Statistics / Hypertension and Blood Pressure

Managing My Blood Pressure

Questions to Ask My Doctor

Measuring Blood Pressure
- How often should I measure my blood pressure?
- How can I measure my blood pressure outside the doctor's office?
- What do I need to know about correctly measuring my blood pressure?

Lifestyle and Habits
- What foods or drinks should I have or avoid to help me keep a healthy blood pressure?
- What types of physical activity are right for me to do on a regular basis?

Blood Pressure Medicines
- If I need to start taking blood pressure medicine, what type is best for me?
- I am currently taking blood pressure medicine. Do I need to adjust my dose or try a new type? How is my progress?
- What are the possible side effects of my current or new medicines?
- How often should I refill my medicine?
- What time of day should I take my blood pressure medicine?
- Should I take it with or without food?
- What should I do if I forget to take my blood pressure medicine?

My Challenges
I will talk to my doctor about any challenges I have measuring or controlling my blood pressure, including:
- ☐ Taking blood pressure medicine/s on time and in the right amount
- ☐ Side effects from my blood pressure medicines
- ☐ Measuring blood pressure on my own
- ☐ Making healthy lifestyle changes

My goal blood pressure is:
_____

Notes
_____

Visit **cdc.gov/bloodpressure** for tips and resources.

National Center for Chronic Disease Prevention and Health Promotion
Division for Heart Disease and Stroke Prevention

Studies & Statistics / Hypertension and Blood Pressure

My Blood Pressure Log

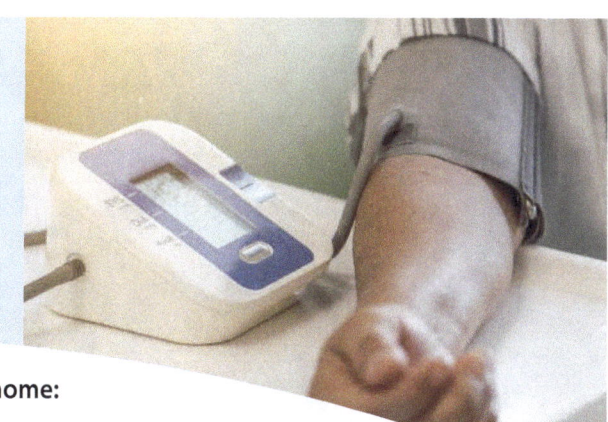

Try these tips for keeping track of your blood pressure at home:
- Always take your blood pressure at the same time every day.
- Take at least two readings, 1 or 2 minutes apart.
- Visit **cdc.gov/bloodpressure** to learn how to correctly measure your blood pressure.

Date	Morning			Evening		
	Time of reading	Reading 1	Reading 2	Time of reading	Reading 1	Reading 2
Sept. 1, 2022	8 a.m.	139/82	141/82	6 p.m.	145/85	142/83

National Center for Chronic Disease Prevention and Health Promotion
Division for Heart Disease and Stroke Prevention

ERECTILE DYSFUNCTION

The following information is a summary of materials featured in the "Men's Health" Whole Health overview. It is meant to be a quick reference for use at the point of care. For more details and a list of references, refer to the overview.

Erectile Dysfunction (ED) is a common condition that many men experience, especially as they age. A study of U.S. men revealed that 52% of men 40-70 years old suffered some level of erectile dysfunction.

A good tool to measure the severity of ED is the International Index of Erectile Function (IIEF). This is a self-administered tool that can be used to follow treatment response during follow-up appointments as well.

Studies have demonstrated a relationship between the severity of ED and abdominal circumference. Having an abdominal circumference over 40 inches increases the risk of ED by two to three times. Abdominal circumference should be measured using a tape measure at the level of the umbilicus. The pant waist size is not a good measure as many men wear their pants below their true waist.

MAINTAIN IDEAL BODY WEIGHT

This is probably the most important thing a man can do. As belly fat increases, there is an increase in activity of the enzyme aromatase, which converts testosterone in the adipose cells into estrogen. A study in Italy showed that exercising and losing weight can significantly improve erectile function. Meeting with a nutritionist or dietician is a good way to start the conversation on better diets and sensible weight-loss plans.

AVOID XENOBIOTICS

Xenobiotics are compounds from the environment that mimic the body's hormones. Research has shown that the average testosterone level in men has gradually dropped over the years; this can influence erectile function. This may be in part due to all the environmental toxins that have accumulated over the years. The main toxins are:

- **Bisphenol A (BPA)**. BPA is found in plastics. To avoid it, don't microwave food in plastic containers. Avoid plastic containers with the numbers 3, 6, or 7 engraved in the triangle on the product. Buy BPA-free water containers. Drinking water out of containers with the numbers 2, 4, 5, or 7 is OK. Do not drink out of Styrofoam containers.
- **Phthalates**. These chemicals are used in plastics, coatings, lubricants, and binders. Many are found in hygiene products such as shampoos and colognes. A useful web site on phthalate-free products is the Guide to Less Toxic Products website
- **Organophosphates**. These are mainly found in pesticides and herbicides. Eat organic when able to avoid exposure to them.

Studies & Statistics / Erectile Dysfunction

EAT WELL

Foods to avoid

- Excessive sugar
- Excessive caffeine
- Red meat and other sources of animal fat
- Excessive dairy products
- Food dyes
- Processed foods

Foods to include

- Green tea
- Multicolored fruits and vegetables
- Nuts (particularly Brazil nuts which are rich in selenium—two a day is plenty)
- Fiber (covered by eating fruits and vegetables)
- Ground flax seed (1 tablespoon a day)
- Soy products (soy milk instead of cow's milk)

CONSIDER DIETARY SUPPLEMENTS

Note: Please refer to the *Passport to Whole Health*, Chapter 15 on Dietary Supplements for more information about how to determine whether or not a specific supplement is appropriate for a given individual. Supplements are not regulated with the same degree of oversight as medications, and it is important that clinicians keep this in mind. Products vary greatly in terms of accuracy of labeling, presence of adulterants, and the legitimacy of claims made by the manufacturer.

Some natural treatments for ED include:

- **L-arginine:** 8 gm along with adenosine monophosphate 200 mcg 1-2 hours before intercourse can help. This was found to be effective and well tolerated.
- **Panax ginseng (Korean or red ginseng)** has been found in a study to improve erectile function to some degree in two-thirds of men studied. The dose studied was 3,000 mcg daily.
- **Oligomeric proanthocyanidins** (OPCs) are substances found in grape seed and pine bark. Small, clinical trials have demonstrated promise.
- **Horny goat weed** is not recommended because of lack of research and the challenges of finding a quality product.

KEEP IN MIND THAT ED MAY BE AN INDICATION OF VASCULAR DISEASE

If ED starts suddenly and there are other risk factors for heart disease, such as diabetes, tobacco use, hypertension, and hyperlipidemia, consider screening for cardiovascular and peripheral vascular disease.

REMEMBER MIND-BODY INFLUENCES

Finally, it is important to recognize the impact that emotions and mental state have on sexual function. It can be helpful to explore those connections and be open to discussing issues related to mental health, referring to a professional counselor or psychologist as appropriate. If Cognitive Therapy is unhelpful, clinical hypnosis or Guided Imagery may be helpful for working with psychological or energetic blocks to healthy sexual function.

RESOURCE LINKS

- Men's Health: https://wholehealth.wisc.edu/overviews/mens-health/
- International Index of Erectile Function (IIEF): http://www.hiv.va.gov/provider/manual-primary-care/urology-tool2.asp
- Guide to Less Toxic Products: http://lesstoxicguide.ca/
- Passport to Whole Health: https://wholehealth.wiscweb.wisc.edu/wp-content/uploads/sites/414/2018/09/Passport-to-Whole-Health-3rd-Edition-2018.pdf

AUTHOR

"Erectile Dysfunction" was written by Robert Z. Edwards, MD (2014, updated 2020).

This Whole Health tool was made possible through a collaborative effort between the University of Wisconsin Integrative Health Program, VA Office of Patient Centered Care and Cultural Transformation, and Pacific Institute for Research and Evaluation.

SCIENCE OF MEDICINE

A History of Developments to Improve *in vitro* Fertilization

by Ashley M. Eskew, MD & Emily S. Jungheim, MD

The central goal of infertility treatment has not changed over time—to help build healthy families.

Ashley Eskew, MD, (left), is Fellow, and Emily S. Jungheim, MD, MSCI, (right), is Associate Professor, Division of Reproductive Endocrinology and Infertility, Department of Obstetrics and Gynecology, Washington University School of Medicine.
Contact: eskewa@wudosis.wustl.edu

Abstract

Methods of *in vitro* fertilization (IVF) have advanced dramatically since the first IVF baby was born in 1978. Originally yielding single-digit success rates, IVF is now successful in nearly 50% of cases in which the woman is younger than 35 years. Here, we describe the improvements in laboratory techniques and advances in our abilities to manipulate reproductive physiology that have facilitated this improvement. Additionally, we describe efforts to ensure safety standards in this competitive field.

A Brief History of *in vitro* Fertilization

Human reproduction research has always been fraught with both scientific and ethical challenges that initially hindered development of treatments for infertility. However, in the 1960s and 1970s, our understanding of the events in human oocyte fertilization grew to the point that *in vitro* fertilization (IVF) of human oocytes became possible. Ultimately, this knowledge led to the widely acclaimed first live birth of a "test tube baby," Louise Brown, in England in 1978.[1] In this sentinel IVF birth, the mother had a natural menstrual cycle, physicians laparoscopically retrieved a single pre-ovulatory oocyte from her ovary, fertilized it *in vitro*, and then transferred the resulting eight-cell embryo into her uterus.

Three years later, the first IVF baby in the U.S., and the 15th worldwide, was born. In this case, rather than rely on the one oocyte that would be produced naturally, the mother was injected for several days with human menopausal gonadotropin to induce several follicles in the ovary to produce oocytes. After this process, termed controlled ovarian stimulation (COS), physicians laparoscopically retrieved the pre-ovulatory oocytes, fertilized them *in vitro*, and then transferred day 3 or day 5 embryos into the mother's uterus. In 1985, the first IVF baby in Missouri was born to a couple who underwent IVF at Washington University, and delivered at what is now Barnes-Jewish Hospital[2]. Since that time, the practice of IVF has continued to evolve at an astounding pace.

Today, IVF accounts for millions of births worldwide and 1-3% of all births every year in the U.S. and Europe.[3] The increasing demand for fertility treatment drives research and development of technologies to optimize IVF regimens and success. In the vast majority of IVF cases, infertile couples undergo treatment to conceive a genetically-related child. However, couples are also undergoing IVF so that their embryos can be genetically tested to decrease transmission of single-gene mutations associated with morbidity.[4,5] Additionally, use of donor sperm and oocytes is becoming increasingly common, and women who are unable to carry a pregnancy are now able to use gestational carriers.

Below, we highlight several of the major milestones that have made IVF an extremely effective tool to care for these patients.

243

Controlled Ovarian Stimulation

The initial studies of IVF conducted in women undergoing natural menstrual cycles yielded on average 0.7 oocytes per retrieval and a 6% per cycle pregnancy rate.[6] In the 1980s, researchers at the Jones Institute in Norfolk, Virginia, began injecting women with gonadotropins to stimulate multiple ovarian follicles to produce oocytes. These oocytes were then fertilized *in vitro,* and the healthiest appearing embryos were implanted in the woman's uterus. This advent of controlled ovarian stimulation (COS) improved average oocyte yields to 2.1–2.6 and average pregnancy rates to 23.5% per cycle in 1982 and 30% in 1983.[4,6] Initially, human chorionic gonadotropin (hCG) was used to trigger ovulation because it is physiologically homologous to luteinizing hormone, which increases rapidly in a natural cycle to trigger ovulation. In early IVF procedures, an important concern was premature ovulation, which would make retrieving oocytes impossible despite careful and labor-intensive COS. However, two innovations to IVF practice, including the use of gonadotropin releasing hormone (GnRH) agonists in the 1980s and of GnRH antagonists in 2001, made it possible to prevent premature ovulation and reliably control oocyte retrieval. Several different medication regimens exist, but all follow the same concept: injectable medications upregulate endogenous hormones to recruit multiple ovarian follicles to yield multiple oocytes at retrieval.[7]

Ovarian Hyperstimulation Syndrome

Two problems occurred as a result of injections of supraphysiologic doses of gonadotropins. First, to improve the chances that a woman would become pregnant with one fetus that would survive to term, physicians began fertilizing multiple oocytes and implanting multiple embryos. This practice sometimes results in women carrying twins and even higher order multiples of fetuses, putting the fetuses at risk of low birth weight and preterm birth. Second, the most common and severe iatrogenic complication of ovarian stimulation is ovarian hyperstimulation syndrome (OHSS). OHSS occurs when the ovaries are excessively stimulated and then either triggered with injected hCG to stimulate ovulation or by the endogenous increase in hCG that occurs when a woman gets pregnant. OHSS is characterized by hemoconcentration from leaky vessels and third spacing of fluid that leads to ascites and electrolyte abnormalities. Symptoms range from mild abdominal distention to renal failure and death as a result of thromboembolic phenomena or end-organ damage. Despite extensive research, the exact pathogenesis of this syndrome remains unclear but is noted to have increasing incidence with an increasing number of developing follicles and elevated levels of estradiol, which is made by the ovarian follicles. To address this concern, in 1979, physicians began monitoring COS by serially measuring the serum estradiol levels and transvaginally assessing ovarian follicles to better monitor for risk factors. Identifying patients at risk allowed physicians to take preventative measures such as adjusting medications appropriately and more frequently monitoring symptoms.[8-10]

The current limitation to COS is that it requires time and labor-intensive monitoring. Additionally, gonadotropin is rapidly degraded in the body, so women have to undergo daily injections for 10 days. However, scientists such as Washington University professor Irving Boime are developing long-acting forms of gonadotropins that may one day reduce the number of required injections and the amount of monitoring.[11]

Embryo Culture

Since the early days of *in vitro* embryo culture, efforts have been directed toward improving the culture system to optimize embryo development and increase the number of high-quality embryos available for transfer. Initially, embryo culture media was fashioned from media intended for culture of somatic cells and supplemented with serum.[12,13] Numerous researchers have optimized media for embryo metabolism and development by supplementing it with various macromolecules, altering the energy substrate composition and amino acid balance, and adding growth factors. For many years, laboratories made their own culture media, but now it is commercially produced, resulting in improved consistency and quality control between different laboratories and practices.[14] Much attention will undoubtedly continue to be directed toward refining culture media to further optimize embryo development and clinical outcomes.

Improvements in embryo culture over the years have allowed us to extend *in vitro* culture of embryos to the blastocyst stage, permitting detailed morphologic assessment of embryos and better selection of embryos for transfer. This has been key to our ability to maximize pregnancy rates in IVF while minimizing the number of embryos transferred and thus minimizing the risk of multiple gestations. Extended culture has also allowed us to perform preimplantation genetic testing of embryos, a process that is best applied when the embryos are far enough developed in culture to sustain removal of several cells for genetic testing.

Improved embryo culture, in combination with improved COS, allow us to generate more embryos than are initially transferred. Today, approximately 50% of IVF cycles performed via COS in our center result in the creation of excess embryos of good quality that can be frozen for the patient's future use. Thus, the woman can often avoid further COS injections and invasive oocyte retrieval. This process is now efficient enough that women facing gonadotoxic treatments such as chemotherapy can preserve future fertility by undergoing COS and having their oocytes retrieved and frozen.

Preimplantation Genetic Testing

Before 1990, options to prevent transmission of genetic defects were limited to invasive techniques such as chorionic villus sampling and amniocentesis, after which termination could be offered if the fetus was found to be affected. Throughout the 1990s, as surplus embryos became available, techniques were developed to utilize the time between days three and five after oocyte fertilization as an opportunity to identify which embryos were affected by chromosomal imbalance or a specific gene disorder before transfer to the uterus.[15] The initial technique was to screen cleavage-stage embryos by fluorescence in situ hybridization, but that was later found to lower birth rates and cause more harm than good.[16,17] Now, we biopsy cells from the trophectoderm of blastocyst-stage embryos, (see Figure 1), and perform one of two types of preimplantation genetic testing. The first, preimplantation genetic diagnosis (PGD) applies when one or both genetic parents carry a mutation, such as those linked to Huntington's disease or cystic fibrosis, and testing is performed to ensure the single-gene trait has not been passed to the embryo. PGD is commonly done by polymerase chain reaction as this method is more accurate than fluorescence in situ hybridization and allows us to obtain sufficient genetic material for evaluation from only a few cells, thus decreasing harm. Although this process requires vitrification of the embryo to allow sufficient time for analysis, recent studies suggest that cycles using frozen and fresh embryos are nearly equally successful, making this a feasible option for couples.[18,19] Importantly, PGD does not appear to increase the risk of obstetric complications, including fetal malformation related to the biopsy procedure.[20]

The other type of testing is preimplantation genetic screening (PGS), which is used to look for embryonic aneuploidy. Although not routinely recommended as a standard of care in IVF as it has not been shown to improve outcomes in low-risk patients, PGS can be beneficial in a select patient population. PGS offers prognostic value for patients who are deemed high risk for embryo aneuploidy (abnormal number of chromosomes), including those of advanced maternal age (≥35 years old) and those diagnosed with recurrent pregnancy loss. Patients should receive genetic counseling

Figure 1: A pipette (left) holding a blastocyst near the inner cell mass (arrow) while a needle (right) biopsies trophectoderm cells.

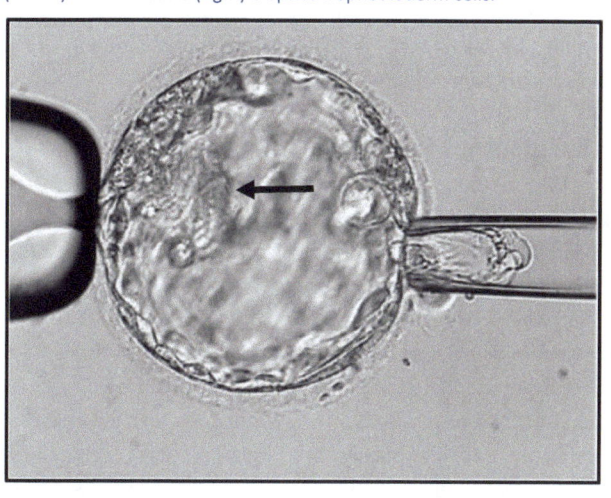

before electing PGS or PGD to ensure they fully understand the risks and limitations of these techniques. Genetics will certainly continue to play a large role in shaping the future of practice in reproductive medicine, and although innumerable advances have been made, there is still work to be done to discern how PGS and PGD are best applied in IVF.

Reducing the Risk of Multiple Gestations Associated with IVF

In the early years of IVF, several embryos were implanted with the hope that at least one would survive, often leading to multiple births. For example, in 2004, 36.6% of women younger than 35 years of age undergoing IVF had a live birth after being implanted with, on average, 2.5 embryos per cycle. As a result, 32.7% of the women delivered twins and 4.9% delivered triplets. Improvements in embryo culture and cryopreservation techniques, in addition to guidelines regarding the number of embryos to be transferred, (see Table 1), have reduced the quantity but increased the quality of embryos transferred, thus reducing the risk of multiples. Thus, in 2014, 48.7% of women younger than 35 undergoing

Table 1
Recommended limits on the numbers of embryos to transfer

Age (years) Prognosis	< 35	35-37	38-40	41-42
Cleavage Stage Embryos				
- Favorable	1	1	≤ 3	≤ 4
- All others	≤ 2	≤ 3	≤ 4	≤ 5
Blastocysts				
- Euploid	1	1	1	1
- Favorable	1	1	≤ 2	≤ 3
- All others	≤ 2	≤ 2	≤ 3	≤ 3

Adapted from ASRM Committee Opinion: Limits on number of embryos to transfer. Fertil Steril 2017.

IVF had a live birth—11.8% of those births were twin deliveries, and 0.4% were triplet deliveries. This reduction in multiples is largely the result of minimizing the number of embryos transferred to just one.

IVF Outcomes Reporting

Efforts to track IVF activity and outcomes started in 1985 and were initially voluntary. However, since Congress passed the Fertility Clinic Success Rate and Certification Act in 1992, clinics have been required to report IVF outcomes data to the Centers for Disease Control (CDC) to provide transparency and protect patients from false claims of IVF success.[21,22] Public reporting of outcomes has become increasingly viewed as a promising strategy to improve health care outcomes.[23] IVF success rates for all reputable clinics are now available on the web from both the CDC and the Society for Assisted Reproductive Technology (SART), an affiliate of the American Society for Reproductive Medicine.[22,24] SART is an excellent resource for both patients and physicians that provides ample information including detailed guides of various ART protocols and procedures, as well as success rates of individual technologies at practices across the country. Their first annual publication was in 1988 and has been increasingly used to help guide continued improvement and evaluation of ART programs. SART reporting differs from that of the CDC in that it includes cycle start information, whereas CDC data only offers outcome statistics for completed cycles.[22,24] More than 90% of clinics are SART members, and the SART registry reports data on more than 95% of ART treatment cycles in the U.S. Between the two reporting systems, a large amount of information is available allowing for detailed analysis of data for transparency and continued opportunities for improvement of patient outcomes. SART also makes it easy for patients to understand the quality of the IVF lab they are entrusting their care to—one of the greatest predictors in their chances of achieving a live birth through IVF.

Conclusion

The field of reproductive endocrinology and infertility has progressed at an astounding pace over the past three decades as we have developed new techniques, medications, testing, and strategies to treat infertile couples. Now, many previously sterile couples are able to conceive, carry, and deliver healthy children of their own. Despite the major advances described here, much attention will remain devoted to assessing the long-term outcomes of the children born as a result of IVF; the oldest child of IVF is merely 38 years old. The central goal of infertility treatment has not changed over time—to help build healthy families.

References

1. Steptoe, PC. Edwards RG. Birth after reimplantation of a human embryo. The Lancet. 1978;312:366.
2. http://www.upi.com/Archives/1985/01/25/First-test-tube-babies-born-in Missouri/8289475477200/
3. Chandra A, Copen CE and Stephen EH (2014) Infertility Service Use in the United States: Data from the National Survey of Family Growth, 1982-2010. National Health Statistics Reports; no 73. Hyattsville, MD: National Center for Health Statistics.
4. Beall SA, DeCherney A. History and challenges surrounding ovarian stimulation in the treatment of infertility. Fertil Steril. 2012;97:795-801.
5. Wang J, Sauer MV. In vitro fertilization (IVF): a review of 3 decades of clinical innovation and technological advancement. Therapeutics and clinical risk management 2006;2:355-64.
6. Edwards RG, Steptoe PC, Purdy JM. Establishing full-term human pregnancies using cleaving embryos grown in vitro. Br J Obstet Gynaecol, 1980;87:737-56.
7. Fritz MA, Speroff L. Clinical Gynecology Endocrinology and Infertility. 8th ed. 2011.
8. Edwards RG, Steptoe PC. Current status of in-vitro fertilisation and implantation of human embryos. Lancet, 1983;2:1265-9.
9. Ylostalo P, Ronnberg L, Jouppila P. Measurement of the ovarian follicle by ultrasound in ovulation induction. Fertil Steril 1979;31:651–5.
10. Smith DH, Picker RH, Sinosich M, Saunders DM. Assessment of ovulation by ultrasound and estradiol levels during spontaneous and induced cycles. Fertil Steril 1980;33:387–90.
11. Fauser BC, Mannaerts BM, Devroey P, Leader A, Boime I, Baird DT. Advances in recombinant DNA techology: corifollitropin alfa, a hybrid molecule with sustained follicle-stimulating activity and reduced injection frequency. Hum Reprod Update. 2009 15(3):309-21.
12. Quinn P, Kerin J, Warnes G. Improved pregnancy rate in human in vitro fertilization with the use of a medium based on the composition of human tubal fluid. Fertil Steril 1985;44:493–8.
13. Menezo Y, Testart J, Perrone D. Serum is not necessary in human in vitro fertilization, early embryo culture, and transfer. Fertil Steril 1984;42:750–5.
14. Swain JE, Carrell D, Cobo A, Meseguer M, Rubio C, Smith GD. Optimizing the culture environment and embryo manipulation to help maintain embryo developmental potential. Fertil Steril 2016;105:571-87.
15. Handyside AH, Kontogianni EH, Hardy K, et al. 1990. Pregnancies from biopsied human preimplantation embryos sexed by Y-specific DNA amplification. Nature, 344:768-70.
16. Fritz MA. Perspectives on the efficacy and indications for preimplantation genetic screening: where are we now? Hum Reprod 2008;23:2617–21.
17. Mastenbroek S, Twisk M, van der Veen F, Repping S. Preimplantation genetic screening: a systematic review and meta-analysis of RCTs. Hum Reprod Update 2011;17:454–66.
18. Preimplantation genetic testing: a Practice Committee opinion. Fertil Steril. 2008:90:S136-S143
19. Schoolcraft WB, Treff NR, Stevens JM, Ferry K, Katz-Jaffe M, Scott RT Jr. Live birth outcome with trophectoderm biopsy, blastocyst vitrification, and single-nucleotide polymorphism microarray-based comprehensive chromosome screening in infertile patients. Fertil Steril 2011;96:638–40.
20. Beukers F, van der Heide M, Middelburg KJ et al. Morphologic abnormalities in 2-year-old children born after in vitro fertilization/intracytoplasmic sperm injection with preimplantation genetic screening: follow- up of a randomized controlled trial. Fertil Steril 2013; 99(2):408-413.
21. The Fertility Clinic Success Rate And Certification Act (FCSRCA) of 1992 (Wyden Law) Requirements. Federal Register 2000;65:53310–6.
22. Centers for Disease Control and Prevention. Assisted reproductive technology (ART). Available at: http://www.cdc.gov/art/artdata/index.html, Accessed: 8/15/2016
23. U.S. Department of Health and Human Services Strategic Plan. Available at: http://www.hhs.gov/secretary/about/priorities/strategicplan2014-2018.pdf, Accessed: 8/15/2016
24. www.sart.org

Disclosure

None reported.

MM

Multiple Sclerosis

Hope Through Research

National Institute of Neurological Disorders and Stroke
National Institutes of Health

What is Multiple Sclerosis?

Multiple Sclerosis (MS) is the most common disabling neurological disease of young adults with symptom onset generally occurring between the ages of 20 to 40 years. In MS, the immune system cells that normally protect us from viruses, bacteria, and unhealthy cells mistakenly attack myelin in the central nervous system (brain, optic nerves, and spinal cord), a substance that makes up the protective sheath (called the myelin sheath) that coats nerve fibers (axons).

MS is a chronic disease that affects people differently. A small number of those with MS will have a mild course with little to no disability, whereas others will have a steadily worsening disease that leads to increased disability over time. Most people with MS, however, will have short periods of symptoms followed by long stretches of relative quiescence (inactivity or dormancy), with partial or full recovery. Women are affected more frequently with MS compared to men. The disease is rarely fatal and most people with MS have a normal life expectancy. New treatments can reduce long-term disability for many people with MS. Currently there are still no cures and no clear ways to prevent the disease from developing.

Myelin and the immune system

MS attacks axons in the central nervous system protected by myelin, which are commonly called **white matter**. MS also damages the nerve cell bodies, which are found in the brain's **gray matter**, as well as the axons themselves in the brain, spinal cord, and optic nerves that transmit visual information from the eye to the brain. As the disease progresses, the outermost layer of the brain, called the cerebral cortex, shrinks (what is known as cortical atrophy).

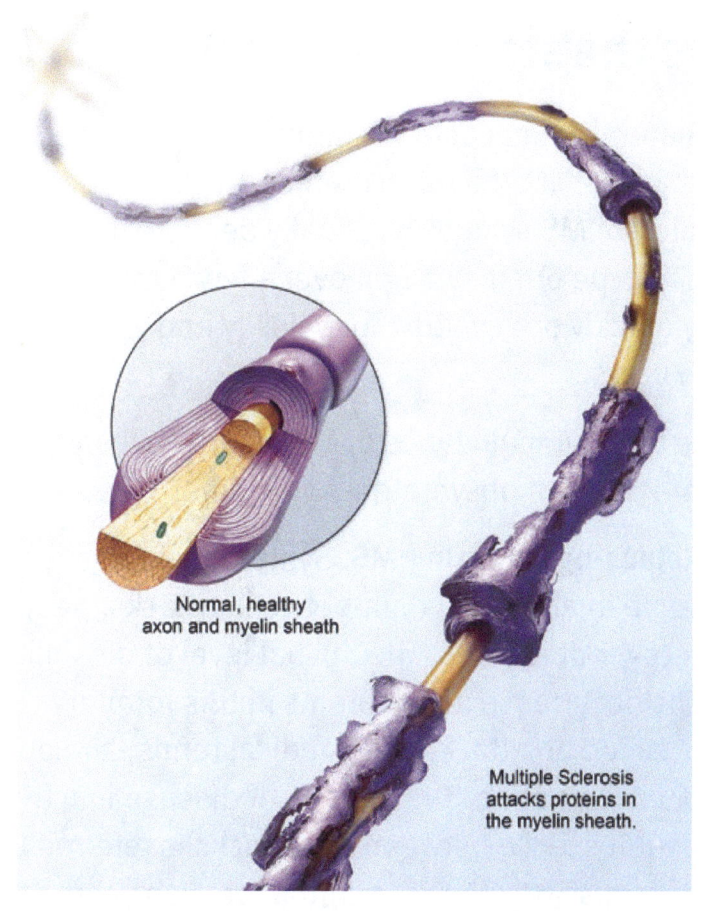

Studies & Statistics / Multiple Sclerosis: Hope Through Research

Myelin is a substance that makes up the protective sheath that insulates nerve fibers. In MS, myelin is damaged. The illustration above shows a normal, healthy myelin sheath, and one damaged by MS.

The term *multiple sclerosis* refers to the distinctive areas of scar tissue (sclerosis—also called plaques or lesions) that result from the attack on myelin by the immune system. These plaques are visible using magnetic resonance imaging in the white and/or gray matter of people who have MS. Plaques can be as small as a pinhead or as large as a golf ball.

During an MS exacerbation, most of the myelin, and to a lesser extent the axons within the affected area, is damaged or destroyed by different types of immune cells (also known as inflammation). The symptoms of MS depend on the severity of the inflammatory reaction as well as the location and extent of the plaques, which primarily appear in the brain stem, cerebellum (involved with balance and coordination of movement, among other functions), spinal cord, optic nerves, and the white matter around the brain ventricles (fluid-filled spaces).

What are the signs and symptoms of MS?

The natural course of MS is different for each person, which makes it difficult to predict. The onset and duration of MS symptoms usually depends on the specific type but may begin over a few days and go away quickly or develop more slowly and gradually over many years.

There are four main types of MS, named according to the progression of symptoms over time:

- **Relapsing-remitting MS.** Symptoms in this type come in attacks and, in-between attacks, people recover or return to their usual level of disability. The occurrence of symptoms in this form of MS is called an attack, or in medical terms, a relapse or exacerbation. The periods of disease inactivity or quiescence between MS attacks is referred to as remission. Weeks, months, or even years may pass before another attack occurs, followed again by a period of inactivity. Most people with MS (approximately 80%) are initially diagnosed with this form of the disease.

- **Secondary-progressive MS.** People with this form of MS usually have had a previous history of MS attacks, but then start to develop gradual and steady symptoms and deterioration in their function over time. Most individuals with severe relapsing-remitting MS may go on to develop secondary progressive MS if they are untreated.

- **Primary-progressive MS.** This type of MS is less common and is characterized by progressively worsening symptoms from the beginning with no noticeable relapses or exacerbations of the disease, although there may be temporary or minor relief from symptoms.

- **Progressive-relapsing MS.** This rarest form of MS is characterized by a steady worsening of symptoms from the beginning, with acute relapses that can occur over time during the disease course.

There are some rare and unusual variants of MS. One of these is **Marburg variant MS** (also called malignant MS), which causes swift and relentless symptoms and decline in function, which can result in significant disability or even death shortly after disease onset. **Balo's concentric sclerosis**, which causes concentric rings of myelin destruction that can be seen on an MRI, is another variant type of MS that can progress rapidly.

Early MS symptoms often include:

- Vision problems such as blurred or double vision, or optic neuritis, which causes pain with eye movement and a rapid loss of vision
- Muscle weakness, often in the hands and legs, and muscle stiffness accompanied by painful muscle spasms
- Tingling, numbness, or pain in the arms, legs, trunk, or face
- Clumsiness, particularly difficulty staying balanced when walking
- Bladder control problems
- Intermittent or more constant dizziness

MS may also cause later symptoms such as:

- Mental or physical fatigue which accompanies the early symptoms during an attack
- Mood changes such as depression or difficulty with emotional expression or control
- Cognitive dysfunction—problems concentrating, multitasking, thinking, learning, or difficulties with memory or judgment

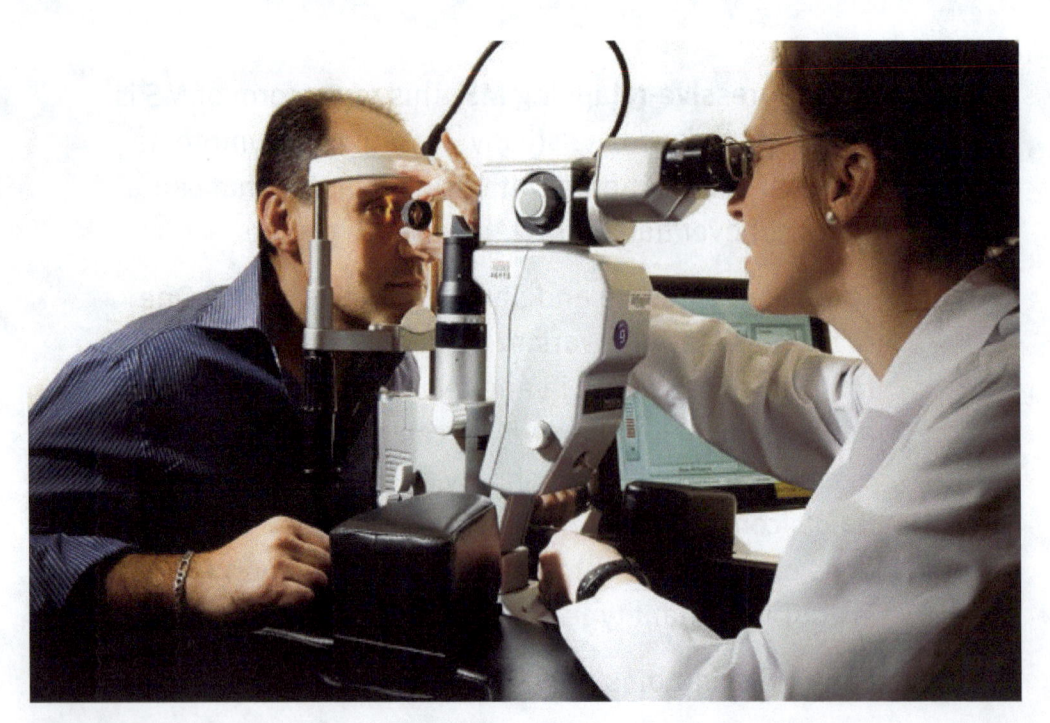

Vision problems, such as blurred or double vision or optic neuritis, are among the early symptoms of MS.

Muscle weakness, stiffness, and spasms may be severe enough to affect walking or standing. In some cases, MS leads to partial or complete paralysis and the use of a wheelchair is not uncommon, particularly in individuals who are untreated or have advanced disease. Many people with MS find that weakness and fatigue are worse when they have a fever or when they are exposed to heat. MS exacerbations may occur following common infections.

Pain is rarely the first sign of MS, but pain often occurs with optic neuritis and trigeminal neuralgia, a disorder that affects one of the nerves that provides sensation to different parts of the face (see Conditions associated with MS section below). Painful limb spasms and sharp pain shooting down the legs or around the abdomen can also be symptoms of MS.

Many individuals with MS may experience difficulties with coordination and balance. Some may have a continuous trembling of the head, limbs, and body, especially during movement.

MS exacerbation

An exacerbation—which is also called a relapse, flare-up, or attack—is a sudden worsening of MS symptoms, or the appearance of new symptoms that lasts for at least 24 hours. MS relapses are thought to be associated with the development of new areas of damage in the brain. Exacerbations are characteristic of relapsing-remitting MS.

An exacerbation may be mild, or severe enough to significantly interfere with life's daily activities. Most exacerbations last from several days to several weeks, although some have lasted for as long as a few months. When the symptoms of the attack subside, an individual with MS is said to be in remission, characterized by disease quiescence.

Conditions associated with MS

Transverse myelitis (an inflammation of the spinal cord) may develop in those with MS. Transverse myelitis can affect spinal cord function over several hours to several weeks before partial or complete recovery. It usually begins as a sudden onset of lower back pain, muscle weakness, abnormal sensations in the toes and feet, or difficulties with bladder control or bowel movements. This can rapidly progress to more severe symptoms, including arm and/or leg paralysis. In most cases, people recover at least some function within the first 12 weeks after an attack begins.

Neuromyelitis optica is a disorder associated with transverse myelitis as well as optic nerve inflammation (also known as optic neuritis). People with this disorder usually have abnormal antibodies (proteins that normally target viruses and bacteria) against a specific channel in optic nerves, the brain stem, or spinal cord, called the aquaporin-4 channel. These individuals respond to certain treatments, which are different than those commonly used to treat MS.

Trigeminal neuralgia is a chronic pain condition that causes sporadic, sudden burning or shock-like facial pain. The condition is more common in young adults with MS and is caused by lesions in the brain stem, the part of the brain that controls facial sensation.

What causes MS?

Researchers are looking at several possible explanations for why the immune system attacks central nervous system myelin, including:

- Fighting an infectious agent (for example, a virus) that has components that mimic components of the brain (called molecular mimicry)

- Destroying brain cells because they are unhealthy

- Mistakenly identifying normal brain cells as foreign

There is also something known as the **blood-brain barrier,** which separates the brain and spinal cord from the immune system. If there is a break in this barrier, it exposes the brain to the immune system. When this happens, the immune system may misinterpret structures in the brain, such as myelin, as "foreign."

Research shows that genetic vulnerabilities combined with environmental factors may cause MS.

Genetic susceptibility

MS itself is not inherited, but susceptibility to MS may be inherited. Studies show that some individuals with MS have one or more family member or relative who also have MS.

Studies & Statistics / Multiple Sclerosis: Hope Through Research

brain stem

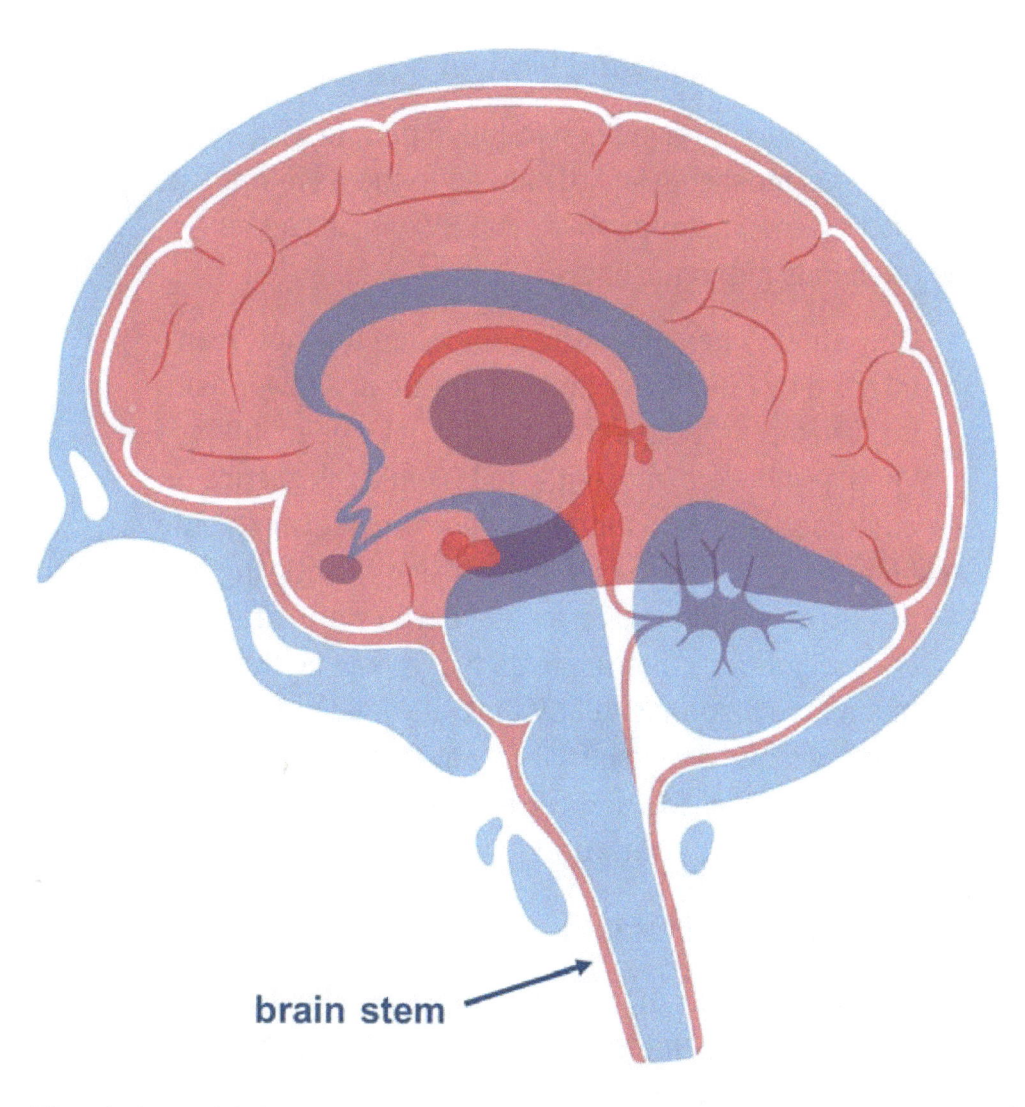

Trigeminal neuralgia is caused by lesions in the brain stem which controls facial sensation.

Current research suggests that dozens of genes and possibly hundreds of variations in the genetic code (called gene variants) combine to create vulnerability to MS. Some of these genes have been identified, and most are associated with functions of the immune system. Many of the known genes are similar to those that have been identified in people with other autoimmune diseases as type 1 diabetes, rheumatoid arthritis, or lupus.

Infectious factors and viruses

Several viruses have been found in people with MS, but the virus most consistently linked to the development of MS is the Epstein-Barr virus (EBV) which causes infectious mononucleosis.

Only about 5 percent of the population has not been infected by EBV. These individuals are at a lower risk for developing MS than those who have been infected. People who were infected with EBV in adolescence or adulthood and who therefore develop an exaggerated immune response to EBV are at a significantly higher risk for developing MS than those who were infected in early childhood. This suggests that it may be the type of immune response to EBV that may lead to MS, rather than EBV infection itself. However, there is still no proof that EBV causes MS and the mechanisms that underlie this process are poorly understood.

Environmental factors

Several studies indicate that people who spend more time in the sun and those with relatively higher levels of vitamin D are less likely to develop MS or have a less severe course of disease and fewer relapses. Bright sunlight helps human skin produce vitamin D. Researchers believe that vitamin D may help regulate the immune system in ways that reduce the risk of MS or autoimmunity in general. People from regions near the equator, where there is a great deal of bright sunlight, generally have a much lower risk of MS than people from temperate areas such as the United States and Canada.

Studies have found that people who smoke are more likely to develop MS and have a more aggressive disease course. People who smoke tend to have more brain lesions and brain shrinkage than non-smokers. The reasons for this are currently unclear.

Aim for a Healthy Weight

Maintaining a Healthy Weight On the Go

A Pocket Guide

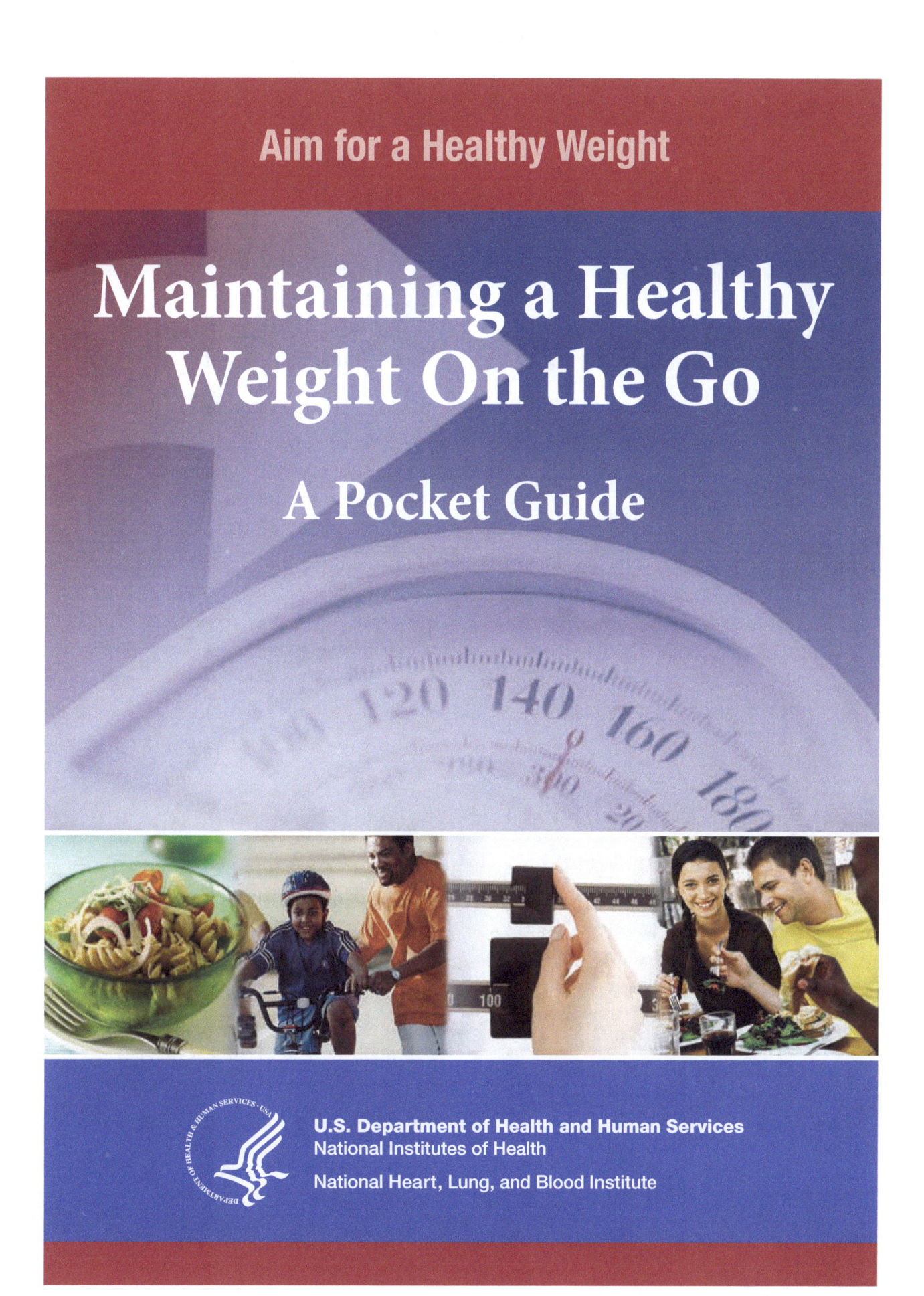

U.S. Department of Health and Human Services
National Institutes of Health
National Heart, Lung, and Blood Institute

Introduction

Importance of Making Healthier Choices While Eating On the Go

According to the National Restaurant Association, American adults buy a meal or snack from a restaurant 5.8 times a week on average. If you are watching your weight, it's hard to always know what calories, fats, and nutrients are in the dishes you order. The information in this booklet provides tips on how to help you select healthier options while eating "on the go" (i.e., dining out or bringing food in). Using the information provided on healthy choices will help you maintain a healthy weight.

Why Is a Healthy Weight Important?

Reaching and maintaining a healthy weight is good for your overall health. It also may help reduce your risk for developing several diseases and conditions. Maintaining a healthy weight has many other benefits, including feeling good about yourself and having more energy to enjoy life.

A person's weight is the result of many things: height, genes, metabolism, behavior, and environment. Maintaining a healthy weight requires keeping a balance. You must balance the calories you get from food and beverages (energy IN) with the calories you use to keep your body going and being physically active (energy OUT).

> The same amount of energy IN and energy OUT over time = weight stays the same
>
> More IN than OUT over time = weight gain
>
> More OUT than IN over time = weight loss

Your energy IN and energy OUT don't have to balance exactly every day. It's the balance over time that will help you maintain a healthy weight in the long run.

For many people, this balance means eating fewer calories and increasing their physical activity. Cutting back on calories is a matter of choice. Making healthy food choices that are lower in fats, especially saturated and *trans* fats, as well as cholesterol, sodium (salt), and added sugar, can help you cut back on calories, as can paying attention to portion size. This pocket guide will provide you with information to make informed food choices, particularly when eating on the go, to help you maintain a healthy weight.

How To Lose Weight and Maintain It

We have all heard the facts . . . to lose weight, you must eat less and move more. But this is often easier said than done. Many people make repeated attempts, often using different fad diets and weight loss gimmicks, and are unsuccessful.

To be successful at weight loss, you need to adopt a new lifestyle. This means making changes such as adopting healthy eating habits, being more physically active, and learning how to change behaviors.

Healthy Eating Plan

A healthy eating plan includes foods from all the basic food groups. It is low in saturated fat, *trans* fat, cholesterol, sodium (salt), and added sugar. It contains enough calories for good health, but not so many that you gain weight. (For more information on the basic food groups, go to http://www.MyPyramid.gov.)

A healthy eating plan:
- Emphasizes fruits, vegetables, whole grains, and fat-free or low-fat milk and milk products
- Includes lean meats, poultry, fish, beans, eggs, and nuts
- Is low in saturated fat, *trans* fat, cholesterol, sodium (salt), and added sugar
- Controls portion size

Choosing Healthier Foods

Foods That Make a Healthy Eating Plan

A healthy eating plan is one that gives your body the nutrients it needs every day while staying within your daily calorie limits. This eating plan also may lower your risk for heart disease and conditions such as high blood pressure or high blood cholesterol.

Foods that can be eaten more often include those that are lower in calories, total fat, saturated and *trans* fats, cholesterol, and sodium (salt). Examples of these foods include fat-free and low-fat milk products; lean meats, fish, and poultry; high-fiber foods such as whole grains, breads, and cereals; fruits; and vegetables. Canola or olive oils and soft margarines made from these oils are heart healthy and can be used in moderate amounts. Unsalted nuts also can be included in a healthy diet, as long as you watch the amount.

Foods higher in fat are typically higher in calories. Foods that should be limited include those with higher amounts of saturated fat, *trans* fat, and cholesterol. These particular fats may raise blood cholesterol levels, which increases the risk of heart disease.

- Saturated fat is found mainly in fresh and processed meats, high-fat milk products (such as cheese, whole milk, cream, butter, and ice cream), lard, and the coconut and palm oils that can be found in many processed foods.

- *Trans* fat is found in foods with partially hydrogenated oils, such as many hard margarines and shortening, commercially fried foods, and some bakery goods.

- Cholesterol is found in foods of animal origin. Major dietary sources include egg yolks, organ meats, cheese, beef, pork, and shrimp. It also may be present in foods that contain an animal-based ingredient, such as eggs, whole milk, or lard.

It's also important to limit foods and beverages with added fat and sugar, such as many desserts, canned fruit packed in syrup, fruit drinks, and sugar-sweetened beverages. These foods and beverages will add calories to your diet while providing limited nutritional benefit.

Fat Matters, But Calories Count

A calorie is a calorie is a calorie, whether it comes from fat or carbohydrate. Any calories eaten in excess can lead to weight gain. You can lose weight by eating fewer calories and by increasing your physical activity.

Reducing the amount of total fat and saturated fat that you eat is one way to limit your overall calorie intake. In fact, 1 gram of fat equals 9 calories, whereas 1 gram of protein or carbohydrate equals less than half the number of calories (4 calories each). By reducing total fat intake, you help reduce your calorie intake.

However, eating fat-free or reduced-fat foods isn't always the answer to reducing your calories. This is especially true when you eat more of the reduced-fat food than you would of the regular item. Many food companies produce fat-free versions of foods that have more calories than the regular versions. For example, if you eat twice as many fat-free cookies, you have increased your overall calorie intake. The following list of foods and their reduced-fat varieties will show you that just because a product is fat free, that doesn't mean it is "calorie free." And calories do count!

Studies & Statistics / Maintaining a Healthy Weight On the Go: A Pocket Guide

Fat-Free or Reduced Fat	Calories	Regular	Calories
Reduced fat peanut butter, 2 Tbsp	187	Regular peanut butter, 2 Tbsp	191
Cookies: Reduced fat chocolate chip cookies, 3 cookies (30 g)	118	*Cookies:* Regular chocolate chip cookies, 3 cookies (30 g)	142
Fat-free fig cookies, 2 cookies (30 g)	102	Regular fig cookies, 2 cookies (30 g)	111
Ice cream: Fat-free vanilla frozen yogurt (<1% fat), ½ cup	100	*Ice cream:* Regular whole milk vanilla frozen yogurt (3–4% fat), ½ cup	104
Light vanilla ice cream (7% fat), ½ cup	111	Regular vanilla ice cream (11% fat), ½ cup	133
Fat-free caramel topping, 2 Tbsp	103	Caramel topping, homemade with butter, 2 Tbsp	103
Low-fat granola cereal, approx. ½ cup (55 g)	213	Regular granola cereal, approx. ½ cup (55 g)	257
Low-fat blueberry muffin, 1 small (2½ inch)	131	Regular blueberry muffin, 1 small (2½ inch)	138
Baked tortilla chips, 1 oz	113	Regular tortilla chips, 1 oz	143
Low-fat cereal bar, 1 bar (1.3 oz)	130	Regular cereal bar, 1 bar (1.3 oz)	140

Source: National Heart, Lung, and Blood Institute. (2005). *Aim for a Healthy Weight* (NIH Publication No. 05-5213), p. 9. Bethesda, MD: U.S. Department of Health and Human Services.

Lower Calorie, Lower Fat Alternatives

The table that follows provides some examples of healthier alternatives for old favorites. When making a food choice, remember to consider vitamins and minerals. Some foods provide most of their calories from sugar and fat, but give you few, if any, vitamins and minerals.

The suggested alternatives are not meant to be an exhaustive list. If a product's package has a Nutrition Facts Panel, we encourage you to read it to find out just how many calories, vitamins, and minerals are in the specific products you decide to buy.

Once you are comfortable identifying foods that are lower in fat and calories, you will be able to make healthier choices when eating on the go.

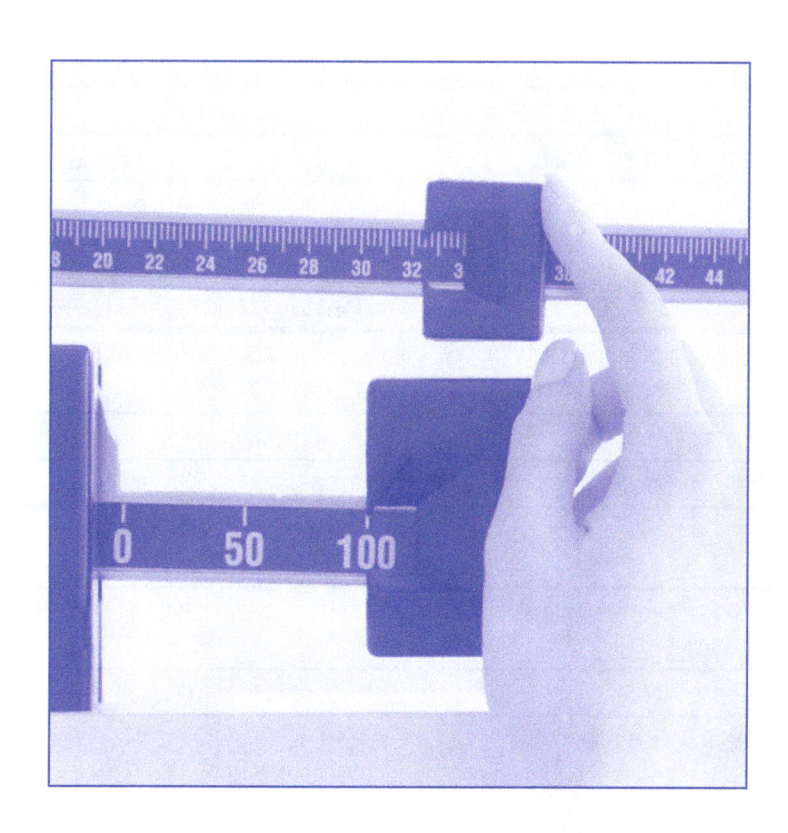

Studies & Statistics / Maintaining a Healthy Weight On the Go: A Pocket Guide

	Instead of . . .	Replace with . . .
Dairy Products	Evaporated whole milk	Evaporated fat-free (skim) or reduced fat (2%) milk
	Whole milk	Low-fat (1%), reduced fat (2%), or fat-free (skim) milk
	Ice cream	Sorbet, sherbet, low-fat or fat-free frozen yogurt, or ice milk (choose lowest calorie variety)
	Whipping cream	Imitation whipped cream (made with fat-free (skim) milk) or low-fat vanilla yogurt
	Sour cream	Plain low-fat yogurt
	Cream cheese	Neufchatel or "light" cream cheese or fat-free cream cheese
	Cheese (cheddar, American, Swiss, jack)	Reduced calorie cheese, low calorie processed cheeses, etc.; fat-free cheese
	Regular (4%) cottage cheese	Low-fat (1%) or reduced fat (2%) cottage cheese
	Whole milk mozzarella cheese	Part skim milk, low moisture mozzarella cheese
	Whole milk ricotta cheese	Part skim milk ricotta cheese
	Coffee cream (half and half) or nondairy creamer (liquid, powder)	Low-fat (1%) or reduced fat (2%) milk or fat-free dry milk powder
Cereals, Grains, and Pasta	Ramen noodles	Rice or noodles (spaghetti, macaroni, etc.)
	Pasta with white sauce (alfredo)	Pasta with red sauce (marinara)
	Pasta with cheese sauce	Pasta with vegetables (primavera)
	Granola	Bran flakes, crispy rice, etc. Cooked grits or oatmeal Whole grains (couscous, barley, bulgar, etc.) Reduced fat granola (choose lowest calorie variety)
Meat, Fish, and Poultry	Cold cuts or lunch meats (bologna, salami, liverwurst, etc.)	Low-fat cold cuts (95% to 97% fat-free lunch meats, low-fat pressed meats)
	Hot dogs (regular)	Lower fat hot dogs
	Bacon or sausage	Canadian bacon or lean ham
	Regular ground beef	Extra lean ground beef such as ground round or ground turkey (read labels)
	Chicken or turkey with skin, duck, or goose	Chicken or turkey without skin (white meat)
	Oil-packed tuna	Water-packed tuna (rinse to reduce sodium content)
	Beef (chuck, rib, brisket)	Beef (round, loin) trimmed of external fat (choose slelect grades)
	Pork (spareribs, untrimmed loin)	Pork tenderloin or trimmed, lean smoked ham

Studies & Statistics / Maintaining a Healthy Weight On the Go: A Pocket Guide

-	Instead of . . .	Replace with . . .
Meat, Fish, and Poultry	Frozen breaded fish or fried fish (homemade or commercial)	Fish or shellfish, unbreaded (fresh, frozen, canned in water)
	Whole eggs	Egg whites or egg substitutes
	Frozen TV dinners (containing more than 13 grams of fat per serving)	Frozen TV dinners (containing less than 13 grams of fat per serving and lowest in sodium)
	Chorizo sausage	Turkey sausage, drained well (read label) Vegetarian sausage (made with tofu)
Baked Goods	Croissants, brioches, etc.	Hard french rolls or soft "brown 'n serve" rolls
	Donuts, sweet rolls, muffins, scones, or pastries	English muffins, bagels, reduced fat or fat-free muffins or scones
	Party crackers	Low-fat crackers (choose lower in sodium) Saltine or soda crackers (choose lowest in sodium)
	Cake (pound, chocolate, yellow)	Cake (angel food, white, gingerbread)
	Cookies	Reduced fat or fat-free cookies (graham crackers, ginger snaps, fig bars) (choose lowest calorie variety)
Snacks and Sweets	Nuts	Popcorn (air-popped or light microwave), fruits, vegetables
	Ice cream, e.g., cones or bars	Frozen yogurt, frozen fruit, or chocolate pudding bars
	Custards or puddings (made with whole milk)	Puddings (made with skim milk)
Fats, Oils, and Salad Dressings	Regular margarine or butter	Light-spread margarines, diet margarine, or whipped butter, tub or squeeze bottle
	Regular mayonnaise	Light or diet mayonnaise or mustard
	Regular salad dressings	Reduced calorie or fat-free salad dressings, lemon juice, or plain, herb-flavored, or wine vinegar
	Butter or margarine on toast or bread	Jelly, jam, or honey on bread or toast
	Oils, shortening, or lard	Nonstick cooking spray for stir-frying or sautéing As a substitute for oil or butter, use applesauce or prune puree in baked goods
Miscellaneous	Canned cream soups	Canned broth-based soups
	Canned beans and franks	Canned baked beans in tomato sauce
	Gravy (homemade with fat and/or milk)	Gravy mixes made with water or homemade with the fat skimmed off and fat-free milk included
	Fudge sauce	Chocolate syrup
	Avocado on sandwiches	Cucumber slices or lettuce leaves
	Guacamole dip or refried beans with lard	Salsa

Source: Adapted from National Heart, Lung, and Blood Institute. (2005). *Aim for a Healthy Weight* (NIH Publication No. 05-5213), pp. 10–11. Bethesda, MD: U.S. Department of Health and Human Services.

Keeping an Eye on Portion Size

Eating fewer calories is not just about choosing healthier foods. It is also about eating less food and paying attention to portion size.

What's the difference between a regular portion and a serving size?

Portion: A "portion" is the amount of food that you choose to eat for a meal or snack. It can be big or small—you decide.

Serving: A "serving" is a measured amount of food or drink, such as one slice of bread or 1 cup of milk. Some foods that most people consume as a single portion actually contain multiple servings (e.g., a 20-ounce soda or a 3-ounce bag of chips).

To see typical portions for various foods, refer to the images below. Also, check out the U.S. Department of Agriculture's MyPyramid at http://www.myPyramid.gov to find out how these food portions fit into a daily eating plan for your recommended calorie level.

Strawberries
½ cup
(½ cup equivalent of fruit)

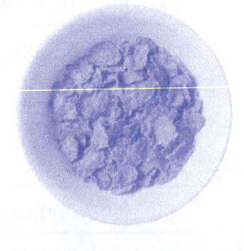

Whole-wheat cereal flakes
1 cup
(1-ounce equivalent of whole grains)

Milk
8 fluid ounces
(counts as 1 cup milk)

Baked sweet potato
1 large
(1-cup equivalent of orange vegetables)

Source: Adapted from the U.S. Department of Agriculture's MyPyramid, online at **http://mypyramid.gov**.

Dining Out/Take-Out: How To Choose

General Tips for Healthy Dining Out and Take-Out

Whether you're trying to maintain weight or lose weight, you can eat healthfully when dining out or bringing food in, if you know how. The following tips will help you move toward healthier eating as you limit your calories, as well as total fat, saturated and *trans* fats, cholesterol, and sodium (salt) when eating prepared foods.

You Are the Customer

- Ask for what you want. Most restaurants will honor your requests.
- Ask questions. Don't be intimidated by the menu—your server will be able to tell you how foods are prepared or suggest substitutions on the menu.
- To reduce portion sizes, try ordering a low-fat appetizer as your main meal, or share an entree with a friend or family member.
- Avoid all-you-can-eat buffets.
- Review the menu online, if possible, and choose the healthiest option before you go to the restaurant.
- General tips: Limiting your calories and fat can be easy as long as you know what to order. Try asking these questions when you call ahead or before you order. Ask the restaurant whether they would, upon request, do the following:
  - Serve fat-free (skim) milk rather than whole milk or cream
  - Reveal the type of cooking oil used
  - Trim visible fat off poultry or meat
  - Leave butter, gravy, or cream sauces off the side dish or entree
  - Serve salad dressing on the side
  - Accommodate special requests if made in advance by telephone or in person

Above all, don't get discouraged. Most restaurants usually have several healthy options to choose from.

Reading the Menu

Choose lower calorie, low-fat cooking methods. Look for terms such as:

- Baked
- Boiled (in wine or lemon juice)
- Broiled
- Grilled
- Lightly sauteed
- Poached
- Roasted
- Steamed in its own juice (au jus)

Be aware of foods high in calories, total fat, and saturated fat. Watch out for terms such as:

- Alfredo
- Au fromage
- Au gratin
- Basted
- Béarnaise
- Breaded
- Butter sauce
- Casserole
- Cheese sauce
- Creamed
- In cream or cream sauce
- Crispy
- Deep fried
- Escalloped
- Fried
- Gravy
- Hollandaise
- Marinated (in oil)
- Pastry crust
- Pot pie

Specific Tips for Healthy Choices

Breakfasts

- Decaf tea or coffee with fat-free or low-fat (1 percent) milk
- Fresh fruit or small glass of 100 percent fruit juice
- Whole-grain bread, bagel, or English muffin with jelly or honey
- Whole-grain cereal with fat-free or low-fat (1 percent) milk
- Oatmeal with fat-free milk topped with fruit
- Omelet made with egg whites or egg substitute
- Multigrain pancakes with fresh fruit or apple butter
- Fat-free yogurt (try adding cereal or fresh fruit)

Beverages

- Water with lemon
- Flavored sparkling water (noncaloric)

- Juice spritzer (half fruit juice and half sparkling water)
- Unsweetened iced tea
- Tomato juice (reduced sodium)
- Fat-free or low-fat (1 percent) milk

Breads

While many yeast breads and breadsticks are low in calories and low in fat, the calories add up when you add butter, margarine, or olive oil to the bread. Also, eating a lot of bread in addition to your meal will fill you up with unwanted calories and not leave enough room for fruits and vegetables.

Appetizers

- Broth-based soups
- Steamed seafood
- Shrimp* cocktail (limit cocktail sauce—it's high in sodium)
- Melons or fresh fruit
- Bean soups
- Salad with reduced-fat dressing (or add lemon juice or vinegar)

Entrees

- Poultry, fish, shellfish, and vegetable dishes
- Pasta with red sauce or with vegetables (primavera)
- Look for terms such as "baked," "broiled," "steamed," "poached," "lightly sauteed," or "lightly stir-fried"
- Ask for sauces and dressings on the side
- Limit the amount of butter, margarine, and salt you use at the table

Salads/Salad Bars

- Lettuce, spinach, and other fresh greens
- Fresh vegetables—tomatoes, mushrooms, carrots, cucumbers, peppers, onions, radishes, and broccoli
- Chickpeas, kidney beans, and other beans
- Skip the nonvegetable choices: deli meats, bacon, egg, cheese, and croutons
- Choose lower calorie, reduced-fat, or fat-free dressing; lemon juice; or vinegar

Side Dishes

- Vegetables and whole-grain side dishes (brown rice, whole wheat pasta, etc.) make good additions to meals and also can be combined for a lower calorie alternative to higher calorie entrees

---

* If you are on a cholesterol-lowering diet, eat shrimp in moderation.

- Ask for side dishes without butter or margarine
- Ask for mustard, salsa, or low-fat yogurt instead of sour cream or butter

Desserts and Coffees
- Fresh fruit
- Fat-free frozen yogurt
- Sherbet or fruit sorbet (these are usually fat free, but check the calorie content)
- Try sharing a dessert
- Ask for fat-free or low-fat (1 percent) milk for your coffee (instead of cream or half-n-half)

Tips for Healthy Eating On the Go

If you're dining out or bringing food in, it's easy to find healthy foods. Knowing about typical American dishes, as well as other ethnic cuisines, can help make your dining experience healthy and enjoyable. The following list includes healthy food choices (lower in calories and fat) and terms to look for when making your on-the-go selections.

Supermarket
Choose More Often . . .

Bringing prepared food home from the supermarket is growing in popularity. Supermarkets often provide a wide selection of foods from various cuisines. Use the suggestions in each of these categories to guide your decision. One thing to keep in mind is portion size. Take-out portions can be just as large as restaurant portions. For more information on portion sizes, refer to Portion Distortion at http://www.nhlbi.nih.gov.

Chinese
Choose More Often . . .
- Zheng (steamed)
- Gun (boiled)
- Kao (roasted)
- Shao (barbecue)
- Poached
- Lightly stir-fried in mild sauce
- Cooked in light wine sauce
- Hot and spicy tomato sauce
- Sweet and sour sauce
- Hot mustard sauce
- Reduced-sodium soy sauce
- Dishes without MSG added
- Spinach or broccoli
- Fresh fish fillets, shrimp, scallops
- Chicken without skin
- Lean beef
- Bean curd (tofu)

- Moo shu vegetables, chicken, or shrimp
- Steamed rice
- Lychee fruit
- Hoisin sauce* with assorted Chinese vegetables: broccoli, mushrooms, onions, cabbage, snow peas, scallions, bamboo shoots, water chestnuts, asparagus
- Oyster sauce* (made from seafood)

French

Choose More Often . . .

- Dinner salad with vinegar or lemon juice (or a reduced-fat dressing)
- Crusty bread without butter
- Fresh fish, shrimp, scallops, steamed mussels (without sauces)
- Chicken without skin
- Rice and noodles without cream or added butter or other fat
- Fresh fruit for dessert

Italian

Choose More Often . . .

- Lightly sauteed with onions
- Shallots
- Peppers and mushrooms
- Artichoke hearts
- Sun-dried tomatoes
- Red sauces—spicy marinara sauce (arrabiata), marinara sauce, or cacciatore
- Light red sauce or light red or white wine sauce
- Light mushroom sauce
- Red clam sauce
- Primavera (no cream sauce)
- Lemon sauce
- Capers
- Herbs and spices—garlic and oregano
- Crushed tomatoes and spices
- Florentine (spinach)
- Grilled (often fish or vegetables)
- Piccata (lemon)
- Manzanne (eggplant)

Middle Eastern

Choose More Often . . .

- Lemon dressing, lemon juice
- Blended or seasoned with Middle Eastern spices
- Herbs and spices (parsley, rosemary, basil, dill, etc.)
- Mashed chickpeas
- Fava beans
- Smoked eggplant

---

* Hoisin and oyster sauces are high in sodium (salt). Choose versions that are lower in sodium, or limit the quantity, particularly if on a low-sodium diet.

Studies & Statistics / Maintaining a Healthy Weight On the Go: A Pocket Guide

- Tomatoes, mushrooms, green peppers, and cucumbers
- Spiced ground meat
- Special garlic sauce
- Basted with tomato sauce
- Garlic
- Chopped parsley and/or onion
- Couscous (grain)
- Rice or bulgur (cracked wheat)
- Stuffed with rice and imported spices
- Grilled on a skewer
- Marinated and barbecued
- Baked
- Charbroiled or charcoal broiled
- Fresh fruit for dessert

Japanese
Choose More Often . . .

- House salad with fresh ginger and cellophane (clear rice) noodles
- Rice
- Nabemono (soup/stew)
- Chicken, fish, or shrimp teriyaki, broiled in sauce
- Soba noodles, often used in soups
- Yakimono (broiled)
- Tofu (or bean curd)
- Grilled vegetables

Indian
Choose More Often . . .

- Tikka (pan roasted)
- Cooked with or marinated in yogurt
- Cooked with green vegetables, onions, tomatoes, peppers, and mushrooms
- With spinach (saag)
- Baked leavened breads
- Masala
- Tandoori
- Paneer
- Cooked with curry, marinated in spices
- Lentils, chickpeas (garbanzo beans)
- Garnished with dried fruits
- Chickpeas (garbanzo) and potatoes
- Basmati rice (pullao)
- Matta (peas)
- Chicken or shrimp kebab

Mexican
Choose More Often . . .

- Shredded spicy chicken
- Rice and black beans
- Rice (particularly brown rice)

- Served with salsa (hot red tomato sauce)
- Served with salsa verde (green chili sauce)
- Covered with enchilada sauce
- Topped with shredded lettuce, diced tomatoes, and onions
- Served with or wrapped in a corn or whole-wheat flour (soft) tortilla
- Grilled
- Marinated
- Picante sauce
- Simmered with vegetarian chili or tomato sauce

Thai

Choose More Often . . .

- Barbecued, sauteed, broiled, boiled, steamed, braised, or marinated
- Charbroiled
- Basil sauce, basil, sweet basil, or basil leaves
- Lime sauce or lime juice
- Chili sauce or crushed dried chili flakes
- Thai spices
- Served in hollowed-out pineapple
- Fish sauce
- Hot sauce
- Napa, bamboo shoots, black mushrooms, ginger, garlic
- Bed of mixed vegetables
- Scallions, onions

Steakhouses

Choose More Often . . .

- Lean broiled beef (no more than 6 ounces)—London broil, filet mignon, round and flank steaks
- Baked potato without added butter, margarine, or sour cream (try low-fat yogurt or mustard)
- Green salad with vinegar or lemon juice (or a reduced-fat dressing)
- Steamed vegetables without added butter or margarine (try lemon juice and herbs)
- Seafood dishes (usually indicated as "surf" on menus)

Fast Food

Choose More Often . . .

- Grilled chicken breast sandwich without mayonnaise
- Single hamburger without cheese
- Grilled chicken salad with reduced-fat dressing
- Garden salad with vinegar or lemon juice (or a reduced-fat dressing)

- Low-fat or fat-free yogurt
- Fat-free muffin or cereal with fat-free or low-fat (1 percent) milk

Deli/Sandwich Shops

Choose More Often . . .

- Fresh sliced vegetables in whole-wheat pita bread with low-fat dressing, yogurt, or mustard
- Bean soup (lentil, minestrone)
- Turkey breast sandwich with mustard, lettuce, and tomato
- Fresh fruit

Saving Money While Eating Out

Another expense of eating out is its effect on your budget. Try these tips for making healthy choices eating out without overspending:

- To reduce costs, start by eating out one less time per week.
- Many restaurants provide portions that are large enough to make two meals out of one entree. Bring half of your meal home for the next day, or if dining with a friend or family member, order one entree to share.
- If you often meet a friend or colleague for lunch at a restaurant, try bringing your lunch instead and meeting outside in the park when the weather permits.

Foods in the Fast Lane

When you eat on the go, you don't have to give up eating fast foods completely. You can eat right and still eat fast foods if you select carefully. Here are some tips on fast foods to choose:

- Order from the dollar or value menu; the portions are often smaller than the regular size.
- Order a small hamburger instead of a larger one. Try ordering a hamburger without cheese and extra sauce.
- Order roast beef for a leaner choice than most burgers.
- Order a baked potato instead of french fries. Be careful of high-fat toppings like sour cream, butter, or cheese.
- Order grilled, broiled, or baked fish or chicken.
- Order fat-free or low-fat milk instead of a milkshake. Or try the low-fat frozen yogurt or low-fat milkshake.
- Order salad. Use vinegar and oil or a low-calorie dressing.
- Create a salad at the salad bar. Choose any raw vegetables, fruits, or beans. Limit toppings high in saturated fat, such as cheese, fried noodles, and bacon bits, as well as salads made with mayonnaise. Also, limit salad dressings high in saturated fat and cholesterol.
- For sandwiches, try whole-wheat bread topped with lettuce, tomato, onion, mustard, and ketchup instead of toppings high in saturated fat, such as cheese, bacon, special sauces, or butter.
- Order thin-crust pizza with vegetable toppings such as peppers, mushrooms, or onions instead of extra cheese, pepperoni, and sausage.

Fast Food Choices

Let's see how small changes can add up to big changes with the following sample fast-food meal:

Typical Meal		**Lower Fat Choice**	
Cheeseburger (313 calories)		Hamburger (265 calories)	
Large french fries (487 calories)		½ small french fries (112 calories)	
12-ounce cola (136 calories)		12-ounce cola (136 calories)	
½ cup vanilla ice cream (137 calories)		Low-fat ice cream cone (146 calories)	
Total saturated fat (g)	13	Total saturated fat (g)	6
Total dietary cholesterol (mg)	71	Total dietary cholesterol (mg)	42
Total fat (g)	46	Total fat (g)	20
Total calories	1,073	Total calories	659

Source: Adapted from National Heart, Lung, and Blood Institute. (2005). *Aim for a Healthy Weight* (NIH Publication No. 05-5213), p. 24. Bethesda, MD: U.S. Department of Health and Human Services.

Obsessive-Compulsive Disorder:

When Unwanted Thoughts or Repetitive Behaviors Take Over

National Institute of Mental Health

Studies & Statistics / Obsessive-Compulsive Disorder

People who are distressed by recurring, unwanted, and uncontrollable thoughts or who feel driven to repeat specific behaviors may have obsessive-compulsive disorder (OCD). The thoughts and behaviors that characterize OCD can interfere with daily life, but treatment can help people manage their symptoms.

What is OCD?

OCD is a common, long-lasting disorder characterized by uncontrollable, recurring thoughts (obsessions) that can lead people to engage in repetitive behaviors (compulsions).

Although everyone worries or feels the need to double-check things on occasion, the symptoms associated with OCD are severe and persistent. These symptoms can cause distress and lead to behaviors that interfere with day-to-day activities. People with OCD may feel the urge to check things repeatedly or perform routines for more than an hour each day as a way of achieving temporary relief from anxiety. If OCD symptoms are not treated, these behaviors can disrupt work, school, and personal relationships and can cause feelings of distress.

OCD symptoms tend to emerge in childhood, around age 10, or in young adulthood, around age 20 to 21, and they often appear earlier in boys than in girls. Most people are diagnosed with OCD by the time they reach young adulthood.

What are the signs and symptoms of OCD?

People with OCD may have obsessions, compulsions, or both.

Obsessions are repeated thoughts, urges, or mental images that cause anxiety. Common obsessions include:

- Fear of germs or contamination
- Fear of forgetting, losing, or misplacing something
- Fear of losing control over one's behavior
- Aggressive thoughts toward others or oneself
- Unwanted, forbidden, or taboo thoughts involving sex, religion, or harm
- Desire to have things symmetrical or in perfect order

Compulsions are repetitive behaviors that a person feels the urge to do in response to an obsessive thought. Common compulsions include:

- Excessive cleaning or handwashing
- Ordering or arranging items in a particular, precise way
- Repeatedly checking things, such as that the door is locked or the oven is off
- Compulsive counting

How do I know if it's OCD?

Not all rituals or habits are compulsions. Everyone double-checks things sometimes. In general, people with OCD:

- Can't control their obsessive thoughts or compulsive behaviors, even when they recognize those thoughts or behaviors as excessive
- Spend at least 1 hour a day on these obsessive thoughts or compulsive behaviors
- Don't get pleasure when performing compulsive behaviors or rituals, but may feel brief relief from the anxiety brought on by obsessive thoughts
- Experience significant problems in daily life due to these thoughts or behaviors

Some individuals with OCD also have a tic disorder. Motor tics are sudden, brief, repetitive movements, such as eye blinking and other eye movements, facial grimacing, shoulder shrugging, and head or shoulder jerking. Common vocal tics include repetitive throat-clearing, sniffing, or grunting sounds. It is common for people with OCD also to have a diagnosed mood disorder or anxiety disorder.

Symptoms of OCD may come and go, ease over time, or worsen. People with OCD may try to help themselves by avoiding situations that trigger their obsessions, or they may use alcohol or drugs to calm themselves. Although most adults with OCD recognize that their compulsive behaviors don't make sense, some adults and most children may not realize that their behavior is out of the ordinary. Parents or teachers typically recognize OCD symptoms in children.

If you think you or your child may have OCD, talk to a health care provider about the possible symptoms. If left untreated, OCD can interfere in all aspects of life.

What causes OCD?

The exact causes of OCD aren't known; however, a variety of factors are associated with an increased chance of developing the disorder.

Genetics is one factor associated with OCD. Studies have shown that having a first-degree relative (parent, sibling, or child) with OCD is associated with an increased chance of developing the disorder. Scientists have not identified any one gene or set of genes that definitively lead to OCD, but studies exploring the connection between genetics and OCD are ongoing.

In addition to genetics, other biological factors may play a role. Brain imaging studies have shown that people with OCD often have differences in the frontal cortex and subcortical structures of the brain, areas of the brain that underlie the ability to control behavior and emotional responses. Researchers also have found that several brain areas, brain networks, and biological processes play a key role in obsessive thoughts, compulsive behavior, and associated fear and anxiety. Research is underway to better understand the connection between OCD symptoms and parts of the brain.

Some studies have reported an association between childhood trauma and obsessive-compulsive symptoms. More research is needed to understand this relationship.

Children who develop a sudden onset or worsening of OCD symptoms after a streptococcal infection may be diagnosed with a condition called Pediatric Autoimmune Neuropsychiatric Disorders Associated with Streptococcal Infections (PANDAS). You can learn more about PANDAS at www.nimh.nih.gov/pandas.

How is OCD treated?

The first step is to talk with your health care provider about your symptoms. Asking questions and providing information to your health care provider can improve your care.

Your health care provider will perform a physical exam and ask you about your health history to make sure that your symptoms are not caused by other illnesses or conditions. Your health care provider may refer you to a mental health professional, such as a psychiatrist, psychologist, social worker, or counselor, for further evaluation or treatment.

Treatment for OCD typically includes specific types of psychotherapy (such as cognitive behavioral therapy), medication, or a combination of the two. A mental health professional can talk about the benefits and risks associated with different treatment options and help identify the best treatment for you.

Sometimes people with OCD also have other mental illnesses, such as anxiety, depression, and body dysmorphic disorder, a disorder in which someone mistakenly believes that a part of their body is abnormal. It is important to consider these other disorders when making decisions about treatment.

It is important to follow your treatment plan because both psychotherapy and medication can take some time to work. Although there is no cure for OCD, current treatments help many people with the disorder manage their symptoms, engage in day-to-day activities, and lead full, active lives.

> For tips on how to talk to your health care provider about your mental health and get the most out of your visit, read the National Institute of Mental Health (NIMH) fact sheet, Taking Control of Your Mental Health: Tips for Talking With Your Health Care Provider, available at www.nimh.nih.gov/talkingtips.

Psychotherapy

Psychotherapy can be an effective treatment for adults and children with OCD. Research shows that certain types of psychotherapy, including cognitive behavioral therapy (CBT) and other related therapies (such as habit reversal training), can be as effective as medication for many people. For others, psychotherapy may be most effective when used in combination with medication.

Research shows that a specific type of CBT called Exposure and Response Prevention (ERP) is effective for reducing compulsive behaviors, even for people who did not respond well to medication. With ERP, people spend time in a situation that triggers their compulsion (such as touching dirty objects) and they are prevented from engaging in their typical compulsion (such as handwashing). Although this approach may cause feelings of anxiety at first, compulsions decrease for most people as they continue treatment.

Children with OCD may need additional help from family members and health care providers when it comes to recognizing and managing their OCD symptoms. Mental health professionals can work with young patients to identify strategies for managing stress and increasing support so that the children are able to manage their OCD symptoms at school and at home.

You can learn more about psychotherapies, including CBT, at www.nimh.nih.gov/psychotherapies.

Studies & Statistics / Obsessive-Compulsive Disorder

Medication

Your health care provider may prescribe medication to help treat OCD. Serotonin reuptake inhibitors (SRIs) are the most common type of medication prescribed for the treatment of OCD.

SRIs, including selective serotonin reuptake inhibitors (SSRIs), are often used to treat depression, and they also are helpful for treating symptoms of OCD. With SRI treatment, it may take up to 8 to 12 weeks before symptoms begin to improve, and treatment for OCD may require higher SRI doses than are typically used in treating depression. For some people, these medications may cause side effects such as headaches, nausea, or difficulty sleeping.

People respond to medication in different ways, but most people with OCD find that medication, often in combination with psychotherapy, can help them manage their symptoms.

Your health care provider can adjust medication doses over time to minimize any side effects or withdrawal symptoms. Do not stop taking your medication without talking to your health care provider first. Your health care provider will work with you to monitor your health and can adjust the treatment plan in a safe and effective way.

The most up-to-date information on medications, side effects, and warnings is available on the U.S. Food and Drug Administration (FDA) website at **www.fda.gov/drugsatfda**.

Other Treatments

In 2018, FDA approved the use of transcranial magnetic stimulation (TMS), most commonly used in treating depression, as an add-on treatment for adults with OCD. You can learn more about brain stimulation therapies, including TMS, on the NIMH website at **www.nimh.nih.gov/braintherapies**.

Beyond Treatment: Things You Can Do

There are several important things you can do to manage stress and anxiety associated with OCD.

- ▶ Create a consistent sleep schedule.
- ▶ Make regular exercise a part of your routine.
- ▶ Eat a healthy, balanced diet.
- ▶ Seek support from trusted family and friends.

Where can I go for help?

If you're not sure where to get help, your health care provider is a good place to start. Your health care provider can refer you to a qualified mental health professional, such as a psychiatrist or psychologist, who has experience treating OCD and can evaluate your symptoms.

You can learn more about getting help and finding a health care provider on the NIMH website at **www.nimh.nih.gov/findhelp**. The Substance Abuse and Mental Health Services Administration (SAMHSA) has an online tool at **https://findtreatment.samhsa.gov** to help you find mental health services in your area.

I know someone who is in crisis. What do I do?

If you or someone you know is having thoughts about wanting to die or is thinking about hurting themselves or someone else, get help quickly.

- Do not leave a person who is in crisis alone.
- Call 911 or go to the nearest hospital emergency room.
- Call the toll-free National Suicide Prevention Lifeline at 1-800-273-TALK (8255) or the toll-free TTY number at 1-800-799-4TTY (4889). You also can text the Crisis Text Line (text HELLO to 741741) or go to the National Suicide Prevention Lifeline website at **https://suicidepreventionlifeline.org**. These services are confidential, free, and available 24/7.

Participating in Clinical Research

Clinical trials are research studies that look at new ways to prevent, detect, or treat diseases and conditions. Although individuals may benefit from being part of a clinical trial, participants should be aware that the primary purpose of a clinical trial is to gain new scientific knowledge so that others may be better helped in the future.

Researchers at NIMH and around the country conduct many studies with patients and healthy volunteers. Talk to your health care provider about clinical trials, their benefits and risks, and whether one is right for you. For more information, visit: **www.nimh.nih.gov/clinicaltrials**.

A FACT SHEET FROM THE OFFICE ON WOMEN'S HEALTH

Osteoporosis

Osteoporosis is a disease of the bones that causes bones to become weak and break easily. Osteoporosis affects mostly older women, but prevention starts when you are younger. No matter your age, you can take steps to build bone mass and prevent bone loss. Broken bones from osteoporosis cause serious health problems and disability in older women.

Q: Who gets osteoporosis?

A: Of the estimated 10 million Americans with osteoporosis, more than 8 million (or 80%) are women.

Osteoporosis is most common in older women. In the United States, osteoporosis affects one in four women 65 or older.

Q: What are the symptoms of osteoporosis?

A: Osteoporosis is called a "silent" disease. You may not have any symptoms of osteoporosis until you break (fracture) a bone. Fractures are most common in the hip, wrist, and spine (vertebrae). Vertebrae support your body, helping you to stand and sit up.

Fractures in the vertebrae can cause the spine to collapse and bend forward. If this happens, you may get any or all of these symptoms:

- Sloping shoulders
- Curve in the back
- Height loss
- Back pain
- Hunched posture

Q: What causes osteoporosis?

A: Osteoporosis is caused by bone loss. Most often, the reason for bone loss is very low levels of the hormone estrogen. Estrogen plays an important role in building and maintaining your bones.

www.womenshealth.gov | 800-994-9662

The most common cause of low estrogen levels is menopause. After menopause, your ovaries make very little estrogen. Some women lose up to 25% of bone mass in the first 10 years after menopause.

Also, your risk for developing osteoporosis is higher if you did not develop strong bones when you were young. Girls develop 90% of their bone mass by age 18. If an eating disorder, poor eating, lack of physical activity, or another health problem prevents you from building bone mass early in life, you will have less bone mass to draw on later in life.

Q: How is osteoporosis diagnosed?

A: Your doctor will do a bone density test to see how strong or weak your bones are. A common test is a central dual-energy x-ray absorptiometry (DXA). A DXA is a special type of x-ray of your bones. This test uses a very low amount of radiation.

Your doctor may also use other screening tools to predict your risk of having low bone density or breaking a bone.

Q: Do I need to be tested for osteoporosis?

A: Your doctor may suggest a bone density test for osteoporosis if:

- You are 65 or older
- You are younger than 65 but have risk factors for osteoporosis. Bone density testing is recommended for older women whose risk of breaking a bone is the same as or greater than that of a 65-year-old white woman with no risk factors other than age. Ask your doctor or nurse whether you need a bone density test before age 65.

Studies & Statistics / Osteoporosis

Q: How is osteoporosis treated?

A: If you have osteoporosis, your doctor may prescribe medicine to prevent more bone loss or build new bone mass. Your doctor may also suggest getting more calcium, vitamin D, and physical activity.

These steps may help prevent fractures, especially in the hip and spine, that can cause serious pain and disability.

Q: How can I prevent osteoporosis?

A: You can take steps to slow the natural bone loss with aging and to prevent your bones from becoming weak and brittle.

- Get enough calcium and vitamin D each day.
- Get active. Choose weight-bearing physical activities like running or dancing to build and strengthen your bones.
- Don't smoke.
- If you drink alcohol, drink in moderation (for women, this is one drink a day at most). Too much alcohol can harm your bones.
- Talk to your doctor about whether you need medicine to prevent bone loss.

Q: Should I take a calcium supplement?

A: It's best to get the calcium your body needs from food. But if you don't get enough calcium from the foods you eat, you may want to consider taking a calcium supplement.

Talk with your doctor or nurse before taking calcium supplements to see which kind is best for you and how much you need to take.

For more information...

about osteoporosis, call the OWH Helpline at 800-994-9662 or contact the following organizations:

Food and Drug Administration (FDA), HHS
888-463-6332 • www.fda.gov

National Institute on Aging (NIA), NIH, HHS
301-496-1752 • www.nia.nih.gov

NIH Osteoporosis and Related Bone Diseases National Resource Center, NIAMS, NIH, HHS
800-624-BONE • www.niams.nih.gov/health_info/bone

American Bone Health
888-266-3015 (Bone Health Hotline)
www.americanbonehealth.org

National Osteoporosis Foundation
800-231-4222 • www.nof.org

The Office on Women's Health is grateful for the additional reviews by:

- National Institute of Arthritis and Musculoskeletal and Skin Diseases staff
- Susan Randall, M.S.N., RN, FNP-BC, Senior Director, Science and Education, National Osteoporosis Foundation

All material contained on this page is free of copyright restrictions and may be copied, reproduced, or duplicated without permission of the Office on Women's Health in the Department of Health and Human Services. Citation of the source is appreciated.

Page last updated: August 30, 2017.

Content last reviewed: October 26, 2016.

www.facebook.com/HHSOWH

www.twitter.com/WomensHealth

www.youtube.com/WomensHealthgov

www.womenshealth.gov | 800-994-9662

Schizophrenia

National Institute of Mental Health

What is schizophrenia?

Schizophrenia is a serious mental illness that affects how a person thinks, feels, and behaves. People with schizophrenia may seem as though they have lost touch with reality, which can be distressing for them and for their family and friends. The symptoms of schizophrenia can make it difficult to participate in usual, everyday activities, but effective treatments are available. Many people who receive treatment can engage in school or work, achieve independence, and enjoy personal relationships.

What are the symptoms of schizophrenia?

It's important to recognize the symptoms of schizophrenia and seek help as early as possible. People with schizophrenia are usually diagnosed between the ages of 16 and 30, after the first episode of psychosis. Starting treatment as soon as possible following the first episode of psychosis is an important step toward recovery. However, research shows that gradual changes in thinking, mood, and social functioning often appear before the first episode of psychosis. Schizophrenia is rare in younger children.

Schizophrenia symptoms can differ from person to person, but they generally fall into three main categories: psychotic, negative, and cognitive.

Psychotic symptoms

Psychotic symptoms include changes in the way a person thinks, acts, and experiences the world. People with psychotic symptoms may lose a shared sense of reality with others and experience the world in a distorted way. For some people, these symptoms come and go. For others, the symptoms become stable over time. Psychotic symptoms include:

- **Hallucinations:** When a person sees, hears, smells, tastes, or feels things that are not actually there. Hearing voices is common for people with schizophrenia. People who hear voices may hear them for a long time before family or friends notice a problem.
- **Delusions:** When a person has strong beliefs that are not true and may seem irrational to others. For example, individuals experiencing delusions may believe that people on the radio and television are sending special messages that require a certain response, or they may believe that they are in danger or that others are trying to hurt them.

- **Thought disorder:** When a person has ways of thinking that are unusual or illogical. People with thought disorder may have trouble organizing their thoughts and speech. Sometimes a person will stop talking in the middle of a thought, jump from topic to topic, or make up words that have no meaning.
- **Movement disorder:** When a person exhibits abnormal body movements. People with movement disorder may repeat certain motions over and over.

Negative symptoms

Negative symptoms include loss of motivation, loss of interest or enjoyment in daily activities, withdrawal from social life, difficulty showing emotions, and difficulty functioning normally. Negative symptoms include:

- Having trouble planning and sticking with activities, such as grocery shopping
- Having trouble anticipating and feeling pleasure in everyday life
- Talking in a dull voice and showing limited facial expression
- Avoiding social interaction or interacting in socially awkward ways
- Having very low energy and spending a lot of time in passive activities. In extreme cases, a person might stop moving or talking for a while, which is a rare condition called *catatonia*.

These symptoms are sometimes mistaken for symptoms of depression or other mental illnesses.

Cognitive symptoms

Cognitive symptoms include problems with attention, concentration, and memory. These symptoms can make it hard to follow a conversation, learn new things, or remember appointments. A person's level of cognitive functioning is one of the best predictors of their day-to-day functioning. Cognitive functioning is evaluated using specific tests. Cognitive symptoms include:

- Having trouble processing information to make decisions
- Having trouble using information immediately after learning it
- Having trouble focusing or paying attention

Risk of violence

Most people with schizophrenia are not violent. Overall, people with schizophrenia are more likely than those without the illness to be harmed by others. For people with schizophrenia, the risk of self-harm and of violence to others is greatest when the illness is untreated. It is important to help people who are showing symptoms to get treatment as quickly as possible.

Schizophrenia vs. dissociative identity disorder

Although some of the signs may seem similar on the surface, schizophrenia is not dissociative identity disorder (which used to be called multiple personality disorder or split personality). People with dissociative identity disorder have two or more *distinct identities* that are present and that alternately take control of them.

What causes schizophrenia?

Several factors may contribute to a person's risk of developing schizophrenia, including:

- **Genetics.** Schizophrenia sometimes runs in families. However, just because one family member has schizophrenia, it does not mean that other members of the family also will have it. Studies suggest that many different genes may increase a person's chances of developing schizophrenia, but that no single gene causes the disorder by itself.
- **Environment.** Research suggests that a combination of genetic factors and aspects of a person's environment and life experiences may play a role in the development of schizophrenia. These environmental factors may include living in poverty, stressful or dangerous surroundings, and exposure to viruses or nutritional problems before birth.
- **Brain structure and function.** Research shows that people with schizophrenia may be more likely to have differences in the size of certain brain areas and in connections between brain areas. Some of these brain differences may develop before birth. Researchers are working to better understand how brain structure and function may relate to schizophrenia.

How is schizophrenia treated?

Current treatments for schizophrenia focus on helping individuals manage their symptoms, improve day-to-day functioning, and achieve personal life goals, such as completing education, pursuing a career, and having fulfilling relationships.

Antipsychotic medications

Antipsychotic medications can help make psychotic symptoms less intense and less frequent. These medications are usually taken every day in a pill or liquid form. Some antipsychotic medications are given as injections once or twice a month.

If a person's symptoms do not improve with usual antipsychotic medications, they may be prescribed clozapine. People who take clozapine must have regular blood tests to check for a potentially dangerous side effect that occurs in 1% to 2% of patients.

People respond to antipsychotic medications in different ways. It is important to report any side effects to a health care provider. Many people taking antipsychotic medications experience side effects such as weight gain, dry mouth, restlessness, and drowsiness when they start taking these medications. Some of these side effects may go away over time, while others may last.

> **You should not stop taking a medication without talking to your health care provider first.** Your health care provider will work with you to adjust your treatment plan in a safe and effective way. Some people may need to try several medications before finding the one that works best for them, so it is important to continue with treatment and to stay hopeful.

You can find the latest information on warnings, patient medication guides, or newly approved medications on the U.S. Food and Drug Administration (FDA) website at **www.fda.gov/drugsatfda**.

Psychosocial treatments

Psychosocial treatments help people find solutions to everyday challenges and manage symptoms while attending school, working, and forming relationships. These treatments are often used together with antipsychotic medication. People who participate in regular psychosocial treatment are less likely to have symptoms reoccur or to be hospitalized.

Examples of this kind of treatment include cognitive behavioral therapy, behavioral skills training, supported employment, and cognitive remediation interventions.

You can find information about psychosocial treatments on the National Institute of Mental Health (NIMH) website at **www.nimh.nih.gov/psychotherapies**.

Family education and support

Educational programs can help family and friends learn about symptoms of schizophrenia, treatment options, and strategies for helping loved ones with the illness. These programs can help friends and family manage their distress, boost their own coping skills, and strengthen their ability to provide support.

Coordinated specialty care

Coordinated specialty care (CSC) programs are recovery-focused programs for people with first episode psychosis, an early stage of schizophrenia. Health professionals and specialists work together as a team to provide CSC, which includes psychotherapy, medication, case management, employment and education support, and family education and support. The treatment team works collaboratively with the individual to make treatment decisions, involving family members as much as possible.

Compared with typical care, CSC is more effective in reducing symptoms, improving quality of life, and increasing involvement in work or school.

Assertive community treatment

Assertive community treatment (ACT) is designed to help individuals with schizophrenia who are likely to experience multiple hospitalizations or homelessness. ACT is usually delivered by a team of health professionals and specialists who work together to provide care to patients in the community.

Treatment for drug and alcohol misuse

It is common for people with schizophrenia to have problems with drugs and alcohol. A treatment program that includes treatment for both schizophrenia and substance use is important for recovery because substance use can interfere with treatment for schizophrenia.

How can I find help?

If you're not sure where to get help, your health care provider is a good place to start. Your health care provider can refer you to a qualified mental health professional, such as a psychiatrist or psychologist who has experience treating schizophrenia. You can learn more about getting help on the NIMH website at **www.nimh.nih.gov/findhelp**.

The Substance Abuse and Mental Health Services Administration (SAMHSA) has an online tool at **https://findtreatment.samhsa.gov** to help you find mental health services in your area. You can find information about treatment facilities that offer coordinated specialty care by using SAMHSA's Early Serious Mental Illness Treatment Locator at **www.samhsa.gov/esmi-treatment-locator**.

For tips on talking with your health care provider about your mental health and getting the most out of your visit, read NIMH's fact sheet, Taking Control of Your Mental Health: Tips for Talking With Your Health Care Provider, available at **www.nimh.nih.gov/talkingtips**.

How can I help a friend or relative with schizophrenia?

It can be difficult to know how to help someone who is experiencing psychosis. Here are some things you can do:

- Help them get treatment and encourage them to stay in treatment.
- Remember that their beliefs or hallucinations seem very real to them.
- Be respectful, supportive, and kind without tolerating dangerous or inappropriate behavior.
- Look for support groups and family education programs, such as those offered by the National Alliance on Mental Illness at **www.nami.org/Support-Education**.

> If your loved one is thinking about attempting suicide or otherwise harming themselves or others, seek help right away:
> - Call 911 or go to the nearest emergency room.
> - Call the National Suicide Prevention Lifeline (Lifeline) at 1-800-273-TALK (8255) or go to the Lifeline website at **https://suicidepreventionlifeline.org**.
> - Text the Crisis Text Line (HELLO to 741741).

What should I know about participating in clinical research?

Clinical trials are research studies that look at new ways to prevent, detect, or treat diseases and conditions. Although individuals may benefit from being part of a clinical trial, participants should be aware that the primary purpose of a clinical trial is to gain new scientific knowledge so that others may be better helped in the future.

Talk to your health care provider about clinical trials, their benefits and risks, and whether one is right for you. For more information, visit **www.nimh.nih.gov/clinicaltrials**.

The Voice of the Patient

A series of reports from the U.S. Food and Drug Administration's (FDA's)
Patient-Focused Drug Development Initiative

Female Sexual Dysfunction

Public Meeting: October 27, 2014
Report Date: June 2015

Center for Drug Evaluation and Research (CDER)
U.S. Food and Drug Administration (FDA)

Introduction

On October 27, 2014, FDA held a public meeting to hear perspectives from women with female sexual dysfunction (FSD) on their condition and on currently available therapies. FDA focused the meeting on the sexual interest and arousal symptoms associated with FSD because disorders of sexual interest and arousal are reported to be the most common forms of FSD and there are no FDA-approved therapies for treating these symptoms. FDA conducted the meeting as part of the agency's Patient-Focused Drug Development initiative, an FDA commitment under the fifth authorization of the Prescription Drug User Fee Act (PDUFA V) to more systematically gather patients' perspectives on their condition and available therapies to treat their condition. As part of this commitment, FDA is holding at least 20 public meetings between Fiscal Years 2013 - 2017, each focused on a specific disease area. More information on this initiative can be found at
http://www.fda.gov/ForIndustry/UserFees/PrescriptionDrugUserFee/ucm326192.htm.

The October 27 patient-focused meeting was part of a two-day FDA workshop to explore important issues with respect to the development of safe and effective drug therapies for FSD. On October 28, 2014, FDA held a scientific meeting with experts to discuss several scientific challenges associated with drug development, including diagnostic criteria, endpoints, and patient-reported outcome instruments. This report focuses on the October 27 patient-focused meeting. The archived webcast and transcript for the October 28 meeting are available on the meeting webpage.

Overview of female sexual dysfunction

Female sexual dysfunction (FSD) is a complex and multi-faceted disorder that has a wide spectrum of symptoms and severity. The term FSD covers a heterogeneous collection of conditions that have previously been classified into four different disorders: hypoactive sexual desire disorder (HSDD) characterized by a reduced or absent interest in sexual activity, female sexual arousal disorder (FSAD) characterized by an inability to attain or maintain sexual excitement, female orgasmic disorder characterized by the difficulty to attain orgasm despite sufficient arousal, and sexual pain disorder characterized by pain during sexual intercourse.

In May 2013, HSDD and FSAD were combined into a single diagnosis of female sexual interest/arousal disorder (FSIAD) in the Fifth Edition of the Diagnostic and Statistical Manual (DSM-5).[1] For a woman to be diagnosed with FSIAD, her symptoms of reduced sexual interest/arousal must have been present for at least six months, and must be severe enough to be a source of personal distress. FSIAD can be lifelong or acquired, range from mild to severe, and may be generalized or situational. There is currently no precise measure of the prevalence of FSIAD. However, one survey of U.S. women found that 12% of women reported experiencing personally distressing sexual problems.[2]

Pharmaceutical treatments for FSD are limited. There are FDA-approved products for treating moderate to severe pain during sexual intercourse related to vulvar and vaginal atrophy associated with menopause; however there are no drugs approved by FDA to specifically treat FSIAD, HSDD, or FSAD. Other prescription products are used off-label by patients, including sildenafil, testosterone or estrogen

---

[1] American Psychiatric Association. (2013). Diagnostic and statistical manual of mental disorders (5th ed.). Washington, DC
[2] Shifren et al. Sexual problems and distress in United States women – prevalence and correlates. Obstet Gynecol. 2008;112:970-8

hormonal therapies, and antidepressants. However, these products have either not demonstrated effectiveness for FSD or have potential safety issues if taken long-term. Non-drug therapies include lubricants, devices, behavioral or couples therapy, and lifestyle modifications.

Drug development for FSIAD is complicated due to many factors, such as the limited understanding of the underlying medical condition that may be responsible for the dysfunction, challenges in diagnosing the condition, difficulty in identifying outcomes that are both meaningful to patients and are measurable, and the complexity associated with designing trials that can reliably assess the drug's efficacy and safety.

Meeting overview

This meeting gave FDA the opportunity to hear directly from patients and patient representatives (including partners, healthcare providers, and patient advocates) about their experiences with female sexual dysfunction and its treatments. Discussion focused on two key topics: (1) the effects of female sexual dysfunction that matter most to patients and (2) patients' perspectives on treatments for female sexual dysfunction. The discussion questions (Appendix 1) were published in a Federal Register notice that announced the meeting.

For each topic, a panel of patients with FSD (Appendix 2) shared comments to begin the dialogue. Panel comments were followed by a facilitated discussion inviting comments from other patients and patient representatives in the audience. An FDA facilitator led the discussion, and a panel of FDA staff (Appendix 2) asked follow-up questions. Participants who joined the meeting via live webcast (referred to in this report as web participants) were also able to contribute comments. In addition, in-person and web participants were periodically invited to respond to polling questions (Appendix 3), which provided a sense of the demographic makeup of participants and how many participants shared a particular perspective on a given topic.[3]

Approximately 50 patients with FSD or patient representatives attended the meeting in-person, and approximately 30 patients or patient representatives provided input through the live webcast. According to their responses to the polling questions, in-person participants represented an even distribution of age (from below 30 to above 70), whereas the majority of web participants were less than 50 years of age. About one-half of in-person participants and most web participants indicated that they have had symptoms for 10 years or less. Most in-person participants reported that they were diagnosed with a form of FSD by a healthcare provider, while most web participants reported that they were not formally diagnosed. Based on the meeting discussion, it appears that in-person participants in general have received more specific care (e.g., from a specialist on sexual health) than is expected in the patient population and they were more familiar with FSD treatments and other aspects of drug development. Some participants voluntarily disclosed that their travel to the meeting was funded. Although meeting participants may not fully represent the population living with FSD, their input reflected a range of experiences with its symptoms and treatments.

---

[3] The polling questions were intended as a discussion aid only, and not for scientific purposes. Polling results should not be interpreted as being representative of the overall FSD patient population.

To supplement the input gathered at the meeting, patients and others were encouraged to submit comments on FSD to a public docket,[4] which was open until December 29, 2014. A total of 110 comments were submitted to the public docket by patients and other stakeholders, including academicians, healthcare professionals, consumer groups, and women's health advocates.

More information, including the archived webcast and meeting transcript, is available on the meeting website: http://www.fda.gov/Drugs/NewsEvents/ucm401167.htm

Report overview and key themes

This report summarizes the input provided by patients and patient representatives at the meeting or through the webcast. It also includes a summary of comments submitted to the public docket. The report is intended to reflect the content of this meeting and the docket comment submissions as they relate to patient perspectives on FSD symptoms, impacts, and current treatments.[5] To the extent possible, the terms used in this summary to describe symptoms, impacts, and treatment experiences reflect the words used by in-person participants, web participants, and docket commenters. The report is not purported to be representative in any way of the views and experiences of the entire FSD patient population or of any specific group of individuals or entities. There may be symptoms, impacts, treatments, or other perspectives on the condition that are not included in the report.

The input from the meeting and docket comments underscores the significant impact that symptoms of FSD can have on women's lives, and the challenges they face in finding safe, effective, and tolerable therapies to manage their condition. It also highlights the range of perspectives on the need for drug therapies for FSIAD. Several key themes emerged from this meeting:

- The women who participated in this meeting conceptualize and experience sexual *interest* (or *desire*, as the term most participants used) distinct from sexual *arousal*. They varied in their experience of reduced or absent interest, reduced or absent arousal, or both. Some, but not all, also experience other aspects of FSD, including pain, dryness, or inability to orgasm, which they believe contributes to their lack of desire. Participants appeared to believe that their most significant symptoms of their condition are multi-faceted and broader than the six specific sexual symptoms of FSIAD outlined in the DSM-5.

- Many participants and docket commenters described a distinct transition from a prior fulfilling sex life to a total loss of interest or arousal. Regardless of their varying beliefs about the causes or triggers of their interest or arousal symptoms, participants stressed the significant distress it causes daily. They described never initiating sexual contact, the measures they take to avoid intimacy, and persistent anxiety. They further described the profound impact their FSD has on their relationships, their self-identity, and their emotional well-being.

---

[4] A *docket* is a repository through which the public can submit electronic and written comments on specific topics to U.S. federal agencies such as FDA. More information can be found at www.regulations.gov.

[5] The public was also able to provide input at the October 27 meeting on other issues related to drug development, through an open public comment session. These comments are available through the meeting transcript and archived webcast, but may not be summarized in this report.

- Participants shared multifaceted views on the concept of a *satisfying sexual event* (a measure used to assess treatment efficacy, described further in the report), largely focusing on their interaction with their partner. Many indicated that although orgasm is important, it is not a necessary component of a satisfying sexual event. Several stressed the importance of feeling desire regardless of whether it is accompanied by a satisfying sexual event.

- Participants and docket commenters shared their complex journeys to find effective and tolerable therapies to address their interest and arousal symptoms. They described their experiences with hormonal therapies and other prescription drugs used off label, investigational therapies studied in a clinical trial, over-the-counter products, non-drug therapies, and couples or behavioral therapy, all varying in their degree of effectiveness.

- Participants had varying perspectives on the best way to adequately manage their condition, particularly with respect to the use of pharmaceutical therapies. Some participants believe that given the significant cultural component of sex and sexuality, interest and arousal effects can and should be primarily addressed through counselling and other behavioral therapies. However, many participants indicated that they see a need to determine and address underlying physiological causes or contributors to their interest and arousal symptoms.

The sections that follow provide greater detail on the experiences and views shared by meeting participants and docket commenters. The patient input generated through this Patient-Focused Drug Development meeting and public docket comments strengthens FDA's understanding of the burden of FSD on patients and the therapies currently used to treat FSD and its symptoms. FDA staff will carefully consider this input as it fulfills its role in the drug development process, including when advising sponsors on their drug development programs and when assessing products under review for marketing approval. For example, Appendix 4 shows how this input may directly support our benefit-risk assessments for products under review. This input may also be of value to the drug development process more broadly. For example, the report may be useful to drug developers as they explore new outcome measures, outcome assessments, and clinical trial designs.

Topic 1: The Effects of Female Sexual Dysfunction that Matter Most to Patients

The first discussion topic focused on patients' experiences with their female sexual dysfunction symptoms and the resulting effects on their daily lives. FDA was particularly interested in hearing about participants' symptoms relating to sexual interest and arousal, how these symptoms affect their sexual experiences, and how their symptoms have changed over time.

Four women with FSD (Appendix 2) provided comments to start the dialogue. Two panelists described beginning to experience interest and/or arousal symptoms within the past five years, and the other two spoke of their experiences dealing with these symptoms for many years. The panelists described the challenges they face living with FSD, and the impact that their condition has on their ability to lead a fulfilling sexual life and maintain relationships. They also described the significant frustration, anxiety, and loss that they have experienced because of their condition.

In the large-group facilitated discussion that followed the panel discussion, most patients with FSD in the audience indicated, by a show of hands, that their experiences were reflected in at least one of the panelists' comments. A summary of the Topic 1 discussion is provided below.

Perspectives on most significant symptoms

The facilitated discussion provided a look into how symptoms manifest and how they have changed over time. The range of symptoms discussed by in-person and web participants is described in more detail below. Note that while FDA focused discussion on sexual interest and arousal symptoms to narrow the meeting scope, this report includes the wider range of symptoms and impacts described at the meeting. Generally speaking, participants appeared to believe that their most significant symptoms are multifaceted and broader than the six specific sexual symptoms outlined in the DSM-5.

Sexual Interest or Desire

FDA began the large group discussion by asking participants how they conceptualize the terms *interest* and *arousal*. One participant described desire as "if you are interested in having sex or receptive to your partner approaching you" and arousal as "when you are getting wet… tingly, when you are having the bodily changes." Several other participants shared similar conceptualizations. However, one participant stressed the challenge in finding consistent, overarching terms given the significant diversity in personal experiences.

Reduction or loss of sexual interest was the most frequently discussed symptom by in-person and web participants. Participants used the terms *desire* (most frequently used), *interest*, *libido*, and *sexual appetite* when describing this aspect of their condition. Their comments focused on thinking about sex, the desire to have sex, and their response to (or avoidance of) their partner's initiation, as illustrated below:

- "I don't even think about sex."
- "I knew I wanted to have sex but I had no desire. I refrained."
- "In a beautiful place with the man I love, my body was like a shell with nothing inside."
- "I am able to grit through [sex], but I do it for [my partner], not for me."

According to the results of a polling question (Appendix 3, Question 6) few in-person and web participants considered "no or reduced sexual/erotic thoughts or fantasies" (one of the diagnostic criteria in the DSM-5) to have a significant impact on daily life.

Several participants commented on the loss of their ability to become aroused. Participants used the terms *arousal, response, stimulated, sexual excitement,* and *becoming lubricated* when describing this aspect of their condition, as illustrated below:

- "The ability to be stimulated by being touched slowly disappeared. Sexual arousal and response time kept taking longer and longer until it became nonexistent."
- "It is not a matter of how much foreplay we do or not. I'll be approached and we can spend forever trying to make something happen."
- "[E]ven if I'm willing when my husband initiates to have sex, I can't stay in the moment necessarily, and then your body stops responding."

The facilitator and FDA panel asked a number of follow-up questions throughout the discussion for a better understanding of patients' experiences with sexual interest and arousal. The topics raised are summarized below.

Onset of interest and arousal symptoms, and changes over time

When asked by show of hands, a few participants indicated that they have been living with their conditions for their entire lives. However, most participants indicated that they had acquired their symptoms, framing their experience as a transition from a fulfilling sex life to a total loss of interest and arousal. Some participants noted a gradual change over the course of several months or years, while for others the change happened "like a switch that went off."

Several participants attributed the onset of their condition (either sudden or gradual) to specific life events, including childbirth, hysterectomy or mastectomy, intrauterine device complications, early-onset menopause, discontinuing hormone therapy, and adverse reactions to medications. Some commented that their lack of interest was related to, or even caused by, other FSD effects. Other participants, however, indicated that they could not pinpoint a possible cause of their symptoms.

Beyond the onset of symptoms, several participants identified other factors that they believe exacerbate or contribute to their symptoms of FSD. Many in-person participants commented on the waxing and waning in symptoms associated with their testosterone treatments (discussed more in Topic 2). A few participants described the impact that stress has on their symptoms. For example, one participant described "the loss of a good job, the illnesses and deaths of my parents, et cetera, added to that ebb and flow in my sex life." A few participants focused their comments on menopause and "the challenge of aging," which "presents an additional issue [to] sexual functioning."

Some participants expressed their belief that there is a natural variation in sexual desire from one person to the next or over the course of time and discussed learning to temper expectations associated with cultural pressures and unrealistic expectations. As one participant explained, "[my husband and I] exposed a war between us sexually that had to do with the stereotypical ideas about men and women that we had personalized to each other." Other participants, however, emphasized that their symptoms do not stem from relationship or communication issues, and are purely physiological. One participant shared, "we don't have any other stressors in our relationship; there are no issues in our life."

Other symptoms and their effect on interest and arousal

Although the focus of the meeting was on interest and arousal, discussion on other FSD symptoms was raised as well, including their relationship to interest and arousal.

- *Reduced or loss of orgasm:* Some participants commented on their inability to achieve orgasm most or all of the time, as well as the subsequent role that orgasm plays in their sexual experience. As one participant explained, "I stopped having desire for sex … [and] although I was alarmed, it wasn't until about four years later when I lost my orgasm that my attention was captured." Some participants commented that although they experience a lack of desire, they do not experience trouble with orgasm. Participants discussed in detail the role that orgasm plays or does not play in a satisfying sexual experience, covered in Topic 2.

- *Pain:* A few participants discussed pain symptoms that manifest whenever they engage in sexual intimacy or intercourse. These participants described the impact that pain can have on their interest and arousal. For example, one participant commented that "as my arousal builds often times I experience just an unbelievable migraine...so some of my low libido might just be [due to] the fact that there is pain waiting at the end." Another participant described the effects of how vaginal dryness and pain affects her interest, stating that "Having sex was not at all appealing. The pain during intercourse was excruciating. Both my desire and interest were overshadowed by my fear of pain." One participant, however, commented that her FSD first manifested as a lack of desire and then progressed to include vaginal dryness.

- *Anxiety:* Several participants commented on the anxiety they feel when facing a sexual encounter. Some described the loop of negative thoughts that constantly runs through their head as they are engaged with their partners, for example wondering "am I going to be able to orgasm during this and is that going to impact how he feels about our relationship," or "I know that I'm not going to be able to respond back." Participants reported these feelings to be a significant deterrent from having sex. In addition, when asked by FDA, about one-half of meeting participants indicated by show of hand that they would place anxiety among the top symptoms of FSD that have the most significant impact on daily life.

- *Other symptoms,* such as hot flashes, sleep disturbances, and mood swings were also mentioned.

Initiation of Sex

Although not asked through polling, most in-person participants referenced having a long-term relationship with a partner. In response to a question asked by FDA, nearly all participants indicated that their partner is the one who typically initiates sexual activity. Participants described engaging in "duty sex" and having sex "out of obligation." As one participant explained, "I might not even want to have sex but if he wants sex then and I give it to him then, yes, I was a good wife today." A web participant commented that "I have to pretend to enjoy for my husband otherwise he won't even approach me to have sex. He has to know that he has pleased me and satisfied me."

Participants also described their reluctance to engage in sexual activity and the measures they take to avoid intimacy "at all costs." One comment resonated with many in-person and web participants: "I found myself avoiding any situations where a sexual experience may occur... going to bed after my husband fell asleep or jumping out of bed in the morning before he got up just so he wouldn't try to initiate sex. I even found myself avoiding simple hugs and kisses."

Overall impact of female sexual dysfunction on daily life

Participants throughout the meeting described the larger impact sexual interest and arousal symptoms have on their lives and the lives of their partners and families, summarized below.

- **Impact on relationships**: Most participants discussed the strain that their FSD placed on their partners and their relationships. A few participants described their partners' reluctance to initiate contact, because of their perceived failure to stimulate sexual response, their fear of rejection, or their fear of causing their partner physical or emotional pain. As one participant's partner commented during the meeting, "It does have a huge impact when your lover, your soul mate, is no longer interested in having sex with you." Another participant shared that her partner "has said to me that he feels stupid at times when he keeps getting shut down. I know he feels rejected." Other participants commented on relationships that have failed because of their FSD. One participant explained, "I lost a major relationship to this issue, and I never want to go back there." A few participants stressed that the negative impact of their condition affects not just relationship with partners, but their relationships with family and friends.

- *Impact on self-esteem and identity:* Participants said that their loss of sexual functioning left them with feelings of low self-esteem and inadequacy. Many noticed a drop in their levels of confidence as it related to their sexuality, attractiveness, and femininity. One participant shared, "I had difficulty coping with my new reality and coming to terms with the discrepancy between who I was and who I became." Another participant commented that her condition "affects things like my self-confidence and how I approach the world and how I feel about myself and what I project to other people."

- *Emotional impacts*: Several participants described the devastation they felt after they failed to regain sexual function and were unable to perform in intimate situations with partners. One participant shared, "I became so frustrated that any attempt to have sexual intercourse would end up in me crying." Other participants discussed the guilt their difficulties caused them to feel when they said, "I can't be the woman he married" and "I feel like I pulled a bait and switch with my poor husband, who is undoubtedly wondering where the old me has run off to." Participants also linked the shame and stigma associated with their condition to the isolation they felt. They described being embarrassed and reluctant to talk about their issues.

Topic 2: Patient Perspectives on Treatments for Female Sexual Dysfunction

The second discussion topic focused on patients' experiences with therapies used to treat FSD, with particular focus on therapies to address interest and arousal. Four patient panelists provided comments to begin the dialogue. Panelists included a woman living with FSD for almost 20 years and who has found hormonal therapies to be effective; a woman in her 30s with a more recent onset of symptoms who has yet to find an effective therapy; a woman living with FSD for twenty-five years and who did not have success with hormonal therapies but who did find benefit by participating in a clinical trial for an investigational drug therapy; and a woman whose management of her condition focuses entirely on her relationships and her consciousness of sex and sexuality.

In the large-group facilitated discussion that followed, nearly all patients in the audience indicated by a show of hands that their experiences were reflected in the panelists' comments. According to the results of a polling question (Appendix 3, Question 8), the majority of in-person participants reported taking prescription medication to treat their symptoms, followed closely by over-the-counter products. Dietary and lifestyle changes were also identified by participants as an important component of therapy. Fewer web participants reported taking prescription medications, although many did report using over-the-counter products and undergoing lifestyle changes. A number of in-person and web participants reported they were not currently doing or taking anything to treat their symptoms.

Throughout the dialogue, participants described in detail the benefits and downsides they have experienced from various therapies and modifications used to manage their condition. Participant experiences and perspectives shared at the meeting are summarized below. This section ends with participants' perspectives on ideal treatments and broader considerations regarding FSD treatment.

Experimental or off-label prescription therapies

Hormonal therapy

Hormonal therapy, particularly testosterone, was discussed at length by several participants at the meeting.[6] Products mentioned included testosterone topical creams or gels, injections, or implanted pellets (these products are not FDA-approved to treat female sexual dysfunction and thus their uses are considered to be off-label). These participants described being prescribed hormonal therapies after blood tests revealed low levels of testosterone for their age range.

Participants described a range of effectiveness for testosterone products. Several described noticeable alleviation of symptoms, including an increase in desire, arousal, and ability to orgasm and described their excitement at discovering that they were interested in initiating sexual contact on their own. Some participants noted variability in effectiveness, or waxing and waning effect, over the course of treatment. A few participants, however, commented that they did not notice benefit or that they briefly experienced benefits but then suddenly ceased responding to treatment.

Participants who used testosterone therapies described experiencing side effects such as acne, unwanted hair growth, and nausea. In addition, participants discussed the downsides to using gels and creams that are odorous and sticky, pellets that require costly surgical procedures, and injections that can cause bruising and bleeding. They discussed their general preference for one type of product over another based on a number of factors such as duration of results, consistency in effect, and convenience. Several participants stated that they did not mind the side effects they experienced when they weighed the benefits against them, while others reported discontinuing use after experiencing downsides with minimal or no improvement of symptoms. A few participants expressed concern about what the long-term effects of testosterone may be, especially if hormone levels were frequently fluctuating. Some participants said that the costs of these treatments not covered by insurance prevented them from continuing treatment even though they had helped to improve their symptoms.

Some participants commented on their success with using estrogen and progestin therapies to treat FSD symptoms, particularly those symptoms associated with menopause or hysterectomy complications. Throughout their treatment regimens they underwent blood testing and updated their dosages periodically under the guidance of their healthcare professionals. These participants noted improvement in both their daily function and sexual responsiveness.

Antidepressants

Several participants described being prescribed antidepressants to address their interest and arousal symptoms. Most of these participants stated that these medications did not relieve their sexual dysfunction symptoms, and only made it more difficult to orgasm. As one participant explained "I had also been prescribed Wellbutrin (bupropion) at the beginning to see if that would maybe help me at least enjoy life. And, it probably made me kinder to my children, but it still didn't give me any better desire." A few women expressed frustration about being prescribed antidepressants to treat their distress associated with FSD, without being treated for their underlying sexual dysfunction symptoms.

---

[6] It should be noted that in-person meeting participants appeared to have more extensive experience with testosterone products than would be expected in the general population of women with FSD.

Other drug therapies

Two participants commented on their experiences with the investigational therapy flibanserin. One participant stated that she took the therapy as part of an open-label (not blinded) clinical trial extension, and one participant noted being part of a clinical trial for flibanserin. These participants described an improvement in sexual desire within a few weeks of use, and described the benefits as having sexual feelings, initiating sex, and enjoying intimacy once again.

Other drug therapies mentioned included muscle relaxants, pain killers, nerve injections, and Viagra (sildenafil). Participants did not report any positive impacts of these therapies on their symptoms.

Non-prescription or non-drug therapies

Participants discussed using or trying a number of non-prescription or non-drug approaches in an attempt to treat their sexual dysfunction, to rule out potential root causes of their symptoms, or to supplement their therapeutic regimens. A summary of these therapies is listed below:

- *Couples therapy*: Participants discussed their experiences with couples therapy, in which they worked on their relationship with their partner in hopes of improving sexual difficulties. Some stressed the benefits they have seen in such therapy, believing that the root of their problems stemmed either from their relationship or from their partner's approach to sex. As one participant explained, "accepting our sexual differences has been part of the whole change." Some said that they did not have any success in resolving their symptoms with couples therapy.

- *Behavioral therapies*: Several participants described practicing behavioral techniques in varying ways during their sexual encounters. One participant described practicing mindfulness, making sure she stays in the moment during intimacy, and refocusing back if she is having difficulty responding. A few participants commented on changing their conceptualization of sexuality and incorporating positive sexuality and sensuality techniques to enhance their sexual experiences. A few participants commented on the benefit of visual or physical stimulation aids (e.g., erotica, devices) for some women. A webcast participant, however, commented on the challenge associated with some partners' perceptions of failure if devices are used.

- *Over-the-counter products* cited by participants included lubricants, use of supplements such as DHEA (dehydroepiandrosterone), Provestra, and male enhancement supplements. Participants generally commented that they did not notice any improvement of desire or arousal symptoms with the use of these products.

- *Physical therapy*: A few participants described trying manual pelvic floor physical therapy, massage, or acupuncture, without success.

Perspectives on an ideal treatment for female sexual dysfunction

Throughout the meeting, participants provided their perspectives on what they would look for in a treatment that addresses their interest and arousal symptoms. Many participants stressed their desire to return to the quality of life they had before they began to experience FSD. For example, participants commented that they want "that part of my life back," "the old me," and "to be the woman my husband married not too long ago." A few participants emphasized the importance of having intimacy in which both parties know, as one participant explained, that "it's not duty sex but that I actually want him." Participants commented on their desire to regain spontaneity in their sex lives, to respond to advances without issue, and to have more satisfying sexual experiences. As one participant concluded, "I want to think about sex. I want to initiate sex. I want to have more of it."

FDA asked participants their perspectives on consistent treatments that would be taken every day versus intermittent treatments that would be taken on specific days. Most participants responded that they would prefer to have a medication that consistently increases their interest and arousal. One participant explained, "I want to always desire my husband and I don't want it to be situational." Another participant, however, stated that constant desire may be too lofty a goal, and that "perfection when it comes to sex" cannot be easily attained. Several participants also commented on wanting to address their sexuality and self-identity more globally. For example, one participant commented that she wants to regain her identity as a woman, which extends beyond thinking about the next sexual event.

Some participants cautioned that the ideal treatment requires understanding of the natural variation among women, the cultural aspects of sex, and their impacts on women's sexual experiences. For example, one participant commented that an ideal treatment would move away from "a broader definition of normal sexuality for both sexes." Another person commented that an ideal treatment would "account for the human waxing and waning of physical and sexual desire and arousal."

Other considerations on drug development for female sexual dysfunction

Given the complex factors underlying drug development for FSD, and in particular treatments targeting interest and arousal, FDA was interested in listening to patient input on some particular issues, summarized below.

Satisfying Sexual Events (SSE) as a clinical endpoint

Evaluating the efficacy of a potential pharmaceutical treatment for sexual interest or arousal symptoms often relies on a measure that assesses changes in the frequency of a woman's *satisfying sexual events* over time. FDA was interested in hearing how participants conceptualize a satisfying sexual event and its importance to their overall sexual experience, with respect to their FSD. Participants largely appeared to believe that having satisfying sexual events was important to them; however they expressed varying perspectives on what they consider the term to mean in the context of their symptoms. Some participants stressed that desire and arousal are important components of a satisfying sexual event, so that they were not simply performing for their partner's benefit.

Participants also had differing views on whether or not orgasms are a necessary component of satisfying sexual events. In a show of hands, many participants indicated that an orgasm is not a necessary part of sexual excitement. As one healthcare provider explained, "sexual excitement is often akin to the building of an orgasm but not necessarily the actual orgasm." Another participant responded, "… for me sex is not just about orgasm… a successful or satisfying event for me is more about feeling connected to [my husband] and being close and feeling arousal." Other participants, however, stated that orgasm is a very important aspect of sexual experience, particularly for women who never experience orgasm. As one participant explained, "for some people who know that orgasm is… an option that they can have relatively easily, then it is not as crucial of a factor. But when it is never a factor then it is a very crucial one."

Tracking symptoms over time

FDA was also interested in hearing participants' experiences and perspectives on tracking symptoms over time and how best to record symptoms. Participants had mixed responses. Some said that they do currently track symptoms because it helps them to better understand the patterns of their dysfunction, guide discussions with their physicians, and track how well their treatments are working (e.g., if they need to get another dose of testosterone). Most participants, however, especially those who were not on a testosterone treatment, indicated they do not systematically track symptoms. As one participant explained, there is "no need to write it down because [my symptoms] are the same every single day." Another commented that she did not see the value of daily tracking in her experience with a clinical trial, viewing the management of her condition as a long-term process of weeks and months rather than daily. Another added that she is opposed to daily recordings because her symptoms are too "depressing and distressing to think about on a daily basis." One participant commented that the considerations on monitoring depend on the nature of the therapy; in the framework of sex therapy "obsessional self-focus [can become the] magnifying problem rather than a useful intervention."

Other issues raised by participants

Throughout the meeting, participants shared experiences and perspectives on several other issues related to FSD, including difficulty in receiving a diagnosis, lack of understanding among healthcare providers, difficulty in accessing treatments, financial burden of treatments, the complexities of sexuality and sexual health, and beliefs that the healthcare system is more cognizant of male sexual dysfunction than female sexual dysfunction.

Summary of Comments Submitted to the Public Docket

FDA received 110 comment submissions to the public docket that supplemented the October 27-28, 2014 public meeting. About one-quarter of submitted comments were contributed by individual patients with FSD or the partners of patients with FSD. Other comments were submitted by academicians, healthcare professionals, consumer groups, women's health advocates, and pharmaceutical industry representatives. Generally speaking, the comments from patients, partners, healthcare providers, and advocates largely reflected the range of input generated at the meeting, and provided greater depth of explanation in areas such as comorbid conditions, contributing factors, and onset of symptoms. The following is a brief summary of the comments on the topics addressed at the October 27 patient-focused meeting,[7] highlighting areas of similarity and difference as compared to the meeting input.

---

[7] Because this report centers on patient perspectives of FSD symptoms, impacts, and treatment, this report focuses on comments pertaining to these subject matters. The comments to the docket covered a wide range of other important topics related to drug development for FSD, such as perspectives on the need for drug therapies, clinical endpoints, the medicalization of women's sexual health, conflicts of interest between healthcare professionals and pharmaceutical companies, marketing influences on the consumer, and the state of female sexual education in the U.S. Comments on these topics were also reviewed and considered by FDA but are not summarized in this report.

Studies & Statistics / The Voice of the Patient: Female Sexual Dysfunction

Submitted comments on symptoms of female sexual dysfunction

Submissions from the docket reinforced the conceptualizations of FSD symptoms that participants described at the October 27 meeting. Commenters emphasized the distress felt from being unable to respond to sexual advances by partners, and reiterated that, as one commenter stated, "sex is more out of obligation than pleasure." For example, one commenter explained that "it is horrible to have someone you love want you, make love to you, and wish that they would stop." Commenters also described employing a variety of tactics to constantly avoid their partners and intimate situations. Below are further highlights of a selection of frequently mentioned symptoms.

- *Onset of reduced or absent sexual interest*: Sexual interest or desire was the most frequently commented upon aspect of FSD in the docket. Most commenters echoed meeting participants' experiences describing a significant change from a former "healthy interest in sex." While a few commented that their libido rises and falls, the majority described a reduction of interest over time until stabilizing at low or absent levels of desire. For some, the loss of interest and arousal was a more abrupt transformation, one that caused their active sex lives to "end overnight." Comments from a few women in their 20s and 30s expressed concerns with suddenly losing interest in sex at such an early stage in their lives. In contrast to the majority of commenters and meeting participants, one woman described living with a lifelong lack of sexual interest, explaining that "although I went through puberty, I did not develop any sexual interest in people. The idea of sex with another person actually disgusted me. I had virtually no libido."

- *Reduced or absent arousal and orgasm:* A few commenters specified that they did not have any issues with desire, but were more distressed by their inability to become aroused and have an orgasm. Commenters described a "lack of physical sensation in former erogenous zones," to the point where "the clitoris does not respond to stimulation." One individual described strong feelings of desire that occur without any downstream physical effects, noting, "I want to have sex with my husband and do so on a regular basis... I just want my 'tingle' back."

- *Contributing factors*: Similar to what was heard at the meeting, almost all commenters were able to pinpoint a specific time when they began to experience symptoms (either gradually or all at once). For some, interest and/or arousal "bottomed out completely" after menopause, hysterectomies, or oophorectomies, and a few mentioned additional symptoms that occurred with menopause, including vaginal dryness, pain, and odor. A few commenters stressed the importance of addressing the effects of menopause and aging on sexual interest and desire. A few commenters described the significance of interest and arousal symptoms as side effects of their antidepressant medication.

    In contrast, several commenters stressed that their FSD symptoms occur independently of other factors, including relationship or emotional problems. As one commenter stated, "I have not noticed any relation to my emotions or anything else in my life. I am just simply not even interested in intercourse in any way much of the time." Another explained, "even when on vacation when stressors are not present, sexual desire does not return, even temporarily."

Submitted comments on the overall impact of female sexual dysfunction on daily life

The submitted comments strongly reiterated the significant impacts that lack of sexual interest and arousal has on many patients' lives more broadly.

- *Impact on relationships*: A common theme in the submitted comments was the toll that FSD symptoms take on partner relationships. Several described the contribution of FSD to divorce, separation, or dissolution of a relationship. Commenters, including the partners of women with FSD, overwhelmingly reiterated the significance of the partner's perceptions of inadequacy, rejection, and frustration. A few commenters described feeling depressed and worried that their partner would leave them for "another woman who can satisfy him."

- *Emotional Impacts:* Commenters reiterated the isolation, guilt, and emotional distress they experience because of their FSD and its impact on relationship and other aspects of life. A healthcare professional said that the constant, unchanging nature of FSD symptoms is what "in part contributes to [the woman's] belief that the symptoms will never get better, there is nothing that will help restore her desire, and leads to isolation and hopelessness." As another commenter explained, "I'm being deprived of having a fulfilling life and marriage because of something I don't seem to have any control over."

Submitted comments on current treatments for female sexual dysfunction

Similar to the meeting input, the submitted comments covered a range of experiences on a multitude of treatments that patients use or have tried in an effort to address their symptoms.

- *Hormonal therapy*: A few commenters described complex treatment regimens consisting of hormone therapies, which often did not help or had benefits that lessened in effect over time. A commenter who used testosterone and estrogen creams said she has some success with "pulsing" her medication (discontinuing and restarting treatment). One commenter described being offered a low dose testosterone therapy by her doctor but said she was "reluctant to take it because of all the warnings that the long term health benefits to women were unknown."

- *Antidepressants*: Comments on the effects of antidepressants largely reflected what was heard at the meeting. Commenters who have had depression described an inability to feel desire or achieve an orgasm while on antidepressants. One commenter stated, "For many years, I blamed the depression for all my problems with sex... In the end, however, what helped me more than anything else was simply getting off the antidepressants, and realizing the effects they'd had on my sexuality for years."

- *Other drug therapies* mentioned included sildenafil and leuprolide, both of which were reported to be unsuccessful in long-term improvement of symptoms for those individuals.

- *Couples therapy and behavioral therapies:* A few commenters shared their experiences and perspectives on counseling to address FSD, with varying perspectives on its effectiveness. One commenter noted that being informed about female sexuality and common misconceptions has helped her to better understand her body and learn to work within her limits.

- *Other products:* A few commenters shared that the dietary supplement and herbal products they have tried did not alleviate symptoms. For example, one individual said, "I was so desperate that I started trying home-remedies and other unsafe herbal products. Although they didn't help my sexual desire, they definitely had adverse effects." One commenter described using marijuana and reported improvements in her sexual experiences.

- *Non-drug therapies:* One commenter discussed the benefits of non-drug lifestyle changes such as stopping smoking, regular exercise, and weight loss.

Submitted comments on ideal treatments for female sexual dysfunction

The submitted comments reflected the varying perspectives shared at the meeting with respect to the best approach for the treatment of FSD, particularly sexual interest and arousal components. Many patients and partners stressed their desire for pharmaceutical treatment options, and a few patients commented that they felt confident in weighing the personal risks and benefits of therapies in order to choose a regimen that works best for them. Several other commenters, however, stressed the need for caution in the push for pharmaceutical treatments and that more focus should be placed on acknowledging the complexity and addressing the psychosocial and cultural aspects of sex and sexuality.

Conclusion

Drug development for female sexual dysfunction is a complex and challenging process, and there are still many scientific issues that need to be resolved in this field. The input received through the October 27 Patient-Focused Drug Development meeting and subsequent October 28 Scientific Workshop enabled FDA and other stakeholders the chance to explore important aspects of drug development for FSD. Importantly, the October 27 patient-focused meeting and accompanying public docket provided FDA an opportunity to listen directly to patients about what aspects of their condition matter most to them, and how their condition affects their sexual experience and their daily life. FDA recognizes that patients have a unique ability to contribute to the understanding of the broader context of this condition, which is important to our role, and that of others, in the drug development process. Of particular value is patient perspective on what they would value in treatment for FSD, which can guide efforts to identify endpoints and develop tools to effectively measure and evaluate the benefit of potential therapies.

FDA is appreciative of the patients and patient representatives who thoughtfully shared their experiences and perspectives on this sensitive topic, including the helplessness and frustration they experience as their conditions affect their relationships, their emotional well-being, and their overall quality of life. The variability in the nature of symptoms and in the current approaches to treatment is considerable. Many participants expressed a strong desire for improvements to their existing treatments and for new treatments that better target the underlying cause of FSD. FDA is committed to supporting the development of safe and effective drug therapies for FSD.

Understanding Sleep

Brain Basics

Studies & Statistics / Understanding Sleep

Introduction

Sleep is an important part of your daily routine—you spend about one-third of your time doing it. Quality sleep—and getting enough of it at the right times—is as essential to survival as food and water. Without sleep you can't form or maintain the pathways in your brain that let you learn and create new memories, and it's harder to concentrate and respond quickly.

Sleep is important to a number of brain functions, including how nerve cells (neurons) communicate with each other. In fact, your brain and body stay remarkably active while you sleep. Recent findings suggest that sleep plays a housekeeping role that removes toxins in your brain that build up while you are awake.

Everyone needs sleep, but its biological purpose remains a mystery. Sleep affects almost every type of tissue and system in the body—from the brain, heart, and lungs to metabolism, immune function, mood, and disease resistance. Research shows that a chronic lack of sleep, or getting poor quality sleep, increases the risk of disorders including high blood pressure, cardiovascular disease, diabetes, depression, and obesity.

Sleep is a complex and dynamic process that affects how you function in ways scientists are now beginning to understand. This booklet describes how your need for sleep is regulated and what happens in the brain during sleep.

Studies & Statistics / Understanding Sleep

ANATOMY OF SLEEP

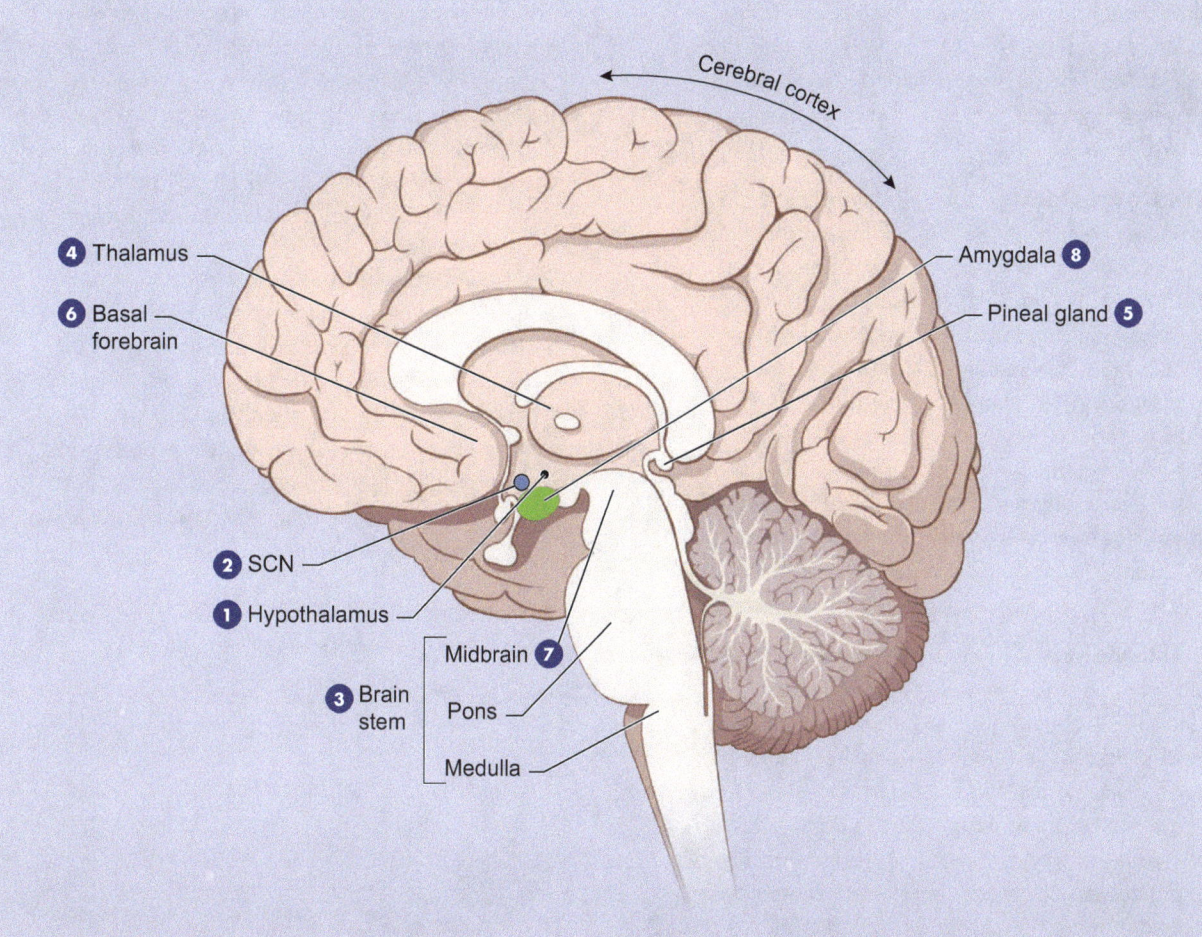

- Cerebral cortex
- **4** Thalamus
- **6** Basal forebrain
- **2** SCN
- **1** Hypothalamus
- **3** Brain stem
- Midbrain **7**
- Pons
- Medulla
- Amygdala **8**
- Pineal gland **5**

Several structures within the brain are involved with sleep. The **hypothalamus** ❶, a peanut-sized structure deep inside the brain, contains groups of nerve cells that act as control centers affecting sleep and arousal. Within the hypothalamus is the **suprachiasmatic nucleus** ❷ (SCN)—clusters of thousands of cells that receive information about light exposure directly from the

313

Studies & Statistics / Understanding Sleep

eyes and control your behavioral rhythm. Some people with damage to the SCN sleep erratically throughout the day because they are not able to match their circadian rhythms with the light-dark cycle. Most blind people maintain some ability to sense light and are able to modify their sleep-wake cycle.

The **brain stem** ❸, at the base of the brain, communicates with the hypothalamus to control the transitions between wake and sleep. (The brain stem includes structures called the pons, medulla, and midbrain.) Sleep-promoting cells within the hypothalamus and the brain stem produce a brain chemical called GABA, which acts to reduce the activity of arousal centers in the hypothalamus and the brain stem. The brain stem (especially the pons and medulla) also plays a special role in REM sleep; it sends signals to relax muscles essential for body posture and limb movements, so that we don't act out our dreams.

The **thalamus** ❹ acts as a relay for information from the senses to the cerebral cortex (the covering of the brain that interprets and processes information from short- to long-term memory). During most stages of sleep, the thalamus becomes quiet, letting you tune out the external world. But during REM sleep, the thalamus is active, sending the cortex images, sounds, and other sensations that fill our dreams.

The **pineal gland** ❺, located within the brain's two hemispheres, receives signals from the SCN and increases production of the hormone melatonin, which helps put you to sleep once the lights go down. People who have lost their sight and cannot coordinate their natural sleep-wake cycle using natural light can stabilize their sleep patterns by taking small amounts of melatonin at the same time each day. Scientists believe that peaks and valleys of melatonin over time are important for matching the body's circadian rhythm to the external cycle of light and darkness.

The **basal forebrain** ❻, near the front and bottom of the brain, also promotes sleep and wakefulness, while part of the **midbrain** ❼ acts as an arousal system. Release of adenosine (a chemical by-product of cellular energy consumption) from cells in the basal forebrain and probably other regions supports your sleep drive. Caffeine counteracts sleepiness by blocking the actions of adenosine.

The **amygdala** ❽, an almond-shaped structure involved in processing emotions, becomes increasingly active during REM sleep.

Sleep Stages

There are two basic types of sleep: rapid eye movement (REM) sleep and non-REM sleep (which has three different stages). Each is linked to specific brain waves and neuronal activity.

You cycle through all stages of non-REM and REM sleep several times during a typical night, with increasingly longer, deeper REM periods occurring toward morning.

1
Stage 1 non-REM sleep is the changeover from wakefulness to sleep. During this short period (lasting several minutes) of relatively light sleep, your heartbeat, breathing, and eye movements slow, and your muscles relax with occasional twitches. Your brain waves begin to slow from their daytime wakefulness patterns.

2
Stage 2 non-REM sleep is a period of light sleep before you enter deeper sleep. Your heartbeat and breathing slow, and muscles relax even further. Your body temperature drops and eye movements stop. Brain wave activity slows but is marked by brief bursts of electrical activity. You spend more of your repeated sleep cycles in stage 2 sleep than in other sleep stages.

3
Stage 3 non-REM sleep is the period of deep sleep that you need to feel refreshed in the morning. It occurs in longer periods during the first half of the night. Your heartbeat and breathing slow to their lowest levels during sleep. Your muscles are relaxed and it may be difficult to awaken you. Brain waves become even slower.

REM
REM sleep first occurs about 90 minutes after falling asleep. Your eyes move rapidly from side to side behind closed eyelids. Mixed frequency brain wave activity becomes closer to that seen in wakefulness. Your breathing becomes faster and irregular, and your heart rate and blood pressure increase to near waking levels. Most of your dreaming occurs during REM sleep, although some can also occur in non-REM sleep. Your arm and leg muscles become temporarily paralyzed, which prevents you from acting out your dreams. As you age, you sleep less of your time in REM sleep. Memory consolidation most likely requires both non-REM and REM sleep.

Sleep Mechanisms

Two internal biological mechanisms—circadian rhythm and homeostasis—work together to regulate when you are awake and sleep.

Circadian rhythms direct a wide variety of functions from daily fluctuations in wakefulness to body temperature, metabolism, and the release of hormones. They control your timing of sleep and cause you to be sleepy at night and your tendency to wake in the morning without an alarm. Your body's biological clock, which is based on a roughly 24-hour day, controls most circadian rhythms. Circadian rhythms synchronize with environmental cues (light, temperature) about the actual time of day, but they continue even in the absence of cues.

Sleep-wake homeostasis keeps track of your need for sleep. The homeostatic sleep drive reminds the body to sleep after a certain time and regulates sleep intensity. This sleep drive gets stronger every hour you are awake and causes you to sleep longer and more deeply after a period of sleep deprivation.

Factors that influence your sleep-wake needs include medical conditions, medications, stress, sleep environment, and what you eat and drink. Perhaps the greatest influence is the exposure to light. Specialized cells in the retinas of your eyes process light and tell the brain whether it is day or night and can advance or delay our sleep-wake cycle. Exposure to light can make it difficult to fall asleep and return to sleep when awakened.

Night shift workers often have trouble falling asleep when they go to bed, and also have trouble staying awake at work because their natural circadian rhythm and sleep-wake cycle is disrupted. In the case of jet lag, circadian rhythms become out of sync with the time of day when people fly to a different time zone, creating a mismatch between their internal clock and the actual clock.

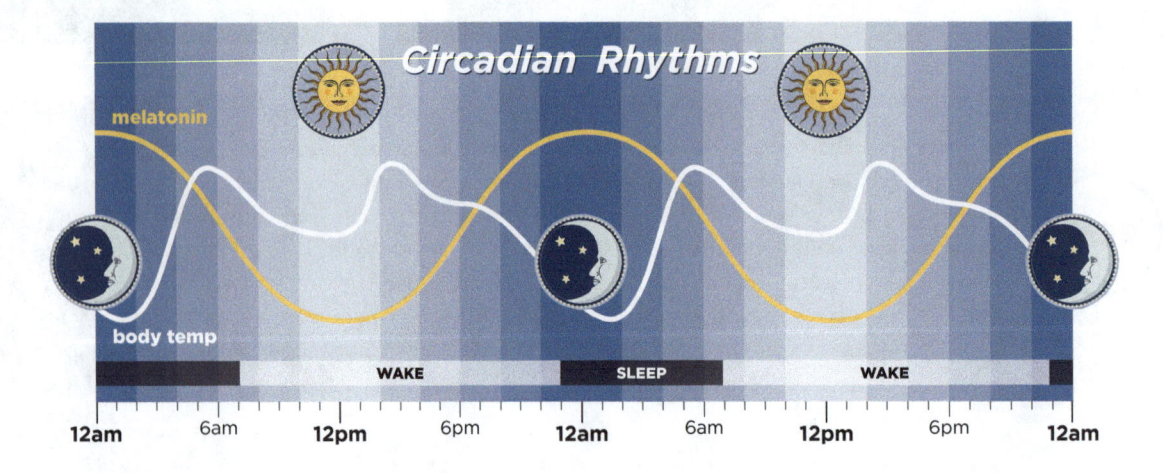

Studies & Statistics / Understanding Sleep

How Much Sleep Do You Need?

Your need for sleep and your sleep patterns change as you age, but this varies significantly across individuals of the same age. There is no magic "number of sleep hours" that works for everybody of the same age. Babies initially sleep as much as 16 to 18 hours per day, which may boost growth and development (especially of the brain). School-age children and teens on average need about 9.5 hours of sleep per night. Most adults need 7-9 hours of sleep a night, but after age 60, nighttime sleep tends to be shorter, lighter, and interrupted by multiple awakenings. Elderly people are also more likely to take medications that interfere with sleep.

In general, people are getting less sleep than they need due to longer work hours and the availability of round-the-clock entertainment and other activities.

Many people feel they can "catch up" on missed sleep during the weekend but, depending on how sleep-deprived they are, sleeping longer on the weekends may not be adequate.

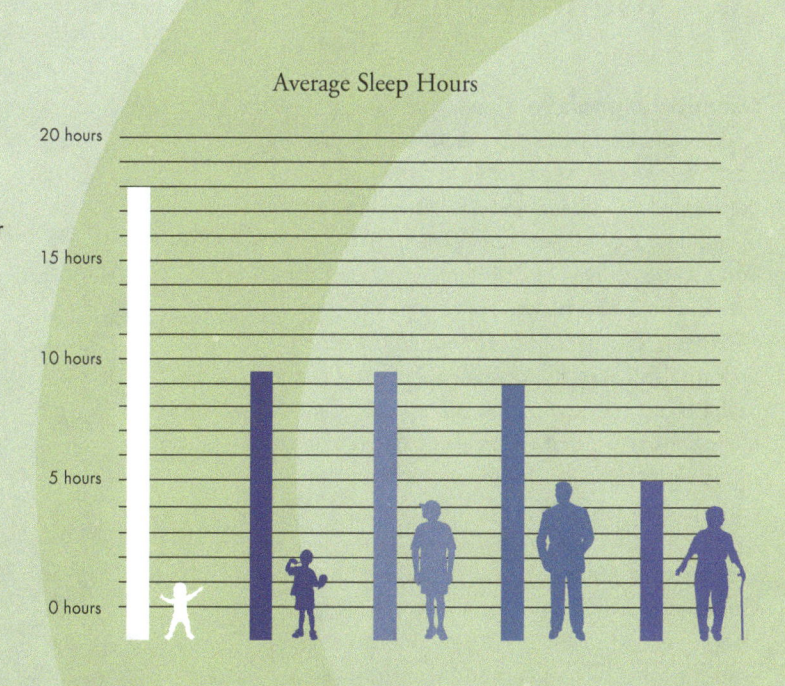

Average Sleep Hours

Dreaming

Everyone dreams. You spend about 2 hours each night dreaming but may not remember most of your dreams. Its exact purpose isn't known, but dreaming may help you process your emotions. Events from the day often invade your thoughts during sleep, and people suffering from stress or anxiety are more likely to have frightening dreams. Dreams can be experienced in all stages of sleep but usually are most vivid in REM sleep. Some people dream in color, while others only recall dreams in black and white.

Studies & Statistics / Understanding Sleep

The Role of Genes and Neurotransmitters

Chemical signals to sleep
Clusters of sleep-promoting neurons in many parts of the brain become more active as we get ready for bed. Nerve-signaling chemicals called neurotransmitters can "switch off" or dampen the activity of cells that signal arousal or relaxation. GABA is associated with sleep, muscle relaxation, and sedation. Norepinephrine and orexin (also called hypocretin) keep some parts of the brain active while we are awake. Other neurotransmitters that shape sleep and wakefulness include acetylcholine, histamine, adrenaline, cortisol, and serotonin.

Genes and sleep
Genes may play a significant role in how much sleep we need. Scientists have identified several genes involved with sleep and sleep disorders, including genes that control the excitability of neurons, and "clock" genes such as Per, Tim, and Cry that influence our circadian rhythms and the timing of sleep. Genome-wide association studies have identified sites on various chromosomes that increase our susceptibility to sleep disorders. Also, different genes have been identified with such sleep disorders as familial advanced sleep-phase disorder, narcolepsy, and restless legs syndrome. Some of the genes expressed in the cerebral cortex and other brain areas change their level of expression between sleep and wake. Several genetic models—including the worm, fruit fly, and zebrafish—are helping scientists to identify molecular mechanisms and genetic variants involved in normal sleep and sleep disorders. Additional research will provide better understanding of inherited sleep patterns and risks of circadian and sleep disorders.

TIPS

For Getting a Good Night's Sleep

Getting enough sleep is good for your health. Here are a few tips to improve your sleep.

- Set a schedule—go to bed and wake up at the same time each day.
- Exercise 20 to 30 minutes a day but no later than a few hours before going to bed.
- Avoid caffeine and nicotine late in the day and alcoholic drinks before bed.
- Relax before bed—try a warm bath, reading, or another relaxing routine.
- Create a room for sleep—avoid bright lights and loud sounds, keep the room at a comfortable temperature, and don't watch TV or have a computer in your bedroom.
- Don't lie in bed awake. If you can't get to sleep, do something else, like reading or listening to music, until you feel tired.
- See a doctor if you have a problem sleeping or if you feel unusually tired during the day. Most sleep disorders can be treated effectively.

Sleep Studies

Your health care provider may recommend a polysomnogram or other test to diagnose a sleep disorder. A polysomnogram typically involves spending the night at a sleep lab or sleep center. It records your breathing, oxygen levels, eye and limb movements, heart rate, and brain waves throughout the night. Your sleep is also video and audio recorded. The data can help a sleep specialist determine if you are reaching and proceeding properly through the various sleep stages. Results may be used to develop a treatment plan or determine if further tests are needed.

Tracking Sleep Through Smart Technology

Millions of people are using smartphone apps, bedside monitors, and wearable items (including smart watches and activity trackers) to informally collect and analyze data about their sleep. Smart technology can record sounds and movement during sleep, journal hours slept, and monitor heart beat and respiration. Using a companion app, data from some devices can be synced to a smartphone or tablet, or uploaded to a PC. Other apps and devices make white noise, produce light that stimulates melatonin production, and use gentle vibrations to help us sleep and wake.

Hope Through Research

Scientists continue to learn about the function and regulation of sleep. A key focus of research is to understand the risks involved with being chronically sleep deprived and the relationship between sleep and disease. People who are chronically sleep deprived are more likely to be overweight, have strokes and cardiovascular disease, infections, and certain types of cancer than those who get enough sleep. Sleep disturbances are common among people with age-related neurological disorders such as Alzheimer's disease and Parkinson's disease. Many mysteries remain about the association between sleep and these health problems. Does the lack of sleep lead to certain disorders, or do certain diseases cause a lack of sleep? These, and many other questions about sleep, represent the future of sleep research.

Case report

Somatic symptom disorder: a diagnostic dilemma

Louise Dunphy, Marta Penna, Jihene EL-Kafsi

Department of General Surgery, Wexham Park Hospital, Slough, UK

Correspondence to
Dr Louise Dunphy;
Louise.Dunphy@doctors.org.uk

Accepted 1 October 2019

SUMMARY

Somatic symptom disorder (SSD) is a diagnosis that was introduced with publication of the Diagnostic and Statistical Manual of Mental Disorders, Fifth Edition (DSM-5) in 2013. It eliminated the diagnoses of somatisation disorder, undifferentiated somatoform disorder, hypochondriasis and pain disorder; most of the patients who previously received these diagnoses are now diagnosed in DSM-5 with SSD. The main feature of this disorder is a patient's concern with physical symptoms for which no biological cause is found. It requires psychiatric assessment to exclude comorbid psychiatric disease. Failure to recognise this disorder may lead the unwary physician or surgeon to embark on investigations or diagnostic procedures which may result in iatrogenic complications. It also poses a significant financial burden on the healthcare service. Patients with non-specific abdominal pain have a poor symptomatic prognosis with continuing use of medical services. Proven treatments include cognitive behavioural therapy, mindfulness therapy and pharmacological treatment using selective serotonin reuptake inhibitors or tricyclic antidepressants. The authors describe the case of a 31-year-old woman with an emotionally unstable personality disorder and comorbid disease presenting to the emergency department with a 3-week history of left-sided abdominal and leg pain. Despite a plethora of investigations, no organic cause for her pain was found. She was reviewed by the multidisciplinary team including surgeons, physicians, neurologists and psychiatrists. A diagnosis of somatoform symptom disorder was subsequently rendered. As patients with SSD will present to general practice and the emergency department rather than psychiatric settings, this case provides a cautionary reminder of furthering the need for appropriate recognition of this condition.

BACKGROUND

Somatisation is present when emotional or psychological distress is manifested as physical symptoms with no biological cause found. To better define these disorders and make them more relevant to the primary setting, the nomenclature for the diagnostic category Diagnostic and Statistical Manual of Mental Disorders, Fifth Edition (DSM-5), previously known as somatoform disorders, was changed to somatic symptom and related disorders from the DSM-4 Text Revision.[1] In contrast to the criteria for somatisation disorder which required a constellation of somatic symptoms including four different pain symptoms, for example, two gastrointestinal, one sexual and one pseudo-neurologic, somatic symptom disorder (SSD) requires the presence of just a single somatic symptom. Subsets of SSD include the following: conversion disorder, factitious disorder, illness anxiety disorder, psychological factors affecting other medical conditions, other specified somatic symptoms and related disorders and unspecified somatic symptoms and related disorders. Increased healthcare utilisation is a significant concern in this patient cohort.

PRESENTATION

A 31-year-old woman with a high Body Mass Index (BMI) presented to the emergency department with a 3-week history of left-sided abdominal and leg pain. She described an episode of nausea and vomiting. Her bowels opened 2 days previously and she denied rectal bleeding or mucus.

She described her abdominal pain as 'sharp, shooting and stabbing' in nature and radiating down her left leg. Her medical history included chronic depression and an emotionally unstable personality disorder. This was her fifth emergency presentation requiring inpatient admission with headache, diplopia, non-specific abdominal and left leg pain over a 12-month period. All investigations including a lumbar puncture and radiology were normal. She reported suicidal ideation in January 2013 resulting in an impulsive opiate overdose. In 2008, she started mobilising with crutches despite no abnormal pathology and progressed to a wheelchair in 2015 despite a normal MRI spine. She reported a 6-year history of intermittent left leg weakness, chronic back pain and constipation. She had a provisional diagnosis of epilepsy with recurrent partial seizures. She declined investigation with an electroencephalogram (EEG). In addition, she described a history of temporary visual loss of her right eye. Ophthalmology review noted normal visual evoked potentials. The clinical impression was of functional reduced visual acuity. She was also diagnosed with asthma, anxiety and migraine. Her surgical history included an appendectomy in 2009. She underwent an examination under anaesthesia and botox injection for an anal fissure. Postoperatively, she developed a seizure and was admitted to Intensive Care Unit (ICU) for observation.

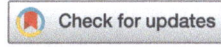

She did not require intubation. She was allergic to aspirin, paracetamol and non-steroidal anti-inflammatory drugs (NSAIDs). Her medications included dihydrocodeine, phenytoin, lamotrigine, sertraline, folic acid, salbutamol and seretide. She was an ex-smoker with a 4.5 pack-year history. She did not consume alcohol. She completed second-level education and was currently unemployed. In addition, she required assistance from her partner to help her dress.

INVESTIGATIONS

Her observations were as follows: heart rate 87 beats/min, blood pressure 127/79 mm Hg, respiratory rate 19 breaths/min, oxygen saturation 95% and temperature 36.4°C. Physical examination confirmed left-sided abdominal tenderness with no evidence of guarding or peritonism. Bowel sounds were present on auscultation. Digital rectal examination was unremarkable. Neurological examination confirmed normal power, tone and reflexes of her upper and lower limbs. Her cranial nerves were intact. Laboratory investigations showed a normal full blood count and a mildly elevated C reactive protein (CRP) (9 mg/L). Urinalysis and her beta human chorionic gonadotropin (bHCG) were negative. A blood gas confirmed normal physiology. Further investigation with a CT abdomen and pelvis with contrast showed no evidence of free air or fluid in the abdomen. The liver, gallbladder and pancreas were unremarkable. Prominent adnexa with multiple cystic lesions were noted bilaterally. No bowel loop distension was observed. The fat halo sign of the colon was non-specific. Normal alignment of the spine and normal height of the vertebral bodies were noted. A transabdominal and transvaginal ultrasound scan (USS) showed a normal sized, shape and position of her uterus. Both ovaries appeared normal and there was no evidence of an adnexal cyst, mass or free fluid. An USS abdomen was unremarkable. A repeat CT of her abdomen due to increased symptom severity failed to identify a cause for her persistent symptoms. She declined further investigation with flexible sigmoidoscopy. She developed weakness and an altered sensation of her left leg. She was reviewed by the neurologist, who reported a 6-year history of recurrent similar presentations, thought functional in origin.

Physical examination confirmed reduced power 3/5 of her left leg. Bilateral symmetrical reflexes and down-going plantars were observed. Cerebellar examination was normal. Cranial nerves I–XII were intact. An MRI head showed normal cerebral and cerebellar parenchyma, ventricles and midline/posterior fossa. An MRI of her thorax and spine showed a prominent central canal/syringomyelia which was unchanged from her MRI in 2017. She developed right-sided myoclonic jerks with increased left leg pain. This event was self-terminated and her lactate was 0.9. She developed severe headache and photophobia, however, a CT head showed no evidence of intracranial haemorrhage, acute infarction, space occupying lesion, brain oedema or hydrocephalus. Her behaviour became aggressive towards medical staff, demanding further investigations, higher dose opioids and an operation to alleviate her abdominal pain.

DIFFERENTIAL DIAGNOSIS

This patient presented with a constellation of symptoms representing features of possible SSD and comorbid psychiatric conditions. She was reviewed by psychiatry. She described a 3-week history of low mood and social withdrawal. She reported changes to her sleep, energy and appetite. She denied suicidal ideation. She stated that her low mood was triggered by her abdominal pain and leg weakness and she was concerned she had a serious health problem. She continued to demand an operation to 'fix her pain'. No change was made to her medications and a psychology review was sought. She was reviewed by the pain team as she was demanding higher dose opioids for pain control.

TREATMENT

She refused to engage with the physiotherapists opting to stay in bed rather than make an effort to mobilise. As there is now global recognition that obesity is a distinct disease that warrants metabolic investigations and management, she was referred to the dietician. She failed to engage with this service and expressed no desire to lose any weight or understand the implications of her high BMI on her health.

OUTCOME

Our patient fulfilled the criteria to render a diagnosis of SSD. She reported a history of distressful symptoms over a period of 6 years resulting in periods of dysfunction and low mood. During this admission, she exhibited disproportionate thoughts and behaviours in response to her symptoms, most notably for her abdominal pain. She would persistently request further investigations including demanding a laparoscopy to 'find something to fix' despite having multiple USS, CT and MRIs which were unchanged from previous admissions.

Following psychological review, she was referred to the 'medically unexplained symptoms' Clinic in the community. After 3 weeks of supportive care and extensive investigations, she was discharged home uneventfully. This case demonstrates the practical and ethical dilemma that confronts physicians and surgeons when such cases are encountered.

DISCUSSION

John Bonica revolutionised the study of pain through his insistence that pain warranted attention as a symptom and not only as an indicator of underlying disease. Historically, somatisation is akin to hysteria and hypochondriasis. In 1908, Stekel introduced the term as 'a deep seated neurosis akin to the mental mechanism of conversion'.[2] Somatisation is an important public health problem because it accounts for significant functional disability and healthcare utilisation. Somatisation describes a constellation of clinical and behavioural features indicating that a patient is experiencing and communicating psychological distress through physical (somatic) symptoms not accounted for by pathological findings. Its aetiology is multifactorial and individual, family and environmental factors have been proposed as predisposing, precipitating or perpetuating in somatisation. Individuals present to primary care or to the emergency department with physical symptoms without an organic cause which may be labelled functional, somatic or medically unexplained symptoms and may prove challenging for physicians to address.

The term 'somatic symptom disorder' was introduced in 2013 with publication of the DSM-5 in 2013. It has a female predilection with an estimated prevalence of 5% in the general population and 25% of individuals develop a chronic somatic illness. Prevalence rates are higher in patients with functional disorders such as fibromyalgia, irritable bowel syndrome and chronic fatigue syndrome. The diagnosis of SSD is not a diagnosis of exclusion, on the contrary, it is a positive diagnosis, based on solid criteria.[3] Diagnostic criteria for SSD include one or more somatic symptoms that are distressing or result in significant disruption of daily life and excessive thoughts, feelings or behaviours related to the somatic symptoms or associated health concerns.[4] Affected individuals experience substantial impairment in social functioning with the risk of progressive social withdrawal and hence a negative impact on the functioning of the entire family.

Subsets of SSD include the following: conversion disorder, factitious disorder, illness anxiety disorder, psychological factors

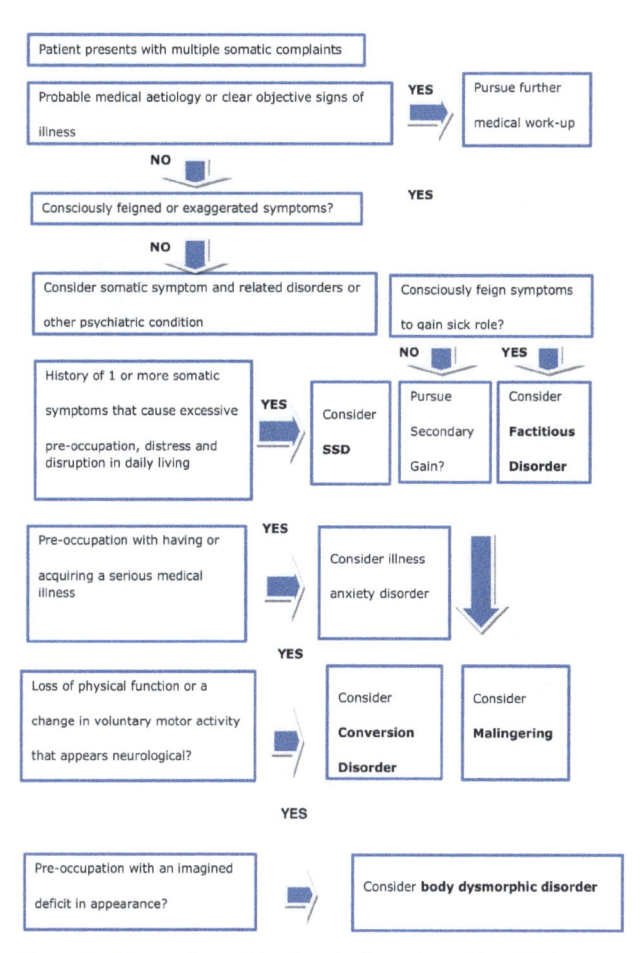

Figure 1 Diagnostic considerations in the patient with multiple unexplained symptoms.

affecting other medical conditions, other specified somatic symptoms and related disorders and unspecified somatic symptoms and related disorders.[4] Medically unexplained symptoms present to most hospital specialities and account for a considerable proportion of consultations by frequent attenders in secondary care.[5] This group of disorders account for one-fifth of presentations to general physicians with headache, fatigue and abdominal pain, for which no biochemical cause can be detected.[6] It has been suggested that patients suffering from medically unexplained symptoms are less aware of their symptoms and use maladaptive coping strategies when coping with problems (figure 1).[7]

Pain is an inherently subjective phenomenon and Henry Beecher's pain research has shown that there is no direct correlation between the amount of tissue damage and the level of pain experienced. Clinical somatisation arises from patients situated at various points along a continuum of distress severity; this distress is manifested in heightened symptom perception and illness behaviour. Several psychosocial factors may be involved in the pathogenesis of SSD, such as developmental factors, physical and sexual abuse, cognitive and perceptual distortions and behavioural abnormalities as well as difficulties with self-expression. Life change has been correlated with the onset of physical and psychological disorders. Family conflict is another recognised risk factor for its pathogenesis. Somatic symptoms manifesting as gastrointestinal symptoms such as nausea, vomiting, abdominal pain, bloating and diarrhoea are common in individuals with a depressive disorder. Pain symptoms include joint pain, back pain, headache and chest pain. Neurologic symptoms include movement disorders, sensory loss, weakness and paralysis. Distress and somatisation are highly correlated.[8] Hypochondriasis often occurs with somatisation. Increasing levels of anxiety, depression and somatisation are associated with higher preprandial and/or postprandial gastrointestinal symptom levels in inflammatory bowel disease. The natural course of the disorder can be variable with periods of flare-ups associated with previous substance abuse, anxiety and affective disorder.[9] There is growing evidence of childhood abuse in women with somatisation disorder and borderline personality disorder. Typically, functional abdominal pain presents as a diffuse or periumbilical pain. Children may present with loss of vision, hearing or mutism. Poloni performed an observational retrospective study to profile clinical and sociodemographic characteristics of patients with medically unexplained physical symptoms.[10] Reported symptoms included headache, seizures, vertigo, fibromyalgia, paraesthesia, visual disturbance and amnesia. The diagnosis was somatoform disorder in 6.3%, conversion disorder in 2.7% and somatoform disorder in 6.3%.[10] Comorbid psychiatric disorders may precede the development of somatic symptoms but often develop during the course of the somatoform disorder. Depression, panic disorder, generalised anxiety disorder, substance misuse and non-psychiatric medical conditions should be considered in the differential diagnosis. The Somatic Symptom Scale shows promise in measuring somatic symptom burden. A common feature of these patients is that they often undergo an extensive, repeated and poorly justified diagnostic work-up, sometimes magnified by 'doctor shopping' in the constant search for different medical opinions.[11]

While it is acknowledged that it is difficult to render an exact diagnosis in this complex group of SSDs, it is important to support effective recognition and response to the needs of this complex patient group. Once patients develop SSD, it may be perpetuated by chronic stressors and maladaptive coping skills. In addition, behaviour related to the symptoms and sick role add another psychological dimension that maintain the disorder.[12] Management requires a multifaceted approach tailored to the individual patient. SSDs are generally chronic, however, 50%–75% of individuals show improvement and 10%–30% deteriorate. Positive prognostic indicators include fewer physical symptoms and better functioning at baseline. Training in the diagnosis and management of this disorder is inadequate in the postgraduate

> **Learning points**
>
> ▸ Somatisation describes a constellation of clinical and behavioural features indicating that a patient is experiencing and communicating psychological distress through physical (somatic) symptoms not accounted for by pathological findings.
> ▸ Somatic symptom disorder (SSD) was derived in part from the somatoform disorders (somatisation disorder, hypochondriasis) which were eliminated from Diagnostic and Statistical Manual of Mental Disorders, Fifth Edition.
> ▸ Anxiety disorders and/or depressive disorders are common in SSD. The key to establishing whether the patient with a medical disorder also has SSD is determining whether the cognitive, emotional and behavioural responses to the medical condition is excessive compared with most other patients with that medical disorder.

curriculum. Scientific research in this field is required. Rehabilitation modelling and behavioural intervention is effective and a bio-psycho-social framework should be used for assessment and intervention. Techniques can be developed to deal with specific symptoms and impairments, for example, distraction, muscular relaxation for headaches, graded physical exercise for muscular problems and fatigue as well as practical management of pseudo-seizures.

Psychological interventions, such as cognitive behavioural therapy is recommended for the management of co-morbid emotional disorders.[13]

A Cochrane review of 21 studies found that all psychological therapies included in the review (cognitive behavioural therapy (CBT), mindfulness, psychodynamic and integrative therapy) were superior in reduction of symptom severity.[14] Longitudinal studies have shown that 90% of SSDs last longer than 5 years.[15] Systematic reviews and meta-analysis have revealed that therapeutic interventions only demonstrate a small-to-moderate effect.[16]

Individuals affected by SSD frequently attend the emergency department and physicians have the unique opportunity to identify this condition according to the DSM criteria and have a positive effect on the patient's prognosis.

Contributors LD wrote the case report. MP performed the literature review. JEL-K edited the final manuscript and approved the paper.

Funding The authors have not declared a specific grant for this research from any funding agency in the public, commercial or not-for-profit sectors.

Competing interests None declared.

Patient consent for publication Obtained.

Provenance and peer review Not commissioned; externally peer reviewed.

ORCID iD
Louise Dunphy http://orcid.org/0000-0001-5499-415X

REFERENCES

1. American Psychiatric Association. *Diagnostic and statistical manual of mental disorders*. 5th edn [DSM-5]. Arlington: American Psychiatric Association, 2013.
2. Bass C. Introduction. In: Bass CM, ed. *Somatization – physical symptoms and psychological illness*. Oxford: Blackwell Scientific, 1990.
3. American Psychiatric Association. Somatic Symptoms and related disorders. In: *Diagnostic and statistical manual of mental disorders*. 5th edn. Airlington, VA: American Psychiatric Publishing, 2013: 318–21.
4. American Psychiatric Association. *Diagnostic and statistical manual of mental disorders*. 5th ed. Washington DC, 2013: 311.
5. Reid S, Wesseley S, Crayford T. Medically unexplained symptoms in frequent attenders of secondary health care: retrospective cohort study. *BMJ* 2001;322:767.
6. De Waal MW, Arnold IA, Eekhof JA, *et al*. Somatoform disorders in general practice - prevalence, functional impairment and comorbidity with anxiety and depressive disorders. *Br J Psychiatry* 2004;184:470–6.
7. Gross AF, Lokko HN, Huffman JC, *et al*. Chapter 229: Approach to the Patient with Multiple Unexplained Somatic Symptoms. In: *Principles and practice of hospital medicine*. 2nd edn, 2017.
8. Kellner R. Somatization – theories and research. *J Nerv Ment Dis* 1990;178:150–60.
9. Lieb R, Zimmermann P, Friis RH, *et al*. The natural course of DSM-IV somatoform disorders and syndromes among adolescents and young adults: a prospective-longitudinal community study. *European Psychiatry* 2002;17:321–31.
10. Poloni N, Ielmini M, Caselli I, *et al*. Medically unexplained physical symptoms in hospitalized patients: a 9-year retrospective observational study. *Frontiers in Psychiatry* 2018;9.
11. Minute M, Cozzi G, Barbi E. An adolescent with disabling abdominal pain. *BMJ* 2016;335.
12. Henningsen P, Zipfel S, Herzog W. Management of functional somatic syndromes. *Lancet* 2007;369:946–55.
13. Whiting P, Bagnall A-M, Sowden AJ, *et al*. Interventions for the treatment and management of chronic fatigue syndrome. *JAMA* 2001;286:1360–8.
14. van Dessel N, den Boeft M, van der Wouden JC, *et al*. Non-pharmacological interventions for somatoform disorders and medically unexplained physical symptoms (MUPS) in adults. *Cochrane Database Syst Rev* 2014:CD011142.
15. Jackson JL, Kroenke K, Prevalence KK. Prevalence, impact, and prognosis of multisomatoform disorder in primary care: a 5-year follow-up study. *Psychosom Med* 2008;70:430–4.
16. Kleinstäuber M, Witthöft M, Hiller W. Efficacy of short-term psychotherapy for multiple medically unexplained physical symptoms: a meta-analysis. *Clin Psychol Rev* 2011;31:146–60.

Copyright 2019 BMJ Publishing Group. All rights reserved. For permission to reuse any of this content visit
https://www.bmj.com/company/products-services/rights-and-licensing/permissions/
BMJ Case Report Fellows may re-use this article for personal use and teaching without any further permission.

Become a Fellow of BMJ Case Reports today and you can:
▶ Submit as many cases as you like
▶ Enjoy fast sympathetic peer review and rapid publication of accepted articles
▶ Access all the published articles
▶ Re-use any of the published material for personal use and teaching without further permission

Customer Service
If you have any further queries about your subscription, please contact our customer services team on +44 (0) 207111 1105 or via email at support@bmj.com.

Visit casereports.bmj.com for more articles like this and to become a Fellow

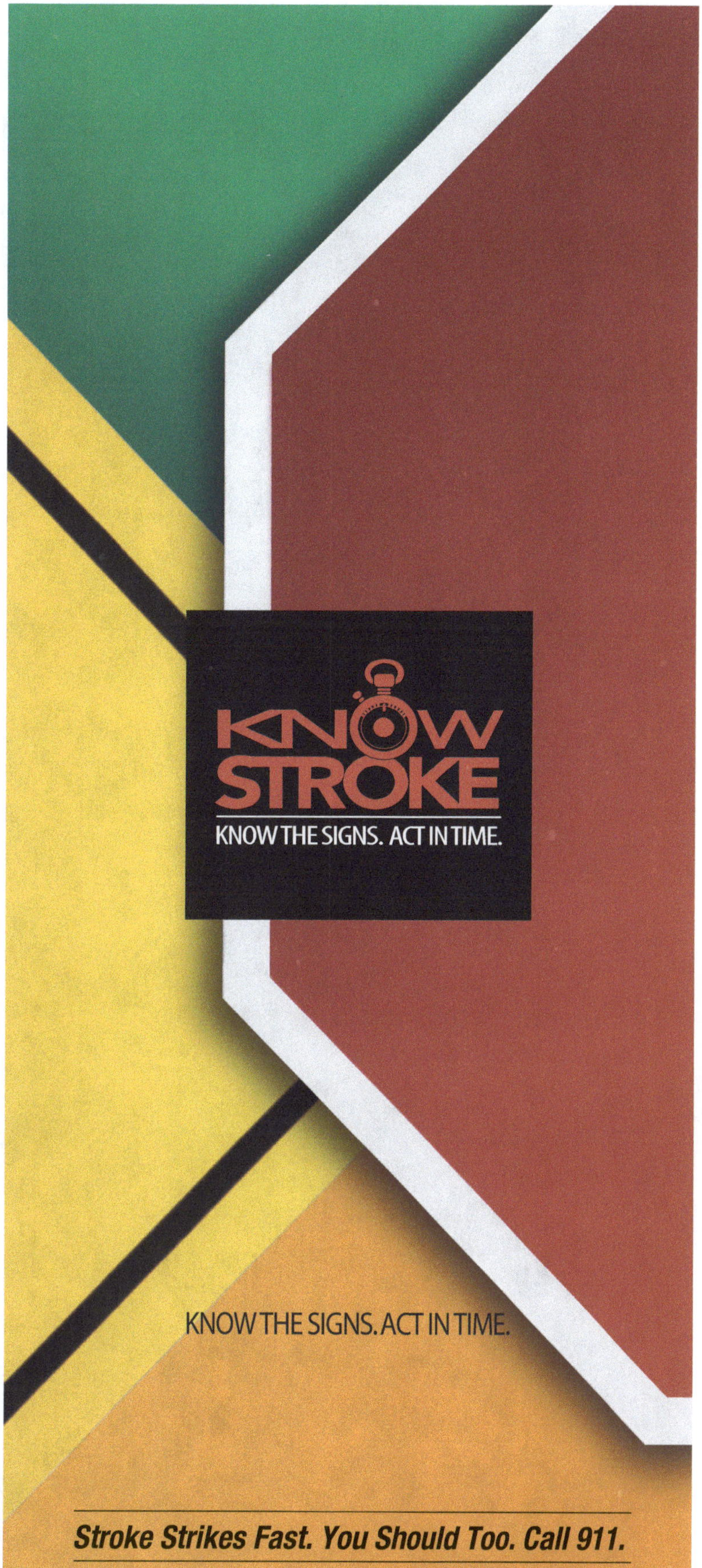
KNOW STROKE
KNOW THE SIGNS. ACT IN TIME.
KNOW THE SIGNS. ACT IN TIME.
Stroke Strikes Fast. You Should Too. Call 911.

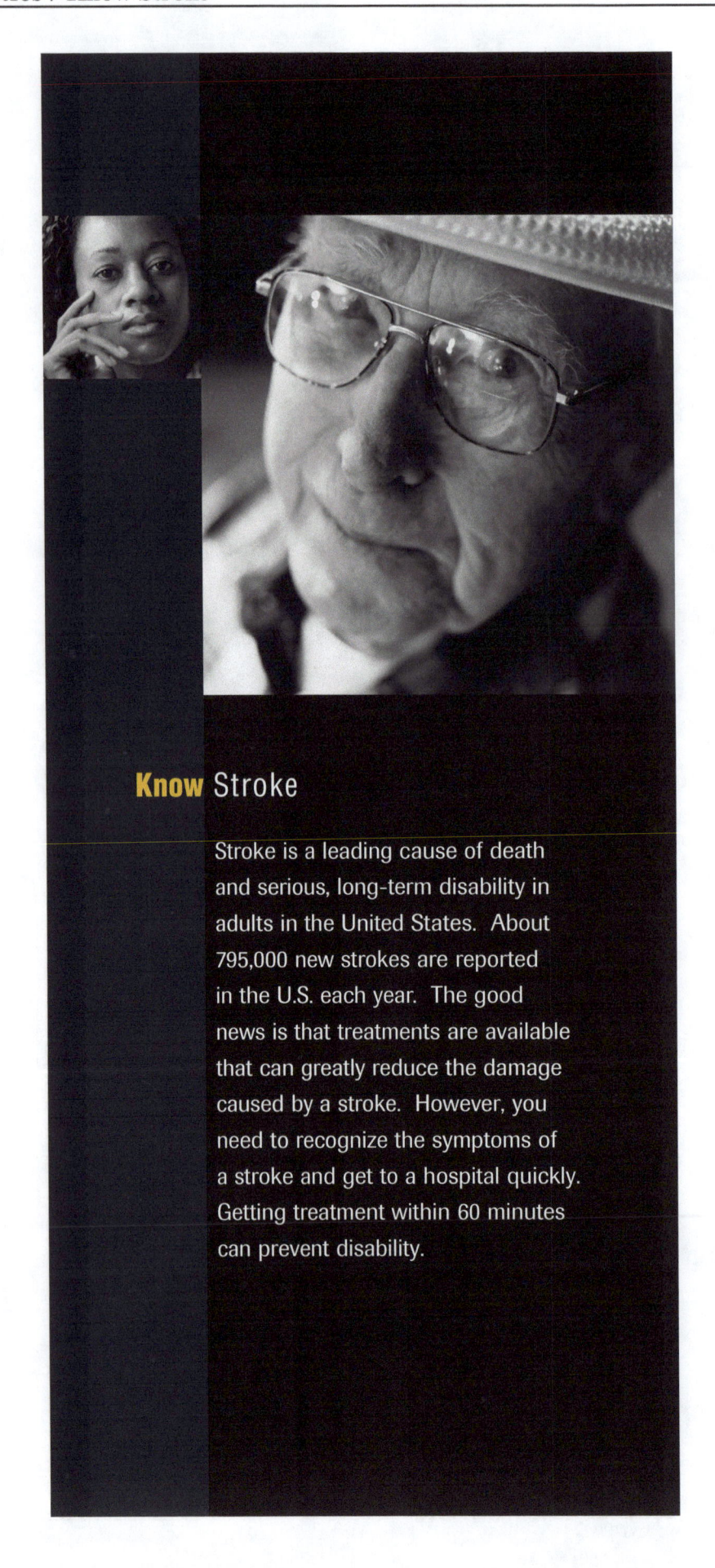

Studies & Statistics / Know Stroke

Know Stroke

Stroke is a leading cause of death and serious, long-term disability in adults in the United States. About 795,000 new strokes are reported in the U.S. each year. The good news is that treatments are available that can greatly reduce the damage caused by a stroke. However, you need to recognize the symptoms of a stroke and get to a hospital quickly. Getting treatment within 60 minutes can prevent disability.

WHAT IS A STROKE?

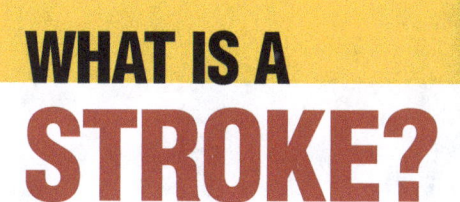

A stroke, sometimes called a "brain attack," occurs when blood flow to the brain is interrupted. When a stroke occurs, brain cells in the immediate area begin to die because they stop getting the oxygen and nutrients they need to function.

What causes a stroke?

There are two major kinds of stroke. The first, called an ischemic stroke, is caused by a blood clot that blocks or plugs a blood vessel or artery in the brain. About 80 percent of all strokes are ischemic. The second, known as a hemorrhagic stroke, is caused by a blood vessel in the brain that breaks and bleeds into the brain. About 20 percent of strokes are hemorrhagic.

What disabilities can result from a stroke?

Although stroke is a disease of the brain, it can affect the entire body. The effects of a stroke range from mild to severe and can include paralysis, problems with thinking, problems with speaking, and emotional problems. Patients may also experience pain or numbness after a stroke.

Studies & Statistics / **Know Stroke**

Know the Signs

Because stroke injures the brain, you may not realize that you are having a stroke. To a bystander, someone having a stroke may just look unaware or confused. Stroke victims have the best chance if someone around them recognizes the symptoms and acts quickly.

TROUBLE WALKING

WEAKNESS ON ONE SIDE

Studies & Statistics / Know Stroke

WHAT ARE THE SYMPTOMS OF A STROKE?

The symptoms of stroke are distinct because they happen quickly:

- Sudden numbness or weakness of the face, arm, or leg (especially on one side of the body)
- Sudden confusion, trouble speaking or understanding speech
- Sudden trouble seeing in one or both eyes
- Sudden trouble walking, dizziness, loss of balance or coordination
- Sudden severe headache with no known cause

What should a bystander do?

If you believe someone is having a stroke – if he or she suddenly loses the ability to speak, or move an arm or leg on one side, or experiences facial paralysis on one side – call 911 immediately.

TROUBLE SEEING

TROUBLE SPEAKING

Studies & Statistics / Know Stroke

Act in Time

Stroke is a medical emergency. Every minute counts when someone is having a stroke. The longer blood flow is cut off to the brain, the greater the damage. Immediate treatment can save people's lives and enhance their chances for successful recovery.

WHY IS THERE A NEED TO ACT FAST?

There are several treatments for stroke. All of them are delivered on an emergency basis. Many ischemic strokes can be treated with a clot-busting drug called t-PA that is most effective within 4.5 hours of stroke onset. There are devices that can extend that window by applying the medicine directly to the clot. There are now ways to mechanically remove blood clots, but again time is of the essence. Even after waking up with a stroke, don't delay; rush to the hospital to be evaluated for treatment. Even a small stroke — a transient ischemic attack — is something to have looked at immediately.

How can I reduce my risk of stroke?

The best treatment for stroke is prevention. Several factors increase your risk of having a stroke:

- High blood pressure
- Diabetes
- Heart disease
- High cholesterol
- Smoking
- Physical inactivity/obesity

If you smoke – quit. If you have high blood pressure, heart disease, diabetes, or high cholesterol, get them under control. If you are overweight, start a healthy diet and exercise regularly.

Results from the 2020 National Survey on Drug Use and Health: Graphics from the Key Findings Report

Center for Behavioral Health Statistics and Quality
Substance Abuse and Mental Health Services Administration
U.S. Department of Health and Human Services

Studies & Statistics / Results from the 2020 National Survey on Drug Use and Health

Past Month General Substance Use and Nicotine Vaping: Among People Aged 12 or Older; 2020

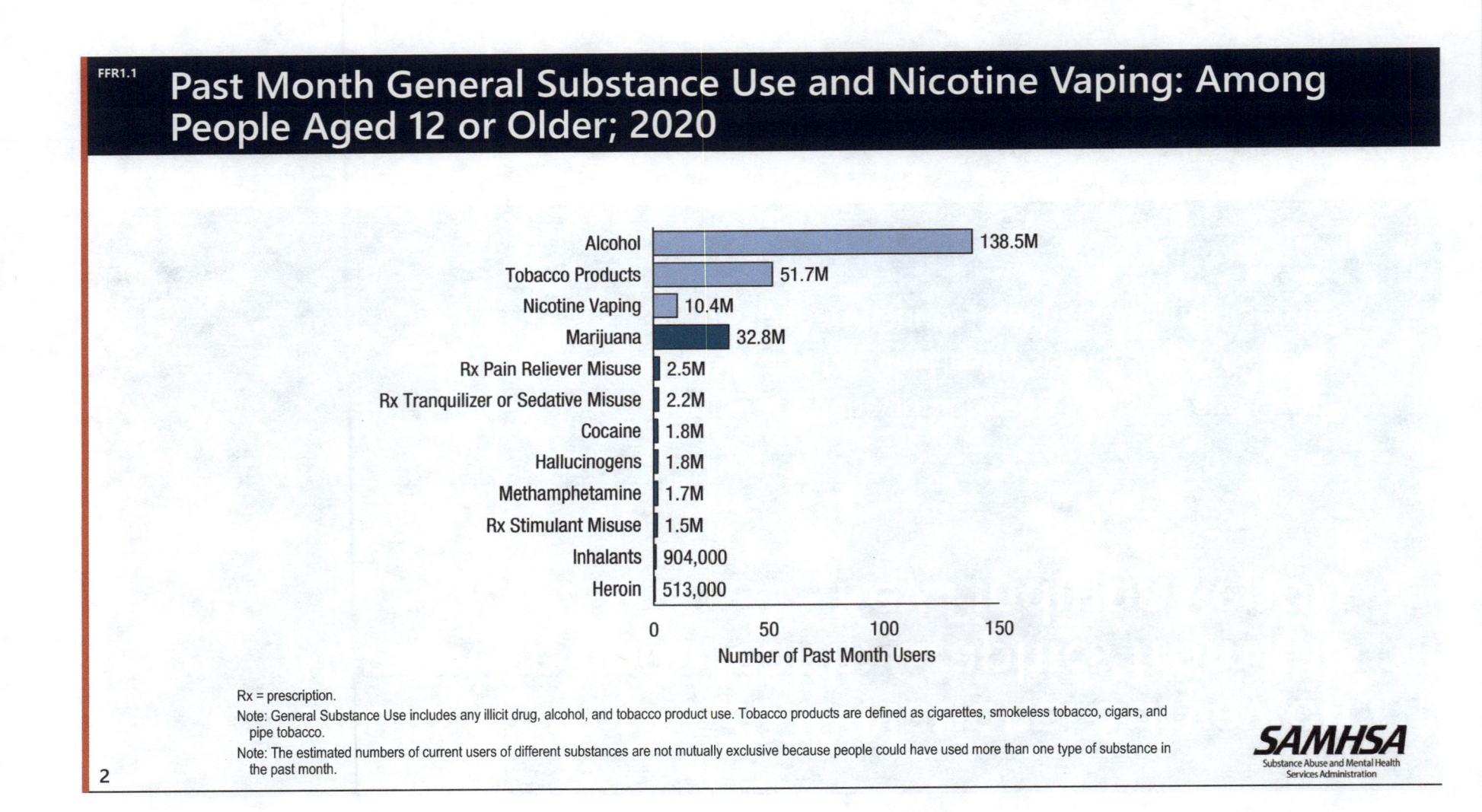

Substance	Number of Past Month Users
Alcohol	138.5M
Tobacco Products	51.7M
Nicotine Vaping	10.4M
Marijuana	32.8M
Rx Pain Reliever Misuse	2.5M
Rx Tranquilizer or Sedative Misuse	2.2M
Cocaine	1.8M
Hallucinogens	1.8M
Methamphetamine	1.7M
Rx Stimulant Misuse	1.5M
Inhalants	904,000
Heroin	513,000

Rx = prescription.
Note: General Substance Use includes any illicit drug, alcohol, and tobacco product use. Tobacco products are defined as cigarettes, smokeless tobacco, cigars, and pipe tobacco.
Note: The estimated numbers of current users of different substances are not mutually exclusive because people could have used more than one type of substance in the past month.

SAMHSA — Substance Abuse and Mental Health Services Administration

Studies & Statistics / Results from the 2020 National Survey on Drug Use and Health

Past Month Tobacco Use and Nicotine Vaping: Among People Aged 12 or Older; 2020

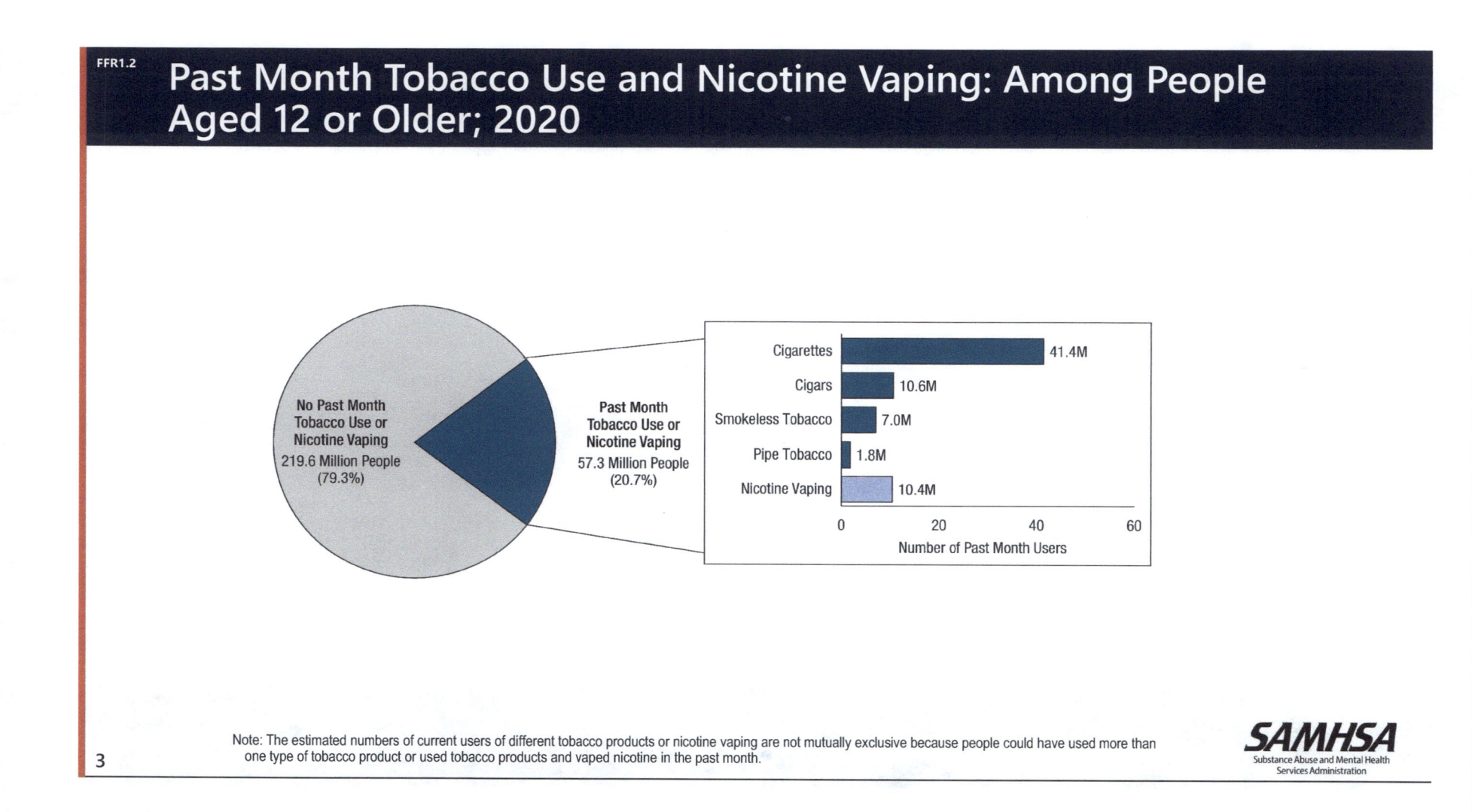

Past Month Tobacco Use or Nicotine Vaping
57.3 Million People (20.7%)

No Past Month Tobacco Use or Nicotine Vaping
219.6 Million People (79.3%)

- Cigarettes: 41.4M
- Cigars: 10.6M
- Smokeless Tobacco: 7.0M
- Pipe Tobacco: 1.8M
- Nicotine Vaping: 10.4M

Number of Past Month Users

Note: The estimated numbers of current users of different tobacco products or nicotine vaping are not mutually exclusive because people could have used more than one type of tobacco product or used tobacco products and vaped nicotine in the past month.

Studies & Statistics / Results from the 2020 National Survey on Drug Use and Health

Past Month Cigarette Use: Among People Aged 12 or Older; 2002-2020

Age	2002	2003	2004	2005	2006	2007	2008	2009	2010	2011	2012	2013	2014	2015	2016	2017	2018	2019	2020
12 or Older	26.0	25.4	24.9	24.9	25.0	24.3	24.0	23.3	23.0	22.1	22.1	21.3	20.8	19.4	19.1	17.9	17.2	16.7	15.0
12 to 17	13.0	12.2	11.9	10.8	10.4	9.9	9.2	9.0	8.4	7.8	6.6	5.6	4.9	4.2	3.4	3.2	2.7	2.3	1.4
18 to 25	40.8	40.2	39.5	39.0	38.5	36.2	35.7	35.8	34.4	33.5	31.8	30.6	28.4	26.7	23.5	22.3	19.1	17.5	13.9
26 or Older	25.2	24.7	24.1	24.3	24.7	24.1	23.8	23.0	22.8	21.9	22.4	21.6	21.5	20.0	20.2	18.9	18.5	18.2	16.7

Age Category: 12 or Older; 12 to 17; 18 to 25; 26 or Older

Note: There is no connecting line between 2019 and 2020 to indicate caution should be used when comparing estimates between 2020 and prior years because of methodological changes for 2020. Due to these changes, significance testing between 2020 and prior years was not performed.

Note: The estimate in 2020 is italicized to indicate caution should be used when comparing estimates between 2020 and prior years because of methodological changes for 2020. Due to these changes, significance testing between 2020 and prior years was not performed.

SAMHSA Substance Abuse and Mental Health Services Administration

Studies & Statistics / Results from the 2020 National Survey on Drug Use and Health

Daily Cigarette Use: Among Past Month Cigarette Smokers Aged 12 or Older; Smoking of One or More Packs of Cigarettes per Day: Among Current Daily Smokers; 2020

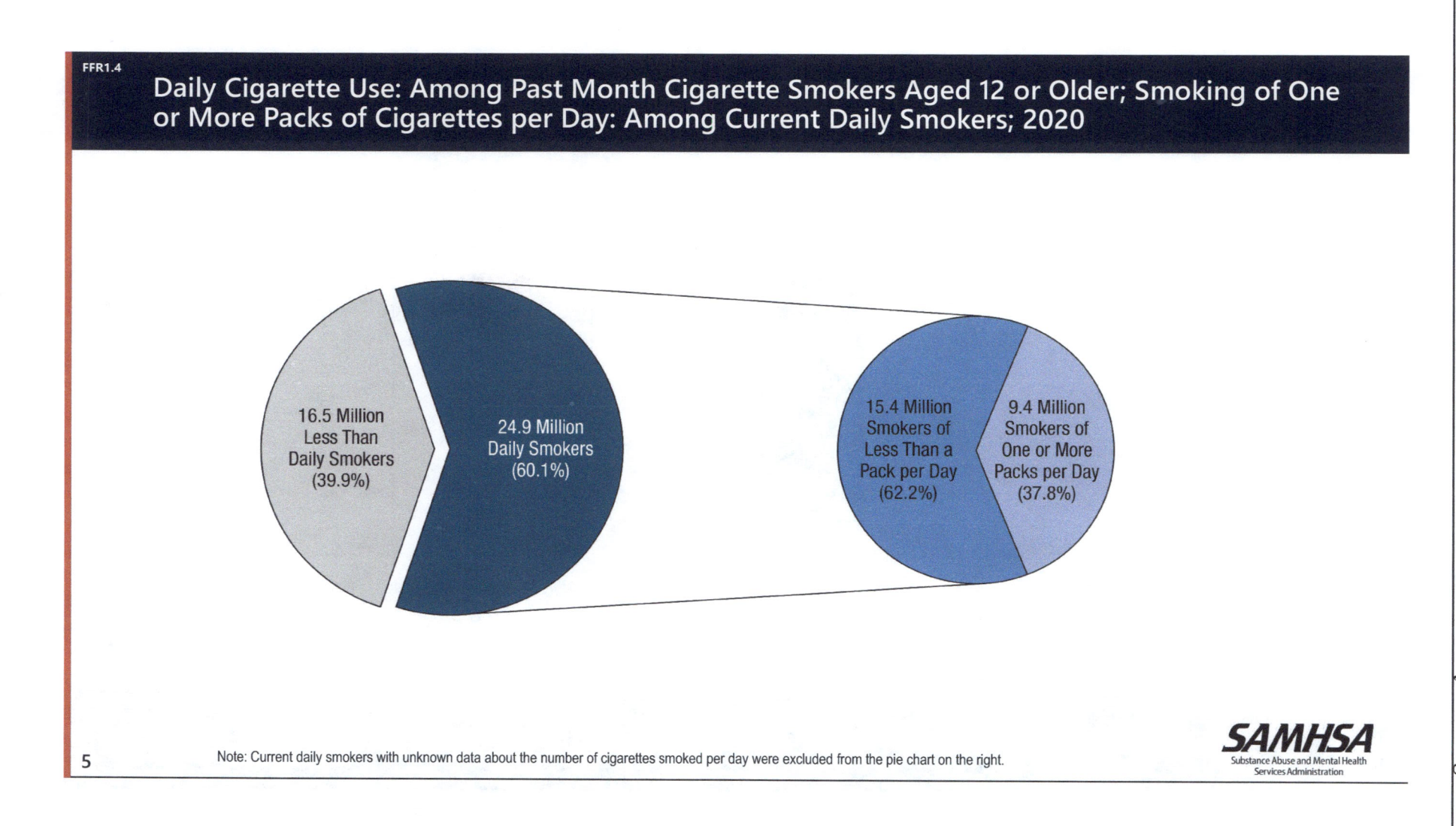

- 24.9 Million Daily Smokers (60.1%)
- 16.5 Million Less Than Daily Smokers (39.9%)

- 15.4 Million Smokers of Less Than a Pack per Day (62.2%)
- 9.4 Million Smokers of One or More Packs per Day (37.8%)

Note: Current daily smokers with unknown data about the number of cigarettes smoked per day were excluded from the pie chart on the right.

SAMHSA — Substance Abuse and Mental Health Services Administration

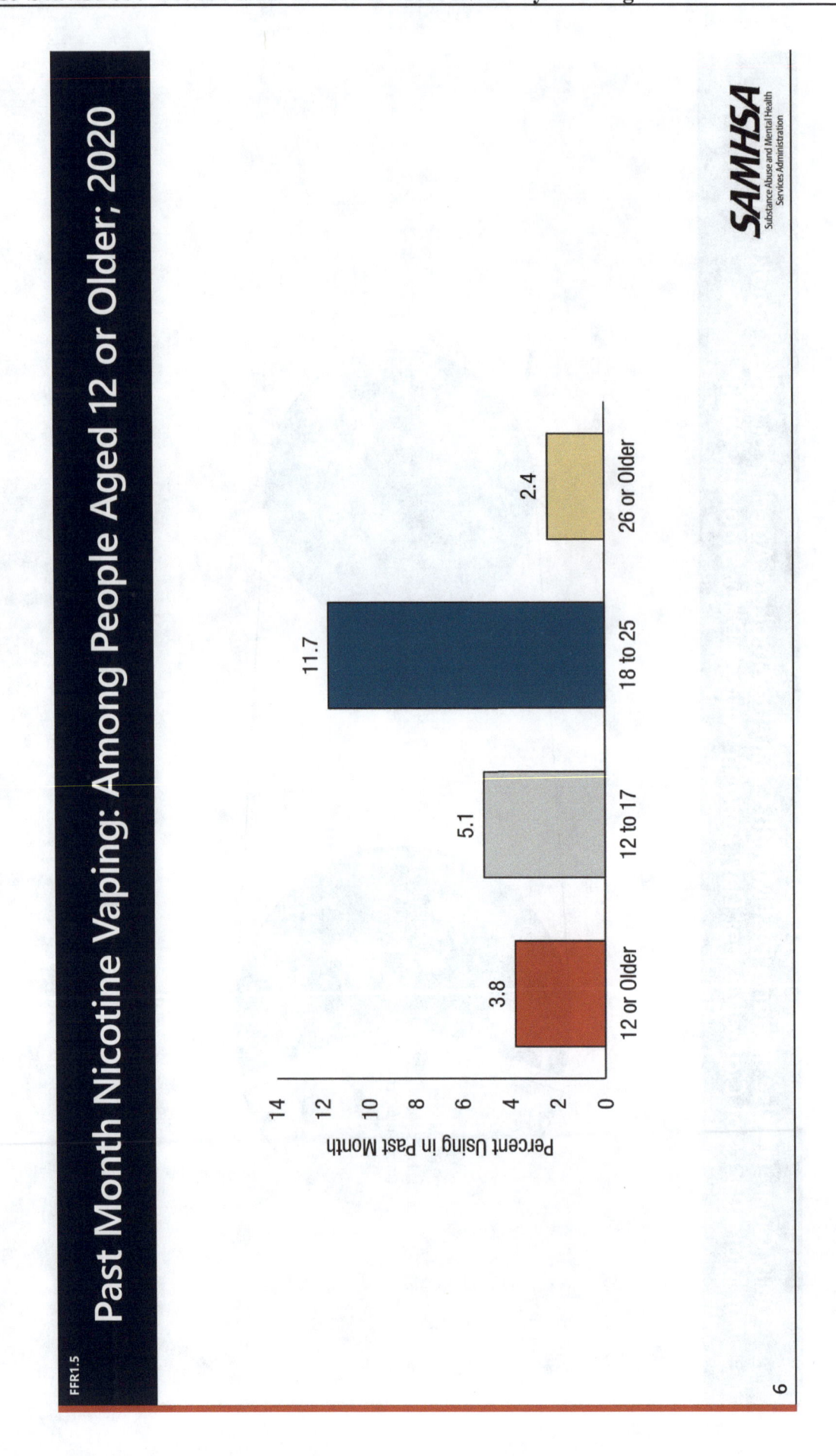

Studies & Statistics / Results from the 2020 National Survey on Drug Use and Health

Past Month Nicotine Vaping: Among People Aged 12 or Older; 2020

Age Group	Percent Using in Past Month
12 or Older	3.8
12 to 17	5.1
18 to 25	11.7
26 or Older	2.4

FFR1.5

SAMHSA
Substance Abuse and Mental Health Services Administration

Studies & Statistics / Results from the 2020 National Survey on Drug Use and Health

Current, Binge, and Heavy Alcohol Use: Among People Aged 12 or Older; 2020

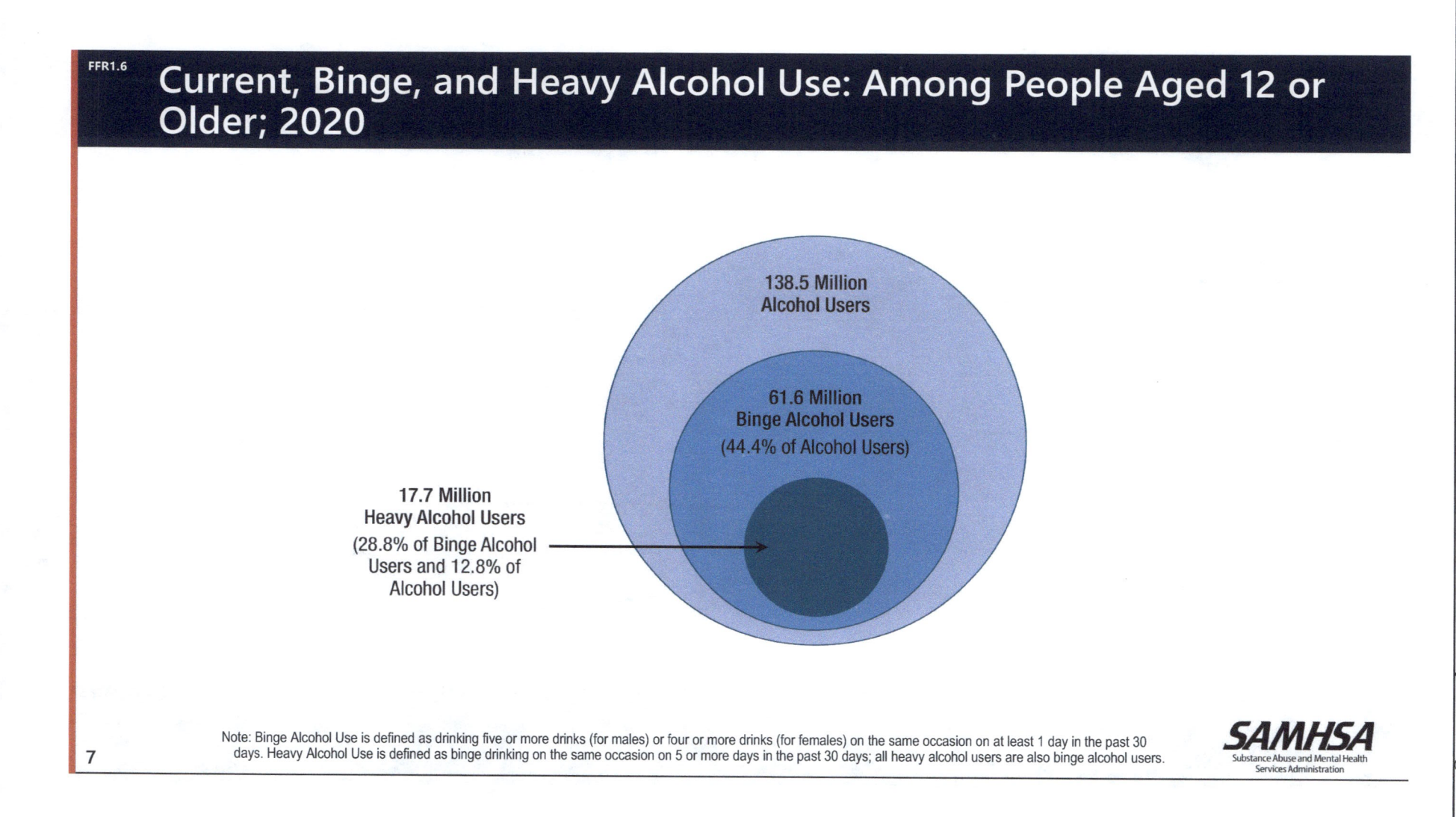

- 138.5 Million Alcohol Users
- 61.6 Million Binge Alcohol Users (44.4% of Alcohol Users)
- 17.7 Million Heavy Alcohol Users (28.8% of Binge Alcohol Users and 12.8% of Alcohol Users)

Note: Binge Alcohol Use is defined as drinking five or more drinks (for males) or four or more drinks (for females) on the same occasion on at least 1 day in the past 30 days. Heavy Alcohol Use is defined as binge drinking on the same occasion on 5 or more days in the past 30 days; all heavy alcohol users are also binge alcohol users.

SAMHSA — Substance Abuse and Mental Health Services Administration

Studies & Statistics / Results from the 2020 National Survey on Drug Use and Health

Past Month Binge Alcohol Use: Among People Aged 12 or Older; 2015-2020

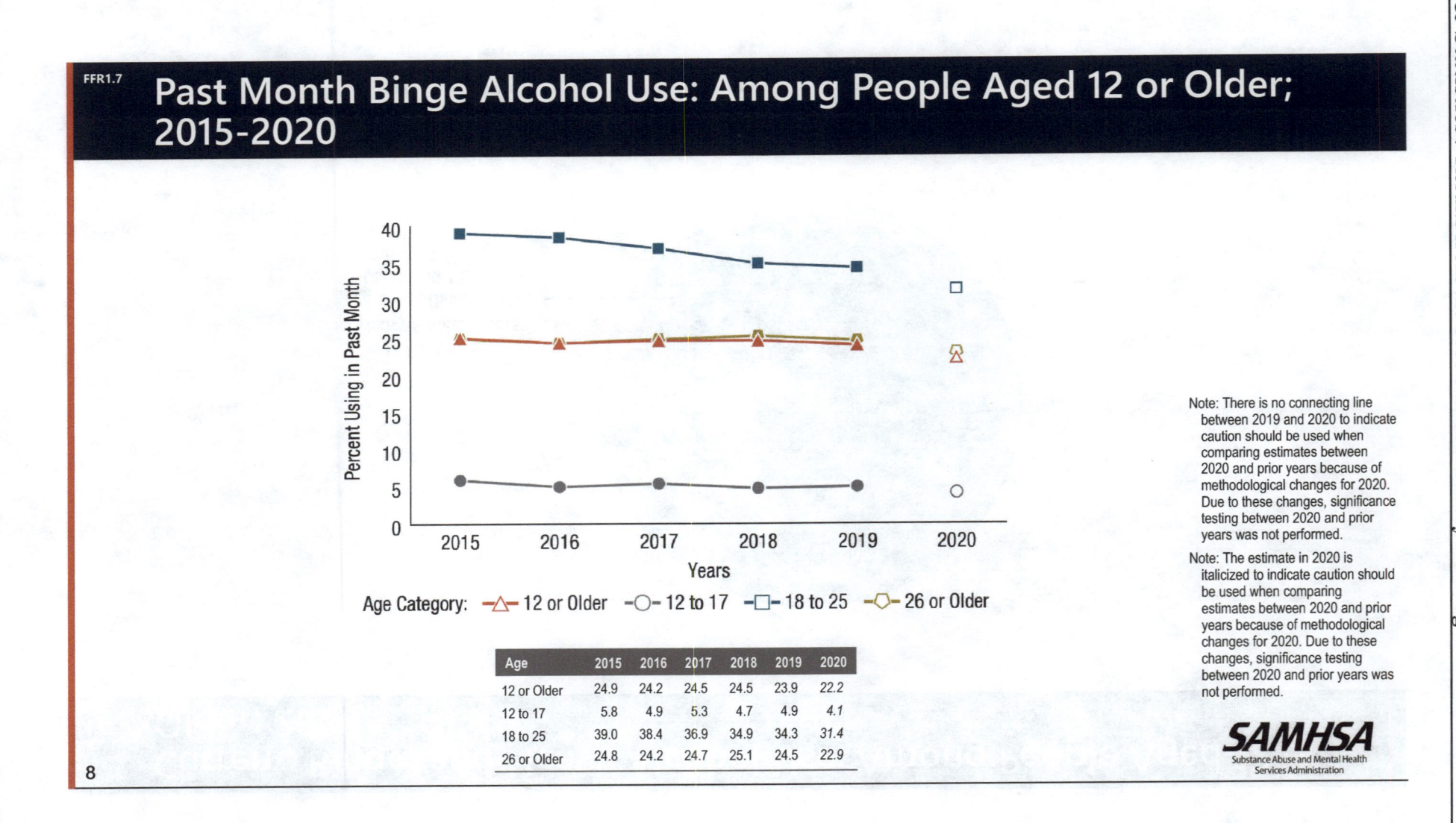

Age	2015	2016	2017	2018	2019	2020
12 or Older	24.9	24.2	24.5	24.5	23.9	22.2
12 to 17	5.8	4.9	5.3	4.7	4.9	4.1
18 to 25	39.0	38.4	36.9	34.9	34.3	31.4
26 or Older	24.8	24.2	24.7	25.1	24.5	22.9

Note: There is no connecting line between 2019 and 2020 to indicate caution should be used when comparing estimates between 2020 and prior years because of methodological changes for 2020. Due to these changes, significance testing between 2020 and prior years was not performed.

Note: The estimate in 2020 is italicized to indicate caution should be used when comparing estimates between 2020 and prior years because of methodological changes for 2020. Due to these changes, significance testing between 2020 and prior years was not performed.

SAMHSA Substance Abuse and Mental Health Services Administration

Studies & Statistics / Results from the 2020 National Survey on Drug Use and Health

Past Month Heavy Alcohol Use: Among People Aged 12 or Older; 2015-2020

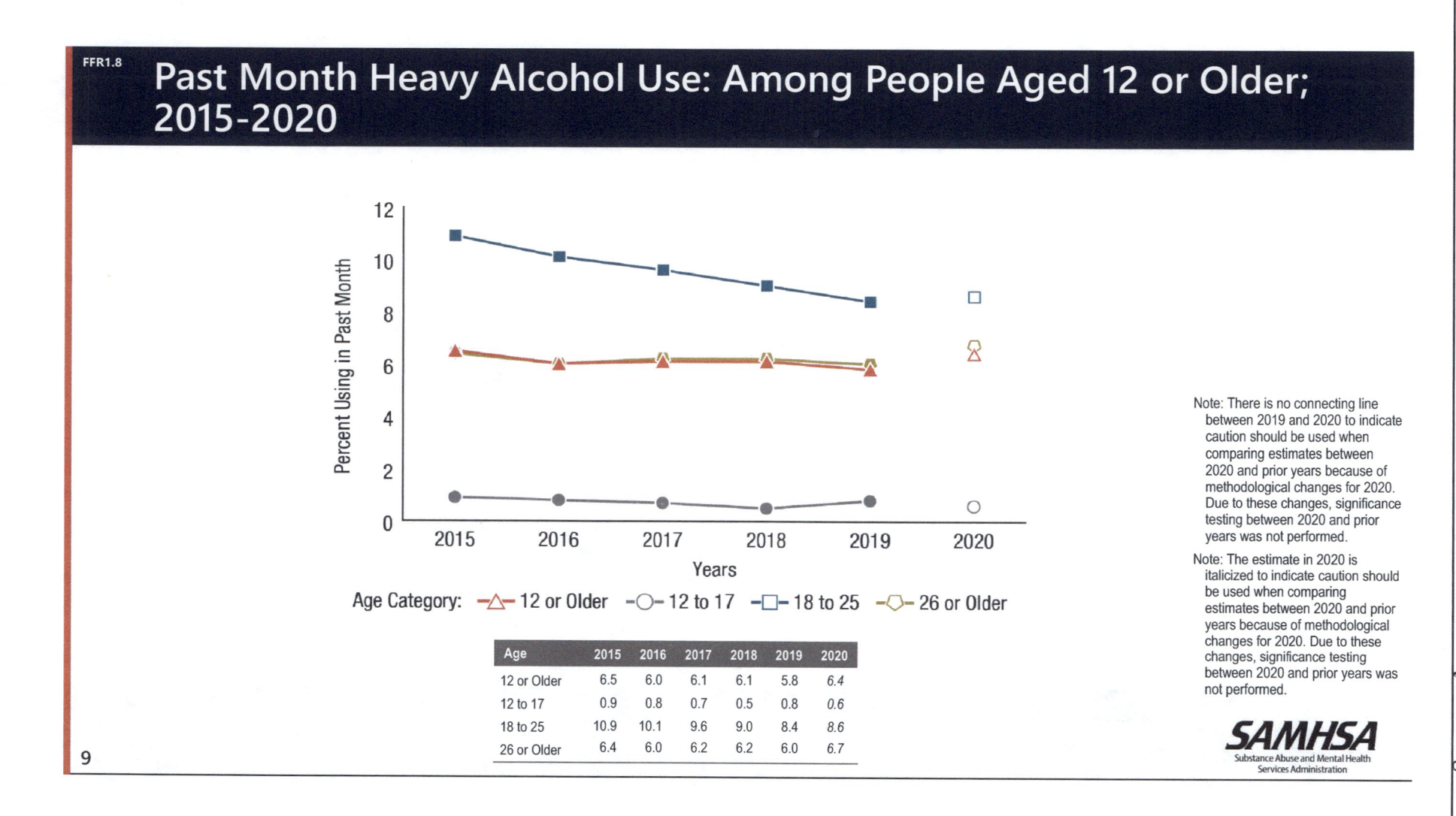

Age	2015	2016	2017	2018	2019	2020
12 or Older	6.5	6.0	6.1	6.1	5.8	6.4
12 to 17	0.9	0.8	0.7	0.5	0.8	0.6
18 to 25	10.9	10.1	9.6	9.0	8.4	8.6
26 or Older	6.4	6.0	6.2	6.2	6.0	6.7

Note: There is no connecting line between 2019 and 2020 to indicate caution should be used when comparing estimates between 2020 and prior years because of methodological changes for 2020. Due to these changes, significance testing between 2020 and prior years was not performed.

Note: The estimate in 2020 is italicized to indicate caution should be used when comparing estimates between 2020 and prior years because of methodological changes for 2020. Due to these changes, significance testing between 2020 and prior years was not performed.

SAMHSA
Substance Abuse and Mental Health Services Administration

Studies & Statistics / Results from the 2020 National Survey on Drug Use and Health

Past Year Illicit Drug Use: Among People Aged 12 or Older; 2020

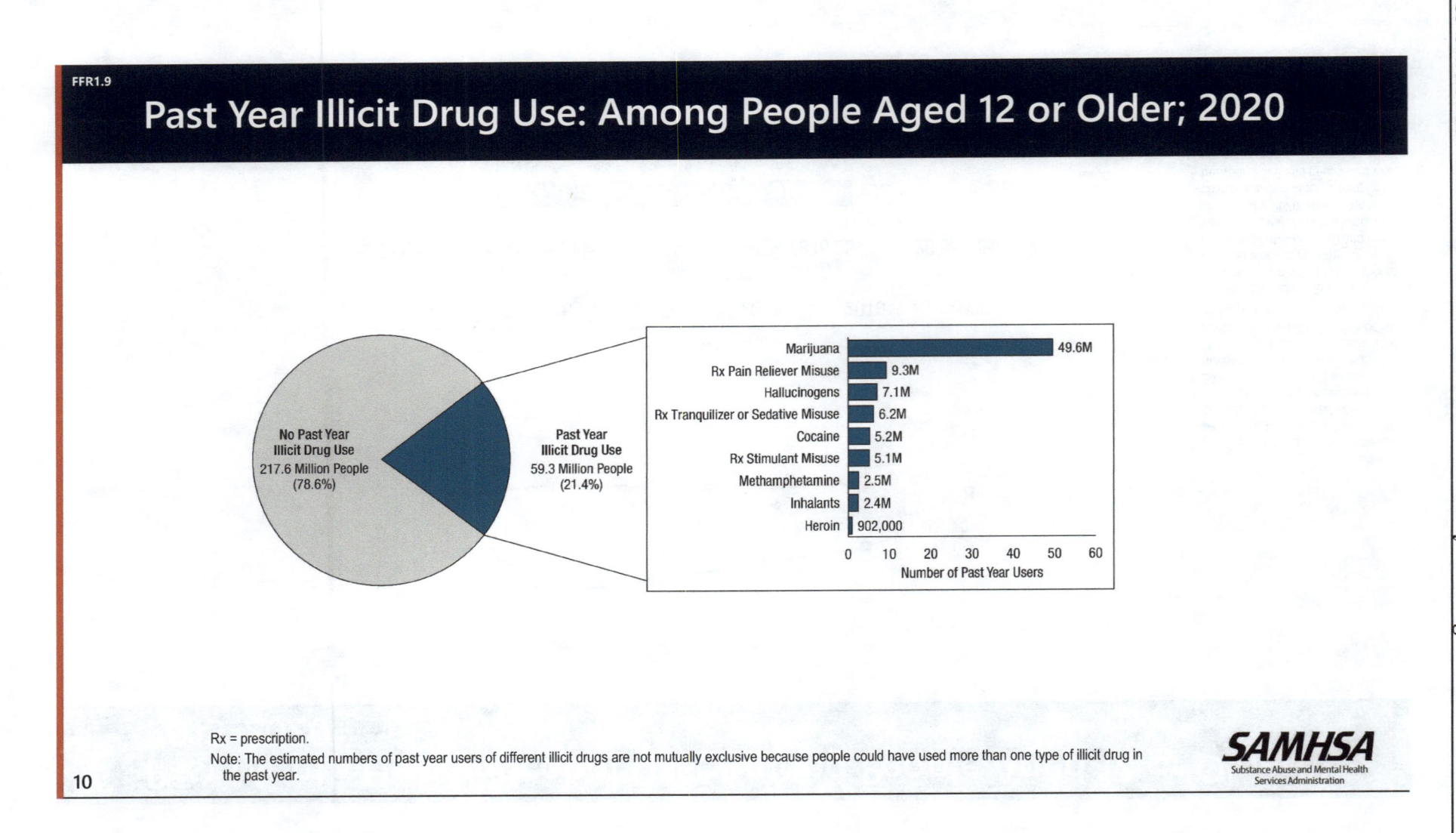

Past Year Illicit Drug Use
59.3 Million People
(21.4%)

No Past Year Illicit Drug Use
217.6 Million People
(78.6%)

- Marijuana: 49.6M
- Rx Pain Reliever Misuse: 9.3M
- Hallucinogens: 7.1M
- Rx Tranquilizer or Sedative Misuse: 6.2M
- Cocaine: 5.2M
- Rx Stimulant Misuse: 5.1M
- Methamphetamine: 2.5M
- Inhalants: 2.4M
- Heroin: 902,000

Number of Past Year Users

Rx = prescription.
Note: The estimated numbers of past year users of different illicit drugs are not mutually exclusive because people could have used more than one type of illicit drug in the past year.

SAMHSA Substance Abuse and Mental Health Services Administration

Studies & Statistics / Results from the 2020 National Survey on Drug Use and Health

FFR1.10 Past Year Illicit Drug Use: Among People Aged 12 or Older; 2015-2020

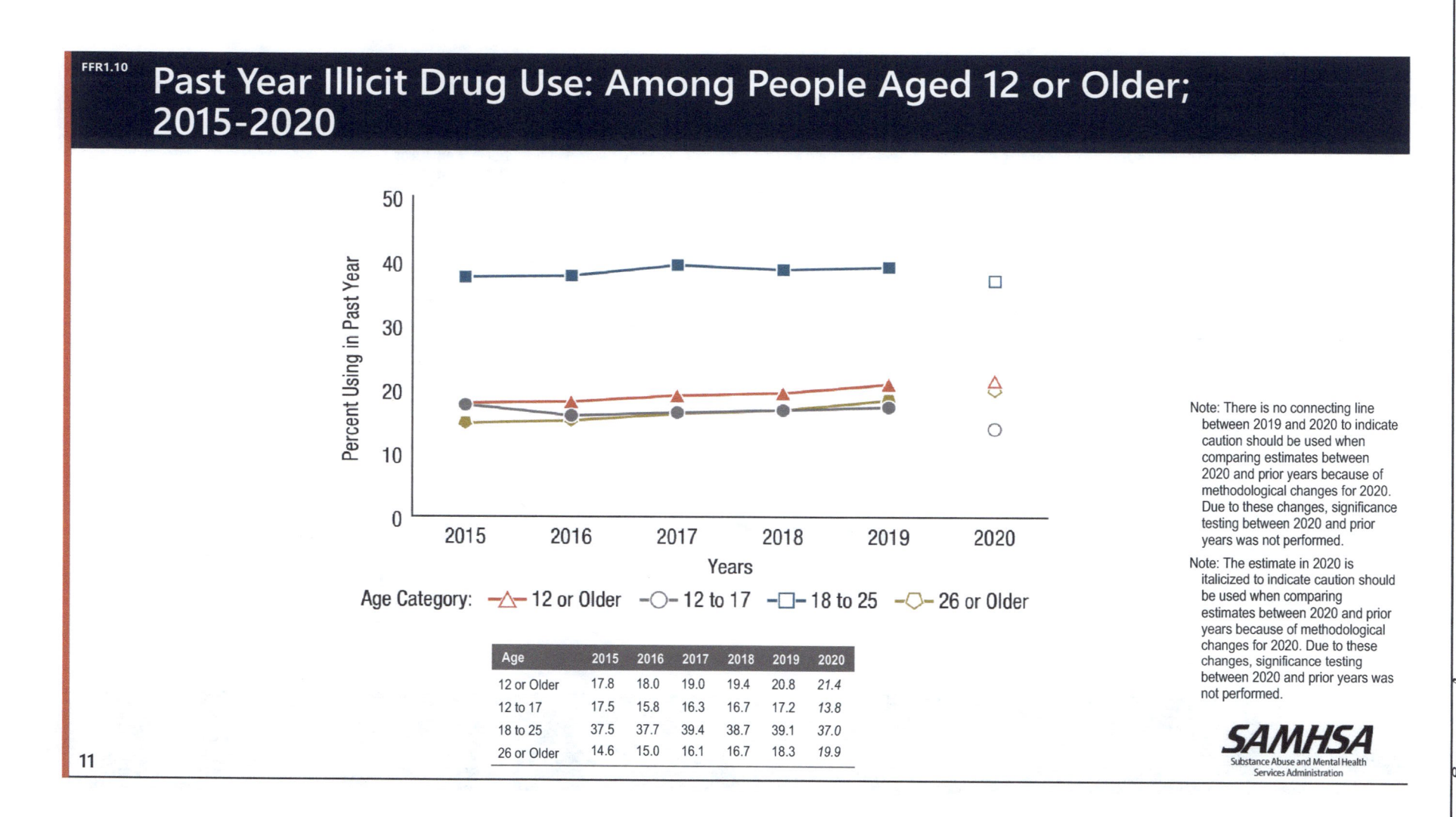

Age	2015	2016	2017	2018	2019	2020
12 or Older	17.8	18.0	19.0	19.4	20.8	21.4
12 to 17	17.5	15.8	16.3	16.7	17.2	13.8
18 to 25	37.5	37.7	39.4	38.7	39.1	37.0
26 or Older	14.6	15.0	16.1	16.7	18.3	19.9

Note: There is no connecting line between 2019 and 2020 to indicate caution should be used when comparing estimates between 2020 and prior years because of methodological changes for 2020. Due to these changes, significance testing between 2020 and prior years was not performed.

Note: The estimate in 2020 is italicized to indicate caution should be used when comparing estimates between 2020 and prior years because of methodological changes for 2020. Due to these changes, significance testing between 2020 and prior years was not performed.

SAMHSA Substance Abuse and Mental Health Services Administration

Studies & Statistics / Results from the 2020 National Survey on Drug Use and Health

Past Year Marijuana Use: Among People Aged 12 or Older; 2002-2020

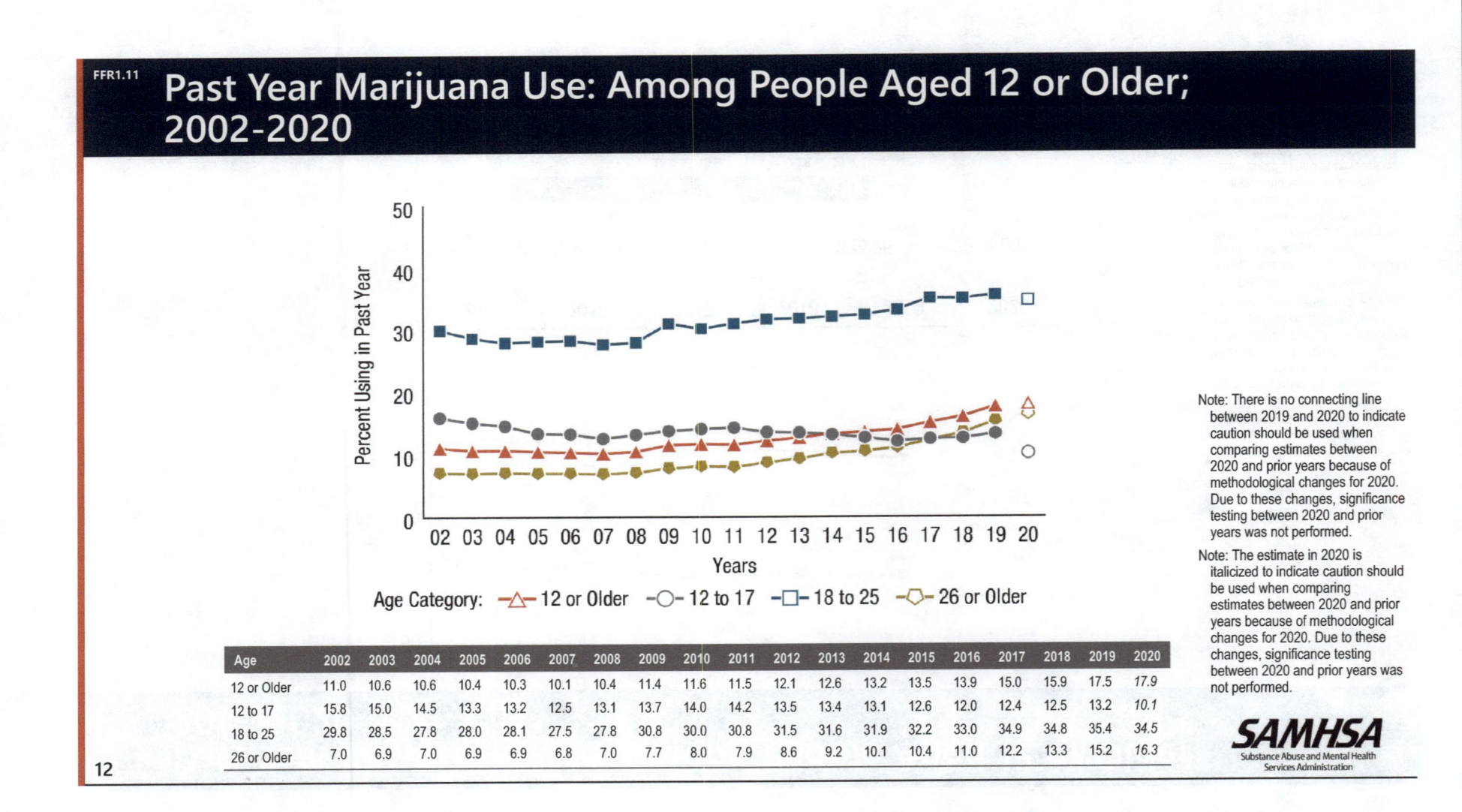

Age Category: — 12 or Older   — 12 to 17   — 18 to 25   — 26 or Older

Age	2002	2003	2004	2005	2006	2007	2008	2009	2010	2011	2012	2013	2014	2015	2016	2017	2018	2019	2020
12 or Older	11.0	10.6	10.6	10.4	10.3	10.1	10.4	11.4	11.6	11.5	12.1	12.6	13.2	13.2	13.9	15.0	15.9	17.5	17.9
12 to 17	15.8	15.0	14.5	13.3	13.2	12.5	13.1	13.7	14.0	14.2	13.5	13.4	13.1	12.6	12.0	12.4	12.5	13.2	10.1
18 to 25	29.8	28.5	27.8	28.0	28.1	27.5	27.8	30.8	30.0	30.8	31.5	31.6	31.9	32.2	33.0	34.9	34.8	35.4	34.5
26 or Older	7.0	6.9	7.0	6.9	6.9	6.8	7.0	7.7	8.0	7.9	8.6	9.2	10.1	10.4	11.0	12.2	13.3	15.2	16.3

Note: There is no connecting line between 2019 and 2020 to indicate caution should be used when comparing estimates between 2020 and prior years because of methodological changes for 2020. Due to these changes, significance testing between 2020 and prior years was not performed.

Note: The estimate in 2020 is italicized to indicate caution should be used when comparing estimates between 2020 and prior years because of methodological changes for 2020. Due to these changes, significance testing between 2020 and prior years was not performed.

SAMHSA Substance Abuse and Mental Health Services Administration

Studies & Statistics / Results from the 2020 National Survey on Drug Use and Health

FFR1.12 Past Year Methamphetamine Use: Among People Aged 12 or Older; 2015-2020

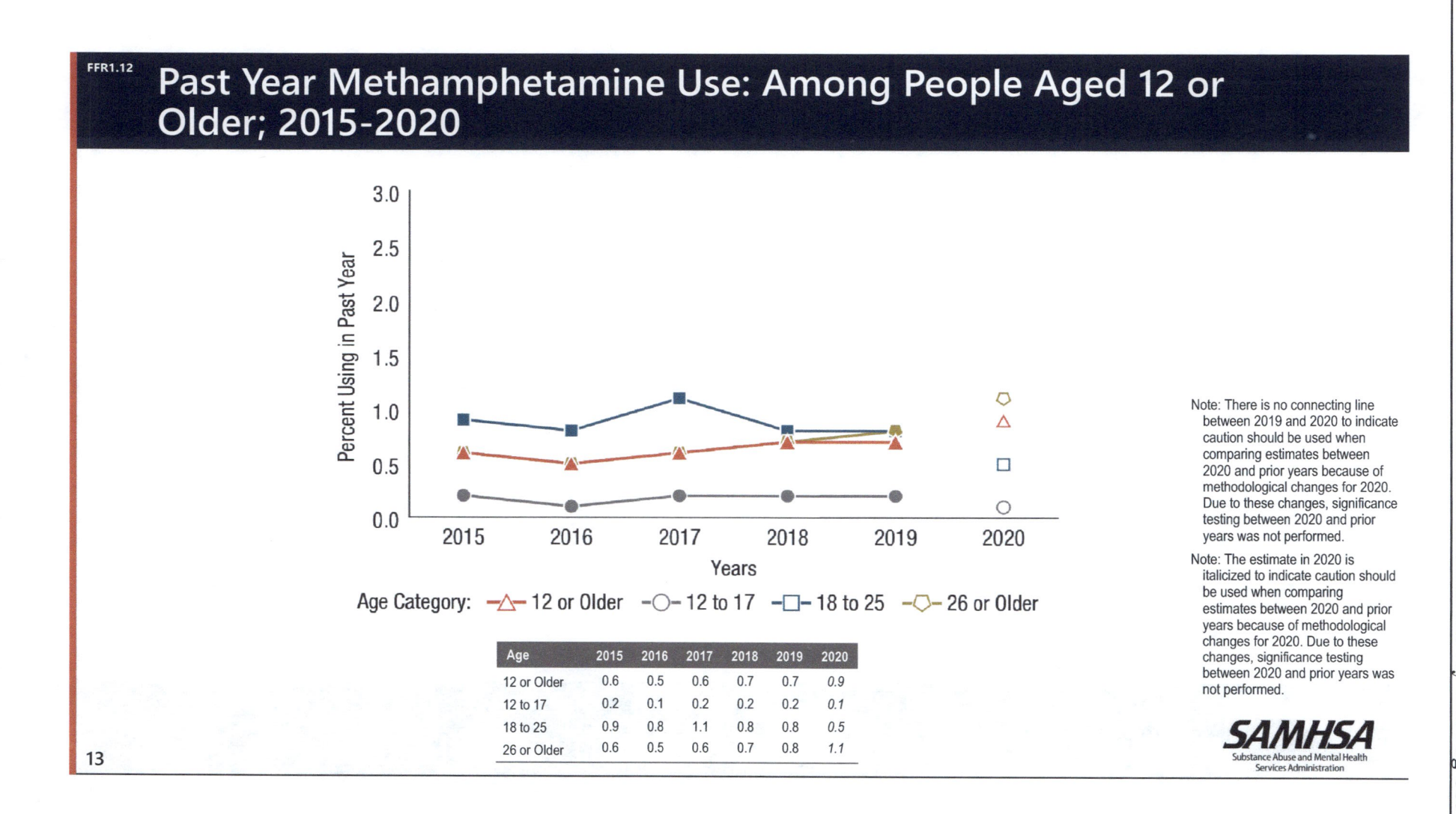

Age	2015	2016	2017	2018	2019	2020
12 or Older	0.6	0.5	0.6	0.7	0.7	0.9
12 to 17	0.2	0.1	0.2	0.2	0.2	0.1
18 to 25	0.9	0.8	1.1	0.8	0.8	0.5
26 or Older	0.6	0.5	0.6	0.7	0.8	1.1

Note: There is no connecting line between 2019 and 2020 to indicate caution should be used when comparing estimates between 2020 and prior years because of methodological changes for 2020. Due to these changes, significance testing between 2020 and prior years was not performed.

Note: The estimate in 2020 is italicized to indicate caution should be used when comparing estimates between 2020 and prior years because of methodological changes for 2020. Due to these changes, significance testing between 2020 and prior years was not performed.

SAMHSA
Substance Abuse and Mental Health Services Administration

Studies & Statistics / Results from the 2020 National Survey on Drug Use and Health

Past Year Hallucinogen Use: Among People Aged 12 or Older; 2015-2020

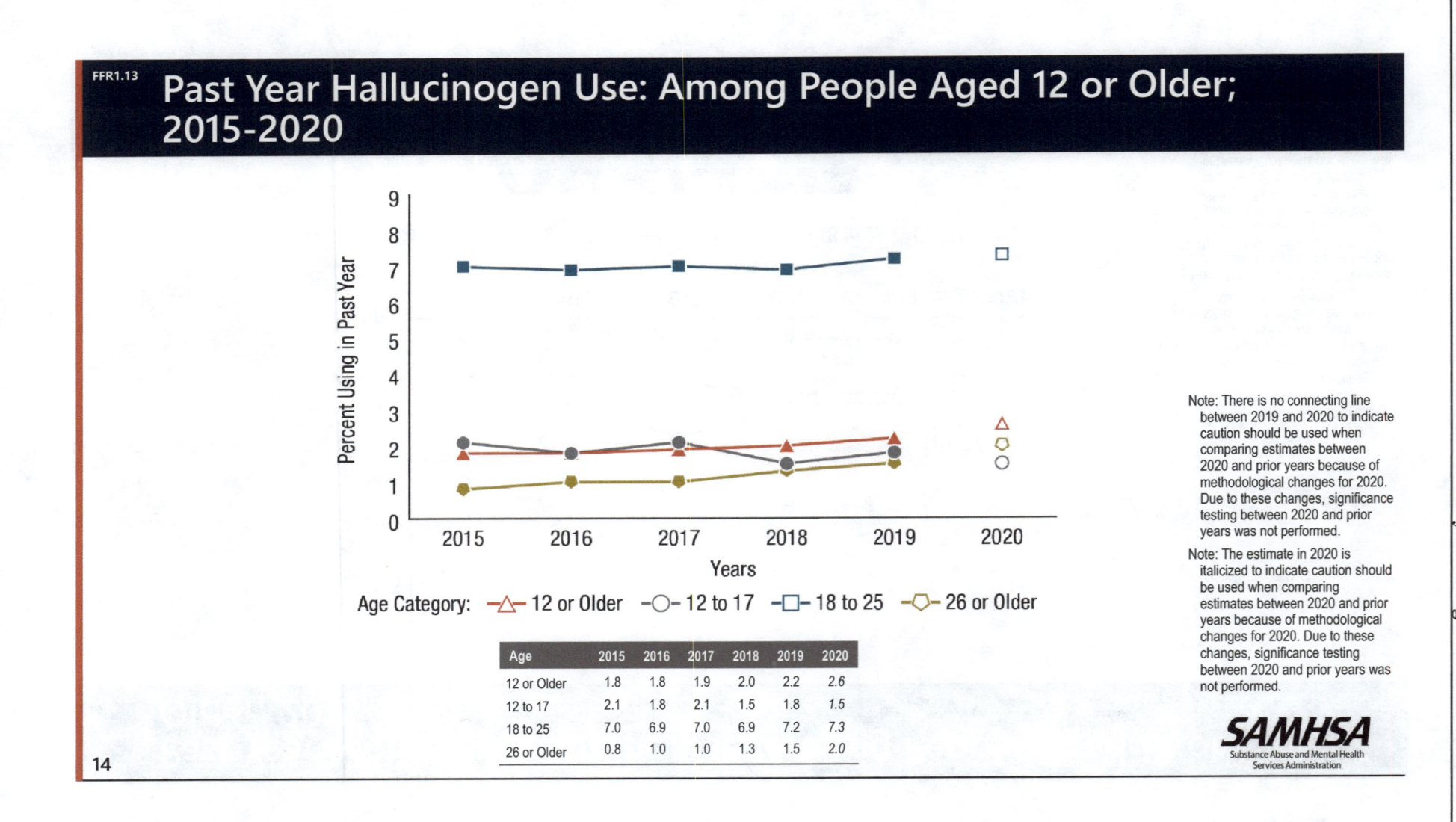

Age	2015	2016	2017	2018	2019	2020
12 or Older	1.8	1.8	1.9	2.0	2.2	2.6
12 to 17	2.1	1.8	2.1	1.5	1.8	1.5
18 to 25	7.0	6.9	7.0	6.9	7.2	7.3
26 or Older	0.8	1.0	1.0	1.3	1.5	2.0

Note: There is no connecting line between 2019 and 2020 to indicate caution should be used when comparing estimates between 2020 and prior years because of methodological changes for 2020. Due to these changes, significance testing between 2020 and prior years was not performed.

Note: The estimate in 2020 is italicized to indicate caution should be used when comparing estimates between 2020 and prior years because of methodological changes for 2020. Due to these changes, significance testing between 2020 and prior years was not performed.

FFR1.13

SAMHSA
Substance Abuse and Mental Health Services Administration

Studies & Statistics / Results from the 2020 National Survey on Drug Use and Health

FFR1.14 Past Year Inhalant Use: Among People Aged 12 or Older; 2015–2020

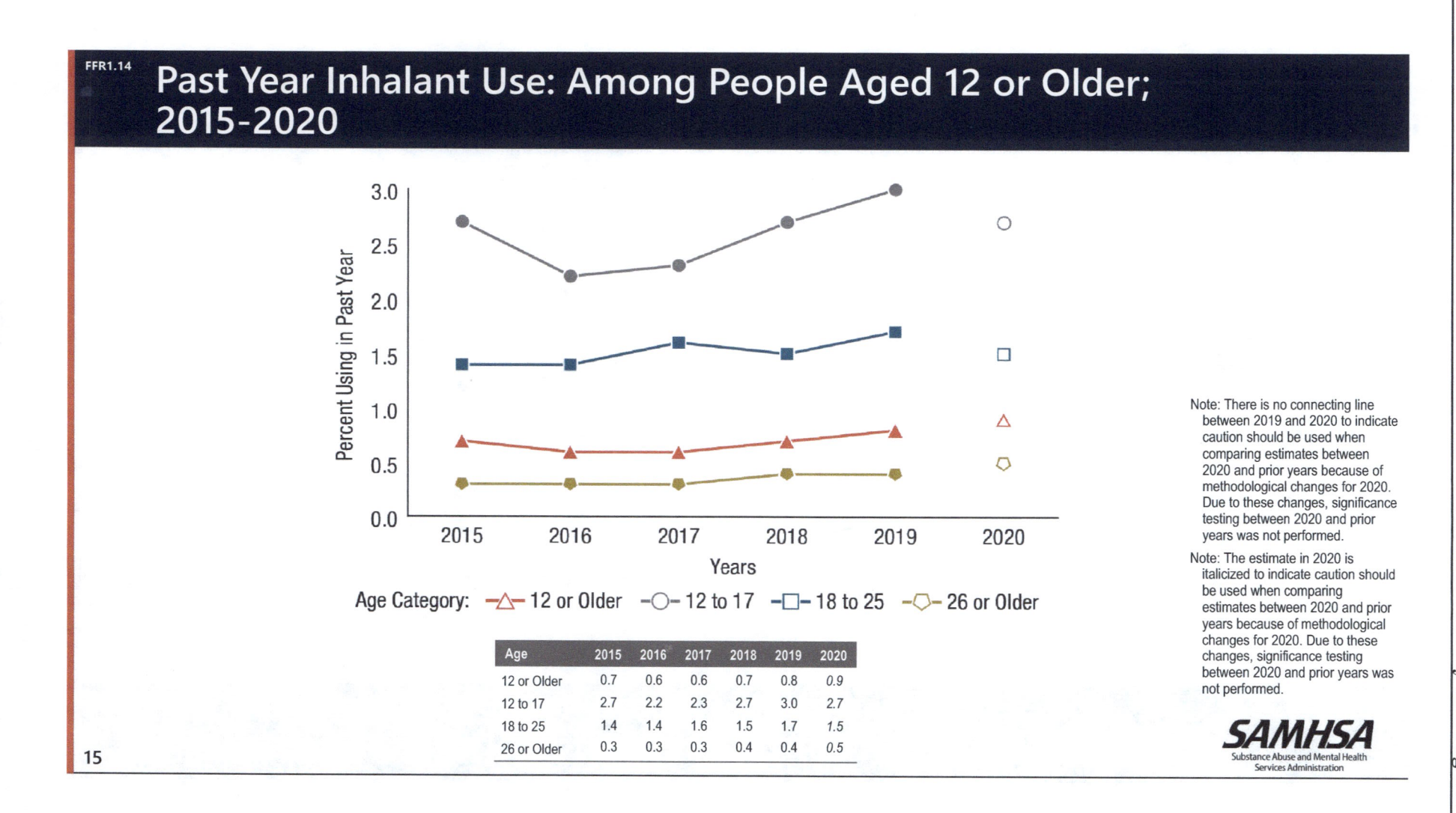

Age	2015	2016	2017	2018	2019	2020
12 or Older	0.7	0.6	0.6	0.7	0.8	0.9
12 to 17	2.7	2.2	2.3	2.7	3.0	2.7
18 to 25	1.4	1.4	1.6	1.5	1.7	1.5
26 or Older	0.3	0.3	0.3	0.4	0.4	0.5

Age Category: — 12 or Older — 12 to 17 — 18 to 25 — 26 or Older

Note: There is no connecting line between 2019 and 2020 to indicate caution should be used when comparing estimates between 2020 and prior years because of methodological changes for 2020. Due to these changes, significance testing between 2020 and prior years was not performed.

Note: The estimate in 2020 is italicized to indicate caution should be used when comparing estimates between 2020 and prior years because of methodological changes for 2020. Due to these changes, significance testing between 2020 and prior years was not performed.

SAMHSA Substance Abuse and Mental Health Services Administration

Studies & Statistics / Results from the 2020 National Survey on Drug Use and Health

FFR1.15 Past Year Prescription Stimulant Misuse: Among People Aged 12 or Older; 2015-2020

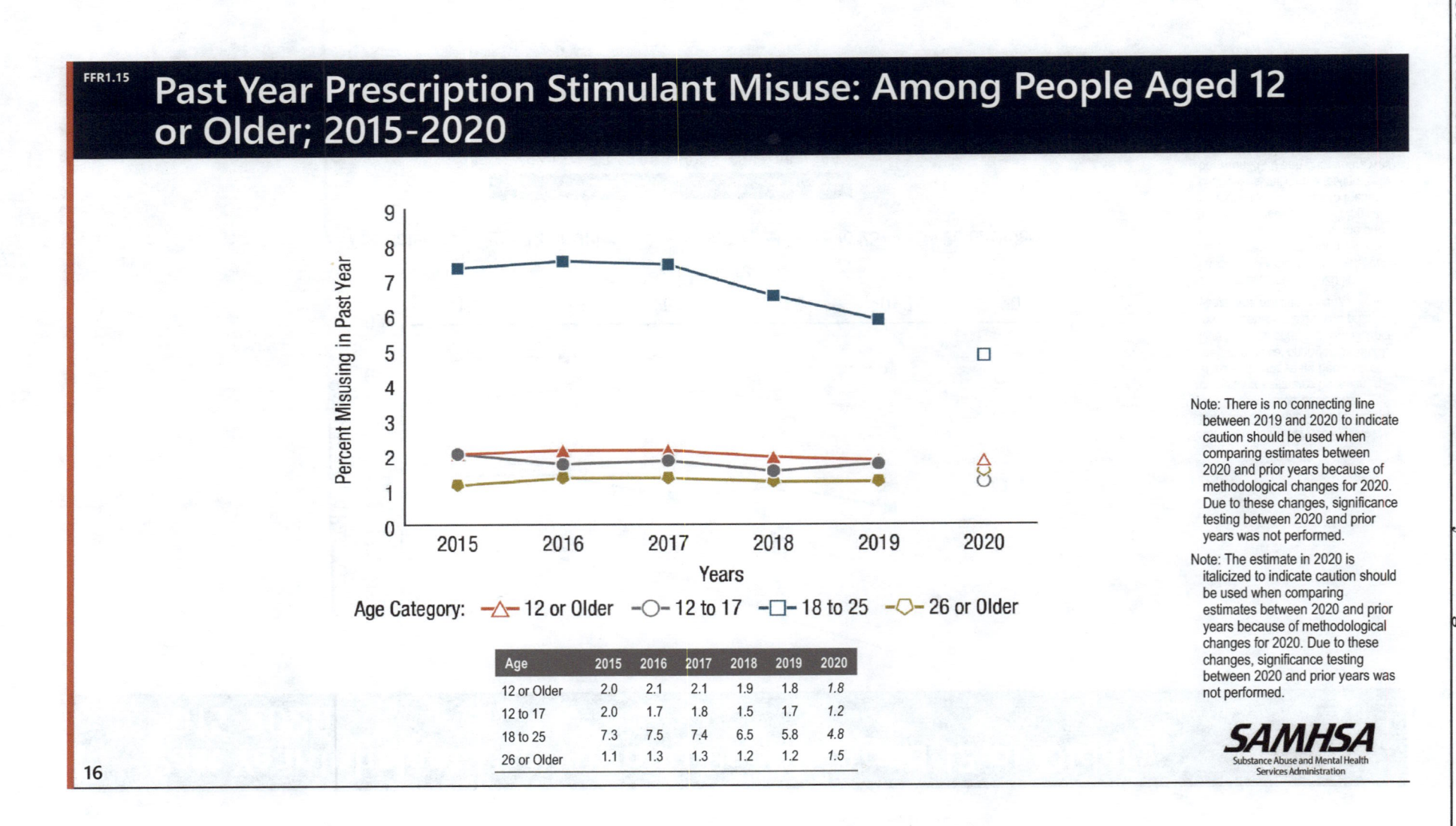

Age	2015	2016	2017	2018	2019	2020
12 or Older	2.0	2.1	2.1	1.9	1.8	*1.8*
12 to 17	2.0	1.7	1.8	1.5	1.7	*1.2*
18 to 25	7.3	7.5	7.4	6.5	5.8	*4.8*
26 or Older	1.1	1.3	1.3	1.2	1.2	*1.5*

Note: There is no connecting line between 2019 and 2020 to indicate caution should be used when comparing estimates between 2020 and prior years because of methodological changes for 2020. Due to these changes, significance testing between 2020 and prior years was not performed.

Note: The estimate in 2020 is italicized to indicate caution should be used when comparing estimates between 2020 and prior years because of methodological changes for 2020. Due to these changes, significance testing between 2020 and prior years was not performed.

SAMHSA — Substance Abuse and Mental Health Services Administration

Studies & Statistics / Results from the 2020 National Survey on Drug Use and Health

FFR1.16 Past Year Prescription Pain Reliever Misuse: Among People Aged 12 or Older; 2015-2020

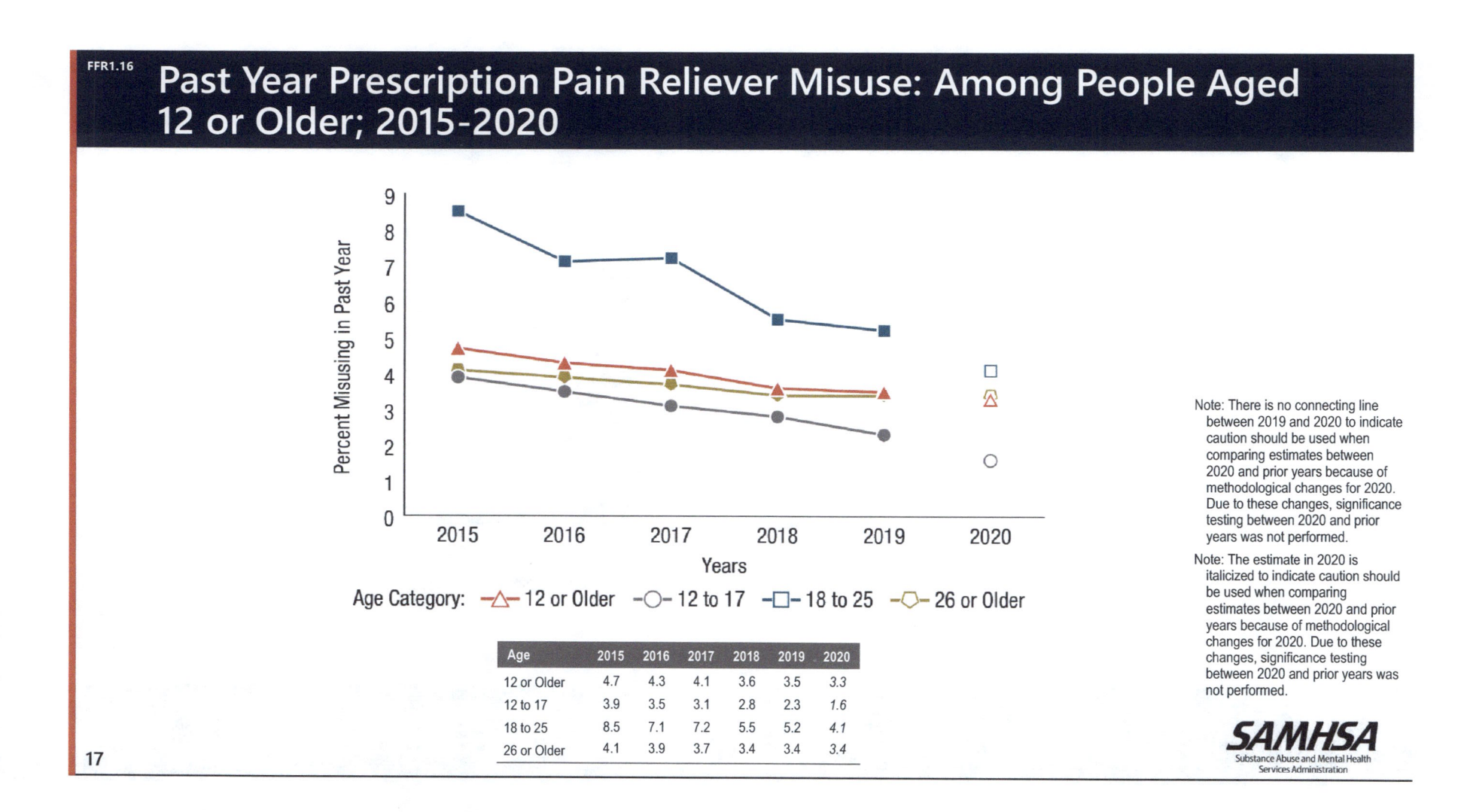

Age	2015	2016	2017	2018	2019	2020
12 or Older	4.7	4.3	4.1	3.6	3.5	3.3
12 to 17	3.9	3.5	3.1	2.8	2.3	1.6
18 to 25	8.5	7.1	7.2	5.5	5.2	4.1
26 or Older	4.1	3.9	3.7	3.4	3.4	3.4

Age Category: —△— 12 or Older —○— 12 to 17 —□— 18 to 25 —⬠— 26 or Older

Note: There is no connecting line between 2019 and 2020 to indicate caution should be used when comparing estimates between 2020 and prior years because of methodological changes for 2020. Due to these changes, significance testing between 2020 and prior years was not performed.

Note: The estimate in 2020 is italicized to indicate caution should be used when comparing estimates between 2020 and prior years because of methodological changes for 2020. Due to these changes, significance testing between 2020 and prior years was not performed.

SAMHSA
Substance Abuse and Mental Health Services Administration

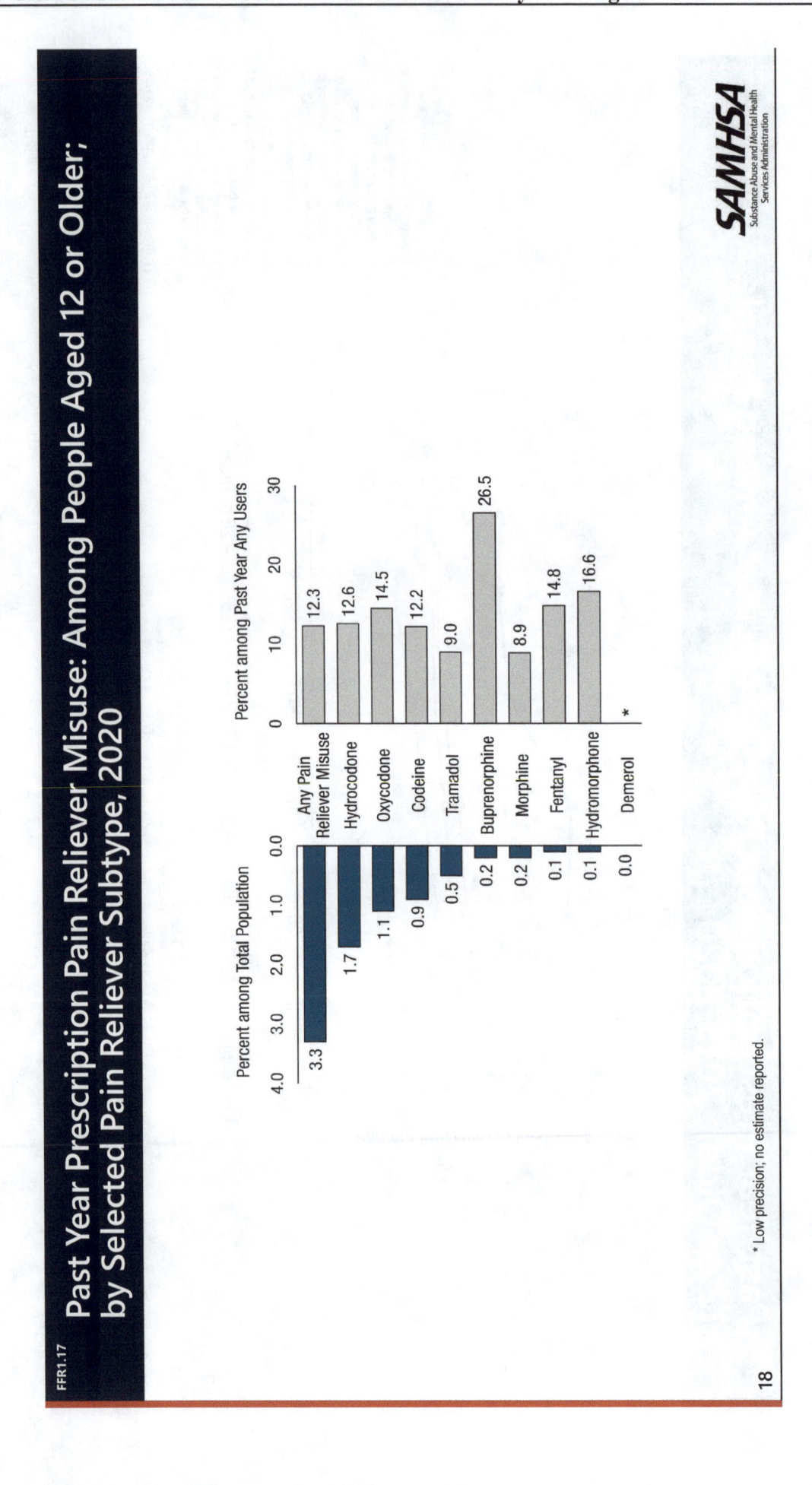

Studies & Statistics / Results from the 2020 National Survey on Drug Use and Health

Past Year Prescription Pain Reliever Misuse: Among People Aged 12 or Older; by Selected Pain Reliever Subtype, 2020

Pain Reliever Subtype	Percent among Total Population	Percent among Past Year Any Users
Any Pain Reliever Misuse	3.3	12.3
Hydrocodone	1.7	12.6
Oxycodone	1.1	14.5
Codeine	0.9	12.2
Tramadol	0.5	9.0
Buprenorphine	0.2	26.5
Morphine	0.2	8.9
Fentanyl	0.1	14.8
Hydromorphone	0.1	16.6
Demerol	0.0	*

* Low precision; no estimate reported.

SAMHSA — Substance Abuse and Mental Health Services Administration

Past Year Opioid Misuse: Among People Aged 12 or Older; 2020

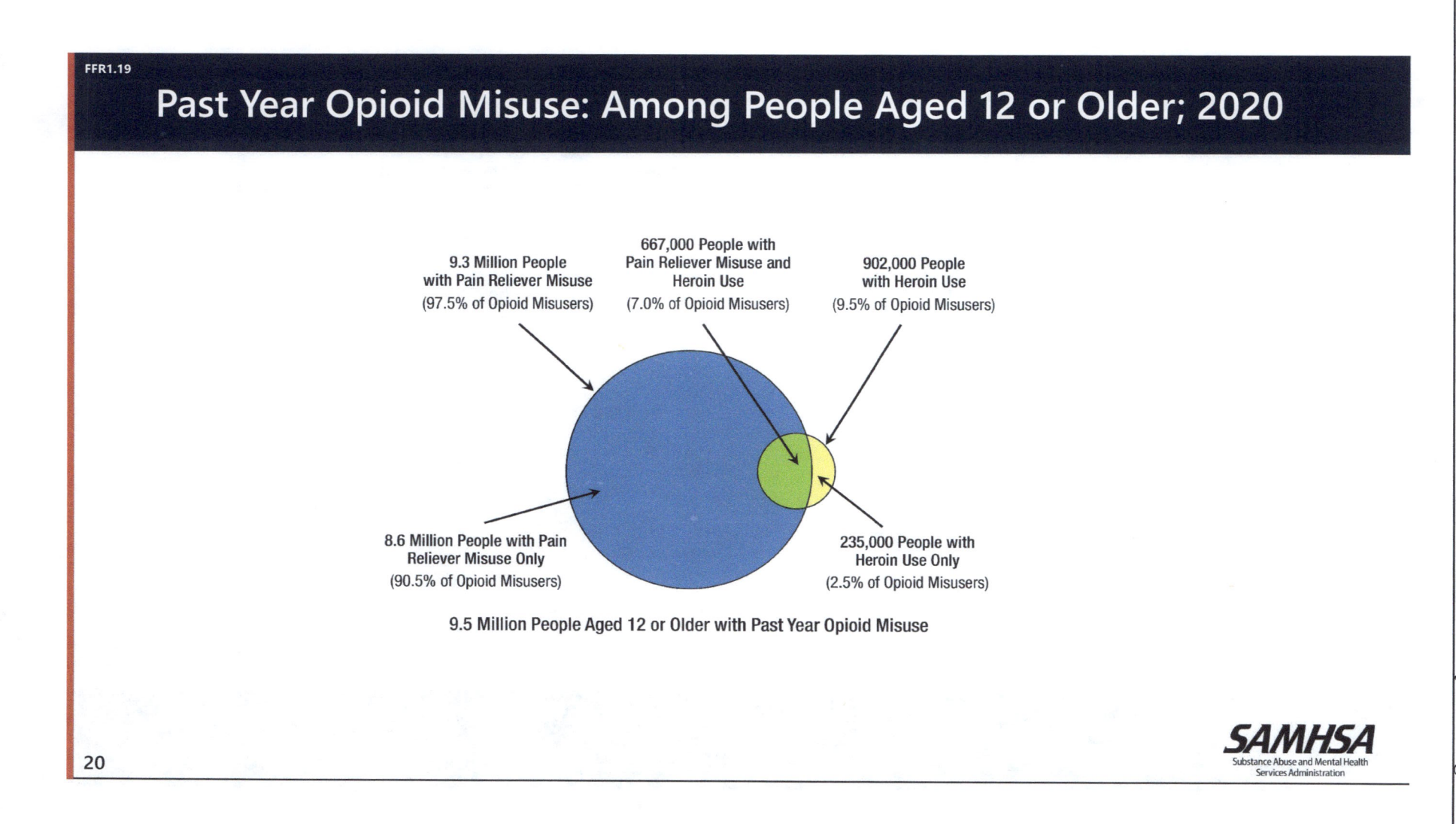

- 9.3 Million People with Pain Reliever Misuse (97.5% of Opioid Misusers)
- 667,000 People with Pain Reliever Misuse and Heroin Use (7.0% of Opioid Misusers)
- 902,000 People with Heroin Use (9.5% of Opioid Misusers)
- 235,000 People with Heroin Use Only (2.5% of Opioid Misusers)
- 8.6 Million People with Pain Reliever Misuse Only (90.5% of Opioid Misusers)
- 9.5 Million People Aged 12 or Older with Past Year Opioid Misuse

Studies & Statistics / Results from the 2020 National Survey on Drug Use and Health

FFR1.30 Major Depressive Episode (MDE) and MDE with Severe Impairment in the Past Year: Among Youths Aged 12 to 17; 2004-2020

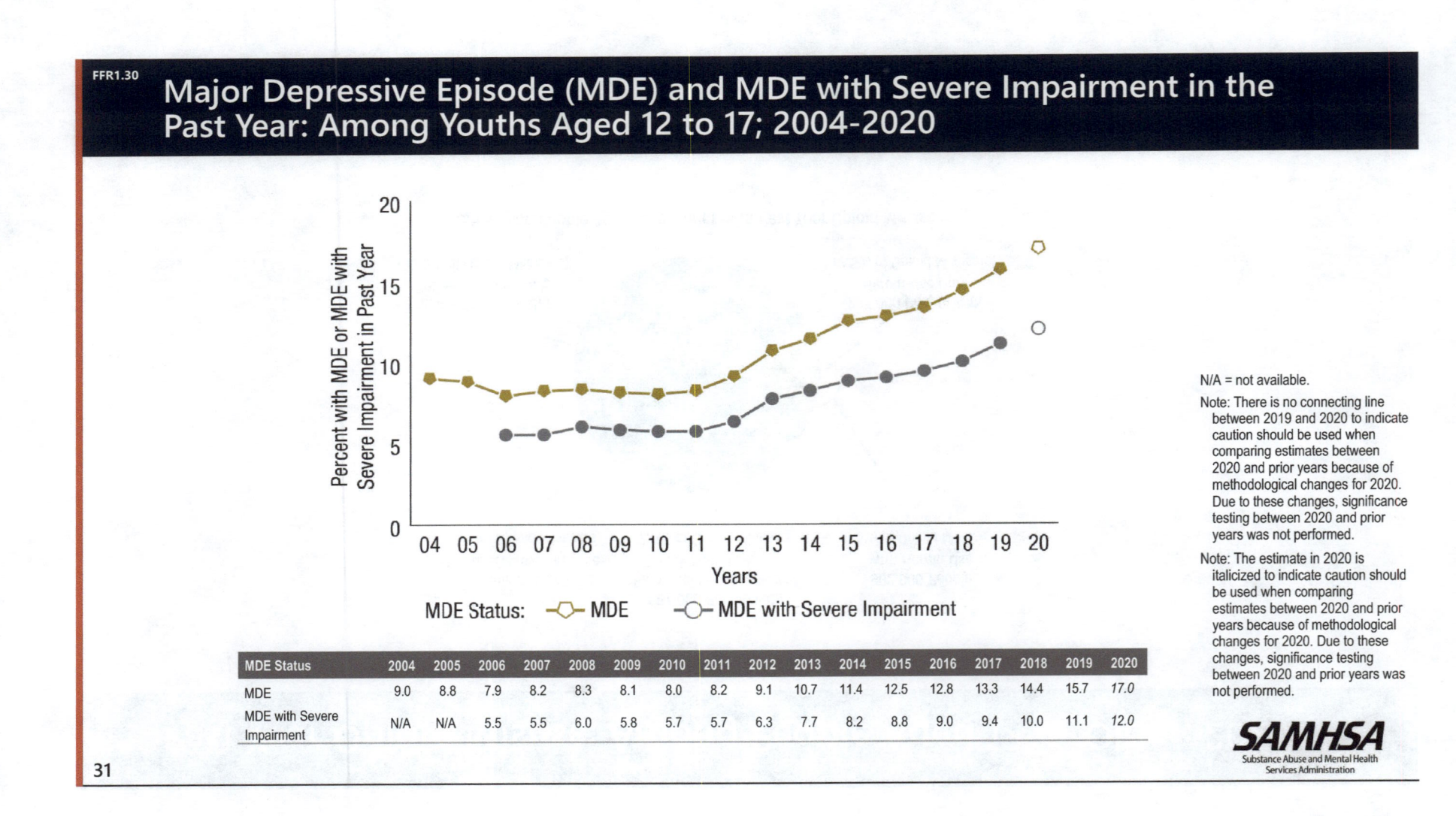

MDE Status	2004	2005	2006	2007	2008	2009	2010	2011	2012	2013	2014	2015	2016	2017	2018	2019	2020
MDE	9.0	8.8	7.9	8.2	8.3	8.1	8.0	8.2	9.1	10.7	11.4	12.5	12.8	13.3	14.4	15.7	17.0
MDE with Severe Impairment	N/A	N/A	5.5	5.5	6.0	5.8	5.7	5.7	6.3	7.7	8.2	8.8	9.0	9.4	10.0	11.1	12.0

N/A = not available.

Note: There is no connecting line between 2019 and 2020 to indicate caution should be used when comparing estimates between 2020 and prior years because of methodological changes for 2020. Due to these changes, significance testing between 2020 and prior years was not performed.

Note: The estimate in 2020 is italicized to indicate caution should be used when comparing estimates between 2020 and prior years because of methodological changes for 2020. Due to these changes, significance testing between 2020 and prior years was not performed.

SAMHSA Substance Abuse and Mental Health Services Administration

Studies & Statistics / Results from the 2020 National Survey on Drug Use and Health

FFR1.31 Major Depressive Episode with Severe Impairment in the Past Year: Among Adults Aged 18 or Older; 2009-2020

Age	2009	2010	2011	2012	2013	2014	2015	2016	2017	2018	2019	2020
18 or Older	4.0	4.2	4.2	4.5	4.3	4.3	4.3	4.3	4.5	4.7	5.3	6.0
18 to 25	5.2	5.2	5.2	5.8	5.7	6.0	6.5	7.0	8.5	8.9	10.3	12.1
26 to 49	4.8	4.7	5.2	5.1	4.9	4.6	4.9	4.7	5.0	5.3	6.1	6.5
50 or Older	2.6	3.5	2.9	3.4	3.2	3.5	3.0	3.0	2.8	2.9	3.2	3.8

Note: There is no connecting line between 2019 and 2020 to indicate caution should be used when comparing estimates between 2020 and prior years because of methodological changes for 2020. Due to these changes, significance testing between 2020 and prior years was not performed.

Note: The estimate in 2020 is italicized to indicate caution should be used when comparing estimates between 2020 and prior years because of methodological changes for 2020. Due to these changes, significance testing between 2020 and prior years was not performed.

SAMHSA Substance Abuse and Mental Health Services Administration

32

Studies & Statistics / Results from the 2020 National Survey on Drug Use and Health

FFR1.32 Serious Mental Illness in the Past Year: Among Adults Aged 18 or Older; 2008-2020

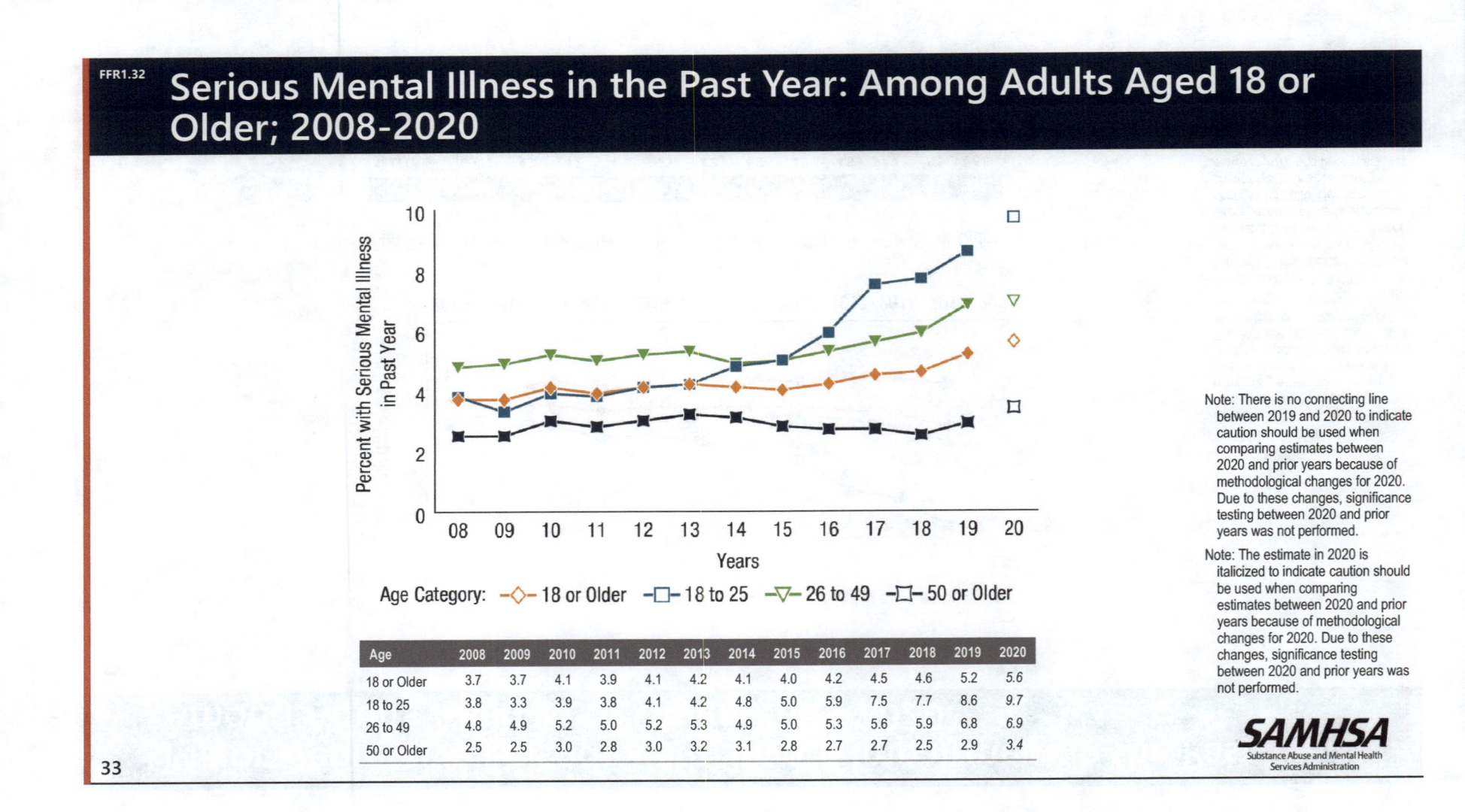

Age	2008	2009	2010	2011	2012	2013	2014	2015	2016	2017	2018	2019	2020
18 or Older	3.7	3.7	4.1	3.9	4.1	4.2	4.1	4.0	4.2	4.5	4.6	5.2	5.6
18 to 25	3.8	3.3	3.9	3.8	4.1	4.2	4.8	5.0	5.9	7.5	7.7	8.6	9.7
26 to 49	4.8	4.9	5.2	5.0	5.2	5.3	4.9	5.0	5.3	5.6	5.9	6.8	6.9
50 or Older	2.5	2.5	3.0	2.8	3.0	3.2	3.1	2.8	2.7	2.7	2.5	2.9	3.4

Note: There is no connecting line between 2019 and 2020 to indicate caution should be used when comparing estimates between 2020 and prior years because of methodological changes for 2020. Due to these changes, significance testing between 2020 and prior years was not performed.

Note: The estimate in 2020 is italicized to indicate caution should be used when comparing estimates between 2020 and prior years because of methodological changes for 2020. Due to these changes, significance testing between 2020 and prior years was not performed.

SAMHSA
Substance Abuse and Mental Health Services Administration

Studies & Statistics / Results from the 2020 National Survey on Drug Use and Health

FFR1.33 Past Year Substance Use Disorder (SUD) and Major Depressive Episode (MDE): Among Youths Aged 12 to 17; 2020

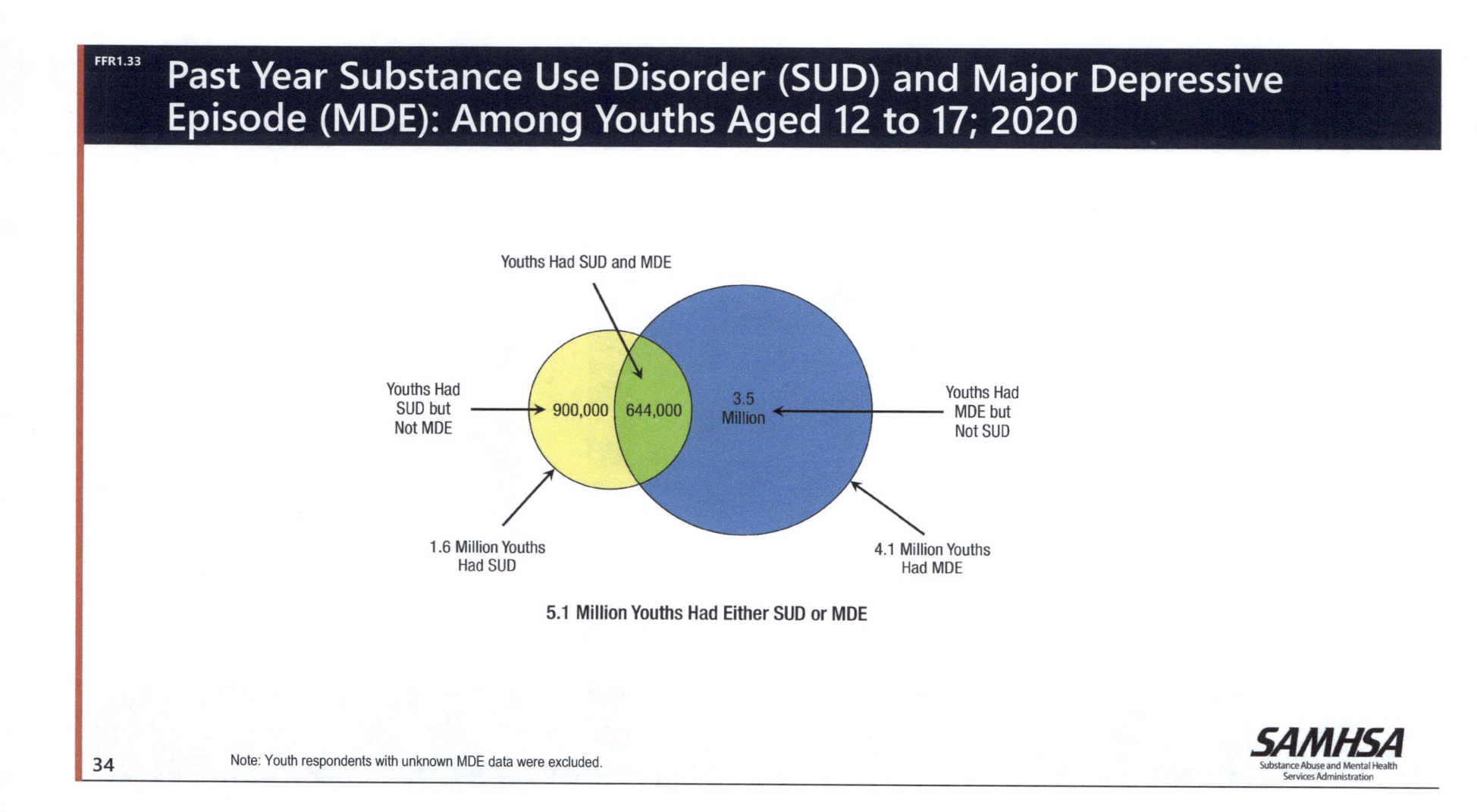

Youths Had MDE but Not SUD: 3.5 Million

4.1 Million Youths Had MDE

Youths Had SUD and MDE: 644,000

Youths Had SUD but Not MDE: 900,000

1.6 Million Youths Had SUD

5.1 Million Youths Had Either SUD or MDE

Note: Youth respondents with unknown MDE data were excluded.

SAMHSA — Substance Abuse and Mental Health Services Administration

Studies & Statistics / Results from the 2020 National Survey on Drug Use and Health

Substance Use: Among Youths Aged 12 to 17; by Past Year Major Depressive Episode (MDE) Status, 2020

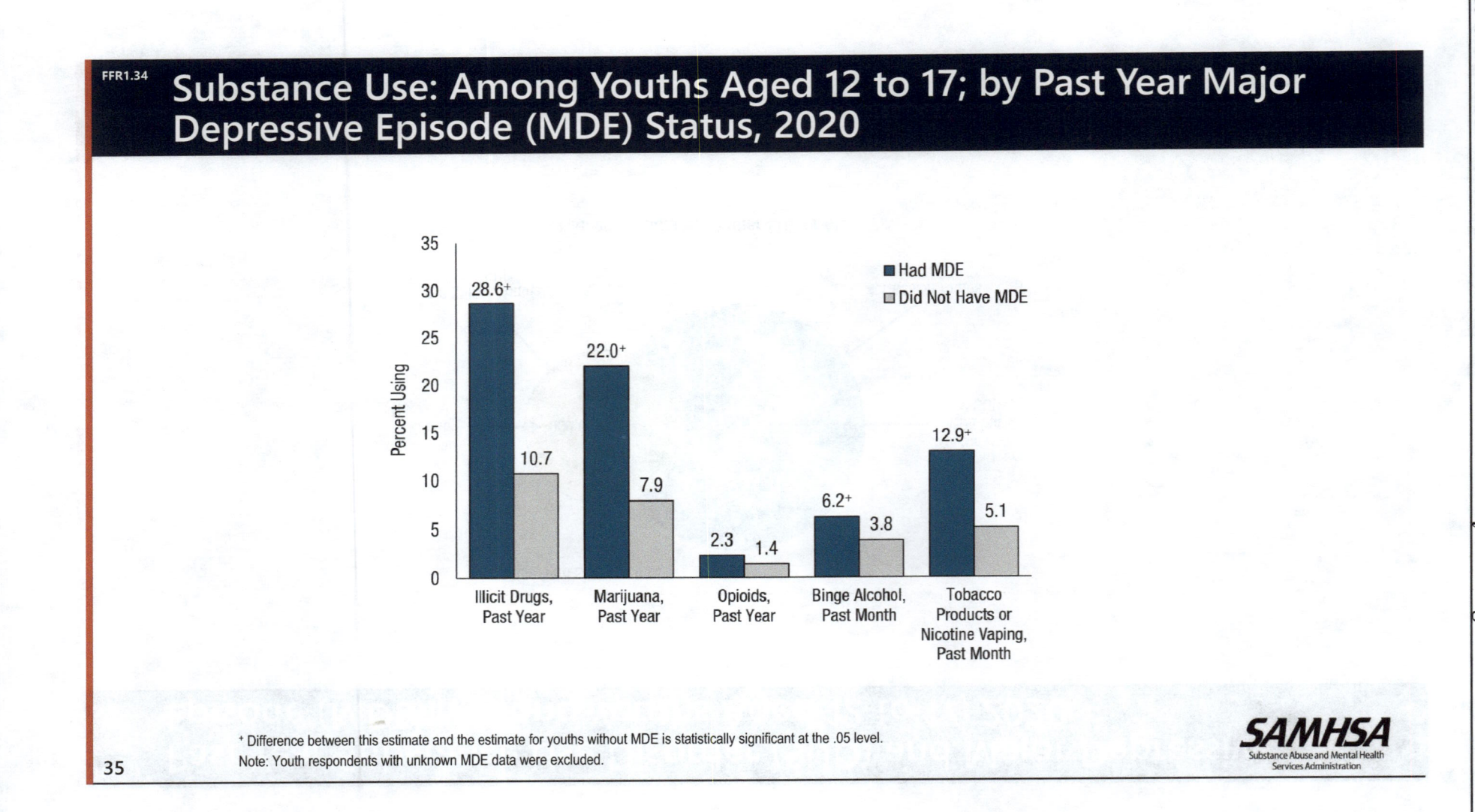

FFR1.34

- Had MDE
- Did Not Have MDE

Substance	Had MDE	Did Not Have MDE
Illicit Drugs, Past Year	28.6+	10.7
Marijuana, Past Year	22.0+	7.9
Opioids, Past Year	2.3	1.4
Binge Alcohol, Past Month	6.2+	3.8
Tobacco Products or Nicotine Vaping, Past Month	12.9+	5.1

Percent Using

+ Difference between this estimate and the estimate for youths without MDE is statistically significant at the .05 level.
Note: Youth respondents with unknown MDE data were excluded.

SAMHSA Substance Abuse and Mental Health Services Administration

Studies & Statistics / Results from the 2020 National Survey on Drug Use and Health

Past Year Substance Use Disorder (SUD) and Any Mental Illness (AMI): Among Adults Aged 18 or Older; 2020

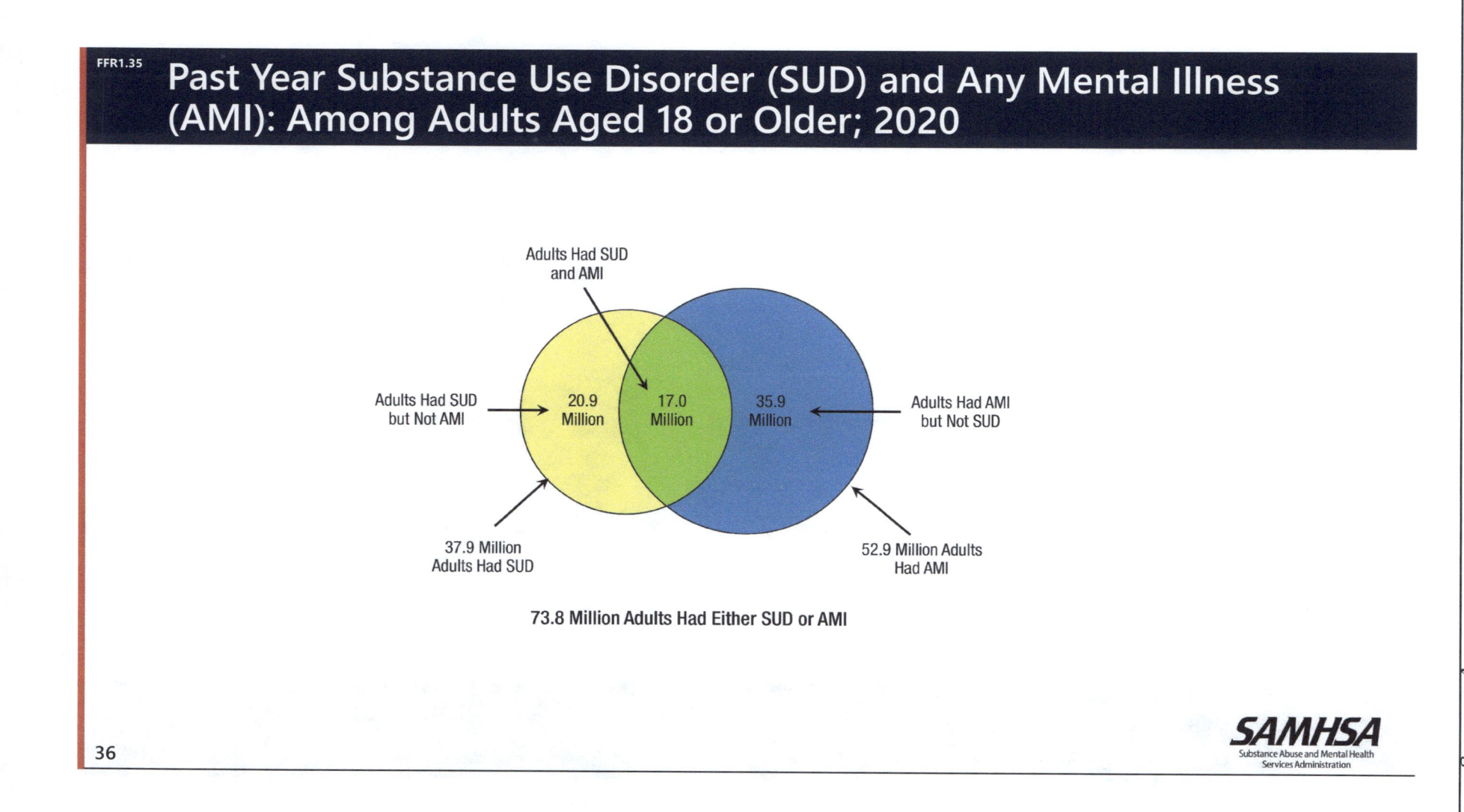

Adults Had AMI but Not SUD → 35.9 Million

52.9 Million Adults Had AMI

Adults Had SUD and AMI → 17.0 Million

Adults Had SUD but Not AMI → 20.9 Million

37.9 Million Adults Had SUD

73.8 Million Adults Had Either SUD or AMI

SAMHSA
Substance Abuse and Mental Health Services Administration

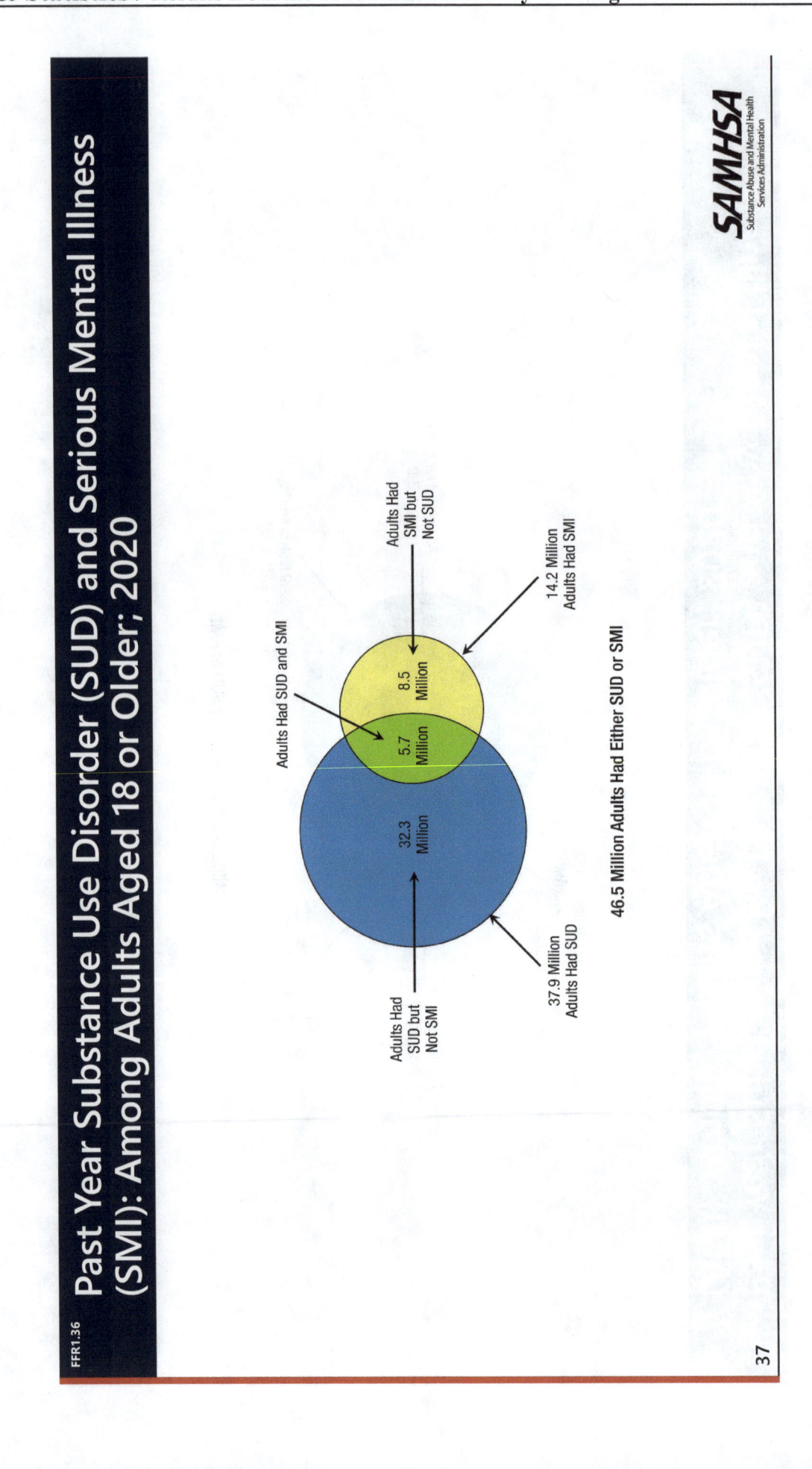

Studies & Statistics / Results from the 2020 National Survey on Drug Use and Health

FFR1.36 Past Year Substance Use Disorder (SUD) and Serious Mental Illness (SMI): Among Adults Aged 18 or Older; 2020

- Adults Had SMI but Not SUD: 8.5 Million
- 14.2 Million Adults Had SMI
- Adults Had SUD and SMI: 5.7 Million
- Adults Had SUD but Not SMI: 32.3 Million
- 37.9 Million Adults Had SUD
- 46.5 Million Adults Had Either SUD or SMI

SAMHSA — Substance Abuse and Mental Health Services Administration

Studies & Statistics / Results from the 2020 National Survey on Drug Use and Health

Substance Use: Among Adults Aged 18 or Older; by Mental Illness Status, 2020

FFR1.37

Legend:
- Any Mental Illness
- Serious Mental Illness
- No Mental Illness

Substance	Any Mental Illness	Serious Mental Illness	No Mental Illness
Illicit Drugs, Past Year	39.8+	47.8+	17.0
Marijuana, Past Year	32.8+	39.2+	14.6
Opioids, Past Year	8.1+	11.6+	2.3
Binge Alcohol, Past Month	28.5+	30.9+	22.8
Tobacco Products or Nicotine Vaping, Past Month	30.9+	37.4+	19.6

Percent Using (y-axis: 0 to 60)

+ Difference between this estimate and the estimate for adults without mental illness is statistically significant at the .05 level.

SAMHSA
Substance Abuse and Mental Health Services Administration

Adults Aged 18 or Older with Serious Thoughts of Suicide, Suicide Plans, or Suicide Attempts in the Past Year: 2020

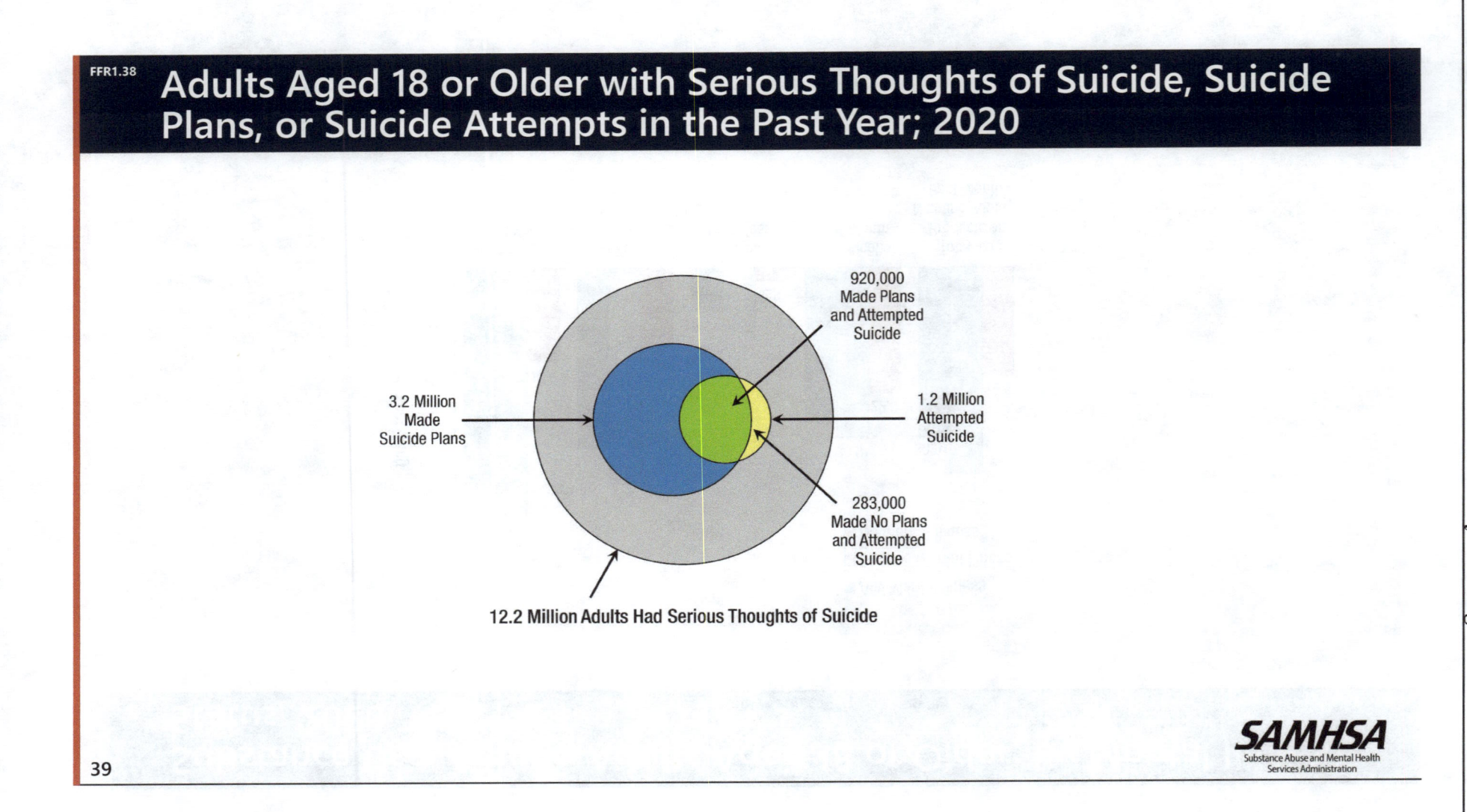

- 12.2 Million Adults Had Serious Thoughts of Suicide
- 3.2 Million Made Suicide Plans
- 920,000 Made Plans and Attempted Suicide
- 1.2 Million Attempted Suicide
- 283,000 Made No Plans and Attempted Suicide

Studies & Statistics / Results from the 2020 National Survey on Drug Use and Health

Had Serious Thoughts of Suicide, Made a Suicide Plan, or Attempted Suicide in the Past Year: Among Adults Aged 18 or Older; 2020

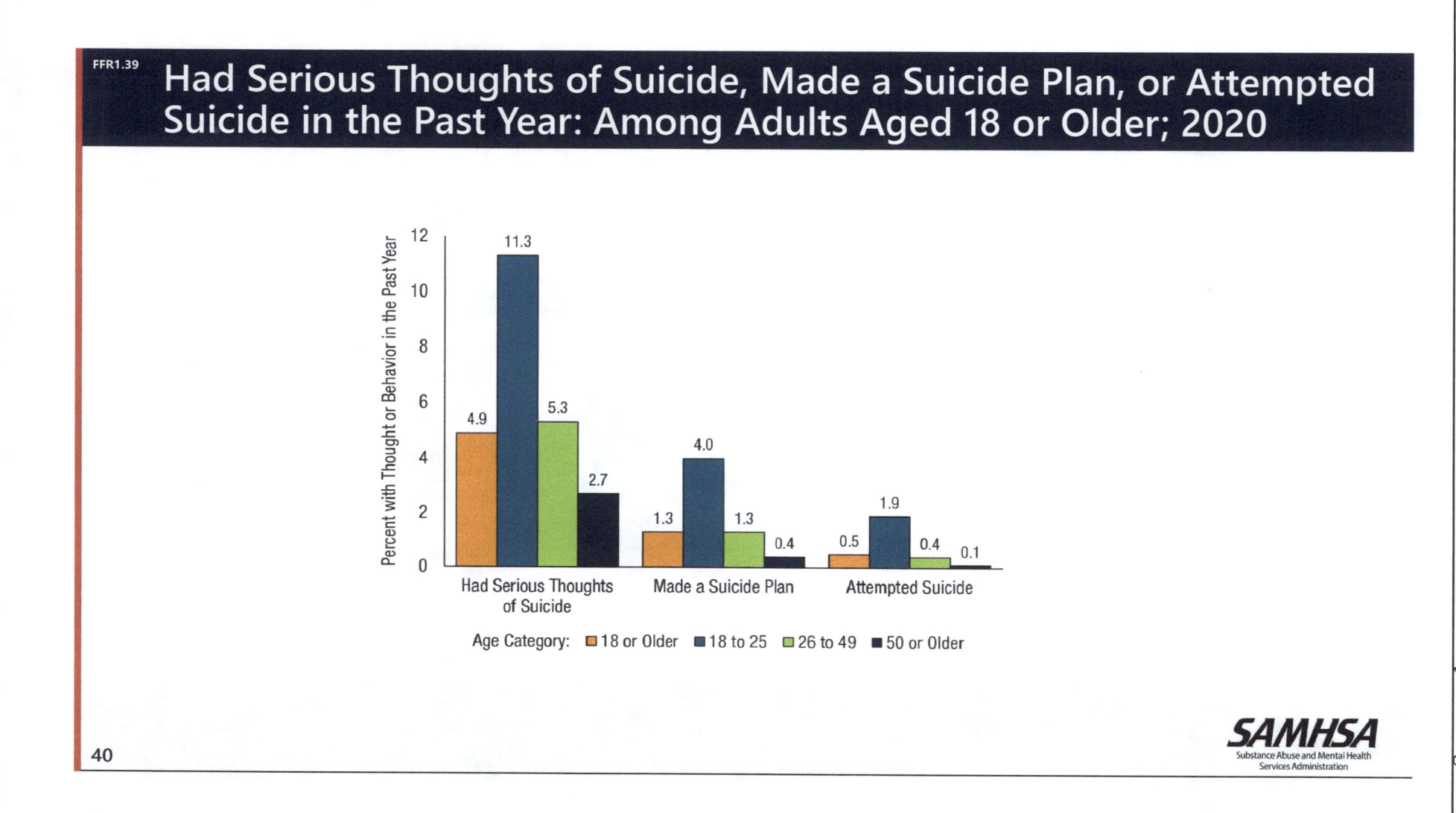

Had Serious Thoughts of Suicide: 18 or Older 4.9; 18 to 25 11.3; 26 to 49 5.3; 50 or Older 2.7

Made a Suicide Plan: 18 or Older 1.3; 18 to 25 4.0; 26 to 49 1.3; 50 or Older 0.4

Attempted Suicide: 18 or Older 0.5; 18 to 25 1.9; 26 to 49 0.4; 50 or Older 0.1

FFR1.39

SAMHSA — Substance Abuse and Mental Health Services Administration

Studies & Statistics / Results from the 2020 National Survey on Drug Use and Health

Youths Aged 12 to 17 with Serious Thoughts of Suicide, Suicide Plans, or Suicide Attempts in the Past Year: 2020

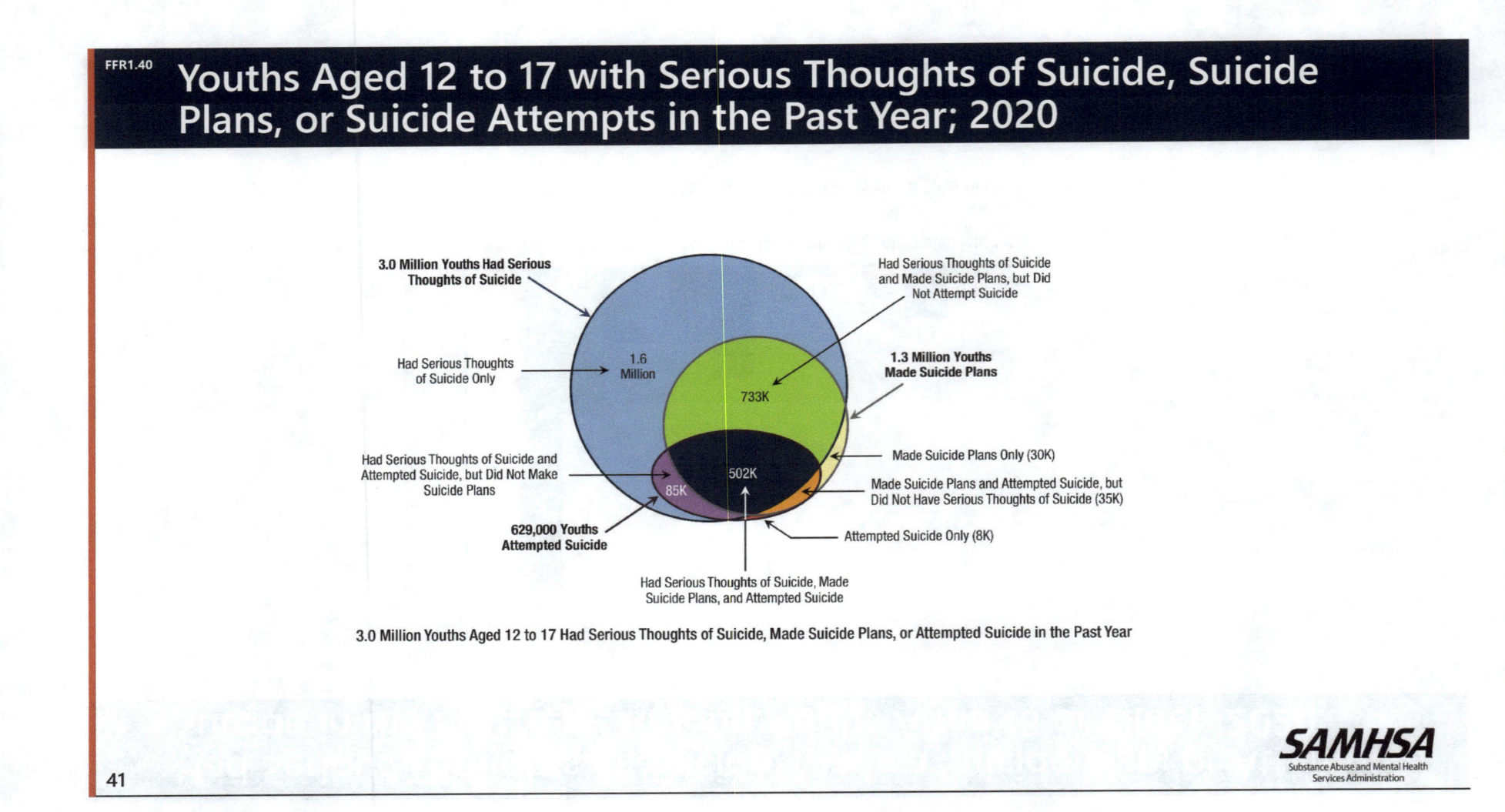

3.0 Million Youths Had Serious Thoughts of Suicide
- Had Serious Thoughts of Suicide Only — 1.6 Million
- Had Serious Thoughts of Suicide and Attempted Suicide, but Did Not Make Suicide Plans — 85K
- Had Serious Thoughts of Suicide and Made Suicide Plans, but Did Not Attempt Suicide — 733K

1.3 Million Youths Made Suicide Plans
- Made Suicide Plans Only — 30K
- Made Suicide Plans and Attempted Suicide, but Did Not Have Serious Thoughts of Suicide — 35K

629,000 Youths Attempted Suicide
- Attempted Suicide Only — 8K
- Had Serious Thoughts of Suicide, Made Suicide Plans, and Attempted Suicide — 502K

3.0 Million Youths Aged 12 to 17 Had Serious Thoughts of Suicide, Made Suicide Plans, or Attempted Suicide in the Past Year

FFR1.40

SAMHSA
Substance Abuse and Mental Health Services Administration

Studies & Statistics / Results from the 2020 National Survey on Drug Use and Health

FFR1.46 Received Treatment in the Past Year for Depression: Among Youths Aged 12 to 17 with a Past Year Major Depressive Episode (MDE) or MDE with Severe Impairment; 2004-2020

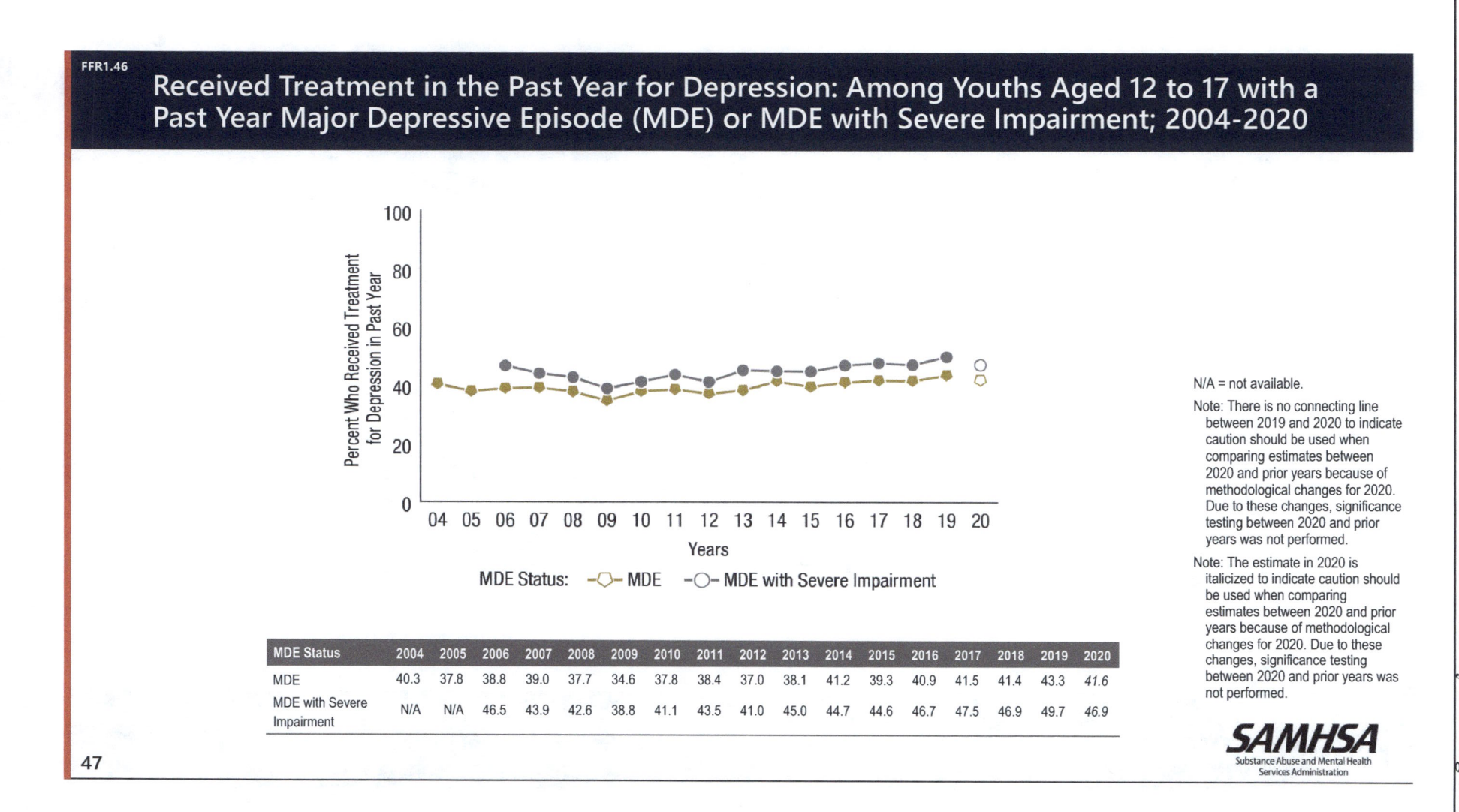

MDE Status	2004	2005	2006	2007	2008	2009	2010	2011	2012	2013	2014	2015	2016	2017	2018	2019	2020
MDE	40.3	37.8	38.8	39.0	37.7	34.6	37.8	38.4	37.0	38.1	41.2	39.3	40.9	41.5	41.4	43.3	41.6
MDE with Severe Impairment	N/A	N/A	46.5	43.9	42.6	38.8	41.1	43.5	41.0	45.0	44.7	44.6	46.7	47.5	46.9	49.7	46.9

N/A = not available.

Note: There is no connecting line between 2019 and 2020 to indicate caution should be used when comparing estimates between 2020 and prior years because of methodological changes for 2020. Due to these changes, significance testing between 2020 and prior years was not performed.

Note: The estimate in 2020 is italicized to indicate caution should be used when comparing estimates between 2020 and prior years because of methodological changes for 2020. Due to these changes, significance testing between 2020 and prior years was not performed.

SAMHSA Substance Abuse and Mental Health Services Administration

Studies & Statistics / Results from the 2020 National Survey on Drug Use and Health

Received Treatment in the Past Year for Depression: Among Adults Aged 18 or Older with a Past Year Major Depressive Episode; 2009-2020

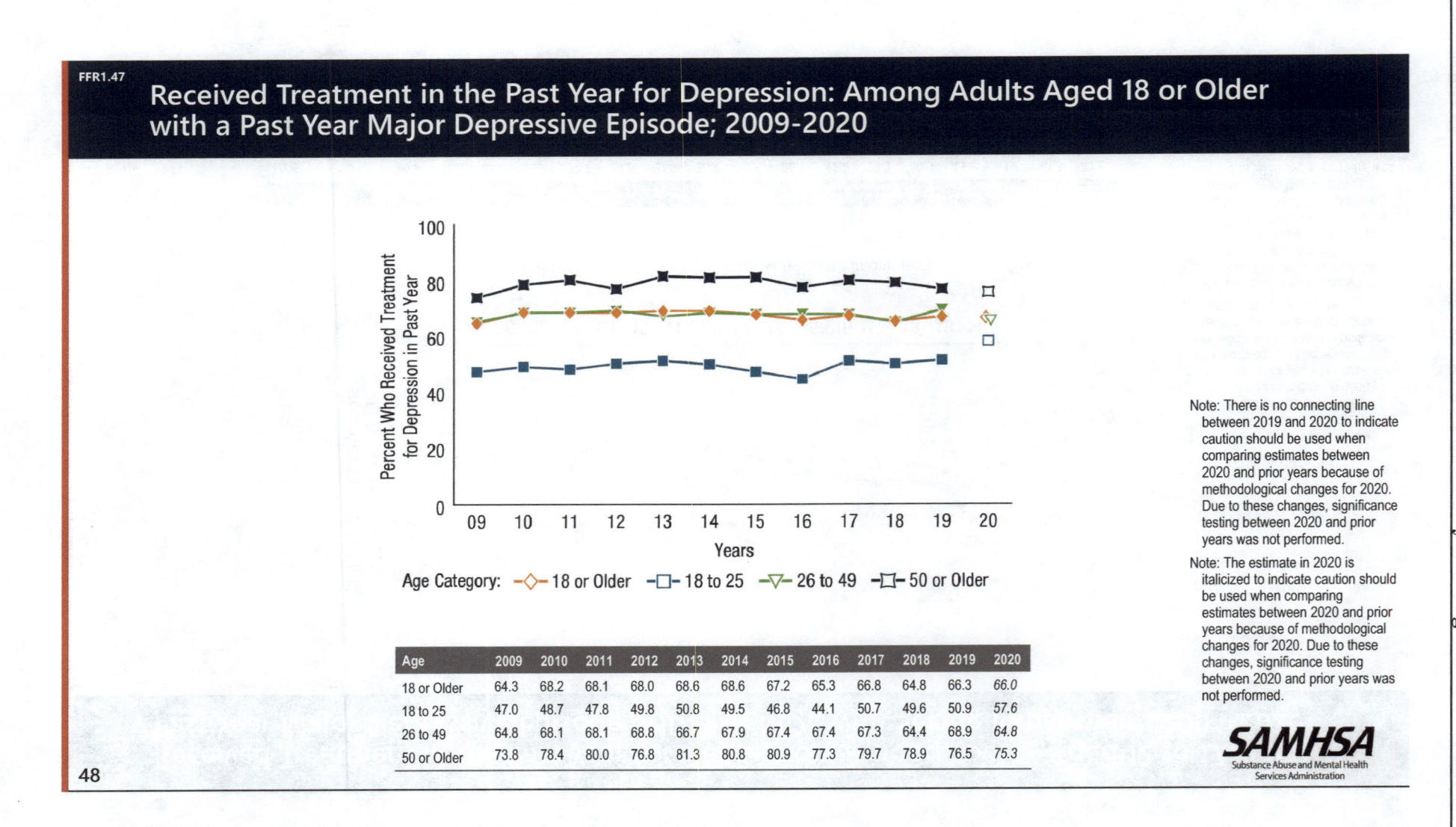

Age	2009	2010	2011	2012	2013	2014	2015	2016	2017	2018	2019	2020
18 or Older	64.3	68.2	68.1	68.0	68.6	68.6	67.2	65.3	66.8	64.8	66.3	66.0
18 to 25	47.0	48.7	47.8	49.8	50.8	49.5	46.8	44.1	50.7	49.6	50.9	57.6
26 to 49	64.8	68.1	68.1	68.8	66.7	67.9	67.4	67.4	67.3	64.4	68.9	64.8
50 or Older	73.8	78.4	80.0	76.8	81.3	80.8	80.9	77.3	79.7	78.9	76.5	75.3

Note: There is no connecting line between 2019 and 2020 to indicate caution should be used when comparing estimates between 2020 and prior years because of methodological changes for 2020. Due to these changes, significance testing between 2020 and prior years was not performed.

Note: The estimate in 2020 is italicized to indicate caution should be used when comparing estimates between 2020 and prior years because of methodological changes for 2020. Due to these changes, significance testing between 2020 and prior years was not performed.

SAMHSA Substance Abuse and Mental Health Services Administration

Studies & Statistics / Results from the 2020 National Survey on Drug Use and Health

FFR1.56 Perceived COVID-19 Pandemic Negative Effect on Emotional or Mental Health: Among Youths Aged 12 to 17; by Past Year Major Depressive Episode (MDE) Status, Quarter 4, 2020

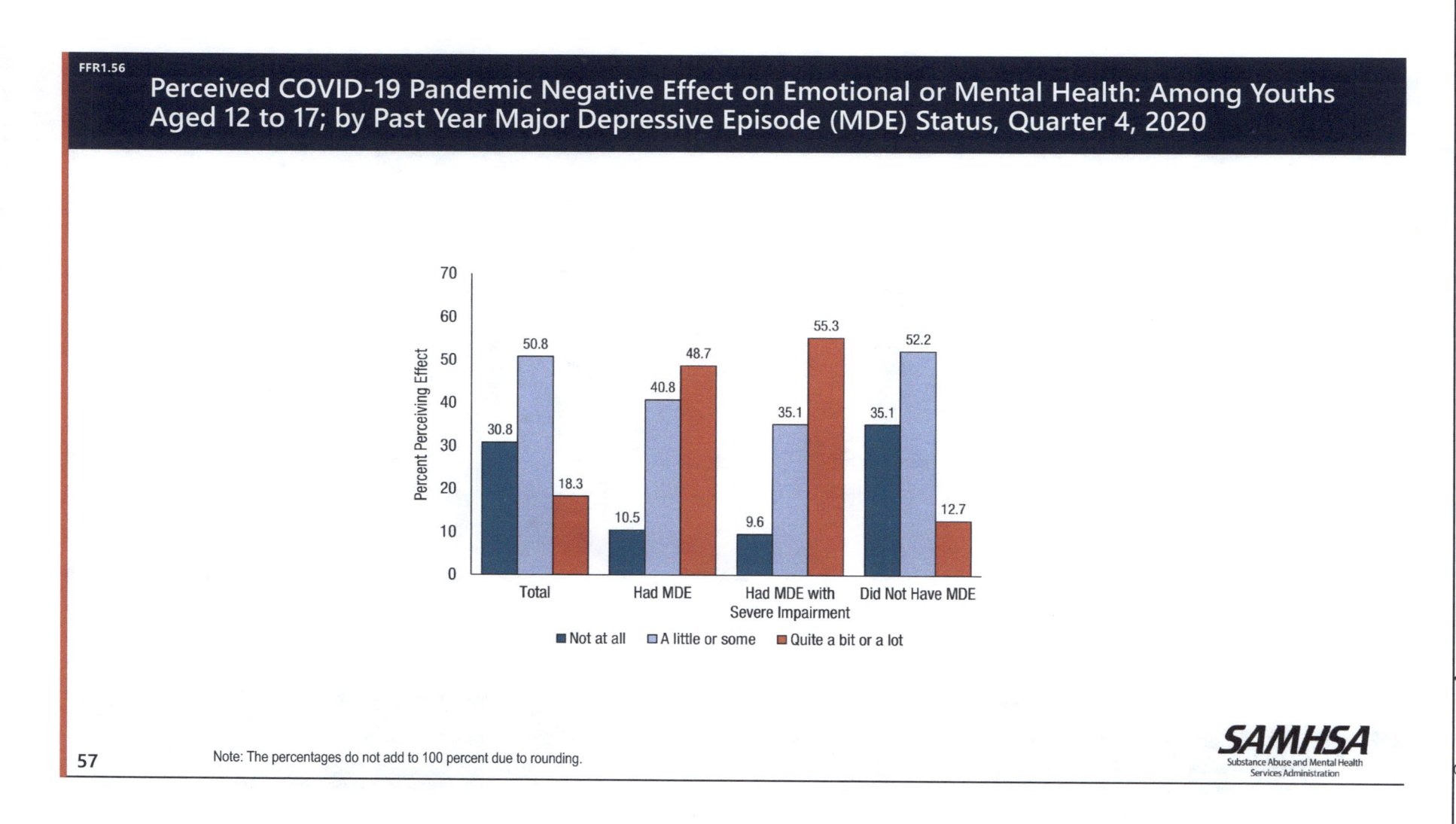

Category	Not at all	A little or some	Quite a bit or a lot
Total	30.8	50.8	18.3
Had MDE	10.5	40.8	48.7
Had MDE with Severe Impairment	9.6	35.1	55.3
Did Not Have MDE	35.1	52.2	12.7

Percent Perceiving Effect

Note: The percentages do not add to 100 percent due to rounding.

SAMHSA — Substance Abuse and Mental Health Services Administration

Studies & Statistics / Results from the 2020 National Survey on Drug Use and Health

FFR1.57 Perceived COVID-19 Pandemic Negative Effect on Emotional or Mental Health: Among Adults Aged 18 or Older; by Past Year Mental Illness Status, Quarter 4, 2020

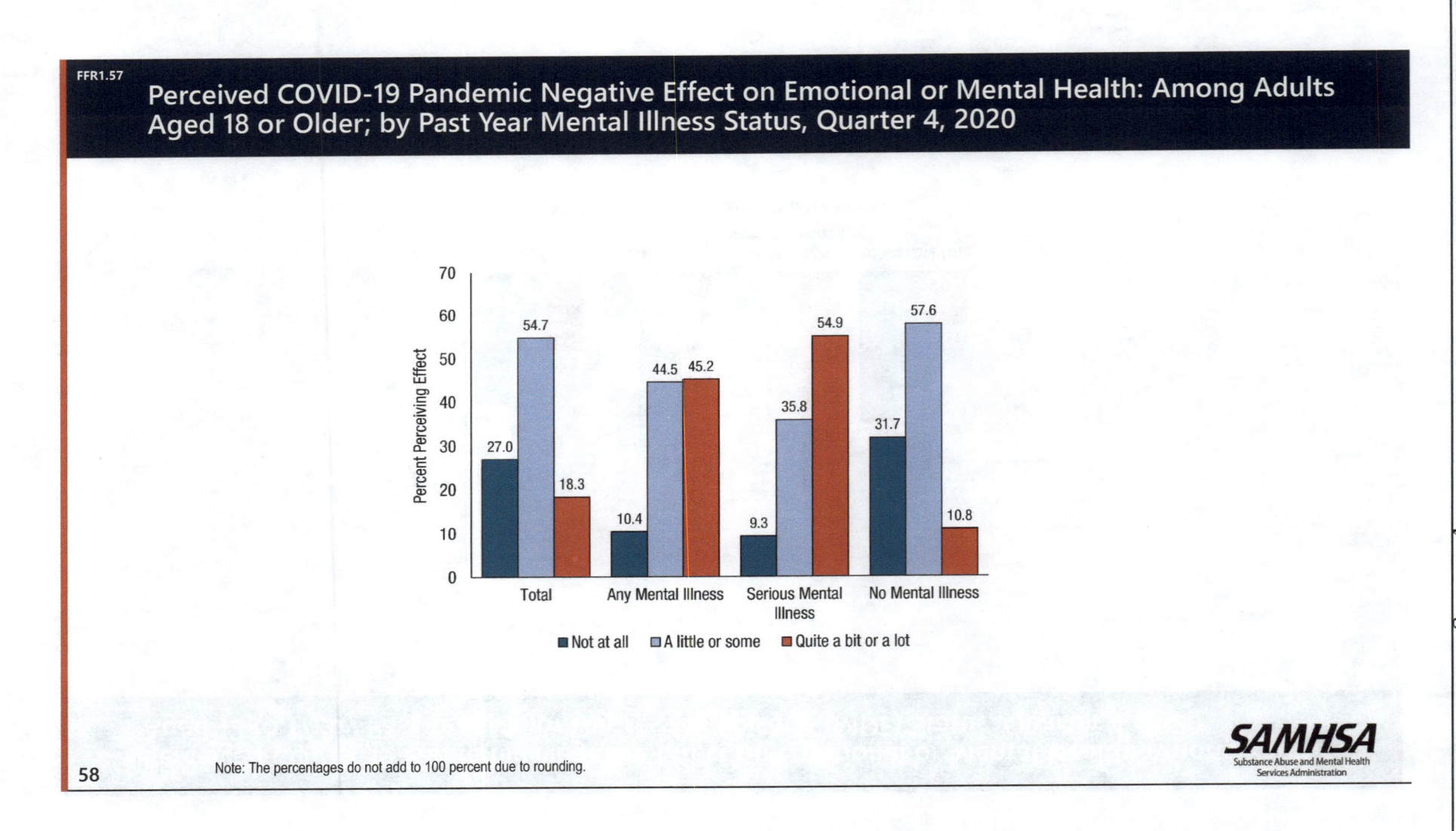

Mental Illness Status	Not at all	A little or some	Quite a bit or a lot
Total	27.0	54.7	18.3
Any Mental Illness	10.4	44.5	45.2
Serious Mental Illness	9.3	35.8	54.9
No Mental Illness	31.7	57.6	10.8

Note: The percentages do not add to 100 percent due to rounding.

SAMHSA — Substance Abuse and Mental Health Services Administration

Studies & Statistics / Results from the 2020 National Survey on Drug Use and Health

Perceived COVID-19 Pandemic Effect on Alcohol Use: Among Past Year Alcohol Users Aged 12 or Older; Quarter 4, 2020

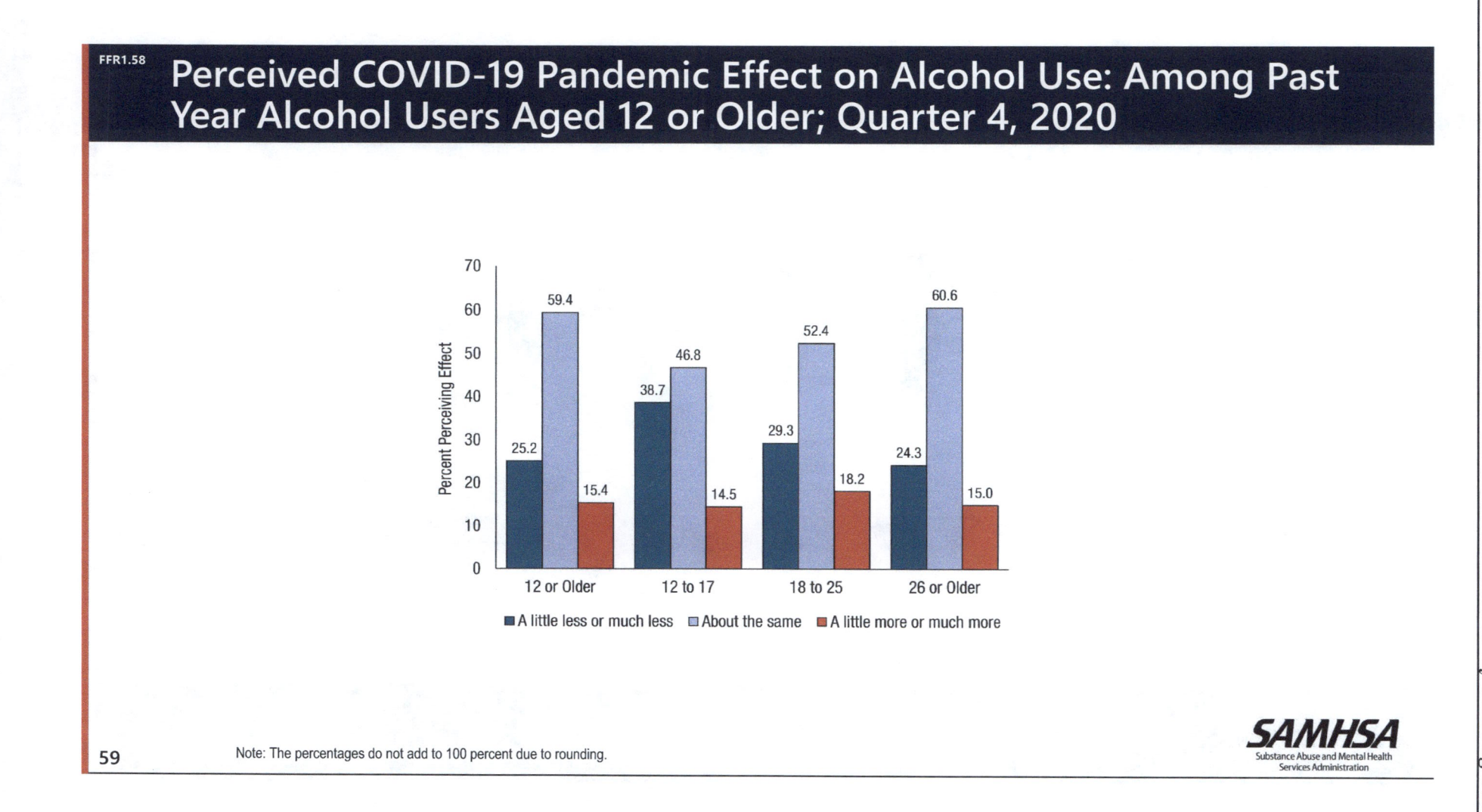

Age Group	A little less or much less	About the same	A little more or much more
12 or Older	25.2	59.4	15.4
12 to 17	38.7	46.8	14.5
18 to 25	29.3	52.4	18.2
26 or Older	24.3	60.6	15.0

Note: The percentages do not add to 100 percent due to rounding.

FFR1.58

Studies & Statistics / Results from the 2020 National Survey on Drug Use and Health

FFR1.59 Perceived COVID-19 Pandemic Effect on Drug Use: Among Past Year Users of Drugs Other than Alcohol Aged 12 or Older; Quarter 4, 2020

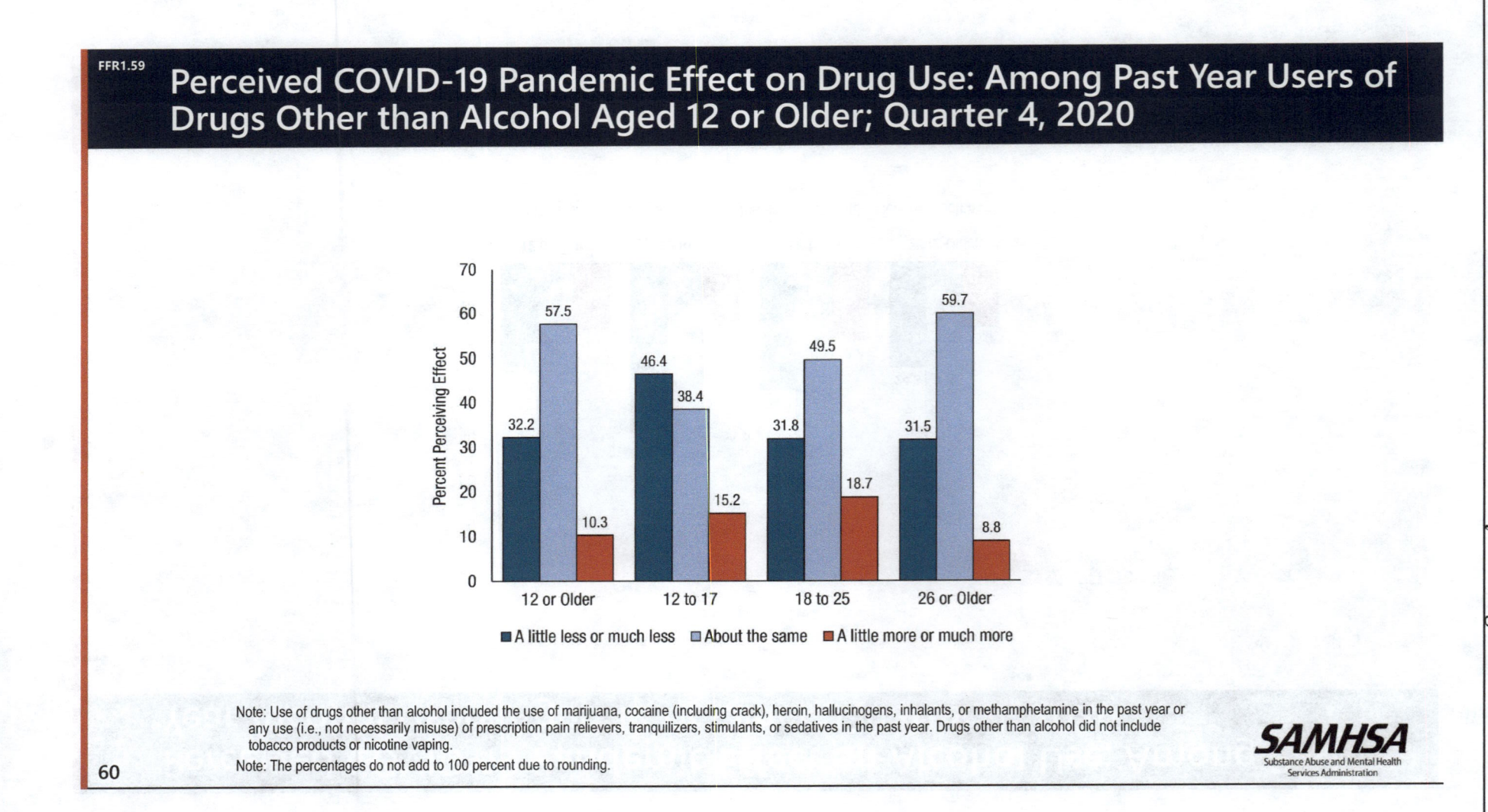

Age Group	A little less or much less	About the same	A little more or much more
12 or Older	32.2	57.5	10.3
12 to 17	46.4	38.4	15.2
18 to 25	31.8	49.5	18.7
26 or Older	31.5	59.7	8.8

Note: Use of drugs other than alcohol included the use of marijuana, cocaine (including crack), heroin, hallucinogens, inhalants, or methamphetamine in the past year or any use (i.e., not necessarily misuse) of prescription pain relievers, tranquilizers, stimulants, or sedatives in the past year. Drugs other than alcohol did not include tobacco products or nicotine vaping.

Note: The percentages do not add to 100 percent due to rounding.

SAMHSA Substance Abuse and Mental Health Services Administration

Studies & Statistics / Results from the 2020 National Survey on Drug Use and Health

Perceived COVID-19 Pandemic Effect on Mental Health Services: Among Adults Aged 18 or Older Who Received Services; Quarter 4, 2020

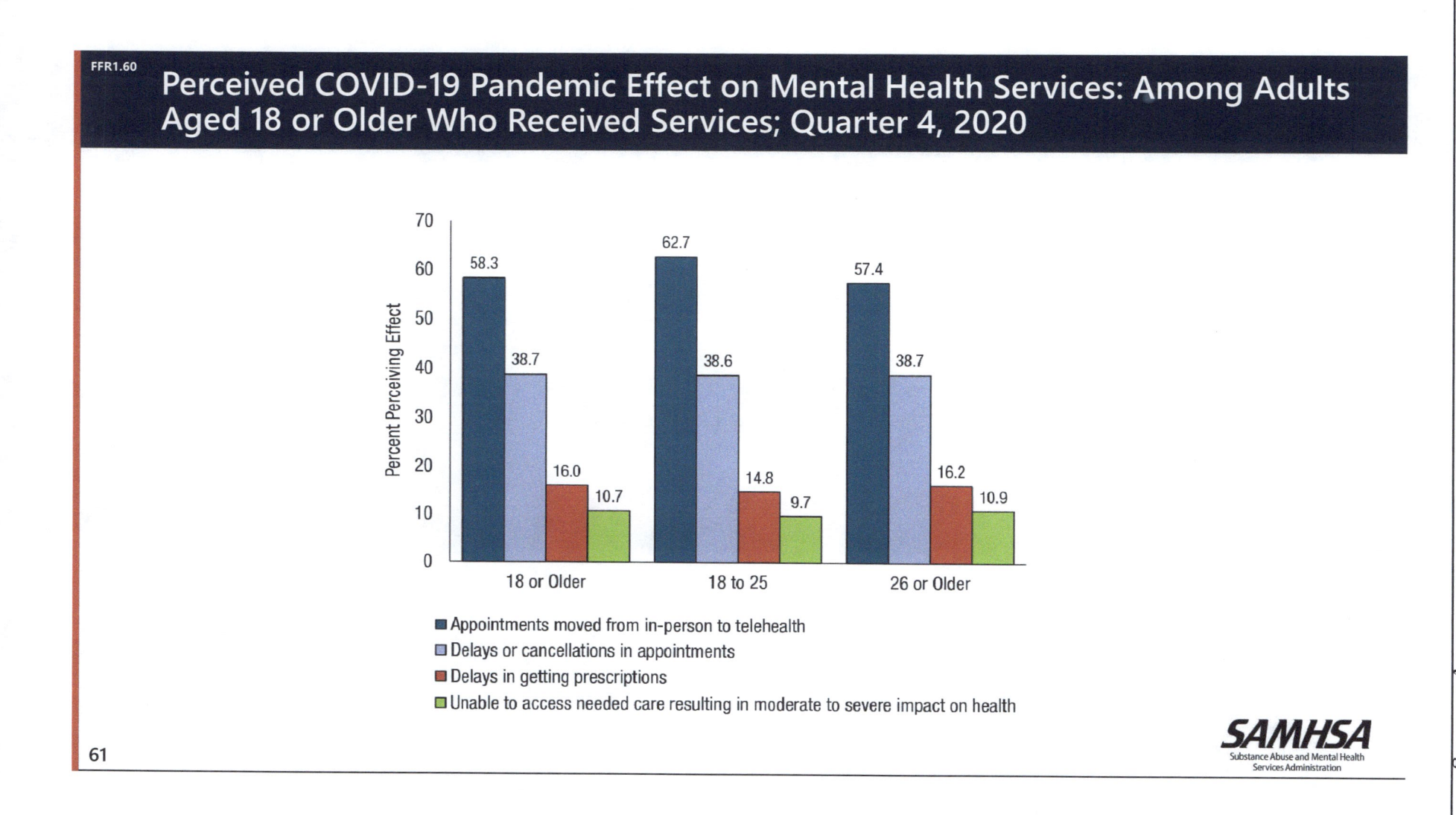

Age Group	Appointments moved from in-person to telehealth	Delays or cancellations in appointments	Delays in getting prescriptions	Unable to access needed care resulting in moderate to severe impact on health
18 or Older	58.3	38.7	16.0	10.7
18 to 25	62.7	38.6	14.8	9.7
26 or Older	57.4	38.7	16.2	10.9

FFR1.60

Suicide Prevention

RESOURCE FOR ACTION

Suicide Can Be Prevented

Like most public health problems, suicide is preventable.[1-3] The National Center for Injury Prevention and Control's vision of "No lives lost to suicide" relies on implementing a comprehensive public health approach to prevention. These efforts rely on timely data and evidence, prompting an update of the 2017 *Preventing Suicide: A Technical Package of Policy, Programs, and Practices*. This 2022 version, now called the *Suicide Prevention Resource for Action* (or *Prevention Resource*, for short), weaves in new evidence that can be implemented and adapted for the community-specific context.

About the Suicide Prevention Resource for Action

> This resource is intended to help communities and states learn about the best available evidence for suicide prevention.

The *Suicide Prevention Resource for Action* maintains the features of the 2017 *Preventing Suicide: A Technical Package of Policy, Programs, and Practices*. It lays out a core set of strategies to achieve and sustain substantial reductions in a specific risk factor or outcome, such as suicide.[4] This resource is intended to help communities and states learn about the best available evidence for suicide prevention. Communities and states can pair this information with their local context and experience to prioritize prevention activities. This resource has three components. The first component is the **strategy** or the preventive actions to achieve the goal of preventing suicide. The second component is the **approach** or the specific ways to advance the strategy. This can be accomplished through policy, programs, and practices, which are the third component and are based on the **evidence** for each of the approaches in preventing suicide or its associated risk factors.

This Prevention Resource represents a select group of strategies based on the best available evidence to help communities and states focus on prevention activities with the greatest potential to prevent suicide. These strategies include:

- Strengthen economic supports
- Create protective environments
- Improve access and delivery of suicide care
- Promote healthy connections
- Teach coping and problem-solving skills
- Identify and support people at risk
- Lessen harms and prevent future risk

Preventing Suicide Is a Priority

Suicide is a critical public health problem in the United States (U.S.).[5]

> **SUICIDE** is a death caused by injuring oneself with the intent to die.
>
> **SUICIDE ATTEMPT** is defined as a *nonfatal act* when someone harms themselves with any intent to end their life but does not die as a result of their actions. A suicide attempt may or may not result in injury.

In recent years, the urgency to prevent suicide has heightened as millions of Americans were impacted by the coronavirus disease 2019 (COVID-19) pandemic and the overdose epidemic. These two major crises have taken a mental, emotional, physical, and economic toll on individuals, families, and communities.[2]

Suicide is not caused by any single factor and suicide prevention will not be achieved by any single strategy or approach.[1,2,6] The public health strategies in this resource focus on preventing the risk of suicide in the first place and lessening the immediate and long-term harms of suicidal behavior by helping those in times of crisis get the services and support they need. These strategies support the goals and objectives of the *National Strategy for Suicide Prevention, The Surgeon General's Call to Action to Implement the National Strategy for Suicide Prevention*, the Action Alliance's priority to strengthen community-based prevention, and the Centers for Disease Control and Prevention's (CDC) comprehensive suicide prevention approach.

Partnering across sectors to leverage expertise and implementing multiple strategies and approaches that are tailored to cultural needs and strengths can address the multiple factors associated with suicide. Commitment, cooperation, and leadership from public health, mental health, education, justice, healthcare, social services, business, labor, and government, among others, can drive significant improvements in suicide prevention.

Suicide is highly prevalent

Suicide presents a major challenge to public health in the U.S. and worldwide. It contributes to premature death, morbidity, lost productivity, and healthcare costs.[1,3] Suicide was responsible for nearly 46,000 deaths in the U.S. in 2020.[7] This is about 1 suicide every 11 minutes.[8] Suicide is a leading cause of death for people ages 10–64 years.[9] Suicide rates rose 30% from 2000 to 2020, including small declines in 2019 and 2020.[7,10]

Suicide rates vary by age, race/ethnicity, and other socio-demographic characteristics. In 2020, suicide was the second leading cause of death for people ages 10–14 years and 25–34 years, the third leading cause for people ages 15–24 years, the fourth leading cause for people ages 34–44 years, the seventh leading cause for people ages 45–54 years, and the ninth leading cause for people ages 55–64 years.[9] Non-Hispanic American Indian or Alaska Native (AI/AN) people have the highest suicide rates, followed by non-Hispanic White people.[10] Racism, historical trauma, and long-lasting inequities such as disproportionate exposure to poverty have contributed to higher suicide rates among non-Hispanic AI/AN youth and other groups who have been marginalized.[11]

Some other population groups disproportionately impacted by higher-than-average suicide rates include veterans, people who live in rural areas, and workers in certain industries and occupations.[12-14] Transition periods are also associated with higher risk of suicide. This includes transitions from work into retirement, from active-duty military status to civilian status, from high school to college, and between levels of healthcare such as from an inpatient psychiatric hospitalization to outpatient care.[15-19]

Suicides reflect only a portion of the problem.[20] Substantially more people are hospitalized or treated in ambulatory settings like emergency departments for nonfatal self-harm such as suicide attempts or

Studies & Statistics / Suicide Prevention: Resource For Action

> Suicide is not caused by any single factor and suicide prevention will not be achieved by any single strategy or approach.

not treated at all.[20] In 2020, 12.2 million American adults seriously thought about suicide, 3.2 million planned a suicide, and 1.2 million attempted suicide.[21] According to recent research, between 1991 and 2017, trends in suicidal ideation and planning among high school students decreased among all sex and racial and ethnic groups except non-Hispanic students of multiple races.[22] Another recent study found that trends in suicide attempts among adolescents from 2009-2019 increased overall, and Black students, both male and female, had the highest prevalence estimates for suicide attempts.[23] Disparities in access to mental health treatment and other factors such as poverty, historical trauma, and adverse childhood experiences (ACEs) may contribute to differences in suicide attempt rates among Black youth.[22] In addition, young people who identify as lesbian, gay, or bisexual have a higher rate of suicidal ideation as compared to their peers who identify as straight. In 2019, suicide attempts were more prevalent among students who reported having sex with persons of the same sex or with both sexes (30%) and students who identified as lesbian, gay, or bisexual (23%).[23] Transgender adolescents are at high risk of suicidal ideation and behavior compared to cisgender adolescents.[24]

Suicide is associated with multiple risk and protective factors

Research indicates that suicide risk varies as a result of the number and intensity of key risk and protective factors experienced.[25] Suicide occurs in response to multiple biological, psychological, interpersonal, environmental, and societal influences that interact with one another, often over time.[3,26,27] The social-ecological model encompasses multiple levels of focus and considers the complex interplay between individual, relationship, community, and societal factors. Characteristics that may increase the likelihood of suicide across populations include:

> Belonging, safety, dignity, and hope can support resilience and healing for individuals and communities, and protect against suicide.

- **Individual risk factors:** Previous suicide attempt, history of depression and other mental illnesses, serious illness such as chronic pain, criminal/legal problems, job/financial problems or loss, impulsive or aggressive tendencies, substance misuse, current or prior history of adverse childhood experiences, sense of hopelessness, violence victimization and/or perpetration
- **Relationship risk factors:** Bullying, family/loved one's history of suicide, loss of relationships, high conflict or violent relationships, social isolation
- **Community risk factors:** Lack of access to healthcare, suicide cluster in the community, stress of acculturation, community violence, historical trauma, discrimination
- **Societal risk factors:** Stigma associated with help-seeking and mental illness, easy access to lethal means of suicide among people at risk, unsafe media portrayals of suicide

The presence of risk factors does not predict suicide or suicide attempts for any given person. Most individuals who experience risk factors or who attempt suicide do not die by suicide. The cumulative effect of several risk factors may serve to increase an individual's vulnerability to suicidal behaviors. The relevance of any given risk factor can vary by age, race, gender, sexual orientation, residential geography, and socio-cultural and economic status.[3,27,28]

Protective factors, or those influences that buffer against the risk for suicide and promote resilience, can also be found across the levels of the social-ecological model. Protective factors that improve resilience include:[3,27,28]

- **Individual protective factors:** Effective coping and problem-solving skills, reasons for living (for example, family, friends, pets, etc.), strong sense of cultural identity
- **Relationship protective factors:** Support from partners, friends, and family, feeling connected to others
- **Community protective factors:** Feeling connected to school, community, and other social institutions, availability of consistent and high quality physical and behavioral healthcare
- **Societal protective factors:** Reduced access to lethal means of suicide among people at risk, cultural, religious, or moral objections to suicide

These protective factors can either counter a specific risk factor or buffer against multiple risks associated with suicide. Belonging, safety, dignity, and hope can support resilience and healing for individuals and communities, and protect against suicide.[29]

Suicide, ACEs, and substance use are connected

Exposure to violence is associated with increased risk of depression, post-traumatic stress disorder, anxiety, suicide attempts, and suicide. Types of violence could include child abuse and neglect, bullying, peer violence, dating violence, sexual violence, and intimate partner violence.[30-37] ACEs, such as physical, sexual, and emotional abuse, or living in homes with violence, mental illnesses, or substance misuse, are also associated with increased risk for suicide attempts and suicide.[33,38] The effects of ACEs are often cumulative. Experiencing more ACEs is associated with greater risk for future poor outcomes when compared to people with fewer ACEs.[39]

Unemployment, poverty, and lower educational attainment are overlapping risk factors for ACEs, substance misuse, and multiple forms of violence and suicide,[40,41] which suggests that efforts to prevent these related issues may also prove beneficial in preventing suicide.[42-44] Similarly, many protective factors overlap and may be shared. Connectedness to one's community,[45] school,[46] family,[47] caring adults,[48,49] and pro-social peers[50] can enhance resilience and help reduce risk for suicide and different forms of violence.

Substance use disorders and suicide risk are associated.[51,52] For example, in a study using the National Death Index data and treatment data from electronic health records of 5 million veterans, researchers found diagnosis of substance use disorder was associated with increased suicide risk.[53] Drinking alcohol at an early age, heavy drinking, and mild to severe alcohol use disorder can all lead to increases in suicidal ideation.[54] The relationship is also cyclical. Losing a loved one to overdose or suicide during childhood can increase the risk for overdose or suicide later in life.[55]

Suicide has far-reaching impacts

Suicide and suicide attempts can contribute to lasting impacts on individuals, families, and communities.[56-59] Studies estimate that the number of individuals impacted by a single suicide attempt ranges from 135–456 individuals.[60,61] Other studies have found that 48–58% of adults in the U.S. know at least one person over their lifetime who died by suicide.[61,62] Research also indicates that people with lived experience, such as having attempted suicide, having suicidal thoughts, or having experienced the loss of a friend or family member to suicide, may suffer long-term health and mental health consequences, such as anger, guilt, and physical impairment.[63-66] Survivors of a loved one's suicide may experience ongoing pain and suffering including complicated grief,[67-69] stigma, depression, anxiety, post-traumatic stress disorder, and increased risk of suicidal ideation and suicide.[64,70-72] The economic toll of suicide on society is immense as well. Suicide cost the U.S. more than $460 billion and self-harm $26 billion in 2019.[73,74]

Studies & Statistics / Suicide Prevention: Resource For Action

STRATEGIES AND APPROACHES
to achieve and sustain substantial reductions in suicide

STRATEGY	APPROACH
❶ Strengthen Economic Supports	• Improve household financial security • Stabilize housing
❷ Create Protective Environments	• Reduce access to lethal means among persons at risk of suicide • Create healthy organizational policies and culture • Reduce substance use through community-based policies and practices
❸ Improve Access and Delivery of Suicide Care	• Cover mental health conditions in health insurance policies • Increase provider availability in underserved areas • Provide rapid and remote access to help • Create safer suicide care through systems change
❹ Promote Healthy Connections	• Promote healthy peer norms • Engage community members in shared activities
❺ Teach Coping and Problem-Solving Skills	• Support social-emotional learning programs • Teach parenting skills to improve family relationships • Support resilience through education programs
❻ Identify and Support People at Risk	• Train gatekeepers • Respond to crises • Plan for safety and follow-up after an attempt • Provide therapeutic approaches
❼ Lessen Harms and Prevent Future Risk	• Intervene after a suicide (postvention) • Report and message about suicide safely

The COVID-19 Pandemic and Suicide Prevention

The COVID-19 pandemic created unprecedented challenges for communities. Some experts noted that COVID-19 created the "perfect storm" for increased suicide risk due to the consequences of physical/social distancing, increases in economic stressors, decreased access to mental health treatment, and decreased access to typical routines and support systems.[81-83] Prior public health crises were associated with increased suicide risk among some populations. Studies suggest increased suicide rates during the 1918–1920 influenza pandemic in the U.S. and in Taiwan and among older adults in Hong Kong during the 2003 severe acute respiratory syndrome pandemic.[84-86]

At the time of this writing (while the world is deeply embedded in the COVID-19 pandemic), it is too early to assess the full impact of the COVID-19 pandemic on suicide. While overall suicide rates declined in 2019 and 2020, they increased among some populations.[7] Studies showed increases in mental distress and substance use for some populations during the pandemic.[87-89] A CDC study conducted in June 2020 indicated that U.S. adults reported significant mental health distress related to COVID-19.[87] The study also showed that specific sub-populations, including younger adults, people from racial and ethnic minority groups, essential workers, and unpaid adult caregivers, reported experiencing disproportionately worse mental health outcomes, increased substance use, and increased suicidal ideation. Early evidence among older adults paints a different picture. A qualitative study of older adults with pre-existing depression showed no difference in depression, anxiety, and suicidal ideation symptom scores. Instead, older adults exhibited resilience and increased use of technology to connect virtually with social supports.[90]

Organizations are developing strategies to respond to the potential risk presented by COVID-19. For example, telehealth is being used to identify, assess, and treat individuals who are at risk for suicide. Evidence-based suicide prevention programs, such as Collaborative Assessment and Management of Suicidality, have been adapted for use with telehealth to support higher demand for mental health services.[91] The effectiveness of telehealth as a treatment modality has been deemed as equivalent to in-person treatment for many mental health diagnoses, including post-traumatic stress disorder and depression, but the effectiveness for specific suicide interventions is less clear at this time.[92-94] The effectiveness of using telehealth alongside existing suicide prevention strategies is a new area of study, as is consideration for access to technology among people who are at increased risk for suicide.

The Action Alliance has convened diverse sectors to coordinate the Mental Health and Suicide Prevention National Response to COVID-19 to create sustainable and comprehensive solutions to the mental health impacts of the COVID-19 pandemic. The National Response is a public-private partnership engaging leaders from academia, business, government, nonprofits, non-governmental organizations, healthcare, public safety, and media and entertainment.[95,96]

Post-Traumatic Stress Disorder

National Institute of Mental Health

Studies & Statistics / Post-Traumatic Stress Disorder

What is post-traumatic stress disorder, or PTSD?

It is natural to feel afraid during and after a traumatic situation. Fear is a part of the body's "fight-or-flight" response, which helps us avoid or respond to potential danger. People may experience a range of reactions after trauma, and most will recover from their symptoms over time. Those who continue to experience symptoms may be diagnosed with post-traumatic stress disorder (PTSD).

Who develops PTSD?

Anyone can develop PTSD at any age. This includes combat veterans and people who have experienced or witnessed a physical or sexual assault, abuse, an accident, a disaster, a terror attack, or other serious events. People who have PTSD may feel stressed or frightened, even when they are no longer in danger.

Not everyone with PTSD has been through a dangerous event. Sometimes, learning that a relative or close friend experienced trauma can cause PTSD.

About 6 of every 100 people will experience PTSD at some point in their lifetime, according to the National Center for PTSD, a U.S. Department of Veterans Affairs program. Women are more likely than men to develop PTSD. Certain aspects of the traumatic event and biological factors (such as genes) may make some people more likely to develop PTSD.

What are the symptoms of PTSD?

Symptoms of PTSD usually begin within 3 months of the traumatic event, but they sometimes emerge later. To meet the criteria for PTSD, a person must have symptoms for longer than 1 month, and the symptoms must be severe enough to interfere with aspects of daily life, such as relationships or work. The symptoms also must be unrelated to medication, substance use, or other illness.

The course of the disorder varies. Although some people recover within 6 months, others have symptoms that last for 1 year or longer. People with PTSD often have co-occurring conditions, such as depression, substance use, or one or more anxiety disorders.

After a dangerous event, it is natural to have some symptoms. For example, some people may feel detached from the experience, as though they are observing things as an outsider rather than experiencing them. A mental health professional—such as a psychiatrist, psychologist, or clinical social worker—can determine whether symptoms meet the criteria for PTSD.

To be diagnosed with PTSD, an adult must have all of the following for at least 1 month:
- At least one re-experiencing symptom
- At least one avoidance symptom
- At least two arousal and reactivity symptoms
- At least two cognition and mood symptoms

Re-experiencing symptoms
- Flashbacks—reliving the traumatic event, including physical symptoms, such as a racing heart or sweating
- Recurring memories or dreams related to the event
- Distressing thoughts
- Physical signs of stress

Thoughts and feelings can trigger these symptoms, as can words, objects, or situations that are reminders of the event.

Avoidance symptoms
- Staying away from places, events, or objects that are reminders of the experience
- Avoiding thoughts or feelings related to the traumatic event

Avoidance symptoms may cause people to change their routines. For example, some people may avoid driving or riding in a car after a serious car accident.

Arousal and reactivity symptoms
- Being easily startled
- Feeling tense, on guard, or on edge
- Having difficulty concentrating
- Having difficulty falling asleep or staying asleep
- Feeling irritable and having angry or aggressive outbursts
- Engaging in risky, reckless, or destructive behavior

Arousal symptoms are often constant. They can lead to feelings of stress and anger and may interfere with parts of daily life, such as sleeping or eating.

Cognition and mood symptoms
- Trouble remembering key features of the traumatic event
- Negative thoughts about oneself or the world
- Exaggerated feelings of blame directed toward oneself or others
- Ongoing negative emotions, such as fear, anger, guilt, or shame
- Loss of interest in previous activities
- Feelings of social isolation
- Difficulty feeling positive emotions, such as happiness or satisfaction

Cognition and mood symptoms can begin or worsen after the traumatic event. They can lead people to feel detached from friends or family members.

How do children and teens react to trauma?

Children and teens can have extreme reactions to traumatic events, but their symptoms may not be the same as those seen in adults. In children younger than age 6, symptoms can include:

- Wetting the bed after having learned to use the toilet
- Forgetting how to talk or being unable to talk
- Acting out the scary event during playtime
- Being unusually clingy with a parent or other adult

Older children and teens usually show symptoms more like those seen in adults. They also may develop disruptive, disrespectful, or destructive behaviors. Older children and teens may feel guilt over not preventing injury or death, or have thoughts of revenge.

For more information on helping children and adolescents cope with traumatic events, see **www.nimh.nih.gov/helpchildrencope**.

Why do some people develop PTSD and other people do not?

Not everyone who lives through a dangerous event develops PTSD—many factors play a part. Some of these factors are present before the trauma; others play a role during and after a traumatic event.

Risk factors that may increase the likelihood of developing PTSD include:

- Exposure to previous traumatic experiences, particularly during childhood
- Getting hurt or seeing people hurt or killed
- Feeling horror, helplessness, or extreme fear
- Having little or no social support after the event
- Dealing with stressors after the event, such as the loss of a loved one, pain and injury, or loss of a job or home
- Having a personal history or family history of mental illness or substance use

Resilience factors that may reduce the likelihood of developing PTSD include:

- Seeking out and receiving support from friends, family, or support groups
- Learning to feel okay with one's actions in response to a traumatic event
- Having a coping strategy for getting through and learning from a traumatic event
- Being prepared and able to respond to upsetting events as they occur, despite feeling fear

How is PTSD treated?

It is important for people with PTSD symptoms to work with a mental health professional who has experience treating PTSD. The main treatments are psychotherapy, medications, or a combination of psychotherapy and medications. An experienced mental health professional can help people find the best treatment plan for their symptoms and needs.

Some people with PTSD, such as those in abusive relationships, may be living through ongoing trauma. In these cases, treatment is usually most effective when it addresses both the traumatic situation and the symptoms of PTSD. People who experience traumatic events or who have PTSD may also experience panic disorder, depression, substance use, or suicidal thoughts. Treatment for these conditions can help with recovery after trauma. Research shows that support from family and friends also can be an essential part of recovery.

For tips to help prepare and guide you in talking to your health care provider about your mental health, visit **www.nimh.nih.gov/talkingtips**.

Psychotherapy

Psychotherapy, sometimes called talk therapy, includes a variety of treatment techniques that mental health professionals use to help people identify and change troubling emotions, thoughts, and behaviors. Psychotherapy can provide support, education, and guidance to people with PTSD and their families. Treatment can take place one on one or in a group setting and usually lasts 6 to 12 weeks but can last longer.

Some types of psychotherapy target PTSD symptoms, while others focus on social, family, or job-related problems. Effective psychotherapies often emphasize a few key components, including learning skills to help identify triggers and manage symptoms.

A common type of psychotherapy called cognitive behavioral therapy can include exposure therapy and cognitive restructuring.

- **Exposure therapy** helps people learn to manage their fear by gradually exposing them, in a safe way, to the trauma they experienced. As part of exposure therapy, people may think or write about the trauma or visit the place where it happened. This therapy can help people with PTSD reduce symptoms that cause them distress.
- **Cognitive restructuring** helps people make sense of the traumatic event. Sometimes people remember the event differently from how it happened, or they may feel guilt or shame about something that is not their fault. Cognitive restructuring can help people with PTSD think about what happened in a realistic way.

Learn more about psychotherapy at **www.nimh.nih.gov/psychotherapies**.

Medications

The U.S. Food and Drug Administration (FDA) has approved two selective serotonin reuptake inhibitors (SSRIs), a type of antidepressant medication, for the treatment of PTSD. SSRIs may help people manage PTSD symptoms, such as sadness, worry, anger, and feeling emotionally numb. Health care providers may prescribe SSRIs and other medications along with psychotherapy. Some medications may help treat specific PTSD symptoms, such as sleep problems and nightmares.

People should work with their health care providers to find the best medication or combination of medications and the right dose. Read the latest medication warnings, patient medication guides, and information on newly approved medications on the FDA website at **www.fda.gov/drugsatfda**.

How can I find help?

The Substance Abuse and Mental Health Services Administration (SAMHSA) provides an online resource for finding mental health services in your area at **https://findtreatment.gov**. For additional resources, visit **www.nimh.nih.gov/findhelp**.

> If you or someone you know is struggling or having thoughts of suicide, call or text the 988 Suicide and Crisis Lifeline at **988** or chat at **988lifeline.org.** In life-threatening situations, call **911.**

What can I do to help myself?

You can get better with treatment. Here are some things you can do to help yourself:

- Talk with your health care provider about treatment options and follow your treatment plan.
- Engage in exercise, mindfulness, or other activities that help reduce stress.
- Try to maintain routines for meals, exercise, and sleep.
- Set realistic goals and focus on what you can manage.
- Spend time with trusted friends or relatives and tell them about things that may trigger symptoms.
- Expect your symptoms to improve gradually, not immediately.
- Avoid the use of alcohol or drugs.

How can I help a loved one with PTSD?

If you know someone who may be experiencing PTSD, the most important thing you can do is to help that person get the right diagnosis and treatment. Some people may need help making an appointment with their health care provider; others may benefit from having someone accompany them to their health care visits.

If a close friend or relative is diagnosed with PTSD, you can encourage them to follow their treatment plan. If their symptoms do not improve after 6 to 8 weeks, you can encourage them to talk about it with their health care provider. You also can:

- Offer emotional support, understanding, patience, and encouragement.
- Learn about PTSD so you can understand what your friend is experiencing.
- Listen carefully. Pay attention to the person's feelings and the situations that may trigger PTSD symptoms.
- Share positive distractions, such as walks, outings, and other activities.

Where can I find more information on PTSD?

The National Center for PTSD, a program of the U.S. Department of Veterans Affairs, is the leading federal center for research and education on PTSD and traumatic stress. You can find information about PTSD, treatment options, getting help, and additional resources for families, friends, and providers at **www.ptsd.va.gov**.

Are there clinical trials studying PTSD?

NIMH supports a wide range of research, including clinical trials that look at new ways to prevent, detect, or treat diseases and conditions—including PTSD. Although individuals may benefit from being part of a clinical trial, participants should be aware that the primary purpose of a clinical trial is to gain new scientific knowledge so that others may be better helped in the future.

Researchers at NIMH and around the country conduct clinical trials with patients and healthy volunteers. Talk to a health care provider about clinical trials, their benefits and risks, and whether one is right for you. For more information, visit **www.nimh.nih.gov/clinicaltrials**.

Studies & Statistics / Post-Traumatic Stress Disorder

Helping Children and Adolescents Cope With Traumatic Events

Every year, children and adolescents experience disasters and other traumatic events. Family, friends, and trusted adults play an essential role in helping youth cope with these experiences.

How do children and adolescents respond to traumatic events?

It is typical for children and adolescents to have a range of reactions after experiencing or witnessing a traumatic event, such as a natural disaster, an act of violence, or a serious accident.

Regardless of age, children and adolescents may:

- Report having physical problems such as stomachaches or headaches.
- Have nightmares or other sleep problems, including refusing to go to bed.
- Have trouble concentrating.
- Lose interest in activities they normally enjoy.
- Have feelings of guilt for not preventing injuries or deaths.
- Have thoughts of revenge.

Young children (age 5 and younger) may:

- Cling to caregivers and/or cry and be tearful.
- Have tantrums, or be irritable or disruptive.
- Suddenly return to behaviors such as bed-wetting and thumb-sucking.
- Show increased fearfulness (for example, fear of the dark, monsters, or being alone).
- Incorporate aspects of the traumatic event into imaginary play.

Older children (age 6 and older) and adolescents may:

- Have problems in school.
- Withdraw or become isolated from family and friends.
- Avoid reminders of the event.
- Use drugs, alcohol, or tobacco.
- Be disruptive, disrespectful, or destructive.
- Be angry or resentful.

Many of these reactions are normal and will lessen with time. If these symptoms last for more than a month, the family should reach out to a health care provider.

What can adults do to help?

How adults respond to trauma can strongly influence how children and adolescents react to trauma. When caregivers and family members take steps to support their own ability to cope, they can provide better care for others.

Caregivers and family members can help by creating a safe and supportive environment, remaining as calm as possible, and reducing stressors. Children and adolescents need to know that their family members love them and will do their best to take care of them.

Do:
- Ensure children and adolescents are safe and that their basic needs are addressed.
- Allow them to be sad or cry.
- Let them talk, write, or draw pictures about the event and their feelings.
- Limit their exposure to repetitive news reports about traumatic events.
- Let them sleep in your room (for a short time) or sleep with a light on if they are having trouble sleeping.
- Try to stick to routines, such as reading bedtime stories, eating dinner together, and playing games.
- Help them feel in control by letting them make some decisions for themselves, such as choosing their meals or picking out their clothes.
- Pay attention to sudden changes in behaviors, speech, language use, or strong emotions.
- Contact a health care provider if new problems develop, particularly if any of the following symptoms occur for more than a few weeks:
  - Having flashbacks (reliving the event)
  - Having a racing heart and sweating
  - Being easily startled
  - Being emotionally numb
  - Being very sad or depressed

Don't:
- Expect children and adolescents to be brave or tough.
- Make them discuss the event before they are ready.
- Get angry if they show strong emotions.
- Get upset if they begin bed-wetting, acting out, or thumb-sucking.
- Make promises you can't keep (such as "You will be OK tomorrow" or "You will go home soon.")

Where can I find help?

The Substance Abuse and Mental Health Services Administration (SAMHSA) offers a Disaster Distress Helpline, which provides immediate crisis counseling for people who are experiencing emotional distress related to any natural or human-caused disaster. The helpline is free, multilingual, confidential, and available 24 hours a day, 7 days a week. You can call or text the helpline at 800-985-5990 or visit the helpline website at **https://disasterdistress.samhsa.gov**.

SAMHSA also provides the Behavioral Health Treatment Services Locator, an online tool for finding mental health services in your area. Find treatment programs in your state at **https://findtreatment.samhsa.gov**. For additional resources, visit **www.nimh.nih.gov/findhelp**.

If you, your child, or someone you know is in immediate distress or is thinking about hurting themselves, call 911 or call the **National Suicide Prevention Lifeline** toll-free at 1-800-273-TALK (8255). You also can text the **Crisis Text Line** (HELLO to 741741) or use the Lifeline Chat on the National Suicide Prevention Lifeline website at **https://suicidepreventionlifeline.org**.

Where can I find more resources?

National Institute of Mental Health:
Coping With Traumatic Events
www.nimh.nih.gov/copingwithtrauma

National Institute of Mental Health:
Child and Adolescent Mental Health
www.nimh.nih.gov/children

Centers for Disease Control and Prevention:
Caring for Children in a Disaster
www.cdc.gov/childrenindisasters

National Child Traumatic Stress Network
www.nctsn.org

NIH Publication No. 22-MH-8066

www.nimh.nih.gov
Follow NIMH on
Social Media @NIMHgov

SECTION TWO:
DEPRESSION RESOURCES

DEPRESSIVE DISORDERS

Depression is one of the most common mental health disorders in the United States and may be caused by a variety of factors. Depression can happen at any age, may co-occur with serious illnesses, and may be caused from medication side effects.

It is important that the individual understands that depression is treatable. It is also important to understand that transient sadness, such as with loss of a family member or pet, a job loss or major life event such as divorce or moving lasting two weeks or less is probably not depression. If this sadness lasts longer than two weeks or gets progressively worse, a physician visit should be scheduled.

Depressive disorders are considered a mental health issue. There are societal, environmental, medical, and economic issues that impact mental health. Homelessness, race and ethnicity, aging, sexual orientation, civil and political unrest, immigration and other factors may all impact the mental health of individuals. Excessive social media use and too much exposure to outside media may also have a negative effect on mental health. Family history of depression, major trauma and stress may increase the risk of depression. Having a chronic disease such as cancer, diabetes or heart disease may lead to depression that requires treatment. Grief and despair may also evolve into depression.

The signs and symptoms of depression vary person to person, making a definitive diagnosis somewhat difficult to make. Some individuals withdraw while others may be irritable or agitated. Behaviors such as sleeping patterns and eating patterns may change with depression. Insomnia, or a constant desire to sleep, and weight gain or loss may be signs of depression. Fatigue, feeling of hopelessness, problems with concentration and poor work performance, sadness and loss of enjoyment of activities, guilt, and recurring thoughts of death or suicide are all considered in the diagnosis of depression.

Once symptoms present and the individual realizes the need for help, a diagnosis needs to be made by a medical professional. While mild cases of depression may be treated with medication from the primary care provider with or without psychotherapy (talk therapy), a referral to a mental health professional may be needed. Knowing what to tell your provider will help to determine your diagnosis.

Antidepressants are often ordered to improve brain chemicals that control mood or stress. A medication that has helped the individual or perhaps a family member with depression may be considered. Several different medications may be tried to determine which one best relieves symptoms. Medications require two to four weeks to work and physical symptoms such as sleep, appetite and ability to concentrate may resolve before mood improvements are noted. Antidepressants should never be stopped suddenly; doses should be slowly tapered down, usually after six months to a year after starting.

Depressive Disorders

Maintaining a healthy lifestyle may prevent or mitigate some types of depression. Social interactions are important as isolationism increases the risk of depression. Talking about problems may actually make things worse if not seeing a professional for counseling. Discussing problems is often seen as a way to give and receive support, but conversations may make the individual more depressed. Distraction through meditation or prayer, making realistic goals, and developing self-esteem may help. Eating a healthy diet and avoiding alcohol, especially to excess, are useful. Exercise and activities are also effective and cost-effective treatments for sadness and may aid in preventing depression. Exercise is good for the body, may prevent other co-morbid diseases, and may be good for mental health. Exercise as both prevention and treatment of depression has been shown through clinical studies to be beneficial. Maintaining good sleep hygiene, such as a regular bedtime and wake-up time is helpful.

Depressive Disorders / Agencies & Associations

Agencies & Associations

1 A.I.M. Agoraphobics in Motion
7636 Emerson
Washington, MI 48094
248-710-5719
aimforrecovery@gmail.com
aimforrecovery.com
AIM is a nonprofit support group organization committed to the support and recovery of people with anxiety disorders, as well as their families.
James Fortune, President
Robert Diedrich, Vice President & Secretary

2 Academy of Psychosomatic Medicine
4800 Hampden Ln
Bethesda, MD 20814
301-718-6520
info@CLpsychiatry.org
apm.org
The Academy of Psychosomatic Medicine represents psychiatrists focused on improving education, medical science, and healthcare for individuals with comorbid psychiatric and general medical conditions. The Academy seeks to promote interdisciplinary education and drive research and public policy with the goal of achieving outstanding clinical care for patients with comorbid psychiatric and general medical conditions throughout the world. They also created the Foundation of the Academy of Psychosom
Philip Biaeler, MD, FACLP, President
Maryland Pao, MD, FACLP, President-Elect

3 Administration for Children and Families
330 C Street SW
Washington, DC 20201
877-696-6775
www.acf.hhs.gov
The Administration for Children & Families (ACF) is a division of the U.S. Department of Health & Human Services (HHS). ACF promotes the economic and social well-being of families, children, individuals and communities.
Jeff Hild, Principal Deputy Assistant Secretary
Larry Handerhan, Chief of Staff

4 American Association of Children's Residential Centers
648 North Plankinton Avenue
Milwaukee, WI 53203
877-332-2272
info@togetherthevoice.org
togetherthevoice.org
The American Association of Children's Residential Centers is a national organization focused on providing residential therapeutic treatment for children and adolescents with behavioral health disorders.
David Wallace, Board President
Robert McCartney, Treasurer

5 American Psychiatric Association
800 Maine Avenue SW
Washington, DC 20024
202-559-3900
apa@psych.org
www.psychiatry.org
A medical specialty society representing a growing membership of psychiatrists. Offers information for psychiatrists, medical students, patients and families.
Saul Levin, MD, MPA, FRCP-E, CEO

6 Anxiety and Depression Association of America
8701 Georgia Avenue
Silver Spring, MD 20910
240-485-1018
information@adaa.org
adaa.org
An international nonprofit organization committed to the use of education and research to promote the prevention, treatment, and cure of anxiety, depressive, obssesive compulsive, and other trauma related disorders. ADAA's mission is to improve the lives of all people with anxiety and mood disorders.
Charles B. Nemeroff, MD, President
Susan K. Gurley, Executive Director

7 Association for Behavioral and Cognitive Therapies
305 Seventh Avenue
New York, NY 10001
212-647-1890
Fax: 212-647-1865
abct.org
A multidisciplinary organization dedicated to utilizing and advancing scientific approaches in the understanding and prevention of human behavioral and cognitive problems.
Mary Jane Eimer, CAE, Executive Director
David Teisler, CAE, Deputy Director

8 Balanced Mind Parent Network
Depression and Bipolar Support Alliance
55 East Jackson Boulevard
Chicago, IL 60604
800-826-3632
community@dbsalliance.org
www.dbsalliance.org
The Balanced Mind provides support, information, and assistance to families raising children with mood disorders and related conditions.
Michael Pollock, CEO
Jessica Chervinko, Development Manager

9 Center for Family Support (CFS)
333 Seventh Avenue
New York, NY 10001
212-629-7939
Fax: 212-239-2211
svernikoff@cfsny.org
www.cfsny.org
The Center for Family Support offers assistance to individuals with developmental and related disabilities, as well as their families, and provides support services and programs that are designed to accommodate individual needs. Offers services throughout New York City, Westchester County, Long Island, and New Jersey.
Steven Vernikoff, Executive Director
Barbara Greenwald, Chief Operating Officer

10 Center for Mental Health Services (CMHS)
Substance Abuse and Mental Health Services Admin.
5600 Fishers Lane
Rockville, MD 20857
240-276-1310
samhsa.gov
Promotes the treatment of mental illness and emotional disorders by increasing accessibility to mental health programs; supporting outreach, treatment, rehabilitation, and support programs and networks; and encouraging the use of scientifically-based information when treating mental disorders. CMHS provides information about mental health via a toll-free number and numerous publications.
Anita Everett, M.D., DFAPA, Director

11 Depression & Bipolar Support Alliance
55 East Jackson Boulevard
Chicago, IL 60604
800-826-3632
info@dbsalliance.org
dbsalliance.org
The Depression and Bipolar Support Alliance is a national organization focused on improving the lives of individuals with depression, bipolar disorder, and other mood disorders. DBSA organizes peer-led support groups; educates patients, families, professionals, and the public on mental health; and works to ensure the availability of quality care for all people.
Roger McIntyre, Chair
Michael Pollock, Chief Executive Officer

12 Freedom From Fear
308 Seaview Avenue
Staten Island, NY 10305
718-351-1717
help@freedomfromfear.org
freedomfromfear.org
A national nonprofit organization whose mission is to aid and counsel individuals suffering from anxiety and depressive disorders through advocacy, education, research, and community support.
Mary Guardino, Founder & Executive Director

13 Help is Here
North Dakota Behavioral Health Division
600 E Boulevard Avenue
Bismarck, ND 58501
701-328-2310
800-472-2622
dhsbhd@nd.gov
www.helpishere.nd.gov
Promotes the support and treatment of mental illness and emotional disorders. Offers mental health services, addiction servces, and recovery centers.

14 Hope for Depression Research Foundation
40 West 57th Street
New York, NY 10019
212-676-3200
Fax: 212-676-3219
hdrf@hopefordepression.org
www.hopefordepression.org
Promotes, and encourages profits for neuroscience research into the treatments, diagnosis, origins, and prevention of depression, and other mood disorders such as anxiety disorders, post-traumatic

Depressive Disorders / Agencies & Associations

stress disorder, postpartum depression, bipolar disorder, and suicide.
Audrey Gruss, Founder & Chairman
Harold W. Koenigsberg, MD, Board Member

15 **Institute for Contemporary Psychotherapy**
33 W 60th St. 212-333-3444
New York, NY 10023 Fax: 212-333-5444
icpnyc.org
The Institute for Contemporary Psychotherapy is a New York City-based mental health treatment and training facility. Consisting of a group of 150 licensed psychotherapists, the Institute focuses on educating the public about the issues surrounding mental health, providing post-graduate training for therapists, and offering therapy at moderate costs.
Ron Taffel, PhD, Chair
Andrea Green-Lewis, LCSW-R, Director of Operations

16 **Mental Health America**
500 Montgomery Street 703-684-7722
Alexandria, VA 22314 800-969-6642
mhanational.org
Mental Health America is a community-based nonprofit organization committed to enabling the mental wellness of all Americans. MHA advocates for greater access to quality health services and seeks to educate individuals on identifying symptoms, as well as intervention and prevention.
Schroeder Stribling, President & CEO
Sachin Doshi, Sr. Dir., Finance & Operations

17 **MindWise Innovations**
270 Bridge Street 781-239-0071
Dedham, MA 02026 Fax: 781-320-9136
info@mindwise.org
www.mindwise.org
Formerly known as Screening For Mental Health, MindWise Innovations provides resources to schools, workplaces, and communities to address mental health issues, eating disorders, substance abuse, and suicide.
Rebecca Ames, LICSW, Senior Clinical Manager
Larry Berkowitz, EdD, Director, Trauma Center

18 **Mood Disorders Center**
600 North Wolfe Street 410-955-5212
Baltimore, MD 21218 877-666-3754
www.hopkinsmedicine.org
The Mood Disorders Center at Johns Hopkins Medicine provides specialized clinical services to patients with mood disorders; conducts research on the causes of mood disorders, treatment responses, and brain function and structure; and educates patients, caregivers, and the public on mood disorders through symposia, publications, community presentations, and the Adolescent Depression Awareness Program.
Karen Swartz, MD, Director

19 **National Alliance on Mental Illness**
4301 Wilson Boulevard 703-524-7600
Arlington, VA 22203 800-950-6264
info@nami.org
nami.org
NAMI is an organization dedicated to raising awareness on mental health and providing support and education for Americans affected by mental illness. NAMI advocates for access to services and treatment and fosters an environment of awareness and understanding for those concerned with mental health.
Shirley J. Holloway, President
Joyce A. Campbell, First Vice President

20 **National Alliance on Mental Illness (NAMI)**
4301 Wilson Boulevard 703-524-7600
Arlington, VA 22203 800-950-6264
nami.org
NAMI is an organization dedicated to raising awareness on mental health and providing support and education for Americans affected by mental illness. NAMI advocates for access to services and treatment and fosters an environment of awareness and understanding for those concerned with mental health.
Joyce A. Campbell, President
Daniel H. Gillison, Jr., CEO

21 **National Association for the Dually Diagnosed (NADD)**
321 Wall Street 845-331-4336
Kingston, NY 12401 info@thenadd.org
thenadd.org
NADD is a nonprofit organization designed to increase awareness of, and provide services for, individuals with developmental disabilities and mental illness. NADD emphasizes the importance of quality mental healthcare for people with mental health needs and offers conferences, information resources, educational programs, and training materials to professionals, parents, and organizations.
Jeanne M. Farr, MA, Chief Executive Officer
Robert J. Fletcher, DSW, Founder & CEO Emeritus

22 **National Center for Complementary and Integrative Health**
9000 Rockville Pike 888-644-6226
Bethesda, MD 20892 TTY: 866-464-3615
info@nccih.nih.gov
nccih.nih.gov
The National Center for Complementary and Integrative Health (NCCIH) is the Federal Government's lead agency for scientific research on the diverse medical and health care systems, practices, and products that are not generally considered part of conventional medicine.
Helene M. Langevin, MD, Director
David Shurtleff, PhD, Deputy Director

23 **National Council for Behavioral Health**
1400 K Street NW communications@thenationalcouncil.org
Washington, DC 20005 thenationalcouncil.org
The National Council for Behavioral Health serves to unify America's behavioral health organizations. The council is dedicated to ensuring that quality mental health and addictions care is readily accessible to all Americans.
Edward Woods, Chair
Charles Ingoglia, President and CEO

24 **National Federation of Families for Children's Mental Health**
15800 Crabbs Branch Way 240-403-1901
Rockville, MD 20855 ffcmh@ffcmh.org
ffcmh.org
The National Federation of Families for Children's Mental Health is a national organization focused on advocating for the rights of children affected by mental health challenges, assisting family-run organizations across the nation, and ensuring that children and families concerned with mental health have access to services.
Lynda Gargan, PhD, Executive Director
Gail Cormier, Project Director

25 **National Institute of Environmental Health Sciences**
111 T.W. Alexander Drive 919-541-3201
Durham, NC 27709 Fax: 919-541-5136
webcenter@niehs.nih.gov
www.niehs.nih.gov
The mission of the NIEHS is to discover how the environment affects people in order to promote healthier lives.
Rick Woychik, PhD, Director
Trevor K. Archer, PhD, Deputy Director

26 **National Institute of Mental Health**
6001 Executive Boulevard 866-615-6464
Bethesda, MD 20892-9663 nimhinfo@nih.gov
nimh.nih.gov
The National Institute of Mental Health conducts clinical research on mental disorders and seeks to expand knowledge on mental health treatments.
Joshua A. Gordon, M.D., Ph. D., Director

27 **Office of Women's Health**
200 Independence Avenue SW 202-690-7650
Washington, DC 20201 800-994-9662
Fax: 202-205-2631
womenshealth@hhs.gov
www.womenshealth.gov
Government agency under the Department of Health & Human Services, with free health information for women.
Dorothy Fink, MD, Deputy Asst. Secretary, Women's Health
Richelle West Marshall, Deputy Director, Ops & Management

28 **PACER Center**
8161 Normandale Boulevard
Bloomington, MN 55437
952-838-9000
800-537-2237
pacer.org
PACER provides information, training, and assistance to parents of children and young adults with all disabilities (physical, learning, cognitive, emotional, and health). Its mission is to help improve the quality of life for young people with disabilities and their families.
Paula F. Goldberg, Co-Founder & Executive Director

29 **Postpartum Support International**
6706 Southwest 54th Avenue
Portland, OR 97219
503-894-9453
800-944-4773
Fax: 503-894-9452
postpartum.net
A nonprofit organization focused on providing support for pregnant, post-loss, and postpartum women across the world. Postpartum Support International seeks to raise awareness about the emotional and mental health issues that women face during pregnancy and postpartum.
Wendy N. Davis, PhD, Executive Director
Lianne Swanson, Executive Administrator

30 **Sutcliffe Clinic**
851 Fremont Avenue
Los Altos, CA 94024
650-941-1698
Fax: 650-434-1953
info@sutcliffedbp.com
www.sutcliffeclinic.com
Sutcliffe Developmental & Behavioral Pediatrics is an organization that specializes in the treatment of ADHD, autism spectrum disorder, anxiety disorders, conduct disorders, learning disabilities, and more. Sutcliffe works with community services, school districts, and primary physicians, and provides family counseling.
Trenna Sutcliffe, MD, MS, Medical Director

31 **Territorial Apprehensiveness (TERRAP) Anxiety & Stress Program**
755 Park Avenue
Huntington, NY 11743
631-549-8867
info@anxietyandpanic.com
anxietyandpanic.com
Helps to treat anxiety and stress disorders through Territorial Apprehensiveness Programs, developed by Dr. Arthur Hardy in the 1960s. The program systematically addresses the behavioral and thought processes of those suffering from stress and anxiety.
Julian Herskowitz, PhD, Director

32 **Thriving Minds**
10524 E. Grand River Avenue
Brighton, MI 48116
810-225-3417
office@thrivingminds.info
www.thrivingmindsbehavioralhealth.com
Thriving Minds is an organization that offers therapy to people with anxiety, behavioral issues, and depression. With locations in Brighton and Chelsea, Thriving Minds uses a mix of research-based interventions, such as Cognitive Behavioral Therapy; parent coaching; and school interventions in order to help children, teens, and adults deal with their anxiety.
Amiee Kotrba, PhD, Owner
Bryce Hella, PhD, Director, Brighton Clinic

33 **United Brain Association**
202-768-8000
info@unitedbrainassociation.org
unitedbrainassociation.org
Non-profit organization that works to find cures through research for over 600 brain and mental health related issues, and disorders.
J.A. Boulton, Founder
Jay Matey, VP & Treasurer

34 **Zur Institute**
321 S. Main Street
Sebastopol, CA 95472
833-961-1344
info@zurinstitute.com
www.zurinstitute.com
Provides quality online continuing education, tools, and services that enhance the ability of psycotherapists, couselors, therapists, social workers, and other health care professionals to meet the needs of those concerned with mental health.
Dr. Ofer Zur, Director

Foundations

35 **Brain & Behavior Research Foundation**
747 Third Avenue
New York, NY 10017
646-681-4888
800-829-8289
info@bbrfoundation.org
www.bbrfoundation.org
The Brain and Behavior Research Foundation awards grants aimed at advancing scientific understandings of mental health treatments and mental disorders such as depression and schizophrenia. The Foundation's mission is to eliminate the suffering caused by mental illness.
Geoffrey A. Simon, Chairman
Miriam E. Katowitz, CPA, Vice President

36 **Centre for Addiction and Mental Health Foundation**
1451 Queen Street West
Toronto, ON, M6R-1A1
416-979-6909
800-414-0471
foundation@camh.ca
www.camh.ca
CAMH Foundation supports people affected by mental health and addiction issues through fundraising, research, education, policy development, clinical care, and the promotion of health.
Deborah Gillis, President & CEO
Gina Daya, CFO

37 **International Foundation for Research and Education on Depression (iFred)**
P.O. Box 17598
Baltimore, MD 21297
Fax: 443-782-0739
info@ifred.org
www.ifred.org
Mission is to alleviate mental health stigma and inspire hope through marketing campaigns, positive imagery, and celebrity engagement.
Kathryn Goetzke, MBA, Founder
Tom Dean, Chair

38 **Jed Foundation**
530 7th Avenue
New York, NY 10018
212-647-7544
Fax: 212-647-7542
jedfoundation.org
JED offers programs to teens and young adults to improve mental health, minimize potential harm, and prevent suicide in the U.S.
Rebecca Benghiat, President & COO
John MacPhee, CEO

Libraries & Resource Centers

39 **Family-to-Family: National Alliance on Mental Illness**
4301 Wilson Boulevard
Arlington, VA 22203
703-524-7600
888-999-6264
info@nami.org
nami.org
The NAMI Family-to-Family Education Program is a free, 8 session course for family caregivers of individuals with severe mental illnesses. The course is taught by trained family members, all instruction and course materials are free to class participants, and over 300,000 family members have graduated from this national program.

40 **National Mental Health Consumers' Self-Help Clearinghouse**
selfhelpclearinghouse@gmail.com
mhselfhelp.org
The Clearinghouse is a peer-run national technical assistance center focused on achieving respect and equality of opportunity for those with mental illnesses. The Clearinghouse helps with the growth of the mental health consumer movement by evaluating mental health services, advocating for mental health reform, and providing consumers with news, information, publications, and consultation services.
Joseph Rogers, Founder & Executive Director
Susan Rogers, Director

Depressive Disorders / Research Centers

Research Centers

41 **Columbia University Pediatric Anxiety and Mood Research Clinic**
1051 Riverside Drive 646-774-8104
New York, NY 10032 childadolescentpsych.cumc.columbia.edu
A research clinic desinged to help children with anxiety, depression, and OCD. The clinic provides evaluations, evidence-based therapy and medications, and a day-treatment program. All evaluation and treatment services are free of charge.
Jeremy Veenstra-VanderWeele, MD, Division Director
Laura Mufson, PhD, Division Associate Director

42 **National Institute of Mental Health**
6001 Executive Boulevard 866-615-6464
Bethesda, MD 20892 TTY: 301-443-8431
nimhinfo@nih.gov
nimh.nih.gov
The National Institute of Mental Health conducts clinical research on mental disorders and seeks to expand knowledge on mental health treatments.
Joshua Gordon, MD, PhD, Director

43 **UAMS Psychiatric Research Institute**
University of Arkansas for Medical Sciences
4224 Shuffield Drive 501-526-8100
Little Rock, AR 72205 psychiatry.uams.edu
Combining research, education and clinical services into one facility, PRI offers inpatiend and outpatient services, with 40 psychiatric beds, therapy options, and specialized treatment for specific disorders, including: addictive eating, anxiety, deppressive and post-traumatic stress disorders. Research focuses on evidence-based care takes into consideration the education of future medical personnel while relying on research scientists to provide innovative forms of treatment.
Donald R. Bobbitt, President
William Bowes, MS, Vice Chancellor, Finance

44 **UCLA Anxiety Disorders Research Center**
Department of Psychology 310-825-9312
Los Angeles, CA 90094 rose@psych.ucla.edu
anxiety.psych.ucla.edu
The purpose of The ADRC is to further our understanding of the factors that place individuals at risk for developing phobias, anxiety disorders and related conditions, and to develop more effective treatments that have long lasting effects and are cost effective.
Michelle G. Craske, Ph.D., Director
Raphael Rose, Ph.D., Associate Director

45 **University of Texas: Mental Health Clinical Research Center**
5323 Harry Hines Boulevard 214-648-3111
Dallas, TX 75390 utsouthwestern.edu
Research activity of major and atypical depression.

46 **Yale Mood Disorders Research Program**
Department of Psychiatry
300 George Street 203-785-2090
New Haven, CT 06511 psychiatry.yale.edu
MDRP is dedicated to understanding the science of mood disorders, including bipolar disorder and depression. The MDRP brings together a multi-disciplinary group of scientists from across the Yale campus in a highly collaborative research effort. Goals of the MDRP include the identification of biological markers for mood disorders and discovery of new treatment strategies.
John H. Krystal, Chair
Rajita Sinha, Chief, Psychology Section

Support Groups & Hotlines

47 **A.I.M. Agoraphobics in Motion**
7636 Emerson 248-710-5719
Washington, MI 48094 aimforrecovery@gmail.com
aimforrecovery.com
AIM is a nonprofit support group organization committed to the support and recovery of people with anxiety disorders, as well as their families.
James Fortune, President
Robert Diedrich, Vice President & Secretary

48 **Balanced Mind Parent Network**
Depression and Bipolar Support Alliance
55 East Jackson Boulevard 800-826-3632
Chicago, IL 60604 community@dbsalliance.org
www.dbsalliance.org
The Balanced Mind provides support, information, and assistance to families raising children with mood disorders and related conditions.
Michael Pollock, CEO
Maria Margaglione, Programs Director

49 **Center for Family Support**
2811 Zulette Avenue 718-518-1500
Bronx, NY 10461 svernikoff@cfsny.org
www.cfsny.org
The Center for Family Support offers assistance to individuals with developmental and related disabilities, as well as their families, and provides support services and programs that are designed to accommodate individual needs. Offers services throughout New York City, Westchester County, Long Island, and New Jersey.
Steven Vernikoff, Executive Director
Barbara Greenwald, Chief Operating Officer

50 **DBSA Support Groups: An Important Step on the Road to Wellness**
Depression and Bipolar Support Alliance
730 North Franklin Street 312-642-0049
Chicago, IL 60654 800-826-3632
dbsalliance.org
Support groups for people with depression or bipolar disorder to discuss the experiences, and helpful treatments.
10 pages
Cheryl T Magrini, MS.Ed, MTS, PhD, Chair
Allen Doederlein, President

51 **Depressed Anonymous**
P.O. Box 17414 502-569-1989
Louisville, KY 40217 depressedanon.com
Formed to provide therapeutic resources for depressed individuals of all ages. Works with the chronically depressed and those recently discharged from health facilities who were treated for depression.

52 **Emotions Anonymous International Service Center**
2233 University Ave W 651-647-9712
Saint Paul, MN 55114 info@emotionsanonymous.org
emotionsanonymous.org
A community-based organization to provide support managing mental health difficulties. Groups meet weekly to share experiences, strength, and hope.
Elaine Weber Nelson, Executive Director

53 **Empty Cradle**
31938 Temecula Parkway 619-573-6515
Temecula, CA 92592 info@emptycradle.org
emptycradle.org
A nonprofit peer support group for parents who have experienced the death of a baby. Focusing on parents in the San Diego and Riverside County area, Empty Cradle supports grieving families through educational resources, monthly meetings, and a network of volunteer parents seeking to offer friendship and emotional support.
Rachel Redhouse, Co-President
John Redhouse, Co-President & Treasurer

54 **Holliswood Hospital Psychiatric Care, Services and Self-Help/Support Groups**
87-37 Palermo Street 718-776-8181
Holliswood, NY 11423 800-486-3005
Fax: 718-776-8572
HolliswoodInfo@libertymgt.com
www.holliswoodhospital.com/
The Holliswood Hospital, a 110-bed private psychiatric hospital located in a quiet residential Queens community, is a leader in providing quality, acute inpatient mental health care for adult, adolescent, geriatric and dually diagnosed patients. Holliswood Hospital treats patients with a broad range of psychiatric disorders. Additionally, specialized services are available for patients with psy-

chiatric diagnoses compounded by chemical dependency, or a history of physical or sexual abuse.
Susan Clayton, Support Group Coordinator
Angela Hurtado, Support Group Coordinator

55 **National Center for Learning Disabilities**
1220 L Street NW   301-966-2234
Washington, DC 20005   ncld.org
The NCLD's mission is to ensure success for all individuals with learning disabilities in school, at work, and in life. They connect parents with resources, guidance, and support to advocate effectively for their children; deliver evidence-based tools, resources, and professional development to educators to improve student outcomes; and develop policies and engage advocates to strengthen educational rights and opportunities.
Margi Booth, Co-Chair
Joe Zimmel, Co-Chair

56 **National Federation of Families for Children's Mental Health**
12320 Parklawn Drive   240-403-1901
Rockville, MD 20852   Fax: 240-403-1909
                                          ffcmh@ffcmh.org
                                          www.ffcmh.org
Provides advocacy at the national level for the rights of children and youth with emotional, behavioral and mental health challenges and their families; provides leadership and technical assistance to a nation-wide network of family run organizations; and collaborates with family run and other child serving organizations to transform mental health care in America.
Lynda Gargan, PhD, Executive Director
Leann Sherman, Project Coordinator

57 **National Health Information Center**
Office of Disease Prevention & Health Promotion
1101 Wootton Pkwy   Fax: 240-453-8281
Rockville, MD 20852   odphpinfo@hhs.gov
                                          www.health.gov/nhic
Supports public health education by maintaining a calendar of National Health Observances; helps connect consumers and health professionals to organizations that can best answer questions and provide up-to-date contact information from reliable sources; updates on a yearly basis toll-free numbers for health information, Federal health clearinghouses and info centers.
Don Wright, MD, MPH, Director

58 **Recovery International**
1415 W. 22nd Street   312-337-5661
Oak Brook, IL 60523   866-221-0302
                                          info@recoveryinternational.org
                                          www.recoveryinternational.org
Recovery International is an organization that uses a peer-to-peer, self-help training system developed by Abraham Low in order to help individuals with mental health issues lead more productive lives.
Sandra K. Wilcoxon, Chief Executive Officer
Joanne Lampey, President

59 **Support4Hope**
PO Box 184   Admin@Support4hope.com
Deer Lodge, TN 37726   www.support4hope.com
Support4Hope is dedicated to support of various mental health issues such as Bipolar Disorder, Depression, Anxiety Disorders, Schizophrenia, Post Traumatic Stress Disorder (PTSD) and the problems that arise from them along with other problems such as Domestic Abuse.

Print Resources

60 **American Journal of Psychiatry**
American Psychiatric Association Publishing
800 Maine Avenue SW, Suite 900   202-459-9722
Washington, DC 20024   800-368-5777
                                          Fax: 202-403-3094
                                          psychiatryonline@psych.org
                                          ajp.psychiatryonline.org
Official journal of the American Psychiatric Association (APA).
Ned H. Kalin, MD, Editor-in-Chief

61 **American Journal of Psychotherapy**
American Psychiatric Association Publishing
800 Maine Avenue SW, Suite 900   202-459-9722
Washington, DC 20024   800-368-5777
                                          Fax: 202-403-3094
                                          psychiatryonline@psych.org
                                          ajp.psychiatryonline.org
Publishes content that aims to advance the theory, science, and clinical practice of psychotherapy.
Holly A. Swartz, MD, Editor-in-Chief

62 **Depression & Anxiety**
Wiley and Hindawi
111 River Street   201-748-6000
Hoboken, NJ 07030-5774   800-567-4797
                                          Fax: 201-748-6088
                                          help@hindawi.com
                                          www.hindawi.com/journals/da
Open-access, peer-reviewed journal covering neurobiology, epidemiology, experimental psychopathology, and treatment aspects of mood and anxiety disorders and related.

63 **International Journal of Depression and Anxiety**
ClinMed International Library
3511 Silverside Road, Suite 105   302-208-7437
Wilmington, DE 19810   contact@clinmedjournals.org
                                          clinmedjournals.org
Open access, peer-reviewed, multidisciplinary journal focusing on treatments for panic attacks, anxiety attacks, phobia, and social phobia.
Photios Anninos, Editor-in-Chief

64 **International Journal of Psychology and Psychoanalysis**
ClinMed International Library
3511 Silverside Road, Suite 105   302-208-7437
Wilmington, DE 19810   contact@clinmedjournals.org
                                          clinmedjournals.org
Open access, peer-reviewed journal focused on cognition, emotions, brain functioning, interpersonal relationships, and the unconscious mind.
Joaquim J.F. Soares, Editor-in-Chief

65 **Journal of Anxiety Disorders**
Elsevier Publishing
1600 John F Kennedy Boulevard   212-989-5800
Philadelphia, PA 19103-2398   800-325-4177
                                          custserv.ehs@elsevier.com
                                          www.sciencedirect.com
Interdisciplinary journal that publishes research papers dealing with all aspects of anxiety disorders for all age groups (child, adolescent, adult and geriatrics).
Deborah Beidel, Author

66 **Journal of Mood & Anxiety Disorders**
Anxiety & Depression Association of America
8701 Georgia Avenue, Suite 412   240-485-1018
Silver Spring, MD 20910   information@adaa.org
                                          adaa.org/professionals/journal
The official journal of the Anxiety & Depression Association of America (ADAA), published with Elsevier. The journal covers neurobiology, epidemiology, experimental psychopathology, pathophysiology, and treatment aspects of mood and anxiety disorders.
Stephen M. Strakowski, MD, Editor-in-Chief

67 **Journal of Psychiatry, Depression & Anxiety**
Herald Scholarly Open Access
2561 Cornelia Road, Suite 205   202-499-9679
Herndon, VA 20171   Fax: 202-217-4195
                                          contact@heraldopenaccess.us
                                          www.heraldopenaccess.us
Online, international, open access, peer-reviewed journal focused primarily on depression and anxiety, but also on other related areas of psychiatry as well.
Sam Vaknin, Editor-in-Chief

Depressive Disorders / Web Sites

Web Sites

68 **Befrienders Worldwide**
www.befrienders.org
Support, helplines, and advice.

69 **Center For Family Support (CFS)**
www.cfsny.org
Devoted to providing support and assistance to individuals with developmental and related disabilities, and to the family members who care for them.

70 **Center For Mental Health Services Knowledge Exchange**
www.mentalhealth.Samhsa.Gov
Information about resources, technical assistance, research, training, networks and other federal clearinghouses.

71 **Center For Mental Health Services Knowledg Knowledge Exchange**
www.mentalhealth.Samhsa.Gov
Information about resources, technical assistance, research, training, networks, and other federal clearinghouses, fact sheets and materials.

72 **Center for Family Support (CFS)**
www.cfsny.org
Devoted to providing support and assistance to individuals with developmental and related disabilities, and to the family members who care for them.

73 **CyberPsych**
www.cyberpsych.org
Hosts the American Psychoanalyists Foundation, American Association of Suicideology, Society for the Exploration of Psychotherapy Intergration, and Anxiety Disorders Association of America. Also subcategories of the anxiety disorders, as well as general information, including panic disorder, phobias, obsessive compulsive disorder (OCD), social phobia, generalized anxiety disorder, post traumatic stress disorder, and phobias of childhood. Book reviews and links to web pages sharing the topics.

74 **Depression and Bipolar Support Alliance**
www.dbsalliance.org
Mental health news updates and local support group information.

75 **EMDR Institute**
www.emdr.com
Discusses EMDR-Eye Movement Desensitization and Reprocessing-as an innovative clinical treatment for trauma, including sexual abuse, domestic violence, combat, crime, and those suffering from a number of other disorders including depressions, addictions, phobias and a variety of self-esteem issues.

76 **Goodwill-Suncoast**
www.goodwill-suncoast.org
A nonprofit, community-based organization that serves individuals diagnosed as developmentally disabled, with a secondary diagnosis of psychiatric difficulties as evidenced by problem behavior.

77 **Healing Well**
www.healingwell.com
A social network and support community for patients, caregivers, and families coping with the daily struggles of diseases, disorders and chronic illness.

78 **Health Central**
www.healthcentral.com
Find clearly explained, medically accurate information regarding conditions, including an overview, symptoms, causes, diagnostic procedures and treatment options. On this site it is possible to ask questions and get information from a neurologist and connect to people who have similar health interests.

79 **Health Finder**
www.health.gov
A government web site, where individuals can find information and tools to help you and those you care about stay healthy.

80 **Internet Mental Health**
www.mentalhealth.com
On-line information and a virtual encyclopedia related to mental disorders, possible causes and treatments. News, articles, on-line diagnostic programs and related links. Designed to improve understanding, diagnosis and treatment of mental illness throughout the world. Awarded the Top Site Award and the NetPsych Cutting Edge Site Award.

81 **Medical News Today**
www.medicalnewstody.com
Offers in-depth health information and the latest news in medical research on a wide variety of medical conditions.

82 **MedicineNet**
www.medicinenet.com
An online resource for consumers providing easy-to-read, authoritative medical and health information.

83 **Meditation, Guided Fantasies, And Other Stress Remedies**
www.selfhelpmagazine.com/articles/stress
Meditative and stress reduction resources for eyes, ears, minds, and hearts.

84 **MedlinePlus**
www.medlineplus.gov
Information regarding a broad range of health,and mental health conditions topics include: Latest news, overview of anatomy and physiology, clinical trials, diagnoses and symptoms, treatment, genetics, plus lots of links to other sites. A service provided by the National Library of Medicine, part of the National Institutes of Health (NIH).

85 **Medscape**
www.medscape.com
Medscape offers specialists, primary care physicians, and other health professionals the Web's most robust and integrated medical information and educational tools.

86 **National Alliance On Mental Illness**
www.nami.org
From its inception in 1979, NAMI has been dedicated to improving the lives of individuals and families affected by mental illness.

87 **National Alliance on Mental Illness (NAMI)**
www.nami.org
From its inception in 1979, NAMI has been dedicated to improving the lives of individuals and families affected by mental illness.

88 **National Association For The Dually Diagno Diagnosed (NADD)**
www.thenadd.org
An association for persons with developmental disabilities and mental health needs.

89 **National Association for the Dually Diagnosed (NADD)**
www.thenadd.org
An association for persons with developmental disabilities and mental health needs.

90 **National Institute of Mental Health**
nimh.nih.gov/health/topics/depression
National Institute of Mental Health offers brochures organized by topic. Depression discusses symptoms, diagnosis, and treatment options.

91 **Planetpsych.com**
www.planetpsych.com
Learn about disorders, their treatments and other topics in psychology. Articles are listed under the related topic areas. Ask a therapist a question for free, or view the directory of professionals in your area. If you are a therapist sign up for the directory. Current features, self-help, interactive, and newsletter archives.

92 **Psych Central**
www.psychcentral.com
Personalized one-stop index for psychology, support, and mental health issues, resources, and people on the Internet.

93 **Psychology Information On-Line: Depression**
www.psychologyinfo.com/depression
Information on diagnosis, therapy, and medication.

94 **Psycom**
www.psycom.net/depression

Medication-oriented site. Clearinghouse on all types of depressive disorders.

95 **SAMHSA - Center for Mental Health Services**
www.samhsa.gov
Information about resources, technical assistance, research, training, networks, and other federal clearinghouses, fact sheets and materials.

96 **UT Southwestern Medical Center**
www.utsouthwestern.edu
Research to find the corticosteroid effects on the human brain, dual-diagnosed patients, and depression in asthma patients.

97 **Verywell Mind**
www.verywellmind.com
Provides up-to-date information on mental health topics. mission is to prioritize mental health and promote balance for day to day living. offers over 5,500 online articles that are researched based, and reviwed by medical professionals.
Kristen Altmeyer, MBA, VP & General Manager
Nick Ingalls, MA, Associate Editorial Director

98 **WebMD**
www.webmd.com
Provides credible information, supportive communities, and in-depth reference material about health subjects. A source for original and timely health information as well as material from well known content providers.

99 **Wing of Madness: A Depression Guide**
www.wingofmadness.com
Accurate information, advice, support, and personal experiences.

100 **Yale School of Medicine**
www.med.yale.edu
Research center dedicated to understanding the science of mood disorders.

101 **Yale University School Of Medicine**
www.med.yale.edu
Research center dedicated to understanding the science of mood disorders.

SECTION THREE:
COMMON COMORBIDITIES OF DEPRESSION

ADJUSTMENT DISORDERS

An adjustment disorder (AD) with depressed mood is a mental health condition resulting from the development of emotional or behaviors symptoms within three months of a disturbing or stressful event. The individual with depressed mood may experience feelings of hopelessness, sadness and lack of interest or "low mood" in daily life. It differs from major depressive disorder (MDD). Stressors may include worrying about money, a major disaster, divorce or relationship issues, personal illness or illness of a family member or friend, death of a loved one, a physical move, changing jobs or schools as well as other situations that are difficult to manage. Bereavement is one area that may complicate the difference between AD and MDD and it may require careful watching before a diagnosis is made.

Differentiating adjustment disorder from major depressive disorder requires a medical or mental health professional and a careful assessment of the individual and the presenting symptoms. Diagnosis of an adjustment disorder relies on taking a careful history from the individual experiencing emotional or behavioral symptoms to determine if there has been a known stressor in the three months preceding the presenting symptoms. Symptoms generally improve within six months when the stressor is removed or a diagnosis pointing to another mental health condition that better explains the symptoms is found. A diagnosis of MDD requires at least five symptoms of depression occurring every day, mostly all day for at least two weeks. Symptoms are often a depressed mood or loss of interest or pleasure in all activities.

Treatment interventions are similar for AD and MDD. Medications such as antidepressants or anxiety medications, cognitive behavior therapy (talk therapy) including individual, group and family therapy, or crisis intervention may be combined based on an individualized plan. Medications are less likely to be used in AD, with talk therapy often being quite successful.

Should symptoms of sadness or depression present, especially after a difficult life event, talking to a medical or mental health professional to get a correct diagnosis is important. Managing symptoms is key to better outcomes.

Adjustment Disorders / Agencies & Associations

Agencies & Associations

102 Alive Alone
PO Box 182
Van Wert, OH 45891
alivalon@bright.net
alivealone.org
Alive Alone is a nonprofit organization dedicated to educating and supporting bereaved parents whose children are deceased. Alive Alone provides a self-help network and publishes bimonthly newsletters to help parents with no surviving children to find friendship and healing, resolve their grief, and work towards a positive future.
Kay Bevington, Founder
Rodney Bevington, Founder

103 American Psychiatric Association
800 Maine Avenue SW   202-559-3900
Washington, DC 20024   apa@psych.org
                                         www.psychiatry.org
A medical specialty society representing a growing membership of psychiatrists. Offers information for psychiatrists, medical students, patients and families.
Saul Levin, MD, MPA, FRCP-E, CEO

104 Bereaved Parents of the USA
5 Vanek Road   979-314-4460
Poughkeepsie, NY 12603-5403   bereavedparentsusa.org
BP/USA is a national nonprofit self-help group that offers support, understanding, compassion and hope especially to the newly bereaved, whether they are granparents, parents or siblings.
Lee Boenig, President
Doris Settle Maxwell, Vice President

105 Center for Family Support
2811 Zulette Avenue   718-518-1500
Bronx, NY 10461   svernikoff@cfsny.org
                                         www.cfsny.org
The Center for Family Support offers assistance to individuals with developmental and related disabilities, as well as their families, and provides support services and programs that are designed to accommodate individual needs. Offers services throughout New York City, Westchester County, Long Island, and New Jersey.
Steven Vernikoff, Executive Director
Barbara Greenwald, Chief Operating Officer

106 Center for Mental Health Services (CMHS)
Substance Abuse and Mental Health Services Adminis
5600 Fishers Lane   240-276-1310
Rockville, MD 20857   www.samhsa.gov
Promotes the treatment of mental illness and emotional disorders by increasing accessibility to mental health programs; supporting outreach, treatment, rehabilitation, and support programs and networks; and encouraging the use of scientifically-based information when treating mental disorders. CMHS provides information about mental health via a toll-free number and numerous publications. Developed for users of mental health services and their families, the general public, policy makers, provider
Anita Everett, MD, DFAPA, Director

107 Compassionate Friends, Inc
1000 Jorie Boulevard   630-990-0010
Oak Brook, IL 60523   877-969-0010
                                         nationaloffice@compassionatefriends.org
                                         compassionatefriends.org
Bereavement support for families grieving the death of a child of any age regardless of cause.
Patrick O'Donnell, President
Lisa Corrao, Chief Operating Officer

108 Empty Cradle
31938 Temecula Parkway   619-573-6515
Temecula, CA 92592   info@emptycradle.org
                                         emptycradle.org
A nonprofit peer support group for parents who have experienced the death of a baby. Focusing on parents in the San Diego and Riverside County area, Empty Cradle supports grieving families through educational resources, monthly meetings, and a network of volunteer parents seeking to offer friendship and emotional support.
Rachel Redhouse, Co-President
John Redhouse, Co-President & Treasurer

109 First Candle
21 Locust Avenue   203-966-1300
New Canaan, CT 06840   firstcandle.org
First Candle is a nonprofit organization dedicated to preventing infant death from Sudden Infant Death Syndrome (SIDS), stillbirth, miscarriage, and other Sudden Unexpected Infant Deaths (SUID). First Candle offers support for bereaved families and promotes research, education, and advocacy programs focused on helping all babies to survive.
Alison Jacobson, Chief Executive Officer
Abby Lundy, Director, Development

110 Friends for Survival, Inc.
PO Box 214463   916-392-0664
Sacramento, CA 95821   800-646-7322
                                         info@friendsforsurvival.org
                                         friendsforsurvival.org
A national nonprofit outreach organization open to those who have lost family or friends by suicide, and also to professionals who work with those who have been touched by a suicide tragedy. Dedicated to providing a variety of peer support services that comfort those in grief, encourage healing and growth, foster the development of skills to cope with a loss and educate the entire community regarding the impact of suicide.

111 Grief Recovery After a Substance Passing (GRASP)
11819 N Deerfield Drive   302-492-7717
Dunlap, IL 61614   administrator@grasphelp.org
                                         grasphelp.org
GRASP provides information resources, offers support, and organizes meetings and events for families or individuals who have experienced the death of a loved one as a result of substance abuse or addiction.
Tamara Olt, Executive Director
Darleen Berg, Chair

112 Institute for Contemporary Psychotherapy
33 W 60th St.   212-333-3444
New York, NY 10023   Fax: 212-333-5444
                                         icpnyc.org
The Institute for Contemporary Psychotherapy is a New York City-based mental health treatment and training facility. Consisting of a group of 150 licensed psychotherapists, the Institute focuses on educating the public about the issues surrounding mental health, providing post-graduate training for therapists, and offering therapy at moderate costs.
Ron Taffel, PhD, Chair
Andrea Green-Lewis, LCSW-R, Director of Operations

113 Mental Health America
500 Montgomery Street   703-684-7722
Alexandria, VA 22314   800-969-6642
                                         mhanational.org
Mental Health America is a community-based nonprofit organization committed to enabling the mental wellness of all Americans. MHA advocates for greater access to quality health services and seeks to educate individuals on identifying symptoms, as well as intervention and prevention.
Schroeder Stribling, President & CEO
Sachin Doshi, Sr. Dir., Finance & Operations

114 National Association for the Dually Diagnosed (NADD)
321 Wall Street   845-331-4336
Kingston, NY 12401   info@thenadd.org
                                         thenadd.org
NADD is a nonprofit organization designed to increase awareness of, and provide services for, individuals with developmental disabilities and mental illness. NADD emphasizes the importance of quality mental healthcare for people with mental health needs and offers conferences, information resources, educational programs, and training materials to professionals, parents, and organizations.
Jeanne M. Farr, MA, Chief Executive Officer
Bruce Davis, President

115 National Organization of Parents of Murdered Children
635 West 7th Street   513-721-5683
Cincinnati, OH 45203   Fax: 513-345-4489
                                         natlpomc@pomc.org
                                         pomc.com

Adjustment Disorders / Print Resources

The organization provides ongoing support services for parents of children who were murdered, as well as other survivors, with the goal of helping them to work towards a healthy future. Monthly meetings, newsletters, and court accompaniment are also offered in many areas. This organization offers guidelines for starting local chapters. Parole Block Program and Second Opinion Services are also available.
Connie Sheely, President
Lori King, Vice President

116 **National Share Office**
42 Jackson Street   800-821-6819
Saint Charles, MO 63301   info@nationalshare.org
www.nationalshare.org
Pregnancy and infant loss support.
Sarah Lawrenz, Executive Drirector
Chris Roberdeau, President

117 **Rainbows**
614 Dempster Street   847-952-1770
Evanston, IL 60201   800-266-3206
info@rainbows.org
rainbows.org
Rainbows is an international, nonprofit organization that fosters emotional healing among children grieving a loss from a life-altering crisis. Rainbows believes that grieving youth deserve supporting, loving listeners as they struggle with their feelings. Available to participants of all races and religions. Serves as an advocate for youth who face life-altering crises.
Lisa Micka, Vice Chair
Stephanie Garrity, Executive Director

118 **UNITE, Inc.**
PO Box 298   484-758-0002
Oxford, PA 19363   administrator@unitegriefsupport.org
unitegriefsupport.org
A nonprofit organization committed to providing support services for those who have lost a baby from miscarriage, stillbirth, ectopic pregnancy or early infant death. UNITE, Inc. organizes grief support groups for parents and offers educational programs, training workshops, literature, referrals, and group development assistance.
Barbara Bond-Moury, Board Chairperson
Denise Paul, Group Facilitators Director

119 **United Brain Association**
202-768-8000
info@unitedbrainassociation.org
unitedbrainassociation.org
Non-profit organization that works to find cures through research for over 600 brain and mental health related issues, and disorders.
J.A. Boulton, Founder
Jay Matey, VP & Treasurer

120 **Zur Institute**
321 S. Main Street   833-961-1344
Sebastopol, CA 95472   info@zurinstitute.com
www.zurinstitute.com
Provides quality online continuing education, tools, and services that enhance the ability of psychotherapists, couselors, therapists, social workers, and other health care professionals to meet the needs of those concerned with mental health.
Dr. Ofer Zur, Director

Foundations

121 **M.I.S.S. Foundation/Center for Loss & Trauma**
PO Box 9195   602-279-6477
Austin, TX 78766   888-455-6477
info@missfoundation.org
missfoundation.org
M.I.S.S. Foundation is committed to supporting those who have experienced the death of a child and using research and education to limit the number of child deaths. The Foundation offers ongoing support for families coping with the loss of a child; provides information, newsletters, referrals, support groups, and online chat room support; and participates in legislative issues, advocacy movements,and community events.
Dr. Joanne Cacciatore, PhD., Founder and Chairman
Kelli Montgomery, Executive Director

Support Groups & Hotlines

122 **Center for Family Support**
2811 Zulette Avenue   718-518-1500
Bronx, NY 10461   svernikoff@cfsny.org
www.cfsny.org
The Center for Family Support offers assistance to individuals with developmental and related disabilities, as well as their families, and provides support services and programs that are designed to accommodate individual needs. Offers services throughout New York City, Westchester County, Long Island, and New Jersey.
Steven Vernikoff, Executive Director
Barbara Greenwald, Chief Operating Officer

123 **Grief Recovery After a Substance Passing (GRASP)**
11819 N Deerfield Drive   302-492-7717
Dunlap, IL 61614   administrator@grasphelp.org
grasphelp.org
GRASP provides information resources, offers support, and organizes meetings and events for families or individuals who have experienced the death of a loved one as a result of substance abuse or addiction.
Tamara Olt, Executive Director
Darleen Berg, Chair

124 **Rainbows**
614 Dempster Street   847-952-1770
Evanston, IL 60201   800-266-3206
info@rainbows.org
rainbows.org
Rainbows is an international, nonprofit organization that fosters emotional healing among children grieving a loss from a life-altering crisis. Rainbows believes that grieving youth deserve supporting, loving listeners as they struggle with their feelings. Available to participants of all races and religions. Serves as an advocate for youth who face life-altering crises.
Lisa Micka, Vice Chair
Stephanie Garrity, Executive Director

Print Resources

125 **American Journal of Psychiatry**
American Psychiatric Association Publishing
800 Maine Avenue SW, Suite 900   202-459-9722
Washington, DC 20024   800-368-5777
Fax: 202-403-3094
psychiatryonline@psych.org
ajp.psychiatryonline.org
Official journal of the American Psychiatric Association (APA).
Ned H. Kalin, MD, Editor-in-Chief

126 **American Journal of Psychotherapy**
American Psychiatric Association Publishing
800 Maine Avenue SW, Suite 900   202-459-9722
Washington, DC 20024   800-368-5777
Fax: 202-403-3094
psychiatryonline@psych.org
ajp.psychiatryonline.org
Publishes content that aims to advance the theory, science, and clinical practice of psychotherapy.
Holly A. Swartz, MD, Editor-in-Chief

127 **International Journal of Psychology and Psychoanalysis**
ClinMed International Library
3511 Silverside Road, Suite 105   302-208-7437
Wilmington, DE 19810   contact@clinmedjournals.org
clinmedjournals.org
Open access, peer-reviewed journal focused on cognition, emotions, brain functioning, interpersonal relationships, and the unconscious mind.
Joaquim J.F. Soares, Editor-in-Chief

Adjustment Disorders / Web Sites

128 Journal of Mental Health Research in Intellectual Disabilities (JMHRID)
321 Wall Street
Kingston, NY 12401
845-331-4336
info@thenadd.org
thenadd.org
Quarterly publication designed to promote interest of professional and parent development with resources for individuals who have the coexistence of mental illness and developmental disabilities.
Bruce Davis, President
Jeanne M. Farr, MA, Chief Executive Officer

Web Sites

129 Alive Alone
www.alivealone.org
An organization for the education and charitable purposes to benefit bereaved parents, whose only child or all children are deceased, by providing a self-help network and publications to promote communication and healing, to assist in resolving their grief, and a means to reinvest their lives for a positive future.

130 At Health
www.AtHealth.com
Providing trustworthy online information, tools, and training that enhance the ability of practitioners to furnish high quality, personalized care to those they serve. For mental health consumers, find practitioners, treatment centers, learn about disorders and medications, news and resources.

131 Bereaved Parents Of The Usa (Bp/Usa)
www.bereavedparentsusa.org
Self-help group that offers support, understanding, compassion and hope especially to the newly bereaved be they bereaved parents, grandparents or siblings struggling to rebuild their lives after the death of their children, grandchildren or siblings.

132 Bill Ferguson's How To Divorce As Friends
www.divorceasfriends.com
Articles, Resources, and Support to help minimize conflict in divorce situations.

133 Center For Family Support (Cfs)
www.cfsny.org
Devoted to providing support and assistance to individuals with developmental and related disabilities, and to the family members who care for them.

134 Center For Loss In Multiple Birth (Climb), Inc.
www.climb-support.org
Support by and for parents who have experienced the death of one or more of their twins or higher multiples during pregnance, birth, in infancy, or childhood. Newsletter, information on specialized topics, pen pals, phone support.

135 Compassionate Friends
www.compassionatefriends.org
Organization for those having lost a child.

136 Counseling For Loss And Life Changes, Inc.
www.counselingforloss.com
Offers individual and family counseling services for grieving people.

137 CyberPsych
www.cyberpsych.org
CyberPsych presents information about psychoanalysis, psychotherapy and topics like anxiety disorders, substance abuse, homophobia, and traumas. It hosts mental health organizations and individuals with content of interest to the public and professional communities. There is also a free therapist finder service.

138 Death And Dying Grief Support
www.forums.grieving.com
Information on grief and loss.

139 Divorce Central
www.divorcecentral.com
Offers helpful advice and suggestions on what to expect emotionally, and how to deal with the emotional effects of divorce.

140 Divorce Information
www.divorceinfo.com
Simply written and covers all the issues.

141 Divorce Magazine
www.divorcemag.com
The printed magazine's commercial site.

142 Divorce Support
www.divorcesupport.com
Covers all aspects of divorce.

143 Empty Cradle
www.emptycradle.org
A peer support group for parents who have experienced the loss of baby due to early pregnancy loss, stillbirth or infant death.

144 First Candle
www.firstcandle.org
For those who have suffered the loss of an infant through SIDS.

145 Friends for Survival
www.friendsforsurvival.org
Assisting anyone who has suffered the loss of a loved one through suicide death.

146 Grief And Bereavement
www.psycom.net/depression.central.grief
Helpful information for those grieving from the loss of a loved one.

147 Grief Recovery After A Substance Passing
www.grasphelp.org
Support and advocacy group for parents who have suffered the death of a child due to substance abuse. Provides opportunity for parents to share theri greif and experiences without shame or recrimination. They will provide information and suggestions for those wanting to start a similar group elsewhere.

148 GriefNet
www.griefnet.org
Internet community of persons dealing with grief, death, and major loss.

149 Healing Well
www.healingwell.com
An online health resource guide to medical news, chat, information and articles, newsgroups and message boards, books, disease-related web sites, medical directories, and more for patients, friends, and family coping with disabling diseases, disorders, or chronic illnesses.

150 Health Central
www.healthcentral.com
Find clearly explained, medically accurate information regarding conditions, including an overview, symptoms, causes, diagnostic procedures and treatment options. On this site it is possible to ask questions and get information from a neurologist and connect to people who have similar health interests.

151 Health Finder
www.health.gov
Searchable, carefully developed web site offering information on over 1000 topics. Developed by the US Department of Health and Human Services, thesite can be used in both English and Spanish.

152 Internet Mental Health
www.mentalhealth.com
Offers online psychiatric diagnosis in the hope of reaching the two-thirds of individuals with mental illness who do not seek treatment.

153 Medical News Today
www.medicalnewstody.com
Offers in-depth health information and the latest news in medical research on a wide variety of medical conditions.

154 MedicineNet
www.medicinenet.com
An online resource for consumers providing easy-to-read, authoritative medical and health information.

155 **MedlinePlus**
www.medlineplus.gov
Information regarding a broad range of health, and mental health conditions topics include: Latest news, overview of anatomy and physiology, clinical trials, diagnoses and symptoms, treatment, genetics, plus lots of links to other sites. A service provided by the National Library of Medicine, part of the National Institutes of Health (NIH).

156 **Medscape**
www.medscape.com
Medscape offers specialists, primary care physicians, and other health professionals the Web's most robust and integrated medical information and educational tools.

157 **Mothers In Sympathy And Support (Miss) Foundation**
www.misschildren.org
Provides immediate and ongoing support to grieving families, empowerment through community volunteerism opportunities, public policy and legislative education, and programs to reduce infant and toddler death through research and education.

158 **National Association For The Dually Diagnosed (NADD)**
www.thenadd.org
An association for persons with developmental disabilities and mental health needs.

159 **National Mental Health Consumers' Self-Help Clearinghouse**
www.mhselfhelp.org
Encourages the development and growth of consumer self-help groups.

160 **National Organization of Parents of Murdered Children**
www.pomc.com
Help for anyone who has suffered the loss of a murdered child.

161 **National SHARE Office**
www.nationalshare.org
Pregnancy and infant loss support.

162 **PlanetPsych**
www.planetpsych.com
Learn about disorders, their treatments and other topics in psychology. Articles are listed under the related topic areas. Ask a therapist a question for free, or view the directory of professionals in your area. If you are a therapist sign up for the directory. Current features, self-help, interactive, and newsletter archives.

163 **Psych Central**
www.psychcentral.com
Personalized one-stop index for psychology, support, and mental health issues, resources, and people on the Internet.

164 **Rainbows**
www.rainbows.org
Group for grieving parents and children.

165 **Relationship Learning Center**
www.relationshipjourney.com
Marriage and relationship counseling and information.

166 **Safe Crossings Foundation**
www.safecrossingsfoundation.org
For children facing a loved one's death.

167 **Shared Parenting Information Group (SPIG)**
www.spig.clara.net/guidline.html
Useful information that helps to decrease the stress associated with separation.

168 **Substance Abuse And Mental Health Services Administration**
www.store.samhsa.gov
Resources on mental disorders as well as treatment and recovery.

169 **Unite, Inc.**
www.unitegriefsupport.org
Grief support after miscarriage, stillbirth and infant death.

170 **Verywell Mind**
www.verywellmind.com
Provides up-to-date information on mental health topics. mission is to prioritize mental health and promote balance for day to day living. offers over 5,500 online articles that are researched based, and reviwed by medical professionals.
Kristen Altmeyer, MBA, VP & General Manager
Nick Ingalls, MA, Associate Editorial Director

171 **WebMD**
www.webmd.com
Provides credible information, supportive communities, and in-depth reference material about health subjects. A source for original and timely health information as well as material from well known content providers.

172 **Widownet**
www.widownet.org
Online information and self-help resource for, and by, widows and widowers. Topics covered include grief, bereavement, recovery, and other information helpful to people who have suffered the death of a spouse or life partner.

AGING

Depression is the most common psychological illness among the elderly. Depression is a serious illness that can affect individuals of all ages including the geriatric population. Untreated depression in the elderly negatively impacts emotional, social, and medical functioning. Depression is not a normal part of aging, but rather a treatable medical condition. A variety of factors contribute to depression in the elderly. The presence of depression in the geriatric population often varies by setting with almost five percent occurring in the community setting, approximately 13 percent in those requiring home healthcare, but increasing to almost 15 percent in long-term care facilities. Admissions to psychiatric acute care facilities in the United States in older adults may be due to depressive disorders in almost half of all individuals admitted.

The diagnosis of depression in the aging population is complicated by a variety of factors. Chronic medical conditions such as Parkinson's Disease or Stroke, Alzheimer's Disease and dementias, and medication interactions and side effects may all make diagnosis more difficult. About 80 percent of older adults have at least one chronic health condition, and half have two or more. Because chronic illness becomes the focus of medical care, the depressive state may be missed or assumed to just be a normal reaction to a diagnosis of chronic illness. Often discussions with family and caregivers are important to recognize changes in behavior that might not be seen as the focus on physiological issues takes precedence.

Geriatric depressive disorders may result from decreases in financial and family resources, social isolation due to age, and physical limitations due to chronic health issues. Major life events such as death of a spouse, friends or family; divorce, living alone, childlessness, stress, and lack of quality interpersonal interactions may all create a climate for depression to develop. Treatment is helpful.

Counseling and psychological therapies are useful in treating depression in the older adult. Modifying thoughts and behaviors contributing to the depression through cognitive-behavioral therapy with mental health professionals is supported by research. Support groups are useful in both treating depressive symptoms but also in providing a social outlet. Counseling and support groups may also be used with medications designed to enhance the quality of life in the older individual with depression.

Medical and mental health professionals should carefully examine the mood and activity level of patients presenting with both normal aging and chronic medical conditions that may contribute to the development of depression.

Aging / Agencies & Associations

Agencies & Associations

173   **ABA Commission on Law and Aging**
1050 Connecticut Avenue N.W.   202-662-8690
Washington, DC 20036   Fax: 202-662-8698
aging@americanbar.org
www.americanbar.org/aging
The Commission examines the issues that affect the elderly as victims of abuse, dispute resolution, international rights, medicare, voting, health care decision-making and other issues arising from the aging prisons populations.
Robyn S. Shapiro, Chair
Lisa P. Gwyther, Commissioner

174   **Academy for Gerontology in Higher Education**
1220 L Street NW   202-842-1275
Washington, DC 20005   membership@geron.org
www.aghe.org
Membership organization comprised of more than 60 institutional members that offer education and research program in the field of aging. Affiliated with the Gerontological Society of America.
Joann Montepare, Society Chair

175   **American Association of Caregiving Youth**
6401 Congress Avenue   561-391-7401
Boca Raton, FL 33487   800-508-9618
info@aacy.org
www.aacy.org
Seeks to raise awareness of and provide services for youth who act as caregivers for their parents and grandparents.
Connie Siskowski, RN, PhD, President

176   **American Association of Retired Persons**
601 E Street NW   202-434-3525
Washington, DC 20049   888-687-2277
TTY: 877-434-7598
member@aarp.org
www.aarp.org
AARP is the nation's leading organization for people aged 50 and older. It serves their needs and interests through information and education, advocacy and community services provided by a network of local chapters and experienced volunteers.
Jo Ann Jenkins, Chief Executive Officer
Scott Frisch, Executive Vice President & COO

177   **Canadian National Seniors Council**
140 Promenade du Portage   800-622-6232
Gatineau, Quebec, K1A   TTY: 800-926-9105
canada.ca/en/national-seniors-council
The council works with older Canadians, stakeholders and experts to advise the Canadian government on matters relating to the health, well-being and quality of life of seniors.
Nora Spinks, Chair

178   **Children of Aging Parents**
PO Box 167   215-355-6611
Richboro, PA 18954   800-227-7294
Fax: 215-355-6824
info@caps4caregivers.org
www.caps4caregivers.org
A nonprofit, charitable organization that assists the nation's nearly 54 million caregivers of the elderly or chronically ill with reliable information, referrals and support, and to heighten public awareness.

179   **Commission on Accreditation of Rehabilitation Facilities**
6951 E Southpoint Road   520-325-1044
Tucson, AZ 85756   888-281-6531
Fax: 520-318-1129
www.carf.org
CARF reviews and grants accreditation services nationally and internationally at the request of a facility or program. Standards are applied to service areas and business practices, and accreditation is ongoing in an effort to encourage service providers to continuously improve services. The CARF group also includes CARF Canada and CARF Europe.
Brian J. Boon, PhD, President & CEO
Jed Johnson, Managing Director, Aging Services

180   **Family Caregiver Alliance/National Center on Caregiving**
101 Montgomery Street   415-434-3388
San Francisco, CA 94104   800-445-8106
www.caregiver.org
Provides caregiver information and assistance via phone or e-mail, as well as fact sheets and publications describing and documenting caregiver needs and services.
Kathleen Kelly, Executive Director
Leah Eskenazi, Director, Operations & Planning

181   **Gerontological Society of America**
1220 L Street NW   202-842-1275
Washington, DC 20005   membership@geron.org
www.geron.org
Nonprofit professional organization with more than 5,500 members in the field of aging. Provides researchers, educators, practitioners and policy makers with opportunities to understand, advance, integrate and use basic and applied research on aging populations. Also runs the National Adult Vaccination Program (www.navp.org).
James Appleby, Chief Executive Officer
Karen Tracy, VP, Strategic Alliances & Communications

182   **Good Shepherd Homecare & Hospice**
3801 Vanesta Drive   785-537-0688
Manhattan, KS 66503   Fax: 785-537-1309
info@hcandh.org
www.goodshepherdhh.org
Aims to be the premier non-profit Homecare & Hospice provider of compassionate, affordable health, wellness and support services.

183   **Goodwill Industries International, Inc.**
15810 Indianola Drive   800-466-3945
Rockville, MD 20855   contactus@goodwill.org
www.goodwill.org
A nonprofit, community-based organization whose mission is to help people achieve self-sufficiency through the dignity and power of work, serving people who are disadvantaged, disabled or elderly. The mission is accomplished through providing independent living skills, affordable housing, and training and placement in community employment. The GoodWill Network includes 160 independent, local locations across the U.S. and Canada.
Ned Helms, Chair
Steven C. Preston, President & CEO

184   **Goodwill Industries-Suncoast**
10596 Gandy Boulevard   727-523-1512
St. Petersburg, FL 33702   888-279-1988
TTY: 727-579-1068
www.goodwill-suncoast.org
A nonprofit, community-based organization whose mission is to help people achieve self-sufficiency through the dignity and power of work, serving people who are disadvantaged, disabled or elderly. The mission is accomplished through providing independent living skills, affordable housing, and training and placement in community employment.
Heather Ceresoli, CPA, Chair
Deborah A. Passerini, President & CEO

185   **Heart Touch Project**
3400 Airport Avenue   310-391-2558
Santa Monica, CA 90405   Fax: 310-391-2168
www.hearttouch.org
Non-profit, educational and service organization devoted to the delivery of compassionate and healing touch to home or hospital-bound men, women, and children.
Shawnee Isaac Smith, Co-Founder
Rene Russo, Co-Founder

186   **Institute for Life Course and Aging**
University of Toronto
246 Bloor Street W.   416-978-0377
Toronto, Ontario, M5S   aging@utoronto.ca
www.grandparentfamily.com
The Institute is a research center under the auspices of the Faculty of Social Work at the University of Toronto.
Prof. Esme Fuller-Thomson, Director
Iulia Park, Program Coordinator

Aging / Agencies & Associations

187 **International Federation on Ageing**
1 Bridgepoint Drive
Toronto, Ontario, M4M
416-342-1655
Fax: 416-639-2165
jbarratt@ifa-fiv.org
www.ifa-fiv.org
The IFA seeks to inform, educate and promote policies and practice to improve the quality of life of older persons around the world.
Greg Shaw, Director, Int'l & Corporate Relations
Jane Barratt, Secretary General

188 **Leading Age**
2519 Connecticut Avenue NW
Washington, DC 20008
202-783-2242
info@LeadingAge.org
www.leadingage.org
National association of more than 5,000 nonprofit nursing homes, continuing care retirement communities, independent living centers, and community service providers.
Katie Smith Sloan, President & CEO
Janine Finck-Boyle, Vice President, Health Policy

189 **Legal Council for Health Justice**
17 N State Street
Chicago, IL 60602
312-427-8990
Fax: 312-427-8419
legalcouncil.org
Provides legal advice and services for persons who are HIV positive or have AIDS, as well as their families. Also serves individuals with disabilities and chronic illnesses, senior citizens, and the homeless.
Tom Yates, Executive Director
Ruth Edwards, Senior Director, Program Services

190 **Mental Health America**
500 Montgomery Street
Alexandria, VA 22314
703-684-7722
800-969-6642
mhanational.org
Mental Health America is a community-based nonprofit organization committed to enabling the mental wellness of all Americans. MHA advocates for greater access to quality health services and seeks to educate individuals on identifying symptoms, as well as intervention and prevention.
Schroeder Stribling, President & CEO
Sachin Doshi, Sr. Dir., Finance & Operations

191 **National Adult Day Services Association**
11350 Random Hills Road
Fairfax, VA 22030
877-745-1440
info@nadsa.org
www.nadsa.org
Aims to be the leading voice of the Adult Day Services industry, representing providers, associations of providers, corporations, educators, students, and retired workers.
Donna Hale, Executive Director & CEO
Lance Roberts, Sr. Director, Membership & Education

192 **National Alliance for Caregiving**
1730 Rhode Island Ave. NW
Washington, DC 20036
202-918-1013
Fax: 202-918-1014
info@caregiving.org
www.caregiving.org
Advocates on behalf of caregivers, as well as conducting research and offering support services.
Jason Resendez, President & CEO
Patrice A. Heinz, Chief Operating Officer

193 **National Council on Aging**
251 18th Street S.
Arlington, VA 22202
info@ncoa.org
www.ncoa.org
The nation's first charitable organization dedicated to promoting the dignity, independence, well-being and contributions of older Americans. The council has a goal of improving the health and economic well-being of 40 million older adults by 2030.
Ramsay Alwin, President & CEO
Alfreda Davis, Chief of Staff

194 **National Hospice & Palliative Care Organization (NHPCO)**
1731 King Street
Alexandria, VA 22314
703-837-1500
Fax: 703-837-1233
www.nhpco.org
The organization seeks to improve end-of-life care, widen access to hospice care, and improve quality of life for the dying and their loved ones.
Ben Marcantonio, COO & Interim CEO
Caleb Tiller, VP, Marketing, Comms. & Membership

195 **National Institute on Aging**
31 Center Drive, MSC 2292
Bethesda, MD 20892
800-222-2225
TTY: 800-222-4225
niaic@nia.nih.gov
www.nia.nih.gov
Seeks to understand the nature of aging, and to extend healthy, active years of life. Free resources are available on topics such as Alzheimer's & dimentia, caregiving, cognitive heath, end of life care, and more.
Richard J. Hodes, MD, Director
Amy Kelley, MD, MSHS, Deputy Director

196 **National Seniors Council**
1100 North Glebe Road
Arlington, VA 22201
571-425-4153
nationalseniorscouncil.org
The council seeks to serve the needs of the new generation of retirees, as an alternative to organizations such as the AARP.
Carole Rhodes, National Director

197 **Senior Resource LLC**
122 C St NW
Washington, DC 20001
888-219-4747
www.seniorresource.com
The company operates Seniorresource.com, which provides information to older adults on needed facilities and services, including through internet directories and an archive of E-zines.

198 **US Administration on Aging**
330 C Street SW
Washington, DC 20201
202-401-4634
aclinfo@acl.hhs.gov
acl.gov/about-acl/administration-aging
The Administration on Aging, an agency in the US Department of Health and Human Services, and under the Administration for Community Living, is one of the nation's largest providers of home and community-based care for older persons and their caregivers.
Alison Barkoff, Acting Administrator & Asst. Secretary
Kelly Cronin, Deputy Administrator

Alabama

199 **AARP Alabama**
400 South Union Street
Montgomery, AL 36104
866-542-8167
alaarp@aarp.org
states.aarp.org/region/alabama
Provides information, events, news, and resources to Alabamians over 50 years of age, and to a membership of over 430,000.
Candi Williams, State Director
Lisa Billingsley, Senior Operations Administrator

Alaska

200 **AARP Alaska**
3601 C Street
Anchorage, AK 99503
866-227-7447
Fax: 907-341-2270
ak@aarp.org
states.aarp.org/region/alaska
Serves 82,000 members in Alaska, providing information, resources, news, and advocacy on matters relevant to individuals aged 50 years and older.
Ken Helander, Advocacy Director
Ann Secrest, Media Contact

Arizona

201 **AARP Arizona**
7250 N 16th Street
Phoenix, AZ 85020
866-389-5649
aarpaz@aarp.org
states.aarp.org/region/arizona
The chapter seeks to enhance the quality of life for all Arizonans, with an emphasis on individuals 50 years and older.
Maria Ramirez-Trillo, Associate State Director
David Parra Luna, Director, Community Outreach

Aging / Agencies & Associations

Arkansas

202   **AARP Arkansas**
1701 Centerview Drive   866-544-5379
Little Rock, AR 72211   Fax: 501-227-7710
araarp@aarp.org
states.aarp.org/region/arkansas
Seeks to redefine and improve life for Arkansans over the age of 50.
Ashley McBride, State President

California

203   **AARP California: Pasadena**
200 S Los Robles Avenue   866-448-3614
Pasadena, CA 91101   Fax: 626-583-8500
caaarp@aarp.org
states.aarp.org/region/california
Provides news, tools, resources, and research to Californians 50 years and older.
Joe Garbanzos, State President
Marisa Guzzardo, Edia Contact, Southern California

204   **AARP California: Sacramento**
1415 L Street   866-448-3614
Sacramento, CA 95814   Fax: 916-446-2223
caaarp@aarp.org
states.aarp.org/region/california
Provides news, tools, resources, and research to Californians 50 years and older.
Joe Garbanzos, State President
Mark Beach, Media Contact, Northern California

Colorado

205   **AARP Colorado**
303 E 17th Avenue   866-554-5376
Denver, CO 80203   Fax: 303-764-5999
coaarp@aarp.org
states.aarp.org/region/colorado
The Colorado chapter seeks to keep Coloradans 50 years and older informed, engaged, and active.
Sara Schueneman, State Director
Angela Cortez, Media Contact

Connecticut

206   **AARP Connecticut**
21 Oak Street   866-295-7279
Hartford, CT 06106   ctaarp@aarp.org
states.aarp.org/region/connecticut
With nearly 600,000 members, the chapter provides recent news, information, and events for residents of Connecticut who are 50 years and older, as well as advocating for positive social change.
Nora Duncan, State Director
Anna Doroghazi, Assoc. State Dir., Advocacy & Outreach

Delaware

207   **AARP Delaware**
222 Delaware Avenue   302-498-6511
Wilmington, DE 19801   866-227-7441
kiapalucci@aarp.org
states.aarp.org/region/delaware
Provides news, advocacy, education, and lifestyle information for residents of Delaware who are 50 years and older.
Lucretia Young, State Director
Kimberly Iapalucci, Media Contact

Florida

208   **AARP Florida: Doral**
3750 Nw 87th Avenue   866-595-7678
Doral, FL 33178   Fax: 786-804-4544
flaarp@aarp.org
states.aarp.org/region/florida
The chapter provides information, research, and events to 2.8 million members, and Floridians 50 years and older.
Ken Thomas, State President
Jamie Champion Mongiovi, Director, Communications

209   **AARP Florida: St. Petersburg**
360 Central Avenue   866-595-7678
St. Petersburg, FL 33701   Fax: 727-369-5191
flaarp@aarp.org
states.aarp.org/region/florida
The chapter provides information, research, and events to 2.8 million members, and Floridians 50 years and older.
Ken Thomas, State President
Jamie Champion Mongiovi, Director, Communications

210   **AARP Florida: Tallahassee**
215 S Monroe St   850-577-5160
Tallahassee, FL 32301   flaarp@aarp.org
states.aarp.org/region/florida
The chapter provides information, research, and events to 2.8 million members, and Floridians 50 years and older.
Ken Thomas, State President
Jamie Champion Mongiovi, Director, Communications

Georgia

211   **AARP Georgia**
999 Peachtree Street NE   866-295-7281
Atlanta, GA 30309   Fax: 404-815-7940
gaaarp@aarp.org
states.aarp.org/region/georgia
The chapter strives to help Georgians 50 years and older.
Debra Tyler-Horton, State Director
Alisa Jackson, Media Contact

Hawaii

212   **AARP Hawaii**
1001 Bishop Street   866-295-7282
Honolulu, HI 96813   Fax: 808-537-2288
hiaarp@aarp.org
states.aarp.org/region/hawaii
With 150,000 members, the chapter advocates at the state level, and provides information, resources, and volunteer opportunities.
Audrey Suga-Nakagawa, Director, Advocacy

Idaho

213   **AARP Idaho**
250 S 5th Street   866-295-7284
Boise, ID 83702   Fax: 208-288-4424
aarpid@aarp.org
states.aarp.org/region/idaho
The chapter advocates for and seeks to improve the lives of residents aged 50 years and older.
Lupe Wissel, State Director
Randy Simon, Media Contact

Illinois

214   **AARP Illinois: Chicago**
222 N LaSalle Street   866-448-3613
Chicago, IL 60601   Fax: 312-372-2204
aarpil@aarp.org
states.aarp.org/region/illinois
Advocates for and provides recent news, events, and lifestyle tips to Illinois residents aged 50 years and older.
Philippe Largent, State Director
Dina Anderson, Media Contact

215   **AARP Illinois: Springfield**
300 W Edwards Street   866-448-3613
Springfield, IL 62704   Fax: 217-522-7803
aarpil@aarp.org
states.aarp.org/region/illinois
Legislative office of the Illinois chapter.
Philippe Largent, State Director
Dina Anderson, Media Contact

Aging / Agencies & Associations

Indiana

216 **AARP Indiana**
One N Capitol Avenue
Indianapolis, IN 46204
866-448-3618
Fax: 317-423-2211
inaarp@aarp.org
states.aarp.org/region/indiana
The chapter seeks to improve life for residents of Indiana aged 50 years and older.
Sarah Waddle, State Director
Jason Tomcsi, Media Contact

Iowa

217 **AARP Iowa**
600 E Court Avenue
Des Moines, IA 50309
866-554-5378
Fax: 515-244-7767
ia@aarp.org
states.aarp.org/region/iowa
Provides news, information, and resources to Iowans aged 50 years and older.
Brad Anderson, State Director
Jeremy Barewin, Media Contact

Kansas

218 **AARP Kansas**
6220 SW 29th Street
Topeka, KS 66614
866-448-3619
Fax: 785-232-1465
ksaarp@aarp.org
states.aarp.org/region/kansas
The chapter provides news, events, and more to Kansans aged 50 years and older.
Maren Turner, Kansas AARP State Media Relations
Mary Tritsch, Media Contact

Kentucky

219 **AARP Kentucky**
10401 Linn Station Road
Louisville, KY 40223
866-295-7275
kyaarp@aarp.org
states.aarp.org/region/kentucky
Provides news and resources for Kentuckians over the age of 50.
Scott Wagenast, Associate State Director

Louisiana

220 **AARP Louisiana: Baton Rouge**
301 Main Street
Baton Rouge, LA 70825
866-448-3620
la@aarp.org
states.aarp.org/region/louisiana
The office seeks to advocate for and provide resources to residents of Louisiana aged 50 and over.
Denise Bottcher, State Director
Andrew Muhl, Director, Advocacy

221 **AARP Louisiana: New Orleans**
3502 S Carrollton Avenue
New Orleans, LA 70118
866-448-3620
la@aarp.org
states.aarp.org/region/louisiana
AARP Louisiana's Community Resource Center.
Denise Bottcher, State Director
Andrew Muhl, Director, Advocacy

Maine

222 **AARP Maine**
53 Baxter Boulevard
Portland, ME 04101
866-554-5380
me@aarp.org
states.aarp.org/region/maine
Seeks to enhance the lives of Mainers aged 50 years and over through advocacy, information sharing, volunteer opportunities, and service. The chapter counts 230,000 members.
Noel Bonam, State Director
Jane Margesson, Director, Communications

Maryland

223 **AARP Maryland**
One Park Place
Annapolis, MD 21401
866-542-8163
Fax: 410-837-0269
md@aarp.org
states.aarp.org/region/maryland
The chapter seeks to enhance the lives of Maryland residents aged 50 and over, as well as caregivers, through resources and a variety of social opportunities.
Jim Campbell, State President
Nancy Carr, Assoc. State Director, Communications

Massachusetts

224 **AARP Massachusetts**
1 Beacon Street
Boston, MA 02108
866-448-3621
Fax: 617-723-4224
ma@aarp.org
states.aarp.org/region/massachusetts
Provides news, events, and resources to Massachusetts residents aged 50 and over.
Mike Festa, State Director
Cindy Campbell, Director, Communications

Michigan

225 **AARP Michigan**
309 N Washington Square
Lansing, MI 48933
866-227-7448
Fax: 517-482-2794
miaarp@aarp.org
states.aarp.org/region/michigan
The chapter seeks to enhance the quality of life for aging residents of Michigan through information, advocacy, and services.
Paula D. Cunningham, State Director

Minnesota

226 **AARP Minnesota**
1919 University Avenue
St. Paul, MN 55104
866-554-5381
aarpmn@aarp.org
states.aarp.org/region/minnesota
Aims to connect aging residents of Minnesota with financial and other resources to enhance quality of life.
Cathy Corkill McLeer, State Director
Erin Parrish, Associate State Director, Advocacy

Mississippi

227 **AARP Mississippi**
141 Township Avenue
Ridgeland, MS 39157
866-554-5382
Fax: 601-898-5429
msaarp@aarp.org
states.aarp.org/region/mississippi
Seeks to improve the lives of Mississippians, particularly those over 50 years of age, through events, news, resources, and advocacy.
Kimberly L. Camobell, Esq, State Director
Ronda Gooden, Media Contact

Missouri

228 **AARP Missouri**
9200 Ward Parkway
Kansas City, MO 64114
866-389-5627
Fax: 816-561-3107
aarpmo@aarp.org
states.aarp.org/region/missouri
Provides information to Missourians aged 50 and over on health, finances, and lifestyle, as well as providing advocacy.
Craig Eichelman, State Director
Jamayla Long, Media Contact

Montana

229 **AARP Montana**
30 W 14th Street
Helena, MT 59601
866-295-7278
mtaarp@aarp.org
states.aarp.org/region/montana

413

Aging / Agencies & Associations

With 135,000 members, the chapter provides advocacy, education, information, resources, and collaborative projects for Montana residents aged 50 and over.
Tim Summers, State Director
Stacia Dahl, Media Contact

Nebraska

230 AARP Nebraska: Lincoln
301 S 13th Street
Lincoln, NE 68508
866-389-5651
Fax: 402-323-6908
neaarp@aarp.org
states.aarp.org/region/nebraska

Works on behalf of over 200,000 members and their families to provide news, services, information, resources, and advocacy for individuals 50 years and older.
Suzan DeCamp, AARP Nebraska State President
Devorah Lanner, Media Contact

231 AARP Nebraska: Omaha
1941 S 42nd Street
Omaha, NE 68105
402-398-9568
omnebraska@aol.com
states.aarp.org/region/nebraska

AARP Nebraska's Information Center.
Suzan DeCamp, AARP Nebraska State President
Devorah Lanner, Media Contact

Nevada

232 AARP Nevada
5820 S Eastern Avenue
Las Vegas, NV 89119
866-389-5652
aarpnv@aarp.org
states.aarp.org/region/nevada

Provides news, information, and resources to 320,000 members, on matters affecting the lives of individuals aged 50 and over.
Maria Dent, State Director
Scott Gulbransen, Media Contact

New Hampshire

233 AARP New Hampshire
45 South Main Street
Concord, NH 03301
866-542-8168
Fax: 603-224-6211
nh@aarp.org
states.aarp.org/region/new-hampshire

Provides information, resources, and advocacy services to 228,000 members, on matters relevant to individuals aged 50 years and older.
Christina FitzPatrick, State Director

New Jersey

234 AARP New Jersey
303 George Street
New Brunswick, NJ 08901
866-542-8165
Fax: 609-987-4634
aarpnJ@aarp.org
states.aarp.org/region/new-jersey

The chapter seeks to educate and advocate for New Jersey residents aged 50 and over, and their families.
Stephanie Hunsinger, State Director

New Mexico

235 AARP New Mexico
535 Cerrillos Road
Santa Fe, NM 87501
866-389-5636
Fax: 505-820-2889
aarpnm@aarp.org
states.aarp.org/region/new-mexico

The chapter advocates on behalf of individuals 50 years and older, monitoring seniors' services, utility rates, transportation services, as well as providing financial planning services to members.
Joseph P. Sanchez, State Director

New York

236 AARP New York: Albany
1 Commerce Plaza
Albany, NY 12260
866-227-7442
nyaarp@aarp.org
states.aarp.org/region/new-york

Provides information, resources, news, and advocacy services to residents of New York who are 50 years and older.
James O'Neal, State President
Erik Kriss, Media Contact

237 AARP New York: New York City
750 Third Avenue
New York, NY 10017
866-227-7442
nyaarp@aarp.org
states.aarp.org/region/new-york

Provides information, resources, news, and advocacy services to residents of New York who are 50 years and older.
James O'Neal, State President
Erik Kriss, Media Contact

238 AARP New York: Rochester
435 E Henrietta Road
Rochester, NY 14620
866-227-7442
nyaarp@aarp.org
states.aarp.org/region/new-york

Provides information, resources, news, and advocacy services to residents of New York who are 50 years and older.
James O'Neal, State President
Erik Kriss, Media Contact

North Carolina

239 AARP North Carolina
5511 Capital Center Drive
Raleigh, NC 27606
866-389-5650
ddickerson@aarp.org
states.aarp.org/region/north-carolina

Advocates for community issues such as health care, employment/income security, retirement planning, utilities, and protection from financial abuse, on behalf of a membership 1.1 million strong.
Michael Oldender, State Director
Audrey Galloway, Manager, Outreach & Federal Advocacy

North Dakota

240 AARP North Dakota
107 W Main Avenue
Bismarck, ND 58501
866-554-5383
Fax: 701-255-2242
aarpnd@aarp.org
states.aarp.org/region/north-dakota

Provides news, information, resources, events, advocacy, and more to North Dakotans aged 50 and over.
Josh Askvig, State Director
Doreen Riedman, Assoc. State Dir., Community Outreach

Ohio

241 AARP Ohio
17 S High Street
Columbus, OH 43215
866-389-5653
Fax: 614-224-9801
ohaarp@aarp.org
states.aarp.org/region/ohio

The chapter shares information, advocates, and performs community services for 1.5 million members, 50 years and older, across the state.
Holly Holtzen, State Director

Oklahoma

242 AARP Oklahoma
126 N Bryant Avenue
Edmond, OK 73034
866-295-7277
Fax: 405-844-7772
ok@aarp.org
states.aarp.org/region/oklahoma

Assists individuals aged 50 and over through advocacy, news, information, resources, and more.
Sean Voskuhl, State Director

Oregon

243 AARP Oregon
1455 SW Portland
Portland, OR 97201
866-554-5360
oraarp@aarp.org
states.aarp.org/region/oregon

Aging / Agencies & Associations

Strives for social change for its 500,000 members, and all individuals 50 years and over, through advocacy and community services.
Bandana Shrestha, State Director
Joyce DeMonnin, Media Contact

Pennsylvania

244 **AARP Pennsylvania: Harrisburg**
30 N 3rd Street 866-389-5654
Harrisburg, PA 17101 Fax: 717-236-4078
aarpa@aarp.org
states.aarp.org/region/pennsylvania
Seeks to enhance the quality of life for 1.8 million members across the state.
Bill Johnston-Walsh, State Director
Steve Gardner, Media Contact

245 **AARP Pennsylvania: Philadelphia**
1650 Market Street 866-389-5654
Philadelphia, PA 19103 Fax: 215-665-8529
aarpa@aarp.org
states.aarp.org/region/pennsylvania
Seeks to enhance the quality of life for 1.8 million members across the state.
Nora Dowd Eisenhower, State Director

Rhode Island

246 **AARP Rhode Island**
10 Orms Street 866-542-8170
Providence, RI 02904 Fax: 401-272-0596
ri@aarp.org
states.aarp.org/region/rhode-island
Provides news, information, resources, advocacy, and community services to those aged 50 and older in the state.
Catherine Taylor, State Director
John Martin, Director, Communications

South Carolina

247 **AARP South Carolina**
2101 Main St 803-765-7381
Columbia, SC 29201 866-389-5655
scaarp@aarp.org
states.aarp.org/region/south-carolina
Seeks to enhance the quality of life for members and individuals aged 50 and older, through information, resources, education, advocacy, and more.
Fuller Cooper, State Director
Nikki Hutchison, Associate State Director, Advocacy

South Dakota

248 **AARP South Dakota**
5101 S Nevada Avenue 866-542-8172
Sioux Falls, SD 57108 sdaarp@aarp.org
states.aarp.org/region/south-dakota
Provides news, information, resources, advocacy, and community services to 110,000 members and those aged 50 and older in the state.
Erik Gaikowski, State Director

Tennessee

249 **AARP Tennessee**
5000 Meridian Blvd. 866-295-7274
Franklin, TN 37067 tnaarp@aarp.org
states.aarp.org/region/tennessee
Strives for positive social change for 660,000 members and individuals aged 50 and over.
Mia McNeil, State Director
Rob Naylor, Director, Communications

Texas

250 **AARP Texas: Austin**
1905 Aldrich Street 866-227-7443
Austin, TX 78723 states.aarp.org/region/texas
The chapter offers news, information, research, and events for individuals aged 50 and over, as well as conducting advocacy on their behalf.
Tina Tran, State Director
Mark Hollis, Associate State Director, Communications

251 **AARP Texas: Dallas**
8140 Walnut Hill Lane 866-227-7443
Dallas, TX 75231 states.aarp.org/region/texas
The chapter offers news, information, research, and events for individuals aged 50 and over, as well as conducting advocacy on their behalf.
Tina Tran, State Director
Mark Hollis, Associate State Director, Communications

252 **AARP Texas: Houston**
2323 S Shepherd Drive 866-227-7443
Houston, TX 77019 states.aarp.org/region/texas
The chapter offers news, information, research, and events for individuals aged 50 and over, as well as conducting advocacy on their behalf.
Tina Tran, State Director
Mark Hollis, Associate State Director, Communications

253 **AARP Texas: San Antonio**
1314 Guadalupe Street 866-227-7443
San Antonio, TX 78207 states.aarp.org/region/texas
The chapter offers news, information, research, and events for individuals aged 50 and over, as well as conducting advocacy on their behalf.
Lisa Rodriguez, State Director
Ismael Herrera, Associate State Director, Outreach

Utah

254 **AARP Utah**
6975 Union Park Center 866-448-3616
Midvale, UT 84047 Fax: 801-561-2209
utaarp@aarp.org
states.aarp.org/region/utah
Serves 211,000 members in 10 regions across the state, with advocacy, communications, programming, and outreach.
Tim Summers, State Director
Danny Harris, Director, Advocacy

Vermont

255 **AARP Vermont**
199 Main Street 866-227-7451
Burlington, VT 05401 Fax: 802-651-9805
vtaarp@aarp.org
states.aarp.org/region/vermont
Seeks to represent the concerns and interests of Vermonters aged 50 and over.
Greg Marchildon, State Director

Virginia

256 **AARP Virginia**
901 E Byrd St 866-542-8164
Richmond, VA 23219 Fax: 804-819-1923
vaaarp@aarp.org
states.aarp.org/region/virginia
Serves Virginians aged 50 and older, and their families, through advocacy, information, resources, and outreach.
Jim Dau, State Director

Washington

257 **AARP D.C.**
100 M Street SE 866-554-5384
Washington, DC 20003 Fax: 202-434-7946
dcaarp@aarp.org
states.aarp.org/region/washington-dc
Provides information, advocacy, and a variety of services to 87,000 members aged 50 and over.
Louis Davis, Jr., State Director
Peter Rankin, Associate State Director, Advocacy

Aging / Foundations

258   **AARP Washington**
18000 International Blvd.
SeaTac, WA 98188
866-227-7457
Fax: 206-517-9350
waaarp@aarp.org
states.aarp.org/region/washington
Serves 900,000 members through information, advocacy, and a variety of services.
Marguerite Ro, State Director

West Virginia

259   **AARP West Virginia**
300 Summers Street
Charleston, WV 25301
866-227-7458
Fax: 304-344-4633
wvaarp@aarp.org
states.aarp.org/region/west-virginia
Provides information, resources, advocacy, and more to individuals aged 50 and over in West Virginia.
Gaylene Miller, State Director
Tom Hunter, Associate State Director, Communications

Wisconsin

260   **AARP Wisconsin**
222 W Washington Avenue
Madison, WI 53703
866-448-3611
Fax: 608-251-7612
wistate@aarp.org
states.aarp.org/region/wisconsin
The chapter advocates for, and provides a variety of services to, its 840,000 members, aged 50 years and over.
Martha Cranley, State Director
Jim Flaherty, Media Contact

Wyoming

261   **AARP Wyoming**
1800 Carey Ave
Cheyenne, WY 82001
866-663-3290
wyaarp@aarp.org
states.aarp.org/region/wyoming
Provides resources, information, and advocates for indviduals in Wyoming aged 50 and older, with an emphasis on health care, retirement, and utility issues.
Stella Montano, State Director
Tom Lacock, Assoc. State Dir., Advocacy & Comm.

Foundations

262   **AARP Foundation**
American Association of Retired Persons
601 E Street NW
Washington, DC 20049
202-434-3525
888-687-2277
TTY: 877-434-7598
www.aarp.org/aarp-foundation
The foundation seeks to assist seniors living in poverty through economic opportunities and social connectedness. Legal services and grants are also offered.
Claire Casey, President

263   **Aging In America**
2975 Westchester Avenue
Purchase, NY 10577
914-205-5030
contact@aginginamerica.org
www.aginginamerica.org
Previously a community-based, social service agency, Aging in America is transitioning into a foundation funding technological innovations in Gerontology.
William T. Smith, PhD, President & CEO
Kathleen Bufano, Executive Assistant

264   **American Federation for Aging Research**
55 W 39th Street
New York, NY 10018
212-703-9977
888-582-2327
Fax: 212-997-0330
info@afar.org
www.afar.org
AFAR supports the science of healthier aging through grants to 4,100 scientists to date.
Stephanie Lederman, Executive Director
Steven N.. Austad, Ph.D, Senior Scientific Director

265   **Archstone Foundation**
301 E Ocean Boulevard
Long Beach, CA 90802
506-590-8655
Fax: 506-495-0317
archstone@archstone.org
archstone.org
The foundation funds initiatives that meet the needs of an aging population, including stopping elder abuse, preventing falls, and compassionate end-of-life care.
Christopher Langston, PhD, President & CEO
Tanisha Davis, MAG, Grants Manager

266   **John A. Hartford Foundation**
55 E 59th Street
New York, NY 10022
212-832-7788
Fax: 212-593-4913
terry.fulmer@johnahartford.org
www.johnahartford.org
The foundation is dedicated to improving care of older adults, including funding in areas such as age-friendly health systems, family caregiving, serious illness and end-of-life, and communications and special projects.
Terry Fulmer, PhD, RN, FAAN, President
Rani E. Snyder, MPA, Program Director

Research Centers

267   **Academy for Gerontology in Higher Education**
1101 14th Street NW
Washington, DC 20005
202-842-1275
membership@geron.org
www.aghe.org
Membership organization comprised of more than 130 colleges and universities that offer education and research program in the field of aging. Affiliated with the Gerontological Society of America.
James Appleby, Chief Executive Officer

268   **American Institutes for Research Center on Aging**
1400 Crystal Drive
Arlington, VA 22202-3289
202-403-5000
Fax: 202-403-5000
www.air.org/center/center-aging
Seeks to improve the lives of the disadvantaged through attention to aging issues, connected to existing work at AIR, and examining emerging issues.
Marilyn Moon, Director

269   **Case Western Reserve University: Center on Aging and Health**
10900 Euclid Avenue
Cleveland, OH 44106
216-368-6472
800-825-2540
dlm5@case.edu
case.edu/nursing/ucah
Research organization conducting, supporting and facilitating research into gerontology and geriatrics.
Diana L Morris, PhD, RN, Executive Director
Evelyn Duffy, DNP, ANP/GNP-BC, Associate Director

270   **Center for Aging Research and Education at the UW-Madison School of Nursing**
Signe Skott Cooper Hall
701 Highland Avenue
Madison, WI 53705
608-265-4330
care@son.wisc.edu
care.nursing.wisc.edu
CARE seeks to prepare healthcare professionals to work with older adults, as well as encouraging inter-professional and campus-community collaborations.
Barbara Bowers, Founding Director
Barbara King, Executive Director

271   **Center on Aging and Work at Boston College**
140 Commonwealth Avenue
Chestnut Hill, MA 02467
617-552-1634
agework@bc.edu
www.bc.edu/research/agingandwork
Conducts research into quality of employment for a multi-generational workforce.
Jacquelyn B. James, PhD, Founder
Christina Matz, Co-Director

272   **Columbia University Robert N. Butler Aging Center**
Mailman School Of Public Health

Aging / Research Centers

722 W 168th Street 212-305-0424
New York, NY 10032 ColumbiaAgingCenter@cumc.columbia.edu
aging.columbia.edu
Clinical research in geriatric/gerontology and long-term care, and promotes the study of aging across the university.
Linda P. Fried, MD, MPH, Interim Co-Director
Kavita Sivaramakrishnan, Interim Co-Director, PhD

273 **De Tornyay Center For Healthy Aging at University of Washington**
School of Nursing
PO Box 357260 206-616-4276
Seattle, WA 98195 206-616-3064
agingctr@u.washington.edu
nursing.uw.edu
Supports gerontology research and education to promote healthy aging.
Basia Belza, PhD, RN, FAAN, Director
Heather Wicklein-Sanchez, Manager

274 **Duke University Center for the Study of Aging and Human Development**
Box 3003 DUMC 919-660-7500
Durham, NC 27710 Fax: 919-668-0453
sites.duke.edu/centerforaging
The center's research focuses on age-related decline, biomarkers of aging, exercise, osteoporosis, Alzheimer's disease, cancer as it relates to aging, viral diseases of aging, later-life depression, caregiver stress, and spirituality and health.
Harvey Jay Cohen, MD, Director
Heather E. Whitson, Deputy Director

275 **George Washington University Center for Aging, Health and Humanities**
1919 Pennsylvania Avenue NW 202-994-7901
Washington, DC 20006 Fax: 202-296-1229
aging@gwu.edu
nursing.gwu.edu
An interdisciplinary space for university faculty to collaborate on aging research, education, scholarship, and innovations.
Melissa Batchelor-Murphy, PhD, Director
Elizabeth Cobbs, MD, Co-Director

276 **Harvey A Friedman Center for Aging Washington University**
Institute for Public Health
600 S Taylor 314-747-9192
St. Louis, MO 63110 centerforaging@wustl.edu
publichealth.wustl.edu/aging
Seeks to provide older adults with the greatest opportunity for health, security, and engagement.
Nancy L. Morrow-Howell, PhD, Director
Natalie Galucia, MSW, Center Manager

277 **Home Instead Center for Successful Aging University of Nebraska Medical Center**
730 S 38th Avenue 402-559-9600
Omaha, NE 68105 webmaster@unmc.edu
www.unmc.edu/homeinsteadcenter
Provides patient care, as well as patient education, and research into promoting independence and aging in place.
Bradley Britigan, MD, Dean, College Of Medicine

278 **Indiana University School of Medicine Center for Aging Research**
545 Barnhill Drive 317-274-8438
Indianapolis, IN 46202 Fax: 317-274-1437
medicine.iu.edu
Research on aging includes brain health, decision-making, physical fitness, transitional and nursing home care, and medication.
Mark Geraci, MD, Chair, Department of Medicine
Samir Gupta, MD, Vice Chair, Research

279 **Jean Mayer USDA Human Nutrition Research Center on Aging at Tufts University**
711 Washington Street 617-556-3000
Boston, MA 02111 hnrca.tufts.edu
Makes research contributions to U.S. and international nutrition and physical activity recommendations for older adults.
Sarah L. Booth, PhD, Director
Xiang-Dong Wang, MD, PhD, Associate Director

280 **Johns Hopkins Center on Aging and Health**
2024 E Monument Street 410-955-0491
Baltimore, MD 21205 Fax: 410-614-9625
coah@jhu.edu
coah.jhu.edu
Sponsored by the Johns Hopkins Schools of Medicine and Public Health, COAH is an interdisciplinary group of research faculty seeking to optimize the health of older adults.
David L. Roth, PhD, Director
Brian Buta, MHS, Program Manager

281 **Kansas State University Center on Aging**
1324 Lovers Lane 785-532-5945
Manhattan, KS 66506 Fax: 785-532-5504
gerontology@k-state.edu
www.he.k-state.edu/aging
Focused on education, research, & outreach in the field of gerontology.
Gayle Doll, Director
Migette Kaup, Chair, Research Committee

282 **Landon Center on Aging University of Kansas Medical Center**
University of Kansas Medical Center
3901 Rainbow Boulevard 913-588-6970
Kansas City, KS 66160 800-766-3777
Fax: 913-945-7544
mchandler@kumc.edu
www2.kumc.edu/coa
Provides support for interdisciplinary research on the issue of age and aging.
Matt Chandler, MBA, Program Director
Diane Clark, Assistant Director

283 **Medical University of South Carolina Center on Aging**
280 Calhoun Street 843-792-0712
Charleston, SC 29425 education.musc.edu/colleges/medicine
Engages in research, services, and education with the aim of promoting health, quality of life, and longevity for seniors.
William Hill, Ph.D, Interim Director

284 **National Academy on an Aging Society**
1220 L Street NW 202-842-1275
Washington, DC 20005 membership@geron.org
www.geron.org
The policy branch of the Gerontological Society of America, the NAAS is a non-partisan institute conducting research on population aging.
James Appleby, Chief Executive Officer
Karen Tracy, VP, Strategic Alliances & Communications

285 **Purdue University: Center for Research on Aging and the Life Course**
1202 W. State Street 765-494-9692
W Lafayette, IN 47907 Fax: 765-494-2180
calc@purdue.edu
www.purdue.edu/aging
Social science research on aging, health and health care delivery.
Kenneth F. Ferraro, PhD, Director
Paige Ebner, Assistant Director

286 **Roy M and Phyllis Gough Huffington Center on Aging**
Baylor College of Medicine
One Baylor Plaza 713-798-4951
Houston, TX 77030 fincher@bcm.edu
www.hcoa.org
Internal unit of Baylor College representing research into the biology of aging.
Hui Zheng, PhD, Director
Ruth Andrea Reeves, MBA, BA, AAS, Center Administrator

287 **Sanders-Brown Center on Aging University of Kentucky**
789 S Limestone Street 859-323-5550
Lexington, KY 40536 linda.vaneldik@uky.edu
www.uky.edu/coa
Investigates healthy brain aging and neurodegenerative disorders through research, education and outreach, and clinical programs.
Linda J. Van Eldik, PhD, Director
Gregory A. Jicha, MD, PhD, Associate Director

Aging / Support Groups & Hotlines

288 **Sanford Center for Aging University Of Nevada, Reno**
Center for Molecular Medicine
1664 North Virginia Street 775-784-4774
Reno, NV 89557 Fax: 775-784-1814
sanford@unr.edu
med.unr.edu/aging
Aims to enhance the quality of life and well-being among older adults through education, research, and outreach.
Peter Reed, PhD, MPH, Director
Hannah Linden, Director, Wellness Programs

289 **Stanford Center on Longevity**
Littlefield Center, Stanford University
365 Lasuen Street 650-736-8643
Stanford, CA 94305 info-longevity@stanford.edu
longevity.stanford.edu
Seeks to advance scientific discoveries, advances in technology, and behavioral and social norms with the goal of enhancing century-long lives.
Laura Carstensen, PhD, Director
Jackie MacDonald, Director, Finance & Operations

290 **Stein Institute for Research on Aging UC San Diego School of Medicine**
9500 Gilman Drive 858-534-6299
La Jolla, CA 92093 Fax: 858-534-5475
aging@ucsd.edu
medschool.ucsd.edu/research/aging
Develops and applies recent advances in biomedical and behavioral science to issues of healthy aging, and reducing the burden of disease and disability in later life.
Dilip V. Jeste, MD, Director
Deborah Kado, MD, MS, Deputy Director, Clinical Research

291 **Tulane University Center For Aging**
1430 Tulane Avenue 504-988-3369
New Orleans, LA 70112 aging-studies@tulane.edu
medicine.tulane.edu
Dedicated to enhancing the quality of life of aging adults through research, education, and innovation.
John W. Deming, MD, Director

292 **University Of North Carolina School of Medicine Center for Aging and Health**
5003 Old Clinic 919-966-5945
Chapel Hill, NC 27599 www.med.unc.edu/aging
Provides care for older patients, provides community resources to families and caregivers, and trains not only geriatricians, but other medical professionals in geriatric medicine.
Ellen Schneider, MBA, Associate Director
June Weston, Project Manager

293 **University Of Wyoming Center on Aging**
1000 E University Avenue 307-766-2829
Laramie, WY 82071 Fax: 307-766-2847
wycoa@uwyo.edu
www.uwyo.edu/wycoa
Seeks to optimize the health and well-being of older adults and caregivers in Wyoming through partnerships, research, community education, and clinical training.
Christine McKibbin, PhD, Director
Catherine Phillips Carrico, PhD, Associate Director

294 **University of Connecticut Center on Aging**
135 Dowling Way 860-679-8400
Farmington, CT 06030 health.uconn.edu/aging
Provides care for older adults, as well as conducting research into the aging process in order to promote health and quality of life.
George A. Kuchel, MD, Director

295 **University of Florida Institute on Aging**
2004 Mowry Road 352-294-5800
Gainesville, FL 32611 info-aging@aging.ufl.edu
aging.ufl.edu
The IOA operates interdisciplinary teams in research, education and health care, dedicated to improving the health, independence, and quality of life for older adults.
Marco Pahor, MD, Director
Stephen Anton, PhD, Associate Director

296 **University of Maryland School of Public Health Center on Aging**
4200 Valley Drive 301-405-2438
College Park, MD 20742 Fax: 301-405-8397
asmaa@umd.edu
sph.umd.edu
An interdisciplinary institution conducting applied and policy research, education, and public service into human aging.
Luisa Franzini, PhD, Director
Jim Hagberg, PhD, Associate Director

297 **University of Pennsylvania Institute on Aging**
3615 Chestnut Street 215-898-7801
Philadelphia, PA 19104 aging@pennmedicine.upenn.edu
www.med.upenn.edu/aging
The mission of the IOA is to improve the health of the elderly by increasing the quality and quantity of clinical and basic research as well as educational programs focusing on normal aging and age-related diseases at the UPSM and across the entire Penn campus.
David A. Wolk, MD, Co-Director
Edward B. Lee, MD, PhD, Co-Director

298 **University of Vermont Larner College of Medicine Center on Aging**
89 Beaumont Avenue 802-656-0292
Burlington, VT 05405 Fax: 802-656-8380
Jeanne.Hutchins@uvm.edu
www.med.uvm.edu/centeronaging
Aims to promote well-being and a high quality of life for older adults, through university collaboration.
Micheal A. LaMantia, MD, MPH, Director

299 **Virginia Commonwealth University Virginia Center on Aging**
900 East Broad Street 804-828-1525
Richmond, VA 23219 804-828-7905
vcoa@vcu.edu
vcoa.chp.vcu.edu
Interdisciplinary center for the study and research of the aged and the aging process.
Tracey Gendron, PhD, MS, Executive Director
Leland Waters, PhD, Associate Director

Support Groups & Hotlines

300 **Caregiver Action Network**
1150 Connecticut Avenue NW 202-454-3970
Washington, DC 20036 info@caregiveraction.org
caregiveraction.org
Aims to improve quality of life for Americans who care for loved ones facing chronic illnesses, disabilities, diseases, or old age.
John Schall, Chief Executive Officer
Chance Browning, Senior Director, Programs

301 **Caregiver Support Services**
PO Box 4291 866-201-6896
Omaha, NE 68104 egreen@caregiversupportservices.org
caregiversupportservices.com
Provides guidance and resources to caregivers.
Eboni Green, President & CEO
Terrence Green, Vice President, Business Development

302 **National Alliance for Caregiving**
1730 Rhode Island Ave. NW 202-918-1013
Washington, DC 20036 Fax: 202-918-1014
info@caregiving.org
www.caregiving.org
Advocates on behalf of caregivers, as well as conducting research and offering support services.
Jason Resendez, President & CEO
Patrice A. Heinz, Chief Operating Officer

303 **National Health Information Center**
Office of Disease Prevention & Health Promotion
1101 Wootton Pkwy Fax: 240-453-8281
Rockville, MD 20852 odphpinfo@hhs.gov
www.health.gov/nhic
Supports public health education by maintaining a calendar of National Health Observances; helps connect consumers and health professionals to organizations that can best answer questions and provide up-to-date contact information from reliable sources; up-

dates on a yearly basis toll-free numbers for health information, Federal health clearinghouses and info centers.
Don Wright, MD, MPH, Director

304 Well Spouse Association
63 W Main Street
Freehold, NJ 07728
732-577-8899
www.wellspouse.org
This association is a nonprofit national self-help organization serving the well spouse of the chronically ill. Members help each other develop coping and survival skills through local support groups (including bereavement), letter and telephone networks, and personal outreach and a quarterly newsletter.
Marilyn Kamp, Executive Director

Print Resources

305 AARP: The Magazine
American Association of Retired Persons
601 East Street NW
Washington, DC 20049
202-434-3525
888-687-2277
TTY: 877-434-7598
member@aarp.org
www.aarp.org
Celebrity interviews. Features on health and finance. Movie reviews and more. All with an eye toward the topics and issues you care about most.
Robert Love, Editor-in-Chief

306 Abstracts in Social Gerontology
National Council on Aging
251 18th Street S.
Arlington, VA 22202
info@ncoa.org
www.ncoa.org
Detailed abstracts are provided for recent major journal articles, books, reports and other materials on many facets of aging, including adult education, demography, family relations, institutional care and work attitudes.
Ramsay Alwin, President & CEO

307 Aging and Health Research
Elsevier Publishing
1600 John F Kennedy Boulevard
Philadelphia, PA 19103-2398
215-239-3900
800-325-4177
Fax: 215-239-3990
custserv.ehs@elsevier.com
www.sciencedirect.com
International, peer-reviewed, open access journal that publishes innovative aging and health research, with the aim of advancing knowledge across disciplines.
Ding Ding, PhD, Editor-in-Chief
Bei Wu, PhD, Editor-in-Chief

308 International Journal of Technology and Aging
Human Sciences Press
233 Spring Street
New York, NY 10013
212-620-8000
800-221-9369
Fax: 212-463-0742
www.springer.com
Designed to serve health-care professionals, researchers, academicians and industries concerned with the convergence of two recent trends, the dramatic advances in technology and the rapidly growing elderly population.

309 Journal of Aging and Health
Sage
1400 L Street NW, Suite 250
Washington, DC 20005
journals.sagepub.com/home/jah
Peer-reviewed journal focusing on the intersection of gerontology and health.
Kyriakos S. Markides, Editor
Brian Downer, Assistant Editor

310 Journal of Geriatric Medicine and Gerontology
ClinMed International Library
3511 Silverside Road, Suite 105
Wilmington, DE 19810
302-208-7437
contact@clinmedjournals.org
clinmedjournals.org
Open access, peer-reviewed journal that publishes information in the areas of clinical, preventative, curative and social aspects of illness in old age.
Ryuichi Morishita, Editor-in-Chief

Digital Resources

311 Innovations
National Council on Aging
251 18th Street S.
Arlington, VA 22202
info@ncoa.org
www.ncoa.org
Explores significant developments in the field of aging through opinion articles, profiles and research summaries. Features articles on social trends, articles on specific aging programs and information on NCOA's activities. Members are free.
Ramsay Alwin, President & CEO

Web Sites

312 Aging.com
www.aging.com
Seeks to provide older adults with information and resources on health & well-being, caregiving, money and financial planning, and lifestyle, through their website.

313 Alliance for Aging Research
www.agingresearch.org
Improving the health and independence of Americans as they age. Promotes medical and behavioral research into the aging process.

314 American Association of Retired Persons
www.aarp.org
AARP is the nation's leading organization for people age 50 and older. It serves their needs and interests through information and education, advocacy and community services provided by a network of local chapters and experienced volunteers. The website features lifestyle and health information for retired persons, as well as entertainment, music, podcasts, and more.

315 American Society on Aging
www.asaging.org
An association of diverse individuals bound together by a common goal: to support the commitment and enhance the knowledge and skills of those who seek to improve the quality of life of older adults and their families.

316 Canadian National Seniors Council
canada.ca/en/national-seniors-council
The council works with older Canadians, stakeholders and experts to advise the Canadian government on matters relating to the health, well-being and quality of life of seniors. The website provides links to reports and other publications featuring research on aging and senior citizens.

317 Caring.com
www.caring.com
Online portal for family caregivers who are caring for aging loved ones.

318 Eldercare Locator
eldercare.acl.gov
Public service run by the U.S. Administration on Aging connecting older adults and their families to services and resources.

319 Gerontological Society of America
www.geron.org
Nonprofit professional organization with more than 5,500 members in the field of aging. Provides researchers, educators, practitioners and policy makers with opportunities to understand, advance, integrate and use basic and applied research on aging populations. The website provides access to publications, including journals, as well as meetings, programs and services, and member benefits.

320 Healing Well
www.healingwell.com
An online health resource guide to medical news, chat, information and articles, newsgroups and message boards, books, dis-

Aging / Web Sites

ease-related web sites, medical directories, and more for patients, friends, and family coping with disabling diseases, disorders, or chronic illnesses.

321 Health Central
www.healthcentral.com
Find clearly explained, medically accurate information regarding conditions, including an overview, symptoms, causes, diagnostic procedures and treatment options. On this site it is possible to ask questions and get information from a neurologist and connect to people who have similar health interests.

322 Health Finder
www.health.gov
Searchable, carefully developed web site offering information on over 1000 topics. Developed by the US Department of Health and Human Services, the site can be used in both English and Spanish.

323 LongTermCare.gov
longtermcare.acl.gov
Provides information on long-term care for patients and caregivers.

324 Lotsa Helping Hands
lotsahelpinghands.com
Platform for creating communities that assist in caring for loved ones, intended for caregivers, friends and family, and volunteers.

325 Medical News Today
www.medicalnewstody.com
Offers in-depth health information and the latest news in medical research on a wide variety of medical conditions.

326 MedicineNet
www.medicinenet.com
An online resource for consumers providing easy-to-read, authoritative medical and health information.

327 MedlinePlus
www.medlineplus.gov
Information regarding a broad range of health,and mental health conditions topics include: Latest news, overview of anatomy and physiology, clinical trials, diagnoses and symptoms, treatment, genetics, plus lots of links to other sites. A service provided by the National Library of Medicine, part of the National Institutes of Health (NIH).

328 Medscape
www.medscape.com
Medscape offers specialists, primary care physicians, and other health professionals the Web's most robust and integrated medical information and educational tools.

329 National Council on Aging
www.ncoa.org
The nation's first charitable organization dedicated to promoting the dignity, independence, well-being and contributions of older Americans. The council has a goal of improving the health and economic well-being of 40 million older adults by 2030. The website provides tools and resources for older adults and caregivers.

330 National Hospice & Palliative Care Organization (NHPCO)
www.nhpco.org
The organization seeks to improve end-of-life care, widen access to hospice care, and improve quality of life for the dying and their loved ones. NHPCO's website offers information on regulations, advocacy, quality and performance, education, and a variety of other resources.

331 National Institute on Aging
www.nia.nih.gov
Conducts research on aging, behavioral and social research, neuroscience and neuropsychology, geriatrics, and clinical gerontology.

332 Next Step in Care
www.nextstepincare.org
Online platform with videos and guides for family caregivers and healthcare providers, as well as other resources.

333 Research Center
www.aarp.org/research/
Online center offering information on consumer issues, demographics, independent living and other items of interest to senior citizens.

334 Seniorresource.com
www.seniorresource.com
Provides information to older adults on needed facilities and services, including through internet directories and an archive of E-zines.

335 US Administration on Aging
acl.gov/about-acl/administration-aging
An agency in the US Department of Health and Human Services, and under the Administration for Community Living, is one of the nation's largest providers of home and community-based care for older persons and their caregivers.

336 Verywell Mind
www.verywellmind.com
Provides up-to-date information on mental health topics. mission is to prioritize mental health and promote balance for day to day living. offers over 5,500 online articles that are researched based, and reviwed by medical professionals.
Kristen Altmeyer, MBA, VP & General Manager
Nick Ingalls, MA, Associate Editorial Director

337 WebMD
www.webmd.com
Provides credible information, supportive communities, and in-depth reference material about health subjects. A source for original and timely health information as well as material from well known content providers.

ALZHEIMER'S DISEASE/DEMENTIA

Depression may result from a diagnosis of Alzheimer's Disease (AD) and/or dementia. Dementia is a clinical diagnosis or syndrome involving cognitive impairment, including memory loss and loss of focus, and is generally associated with old age, but earlier ages may develop symptoms. Alzheimer's is the most common cause of dementia and accounts for 60-80 percent of cases. Alzheimer's disease is a type of dementia with symptoms of memory, thinking and behavior impairment, and symptoms may become severe to the point of interfering with activities of daily living. The disease worsens over time and may result in a shortened life span.

Depression is often associated with both dementia and AD and may begin in the early stages of diagnosis. Identifying depression can be difficult, since the diagnosis may cause some of the same depressive symptoms. Apathy, loss of interest in daily life, social withdrawal and isolation, and trouble concentrating are symptoms of both depression and the cognitive impairment seen in dementia and AD. Depression may be less severe in individuals with AD and symptoms may come and go. A medical professional or mental health professional should be involved in the clinical evaluation and diagnosis when depression is suspected in individuals with dementia and/or AD. Diagnosis of depression in dementias and AD relies less on verbal discussions and expression and more on irritability and social isolation. Family and caregiver input is solicited.

Treatment of depression for individuals diagnosed with dementia and/or AD includes medications, counseling, and assisting both the individual and the caregiver to return to activities that bring pleasure and happiness where possible. Support groups are often helpful, especially in the early stages of the disease. Individual counseling is also an option if support groups are too overwhelming or if the individual is not comfortable in the setting. Routine schedules, taking advantage of "good" days, getting appropriate exercise usually earlier in the day, involving the individual as possible in family activities and providing ongoing reassurance of love and respect all contribute to enhancing the quality of life of individuals with dementias or AD.

Seeking help for a diagnosis of depression as a result of a dementia or Alzheimer's Disease diagnosis in a timely fashion may contribute to a better quality of life. Family members and caregivers should also be alert to depression resulting from a loved one's diagnosis and seek support.

Alzheimer's Disease/Dementia / Agencies & Associations

Agencies & Associations

338 Alzheimer Society of Alberta and Northwest Territories
10430 - 61 Avenue 780-488-2266
Edmonton, Alberta, T6H-2J3 866-950-5465
Fax: 780-488-3055
reception@alzheimer.ab.ca
www.alzheimer.ca/en/ab
Provides support, education, and advocacy for all those affected by Alzheimer's disease in Alberta and the Northwest Territories, including patients, caregivers, patients' families, and the community.
George Andrews, President & CEO
Christene Gordon, VP, Programs & Partnerships

339 Alzheimer Society of British Columbia
828 W 8th Avenue Street 604-681-6530
Vancouver, BC, V5C-1E2 800-667-3742
Fax: 604-669-6907
info@alzheimerbc.org
www.alzheimer.ca/en/bc
Provides support, education, and advocacy for all those affected by Alzheimer's disease in British Columbia, including patients, caregivers, patients' families, and the community.
Jen Lyle, CEO
Paul Brill, Director, Marketing & Communications

340 Alzheimer Society of Canada
20 Eglinton Avenue W 416-488-8772
Toronto, Ontario, M4R-1K8 800-618-8816
Fax: 416-488-3778
info@alzheimer.ca
www.alzheimer.ca
Identifies, develops and facilitates national priorities that enable its members to effectively alleviate the personal and social consequences of Alzheimer's disease and related disorders; promotes research and leads the search for a cure.
Christopher Barry, Chief Executive Officer
Gail Black-Elliot, Chief Development Officer

341 Alzheimer Society of Manitoba
10 - 120 Donald Street 204-943-6622
Winnipeg, Manitoba, R3C-4G2 800-378-6699
Fax: 833-638-0760
alzmb@alzheimer.mb.ca
alzheimer.mb.ca
Provides support, education, and advocacy for all those affected by Alzheimer's disease in Manitoba, including patients, caregivers, patients' families, and the community.
Wendy Schettler, Chief Executive Officer
Rebecca Krowelski, Marketing & Communications Director

342 Alzheimer Society of New Brunswick
320 Maple Street 506-459-4280
Fredericton, NB, E3A-3R4 800-664-8411
Fax: 506-452-0313
info@alzheimernb.ca
alzheimer.ca/en/nb
Provides support, education, and advocacy for all those affected by Alzheimer's disease in New Brunswick, including patients, caregivers, patients' families, and the community.

343 Alzheimer Society of Newfoundland & Labrador
835 Topsail Road 709-576-0608
Mount Pearl, NL, A1N-3J6 877-776-0608
Fax: 709-576-0798
info@alzheimernl.ca
alzheimer.ca/en/nl
Provides support, education, and advocacy for all those affected by Alzheimer's disease in Newfoundland and Labrador, including patients, caregivers, patients' families, and the community.

344 Alzheimer Society of Nova Scotia
112-2719 Gladstone Street 902-422-7961
Halifax, Nova Scotia, B3K-4W6 800-611-6345
Fax: 902-422-7971
alzheimer@asns.ca
alzheimer.ca/en/ns
Provides support, education, and advocacy for all those affected by Alzheimer's disease in Nova Scotia, including patients, caregivers, patients' families, and the community.

345 Alzheimer Society of Ontario
20 Eglinton Avenue W 416-967-5900
Toronto, Ontario, M4R-1K8 800-879-4226
Fax: 416-967-3826
staff@alzon.ca
alzheimer.ca/en/on
Provides support, education, and advocacy for all those affected by Alzheimer's disease in Ontario, including patients, caregivers, patients' families, and the community.

346 Alzheimer Society of Prince Edward Island
166 Fitzroy Street 902-628-2257
Charlottetown, PE, C1A-1S1 society@alzpei.ca
alzheimer.ca/en/pei
Provides support, education, and advocacy for all those affected by Alzheimer's disease in Prince Edward Island, including patients, caregivers, patients' families, and the community.
Nelson Hagerman, President
Val Maclean, Treasurer

347 Alzheimer Society of Saskatchewan
2550 - 12th Avenue 306-949-4141
Regina, Saskatchewan, S4P-3X1 800-263-3367
Fax: 306-949-3069
info@alzheimer.sk.ca
www.alzheimer.ca/en/sk
Provides support, education, and advocacy for all those affected by Alzheimer's disease in Saskatchewan, including patients, caregivers, patients' families, and the community.
Joanne Bracken, CEO
Leslie Quennell, Dir., Public Awareness & Comms.

348 Alzheimer Society of Toronto
20 Eglinton Ave. West 416-322-6560
Toronto, ON, M4R-1K8 write@alz.to
alz.to
Provides information, programs, and educational resources to individuals living with dementia, and their families and caregivers. Serves the Greater Toronto Area.
Kari Quinn-Humphrey, Interim CEO
Kristy McKay, Dir., Community Support Services

349 Alzheimer's Association
225 N. Michigan Avenue
Chicago, IL 60601 www.act.alz.org
Dedicated to research for the prevention, cure, and treatment of Alzheimer's disease and related disorders, and to providing support and assistance to patients and their families.
Sarah Lorance, Chair
Joanne Pike, Ph.D, Chief Executive Officer

350 American Neuropsychiatric Association
P.O. Box 1804 703-960-6500
Alexandria, VA 22313 Fax: 703-960-6603
anpaoffice@gmail.com
anpaonline.org
The American Neuropsychiatric Association (ANPA) represents professionals in behavioral neurology, neuropsychiatry, neuropsychology, and the clinical neurosciences.
Margaret Roberts, Acting Administrative Director

351 Center for Mental Health Services (CMHS)
Substance Abuse and Mental Health Services Adminis
5600 Fishers Lane 240-276-1310
Rockville, MD 20857 samhsa.gov
Promotes the treatment of mental illness and emotional disorders by increasing accessibility to mental health programs; supporting outreach, treatment, rehabilitation, and support programs and networks; and encouraging the use of scientifically-based information when treating mental disorders. CMHS provides information about mental health via a toll-free number and numerous publications. Developed for users of mental health services and their families, the general public, policy makers, provider
Anita Everett, MD, DFAPA, Director

Alzheimer's Disease/Dementia / Agencies & Associations

352 **Federation of Quebec Alzheimer Societies**
507-460 Rue Sainte-Catherine Ouest
Montreal, Quebec, H4A-1A7
514-369-7891
888-636-6473
info@alzheimerquebec.ca
alzheimer.ca/en/federationquebecoise
Provides support, education, and advocacy for all those affected by Alzheimer's disease in Quebec, including patients, caregivers, patients' families, and the community.
Luc Pinard, President
Charles Cyr-Gill, Vice President

353 **Mental Health America**
500 Montgomery Street
Alexandria, VA 22314
703-684-7722
800-969-6642
mhanational.org
Mental Health America is a community-based nonprofit organization committed to enabling the mental wellness of all Americans. MHA advocates for greater access to quality health services and seeks to educate individuals on identifying symptoms, as well as intervention and prevention.
Schroeder Stribling, President & CEO
Sachin Doshi, Sr. Dir., Finance & Operations

354 **National Institute on Aging**
P.O. Box 8057
Gaithersburg, MD 20898
800-222-2225
niaic@nia.nih.gov
www.nia.nih.gov
Seeks to understand the nature of aging, and to extend healthy, active years of life. Free resources are available on topics such as Alzheimer's & dimentia, caregiving, cognitive heath, end of life care, and more.
Richard J. Hodes, M.D., Director
Amy Kelley, M.D., M.S.H.S., Deputy Director

355 **United Brain Association**
202-768-8000
info@unitedbrainassociation.org
unitedbrainassociation.org
Non-profit organization that works to find cures through research for over 600 brain and mental health related issues, and disorders.
J.A. Boulton, Founder
Jay Matey, VP & Treasurer

Alabama

356 **Alzheimer's Association: Alabama**
1 Metroplex Drive
Birmingham, AL 35209
205-379-8065
800-272-3900
jcmiller@alz.org
www.alz.org/al
Jessica Miller, Executive Director
Billy Curtis, Director, Programs

Alaska

357 **Alzheimer's Association: Alaska**
206-245-6431
800-272-3900
jwilgus@alz.org
www.alz.org/alaska
Jim Wilgus, Regional Leader
Elizabeth Bolling, Public Policy Manager

Arizona

358 **Alzheimer's Association: Desert Southwest**
340 E Palm Lane
Phoenix, AZ 85004
602-528-0545
800-272-3900
tgspitz@alz.org
www.alz.org/dsw
Serving the state of Arizona and Southern Nevada offices in Phoenix, Tucson, Sun City, Prescott and Las Vegas.
Terri Spitz, Executive Director
Kinsey McManus, Programs Director

359 **Alzheimer's Association: Northern Arizona**
3111 Clearwater Drive
Prescott, AZ 86305
928-771-9257
800-272-3900
alramirez@alz.org
www.alz.org/dsw
Alexis Ramirez, Community Engagement Coordinator
Susie James, Helpline Manager

360 **Alzheimer's Association: Southern Arizona**
2990 N Swan Road
Tucson, AZ 85712
520-322-6601
800-272-3900
rbuenobarron@alz.org
www.alz.org/dsw
Raul Bueno, Community Engagement Coordinator
Nallelhy Ballesteros, Program Manager

Arkansas

361 **Alzheimer's Association: Arkansas**
11300 N. Rodney Parham Road
Little Rock, AR 72212
501-265-0027
800-272-3900
kedickins@alz.org
www.alz.org/arkansas
Kirsten Dickens, Executive Director
Taco Price, Director, Programs

California

362 **Alzheimer's Association: Cali. - Southland**
1401 Commericial Way
Baskersfield, CA 93309
661-912-3053
800-272-3900
mbarron@alz.org
www.alz.org/socal
Meg Barron, Regional Leader & Executive Director

363 **Alzheimer's Association: California - Central Coast**
1528 Chapala Street
Santa Barbara, CA 93101
805-892-4259
800-272-3900
Fax: 805-892-4250
lmleonard@alz.org
www.alz.org/cacentralcoast
Lindsey Leonard, Executive Director
Karen Ortiz, Director, Development

364 **Alzheimer's Association: Northern California**
2290 North First Street
San Jose, CA 95131
408-372-9900
800-272-3900
www.alz.org/norcal
Elizabeth Edgerly, PhD, Executive Director
Shelley Dombroski, Senior Regional Director

365 **Alzheimer's Association: Orange County**
38 Executive Park
Irvine, CA 92614
949-426-8544
800-272-3900
dblevy@alz.org
www.alz.org/oc
Deborah Levy, Executive Director
Gregory Mathes, Director, Programs

366 **Alzheimer's Association: San Diego**
5075 Shoreham Place
San Diego, CA 92122
619-678-8322
800-272-3900
klcroskrey@alz.org
www.alz.org/sandiego
Janet Hamada Kelley, Executive Director
Ana Gonzalez Seda, MPH, Director, Programs

Colorado

367 **Alzheimer's Association: Boulder and Mountain Region**
5353 Manhattan Circle
Boulder, CO 80303
303-813-1669
800-272-3900
Fax: 720-974-1583
rpatrick@alz.org
www.alz.org/co
Serving residents in Boulder, Broomfield, Chaffee, Clear Creek, Eagle, Gilpin, Lake, Park, Pitkin, and Summit counties.
Ralph Patrick, Regional Director
Jeff Bird, Executive Director

Alzheimer's Disease/Dementia / Agencies & Associations

368 Alzheimer's Association: Great Denver Region
455 N. Sherman Street
Denver, CO 80203
303-813-1669
800-272-3900
Fax: 303-813-1670
toclark@alz.org
www.alz.org/co

Serving residents in Adams, Arapahoe, Denver, Douglas, and Jefferson Counties.
Tom Clark, Community Engagement Manager

369 Alzheimer's Association: Northeastern Colorado Region
P.O. Box 336672
Greeley, CO 80633
303-795-5465
Fax: 970-346-9025
www.alz.org/c

Serving residents in Cheyenne, Elbert, Kit Carson, Lincoln, Logan, Morgan, Phillips, Sedgwick, Washington, Weld, and Yuma Counties.
Sarah Gostenik, Regional Director

370 Alzheimer's Association: Northern Colorado Region
5010 Aspen Drive
Littleton, CO 80123
303-795-5465
800-272-3900
Fax: 303-794-0487
alhoffman@alz.org
www.alz.org/co

Serving residents in Grand, Jackson, Larimer, Moffat, Rio Blanco, and Routt Counties.
Angel Hoffman, Regional Director

371 Alzheimer's Association: Southern and Central Colorado Region
1520 N Union Blvd.
Colorado Springs, CO 80909
303-795-5465
Fax: 719-266-8798
rmjaramillo@alz.org
www.alz.org/co

Serving residents in Alamosa, Baca, Bent, Conejos, Costilla, Crowley, Custer, El Paso, Fremont, Kiowa, Las Animas, Mineral, Otero, Prowers, Pueblo, Rio Grande, Saguache, and Teller counties.
RoseMary Jaramillo, Regional Director

372 Alzheimer's Association: Western Colorado Region
2232 N. 7th Ave.
Grand Junction, CO 81501
303-795-5465
Fax: 970-243-6924
wlbandel@alz.org
www.alz.org/co

Serving residents in Archuleta, Delta, Dolores, Gunnison, Hinsdale, La Plata, Montezuma, Mesa, Montrose, Ouray, San Juan, and San Miguel counties.
Woo Bandel, Community Engagement Manager

Connecticut

373 Alzheimer's Association: Connecticut
200 Executive Blvd
Southington, CT 06489
860-406-3040
Fax: 860-571-8613
ckovel@alz.org
www.alz.org/ct

Ginny Hanbridge, Executive Director

Delaware

374 Alzheimer's Association: Delaware
399 Market St.
Philadelphia, PA 19106
800-272-3900
klfransel@alz.org
www.alz.org/delval

Kristina Fransel, Executive Director
Abbey Hunton, Sr. Dir., Marketing & Communications

District of Columbia

375 Alzheimer's Association: National Capital Area
8180 Greensboro Drive
McLean, VA 22102
703-359-4440
Fax: 703-359-4441
kgrooper@alz.org
www.alz.org/nca

Kate Rooper, Chapter President & CEO
Ana Nelson, VP, Programs & Services

Florida

376 Alzheimer's Association: Central and North Florida
2170 W State Rd 434
Longwood, FL 32779
407-951-7992
800-272-3900
Fax: 407-951-7993
jhmarshall@alz.org
www.alz.org/cnfl

Jessica Marshall, Executive Director
Deann Marasco, Regional Director, Health Systems

377 Alzheimer's Association: Florida Gulf Coast
14010 Roosevelt Blvd.
Clearwater, FL 33762
727-578-2558
800-272-3900
Fax: 727-578-2286
admcauley@alz.org
www.alz.org/flgulfcoast

Angela McAuley, Regional Leader

378 Alzheimer's Association: Southeast Florida
100 W. Cypress Creek Rd.
Ft. Lauderdale, FL 33309
954-786-1533
800-272-3900
Fax: 954-497-4049
twpaige@alz.org
www.alz.org/seflorida

Tracey Wekar-Paige, Executive Director

Georgia

379 Alzheimer's Association: Georgia
41 Perimeter Center East
Atlanta, GA 30345
404-728-1181
800-272-3900
Fax: 404-636-9768
lidavidson@alz.org
www.alz.org/georgia

Linda Davidson, Executive Director

Hawaii

380 Alzheimer's Association: Hawaii
677 Ala Moana Boulevard
Honolulu, HI 96813
808-591-2771
800-272-3900
Fax: 808-591-9071
alohainfo@alz.org
www.alz.org/hawaii

LJ R. Duenas, Executive Director

Idaho

381 Alzheimer's Association: Greater Idaho
P.O. Box 4746
Boise, ID 83711
208-206-0041
800-272-3900
Fax: 866-201-5957
www.alz.org/idaho

Illinois

382 Alzheimer's Association: Illinois
8430 W. Bryn Mawr
Chicago, IL 60631
847-933-2413
800-272-3900
djervier@alz.org
www.alz.org/illinois

Delia Jervier, Chapter Executive

Indiana

383 Alzheimer's Association: Greater Indiana
50 E 91st St.
Indianapolis, IN 46240
317-575-9620
800-272-3900
Fax: 317-575-9624
nmsutton@alz.org
www.alz.org/indiana

Natalie Sutton, Chapter Executive

Alzheimer's Disease/Dementia / Agencies & Associations

Iowa

384 **Alzheimer's Association: Iowa**
1415 28th St.
West Des Moines, IA 50266
515-440-2722
800-272-3900
Fax: 515-440-6385
dabickford@alz.org
www.alz.org/iowa

Serves the following counties: Adair, Clarke, Dallas, Decatur, Guthrie, Jasper, Lucas, Madison, Marion, Polk, Ringgold, Union, Warren and Wayne.
Doug Bickford, Executive Director

Kansas

385 **Alzheimer's Association: Central and Western Kansas**
1820 East Douglas
Wichita, KS 67214
316-267-7333
800-272-3900
Fax: 316-267-6369
lbelton@alz.org
www.alz.org/cwkansas
Juliette B. Bradley, Kansas State Director of Communications

386 **Alzheimer's Association: Heart of America**
3846 W. 75th Street
Prairie Village, KS 66208
913-831-3888
800-272-3900
kjjackson@alz.org
www.alz.org/kansascity

Ken Jackson, Executive Director

Kentucky

387 **Alzheimer's Association: Greater Kentucky and Soutern Indiana**
2808 Palumbo Dr.
Lexington, KY 40509
859-266-5283
800-272-3900
Fax: 859-268-4764
ShWhite@alz.org
www.alz.org/kyin

Shannon White, Chapter Executive

Maine

388 **Alzheimer's Association: Maine**
383 Us Route One
Scarborough, ME 04074
207-772-0115
800-272-3900
dwyman@alz.org
www.alz.org/maine

Drew Wyman, Executive Director
Amy Angelo, Program Manager

Maryland

389 **Alzheimer's Association: Greater Maryland**
502 Washington Avenue
Towson, MD 21204
410-561-9099
800-272-3900
djmcshea@alz.org
www.alz.org/maryland

David McShea, Executive Director

Massachusetts

390 **Alzheimer's Association: Massachusetts and New Hampshire**
309 Waverley Oaks Road
Waltham, MA 02452
617-868-6718
800-272-3900
Fax: 617-868-6720
www.alz.org/manh

Michigan

391 **Alzheimer's Association: Greater Michigan**
25200 Telegraph Rd.
Southfield, MI 48033
248-351-0280
800-272-3900
jlepard@alz.org
www.alz.org/gmc

Jennifer Lepard, President & CEO
Kathryn Ribant Payne, Communications Director

Minnesota

392 **Alzheimer's Association: Minnesota and North Dakota**
7900 West 78th Street
Minneapolis, MN 55439
952-830-0512
800-272-3900
Fax: 952-830-0513
sjparriott@alz.org
www.alz.org/mnnd

Susan Parriott, CEO

Mississippi

393 **Alzheimer's Association: Mississippi**
601-331-6115
800-272-3900
capolk@alz.org
www.alz.org/ms

Chad Polk, Executive Director
Kristen White, LMSW, Program Coordinator

Missouri

394 **Alzheimer's Association: Greater Missouri**
9370 Olive Blvd.
St. Louis, MO 63132
800-272-3900
www.alz.org/greatermissouri

Montana

395 **Alzheimer's Association: Montana**
3010 11th Ave N
Billings, MT 59101
406-252-3053
800-272-3900
jfunyak@alz.org
www.alz.org/montana

Jami Funyak, Executive Director
Melanie Williams, Program Director, Programs & Edu.

Nebraska

396 **Alzheimer's Association: Nebraska**
402-260-7912
800-272-3900
sstephens@alz.org
www.alz.org/nebraska

Sharon Stephens, Executive Director
Julie Chytil, Director, Programs

Nevada

397 **Alzheimer's Association: Northern Nevada**
639 Isbell Road
Reno, NV 89509
775-786-8061
800-272-3900
www.alz.org/norcal

Elizabeth Edgerly, PhD, Executive Director
Shelley Dombroski, Senior Regional Director

398 **Alzheimer's Association: Southern Nevada**
5190 S Valley View Boulevard
Las Vegas, NV 89118
702-248-2770
800-272-3900
Fax: 702-248-2771
cbaumis@alz.org
www.alz.org/dsw

Johna Meints, Community Engagement Coordinator
Caroline Baumis, Program Manager

New Jersey

399 **Alzheimer's Association: Greater New Jersey**
23 Vreeland Road
Florham Park, NJ 07932
732-504-2347
800-272-3900
criccifrancione@alz.org
www.alz.org/nj

Cheryl Ricci-Francione, Executive Director
Robyn Kohn, Director, Programs & Services

425

Alzheimer's Disease/Dementia

New Mexico

400 **Alzheimer's Association: New Mexico**
6731 Academy Rd NE
Albuquerque, NM 87109
505-266-4473
800-272-3900
Fax: 505-266-0108
tisheahan@alz.org
www.alz.org/newmexico

Tim Sheahan, Executive Director
Ron D. Eppes, Program Director

New York

401 **Alzheimer's Association: Hudson Valley**
2649 South Road
Poughkeepsie, NY 12601
845-471-2655
800-272-3900
Fax: 845-471-8960
dsobel@alz.org
www.alz.org/hudsonvalley

David Sobel, Executive Director
Meg Boyce, Director, Programs & Services

402 **Alzheimer's Association: Central New York**
P.O. Box 12226
Syracuse, NY 13218
315-472-4201
800-272-3900
Fax: 315-472-4202
cny-info@alz.org
www.alz.org/centralnewyork

Catherine James, CEO
Kristen Campbell, LMSW, Director, Programs & Services

403 **Alzheimer's Association: Long Island**
300 Broadhollow Road
Melville, NY 11747
631-629-6950
800-272-3900
ddavidson@alz.org
www.alz.org/longisland

Doug Davidson, Executive Director
Kate Anastasia, Program Director

404 **Alzheimer's Association: New York City**
60 East 42nd Street
New York, NY 10165
646-418-4466
800-272-3900
NYCinfo@alz.org
www.alz.org/nyc

Christopher Smith, Executive Director
Gwen Bolden, Program Operations Specialist

405 **Alzheimer's Association: Northeastern New York**
1003 New Loudon Road
Cohoes, NY 12047
518-867-4999
800-272-3900
Fax: 518-867-4997
www.alz.org/northeasternny

Elizabeth Smith-Boivin, Executive Director & CEO
Shannon Lawler, Director, Programs & Services

406 **Alzheimer's Association: Rochester and Finger Lakes Region**
200 Meridian Centre Blvd.
Rochester, NY 14618
800-272-3900
inforochny@alz.org
www.alz.org/rochesterny

Teresa Galbier, Chapter Executive
Amanda Drobnica, Senior Director, Programs & Services

407 **Alzheimer's Association: Western New York**
6400 Sheridan Drive
Amherst, NY 14421
716-626-0600
800-272-3900
program.wny@alz.org
www.alz.org/wny

Jill Horner, Executive Director
Lauren Ashburn, Associate Director, Advocacy

North Carolina

408 **Alzheimer's Association: Eastern North Carolina**
5171 Glenwood Avenue
Raleigh, NC 27612
919-803-8285
800-272-3900
Fax: 866-586-6307
encinfo@alz.org
www.alz.org/nc

Madison Buchanan, Program Manager

Ohio

409 **Alzheimer's Association: Greater Cincinnati**
800-272-3900
anbarnett@alz.org
www.alz.org/cincinnati

410 **Alzheimer's Association: Central Ohio**
1379 Dublin Road
Columbus, OH 43215
614-457-6003
800-272-3900
vmcgrail@alz.org
www.alz.org/centralohio

Vince McGrail, Executive Director
Katie Kirby, Director, Public Relations & Comms.

411 **Alzheimer's Association: Cleveland Area**
23215 Commerce Park Drive
Beachwood, OH 44122
216-721-8457
800-272-3900
Fax: 216-831-8585
www.alz.org/cleveland

Cheryl Kanetsky, Interim Executive Director

412 **Alzheimer's Association: Greater East Ohio**
408 Ninth St. SW
Canton, OH 44707
330-966-7343
800-272-3900
Fax: 330-966-7757
ckanetsky@alz.org
www.alz.org/eastohio

Cheryl Kanetsky, Interim Executive Director
Mary Ertle, Program Director

413 **Alzheimer's Association: Miami Valley**
6077 Far Hills Ave.
Dayton, OH 45459
937-291-3332
800-272-3900
Fax: 937-291-0463
mvprograms@alz.org
www.alz.org/dayton

414 **Alzheimer's Association: Northwest Ohio**
480 Dussel Dr.
Maumee, OH 43537
419-537-1999
800-272-3900
Fax: 419-536-5591
jpechlivanos@alz.org
www.alz.org/nwohio

Julia Faulkner Pechlivanos, Executive Director

Oklahoma

415 **Alzheimer's Association: Oklahoma**
6601 N. Broadway Ext.
Oklahoma City, OK 73116
405-319-0780
800-272-3900
www.alz.org/oklahoma

Oregon

416 **Alzheimer's Association: Oregon and SW Washington**
5285 Meadows Road
Lake Oswego, OR 97035
503-416-0201
800-272-3900
www.alz.org/orswwa

Pennsylvania

417 **Alzheimer's Association: Delaware Valley**
399 Market St.
Philadelphia, PA 19106
800-272-3900
klfransel@alz.org
www.alz.org/delval

Kristina Fransel, Executive Director
Abbey Hunton, Senior Director, Marketing & Comms.

418 **Alzheimer's Association: Greater Pennsylvania**
2595 Interstate Drive
Harrisburg, PA 17110
717-651-5020
800-272-3900
cjacobs@alz.org
www.alz.org/pa

Clay Jacobs, Executive Director
Sara Murphy, VP, Programs & Services

Alzheimer's Disease/Dementia / Agencies & Associations

Rhode Island

419 Alzheimer's Association: Rhode Island
245 Waterman Street
Providence, RI 02906
800-272-3900
Donna.McGowan@alz.org
www.alz.org/ri

Jacqueline Waldon, CPA, President
Thomas Enright, Esq., Vice President

South Carolina

420 Alzheimer's Association: South Carolina
123 W. Antrim Drive
Greenville, SC 29607
800-272-3900
calewine@alz.org
www.alz.org/sc

Cindy Alewine, President & CEO
Sam Wiley, VP, Programs

South Dakota

421 Alzheimer's Association: South Dakota
5915 S. Remington Place
Sioux Falls, SD 57108
605-339-4543
800-272-3900
www.alz.org/sd

Tennessee

422 Alzheimer's Association: East Tennessee
9050 Executive Park Drive
Knoxville, TN 37923
800-272-3900
skthompson@alz.org
www.alz.org/tn

Sara Dickson, Development Manager

423 Alzheimer's Association: Middle Tennessee
1801 West End Ave., Suite 200
Nashville, TN 37203
800-272-3900
dcbunn@alz.org
www.alz.org/tn

Dawne Bunn, Executive Director
Misa Acox, Director, Communications

424 Alzheimer's Association: Northeast Tennessee
P.O. Box 41428
Nashville, TN 37204
800-272-3900
www.alz.org/tn

George Jensen, Chair
Sarah Wood, Local Contact

425 Alzheimer's Association: Southeast Tennessee
7625 Hamilton Park Dr.
Chattanooga, TN 37421
800-272-3900
afrench@alz.org
www.alz.org/tn

Amy French, Programs Manager

Texas

426 Alzheimer's Alliance: Dallas and Northeast Texas
5000 Quorum Drive
Dallas, TX 75254
800-272-3900
madenzin@alz.org
www.alztexark.org/dallasnetexas

Mark Denzin, Executive Director
Kathy Shockley, MA, LNHA, Program Director

427 Alzheimer's Association: Capital of Texas
5508 Highway 290 West
Austin, TX 78735
512-592-0990
800-272-3900
Fax: 512-692-3813
ataurins@alz.org
www.alz.org/texascapital

Andrea Taurins, Executive Director
Christine Casebeer, Development Director

428 Alzheimer's Association: Houston and Southeast Texas
6055 South Loop East
Houston, TX 77087-1005
713-314-1313
800-272-3900
Fax: 713-314-1316
relbein@alz.org
www.alz.org/texas

Richard Elbein, CEO
Alexis Eaton, Chief Development Officer

429 Alzheimer's Association: North Central Texas
2630 West Freeway
Fort Worth, TX 76102
817-336-4949
800-272-3900
www.alz.org

Brenda Shuttlesworth, Executive Director
Jenna Perales, LMSW, Director, Program Services

430 Alzheimer's Association: San Antonio and South Texas
1100 Northwest Loop 410
San Antonio, TX 78213
800-272-3900
gsciuto@alz.org
www.alz.org

Gregory Sciuto, Executive Director
Ginny Funk, Director, Programs

431 Alzheimer's Association: West Texas
110 Mesa Park Dr.
El Paso, TX 79912
915-544-1799
800-272-3900
westtexas@alz.org
www.alz.org/westtexas

Dave Hernandez, Chapter Executive
Maria Llamas, Director, Programs

Utah

432 Alzheimer's Association: Utah
12894 S. Pony Express Road
Draper, UT 84020
801-265-1944
800-272-3900
stkulp@alz.org
www.alz.org/utah

Stacie Kulp, Executive Director
Raven Albertson, Program Director

Vermont

433 Alzheimer's Association: Vermont
75 Talcott Road
Williston, VT 05495
802-316-3839
800-272-3900
www.alz.org/vermont

Howard Goodrow, Executive Director
Jordan Cotto, Program Manager

Virginia

434 Alzheimer's Association: Central and Western Virginia
355 Rio Road West
Charlottesville, VA 22901
434-973-6122
800-272-3900
alzcwva@alz.org
www.alz.org/cwva

Lissa Greenlee, Executive Director
Jeanne Snyder, Community Executive

435 Alzheimer's Association: Greater Richmond
4600 Cox Road
Glen Allen, VA 23060
804-967-2580
800-272-3900
Fax: 804-967-2588
lagreenlee@alz.org
www.alz.org/grva

Lissa Greenlee, Executive Director
Tabitha Cox, Regional Office Operations Manager

436 Alzheimer's Association: Southeastern Virginia
6350 Center Drive
Norfolk, VA 23502
757-459-2405
800-272-3900
Fax: 757-461-7902
kmcdonough@alz.org
www.alz.org/seva

Katie McDonough, LCSW, Executive Director
Douglas Panto, Community Programs Manager

437 Alzheimer's Association: West Virginia
1601 2nd Avenue
Charleston, WV 25387
304-343-2717
800-272-3900
Fax: 304-343-2723
wvinfo@alz.org
www.alz.org/wv

Sharon M. Covert, Executive Director
Teresa Morris, Program Director

Alzheimer's Disease/Dementia / Foundations

Washington

438 **Alzheimer's Association: Washington State**
19031 33rd Ave West
Lynnwood, WA 98036
206-363-5500
800-272-3900
Fax: 206-363-5700
jwilgus@alz.org
www.alz.org/alzwa

Jim Wilgus, Executive Director
Brad Forbes, Director, Public Policy

West Virginia

439 **Alzheimer's Association: West Virginia**
1601 2nd Avenue
Charleston, WV 25387
304-343-2717
800-272-3900
Fax: 304-343-2723
wvinfo@alz.org
www.alz.org/wv

Sharon M. Covert, Executive Director
Teresa Morris, Program Director

Wisconsin

440 **Alzheimer's Association: Wisconsin**
2700 Vernon Ave.
Green Bay, WI 54304
920-469-2110
800-272-3900
Fax: 920-469-2131
dgrams@alz.org
www.alz.org/wi

Dave Grams, Executive Director
Wendy Betley, Senior Program Director

Wyoming

441 **Alzheimer's Association: Wyoming**
2232 Dell Range Blvd.
Cheyenne, WY 82009
307-316-2892
800-272-3900
debianchi@alz.org
www.alz.org/wyoming

Debra Antista-Bianchi, MPH, MS, Executive Director
Robin McIntyre, Development Manager

Foundations

442 **Alzheimer's Foundation of America**
322 Eighth Avenue
New York, NY 10001
866-232-8484
info@alzfdn.org
alzfdn.org

Offers support and resources to individuals, families, and caregivers affected by Alzheimer's disease, and funds research for advanced treatment and a cure.
Bert E. Brodsky, Founder & Chair
Charles J. Fuschillo Jr., President & CEO

443 **John Douglas French Alzheimer's Foundation**
1191 Brookmere Road
Pasadena, CA 91105
213-219-3575
cheryl@jdfaf.org
www.jdfaf.org

Provides seed money for promising research including the cause cure and prevention of Alzheimer's disease. Also gives funding to scientists who might not otherwise be funded.
B.J. Kirwan Hanna, Chair
Cheryl Mae Craft, Ph.D., President & CEO

Libraries & Resource Centers

444 **Alzheimer's Disease & Related Dementias**
National Institute on Aging
P.O. Box 8057
Gaithersburg, MD 20898
800-438-4380
adear@nia.nih.gov
www.nia.nih.gov/health/alzheimers

A service of the National Institute on Aging, the center distributes information on Alzheimer's disease, on current research activities and on services available to patients and family members. Offers a free list of publications available upon request.
Nina Silverberg, Program Director, Alzheimer's

445 **Green-Field Library-Alzheimer's Association**
225 N. Michigan Avenue
Chicago, IL 60601
847-324-0356
800-272-3900
Fax: 866-699-1238
TTY: 312-335-5886
TDD: 312-335-8700
greenfield@alz.org
www.alz.org

Located at the national Alzheimer's Association in Chicago this library offers a sizable collection of videos on a variety of subjects that may interest the Alzheimer's patient family members and caregivers.
Richard Hovland, COO

Research Centers

446 **Aging and Alzheimer's Disease Center Oregon Health Sciences University**
3303 S Bond Avenue
Portland, OR 97239
503-494-7772
www.ohsu.edu/research/alzheimers

Researches causes and consequences of Alzheimer's disease and ways of clinical services. Publishes a newsletter twice a year.
Peter Barr-Gillespie, PhD, Chief Research Officer
Danny Jacobs, OHSU President

447 **Alzheimer's Disease & Memory Disorders Center**
ADMDC
One Baylor Plaza
Houston, TX 77030
713-798-4734
Fax: 713-798-7434
neurons@bcm.edu
www.bcm.edu/neurology/admdc

Researchers work to translate advances into improved care and diagnosis for Alzheimer's Disease and other memory disorders.
Everton A. Edmondson, MD, Professor
Doris Hichi Kung, DO, Associate Professor

448 **Alzheimer's Disease Center University of Alabama at Birmingham**
University of Alabama at Birmingham
1720 2nd Avenue S
Birmingham, AL 35294
205-934-4011
TTY: 205-996-2691
icar@uab.edu
www.uab.edu

Researchers work to translate advances into improved care and diagnosis for Alzheimer's patients.
Erik Roberson, MD, Director

449 **Alzheimer's Disease Center Kentucky University**
Sanders-Brown Center on Aging
789 S Limestone
Lexington, KY 40536
859-323-5550
www.medicine.uky.edu

Researchers work to translate advances into improved care and diagnosis for Alzheimer's patients.
Linda J. Van Eldik, Ph.D., Director
Vince J Kellen, Chief Information Officer

450 **Alzheimer's Disease Center Mayo Clinic Mayo Medical School**
Mayo Medical School
3033 41st NW
Rochester, MN 55901
507-284-1324
Fax: 507-538-0878
mcsaadrcdatasharing@mayo.edu
www.mayoclinic.com

Researchers work to translate advances into improved care and diagnosis for Alzheimer's patients.
John H. Noseworhty, M.D., President & CEO

451 **Alzheimer's Disease Center: Boston University**
Boston University School of Medicine
72 E Concord Street
Boston, MA 02118
617-638-5426
888-458-2823
Fax: 617-414-1197
buad@bu.edu
www.bu.edu/alzresearch

Researchers work to translate advances into improved care and diagnosis for Alzheimer's patients.
Neil W. Kowall, Director
Richard Fine, Associate Director

Alzheimer's Disease/Dementia / Research Centers

452 **Alzheimer's Disease Center: Johns Hopkins University School of Medicine**
Johns Hopkins University Department of Pathology
720 Rutland Avenue 410-502-5164
Baltimore, MD 21205 Fax: 410-955-9777
edelman1@jhmi.edu
www.alzresearch.org
Researchers work to translate advances into improved care and diagnosis for Alzheimer's patients.
Marilyn Albert, Director
Philip Wong, Associate Director

453 **Alzheimer's Disease Center: University of California, Davis**
4860 Y Street 916-734-5496
Sacramento, CA 95817 wjjagust@lbl.gov
alzheimer.ucdavis.edu/
Researchers work to translate advances into improved care and diagnosis for Alzheimer's patients.
Charles DeCarli, M.D., Clinical Core Director

454 **Alzheimer's Disease Center: University of Alabama at Birmingham**
1720 7th Avenue S 205-934-3847
Birmingham, AL 35294 Fax: 205-975-7365
adbrain@uab.edu
www.main.uab.edu/adc
Researchers work to translate advances into improved care and diagnosis for Alzheimer's patients.
Daniel Marson, Director
J. Michael Wyss, Associate Director

455 **Alzheimer's Disease Center: Washington University**
1660 S Columbian Way 206-764-2069
Seattle, WA 98108 800-317-5382
Fax: 206-768-5456
wamble@u.washington.edu
www.depts.washington.edu/adrcweb
Researchers work to translate advances into improved care and diagnosis for Alzheimer's patients.
Sydney Lewis, Education & Outreach Coordinator
Nancy Brown, Lead Psychometrist

456 **Alzheimer's Disease Research Center Washington University School of Medicine**
Washington University School of Medicine
4488 Forest Park Avenue 314-286-2683
St Louis, MO 63108 Fax: 314-286-2763
morrisj@abraxas.wustl.edu
www.adrc.wustl.edu
Researchers work to translate advances into improved care diagnosis and treatment for Alzheimer's patients.
John Morris, Director
Virginia D. Buckles, Executive Director

457 **Alzheimer's Disease Research Center Duke University**
Bryan ADRC
2200 W Main Street Suite A200 919-668-0820
Durham, NC 27705 866-444-2372
kwe@duke.edu
adrc.mc.duke.edu
Researchers work to translate advances into improved care and diagnosis for Alzheimer's patients.
Kathleen A. Welsh-Bohmer, Director
James Robert Burke, Associate Director

458 **Alzheimer's and Memory Disorders Clinic**
1120 15th Street 706-721-4581
Augusta, GA 30912 www.augusta.edu
Clinical and basic research of Alzheimer's disease.

459 **Brain Health and Memory Center Research**
Case Western Reserve University
10900 Euclid Avenue 216-368-2000
Cleveland, OH 44106 www.case.edu
Researchers work to translate advances into improved care and diagnosis for Alzheimer's patients.
Cathy Sila, MD, Chair

460 **Center for Cognitive Neuroscience and Aging**
Center on Aging
1695 NW 9th Avenue 305-355-9080
Miami, FL 33136 Fax: 305-355-9076
CNSA@miami.edu
med.miami.edu
Focuses on brain disorders such as Alzheimer's research.
Alexandra Amaya, Research Associate
Yuleidys Feito, Clinic Coordinator

461 **Cognitive Neurology and Alzheimer's Disease Center**
CNADC
320 E Superior Street 312-908-9339
Chicago, IL 60611 Fax: 312-908-8789
CNADC-Admin@northwestern.edu
www.brain.northwestern.edu
Researchers work to translate advances into improved care and diagnosis for Alzheimer's patients.
Megan Atchu, Research Administrator
Kevin Connolly, Business Administrator

462 **Cornell University: Winifred Masterson Burke Medical Research-Dementia**
1300 York Avenue 212-746-5454
New York, NY 10065 Fax: 212-821-0576
publicaffairs@med.cornell.edu
www.med.cornell.edu
Clinical and basic studies in metabolic aspects of the nervous system especially Alzheimer's disease.
David J. Skorton, MD, President
Thomas H. Blair, III, Senior Director Administrator

463 **Department of Psychology**
1835 Neil Avenue 614-292-8185
Columbus, OH 43210 Fax: 614-292-6798
ASC-psychmainoffice@osu.edu
www.psy.ohio-state.edu
Specializes in brain disorders such as Alzheimer's disease. Research programs include: Attiudes and Persuasion, Social Behaviour, Social Cognition, Cognitive Neuroscience, and Decision Psychology.
Richard Petty, Chair
Scott Burch, Behavioral Neurosciences Area Assistant

464 **Duke University Center for the Study of Aging and Human Development**
Duke University
Box 3003 919-660-7500
Durham, NC 27710 Fax: 919-668-0453
webmaster@geri.duke.edu
www.geri.duke.edu
Basic and clinical research into geriatrics and gerontology focusing on a number of chronic diseases in the elderly including osteoporosis, cancer, heart disease, infectious diseases, Alzheimer's disease and other disorders leading to dysmobility.
Harvey Jay Cohen, MD, Director
Linda K. George, Associate Director

465 **Duke University Clinical Research Institute**
Headquarters
2400 Pratt Street 919-668-8700
Durham, NC 27705 www.dcri.duke.edu
Multidisciplinary clinical research into the cause and prevention of human diseases such as Alzheimer's.
Robert Harrington, Director

466 **Goizueta Alzheimer's Disease Research Center**
6 Executive Park Drive NE 404-712-0367
Atlanta, GA 30329 www.alzheimers.emory.edu
Researchers work to translate advances into improved care and diagnosis for Alzheimer's patients.
Allan Levey, MD, PhD, Director
James Lah, MD, PhD, Associate Director

467 **Icahn School of Medicine at Mount Sinai**
Alzheimer's Disease Research Center
One Gustave L Levy Place 212-241-6500
New York, NY 10029 mary.sano@mssm.edu
www.mssm.edu
Focuses on Alzheimer's disease research.
Kenneth Davis, MD, Chief Executive Officer
David Muller, MD, Dean, Medical Education

429

Alzheimer's Disease/Dementia / Support Groups & Hotlines

468 Indiana University Center for Aging Research
The Center for Aging Research
1050 Wishard Blvd   317-630-6083
Indianapolis, IN 46202   Fax: 317-423-5695
www.medicine.iupui.edu/iucar/?
Researchers work to translate advances into improved care and diagnosis for Alzheimer's patients.
Christopher Callahan, Director
Douglas Miller, Associate Director

469 Indiana University: Human Genetics Center of Medical & Molecular Genetics
School of Medicine
410 West 10th Street   317-274-2240
Indianapolis, IN 46202   iusm@iu.edu
www.medicine.iu.edu
Comprised of a core group of scientists with primary appointments in the Department and a group of molecular biologists from other departments who hold joint appointments in Medical and Molecular Genetics.
Wayne C. Forrester, PhD, Director of Genetics
Tatiana Foroud, PhD, Executive Associate Dean

470 Institute for Basic Research in Developmental Disabilities
44 Holland Avenue   866-946-9733
Albany, NY 12229   info@opwdd.ny.gov
www.opwdd.ny.gov/institute-for-basic-res
Kerri E. Neifeld, Commissioner

471 Long Island Alzheimers & Dementia Center
1025 Old Country Road   516-767-6856
Westbury, NY 11590   Fax: 516-767-6856
info@liaf.org
www.liaf.org
Researchers work to translate advances into improved care and diagnosis for Alzheimer's and Dementia patients
Tori Cohen, Executive Director
Gregg Suchow, Executive Assistant

472 Massachusetts Alzheimers Disease Research Center
Massachusetts ADRC
16th Street   617-278-0600
Charlestown, MA 02129   www.madrc.org
Multi-institutional consortium of Harvard affiliated facilities that encompasses five Core units: an Administrative Core, a Clinical Core, a Database Management and Statistics Core, a Neuropathology Core, and an Education and Information Transfer Core. The ADRC also supports four specific research projects funded for 3-5 years, and annually designates three or four pilot research projects that are funded for 1 year.
Bradley T. Hyman, MD, PhD, Center Director
M.Teresa Gomez-Isla, MD, PhD, Assistant Center Director

473 Michigan Alzheimer's Disease Research Center
University of Michigan
2101 Commonwealth Blvd.,   734-936-8803
Ann Arbor, MI 48105   MADC@med.umich.edu
www.med.umich.edu/alzheimers
Researchers work to translate advances into improved care and diagnosis for Alzheimer's patients.
Sid Gilman, M.D., Director
Bruno Giordani Ph.D., Core Director

474 Penn Memory Center
Perelman Center For Advanced Medicine
3400 Civic Center Boulevard   215-662-7810
Philadelphia, PA 19104   Fax: 215-615-4695
pennmemorycenter.org
Researchers work to translate advances into improved care and diagnosis for Alzheimer's patients.
John Karlawish, MD, Director

475 Taub Institute for Research on Alzheimers Disease and the Aging Brain
630 West 168th Street   212-305-1818
New York, NY 10032   Fax: 212-342-2849
taubinstitute@columbia.edu
columbianeuroresearch.org
Researchers work to translate advances into improved care and diagnosis for Alzheimer's patients.
Michael L. Shelanski, Co-Director
Richard Mayeux, Co-Director

476 UC San Diego Center for Healthy Aging
University of California San Diego
9500 Gilman Drive   858-534-6299
La Jolla, CA 92093-0664   Fax: 858-534-5475
aging@ucsd.edu
healthyaging.uscd.edu
Research on aging and Alzheimer's disease.
Alison A. Moore, MD, MPH, Interim Director
Anthony Molina, PhD, Interim Scientific Director

477 UI Health
University of Illinois College of Medicine
1740 W Taylor Street   866-600-2273
Chicago, IL 60612   www.hospital.uillinois.edu
A unit of the University of Illinois College of Medicine at Rockford serves faculty students health care providers human services agencies and other community organizations throughout Illinois with demographic health social and economic data. The skills data and resources available to faculty and students at the college are also available to individuals and organizations needing assistance.
Michael B. Zenn, MBA, Chief Executive Officer
Jon Rodosta, MD, Chief Medical Officer

478 University of Chicago Dept of Neurology
University of Chicago
5841 S Maryland Avenue   773-702-6222
Chicago, IL 60637   neurology.uchicago.edu
Covers Translational Neuroscience Research and research programs in neuroimmunology neuromuscular disease and neurovirology provided the initial foundation and brought national recognition.
Shyam Prabhakaran, Chair

479 University of Maryland: Division of Infectious Diseases
UM Baltimore Department of Medicine
655 West Baltimore Street 410-328-2488
Baltimore, MD 21201   Fax: 410-328-8688
cwallace@som.umaryland.edu
www.medschool.umaryland.edu
Focuses research on elderly studies including drug use treatments and infectious diseases of the aged.
Stephen N. Davis, Professor & Chair

480 Yeshiva University: Resnick Gerontology Center
Albert Einstein College of Medicine
Jack and Pearl Resnick Campus   718-430-2000
Bronx, NY 10467   www.einsteinmed.edu
Alzheimer's disease and other dementia studies.
Joe Verghese, Director
Yousin Suh, PhD, Professor

Support Groups & Hotlines

481 Alzheimer's Association Autopsy Assistance Network
Alzheimer s Association
Western/Central Washington Chapter   206-363-5500
Seattle, WA 98125   800-848-7097
Fax: 206-363-5700
rowena.rye@alz.org
http://alzwa.org/resources6.htm
The primary purposes of the Autopsy Assistance Network are: to provide families with information regarding autopsy; to assist in obtaining a confirmed diagnosis; provide tissue for Alzheimer's disease research; and establish diagnosis for purpose of clinical and epidemiological studies.
Nancy Dapper, Executive Director
Rowena Rye, Community Resources

482 Alzheimer's Support Group
Columbus Health Rehabilitation Center
2100 Midway Street   812-372-8447
Columbus, IN 47201   Fax: 812-375-5117
www.columbushrc.com/

Alzheimer's Disease/Dementia / Web Sites

The skilled Nursing Center includes a separate unit dedicated to the care of residents with Alzheimer's disease and other forms of dementia. The Alzheimer's program is designed to celebrate the spirit of their residents, striving to offer a comfortable and compassionate environment that emphasizes positive life experiences and active involvement in a daily routine.
Mike Spencer, Executive Director

483   Holliswood Hospital Psychiatric Care, Services and Self-Help/Support Groups
87-37 Palermo Street   718-776-8181
Holliswood, NY 11423   800-486-3005
                     Fax: 718-776-8572
HolliswoodInfo@libertymgt.com
www.holliswoodhospital.com/

The Holliswood Hospital, a 110-bed private psychiatric hospital located in a quiet residential Queens community, is a leader in providing quality, acute inpatient mental health care for adult, adolescent, geriatric and dually diagnosed patients. Holliswood Hospital treats patients with a broad range of psychiatric disorders. Additionally, specialized services are available for patients with psychiatric diagnoses compounded by chemical dependency, or a history of physical or sexual abuse.
Susan Clayton, Support Group Coordinator
Angela Hurtado, Support Group Coordinator

484   National Health Information Center
Office of Disease Prevention & Health Promotion
1101 Wootton Pkwy   Fax: 240-453-8281
Rockville, MD 20852   odphpinfo@hhs.gov
                     www.health.gov/nhic

Supports public health education by maintaining a calendar of National Health Observances; helps connect consumers and health professionals to organizations that can best answer questions and provide up-to-date contact information from reliable sources; updates on a yearly basis toll-free numbers for health information, Federal health clearinghouses and info centers.
Don Wright, MD, MPH, Director

Print Resources

485   Alzheimer Disease and Associated Disorders: An International Journal
Raven Press
1185 Ave of the Americas   212-930-9500
New York, NY 10036   800-777-2295
                     journals.lww.com

A leading international forum for reports of new research findings and new approaches to diagnosis and treatments. Contributions are offered from all scientific and medical fields.
Dr. Jose Luchsinger-Stuart, Editor-in-Chief

486   Alzheimer's & Dementia: The Journal of the Alzheimer's Association
Alzheimer's Association
225 North Michigan Avenue   314-447-8871
Chicago, IL 60601   800-654-2452
                     www.alz.org

A peer-reviewed journal that publishes reviews, clinical trials, and investigations on dementia research.
Donna M. Wilcock, PhD, Editor-in-Chief

487   Journal of Alzheimer's Disease (JAD)
IO Press
                  george.perry@j-alz.com
                     www.j-alz.com

An international multidisciplinary journal that publishes research reports, reviews, and hypotheses on Alzheimer's disease.
George Perry, PhD, Editor-in-Chief
Beth Kumar, Managing Editor

488   Journal of Neuropsychiatry and Clinical Neurosciences
American Neuropsychiatric Association
P.O. Box 97   anpaoffice@gmail.com
Abilene, KS 67410-1707   neuro.psychiatryonline.org

Publishes peer-reviewed articles on neuroscience and behavioral disrders, and addresses subjects like Alzheimer's disease, traumatic brain injury, Parkinson's disease, epilepsy, and seizure disorders.
David B. Arciniegas, M.D., Editor
C. Alan Anderson, M.D., Deputy Editor

Web Sites

489   Alzheimer Research Forum
                     www.alzforum.org
The web's most dynamic scientific community dedicated to understanding alzheimer's disease and related disorders.

490   Alzheimer Support
                  www.alzheimersupport.com
Serves Alzheimer's sufferers and their loved ones by reporting the latest news in research and treatment, making hard-to-find, recommended nutritional supplements available at manufacturer-direct low prices, and, most importantly, donating profits from each purchase to fund Alzheimer's medical research.

491   Alzheimer's Association
                       www.alz.org
The leading, global voluntary health organization in Alzheimer care and support, and the largest private, nonprofit funder of Alzheimer research.

492   Alzheimer's Disease International
                     www.alz.co.uk/adi
The international federation of 73 Alzheimer associations around the world, in relations with the World Health Organization.

493   Healing Well
                     www.healingwell.com
A social network and support community for patients, caregivers, and families coping with the daily struggles of diseases, disorders and chronic illness.

494   Health Central
                     www.healthcentral.com
Find clearly explained, medically accurate information regarding conditions, including an overview, symptoms, causes, diagnostic procedures and treatment options. On this site it is possible to ask questions and get information from a neurologist and connect to people who have similar health interests.

495   Health Finder
                       www.health.gov
Searchable, carefully developed web site offering information on over 1000 topics. Developed by the US Department of Health and Human Services, thesite can be used in both English and Spanish.

496   MEDLINEplus Health Information
                  www.nlm.nih.gov/medlineplus
MedlinePlus is the National Institutes of Health's Web site for patients and their families and friends.

497   Medical News Today
                    www.medicalnewstody.com
Offers in-depth health information and the latest news in medical research on a wide variety of medical conditions.

498   MedicineNet
                     www.medicinenet.com
An online resource for consumers providing easy-to-read, authoritative medical and health information.

499   MedlinePlus
                     www.medlineplus.gov
Information regarding a broad range of health,and mental health conditions topics include: Latest news, overview of anatomy and physiology, clinical trials, diagnoses and symptoms, treatment, genetics, plus lots of links to other sites. A service provided by the National Library of Medicine, part of the National Institutes of Health (NIH).

500   Medscape
                     www.medscape.com
Medscape offers specialists, primary care physicians, and other health professionals the Web's most robust and integrated medical information and educational tools.

Alzheimer's Disease/Dementia / Web Sites

501 MyHealthfinder
www.healthfinder.gov
Searchable, carefully developed web site offering information on over 1000 topics. Developed by the US Department of Health and Human Services, the site can be used in both English and Spanish.

502 Neurology Channel
www.healthcommunities.com
Find clearly explained, medically accurate information regarding conditions, including an overview, symptoms, causes, diagnostic procedures and treatment options. On this site it is possible to ask questions and get information from a neurologist and connect to people who have similar health interests.

503 Verywell Mind
www.verywellmind.com
Provides up-to-date information on mental health topics. mission is to prioritize mental health and promote balance for day to day living. offers over 5,500 online articles that are researched based, and reviwed by medical professionals.
Kristen Altmeyer, MBA, VP & General Manager
Nick Ingalls, MA, Associate Editorial Director

504 WebMD
www.webmd.com
Provides credible information, supportive communities, and in-depth reference material about health subjects. A source for original and timely health information, as well as material from well-known content providers.

ANXIETY DISORDERS

Anxiety is a normal reaction to stress and refers to anticipation of a future concern, or a "what if." Worry about health, money or family problems occasionally is normal but in anxiety disorders the worry never goes away. Anxiety disorders are the most common form of mental disorders impacting almost 30 percent of adults at some point in their lives. In individuals with anxiety disorders, the anxiety never goes away and can get worse over time. Symptoms interfere with activities of daily life such as relationships, work performance, and school performance. Types of anxiety disorders include generalized anxiety disorder, social anxiety disorder, panic disorder, and a variety of phobia-related disorders.

Typical symptoms of generalized anxiety disorder include feelings of restlessness, being "wound-up" or irritable, easily fatigued, headaches, muscle aches and unexplained pain and sleep problems. Individuals who have panic attacks have panic disorder. Characterized by sudden bouts of intense fear, sense of losing control even without clear danger or generalized discomfort, panic attacks may cause racing or pounding heart, chest pain, sweating and feelings of impending doom or being out of control. They may occur several times a day or only a few times a year.

An intense fear or feeling of being watched and judged by others is described as a social anxiety disorder. The fear of social situations may prevent going to work, school or doing everyday activities. An intense fear or aversion to something is the definition of a phobia. Often the fear associated with the phobia is disproportionate to the actual danger of the situation. Simple phobias may include flying, heights, spiders, receiving injections or seeing blood. Social anxiety disorder, previously called social phobia, causes individuals to avoid social settings. Agoraphobia, may include using public transportation, fear of open or closed spaces, being in a crowd or being outside of the home and the individual may have a panic-like reaction to these types of situations. Selective mutism is a rare disorder where individuals do not speak in public, may be accompanied by extreme shyness and withdrawal, and may run in tandem with other anxiety disorders.

Both environmental and genetic factors contribute to the development of anxiety disorder. Thyroid and heart conditions as well as other physical health issues may produce or aggravate anxiety symptoms. Anxiety disorders tend to run in families. If anxiety is present, there is a chance of developing depression. If major depression is already present, anxiety may develop and become persistent.

Anxiety disorders are usually treated with psychotherapy, medication or a combination of the two. Medical and mental health professionals will develop an individualized treatment plan to address the individual's needs. Talk therapy, or psychotherapy, cognitive behavioral therapy, acceptance, and commitment therapy (mindfulness and goal setting to reduce discomfort), are helpful. Medication use is directed at symptom management and may include anti-anxiety medications, anti-depressants and beta blockers. Support groups, either in person or online, may be of benefit but should never be used in place of professional therapy. With proper management, anxiety is controllable.

Anxiety Disorders / Agencies & Associations

Agencies & Associations

505 **A.I.M. Agoraphobics in Motion**
7636 Emerson
Washington, MI 48094
248-710-5719
aimforrecovery@gmail.com
aimforrecovery.com
AIM is a nonprofit support group organization committed to the support and recovery of people with anxiety disorders, as well as their families.
James Fortune, President
Robert Diedrich, Vice President & Secretary

506 **Academy of Psychosomatic Medicine**
4800 Hampden Ln
Bethesda, MD 20814
301-718-6520
info@CLpsychiatry.org
apm.org
The Academy of Psychosomatic Medicine represents psychiatrists focused on improving education, medical science, and healthcare for individuals with comorbid psychiatric and general medical conditions. The Academy seeks to promote interdisciplinary education and drive research and public policy with the goal of achieving outstanding clinical care for patients with comorbid psychiatric and general medical conditions throughout the world. They also created the Foundation of the Academy of Psychosom
Philip Biaeler, MD, FACLP, President
Maryland Pao, MD, FACLP, President-Elect

507 **Adventure Camp**
Advanced Therapeutic Solutions
600 W 22nd Street
Oak Brook, IL 60523
630-230-6505
www.selectivemutismtreatment.net
A summer camp designed to help children with selective mutism. This exposure therapy program is designed to simulate a classroom environment, and each child is assigned a counselor for one-on-one therapy.
Carmen M. Tumialan Lyna, PhD, Clinical Psychologist/Owner

508 **Agoraphobics Building Independent Lives**
2008 Bremo Road
Richmond, VA 23226
804-257-5591
866-400-6428
info@mhav.org
mhav.org
A nonprofit organization for people dealing with anxiety and panic disorders, incorporated in the State of Virginia. It has support groups nationwide.
Bruce Cruser, Executive Director
Jenny Sappington, Outreach Coordinator

509 **American Psychiatric Association**
800 Maine Avenue SW
Washington, DC 20024
202-559-3900
apa@psych.org
www.psychiatry.org
A medical specialty society representing a growing membership of psychiatrists. Offers information for psychiatrists, medical students, patients and families.
Saul Levin, MD, MPA, FRCP-E, CEO

510 **Anxiety and Depression Association of America**
8701 Georgia Avenue
Silver Spring, MD 20910
240-485-1030
information@adaa.org
adaa.org
An international nonprofit organization committed to the use of education and research to promote the prevention, treatment, and cure of anxiety, depressive, obssesive compulsive, and other trauma related disorders. ADAA's mission is to improve the lives of all people with anxiety and mood disorders.
Charles B. Nemeroff, MD, President
Susan K. Gurley, JD, Executive Director

511 **Center for Mental Health Services (CMHS)**
Substance Abuse and Mental Health Services Adminis
5600 Fishers Lane
Rockville, MD 20857
240-276-1310
samhsa.gov
Promotes the treatment of mental illness and emotional disorders by increasing accessibility to mental health programs; supporting outreach, treatment, rehabilitation, and support programs and networks; and encouraging the use of scientifically-based information when treating mental disorders. CMHS provides information about mental health via a toll-free number and numerous publications. Developed for users of mental health services and their families, the general public, policy makers, provider
Anita Everett, MD, DFAPA, Director

512 **Children's and Adult Center for OCD and Anxiety**
3138 Butler Pike
Plymouth Meeting, PA 19462
childrenscenterocdandanxiety.com
A center comprising five private practice psychologists delivering treatment and therapy to children and adults with OCD, Separation Anxiety, and other mental health disorders. They also offer parent workshops on skills and strategies to help their child cope with anxiety.
Tamar Chansky, PhD, Founder

513 **Children's and Adult Center for OCD an Anxiety**
3138 Butler Pike
Plymouth Meeting, PA 19462
484-530-0778
childrenscenterocdandanxiety.com
A center comprising five private practice psychologists delivering treatment and therapy to children and adults with OCD, Separation Anxiety, and other mental health disorders. They also offer parent workshops on skills and strategies to help their child cope with anxiety.
Tamar Chansky, PhD, Founder

514 **Depression & Bipolar Support Alliance**
55 East Jackson Boulevard
Chicago, IL 60604
800-826-3632
info@dbsalliance.org
dbsalliance.org
The Depression and Bipolar Support Alliance is a national organization focused on improving the lives of individuals with depression, bipolar disorder, and other mood disorders. DBSA organizes peer-led support groups; educates patients, families, professionals, and the public on mental health; and works to ensure the availability of quality care for all people.
Roger McIntyre, Chair
Michael Pollock, Chief Executive Officer

515 **Freedom From Fear**
308 Seaview Avenue
Staten Island, NY 10305
718-351-1717
help@freedomfromfear.org
freedomfromfear.org
A national nonprofit organization, the mission of Freedom From Fear is to aid and counsel individuals suffering from anxiety and depressive disorders through advocacy, education, research, and community support.
Mary Guardino, Founder and Executive Director

516 **Goodwill's Community Employment Services**
Goodwill Industries-Suncoast, Inc.
10596 Gandy Blvd.
St. Petersburg, FL 33702
727-523-1512
888-279-1988
TDD: 727-579-1068
goodwill-suncoast.org
The St. Petersburg headquarters serves ten counties in the state of Florida. Their mission is to help people with disabilities gain employment through training programs, employment services, and affordable housing.
Sandra Young, Chair
Louise Lopez, Sr. Vice Chair

517 **Help is Here**
North Dakota Behavioral Health Division
600 E Boulevard Avenue
Bismarck, ND 58501
701-328-2310
800-472-2622
dhsbhd@nd.gov
www.helpishere.nd.gov
Promotes the support and treatment of mental illness and emotional disorders. Offers mental health services, addiction servces, and recovery centers.

518 **Hope for Depression Research Foundation**
40 West 57th Street
New York, NY 10019
212-676-3200
Fax: 212-676-3219
hdrf@hopefordepression.org
www.hopefordepression.org
Promotes, and encourages profits for neuroscience research into the treatments, diagnosis, origins, and prevention of depression, and other mood disorders such as anxiety disorders, post-traumatic

Anxiety Disorders / Agencies & Associations

stress disorder, postpartum depression, bipolar disorder, and suicide.
Audrey Gruss, Founder & Chairman
Harold W. Koenigsberg, MD, Board Member

519 Institute for Contemporary Psychotherapy
33 W 60th St. 212-333-3444
New York, NY 10023 Fax: 212-333-5444
icpnyc.org
The Institute for Contemporary Psychotherapy is a New York City-based mental health treatment and training facility. Consisting of a group of 150 licensed psychotherapists, the Institute focuses on educating the public about the issues surrounding mental health, providing post-graduate training for therapists, and offering therapy at moderate costs.
Ron Taffel, PhD, Chair
Andrea Green-Lewis, LCSW-R, Director of Operations

520 Mental Health America
500 Montgomery Street 703-684-7722
Alexandria, VA 22314 800-969-6642
mhanational.org
Mental Health America is a community-based nonprofit organization committed to enabling the mental wellness of all Americans. MHA advocates for greater access to quality health services and seeks to educate individuals on identifying symptoms, as well as intervention and prevention.
Schroeder Stribling, President & CEO
Sachin Doshi, Sr. Dir., Finance & Operations

521 National Alliance on Mental Illness
4301 Wilson Boulevard 703-524-7600
Arlington, VA 22203 800-950-6264
info@nami.org
nami.org
NAMI is an organization dedicated to raising awareness on mental health and providing support and education for Americans affected by mental illness. NAMI advocates for access to services and treatment and fosters an environment of awareness and understanding for those concerned with mental health.
Shirley J. Holloway, President
Joyce A. Campbell, First Vice President

522 National Association for the Dually Diagnosed (NADD)
321 Wall Street 845-331-4336
Kingston, NY 12401 info@thenadd.org
thenadd.org
NADD is a nonprofit organization designed to increase awareness of, and provide services for, individuals with developmental disabilities and mental illness. NADD emphasizes the importance of quality mental healthcare for people with mental health needs and offers conferences, information resources, educational programs, and training materials to professionals, parents, and organizations.
Jeanne M. Farr, MA, Chief Executive Officer
Bruce Davis, President

523 National Association of Parents with Children in Special Education
3642 East Sunnydale Drive 800-754-4421
Chandler Heights, AZ 85142 contact@napcse.org
napcse.org
The NAPCSE is dedicated to ensuring quality education for all children and adolescents with special needs. NAPCSE provides resources, support, and assistance to parents with children in special education.
Dr. George Giuliani, President

524 National Council for Behavioral Health
1400 K Street NW communications@thenationalcouncil.org
Washington, DC 20005 thenationalcouncil.org
The National Council for Behavioral Health serves to unify America's behavioral health organizations. The council is dedicated to ensuring that quality mental health and addictions care is readily accessible to all Americans.
Edward Woods, Chair
Charles Ingoglia, President and CEO

525 Recovery International
1415 W. 22nd Street 312-337-5661
Oak Brook, IL 60523 866-221-0302
info@recoveryinternational.org
www.recoveryinternational.org
Recovery International is an organization that uses a peer-to-peer, self-help training system developed by Abraham Low in order to help individuals with mental health issues lead more productive lives.
Sandra K. Wilcoxon, Chief Executive Officer
Joanne Lampey, President

526 SMart Center: Selective Mutism, Anxiet & Related Disorders Treatment Center
261 Old York Road 215-887-5748
Jenkintown, PA 19046 selectivemutismcenter.org
A center that provides treatment and support to children and young adults with selective mutism and other social communication issues. The SMart Center uses the evidence-based Social Communication Anxiety Treatment (S-CAT) program, and also offers products, services, and events for parents, professionals, researchers, and educators.
Dr. Elisa Shipon-Blum, President and Director
William Lavalle, PsyD, Director of Clinical Training

527 Selective Mutism Association (SMA)
info@selectivemutism.org
www.selectivemutism.org
An organization that increases awareness and education about selective mutism. SMA supports families and professionals through an annual conference, expert chat sessions, professional training, online resources, and providing connections with research institutions.
Rachel A. Merson, President
Pamela Martis Zambriski, Treasurer

528 Sutcliffe Clinic
851 Fremont Avenue 650-941-1698
Los Altos, CA 94024 info@sutcliffedbp.com
www.sutcliffeclinic.com
Sutcliffe Developmental & Behavioral Pediatrics is an organization that specializes in the treatment of ADHD, autism spectrum disorder, anxiety disorders, conduct disorders, learning disabilities, and more. Sutcliffe works with community services, school districts, and primary physicians, and provides family counseling.
Trenna Sutcliffe, MD, MS, Medical Director

529 Territorial Apprehensiveness (TERRAP) Anxiety & Stress Program
755 Park Avenue 631-549-8867
Huntington, NY 11743 info@anxietyandpanic.com
anxietyandpanic.com
Helps to treat anxiety and stress disorders through Territorial Apprehensiveness Programs, developed by Dr. Arthur Hardy in the 1960s. The program systematically addresses the behavioral and thought processes of those suffering from stress and anxiety.
Julian Herskowitz, PhD, Director

530 Thriving Minds
10524 E Grand River Avenue 810-225-3417
Brighton, MI 48116 office@thrivingminds.info
www.thrivingmindsbehavioralhealth.com
Thriving Minds is an organization that offers therapy to people with anxiety, behavioral issues, and depression. With locations in Brighton and Chelsea, Thriving Minds uses a mix of research-based interventions, such as Cognitive Behavioral Therapy; parent coaching; and school interventions in order to help children, teens, and adults deal with their anxiety.
Amiee Kotrba, PhD, Owner
Bryce Hella, PhD, Director, Brighton Clinic

531 United Brain Association
202-768-8000
info@unitedbrainassociation.org
unitedbrainassociation.org
Non-profit organization that works to find cures through research for over 600 brain and mental health related issues, and disorders.
J.A. Boulton, Founder
Jay Matey, VP & Treasurer

435

Anxiety Disorders / Foundations

Foundations

532 Brain & Behavior Research Foundation
747 Third Avenue
New York, NY 10017
646-681-4888
800-829-8289
info@bbrfoundation.org
www.bbrfoundation.org

The Brain and Behavior Research Foundation awards grants aimed at advancing scientific understandings of mental health treatments and mental disorders such as depression and schizophrenia. The Brain and Behavior Research Foundation's mission is to eliminate the suffering caused by mental illness.
Donald M. Boardman, Treasurer
Jeffrey Borenstein, MD, President and CEO

Libraries & Resource Centers

533 Family-to-Family: National Alliance on Mental Illness
4301 Wilson Boulevard
Arlington, VA 22203
703-524-7600
888-999-6264
info@nami.org
nami.org

The NAMI Family-to-Family Education Program is a free, 8 session course for family caregivers of individuals with severe mental illnesses. The course is taught by trained family members, all instruction and course materials are free to class participants, and over 300,000 family members have graduated from this national program.

Research Centers

534 Anxiety and Phobia Treatment Center
79 East Post Road
White Plains, NY 10601
914-286-4430
www.phobia-anxiety.org

Treatment for individuals suffering from phobias and other anxiety disorders. Specializes in the use of cognitive-behavioral therapy and exposure therapy.
Judy Lake Chess, LMSW, Coordinator
Thomas Cirolia, LCSW, Group Leader

535 Columbia University Pediatric Anxiety and Mood Research Clinic
1051 Riverside Drive
New York, NY 10032
646-774-8104
childadolescentpsych.cumc.columbia.edu

A research clinic desinged to help children with anxiety, depression, and OCD. The clinic provides evaluations, evidence-based therapy and medications, and a day-treatment program. All evaluation and treatment services are free of charge.
Jeremy Veenstra-VanderWeele, MD, Division Director
Laura Mufson, PhD, Division Associate Director

536 National Institute of Mental Health
6001 Executive Boulevard
Bethesda, MD 20892
866-615-6464
TTY: 301-443-8431
nimhinfo@nih.gov
nimh.nih.gov

The National Institute of Mental Health conducts clinical research on mental disorders and seeks to expand knowledge on mental health treatments.
Joshua Gordon, MD, PhD, Director

537 Selective Mutism Research Institute
505 North Old York Road
Jenkintown, PA 19046
Research@SelectiveMutismCenter.org
selectivemutismresearchinstitute.org

A nonprofit organization dedicated to raising better awareness, treatment, and resources for children dealing with selective mutism and other social communication anxiety.
Dr. Elisa Shipon-Blum, President & Director

538 UAMS Psychiatric Research Institute
4224 Shuffield Drive
Little Rock, AR 72205
501-526-8100
kramerteresal@uams.edu
www.psychiatry.uams.edu

Combining research, education and clinical services into one facility, PRI offers inpatiend and outpatient services, with 40 psychiatric beds, therapy options, and specialized treatment for specific disorders, including: addictive eating, anxiety, deppressive and post-traumatic stress disorders. Research focuses on evidence-based care takes into consideration the education of future medical personnel while relying on research scientists to provide innovative forms of treatment.
John Fortney PhD, Director
Geoff Curran PhD, Associate Director

539 UCLA Anxiety Disorders Research Center
Department of Psychology
Los Angeles, CA 90094
310-825-9312
rose@psych.ucla.edu
anxiety.psych.ucla.edu

The purpose of The ADRC is to further our understanding of the factors that place individuals at risk for developing phobias, anxiety disorders and related conditions, and to develop more effective treatments that have long lasting effects and are cost effective.
Michelle G. Craske, Ph.D., Director
Raphael Rose, Ph.D., Associate Director

Support Groups & Hotlines

540 Agoraphobics Building Independent Lives
2008 Bremo Road
Richmond, VA 23226
804-257-5591
866-400-6428
info@mhav.org
mhav.org

A nonprofit organization for people dealing with anxiety and panic disorders, incorporated in the State of Virginia. It has support groups nationwide.
Bruce Cruser, Executive Director
Jenny Sappington, Outreach Coordinator

541 Center for Family Support
2811 Zulette Avenue
Bronx, NY 10461
718-518-1500
svernikoff@cfsny.org
www.cfsny.org

The Center for Family Support offers assistance to individuals with developmental and related disabilities, as well as their families, and provides support services and programs that are designed to accommodate individual needs. Offers services throughout New York City, Westchester County, Long Island, and New Jersey.
Steven Vernikoff, Executive Director
Barbara Greenwald, Chief Operating Officer

542 Emotions Anonymous International Service Center
PO Box 4245
St. Paul, MN 55104
651-647-9712
director@emotionsanonymous.org
emotionsanonymous.org

A community-based organization to provide support managing mental health difficulties. Groups meet weekly to share experiences, strength, and hope.
Elaine Weber Nelson, Executive Director
Scott J., President

543 Freedom From Fear
308 Seaview Avenue
Staten Island, NY 10305
718-351-1717
help@freedomfromfear.org
freedomfromfear.org

A national nonprofit organization, the mission of Freedom From Fear is to aid and counsel individuals suffering from anxiety and depressive disorders through advocacy, education, research, and community support.
Mary Guardino, Founder and Executive Director

544 Holliswood Hospital Psychiatric Care, Services and Self-Help/Support Groups
87-37 Palermo Street
Holliswood, NY 11423
718-776-8181
800-486-3005
Fax: 718-776-8572
HolliswoodInfo@libertymgt.com
www.holliswoodhospital.com/

The Holliswood Hospital, a 110-bed private psychiatric hospital located in a quiet residential Queens community, is a leader in providing quality, acute inpatient mental health care for adult, adolescent, geriatric and dually diagnosed patients. Holliswood Hospital treats patients with a broad range of psychiatric disorders. Additionally, specialized services are available for patients with psy-

chiatric diagnoses compounded by chemical dependency, or a history of physical or sexual abuse.
Susan Clayton, Support Group Coordinator
Angela Hurtado, Support Group Coordinator

545 **Support4Hope**
PO Box 184
Deer Lodge, TN 37726
Admin@Support4hope.com
www.support4hope.com
Support4Hope is dedicated to support of various mental health issues such as Bipolar Disorder, Depression, Anxiety Disorders, Schizophrenia, Post Traumatic Stress Disorder (PTSD) and the problems that arise from them along with other problems such as Domestic Abuse.

Print Resources

546 **American Journal of Psychiatry**
American Psychiatric Association Publishing
800 Maine Avenue SW, Suite 900
Washington, DC 20024
202-459-9722
800-368-5777
Fax: 202-403-3094
psychiatryonline@psych.org
ajp.psychiatryonline.org
Official journal of the American Psychiatric Association (APA).
Ned H. Kalin, MD, Editor-in-Chief

547 **American Journal of Psychotherapy**
American Psychiatric Association Publishing
800 Maine Avenue SW, Suite 900
Washington, DC 20024
202-459-9722
800-368-5777
Fax: 202-403-3094
psychiatryonline@psych.org
ajp.psychiatryonline.org
Publishes content that aims to advance the theory, science, and clinical practice of psychotherapy.
Holly A. Swartz, MD, Editor-in-Chief

548 **Depression & Anxiety**
Wiley and Hindawi
111 River Street
Hoboken, NJ 07030-5774
201-748-6000
800-567-4797
Fax: 201-748-6088
help@hindawi.com
www.hindawi.com/journals/da
Open-access, peer-reviewed journal covering neurobiology, epidemiology, experimental psychopathology, and treatment aspects of mood and anxiety disorders and related.

549 **International Journal of Depression and Anxiety**
ClinMed International Library
3511 Silverside Road, Suite 105
Wilmington, DE 19810
302-208-7437
contact@clinmedjournals.org
clinmedjournals.org
Open access, peer-reviewed, multidisciplinary journal focusing on treatments for panic attacks, anxiety attacks, phobia, and social phobia.
Photios Anninos, Editor-in-Chief

550 **International Journal of Psychology and Psychoanalysis**
ClinMed International Library
3511 Silverside Road, Suite 105
Wilmington, DE 19810
302-208-7437
contact@clinmedjournals.org
clinmedjournals.org
Open access, peer-reviewed journal focused on cognition, emotions, brain functioning, interpersonal relationships, and the unconscious mind.
Joaquim J.F. Soares, Editor-in-Chief

551 **Journal of Anxiety Disorders**
Elsevier Publishing
1600 John F Kennedy Boulevard
Philadelphia, PA 19103-2398
215-239-3900
800-325-4177
Fax: 215-239-3990
custserv.ehs@elsevier.com
www.sciencedirect.com
Interdisciplinary journal that publishes research papers dealing with all aspects of anxiety disorders for all age groups (child, adolescent, adult and geriatrics).
Deborah Beidel, Author

552 **Journal of Mood & Anxiety Disorders**
Anxiety & Depression Association of America
8701 Georgia Avenue, Suite 412
Silver Spring, MD 20910
240-485-1018
information@adaa.org
adaa.org/professionals/journal
The official journal of the Anxiety & Depression Association of America (ADAA), published with Elsevier. The journal covers neurobiology, epidemiology, experimental psychopathology, pathophysiology, and treatment aspects of mood and anxiety disorders.
Stephen M. Strakowski, MD, Editor-in-Chief

553 **Journal of Psychiatry, Depression & Anxiety**
Herald Scholarly Open Access
2561 Cornelia Road, Suite 205
Herndon, VA 20171
202-499-9679
Fax: 202-217-4195
contact@heraldopenaccess.us
www.heraldopenaccess.us
Online, international, open access, peer-reviewed journal focused primarily on depression and anxiety, but also on other related areas of psychiatry as well.
Sam Vaknin, Editor-in-Chief

554 **National Mental Health Consumers' Self-Help Clearinghouse**
selfhelpclearinghouse@gmail.com
mhselfhelp.org
The Clearinghouse is a peer-run national technical assistance center focused on achieving respect and equality of opportunity for those with mental illnesses. The Clearinghouse helps with the growth of the mental health consumer movement by evaluating mental health services, advocating for mental health reform, and providing consumers with news, information, publications, and consultation services.
Joseph Rogers, Founder and Executive Director
Susan Rogers, Director

Web Sites

555 **A Guide To Psychology & Its Practice**
www.guidetopsychology.com
Free information on various types of psychology.

556 **Agoraphobia: For Friends/Family**
www.panicdisorder.about.com

557 **Anxiety And Phobia Treatment Center**
www.healthanxiety.org
Treatment groups for individuals suffering from phobias.

558 **Anxiety Disorders**
www.healthyminds.org
American Psychiatric Association publication diagnostic criteria and treatment.

559 **Anxiety Panic Hub**
www.panicattacks.com.au
Information, resources and support.

560 **Career Assessment & Planning Services**
www.goodwill-suncoast.org
A comprehensive assessment for the developmentally disabled persons who may be unemployed or underemployed.

561 **Caregivers Series**
www.bcm.tmc.edu/civitas/caregivers.html
Sophisticated articles describing the effects of childhood trauma on brain development and relationships.

562 **Center For Mental Health Services Knowledge Exchange**
www.mentalhealth.Samhsa.Gov
Information about resources, technical assistance, research, training, networks and other federal clearinghouses.

563 **CyberPsych**
www.cyberpsych.org
Presents information about psychoanalysis, psychotherapy and special topics such as anxiety disorders, the problematic use of alcohol, homophobia, and the traumatic effects of racism. Explains in detail what anxiety it is how it is treated and the symptoms associated with anxiety.

Anxiety Disorders / Web Sites

564 Healing Well
www.healingwell.com
An online health resource guide to medical news, chat, information and articles, newsgroups and message boards, books, disease-related web sites, medical directories, and more for patients, friends, and family coping with disabling diseases, disorders, or chronic illnesses.

565 Health Central
www.healthcentral.com
Find clearly explained, medically accurate information regarding conditions, including an overview, symptoms, causes, diagnostic procedures and treatment options. On this site it is possible to ask questions and get information from a neurologist and connect to people who have similar health interests.

566 Health Finder
www.health.gov
Searchable, carefully developed web site offering information on over 1000 topics. Developed by the US Department of Health and Human Services, thesite can be used in both English and Spanish.

567 Internet Mental Health
www.mentalhealth.com
On-line information and a virtual encyclopedia related to mental disorders, possible causes and treatments. News, articles, on-line diagnostic programs and related links. Designed to improve understanding, diagnosis and treatment of mental illness throughout the world. Awarded the Top Site Award and the NetPsych Cutting Edge Site Award.

568 Mayo Clinic
www.mayoclinic.com
Provides information on obsessive-compulsive disorder and anxiety.

569 Medical News Today
www.medicalnewstody.com
Offers in-depth health information and the latest news in medical research on a wide variety of medical conditions.

570 MedicineNet
www.medicinenet.com
An online resource for consumers providing easy-to-read, authoritative medical and health information.

571 Meditation, Guided Fantasies, And Other Stress Remedies
www.selfhelpmagazine.com/articles/stress
Meditative and stress reduction resources for eyes, ears, minds, and hearts.

572 MedlinePlus
www.medlineplus.gov
Information regarding a broad range of health,and mental health conditions topics include: Latest news, overview of anatomy and physiology, clinical trials, diagnoses and symptoms, treatment, genetics, plus lots of links to other sites. A service provided by the National Library of Medicine, part of the National Institutes of Health (NIH).

573 Medscape
www.medscape.com
Medscape offers specialists, primary care physicians, and other health professionals the Web's most robust and integrated medical information and educational tools.

574 National Alliance On Mental Illness
www.nami.org
From its inception in 1979, NAMI has been dedicated to improving the lives of individuals and families affected by mental illness.

575 National Association For The Dually Diagnosed (NADD)
www.thenadd.org
An association for persons with developmental disabilities and mental health needs.

576 National Institute Of Health
www.nimh.nih.gov/anxiety/anxiety/ocd
Information on anxiety disorders and OCD.

577 National Panic/Anxiety Disorder Newsletter
www.npadnews.com
This resource was founded by Phil Darren who collects and collates information of recovered anxiety disorder sufferers who want to distribute some of the lessons that they learned with a view to helping others.

578 Panic Disorder
www.lexington-on-line.com
Explains development and treatment of panic disorder.

579 Planetpsych.com
www.planetpsych.com
Learn about disorders, their treatments and other topics in psychology. Articles are listed under the related topic areas. Ask a therapist a question for free, or view the directory of professionals in your area. If you are a therapist sign up for the directory. Current features, self-help, interactive, and newsletter archives.

580 Psych Central
www.psychcentral.com
Personalized one-stop index for psychology, support, and mental health issues, resources, and people on the Internet.

581 Selective Mutism Foundation
www.selectivemutismfoundation.org
Promotes awareness and understanding for individuals and families affected by mutism.

582 Territorial Apprehensiveness Programs (TERRAP)
www.terraphouston.com
Formed to disseminate information concerning the recognition, causes and treatment of anxieties, fears and phobias.
Shirley Riff, Director

583 Verywell Mind
www.verywellmind.com
Provides up-to-date information on mental health topics. mission is to prioritize mental health and promote balance for day to day living. offers over 5,500 online articles that are researched based, and reviwed by medical professionals.
Kristen Altmeyer, MBA, VP & General Manager
Nick Ingalls, MA, Associate Editorial Director

584 WebMD
www.webmd.com
Provides credible information, supportive communities, and in-depth reference material about health subjects. A source for original and timely health information as well as material from well known content providers.

ARTHRITIS

Arthritis causes discomfort and limited range of motion, up to and including complete loss of motion and extreme pain. Medical treatment is mainly focused on symptom-management, considered palliative in nature, although research is focusing on more direct and curative treatments. Arthritis is composed of over 100 different types of joint diseases with over 58 million adults affected in the United States, and 10 million reporting anxiety or depression as part of their disease. Joint inflammation may be present; swelling around the joint is often evident; range of motion of the joints may be negatively impacted; and pain, often related to exercise or even daily activities, may occur. Fatigue, fever, and other symptoms may exhibit as interference with the immune system may lead to secondary side effects.

The most common type of arthritis is osteoarthritis, or the "wear and tear" arthritis, where overuse of a joint leads to joint degeneration; followed by rheumatoid arthritis, an autoimmune disease where the immune system attacks healthy cells by mistake, leading to inflammation over large areas of the body. Psoriatic arthritis, a form of arthritis with a skin rash (psoriasis) causes inflamed, swollen, and painful joints. Gout is a form of arthritis with crystals of uric acid congregating in the joints leading to pain and limited range of motion. Ankylosing spondylitis is an arthritis that mainly affects the spine. The autoimmune system may also attack the synovium and cartilage of the joints. All forms of arthritis are generally considered painful and limit mobility of joints or the body as a whole.

Depression in people with arthritis related diseases are often two times, to as much as ten times, the rate found in the general population. Depression related to arthritis can also lower the pain threshold, making pain worse, and is associated with arthritis leading to more limitations in activities of daily life, and may lead to other health problems. Living with daily pain is physically and emotionally stressful and brain chemicals may be impacted, disrupting your body's balance bringing on depression.

The link between arthritis and depression is real. Having arthritis of any type leads to fatigue, inflammation, and pain. If there is a comorbid condition like diabetes or heart disease, the lifestyle the individual once had may disappear. Depression and arthritis combined may lead to less exercise, limitations in social interactions and increased pain, and prevent the individual from leading a productive life.

Treating arthritis and managing depression are critical. Treatments for arthritis begin with a comprehensive wellness plan that may include medications, physical therapy, natural pain relief measures including heat and cold, counseling (cognitive behavioral therapy), massage, acupuncture, hypnotherapy, biofeedback, and other interventions. Working with medical professionals and mental health professionals will help address depression brought on by arthritis.

Arthritis / Agencies & Associations

Agencies & Associations

585 American Chronic Pain Association
11936 W. 119th Street   913-991-4740
Overland Park, KS 66213   www.acpanow.com
The ACPA facilitates peer support and education for individuals with chronic pain in its many forms, in order to increase quality of life. Also raises awareness among the healthcare community, and with policy makers.
Penney Cowan, Founder
Trupti Gokani, MD, President

586 American Juvenile Arthritis Organization
Arthritis Foundation
1355 Peachtree Street NE   800-283-7800
Atlanta, GA 30309   www.arthritis.org
A council established by the Arthritis Foundation which serves the special needs of the 300,000 young people with arthritis and their families. Provides information, inspiration and advocacy by identifying the needs of children with arthritis and speaks out on their behalf.
Steven Taylor, President & CEO
Kelly Martin, Sr. Vice President, Operations

587 Arthritis Society Canada
393 University Avenue   416-979-7228
Toronto Ontario, M5G   800-321-1433
   Fax: 416-979-8366
   info@arthritis.ca
   www.arthritis.ca
Promotes, evaluates, and funds research in the areas of causes, prevention, treatment, and cures of arthritis.
Trish Barbato, President & CEO
Sian Bevan, PhD, Chief Science Officer

588 Myositis Association of America
6950 Columbia Gateway Drive   800-821-7356
Columbia, MD 21046   tma@myositis.org
   www.myositis.org
The MMA seeks to improve the lives of individuals affected by myositis, an inflammation of the muscles, through funding research and increasing public awareness.
Rhonda Buckley-Bishop, Interim Executive Director
Aisha Morrow, Senior Manager, Operations

589 National Institute of Arthritis & Musculoskeletal & Skin Diseases
National Institutes of Health
9000 Rockville Pike   301-495-4484
Bethesda, MD 20892   877-226-4267
   Fax: 301-718-6366
   TTY: 301-565-2966
   NIAMSinfo@mail.nih.gov
   www.niams.nih.gov
Supports research into the causes, treatment, and prevention of arthritis and musculoskeletal and skin diseases, the training of basic and clinical scientists to carry out this research, and the dissemination of information on research programs.
Lindsey A. Criswell, MD, MPH, DSc, Director

Foundations

590 Arthritis Foundation
1355 Peachtree Street NE   800-283-7800
Atlanta, GA 30309   www.arthritis.org
A nonprofit organization that depends on volunteers to provide services to help people with arthritis. Supports research to find ways to cure and prevent arthritis and provides services to improve the quality of life for those affected by arthritis. Provides help through information, referrals, speakers bureaus, forums, self-help courses, and various support groups and programs nationwide.
Steven Taylor, President & CEO
Kelly Martin, Sr. Vice President, Operations

Research Centers

591 Affiliated Children's Arthritis Centers of New England
New England Medical Center
750 Washington Street   617-636-7285
Boston, MA 02111   Fax: 617-350-8388
Research organization comprised of a network of 15 territory pediatric centers throughout New England and based at the Floating Hospital of New England Medical Center.
Jane G Schaller MD, Coordinator

592 Arthritis and Musculoskeletal Center: UAB Heersink School of Medicine
The University of Alabama at Birmingham
1720 2nd Avenue S   205-934-4011
Birmingham, AL 35294   sledbetter@uabmc.edu
   www.uab.edu
Arthritis and related rheumatic disorders are studied.
Stephanie Stafford Ford, Clinical Research Administrator

593 Boston University Arthritis Center
Boston University School of Medicine
72 East Concord Street   617-358-9650
Boston, MA 02118   Fax: 617-358-9653
   rhuem@bu.edu
   www.bumc.bu.edu
The research efforts of the Rheumatology Section relate to basic biologic mechanisms in the pathogenesis of scleroderma vasculitis amyloidosis osteoarthritis and systemic lupus erythematosus. There are concordant research efforts in clinical investigation of these disorders including testing of novel therapies.
Alice Anderson, Academic & Clinical Affairs Manager
Sharon Tomlinson, Administrative Manager

594 Boston University Clinical & Translational Science Institute
72 E Concord Street   617-358-7274
Boston, MA 02118   ctsi@bu.edu
   www.ctsi.bu.edu
Integral unit of the University Hospital specializing in arthritis and connective tissue studies.
George O'Connor, MD, Clinical Research Director

595 Brigham and Women's Orthopedica and Arthritis Center
Brigham and Women's Hospital
75 Francis Street   617-732-5500
Boston, MA 02115   800-294-9999
   www.brighamandwomens.org
Research studies into arthritis and rheumatic diseases.
Matthew Lian MD, Director

596 Central Missouri Regional Arthritis Center Stephen's College Campus
Stephen's College Campus
1205 University Ave   573-882-1498
Columbia, MO 65211   Fax: 573-884-5768
   TDD: 0
   richardsjo@missouri.edu
   www.moarthritis.org
Research into arthritis and rheumatic diseases.
Liz Raine, MPH, CHES,, Health Educator
Beth Richards ,BS,TRS, Director

597 Department of Pediatrics, Division of Rheumatology
Duke University School of Medicine
T909 Children's Health Center   919-684-6575
Durham, NC 27710   Fax: 919-684-6616
   rheum.pediatrics.duke.edu
Clinical and laboratory pediatric rheumatoid studies.
Laura Schanberg MD, Cochairman
Egla Rabinovich MD, Co-Chairman

598 Hahnemann University Hospital, Orthopedic Wellness Center
Hahnemann University Hospital
230 N Broad St   215-762-4325
Philadelphia, PA 19102   Fax: 215-762-8109
   www.hahnemannhospital.com
Research activity at Hahnemann University into the areas of arthritis.
Dr. Arnold Berman, Director

Arthritis / Web Sites

599 **Medical University of South Carolina**
171 Ashley Avenue 843-792-2300
Charleston, SC 29425 www.web.musc.edu
Offers basic and clinical research on various types of arthritis.
David J. Cole, MD, MUSC President

600 **Medical University of South Carolina: Division of Rheumatology & Immunology**
96 Jonathan Lucas Street 843-792-1991
Charleston, SC 29403 Fax: 843-792-7121
www.musc.edu
Offers basic and clinical research on various types of arthritis.
Richard M Silver, Division Director/Professor
Gary S Gilkeson, Vice Chairman Research

601 **Multipurpose Arthritis and Musculoskeletal Disease Center**
School of Medicine Rheumatology Division
545 Barnhill Drive 317- 27- 843
Indianapolis, IN 46202 Fax: 317-274-1437
medicine.iupui.edu
The mission of this center is to pursue major biomedical research interests relevant to the rheumatic diseases. Current areas of emphasis include articular cartilage biology pathogenesis and treatment of various forms of amyloidosis the pathogenesis of dermatomyositis and immunologic and biochemical markers of cartilage breakdown and repair.
Bernetta Hartman, Executive Assistant to the Chairman
Martin Friedman, VP Medicine Specialties Division, IUHP

602 **National Institute of Arthritis & Musculoskeletal & Skin Diseases**
National Institutes of Health
9000 Rockville Pike 301-495-4484
Bethesda, MD 20892 877-226-4267
Fax: 301-718-6366
TTY: 301-565-2966
NIAMSinfo@mail.nih.gov
www.niams.nih.gov
Supports research into the causes, treatment, and prevention of arthritis and musculoskeletal and skin diseases, the training of basic and clinical scientists to carry out this research, and the dissemination of information on research programs.
Lindsey A. Criswell, MD, MPH, DSc, Director

603 **Oklahoma Medical Research Foundation**
825 NE 13th Street 405-271-6673
Oklahoma City, OK 73104 800-522-0211
Fax: 405-271-OMRF
contact@omrf.org
www.omrf.org
Focuses on arthritis and muscoloskeletal disease research.
Andrew Weyrich, MD, President
Judith James, EVP & Chief Medical Officer

604 **Rosalind Russell Medical Research Center for Arthritis at UCSF**
350 Parnassus Avenue 415-476-1141
San Francisco, CA 94117 Fax: 415-476-3526
rrac@medicine.ucsf.edu
www.rosalindrussellcenter.ucsf.edu
Arthritis research and its probable causes.
Ephraim P Engelman MD, Director
David Wofsy, Associate Director

605 **Shirley Ryan AbilityLab**
355 E Erie Street 312-238-1000
Chicago, IL 60611 800-354-7342
TTY: 312-238-1059
www.sralab.org
Expertise in treating a range of conditions from the most complex conditions including cerebral palsy spinal cord injury stroke and traumatic brain injury to the more common such as arthritis chronic pain and sports injuries.
Edward B Case, Executive Vice President and Chief Finan
Joanne C Smith, President and Chief Executive Officer

606 **University of Michigan: Orthopaedic Research Laboratories**
University of Michigan Mott Hospital
109 Zina Pitcher Place 734-936-7417
Ann Arbor, MI 48109 Fax: 734-647-0003
www.orl.med.umich.edu
Develops and studies the causes and treatments for arthritis including new devices and assistive aids.
Dr SA Goldstein, Director

607 **Warren Grant Magnuson Clinical Center**
National Institute of Health
9000 Rockville Pike 301-496-2563
Bethesda, MD 20892 800-411-1222
Fax: 301-480-9793
TTY: 866-411-1010
prpl@mail.cc.nih.gov
www.clinicalcenter.nih.gov
Established in 1953 as the research hospital of the National Institutes of Health. Designed so that patient care facilities are close to research laboratories so new findings of basic and clinical scientists can be quickly applied to the treatment of patients. Upon referral by physicians, patients are admitted to NIH clinical studies.
John Gallin, Director
David Henderson, Deputy Director for Clinical Care

Support Groups & Hotlines

608 **Arthritis Foundation Information Helpline**
1355 Peachtree Street NE 800-283-7800
Atlanta, GA 30309 www.arthritis.org
Offers information and referrals, counseling, physicians information and more to persons living with arthritis.
Steven Taylor, President & CEO

609 **Kids on the Block Arthritis Programs**
Arthritis Foundation
PO Box 19000 404-872-7100
Atlanta, GA 31126 800-283-7800
Fax: 404-872-0457
State and local programs that use puppetry to help children understand what it is like for children and adults who have arthritis.

610 **National Health Information Center**
Office of Disease Prevention & Health Promotion
1101 Wootton Pkwy Fax: 240-453-8281
Rockville, MD 20852 odphpinfo@hhs.gov
www.health.gov/nhic
Supports public health education by maintaining a calendar of National Health Observances; helps connect consumers and health professionals to organizations that can best answer questions and provide up-to-date contact information from reliable sources; updates on a yearly basis toll-free numbers for health information, Federal health clearinghouses and info centers.
Don Wright, MD, MPH, Director

Print Resources

611 **Arthritis Today**
Arthritis Foundation
1330 W Peachtree Strt NW 404-872-7100
Atlanta, GA 30309 800-933-0032
Fax: 404-872-9559
www.arthritis.org
The authoritative and respected source of information for persons with arthritis, their families and health professionals who manage their care. As the official magazine of the Arthritis Foundation, it is backed by the Foundation's experience of 44 years and leadership in the fight against arthritis. This magazine gives its readers the advice, information and inspiration they need to live better with arthritis.

Web Sites

612 **American Juvenile Arthritis Organization**
www.arthritis.com
Serves the special needs of young people with arthritis and their families. Provides information, inspiration and advocacy.

613 **Arthritis Foundation**
www.arthritis.org

Arthritis / Web Sites

Provides services to help through information, referrals, speakers bureaus, forums, self-help courses, and various support groups and programs nationwide.

614   Healing Well

www.healingwell.com

An online health resource guide to medical news, chat, information and articles, newsgroups and message boards, books, disease-related web sites, medical directories, and more for patients, friends, and family coping with disabling diseases, disorders, or chronic illnesses.

615   Health Central

www.healthcentral.com

Find clearly explained, medically accurate information regarding conditions, including an overview, symptoms, causes, diagnostic procedures and treatment options. On this site it is possible to ask questions and get information from a neurologist and connect to people who have similar health interests.

616   Health Finder

www.health.gov

Searchable, carefully developed web site offering information on over 1000 topics. Developed by the US Department of Health and Human Services, the site can be used in both English and Spanish.

617   Medical News Today

www.medicalnewstody.com

Offers in-depth health information and the latest news in medical research on a wide variety of medical conditions.

618   MedicineNet

www.medicinenet.com

An online resource for consumers providing easy-to-read, authoritative medical and health information.

619   MedlinePlus

www.medlineplus.gov

Information regarding a broad range of health, and mental health conditions topics include: Latest news, overview of anatomy and physiology, clinical trials, diagnoses and symptoms, treatment, genetics, plus lots of links to other sites. A service provided by the National Library of Medicine, part of the National Institutes of Health (NIH).

620   Medscape

www.medscape.com

Medscape offers specialists, primary care physicians, and other health professionals the Web's most robust and integrated medical information and educational tools.

621   National Arthritis & Musculoskeletal & Skin Diseases Information Clearinghouse

www.niams.nih.gov

The mission of the National Institute of Arthritis and Musculoskeletal and Skin Diseases is to support research into the causes, treatment, and prevention of arthritis and musculoskeletal and skin diseases; the training of basic and clinical scientists to carry out this research; and the dissemination of information on research progress in these diseases.

622   WebMD

www.webmd.com

Provides credible information, supportive communities, and in-depth reference material about health subjects. A source for original and timely health information as well as material from well known content providers.

ASTHMA

Asthma is a disease of the respiratory system. The respiratory system is responsible for moving oxygen throughout the body and removing waste gases like carbon dioxide. The organs that help you breathe and get sufficient oxygen for organ health include the airway, lungs and blood vessels. The cause of asthma is still unknown, but certain factors play a role in development, including family history, allergies, infections, smoking, occupational exposure, and obesity. Asthma occurs in over 22 million people in the United States, and 4,000 people die every year from the disease. Poor asthma management can be life-threatening, and any real or perceived shortness of breath or difficulty breathing (dyspnea) may contribute to depressive symptoms.

Asthma makes breathing difficult and while there is no cure, it can be treated to insure a healthier life. Stress and strong emotions can trigger asthma attacks and there is a link between the disease, anxiety, and depression. Strong emotions such as anger, fear, yelling and crying, often change breathing patterns causing changes in the muscles involved in respiration. Severe asthma can lead to oxygen desaturation and fatigue. Even mild asthma can lead to hyperventilation due to perceived inability to breathe causing psychological symptoms.

Anxiety and depression may be associated with poor asthma control. Developing a treatment plan with the physician and strictly following the plan can control asthma and may prevent the development of depression related to poor control of the disease. During an asthma attack, the airways become swollen and inflamed causing the bronchial tubes to narrow. It becomes difficult to take in sufficient air, leading to wheezing, coughing and trouble breathing. An asthma attack may be life-threatening if not treated promptly. If symptoms do not improve after using a rescue (quick-acting) inhaler, emergency treatment may be indicated.

Major depressive disorders are often correlated with asthma, in part due to the chronic nature of asthma and the threats posed by the disease. Individuals with both asthma and depressive disorders are at greater risk of not maintaining appropriate lung function and having a poor, respiratory-related quality of life. Not managing depression in the asthma patient may result in non-compliance with the asthma care protocol necessary to protect life. Chronic fear of not being able to breathe or realized shortness of breath can negatively impact quality of life leading to depressive disorders and anxiety.

Asthma / Agencies & Associations

Agencies & Associations

623 Administration for Children and Families
330 C Street SW
Washington, DC 20201
877-696-6775
www.acf.hhs.gov
The Administration for Children & Families (ACF) is a division of the U.S. Department of Health & Human Services (HHS). ACF promotes the economic and social well-being of families, children, individuals and communities.
Jeff Hild, Principal Deputy Assistant Secretary
Larry Handerhan, Chief of Staff

624 Agency for Healthcare Research and Quality
5600 Fishers Lane
Rockville, MD 20857
301-427-1104
www.ahrq.gov
The Agency for Healthcare Research and Quality's (AHRQ) mission is to produce evidence to make health care safer, higher quality, more accessible, equitable, and affordable, and to work within the U.S. Department of Health and Human Services and with other partners to make sure that the evidence is understood and used.
Robert Otto Valdez, PhD, MHSA, Acting Director
Howard E. Holland, Director, Communications

625 Agency for Toxic Substances and Disease Registry
1600 Clifton Rd. NE
Atlanta, GA 30329
800-232-4636
www.atsdr.cdc.gov
The Agency for Toxic Substances and Disease Registry (ATSDR), based in Atlanta, Georgia, is a federal public health agency of the U.S. Department of Health and Human Services. ATSDR serves the public by using the best science, taking responsive public health actions, and providing trusted health information to prevent harmful exposures and diseases related to toxic substances.
Robin M. Ikeda, MD, MPH, Acting Director

626 Allergy & Asthma Network
10304 Eaton Place
Fairfax, VA 22030
800-878-4403
info@allergyasthmanetwork.org
www.allergyasthmanetwork.org
Non-profit membership organization dedicated to eliminating suffering and death due to asthma, allergies and related conditions through education, advocacy, community outreach, and research.
Lynda Mitchell, MA, CAE, Interim CEO
Charmayne Anderson, MPA, Director, Advocacy

627 American Academy of Allergy, Asthma & Immunology
555 East Wells Street
Milwaukee, WI 53202
414-272-6071
Fax: 414-272-6070
info@aaaai.org
www.aaaai.org
Strives to serve the public through information on asthma and allergies, as well as referrals to allergists.
Jonathan A. Bernstein, MD, President
Frank S. Virant, MD, Secretary-Treasurer

628 American Lung Association
55 W. Wacker Drive
Chicago, IL 60601
800-586-4872
info@lung.org
www.lung.org
The mission of the American Lung Association is to prevent lung disease and promote lung health by fighting disease in all its forms, with special emphasis on asthma, tobacco control and environmental health.
Harold P. Wimmer, National President & CEO
Albert Rizzo, MD, FACP, Chief Medical Officer

629 Asthma Canada
124 Merton Street
Toronto, Ontario, M4S
416-787-4050
866-787-4050
Fax: 416-787-5807
info@asthma.ca
www.asthma.ca
National, volunteer-led organization devoted to enhancing the quality of life for individuals with athsma and respiratory allergies.
Jenna Reynolds, Interim CEO & Dir., Programs & Services
Zhen Liu, Director, Operations & Administration

630 Birth Defect Research for Children, Inc.
976 Lake Baldwin Lane
Celebration, FL 32814
407-895-0802
staff@birthdefects.org
www.birthdefects.org/allergies
A non-profit organization providing parents and soon-to-be parents with information resources about birth defects, and support services for their children. Offers fact sheets on allergies.

631 Canadian Society of Allergy and Clinical Immunology
207 Bank St
Ottawa, ON, K2P
613-265-7571
info@csaci.ca
www.csaci.ca
Promotes the advancement of the knowledge and practice of allergy, clinical immunology, and asthma for optimal patient care.
Anne Ellis, MD, MSc, FRCPC, President
Jasmin Lidington, Executive Director

632 Centers for Disease Control & Prevention: Division of Adolescent & School Health
1600 Clifton Road
Atlanta, GA 30329
800-232-4636
TTY: 888-232-6348
www.cdc.gov/HealthyYouth
CDC promotes the health and well-being of children and adolescents to enable them to become healthy and productive adults.

633 Centers for Medicare & Medicaid Services
7500 Security Boulevard
Baltimore, MD 21244
www.cms.gov
U.S. federal agency which administers Medicare, Medicaid, and the State Children's Health Insurance Program.
Chiquita Brooks-Lasure, Acting Administrator
Jonathan Blum, Principal Deputy Administrator & COO

634 National Human Genome Research Institute
Building 31, Room 4B09
Bethesda, MD 20892
301-402-0911
Fax: 301-402-2218
www.genome.gov
The National Human Genome Research Institute began as the National Center for Human Genome Research (NCHGR), which was established in 1989 to carry out the role of the National Institutes of Health (NIH) in the International Human Genome Project (HGP).
Eric D. Green, MD, PhD, Director
Nicole C. Lockhart, PhD, Program Director

635 National Institute for Occupational Safety and Health
Patriots Plaza 1
395 E Street SW
Washington, DC 20201
800-232-4636
www.cdc.gov/niosh
The National Institute for Occupational Safety and Health (NIOSH) is the U.S. federal agency that conducts research and makes recommendations to prevent worker injury and illness.
John Howard, MD, Director
Leah Ford, Chief of Staff

636 National Institute of Allergy and Infectious Diseases
NIAID Office of Communications & Govt Relations
5601 Fishers Lane
Bethesda, MD 20892
301-496-5717
866-284-4107
Fax: 301-402-3573
TDD: 800-877-8339
ocpostoffice@niaid.nih.gov
www.niaid.nih.gov
Conducts and supports research on allergies; focused on understanding what happens to the body during the allergic process. Educates patients and health care workers in controlling allergic disease; offers various research centers that conduct and evaluate educational programs focused on methods to control allergic diseases.
Hugh Auchincloss, MD, Acting Director

637 National Institute of Biomedical Imaging and Bioengineering
9000 Rockville Pike
Bethesda, MD 20892
301-496-3500
info@nibib.nih.gov
www.nibib.nih.gov
The mission of the National Institute of Biomedical Imaging and Bioengineering (NIBIB) is to improve health by leading the devel-

opment and accelerating the application of biomedical technologies.
Bruce J. Tromberg, PhD, Director
Jill Heemskerk, PhD, Deputy Director

638   National Institute of Nursing Research
31 Center Drive
Bethesda, MD 20892
301-496-0207
Fax: 301-496-8845
info@ninr.nih.gov
www.ninr.nih.gov

The mission of the National Institute of Nursing Research (NINR) is to promote and improve the health of individuals, families, communities, and populations.
Shannon N. Zenk, PhD, MPH, RN, FAAN, Director
Olga Acosta, Executive Officer

639   U.S. Food and Drug Administration
10903 New Hampshire Avenue
Silver Spring, MD 20993
888-463-6332
www.fda.gov

FDA is responsible for protecting the public health by assuring the safety, efficacy and security of human and veterinary drugs, biological products, medical devices, the nation's food supply, cosmetics, and products that emit radiation.
Janet Woodcock, MD, Acting Commissioner
Namandj N. Bumpus, Chief Scientist

Foundations

640   American Academy of Allergy, Asthma & Immunology Foundation
555 East Wells Street
Milwaukee, WI 53202
414-272-6071
Fax: 414-272-6070
lwiensch@aaaai.org
www.aaaaifoundation.org

Funds research in an effort to prevent and cure asthma and allergic/immunologic diseases.
Karen Michaels, Director
Katie Tetzlaff, Program Manager, Awards

641   American College of Allergy, Asthma & Immunology Foundation
85 West Algonquin Road
Arlington Heights, IL 60005
847-427-1200
Fax: 847-427-9656
mail@acaai.org
college.acaai.org/acaai-foundation

Funds faculty research grants and travel scholarships.

642   Asthma and Allergy Foundation of America
1235 South Clark Street
Arlington, VA 22202
202-466-7643
800-727-8462
Fax: 202-466-8940
info@aafa.org
www.aafa.org

The AAFA is a non-profit patient organization dedicated to improving the quality of life for people with asthma and allergies and their caregivers, through education, advocacy, funding, and research.
Ritesh Patel, Chair
Kenneth Mendez, Chief Executive Officer

643   Asthma and Allergy Foundation of America: St. Louis Chapter
5501 Delmar Blvd.
St. Louis, MO 63112
314-645-2422
Fax: 314-692-2022
admin@aafastl.org
www.aafastl.org

Serves patients of all ages in St. Louis and surrounding counties who are affected by asthma and allergies, and also provides resources to healthcare professionals, caregivers and childcare providers. Offers the BREATH asthma and allergy management program for children.
Chris Martinez, MIB, CFRE, CEO
Jackie O'Guin, Administrative Director

644   National Science Foundation
2415 Eisenhower Ave.
Alexandria, VA 22314
703-292-5111
TDD: 703-292-5090
info@nsf.gov
www.nsf.gov

NSF is the only federal agency whose mission includes support for all fields of fundamental science and engineering, except for medical sciences.
Sethuraman Panchanathan, Director
Karen A. Marrongelle, Chief Operating Officer

Research Centers

645   American College of Allergy, Asthma & Immunology
85 West Algonquin Road
Arlington Heights, IL 60005
847-427-1200
Fax: 847-427-9656
mail@acaai.org
www.acaai.org

Focuses on research and public awareness of allergies, asthma, and immunology. Distributes informational brochures and pamphlets, offers referrals and counseling services, as well as patient care.
Todd A. Mahr, MD, FACAAI, Executive Medical Director

646   Brigham and Women's Hospital: Rheumatology Immunology, and Allergy Division
75 Francis Street
Boston, MA 02115
61-73-550
Fax: 617-525-1001
TTY: 617-732-6458
www.brighamandwomens.org

Internationally renowned for excellence in clinical care clinical investigation and basic research. A faculty of 36 board certified rheumatologists and allergists provide eldtive urgent and emergency consultations as necessary.
Michael B Brenner MD, Division Chief
Jonathan S Coblyn, Clinical Director Rheumatology

647   Childrens Hospital Immunology Division Children's Hospital
Children's Hospital
300 Longwood Avenue
Boston, MA 02115
61-35-600
www.childrenshospital.org

Organizational research unit of the Children's Hospital that focuses on the causes prevention and treatments of asthma infections and allergies.
Dr. James Mandell, CEO
Sandra Fenwick, President & COO

648   Clinical Immunology, Allergy, and Rheumatology
Tulane Medical School
1700 Perdido Street
New Orleans, LA 70112
504-988-5187
Fax: 504-988-3686
medsch@tulane.edu
www.som.tulane.edu/medciar

Mauel Lopez MD, Director

649   Duke Asthma, Allergy and Airway Center
4309 Medical Park Drive
Durham, NC 27704
919-620-7300
www.aaac.duhs.duke.edu/

Raffeal Rau, President
Dr Monica Kraft, Director

650   Johns Hopkins University: Asthma and Allergy Center
5501 Hopkins Bayview Circle
Baltimore, MD 21224
410-550-2101
Fax: 410-550-3256
jhuallergy@jhmi.edu
www.hopkinsmedicine.org/allergy

Studies of allergic diseases and individuals with allergic disease pulmonary diseases and diseases involving inflammation and immunological processes.
Bruce S Bochner, Director
Peter S Creticos, Clinical Director

651   National Center for Complementary and Integrative Health
9000 Rockville Pike
Bethesda, MD 20892
888-644-6226
TTY: 866-464-3615
info@nccih.nih.gov
nccih.nih.gov

The National Center for Complementary and Integrative Health (NCCIH) is the Federal Government's lead agency for scientific research on the diverse medical and health care systems, practices, and products that are not generally considered part of conventional medicine.
Helene M. Langevin, MD, Director
David Shurtleff, PhD, Deputy Director

Asthma / Support Groups & Hotlines

652 National Institute of Environmental Health Sciences
111 T.W. Alexander Drive
Durham, NC 27709
919-541-3201
Fax: 919-541-5136
webcenter@niehs.nih.gov
www.niehs.nih.gov

The mission of the NIEHS is to discover how the environment affects people in order to promote healthier lives.
Rick Woychik, PhD, Director
Trevor K. Archer, PhD, Deputy Director

653 National Institute of General Medical Sciences
45 Center Drive
Bethesda, MD 20892
301-496-7301
info@nigms.nih.gov
www.nigms.nih.gov

The National Institute of General Medical Sciences (NIGMS) supports basic research that increases understanding of biological processes and lays the foundation for advances in disease diagnosis, treatment and prevention.
Jon R. Lorsch, PhD, Director
Dorit Zuk, PhD, Acting Deputy Director

654 National Jewish Division of Immunology
National Jewish Medical and Research Center
1400 Jackson Street
Denver, CO 80206
303-398-1337
80-42-889
Fax: 303-270-2125
harbeckr@njc.org
www.njc.org

The only medical center in the country whose research and patient care resources are dedicated to respiratory and immunologic diseases.
John Cambier, Chairman
Ronald J Harbeck, Medical Director

655 Northwestern University: Division of Allergy and Immunology
The Feinberg School of Medicine
251 East Huron Street
Chicago, IL 60611
312-926-6895
Fax: 312-926-6905
rpschleimer@northwestern.edu
www.medicine.northwestern.edu

A referral center of local regional and national stature. Areas of clinical excellence include asthma allergic bronchopulmonary aspergillosis idiopathic anaphylaxis drug allergy occupational immunologic lung disease and allergen immunotherapy.
Douglas E Vaughan MD, Chair
James Foody MD, Vice Chair Clinical Affairs

656 University of Virginia: General Clinical Research Center
University of Virginia Health System
2515 Lee Street
Charlottesville, VA 22908
434-924-2394
Fax: 434-924-9960
www.healthsystem.virginia.edu/

Focuses on asthmatic disorders.
Arthur Garso Jr MD MPH, Principal Investigator
Eugene J Barrett, Program Director

657 University of Wisconsin: Asthma, Allergy and Pulmonary Research Center
600 Highland Avenue
Madison, WI 53792
608-263-6400
Fax: 608-263-6401
www.medicine.wisc.edu

Sheri L Lawrence, MBA, Administrator
Sharon Gehl, MBA, Associate Administrator

Support Groups & Hotlines

658 National Health Information Center
Office of Disease Prevention & Health Promotion
1101 Wootton Pkwy
Rockville, MD 20852
Fax: 240-453-8281
odphpinfo@hhs.gov
www.health.gov/nhic

Supports public health education by maintaining a calendar of National Health Observances; helps connect consumers and health professionals to organizations that can best answer questions and provide up-to-date contact information from reliable sources; updates on a yearly basis toll-free numbers for health information, Federal health clearinghouses and info centers.
Don Wright, MD, MPH, Director

659 Physician Referral and Information Line
American Academy of Allergy Asthma and Immunology
555 East Wells Street
Milwaukee, WI 53202
414-272-6071
800-822-2762
Fax: 414-272-6070
www.aaaai.org

Referral line offering information on allergy and asthma, referral to an allergy/immunology specialist.

660 Support for Asthmatic Youth
Asthma and Allergy Foundation of America
1080 Glen Cove Avenue
Glen Head, NY 11545
516-625-5735
Fax: 516-625-2976

A network of educational/support groups for adolescents between the ages of 9 and 17. All meetings are free and feature guest speakers, informational programs, games and other fun activities.
Renee Theodorakis MA, Director Adolescent Services

Print Resources

661 Allergy & Asthma Today
Allergy & Asthma Network
8229 Boone Boulevard
Vienna, VA 22182
800-878-4403
info@allergyasthmanetwork.org
www.allergyasthmanetwork.org

Medically reviewed magazine for people living with asthma, allergies and other respiratory conditions. Free with Allergy & Asthma Network membership.
40 pages
Gary Fitzgerald, Managing Editor
Paul Tury, Creative Director

662 Controlling Asthma
American Lung Association
1740 Broadway
New York, NY 10019
212-315-8700

For parents of children with asthma, this newsmagazine tells how parents can help their child deal with the many problems presented by asthma.
16 pages

Web Sites

663 Allergy & Asthma Network
www.allergyasthmanetwork.org
Non-profit membership organization dedicated to eliminating suffering and death due to asthma, allergies and related conditions through education, advocacy, community outreach, and research.

664 American Academy of Allergy, Asthma & Immunology
www.aaaai.org
Strives to serve the public through information on asthma and allergies, as well as referrals to allergists.

665 American College of Allergy, Asthma & Immunology
www.acaai.org
Focuses on research and public awareness of allergies, asthma, and immunology. Distributes informational brochures and pamphlets, offers referrals and counseling services, as well as patient care.

666 American Lung Association
www.lung.org
Offers research, medical updates, fund-raising, educational materials and public awareness campaigns relating to lung disease causes.

667 Asthma and Allergy Foundation of America
www.aafa.org
The AAFA is a non-profit patient organization dedicated to improving the quality of life for people with asthma and allergies and their caregivers, through education, advocacy, funding, and research.

668 Gazoontite
www.gazoontite.com
Provides links to websites involving asthma and also asthma-related products, such as books and guides.

Asthma / Web Sites

669 **Healing Well**
www.healingwell.com
An online health resource guide to medical news, chat, information and articles, newsgroups and message boards, books, disease-related web sites, medical directories, and more for patients, friends, and family coping with disabling diseases, disorders, or chronic illnesses.

670 **Healingwell**
www.healingwell.com
A social network and support community for patients, caregivers, and families coping with the daily struggles of diseases, disorders and chronic illness.

671 **Health Central**
www.healthcentral.com
Find clearly explained, medically accurate information regarding conditions, including an overview, symptoms, causes, diagnostic procedures and treatment options. On this site it is possible to ask questions and get information from a neurologist and connect to people who have similar health interests.

672 **Health Finder**
www.health.gov
A government web site where individuals can find information and tools to help you and those you care about stay healthy.

673 **Medical News Today**
www.medicalnewstody.com
Offers in-depth health information and the latest news in medical research on a wide variety of medical conditions.

674 **MedicineNet**
www.medicinenet.com
An online resource for consumers providing easy-to-read, authoritative medical and health information.

675 **MedlinePlus**
www.medlineplus.gov
Information regarding a broad range of health,and mental health conditions topics include: Latest news, overview of anatomy and physiology, clinical trials, diagnoses and symptoms, treatment, genetics, plus lots of links to other sites. A service provided by the National Library of Medicine, part of the National Institutes of Health (NIH).

676 **Medscape**
www.medscape.com
Medscape offers specialists, primary care physicians, and other health professionals the Web's most robust and integrated medical information and educational tools.

677 **WebMD**
www.webmd.com
Provides credible information, supportive communities, and in-depth reference material about health subjects. A source for original and timely health information as well as material from well known content providers.

ATTENTION DEFICIT HYPERACTIVITY DISORDER (ADHD)

Attention-deficit hyperactivity disorder (ADHD) is a condition characterized by an inability to focus attention or to inhibit impulsive, hyperactive behavior. It is associated with poor academic performance and behavioral problems in children but also may be diagnosed in adults under certain conditions. ADHD is often diagnosed in childhood, with up to 10 percent demonstrating related behaviors, but many continue to show symptoms well into adulthood. The cause of ADHD is unknown but there is believed to be a genetic relationship within families. Psychotherapy and psychological interventions have been shown to help with ADHD. It may be managed by counseling, medications, behavioral therapy, and other treatments.

A disproportionate number of adults with ADHD also demonstrate depression. One in three people diagnosed with ADHD also have depression or have experienced a depressive episode, and almost 20 percent of adults are affected by ADHD and depression. While ADHD is a broad term, trouble paying attention, getting distracted easily, struggling to organize thoughts in a coherent manner, feeling restless and interrupting others are hallmark signs of ADHD. Depression symptoms may overlap with ADHD symptoms. Trouble paying attention, persistent feelings of sadness, anxiety, irritability, restlessness and frustration, trouble sleeping and fatigue are examples. The medications used in ADHD therapy may also produce side effects that mimic depression.

Unlike some other mental health conditions, individuals may be misdiagnosed with depression when in reality they are suffering from ADHD. The two conditions are often mistaken. Moods that change with a change in activity or a different situation may be labeled depression when inconsistent feelings of depression or boredom are not clinical depression. Often individuals with ADHD may also exhibit an anxiety disorder.

In some individuals, ADHD and depression are not considered causative, but for others, depression is a result of ADHD. People with ADHD my experience low self-esteem and poor self image because they are overwhelmed by life at every turn. Struggling to complete tasks may lead to depressive feelings that contribute to feelings of worthlessness and depression.

Proper diagnosis and treatment of ADHD with or without the presence of depression can help manage symptoms and create a better quality of life. Seek out medical professionals and mental health professionals if you have a diagnosis of either ADHD or depression or if you are experiencing signs of ADHD or depression. ADHD medications are unlikely to help with depression and anti-depressants cannot treat ADHD. The goal is to reduce the impact of either disease on activities of daily life.

Attention Deficit Hyperactivity Disorder (ADHD) / Agencies & Associations

Agencies & Associations

678 American Psychiatric Association
800 Maine Avenue SW
Washington, DC 20024
202-559-3900
apa@psych.org
www.psychiatry.org
A medical specialty society representing a growing membership of psychiatrists. Offers information for psychiatrists, medical students, patients and families.
Saul Levin, MD, MPA, FRCP-E, CEO

679 Attention Deficit Disorder Association
PO Box 7557
Wilmington, DE 19803
800-939-1019
add.org
Provides information, support groups, publications, workshops, and networking opportunities for people with Attention Deficit Hyperactivity Disorder. Strives to improve the lives of those with ADHD.
Duane Gordon, President
Annette Tabor, Education Committee Chair

680 Canadian ADHD Resource Alliance
366 Adelaide Street E
Toronto, Ontario, M5A
416-637-8582
niamh.mcgarry@caddra.ca
www.caddra.ca
Non-profit organization for healthcare and research professionals with interests in the study of ADHD.
Niamh McGarry, Executive Director
Stacey D. Espinet, Education Project Manager

681 Center for Family Support
2811 Zulette Avenue
Bronx, NY 10461
718-518-1500
svernikoff@cfsny.org
www.cfsny.org
The Center for Family Support offers assistance to individuals with developmental and related disabilities, as well as their families, and provides support services and programs that are designed to accommodate individual needs. Offers services throughout New York City, Westchester County, Long Island, and New Jersey.
Steven Vernikoff, Executive Director
Barbara Greenwald, Chief Operating Officer

682 Center for Mental Health Services (CMHS)
Substance Abuse and Mental Health Services Adminis
5600 Fishers Lane
Rockville, MD 20857
240-276-1310
samhsa.gov
Promotes the treatment of mental illness and emotional disorders by increasing accessibility to mental health programs; supporting outreach, treatment, rehabilitation, and support programs and networks; and encouraging the use of scientifically-based information when treating mental disorders. CMHS provides information about mental health via a toll-free number and numerous publications. Developed for users of mental health services and their families, the general public, policy makers, provider
Anita Everett, MD, DFAPA, Director

683 Center for Parent Information & Resources
SPAN
35 Halsey Street
Newark, NJ 07102
973-642-8100
mrodriguez@spanadvocacy.org
www.parentcenterhub.org
Serves as a central hub of information and products for Parent Centers that serve children with disabilities. Coordinates training, provides an e-newsletter twice a month, and produces specially designed databases.
Carolyn Hayer, Director
Myriam Alizo, Assistant Program Director

684 Children & Adults with Attention Deficit /Hyperactivity Disorder
4221 Forbes Blvd
Lanham, MD 20706
301-306-7070
Fax: 301-306-7090
customer_service@chadd.org
www.chadd.org
CHADD's primary objectives are: to provide a support network for parents and caregivers; to provide a forum for continuing education; to be a community resource and disseminate accurate evidence-based information about AD/HD to parents, educators and adults.
Laurie Kulikosky, CAE, Chief Executive Officer
Dr. L. Eugene Arnold, Resident Expert

685 Children and Adults with AD/HD (CHADD)
4221 Forbes Boulevard
Lanham, MD 20706
301-306-7070
customer_service@chadd.org
chadd.org
National nonprofit organization serving individuals with Attention Deficit Hyperactivity Disorder (ADHD) and their families. Offers support and information for individuals, parents, teachers, professionals, and others, and advocates for the rights of people with ADHD. Available on Facebook and Twitter.
Patricia M. Hudak, PCC, BCC, President
Laurie Kulikosky, Chief Execuitve Officer

686 Council for Exceptional Children
3100 Clarendon Blvd
Arlington, VA 22201
888-232-7733
cecontarioboard@gmail.com
exceptionalchildren.org
Advocates appropriate policies, standards and development for individuals with special needs. Provides professional development for special educators.
Donna Zuccato, President
Dr. Sue Ball, Vice President

687 Feingold Association of the US
10955 Windjammer Drive S
Indianapolis, IN 46256
631-369-9340
membership@feingold.org
feingold.org
Helps families of children with learning and behavior problems, including attention deficit disorder. Also helps chemically-sensitive and salicylate-sensitive adults. Program is based upon a diet which primarily eliminates certain synthetic food additives.

688 Goodwill Industries International, Inc.
15810 Indianola Drive
Rockville, MD 20855
contactus@goodwill.org
www.goodwill.org
A nonprofit, community-based organization whose mission is to help people achieve self-sufficiency through the dignity and power of work, serving people who are disadvantaged, disabled or elderly. The mission is accomplished through providing independent living skills, affordable housing, and training and placement in community employment. The GoodWill Network includes 160 independent, local locations across the U.S. and Canada.
Ned Helms, Chair
Steven C. Preston, President & CEO

689 Help is Here
North Dakota Behavioral Health Division
600 E Boulevard Avenue
Bismarck, ND 58501
701-328-2310
800-472-2622
dhsbhd@nd.gov
www.helpishere.nd.gov
Promotes the support and treatment of mental illness and emotional disorders. Offers mental health services, addiction servces, and recovery centers.

690 Institute for Contemporary Psychotherapy
33 W 60th St.
New York, NY 10023
212-333-3444
Fax: 212-333-5444
icpnyc.org
The Institute for Contemporary Psychotherapy is a New York City-based mental health treatment and training facility. Consisting of a group of 150 licensed psychotherapists, the Institute focuses on educating the public about the issues surrounding mental health, providing post-graduate training for therapists, and offering therapy at moderate costs.
Ron Taffel, PhD, Chair
Andrea Green-Lewis, LCSW-R, Director of Operations

691 Learning Disabilities Association of America
4068 Mount Royal Boulevard
Allison Park, PA 15101
412-341-1515
info@LDAAmerica.org
www.ldaamerica.org
An information and referral center for parents and professionals dealing with learning disabilities.
Cindy Cipoletti, Executive Director
Tracy Gregoire, Director, Healthy Children Project

692 Mental Health America
500 Montgomery Street
Alexandria, VA 22314
703-684-7722
800-969-6642
mhanational.org

Attention Deficit Hyperactivity Disorder (ADHD) / Research Centers

Mental Health America is a community-based nonprofit organization committed to enabling the mental wellness of all Americans. MHA advocates for greater access to quality health services and seeks to educate individuals on identifying symptoms, as well as intervention and prevention.
Schroeder Stribling, President & CEO
Sachin Doshi, Sr. Dir., Finance & Operations

693 **National Alliance on Mental Illness**
4301 Wilson Boulevard 703-524-7600
Arlington, VA 22203 800-950-6264
info@nami.org
nami.org
NAMI is an organization dedicated to raising awareness on mental health and providing support and education for Americans affected by mental illness. NAMI advocates for access to services and treatment and fosters an environment of awareness and understanding for those concerned with mental health.
Shirley J. Holloway, President
Joyce A. Campbell, First Vice President

694 **National Association for the Dually Diagnosed (NADD)**
321 Wall Street 845-331-4336
Kingston, NY 12401 info@thenadd.org
thenadd.org
NADD is a nonprofit organization designed to increase awareness of, and provide services for, individuals with developmental disabilities and mental illness. NADD emphasizes the importance of quality mental healthcare for people with mental health needs and offers conferences, information resources, educational programs, and training materials to professionals, parents, and organizations.
Jeanne M. Farr, MA, Chief Executive Officer
Bruce Davis, President

695 **National Association of Parents with Childen in Special Education**
3642 East Sunnydale Drive 800-754-4421
Chandler Heights, AZ 85142 contact@napcse.org
napcse.org
The NAPCSE is dedicated to ensuring quality education for all children and adolescents with special needs. NAPCSE provides resources, support, and assistance to parents with children in special education.
Dr. George Giuliani, President

696 **National Center for Learning Disabilities**
1220 L Street NW 301-966-2234
Washington, DC 20005 info@ncld.org
www.ncld.org
Nonprofit organization committed to improving the lives of the estimated one in ten children with learning disabilities, and raising public awareness and understanding.
Jacqueline Rodriguez, PhD, Chief Executive Officer
Kena Mayberry, PhD, Chief Operating Officer

697 **National Federation of Families for Children's Mental Health**
15800 Crabbs Branch Way 240-403-1901
Rockville, MD 20855 ffcmh@ffcmh.org
ffcmh.org
The National Federation of Families for Children's Mental Health is a national organization focused on advocating for the rights of children affected by mental health challenges, assisting family-run organizations across the nation, and ensuring that children and families concerned with mental health have access to services.
Lynda Gargan, PhD, Executive Director
Gail Cormier, Project Director

698 **National Institute of Mental Health**
6001 Executive Boulevard 866-615-6464
Bethesda, MD 20892 nimhinfo@nih.gov
nimh.nih.gov
The National Institute of Mental Health conducts clinical research on mental disorders and seeks to expand knowledge on mental health treatments.
Joshua Gordon, MD, PhD, Director

699 **National Mental Health Consumers' Self-Help Clearinghouse**
selfhelpclearinghouse@gmail.com
mhselfhelp.org

The Clearinghouse is a peer-run national technical assistance center focused on achieving respect and equality of opportunity for those with mental illnesses. The Clearinghouse helps with the growth of the mental health consumer movement by evaluating mental health services, advocating for mental health reform, and providing consumers with news, information, publications, and consultation services.
Joseph Rogers, Founder and Executive Director
Susan Rogers, Director

700 **PACER Center**
8161 Normandale Boulevard 952-838-9000
Bloomington, MN 55437 800-537-2237
pacer.org
PACER provides information, training, and assistance to parents of children and young adults with all disabilities (physical, learning, cognitive, emotional, and health). Its mission is to help improve the quality of life for young people with disabilities and their families.
Paula F. Goldberg, Co-Founder & Executive Director

701 **Sutcliffe Clinic**
851 Fremont Avenue 650-941-1698
Los Altos, CA 94024 info@sutcliffedbp.com
www.sutcliffeclinic.com
Sutcliffe Developmental & Behavioral Pediatrics is an organization that specializes in the treatment of ADHD, autism spectrum disorder, anxiety disorders, conduct disorders, learning disabilities, and more. Sutcliffe works with community services, school districs, and primary physicians, and provides family counseling.
Trenna Sutcliffe, MD, MS, Medical Director

702 **United Brain Association**
202-768-8000
info@unitedbrainassociation.org
unitedbrainassociation.org
Non-profit organization that works to find cures through research for over 600 brain and mental health related issues, and disorders.
J.A. Boulton, Founder
Jay Matey, VP & Treasurer

Foundations

703 **Brain & Behavior Research Foundation**
747 Third Avenue 646-681-4888
New York, NY 10017 800-829-8289
info@bbrfoundation.org
www.bbrfoundation.org
The Brain and Behavior Research Foundation awards grants aimed at advancing scientific understandings of mental health treatments and mental disorders such as depression and schizophrenia. The Brain and Behavior Research Foundation's mission is to eliminate the suffering caused by mental illness.
Donald M. Boardman, Treasurer
Jeffrey Borenstein, MD, President and CEO

Libraries & Resource Centers

704 **HEATH Resource Center**
George Washington University
800 21st Street, NW 202-994-5300
Washington, DC 20052 Fax: 202-242-9922
shcadmin@gwu.edu
healthcenter.gwu.edu
Serves as a national clearinghouse on postsecondary education for individuals with disabilities.
Anthony Bradley, Senior Patient Specialist
Rosa Green, Administrative Supervisor

Research Centers

705 **UCLA Anxiety Disorders Research Center**
Department of Psychology 310-825-9312
Los Angeles, CA 90094 rose@psych.ucla.edu
anxiety.psych.ucla.edu

Attention Deficit Hyperactivity Disorder (ADHD) / Support Groups & Hotlines

The purpose of The ADRC is to further our understanding of the factors that place individuals at risk for developing phobias, anxiety disorders and related conditions, and to develop more effective treatments that have long lasting effects and are cost effective.
Michelle G. Craske, Ph.D., Director
Raphael Rose, Ph.D., Associate Director

Support Groups & Hotlines

706 Attention Deficit Information Network
475 Hillside Ave 617-455-9895
Needham, MA 02194
Offers support and information to families of children with attention deficit disorder, adults with ADD and professionals through an international network of 60 parent and adult chapters.

707 Children and Adults with AD/HD (CHADD)
4221 Forbes Boulevard 301-306-7070
Lanham, MD 20706 customer_service@chadd.org
chadd.org
Nonprofit organization serving individuals with AD/HD and their families. Over 16,000 members in 200 local chapters throughout the United States. Chapters offer support for individuals, parents, teachers, professionals, and others. Available on Facebook and Twitter.
Patricia M. Hudak, PCC, BCC, President
Rhonda Buckley, Interim CEO

708 National Center for Learning Disabilities
1220 L Street NW 301-966-2234
Washington, DC 20005 ncld.org
The NCLD's mission is to ensure success for all individuals with learning disabilities in school, at work, and in life. They connect parents with resources, guidance, and support to advocate effectively for their children; deliver evidence-based tools, resources, and professional development to educators to improve student outcomes; and develop policies and engage advocates to strengthen educational rights and opportunities.
Margi Booth, Co-Chair
Joe Zimmel, Co-Chair

709 National Health Information Center
Office of Disease Prevention & Health Promotion
1101 Wootton Pkwy Fax: 240-453-8281
Rockville, MD 20852 odphpinfo@HHS.gov
www.health.gov/nhic
Supports public health education by maintaining a calendar of National Health Observances; helps connect consumers and health professionals to organizations that can best answer questions and provide up-to-date contact information from reliable sources; updates on a yearly basis toll-free numbers for health information, Federal health clearinghouses and info centers.
Don Wright, MD, MPH, Director

Print Resources

710 ADDitude Magazine
ADD Warehouse
300 NW 70th Avenue 954-792-8944
Plantation, FL 33317 800-233-9273
sales@addwarehouse.com
addwarehouse.com
Provides valuable resource information for professionals-teachers, healthcare providers, employers and others-who interact with AD/HD people everyday.
Harvey C Parker, Owner

711 American Journal of Psychiatry
American Psychiatric Association Publishing
800 Maine Avenue SW, Suite 900 202-459-9722
Washington, DC 20024 800-368-5777
Fax: 202-403-3094
psychiatryonline@psych.org
ajp.psychiatryonline.org
Official journal of the American Psychiatric Association (APA).
Ned H. Kalin, MD, Editor-in-Chief

712 American Journal of Psychotherapy
American Psychiatric Association Publishing
800 Maine Avenue SW, Suite 900 202-459-9722
Washington, DC 20024 800-368-5777
Fax: 202-403-3094
psychiatryonline@psych.org
ajp.psychiatryonline.org
Publishes content that aims to advance the theory, science, and clinical practice of psychotherapy.
Holly A. Swartz, MD, Editor-in-Chief

713 Attention
Children & Adults with Attention Deficit Disorder
8181 Professional Place 301-306-7070
Landover, MD 20785 800-233-4050
Fax: 301-306-7090
TTY: 301-429-0641
www.chadd.org

714 Attention Magazine
Children and Adults with AD/HD (CHADD)
4221 Forbes Boulevard 301-306-7070
Lanham, MD 20706 chadd.org
A bi-monthly magazine for members of CHADD that offers practical information, clinical insights, and strategies for managing ADHD. Attention manazine also offers a digital edition subscription.
Dr L. Eugene Arnold, MD, MEd, Resident Expert
Sarah Brown, MA, NRC Program Manager

715 Learning Disabilities: A Multidisciplinary Journal
Learning Disabilities Association of America
4068 Mount Royal Boulevard 412-341-1515
Allison Park, PA 15101 info@LDAAmerica.org
ldaamerica.org
The most current research designed for professionals in the field of LD.
Kevin Gailey, Chair
Cindy Cipoletti, Executive Director

Digital Resources

716 National Resource Center on ADHD
Children and Adults with AD/HD
4221 Forbes Boulevard 301-306-7070
Lanham, MD 20706 chadd.org/about/about-nrc/
The National Resource Center, a program of CHADD, is a resource platform focused on disseminating the latest science-based information on ADHD. The NRC provides comprehensive information and program activities for children and adults with ADHD, parents, caregivers, professionals, and other members of the public.
Dr L. Eugene Arnold, MD, MEd, Resident Expert
Zuali Malsawma, NRC Director

Web Sites

717 Advocating For Your Child
www.adhdnews.com/Advocate.html

718 American Academy Of Pediatrics Practice Guidelines
www.aap.org
Site serves the purpose of giving the public guidelines for diagnosing and evaluating children with possible ADHD.

719 Answers To Your Questions About ADD
www.addvance.com
Provides answers to questions about ADD, ADHD for families and individuals at every stage of life from preschool through retirement years.

720 Attention Deficit Disorder And Parenting Site
www.LD-ADD.comAttention Deficit Disorder

721 Attention Deficit Disorder Association
www.add.org
Provides information, resources and networking to adults with ADHD and to the professionals who work with them.

452

Attention Deficit Hyperactivity Disorder (ADHD) / Web Sites

722 **Attention Deficit Hyperactivity Disorder**
www.nimh.nih.gov/publicat/adhd.cfm
Thirty page booklet.

723 **Babycenter**
www.babycenter.com/rcindex.html

724 **Center For Family Support (CFS)**
www.cfsny.org
Devoted to providing support and assistance to individuals with developmental and related disabilities, and to the family members who care for them.

725 **Children/Adults With Attention Deficit/ Hyperactivity**
www.CHADD.org

726 **CyberPsych**
www.cyberpsych.org
Hosts the American Psychoanalysts Foundation, American Association of Suicideology, Society for the Exploration of Psychotherapy Intergration, and Anxiety Disorders Association of America. Also subcategories of the anxiety disorders, as well as general information, including panic disorder, phobias, obsessive compulsive disorder (OCD), social phobia, generalized anxiety disorder, post traumatic stress disorder, and phobias of childhood. Book reviews and links to web pages sharing the topics.

727 **Happy Healthy Lifestyle Magazine For People with Attention Deficit Disorder**
www.additudemag.com

728 **Healing Well**
www.healingwell.com
An online health resource guide to medical news, chat, information and articles, newsgroups and message boards, books, disease-related web sites, medical directories, and more for patients, friends, and family coping with disabling diseases, disorders, or chronic illnesses.

729 **Health Central**
www.healthcentral.com
Find clearly explained, medically accurate information regarding conditions, including an overview, symptoms, causes, diagnostic procedures and treatment options. On this site it is possible to ask questions and get information from a neurologist and connect to people who have similar health interests.

730 **Health Finder**
www.health.gov
A government web site, where individuals can find information and tools to help you and those you care about stay healthy.

731 **Internet Mental Health**
www.mentalhealth.com
Offers online psychiatric diagnosis in the hope of reaching the two-thirds of individuals with mental illness who do not seek treatment.

732 **Medical News Today**
www.medicalnewstody.com
Offers in-depth health information and the latest news in medical research on a wide variety of medical conditions.

733 **MedicineNet**
www.medicinenet.com
An online resource for consumers providing easy-to-read, authoritative medical and health information.

734 **MedlinePlus**
www.medlineplus.gov
Information regarding a broad range of health, and mental health conditions topics include: Latest news, overview of anatomy and physiology, clinical trials, diagnoses and symptoms, treatment, genetics, plus lots of links to other sites. A service provided by the National Library of Medicine, part of the National Institutes of Health (NIH).

735 **Medscape**
www.medscape.com
Medscape offers specialists, primary care physicians, and other health professionals the Web's most robust and integrated medical information and educational tools.

736 **National Alliance On Mental Illness**
www.nami.org
From its inception in 1979, NAMI has been dedicated to improving the lives of individuals and families affected by mental illness.

737 **National Association For The Dually Diagno Diagnosed (NADD)**
www.thenadd.org
An association for persons with developmental disabilities and mental health needs.

738 **National Information Center For Children and Youth**
www.nichcy.org
Excellent information in English and Spanish.

739 **One ADD Place**
www.oneaddplace.com

740 **Planetpsych.com**
www.planetpsych.com
Learn about disorders, their treatments and other topics in psychology. Articles are listed under the related topic areas. Ask a therapist a question for free, or view the directory of professionals in your area. If you are a therapist sign up for the directory. Current features, self-help, interactive, and newsletter archives.

741 **Psych Central**
www.psychcentral.com
Personalized one-stop index for psychology, support, and mental health issues, resources, and people on the Internet.

742 **Special Education Rights and Respnsibilities**
www.adhdnews.com/sped.html
Writing IEP's and TIEPS. Pursuing special education services.

743 **Substance Abuse And Mental Health Services Administration**
www.store.samhsa.gov
Resources on mental disorders as well as treatment and recovery.

744 **Verywell Mind**
www.verywellmind.com
Provides up-to-date information on mental health topics. mission is to prioritize mental health and promote balance for day to day living. offers over 5,500 online articles that are researched based, and reviwed by medical professionals.
Kristen Altmeyer, MBA, VP & General Manager
Nick Ingalls, MA, Associate Editorial Director

745 **WebMD**
www.webmd.com
Provides credible information, supportive communities, and in-depth reference material about health subjects. A source for original and timely health information as well as material from well known content providers.

BIPOLAR & RELATED DISORDERS

Formerly called manic-depressive illness or manic depression, bipolar disorder is a mental illness that impacts energy, mood, concentration, and activity levels, making it difficult to carry out day-to-day tasks. The three types of bipolar disorder are Bipolar I disorder, Bipolar II disorder and cyclothymic disorder, also called cyclothymia. All three types have evident changes in mood, energy and activity levels ranging from manic episodes with periods of feeling extremely "up"; irritable, elated or energized behaviors; to depressive episodes with sad, hopeless or indifferent periods described as "down" periods. Hypomanic episodes are described as less severe manic episodes.

Individuals experience mood fluctuations, but these moods rarely last more than a few hours and are not extreme in nature. Bipolar I disorder is characterized by manic episodes lasting at least 7 days with behaviors occurring nearly every day for much of the day. Symptoms may be so severe that immediate medical care may be needed. Depressive periods follow lasting at least two weeks. Episodes of depression may include both manic and depressive periods. Bipolar II disorder is like Bipolar I disorder but less severe with depressive episodes and hypomanic episodes. Cyclothymic disorder is recurring hypomanic and depressive symptoms that are much less intense and do not last long enough to qualify as episodes. Individuals with symptoms of bipolar disorder that do not match any of the three categories are said to have specified and unspecified bipolar and related disorders.

Diagnosis requires medical or mental health professionals' intervention as the disorder usually requires lifetime treatment. Signs and symptoms include intense emotional periods and changes in sleep and activity levels. Behaviors may occur that are not the norm for the individual. Talking fast, having racing thoughts, and feeling able to do many things (often to excess) characterize the manic episode. The depressive episode is evident when the individual feels slow, restless, "down" and sad, and has trouble sleeping, feels hopeless, and has a lack of interest in activities and may voice thoughts of suicide.

People with bipolar disorders may also have other disorders such as anxiety disorders, attention-deficit/hyperactivity disorder (ADHD), eating disorders, and may abuse drugs and alcohol. Psychoses, having hallucinations and delusions for example, may create psychotic episodes during manic moods where the individual may feel they have special powers, or during a depressive mood may believe they are financially ruined. Genetics may play a role in developing bipolar disorders. Individuals diagnosed with bipolar disorder have a relative with the disorder in 80-90 percent of cases.

Treatment involves medications and psychotherapy or talk therapy. Electroconvulsive therapy (ECT) may be used in severe cases not helped by other interventions. Repetitive transcranial magnetic stimulation (rTMS) is similar to ECT but not as powerful. Light therapy is an evidence-based treatment for seasonal affective disorder (SAD) and may treat bipolar disorder that worsens seasonally. Long-term treatment will allow the individual to manage the symptoms of bipolar and related disorders and live a healthy life.

Bipolar & Related Disorders / Agencies & Associations

Agencies & Associations

746 Academy of Psychosomatic Medicine
4800 Hampden Ln
Bethesda, MD 20814
301-718-6520
info@CLpsychiatry.org
apm.org

The Academy of Psychosomatic Medicine represents psychiatrists focused on improving education, medical science, and healthcare for individuals with comorbid psychiatric and general medical conditions. The Academy seeks to promote interdisciplinary education and drive research and public policy with the goal of achieving outstanding clinical care for patients with comorbid psychiatric and general medical conditions throughout the world. They also created the Foundation of the Academy of Psychosom

Philip Biaeler, MD, FACLP, President
Maryland Pao, MD, FACLP, President-Elect

747 American Psychiatric Association
800 Maine Avenue SW
Washington, DC 20024
202-559-3900
apa@psych.org
www.psychiatry.org

A medical specialty society representing a growing membership of psychiatrists. Offers information for psychiatrists, medical students, patients and families.

Saul Levin, MD, MPA, FRCP-E, CEO

748 Center for Mental Health Services (CMHS)
Substance Abuse and Mental Health Services Adminis
5600 Fishers Lane
Rockville, MD 20857
240-276-1310
samhsa.gov

Promotes the treatment of mental illness and emotional disorders by increasing accessibility to mental health programs; supporting outreach, treatment, rehabilitation, and support programs and networks; and encouraging the use of scientifically-based information when treating mental disorders. CMHS provides information about mental health via a toll-free number and numerous publications. Developed for users of mental health services and their families, the general public, policy makers, provider

Anita Everett, MD, DFAPA, Director

749 Depression & Bipolar Support Alliance
55 East Jackson Boulevard
Chicago, IL 60604
800-826-3632
info@dbsalliance.org
dbsalliance.org

The Depression and Bipolar Support Alliance is a national organization focused on improving the lives of individuals with depression, bipolar disorder, and other mood disorders. DBSA organizes peer-led support groups; educates patients, families, professionals, and the public on mental health; and works to ensure the availability of quality care for all people.

Roger McIntyre, Chair
Michael Pollock, Chief Executive Officer

750 Hope for Depression Research Foundation
40 West 57th Street
New York, NY 10019
212-676-3200
Fax: 212-676-3219
hdrf@hopefordepression.org
www.hopefordepression.org

Promotes, and encourages profits for neuroscience research into the treatments, diagnosis, origins, and prevention of depression, and other mood disorders such as anxiety disorders, post-traumatic stress disorder, postpartum depression, bipolar disorder, and suicide.

Audrey Gruss, Founder & Chairman
Harold W. Koenigsberg, MD, Board Member

751 Institute for Contemporary Psychotherapy
33 W 60th St.
New York, NY 10023
212-333-3444
Fax: 212-333-5444
icpnyc.org

The Institute for Contemporary Psychotherapy is a New York City-based mental health treatment and training facility. Consisting of a group of 150 licensed psychotherapists, the Institute focuses on educating the public about the issues surrounding mental health, providing post-graduate training for therapists, and offering therapy at moderate costs.

Ron Taffel, PhD, Chair
Andrea Green-Lewis, LCSW-R, Director of Operations

752 Mental Health America
500 Montgomery Street
Alexandria, VA 22314
703-684-7722
800-969-6642
mhanational.org

Mental Health America is a community-based nonprofit organization committed to enabling the mental wellness of all Americans. MHA advocates for greater access to quality health services and seeks to educate individuals on identifying symptoms, as well as intervention and prevention.

Schroeder Stribling, President & CEO
Sachin Doshi, Sr. Dir., Finance & Operations

753 Mood Disorders Center
Department of Psychiatry and Behavioral Sciences a
600 North Wolfe Street
Baltimore, MD 21218
410-955-5212
877-666-3754
www.hopkinsmedicine.org/psychiatry/speci

The Mood Disorders Center at Johns Hopkins Medicine provides specialized clinical services to patients with mood disorders; conducts research on the causes of mood disorders, treatment responses, and brain function and structure; and educates patients, caregivers, and the public on mood disorders through symposia, publications, community presentations, and the Adolescent Depression Awareness Program.

J. Raymond DePaulo, MD, Co-Director
Kay Redfield Jamison, PhD, Co-Director

754 National Alliance on Mental Illness
4301 Wilson Boulevard
Arlington, VA 22203
703-524-7600
800-950-6264
info@nami.org
nami.org

NAMI is an organization dedicated to raising awareness on mental health and providing support and education for Americans affected by mental illness. NAMI advocates for access to services and treatment and fosters an environment of awareness and understanding for those concerned with mental health.

Shirley J. Holloway, President
Joyce A. Campbell, First Vice President

755 National Association for the Dually Diagnosed (NADD)
321 Wall Street
Kingston, NY 12401
845-331-4336
info@thenadd.org
thenadd.org

NADD is a nonprofit organization designed to increase awareness of, and provide services for, individuals with developmental disabilities and mental illness. NADD emphasizes the importance of quality mental healthcare for people with mental health needs and offers conferences, information resources, educational programs, and training materials to professionals, parents, and organizations.

Jeanne M. Farr, MA, Chief Executive Officer
Bruce Davis, President

756 National Mental Health Consumers' Self-Help Clearinghouse
selfhelpclearinghouse@gmail.com
mhselfhelp.org

The Clearinghouse is a peer-run national technical assistance center focused on achieving respect and equality of opportunity for those with mental illnesses. The Clearinghouse helps with the growth of the mental health consumer movement by evaluating mental health services, advocating for mental health reform, and providing consumers with news, information, publications, and consultation services.

Joseph Rogers, Founder and Executive Director
Susan Rogers, Director

757 United Brain Association
202-768-8000
info@unitedbrainassociation.org
unitedbrainassociation.org

Non-profit organization that works to find cures through research for over 600 brain and mental health related issues, and disorders.

J.A. Boulton, Founder
Jay Matey, VP & Treasurer

Foundations

758 **Brain & Behavior Research Foundation**
747 Third Avenue
New York, NY 10017
646-681-4888
800-829-8289
info@bbrfoundation.org
www.bbrfoundation.org

The Brain and Behavior Research Foundation awards grants aimed at advancing scientific understandings of mental health treatments and mental disorders such as depression and schizophrenia. The Brain and Behavior Research Foundation's mission is to eliminate the suffering caused by mental illness.
Donald M. Boardman, Treasurer
Jeffrey Borenstein, MD, President and CEO

759 **International Bipolar Foundation**
1050 Rosecrans Street
San Diego, CA 92106
858-598-5967
Fax: 858-598-5158
info@ibpf.org
ibpf.org

mission is to advocate, educate, and support individuals living with bipolar disorder.
Mike Griffiths, MD, Chairman
Susan Berger, Treasurer

Libraries & Resource Centers

760 **Family-to-Family: National Alliance on Mental Illness**
4301 Wilson Boulevard
Arlington, VA 22203
703-524-7600
888-999-6264
info@nami.org
nami.org

The NAMI Family-to-Family Education Program is a free, 8 session course for family caregivers of individuals with severe mental illnesses. The course is taught by trained family members, all instruction and course materials are free to class participants, and over 300,000 family members have graduated from this national program.

Research Centers

761 **Bipolar Clinic and Research Program**
The Massachusetts General Hospital Bipolar Clinic
50 Staniford Street
Boston, MA 02114
617-726-5855
www.massgeneral.org

Dedicated to providing quality clinical care, conducting clinically informative research, and educating our colleagues, patients, as well as the community.
Michael Jellinek, MD, President
Laurie Ansorge Ball, Executive Director, MGH Departmen

762 **Bipolar Disorders Clinic**
Standford School of Medicine
401 Quarry Road
Stanford, CA 94305
650-723-3305
bipolar.stanford.edu

Offers an on-going clinical treatment, manage clinical trials and neuroimaging studies, lecture and teach seminar courses at Stanford University and train residents in the School of Medicine.
Terrence A Ketter, MD, Chief, Bipolar Disorders Clinic
Shelley Hill, MS, Clinical Research Coordinator

763 **Bipolar Research Program at University of Pennsylvania**
3535 Market Street
Philadelphia, PA 19104
215-898-4301
www.med.upenn.edu/psych/bipolar_research

Offers and conducts research on treatments for bipolar disorders. The program provides comprehensive care for persons with bipolar affective disorder (manic depressive illness), seasonal affective disorder, and rapid cycling bipolar disorder. Services offered for individuals who are in the ages of 18 or older include evaluations, consultations, and ongoing treatment options.
Laszlo Gyulai, MD, Program Director
Chang-Gyu Hahn, MD, Ph.D., Clinical Team Member

764 **Epidemiology-Genetics Program in Psychiatr**
John Hopkins University School of Medicine
PO Box 1997
Baltimore, MD 21203
888-289-4095
www.hopkinsmedicine.org

The research program is to help characterize the genetic (biochemical) developmental, and environmental components of bipolar disorder. The hope is that once scientists understand the biological causes of this disorder new medications and treatments can be developed.

765 **National Institute of Mental Health**
6001 Executive Boulevard
Bethesda, MD 20892
866-615-6464
nimhinfo@nih.gov
nimh.nih.gov

The National Institute of Mental Health conducts clinical research on mental disorders and seeks to expand knowledge on mental health treatments.
Joshua Gordon, MD, PhD, Director

766 **UAMS Psychiatric Research Institute**
4224 Shuffield Drive
Little Rock, AR 72205
501-526-8100
kramerteresal@uams.edu
www.psychiatry.uams.edu

Combining research, education and clinical services into one facility, PRI offers inpatient and outpatient services, with 40 psychiatric beds, therapy options, and specialized treatment for specific disorders, including: addictive eating, anxiety, deppressive and post-traumatic stress disorders. Research focuses on evidence-based care takes into consideration the education of future medical personnel while relying on research scientists to provide innovative forms of treatment.
Dan Rahn, MD, Chancellor

767 **UCLA Anxiety Disorders Research Center**
Department of Psychology
Los Angeles, CA 90094
310-825-9312
rose@psych.ucla.edu
anxiety.psych.ucla.edu

The purpose of The ADRC is to further our understanding of the factors that place individuals at risk for developing phobias, anxiety disorders and related conditions, and to develop more effective treatments that have long lasting effects and are cost effective.
Michelle G. Craske, Ph.D., Director
Raphael Rose, Ph.D., Associate Director

768 **Yale Mood Disorders Research Program**
Department of Psychiatry
300 George Street
New Haven, CT 06511
203-785-2090
psychiatry.yale.edu

MDRP is dedicated to understanding the science of mood disorders, including bipolar disorder and depression. The MDRP brings together a multi-disciplinary group of scientists from across the Yale campus in a highly collaborative research effort. Goals of the MDRP include the identification of biological markers for mood disorders and discovery of new treatment strategies.
John H Krystal, Chair
Rajita Sinha, Chief, Psychology Section

Support Groups & Hotlines

769 **Balanced Mind Parent Network**
Depression and Bipolar Support Alliance
55 East Jackson Boulevard
Chicago, IL 60604
800-826-3632
community@dbsalliance.org
www.dbsalliance.org

The Balanced Mind provides support, information, and assistance to families raising children with mood disorders and related conditions.
Michael Pollock, CEO
Maria Margaglione, Programs Director

770 **Center for Family Support**
2811 Zulette Avenue
Bronx, NY 10461
718-518-1500
svernikoff@cfsny.org
www.cfsny.org

The Center for Family Support offers assistance to individuals with developmental and related disabilities, as well as their families, and provides support services and programs that are designed to accommodate individual needs. Offers services throughout New York City, Westchester County, Long Island, and New Jersey.
Steven Vernikoff, Executive Director
Barbara Greenwald, Chief Operating Officer

Bipolar & Related Disorders / Print Resources

771 **DBSA Support Groups: An Important Step on the Road to Wellness**
Depression and Bipolar Support Alliance
730 North Franklin Street   312-642-0049
Chicago, IL 60654   800-826-3632
                                       dbsalliance.org
Support groups for people with depression or bipolar disorder to discuss the experiences, and helpful treatments.
10 pages
Cheryl T Magrini,MS.Ed,MTS,PhD, Chair
Allen Doederlein, President

772 **Holliswood Hospital Psychiatric Care, Services and Self-Help/Support Groups**
87-37 Palermo Street   718-776-8181
Holliswood, NY 11423   800-486-3005
                                      Fax: 718-776-8572
                       HolliswoodInfo@libertymgt.com
                              www.holliswoodhospital.com/
The Holliswood Hospital, a 110-bed private psychiatric hospital located in a quiet residential Queens community, is a leader in providing quality, acute inpatient mental health care for adult, adolescent, geriatric and dually diagnosed patients. Holliswood Hospital treats patients with a broad range of psychiatric disorders. Additionally, specialized services are available for patients with psychiatric diagnoses compounded by chemical dependency, or a history of physical or sexual abuse.
Susan Clayton, Support Group Coordinator
Angela Hurtado, Support Group Coordinator

773 **Recovery International**
1415 W. 22nd Street   312-337-5661
Oak Brook, IL 60523   866-221-0302
                              info@recoveryinternational.org
                              www.recoveryinternational.org
Recovery International is an organization that uses a peer-to-peer, self-help training system developed by Abraham Low in order to help individuals with mental health issues lead more productive lives.
Sandra K. Wilcoxon, Chief Executive Officer
Joanne Lampey, President

774 **Support4Hope**
PO Box 184   Admin@Support4hope.com
Deer Lodge, TN 37726   www.support4hope.com
Support4Hope is dedicated to support of various mental health issues such as Bipolar Disorder, Depression, Anxiety Disorders, Schizophrenia, Post Traumatic Stress Disorder (PTSD) and the problems that arise from them along with other problems such as Domestic Abuse.

775 **www.befrienders.org**
Samaritans International
Support, helplines, and advice.

Print Resources

776 **American Journal of Psychiatry**
American Psychiatric Association Publishing
800 Maine Avenue SW, Suite 900   202-459-9722
Washington, DC 20024   800-368-5777
                                       Fax: 202-403-3094
                              psychiatryonline@psych.org
                              ajp.psychiatryonline.org
Official journal of the American Psychiatric Association (APA).
Ned H. Kalin, MD, Editor-in-Chief

777 **American Journal of Psychotherapy**
American Psychiatric Association Publishing
800 Maine Avenue SW, Suite 900   202-459-9722
Washington, DC 20024   800-368-5777
                                       Fax: 202-403-3094
                              psychiatryonline@psych.org
                              ajp.psychiatryonline.org
Publishes content that aims to advance the theory, science, and clinical practice of psychotherapy.
Holly A. Swartz, MD, Editor-in-Chief

778 **International Journal of Psychology and Psychoanalysis**
ClinMed International Library
3511 Silverside Road, Suite 105   302-208-7437
Wilmington, DE 19810   contact@clinmedjournals.org
                                       clinmedjournals.org
Open access, peer-reviewed journal focused on cognition, emotions, brain functioning, interpersonal relationships, and the unconscious mind.
Joaquim J.F. Soares, Editor-in-Chief

779 **Journal of Psychiatry, Depression & Anxiety**
Herald Scholarly Open Access
2561 Cornelia Road, Suite 205   202-499-9679
Herndon, VA 20171   Fax: 202-217-4195
                              contact@heraldsopenaccess.us
                              www.heraldopenaccess.us
Online, international, open access, peer-reviewed journal focused primarily on depression and anxiety, but also on other related areas of psychiatry as well.
Sam Vaknin, Editor-in-Chief

Web Sites

780 **Bipolar Disorders Treatment Information Center**
                                       www.miminc.org
Provides information on mood stabilizers other than lithium for bipolar disorders.

781 **Bpso-Bipolar Significant Others**
                                       www.bpso.org
Informational site intended to provide information and support to the spouses, families, friends and other loved ones of those who suffer from bi-polar.

782 **Center For Mental Health Services Knowledg Knowledge Exchange**
                                       www.mentalhealth.Samhsa.Gov
Information about resources, technical assistance, research, training, networks, and other federal clearinghouses, fact sheets and materials.

783 **Depression & Bi-Polar Support Alliance**
                                       www.dbsalliance.org
Mental health news updates and local support group information.

784 **Healing Well**
                                       www.healingwell.com
An online health resource guide to medical news, chat, information and articles, newsgroups and message boards, books, disease-related web sites, medical directories, and more for patients, friends, and family coping with disabling diseases, disorders, or chronic illnesses.

785 **Health Central**
                                       www.healthcentral.com
Find clearly explained, medically accurate information regarding conditions, including an overview, symptoms, causes, diagnostic procedures and treatment options. On this site it is possible to ask questions and get information from a neurologist and connect to people who have similar health interests.

786 **Health Finder**
                                       www.health.gov
Searchable, carefully developed web site offering information on over 1000 topics. Developed by the US Department of Health and Human Services, thesite can be used in both English and Spanish.

787 **Internet Mental Health**
                                       www.mentalhealth.com
Offers online psychiatric diagnosis in the hope of reaching the two-thirds of individuals with mental illness who do not seek treatment.

788 **Medical News Today**
                                       www.medicalnewstody.com
Offers in-depth health information and the latest news in medical research on a wide variety of medical conditions.

789 **MedicineNet**
                                       www.medicinenet.com

Bipolar & Related Disorders / Web Sites

An online resource for consumers providing easy-to-read, authoritative medical and health information.

790 MedlinePlus

www.medlineplus.gov

Information regarding a broad range of health, and mental health conditions topics include: Latest news, overview of anatomy and physiology, clinical trials, diagnoses and symptoms, treatment, genetics, plus lots of links to other sites. A service provided by the National Library of Medicine, part of the National Institutes of Health (NIH).

791 Medscape

www.medscape.com

Medscape offers specialists, primary care physicians, and other health professionals the Web's most robust and integrated medical information and educational tools.

792 National Alliance On Mental Illness

www.nami.org

From its inception in 1979, NAMI has been dedicated to improving the lives of individuals and families affected by mental illness.

793 National Association For The Dually Diagnosed (NADD)

www.thenadd.org

An association for persons with developmental disabilities and mental health needs.

794 National Mental Health Consumers' Self-Help Clearinghouse

www.mhselfhelp.org

Encourages the development and growth of consumer self-help groups.

795 Planetpsych.com

www.planetpsych.com

Learn about disorders, their treatments and other topics in psychology. Articles are listed under the related topic areas. Ask a therapist a question for free, or view the directory of professionals in your area. If you are a therapist sign up for the directory. Current features, self-help, interactive, and newsletter archives.

796 Psych Central

www.psychcentral.com

Personalized one-stop index for psychology, support, and mental health issues, resources, and people on the Internet.

797 Self Help Magazine

www.shpm.com

Articles and discussion forums, resource links.

798 Substance Abuse And Mental Health Services Administration

www.store.samhsa.gov

Resources on mental disorders as well as treatment and recovery.

799 Suncoast Residential Training Center

www.goodwill-suncoast.org

Group home that serves individuals diagnosed as developmentally disabled, with a secondary diagnosis of psychiatric difficulties as evidenced by problem behavior.

800 Verywell Mind

www.verywellmind.com

Provides up-to-date information on mental health topics. mission is to prioritize mental health and promote balance for day to day living. offers over 5,500 online articles that are researched based, and reviwed by medical professionals.

Kristen Altmeyer, MBA, VP & General Manager
Nick Ingalls, MA, Associate Editorial Director

801 WebMD

www.webmd.com

Provides credible information, supportive communities, and in-depth reference material about health subjects. A source for original and timely health information as well as material from well known content providers.

802 Yale University School Of Medicine

www.med.yale.edu

Research center dedicated to understanding the science of mood disorders.

DIABETES MELLITUS

Individuals with diabetes are two to three times more likely to experience depression than those without diabetes. Diabetes occurs when blood sugar, also known as blood glucose, is too high. Too much glucose in the blood can result in health problems unless managed through lifestyle modifications or medications. Blood glucose is used by the body as the main source of energy and comes from food. A hormone made by the pancreas called insulin is necessary to regulate and mobilize glucose from food into the cells for energy. If the pancreas does not manufacture sufficient insulin, then glucose stays in the circulating blood, depriving the cells of the energy needed to fuel body functions.

Diabetes is a serious disease affecting almost 35 million people, or over 10 percent of the population in the United States, with one in four not realizing they have the disease. Approximately 25 percent of people aged 65 and older are affected. The cost of diagnosed diabetes in the U.S. is approaching $350 million.

Diabetes can affect any age group, with type 1 disease that requires insulin daily for survival, primarily impacting children and young adults. Approximately 90-95 percent of diabetes diagnosed in adults is type 2 diabetes, and can develop at any age, but is more common after the age of 40. Treatment may be diet management, oral medications, and injectables. Prevention of type 2 diabetes is possible by maintaining a healthy weight, eating a healthy diet, getting sufficient exercise, and not smoking.

Diabetes is a serious disease, especially if managed poorly. Complications may be disabling and life-threatening. Complications may include Alzheimer's disease, with the presence of type 2 diabetes increasing the risk of dementia when there is poor glucose control. Depression is common in type 1 and type 2 diabetes and may negatively impact diabetes management. Cardiovascular disease, digestive issues, erectile dysfunction, and organ damage may also occur. Hearing impairment, which also increases the risk of cognitive dementia, may occur due to nerve damage from the disease. Stress, anxiety and feelings of worry are 20 percent more likely to occur in people with diabetes and may make managing the disease more difficult.

Treatment varies by type of diabetes diagnosed, but eating healthy and getting sufficient physical activity need to be practiced regardless. A diagnosis of prediabetes gives the individual the chance to bring blood sugar levels back to normal or keep them from rising further, and may decrease the risk of developing type 2 diabetes. Type 1 diabetes cannot be prevented. A healthy lifestyle, normal body weight and appropriate activity may contribute to the prevention of type 2 diabetes.

Diabetes Mellitus / Agencies & Associations

Agencies & Associations

803 **American Association of Diabetes Care & Education Specialists**
125 S. Wacker Dr. 800-338-3633
Chicago, IL 60606 www.diabeteseducator.org
An independent, multidisciplinary organization of health professionals involved in teaching persons with diabetes. The mission is to enhance the competence of health professionals who teach persons with diabetes and advance the specialty practice of diabetes.
Charles Macfarlane, Chief Executive Officer
Crystal Broj, Chief Technology and Innovation Officer

804 **American Diabetes Association**
2451 Crystal Drive 888-342-2383
Arlington, VA 22202 askada@diabetes.org
www.diabetes.org
Voluntary organization concerned with diabetes and its complications. The mission of the organization is to prevent and cure diabetes and to improve the lives of persons with diabetes. Offers a network of offices nationwide.
Charles Henderson, Chief Executive Officer
Robert A. Gabbay, MD, PhD, Chief Science & Medical Officer

805 **American Diabetes Association: New England**
617-482-4580
ADANewEngland@diabetes.org
www.diabetes.org

806 **Canadian Diabetes Educator Certification Board**
13909 Hurontario Street 905-838-4898
Caledon, ON L7C Fax: 905-583-8489
www.cdecb.ca
Dedicated to promoting excellence in the field of diabetes education through the development, maintenance, and protection of the certified Diabetes Educator credential and the certification process.

807 **Diabetes Action Network for the Blind**
200 East Wells Street 573-268-6989
Baltimore, MD 21230 debbiewunder@charter.net
www.nfb.org
DAN is a division of the National Federation of the Blind. It is a support and information organization of persons losing vision due to diabetes. Provides personal contact and resource information with other blind diabetics about non-visual techniques of independently managing diabetes and monitoring glucose levels.
Debbie Wunder, President

808 **Diabetes Control Program**
California Department of Health Services
PO Box 997377 916-558-1784
Sacramento, CA 95899 www.cdph.ca.gov
Our mission is to prevent diabetes and its complications in California's diverse communities.
Susan Lopez-Payan, Consltant

809 **Division of Diabetes Translation**
National Center for Chronic Disease Prevention
1600 Clifton Rd 800-232-4636
Atlantia, GA 30333 Fax: 770-488-5966
TTY: 888-232-6348
cdcinfo@cdc.gov
www.cdc.gov/diabetes
The Division of Diabetes Translation's (DDT) goal is to reduce the burden of diabetes in the United States. The division works to achieve this goal by combining support for public health-oriented diabetes prevention and control programs (DPCPs) and translating diabetes research findings into widespread clinical and public health practice.

810 **Joslin Center at University of Maryland Medicine**
301 Hospital Drive 410-787-4940
Glen Brunie, MD 21261 800-492-5538
TDD: 800735225800
www.umm.edu/joslindiabetes
The Joslin Center at University of Maryland Medicine meets the highest standards of care for people with diabetes. Its programs reflect a philosophy which have been the hallmark of Joslin's care — a comprehensive team approach to diabetes treatment with programs designed to help children and adults with diabetes take charge of their own health and well-being.
Thomas W Donner, MD, Director

811 **Naomi Berrie Diabetes Center at Columbia University Medical Center**
Russ Berrie Medical Science Pavillion
1150 St. Nicholas Avenue 212-851-5494
New York, NY 10032 Fax: 212-851-5459
diabetes@columbia.edu
nbdiabetes.org
The special focus of the Naomi Berrie Diabetes Center is on families — a concept that differentiates it from almost every other diabetes treatment facility in America. People with diabetes are strongly encouraged to involve their entire families in the treatment process.
Robin Goland, MD, Co-Director
Rudolph Liebel, Co-Director

812 **National Diabetes Information Clearinghouse**
One Information Way 800-860-8747
Bethesda, MD 20892 Fax: 703-738-4929
TTY: 866-8569-116
ndic@info.niddk.nih.gov
diabetes.niddk.nih.gov
To serve as a diabetes informational, educational, and referral resource for health professionals and the public. NDIC is a service of the NIDDK.

813 **National Institute of Diabetes & Digestive & Kidney Diseases**
Office of Communications and Public Liaison, NIH
31 Center Drive 800-860-8747
Bethesda, MD 20892 TTY: 866-569-1162
healthinfo@niddk.nih.gov
www.niddk.nih.gov
Research areas include diabetes, digestive diseases, endocrine and metabolic diseases, hematologic diseases, kidney disease, liver disease, urologic diseases, as well as matters relating to nutrition and obesity.
Griffin P. Rodgers, MD, MACP, Director
Gregory Germino, MD, Deputy Director

814 **Schulze Diabetes Institute**
University of Minnesota
420 Delaware Street SE 612-626-1999
Minneapolis, MN 55455 diitinfo@umn.edu
www.med.umn.edu
Formerly the Diabetes Institute for Immunology and Transplantation
David Sutherland MD, PhD, Director
Bernard Hering, Director

815 **Tallahassee Memorial Diabetes Center**
Tallahassee Memorial Health Care
1300 Miccosukee Road 850-431-5404
Tallahassee, FL 32308 800-662-4278
Fax: 850-431-6325
www.tmh.org/diabetes
TMH provides comprehensive, patient-centered services to both children and adults. The Diabetes Center uses a team approach that involves the patient, physicians, nurse educators, registered dietitians with access to a diabetes counselor and registered pharmacists and social worker.
Nancy Smith, Diabetes Nutrition Educator

Alabama

816 **American Diabetes Association: Alabama**
3918 Montclair Rd 250-870-5172
Birmingham, AL 35213 www.diabetes.org

Alaska

817 **American Diabetes Association: Alaska**
200 W 34th Ave #952 907-272-1424
Anchorage, AK 99503 www.diabetes.org

Diabetes Mellitus / Agencies & Associations

Arizona

818 American Diabetes Association: New Mexico & Arizona
602-861-4731
adunn@diabetes.org
www.diabetes.org

California

819 American Diabetes Association: Nevada & California (Southern)
323-966-2890
ADASOCAL@diabetes.org
www.diabetes.org

820 American Diabetes Association: Northern California
510-654-4499
adabayarea@diabetes.org
www.diabetes.org

Delaware

821 American Diabetes Association: Delaware
ADAEastPA@diabetes.org
www.diabetes.org

822 American Diabetes Association: Eastern Pennsylvania & Delaware
610-828-5003
ADAEastPA@diabetes.org
www.diabetes.org

District of Columbia

823 American Diabetes Association: District of Columbia
202-331-8303
ADAWashDC@diabetes.org
www.diabetes.org

Florida

824 American Diabetes Association: Florida
407-660-1926
ADAFL@diabetes.org
www.diabetes.org

Hawaii

825 American Diabetes Association: Hawaii
808-947-5979
ADAHawaii@diabetes.org
www.diabetes.org

Illinois

826 American Diabetes Association: Illinois
312-346-1805
ADAIL@diabetes.org
www.diabetes.org

Iowa

827 American Diabetes Association: Nebraska, Iowa & South Dakota
317-352-9226
ADAIN@diabetes.org
www.diabetes.org

Kansas

828 American Diabetes Association: Kansas
317-352-9226
ADAIN@diabetes.org
www.diabetes.org

Louisiana

829 American Diabetes Association: Mississippi & Louisiana
504-889-0278
ADALA_MS@diabetes.org
www.diabetes.org

Maryland

830 American Diabetes Association: Maryland
410-265-0075
ADAMD@diabetes.org
www.diabetes.org

Michigan

831 American Diabetes Association: Michigan
248-433-3830
ADAMI@diabetes.org
www.diabetes.org

Minnesota

832 American Diabetes Association: Minnesota & North Dakota
763-593-5333
ADAMN_WI_ND@diabetes.org
www.diabetes.org

833 American Diabetes Association: North Dakota & Minnesota
763-593-5333
ADAMN_WI_ND@diabetes.org
www.diabetes.org

Mississippi

834 American Diabetes Association: Mississippi & Louisiana
504-889-0278
ADALA_MS@diabetes.org
www.diabetes.org

Missouri

835 American Diabetes Association: Missouri
1944-A Sunshine
Springfield, MO 65804
317-352-9226
ADAIN@diabetes.org
www.diabetes.org

Nebraska

836 American Diabetes Association: Nebraska, Iowa & South Dakota
317-352-9226
ADAIN@diabetes.org
www.diabetes.org

Nevada

837 American Diabetes Association: Nevada & California (Southern)
323-966-2890
ADASOCAL@diabetes.org
www.diabetes.org

New Mexico

838 American Diabetes Association: New Mexico & Arizona
602-861-4731
adunn@diabetes.org
www.diabetes.org

New York

839 American Diabetes Association: New York (Greater NYC and New Jersey)
703-549-1500
www.diabetes.org

North Dakota

840 American Diabetes Association: Minnesota & North Dakota
763-593-5333
ADAMN_WI_ND@diabetes.org
www.diabetes.org

Diabetes Mellitus / Foundations

Ohio

841 American Diabetes Association: Northeast Ohio
316-328-9989
ADAOH@diabetes.org
www.diabetes.org

842 American Diabetes Association: Ohio
317-352-9226
ADAIN@diabetes.org
www.diabetes.org

Oklahoma

843 American Diabetes Association: Oklahoma
918-492-3839
ADAOK@diabetes.org
www.diabetes.org

Oregon

844 American Diabetes Association: Oregon
503-736-2770
ADAOR_WA@diabetes.org
www.diabetes.org

Pennsylvania

845 American Diabetes Association: Eastern Pennsylvania & Delaware
610-828-5003
ADAEastPA@diabetes.org
www.diabetes.org

846 American Diabetes Association: Western Pennsylvania
412-824-1181
ADAWestPA@diabetes.org
www.diabetes.org

Rhode Island

847 American Diabetes Association: Rhode Island
146 Clifford St
Providence, RI 02903
401-351-0498
888-342-2383
Fax: 401-351-1674
www.jdf.org

South Dakota

848 American Diabetes Association: Nebraska, Iowa & South Dakota
317-352-9226
ADAIN@diabetes.org
www.diabetes.org

Tennessee

849 American Diabetes Association: Tennessee
317-352-9226
ADAIN@diabetes.org
www.diabetes.org

Texas

850 American Diabetes Association: Texas
713-977-7706
ADACSTX@diabetes.org
www.diabetes.org

Virginia

851 American Diabetes Association: Virginia/West Virginia
757-424-6662
ADAVA_WV_NC@diabetes.org
diabetes.org

Washington

852 American Diabetes Association: Washington
206-282-4616
ADAWA@diabetes.org
www.diabetes.org

West Virginia

853 American Diabetes Association: Virginia/West Virginia
757-424-6662
ADAVA_WV_NC@diabetes.org
diabetes.org

Foundations

854 **Diabetes Youth Foundation of Indiana**
5050 East 211th Street
Noblesville, IN 46060-9212
317-750-9310
Fax: 317-877-1846
dyfjulie@yahoo.com
www.dyfi.org

This nonprofit group whose mission is to improve the lives of children with diabetes and their families.
Julie Shutt, Executive Director
Rick Crosslin, Camp Director

855 **JDRF: Greater Palm Beach County Chapter**
1450 Centrepark Boulevard
West Palm Beach, FL 33401
561-686-7701
Fax: 561-686-7702
greaterpalmbeach@jdrf.org
www.jdrf.org/greaterpalmbeach

Lora Hazelwood, Executive Director
Esther Swann, Special Events Coordinator

856 **Juvenile Diabetes Research Foundation Canada**
235 Yorkland Blvd.
Toronto, Ontario, M2J
647-789-2000
877-287-3533
Fax: 416-491-2111
general@jdrf.ca
www.jdrf.ca

JDRF Canada concentrates on research projects in three areas: Cure, Treat, and Prevent.
Dave Prowten, President & CEO
Susan Delisle, VP, Philanthropy & Corporate Partnership

857 **Juvenile Diabetes Research Foundation International**
26 Broadway
New York, NY 10004
800-533-2873
Fax: 212-785-9595
info@jdrf.org
www.jdrf.org

Focuses energies on fund-raising, referrals, educational materials and information pertaining to juvenile diabetes.
Aaron J. Kowalski, PhD, President & CEO
Sandra Hijikata, Chief Development Officer

Alabama

858 **JDRF: Birmingham**
14 Office Park Circle
Birmingham, AL 35223
205-871-0333
Fax: 205-871-0355
www.jdrf.org/alabama

Karin Scott, Executive Director
Sarah Hendren, Special Events Manager

Arizona

859 **JDRF: Phoenix Chapter**
4343 E Camelback Road
Phoenix, AZ 85018
602-224-1800
Fax: 602-224-1801
desertsouthwest@jdrf.org
www.jdrf.org/arizona

Marci Zimmerman, Executive Director
Valerie Jones, Associate Executive Director

Diabetes Mellitus / Foundations

Arkansas

860 **JDRF: Northwest Arkansas Branch**
4241 Gabel Dr
Fayetteville, AR 72703
479-443-9190
Fax: 479-443-2692
nwarkansas@jdrf.org
www.nwark.jdrf.org

Deb Euculano, Special Events Manager

California

861 **JDRF: Bakersfield Chapter**
712 19th Street
Bakersfield, CA 93301
661-636-1305
Fax: 661-636-1307
www.jdrf-bakersfield.org

Allison Perkins Thomas, Bakersfield Branch Manager
Arnold Donald, President/CEO Corporate Office (NY)

862 **JDRF: Inland Empire Chapter**
1001 East Cooley Drive
Colton, CA 92324
909-424-0100
Fax: 909-424-0044
inlandempire@jdrf.org
www.inlandempire.jdrf.org

Jamie Brunelle, Board of Directors
Evelyn Edinin, Board of Directors

863 **JDRF: Los Angeles Chapter**
800 West Sixth Street
Los Angeles, CA 90017
213-233-9901
Fax: 213-622-6276
losangeles@jdrf.org
www.jdrf.org/losangeles

Mark Rieck, Executive Director
Dennis Ellman Esq, Board of Directors President

864 **JDRF: Northern California Inland Chapter**
1329 Howe Avenue
Sacramento, CA 95825
916-920-0790
Fax: 916-920-0367
northernca@jdrf.org
www.jdrf.org/norcal

Victoria Webster, Executive Director
Molly Atkinson, Special Events Coordinator

865 **JDRF: Orange County Chapter**
17992 Mitchell South
Irvine, CA 92614
949-553-0363
Fax: 949-553-8813
orangecounty@jdrf.org
www.jdrfoc.org

Louise Cummings, Executive Director
John Giovannone, President

866 **JDRF: San Diego Chapter**
5677 Oberlin Drive
San Diego, CA 92121
858-597-0240
Fax: 858-597-2072
sandiego@jdrf.org
www.jdrf-sandiego-news.org

Linda Riley, Executive Director
Katherine Griswold, Special Events Manager

Colorado

867 **JDRF: Colorado Springs Chapter**
3710 Sinton Road
Colorado Springs, CO 80907
719-633-8110
Fax: 719-633-8155
lpage@jdrf.org
www.jdrfcoloradosprings.org

Lynn Page, Branch Manager
Andi Chernushin, President

868 **JDRF: Rocky Mountain Chapter**
5613 DTC Parkway
Greenwood Village, CO 80111
303-779-0525
Fax: 303-720-1630
RockyMountain@jdrf.org
www.jdrf.org/rockymountain

James Buckles, Executive Director
Nancy L Walters, Special Events Director

Connecticut

869 **JDRF: Fairfield County Chapter**
200 Connecticut Avenue
Norwalk, CT 06854
203-854-0658
Fax: 203-854-0798
fairfield@jdrf.org
www.jdrf.org/fairfieldcounty

Barbara Rose, Executive Director
Michelle Tighe, Special Events Coordinator

870 **JDRF: Greater New Haven Chapter**
2969 Whitney Avenue
Hamden, CT 06518
203-248-1880
Fax: 203-248-1820
www.jdrf.org/greaternewhaven

Mary K Kessler, Executive Director
Will Martinez, Board of Directors President

871 **JDRF: North Central CT & Western MA**
18 North Main Street
West Hartford, CT 06107
860-561-1153
Fax: 860-561-3440
northcentralct@jdrf.org
www.jdrf.org/index.cfm?page_id=100619

Mary Ann Slomski, Executive Director
Ellen Kellie, Special Events Coordinator

Delaware

872 **JDRF: Delaware Chapter**
100 West 10th Street
Wilmington, DE 19801
302-888-1117
Fax: 302-888-1878
delaware@jdrf.org
www.jdrf.org/delaware

Ellen Rubesin, Executive Director
Stephanie Bucksner, Special Events Coordinator

Florida

873 **JDRF: Central Florida Chapter**
279 Douglas Avenue
Altamonte Springs, FL 32714
407-774-2166
Fax: 407-774-2168
centralflorida@jdrf.org
www.jdrf.org/centralflorida

Kendra Presley, Special Events Manager
Gwen Bell, Office Manager

874 **JDRF: Florida Sun Coast Chapter**
3333 Clark Road
Sarasota, FL 34231
941-929-0621
Fax: 941-929-0602
floridasuncoast@jdrf.org
www.jdrf.org/index.cfm

Sara Rankin, Executive Director
Jeannie Kawcak, Special Events Coordinator

875 **JDRF: North Florida Chapter**
8400 Baymeadows Way
Jacksonville, FL 32256
904-739-2101
Fax: 904-739-2693
northflorida@jdrf.org
www.jdrf.org/northflorida

Brooks Biagini, Executive Director
Wendy Smit, Special Events Assistant

876 **JDRF: South Florida Chapter**
3411 NW 9th Avenue
Fort Lauderdale, FL 33309
954-565-4775
Fax: 954-565-4767
southflorida@jdrf.org
www.jdrf.org/chapters/FL/South-Florida

Ingrid Velarde, Special Events Coordinator
Katelyn Tolzien, Special Events Coordinator

877 **JDRF: Tampa Bay Chapter**
5959 Central Avenue
Saint Petersburg, FL 33710
727-344-2873
Fax: 727-384-9009
tampabay@jdrf.org
www.jdf.org

Arnold Donald, President/CEO Corporate Office
Robin Harding, EVP Development & COO

Diabetes Mellitus / Foundations

Georgia

878 **JDRF: Georgia Chapter**
400 Perimeter Center Terrace
Atlanta, GA 30346
404-420-5990
Fax: 404-420-5995
georgia@jdrf.org
www.jdrfgeorgia.org/

Rob Shaw, Executive Director
Scott Whiteside, EVP/General Manager

Hawaii

879 **JDRF: Hawaii Chapter**
1019 Waimanu Street
Honolulu, HI 96814
808-988-1000
Fax: 808-597-8758
www.jdf.org

Arnold Donald, President/CEO Corporate
Robin Harding, EVP/Develpment & COO Corporate

Illinois

880 **JDRF: Greater Chicago Chapter**
500 North Dearborn Street
Chicago, IL 60610
312-670-0313
Fax: 312-670-0250
illinois@jdrf.org
www.jdrfillinois.org

Amy Franze, Executive Director
Janine Tobola, Director Office Operations

Indiana

881 **JDRF: Indiana State Chapter**
8465 Keystone Crossing
Indianapolis, IN 46240
317-202-0352
Fax: 317-202-0357
indianastate@jdrf.org
www.jdrf.org/indiana

Henry Rodriguez MD, Chapter President

882 **JDRF: Northern Indiana Chapter**
2004 Ironwood Circle
South Bend, IN 46635
574-273-1810
Fax: 574-273-1870
northernindiana@jdrf.org
www.jdrf.org

Arnold Donald, President/CEO Corporate
Robin Harding, EVP/Development & COO Corporate

Iowa

883 **JDRF: Eastern Iowa Chapter**
701 10th Street SE
Cedar Rapids, IA 52403
319-393-3850
Fax: 319-393-3852
easterniowa@jdrf.org
www.jdrf.org/easterniowa

Ann Elise Walsh, Special Events Manager
Mary Henry, Special Events Coordinator

884 **JDRF: Greater Iowa Chapter**
5444 NW 96th Street
Johnston, IA 50131
515-986-1512
Fax: 515-986-1513
www.jdrf.org/greateriowa

Jean Howieson, Special Events Director
Judy Greaves, Office Administrator

Kentucky

885 **JDRF: Kentuckiana Chapter**
133 Evergreen Road
Louisville, KY 40243
502-485-9397
866-485-9397
Fax: 502-485-9591
kentuckiana@jdrf.org
www.jdf.org/chapters/ky/kentuckiana

Twynette S Davidson, Executive Director
Joe Salvagne, Chapter President

Louisiana

886 **JDRF: Baton Rouge Chapter**
9457 Brookline Avenue
Baton Rouge, LA 70809
225-932-9511
Fax: 225-932-9514
www.jdrf.org/batonrouge

Kristy Andries, President/Development Chair
Danielle Graham, Special Events Assistant

887 **JDRF: Louisiana Chapter**
2201 Veterans Memorial Bouelvard
Metairie, LA 70002
504-828-2873
Fax: 504-828-4922
louisiana@jdrf.org
www.jdrf.org/louisiana

Sam Robinson, President Board of Directors
Becky Spinnato, Vice President Fundraising

888 **JDRF: Shreveport Chapter**
2001 East 70th Street
Shreveport, LA 71105
318-798-1195
Fax: 318-798-1194
jburns@jdrf.org
www.jdrf.org/shreveport

Jeff Knutson, President Board of Directors
Craig Floyd, Vice President Fundraising

Maryland

889 **JDRF: Maryland Chapter**
200 East Joppa Road
Towson, MD 21286
410-823-0073
Fax: 410-823-0416
www.jdrf.org/maryland/

Rebecca Maude, Executive Director
Dotty Raynor, Outreach Manager

Massachusetts

890 **JDRF: New England/Bay State Chapter**
20 Walnut Street
Wellesley, MA 02481
781-431-0700
Fax: 781-431-8836
www.jdrf.org/baystate

Heidi Daniels, New England Chapter Executive Director
Virginia Irving, Associate Executive Director

891 **JDRF: New England/Maine Chapter**
33 Silver Street
Portland, ME 04101
207-761-0133
Fax: 207-761-1687
www.jdrf.org/maine

Heidi Daniels, New England Chapter Executive Director
Emily Hampton Burgo, Branch Manager

Michigan

892 **JDRF: Metropolitan Detroit/SE Michigan**
24359 Northwestern Highway
Southfield, MI 48075
248-355-1133
Fax: 248-355-1188
metrodetroit@jdrf.org
www.jdrfdetroit.org

Rita L Combest, Development Director
Susan Kossik, Development Manager

893 **JDRF: West Michigan Chapter**
5075 Cascade Road SE
Grand Rapids, MI 49546
616-957-1838
Fax: 616-957-1169
westmichigan@jrdf.org
www.jdrf.org/westmichigan

Annette Guilfoyle, Executive Director
Maxine Gray, Special Events Coordinator

Minnesota

894 **JDRF: Minnesota Chapter**
2626 East 82nd Street
Bloomington, MN 55425
952-851-0770
800-663-1860
Fax: 952-851-0766
minnesota@jdrf.org
www.jdrf.org/minnesota

Jackie Casey, Executive Director
Angie McCarthy, Special Events Manager

Diabetes Mellitus / Foundations

Missouri

895 **JDRF: St. Louis Chapter**
225 S Meramec Avenue
Clayton, MO 63105
314-726-6778
Fax: 314-726-6778
metrostlouis@jdrf.org
www.jdrfstl.org

M Marie Davis, Executive Director
William Schmitt, Corporate Development

Nebraska

896 **JDRF: Lincoln Chapter**
1540 S 70th Street
Lincoln, NE 68506
402-484-8300
Fax: 402-484-8302
lincoln@jdrf.org
www.jdrf.org/lincoln

Deb Gokie, Executive Director
Maggie Pavelka, Special Events Assistant

897 **JDRF: Omaha Council Bluffs Chapter**
9202 W Dodge Road
Omaha, NE 68114
402-397-2873
Fax: 402-572-3343
omaha@jdrf.org
www.jdrf.org/omaha

Shawn Reynolds, Executive Director
Melissa Shapiro, Special Events Coordinator

Nevada

898 **JDRF: Nevada Chapter**
5542 S Fort Apache Road
Las Vegas, NV 89148
702-732-4795
Fax: 702-732-1635
www.jdrf.org/nevada

Stuart Mason, Nevada Chapter Co-Founder
Flora Mason, Nevada Chapter Co-Founder

899 **JDRF: Northern Nevada Branch**
5335 Kietzke Lane
Reno, NV 89511
775-786-1881
Fax: 775-827-0131
northernnevada@jdrf.org
www.jdrf.org/northernnevada

Molly Dillon, Branch Manager
Arnie Pitts, Board of Directors President

New Hampshire

900 **JDRF: New England/New Hampshire Chapter**
2 Wellman Avenue
Nashua, NH 03064
603-595-2595
Fax: 603-595-2073
newhampshire@jdrf.org
www.jdrf.org/newhampshire

Brooke Edwards, Special Events Coordinator
Heidi Daniels, New England Chapter Executive Director

New Jersey

901 **JDRF: Central Jersey Chapter**
740 Broad Street
Shrewsbury, NJ 07702
732-219-6654
Fax: 732-219-8722
centraljersey@jdrf.org
www.jdrf.org/chapters/NJ/Central-Jersey

Lori McLane, Executive Director
Beckie Burlew, Special Events Coordinator

902 **JDRF: Mid-Jersey Chapter**
28 Kennedy Boulevard
East Brunswick, NJ 08816
732-296-7171
Fax: 732-296-1433
midjersey@jdrf.org
www.jdrf.org/NJ/Mid-Jersey

Elizabeth Giardina Preston, Chapter Executive Director
Sandra Hilsenrath, Special Events Coordinator

903 **JDRF: Rockland County/Northern New Jersey Chapter**
560 Sylvan Avenue
Englewood Cliffs, NJ 07632
201-568-4838
Fax: 201-568-5360
rockland@jdrf.org
www.jdrf.org/northernnj

Douglas Rouse, Executive Director
Allison Hartstone, Special Events Coordinator

904 **JDRF: South Jersey Chapter**
1415 Route 70 E
Cherry Hill, NJ 08034
856-429-1101
Fax: 856-429-1105
southjersey@jdrf.org
www.jdrf.org/southjersey

Stephen Blocher, Executive Director
Robin Berger, Special Events Coordinator

New Mexico

905 **JDRF: Albuquerque Chapter**
2501 San Pedro NE
Albuquerque, NM 87110
505-255-4005
Fax: 505-260-1430
newmexico@jdrf.org
www.jdrf.org/newmexico

Joann Perrine, Branch Manager
Elizabeth Romero, Fundraising Assistant

New York

906 **JDRF: Buffalo/Western New York Chapter**
331 Alberta Drive
Buffalo, NY 14226
716-833-2873
Fax: 716-833-0199
westernny@jdrf.org
www.jdrf.org/westernny

Karen Swierski, Executive Director
Jennifer Hickok, Special Events Manager

907 **JDRF: Hudson Valley Chapter**
Hollowbrook Office Park
Wappinger Falls, NY 12590
845-297-8600
Fax: 845-297-7887
hudsonvalley@jdrf.org
www.letscurediabetes.com

Charlie Lawrence, Branch Manager
Linda Delia, Events Assistant

908 **JDRF: Long Island/South Shore Chapter**
532 Broadhollow Road
Melville, NY 11747
631-414-1126
Fax: 631-414-1133
longisland@jdrf.org
www.jdrf.org/longisland

Barbara Rogus, Executive Director
Christina Colandro, Special Events Manager

909 **JDRF: New York Chapter**
432 Park Avenue S
New York, NY 10016
212-689-2860
Fax: 212-689-4038
newyorkchapter@jdrf.org
www.nyc.jdrf.org

Mania Boyder, New York City Chapter Executive Director

910 **JDRF: Northeastern New York Chapter**
6 Greenwood Drive
East Greenbush, NY 12061
518-477-2873
Fax: 518-477-7004
northeastny@jdrf.org
www.jdrf.org/NortheasternNY

Bev Kennedy, Executive Director
Darlene Robbiano, Special Events Manager

911 **JDRF: Rochester Branch/Western New York Chapter**
1200-A Scottsville Road
Rochester, NY 14624
585-546-1390
Fax: 585-546-1404
www.jdrf.org/rochester

Mary Anne Fox, Executive Director
Lisa Swindon, Senior Development Coordinator

912 **JDRF: Westchester County Chapter**
30 Glenn Street
White Plains, NY 10603
914-686-7700
Fax: 914-686-7701
westchester@jdrf.org
www.jdrf.org/westchester

Katherine Cintron, Executive Director
Dejan Popovich, Special Events Coordinator

Diabetes Mellitus / Foundations

North Carolina

913 **JDRF: Charlotte Chapter**
205 Regency Executive Park Drive
Charlotte, NC 28217
704-561-0828
Fax: 704-561-9920
charlotte@jdrf.org
www.gwc.jdrf.org

Brenning Johnston, Volunteer Coordinator

914 **JDRF: Piedmont Triad Chapter**
1401-B Old Mill Circle
Winston-Salem, NC 27103
336-768-1027
Fax: 336-768-1029
piedmont@jdrf.org
www.jdrf.org/triad

Brad Calloway, President Board of Directors
Tom Brinkley, VP Fundraising & Development

915 **JDRF: Triangle/Eastern North Carolina Chapter**
2210 Millbrook Road
Raleigh, NC 27604
919-431-8330
Fax: 919-431-8373
triangle@jdrf.org
www.jdrftriangle.org

Jim Burson, Chapter President
Courtney Davies, Executive Director

Ohio

916 **JDRF: Akron/Canton Chapter**
5000 Rockside Road
Canton, OH 44131
888-718-3061
Fax: 216-328-8340
jcallahan@jdrf.org
www.jdrf.org/chapters/OH/Northeast-Ohio

Laura E Maciag, Executive Director
Danielle Thompson, Special Events Manager

917 **JDRF: Greater Cincinnati Chapter**
8041 Hosbrook Road
Cincinnati, OH 45236
513-793-3223
Fax: 513-936-5333
cincinnati@jdrf.org
www.jdrf.org/cincinnati

Bill Rice, Executive Director
Bethe Ferguson, Special Events Coordinator

918 **JDRF: Mid-Ohio Chapter**
1550 Old Henderson Rd
Columbus, OH 43220
614-464-2873
Fax: 614-464-2877
midohio@jdrf.org
www.jdrf.org/midohio

Staci Perkins, Executive Director
Roberta Smedes, Office Manager

919 **JDRF: Toledo/Northwest Ohio Chapter**
3450 W Central Avenue
Toledo, OH 43606
419-873-1377
800-533-2873
Fax: 419-720-6339
northwestohio@jdrf.org
www.jdrf.org/northwestohio

Megan Meyer, Executive Director
Marna Cousino, Special Events Coordinator

Oklahoma

920 **JDRF: Central Oklahoma Chapter**
2601 NW Expressway
Oklahoma City, OK 73112
405-810-0070
888-533-9255
Fax: 405-810-0078
oklahoma@jdrf.org
www.jdrf.org/centralok

Renee MacDonald, Executive Director
Shannon Scott, Special Events Coordinator

921 **JDRF: Tulsa Green County Chapter**
4606 E 67th Street
Tulsa, OK 74136
918-481-5807
Fax: 918-481-5823
tulsa@jdrf.org
www.jdrf.org/tulsa-green

Brandi Sullivan, Executive Director
Angela Peterson, Special Events Coordinator

Oregon

922 **JDRF: Oregon/SW Washington Chapter**
7460 SW Hunziker Street
Portland, OR 97223
503-643-1995
866-598-9074
Fax: 503-598-9087
oregon-washington@jdrf.org
www.jdrf.org/oregon

Ashleigh Farleigh, Special Events Manager
Debbie Secor, Special Events Assistant

Pennsylvania

923 **JDRF: Berks County Chapter**
619 Wellington Avenue
West Lawn, PA 19609
610-775-4169

Tammy A. Edwards, Contact

924 **JDRF: Central Pennsylvania Chapter**
119 Aster Drive
Harrisburg, PA 17112
717-901-6489
Fax: 717-901-6573
centralpa@jdrf.org
www.jdrf.org/centralpa

Susan Harral, Executive Director
Kate Severs, Special Events Assistant

925 **JDRF: Northwestern Pennsylvania Chapter**
1700 Peach St
Erie, PA 16501
814-452-0635
Fax: 814-452-0645
northwestpa@jdrf.org
www.jdrf.org/northwestpa

Douglas K White, Executive Director
Amy Bement, Special Events Assistant

926 **JDRF: Philadelphia Chapter**
225 City Line Avenue
Bala Cynwyd, PA 19004
610-664-9255
Fax: 610-664-9585
philadelphia@jdrf.org
www.jdrf.org/philadelphia

Ellen Rubesin, Executive Director
Kathy Farren, Special Events Director

927 **JDRF: Western Pennsylvania**
960 Penn Avenue
Pittsburgh, PA 15222
412-471-1414
888-528-8788
Fax: 412-471-1417
westernpa@jdrf.org
www.jdrf.org/westernpa

David R Donahue, Executive Director
Kimberly A McElroy, Office Manager

South Carolina

928 **JDRF: Low Country Chapter**
520 Folly Road
Charleston, SC 29412
843-345-0369
Fax: 843-406-7957
dmenefee@jdrf.org
www.jdrf.org/lowcountry

Pam Nestor McAdams, Events/Walk Director South Coastal Chptr

929 **JDRF: Palmetto Chapter**
810 Dutch Square Blvd
Columbia, SC 29210
803-782-1477
Fax: 803-782-8975
palmetto@jdrf.org
www.jdrfpalmetto.org/about.aspx

Michael Slapnik, President
Dana Bruce, Executive Director

South Dakota

930 **JDRF: Sioux Falls Chapter**
PO Box 88540
Sioux Falls, SD 57109
605-338-2295

Diabetes Mellitus / Research Centers

Tennessee

931 **JDRF: East Tennessee Chapter**
355 Trane Lane
Knoxville, TN 37919
865-544-0768
Fax: 865-544-4312
EastTennessee@jdrf.org
www.easttennessee.jdrf.org

932 **JDRF: Middle Tennessee Chapter**
105 Westpark Drive
Nashville, TN 37027
615-383-6781
Fax: 615-383-4284
MidTennessee@jrdf.org
www.midtennessee.jdrf.org

Joe Bide, Vice President

Texas

933 **JDRF: Dallas Chapter**
9400 North Central Expressway
Dallas, TX 75231
214-373-9808
Fax: 214-373-6337
dallas@jrdf.org
www.jdrfdallas.org

Dave Johnson, President
Michael Keith, Treasurer

934 **JDRF: Greater Fort Worth/Arlington Chapter**
3840 Hulen Street
Fort Worth, TX 76107
817-332-2601
Fax: 817-332-5641
grfortworth@jdrf.org
www.jdf.org

935 **JDRF: Houston/Gulf Coast Chapter**
2425 Fountain View
Houston, TX 77057
713-334-4400
Fax: 713-334-4040
houston@jdrf.org
www.jdf.org

936 **JDRF: South Central Texas Chapter**
8700 Crownhill Boulevrad
San Antonio, TX 78209
210-822-5336
Fax: 210-822-1443
scentraltexas@jdrf.org
www.sctx-jdrf.org

Doug Koskie, President
Brigitte West, Secretary

937 **JDRF: West Texas Chapter**
Clay Desta Towers, 10 Desta Drive
Midland, TX 79705
432-570-5643
Fax: 432-682-0765
westtexas@jdrf.org
www.jdf.org

Virginia

938 **JDRF: Greater Blue Ridge Chapter**
3959 Electric Road
Roanoke, VA 24018
540-772-1975
888-849-0510
Fax: 540-772-6672
www.jdrfgreaterblueridge.org

Mary Lou Bruce, Board President
Annette Kirby, Secretary

Washington

939 **JDRF: Capitol Chapter**
1400 K Street NW
Washington, DC 20005
202-371-0044
Fax: 202-371-0046
www.jdrfcapitol.org

Pam Gatz, Executive Director
Carrie Hamilton, Special Events Director

940 **JDRF: Seattle Chapter**
1333 N Northlake Way
Seattle, WA 98103
206-545-1510
Fax: 206-545-1511
www.jdf.org

941 **JDRF: Seattle Guild**
1215 Fourth Avenue
Seattle, WA 98161
206-343-0873
Fax: 206-343-7015
terickson@jdrf.org
www.jdrfnorthwest.org

Nadie Heichel, Executive Director
Becky Baumgardner, Office Manager

942 **JDRF: Spokane County Area Chapter**
9 South Washington
Spokane, WA 99201
509-459-6307
Fax: 509-459-6392
inlandnw@jdrf.org
http://www.jdrf.org/index.cfm

Kay C Dightman, Contact

West Virginia

943 **JDRF: Huntington Chapter**
PO Box 2903
Huntington, WV 25728
304-525-4533

Wisconsin

944 **JDRF: Greater Madison Chapter**
434 S. Yellowstone Drive
Madison, WI 53719
608-833-2873
Fax: 608-833-9214
westernwi@jdrf.org
www.jdrfwesternwisconsin.org/

Douglas Berry, President
Aaron Weinbe Swenson, Treasurer

945 **JDRF: Northeast Wisconsin Chapter**
1800 Appleton Road
Menasha, WI 54952
920-997-0038
Fax: 920-997-0039
northeastwi@jdrf.org
www.jdrf.org

Julie Kersten, Executive Director
Dana Paschen, Special Events Coordinator

946 **JDRF: Southeastern Chapter**
3333 North Mayfair Road
Wauwatosa, WI 53222
414-453-4673
Fax: 414-453-4919
southeastwi@jdrf.org
www.sewi.jdrf.org/

Libraries & Resource Centers

947 **Health Science Library**
Marshall University
1600 Medical Center Drive
Huntington, WV 25701
304-691-1700
www.musom.marshall.edu/library
The Health Sciences Library's primary mission is serving the informational needs of the students, faculty, and staff at Marshall University and the Cabell-Huntington Hospital. The Library also plays an important role in providing information services to hospitals and healthcare professionals in the Huntington and the Tri-State area.
Edward Dzierzak, Director

Research Centers

948 **Barbara Davis Center for Childhood Diabetes**
13001 E 17th Place
Aurora, CO 80045
303-724-2323
Fax: 303-724-6839
www.uchsc.edu/misc/diabetes
Research and educational organization.
Marian Rewers, Clinical Director
George S Eisenbarth, Executive Director

949 **Baylor College of Medicine: Children's General Clinical Research Center**
One Baylor Plaza
Houston, TX 77030
713-798-4780
Fax: 713-790-1345
pedi-webmaster@bcm.edu
www.bcm.edu/pediatrics

Diabetes Mellitus / Research Centers

Offers research into juvenile aspects of immunology and infectious diseases including diabetes research activities.
Lisa Bomgaars, Medical Director
Mark A Ward, Director

950 **Benaroya Research Institute Virginia Mason Medical Center**
Virginia Mason Medical Center
1201 9th Avenue
Seattle, WA 98101
206-583-6525
Fax: 206-223-7543
info@benaroyaresearch.org
www.benaroyaresearch.org
Immunology and diabetes research.
Robert B Lemon, Chair
Gerald Nepom, Director

951 **Diabetes Education and Research Center The Franklin House**
The Franklin House
PO Box 897
Philadelphia, PA 19105
215-829-3426
Fax: 215-829-5807
www.diabeteseducationandresearchcenter.o
Is a non-profit organization serving the needs of people living in Philadelphia PA and surrounding communities. The goal of the Foundation is to improve the health of people with diabetes.

952 **Diabetes Research and Training Center: University of Alabama at Birmingham**
Department of Medicine
1530 3rd Avenue S
Birmingham, AL 35294
205-934-4011
Fax: 205-934-4389
TTY: 205-934-4642
www.main.uab.edu
The DRTC works to develop and evaluate new models of diabetes care and to facilitate translational diabetes research.
Dr Carol Garrison, President
William Ferniany, CEO

953 **Division on Endocrinology Northwestern University Feinberg School**
Northwestern University Feinberg School of Medicin
251 East Huron Street
Chicago, IL 60611
312-926-6895
Fax: 312-503-7757
help@medicine.northwestern.edu
www.medicine.northwestern.edu
Nonprofit organization focusing research activities on endocrinology metabolism nutrition and specializing in diabetes.
Joe Bass, MD, PhD, Chief of the Division of Endocrinology
Grazia Aleppo, MD, Director, Endocrinology Clinical Practic

954 **Endocrinology Research Laboratory Cabrini Medical Center**
Cabrini Medical Center
227 E 19th Street
New York, NY 10003
212-222-7464
www.cabrininy.org
Focuses on the effects of insulin and insulin-like growth factors on human body functions.
Dr Leonid Poretsky, Director

955 **Indiana University: Area Health Education Center**
714 N Senate Avenue
Indianapolis, IN 46202
317-278-8893
Fax: 317-278-0392
ahec@iupui.edu
www.ahec.iupui.edu
A collaborative statewide system for community-based primary health care professions education that fosters the continuing improvement of health care services for all citizens in Indiana.
Richard D Kiovsky, MD, Director
Jonathan C Barclay, Associate Director

956 **Indiana University: Center for Diabetes Research**
340 West 10th Street
Indianapolis, IN 46202
317-274-8157
Fax: 317-274-1437
rconsidi@iupui.edu
www.medicine.iu.edu
Our goal is to promote the training of scientists whose research will develop new understandings of the basis of the disease and its complications and to cultivate basic science research that can speed the discovery of more effective therapies.
Robert Considine, Associate Professor of Medicine
D Craig Brater MD, Dean

957 **Indiana University: Pharmacology Research Laboratory**
Division of Clinical Pharmacology
1001 W 10th Street
Indianapolis, IN 46202
317-630-8795
Fax: 317-630-8185
www.medicine.iupui.edu/clinpharm
We will train highly skilled compassionate and altruistic professionals both generalists and specialists to be future leaders in medical practice academia and industry.
David A Flockhart, Division Director
John T Callaghan, Associate Professor of Medicine

958 **International Diabetes Center at Nicollet**
3800 Park Nicollet Boulevard
Saint Louis Park, MN 55416
952-993-3393
888-825-6315
Fax: 952-993-1302
idcdiabetes@parknicollet.com
www.parknicollet.com/diabetes
Research center which improves the quality of life of individuals with diabetes and those at risk of developing diabetes by undertaking clinical care education research and outreach activities that stimulate and support health.
Richard Berg MD, Executive Director

959 **Joslin Diabetes Center**
One Joslin Place
Boston, MA 02215
617-732-2400
800-567-5461
Fax: 617-322-40
diabetes@joslin.harvard.edu
www.joslin.org
An internationally recognized leader in diabetes and endocrine disease treatment research and patient and professional education affiliated with Harvard Medical School. In addition to its headquarters in Boston's Longwood Medical area Joslin has affiliated treatment centers across the nation. Established in 1898.
John L Brooks, Chairman of the Board
Martin J Abrahamson, Senior VP, Medical Director

960 **Metabolic Research Institute**
1515 N Flagler Drive
West Palm Beach, FL 33401
561-802-3060
Fax: 561-802-3260
www.metabolic-institute.com
The Metabolic Research Institute specializes in clinical studies involving endocrinology disorders complications of endocrinology disorders metabolic problems and selected renal disease.
William A Kaye, Co-Director
Barry Horowitz, Co-Director

961 **Sansum Diabetes Research Institute**
2219 Bath Street
Santa Barbara, CA 93105
805-682-7638
Fax: 805-682-3332
info@sansum.org
www.sansum.org
A research institute devoted to the prevention treatment and cure of diabetes.
Lois Jovanovich, CEO & Chief Scientific Officer
Wendy Bevier, Associate Investigator

962 **University of Chicago: Comprehensive Diabetes Center**
5841 S Maryland Avenue
Chicago, IL 60637
773-702-2371
800-989-6740
diabetes@uchospitals.edu
www.kovlerdiabetescenter.org
The University of Chicago Kovler Diabetes Center offers a unique fully comprehensive approach to diagnosing and treating diabetes. Focuses on children adolescents and adults with diabetes as well as individuals at the highest risk for serious complications.
Louis H Philipson, Medical Director
Christopher Rhodes, Kovler Diabetes Center Pediatric Program

963 **University of Colorado: General Clinical Research Center, Pediatric**
13001 E 17th Place
Aurora, CO 80045
720-777-2957
www.uchsc.edu/pedsgcrc
Focuses on developmental studies and diabetes research.
Ronald J Sokol, Program Director
Philip S Zeitler, Associate Program Director

964 **University of Iowa: Diabetes Research Center**
Department of Internal Medicine
200 Hawkins Drive
Iowa City, IA 52242
319-353-7842
www.int-med.uiowa.edu

Diabetes Mellitus / Research Centers

The Diabetes Research Center combines the talents of experienced clinical investigators molecular biologists and vascular physiologists in an integrated multidisciplinary approach toward the study and treatment of abnormalities of vascular reactivity which characterize diabetes mellitus.
Ken Kates, Chief Executive Officer
John Swenning, Associate Director

965 **University of Kansas Cray Diabetes Center**
3901 Rainbow Boulevard 913-588-5000
Kansas City, KS 66160 Fax: 913-588-4023
TTY: 913-588-7963
geaks@kumc.edu
www.kumc.edu
The KU Medical Center is a complex institution whose basic functions include research education patient care and community service involving multiple constituencies at state and national levels.
Barbara Atkinson, Executive Vice Chancellor

966 **University of Massachusetts: Diabetes and Endocrinology Research Center**
55 Lake Avenue N 508-856-8989
Worcester, MA 01655 evelyn.vignola@umassmed.edu
www.umassmed.edu
UMMS has exploded onto the national scene as a major center for research, and in the past four decades, UMMS researchers have made pivotal advances in HIV, cancer, diabetes, infectious disease and in understanding the molecular basis of disease.
Micheal F Collins MD, Senior VP
Michael P Czech, Professor and Chair

967 **University of Miami: Diabetes Research Institute**
200 S Park Road 954-964-4040
Hollywood, FL 33021 800-321-3437
Fax: 954-964-7036
info@drif.org
www.diabetesresearch.org
The Diabetes Research Institute (DRI) is an innovator in many fields of diabetes research but one of its primary strengths lies in islet cell transplantation, a cellular therapy that restores insulin production to normalize blood sugar control.
Thomas D Stern, Chairman
Camillo Ricordi, DRI Scientific Director

968 **University of New Mexico General Clinical Research Center**
University of New Mexico Hospital
The University of New Mexico 505-277-0111
Albuquerque, NM 87131 Fax: 505-272-0266
mburge@salud.unm.edu
hsc.unm.edu/som/gcrc
Diabetes research.
Steve McKernan, CEO
Richard Larson, Vice President for Research

969 **University of Pennsylvania Diabetes and Endocrinology Research Center**
700 Clinical Research Building (CRB 215-898-4365
Philadelphia, PA 19104 Fax: 215-898-5408
www.med.upenn.edu/idom/derc
The Penn Diabetes and Endocrinology Research Center (DERC) participates in the nationwide inter-disciplinary program established over two decades ago by the NIDDK to foster research and training in the areas of diabetes and related endocrine and metabolic disorders.
Mitchell A Lazar, Director
Morris J Birnbaum, Co Director

970 **University of Pittsburgh: Department of Molecular Genetics and Biochemistry**
200 Lothrop Street 412-648-9570
Pittsburgh, PA 15261 Fax: 412-624-8997
info@mmg.pitt.edu
www.mgb.pitt.edu
MMG students and fellows routinely publish their research in outstanding journals, present their science at international conferences and go on to achieve positions at prestigious laboratories and institutions.
J Richard Chaillet, Associate Professor
Bruce A McClane, Professor

971 **University of Tennessee: General Clinical Research Center**
1265 Union Avenue 901-516-2212
Memphis, TN 38104 Fax: 901-516-7013
www.utmem.edu/crc
Congress directed the National Institutes of Health to establish clinical research centers throughout the United States to launch an all-out attack on human diseases.
Bruce S Alpert MD, Program Director
Teresa Carr, Research Nurses

972 **University of Texas General Clinical Research Center**
7400 Merton Minter Boulevard 409-772-1950
San Antonio, TX 78229 Fax: 409-772-8097
public.affairs@utmb.edu
www.utmb.edu/gcrc
Focuses on diabetes and infectious disease research.
Michael Lich MD, Program Director
Garland D Anderson, Principal Investigator

973 **University of Washington Diabetes: Endocrinology Research Center**
DVA Puget Sound Health Care System
1660 S Columbian Way 206-616-4860
Seattle, WA 98108 Fax: 206-764-2693
derc@u.washington.edu
www.depts.washington.edu/diabetes
The primary purpose of the DERC is to facilitate and enhance the diabetes-related research of approximately 100 Affiliate Investigators at the University of Washington
Jerry P Palmer MD, Director
David E Cummings, Deputy Director

974 **Vanderbilt University Diabetes Center**
1211 Medical Center Drive 615-322-5000
Nashville, TN 37232 Fax: 615-936-1667
dc.brown@vanderbilt.edu
www.mc.vanderbilt.edu/diabetes/vdc
The Vanderbilt Diabetes Center provides complete care for children and adults with diabetes under one roof
Joe C Davis, Chair in Biomedical Sciences
Alvin C Powers, Director Vanderbilt Diabetes Center

975 **Veterans Affairs Medical Center: Research Service**
500 Foothill Drive 801-582-1565
Salt Lake City, UT 84148 Fax: 801-584-1289
www.va.gov
Diabetes and cancer research.
James Floyd, Director
Byron Bair, Director

976 **Warren Grant Magnuson Clinical Center**
National Institute of Health
9000 Rockville Pike 301-496-4000
Bethesda, MD 20892 800-411-1222
Fax: 301-480-9793
TTY: 866-411-1010
prpl@mail.cc.nih.gov
clinicalcenter.nih.gov
Established in 1953 as the research hospital of the National Institutes of Health. Designed so that patient care facilities are close to research laboratories so new findings of basic and clinical scientists can be quickly applied to the treatment of patients. Upon referral by physicians, patients are admitted to NIH clinical studies.
John Gallin, Director
David Henderson, Deputy Director for Clinical Care

977 **Washington University: Diabetes Research and Training Center**
School of Medicine
660 S Euclid Avenue 314-362-0558
Saint Louis, MO 63110 Fax: 314-747-2692
drtc.im.wustl.edu
DRTC investigators were involved in conducting 60 investigator-initiated diabetes-related clinical research protocols on the WU GCRC
Jean Schaffer MD, Professor of Medicine
Kristin E Mondy, Medicine/Infectious Diseases

Diabetes Mellitus / Support Groups & Hotlines

Support Groups & Hotlines

978 American Diabetes Association
2451 Crystal Drive
Arlington, VA 22202
888-342-2383
askada@diabetes.org
www.diabetes.org
Voluntary organization concerned with diabetes and its complications. The mission of the organization is to prevent and cure diabetes and to improve the lives of persons with diabetes. Offers a network of offices nationwide.
Tracey D. Brown, MBA, BChE, Chief Executive Officer
Eloise Scavella, MA, Chief Operating & Strategy Officer

979 National Health Information Center
Office of Disease Prevention & Health Promotion
1101 Wootton Pkwy
Rockville, MD 20852
Fax: 240-453-8281
odphpinfo@hhs.gov
www.health.gov/nhic
Supports public health education by maintaining a calendar of National Health Observances; helps connect consumers and health professionals to organizations that can best answer questions and provide up-to-date contact information from reliable sources; updates on a yearly basis toll-free numbers for health information, Federal health clearinghouses and info centers.
Don Wright, MD, MPH, Director

Print Resources

980 Countdown
Juvenile Diabetes Foundation International
432 Park Avenue S
New York, NY 10016
212-889-7575
Fax: 212-725-7259
Offers the latest news and information in diabetes research and treatment to everyone from an international arena of diabetes investigators to parents of small children with diabetes, from physicians to school teachers, from pharmacists to corporate executives.
Sandy Dylak, Editor

981 Diabetes
American Diabetes Association
2451 Crystal Drive
Arlington, VA 22202
800-342-2383
Fax: 703-549-6995
www.diabetes.org
A peer-reviewed journal focusing on laboratory research.
Brenda Montgomery, President, Health Care & Education

982 Diabetes Care
American Diabetes Association
2451 Crystal Drive
Arlington, VA 22202
800-342-2383
Fax: 703-549-6995
www.diabetes.org
A peer-reviewed journal emphasizing reviews, commentaries and original research on topics of interest to clinicians.
Brenda Montgomery, President, Health Care & Education

983 Diabetes Forecast
American Diabetes Association
2451 Crystal Drive
Arlington, VA 22202
800-342-2383
Fax: 703-549-6995
www.diabetes.org
The monthly lifestyle magazine for people with diabetes, featuring complete, in-depth coverage of all aspects of living with diabetes.
Brenda Montgomery, President, Health Care & Education

984 Diabetes Spectrum: From Research to Practice
American Diabetes Association
2451 Crystal Drive
Arlington, VA 22202
800-342-2383
Fax: 703-549-6995
www.diabetes.org
A journal translating research into practice and focusing on diabetes education and counseling.
Brenda Montgomery, President, Health Care & Education

985 International Journal of Diabetes and Clinical Research
ClinMed International Library
3511 Silverside Road, Suite 105
Wilmington, DE 19810
302-208-7437
contact@clinmedjournals.org
clinmedjournals.org
Open access, peer-reviewed journal focused on areas such as the pathogenesis of diabetes and its complications, normal and pathologic pancreatic islet function and intermediary metabolism, pharmacological mechanisms of drug and hormone action, and biochemical and molecular aspects of normal and abnormal biological processes.
Masayoshi Yamaguchi, Editor-in-Chief

986 Joslin Magazine
Joslin Diabetes Center
1 Joslin Place
Boston, MA 02215
617-732-2400
Fax: 617-732-2562
diabetes@joslin.harvard.edu
www.joslin.org

987 Voice of the Diabetic
Ed Bryant, author
National Federation of the Blind
200 East Wells Street
Baltimore, MD 21230
410-659-9314
Fax: 410-685-5653
www.nfb.org
The leading publication in the diabetes field. Each issue addresses the problems and concerns of diabetes, with a special emphasis for those who have lost vision due to diabetes. Available in print and on cassette.
28 pages
Eileen Ley, Director of Publishing
Elizabeth Lunt, Editor

Web Sites

988 American Association of Diabetes Care & Education Specialists
125 S. Wacker Dr.
Chicago, IL 60606
800-338-3633
www.diabeteseducator.org
An independent, multidisciplinary organization of health professionals involved in teaching persons with diabetes. The mission is to enhance the competence of health professionals who teach persons with diabetes and advance the specialty practice of diabetes.

989 American Diabetes Association
www.diabetes.org
Voluntary organization concerned with diabetes and its complications. The mission of the organization is to prevent and cure diabetes and to improve the lives of persons with diabetes. Offers a network of offices nationwide.

990 Diabetes Dictionary
diabetes.niddk.nih.gov
A publication of National Diabetes Information Clearinghouse. The Clearinghouse provides information about diabetes to people with diabetes and to their families, health care professionals, and the public. The NDIC answers inquiries, develops and distributes publications, and works closely with professional and patient organizations and Government agencies to coordinate resources about diabetes.

991 Diabetes Exercise
www.diabetes-exercise.org
Exists to enhance the quality of life for people with diabetes through exercise and physical fitness.

992 Healing Well
www.healingwell.com
An online health resource guide to medical news, chat, information and articles, newsgroups and message boards, books, disease-related web sites, medical directories, and more for patients, friends, and family coping with disabling diseases, disorders, or chronic illnesses.

993 Health Central
www.healthcentral.com
Find clearly explained, medically accurate information regarding conditions, including an overview, symptoms, causes, diagnostic procedures and treatment options. On this site it is possible to ask questions and get information from a neurologist and connect to people who have similar health interests.

994 Health Finder
www.health.gov

Searchable, carefully developed web site offering information on over 1000 topics. Developed by the US Department of Health and Human Services, the site can be used in both English and Spanish.

995 Lifeclinic.Com

www.lifeclinic.com

Online information about blood pressure, hypertension, diabetes, cholesterol, stroke, heart failure and more. Maintains current, up-to-date and accurate information for patients to help them manage their conditions better and to improve communications between them and their doctors.

996 Medical News Today

www.medicalnewstody.com

Offers in-depth health information and the latest news in medical research on a wide variety of medical conditions.

997 MedicineNet

www.medicinenet.com

An online resource for consumers providing easy-to-read, authoritative medical and health information.

998 MedlinePlus

www.medlineplus.gov

Information regarding a broad range of health,and mental health conditions topics include: Latest news, overview of anatomy and physiology, clinical trials, diagnoses and symptoms, treatment, genetics, plus lots of links to other sites. A service provided by the National Library of Medicine, part of the National Institutes of Health (NIH).

999 Medscape

www.medscape.com

Medscape offers specialists, primary care physicians, and other health professionals the Web's most robust and integrated medical information and educational tools.

1000 National Diabetes Information Clearinghouse

www.niddk.nih.gov

Offers various materials, resources, books, pamphlets and more for persons and families in the area of diabetes.

1001 WebMD

www.webmd.com

Provides credible information, supportive communities, and in-depth reference material about health subjects. A source for original and timely health information as well as material from well known content providers.

DISRUPTIVE, IMPULSE-CONTROL & CONDUCT DISORDERS

Disruptive, impulse control and conduct disorders are disorders related to difficulties in behavior control, specifically aggressive behaviors, self-control, and impulses. These behaviors are seen as a threat to other's safety and/or societal norms.

It is more likely to be seen in children and adolescents. For example, symptoms may include fighting with others, destroying property, stealing, lying, and defying rules. The disorders are:

- Oppositional defiant disorder: a disorder with a desire to oppose authority figures
- Conduct disorder: a disorder involving aggression toward others, animals, and destruction of property with legal consequences
- Intermittent explosive disorder: demonstrating frequent angry outbursts disproportionate to the trigger event, causing problems at work or home
- Kleptomania: a compulsion to steal unwanted or unneeded objects not for gain
- Pyromania: an impulse disorder where the individual sets fires even knowing it is harmful (not to be confused with fire-setting, which is motivated by curiosity)
- Other specified and unspecified disruptive, impulse-control and conduct disorders

Unlike other mental health conditions, these disorders are directed outward and affect other people. With most other mental health conditions like depression and anxiety, the person's distress is directed inward. Treatment requires an individualized plan developed by both medical and mental health professionals and may include medications and therapy. Parent and caregiver management training may be employed for support persons to learn skills and techniques to respond to challenging behaviors as a result of these disorders.

Disruptive, Impulse-Control & Conduct Disorders / Agencies & Associations

Agencies & Associations

1002 American Association of Children's Residential Centers
648 North Plankinton Avenue
Milwaukee, WI 53203
877-332-2272
info@togetherthevoice.org
togetherthevoice.org

The American Association of Children's Residential Centers is a national organization focused on providing residential therapeutic treatment for children and adolescents with behavioral health disorders.
David Wallace, Board President
Robert McCartney, Treasurer

1003 American Psychiatric Association
800 Maine Avenue SW
Washington, DC 20024
202-559-3900
apa@psych.org
www.psychiatry.org

A medical specialty society representing a growing membership of psychiatrists. Offers information for psychiatrists, medical students, patients and families.
Saul Levin, MD, MPA, FRCP-E, CEO

1004 Association for Behavioral and Cognitive Therapies
305 Seventh Avenue
New York, NY 10001
212-647-1890
Fax: 212-647-1865
abct.org

A multidisciplinary organization dedicated to utilizing and advancing scientific approaches in the understanding and prevention of human behavioral and cognitive problems.
Mary Jane Eimer, CAE, Executive Director
David Teisler, CAE, Deputy Director

1005 Balanced Mind Parent Network
Depression and Bipolar Support Alliance
55 East Jackson Boulevard
Chicago, IL 60604
800-826-3632
community@dbsalliance.org
www.dbsalliance.org

The Balanced Mind provides support, information, and assistance to families raising children with mood disorders and related conditions.
Michael Pollock, CEO
Jessica Chervinko, Development Manager

1006 Center for Family Support
2811 Zulette Avenue
Bronx, NY 10461
718-518-1500
svernikoff@cfsny.org
www.cfsny.org

The Center for Family Support offers assistance to individuals with developmental and related disabilities, as well as their families, and provides support services and programs that are designed to accommodate individual needs. Offers services throughout New York City, Westchester County, Long Island, and New Jersey.
Steven Vernikoff, Executive Director
Barbara Greenwald, Chief Operating Officer

1007 Center for Mental Health Services (CMHS)
Substance Abuse and Mental Health Services Adminis
5600 Fishers Lane
Rockville, MD 20857
240-276-1310
samhsa.gov/about-us/who-we-are/offices-c

Promotes the treatment of mental illness and emotional disorders by increasing accessibility to mental health programs; supporting outreach, treatment, rehabilitation, and support programs and networks; and encouraging the use of scientifically-based information when treating mental disorders. CMHS provides information about mental health via a toll-free number and numerous publications. Developed for users of mental health services and their families, the general public, policy makers, provider
Anita Everett, MD, DFAPA, Director

1008 Child & Family Center
Menninger Clinic
21545 Centre Pointe Parkway
Santa Clarita, CA 91350
661-259-9439
800-351-9058
webmaster@menninger.edu
www.childfamilycenter.org/

The Center's goals: to further develop emerging understanding of the impact of childhood maltreatment and abuse; to chart primary prevention strategies that will foster healthy patterns of caregiving and attachment and reduce the prevalence of maltreatment and abuse; to develop secondary prevention strategies that will promote early detection of attachment-related problems and effective interventions to avert the development of chronic and severe disorders; and to develop more effective treatmen
Nikki Buckstead, Chief Executive Officer
Ana DeGuzman-Silva, Executive Assistant

1009 Goodwill's Community Employment Services
Goodwill Industries-Suncoast, Inc.
10596 Gandy Blvd.
St. Petersburg, FL 33702
727-523-1512
888-279-1988
TDD: 727-579-1068
goodwill-suncoast.org

The St. Petersburg headquarters serves ten counties in the state of Florida. Their mission is to help people with disabilities gain employment through training programs, employment services, and affordable housing.
Sandra Young, Chair
Louise Lopez, Sr. Vice Chair

1010 Help is Here
North Dakota Behavioral Health Division
600 E Boulevard Avenue
Bismarck, ND 58501
701-328-2310
800-472-2622
dhsbhd@nd.gov
www.helpishere.nd.gov

Promotes the support and treatment of mental illness and emotional disorders. Offers mental health services, addiction servces, and recovery centers.

1011 Mental Health America
500 Montgomery Street
Alexandria, VA 22314
703-684-7722
800-969-6642
mhanational.org

Mental Health America is a community-based nonprofit organization committed to enabling the mental wellness of all Americans. MHA advocates for greater access to quality health services and seeks to educate individuals on identifying symptoms, as well as intervention and prevention.
Schroeder Stribling, President & CEO
Sachin Doshi, Sr. Dir., Finance & Operations

1012 National Association for the Dually Diagnosed (NADD)
321 Wall Street
Kingston, NY 12401
845-331-4336
info@thenadd.org
thenadd.org

NADD is a nonprofit organization designed to increase awareness of, and provide services for, individuals with developmental disabilities and mental illness. NADD emphasizes the importance of quality mental healthcare for people with mental health needs and offers conferences, information resources, educational programs, and training materials to professionals, parents, and organizations.
Jeanne M. Farr, MA, Chief Executive Officer
Bruce Davis, President

1013 National Mental Health Consumers' Self-Help Clearinghouse
selfhelpclearinghouse@gmail.com
mhselfhelp.org

The Clearinghouse is a peer-run national technical assistance center focused on achieving respect and equality of opportunity for those with mental illnesses. The Clearinghouse helps with the growth of the mental health consumer movement by evaluating mental health services, advocating for mental health reform, and providing consumers with news, information, publications, and consultation services.
Joseph Rogers, Founder and Executive Director
Susan Rogers, Director

1014 Shulman Center for Compulsive Theft, Spending & Hoarding
PO Box 250008
Franklin, MI 48025
248-358-8508
terrenceshulman@theshulmancenter.com
theshulmancenter.com

The Shulman Center provides counseling and professional services designed to help individuals with compulsive stealing, spending, and hoarding disorders. The Shulman Center supports individuals, families, companies, and communities through education, assessment, and treatment.
Terrence Shulman, JD, LMSW, CPC, Founder and Director

Disruptive, Impulse-Control & Conduct Disorders / Web Sites

Foundations

1015 TLC Foundation for Body-Focused Repetitive Behaviors
716 Soquel Avenue
Santa Cruz, CA 95062
831-457-1004
info@bfrb.org
www.bfrb.org
The TLC Foundation, formerly The Trichotillomania Learning Center, serves to raise awareness on trichotillomania and related body-focused repetitive disorders, support research, and disseminate scientifically-based information about trichotillomania, and offer support services for individuals and families affected by the disorders. The TLC Foundation aims to eliminate the suffering caused by trichotillomania and body-focused repetitive behaviors.
John Piacentini, Ph.D, President & Chair
Suzanne Mouton-Odum, VP & Vice Chair

Libraries & Resource Centers

1016 Family-to-Family: National Alliance on Mental Illness
4301 Wilson Boulevard
Arlington, VA 22203
703-524-7600
888-999-6264
info@nami.org
nami.org
The NAMI Family-to-Family Education Program is a free, 8 session course for family caregivers of individuals with severe mental illnesses. The course is taught by trained family members, all instruction and course materials are free to class participants, and over 300,000 family members have graduated from this national program.

Research Centers

1017 Impulse Control Disorders Clinic
University of Minnesota
231 Pillsbury Drive, South East.
Minneapolis, MN 55455
612-625-2008
800-752-1000
TTY: 612-625-9051
A group of doctors and trainees engaged in research in Impulse-Control Disorders (ICD) and Obsessive-Compulsive Disorder (OCD) and treating patients in a specialty clinic. Conducts research to elucidate pathophysiological links to the ICD and OCD and conducts clinical trials to come up with better and improved treatments for patients.

Support Groups & Hotlines

1018 Common Ground Sanctuary
1410 S. Telegraph
Bloomfield Hills, MI 48302
248-456-8150
800-231-1127
www.commongroundsanctuary.org
A 24-hour nonprofit agency dedicated to helping youths, adults and families in crisis. Through its crisis line and in person through various programs, Common Ground Sanctuary provides professional and compassionate service to more than 40,000 people a year, with most services provided free of charge. Mission is to provide a lifeline for individuals and families in crisis, victims of crime, persons with mental illness, people trying to cope with critical situations and runaway and homeless youth.
Tony Rothschild, President & CEO
Steve Mitchell, Board Chair

1019 Gam-Anon Family Groups International Servi Office, Inc.
PO Box 307
Massapequa Park, NY 11762
718-352-1671
gamanonoffice@gam-anon.org
gam-anon.org
A 12-step self-help fellowship of men and women who have been affected by the gambling problems of a loved one. Their program works through literature and meetings. At meetings individuals learn how other members applied the Gam-Anon program to find serenity and a more normal way of thinking and living.

1020 Gamblers Anonymous
PO Box 17173
Los Angeles, CA 90017
626-960-3500
isomain@gamblersanonymous.org
gamblersanonymous.org
Fellowship of men and women who share their experience, strength and hope with each other so that they may solve their common problem and help others recover from a gambling problem.

1021 Kleptomaniacs Anonymous
The Shulman Center for Compulsive Theft, Spending
PO Box 250008
Franklin, MI 48025
248-358-8508
kleptomaniacsanonymous.com
Kleptomaniacs And Shoplifters Anonymous (CASA) is a unique, independent and secular weekly self-help group.
Terrence Shulman, JD, LMSW, Founder/Director

1022 TLC Foundation for Body-Focused Repetitive Behaviors
716 Soquel Avenue
Santa Cruz, CA 95062
831-457-1004
info@bfrb.org
www.bfrb.org
The TLC Foundation, formerly The Trichotillomania Learning Center, serves to raise awareness on trichotillomania and related body-focused repetitive disorders, support research, and disseminate scientifically-based information about trichotillomania, and offer support services for individuals and families affected by the disorders. The TLC Foundation aims to eliminate the suffering caused by trichotillomania and body-focused repetitive behaviors.

Print Resources

1023 American Journal of Psychiatry
American Psychiatric Association Publishing
800 Maine Avenue SW, Suite 900
Washington, DC 20024
202-459-9722
800-368-5777
Fax: 202-403-3094
psychiatryonline@psych.org
ajp.psychiatryonline.org
Official journal of the American Psychiatric Association (APA).
Ned H. Kalin, MD, Editor-in-Chief

1024 American Journal of Psychotherapy
American Psychiatric Association Publishing
800 Maine Avenue SW, Suite 900
Washington, DC 20024
202-459-9722
800-368-5777
Fax: 202-403-3094
psychiatryonline@psych.org
ajp.psychiatryonline.org
Publishes content that aims to advance the theory, science, and clinical practice of psychotherapy.
Holly A. Swartz, MD, Editor-in-Chief

1025 International Journal of Psychology and Psychoanalysis
ClinMed International Library
3511 Silverside Road, Suite 105
Wilmington, DE 19810
302-208-7437
contact@clinmedjournals.org
clinmedjournals.org
Open access, peer-reviewed journal focused on cognition, emotions, brain functioning, interpersonal relationships, and the unconscious mind.
Joaquim J.F. Soares, Editor-in-Chief

Web Sites

1026 Anger And Aggressions
www.mentalhelp.net/psyhelp/chap7
Therapeutic approaches.

1027 Center For Family Support (CFS)
www.cfsny.org
Devoted to providing support and assistance to individuals with developmental and related disabilities, and to the family members who care for them.

1028 Center For Mental Health Services Knowledge Exchange
www.ncwd-youth.info/node/245
Information about resources, technical assistance, research, training, networks and other federal clearinghouses, fact sheets and materials.

1029 Controlling Anger-Before It Controls You
www.apa.org/pubinfo/anger.html
From the American Psychological Association.

477

Disruptive, Impulse-Control & Conduct Disorders / Web Sites

1030 CyberPsych
www.cyberpsych.org
Presents information about psychoanalysis, psychotherapy and special topics such as anxiety disorders, the problematic use of alcohol, homophobia, and the traumatic effects of racism. Includes an archive of older site content.

1031 Get Your Angries Out
www.members.aol.com/AngriesOut
Guidelines for kids, teachers, and parents.

1032 Healing Well
www.healingwell.com
An online health resource guide to medical news, chat, information and articles, newsgroups and message boards, books, disease-related web sites, medical directories, and more for patients, friends, and family coping with disabling diseases, disorders, or chronic illnesses.

1033 Health Central
www.healthcentral.com
Find clearly explained, medically accurate information regarding conditions, including an overview, symptoms, causes, diagnostic procedures and treatment options. On this site it is possible to ask questions and get information from a neurologist and connect to people who have similar health interests.

1034 Health Finder
www.health.gov
Searchable, carefully developed web site offering information on over 1000 topics. Developed by the US Department of Health and Human Services, thesite can be used in both English and Spanish.

1035 Internet Mental Health
www.mentalhealth.com
Offers online psychiatric diagnosis in the hope of reaching the two-thirds of individuals with mental illness who do not seek treatment.

1036 Medical News Today
www.medicalnewstody.com
Offers in-depth health information and the latest news in medical research on a wide variety of medical conditions.

1037 MedicineNet
www.medicinenet.com
An online resource for consumers providing easy-to-read, authoritative medical and health information.

1038 MedlinePlus
www.medlineplus.gov
Information regarding a broad range of health,and mental health conditions topics include: Latest news, overview of anatomy and physiology, clinical trials, diagnoses and symptoms, treatment, genetics, plus lots of links to other sites. A service provided by the National Library of Medicine, part of the National Institutes of Health (NIH).

1039 Medscape
www.medscape.com
Medscape offers specialists, primary care physicians, and other health professionals the Web's most robust and integrated medical information and educational tools.

1040 Mental Health Matters
ryan@mhmatters.com
mental-health-matters.com
Mental Health Matters serves as a source of information about mental health issues. Provides mental health consumers, professionals, and students with resources on disorders, symptoms, treatment, and medications.
Sean Bennick, Editor

1041 National Association For The Dually Diagnosed (NADD)
www.thenadd.org
An association for persons with developmental disabilities and mental health needs.

1042 National Mental Health Consumers' Self-Help Clearinghouse
www.mhselfhelp.org
A national consumer technical assistance center, has played a major role in the development of the mental health consumer movement.

1043 Planetpsych.com
www.planetpsych.com
Learn about disorders, their treatments and other topics in psychology. Articles are listed under the related topic areas. Ask a therapist a question for free, or view the directory of professionals in your area. If you are a therapist sign up for the directory. Current features, self-help, interactive, and newsletter archives.

1044 Psych Central
www.psychcentral.com
Personalized one-stop index for psychology, support, and mental health issues, resources, and people on the Internet.

1045 Stop Biting Nails
www.stopbitingnails.com
Online organization created for those who bite their nails. Created a product which is used to prevent nailbiting.

1046 Substance Abuse And Mental Health Services Administration
www.store.samhsa.gov
Resources on mental disorders as well as treatment and recovery.

1047 Verywell Mind
www.verywellmind.com
Provides up-to-date information on mental health topics. mission is to prioritize mental health and promote balance for day to day living. offers over 5,500 online articles that are researched based, and reviwed by medical professionals.
Kristen Altmeyer, MBA, VP & General Manager
Nick Ingalls, MA, Associate Editorial Director

1048 WebMD
www.webmd.com
Provides credible information, supportive communities, and in-depth reference material about health subjects. A source for original and timely health information as well as material from well known content providers.

DISSOCIATIVE DISORDERS (DD)

Dissociative disorders (DD) are characterized by a disconnection and lack of continuity in thoughts, surroundings, memories, actions, and identity. As many as three-fourths of people experience at least one episode of depersonalization or derealization in their lifetime. Women are more likely than men to exhibit DD symptoms. Dissociative disorders often develop as a response to traumas. Depression and anxiety are often related conditions. The individual with DD may also suffer from posttraumatic stress disorder (PTSD), borderline personality disorder or substance use disorders.

Individuals with dissociative disorders attempt to escape reality using unhealthy actions that are often involuntary and may interfere with functioning in daily life. Emotion, perception, behavior, and sense of self are also issues seen in the disorder. Symptoms of dissociative disorder can disrupt every area of mental function. There are three types of DD: dissociative identity disorder, dissociative amnesia, and depersonalization/derealization disorder. Mild, common dissociation may include daydreaming, getting overly involved in a book or movie, and highway hypnosis in which the individual loses touch with the immediate surroundings. During a traumatic event such as being victim of a crime or being involved in an accident or disaster, dissociation may allow the individual to tolerate a situation too horrible to ordinarily manage. It may make it difficult to recall events later.

Dissociative identity disorder is overwhelmingly a result of traumatic events or abuse that occurred in childhood. It was previously called multiple personality disorder where two or more distinct entities exist in one person. Ongoing gaps in memories are a hallmark sign. Symptoms may cause significant problems or distress in social and work settings. People around the individual with dissociative identity disorder may notice that personal preferences such as food choices, activities and dress may suddenly change or shift. Functional problems may be minimal to significant. There is a greater risk of suicide in the individual with DD.

Depersonalization/derealization disorder involves detachment from the mind, self, or body; for example, feeling they are outside their body watching events happen. Derealization is when the individual feels that the people in the world around them are not real. Dissociative amnesia is evident when the individual cannot recall information about oneself. It is not a normal type of forgetting, but rather related to a stressful or traumatic event in the past.

With treatment involving psychotherapy, cognitive behavioral therapy and occasionally hypnosis, individuals can gain control over their dissociative symptoms. There are no medications specifically to treat DD, but anti-depressants may be used if depression is noted as part of the disorder and anti-anxiety medications if anxiety is present.

Dissociative Disorders (DD) / Agencies & Associations

Agencies & Associations

1049 Academy of Psychosomatic Medicine
4800 Hampden Ln
Bethesda, MD 20814
301-718-6520
info@CLpsychiatry.org
apm.org

The Academy of Psychosomatic Medicine represents psychiatrists focused on improving education, medical science, and healthcare for individuals with comorbid psychiatric and general medical conditions. The Academy seeks to promote interdisciplinary education and drive research and public policy with the goal of achieving outstanding clinical care for patients with comorbid psychiatric and general medical conditions throughout the world. They also created the Foundation of the Academy of Psychosom
Philip Biaeler, MD, FACLP, President
Maryland Pao, MD, FACLP, President-Elect

1050 American Psychiatric Association
800 Maine Avenue SW
Washington, DC 20024
202-559-3900
apa@psych.org
www.psychiatry.org

A medical specialty society representing a growing membership of psychiatrists. Offers information for psychiatrists, medical students, patients and families.
Saul Levin, MD, MPA, FRCP-E, CEO

1051 Center for Family Support
2811 Zulette Avenue
Bronx, NY 10461
718-518-1500
svernikoff@cfsny.org
www.cfsny.org

The Center for Family Support offers assistance to individuals with developmental and related disabilities, as well as their families, and provides support services and programs that are designed to accommodate individual needs. Offers services throughout New York City, Westchester County, Long Island, and New Jersey.
Steven Vernikoff, Executive Director
Barbara Greenwald, Chief Operating Officer

1052 Center for Mental Health Services (CMHS)
Substance Abuse and Mental Health Services Adminis
5600 Fishers Lane
Rockville, MD 20857
240-276-1310
samhsa.gov/about-us/who-we-are/offices-c

Promotes the treatment of mental illness and emotional disorders by increasing accessibility to mental health programs; supporting outreach, treatment, rehabilitation, and support programs and networks; and encouraging the use of scientifically-based information when treating mental disorders. CMHS provides information about mental health via a toll-free number and numerous publications. Developed for users of mental health services and their families, the general public, policy makers, provider
Anita Everett, MD, DFAPA, Director

1053 Help is Here
North Dakota Behavioral Health Division
600 E Boulevard Avenue
Bismarck, ND 58501
701-328-2310
800-472-2622
dhsbhd@nd.gov
www.helpishere.nd.gov

Promotes the support and treatment of mental illness and emotional disorders. Offers mental health services, addiction servces, and recovery centers.

1054 Hope for Depression Research Foundation
40 West 57th Street
New York, NY 10019
212-676-3200
Fax: 212-676-3219
hdrf@hopefordepression.org
www.hopefordepression.org

Promotes, and encourages profits for neuroscience research into the treatments, diagnosis, origins, and prevention of depression, and other mood disorders such as anxiety disorders, post-traumatic stress disorder, postpartum depression, bipolar disorder, and suicide.
Audrey Gruss, Founder & Chairman
Harold W. Koenigsberg, MD, Board Member

1055 Institute for Contemporary Psychotherapy
33 W 60th St.
New York, NY 10023
212-333-3444
Fax: 212-333-5444
icpnyc.org

The Institute for Contemporary Psychotherapy is a New York City-based mental health treatment and training facility. Consisting of a group of 150 licensed psychotherapists, the Institute focuses on educating the public about the issues surrounding mental health, providing post-graduate training for therapists, and offering therapy at moderate costs.
Ron Taffel, PhD, Chair
Andrea Green-Lewis, LCSW-R, Director of Operations

1056 International Society for the Study of Trauma and Dissociation
4201 Wilson Boulevard
Arlington, VA 22203
844-994-7783
info@isst-d.org
isst-d.org

ISSTD seeks to provide educational resources, programs, conferences, and publications on the prevalence and consequences of chronic trauma and dissociation.

1057 Mental Health America
500 Montgomery Street
Alexandria, VA 22314
703-684-7722
800-969-6642
mhanational.org

Mental Health America is a community-based nonprofit organization committed to enabling the mental wellness of all Americans. MHA advocates for greater access to quality health services and seeks to educate individuals on identifying symptoms, as well as intervention and prevention.
Schroeder Stribling, President & CEO
Sachin Doshi, Sr. Dir., Finance & Operations

1058 National Association for the Dually Diagnosed (NADD)
321 Wall Street
Kingston, NY 12401
845-331-4336
info@thenadd.org
thenadd.org

NADD is a nonprofit organization designed to increase awareness of, and provide services for, individuals with developmental disabilities and mental illness. NADD emphasizes the importance of quality mental healthcare for people with mental health needs and offers conferences, information resources, educational programs, and training materials to professionals, parents, and organizations.
Jeanne M. Farr, MA, Chief Executive Officer
Bruce Davis, President

1059 National Mental Health Consumers' Self-Help Clearinghouse
selfhelpclearinghouse@gmail.com
mhselfhelp.org

The Clearinghouse is a peer-run national technical assistance center focused on achieving respect and equality of opportunity for those with mental illnesses. The Clearinghouse helps with the growth of the mental health consumer movement by evaluating mental health services, advocating for mental health reform, and providing consumers with news, information, publications, and consultation services.
Joseph Rogers, Founder and Executive Director
Susan Rogers, Director

1060 Sidran Traumatic Stress Institute
370 Linwood Street
New Britain, CT 06052
410-825-8888
admin@sidran.org
sidran.org

Sidran Institute provides useful, practical information for child and adult survivors of any type of trauma, for families/friends, and for the clinical and frontline service providers who assist in their recovery. Sidran's philosophy of education through collaboration brings together great minds (providers, survivors, and loved ones) to develop comprehensive programs to address the practical, emotional, spiritual, and medical needs of trauma survivors.
Esther Giller, President and Director
Ruta Mazelis, Editor, The Cutting Edge/Trainer

1061 United Brain Association
202-768-8000
info@unitedbrainassociation.org
unitedbrainassociation.org

Non-profit organization that works to find cures through research for over 600 brain and mental health related issues, and disorders.
J.A. Boulton, Founder
Jay Matey, VP & Treasurer

Dissociative Disorders (DD) / Web Sites

Libraries & Resource Centers

1062 **Family-to-Family: National Alliance on Mental Illness**
4301 Wilson Boulevard 703-524-7600
Arlington, VA 22203 888-999-6264
info@nami.org
nami.org
The NAMI Family-to-Family Education Program is a free, 8 session course for family caregivers of individuals with severe mental illnesses. The course is taught by trained family members, all instruction and course materials are free to class participants, and over 300,000 family members have graduated from this national program.

Research Centers

1063 **UCLA Anxiety Disorders Research Center**
Department of Psychology 310-825-9312
Los Angeles, CA 90094 rose@psych.ucla.edu
anxiety.psych.ucla.edu
The purpose of The ADRC is to further our understanding of the factors that place individuals at risk for developing phobias, anxiety disorders and related conditions, and to develop more effective treatments that have long lasting effects and are cost effective.
Michelle G. Craske, Ph.D., Director
Raphael Rose, Ph.D., Associate Director

Support Groups & Hotlines

1064 **Support4Hope**
PO Box 184
Deer Lodge, TN 37726 Admin@Support4hope.com
www.support4hope.com
Support4Hope is dedicated to support of various mental health issues such as Bipolar Disorder, Depression, Anxiety Disorders, Schizophrenia, Post Traumatic Stress Disorder (PTSD) and the problems that arise from them along with other problems such as Domestic Abuse.

Print Resources

1065 **American Journal of Psychiatry**
American Psychiatric Association Publishing
800 Maine Avenue SW, Suite 900 202-459-9722
Washington, DC 20024 800-368-5777
Fax: 202-403-3094
psychiatryonline@psych.org
ajp.psychiatryonline.org
Official journal of the American Psychiatric Association (APA).
Ned H. Kalin, MD, Editor-in-Chief

1066 **American Journal of Psychotherapy**
American Psychiatric Association Publishing
800 Maine Avenue SW, Suite 900 202-459-9722
Washington, DC 20024 800-368-5777
Fax: 202-403-3094
psychiatryonline@psych.org
ajp.psychiatryonline.org
Publishes content that aims to advance the theory, science, and clinical practice of psychotherapy.
Holly A. Swartz, MD, Editor-in-Chief

1067 **International Journal of Psychology and Psychoanalysis**
ClinMed International Library
3511 Silverside Road, Suite 105 302-208-7437
Wilmington, DE 19810 contact@clinmedjournals.org
clinmedjournals.org
Open access, peer-reviewed journal focused on cognition, emotions, brain functioning, interpersonal relationships, and the unconscious mind.
Joaquim J.F. Soares, Editor-in-Chief

Web Sites

1068 **CyberPsych**
www.cyberpsych.org
Hosts the American Psychoanalyists Foundation, American Association of Suicideology, Society for the Exploration of Psychotherapy Intergration, and Anxiety Disorders Association of America. Also subcategories of the anxiety disorders, as well as general information, including panic disorder, phobias, obsessive compulsive disorder (OCD), social phobia, generalized anxiety disorder, post traumatic stress disorder, and phobias of childhood. Book reviews and links to web pages sharing the topics.

1069 **False Memory Syndrome Facts**
www.fmsf.com
Access to literature.

1070 **Healing Well**
www.healingwell.com
An online health resource guide to medical news, chat, information and articles, newsgroups and message boards, books, disease-related web sites, medical directories, and more for patients, friends, and family coping with disabling diseases, disorders, or chronic illnesses.

1071 **Health Central**
www.healthcentral.com
Find clearly explained, medically accurate information regarding conditions, including an overview, symptoms, causes, diagnostic procedures and treatment options. On this site it is possible to ask questions and get information from a neurologist and connect to people who have similar health interests.

1072 **Health Finder**
www.health.gov
Searchable, carefully developed web site offering information on over 1000 topics. Developed by the US Department of Health and Human Services, thesite can be used in both English and Spanish.

1073 **International Society For The Study Of Dissociation**
www.isst-D.Org
A non-profit, professional society that promotes research and training in the identification and treatment of dissociative disorders, provides professional and public education about dissociative states, and serves as a catalyst for international communication and cooperation among clinicians and researchers working in this field.

1074 **International Society for the Study of Dissociation**
www.issd.org
Association that promotes research and training in the identification of treatment of multiple personality.

1075 **Internet Mental Health**
www.mentalhealth.com
Offers online psychiatric diagnosis in the hope of reaching the two-thirds of individuals with mental illness who do not seek treatment.

1076 **Medical News Today**
www.medicalnewstody.com
Offers in-depth health information and the latest news in medical research on a wide variety of medical conditions.

1077 **MedicineNet**
www.medicinenet.com
An online resource for consumers providing easy-to-read, authoritative medical and health information.

1078 **MedlinePlus**
www.medlineplus.gov
Information regarding a broad range of health,and mental health conditions topics include: Latest news, overview of anatomy and physiology, clinical trials, diagnoses and symptoms, treatment, genetics, plus lots of links to other sites. A service provided by the National Library of Medicine, part of the National Institutes of Health (NIH).

1079 **Medscape**
www.medscape.com

Dissociative Disorders (DD) / Web Sites

Medscape offers specialists, primary care physicians, and other health professionals the Web's most robust and integrated medical information and educational tools.

1080 Planetpsych.com

www.planetpsych.com

Learn about disorders, their treatments and other topics in psychology. Articles are listed under the related topic areas. Ask a therapist a question for free, or view the directory of professionals in your area. If you are a therapist sign up for the directory. Current features, self-help, interactive, and newsletter archives.

1081 Psych Central

www.psychcentral.com

Personalized one-stop index for psychology, support, and mental health issues, resources, and people on the Internet.

1082 Substance Abuse And Mental Health Services Administration

www.store.samhsa.gov

Resources on mental disorders as well as treatment and recovery.

1083 Trauma Resource Area

www.sidran.org

Resources and Articles on Dissociative Experiences Scale and Dissociative Identity Disorder, PsychTrauma Glossary and Traumatic Memories.

1084 Verywell Mind

www.verywellmind.com

Provides up-to-date information on mental health topics. mission is to prioritize mental health and promote balance for day to day living. offers over 5,500 online articles that are researched based, and reviwed by medical professionals.

Kristen Altmeyer, MBA, VP & General Manager
Nick Ingalls, MA, Associate Editorial Director

1085 WebMD

www.webmd.com

Provides credible information, supportive communities, and in-depth reference material about health subjects. A source for original and timely health information as well as material from well known content providers.

FEEDING & EATING DISORDERS

Feeding and eating disorders affect up to five percent of the population and are defined by severe, persistent difficulties with eating related to distressing thoughts and emotions. Eating disorders are not a choice but rather a type of mental illness. Types of eating disorders may include anorexia nervosa, binge eating disorder, bulimia, restrictive food intake disorder and others. Symptoms may be similar in the disorders and individuals may appear healthy. Developing most often in adolescence and young adulthood, eating disorders may affect both men and women at any age. Often eating disorders occur in the presence of other psychiatric disorders, including depression. Genes and heredity may play a role in creating a higher risk for food related issues. Several factors involving biological, psychological, and social variables have been identified as contributing to the condition.

There are a variety of eating disorders, with anorexia begin the more prevalent. Anorexia has the highest mortality of any mental illness, other than opioid use disorder. It is characterized by self-starvation and excessive weight loss. Depression, irritability, anxiety and fatigue are common symptoms, along with dizziness and fainting, muscle weakness and wasting, stress fractures, severe constipation and loss of menstrual periods. Individuals with bulimia nervosa alternate restrictive dieting with binge eating. Binging is usually secretive and may bring on excessive laxative misuse and compulsive exercise. Binge eating disorder features episodes of excessive eating leading to obesity, diabetes, and cardiovascular disease. Other specified feeding and eating disorders are periods of behavior that cause distress and impair interactions with others, including impaired work performance. Avoidant restrictive food intake disorder (ARFID) results in an inability to meet nutritional needs and extreme picky eating. Anxiety is often a component of ASFID and depression may occur. Pica refers to the individual eating things with no nutritional value such as paper, soap, and charcoal. Rumination disorder involves repeated regurgitation and re-chewing of food deliberately brought up after eating.

Eating disorders may be successfully treated with a comprehensive management plan. Treatment must address the physical, psychological, behavioral, and nutritional components of the disorder, including addressing any medical complications as a result of the behavior. Malnutrition or purging behaviors that damage the gastrointestinal system and cardiovascular system must be treated. The goals of treatment are to restore adequate and healthy nutrition, achieve a healthy weight, control excessive exercise and treat mental disorders such as depression and anxiety. Outpatient cognitive behavioral therapy, nutritional counseling, hospitalization and in rare instances, forced nutrition may be needed to control the disorder. The treatment team may consist of a psychiatrist, individual and family therapists, a dietician, a nurse, and other physician specialists based on the needs of the patient including medical complications from the disorder.

Feeding & Eating Disorders / Agencies & Associations

Agencies & Associations

1086 Academy for Eating Disorders
11130 Sunrise Valley Drive
Reston, VA 20191
703-234-4078
Fax: 703-435-4390
info@aedweb.org
www.aedweb.org
AED is an association of multidisciplinary professionals promoting effective treatment, developing prevention initiatives, advocating for the field, stimulating research and sponsoring an annual conference.
Jennifer J. Thomas, PhD, FAED, President
Erin Quinn, Operations Director

1087 Academy of Nutrition & Dietetics
120 South Riverside Plaza
Chicago, IL 60606
312-899-0040
800-877-1600
media@eatright.org
www.eatright.org
Serves the public through the promotion of optimal nutrition, health, and well-being. Formerly the American Dietetic Association.
Ellen R. Shaley, President
Patricia M. Babjak, Chief Executive Officer

1088 Administration for Children and Families
330 C Street SW
Washington, DC 20201
877-696-6775
www.acf.hhs.gov
The Administration for Children & Families (ACF) is a division of the U.S. Department of Health & Human Services (HHS). ACF promotes the economic and social well-being of families, children, individuals and communities.
Jeff Hild, Principal Deputy Assistant Secretary
Larry Handerhan, Chief of Staff

1089 Agency for Healthcare Research and Quality
5600 Fishers Lane
Rockville, MD 20857
301-427-1104
www.ahrq.gov
The Agency for Healthcare Research and Quality's (AHRQ) mission is to produce evidence to make health care safer, higher quality, more accessible, equitable, and affordable, and to work within the U.S. Department of Health and Human Services and with other partners to make sure that the evidence is understood and used.
Robert Otto Valdez, PhD, MHSA, Acting Director
Howard E. Holland, Director, Communications

1090 American Psychiatric Association
800 Maine Avenue SW
Washington, DC 20024
202-559-3900
apa@psych.org
www.psychiatry.org
A medical specialty society representing a growing membership of psychiatrists. Offers information for psychiatrists, medical students, patients and families.
Saul Levin, MD, MPA, FRCP-E, CEO

1091 Association of Gastrointestinal Motility Disorders
140 Pleasant Street
Lexington, MA 02421
781-275-1300
Fax: 781-275-1304
digestive.motility@gmail.com
www.agmdhope.org
A non-profit international organization which serves as an integral educational resource concerning digestive motility diseases and disorders. Also functions as an important information base for members of the medical and scientific communities. Also provides a forum for patients suffering from digestive motility diseases and disorders as well as their families and members of the medical, scientific, and nutritional communities.
Mary Angela DeGrazia-DiTucci, President/Patient/Founder

1092 Bulimia Anorexia Nervosa Association
1500 Ouellette Avenue
Windsor, Ontario, N8X
519-969-2112
855-969-5530
Fax: 519-969-0227
www.bana.ca
BANA facilitates, advocates, and coordinates support for any individual directly or indirectly affected by eating disorders, and raises public awareness through improved communication and the provision of education within the community.
Kelly Gosselin, BACo, President
Dana Levin, PhD, Vice President

1093 Center for Family Support
2811 Zulette Avenue
Bronx, NY 10461
718-518-1500
www.cfsny.org
The Center for Family Support offers assistance to individuals with developmental and related disabilities, as well as their families, and provides support services and programs that are designed to accommodate individual needs. Offers services throughout New York City, Westchester County, Long Island, and New Jersey.
Steven Vernikoff, Executive Director
Barbara Greenwald, Chief Operating Officer

1094 Center for Mental Health Services (CMHS)
Substance Abuse and Mental Health Services Adminis
5600 Fishers Lane
Rockville, MD 20857
240-276-1310
samhsa.gov
Promotes the treatment of mental illness and emotional disorders by increasing accessibility to mental health programs; supporting outreach, treatment, rehabilitation, and support programs and networks; and encouraging the use of scientifically-based information when treating mental disorders. CMHS provides information about mental health via a toll-free number and numerous publications. Developed for users of mental health services and their families, the general public, policy makers, provider
Anita Everett, MD, DFAPA, Director

1095 Center for the Study of Anorexia and Bulimia
33 West 60th Street
New York, NY 10023
212-333-3444
www.icpnyc.org/csab/
Established as a division of the Institute for Contemporary Psychotherapy in 1979 and is the oldest non-profit eating disorders clinic in New York City. Using an eclectic approach, the professional staff and affiliates are on the cutting edge of treatment in their field. The treatment staff includes social workers, psychologists, registered nurses and nutritionists, all with special training in the treatment of eating disorders.
Jill M Pollack, Director
Jill E Daino, Co-Director

1096 Centers for Disease Control & Prevention: Division of Adolescent & School Health
1600 Clifton Road
Atlanta, GA 30329
800-232-4636
TTY: 888-232-6348
www.cdc.gov/HealthyYouth
CDC promotes the health and well-being of children and adolescents to enable them to become healthy and productive adults.

1097 Centers for Medicare & Medicaid Services
7500 Security Boulevard
Baltimore, MD 21244
www.cms.gov
U.S. federal agency which administers Medicare, Medicaid, and the State Children's Health Insurance Program.
Chiquita Brooks-Lasure, Acting Administrator
Jonathan Blum, Principal Deputy Administrator & COO

1098 Council on Size and Weight Discrimination (CSWD)
PO Box 305
Mount Marion, NY 12456
845-750-7710
Fax: 845-802-0000
info@cswd.org
cswd.org
The Council on Size and Weight Discrimination is a not-for-profit group aiming to change dominant perceptions about weight. CSWD advocates for the rights of larger people, particularly in the areas of media image, job discrimination, and medical treatment.
Miriam Berg, President
Lynn McAfee, Director of Medical Advocacy

1099 Eating Disorders Coalition for Research, Policy and Action
PO Box 96503-98807
Washington, DC 20090
202-543-9570
Fax: 202-543-9570
www.eatingdisorderscoalition.org
Advocates at the federal level on behalf of people with eating disorders, their families, and professionals working with these populations. Promotes federal support for improved access to care.
Christine Peat, PhD, President
Laura Donahue, Vice President

1100 Healthy Weight Network
402 S 14th Street
Hettinger, ND 58639
701-567-2646
Fax: 701-567-2602
www.healthyweight.net

Feeding & Eating Disorders / Agencies & Associations

Promotes information and resources pertaining to the Health at Any Size paradigm.
Frances M. Berg, MS, Founder/Editor

1101 Help is Here
North Dakota Behavioral Health Division
600 E Boulevard Avenue 701-328-2310
Bismarck, ND 58501 800-472-2622
dhsbhd@nd.gov
www.helpishere.nd.gov
Promotes the support and treatment of mental illness and emotional disorders. Offers mental health services, addiction servces, and recovery centers.

1102 Institute for Contemporary Psychotherapy
33 W 60th St. 212-333-3444
New York, NY 10023 Fax: 212-333-5444
icpnyc.org
The Institute for Contemporary Psychotherapy is a New York City-based mental health treatment and training facility. Consisting of a group of 150 licensed psychotherapists, the Institute focuses on educating the public about the issues surrounding mental health, providing post-graduate training for therapists, and offering therapy at moderate costs.
Ron Taffel, PhD, Chair
Andrea Green-Lewis, LCSW-R, Director of Operations

1103 International Association of Eating Disorders Professionals Foundation
PO Box 1295 800-800-8126
Pekin, IL 61555 iaedpmembers@earthlink.net
iaedp.com
IAEDP Foundation seeks to strengthen the level of quality among professionals who treat individuals with eating disorders. The Foundation provides training, education, and certifications; encourages professional and ethical standards; raises awareness on eating disorders; and participates in prevention efforts.
Bonnie Harken, Managing Director
Blanche Williams, Director, International Dev.

1104 Jessie's Legacy
1111 Lonsdale Avenue 604-988-5281
North Vancouver, BC, V7M jessieslegacy@familyservices.bc.ca
jessieslegacy.com
A program of Family Services of the North Shore, Jessie's Legacy seeks to support youth, families, and professionals involved in body image and eating disorders in BC.
Joanna Zelichowska, Manager

1105 Mental Health America
500 Montgomery Street 703-684-7722
Alexandria, VA 22314 800-969-6642
mhanational.org
Mental Health America is a community-based nonprofit organization committed to enabling the mental wellness of all Americans. MHA advocates for greater access to quality health services and seeks to educate individuals on identifying symptoms, as well as intervention and prevention.
Schroeder Stribling, President & CEO
Sachin Doshi, Sr. Dir., Finance & Operations

1106 MindWise Innovations
270 Bridge Street 781-239-0071
Dedham, MA 02026 Fax: 781-320-9136
info@mindwise.org
www.mindwise.org
Formerly known as Screening For Mental Health, MindWise Innovations provides resources to schools, workplaces, and communities to address mental health issues, eating disorders, substance abuse, and suicide.
Rebecca Ames, LICSW, Senior Clinical Manager
Larry Berkowitz, EdD, Director, Trauma Center

1107 Multiservice Eating Disorders Association
1320 Centre Street 617-558-1881
Newton, MA 02459 888-350-4049
info@medainc.org
medainc.org
MEDA is a nonprofit organization dedicated to the prevention and treatment of eating disorders and disordered eating. MEDA'S mission is to prevent the continuing spread of eating disorders through educational awareness and early detection. MEDA serves as a support network and resource for clients, loved ones, clinicians, educators and the general public.
Rebecca Manley, MS, Founder
Leslie Bernstein, Chair

1108 National Alliance for Eating Disorders
4400 North Congress Avenue 866-662-1235
West Palm Beach, FL 33407 allianceforeatingdisorders.com
The National Alliance for Eating Disorders (formerly The Alliance for Eating Disorders Awareness) is the leading national nonprofit organization providing referrals, education, and support for all eating disorders.
Judy Rifkin, Chair
Johanna Kandel, Founder and CEO

1109 National Alliance on Mental Illness
4301 Wilson Boulevard 703-524-7600
Arlington, VA 22203 800-950-6264
info@nami.org
nami.org
NAMI is an organization dedicated to raising awareness on mental health and providing support and education for Americans affected by mental illness. NAMI advocates for access to services and treatment and fosters an environment of awareness and understanding for those concerned with mental health.
Shirley J. Holloway, President
Joyce A. Campbell, First Vice President

1110 National Association for the Dually Diagnosed (NADD)
321 Wall Street 845-331-4336
Kingston, NY 12401 info@thenadd.org
thenadd.org
NADD is a nonprofit organization designed to increase awareness of, and provide services for, individuals with developmental disabilities and mental illness. NADD emphasizes the importance of quality mental healthcare for people with mental health needs and offers conferences, information resources, educational programs, and training materials to professionals, parents, and organizations.
Jeanne M. Farr, MA, Chief Executive Officer
Bruce Davis, President

1111 National Association of Anorexia Nervosa and Associated Disorders
PO Box 409047 888-375-7767
Chicago, IL 60640 hello@anad.org
www.anad.org
Works to prevent eating disorders and provides numerous programs — all free — to help victims and families including hotlines, support groups, referrals, information packets and newsletters. Educational/prevention programs include presentations and early detection.
Kristen Portland, MA, Executive Director
Jason Wood, Marketing & Communications Manager

1112 National Association of Anorexia Nervosa a Associated Disorders (ANAD)
PO Box 409047 888-375-7767
Chicago, IL 60640 hello@anad.org
anad.org
A nonprofit organization dedicated to preventing anorexia nervosa, bulimia nervosa, binge eating disorder, and other eating disorders. ANAD serves as a clearinghouse of information with the goal of raising awareness and supports research and educational programs focused on understanding and preventing eating disorders.
Maria Rago, President
Matt DeBoer, CFP, Treasurer

1113 National Association to Advance Fat Acceptance (NAAFA)
PO Box 61586 916-558-6880
Las Vegas, NV 89160 admin@naafa.org
naafa.org
A nonprofit organization committed to defending the rights of fat people and improving their quality of life. NAAFA opposes discrimination against fat people, including discrimination in adver-

Feeding & Eating Disorders / Agencies & Associations

tising, employment, fashion, medicine, insurance, social acceptance, the media, schooling, and public accommodations.
Tigress Osborn, Chair
Amanda Cooper, Public Relations Director

1114 National Center for Complementary and Integrative Health
9000 Rockville Pike   888-644-6226
Bethesda, MD 20892   TTY: 866-464-3615
info@nccih.nih.gov
nccih.nih.gov

The National Center for Complementary and Integrative Health (NCCIH) is the Federal Government's lead agency for scientific research on the diverse medical and health care systems, practices, and products that are not generally considered part of conventional medicine.
Helene M. Langevin, MD, Director
David Shurtleff, PhD, Deputy Director

1115 National Eating Disorder Information Centre
ES 7-421, 200 Elizabeth Street   416-340-4156
Toronto, Ontario, M5G   866-633-4220
Fax: 416-340-4736
nedic@uhn.ca
www.nedic.ca

NEDIC promotes healthy lifestyles, including both healty eating and appropriate, enjoyable exercise, through outreach and education, direct client support, and other programs.
Suzanne Phillips, Program Manager
Ary Maharaj, Outreach & Education Coordinator

1116 National Eating Disorders Association
333 Mamaroneck Avenue   212-575-6200
White Plains, NY 10605   800-931-2237
info@NationalEatingDisorders.org
www.nationaleatingdisorders.org

NEDA aims to eliminate eating disorders and body dissatisfaction through prevention efforts, education, referral and support services, advocacy training, and research.
Elizabeth Thompson, Chief Executive Officer
Jessica Scheer, Chief Operating Officer

1117 National Human Genome Research Institute
Building 31, Room 4B09   301-402-0911
Bethesda, MD 20892   Fax: 301-402-2218
www.genome.gov

The National Human Genome Research Institute began as the National Center for Human Genome Research (NCHGR), which was established in 1989 to carry out the role of the National Institutes of Health (NIH) in the International Human Genome Project (HGP).
Eric D. Green, MD, PhD, Director
Nicole C. Lockhart, PhD, Program Director

1118 National Institute for Occupational Safety and Health
Patriots Plaza 1
395 E Street SW   800-232-4636
Washington, DC 20201   www.cdc.gov/niosh

The National Institute for Occupational Safety and Health (NIOSH) is the U.S. federal agency that conducts research and makes recommendations to prevent worker injury and illness.
John Howard, MD, Director
Leah Ford, Chief of Staff

1119 National Institute of Environmental Health Sciences
111 T.W. Alexander Drive   919-541-3201
Durham, NC 27709   Fax: 919-541-5136
webcenter@niehs.nih.gov
www.niehs.nih.gov

The mission of the NIEHS is to discover how the environment affects people in order to promote healthier lives.
Rick Woychik, PhD, Director
Trevor K. Archer, PhD, Deputy Director

1120 National Institute of Mental Health Eating Disorders Research Program
6001 Executive Boulevard   301-443-8942
Bethesda, MD 20892   866-615-6464
TTY: 301-443-8431
mchavez1@mail.nih.gov
nimh.nih.gov

The program supports studies and research on eating disorders in areas including assessment, risk factors, and intervention development.
Mark Chavez, PhD, Program Chief

1121 National Mental Health Consumers' Self-Help Clearinghouse
selfhelpclearinghouse@gmail.com
mhselfhelp.org

The Clearinghouse is a peer-run national technical assistance center focused on achieving respect and equality of opportunity for those with mental illnesses. The Clearinghouse helps with the growth of the mental health consumer movement by evaluating mental health services, advocating for mental health reform, and providing consumers with news, information, publications, and consultation services.
Joseph Rogers, Founder and Executive Director
Susan Rogers, Director

1122 Office of Women's Health
200 Independence Avenue SW   202-690-7650
Washington, DC 20201   800-994-9662
Fax: 202-205-2631
womenshealth@hhs.gov
www.womenshealth.gov

Government agency under the Department of Health & Human Services, with free health information for women.
Dorothy Fink, MD, Deputy Asst. Secretary, Women's Health
Richelle West Marshall, Deputy Director, Ops & Management

1123 TOPS Take Off Pounds Sensibly
4575 South 5th Street   414-482-4620
Milwaukee, WI 53207   tops.org

TOPS is a nonprofit network of weight loss support groups and wellness education organizations. Promotes healthy lifestyles and sensible approaches to weight management. Provides meetings, educational tools and programs based on positive reinforcement and motivation. Supports people of all ages, sizes, and shapes.

1124 U.S. Food and Drug Administration
10903 New Hampshire Avenue   888-463-6332
Silver Spring, MD 20993   www.fda.gov

FDA is responsible for protecting the public health by assuring the safety, efficacy and security of human and veterinary drugs, biological products, medical devices, the nation's food supply, cosmetics, and products that emit radiation.
Janet Woodcock, MD, Acting Commissioner
Namandj N. Bumpus, Chief Scientist

1125 Up Against Eating Disorders
upagainsted.com

Provides services to loved ones of people with eating disorders, and training to treatment professionals.
Joe Kelly, Founder

1126 Weight-Control Information Network
National Institutes of Health
31 Center Drive   800-860-8747
Bethesda, MD 20892   TTY: 866-569-1162
healthinfo@niddk.nih.gov
www.win.niddk.nih.gov

WIN provides the general public, health professionals, and the media with up-to-date, science-based information on obesity, weight control, physical activity, and related nutritional issues.

Massachusetts

1127 Massachusetts Eating Disorder Association
1320 Centre Street   617-558-1881
Newton, MA 02459   888-350-4049
Fax: 617-297-9518
www.medainc.org

A nonprofit organization dedicated to the treatment and prevention of eating disorders. MEDA provides help line resource and referral, assessments, client consultations, individual therapy, support groups and an intensive evening treatment program.
Rebecca Manley, Founder
Monika Ostroff, Executive Director

Pennsylvania

1128 **Pennsylvania Educational Network for Eating Disorders**
4801 McKnight Road
Pittsburgh, PA 15237
412-215-7967
www.pened.org
PENED is a nonprofit organization providing education, support, and referral information to the general and professional public.
Anita Sincro Maier, Therapist
Ralph F. Wilps, Therapist

Foundations

1129 **Brain & Behavior Research Foundation**
747 Third Avenue
New York, NY 10017
646-681-4888
800-829-8289
info@bbrfoundation.org
www.bbrfoundation.org
The Brain and Behavior Research Foundation awards grants aimed at advancing scientific understandings of mental health treatments and mental disorders such as depression and schizophrenia. The Brain and Behavior Research Foundation's mission is to eliminate the suffering caused by mental illness.
Donald M. Boardman, Treasurer
Jeffrey Borenstein, MD, President and CEO

1130 **International Association of Eating Disorders Professionals Foundation**
PO Box 1295
Pekin, IL 61555
309-346-3341
800-800-8126
Fax: 309-346-2874
iaedpmembers@earthlink.net
www.iaedp.com
IAEDP Offers professional counseling and assistance to the medical community, courts, law enforcement officials and social welfare agencies.
Bonnie Harken, Managing Director
Blanche Williams, Director, International Development

1131 **WithAll**
5354 Parkdale Drive
St Louis Park, MN 55416
612-217-0533
www.withall.org
The WithAll Foundation is dedicated to the prevention and treatment of eating disorders. They are committed to preventing the tragic loss of life to anorexia nervosa and bulimia and to raising public awareness of those dangerous illnesses.
Lisa Radzak, Executive Director
Lindsay Crye, Associate Director

Libraries & Resource Centers

1132 **Family-to-Family: National Alliance on Mental Illness**
4301 Wilson Boulevard
Arlington, VA 22203
703-524-7600
888-999-6264
info@nami.org
nami.org
The NAMI Family-to-Family Education Program is a free, 8 session course for family caregivers of individuals with severe mental illnesses. The course is taught by trained family members, all instruction and course materials are free to class participants, and over 300,000 family members have graduated from this national program.

1133 **Multiservice Eating Disorders Association**
1320 Centre Street
Newton, MA 02459
617-558-1881
888-350-4049
info@medainc.org
medainc.org
MEDA is a nonprofit organization dedicated to the prevention and treatment of eating disorders and disordered eating. MEDA'S mission is to prevent the continuing spread of eating disorders through educational awareness and early detection. MEDA serves as a support network and resource for clients, loved ones, clinicians, educators and the general public.
Rebecca Manley, MS, Founder
Leslie Bernstein, Chair

1134 **National Eating Disorders Association**
3308 Preston Road
Plano, TX 10036
212-575-6200
800-931-2237
info@nationaleatingdisorders.org
nationaleatingdisorders.org
NEDA offers a national information phone line, an international treatment referral directory, and a support group directory. The organization sponsors an annual conference; provides resources on eating disorders for individuals, parents, and educators; funds research; and raises awareness of eating disorders.
Geoffrey Craddock, Chair
Elizabeth Thompson, Chief Executive Officer

1135 **Weight-Control Information Network**
National Institutes of Health
31 Center Drive
Bethesda, MD 20892
800-860-8747
TTY: 866-569-1162
healthinfo@niddk.nih.gov
www.win.niddk.nih.gov
WIN provides the general public, health professionals, and the media with up-to-date, science-based information on obesity, weight control, physical activity, and related nutritional issues. WIN provides tip sheets, fact sheets, and brochures for a range of audiences. Some of WIN's content is available in Spanish.

Research Centers

1136 **Academy for Eating Disorders**
11130 Sunrise Valley Drive
Reston, VA 20191
703-234-4079
Fax: 703-435-4390
info@aedweb.org
www.aedweb.org
AED is an association of multidisciplinary professionals promoting effective treatment, developing prevention initiatives, advocating for the field, stimulating research and sponsoring an annual conference.
Jennifer J. Thomas, PhD, FAED, President
Erin Quinn, Operations Director

1137 **Center for the Study of Anorexia and Bulimia**
1841 Broadway at 60th Street
New York, NY 10023
212-333-3444
Fax: 212-333-5444
www.icpnyc.org
The Institute is composed of a group of 150 professionally trained licensed psychotherapists who offer a full range of psychotherapeutic services including individual and group psychotherapy and psychoanalysis in addition to more specialized treatment services.
Jim M Pollack CSW, Executive Director/Director of Treatment
Ron Taffel, Chair

1138 **Division of Digestive & Liver Diseases of Cloumbia University**
630 W 168th Street
New York, NY 10032
212-305-5960
Fax: 212-305-8466
hjw14@columbia.edu
www.cumc.columbia.edu
The Division's faculty members are devoted to research and the clinical care of patients with gastrointestinal, liver and nutritional disorders. The Division is also responsible for the Gastroenterology Training Program at the medical center and for teaching medical students, interns, residents, fellows and attending physicians aspects of gastrointestinal and liver diseases.
Howard J Worman MD, Division Director
Karen Wisdom, Director

1139 **Harris Center for Education and Advocacy in Eating Disorders**
2 Longfellow Place
Boston, MA 02114
617-726-8470
Fax: 617-726-1595
www.harriscentermgh.org
Conducts research provides a newsletter and information.
David B Herzog MD, Director
David B Herzog, Director

1140 **Obesity Research Center**
St. Luke's-Roosevelt Hospital
1111 Amsterdam Ave., Babcock 10
New York, NY 10025
212-523-4161
www.nyorc.org/

Feeding & Eating Disorders / Support Groups & Hotlines

Helps reduce the the incidence of obesity and related diseases through leadership in basic research, clinical research, epidemiology and public health, patient care, and public education.
Lee C Bollinger, President
John H Coatsworth, Provost

1141 **St. Joseph's Medical Center**
7601 Osler Drive 410-337-1000
Towson, MD 21204 www.stjosephtowson.com
John Tolmie, President/CEO

1142 **UAMS Psychiatric Research Institute**
4224 Shuffield Drive 501-526-8100
Little Rock, AR 72205 kramerteresal@uams.edu
www.psychiatry.uams.edu
Combining research, education and clinical services into one facility, PRI offers inpatient and outpatient services, with 40 psychiatric beds, therapy options, and specialized treatment for specific disorders, including: addictive eating, anxiety, deppressive and post-traumatic stress disorders. Research focuses on evidence-based care takes into consideration the education of future medical personnel while relying on research scientists to provide innovative forms of treatment.
Dan Rahn, MD, Chancellor

1143 **University of Pennsylvania Weight and Eating Disorders Program**
3535 Market Street 215-898-7314
Philadelphia, PA 19104 www.med.upenn.edu/weight/
Conducts a wide variety of studies on the causes and treatment of weight-related disorders.
Dwight L. Evans, MD, Chair

Support Groups & Hotlines

1144 **AABA Support Group**
Chippenham Medical Center
7101 Jahnke Rd. 804-320-3911
Richmond, VA 23225
Elliot Spanier, Contact

1145 **About Kids GI Disorders**
IFFGD
PO Box 170864 414-964-1799
Milwaukee, WI 53217 888-964-2001
Fax: 414-964-7176
iffgd@iffgd.org
www.aboutkidsgi.org
About Kids is the pediatric branch of the International Foundation for Functional Gastrointestinal Disorders (IFFGD), a registered nonprofit education and research organization founded in 1991. Their mission is to inform, assist, and support those affected by gastrointestinal (GI) disorders, addressing issues of digestive health in children through support of education and research. IFFGD promotes awareness among the public, health care providers, researchers, and regulators.
Nancy J Norton, President/Founder

1146 **Coconut Creek Eating Disorders Support Group**
Renfrew Center
7700 NW 48th Avenue 954-698-9222
Coconut Creek, FL 33073 877-367-3383
Fax: 954-698-9007
www.renfrew.org
Samuel Menagad, Director

1147 **Common Ground Sanctuary**
1410 S. Telegraph 248-456-8150
Bloomfield Hills, MI 48302 800-231-1127
www.commongroundsanctuary.org
A 24-hour nonprofit agency dedicated to helping youths, adults and families in crisis. Through its crisis line and in person through various programs, Common Ground Sanctuary provides professional and compassionate service to more than 40,000 people a year, with most services provided free of charge. Mission is to provide a lifeline for individuals and families in crisis, victims of crime, persons with mental illness, people trying to cope with critical situations and runaway and homeless youth.
Tony Rothschild, President & CEO
Steve Mitchell, Board Chair

1148 **Eating Disorder Resource Center**
330 W 58th Street 212-989-3987
New York, NY 10019 info@edrcnyc.org
www.edrcnyc.org
A specialized treatment program for women and men who were suffering from bulimia. Now EDRC treats eating disorders of all kinds, offering individual, group, family and couples treatment for those challenged by bulimia, binge eating disorder, anorexia and other kinds of body dysmorphia.
Judith Brisman, Director & Founder
Senna Lauer, Marketing Assistant

1149 **Eating Disorders Anonymous**
P.O. Box 5243 info@eatingdisordersanonymous.org
Chico, CA 95927 eatingdisordersanonymous.org
EDA provides support group services for people recovering from eating disorders.

1150 **Eating Disorders Association of New Jersey**
10 Station Place 800-522-2230
Metuchen, NJ 08840 Fax: 732-906-9307
info@edanj.org
www.edanj.org
A non-profit state organization whose mission is to provide supportive services and resources to indivudals affected by eating disorders, including family members and friends.

1151 **First Presbyterian Church in the City of New York Support Groups**
First Presbyterian Church in the City of New York
12 West 12th Street 212-675-6150
New York, NY 10011 fpcnyc@fpcnyc.org
www.fpcnyc.org
The First Presbyterian Church in the City of New York provides numerous programs and supports groups for both adults and children including an educational program for children.
Jon M Walton, Senior Pastor
Sarah Segal Mccaslin, Associate Pastor

1152 **Food Addicts Anonymous**
529 N W Prima Vista Blvd. 772-878-9657
Port St. Lucie, FL 34983 faawso@bellsouth.net
foodaddictsanonymous.org
The FAA program is based on the belief that food addiction is a bio-chemical disease. We share our experience, strength, and hope with others allows us to recover from this disease.
Linda Closy, Manager

1153 **Holliswood Hospital Psychiatric Care, Services and Self-Help/Support Groups**
87-37 Palermo Street 718-776-8181
Holliswood, NY 11423 800-486-3005
Fax: 718-776-8572
HolliswoodInfo@libertymgt.com
www.holliswoodhospital.com/
The Holliswood Hospital, a 110-bed private psychiatric hospital located in a quiet residential Queens community, is a leader in providing quality, acute inpatient mental health care for adult, adolescent, geriatric and dually diagnosed patients. Holliswood Hospital treats patients with a broad range of psychiatric disorders. Additionally, specialized services are available for patients with psychiatric diagnoses compounded by chemical dependency, or a history of physical or sexual abuse.
Susan Clayton, Support Group Coordinator
Angela Hurtado, Support Group Coordinator

1154 **National Association of Anorexia Nervosa and Associated Disorders Helpline**
PO Box 409047 888-375-7767
Chicago, IL 60640 hello@anad.org
www.anad.org
Works to prevent eating disorders and provides numerous programs — all free — to help victims and families including hotlines, support groups, referrals, information packets, and online content.

Feeding & Eating Disorders / Web Sites

Educational/prevention programs include presentations and early detection.
Kirsten Portland, MA, Executive Director
Jason Wood, Marketing & Communications Manager

1155 **National Eating Disorder Information Centre Helpline**
ES 7-421, 200 Elizabeth Street 416-340-4156
Toronto, Ontario, M5G 866-633-4220
Fax: 416-340-4736
nedic@uhn.ca
www.nedic.ca

NEDIC promotes healthy lifestyles, including both healty eating and appropriate, enjoyable exercise, through outreach and education, direct client support, and other programs, including a helpline.
Suzanne Phillips, Program Manager
Ary Maharaj, Outreach & Education Coordinator

1156 **National Eating Disorders Association Helpline**
333 Mamaroneck Avenue 212-575-6200
White Plains, NY 10605 800-931-2237
info@NationalEatingDisorders.org
www.nationaleatingdisorders.org

NEDA aims to eliminate eating disorders and body dissatisfaction through prevention efforts, education, referral and support services, advocacy training, and research. Also provides a Helpline.
Elizabeth Thompson, Chief Executive Officer
Jessica Scheer, Chief Operating Officer

1157 **National Health Information Center**
Office of Disease Prevention & Health Promotion
1101 Wootton Pkwy Fax: 240-453-8281
Rockville, MD 20852 odphpinfo@hhs.gov
www.health.gov/nhic

Supports public health education by maintaining a calendar of National Health Observances; helps connect consumers and health professionals to organizations that can best answer questions and provide up-to-date contact information from reliable sources; updates on a yearly basis toll-free numbers for health information, Federal health clearinghouses and info centers.
Don Wright, MD, MPH, Director

1158 **Overeaters Anonymous General Service Offic**
6075 Zenith Court, NorthEast 505-891-2664
Rio Rancho, NM 87144 info@oa.org
oa.org

OA offers a program of recovery from compulsive eating using the Twelve Steps and Twelve Traditions of OA. It addresses physical, emotional and spiritual well-being.

1159 **Richmond Support Group**
Warwick Medical & Professional Ctr 804-320-7881
Richmond, VA

Print Resources

1160 **American Journal of Psychiatry**
American Psychiatric Association Publishing
800 Maine Avenue SW, Suite 900 202-459-9722
Washington, DC 20024 800-368-5777
Fax: 202-403-3094
psychiatryonline@psych.org
ajp.psychiatryonline.org

Official journal of the American Psychiatric Association (APA).
Ned H. Kalin, MD, Editor-in-Chief

1161 **American Journal of Psychotherapy**
American Psychiatric Association Publishing
800 Maine Avenue SW, Suite 900 202-459-9722
Washington, DC 20024 800-368-5777
Fax: 202-403-3094
psychiatryonline@psych.org
ajp.psychiatryonline.org

Publishes content that aims to advance the theory, science, and clinical practice of psychotherapy.
Holly A. Swartz, MD, Editor-in-Chief

1162 **BASH Magazine**
Bulimia Anorexia Self-Help/Behavior Adaptation
PO Box 39903 800-762-3334
Saint Louis, MO 63139

A journal of eating and mood disorders.

1163 **Food & Nutrition**
120 South Riverside Plaza 312-899-0040
Chicago, IL 60606 foodandnutrition@eatright.org
www.eatright.org

Formerly the ADA Times, Food & Nutrition is the member and professional magazine of the Academy of Nutrition & Dietetics.

1164 **Journal of Psychiatry, Depression & Anxiety**
Herald Scholarly Open Access
2561 Cornelia Road, Suite 205 202-499-9679
Herndon, VA 20171 Fax: 202-217-4195
contact@heraldopenaccess.us
www.heraldopenaccess.us

Online, international, open access, peer-reviewed journal focused primarily on depression and anxiety, but also on other related areas of psychiatry as well.
Sam Vaknin, Editor-in-Chief

1165 **Journal of the Academy of Nutrition and Dietetics**
120 South Riverside Plaza 312-899-4831
Chicago, IL 60606 journal@eatright.org
www.eatright.org

Official research publication of the Academy of Nutrition and Dietetics.
Linda G. Snetselaar, Editor-in-Chief
Marilyn Anderson, Assistant to the Editor-in-Chief

Web Sites

1166 **Academy of Nutrition & Dietetics**
www.eatright.org
Offers information and support to allergy sufferers. Serves the public through the promotion of optimal nutrition, health, and well-being. Formerly the American Dietetic Association.

1167 **Anorexia Nervosa & Related Eating Disorders**
www.anred.com
A nonprofit organization that provides information about anorexia nervosa, bulimia nervosa, binge eating disorder, and other less-well-known food and weight disorders.

1168 **Anorexia Nervosa And Related Eating Disorders**
www.anred.com
Online resource providing information about eating disorders and how to recover from them.

1169 **Anorexia Nervosa General Information**
www.mentalhelp.net
Introductory text on Anorexia Nervosa.

1170 **Bulimia: News & Discussion Forum**
www.bulimia.us.com
Eating disorders forum with news and information about bulimia, anorexia, male and teen eating disorders; treatment, help and resources information, events and inspirational stories.

1171 **Close To You**
www.closetoyou.org/eatingdisorders
Information about eating disorders, anorexia, bulimia, binge eating disorder, and compulsive overeating.

1172 **CyberPsych**
www.cyberpsych.org
Hosts the American Psychoanalysts Foundation, American Association of Suicideology, Society for the Exploration of Psychotherapy Intergration, and Anxiety Disorders Association of America. Also subcategories of the anxiety disorders, as well as general information, including panic disorder, phobias, obsessive compulsive disorder (OCD), social phobia, generalized anxiety disorder, post traumatic stress disorder, and phobias of childhood. Book reviews and links to web pages sharing the topics.

1173 **Eating Disorders Awareness And Prevention**
www.edap.org
A source of educational brochures and curriculum materials.

Feeding & Eating Disorders / Web Sites

1174 GERD Information Resource Center
www.gerd.com
A resource center with educational resources on Gastroesophageal Reflux Disease (GERD).

1175 Gastroenterology Therapy Online
www.gastrotherapy.com
An informational website with resources for many kinds of diseases.

1176 Gurze Bookstore
www.gurze.com
Hundreds of books on eating disorders.

1177 Healing Well
www.healingwell.com
An online health resource guide to medical news, chat, information and articles, newsgroups and message boards, books, disease-related web sites, medical directories, and more for patients, friends, and family coping with disabling diseases, disorders, or chronic illnesses.

1178 Health Central
www.healthcentral.com
Find clearly explained, medically accurate information regarding conditions, including an overview, symptoms, causes, diagnostic procedures and treatment options. On this site it is possible to ask questions and get information from a neurologist and connect to people who have similar health interests.

1179 Health Finder
www.health.gov
Searchable, carefully developed web site offering information on over 1000 topics. Developed by the US Department of Health and Human Services, the site can be used in both English and Spanish.

1180 Medical News Today
www.medicalnewstody.com
Offers in-depth health information and the latest news in medical research on a wide variety of medical conditions.

1181 MedicineNet
www.medicinenet.com
An online resource for consumers providing easy-to-read, authoritative medical and health information.

1182 MedlinePlus
www.medlineplus.gov
Information regarding a broad range of health,and mental health conditions topics include: Latest news, overview of anatomy and physiology, clinical trials, diagnoses and symptoms, treatment, genetics, plus lots of links to other sites. A service provided by the National Library of Medicine, part of the National Institutes of Health (NIH).

1183 Medscape
www.medscape.com
Medscape offers specialists, primary care physicians, and other health professionals the Web's most robust and integrated medical information and educational tools.

1184 Mirror, Mirror
www.mirror-mirror.org/eatdis.html
Relapse prevention for eating disorders.

1185 National Association for Anorexia Nervosa and Associated Disorders
www.anad.org
ANAD provides educational/prevention programs include presentations and early detection packets for schools and community groups, sponsoring local and national training conferences for health professionals, and working with electronic and print media. Undertakes and encourages research, fights insurance discrimination.

1186 National Association of Anorexia Nervosa and Associated Disorders
www.anad.org
Works to prevent eating disorders and provides numerous programs — all free — to help victims and families including hotlines, support groups, referrals, information packets, and online content. Educational/prevention programs include presentations and early detection.

1187 National Eating Disorders Association
www.nationaleatingdisorders.org
NEDA aims to eliminate eating disorders and body dissatisfaction through prevention efforts, education, referral and support services, advocacy training, and research.

1188 National Eating Disorders Organization
www.kidsource.com/nedo
Educational materials on dynamics, causative factors and evaluating treatment options.

1189 Peace, Love, And Hope
www.healthyplace.com/Communities/
Information on body dysmorphic disorder.

1190 PlanetPsych.com
www.planetpsych.com
Learn about disorders, their treatments and other topics in psychology. Articles are listed under the related topic areas. Ask a therapist a question for free, or view the directory of professionals in your area. If you are a therapist sign up for the directory. Current features, self-help, interactive, and newsletter archives.

1191 Psych Central
www.psychcentral.com
Personalized one-stop index for psychology, support, and mental health issues, resources, and people on the Internet.

1192 Something Fishy Music And Publishing
www.something-fishy.com
Continuously educating the world on eating disorders to encourage every sufferer towards recovery.

1193 Substance Abuse And Mental Health Services Administration
www.store.samhsa.gov
Resources on mental disorders as well as treatment and recovery.

1194 Verywell Mind
www.verywellmind.com
Provides up-to-date information on mental health topics. mission is to prioritize mental health and promote balance for day to day living. offers over 5,500 online articles that are researched based, and reviewed by medical professionals.
Kristen Altmeyer, MBA, VP & General Manager
Nick Ingalls, MA, Associate Editorial Director

1195 WebMD
www.webmd.com
Provides credible information, supportive communities, and in-depth reference material about health subjects. A source for original and timely health information as well as material from well known content providers.

1196 Weight-Control Information Network
www.win.niddk.nih.gov
The Weight-control Information Network (WIN) provides the general public, health professionals, and the media with up-to-date, science-based information on obesity, weight control, physical activity, and related nutritional issues. WIN provides tip sheets, fact sheets, and brochures for a range of audiences. Some of WIN's content is available in Spanish.

HEART DISEASE

Depression and heart disease have a strong relationship, but no real cause is known. At least 25 percent of individuals with cardiac disease also experience depression and depressed individuals often develop cardiac disease. Adults with depressive disorders have almost a 70 percent greater risk of developing coronary artery disease (CAD) and individuals with CAD are almost 60 percent more likely to have a future coronary event such as heart attack or cardiac death. Depressive episodes may also develop after major medical trauma, including heart surgery. Approximately 350 people suffer from depression globally and almost 18 million die of heart disease annually, making it the number one cause of death. Mood disorders, including major depression or bipolar disorder, have been shown to worsen the prognosis of cardiac patients. Anxiety disorders, chronic stress, and post-traumatic stress disorder (PTSD) may also affect the individual with heart disease as mental health issues affect psychological and mental well-being.

Depressed people may engage in unhealthy behaviors that contribute to heart disease risk. If individuals are feeling depressed, they may overindulge in eating unhealthy foods or skip exercise. Stress, feeling anxious or overwhelmed may lead to poor lifestyle choices and increases heart rate and blood pressure. Individuals may sleep too much or too little, smoke and consume excessive alcohol, increasing the risk of heart disease. Issues with mental health, including depression, are clearly linked to physiologic effects on the body.

Treatment involves identification of depression, stress or anxiety and defining ways to manage it. Choosing healthy habits, including physical activity, may improve mood. If feelings of depression are short-term, lasting a few days, simple changes may be all that are needed. If feelings of depression, anxiety, or hopelessness last longer than two weeks, it is important to seek medical and mental health professionals to help manage symptoms. Talk therapy and medications may be included in a plan of care that addresses healthy lifestyle individualized to each person. Self-care is an important part of managing heart disease and the relationship with depression.

Heart Disease / Agencies & Associations

Agencies & Associations

1197 **American Autoimmune Related Diseases Association**
19176 Hall Road
Clinton Township, MI 48038
586-776-3900
hello@autoimmune.org
autoimmune.org
Awareness, education, referrals for patients with any type of autoimmune disease.
Molly Murray, CAE, President & CEO
Laura Simpson, MBA, Chief Operating Officer

1198 **American Heart Association**
7272 Greenville Avenue
Dallas, TX 75231
800-242-8721
www.heart.org
The American Heart Association is the nation's oldest, largest volunteer organization devoted to fighting cardiovascular diseases and stroke. Funds research and raises public awareness of heart diseases.
Nancy Brown, CEO
Michelle A. Albert, MD, MPH, FACC, President

1199 **Canadian Adult Congenital Heart Network**
222 Queen Street
Ottawa, Ontario, K1P
877-569-3407
cachnet@ccs.ca
www.cachnet.org
Organization founded to share knowledge and skills among congenital heart disease professionals in order to create a community committed to caring for individuals with congenital heart disease.
Ariane Marelli, MD, President
Candice Silversides, MD, Vice President

1200 **Children's Heart Society**
12122 68 Street NW
Edmonton, Alberta, T5B
780-454-7665
childrensheart@shaw.ca
www.childrensheart.ca
Supports families of children with acquired and congenital heart disease.
Cameron Kerr, President
Gerry Cruz, Vice President

1201 **National Heart, Lung & Blood Institute**
31 Center Drive
Bethesda, MD 20892
nhlbiinfo@nhlbi.nih.gov
www.nhlbi.nih.gov
Trains, conducts research, and educates in order to promote the prevention and treatment of heart, lung, and blood disorders.
Gary H. Gibbons, MD, Director
Amy Patterson, MD, Immediate Office of the Director

1202 **Pulmonary Hypertension Association**
801 Roeder Road
Silver Spring, MD 20910
301-565-3004
800-748-7274
www.phassociation.org
A nonprofit organization funded and for pulmonary hypertension patients.
Matt Granato, President & CEO
Elizabeth Joseloff, VP, Quality Care & Research

1203 **Pulmonary Hypertension Association (PHA)**
801 Roeder Road
Silver Spring, MD 20910
301-565-3004
800-748-7274
www.PHAssociation.org
A non-profit organization for pulmonary hypertension patients, families, caregivers and PH-treating medical professionals. PHA works to provide support, education, and find a cure for pulmonary hypertension.
Matt Granato, President & CEO
Elizabeth Joseloff, VP, Quality Care & Research

Research Centers

1204 **Arizona Heart Institute**
2632 N 20th Street
Phoenix, AZ 85006
602-266-2200
800-345-4278
Fax: 602-604-5047
www.azheart.com
Edward Diethrich, Medical Director and Founder

1205 **Baylor College of Medicine: Debakey Heart Center**
Texas Medical Center
1 Baylor Plaza
Houston, TX 77030
713-798-4710
Fax: 713-798-3692
president@bcm.edu
www.bcm.tmc.edu
Research activities have an emphasis on therapeutic intervention and prevention of heart disease.
James T Hackett, Chair
Paul Klotman MD, President

1206 **Bees-Stealy Research Foundation**
2001 4th Avenue
San Diego, CA 92101
619-235-8744
Fax: 619-234-8190
Basic cardiac research.
HD Peabody Jr, Director

1207 **Bockus Research Institute Graduate Hospital**
Graduate Hospital
415 S 19th Street
Philadelphia, PA 19146
215-893-2000
Offers research in cardiovascular diseases with emphasis on muscle tissue studies.
Dr Robert Cox, Director

1208 **Boston University, Whitaker Cardiovascular Institute**
715 Albany Street
Boston, MA 02118
617-638-4887
Fax: 617-638-4066
www.bumc.bu.edu
Offers basic and clinical care research relating to cardiovascular diseases.
Gary J Balady MD, Clinical Investigator

1209 **Cardiovascular Research and Training Center University of Alabama**
THT Room 311
Birmingham, AL 35294
205-934-3624
Fax: 205-345-96
Robert C Bueourge, Director

1210 **Children's Heart Institute of Texas**
PO Box 3966
Corpus Christi, TX 78463
512-887-4505
Fax: 512-887-0539
Offers research and statistical information on pediatric cardiology.
Laura Berlanga, Director

1211 **Cleveland Clinic Lerner Research Institute**
9500 Euclid Avenue
Cleveland, OH 44195
216-444-3900
Fax: 216-444-3279
dicorlp@ccf.org
www.lerner.ccf.org
Research institute focusing on diseases of the cardiovascular system.
Paul E DiCorleto PhD, Institute Chairman
Guy M Chisolm, III, PhD, Institute Vice-Chair

1212 **Columbia University Irving Center for Clinical Research Adult Unit**
Presbyterian Hospital
116 Street and Broadway
New York, NY 10027
212-854-1754
Fax: 212-053-13
askcuit@columbia.edu
www.columbia.edu
Research center focusing on pulmonary diseases.
Lee C Bollinger, President
John H Coatsworth, Provost

1213 **Creighton University Cardiac Center**
3006 Webster Street
Omaha, NE 68131
402-280-4566
800-237-7828
Fax: 402-280-4938
thecardiaccenter.creighton.edu
Research into the clinical aspects of cardiology and heart disease.
Tami Ward, Nurse Practitioner
Kimberly Harm, Nurse Practitioner

1214 **Duke University Pediatric Cardiac Catheterization Laboratory**
T901/Children's Health Center
Durham, NC 27705
919-681-4080
Fax: 919-681-2714
john.rhodes@duke.edu
pediatrics.duke.edu
Research into pediatric cardiology.
Joseph St Geme, III, MD, Chair
Kay Marshall, Chief Administrator

Heart Disease / Research Centers

1215 Florida Heart Research Institute
4770 Biscayne Boulevard
Miami, FL 33137
305-674-3020
Fax: 305-535-3642
pak@floridaheart.org
www.miamiheartresearch.org

General cardiovascular research.
Kathleen T DuCasse, Chief Executive Officer

1216 Framingham Heart Study
73 Mount Wayte Avenue
Framingham, MA 01702
508-935-3418
Fax: 508-626-1262
LLehmann1@partners.org
www.framinghamheartstudy.org

Lisa Soleymani Lehmann, MD, Chair

1217 General Clinical Research Center at Beth Israel Hospital
330 Brookline Avenue
Boston, MA 02215
617-667-7000
800-667-5356
TDD: 800-439-0183
www.bidmc.org

Studies into cardiology pulmonary disorders and heart disease.
Stephen B Kay, Chair
Kevin Tabb, MD, President & Chief Executive Officer

1218 General Clinical Research Center: University of California at LA
Center for Health Sciences
10833 Le Conte Avenue
Los Angeles, CA 90095
310-825-7177
Fax: 310-206-5012
www.gcrc.medsch.ucla.edu

Cardiovascular and heart disease disorders and illness research.
Isidro Salus MD, Program Director
Gerald Levey, Principal Investigator

1219 Hahnemann University Likoff Cardiovascular Institute
Broad & Vine Streets
Philadelpia, PA 19102
215-854-8100

Diseases of the heart and vessels.
William S Frankl MD, Director

1220 Harvard Throndike Laboratory Harvard Medical Center
Harvard Medical Center
330 Brookline Avenue
Boston, MA 02215
617-735-3020
Fax: 617-735-4833

Dr James Morgan, Director

1221 Heart Disease Research Foundation
50 Court Street
Brooklyn, NY 11201
718-649-6210

Robert A Teters, Director

1222 Heart Research Foundation of Sacramento
1007 39th Street
Sacramento, CA 95816
916-456-3365
www.hrfsac.org

Dr Frink, Founder/Principal Investigator

1223 Hope Heart Institute
1380 112th Ave. NE
Bellvue, WA 98004
425-456-8700
Fax: 425-456-8701
info@hopeheart.org
www.hopeheart.org

Heart and blood vessel research.
Dr Lester R Sauvage MD, Founder
Cherie Skager, Interim Executive Director

1224 John L McClellan Memorial Veterans' Hospital Research Office
4300 W 7th Street
Little Rock, AR 72205
501-257-1000
Fax: 501-671-2510
www2.va.gov

Karl David Straub MD, Chief Staff

1225 Krannert Institute of Cardiology
1801 N Senate Boulevard
Indianapolis, IN 46202
317-962-0500
800-843-2786
Fax: 317-962-0501
medicine.iupui.edu/krannert

The cardiovascular program at the Indiana University School of Medicine is recognized throughout the world for its commitment to excellence in patient care research and education. While we're known for our experience and ability to take care of the most complex cardiovascular problems we are equally focused on prevention and early detection.
Peng-Sheng Chen, MD, Division Director
Eric Williams, MD, Associate Dean

1226 Loyola University of Chicago Cardiac Transplant Program
2160 S 1st Avenue
Maywood, IL 60153
708-216-9000
888-584-7888
Fax: 708-216-4918
www.loyolamedicine.org/

Loyola University Health System is committed to excellence in patient care and the education of health professionals. They believe that our Catholic heritage and Jesuit traditions of ethical behavior academic distinction and scientific research lead to new knowledge and advance our healing mission in the communities we serve.
Larry M Goldberg, President & CEO
Wendy S Leutgens, Senior Vice President and COO

1227 Medstar Georgetown University Hospital Facility
3800 Reservoir Road, NW
Washington, DC 20007
202-444-2000
www.georgetownuniversityhospital.org

Studies of medical sciences with particular emphasis on heart disease.
Michael Sachtleben, SVP & COO
Reggie Pearson, VP, Operations

1228 Mount Sinai Medical Center
4300 Alton Road
Miami Beach, FL 33140
305-674-2121
Fax: 305-743-09
www.msmc.com

General cardiovascular research.
Steven D Sonenreich, President & Chief Executive Officer

1229 Oklahoma Medical Research Foundation: Cardiovascular Research Program
825 NE 13th Street
Oklahoma City, OK 73104
405-271-6673
800-522-0211
Fax: 405-271-3980
contact@omrf.org
www.omrf.ouhsc.edu

The Cardiovascular Biology Research Program investigates fundamental mechanisms involved in blood coagulation inflammation and atherogenesis with special emphasis on the regulation of theses processes.
Dr Stephen M Prescott, President
Mike D Morgan, Executive Vice President & COO

1230 Pennsylvania State University Artificial Heart Research Project
Milton S Hershey Medical Center
500 University Drive
Hershey, PA 17033
717-531-8407
Fax: 717-531-5011
www.psu.edu

William S Pierce MD, Director

1231 Preventive Medicine Research Institute
900 Bridgeway
Sausalito, CA 94965
415-332-2525
Fax: 415-325-30
Tandis@pmri.org
www.pmri.org

Nonprofit organization focusing on prevention and treatment of heart disease through modification of diet exercise and relaxation techniques.
Dean Ornish, MD, Founder & President
Anne Ornish, Vice President, Director of Program Deve

1232 Purdue University William A Hillenbrand Biomedical Engineering Center
AA Potter Engineering Center
206 S. Martin Jischke Drive
W Lafayette, IN 47907
765-494-2995
877-598-4233
Fax: 765-494-6628
WeldonBME@purdue.edu
engineering.purdue.edu/BME

Cardiology and heart disease research.
Brian J Knoy, Director of Development
Kathryn Copper, Secretary

493

Heart Disease / Research Centers

1233 Rockefeller University Laboratory of Cardiac Physiology
1230 York Avenue
New York, NY 10065
212-327-8000
Fax: 212-327-7974
pubinfo@rockefeller.edu
www.rockefeller.edu
Causes of cardiac arrhythmias and prevention of heart disease.
David Rockefeller, Honorary Chair
Russell L Carson, Chair

1234 San Francisco Heart & Vascular Institute
1900 Sullivan Avenue
Daly City, CA 94015
650-991-6712
800-82H-EART
Fax: 650-755-7315
www.sfhi.com
At Seton Medical Center we are committed to providing a full range of high quality services and state-of-the-art cardiovascular treatments for our patients. Our medical nursing and social services staff provide quality care and compassion as a coordinated team focusing on the medical emotional and spiritual needs of patients and their families.
Colman J Ryan, MD, Executive Medical Director
Michael Girolami, MD, Chief of Cardiology

1235 Specialized Center of Research in Ischemic Heart Disease
1802 6th Avenue South
Birmingham, AL 35294
205-934-4011
800-822-8816
www.health.uab.edu
Coronary artery disease.
Will Ferniany, CEO
Becky Armstrong, Program Manager

1236 Texas Heart Institute St Lukes Episcopal Hospital
St Lukes Episcopal Hospital
6770 Bertner Avenue
Houston, TX 77030
832-355-4011
800-292-2221
Fax: 713-791-3089
www.texasheartinstitute.org
Denton A Cooley MD, President Emeritus
James T Willerson MD, President, Medical Director

1237 University of Alabama at Birmingham: Congenital Heart Disease Center
1720 2nd Avenue South
Birmingham, AL 35294
205-934-4011
Fax: 205-934-7514
TDD: 205-934-4642
www.uab.edu
Ray L Watts, MD, President
Linda Lucas, PhD, Provost

1238 University of California San Diego General Clinical Research Center
UCSD Medical Center
200 W Arbor Drive
San Diego, CA 92103
619-543-3102
858-657-7000
Fax: 619-435-36
www.health.ucsd.edu
General clinical research.
Paul Viviano, Chief Executive Officer
Margarita Baggett, Interim Chief Operating Officer

1239 University of California: Cardiovascular Research Laboratory
Center for Health Sciences
UCLA Medical Center
Los Angeles, CA 90024
310-825-6824
Fax: 310-206-5777
Cellular and subcellular cardiac conditions.
Dr. Glenn Langer, Director

1240 University of Cincinnati Department of Pathology & Laboratory Medicine
234 Goodman Street
Cincinnati, OH 45219
513-584-7284
Fax: 513-584-3892
pathology@uc.edu
pathology.uc.edu
Fred V Lucas, MD, Chair of Pathology
James Hill, Business Manager

1241 University of Iowa: Iowa Cardiovascular Center
College of Medicine
200 Hawkins Drive
Iowa City, IA 52242
319-335-8588
Fax: 319-335-6969
www.int-med.uiowa.edu

The purpose is to coordinate the cardiovascular programs of the College into a more cohesive unit to permit us to 1) utilize our cardiovascular resources optimally 2) intensify expand and integrate basic and clinical research programs in areas related to cardiovascular research and 3) evaluate the role of new measures for prevention diagnosis and treatment of cardiovascular disease.
Barry London, MD, PhD, Director Cardiovascular Medicine

1242 University of Michigan Pulmonary and Critical Care Division
University Hospital
1500 E Medical Center Drive
Ann Arbor, MI 48109
734-647-9342
888-287-1084
Fax: 734-763-4585
www2.med.umich.edu/healthcenters/clinic_
Kevin Michael Chan, MD, Division Director

1243 University of Michigan: Cardiovascular Medicine
325 Briarwood Circle
Ann Arbor, MI 48108
734-647-9000
Fax: 734-936-0133
www2.med.umich.edu/departments/cvc/servi
Focuses on the diagnosis, treatment and prevention of cardiovascular and heart diseases.
Kim Allen Eagle, MD, Division Director

1244 University of Missouri Columbia Division of Cardiothoracic Surgery
School of Medicine
Columbia, MO 65212
573-882-2121
Fax: 573-884-0437
AldenM@missouri.edu
www.missouri.edu
Cardiac surgery research.
Mike Alden, Director
Brian Foster, Provost

1245 University of Pennsylvania Muscle Institute
School of Medicine
700A Clinical Research Building
Philadelphia, PA 19104
215-573-9758
Fax: 215-898-2653
www.med.upenn.edu/pmi/
Studies in tissue science.
E. Michael Ostap, PhD, Director

1246 University of Pittsburgh: Human Energy Research Laboratory
4200 Fifth Avenue
Pittsburgh, PA 15260
412-624-4141
www.pitt.edu
Focuses on exercise and cardiac rehabilitation.
Mark A Nordenberg, Chancellor
Patricia E Beeson, Provost and Senior Vice Chancellor

1247 University of Rochester: Clinical Research Center
601 Elmwood Avenue
Rochester, NY 14642
585-275-2907
Fax: 585-256-3805
germaine_reinhardt@urmc.rochester.edu
www.urmc.rochester.edu/crc/
Studies of normal tissue functions pertaining to heart diseases.
Thomas A Pearson, MD, MPH, PhD, Director, Principal Investigator
Giovanni Schifitto , MD, Program Director

1248 University of Southern California: Coronary Care Research
1200 N State Street
Los Angeles, CA 90033
213-226-7242
Dr. L Julian Haywood, Director

1249 University of Tennessee: Division of Cardiovascular Diseases
920 Madison Avenue
Memphis, TN 38163
901-448-5750
Fax: 901-448-8084
www.utmem.edu/cardiology
Cardiovascular system disorders including heart disease prevention and treatment.
Karl T Weber MD, Director

1250 University of Texas Southwestern Medical Center at Dallas
University of Texas
5323 Harry Hines Boulevard
Dallas, TX 75390
214-648-3111
Fax: 214-483-11
www.utsouthwestern.edu
Cardiology department research.
Daniel K Podolsky, MD, President
J. Gregory Fitz, MD, Executive Vice President

Heart Disease / Web Sites

1251 **University of Utah: Artificial Heart Research Laboratory**
50 North Medical Drive 801-581-2121
Salt Lake City, UT 84132 Fax: 801-581-4044
healthsciences.utah.edu
Cardiac and blood vessel research.
Allen Stephens, Associate Director

1252 **University of Utah: Cardiovascular Genetic Research Clinic**
420 Chipeta Way 801-581-3888
Salt Lake City, UT 84132 Fax: 801-581-6862
www.medicine.utah.edu/internalmedicine/c
Cardiovascular genetics research.
Dr Roger Williams, Founder

1253 **Urban Cardiology Research Center**
2300 Garrison Boulevard 410-945-8600
Baltimore, MD 21216
Causes diagnosis and treatment of cardiovascular diseases.
Arthur White MD, Director

1254 **Warren Grant Magnuson Clinical Center**
National Institute of Health
10 Center Drive MSC 1078 301-496-3311
Bethesda, MD 20892 800-411-1222
Fax: 301-496-2390
TTY: 866-411-1010
mmichael@cc.nih.gov
www.dnrc.nih.gov/reports/programs/ncc.as
Established in 1953 as the research hospital of the National Institutes of Health. Designed so that patient care facilities are close to research laboratories so new findings of basic and clinical scientists can be quickly applied to the treatment of patients. Upon referral by physicians, patients are admitted to NIH clinical studies.
Madeline Michael, Chief, Clinical Nutrition Services

1255 **Yeshiva University General Clinical Research Center**
500 West 185th Street 212-960-5400
New York, NY 10033 www.yu.edu
Cardiovascular research.
Dr Henry Kressel, Chairman
Richard M Joel, President

Support Groups & Hotlines

1256 **Mended Hearts**
8150 N. Central Expressway 214-206-9259
Dallas, TX 75206 888-432-7899
Fax: 214-295-9552
info@mendedhearts.org
www.mendedhearts.org
Mutual support for persons who have heart disease, their families, friends, and other interested persons.
Gordon Littlefield, President of the Board
Donnette Smith, Executive Vice President

1257 **Mitral Valve Prolapse Program of Cincinnati Support Group**
10525 Montgomery Road 513-745-9911
Cincinnati, OH 45242 kscordo@wright.edu
www.nursing.wright.edu
Brings together persons frightened by their symptoms in order to learn to better cope with MVP. Fosters use of non-drug therapies. Supervised exercise sessions, diagnostic evaluations and specialized testing. Information and referrals, conferences, literature, group meetings, MVP Hot Line, and assistance in starting groups.

1258 **National Health Information Center**
Office of Disease Prevention & Health Promotion
1101 Wootton Pkwy Fax: 240-453-8281
Rockville, MD 20852 odphpinfo@hhs.gov
www.health.gov/nhic
Supports public health education by maintaining a calendar of National Health Observances; helps connect consumers and health professionals to organizations that can best answer questions and provide up-to-date contact information from reliable sources; updates on a yearly basis toll-free numbers for health information, Federal health clearinghouses and info centers.
Don Wright, MD, MPH, Director

1259 **National Society for MVP and Dysautonomia**
880 Montclair Road 205-595-8229
Birmingham, AL 35213 866-595-8229
Fax: 205-595-8222
nancysawyermd@bellsouth.net
Assists individuals suffering from mitral valve prolapse syndrome and dysautonomia to find support and understanding. Education on symptoms and treatment. Other areas of focus are Fibromyalgia and Sjogren's Syndrome.
Nancy Sawyer, MD

1260 **Society of Mitral Valve Prolapse Syndrome**
PO Box 431 630-250-9327
Itasca, IL 60143 Fax: 630-773-0478
bonnie0107@aol.com
www.mitralvalveprolapse.com/
Provides support and education to patients, families and friends about mitral valve prolapse syndrome.
Jim Durante, Co-Founder
Bonnie Durante, Co-Founder

Print Resources

1261 **International Archives of Cardiovascular Diseases**
ClinMed International Library
3511 Silverside Road, Suite 105 302-208-7437
Wilmington, DE 19810 contact@clinmedjournals.org
clinmedjournals.org
Open access, peer-reviewed journal focused on clinical areas of cardiovascular medicine.
Richard Kones, Editor-in-Chief

Web Sites

1262 **American Heart Association**
www.heart.org
Supports research, education and community service programs with the objective of reducing premature death and disability from cardiovascular diseases and stroke; coordinates the efforts of health professionals, and other engaged in the fight against heart and circulatory disease.

1263 **Healing Well**
www.healingwell.com
An online health resource guide to medical news, chat, information and articles, newsgroups and message boards, books, disease-related web sites, medical directories, and more for patients, friends, and family coping with disabling diseases, disorders, or chronic illnesses.

1264 **Health Central**
www.healthcentral.com
Find clearly explained, medically accurate information regarding conditions, including an overview, symptoms, causes, diagnostic procedures and treatment options. On this site it is possible to ask questions and get information from a neurologist and connect to people who have similar health interests.

1265 **Health Finder**
www.health.gov
Searchable, carefully developed web site offering information on over 1000 topics. Developed by the US Department of Health and Human Services, the site can be used in both English and Spanish.

1266 **Lifeclinic.Com**
www.lifeclinic.com
Online information about blood pressure, hypertension, diabetes, cholesterol, stroke, heart failure and more. Maintains current, up-to-date and accurate information for patients to help them manage their conditions better and to improve communications between them and their doctors.

1267 **Medical News Today**
www.medicalnewstody.com
Offers in-depth health information and the latest news in medical research on a wide variety of medical conditions.

Heart Disease / Web Sites

1268 MedicineNet

www.medicinenet.com

An online resource for consumers providing easy-to-read, authoritative medical and health information.

1269 MedlinePlus

www.medlineplus.gov

Information regarding a broad range of health, and mental health conditions topics include: Latest news, overview of anatomy and physiology, clinical trials, diagnoses and symptoms, treatment, genetics, plus lots of links to other sites. A service provided by the National Library of Medicine, part of the National Institutes of Health (NIH).

1270 Medscape

www.medscape.com

Medscape offers specialists, primary care physicians, and other health professionals the Web's most robust and integrated medical information and educational tools.

1271 National Heart, Lung and Blood Institute

www.nhlbi.nih.gov

Primary responsibility of this organization is the scientific investigation of heart, blood vessel, lung and blood disorders. Oversees research, demonstration, prevention, education, control and training activities in these fields and emphasizes the prevention and control of heart diseases.

1272 WebMD

www.webmd.com

Provides credible information, supportive communities, and in-depth reference material about health subjects. A source for original and timely health information as well as material from well known content providers.

HYPERTENSION

When an individual experiences stress, anxiety or depression, heart rate and blood pressure rise. Blood puts pressure on the artery walls that carry blood from the heart to other parts of the body.

Blood pressure may rise and fall during the day. It is measured using two values. The systolic blood pressure is the pressure in your arteries during heart beat and the second number, the diastolic blood pressure, measures the pressure in the arteries when the heart rests between beats. There are ranges of normal blood pressures by age, but a reading around 120/80 mmHg is considered normal range. Hypertension, or high blood pressure, is said to exist when the blood pressure is measured and found to be outside the ranges of normal for the individual. An occasional high reading is not hypertension; hypertension is said to exist when readings are consistently higher than normal. Hypertension increases the risk for heart disease and a defined relationship between heart disease and depression has been found.

High blood pressure develops over time and can happen because of unhealthy lifestyle choices. Damage to arteries from high blood pressure can lead to heart disease, heart attack, heart failure, stroke and brain problems and kidney disease.

Often lowering blood pressure to normal ranges can be managed with lifestyle changes, including eating a healthy diet, getting sufficient exercise, keeping a healthy weight, stopping smoking, and managing stress. Medications may be used if lifestyle changes do not lower high blood pressure. Preventing or managing hypertension protects against heart disease and stroke, often referred to as cardiovascular disease.

Hypertension / Agencies & Associations

Agencies & Associations

1273 **National Heart, Lung & Blood Institute**
31 Center Drive
Bethesda, MD 20892
nhlbiinfo@nhlbi.nih.gov
www.nhlbi.nih.gov
Trains, conducts research, and educates in order to promote the prevention and treatment of heart, lung, and blood disorders.
Gary H. Gibbons, MD, Director
Nakela Cook, MD, MPH, FACC, Chief of Staff

1274 **National Stroke Association**
7272 Greenville Ave.
Dallas, TX 75231
800-242-8721
www.stroke.org
A national organization whose sole purpose is to reduce the incidence and impact of stroke through prevention, treatment, rehabilitation and research and support for stroke survivors and their families.

1275 **Pulmonary Hypertension Association (PHA)**
801 Roeder Road
Silver Spring, MD 20910
301-565-3004
800-748-7274
www.PHAssociation.org
A non-profit organization for pulmonary hypertension patients, families, caregivers and PH-treating medical professionals. PHA works to provide support, education, and find a cure for pulmonary hypertension.
Matt Granato, President & CEO
Elizabeth Joseloff, VP, Quality Care & Research

Research Centers

1276 **Creighton University Midwest Hypertension Research Center**
601 N 30th Street
Omaha, NE 68131
402-280-4507
Fax: 402-280-4101
Dr William PhD, Director

1277 **Hahnemann University: Division of Surgical Research**
230 N Broad Street
Philadelphia, PA 19102
215-762-7000
866-884-4HUH
Fax: 215-762-8109
www.hahnemannhospital.com
Studies hypertension and management of stress ulcers.
Teuro Matsum Carretero, Division Head
William H Beierwaltes, Scientist

1278 **Henry Ford Hospital: Hypertension and Vascular Research Division**
2799 W Grand Boulevard
Detroit, MI 48202
313-972-1693
Fax: 313-876-1479
ocarret1@hfhs.org
www.hypertensionresearch.org
Basic biomedical research seeks to understand: The role of vasoconstrictors and vasodilators (angiotensin II bradykinin nitric oxide natriuretic peptides) in the regulation of blood pressure development of hypertension and development of target organ damage (myocardial infarction heart failure vascular injury and renal disease); The generation of reactive oxygen species by blood vessels and kidney cells and how this contributes to target organ damage; and The mechanisms by which therape
William H Beierwaltes, Ph.D., Faculty
Oscar A Carretero, Faculty

1279 **Indiana University: Hypertension Research Center**
425 University Boulevard
Indianapolis, IN 46202
317-274-4591
800-274-4862
Fax: 317-278-0673
www.indiana.edu/medical
The mission of the Center is to conduct research in the causes diagnosis treatment and prevention of high blood pressure and its complications.
Dr Myron Rom MPH, Director
Eric Schips, Divisional Administrator

1280 **New York University General Clinical Research Center**
NYU Medical Center
550 First Avenue
New York, NY 10016
212-263-7300
Fax: 212-263-8501
www.med.nyu.edu
Focuses in the areas of hypertension and studies into endocrinology.
Robert I Grossman, MD, Dean & CEO
Steven B Abramson, MD, Senior Vice President and Vice Dean for

1281 **University of Michigan: Division of Hypertension**
1500 E Medical Center
Ann Arbor, MI 48109
734-615-0863
855-855-0863
www.med.umich.edu
Excellence in medical education patient care and research.
Douglas L Stoulil, Study Coordinator

1282 **University of Minnesota: Hypertensive Research Group**
611 Beacon Street SE
Minneapolis, MN 55455
612-624-1438
Research pertaining to hypertension and stress disorders.
Jack Massry, Head

1283 **University of Southern California: Division of Nephrology**
2025 Zonal Avenue
Los Angeles, CA 90033
323-442-5100
Fax: 213-226-3958
www.usc.edu/health/internal/divisions/ne
Research into hypertension and sleep disorders.
Gbemisola A Adeseun, MD, MPH, Faculty
Vito M Campese, MD, Faculty

1284 **University of Virginia: Hypertension and Atherosclerosis Unit**
Medical Center
Charlottesville, VA 22908
804-924-8470
Fax: 804-924-2581
Dr Carlos DVM, Director

1285 **Wake Forest University: Arteriosclerosis Research Center**
Department of Comparative Medicine
300 S Hawthorne Road
Winston-Salem, NC 27103
336-764-3600
Fax: 336-764-5818
Hypertension research.
Thomas Clark

Support Groups & Hotlines

1286 **National Health Information Center**
Office of Disease Prevention & Health Promotion
1101 Wootton Pkwy
Rockville, MD 20852
Fax: 240-453-8281
odphpinfo@hhs.gov
www.health.gov/nhic
Supports public health education by maintaining a calendar of National Health Observances; helps connect consumers and health professionals to organizations that can best answer questions and provide up-to-date contact information from reliable sources; updates on a yearly basis toll-free numbers for health information, Federal health clearinghouses and info centers.
Don Wright, MD, MPH, Director

Print Resources

1287 **American Journal of Hypertension**
American Society of Hypertension
45 Main Street
New York, NY 11201
212-696-9099
Fax: 347-916-0267
ash@ash-us.org
www.ash-us.org

1288 **Ethnicity & Disease**
International Society on Hypertension in Blacks
2045 Manchester Street NE
Atlanta, GA 30324
404-875-6263
Fax: 404-875-6334
member@ishib.org
www.ishib.org
International journal on ethnic minority population differences in diease patterns. Provides a comprehensive source of information on the causal relationships in the etiology of common illnesses through the study of ethnic patterns of disease.
John Willey, Publisher
Melanie T Cockfield, Director Administration

1289 **Ethnicity Disease**
International Society on Hypertension in Blacks

2045 Manchester Street NE 404-875-6263
Atlanta, GA 30324 Fax: 404-875-6334
member@ishib.org
www.ishib.org
Determined to accomplish the overall mission to improving the health and life expectancy of ethnic minority populations around the world. Publishes a quarterly journal and holds an annual conference.
150 pages
Christopher T Fitzpatrick, CEO
Melanie T Cockfield, Director Administration

1290 Journal of Hypertension and Management
ClinMed International Library
3511 Silverside Road, Suite 105 302-208-7437
Wilmington, DE 19810 contact@clinmedjournals.org
clinmedjournals.org
Open access, peer-reviewed journal that publishes clinical information in all the aspects of arterial blood pressure.
Stefano Omboni, Editor-in-Chief

1291 Magazine of the National Institute of Hypertension Studies
13217 Livernois Avenue 313-931-3427
Detroit, MI 48238
Association news.

Web Sites

1292 American Society of Hypertension
www.ash-us.org
To organize and conduct educational seminars, materials, and products in all aspects of hypertension and other cardiovascular diseases.

1293 Healing Well
www.healingwell.com
An online health resource guide to medical news, chat, information and articles, newsgroups and message boards, books, disease-related web sites, medical directories, and more for patients, friends, and family coping with disabling diseases, disorders, or chronic illnesses.

1294 Health Central
www.healthcentral.com
Find clearly explained, medically accurate information regarding conditions, including an overview, symptoms, causes, diagnostic procedures and treatment options. On this site it is possible to ask questions and get information from a neurologist and connect to people who have similar health interests.

1295 Health Finder
www.health.gov
Searchable, carefully developed web site offering information on over 1000 topics. Developed by the US Department of Health and Human Services, thesite can be used in both English and Spanish.

1296 Hypertension: Journal of the American Heart Association
hyper.ahajournals.org
Lists current issues of journals about hypertension and the American Heart Association.

1297 Inter-American Society of Hypertension
www.iashonline.org
Website hosted by IASH, a non-profit professional organization devoted to the understanding, prevention and control of hypertension and vascular diseases in the American population. Members from 20 different countries in the Americas as well as Europe, Australia and Asia. Stimulates research and the exchange of ideas in hypertension and vascular diseases amoung physicians and scientists. Promotes the detection, control and prevention of hypertension and other cardiovascular risk factors.

1298 Lifeclinic.Com
www.lifeclinic.com
Online information about blood pressure, hypertension, diabetes, cholesterol, stroke, heart failure and more. Maintains current, up-to-date and accurate information for patients to help them manage their conditions better and to improve communications between them and their doctors.

1299 Mayo Clinic Health Oasis
www.mayohealth.org
Mission is to empower people to manage their health, by providing useful and up-to-date information and tools that reflect the expertise and standard of excellence of the Mayo Clinic.

1300 Medical News Today
www.medicalnewstody.com
Offers in-depth health information and the latest news in medical research on a wide variety of medical conditions.

1301 MedicineNet
www.medicinenet.com
An online resource for consumers providing easy-to-read, authoritative medical and health information.

1302 MedlinePlus
www.medlineplus.gov
Information regarding a broad range of health,and mental health conditions topics include: Latest news, overview of anatomy and physiology, clinical trials, diagnoses and symptoms, treatment, genetics, plus lots of links to other sites. A service provided by the National Library of Medicine, part of the National Institutes of Health (NIH).

1303 Medscape
www.medscape.com
Medscape offers specialists, primary care physicians, and other health professionals the Web's most robust and integrated medical information and educational tools.

1304 National Heart, Lung & Blood Institute
www.nhlbi.nih.gov
A website maintained by the National Institute of Health offering general information regarding the heart, lungs, and blood.

1305 WebMD
www.webmd.com
Provides credible information, supportive communities, and in-depth reference material about health subjects. A source for original and timely health information as well as material from well known content providers.

IMPOTENCE

Impotence is an inability to have sexual intercourse due to a lack of achieving and/or maintaining an erection and may impact as many as three million men annually in the United States. This may be due to a physical abnormality or psychological state. Impotence is also referred to as erectile dysfunction (ED) and may cause stress on relationships from low self-confidence. Physical causes of ED may include chronic illnesses such as type 2 diabetes, heart disease, high blood pressure, chronic kidney disease, Peyronie's disease, and injury from treatments for prostate cancer, including surgery and radiation. Men with ED often feel sad and angry and are twice as likely to develop clinical depression. Depression that is seen in individuals with ED is treatable. Common symptoms of depression that may contribute to ED are low self-esteem, fatigue, and loss of interest in previously pleasurable activities, sleep disturbances, apathy, and the way individuals feel about themselves and their lives. Symptoms of depression may last months or years and contribute to the psychological basis for impotence. Anxiety and stress also play a role in ED.

The first step in addressing impotence is to determine if it is due to physical or psychological factors. Being honest about ED is critical. Often sexual performance is a subject that is difficult to address. Talking with a medical doctor will begin the process of ruling out a physical cause for ED. Treatment and control of chronic illness that may contribute to ED may be sufficient to minimize ED. If no physical cause is determined, a referral to a mental health professional may occur. Treatments may include medications such as antidepressants (although these drugs may cause or worsen ED) and talk therapy. During talk therapy, the mental health professional assists the individual in identifying issues related to depression and ED. Couples therapy, individual therapy, and group therapy may all be considered.

Ongoing treatment of ED involves achieving healthy behaviors such as lowering stress, getting exercise and maintaining a healthy weight, and considering alternative medications if the physician determines prescribed medications are worsening ED. Pills, drugs inserted into the tip of the penis, or injections into the penis may help in about 80 percent of cases of ED. Mechanical means to restore erections may include vacuum devices and penile implants, a prosthesis inserted into the penis during surgery. A physician specialist in urology may be consulted.

Sexual performance is important in quality of life. Seeking help should not be limited by feelings of embarrassment or shame when options for treatment are available.

Impotence / Agencies & Associations

Agencies & Associations

1306 **American Urological Association (AUA)**
1000 Corporate Boulevard
Linthicum, MD 21090
410-689-3700
800-828-7866
Fax: 410-689-3800
aua@auanet.org
www.auanet.org
Supports urological research through funding and advocacy; offers educational opportunities for urologists; and advocates for quality patient care on a federal level. Provides information on impotence and erectile dysfunction to the general public.
Edward M. Messing, MD, FACS, President
Mike Sheppard, CPA, CAE, CEO

1307 **Canadian Urological Association (CUA)**
185 Dorval Avenue
Dorval, QC, H9S-SJ9
514-395-0376
Fax: 514-395-1664
corporate.office@cua.org
www.cua.org
A member-based organization that represents the Canadian urologic community; provides professional development for urologists; and offers advocacy, education, and research in the field of urologic care.
Tiffany Pizioli, CEO
Dr. Armen Aprikian, President

1308 **Center for Healthy Sex**
10700 Santa Monica Boulevard
Los Angeles, CA 90025
310-843-9902
info@centerforhealthysex.com
centerforhealthysex.com
A therapy center that specializes in the treatment of sexual dysfunction, sexual aversion/anorexia, sex addiction, and love addiction.
Alexandra Katehakis, Founder and Clinical Director

1309 **Center for Reconstructive Urology**
333 City Boulevard West
Orange, CA 92868
714-456-2951
Fax: 714-456-7263
www.centerforreconstructiveurology.org
A regional, national, and international tertiary referral center committed to the treatment of male urethra disorders.
Joel Gelman, MD, Director

1310 **National Institute of Diabetes & Digestive & Kidney Diseases**
31 Center Drive
Bethesda, MD 20892
800-860-8747
TTY: 866-569-1162
healthinfo@niddk.nih.gov
www.niddk.nih.gov
Research areas include diabetes, digestive diseases, endocrine and metabolic diseases, hematologic diseases, kidney disease, liver disease, urologic diseases, as well as matters relating to nutrition and obesity.
Griffin P. Rodgers, Director
Gregory Germino, Deputy Director

1311 **Sexual Medicine Society of North America**
14305 Southcross Drive
Burnsville, MN 55306
952-683-1917
info@smsna.org
www.smsna.org
A nonprofit professional association of physicians, researchers, nurses, and assistants who are dedicated to treating human sexual function and dysfunction.
David Casalod, Executive Director
Tessa Benitez, Associate Executive Director

Foundations

1312 **Canadian Men's Health Foundation**
609 W. Hastings St.
Vancouver, BC V6B-4W4
604-737-2990
info@menshealthfoundation.ca
menshealthfoundation.ca
Offers e-health resources to reduce men's risk for chronic diseases. Provides medically reviewed information on erectile dysfunction, including causes, symptoms, prevention, and treatment.
Dr. S. Larry Goldenberg, Founder
TC Carling, President & CEO

1313 **Urology Care Foundation**
100 Corporate Blvd.
Linthicum, MD 21090
410-689-3700
800-828-7866
info@UrologyCareFoundation.org
www.urologyhealth.org
The Urology Care Foundation is committed to promoting urology research and education. They work with researchers, healthcare professionals, patients and caregivers to improve patients' lives.
Harris M. Nagler, MD, FACS, President
Gopal H. Badlani, MD, Secretary

Research Centers

1314 **Male Sexual Dysfunction Clinic**
3401 N Central Avenue
Chicago, IL 60634
800-788-2873
800-788-2873
Fax: 847-231-4130
www.msdclinic.com
Helping men overcome male sexual dysfunctions such as impotence since 1981.

1315 **New York Male Reproductive Center: Sexual Dysfunction Unit**
161 Fort Washington Avenue
New York, NY 10032
212-305-0123
Fax: 212-305-0126
The New York Male Reproductive Center at Columbia-Presbyterian Medical Center offers state-of-the-art diagnosis and treatment for impotence. Treatments include surgical and non-surgical procedures.

Support Groups & Hotlines

1316 **Impotents Anonymous**
8630 Fenton Street
Silver Spring, MD 20910
301-588-5777
Serves as an educational organization providing concerned individuals with information regarding impotence.

1317 **National Health Information Center**
Office of Disease Prevention & Health Promotion
1101 Wootton Pkwy
Rockville, MD 20852
Fax: 240-453-8281
odphpinfo@hhs.gov
www.health.gov/nhic
Supports public health education by maintaining a calendar of National Health Observances; helps connect consumers and health professionals to organizations that can best answer questions and provide up-to-date contact information from reliable sources; updates on a yearly basis toll-free numbers for health information, Federal health clearinghouses and info centers.
Don Wright, MD, MPH, Director

Print Resources

1318 **International Archives of Urology and Complications**
ClinMed International Library
3511 Silverside Road, Suite 105
Wilmington, DE 19810
302-208-7437
contact@clinmedjournals.org
clinmedjournals.org
Open access, peer-reviewed journal focused on sub-fields of urology, including andrology, female urology, reconstructive surgery, medical oncology, surgical oncology, radiology, incontinence, transplantation, endourology, pathology, infertility, and relevant urology complications.
Ajay Singla, Editor-in-Chief

1319 **Journal of Urology**
American Urological Association
1000 Corporate Boulevard
Linthicum, MD 21090
410-689-3700
800-828-7866
Fax: 410-689-3800
www.auajournals.org
Cited as the most widely read and highly cited journal in the field, The Journal of Urology is accessible to members of the American Urological Association. Topics covered include male infertility and erectile dysfunction or impotence.
D. Robert Siemens, Editor
Toby C. Chai, Associate Editor

Web Sites

1320 Healing Well
www.healingwell.com
An online health resource guide to medical news, chat, information and articles, newsgroups and message boards, books, disease-related web sites, medical directories, and more for patients, friends, and family coping with disabling diseases, disorders, or chronic illnesses.

1321 Health Central
www.healthcentral.com
Find clearly explained, medically accurate information regarding conditions, including an overview, symptoms, causes, diagnostic procedures and treatment options. On this site it is possible to ask questions and get information from a neurologist and connect to people who have similar health interests.

1322 Health Finder
www.health.gov
Searchable, carefully developed web site offering information on over 1000 topics. Developed by the US Department of Health and Human Services, thesite can be used in both English and Spanish.

1323 Medical News Today
www.medicalnewstody.com
Offers in-depth health information and the latest news in medical research on a wide variety of medical conditions.

1324 MedicineNet
www.medicinenet.com
An online resource for consumers providing easy-to-read, authoritative medical and health information.

1325 MedlinePlus
www.medlineplus.gov
Information regarding a broad range of health,and mental health conditions topics include: Latest news, overview of anatomy and physiology, clinical trials, diagnoses and symptoms, treatment, genetics, plus lots of links to other sites. A service provided by the National Library of Medicine, part of the National Institutes of Health (NIH).

1326 Medscape
www.medscape.com
Medscape offers specialists, primary care physicians, and other health professionals the Web's most robust and integrated medical information and educational tools.

1327 MyHealthfinder
www.healthfinder.gov
Searchable, carefully developed web site offering information on over 1000 topics. Developed by the US Department of Health and Human Services, the site can be used in both English and Spanish.

1328 WebMD
www.webmd.com
Provides credible information, supportive communities, and in-depth reference material about health subjects. A source for original and timely health information, as well as material from well-known content providers.

INFERTILITY

A decline in human fertility over the past few decades has occurred with infertility affecting about 15 in every 100 couples. There is a direct correlation between mental health, unhealthy habits and poor lifestyle choices on fertility and other diseases. Infertility is defined as 12 months with regular, unprotected vaginal sex without being able to conceive, or six months if the woman is over the age of 35. The inability to conceive is a life crisis that often leads to mental health issues. There is a significant awareness of the emotional impact of both infertility and its treatments, including depression, stress, and anxiety. When treatments fail, feelings of loss and grief often occur leading particularly to depression. Both males and females may develop depression, especially if they are found to be the person unable to contribute to reproduction.

The first step in addressing the inability to get pregnant is to discuss the situation with an Obstetrician/Gynecologist (OBGYN) to determine if there are physical issues interfering with conception. Both the female and male partner need to be examined and tested, as either partner may be the cause of the infertility. Close to 40 percent of women with infertility have a mental health diagnosis, most often depression or anxiety. While some research has shown a link between infertility and anxiety and depression, the reason is not clear. Often individuals do not express their issues with sadness and depression, thus not getting the help needed. A significant issue is that infertility treatments such as in vitro fertilization may be painful, often take years and still may not be effective. An ongoing state of stress is not healthy and the development of depression may occur. A referral to a mental health professional may be needed. Some studies have shown that mental health interventions to lower distress may be associated with increases in pregnancy rates.

Treatments may include both medications safe to use when trying to get pregnant and talk therapy, including couples therapy, individual therapy, and group therapy. Individuals may be encouraged to cry and be angry and not shut off feelings and allowing your spouse or partner permission to cope differently. Effective communication between spouses and partners helps alleviate stress and may improve depressive symptoms.

Seeking help with infertility should include addressing the mental issues surrounding this life-altering event. Asking the OBGYN for a referral to a mental health professional is a healthy coping strategy.

Infertility / Agencies & Associations

Agencies & Associations

1329 American Pregnancy Association
800-672-2296
info@americanpregnancy.org
www.americanpregnancy.org
Provides the public with information about reproductive disease and supports families during struggles with pregnancy, infertility, and adoption. Exists to serve the unique needs of men and women confronting infertility issues.

1330 American Society for Reproductive Medicine
J. Benjamin Younger Office of Public Affairs
726 7th St. SE
Washington, DC 20003
202-863-4985
asrm@asrm.org
www.asrm.org
A private, non-profit medical organization devoted to advancing the knowledge, understanding, and expertise in all phases of reproductive medicine and biology. Offers patient education brochures, recommended readings and support. Publishes professional journal and consumer publications.
Michael A. Thomas, MD, President
Jared C. Robins, MD, MBA, Executive Director

1331 American Urological Association
1000 Corporate Boulevard
Linthicum, MD 21090
410-689-3700
866-746-4282
aua@AUAnet.org
www.auanet.org
An association of professionals who promote high standards of urological care, including male infertility. The Association provides support for urologists through education, funding for research, and networking/information sharing opportunities.
Randall B. Meacham, MD, President
Stephen Y. Nakada, MD, President-Elect

1332 Canadian Society of Nephrology
P.O. Box 25255 RDP
Montreal, QC, H1E-7P9
514-643-4985
info@csnscn.ca
www.csnscn.ca
Mission is to support Canadian Nephrologists by offering professional development and educational opportunities; advancing the care of individuals living with, or at risk for, kidney disease; and fostering scholarly advancement in the field of kidney health in Canada.
Dr. Claudio Rigatto, President
Dr. Manish Sood, Secretary/Treasurer

1333 HealthyWomen
P.O. Box 336
Middletown, NJ 07748
732-530-3425
877-986-9472
info@healthywomen.org
www.healthywomen.org
Independent, non-profit organization seeking to educate women in all areas of health, to allow them to make informed choices. The HealthyWomen website features numerous tools and health calculators, plus other media.
Beth Battaglino, CEO
Julia M. Amadio, Chair

1334 International Council on Infertility Information Dissemination
5765 F. Burke Centre Parkway
Burke, VA 22015
703-379-9178
Fax: 703-379-1593
INCIIDinfo@inciid.org
www.inciid.org
Provides information on infertility, pregnancy loss, adoption, high risk pregnancy and parenting.

1335 National Women's Health Network
1413 K. Street NW
Washington, DC 20005
202-682-2640
Fax: 202-682-2648
nwhn@nwhn.org
www.nwhn.org
Non-profit organization advocating for national policies that protect and promote all women's health, and providing evidence-based independent information.
Teri Bordenave, Interim Executive Director
Adele Costa, Director, Communications

1336 RESOLVE: New England
395 Totten Pond Road
Waltham, MA 02451
781-890-2225
admin@resolvenewengland.org
resolvenewengland.org
Resolve New England (RNE) provides support for all those struggling with fertility and family building in Connecticut, Maine, Massachusetts, New Hampshire, Rhode Island, and Vermont.
Jennifer Redmond, President
Kate Weldon LeBlanc, Executive Director

1337 RESOLVE: The National Infertility Association
1660 International Drive
McLean, VA 22102
703-556-7172
Fax: 703-506-3266
info@resolve.org
www.resolve.org
A nationwide non-profit organization serving the unique needs of those striving to build a family. Provides informed help to people who are experiencing infertility.
Barbara Collura, President & CEO
Betsy Campbell, Chief Engagement Officer

1338 Society for the Study of Reproduction
11130 Sunrise Valley Drive
Reston, VA 20191
703-885-3502
Fax: 703-234-4147
www.ssr.org
International scientific society promotes the study of reproductive biology by fostering interdisciplinary communication within the science by holding conferences and by publishing meritorious studies.
Julie Utano, Executive Director
Erika Martin, Membership Manager

1339 Wayfinder Family Services
5300 Angeles Vista Boulevard
Los Angeles, CA 90043
323-295-4555
800-352-2290
www.lilliput.org
Formerly known as Lilliput, Wayfinder Family Serivces is an adoption agency that bridges the gap between the public and private sectors of foster care.
Jay Allen, President & CEO
Glenn A. Sonnenberg, Chair

Foundations

1340 Fertility Friends Foundation
2225 Sheppard Ave. E.
Toronto, ON, M2J-5C2
info@fertilityfriendsfoundation.com
fertilityfriendsfoundation.com
A registered charity that offers support to Canadians struggling with infertility through educational resources, fundraising, and grants.
Chloe Roumain, Founder & President
Frederick Dzineku, Founder & Board Member

1341 Fertility Matters Canada (FMC)
P.O. Box 25077
Moncton, NB, E1C-9M9
info@fertilitymatters.ca
fertilitymatters.ca
A national charitable organization that helps Canadians access fertility treatments through awareness, information, and education.
Carolynn Dube, Executive Director
Dr. Ari Baratz, President

1342 Hope for Fertility Foundation
info@hopeforfertility.org
www.hopeforfertility.org
A non-profit organization that offers financial support to couples struggling with infertility treatments, surrogacy, and/or adoption costs.
Angela Williams, President
McCall Weekes, Vice President, Fundraising

1343 Hysterectomy Educational Resources & Services (HERS) Foundation
610-667-7757
Fax: 610-667-8096
hers@hersfoundation.org
www.hersfoundation.com
A nonprofit foundation which provides information about the alternatives to hysterectomy, the risks of the alternatives, and the consequences of the surgery. HERS provides copies of a medical

Infertility / Print Resources

journals, a quarterly newsletter, and a free lending library of books, videos and audio tapes.

Research Centers

1344 **Fertility Clinic at the Shepherd Spinal Center**
Shepherd Spinal Center
2020 Peachtree Road NW   404-352-2020
Atlanta, GA 30309   www.shepherd.org
This clinic makes it possible for paralyzed men to father children.
Gary Ulicny, Chief Executive Officer

1345 **Fertility and Women's Health Care Center**
130 Maple Street   413-781-8220
Springfield, MA 01103   Fax: 413-732-9088
Conducts basic and clinical studies of male and female infertility.
Ronald K. Burke, MD, Head

1346 **Melpomene Institute for Women's Health Research**
550 Rice Street   651-789-0140
Saint Paul, MN 55103   Fax: 651-292-9417
                                 www.melpomene.org
Focuses on women's health including fertility issues.
Judy Mahle Lutter, President

1347 **University of California: UCLA Population Research Center**
4284 Public Affairs Building   310-206-7566
Los Angeles, CA 90095   Fax: 310-825-8762
                                 stats@ccpr.ucla.edu
                                 www.ccpr.ucla.edu
Clinical investigations of overpopulation and infertility.
Judith A. Seltzer, Director
Jennie Brand, Associate Director

1348 **University of Michigan Reproductive Sciences Program**
1500 East Medical Center Drive   734-764-8123
Ann Arbor, MI 48109   Fax: 734-763-5992
                                 juckno@umich.edu
                 www.med.umich.edu/OBGYN/research/rsp/
Research done into reproductive medicine and infertility treatments.
Timothy R. Johnson, Chair
Janet Hall, Clinical Department Administrator

1349 **Vanderbilt University: Center for Fertility and Reproductive Research**
Nashville, TN 37232   615-322-6576
                                 Fax: 615-343-4902
Reproductive biology and fertility research.

1350 **Wayne State University: University Women's Care**
26400 W 12 Mile Road   248-352-8200
Southfield, MI 48034   Fax: 248-356-8224
                                 wayne.edu
Reproductive endocrine infertility and gynecologic surgery research. The research spans the woman's life cycle. Research projects include: endometriosis, polycystic ovary syndrome, sexual dysfunction, fibroids and menopause. Additional studies pertaining to women's health and male infertility.

Support Groups & Hotlines

1351 **National Health Information Center**
Office of Disease Prevention & Health Promotion
1101 Wootton Pkwy   Fax: 240-453-8281
Rockville, MD 20852   odphpinfo@hhs.gov
                                 www.health.gov/nhic
Supports public health education by maintaining a calendar of National Health Observances; helps connect consumers and health professionals to organizations that can best answer questions and provide up-to-date contact information from reliable sources; updates on a yearly basis toll-free numbers for health information, Federal health clearinghouses and info centers.
Don Wright, MD, MPH, Director

1352 **National Infertility Network Exchange**
P.O. Box 204   516-794-5772
East Meadow, NY 11554   Fax: 516-794-0008
                                 www.nine-infertility.org/
The National Infertility Network Exchange (NINE) is a national, notfor profit organization for persons and couples with impaired fertility. NINE supportes the decision of legal and medical means to build families as well as the decision to remain childfree.

Print Resources

1353 **Biology of Reproduction**
Society for the Study of Reproduction
11130 Sunrise Valley Drive   703-885-3502
Reston, VA 20191   Fax: 703-234-4147
                                 info@ssr.org
                                 academic.oup.com/biolreprod
This peer-reviewed journal is the official journal of the Society for the Study of Reproduction.
250 pages Monthly
Romana Nowak, PhD, Editor-in-Chief
Mary Zelinski, PhD, Co-Editor-in-Chief

1354 **Family Building Magazine**
RESOLVE: National Infertility Association
1310 Broadway   617-623-1156
Somerville, MA 02144   888-623-0744
                                 Fax: 617-623-0252
                                 info@resolve.org
                                 www.resolve.org
Offers various information on the newest technology and advances in infertility treatments, support groups, helplines, centers and in depth articles written by professionals in the field.
15-18 pages
Bonny Gilbert, Executive Director

1355 **Fertility and Sterility**
American Society for Reproductive Medicine
726 7th St. S.E.   202-863-4985
Washington, DC 20003   asrm@asrm.org
                                 www.asrm.org
A journal for health professionals who treat infertility, sterility and the physiology of reproduction.
Kurt Barnhart, M.D., M.S.C.E., Editor-in-Chief
Micah J. Hill, D.O., Media Editor

1356 **Fertility and Sterility Journal**
American Society for Reproductive Medicine
726 7th St. SE   202-863-4985
Washington, DC 20003   asrm@asrm.org
                                 www.asrm.org
Publishes original research on reproductive endocrinology, physiology, immunology, genetics, and menopause.
Kurt Barnhart, M.D., M.S.C.E., Editor-in-Chief

1357 **Infertility and Adoption**
RESOLVE: National Infertility Association
1310 Broadway   617-623-1156
Somerville, MA 02144   888-623-0744
                                 Fax: 617-623-0252
                                 info@resolve.org
                                 www.resolve.org
Published by RESOLVE: The National Infertility Association.
Bonny Gilbert, Executive Director
Roy Sokol, Author

1358 **International Archives of Urology and Complications**
ClinMed International Library
3511 Silverside Road, Suite 105 302-208-7437
Wilmington, DE 19810   contact@clinmedjournals.org
                                 clinmedjournals.org
Open access, peer-reviewed journal focused on sub-fields of urology, including andrology, female urology, reconstructive surgery, medical oncology, surgical oncology, radiology, incontinence, transplantation, endourology, pathology, infertility, and relevant urology complications.
Ajay Singla, Editor-in-Chief

Infertility / Web Sites

1359 **Journal of Urology**
American Urological Association
1000 Corporate Boulevard
Linthicum, MD 21090
410-689-3700
800-828-7866
Fax: 410-689-3800
www.auajournals.org
Cited as the most widely read and highly cited journal in the field, The Journal of Urology is accessible to members of the American Urological Association. Topics covered include male infertility and erectile dysfunction or impotence.
D. Robert Siemens, Editor
Toby C. Chai, Associate Editor

Web Sites

1360 **Adopt-A-Special-Kid America**
www.adoptaspecialkid.org
Adopt-A-Special-Kid provides information on adoption of children with special needs.

1361 **American Society for Reproductive Medicine**
www.reproductivefacts.org
A private, non-profit medical organization devoted to advancing the knowledge, understanding and expertise in all phases of reproductive medicine and biology. Offers patient education brochures, recommended readings and support. Publishes professional journal and consumer publications, and runs the ReproductiveFacts.org website for patients.

1362 **Center for Disease Control**
cdc.gov/reproductivehealth/infertility
Reproductive health information source. Also a resource for the Society of Reproductive Technology. Invitro fertilization data reports and men's reproductive health.

1363 **Healing Well**
www.healingwell.com
An online health resource guide to medical news, chat, information and articles, newsgroups and message boards, books, disease-related web sites, medical directories, and more for patients, friends, and family coping with disabling diseases, disorders, or chronic illnesses.

1364 **Health Central**
www.healthcentral.com
Find clearly explained, medically accurate information regarding conditions, including an overview, symptoms, causes, diagnostic procedures and treatment options. On this site it is possible to ask questions and get information from a neurologist and connect to people who have similar health interests.

1365 **Health Finder**
www.health.gov
Searchable, carefully developed web site offering information on over 1000 topics. Developed by the US Department of Health and Human Services, thesite can be used in both English and Spanish.

1366 **HealthyWomen**
www.healthywomen.org
Independent, non-profit organization seeking to educate women in all areas of health, to allow them to make informed choices. The HealthyWomen website features numerous tools and health calculators, plus other media.

1367 **Infertility Books**
www.infertilitybooks.com
Nonprofit site includes book titles regarding infertility and a short explanation of each book and how to get it.

1368 **International Council on Infertility Information Dissemination**
www.inciid.org
A nonprofit organization that helps individuals and couples explore their family-building options.

1369 **Internet Health Resources**
www.ihr.com/infertility
This web site provides extensive information about IVF, ICSI, infertility clinics, donor egg and surrogacy services, sperm banks, pharmacies, infertility books and videotapes, sperm testing, infertility newsgroups and support organizations, and drugs and medications.

1370 **Medical News Today**
www.medicalnewstody.com
Offers in-depth health information and the latest news in medical research on a wide variety of medical conditions.

1371 **MedicineNet**
www.medicinenet.com
An online resource for consumers providing easy-to-read, authoritative medical and health information.

1372 **MedlinePlus**
www.medlineplus.gov
Information regarding a broad range of health,and mental health conditions topics include: Latest news, overview of anatomy and physiology, clinical trials, diagnoses and symptoms, treatment, genetics, plus lots of links to other sites. A service provided by the National Library of Medicine, part of the National Institutes of Health (NIH).

1373 **Medscape**
www.medscape.com
Medscape offers specialists, primary care physicians, and other health professionals the Web's most robust and integrated medical information and educational tools.

1374 **MyHealthfinder**
www.healthfinder.gov
Searchable, carefully developed web site offering information on over 1000 topics. Developed by the US Department of Health and Human Services, the site can be used in both English and Spanish.

1375 **National Institutes of Health**
www.medlineplus.gov
Information regarding all aspects of infertility. Some of the topics include: Latest news, overview of anatomy and physiology, clinical trails, diagnoses and symptoms, treatment, genetics, plus lots of links to other sites. Type infertility into the search engine.

1376 **Progyny**
progyny.com
A support sytem concerned with helping reach a goal of finding the perfect doctor, the diagnosis, as well as the treatment.

1377 **RESOLVE**
www.resolve.org
Provides help to people who are experiencing the infertility crisis and strives to increase the visibility of infertility issues via concerted advocacy and public education.

1378 **Uterine Artery Embolization**
www.uterinearteryembolization.com
Provides information on Uterine Artery Embolization, or Uterine Fibroid Embolization as an alternative to hysterectomy or myomectomy as a treatment for uterine fibroids.

1379 **WebMD**
www.webmd.com
Provides credible information, supportive communities, and in-depth reference material about health subjects. A source for original and timely health information, as well as material from well-known content providers.

MULTIPLE SCLEROSIS (MS)

Multiple sclerosis (MS) is a chronic disease that impacts the brain, optic nerves, and spinal cord. Approximately one in every 750 individuals in the United States has MS. It negatively impacts the central nervous system that controls life functions. Common symptoms are fatigue, sexual problems, bladder and bowel problems, mood and thought changes, muscular changes, and vision changes. Early symptoms may be the same in both men and women. The most obvious first sign is change in vision or optic neuritis. This is a more easily recognized symptom than numbness and tingling that often occur in MS but that can also occur in other diagnoses. An individual with benign MS may go without symptoms for as long as 15 years but those with malignant or fulminate MS, a rapid and progressive disease course, will experience severe relapses within five years after diagnosis. Without treatment, a relapsing form of MS, will transition to a progressive form of MS within 10 years. Medications for MS are used to modify the disease course, treat relapses, and manage symptoms.

One of the most common symptoms in MS is depression. A low mood may only be intermittent and is normal grief and emotions around a life altering condition. If symptoms occur such as feeling down, hopeless and depressed coupled with a lack of interest in things that used to be pleasurable, it may be depression and the individual needs to discuss these feelings with the MS treatment team. A referral to a mental health professional may be indicated. Left untreated, depression negatively impacts quality of life and makes symptoms such as fatigue, pain and cognitive changes feel worse. Depression is most evident following diagnosis or during a major change in function due to the disease.

Daily exercise, reducing stress, staying active with family and friends, writing in a journal about thoughts and feelings and staying away from addictive substance such as alcohol are coping strategies for depression. Clinical depression may require medications and talk therapy under the supervision of the MS treatment team and mental health professionals.

Multiple Sclerosis (MS) / Agencies & Associations

Agencies & Associations

1380 **American Chronic Pain Association**
11936 W. 119th Street 913-991-4740
Overland Park, KS 66213 www.acpanow.com
The ACPA facilitates peer support and education for individuals with chronic pain in its many forms, in order to increase quality of life. Also raises awareness among the healthcare community, and with policy makers.
Penney Cowan, Founder
Trupti Gokani, MD, President

1381 **Multiple Sclerosis Association of America**
375 Kings Highway N 800-532-7667
Cherry Hill, NJ 08034 Fax: 856-661-9797
msaa@mymsaa.org
www.mymsaa.org
A national non-profit organization dedicated to enriching the quality of life for everyone affected by multiple sclerosis.
Jennifer L. Schwartz, Esq., Chair
Eric K. Bossard, Vice Chair

1382 **National Institute of Neurological Disorders and Stroke**
NIH Neurological Institute 800-352-9424
Bethesda, MD 20824 www.ninds.nih.gov
Seeks to reduce the burden of neurological disease affecting individuals from all walks of life.
Walter Koroshetz, MD, Director
Amy B. Adams, Director, Office of Scientific Liaison

1383 **National Multiple Sclerosis Society: Pacific South Coast**
10089 Willow Creek Rd. 714-689-9603
San Diego, CA 92131 800-344-4867
renata.sahagian@nmss.org
www.nationalmssociety.org/Chapters/CAS
Renata Sahagian, President

1384 **National Multiple Sclerosis Society: Pennsylvania Keystone Chapter**
1501 Reedsdale Street 412-261-6347
Pittsburgh, PA 15233 800-344-4867
anne.mageras@nmss.org
www.nationalmssociety.org/Chapters/PAX
Anne Mageras, President

1385 **National Multiple Sclerosis Society**
New York, NY 800-344-4867
www.nationalmssociety.org
Serves persons with MS, their families, health professionals and the interested public. Provides funding for research, public and professional education, advocacy and the design of rehabilitative and psychosocial programs.
Sylvia Lawry, Founder
Cynthia Zagieboylo, President & CEO

1386 **National Multiple Sclerosis Society: Wyoming Chapter**
900 S. Broadway 800-344-4867
Denver, CO 80209 robyn.moore@nmss.org
www.nationalmssociety.org/Chapters/COC
Robyn Moore, President

1387 **National Multiple Sclerosis Society: Idaho Chapter**
P.O. Box 54879 800-344-4867
Los Angeles, CA 90054 www.nationalmssociety.org/Chapters/UTU
Melissa Matthews, President

1388 **National Multiple Sclerosis Society: New Jersey Metro Chapter**
1480 U.S. Highway 9 North 201-977-6055
Woodbridge, NJ 07095 800-344-4867
Yasmin.Nielsen@nmss.org
www.nationalmssociety.org/Chapters/NJM
Yasmin Nielsen, President

1389 **National Multiple Sclerosis Society: North Florida Chapter**
8940 Western Way 800-344-4867
Jacksonville, FL 32256 heidi.katz@nmss.org
www.nationalmssociety.org/Chapters/FLN
Heidi Katz, President

1390 **National Multiple Sclerosis Society: Ohio Chapter**
6133 Rockside Rd 800-344-4867
Independence, OH 44131 julie.leggett@nmss.org
www.nationalmssociety.org/chapters/OHO/i
Julie Leggett, President

1391 **National Multiple Sclerosis Society: Texas Chapter**
1050 N. Post Oak Road 800-344-4867
Houston, TX 77055 linda.bates@nmss.org
www.nationalmssociety.org/Chapters/TXH
Linda Bates, President, South Central Chapter

1392 **National Multiple Sclerosis Society: Utah Chapter**
P.O. Box 54879 800-344-4867
Los Angeles, CA 90054 www.nationalmssociety.org
Melissa Matthews, President

Foundations

1393 **Multiple Sclerosis Foundation**
6520 N Andrews Avenue 954-776-6805
Fort Lauderdale, FL 33309 888-673-6287
Fax: 954-351-0630
support@msfocus.org
www.msfocus.org
The foundation offers free services including educational programs, homecare, support groups, assistive technology for individuals with MS.
Charles Eader, President
John Blackstock, Secretary

Libraries & Resource Centers

1394 **St. Agnes Hospital Medical: Health Science Library**
305 North Street 914-681-4500
White Plains, NY 10605 Fax: 914-328-6408
Labe C Scheinberg MD, Director

Research Centers

1395 **Brigham and Women's Hospital: Center for Neurologic Diseases**
LMRC Building
75 Francis Street 617-732-5500
Boston, MA 02115 800-294-9999
TTY: 617-732-6458
www.brighamandwomens.org
Offers research relating to Multiple Sclerosis and other autoimmune diseases.
Dennis J. Selkoe, Co-Director
Howard L. Weiner, Co-Director

1396 **Center for Neuroimmunology: University of Alabama at Birmingham**
1720 7th Ave S 205-934-0683
Birmingham, AL 35294 Fax: 205-996-4039
www.main.uab.edu/neurology
Evaluate and treat acute and chronic neurological and neuromuscular diseases which are caused by autoimmune mechanisms or linked to presumed abnormalities affecting the immune system.
Khurram Bashir, Director

1397 **Jimmie Heuga Center**
27 Main Street 970-926-1290
Edwards, CO 81632 800-367-3101
Fax: 970-926-1295
info@mscando.org
www.mscando.org
Conducts research and studies on multiple sclerosis patients.
Kim Lennox Sharkey, Chief Executive Officer
Carrie Van Beek, Office Coordinator

1398 **Neuromuscular Treatment Center: Univ. of Texas Southwestern Medical Center**
Department of Neurology 214-648-3111
Dallas, TX 75390 www.utsouthwestern.edu

Basic and clinical studies of myasthenia gravis.
Daniel K Podolsky MD, President
Diane Jeffries, Director

1399 Rush University Multiple Sclerosis Center
1653 W. Congress Parkway
Chicago, IL 60612
312-942-5000
888-352-RUSH
TTY: 312-942-2207
complaint@jointcommission.org
www.rush.edu
The Multiple Sclerosis Center combines comprehensive treatment with clinical and laboratory research to provide the highest quality patient care.
Floyd A Davis, Director

Support Groups & Hotlines

1400 MS Toll-Free Information Line
National Multiple Sclerosis Society
733 3rd Avenue
New York, NY 10017
800-344-4867
Offers public and professional information, brochures and referrals to MS patients, their families and health care professionals.

1401 MSWorld
1943 Morrill Street
Sarasota, FL 34236
415-701-1117
877-710-0302
msworld@msworld.org
www.msworld.org/
MSWorld is for people with multiple sclerosis their families and friends, offer support via chat, e-mail, message boards, magazines.
Kathleen Wilson, Founder/President

1402 Multiple Sclerosis Action Group
National Multiple Sclerosis Society
733 3rd Avenue
New York, NY 10017
409-883-2282
800-344-4867
msag@erasems.com
www.nationalmssociety.org/index.aspx
Richard J Mengel, Treasurer
Fred J Lublin, Director

1403 National Health Information Center
Office of Disease Prevention & Health Promotion
1101 Wootton Pkwy
Rockville, MD 20852
Fax: 240-453-8281
odphpinfo@hhs.gov
www.health.gov/nhic
Supports public health education by maintaining a calendar of National Health Observances; helps connect consumers and health professionals to organizations that can best answer questions and provide up-to-date contact information from reliable sources; updates on a yearly basis toll-free numbers for health information, Federal health clearinghouses and info centers.
Don Wright, MD, MPH, Director

1404 Traditional Tibetan Healing
13 Harrison Street
Sommerville, MA 2143
617-666-8635
866-628-6504
Kelob@gte.net
www.tibetanherbalhealing.com/
To rid mankind from chronic illnesses using alternative methods.
Keyzon Bhutti, Chief Physician

Print Resources

1405 Inside MS
National Multiple Sclerosis Society
733 3rd Avenue
New York, NY 10017
212-986-3240
800-344-4867
Fax: 212-986-7981
www.nationalmssociety.org
Full color quarterly magazine on living well with multiple sclerosis. Articles by people with MS; daily living, achievments, news, treatments, research, advocacy, humor, travel, helpful resources, large type. The magazine is a benefit of membership.
64 pages
Eli Rubenstein, Chairman of the Board
Cynthia Zagieboylo, Chapter President

Web Sites

1406 Healing Well
www.healingwell.com
An online health resource guide to medical news, chat, information and articles, newsgroups and message boards, books, disease-related web sites, medical directories, and more for patients, friends, and family coping with disabling diseases, disorders, or chronic illnesses.

1407 Health Central
www.healthcentral.com
Find clearly explained, medically accurate information regarding conditions, including an overview, symptoms, causes, diagnostic procedures and treatment options. On this site it is possible to ask questions and get information from a neurologist and connect to people who have similar health interests.

1408 Health Finder
www.health.gov
Searchable, carefully developed web site offering information on over 1000 topics. Developed by the US Department of Health and Human Services, the site can be used in both English and Spanish.

1409 Medical News Today
www.medicalnewstody.com
Offers in-depth health information and the latest news in medical research on a wide variety of medical conditions.

1410 MedicineNet
www.medicinenet.com
An online resource for consumers providing easy-to-read, authoritative medical and health information.

1411 MedlinePlus
www.medlineplus.gov
Information regarding a broad range of health,and mental health conditions topics include: Latest news, overview of anatomy and physiology, clinical trials, diagnoses and symptoms, treatment, genetics, plus lots of links to other sites. A service provided by the National Library of Medicine, part of the National Institutes of Health (NIH).

1412 Medscape
www.medscape.com
Medscape offers specialists, primary care physicians, and other health professionals the Web's most robust and integrated medical information and educational tools.

1413 Multiple Sclerosis Foundation
www.msfocus.org
Dedicated to helping create a brighter tomorrow for those with MS, the foundation offers a wide array of free services including: national toll-free support, educational programs, homecare, support groups, assitive technology, publications, a comprehensive website and more to improve the quality of life for those affected by MS.

1414 National Multiple Sclerosis Society
www.nmss.org
The Society helps people affected by MS by funding cutting-edge research, driving change through advocacy, facilitating professional education, and providing programs and services that help people with MS and their families move their lives forward.

1415 WebMD
www.webmd.com
Provides credible information, supportive communities, and in-depth reference material about health subjects. A source for original and timely health information as well as material from well known content providers.

511

OBESITY

Obesity and depression are closely linked, with almost 50 percent of adults with depression experiencing obesity. Those individuals are more likely to be depressed than those who are not obese. Obesity is higher in non-Hispanic white women; in women in every age group, women with depression were more likely to also be obese. As the severity of depression increases, the level of obesity often increases. Approximately 55 percent of adults taking antidepressant medications and still reporting depressive symptoms, were, by definition, obese. Physical consequences of obesity include many chronic conditions including type 2 diabetes, heart issues and osteoarthritis. Individuals living with obesity often experience mood and anxiety disorders.

Mental health issues for patients living with obesity are both practical and societal. Quality of life may be negatively impacted including work limitations and occupational functioning due to body size and chronic ailments. Physical limitations may lead to social isolation, difficulty coping with life, and loneliness, with chronic pain often linked to depression. Weight bias and discrimination are challenges faced by the obese individual. They may be perceived as lazy, unattractive, and undisciplined leading to a poor body image and heightened inflammation in the body correlated with developing depression. Chronic stress, anxiety, and depression, including bipolar disorder, may cause the use of food as a coping mechanism leading to even more weight gain. Serotonin deficiency linked with depressed mood, poor sleep patterns and anxiety has been shown to increase carbohydrate cravings and weight gain. Depression may also diminish the desire to engage in healthy activities and exercise.

While treatment is effective, individuals may face stigmatizing attitudes when seeking out resources. Both obesity and mental health issues can keep people in a vicious cycle of learning to deal with the obesity and mental health disability. Many medications for depression and other mental health disorders cause weight gain as a side effect. Traditional obesity interventions such as healthy nutrition and a physical activity plan may be difficult for someone struggling with low mood, clinical depression, or anxiety. A balanced treatment plan developed by a caring team can lead to improvements in both weight management and depression.

Obesity / Agencies & Associations

Agencies & Associations

1416 **American Obesity Treatment Association**
117 Anderson Court
Dothan, AL 36303
334-403-4057
info@americanobesity.org
americanobesity.org
Provides obesity awareness and prevention information.
Cesar Cuneo, President & Founder
Gonzalo Tovar, Vice President

1417 **National Association to Advance Fat Acceptance (NAAFA)**
PO Box 61586
Las Vegas, NV 89160
naafa.org
Non-profit organization committed to improving the lives of fat individuals and reducing discrimination.
Tigress Osborn, Board Chair
Amanda Cooper, Public Relations Director

1418 **Obesity Canada**
2-126 Li Ka Shing Center for Health
Edmonton, Alberta, T6G
780-492-8361
info@obesitynetwork.ca
www.obesitycanada.ca
An organization of researchers, clinicians and other health professionals dedicated to reducing the mental, physical and economic burden of obesity in Canadians.

1419 **Research Chair in Obesity, Universite Laval**
2725 Chemin Sainte-Foy
Quebec, Canada, G1V
418-656-8711
Fax: 418-656-4929
obesity.chair@crhl.ulaval.ca
www.iucpq.qc.ca
Shares communication about nutrition, energy metabolism, obesity, lipid metabolism and cardiovascular research. Provides continuing education about obesity to health professionals, physicians and to the public regarding the causes, the complications and the treatment of obesity.
Denis Richard, PhD, Chair

1420 **Weight-Control Information Network**
National Institutes of Health
31 Center Drive
Bethesda, MD 20892
800-860-8747
TTY: 866-569-1162
healthinfo@niddk.nih.gov
www.win.niddk.nih.gov
WIN provides the general public, health professionals, and the media with up-to-date, science-based information on obesity, weight control, physical activity, and related nutritional issues.

Libraries & Resource Centers

1421 **Weight-Control Information Network**
National Institutes of Health
31 Center Drive
Bethesda, MD 20892
800-860-8747
TTY: 866-569-1162
healthinfo@niddk.nih.gov
www.win.niddk.nih.gov
WIN provides the general public, health professionals, and the media with up-to-date, science-based information on obesity, weight control, physical activity, and related nutritional issues. WIN provides tip sheets, fact sheets, and brochures for a range of audiences. Some of WIN's content is available in Spanish.

Research Centers

1422 **Harvard Clinical Nutrition Research Center**
Harvard Medical School
Boston, MA 02215
617-998-8803
Fax: 617-998-8804
allan_walker@hms.harvard.edu
nutrition.med.harvard.edu
Mission is to derive the benefit of continuity in assessing the effectiveness of the Center from year to year while still allowing flexibility for new insights as the Center's activities evolve.
W Allan Walker, Director
George Blackburn, Associate Director

1423 **Minnesota Obesity Center**
1334 Eckles Avenue
St Paul, MN 55108
763-807-0559
mnoc@tc.umn.edu
www.mnoc.umn.edu
Mission is to find ways to prevent weight gain obesity and its complications. The Center incorporates 46 Participating Investigators who are studying the causes and treatments of obesity. Provides the general public with a source of information on the happenings of the Center and on the current developments in the field of obesity.
Catherine C Welch, Program Coordinator

1424 **New York Obesity/Nutrition Research Center**
31 Center Drive MSC 2560
Bethesda, MD 20892
301-496-3583
www2.niddk.nih.gov
Griffin P Rodgers, Director

1425 **Obesity Research Center St. Luke's-Roosevelt Hospital**
St. Luke's-Roosevelt Hospital
1090 Amsterdam Avenue
New York, NY 10025
212-523-4196
Fax: 212-523-3416
dg108@columbia.edu
www.nyorc.org
The mission of the New York Obesity Research Center is to help reduce the incidence of obesity and related diseases through leadership in basic research clinical research epidemiology and public health patient care and public education.
Dr Xavier Pi-Sunyer, Director
Janet Crane, Dietitians

Support Groups & Hotlines

1426 **Greater New York Metro Intergroup of Overeaters Anonymous**
Madison Square Station
New York, NY 10159
212-946-4599
office@oanyc.org
www.oanyc.org

Tom M, Chairman
Raina M, Vice chairman

1427 **National Health Information Center**
Office of Disease Prevention & Health Promotion
1101 Wootton Pkwy
Rockville, MD 20852
Fax: 240-453-8281
odphpinfo@hhs.gov
www.health.gov/nhic
Supports public health education by maintaining a calendar of National Health Observances; helps connect consumers and health professionals to organizations that can best answer questions and provide up-to-date contact information from reliable sources; updates on a yearly basis toll-free numbers for health information, Federal health clearinghouses and info centers.
Don Wright, MD, MPH, Director

1428 **Overeaters Anonymous**
6075 Zenith Court NE
Rio Rancho, NM 87144
505-891-2664
www.oa.org
A fellowship of individuals who meet in order to help solve their eating behaviors.

Print Resources

1429 **CheckUp**
Medical University of South Carolina
67 President Street
Charleston, SC 29425
843-792-2273
800-424-6872
Fax: 843-792-5432
www.muschealth.com/weight
Provides health information about screenings, treatments, medical advances and services available through MUSC, as well as advice about nutrition and prevention.
Susan Kammeraad-Campbell, Managing Editor
Damon Simmons, Art Director

1430 **Journal of Obesity and Weight-loss Medication**
ClinMed International Library
3511 Silverside Road, Suite 105
Wilmington, DE 19810
302-208-7437
contact@clinmedjournals.org
clinmedjournals.org

Open access, peer-reviewed journal that publishes information on basic to advanced research in obesity management and weight-loss medications.
Timothy Koch, Editor-in-Chief

1431 Official Journal of NAASO
NAASO
8757 Georgia Avenue
Silver Spring, MD 20910
301-563-6526
Fax: 301-563-6595
www.obesity.org

Promotes research, education and advocacy to better understand, prevent and treat obesity and improve the lives of those affected.
Barbara E. Corkey, Editor-In-Chief
Deborah Moskowitz, Managing Editor

1432 Progress Notes
Medical University of South Carolina
67 President Street
Charleston, SC 29425
843-792-2273
800-922-5250
Fax: 843-792-5432
www.muschealth.com/weight

Designed to inform the medical community developments at the Medical University of South Carolina and as a continuing medical education resource for practicing physicians and faculty.
Susan Kammeraad-Campbell, Managing Editor
Lynne Barber Associate Editor, Alex Sargent, Associate Editor

Web Sites

1433 Boston Obesity Nutrition Research Center (BONRC)
www.bmc.org
Provides resources and support for studies in the area of obesity and nutrition. Comprised of four research cores located within the Boston area. In the areas of adipocytes, epidemiology and statistics, body composition, energy expenditure and genetic analyses, and transgenic animal models.

1434 Center for Human Nutrition
www.uchsc.edu/nutrition
A interdisciplinary team encompassing basic and clinical research, post-graduate training and career development of nutrition professionals, and commuity outreach. The research conducted at the CHN focuses on obesity prevention and treatment, nutrient metabolism, and micronutrient status in children. Activities conducted aim to improve the quallity of life by promoting physical activity and nutritional awareness.

1435 Clinical Nutrition Research Unit (CNRU)
depts.washington.edu/uwnorc
Promotes and enhances the interdisciplinary nutrition research and education at the Univeristy of Washington. By providing a number of Core Facilities, the CNRU attempts to integrate and co-ordinate the abundant ongoing activities with the goals of fostering new interdisciplinary research collaborations, stimulating new research activities, improving nutrition education at multiple levels, and facilitating the nutritional management of patients.

1436 Healing Well
www.healingwell.com
An online health resource guide to medical news, chat, information and articles, newsgroups and message boards, books, disease-related web sites, medical directories, and more for patients, friends, and family coping with disabling diseases, disorders, or chronic illnesses.

1437 Health Central
www.healthcentral.com
Find clearly explained, medically accurate information regarding conditions, including an overview, symptoms, causes, diagnostic procedures and treatment options. On this site it is possible to ask questions and get information from a neurologist and connect to people who have similar health interests.

1438 Health Finder
www.health.gov
Searchable, carefully developed web site offering information on over 1000 topics. Developed by the US Department of Health and Human Services, thesite can be used in both English and Spanish.

1439 Medical News Today
www.medicalnewstody.com
Offers in-depth health information and the latest news in medical research on a wide variety of medical conditions.

1440 MedicineNet
www.medicinenet.com
An online resource for consumers providing easy-to-read, authoritative medical and health information.

1441 MedlinePlus
www.medlineplus.gov
Information regarding a broad range of health,and mental health conditions topics include: Latest news, overview of anatomy and physiology, clinical trials, diagnoses and symptoms, treatment, genetics, plus lots of links to other sites. A service provided by the National Library of Medicine, part of the National Institutes of Health (NIH).

1442 Medscape
www.medscape.com
Medscape offers specialists, primary care physicians, and other health professionals the Web's most robust and integrated medical information and educational tools.

1443 New York Obesity/Nutrition Research Center (ONRC)
www.niddk.nih.gov
Funded by the National Institute of Diabetes and Digestive and Kidney Diseases (NIDDK). A combined effort by Columbia ane Cornell Universities. Provides participating investigators of funded projects relevant to obesity research with valuable laboratory, technical, and educational services that otherwise would not be available to them, thereby improving the productivity an efficiency of their operations.

1444 North American Association for the Study of Obesity
www.obesity.org
The leading scientific society dedicated to the study of obesity. Committed to encouraging research on the causes and treatment of obesity, and to keeping the medical community and public informed of new advances.

1445 Research Chair on Obesity
obesity.chair.ulaval.ca
Ever since 1997, the Research Chair in Obesity is dedicated to support and launch initiatives leading to a better understanding of obesity through research on the mechanisms of body weight regulation, to facilitate communication between researchers, to promote the training of highly qualified personnel, to contribute to continuing education for health professionals, and to inform the public on the causes, consequences, treatments, and prevention of obesity.

1446 University of Pittsburgh Obesity/Nutrition Research Center
www.pitt.edu/~mdm2/ONRCWeb
Goal is to develop more effective interventions for the prevention and treatment of obesity. Exists to support research functions for investigators studying the broad areas of obesity and nutrition. Focuses on behavioral aspects of obesity and behavioral treatment of this disease.

1447 Vanderbilt Clinical Nutrition Research Unit (CNRU)
www.vanderbilt.edu/nutrition/index.html
A core center grant funded by the National Institute of Diabetes and Digestive and Kidney Diseases (NIDDK). Nutrition research is carried out by faculty members i most academic departments and extends from basic laboratory research to clinical and applied research. Maintains service facilities to support both basic and clinical research. Supports research cores that bring nutrition investigators together to discuss their work.

1448 WebMD
www.webmd.com
Provides credible information, supportive communities, and in-depth reference material about health subjects. A source for original and timely health information as well as material from well known content providers.

Obesity / Web Sites

1449 Weight-Control Information Network

www.win.niddk.nih.gov

The Weight-control Information Network (WIN) provides the general public, health professionals, and the media with up-to-date, science-based information on obesity, weight control, physical activity, and related nutritional issues. WIN provides tip sheets, fact sheets, and brochures for a range of audiences. Some of WIN's content is available in Spanish.

OBSESSIVE-COMPULSIVE DISORDER (OCD)

Obsessive-compulsive disorder (OCD) is one of the most common mental health issues leading to distress and disability in functions of daily life. Studies have shown that 25-50 percent of individuals with OCD also meet the diagnostic criteria for major depressive disorders. The individual has uncontrollable, recurring thoughts (obsessions) and/or behaviors (compulsions) that must be repeated over and over. Example of obsessions are fear of germs, aggressive thoughts toward self and others, having things perfectly orderly and becoming upset if things are changed, and unwanted thoughts often about sex or religion. Compulsions are repetitive behaviors as a result of obsessive thoughts. Excessive handwashing, excessive cleaning, ordering things in a certain way, repeatedly checking, for example, if the oven is off, and compulsive counting are examples of symptoms of OCD. Developing clinical depression, depression lasting at least two weeks with loss of interest in daily life, is common with OCD.

Individuals with OCD cannot control thoughts and actions, even when recognizing that the thoughts and actions are excessive. They spend at least an hour or more every day on these behaviors but get no pleasure from the action or ritual. These thoughts and behaviors can create significant problems in daily life. Often those experiencing OCD keep their rituals hidden, resulting in withdrawal from others and becoming introverted. Only when the symptoms become severe leading to depression that the individual seeks mental health support. Depression may occur before or at the same time as the onset of OCD. Depression may interfere with the treatment of OCD and many times chronic depression worsens the anxieties associated with OCD.

OCD is usually treated with medications and psychotherapy. Treatment may take an extended time and individuals may continue to experience symptoms even with treatment. An integrated approach to OCD treatment is important as individuals may also have other mental disorders including depression, anxiety, and body dysmorphic disorder (a feeling that a part of the body is abnormal). A variety of medications may be used and psychotherapy is an effective treatment. Cognitive behavior therapy (CBT) and other related therapies may be as effective as medication in some individuals. Recently Transcranial Magnetic Stimulation (TMS) has been approved as an adjunct in the treatment of OCD in adults. Research into OCD treatment is ongoing. Treatment must be personalized.

Obsessive-Compulsive Disorder (OCD) / Agencies & Associations

Agencies & Associations

1450 **American Psychiatric Association**
800 Maine Avenue SW
Washington, DC 20024
202-559-3900
apa@psych.org
www.psychiatry.org
A medical specialty society representing a growing membership of psychiatrists. Offers information for psychiatrists, medical students, patients and families.
Saul Levin, MD, MPA, FRCP-E, CEO

1451 **Anxiety and Depression Association of America**
8701 Georgia Avenue
Silver Spring, MD 20910
240-485-1001
information@adaa.org
adaa.org
An international nonprofit organization committed to the use of education and research to promote the prevention, treatment, and cure of anxiety, depressive, obsessive compulsive, and other trauma related disorders. ADAA's mission is to improve the lives of all people with anxiety and mood disorders.
Charles B. Nemeroff, MD, President
Susan K. Gurley, JD, Executive Director

1452 **Center for Family Support**
2811 Zulette Avenue
Bronx, NY 10461
718-518-1500
svernikoff@cfsny.org
www.cfsny.org
The Center for Family Support offers assistance to individuals with developmental and related disabilities, as well as their families, and provides support services and programs that are designed to accommodate individual needs. Offers services throughout New York City, Westchester County, Long Island, and New Jersey.
Steven Vernikoff, Executive Director
Barbara Greenwald, Chief Operating Officer

1453 **Center for Mental Health Services (CMHS)**
Substance Abuse and Mental Health Services Adminis
5600 Fishers Lane
Rockville, MD 20857
240-276-1310
samhsa.gov/about-us/who-we-are/offices-c
Promotes the treatment of mental illness and emotional disorders by increasing accessibility to mental health programs; supporting outreach, treatment, rehabilitation, and support programs and networks; and encouraging the use of scientifically-based information when treating mental disorders. CMHS provides information about mental health via a toll-free number and numerous publications. Developed for users of mental health services and their families, the general public, policy makers, provider
Anita Everett, MD, DFAPA, Director

1454 **Children's and Adult Center for OCD and Anxiety**
3138 Butler Pike
Plymouth Meeting, PA 19462
childrenscenterocdandanxiety.com
A center comprising five private practice psychologists delivering treatment and therapy to children and adults with OCD, Separation Anxiety, and other mental health disorders. They also offer parent workshops on skills and strategies to help their child cope with anxiety.
Tamar Chansky, PhD, Founder

1455 **Goodwill's Community Employment Services**
Goodwill Industries-Suncoast, Inc.
10596 Gandy Blvd.
St. Petersburg, FL 33702
727-523-1512
888-279-1988
TDD: 727-579-1068
goodwill-suncoast.org
The St. Petersburg headquarters serves ten counties in the state of Florida. Their mission is to help people with disabilities gain employment through training programs, employment services, and affordable housing.
Sandra Young, Chair
Louise Lopez, Sr. Vice Chair

1456 **Help is Here**
North Dakota Behavioral Health Division
600 E Boulevard Avenue
Bismarck, ND 58501
701-328-2310
800-472-2622
dhsbhd@nd.gov
www.helpishere.nd.gov
Promotes the support and treatment of mental illness and emotional disorders. Offers mental health services, addiction servces, and recovery centers.

1457 **Institute for Contemporary Psychotherapy**
33 W 60th St.
New York, NY 10023
212-333-3444
Fax: 212-333-5444
icpnyc.org
The Institute for Contemporary Psychotherapy is a New York City-based mental health treatment and training facility. Consisting of a group of 150 licensed psychotherapists, the Institute focuses on educating the public about the issues surrounding mental health, providing post-graduate training for therapists, and offering therapy at moderate costs.
Ron Taffel, PhD, Chair
Andrea Green-Lewis, LCSW-R, Director of Operations

1458 **International OCD Foundation**
P.O.Box 961029
Boston, MA 02196
617-973-5801
info@ocfoundation.org
ocfoundation.org
An international not-for-profit organization made up of people with Obsessive Compulsive Disorder and related disorders, as well as their families, friends, professionals and others.
Matthew Antonelli, Interim Executive Director
Stephanie Cogen, MPH, MSW, Program Director

1459 **Mental Health America**
500 Montgomery Street
Alexandria, VA 22314
703-684-7722
800-969-6642
mhanational.org
Mental Health America is a community-based nonprofit organization committed to enabling the mental wellness of all Americans. MHA advocates for greater access to quality health services and seeks to educate individuals on identifying symptoms, as well as intervention and prevention.
Schroeder Stribling, President & CEO
Sachin Doshi, Sr. Dir., Finance & Operations

1460 **National Alliance on Mental Illness**
4301 Wilson Boulevard
Arlington, VA 22203
703-524-7600
800-950-6264
info@nami.org
nami.org
NAMI is an organization dedicated to raising awareness on mental health and providing support and education for Americans affected by mental illness. NAMI advocates for access to services and treatment and fosters an environment of awareness and understanding for those concerned with mental health.
Shirley J. Holloway, President
Joyce A. Campbell, First Vice President

1461 **National Association Of Parents With Children in Special Education**
3642 East Sunnydale Drive
Chandler Heights, AZ 85142
800-754-4421
contact@napcse.org
napcse.org
The NAPCSE is dedicated to ensuring quality education for all children and adolescents with special needs. NAPCSE provides resources, support, and assistance to parents with children in special education.
Dr. George Giuliani, President

1462 **National Association for the Dually Diagnosed (NADD)**
321 Wall Street
Kingston, NY 12401
845-331-4336
info@thenadd.org
thenadd.org
NADD is a nonprofit organization designed to increase awareness of, and provide services for, individuals with developmental disabilities and mental illness. NADD emphasizes the importance of quality mental healthcare for people with mental health needs and offers conferences, information resources, educational programs, and training materials to professionals, parents, and organizations.
Jeanne M. Farr, MA, Chief Executive Officer
Bruce Davis, President

1463 **National Council for Behavioral Health**
1400 K Street NW
Washington, DC 20005
communications@thenationalcouncil.org
thenationalcouncil.org

Obsessive-Compulsive Disorder (OCD) / Print Resources

The National Council for Behavioral Health serves to unify America's behavioral health organizations. The council is dedicated to ensuring that quality mental health and addictions care is readily accessible to all Americans.
Tim Swinfard, Chair
Charles Ingoglia, President and CEO

1464 **National Institute of Mental Health**
6001 Executive Boulevard 866-615-6464
Bethesda, MD 20892 nimhinfo@nih.gov
nimh.nih.gov
The National Institute of Mental Health conducts clinical research on mental disorders and seeks to expand knowledge on mental health treatments.
Joshua Gordon, MD, PhD, Director

1465 **Sutcliffe Clinic**
851 Fremont Avenue 650-941-1698
Los Altos, CA 94024 info@sutcliffedbp.com
www.sutcliffeclinic.com
Sutcliffe Developmental & Behavioral Pediatrics is an organization that specializes in the treatment of ADHD, autism spectrum disorder, anxiety disorders, conduct disorders, learning disabilities, and more. Sutcliffe works with community services, school districs, and primary physicians, and provides family counseling.
Trenna Sutcliffe, MD, MS, Medical Director

1466 **Territorial Apprehensiveness (TERRAP) Anxiety & Stress Program**
755 Park Avenue 631-549-8867
Huntington, NY 11743 info@anxietyandpanic.com
anxietyandpanic.com
Helps to treat anxiety and stress disorders through Territorial Apprehensiveness Programs, developed by Dr. Arthur Hardy in the 1960s. The program systematically addresses the behavioral and thought processes of those suffering from stress and anxiety.
Julian Herskowitz, PhD, Director

1467 **United Brain Association**
202-768-8000
info@unitedbrainassociation.org
unitedbrainassociation.org
Non-profit organization that works to find cures through research for over 600 brain and mental health related issues, and disorders.
J.A. Boulton, Founder
Jay Matey, VP & Treasurer

Foundations

1468 **Brain & Behavior Research Foundation**
747 Third Avenue 646-681-4888
New York, NY 10017 800-829-8289
info@bbrfoundation.org
www.bbrfoundation.org
The Brain and Behavior Research Foundation awards grants aimed at advancing scientific understandings of mental health treatments and mental disorders such as depression and schizophrenia. The Brain and Behavior Research Foundation's mission is to eliminate the suffering caused by mental illness.
Donald M. Boardman, Treasurer
Jeffrey Borenstein, MD, President and CEO

1469 **International OCD Foundation, Inc.**
P.O. Box 961029 617-973-5801
Boston, MA 02196 info@iocdf.org
iocdf.org
An organization for people with obsessive-compulsive disorder, as well as their families and friends. The Foundation aims to educate the public and professional communities about OCD and related disorders, work towards achieving increased accessibility to effective treatment, and support research into the causes and treatment methods of OCD.
Susan Boaz, President
David Calusdian, Vice President

Libraries & Resource Centers

1470 **Family-to-Family: National Alliance on Mental Illness**
4301 Wilson Boulevard 703-524-7600
Arlington, VA 22203 888-999-6264
info@nami.org
nami.org
The NAMI Family-to-Family Education Program is a free, 8 session course for family caregivers of individuals with severe mental illnesses. The course is taught by trained family members, all instruction and course materials are free to class participants, and over 300,000 family members have graduated from this national program.

Research Centers

1471 **UAMS Psychiatric Research Institute**
4224 Shuffield Drive 501-526-8100
Little Rock, AR 72205 kramerteresal@uams.edu
www.psychiatry.uams.edu
Combining research, education and clinical services into one facility, PRI offers inpatient and outpatient services, with 40 psychiatric beds, therapy options, and specialized treatment for specific disorders, including: addictive eating, anxiety, deppressive and post-traumatic stress disorders. Research focuses on evidence-based care takes into consideration the education of future medical personnel while relying on research scientists to provide innovative forms of treatment.
Dan Rahn, MD, Chancellor

Support Groups & Hotlines

1472 **Obsessive-Compulsive Anonymous**
PO Box 215 516-739-0662
New Hyde Park, NY 11040 west24th@aol.com
obsessivecompulsiveanonymous.com
Is a fellowship of people who share their Experience, Strength, and Hope with each other that they may solve their common problem and help others to recover from OCD.

1473 **Support4Hope**
PO Box 184 Admin@Support4hope.com
Deer Lodge, TN 37726 www.support4hope.com
Support4Hope is dedicated to support of various mental health issues such as Bipolar Disorder, Depression, Anxiety Disorders, Schizophrenia, Post Traumatic Stress Disorder (PTSD) and the problems that arise from them along with other problems such as Domestic Abuse.

Print Resources

1474 **American Journal of Psychiatry**
American Psychiatric Association Publishing
800 Maine Avenue SW, Suite 900 202-459-9722
Washington, DC 20024 800-368-5777
Fax: 202-403-3094
psychiatryonline@psych.org
ajp.psychiatryonline.org
Official journal of the American Psychiatric Association (APA).
Ned H. Kalin, MD, Editor-in-Chief

1475 **American Journal of Psychotherapy**
American Psychiatric Association Publishing
800 Maine Avenue SW, Suite 900 202-459-9722
Washington, DC 20024 800-368-5777
Fax: 202-403-3094
psychiatryonline@psych.org
ajp.psychiatryonline.org
Publishes content that aims to advance the theory, science, and clinical practice of psychotherapy.
Holly A. Swartz, MD, Editor-in-Chief

1476 **International Journal of Psychology and Psychoanalysis**
ClinMed International Library

Obsessive-Compulsive Disorder (OCD) / Web Sites

3511 Silverside Road, Suite 105
Wilmington, DE 19810
302-208-7437
contact@clinmedjournals.org
clinmedjournals.org

Open access, peer-reviewed journal focused on cognition, emotions, brain functioning, interpersonal relationships, and the unconscious mind.

Joaquim J.F. Soares, Editor-in-Chief

1477 Journal of Psychiatry, Depression & Anxiety
Herald Scholarly Open Access
2561 Cornelia Road, Suite 205
Herndon, VA 20171
202-499-9679
Fax: 202-217-4195
contact@heraldopenaccess.us
www.heraldopenaccess.us

Online, international, open access, peer-reviewed journal focused primarily on depression and anxiety, but also on other related areas of psychiatry as well.

Sam Vaknin, Editor-in-Chief

Web Sites

1478 A Guide To Psychlogy & Its Practice
www.guidetopsychology.com
Free information on various types of psychology.

1479 Center For Mental Health Services Knowledge
www.mentalhealth.Samhsa.Gov
Information about resources, technical assistance, research, training, networks and other federal clearinghouses.

1480 CyberPsych
www.cyberpsych.org
Presents information about psychoanalysis, psychotherapy and special topics such as anxiety disorders, the problematic use of alcohol, homophobia, and the traumatic effects of racism. Explains in detail what anxiety it is how it is treated and the symptoms associated with anxiety.

1481 Guidelines For Families Coping With OCD
www.ocdhope.com/gdlines.html

1482 Healing Well
www.healingwell.com
An online health resource guide to medical news, chat, information and articles, newsgroups and message boards, books, disease-related web sites, medical directories, and more for patients, friends, and family coping with disabling diseases, disorders, or chronic illnesses.

1483 Health Central
www.healthcentral.com
Find clearly explained, medically accurate information regarding conditions, including an overview, symptoms, causes, diagnostic procedures and treatment options. On this site it is possible to ask questions and get information from a neurologist and connect to people who have similar health interests.

1484 Health Finder
www.health.gov
Searchable, carefully developed web site offering information on over 1000 topics. Developed by the US Department of Health and Human Services, thesite can be used in both English and Spanish.

1485 Internet Mental Health
www.mentalhealth.com
Offers online psychiatric diagnosis in the hope of reaching the two-thirds of individuals with mental illness who do not seek treatment.

1486 Mayo Clinic
www.mayoclinic.com
Provides information on obsessive-compulsive disorder and anxiety.

1487 Medical News Today
www.medicalnewstody.com
Offers in-depth health information and the latest news in medical research on a wide variety of medical conditions.

1488 MedicineNet
www.medicinenet.com
An online resource for consumers providing easy-to-read, authoritative medical and health information.

1489 MedlinePlus
www.medlineplus.gov
Information regarding a broad range of health,and mental health conditions topics include: Latest news, overview of anatomy and physiology, clinical trials, diagnoses and symptoms, treatment, genetics, plus lots of links to other sites. A service provided by the National Library of Medicine, part of the National Institutes of Health (NIH).

1490 Medscape
www.medscape.com
Medscape offers specialists, primary care physicians, and other health professionals the Web's most robust and integrated medical information and educational tools.

1491 National Alliance On Mental Illness
www.nami.org
From its inception in 1979, NAMI has been dedicated to improving the lives of individuals and families affected by mental illness.

1492 National Association For The Dually Diagno Diagnosed (NADD)
www.thenadd.org
An association for persons with developmental disabilities and mental health needs.

1493 National Institute Of Health
www.nimh.nih.gov/anxiety/anxiety/ocd
Information on anxiety disorders and OCD.

1494 Obsessive-Compulsive Disorder
www.nimh.nih.gov/publicat/ocdmenu.cfm
Introductory handout with treatment recommendations.

1495 Obsessive-Compulsive Foundation
Obsessive-Compulsive Foundation
An international not-for-profit organization composed of people with obsessive compulsive disorder and related disorders, their families, friends, professionals and other concerned individuals.

1496 Verywell Mind
www.verywellmind.com
Provides up-to-date information on mental health topics. mission is to prioritize mental health and promote balance for day to day living. offers over 5,500 online articles that are researched based, and reviwed by medical professionals.

Kristen Altmeyer, MBA, VP & General Manager
Nick Ingalls, MA, Associate Editorial Director

1497 WebMD
www.webmd.com
Provides credible information, supportive communities, and in-depth reference material about health subjects. A source for original and timely health information as well as material from well known content providers.

OSTEOPOROSIS

Osteoporosis is a major public health problem affecting 1 in 3 women and 1 in 5 men over the age of 50. Individuals with osteoporosis are very likely to have a broken bone due to the disease at some point. It is estimated that over 200 million women worldwide have osteoporosis. The condition is often silent until a fracture occurs. Bone density measurements may indicate osteopenia, a precursor to osteoporosis. Bones lose strength over time with bone mass not increasing after the age of 30. Bones become porous and fragile and the risk of painful, fragility fractures increase. Twenty-five percent of older patients who sustain a hip fracture die within six months of the fracture. One-half of the survivors of hip fracture need some help with their daily living activities, and as many as a quarter of these patients need care in a nursing home. Individuals with hip fracture experience a loss of independence with 40 percent unable to walk, almost 60 percent needing walking assistance a year post fracture, and 80 percent face some level of restriction such as driving and grocery shopping.

Risk factors for osteoporosis may include depression and mental health issues, family history, ovaries removed before periods stopped, early menopause, insufficient calcium and/or vitamin D throughout life, smoking, insufficient exercise or extended bedrest, certain medications for arthritis and asthma, some cancer drugs, and a small body frame. The emotional impacts of osteoporosis are significant. The disease reduces overall quality of life, often leading to depression and isolation as individuals are unable to maintain the activities they previously enjoyed. This long-term loss of independence and mobility causes physical, psychological, and financial strain on the individual, their relatives, and friends. Osteoporosis is like other chronic diseases, often causing depression, anxiety, and feelings of hopelessness.

Prevention of osteoporosis is possible by leading a bone-healthy lifestyle throughout life. The highest peak bone mass occurs in childhood and the more bone mass as the individual enters adulthood, the less likely fractures will occur. Around the age of 50 with the decline in estrogen at menopause, bone loss occurs rapidly. It is important to eat a healthy diet with calcium and protein, getting enough vitamin D through 15 minutes of sun exposure daily without sunscreen, and eating oily fish, eggs, and fortified foods, maintaining a healthy weight (not being too thin), avoiding smoking and drinking. Weight-bearing exercise as well as exercises to strengthen balance and muscle strength are important. Treatment options include anti-resorptive agents to reduce bone destruction and anabolic agents to stimulate bone formation. Treatments may decrease the risk of hip fracture by up to 40 percent, vertebral fractures by up to 70 percent and in some cases, reduce the risk for non-vertebral fractures up to 20 percent.

Preventing or managing osteoporosis requires a medical team to manage the disease and its side effects. Should depression occur, mental health professionals should join the team managing the individual's disease. Medication and talk therapy, including individual and group therapy, may be needed.

Osteoporosis / Agencies & Associations

Agencies & Associations

1498 **American Association of Clinical Endocrinologists**
Fax: 240-547-0026
www.aace.com
A professional community of physicians specializing in endocrinology, diabetes, and metabolism. Referrals and patient information available.
S. Sethu K. Reddy, MD, MBA, FRCPC, President
Scott D. Isaacs, MD, FACP, FACE, Treasurer

1499 **American Chronic Pain Association**
11936 W. 119th Street   913-991-4740
Overland Park, KS 66213   www.acpanow.com
The ACPA facilitates peer support and education for individuals with chronic pain in its many forms, in order to increase quality of life. Also raises awareness among the healthcare community, and with policy makers.
Penney Cowan, Founder
Trupti Gokani, MD, President

1500 **American Physical Therapy Association**
3030 Potomac Avenue   703-684-2782
Alexandria, VA 22305   800-999-2782
                             www.apta.org
The American Physical Therapy Association (APTA) is an individual membership professional organization representing more than 100,000 member physical therapists (PTs), physical therapist assistants (PTAs), and students of physical therapy.
Roger Herr, PT, MPA, President
Susan Appling, PT, DPT, PhD, Vice President

1501 **National Association of Chronic Disease Directors**
325 Swanton Way   info@chronicdisease.org
Decatur, GA 30030   www.chronicdisease.org
Non-profit public health organization committed to serving the chronic disease program directors of each state and jurisdiction in the United States.
John W. Robitscher, CEO
Tamika Smith, Chief Operations Officer

1502 **Nurse Practitioners in Women's Health**
PO Box 15837   202-543-9693
Washington, DC 20003   info@npwh.org
                             www.npwh.org
Ensures the delivery and accessibility of primary and specialty healthcare to women of all ages by women's health and women's health focused nurse practitioners.
Shawana Moore, DNP, MSN, CRNP, Chair
Allyssa Harris, RN, PhD, WHNP-BC, Secretary

1503 **Osteoporosis Canada**
201 250 Ferrand Dr.   416-696-2663
Toronto, Ontario, M3C   800-463-6842
                             Fax: 416-696-2673
                             www.osteoporosis.ca
National organization serving people who have, or are at risk for osteoporosis.
Famida Jiwa, President & CEO
Laurie Georges, Director, Finance & HR

1504 **Society For Post-Acute and Long-Term Care Medicine**
9891 Broken Land Parkway   410-740-9743
Columbia, MD 21046   800-876-2632
                             Fax: 410-740-4572
                             info@paltc.org
                             www.paltc.org
Provides education, advocacy, information and professional development to promote the delivery of standardized post-acute and long-term care medicine.
Milta Little, DO, CMD, President
Rajeev Kumar, MD, FACP, CMD, Vice President

Foundations

1505 **Bone Health & Osteoporosis Foundation**
251 18th Street S   800-231-4222
Arlington, VA 22202   info@bonehealthandosteoporosis.org
                             www.bonehealthandosteoporosis.org
The nation's leading resource for people seeking current and accurate medical information on the causes, prevention, detection and treatment of osteoporosis.
Claire Gill, CEO
Debra Erikson, Chief Administrative Officer

Libraries & Resource Centers

1506 **NIH Osteoporosis and Related Bone Diseases - National Resource Center**
2 AMS Circle   202-223-0344
Bethesda, MD 20892   800-624-2663
                             Fax: 202-293-2356
                             TTY: 202-466-4315
                             www.osteo.org
Provides patients, health professionals and the public with an important link to resources and information on osteoporosis, Paget's disease of bone, osteogenesis imperfecta, and other metabolic bone diseases. The National Resource Center's mission is to expand awareness and enhance knowledge and understanding of the prevention, early detection, and treatment of these diseases.

Research Centers

1507 **Medical College of Pennsylvania Center for the Mature Woman**
3300 Henry Avenue   215-842-6000
Philadelphia, PA 19129
our purpose is to provide consumers information to help them get high quality services and products at the best possible prices.
Jon Schneider, MD, Director

1508 **Osteoporosis Center Memorial Hospital/Advanced Medical Diagn**
Memorial Hospital/Advanced Medical Diagnostic
1700 Coffee Road   209-526-4500
Modesto, CA 95355   www.memorialmedicalcenter.org
Memorial Medical Center is part of Memorial Hospitals Association a not-for-profit organization that exists to maintain and improve the health status of citizens in the greater Stanislaus County.
David Benn, Director
Bev Finley, Director

1509 **Regional Bone Center Helen Hayes Hospital**
Helen Hayes Hospital
51-55 Route 9W   845-786-4000
W Haverstraw, NY 10993   1 8-8 7- 734
                             Fax: 845-947-3097
                             TTY: 845-947-3187
                             info@helenhayeshospital.org
                             www.helenhayeshospital.org
The mission of the Regional Bone conduct a broad-based research program focused on the elucidation of cellular mechanisms underlying metabolic bone disease and the development of new treatments for bone disease.
David W Dempster PhD, Director
Adrienne Tewksbury, Grants Administrator

1510 **University of Connecticut Osteoporosis Center**
263 Farmington Avenue   860-679-2000
Farmington, CT 06030   800-535-6232
                             Fax: 860-679-1258
                             www.uchc.edu
Jay R Lieberman, Director

Support Groups & Hotlines

1511 **Bone Health & Osteoporosis Foundation**
251 18th Street S   800-231-4222
Arlington, VA 22202   info@bonehealthandosteoporosis.org
                             www.bonehealthandosteoporosis.org
Dedicated to reducing the widespread prevalence of osteoporosis through programs of research, education and advocacy. Provides referrals to existing support groups, as well as free resources, training and materials to assist people to start groups.
Elizabeth Thompson, CEO
Susan Greenspan, MD, President

1512 **National Health Information Center**
Office of Disease Prevention & Health Promotion
1101 Wootton Pkwy
Rockville, MD 20852
Fax: 240-453-8281
odphpinfo@hhs.gov
www.health.gov/nhic
Supports public health education by maintaining a calendar of National Health Observances; helps connect consumers and health professionals to organizations that can best answer questions and provide up-to-date contact information from reliable sources; updates on a yearly basis toll-free numbers for health information, Federal health clearinghouses and info centers.
Don Wright, MD, MPH, Director

Web Sites

1513 **Bone Health & Osteoporosis Foundation**
www.bonehealthandosteoporosis.org
The National Osteoporosis Foundation is dedicated to preventing osteoporosis, promoting strong bones, and reducing human suffering through education, advocacy and research.
Claire Gill, CEO
Lindsey West, MPH, Chief Program Officer

1514 **Healing Well**
www.healingwell.com
An online health resource guide to medical news, chat, information and articles, newsgroups and message boards, books, disease-related web sites, medical directories, and more for patients, friends, and family coping with disabling diseases, disorders, or chronic illnesses.

1515 **Health Central**
www.healthcentral.com
Find clearly explained, medically accurate information regarding conditions, including an overview, symptoms, causes, diagnostic procedures and treatment options. On this site it is possible to ask questions and get information from a neurologist and connect to people who have similar health interests.

1516 **Health Finder**
www.health.gov
Searchable, carefully developed web site offering information on over 1000 topics. Developed by the US Department of Health and Human Services, the site can be used in both English and Spanish.

1517 **Medical News Today**
www.medicalnewstody.com
Offers in-depth health information and the latest news in medical research on a wide variety of medical conditions.

1518 **MedicineNet**
www.medicinenet.com
An online resource for consumers providing easy-to-read, authoritative medical and health information.

1519 **MedlinePlus**
www.medlineplus.gov
Information regarding a broad range of health,and mental health conditions topics include: Latest news, overview of anatomy and physiology, clinical trials, diagnoses and symptoms, treatment, genetics, plus lots of links to other sites. A service provided by the National Library of Medicine, part of the National Institutes of Health (NIH).

1520 **Medscape**
www.medscape.com
Medscape offers specialists, primary care physicians, and other health professionals the Web's most robust and integrated medical information and educational tools.

1521 **NIH Osteoporosis and Related Bone Disease**
www.bones.nih.gov
Provides patients, health professionals, and the public with an important link to resources and information on metabolic bone diseases. The center is dedicated to increasing the awareness, knowledge, and understanding of physicians, health professionals, patients, underserved and at-risk populations, and the general public about the prevention, early detection, and treatment of osteoporosis and related bone diseases.

1522 **WebMD**
www.webmd.com
Provides credible information, supportive communities, and in-depth reference material about health subjects. A source for original and timely health information as well as material from well known content providers.

SCHIZOPHRENIA SPECTRUM & OTHER PSYCHOTIC DISORDERS

Individuals are generally diagnosed with schizophrenia between the ages of 16 and 30, after the first episode of psychosis. Schizophrenia is characterized by at least two or more of the following symptoms: delusions, hallucinations, disorganized speech and loss of train of thought, grossly disorganized or catatonic (unable to move) behavior and negative symptoms such as flat affect, loss of motivation and withdrawal from social interactions. Individuals are said to be on the schizophrenia spectrum if they experience delusions, beliefs that do not align with reality, and hallucinations—seeing and hearing things or people that are not there for six months or more. Depressive symptoms are frequently seen in individuals with schizophrenia, and may be referred to as schizoaffective disorder, a combination of schizophrenia symptoms and mood disorder symptoms such as depression or mania. Schizophrenia and depression are commonly seen together, with feelings of anxiety and low mood present.

Approximately 10,000 people around the world have schizophrenia with almost 30 percent of them also being diagnosed with depression. Schizoaffective disorder, depressed type; depression with features of psychosis, and schizophrenia with episodes of depression are determined by how symptoms occur.

Often periods of psychosis, periods when the brain cannot tell what is real versus what is not, are experienced before a diagnosis of schizophrenia is made. Psychosis is the most severe mental disorder, in which the individual loses contact with reality and suffers from such symptoms as delusions and hallucinations. Psychosis is a symptom not an illness. Approximately 20 percent of individuals diagnosed with major depression also have psychotic symptoms. When depression and psychosis occur together, it may be called depressive psychosis, delusional depression, psychotic depression, or major depressive disorder with or without mood-congruent psychotic features. Urgent referral to a mental health professional is recommended at the first sign of psychosis.

Determining diagnosis and treatment options requires a team of medical and mental health professionals. Treatment involves managing symptoms including psychoses in schizophrenia and mood in major depressive disorder. Antipsychotics, antidepressants, and mood stabilizers may treat schizoaffective disorders. Psychotherapy, including cognitive behavioral therapy (CBT) and electroconvulsive therapy (ECT) may be used.

It is common to have schizophrenia and major depressive disorder (MDD), commonly referred to as schizoaffective disorder. Symptoms will determine diagnosis and treatment by the care team.

Schizophrenia Spectrum & Other Psychotic Disorders / Agencies & Associations

Agencies & Associations

1523 American Psychiatric Association
800 Maine Avenue SW
Washington, DC 20024
202-559-3900
apa@psych.org
www.psychiatry.org
A medical specialty society representing a growing membership of psychiatrists. Offers information for psychiatrists, medical students, patients and families.
Saul Levin, MD, MPA, FRCP-E, CEO

1524 Brain & Behavior Research Foundation
747 Third Avenue
New York, NY 10017
646-681-4888
800-829-8289
info@bbrfoundation.org
www.bbrfoundation.org
The Brain and Behavior Research Foundation awards grants aimed at advancing scientific understandings of mental health treatments and mental disorders such as depression and schizophrenia. The Brain and Behavior Research Foundation's mission is to eliminate the suffering caused by mental illness.
Donald M. Boardman, Treasurer
Jeffrey Borenstein, MD, President and CEO

1525 Center for Family Support
2811 Zulette Avenue
Bronx, NY 10461
718-518-1500
svernikoff@cfsny.org
www.cfsny.org
The Center for Family Support offers assistance to individuals with developmental and related disabilities, as well as their families, and provides support services and programs that are designed to accommodate individual needs. Offers services throughout New York City, Westchester County, Long Island, and New Jersey.
Steven Vernikoff, Executive Director
Barbara Greenwald, Chief Operating Officer

1526 Center for Mental Health Services (CMHS)
Substance Abuse and Mental Health Services Adminis
5600 Fishers Lane
Rockville, MD 20857
240-276-1310
samhsa.gov/about-us/who-we-are/offices-c
Promotes the treatment of mental illness and emotional disorders by increasing accessibility to mental health programs; supporting outreach, treatment, rehabilitation, and support programs and networks; and encouraging the use of scientifically-based information when treating mental disorders. CMHS provides information about mental health via a toll-free number and numerous publications. Developed for users of mental health services and their families, the general public, policy makers, provider
Anita Everett, MD, DFAPA, Director

1527 Goodwill's Community Employment Services
Goodwill Industries-Suncoast, Inc.
10596 Gandy Blvd.
St. Petersburg, FL 33702
727-523-1512
888-279-1988
TDD: 727-579-1068
goodwill-suncoast.org
The St. Petersburg headquarters serves ten counties in the state of Florida. Their mission is to help people with disabilities gain employment through training programs, employment services, and affordable housing.
Sandra Young, Chair
Louise Lopez, Sr. Vice Chair

1528 Institute for Contemporary Psychotherapy
33 W 60th St.
New York, NY 10023
212-333-3444
Fax: 212-333-5444
icpnyc.org
The Institute for Contemporary Psychotherapy is a New York City-based mental health treatment and training facility. Consisting of a group of 150 licensed psychotherapists, the Institute focuses on educating the public about the issues surrounding mental health, providing post-graduate training for therapists, and offering therapy at moderate costs.
Ron Taffel, PhD, Chair
Andrea Green-Lewis, LCSW-R, Director of Operations

1529 International Society for the Study of Trauma and Dissociation
4201 Wilson Blvd
Arlington, VA 22203
844-994-7783
Fax: 888-966-0310
info@isst-d.org
www.isst-d.org
The International Society for the Study of Trauma and Dissociation is a non-profit, professional association organized to develop clinically effective and empirically based resources and responses to trauma and dissociation.

1530 Mental Health America
500 Montgomery Street
Alexandria, VA 22314
703-684-7722
800-969-6642
mhanational.org
Mental Health America is a community-based nonprofit organization committed to enabling the mental wellness of all Americans. MHA advocates for greater access to quality health services and seeks to educate individuals on identifying symptoms, as well as intervention and prevention.
Schroeder Stribling, President & CEO
Sachin Doshi, Sr. Dir., Finance & Operations

1531 National Alliance on Mental Illness
4301 Wilson Boulevard
Arlington, VA 22203
703-524-7600
800-950-6264
info@nami.org
nami.org
NAMI is an organization dedicated to raising awareness on mental health and providing support and education for Americans affected by mental illness. NAMI advocates for access to services and treatment and fosters an environment of awareness and understanding for those concerned with mental health.
Shirley J. Holloway, President
Joyce A. Campbell, First Vice President

1532 National Association for the Dually Diagnosed (NADD)
321 Wall Street
Kingston, NY 12401
845-331-4336
info@thenadd.org
thenadd.org
NADD is a nonprofit organization designed to increase awareness of, and provide services for, individuals with developmental disabilities and mental illness. NADD emphasizes the importance of quality mental healthcare for people with mental health needs and offers conferences, information resources, educational programs, and training materials to professionals, parents, and organizations.
Jeanne M. Farr, MA, Chief Executive Officer
Bruce Davis, President

1533 National Institute of Mental Health
6001 Executive Boulevard
Bethesda, MD 20892
866-615-6464
nimhinfo@nih.gov
nimh.nih.gov
The National Institute of Mental Health conducts clinical research on mental disorders and seeks to expand knowledge on mental health treatments.
Joshua Gordon, MD, PhD, Director

1534 National Mental Health Consumers' Self-Help Clearinghouse
selfhelpclearinghouse@gmail.com
mhselfhelp.org
The Clearinghouse is a peer-run national technical assistance center focused on achieving respect and equality of opportunity for those with mental illnesses. The Clearinghouse helps with the growth of the mental health consumer movement by evaluating mental health services, advocating for mental health reform, and providing consumers with news, information, publications, and consultation services.
Joseph Rogers, Founder and Executive Director
Susan Rogers, Director

1535 United Brain Association
202-768-8000
info@unitedbrainassociation.org
unitedbrainassociation.org
Non-profit organization that works to find cures through research for over 600 brain and mental health related issues, and disorders.
J.A. Boulton, Founder
Jay Matey, VP & Treasurer

Schizophrenia Spectrum & Other Psychotic Disorders / Support Groups & Hotlines

Foundations

1536 **Brain & Behavior Research Foundation**
747 Third Avenue
New York, NY 10017
646-681-4888
800-829-8289
info@bbrfoundation.org
www.bbrfoundation.org
Awards funding and grants to scientists around the world in order to advance brain and behavioral science.
Geoffrey A. Simon, Chair
Donald M. Boardman, Treasurer

Libraries & Resource Centers

1537 **Family-to-Family: National Alliance on Mental Illness**
4301 Wilson Boulevard
Arlington, VA 22203
703-524-7600
888-999-6264
info@nami.org
nami.org
The NAMI Family-to-Family Education Program is a free, 12-week course for family caregivers of individuals with severe mental illnesses. The course is taught by trained family members, all instruction and course materials are free to class participants, and over 300,000 family members have graduated from this national program.

Research Centers

1538 **Brain & Behavior Research Foundation**
747 Third Avenue
New York, NY 10017
646-681-4888
800-829-8289
info@bbrfoundation.org
www.bbrfoundation.org
Awards funding and grants to scientists around the world in order to advance brain and behavioral science.
Geoffrey A. Simon, Chair
Donald M. Boardman, Treasurer

1539 **Huxley Insititute-American Schizophrenic Association**
86-B Dorchester Drive
Lakewood, NJ 08701
www.schizohprenia.org
The ASA works to bring effective, low-cost treatment to patients woth schizophrenia and help them in a cooperative effort to cope with the disorder.
Abram Carpenter Jr, Director
Vito J Seskunas, Deputy Director for Administration

1540 **Maryland Psychiatric Research Center**
655 W. Baltimore Street
Baltimore, MD 21201
410-402-7666
Fax: 410-788-3837
www.mprc.umaryland.edu/default.asp
Providing treatment to patients with schizophrenia and related disorders educating professionals and consumers about schizophrenia and conducting basic and translational research into the manifestations causes and treatment of schizophrenia.
Robert Buchanan, MD, Interim Director
Vito J Seskunas, Deputy Director for Administration

1541 **Schizophrenia Research Branch: Division of Clinical and Treatment Research**
5600 Fisher Lane, Parklawn Building
Rockville, MD 20857
301-443-4707
Fax: 301-443-6000
Plans, supports, and conducts programs of research, research training, and resource development of schizophrenia and related disorders. Reviews and evaluates research developments in the field and recommends new program directors. Collaborates with organizations in and outside of the National Institue of Mental Health (NIMH) to stimulate work in the field through conferences and workshops.

1542 **Tennessee Neuropsychiatric Institute Middle Tennessee Mental Health Institute**
Middle Tennessee Mental Health Institute
221 Stewarts Ferry Pike
Nashville, TN 37217
615-902-7535
Michael Eber Andreassen MD, Director

1543 **UCLA Anxiety Disorders Research Center**
Department of Psychology
Los Angeles, CA 90094
310-825-9312
rose@psych.ucla.edu
anxiety.psych.ucla.edu
The purpose of The ADRC is to further our understanding of the factors that place individuals at risk for developing phobias, anxiety disorders and related conditions, and to develop more effective treatments that have long lasting effects and are cost effective.
Michelle G. Craske, Ph.D., Director
Raphael Rose, Ph.D., Associate Director

1544 **University of Iowa Mental Health Clinical Research Center**
University of Iowa Hospitals & Clinics
200 Hawkins Drive
Iowa City, IA 52242
319-356-1553
877-575-2864
Fax: 319-353-8300
www.iowa-mhcrc.psychiatry.uiowa.edu
Schizophrenia studies and other cognitive disorder research.
Nancy C

Support Groups & Hotlines

1545 **Common Ground Sanctuary**
1410 S. Telegraph
Bloomfield Hills, MI 48302
248-456-8150
800-231-1127
www.commongroundsanctuary.org
A 24-hour nonprofit agency dedicated to helping youths, adults and families in crisis. Through its crisis line and in person through various programs, Common Ground Sanctuary provides professional and compassionate service to more than 40,000 people a year, with most services provided free of charge. Mission is to provide a lifeline for individuals and families in crisis, victims of crime, persons with mental illness, people trying to cope with critical situations and runaway and homeless youth.
Tony Rothschild, President & CEO
Steve Mitchell, Board Chair

1546 **Holliswood Hospital Psychiatric Care, Services and Self-Help/Support Groups**
87-37 Palermo Street
Holliswood, NY 11423
718-776-8181
800-486-3005
Fax: 718-776-8572
HolliswoodInfo@libertymgt.com
www.holliswoodhospital.com/
The Holliswood Hospital, a 110-bed private psychiatric hospital located in a quiet residential Queens community, is a leader in providing quality, acute inpatient mental health care for adult, adolescent, geriatric and dually diagnosed patients. Holliswood Hospital treats patients with a broad range of psychiatric disorders. Additionally, specialized services are available for patients with psychiatric diagnoses compounded by chemical dependency, or a history of physical or sexual abuse.
Susan Clayton, Support Group Coordinator
Angela Hurtado, Support Group Coordinator

1547 **National Health Information Center**
Office of Disease Prevention & Health Promotion
1101 Wootton Pkwy
Rockville, MD 20852
Fax: 240-453-8281
odphpinfo@hhs.gov
www.health.gov/nhic
Supports public health education by maintaining a calendar of National Health Observances; helps connect consumers and health professionals to organizations that can best answer questions and provide up-to-date contact information from reliable sources; updates on a yearly basis toll-free numbers for health information, Federal health clearinghouses and info centers.
Don Wright, MD, MPH, Director

1548 **Support4Hope**
PO Box 184
Deer Lodge, TN 37726
Admin@Support4hope.com
www.support4hope.com
Support4Hope is dedicated to support of various mental health issues such as Bipolar Disorder, Depression, Anxiety Disorders, Schizophrenia, Post Traumatic Stress Disorder (PTSD) and the problems that arise from them along with other problems such as Domestic Abuse.

Schizophrenia Spectrum & Other Psychotic Disorders / Print Resources

Print Resources

1549 **American Journal of Psychiatry**
American Psychiatric Association Publishing
800 Maine Avenue SW, Suite 900
Washington, DC 20024
202-459-9722
800-368-5777
Fax: 202-403-3094
psychiatryonline@psych.org
ajp.psychiatryonline.org
Official journal of the American Psychiatric Association (APA).
Ned H. Kalin, MD, Editor-in-Chief

1550 **American Journal of Psychotherapy**
American Psychiatric Association Publishing
800 Maine Avenue SW, Suite 900
Washington, DC 20024
202-459-9722
800-368-5777
Fax: 202-403-3094
psychiatryonline@psych.org
ajp.psychiatryonline.org
Publishes content that aims to advance the theory, science, and clinical practice of psychotherapy.
Holly A. Swartz, MD, Editor-in-Chief

1551 **Dissociation**
ISSMP&D
5700 Old Orchard Road
Skokie, IL 60077
847-966-4322
Fax: 847-966-9418
A professional journal offering the latest information about the issues and research into multiple personalities and related disorders.

1552 **International Journal of Psychology and Psychoanalysis**
ClinMed International Library
3511 Silverside Road, Suite 105
Wilmington, DE 19810
302-208-7437
contact@clinmedjournals.org
clinmedjournals.org
Open access, peer-reviewed journal focused on cognition, emotions, brain functioning, interpersonal relationships, and the unconscious mind.
Joaquim J.F. Soares, Editor-in-Chief

1553 **Journal of Psychiatry, Depression & Anxiety**
Herald Scholarly Open Access
2561 Cornelia Road, Suite 205
Herndon, VA 20171
202-499-9679
Fax: 202-217-4195
contact@heraldsopenaccess.us
www.heraldopenaccess.us
Online, international, open access, peer-reviewed journal focused primarily on depression and anxiety, but also on other related areas of psychiatry as well.
Sam Vaknin, Editor-in-Chief

1554 **Schizophrenia Bulletin**
Superintendent of Documents/NIMH Journal
PO Box 371954
Pittsburgh, PA 15250
202-512-2250
Serves as a forum for multidisciplinary exchange of information about schizophrenia and is exclusively devoted to the exploration of this severe disorder.

1555 **Schizophrenia Research**
1600 John F Kennedy Boulevard
Philadelphia, PA 19103
212-633-3730
800-545-2522
usbkinfo@elsevier.com
elsevier.com
The journal of choice for international researchers and clinicians to share their work with the global schizophrenia research community. Publishes novel papers that really contribute to understanding the biology and treatment of schizophrenic disorders; Schizophrenia Research brings together biological, clinical and psychological research in order to stimulate the synthesis of findings from all disciplines involved in improving patient outcomes in schizophrenia.
H.A Nasrallah, Editor-in-Chief
L.E DeLisi, Editor-in-Chief

Web Sites

1556 **Brain & Behavior Research Foundation**
www.bbrfoundation.org
The Brain and Behavior Research Foundation awards grants aimed at advancing scientific understandings of mental health treatments and mental disorders such as depression and schizophrenia. The Brain and Behavior Research Foundation's mission is to eliminate the suffering caused by mental illness.
Herbert Pardes, MD, Treasurer
Jeffrey Borenstein, MD, President and CEO

1557 **CyberPsych**
www.cyberpsych.org
Presents information about psychoanalysis, psychotherapy and special topics such as anxiety disorders, the problematic use of alcohol, homophobia, and the traumatic effects of racism.

1558 **Epidemology-Genetics Program In Psychiatry**
www.hopkinsmedicine.org/epigen
Research program to help characterize the genetic, developmental and environmental componenets of bipolar disorder and schizophrenia.

1559 **Healing Well**
www.healingwell.com
An online health resource guide to medical news, chat, information and articles, newsgroups and message boards, books, disease-related web sites, medical directories, and more for patients, friends, and family coping with disabling diseases, disorders, or chronic illnesses.

1560 **Health Central**
www.healthcentral.com
Find clearly explained, medically accurate information regarding conditions, including an overview, symptoms, causes, diagnostic procedures and treatment options. On this site it is possible to ask questions and get information from a neurologist and connect to people who have similar health interests.

1561 **Health Finder**
www.health.gov
Searchable, carefully developed web site offering information on over 1000 topics. Developed by the US Department of Health and Human Services, the site can be used in both English and Spanish.

1562 **International Society for the Study of Dissociation**
www.issd.org
Association that promotes research and training in the identification of treatment of multiple personality.

1563 **Internet Mental Health**
www.mentalhealth.com
Offers online psychiatric diagnosis in the hope of reaching the two-thirds of individuals with mental illness who do not seek treatment.

1564 **Medical News Today**
www.medicalnewstody.com
Offers in-depth health information and the latest news in medical research on a wide variety of medical conditions.

1565 **MedicineNet**
www.medicinenet.com
An online resource for consumers providing easy-to-read, authoritative medical and health information.

1566 **MedlinePlus**
www.medlineplus.gov
Information regarding a broad range of health,and mental health conditions topics include: Latest news, overview of anatomy and physiology, clinical trials, diagnoses and symptoms, treatment, genetics, plus lots of links to other sites. A service provided by the National Library of Medicine, part of the National Institutes of Health (NIH).

1567 **Medscape**
www.medscape.com
Medscape offers specialists, primary care physicians, and other health professionals the Web's most robust and integrated medical information and educational tools.

1568 **National Alliance On Mental Illness**
www.naminys.org
From its inception in 1979, NAMI has been dedicated to improving the lives of individuals and families affected by mental illness.

Schizophrenia Spectrum & Other Psychotic Disorders / Web Sites

1569 National Alliance for the Mentally Ill
www.nami.org
Mental health organization dedicated to building better lives for the millions of Americans affected by mental illness.

1570 PlanetPsych
www.planetpsych.com
The online resource for mental health information.

1571 Psych Central
www.psychcentral.com
The Internet's largest and oldest independent mental health social network created and run by mental health professionals to guarantee reliable, trusted information and support communities to you.

1572 Schizophrenia
www.schizophrenia.com
A non-profit community providing in-depth information, support and education related to schizophrenia, a disorder of the brain and mind.

1573 Schizophrenia Therapy Online Resource Center
www.schizophreniatherapy.com
A website which provides effective and lasting alternatives to traditional treatment for individuals suffering with schizophrenia. Offers an effective and full continium of services ranging from psychopharmacology to individual and group psychotherapy to social rehabilitation, supported work experience, assertive community training and supported housing.

1574 Substance Abuse And Mental Health Services Administration
www.store.samhsa.gov
Resources on mental disorders as well as treatment and recovery.

1575 Verywell Mind
www.verywellmind.com
Provides up-to-date information on mental health topics. mission is to prioritize mental health and promote balance for day to day living. offers over 5,500 online articles that are researched based, and reviwed by medical professionals.
Kristen Altmeyer, MBA, VP & General Manager
Nick Ingalls, MA, Associate Editorial Director

1576 WebMD
www.webmd.com
Provides credible information, supportive communities, and in-depth reference material about health subjects. A source for original and timely health information as well as material from well known content providers.

SEXUAL DISORDERS

Sexual disorders are also referred to as sexual dysfunction, when the individual has trouble having or enjoying sex and is bothered by the situation. Sex can be important to quality of life and dealing with sexual dysfunction can be difficult physically and emotionally. These disorders are very common and, in most instances, very treatable. Common causes of sexual disorders include stress, mental health issues like depression, fear and anxiety about sex, hormone levels, certain medication and treatments, substance use and abuse, relationship problems, menopause, recent pregnancy, medical problems including cancer, diabetes, multiple sclerosis, and heart problems. Depression can both cause and be a result of sexual dysfunction. Up to half of individuals with untreated depression may experience sexual dysfunction.

Depression in women may lead to sexual disorders and are often related to pregnancy, the postpartum period, perimenopause, and the menstrual cycle as they are all closely associated to physical and hormonal changes. Sexual disorders in men may lead to depression related to lack of performance. Men may appear to be angry or aggressive rather than sad and are less likely to talk about or seek help. The primary forms of sexual disorders include hypoactive sexual desire disorder (HSDD), genital arousal disorder, orgasm disorder, erectile dysfunction, premature ejaculation, and vulvodynia, and in all a component of mental health, including depression, may be seen.

Treatment of sexual disorders is based on type, cause, and symptoms. A physical examination to determine if there are physical factors causing dysfunction is followed by a definitive plan of care including medications and other interventions and talk therapy.

Sexual Disorders / Agencies & Associations

Agencies & Associations

1577 **American Association of Sexuality Educators, Counselors And Therapists**
35 E Wacker Drive
Chicago, IL 60601
202-449-1099
info@aasect.org
www.aasect.org

(AASECT) A nonprofit professional organization for sexuality educators, cousnelors, sex therapists, physicians, social workers, and psychologists. Members of the association advance the fields of sexual therapy, counseling, and education.
Kellie Braband, Executive Director
Rosalyn Dischavio, EdD, MA, President

1578 **American Psychiatric Association**
800 Maine Avenue SW
Washington, DC 20024
202-559-3900
apa@psych.org
www.psychiatry.org

A medical specialty society representing a growing membership of psychiatrists. Offers information for psychiatrists, medical students, patients and families.
Saul Levin, MD, MPA, FRCP-E, CEO

1579 **American Sexual Health Association (ASHA)**
PO Box 13827
Research Triangle Park, NC 27709
919-361-8400
info@ashasexualhealth.org
www.ashasexualhealth.org

A nonprofit organization that aims to foster healthy sexual behaviours. ASHA's objectives are to educate individuals with scientifically based information, collaborate with other organizations, and advocate for beneficial changes in sexual health policy.
Lynn Barclay, President and CEO
Deborah Arrindell, Vice President, Health Policy

1580 **American Society for Reproductive Medicine**
1209 Montgomery Highway
Birmingham, AL 35216
205-978-5000
asrm@asrm.org
www.asrm.org

A nonprofit, multidisciplinary organization composed of urologists, obstetricians/gynecologists, embryologists, mental health professionals, nurses, reproductive endocrinologists, and other reproductive health professionals. The society aims to advance the science and practice of reproductive medicine through education, research, and advocacy.
Marcelle I. Cedars, MD, President
Michael A. Thomas, MD, President Elect

1581 **American Urological Association**
1000 Corporate Boulevard
Linthicum, MD 21090
410-689-3700
866-746-4282
aua@AUAnet.org
www.auanet.org

An association of professionals who promote high standards of urological care, including male infertility. The Association provides support for urologists through education, funding for research, and networking/information sharing opportunities.
Randall B. Meacham, MD, President
Stephen Y. Nakada, MD, President-Elect

1582 **Center for Family Support**
2811 Zulette Avenue
Bronx, NY 10461
718-518-1500
svernikoff@cfsny.org
www.cfsny.org

The Center for Family Support offers assistance to individuals with developmental and related disabilities, as well as their families, and provides support services and programs that are designed to accommodate individual needs. Offers services throughout New York City, Westchester County, Long Island, and New Jersey.
Steven Vernikoff, Executive Director
Barbara Greenwald, Chief Operating Officer

1583 **Center for Healthy Sex**
10700 Santa Monica Boulevard
Los Angeles, CA 90025
310-843-9902
info@centerforhealthysex.com
centerforhealthysex.com

A therapy center that specializes in the treatment of sexual dysfunction, sexual aversion/anorexia, sex addiction, and love addiction.
Alexandra Katehakis, Founder and Clinical Director

1584 **Center for Mental Health Services (CMHS)**
Substance Abuse and Mental Health Services Adminis
5600 Fishers Lane
Rockville, MD 20857
240-276-1310
samhsa.gov/about-us/who-we-are/offices-c

Promotes the treatment of mental illness and emotional disorders by increasing accessibility to mental health programs; supporting outreach, treatment, rehabilitation, and support programs and networks; and encouraging the use of scientifically-based information when treating mental disorders. CMHS provides information about mental health via a toll-free number and numerous publications. Developed for users of mental health services and their families, the general public, policy makers, provider
Anita Everett, MD, DFAPA, Director

1585 **Center for Women's Health**
3181 S.W. Sam Jackson Park Road
Portland, OR 97239
503-494-8311
www.ohsu.edu/womens-health

A center dedicated to providing services in many areas of women's health, including women's sexual health.
Danny Jacobs, MD, MPH, FACS, President
David B. Jacoby, MD, Executive Vice President

1586 **Institute for Contemporary Psychotherapy**
33 W 60th St.
New York, NY 10023
212-333-3444
Fax: 212-333-5444
icpnyc.org

The Institute for Contemporary Psychotherapy is a New York City-based mental health treatment and training facility. Consisting of a group of 150 licensed psychotherapists, the Institute focuses on educating the public about the issues surrounding mental health, providing post-graduate training for therapists, and offering therapy at moderate costs.
Ron Taffel, PhD, Chair
Andrea Green-Lewis, LCSW-R, Director of Operations

1587 **International Society for the Study of Women's Sexual Health (ISSWSH)**
14305 Southcross Dr.
Burnsville, MN 55306
952-683-9025
952-314-8212
info@isswsh.org
www.isswsh.org

The ISSWSH promotes communication among scholars, researchers, and practitioners about women's sexual function and sexual experience; supports high standards of ethics and professionalism in research, education, and clinical practice of women's sexuality; and provides the public with accurate information about women's sexuality and sexual health.
Tessa Benitez, Executive Director
Bobbi Hahn, Association Manager

1588 **Mental Health America**
500 Montgomery Street
Alexandria, VA 22314
703-684-7722
800-969-6642
mhanational.org

Mental Health America is a community-based nonprofit organization committed to enabling the mental wellness of all Americans. MHA advocates for greater access to quality health services and seeks to educate individuals on identifying symptoms, as well as intervention and prevention.
Schroeder Stribling, President & CEO
Sachin Doshi, Sr. Dir., Finance & Operations

1589 **National Association for the Dually Diagnosed (NADD)**
321 Wall Street
Kingston, NY 12401
845-331-4336
info@thenadd.org
thenadd.org

NADD is a nonprofit organization designed to increase awareness of, and provide services for, individuals with developmental disabilities and mental illness. NADD emphasizes the importance of quality mental healthcare for people with mental health needs and offers conferences, information resources, educational programs, and training materials to professionals, parents, and organizations.
Jeanne M. Farr, MA, Chief Executive Officer
Bruce Davis, President

1590 **National Mental Health Consumers' Self-Help Clearinghouse**
selfhelpclearinghouse@gmail.com
mhselfhelp.org

The Clearinghouse is a peer-run national technical assistance center focused on achieving respect and equality of opportunity for

those with mental illnesses. The Clearinghouse helps with the growth of the mental health consumer movement by evaluating mental health services, advocating for mental health reform, and providing consumers with news, information, publications, and consultation services.
Joseph Rogers, Founder and Executive Director
Susan Rogers, Director

1591 **Sexual Medicine Society of North America**
14305 Southcross Drive
Burnsville, MN 55306
952-683-1917
info@smsna.org
www.smsna.org
A nonprofit professional association of physicians, researchers, nurses, and assistants who are dedicated to treating human sexual function and dysfunction.
David Casalod, Executive Director
Tessa Benitez, Associate Executive Director

Foundations

1592 **Urology Care Foundation**
1000 Corporate Boulevard
Linthicum, MB 21090
410-689-3700
800-828-7866
info@UrologyCareFoundation.org
www.urologyhealth.org
Associated with the American Urological Association, the Urology Care Foundation is a nonprofit organization that partners with urological health professionals, reserchers, patients, caregivers, and families to support the treatment of urological diseases such as male erectile dysfunction.
Harris M. Nagler, MD, FACS, President
Gopal H. Badlani, MD, Secretary

Support Groups & Hotlines

1593 **Holliswood Hospital Psychiatric Care, Services and Self-Help/Support Groups**
87-37 Palermo Street
Holliswood, NY 11423
718-776-8181
800-486-3005
Fax: 718-776-8572
HolliswoodInfo@libertymgt.com
www.holliswoodhospital.com/
The Holliswood Hospital, a 110-bed private psychiatric hospital located in a quiet residential Queens community, is a leader in providing quality, acute inpatient mental health care for adult, adolescent, geriatric and dually diagnosed patients. Holliswood Hospital treats patients with a broad range of psychiatric disorders. Additionally, specialized services are available for patients with psychiatric diagnoses compounded by chemical dependency, or a history of physical or sexual abuse.
Susan Clayton, Support Group Coordinator
Angela Hurtado, Support Group Coordinator

Print Resources

1594 **American Journal of Psychiatry**
American Psychiatric Association Publishing
800 Maine Avenue SW, Suite 900
Washington, DC 20024
202-459-9722
800-368-5777
Fax: 202-403-3094
psychiatryonline@psych.org
ajp.psychiatryonline.org
Official journal of the American Psychiatric Association (APA).
Ned H. Kalin, MD, Editor-in-Chief

1595 **American Journal of Psychotherapy**
American Psychiatric Association Publishing
800 Maine Avenue SW, Suite 900
Washington, DC 20024
202-459-9722
800-368-5777
Fax: 202-403-3094
psychiatryonline@psych.org
ajp.psychiatryonline.org
Publishes content that aims to advance the theory, science, and clinical practice of psychotherapy.
Holly A. Swartz, MD, Editor-in-Chief

1596 **Journal of Sexual Medicine**
Oxford University Press
198 Madison Avenue
New York, NY 10016
academic.oup.com/jsm
An official journal of the International Society for Sexual Medicine, it publishes multidisciplinary basic science and clinical research on male, female, and couple's sexual function and dysfunction.
John P. Mulhall, MD, Editor-in-Chief

Web Sites

1597 **Healing Well**
www.healingwell.com
An online health resource guide to medical news, chat, information and articles, newsgroups and message boards, books, disease-related web sites, medical directories, and more for patients, friends, and family coping with disabling diseases, disorders, or chronic illnesses.

1598 **Health Central**
www.healthcentral.com
Find clearly explained, medically accurate information regarding conditions, including an overview, symptoms, causes, diagnostic procedures and treatment options. On this site it is possible to ask questions and get information from a neurologist and connect to people who have similar health interests.

1599 **Health Finder**
www.health.gov
Searchable, carefully developed web site offering information on over 1000 topics. Developed by the US Department of Health and Human Services, thesite can be used in both English and Spanish.

1600 **Internet Mental Health**
www.mentalhealth.com
Offers online psychiatric diagnosis in the hope of reaching the two-thirds of individuals with mental illness who do not seek treatment.

1601 **Medical News Today**
www.medicalnewstody.com
Offers in-depth health information and the latest news in medical research on a wide variety of medical conditions.

1602 **MedicineNet**
www.medicinenet.com
An online resource for consumers providing easy-to-read, authoritative medical and health information.

1603 **MedlinePlus**
www.medlineplus.gov
Information regarding a broad range of health,and mental health conditions topics include: Latest news, overview of anatomy and physiology, clinical trials, diagnoses and symptoms, treatment, genetics, plus lots of links to other sites. A service provided by the National Library of Medicine, part of the National Institutes of Health (NIH).

1604 **Medscape**
www.medscape.com
Medscape offers specialists, primary care physicians, and other health professionals the Web's most robust and integrated medical information and educational tools.

1605 **PlanetPsych.com**
www.planetpsych.com
Online resource for mental health information.

1606 **Psych Central**
www.psychcentral.com
The Internet's largest and oldest independent mental health social network created and run by mental health professionals to guarantee reliable, trusted information and support communities to you.

1607 **Sexual Disorders**
www.priory.com/sex.html
Diagnoses and treatments.

Sexual Disorders / Web Sites

1608 Shrinktank

www.shrinktank.com

Psychology-related programs, shareware and freeware.

1609 Substance Abuse And Mental Health Services Administration

www.store.samhsa.gov

Resources on mental disorders as well as treatment and recovery.

1610 Vaginismus.Com

www.vaginismus.com

An online resource for individuals who suffer from sexual pain. Vaginismus.com offers products, materials in a variety of languages, and a forum for people with Vaginismus to connect with each other.

1611 Verywell Mind

www.verywellmind.com

Provides up-to-date information on mental health topics. mission is to prioritize mental health and promote balance for day to day living. offers over 5,500 online articles that are researched based, and reviwed by medical professionals.

Kristen Altmeyer, MBA, VP & General Manager
Nick Ingalls, MA, Associate Editorial Director

1612 WebMD

www.webmd.com

Provides credible information, supportive communities, and in-depth reference material about health subjects. A source for original and timely health information as well as material from well known content providers.

SLEEP-WAKE DISORDERS

Sleep-wake disorders, also referred to as sleep disorders, are problems with the quality, timing and amount of sleep that interferes with daytime functioning and may also cause daytime distress. It is estimated that 50 million Americans have chronic sleep disorders. These disorders often occur with medical conditions and mental health conditions, especially depression, anxiety, and cognitive disorders. Sleep issues may also be an indicator of bipolar disorder. Insomnia is the most common sleep-wake disorder. Sleep apnea, parasomnias (abnormal movements, talk or experience that interrupts sleep), narcolepsy (uncontrollable daytime sleepiness) and restless leg syndrome are additional sleep-wake disorders. Sleep difficulties may be linked to both physical and emotional issues. Sleep problems can contribute to or make mental health conditions worse as sleep is a basic need critical to health. One third of adults report insomnia symptoms. The amount of sleep needed varies by age and by individual. An average of 7-9 hours per night of restful sleep is recommended. Approximately one-third of adults get less than six hours of sleep per night and less than 30 percent of high school students get 8 hours of sleep. Over a third of Americans report poor or only fair sleep quality.

Sleep is necessary for optimal brain functioning and insufficient sleep has potential consequences including fatigue and decreased energy, irritability and problems focusing. Sleep problems often coexist with depression or anxiety, and depression and anxiety can lead to sleep problems.

Sleep-wake disorders can be improved with regular sleep habits. If regular sleep does not improve sleep problems, evaluation and treatment by a physician is indicated. Sleep hygiene, or promoting healthy sleep, includes a regular sleep schedule, a calming activity such as reading before bedtime, avoiding electronics at bedtime, having a peaceful bedroom environment, getting sufficient exercise, and avoiding alcohol, caffeine, and heavy meals at night.

Prescribed sleep medications may help achieve sleep, but medications may be habit forming. Over-the-counter sleep medicines contain antihistamines, commonly used to treat allergies and are not addictive. In the aging population, antihistamines may contribute to confusion, urinary retention, and falls, and should be used cautiously. Complementary health approaches including meditation, relaxation techniques, melatonin, herbs, and dietary supplements may be used. Some may be safe and effective but others have nothing to validate effectiveness. All complementary health approaches should be discussed with the physician. Light therapy, or phototherapy, may be helpful in individuals with delayed sleep phase syndrome. Exercise is associated with improved sleep quality but discuss all exercise plans with the physician before beginning.

Healthy sleep is important to optimal functioning and may help prevent depressive symptoms. Many mental health conditions are worsened by sleep problems.

Sleep-Wake Disorders / Agencies & Associations

Agencies & Associations

1613 **American Chronic Pain Association**
11936 W. 119th Street 913-991-4740
Overland Park, KS 66213-2216 ACPA@theacpa.org
www.acpanow.com
The ACPA facilitates peer support and education for individuals with chronic pain in its many forms, in order to increase quality of life. Also raises awareness among the healthcare community, and with policy makers.
Trupti Gokani, MD, President
Kathy Sapp, Chief Executive Officer

1614 **American Sleep Apnea Association**
1414 NE 42nd St. contact@sleepapnea.org
Seattle, WA 98105 www.sleepapnea.org
Offers help and information to persons with sleep apnea and their families.
Martinique Edwards, Staff Writer
Tochukwu Ikpeze, Staff Writer

1615 **Canadian Sleep Society**
info@css-scs.ca
css-scs.ca
A national organization that advocates for sleep health through funding research, offering patient information brochures in French and English, and providing training/educational oppportunities to members.
Celyne Bastien, PhD, President
Najib Ayas, MD, MPH, Secretary/Treasurer

1616 **Mental Health America**
500 Montgomery Street 703-684-7722
Alexandria, VA 22314 800-969-6642
mhanational.org
Mental Health America is a community-based nonprofit organization committed to enabling the mental wellness of all Americans. MHA advocates for greater access to quality health services and seeks to educate individuals on identifying symptoms, as well as intervention and prevention.
Schroeder Stribling, President & CEO
Sachin Doshi, Sr. Dir., Finance & Operations

1617 **Narcolepsy Network**
3242 NE 3rd Avenue #1101 401-667-2523
Camas, WA 98607 888-292-6522
info@narcolepsynetwork.org
narcolepsynetwork.org
Offers help and information to persons with narcolepsy and their families.
Keith Harper, President
Paul Reynolds, Vice President

1618 **National Institute of Neurological Disorders and Stroke**
P.O. Box 5801 800-352-9424
Bethesda, MD 20824 www.ninds.nih.gov
Seeks to reduce the burden of neurological disease affecting individuals from all walks of life.
Walter Koroshetz, MD, Director
Amy Bany Adams, PhD, Acting Principal Deputy Director

1619 **Sleep Research Society (SRS)**
2510 N Frontage Road 630-737-9702
Darien, IL 60561 coordinator@srsnet.org
www.sleepresearchsociety.org
Facilitates communication among research workers in the field of sleep medicine.
Namni Goel, PhD, President
Stephanie J. Crowley, PhD, Secretary & Treasurer

Foundations

1620 **National Sleep Foundation**
2001 Massachusetts Ave., N.W. 703-243-1697
Washington, DC 20036 www.thensf.org
The National Sleep Foundation promotes sleep health as a "crucial measure of overall health" through education and advocacy.
Temitayo O. Oyegbile-Chidi, MD, PhD, Chair
Thomas C. DiSalvi, CDS, Vice Chair

1621 **Sleep Research Society Foundation**
2510 North Frontage Road 630-737-9702
Darien, IL 60561 coordinator@srsnet.org
sleepresearchsociety.org/foundation/
The Sleep Research Society Foundation funds research and education opportunities in the field of sleep.
Namni Goel, PhD, President
Stephanie J. Crowley, PhD, Secretary & Treasurer

Libraries & Resource Centers

1622 **SleepFoundation.org**
1414 NE 42nd St. 877-672-8966
Seattle, WA 98105 www.sleepfoundation.org
Information for millions of Americans who suffer from sleep disorders, and to prevent the catastrophic accidents that are related to poor or disordered sleep through research, education and the dissemination of information.
Keith Cushner, Executive Director, Product
Logan Foley, Managing Editor, Health & Product

Research Centers

1623 **Baylor College of Medicine: Sleep Disorder and Research Center**
6620 Main St 713-798-1000
Houston, TX 77030 800-229-5671
Fax: 713-796-9718
baylorclinicweb@bcm.edu
www.baylorclinic.com
Internal unit of the College that focuses on research into sleep and sexual dysfunction in males.
Shyam Subramanian, Medical Director
Charlie Lan, Assistant Professor of Medicine

1624 **Capital Regional Sleep-Wake Disorders Center**
St. Peter's Hospital and Albany Medical Center
25 Hackett Boulevard 518-436-9253
Albany, NY 12208

1625 **Center for Narcolepsy Research at the University of Illinois at Chicago**
University of Illinois
845 S Damen Avenue 312-996-5176
Chicago, IL 60612 Fax: 312-996-7008
CNSHR@listserv.uic.edu
www.uic.edu/depts/cnr
Provides information to health professionals and people with sleep disorders regarding diagnosis and treatment.
6-8 pages
David W. Carley, Director
Julie Law, Center Administrator

1626 **Center for Research in Sleep Disorders Affiliated with Mercy Hospital**
Mercy Hospital of Hamilton/Fairfield
1275 E Kemper Road 513-671-3101
Cincinnati, OH 45246

1627 **Center for Sleep & Wake Disorders: Miami Valley Hospital**
One Wyoming Street 937-208-8000
Dayton, OH 45409 www.miamivalleyhospital.org
Offering the largest variety of sleep disorder testing available in the area, it also offers comprehensive sleep care and care of related issues with a sleep lab, clinical treatment, pulmonary treatment, and behavioral treatment in the same facility.
Kevin Huban, Director
Amy Cline, Administrative Director

1628 **Center for Sleep Medicine of the Mount Sinai Medical Center**
One Gustave L.Levy Place 212-241-6500
New York, NY 10029 Fax: 212-875-84
www.mountsinai.org

Sleep-Wake Disorders / Research Centers

The Center for Sleep Medicine at The Mount Sinai Medical Center is a comprehensive program dedicated to the diagnosis and treatment of all aspects of sleep pathology including breathing-related sleep disorders, periodic limb movements in sleep, insomnia. and narcolepsy. Mechanical (CPAP BiPAP ventilator), surgical, dental, and pharmacologic therapies are available.
E. Neil Schachter, Professor
Gwen S. Skloot, Associates Professor

1629 Geisinger Wyoming Valley Medical Center: Sleep Disorders Center
1000 E Mountain Drive   570-819-5770
Wilkes-Barre, PA 18711   www.geisinger.org
Sleep team operates service sleep centers and laboratories to diagnose and treat a broad range of sleep disorders. Geisinger sleep centers are conveniently located in Danville, Bloomsburg, Shamokin, Wilkes-Barre and Mt. Pocono.
Andrew Paul Matragrano, Director
Stephanie Schaefer, Nurse Practitioner

1630 Johns Hopkins University: Sleep Disorders Francis Scott Key Medical Center
Francis Scott Key Medical Center
601 N Caroline Street   410-550-0545
Baltimore, MD 21287   www.hopkinshospital.org
The Johns Hopkins University Sleep Disorders Center is a tertiary care center for patients with sleep/wake disorders and medical disorders associated with sleep.
Phillip L. Smith, Director

1631 Knollwoodpark Hospital Sleep Disorders Center
5600 Girby Road   251-660-5120
Mobile, AL 36693   Fax: 251-660-5245
71054.2530@compuserve.com
www.southalabama.edu/usakph

1632 Loma Linda University Sleep Disorders Clinic
VA Hospital Medical Services Center
11201 Benton Street   909-825-7084
Loma Linda, CA 92357   800-741-8387
Fax: 909-963-64
www.lom.med.va.gov
Ralph Downey III, M.D., Director

1633 Methodist Hospital Sleep Center Winona Memorial Hospital
Rehab Centers
6565 Fannin Street   713-441-7854
Houston, TX 77030   Fax: 713-790-2612
www.methodisthealth.com
Marc L. Boom, President & CEO
David M. Underwood, Vice Chairman

1634 MidWest Medical Center: Sleep Disorders Center
Winona Memorial Hospital
Indianapolis, IN 46208   317-927-2100
Fax: 317-927-2914

1635 Northwest Ohio Sleep Disorders Center Toledo Hospital
Toledo Hospital
2142 N Cove Boulevard   419-471-5629
Toledo, OH 43606
Frank O. Horton III, M.D., Director

1636 Ohio Sleep Medicine Institute
4220 Bradenton Avenue   614-766-0773
Dublin, OH 43017   Fax: 614-766-2599
info@sleepmedicine.com
www.sleepmedicine.com
A comprehensive accredited sleep disorders center that is dedicated to excellence in sleep medicine care. Offers evaluation, diagnosis and treatment for adults and children with sleep apnea, insomnia, restless legs syndrome, narcolepsy, parasomnias, circadian rhythms disorders, shift work, fatigue and other sleep problems.
Betty Palmer, Director

1637 Penn Center for Sleep Disorders: Hospital of the University of Pennsylvania
3400 Spruce Street   215-662-7772
Philadelphia, PA 19104   Fax: 215-349-8038
Joanne Getsy, M.D., Director

1638 Presbyterian-University Hospital: Pulmonary Sleep Evaluation Center
DeSoto At O'Hara Street   412-647-3475
Pittsburgh, PA 15213
Mark Sanders, M.D., Director

1639 Scripps Clinic Sleep Disorders Center Scripps Clinic
Scripps Clinic
10666 N Torrey Pines Road   858-455-9100
La Jolla, CA 92037   Fax: 858-828-64
malcoRN@scrippsclinic.com
www.scripps.org
The Scripps Clinic Sleep Center provides evaluation diagnosis and treatment of a full range of sleep disorders such as Circadian rhythm disorders, insomnia, narcolepsy, night terror, nightmares, restless legs syndrome, sleep apnea, sleepwalking, and snoring.
Dan Dworsky, M.D., Medical Director
Merrill M. Mitle, M.D., Scientific Director

1640 Sleep Alertness Center: Lafayette Home Hospital
2400 S Street   765-447-6811
Lafayette, IN 47904

1641 Sleep Center: Community General Hospital
750 East Adams Street   315-464-5540
Syracuse, NY 13210   www.cgh.org
The Sleep Center at Community General Hospital is a specialized facility providing accurate diagnosis and recommending treatment of sleep-related problems.

1642 Sleep Disorders Center Bethesda Oak Hospital
619 Oak Street   513-569-5400
Cincinnati, OH 45206   www.trihealth.com

1643 Sleep Disorders Center Columbia Presbyterian Medical Center
The University Hospital of Columbia & Cornell
161 Fort Washington Avenue   212-305-1860
New York, NY 10032   Fax: 212-305-5496
www.sleepnyp.com
A highly specialized outpatient facility for the evaluation and treatment of patients with problems related to sleep and wakefulness.
Neil B. Kavey, Medical Director
Andrew Tucker, Director

1644 Sleep Disorders Center Dartmouth Hitchcock Medical Center
Darthmouth Hitchcock medical Center
One Rope Ferry Road   603-650-1200
Hanover, NH 03755   877-367-1797
Fax: 603-650-1202
Joanne.MacQuarrie@dartmouth.edu
dms.dartmouth.edu
Provides consultation and testing for all varieties of sleep-related disturbances, including snoring, sleep apnea, narcolepsy, restless legs syndrome, periodic limb movement disorder, insomnia, parasomnias and circadian rhythm disorders.
Glen Greenough, Fellowship Director

1645 Sleep Disorders Center Lankenau Hospital
100 E Lancaster Avenue   610-645-3400
Wynnewood, PA 19096   Fax: 610-645-2291

1646 Sleep Disorders Center Ohio State University Medical Center
410 W.10th Ave   614-257-2500
Columbus, OH 43210   800-293-5123
Fax: 614-257-2551
webmaster@osumc.edu
medicalcenter.osu.edu
Ulysses J. Magalang, M.D., Medical Director

1647 Sleep Disorders Center at California: Pacific Medical Center
2340 Clay Street   415-923-3336
San Francisco, CA 94115   Fax: 415-923-3584
76307.2221@compuserve.com

Sleep-Wake Disorders / Research Centers

1648 **Sleep Disorders Center of Metropolitan Toronto**
500 Alden Road 905-475-5155
Markham Ontario, CA M6B 888-401-5155
Fax: 647-436-7607
sleep@compuserve.com
www.sdc.ca

Jeffrey Lips, M.D., Director

1649 **Sleep Disorders Center of Rochester: St. Mary's Hospital**
2110 Clinton Avenue S 716-442-4141
Rochester, NY 14618
Donald Green, M.D.

1650 **Sleep Disorders Center of Western New York Millard Fillmore Hospital**
726 Exchange Street 716-859-5600
Buffalo, NY 14210 Fax: 716-887-5332
gates.kaleidahealth.org

Daniel Rifkin, Director

1651 **Sleep Disorders Center: Cleveland Clinic Foundation**
9500 Euclid Avenue 216-636-5860
Cleveland, OH 44195 800-223-2273
Fax: 216-445-1022
TTY: 216-444-0261
my.clevelandclinic.org

Accredited by the American Academy of Sleep Medicine, the Cleveland Clinic Sleep Disorders Center is staffed by physicians specializing in sleep disorders from a variety of disciplines, including adult and child neurology, pulmonary and critical care medicine, psychology, psychiatry, otolaryngology and dentistry.

1652 **Sleep Disorders Center: Community Medical Center**
1822 Mulberry Street 717-969-8931
Scranton, PA 18510
John Goodnow, Director

1653 **Sleep Disorders Center: Crozer-Chester Medical Center**
Sleep Disorders Center
175 E Chester Pike 610-447-2689
Ridley Park, PA 19078 www.crozer.org

A multidisciplinary facility for the investigation and treatment of sleep problems

1654 **Sleep Disorders Center: Good Samaritan Medical Center**
1020 Franklin Street 814-533-1661
Johnstown, PA 15905

1655 **Sleep Disorders Center: Kettering Medical Center**
3935 Southern Boulevard 937-395-8805
Kettering, OH 45439 Fax: 937-395-8821
www.kmcnetwork.org

Donna Arand, Ph.D., Clinical Director
George G. Burton, M.D., Medical Director

1656 **Sleep Disorders Center: Medical College of Pennsylvania**
3200 Henry Avenue 215-842-4250
Philadelphia, PA 19129
June M. Fry, M.D., Ph.D., Director

1657 **Sleep Disorders Center: Newark Beth Israel Medical Center**
201 Lyons Avenue at Osborne Terrace 973-926-2973
Newark, NJ 07112 www.sbhcs.com

Evaluates a wide range of disorders, including sleep apnea, snoring, insomnia, narcolepsy, sleep-wake schedule disorders, and male impotency. The center also provides board-certified consultants in sleep medicine, neurology, urology, endocrinology, psychiatry, cardiology, and ear, nose, and throat surgery, in addition to certified sleep technologists.
Monroe S. Karetzky, M.D.

1658 **Sleep Disorders Center: Rhode Island Hospital**
70 Catamore Boulevard 401-431-5420
E Providence, RI 02914 Fax: 401-431-5429
www.lifespan.org

1659 **Sleep Disorders Center: St. Vincent Medical Center**
2213 Cherry Street 419-321-4980
Toledo, OH 43608

1660 **Sleep Disorders Center: University Hospital, SUNY at Stony Brook**
240 Middle Country Road 631-444-2500
Smithtown, NY 11787 Fax: 631-444-2580
uhmc-xweb1.uhmc.sunysb.edu/sleepdisorder

1661 **Sleep Disorders Center: Winthrop, University Hospital**
259 First Street 516-663-0333
Mineola, NY 11501 www.winthrop.org
Steven H. Feinsilver, M.D.

1662 **Sleep Disorders Unit Beth Israel Deaconess Medical Center**
330 Brookline Avenue 617-667-3237
Boston, MA 02215 www.bidmc.org
Jean K. Matheson, M.D.

1663 **Sleep Laboratory**
St Joseph's Hospital
301 Prospect Ave 315-703-2138
Syracuse, NY 13203 888-785-6371
Fax: 315-755-77
www.sjhsyr.org

The Sleep Lab focuses on diagnosing and treating Obstructive Sleep Apnea and sleep-related breathing disorders, and has the largest number of sleep-credentialed physicians and registered sleep technologists of any sleep lab in the area.
Edward T. Downing, Director

1664 **Sleep Laboratory, Maine Medical Center**
22 Bramhall Street 207-871-2279
Portland, ME 04102

1665 **Sleep Medicine Associates of Texas**
5477 Glen Lakes Drive 214-750-7776
Dallas, TX 13210 Fax: 214-750-4621
www.sleepmed.com

First, largest and longest-standing accredited sleep center in North Texas.
Philipp Becker, President/Founding Partner
Andrew O. Jamieson, M.D., Chair/Co-Founding Partner

1666 **Sleep and Chronobiology Center: Western Psychiatric Institute and Clinic**
3811 Ohara Street 412-624-2246
Pittsburgh, PA 15213
Charles F. Reynolds III, M.D., Director

1667 **Sleep/Wake Disorders Center Montefiore Sleep Disorders Center**
111 E 210th Street 718-920-4321
Bronx, NY 10467 Fax: 718-798-4352
www.montefiore.org

Provides outstanding clinical care for patients with disorders that affect the sleep-wake cycle and are committed to performing high quality research and to making outstanding contributions to the areas of clinical research that includes the entire spectrum of sleep medicine.
Michael J. Thorpy, M.D., Director
Karen Ballab, M.D., Associate Director

1668 **Sleep/Wake Disorders Center: Community Hospitals of Indianapolis**
1500 N Ritter Avenue 317-355-4275
Indianapolis, IN 46219 Fax: 317-351-2785
Marvin E. Vollmer, M.D.

1669 **Sleep/Wake Disorders Center: Hampstead Hospital**
218 East Road 603-329-5311
Hampstead, NH 03841 info@hampsteadhospital.com
Kathi Collins, CEO
Steven Finnegan, COO

1670 **Sleep/Wake Disorders Center: New York Hospital-Cornell Medical Center**
520 E 70th Street 212-746-2623
New York, NY 10021 Fax: 212-746-5509
www.weillcornell.org

Charles Poll, M.D., Director

1671 **Stanford University Center for Narcolepsy**
Dept. of Psychiatry & Behavioral Sciences

450 Broadway Street 650-725-6517
Redwood City, CA 94063 Fax: 650-498-7761
med.stanford.edu
Dr. Emanuel Mignot, Director
Marlene Iry, Admin Associate

1672 **Thomas Jefferson University: Sleep Disorders Center**
Jefferson Medical College
1020 Walnut Street 215-955-6000
Philadelphia, PA 19107 800-JEF-FNOW
Fax: 215-955-9783
www.jefferson.edu
A comprehensive clinical, research and educational program in sleep and sleep disorders medicine.
Karl Doghram, M.D., Medical Director

Support Groups & Hotlines

1673 **Narcolepsy Institute/Montefiore Medical Center**
111 E 210th Street 718-920-6799
Bronx, NY 10467 Fax: 718-654-9580
MGoswami@aol.com
www.narcolepsyinstitute.org
The Narcolepsy Institute provides psychosocial support services for narcolepsy.
Dr. Meeta Goswami, Director

1674 **Narcolepsy Network**
3242 NE 3rd Avenue #1101 401-667-2523
Camas, WA 98607 888-292-6522
info@narcolepsynetwork.org
www.narcolepsynetwork.org
Provides advocacy and education, supports research. Newsletter, conferences, phone support, and group development guidelines.
Keith Harper, President
Paul Reynolds, Vice President

1675 **National Health Information Center**
Office of Disease Prevention & Health Promotion
1101 Wootton Pkwy Fax: 240-453-8281
Rockville, MD 20852 odphpinfo@hhs.gov
www.health.gov/nhic
Supports public health education by maintaining a calendar of National Health Observances; helps connect consumers and health professionals to organizations that can best answer questions and provide up-to-date contact information from reliable sources; updates on a yearly basis toll-free numbers for health information, Federal health clearinghouses and info centers.
Don Wright, MD, MPH, Director

Print Resources

1676 **American Journal of Psychiatry**
American Psychiatric Association Publishing
800 Maine Avenue SW, Suite 900 202-459-9722
Washington, DC 20024 800-368-5777
Fax: 202-403-3094
psychiatryonline@psych.org
ajp.psychiatryonline.org
Official journal of the American Psychiatric Association (APA).
Ned H. Kalin, MD, Editor-in-Chief

1677 **Journal of Psychiatry, Depression & Anxiety**
Herald Scholarly Open Access
2561 Cornelia Road, Suite 205 202-499-9679
Herndon, VA 20171 Fax: 202-217-4195
contact@heraldsopenaccess.us
www.heraldopenaccess.us
Online, international, open access, peer-reviewed journal focused primarily on depression and anxiety, but also on other related areas of psychiatry as well.
Sam Vaknin, Editor-in-Chief

1678 **Journal of Sleep Disorders and Management**
ClinMed International Library
3511 Silverside Road, Suite 105 302-208-7437
Wilmington, DE 19810 contact@clinmedjournals.org
clinmedjournals.org
Open access, peer-reviewed journal focused on clinical, preventative, curative and social aspects of sleep medicine.
Scicchitano Pietro, Editor-in-Chief

1679 **Sleep Health: Journal of the National Sleep Foundation**
National Sleep Foundation
2001 Massachusetts Ave., N.W. 703-243-1697
Washington, DC 20036 www.sleephealthjournal.org
This multidisciplinary journal publishes original, evidence-based research, review articles, reports, and commentaries on sleep-related topics.
Orfeu M. Buxton, PhD, Editor-in-Chief
Kelly Baron, PhD, MPH, Senior Associate Editor

Web Sites

1680 **American Sleep Apnea Association**
www.sleeppapnea.org
The American Sleep Apnea Association, founded in 1990, is a 501(c)(3) nonprofit organization that promotes awareness of sleep apnea, works for continuing improvements in treatments for this serious disorder, and advocates for the interests of sleep apnea patients.

1681 **American Sleep Disorders Association**
www.aasm.org
Provides full diagnostic and treatment services to improve the quality of care for patients with all types of sleep disorders.

1682 **Healing Well**
www.healingwell.com
An online health resource guide to medical news, chat, information and articles, newsgroups and message boards, books, disease-related web sites, medical directories, and more for patients, friends, and family coping with disabling diseases, disorders, or chronic illnesses.

1683 **Health Central**
www.healthcentral.com
Find clearly explained, medically accurate information regarding conditions, including an overview, symptoms, causes, diagnostic procedures and treatment options. On this site it is possible to ask questions and get information from a neurologist and connect to people who have similar health interests.

1684 **Health Finder**
www.health.gov
Searchable, carefully developed web site offering information on over 1000 topics. Developed by the US Department of Health and Human Services, thesite can be used in both English and Spanish.

1685 **MGH Neurology WebForums**
Online. Provides both unmoderated message boards and chat rooms for specific neurological disorders.

1686 **Medical News Today**
www.medicalnewstody.com
Offers in-depth health information and the latest news in medical research on a wide variety of medical conditions.

1687 **MedicineNet**
www.medicinenet.com
An online resource for consumers providing easy-to-read, authoritative medical and health information.

1688 **MedlinePlus**
www.medlineplus.gov
Information regarding a broad range of health,and mental health conditions topics include: Latest news, overview of anatomy and physiology, clinical trials, diagnoses and symptoms, treatment, genetics, plus lots of links to other sites. A service provided by the National Library of Medicine, part of the National Institutes of Health (NIH).

1689 **Medscape**
www.medscape.com
Medscape offers specialists, primary care physicians, and other health professionals the Web's most robust and integrated medical information and educational tools.

539

Sleep-Wake Disorders / Web Sites

1690 MyHealthfinder
www.healthfinder.gov
Searchable, carefully developed web site offering information on over 1000 topics. Developed by the US Department of Health and Human Services, the site can be used in both English and Spanish.

1691 Neurology Channel
www.healthcommunities.com
Find clearly explained, medically accurate information regarding conditions, including an overview, symptoms, causes, diagnostic procedures and treatment options. On this site it is possible to ask questions and get information from a neurologist and connect to people who have similar health interests.

1692 Sleep Research Society (SRS)
www.sleepresearchsociety.org
Facilitates communication among research workers in this field, but does not sponsor research investigations on its own.

1693 SleepFoundation.org
www.sleepfoundation.org
Information for millions of Americans who suffer from sleep disorders, and to prevent the catastrophic accidents that are related to poor or disordered sleep through research, education and the dissemination of information.

1694 Verywell Mind
www.verywellmind.com
Provides up-to-date information on mental health topics. mission is to prioritize mental health and promote balance for day to day living. offers over 5,500 online articles that are researched based, and reviwed by medical professionals.
Kristen Altmeyer, MBA, VP & General Manager
Nick Ingalls, MA, Associate Editorial Director

1695 WebMD
www.webmd.com
Provides credible information, supportive communities, and in-depth reference material about health subjects. A source for original and timely health information, as well as material from well-known content providers.

SOMATIC SYMPTOM & RELATED DISORDERS

When individuals experience a heightened focus on physical symptoms such as weakness or shortness of breath that results in major distress or problems functioning, they may be experiencing somatic symptom disorder (SSD).

The prevalence of somatic symptom disorder (SSD) is evident in almost 20 percent of the primary care population with a higher representation in females. Excessive thoughts, behaviors and feelings related to the perceived physical symptoms convinces the person that they are sick. While the etiology of SSD is unclear, risk factors may include childhood neglect, sexual abuse, lifestyle, and substance use and abuse. Physical symptoms may or may not be associated with a diagnosed medical condition. A lack of definitive diagnosis of a medical condition is not sufficient to diagnose somatic symptom disorder, rather it is the extent to which behaviors and thoughts related to the illness are out of proportion, lasting more than six months. Diagnosis involves identifying one or more physical symptoms causing the disruption in daily activities coupled with at least one other measure. These measures include ongoing thoughts out of proportion with the seriousness of the symptoms, excessive time and energy spent on health concerns, a high level of anxiety about health, with at least one of these measures constantly present.

Related disorders may include illness anxiety disorder, formerly known as hypochondrias, where the individual is constantly worrying about having or getting an illness. They may go to extremes to avoid health risks and may visit multiple physicians for the perceived illness. Conversion disorder is a functional neurological symptom disorder that affects an individuals' perception, sensation, or movement with no physical cause. People with conversion disorder often experience depression or anxiety disorders. Factitious disorder involves faking physical or mental illness when not really sick. Individuals may also fabricate an illness or injury in another person either with or without any benefit from the situation they create.

SSD is often associated with depression and anxiety but more severe personality disorders may develop such as avoidant, paranoid, self-defeating and obsessive-compulsive disorder. Psychosocial stressors such as job loss or unemployment and impaired occupational functioning may also contribute to SSD.

The first step in diagnosis is seeing a physician to determine if symptoms are representative of a medical condition. If nothing is found, the individual may have trouble accepting the fact. Too often, individuals are told "it's all in your head" with no referral to a mental health professional for follow-up. The primary care physician and a mental health professional should remain in contact as treatment regimens are planned. Treatments consist of controlling symptoms to promote optimal functioning in activities of daily living and avoid unnecessary tests and treatments. Talk therapy and anti-depressant or anti-anxiety medications may be indicated if significant depression or anxiety is also present.

Somatic Symptom & Related Disorders / Agencies & Associations

Agencies & Associations

1696 Academy of Psychosomatic Medicine
4800 Hampden Ln
Bethesda, MD 20814
301-718-6520
info@CLpsychiatry.org
apm.org

The Academy of Psychosomatic Medicine represents psychiatrists focused on improving education, medical science, and healthcare for individuals with comorbid psychiatric and general medical conditions. The Academy seeks to promote interdisciplinary education and drive research and public policy with the goal of achieving outstanding clinical care for patients with comorbid psychiatric and general medical conditions throughout the world. They also created the Foundation of the Academy of Psychosom
Philip Biaeler, MD, FACLP, President
Maryland Pao, MD, FACLP, President-Elect

1697 American Psychiatric Association
800 Maine Avenue SW
Washington, DC 20024
202-559-3900
apa@psych.org
www.psychiatry.org

A medical specialty society representing a growing membership of psychiatrists. Offers information for psychiatrists, medical students, patients and families.
Saul Levin, MD, MPA, FRCP-E, CEO

1698 Center for Family Support
2811 Zulette Avenue
Bronx, NY 10461
718-518-1500
svernikoff@cfsny.org
www.cfsny.org

The Center for Family Support offers assistance to individuals with developmental and related disabilities, as well as their families, and provides support services and programs that are designed to accommodate individual needs. Offers services throughout New York City, Westchester County, Long Island, and New Jersey.
Steven Vernikoff, Executive Director
Barbara Greenwald, Chief Operating Officer

1699 Center for Mental Health Services (CMHS)
Substance Abuse and Mental Health Services Adminis
5600 Fishers Lane
Rockville, MD 20857
240-276-1310
samhsa.gov/about-us/who-we-are/offices-c

Promotes the treatment of mental illness and emotional disorders by increasing accessibility to mental health programs; supporting outreach, treatment, rehabilitation, and support programs and networks; and encouraging the use of scientifically-based information when treating mental disorders. CMHS provides information about mental health via a toll-free number and numerous publications. Developed for users of mental health services and their families, the general public, policy makers, provider
Anita Everett, MD, DFAPA, Director

1700 Goodwill's Community Employment Services
Goodwill Industries-Suncoast, Inc.
10596 Gandy Blvd.
St. Petersburg, FL 33702
727-523-1512
888-279-1988
TDD: 727-579-1068
goodwill-suncoast.org

The St. Petersburg headquarters serves ten counties in the state of Florida. Their mission is to help people with disabilities gain employment through training programs, employment services, and affordable housing.
Sandra Young, Chair
Louise Lopez, Sr. Vice Chair

1701 Institute for Contemporary Psychotherapy
33 W 60th St.
New York, NY 10023
212-333-3444
Fax: 212-333-5444
icpnyc.org

The Institute for Contemporary Psychotherapy is a New York City-based mental health treatment and training facility. Consisting of a group of 150 licensed psychotherapists, the Institute focuses on educating the public about the issues surrounding mental health, providing post-graduate training for therapists, and offering therapy at moderate costs.
Ron Taffel, PhD, Chair
Andrea Green-Lewis, LCSW-R, Director of Operations

1702 Mental Health America
500 Montgomery Street
Alexandria, VA 22314
703-684-7722
800-969-6642
mhanational.org

Mental Health America is a community-based nonprofit organization committed to enabling the mental wellness of all Americans. MHA advocates for greater access to quality health services and seeks to educate individuals on identifying symptoms, as well as intervention and prevention.
Schroeder Stribling, President & CEO
Sachin Doshi, Sr. Dir., Finance & Operations

1703 National Association for the Dually Diagnosed (NADD)
321 Wall Street
Kingston, NY 12401
845-331-4336
info@thenadd.org
thenadd.org

NADD is a nonprofit organization designed to increase awareness of, and provide services for, individuals with developmental disabilities and mental illness. NADD emphasizes the importance of quality mental healthcare for people with mental health needs and offers conferences, information resources, educational programs, and training materials to professionals, parents, and organizations.
Jeanne M. Farr, MA, Chief Executive Officer
Robert J. Fletcher, DSW, Founder and CEO Emeritus

1704 National Mental Health Consumers' Self-Help Clearinghouse
selfhelpclearinghouse@gmail.com
mhselfhelp.org

The Clearinghouse is a peer-run national technical assistance center focused on achieving respect and equality of opportunity for those with mental illnesses. The Clearinghouse helps with the growth of the mental health consumer movement by evaluating mental health services, advocating for mental health reform, and providing consumers with news, information, publications, and consultation services.
Joseph Rogers, Founder and Executive Director
Susan Rogers, Director

1705 United Brain Association
202-768-8000
info@unitedbrainassociation.org
unitedbrainassociation.org

Non-profit organization that works to find cures through research for over 600 brain and mental health related issues, and disorders.
J.A. Boulton, Founder
Jay Matey, VP & Treasurer

Print Resources

1706 American Journal of Psychiatry
American Psychiatric Association Publishing
800 Maine Avenue SW, Suite 900
Washington, DC 20024
202-459-9722
800-368-5777
Fax: 202-403-3094
psychiatryonline@psych.org
ajp.psychiatryonline.org

Official journal of the American Psychiatric Association (APA).
Ned H. Kalin, MD, Editor-in-Chief

1707 American Journal of Psychotherapy
American Psychiatric Association Publishing
800 Maine Avenue SW, Suite 900
Washington, DC 20024
202-459-9722
800-368-5777
Fax: 202-403-3094
psychiatryonline@psych.org
ajp.psychiatryonline.org

Publishes content that aims to advance the theory, science, and clinical practice of psychotherapy.
Holly A. Swartz, MD, Editor-in-Chief

1708 Journal of Psychiatry, Depression & Anxiety
Herald Scholarly Open Access
2561 Cornelia Road, Suite 205
Herndon, VA 20171
202-499-9679
Fax: 202-217-4195
contact@heraldopenaccess.us
www.heraldopenaccess.us

Online, international, open access, peer-reviewed journal focused primarily on depression and anxiety, but also on other related areas of psychiatry as well.
Sam Vaknin, Editor-in-Chief

Web Sites

1709 Healing Well
www.healingwell.com
An online health resource guide to medical news, chat, information and articles, newsgroups and message boards, books, disease-related web sites, medical directories, and more for patients, friends, and family coping with disabling diseases, disorders, or chronic illnesses.

1710 Health Central
www.healthcentral.com
Find clearly explained, medically accurate information regarding conditions, including an overview, symptoms, causes, diagnostic procedures and treatment options. On this site it is possible to ask questions and get information from a neurologist and connect to people who have similar health interests.

1711 Health Finder
www.health.gov
Searchable, carefully developed web site offering information on over 1000 topics. Developed by the US Department of Health and Human Services, thesite can be used in both English and Spanish.

1712 Internet Mental Health
www.mentalhealth.com
Offers online psychiatric diagnosis in the hope of reaching the two-thirds of individuals with mental illness who do not seek treatment.

1713 Mbp Expert Services
www.mbpexpert.com
Expert services from Louisa J Lasher, MA, provides Munchausen by Proxy maltreatment training, case consultation, technical assistance, and expert witness services in an objective manner and in the best interest of the child or children involved.

1714 Medical News Today
www.medicalnewstody.com
Offers in-depth health information and the latest news in medical research on a wide variety of medical conditions.

1715 MedicineNet
www.medicinenet.com
An online resource for consumers providing easy-to-read, authoritative medical and health information.

1716 MedlinePlus
www.medlineplus.gov
Information regarding a broad range of health,and mental health conditions topics include: Latest news, overview of anatomy and physiology, clinical trials, diagnoses and symptoms, treatment, genetics, plus lots of links to other sites. A service provided by the National Library of Medicine, part of the National Institutes of Health (NIH).

1717 Medscape
www.medscape.com
Medscape offers specialists, primary care physicians, and other health professionals the Web's most robust and integrated medical information and educational tools.

1718 Mothers Against Munchausen Syndrome By Proxy Allegations
www.msbp.com
Begun in response to the fast growing number of false allegations of Munchausen Syndrome by Proxy.

1719 Munchause Syndrome
www.munchausen.com
Dr. Marc Feldman's Munchausen Syndrome, Malingering, Factitious Disorder, & Munchausen by Proxy page. Includes articles, related book list, personal stories and links.

1720 Planetpsych.com
www.planetpsych.com
Online resource for mental health information

1721 Psych Central
www.psychcentral.com
The Internet's largest and oldest independent mental health social network created and run by mental health professionals to guarantee reliable, trusted information and support communities to you.

1722 Substance Abuse And Mental Health Services Administration
www.store.samhsa.gov
Resources on mental disorders as well as treatment and recovery.

1723 Verywell Mind
www.verywellmind.com
Provides up-to-date information on mental health topics. mission is to prioritize mental health and promote balance for day to day living. offers over 5,500 online articles that are researched based, and reviwed by medical professionals.
Kristen Altmeyer, MBA, VP & General Manager
Nick Ingalls, MA, Associate Editorial Director

1724 WebMD
www.webmd.com
Provides credible information, supportive communities, and in-depth reference material about health subjects. A source for original and timely health information as well as material from well known content providers.

STROKE

The leading cause of disability in the United States is stroke, and it is the fifth most common cause of death.

Stroke occurs when arteries in or leading to the brain bursts, called hemorrhagic stroke, or the artery is blocked by a clot, called an ischemic stroke. If blood does not get to the brain, the brain cells die. A transient ischemic attack, or TIA or mini-stroke, occurs when blockage of the artery is caused by a temporary clot. Ischemic stroke, when caught early (usually within 4 hours of the event) and treated with clot-dissolving drugs may prevent disabling physical damage as the area of the brain affected may cause speech and mobility problems long term. Hemorrhagic stroke occurs in about 13 percent of strokes and may require treatment with interventional radiology or surgery to "clip" the area of bleed. It must be done quickly to restore blood flow to the area before permanent damage is done.

Depression is common in stroke survivors often caused by biochemical changes in the brain or the disabilities caused from untreated stroke. Depending on the area of the brain affected, survivors may not feel positive emotions. Rehabilitation to address physical limitations from the stroke is challenging and patients may feel hopeless, sad, or anxious. Treatment requires a stroke team with both medical and mental health professionals and may involve medications and therapy. Treating depression improves the individual's mood and boosts both medical and cognitive recovery. Social support is important and family, friends and stroke support groups play a major role in returning the individual for the optimal level of functioning based on the stroke and its aftermath. The goal of stroke care is to assist the individual to achieve optimal outcomes so that activities of daily living are possible.

Stroke / Agencies & Associations

Agencies & Associations

1725 American Heart Association
7272 Greenville Avenue
Dallas, TX 75231
214-570-5943
800-242-8721
www.heart.org

The American Heart Association is the nation's oldest, largest voluntary organization devoted to fighting cardiovascular diseases and stroke. Funds research and raises public awareness of heart diseases.
Michelle A. Albert, President
Nancy Brown, Chief Executive Officer

1726 American Stroke Association
7272 Greenville Avenue
Dallas, TX 75231
800-242-8721
www.stroke.org

Dedicated to the prevention, diagnosis, and treatment of stroke. Funds research on stroke and advises the public on how to detect and avoid stroke.
Nancy Brown, Chief Executive Officer

1727 March of Dimes Canada
885 Don Mills Road
Toronto, Ontario, M3C-1V9
416-425-3463
800-263-3463
Fax: 416-425-1920
www.marchofdimes.ca

A national service offering support, education and community programs for stroke survivors, their caregivers and families.
Elizabeth Cherot, MD, President & CEO
Alan Brogdon, SVP, Chief Operating Officer

1728 National Heart, Lung & Blood Institute
31 Center Drive
Bethesda, MD 20892
nhlbiinfo@nhlbi.nih.gov
www.nhlbi.nih.gov

Trains, conducts research, and educates in order to promote the prevention and treatment of heart, lung, and blood disorders.
Gary H. Gibbons, MD, Director

1729 National Institute of Neurological Disorders and Stroke
P.O. Box 5801
Bethesda, MD 20824
800-352-9424
www.ninds.nih.gov

Seeks to reduce the burden of neurological disease affecting individuals from all walks of life.
Walter Koroshetz, MD, Director
Amy Bany Adams, PhD, Acting Principal Deputy Director

Foundations

1730 American Stroke Foundation
6405 Metcalf Ave.
Overland Park, KS 66202
913-649-1776
www.americanstroke.org

The vision of the American Stroke Foundation is to reach out to stroke survivors and their families across America and empower them to reclaim hope for life after stroke.
Jane Savidge, Executive Director
Susan Suzuki, Administrative Assistant

1731 Heart and Stroke Foundation of Canada
2300 Yonge St.
Toronto, Ontario, M4P-1E4
888-473-4636
www.heartandstroke.ca

Leading authority on cardiovascular disease, providing resources for individuals and funding scientific research on heart disease and stroke.
Doug Roth, Chief Executive Officer

Research Centers

1732 Cerebral Blood Flow Laboratories Veterans Administration Medical Center
Veterans Administration Medical Center
2002 Holcombe Boulevard
Houston, TX 77030
713-795-5807
Fax: 713-957-01

Offers research in cerebrovascular disorders and risk factors for stroke.
John S. Meyer, M.D., Director

1733 Comprehensive Stroke Center of Oregon
University of Oregon Health Sciences Center
3181 SW Sam Jackson Park Road
Portland, OR 97239
503-494-7225
www.ohsu.edu

The Oregon Stroke Center (OSC) was established over 20 years ago to provide comprehensive treatment and prevention services to stroke patients throughout the Northwest. Recognized as a national leader in acute stroke treatment, the OSC mobile stroke team provides novel stroke treatments to multiple Portland hospitals. In addition to clinical care, the OSC is actively involved in clinical and basic research and provides extensive stroke related education to the public and providers.
Wayne Clark, M.D., Professor
Helmi Lutsep, M.D., Professor

1734 Departments of Neurology & Neurosurgery: University of California, San Francisco
UCSF Medical Center
505 Parnassus Avenue
San Francisco, CA 94143
415-476-1537
Fax: 415-476-0616
bill.dillon@radiology.ucsf.edu
www.radiology.ucsf.edu

The Department of Radiology & Biomedical Imaging at the University of California, San Francisco combines clinical excellence, trailblazing research, and outstanding education in a leading academic health sciences institution. The faculty includes some of the foremost names in diagnostic and interventional radiology today.
Dr. Ronald Arenson, Chairman
Catherine Garzio, Director of Administration

1735 Hospital of the University of Pennsylvania
3400 Spruce Street
Philadelphia, PA 19104
215-662-4000
800-789-PENN
Fax: 215-903-09
pleasure@email.chop.edu
www.pennmedicine.org

The Hospital of the University of Pennsylvania (HUP) is world-renowned for its clinical and research excellence, forging the way for newer and better ways to diagnose and treat illnesses and disorders. The world-class faculty and staff of the Hospital of the University of Pennsylvania are dedicated to superior patient care, education and research for a better, healthier future. Their significant and groundbreaking contributions to medicine are recognized both nationally and internationally.
David E. Pleasure, M.D., Director

1736 Massachusetts General Departments of Neurology and Neurosurgery
Massachusetts General Hospital
55 Fruit Street
Boston, MA 02114
617-726-2000
www.massgeneral.org

Mission is to be the preeminent academic neurology department in the US by: providing outstanding clinical care while rapidly discovering new treatments to reduce and eliminate the devastating impact of neurological disorders; training the very best neurologists and scientists of the future, and improving the health and well-being of the diverse communities they serve.
Peter Slavin, Director
Robert Ackerman, Doctor

1737 Stroke Research and Treatment Center UAB Medical Center
Medical Center
1530 3rd Ave S
Birmingham, AL 35294
205-934-9999
800-822-6478
Fax: 205-996-4039
www.main.uab.edu/neurology

The nationally-ranked UAB Department of Neurology is home to eight comprehensive divisions and seven centers offering an array of clinical activities. Over 26,000 patients are cared for annually through state-of-the-art subspecialty care and innovative treatments. Residents have the opportunity to work in various neurology fields with 50 clinical and research faculty members.
Andrei V. Alexandrov, M.D., Director, Comprehensive Stroke Research

1738 University of Iowa College of Medicine
451 Newton Road
Iowa City, IA 52242
319-335-6707
www.medicine.uiowa.edu

The Roy J. and Lucille A. Carver College of Medicine is a highly ranked medical school where students learn to become accom-

plished clinicians and top-flight researchers and educators. Students come to Iowa to study medicine in a program that uses case-based learning as the basis of their education. With its emphasis on problem-solving skills, early exposure to patients, and enhanced community-based experiences, UI medical students typically earn impressive scores on Step 1 of the U.S. Medical Li
Debra A. Schwinn, MD, Dean
Donna L. Hammond, PhD, Executive Associate Dean

1739 **University of Maryland Center for Studies of Cerebrovascular Disease & Stroke**
16 S Utah Street 410-328-4323
Baltimore, MD 21201 Fax: 410-328-1149
Thomas R Price MD, Principal Investor

1740 **University of Miami School of Medicine Department of Neurology**
1120 NW 14th Street 305-243-6732
Miami, FL 33136 877-243-4340
Fax: 305-243-1632
RSacco@med.miami.edu
www.med.miami.edu
Ralph L. Sacco, MD, Chairman-Department of Neurology
Myron D. Ginsberg, MD, Professor

1741 **Wake Forest University: Cerebrovascular Research Center**
Department of Neurology
300 S Hawthorne Road 336-748-2338
Winston-Salem, NC 27103 Fax: 336-748-5477
Cerebrovascular research.
Dr. James Toole, Director

1742 **Washington University School of Medicine**
660 S Euclid Avenue 314-362-5000
Saint Louis, MO 63110 www.medicine.wustl.edu
Washington University School of Medicine is a leader in improving human health throughout the world. As noted leaders in patient care, research and education, their faculty members have contributed many discoveries and innovations to the field of science since the founding of the School of Medicine in 1891. The School of Medicine is one of seven schools of Washington University in St. Louis.
Larry J. Shapiro, M.D, Executive Vice Chancellor

Support Groups & Hotlines

1743 **National Health Information Center**
Office of Disease Prevention & Health Promotion
1101 Wootton Pkwy Fax: 240-453-8281
Rockville, MD 20852 odphpinfo@hhs.gov
www.health.gov/nhic
Supports public health education by maintaining a calendar of National Health Observances; helps connect consumers and health professionals to organizations that can best answer questions and provide up-to-date contact information from reliable sources; updates on a yearly basis toll-free numbers for health information, Federal health clearinghouses and info centers.
Don Wright, MD, MPH, Director

Print Resources

1744 **Stroke Connection**
7272 Greenville Ave. 800-242-8721
Dallas, TX 75231 www.americanstroke.org
Official magazine of the American Stroke Foundation. Supports stroke survivors, their families, caregivers and friends by providing resources, services, education and information that improves the quality of life.

Web Sites

1745 **American Heart Association**
www.heart.org
A national organization whose primary concern is the reduction of death and disability due to cardiovascular diseases and stroke.

1746 **Healing Well**
www.healingwell.com
An online health resource guide to medical news, chat, information and articles, newsgroups and message boards, books, disease-related web sites, medical directories, and more for patients, friends, and family coping with disabling diseases, disorders, or chronic illnesses.

1747 **Health Central**
www.healthcentral.com
Find clearly explained, medically accurate information regarding conditions, including an overview, symptoms, causes, diagnostic procedures and treatment options. On this site it is possible to ask questions and get information from a neurologist and connect to people who have similar health interests.

1748 **Health Finder**
www.health.gov
Searchable, carefully developed web site offering information on over 1000 topics. Developed by the US Department of Health and Human Services, thesite can be used in both English and Spanish.

1749 **Medical News Today**
www.medicalnewstody.com
Offers in-depth health information and the latest news in medical research on a wide variety of medical conditions.

1750 **MedicineNet**
www.medicinenet.com
An online resource for consumers providing easy-to-read, authoritative medical and health information.

1751 **MedlinePlus**
www.medlineplus.gov
Information regarding a broad range of health,and mental health conditions topics include: Latest news, overview of anatomy and physiology, clinical trials, diagnoses and symptoms, treatment, genetics, plus lots of links to other sites. A service provided by the National Library of Medicine, part of the National Institutes of Health (NIH).

1752 **Medscape**
www.medscape.com
Medscape offers specialists, primary care physicians, and other health professionals the Web's most robust and integrated medical information and educational tools.

1753 **MyHealthfinder**
www.healthfinder.gov
Searchable, carefully developed web site offering information on over 1000 topics. Developed by the US Department of Health and Human Services, the site can be used in both English and Spanish.

1754 **National Heart, Lung & Blood Institute**
www.nhlbi.nih.gov
Primary responsibility of this organization is the scientific investigation of heart, blood vessel, lung and blood disorders. Oversees research, demonstration, prevention, education and training activities in these fields and emphasizes the control of stroke.

1755 **National Stroke Association**
www.stroke.org
A national organization whose sole purpose is to reduce the incidence and impact of stroke through prevention, treatment, rehabilitation and research, and support for stroke survivors and their families. Educational resources on all aspects of stroke available on website.

1756 **Neurology Channel**
www.healthcommunities.com
Find clearly explained, medically accurate information regarding conditions, including an overview, symptoms, causes, diagnostic procedures and treatment options. On this site it is possible to ask questions and get information from a neurologist and connect to people who have similar health interests.

1757 **WebMD**
www.webmd.com
Provides credible information, supportive communities, and in-depth reference material about health subjects.

SUBSTANCE-RELATED & ADDICTIVE DISORDERS

Substance-related and addictive disorders, also referred to as substance use disorders (SUD), are treatable mental health disorders that affect the individual's brain leading to changes in behavior. Depression and anxiety may also exist in connection with SUD. Changes in behavior may include overuse of legal and illegal drugs, alcohol or medications causing mild to moderate symptoms. Addiction is the most severe form of substance abuse and differs from SUD in that it is a chronic disease that is incredibly difficult to control. Substance use disorder combines the categories of substance abuse and substance dependence on a scale from mild to severe. Substance use disorders are defined as primary, progressive, chronic, relapsing and treatable diseases. Addictions remold the brain to assign more value to compulsions than health, work family and even life.

Individuals often link substance dependence with addiction, when in fact, dependance can be a normal body response to a substance. Addictive disorders, in addition to substance-related disorder, include behavioral disorders such as gambling disorder and internet gaming disorder. For example, gambling disorder is similar to substance use disorder in clinical expression, comorbidity, physiology, brain origin and treatment. Additional behavioral disorders, including general use of the internet and social media, are being researched to determine if these activities can rise to the level of behavioral disorders. Regardless of formal diagnoses, any behavior that interferes with activities of daily life to the detriment of self and others should be monitored.

Alcohol use disorder remains the most common substance use disorder, encouraged by both the social aspects of alcohol consumption and the perceived health benefits of a daily glass of wine. In adults reporting alcohol dependence, over half also experienced anxiety or depression, and one-third experienced a personality disorder. Tobacco use disorder causes almost half a million deaths each year and may do damage to nearly every organ in the human body.

Opioids, even when used correctly for pain control, may be addictive if continued for too long and are used for the euphoria created by the drug after the pain subsides. Opioid abuse may lead to the use of other chemicals. Marijuana is the most-used drug in the United States after alcohol and tobacco, and over 4 million people 12 and up met the criteria for substance use disorder based on the drug.

Substance use disorder and addiction are complicated diseases that are highly personalized to the individual. The physiological and emotional makeup of the person may result in some people being able to resist substance abuse and behavioral abuse while others experience crippling addiction. The individual will most likely need the assistance of mental health professionals to address the impact of SUD.

Substance-Related & Addictive Disorders / Agencies & Associations

Agencies & Associations

1758 **AMERSA**
P.O. Box 952
Charlestown, RI 02813
401-230-2165
doreen@amersa.org
amersa.org
The Association for Multidisciplinary Education and Research in Substance use and Addiction (AMERSA) is a nonprofit organization of healthcare professionals dedicated to improving education and clinical care in the management of problems related to substance abuse.
Rebecca Northup, Executive Director

1759 **Academy of Psychosomatic Medicine**
4800 Hampden Ln
Bethesda, MD 20814
301-718-6520
info@CLpsychiatry.org
apm.org
The Academy of Psychosomatic Medicine represents psychiatrists focused on improving education, medical science, and healthcare for individuals with comorbid psychiatric and general medical conditions. The Academy seeks to promote interdisciplinary education and drive research and public policy with the goal of achieving outstanding clinical care for patients with comorbid psychiatric and general medical conditions throughout the world. They also created the Foundation of the Academy of Psychosom
Philip Biaeler, MD, FACLP, President
Maryland Pao, MD, FACLP, President-Elect

1760 **Adult Children of Alcoholics World Service Organization, Inc.**
P.O. Box 811
Lakewood, CA 90714
310-534-1815
adultchildren.org
Adult Children of Alcoholics is a 12 Step, 12 Tradition program for adult women and men who grew up in alcoholic or otherwise dysfunctional homes, and for adults who have experienced abuse or neglect in the past. The program involves ACA members meeting with each other in a mutually respectful, safe environment and sharing their experiences, as well as applying the program's 12 Steps for recovery to their own lives.

1761 **African American Family Services (AAFS)**
310 Groveland Avenue S
Minneapolis, MN 55403
612-813-5034
Fax: 651-925-0044
dgrogan@aafs.org
www.aafs.net
African American Family Services works with individuals, families and communities affected by addiction and mental illness. Provides culturally-specific mental health services.
Thomas Adams, Chief Executive Officer
Harvey Linder, MD, Behavioral Health Director

1762 **American Academy of Addiction Psychiatry (AAAP)**
400 Massasoit Avenue
East Providence, RI 02914
401-524-3076
Fax: 401-272-0922
aaap.org
An organization of healthcare professionals dedicated to helping those with mental health disorders. Promotes the use of evidence-based research in the assessment and treatment of substance abuse and mental disorders, as well as in public policy and clinical practice. Provides education to healthcare professionals and the public on patient care, recovery, and the safe treatment of those suffering from substance abuse disorders.
Larissa Mooney, MD, President
Kathryn Cates-Wessel, CEO

1763 **American Chronic Pain Association**
11936 W. 119th Street
Overland Park, KS 66213-2216
913-991-4740
ACPA@theacpa.org
www.theacpa.org
The ACPA facilitates peer support and education for individuals with chronic pain in its many forms, in order to increase quality of life. Also raises awareness in the healthcare community.
Trupti Gokani, MD, President
Kathy Sapp, Chief Executive Officer

1764 **American Psychiatric Association**
800 Maine Avenue SW
Washington, DC 20024
202-559-3900
apa@psych.org
www.psychiatry.org
A medical specialty society representing a growing membership of psychiatrists. Offers information for psychiatrists, medical students, patients and families.
Saul Levin, MD, MPA, FRCP-E, CEO

1765 **American Public Human Services Association**
1300 17th St. N
Arlington, VA 22209
202-682-0100
Fax: 202-289-6555
memberservice@aphsa.org
aphsa.org
APHSA is a nonprofit organization dedicated to improving health and human services by supporting state and local agencies, and working with partners and policymakers to drive effective policies.
Tracy Wareing Evans, President & CEO
Ray Davidson, Chief Operating Officer

1766 **American Society of Addiction Medicine**
11400 Rockville Pike
Rockville, MD 20852
301-656-3920
Fax: 301-656-3815
email@asam.org
asam.org
ASAM's mission is to support the practice of Addiction Medicine and to improve the quality of care and treatment for people struggling with addiction.
Brian Hurley, MD, MBA, President
Stephen M. Taylor, MD, President-Elect

1767 **Center for Family Support (CFS)**
333 Seventh Avenue
New York, NY 10001
888-813-5014
svernikoff@cfsny.org
www.cfsny.org
The Center for Family Support offers assistance to individuals with developmental and related disabilities, as well as their families, and provides support services and programs that are designed to accommodate individual needs. Offers services throughout New York City, Westchester County, Long Island, and New Jersey.
Steven Vernikoff, Executive Director
Barbara Greenwald, Chief Operating Officer

1768 **Center for Mental Health Services (CMHS)**
Substance Abuse and Mental Health Services Admin.
5600 Fishers Lane
Rockville, MD 20857
240-276-1310
samhsa.gov
Promotes the treatment of mental illness and emotional disorders by increasing accessibility to mental health programs; supporting outreach, treatment, rehabilitation, and support programs and networks; and encouraging the use of scientifically-based information when treating mental disorders. CMHS provides information about mental health via a toll-free number and numerous publications.
Anita Everett, M.D., DFAPA, Director

1769 **Center for Substance Abuse Prevention: Substance Abuse & Mental Health Services**
5600 Fishers Lane
Rockville, MD 20857
240-276-2420
877-726-4727
TTY: 800-487-4889
www.samhsa.gov
Connects people and resources with strategies and programs designed to encourage efforts aimed at reducing and eliminating alcohol, tobacco and other drug problems in society. Works with federal, state, public and private organizations to develop prevention programs.
Jennifer Fan, Pharm.D., J.D., Acting Director

1770 **Cocaine Anonymous World Services**
21720 S. Wilmington Ave
Long Beach, CA 90810-1641
310-559-5833
Fax: 310-559-2554
cawso@ca.org
www.ca.org
Members are recovering from addiction, and offer support and maintain their sobriety by working together.

1771 **Community Anti-Drug Coalitions of America (CADCA)**
500 Montgomery Street
Alexandria, VA 22314
703-706-0560
Fax: 703-706-0565
international@cadca.org
cadca.org

Substance-Related & Addictive Disorders / Agencies & Associations

Community Anti-Drug Coalition of America is a national organization representing the interests of over 5,000 anti-drug coalitions across the United States. CADCA participates in public policy advocacy and provides community coalitions with marketing programs, technical assistance and training, and special events with the purpose of making communities safe and drug-free.
Mary Bono, Chairman
Larry P. Cote, Vice Chairman

1772 Drug Abuse Resistance Education of America
P.O. Box 512090   310-215-0575
Los Angeles, CA 90051   800-223-3273
Fax: 310-215-0180
dare.org
Provides information, resources, tips, warning signs and other information for parents and kids to help keep children off drugs.
Francisco X. Pegueros, President & CEO
Thomas Hazelton, President, Development

1773 FASD United
P.O. Box 251   202-785-4585
McLean, VA 22101   fasdunited.org
Educates the public about the risks associated with alcohol use during pregnancy, including Fetal Alcohol Spectrum Disorders, which causes birth defects and developmental disabilities in children. Dedicated to preventing alcohol consumption during pregnancy and reducing the number of birth defects. Provides support for individuals and families concerned with Fetal Alcohol Spectrum Disorders.
Tom Donaldson, President & CEO
Jennifer Wisdahl, Chief Operating Officer

1774 Goodwill Industries-Suncoast, Inc.
727-523-1512
888-279-1988
TTY: 727-579-1068
goodwill-suncoast.org
A nonprofit, community-based organization whose mission is to help people achieve self-sufficiency through the dignity and power of work, serving people who are disadvantaged, disabled or elderly. The mission is accomplished through providing independent living skills, affordable housing, and training and placement in community employment.
Sandra Young, Chair
Deborah A. Passerini, President & CEO

1775 Grief Recovery After a Substance Passing (GRASP)
11819 N. Deerfield Dr.   302-492-7717
Dunlap, IL 61614   administrator@grasphelp.org
grasphelp.org
GRASP provides information resources, offers support, and organizes meetings and events for families or individuals who have experienced the death of a loved one as a result of substance abuse or addiction.
Tamara Olt, Executive Director
Darleen Berg, Chair

1776 Help is Here
North Dakota Behavioral Health Division
600 E Boulevard Avenue   701-328-2310
Bismarck, ND 58501   800-472-2622
dhsbhd@nd.gov
www.helpishere.nd.gov
Promotes the support and treatment of mental illness and emotional disorders. Offers mental health services, addiction servces, and recovery centers.

1777 Indian Health Service
5600 Fishers Lane   605-226-7456
Rockville, MD 20857   800-225-0241
www.ihs.gov
Provides a comprehensive program of alcoholism and substance abuse prevention and treatment for Native Americans and Alaskan natives.

1778 Institute for Contemporary Psychotherapy
33 W 60th St.   212-333-3444
New York, NY 10023   Fax: 212-333-5444
icpnyc.org

The Institute for Contemporary Psychotherapy is a New York City-based mental health treatment and training facility. Consisting of a group of 150 licensed psychotherapists, the Institute focuses on educating the public about the issues surrounding mental health, providing post-graduate training for therapists, and offering therapy at moderate costs.
Ron Taffel, PhD, Chair
Andrea Green-Lewis, LCSW-R, Director of Operations

1779 Lawyers Concerned for Lawyers
2550 University Avenue W.   651-646-5590
Saint Paul, MN 55114   866-525-6466
help@mnlcl.org
www.mnlcl.org
A non-profit organization of recovering lawyers, judges, law students, and concerned others. Educates and arranges interventions and offers lawyer-only AA meetings.
Joan Bibelhausen, Executive Director
Judith Rush, Outreach Manager

1780 Mental Health America
500 Montgomery Street   703-684-7722
Alexandria, VA 22314   800-969-6642
Fax: 703-684-5968
mhanational.org
Mental Health America is a community-based nonprofit organization committed to enabling the mental wellness of all Americans. MHA advocates for greater access to quality health services and seeks to educate individuals on identifying symptoms, as well as intervention and prevention.
Schroeder Stribling, President & CEO

1781 MindWise Innovations
270 Bridge Street   781-239-0071
Dedham, MA 02026   SOS@mindwise.org
www.mindwise.org
Formerly known as Screening For Mental Health, MindWise Innovations provides resources to schools, workplaces, and communities to address mental health issues, substance abuse, and suicide.

1782 Mothers Against Drunk Driving (MADD)
511 E. John Carpenter Freeway   877-275-6233
Irving, TX 75062   www.madd.org
Founded by a small group of mothers and currently one of the largest crime victims organizations in the world. Resources available online.
Ellen Willmott, Interim CEO
Andrew Robinson, Chair

1783 NCADD
28 East Ostend Street   adminl@ncadd.us
Baltimore, MD 21230   www.ncadd.org
The National Council on Alcoholism and Drug Dependence, Inc. (NCADD) is a national leading organization dedicated to fighting the addiction epidemic, providing awareness, support, and resources.

1784 National Alliance on Mental Illness (NAMI)
4301 Wilson Boulevard   703-524-7600
Arlington, VA 22203   800-950-6264
nami.org
NAMI is an organization dedicated to raising awareness on mental health and providing support and education for Americans affected by mental illness. NAMI advocates for access to services and treatment and fosters an environment of awareness and understanding for those concerned with mental health.
Joyce A. Campbell, President
Daniel H. Gillison, Jr., CEO

1785 National Association for Children of Alcoholics (NACOA)
10920 Connecticut Avenue   301-468-0985
Kensington, MD 20895   888-554-2627
info@nacoa.org
www.nacoa.org
Advocates for all children and families affected by alcohol and other drug dependencies. Programs, training, and other resources are available.
Denise Bertin Epp, MS, RN, CEO

Substance-Related & Addictive Disorders / Agencies & Associations

1786 **National Association of Addiction Treatment Providers (NAATP)**
P.O. Box 271686
Louisville, CO 80027
888-574-1008
info@naatp.org
naatp.org
NAATP ensures the availability and accessibility of high quality addiction treatment across the country through leadership, advocacy, training, and other member support services.
Marvin Ventrell, JD, CEO

1787 **National Association of Alcoholism and Drug Abuse Counselors (NAADAC)**
44 Canal Center Plaza
Alexandria, VA 22314
703-741-7686
Fax: 703-741-7698
naadac@naadac.org
www.naadac.org
Largest membership organization serving addiction counselors, educators and other addiction-focused health care professionals who specialize in addiction prevention, treatment and education.
Cynthia Moreno Tuohy, BSW, SAP, Executive Director
Jessica Gleason, JD, Deputy Director

1788 **National Association of State Alcohol/Drug Abuse Directors**
1919 Pennsylvania Avenue NW
Washington, DC 20006
202-293-0090
Fax: 202-293-1250
dcoffice@nasadad.org
nasadad.org
The National Association of State Alcohol and Drug Abuse Directors is a private, not-for-profit organization focused on the promotion of educational and scientific materials on alcohol, drug abuse, and related fields. NASADAD seeks to support and further the development of effective alcohol and other drug abuse treatment programs in the United States.
Sara Goldsby, President
Robert Morrison, Executive Director

1789 **National Association on Drug Abuse Problems**
355 Lexington Avenue
New York, NY 10017
212-986-1170
info@nadap.org
www.nadap.org
Private non-profit corporation providing skills, evaluation, job training and job placement to recovering drug addicts in the metropolitan New York area.
John A. Darin, President & CEO
Gary Stankowski, EVP, COO & CCO

1790 **National Coalition for the Homeless**
2201 P Street Northwest
Washington, DC 20037
202-462-4822
info@nationalhomeless.org
nationalhomeless.org
The National Coalition for the Homeless is an organization serving to protect the needs of those experiencing homelessness, while striving to prevent and end homelessness. NCH promotes effective treatment, services, and programs for those struggling with homelessness as well as substance abuse problems.
Barbara Anderson, Treasurer
Donald Whitehead, Executive Director

1791 **National Council for Behavioral Health**
1400 K Street NW
Washington, DC 20005
202-684-7457
communications@thenationalcouncil.org
www.thenationalcouncil.org
The National Council for Behavioral Health serves to unify America's behavioral health organizations. The council is dedicated to ensuring that quality mental health and addictions care is readily accessible to all Americans.
Edward Woods, Chair
Charles Ingoglia, President & COO

1792 **National Crime Prevention Council**
1100 15th Street, NW
Washington, DC 20005
www.ncpc.org
Organization working to prevent crime and drug use by developing materials for parents and children, teaching strategies to communities, and raising awareness by coodinating with local agencies.
Paul DelPonte, Executive Director

1793 **National Families in Action (NFIA)**
P.O. Box 45339
San Francisco, CA 94145-0339
nfia@nationalfamilies.org
www.nationalfamilies.org
Non-profit organization that obtained the nation's first state laws banning the sale of drug paraphernalia. Leads a national effort to help parents replicate Georgia's laws in other states to prevent the marketing of drugs and drug use to children.
Bill Carter, Board Chairman
Sue Rusche, President & CEO

1794 **National Institute on Alcohol Abuse and Alcoholism (NIAAA)**
National Institute on Health
9000 Rockville Pike
Rockville, MD 20892
301-443-3860
niaaaweb-r@exchange.nih.gov
www.niaaa.nih.gov
NIAAA seeks to reduce alcohol-related problems by conducting scientific research in a range of areas, including neuroscience, treatment, prevention, and epidemiology; working with other research institutes, federal programs, and organizations focused on the issues surrounding alcohol abuse; and disseminating information to healthcare providers, researchers, policymakers, and the public.
George F. Koob, PhD, Director
Patricia A. Powell, Deputy Director

1795 **National Institute on Drug Abuse (NIDA)**
251 Bayview Blvd.
Baltimore, MD 21224
443-740-2463
800-535-8254
www.nida.nih.gov
NIDA's mission is to lead the Nation in bringing the power of science to bear on drug abuse and addiction.
Amy H. Newman, Ph.D., Scientific Director
Lorenzo Leggio, M.D., Ph.D., Deputy Scientific Director

1796 **Office of Women's Services: Substance Abuse & Mental Health Services**
5600 Fishers Lane
Rockville, MD 20857
877-726-4727
www.samhsa.gov
Provides leadership and guidance in creating and maintaining an agency-wide focus for addressing the substance abuse and mental health needs of women.

1797 **Partnership to End Addiction**
711 Third Avenue
New York, NY 10017
212-841-5200
contact@toendaddiction.org
www.drugfree.org
Dedicated to transforming how addiction is addressed by the nation, from prevention to recovery.
Creighton Drury, CEO
Emily Feinstein, J.D., Executive Vice President

1798 **Recovered**
224 West 35th Street
New York, NY 10001
info@recovered.org
recovered.org
An organization of writers and editors dedicated to raising awareness on susbtance abuse.

1799 **Remove Intoxicated Drivers (RID-USA)**
P.O. Box 520
Schenectady, NY 12301
518-372-0034
ridusa@verizon.net
rid-usa.org
Volunteers working to deter impaired driving, to help its victims obtain justice, restitution and peace of mind while navigating the criminal justice systems, and to curb the alcohol abuse which leads to drunk driving.
Doris Aiken, Founder

1800 **Section for Psychiatric and Substance Abuse Services (SPSPAS)**
155 North Wacker Drive
Chicago, IL 60606
312-422-3000
800-424-4301
www.aha.org
A membership section that represents over 1,660 behavioral health providers and professionals who are members of the American Hospital Association (AHA). The Section applies AHA policy, advocacy, and service efforts to advance understandings of behavioral health care and to emphasize its importance.
Richard J. Pollack, President & CEO
Michelle Hood, EVP & COO

1801 **Substance Abuse and Mental Health Services Administration (SAMHSA)**
5600 Fishers Lane
Rockville, MD 20857
877-726-4727
TTY: 800-487-4889
www.samhsa.gov

Substance-Related & Addictive Disorders / Agencies & Associations

Part of the U.S. Department of Health and Human Services, SAMHSA promotes, monitors, evaluates and coordinates programs for the prevention and treatment of alcoholism and alcohol abuse.
Miriam E. Delphin-Rittmon, Ph.D., Asststistant Secretary, Mental Health

Alabama

1802 Alabama Department of Mental Health: Div. of Mental Health & Substance Abuse
100 North Union Street
Montgomery, AL 36130
334-242-3642
Alabama.DMH@mh.alabama.gov
www.mh.alabama.gov

Alaska

1803 Alaska Department of Health: Office of Substance Abuse and Addiction Prevention
3601 C Street
Anchorage, AK 99503
907-269-7800
osmap@alaska.gov
health.alaska.gov/Pages/default.aspx
Heidi Hedberg, Commissioner

Delaware

1804 Delaware Division of Substance Abuse and Mental Health (DSAMH)
Alcohol And Drug Services
1901 N. Du Pont Highway
New Castle, DE 19720
302-255-9399
DHSSInfor@state.de.us
dhss.delaware.gov/dsamh/
Renata J. Henry, Director

Florida

1805 Alcohol and Drug Abuse Program
Department of Children and Families
P.O. Box 1770
Ocala, FL 34478-1770
850-300-4323
Fax: 866-886-4342
myflfamilies.com/service-programs/samh/
The Substance Abuse and Mental Health (SAMH) Program, within the Florida Department of Children and Families, is the single state authority on substance abuse and mental health as designated by the federal Substance Abuse and Mental Health Services Administration (SAMHSA). The Department's SAMH Program oversees a statewide system of care for the prevention, treatment, and recovery of children and adults with serious mental illnesses and/or substance abuse disorders.

Georgia

1806 Alcohol and Drug Services
Addictive Diseases Program
Two Peachtree Street NW
Atlanta, GA 30303
404-657-2331
dbhdd.georgia.gov/be-supported/help-subs
DBHDD contracts with providers in all 6 regions to provide outpatient and residential substance abuse treatment to men and women who are struggling with the disease of addiction

Hawaii

1807 Alcohol and Drug Abuse Division
Department of Health
601 Kamokila Blvd.
Kapoleiu, HI 96707
808-692-7506
health.hawaii.gov/substance-abuse/
The mission of the Department of Health is to protect and improve the health and environment for all people in Hawai'i.
Loretta J. Fuddy, Director
Keith Yamamoto, Asst. Director

Illinois

1808 Illinois Department of Alcoholism and Susbstance Abuse
Department of Human Services
2605 Woodlawn Rd
Sterling, IL 61081
815-632-4045
www.dhs.state.il.us

Indiana

1809 Indiana Division of Addiction Services
800-901-1133
www.in.gov/fssa/dmha/home/

Iowa

1810 Department of Public Health: Division of Substance Abuse
Lucas State Office Bldg.
Des Moines, IA 50319
515-281-7689
866-227-9878
Fax: 515-281-4535
www.idph.state.ia.us
The Iowa Department of Public Health (IDPH) partners with local public health, policymakers, health care providers, business and many others to fulfill their mission of promoting and protecting the health of Iowans.
DeAnn Decker, Bureau Chief

Louisiana

1811 Alcohol and Drug Abuse Council of South Louisiana
1155 St. Charles Street
Houma, LA 70360
985-879-2273
Fax: 985-879-3766
ftoups@adacsl.org
www.dhh.louisiana.gov

Massachusetts

1812 Bureau of Substance Addiction Services
250 Washington Street
Boston, MA 02108
617-624-5111
800-327-5050
Fax: 617-624-5185
TTY: 888-448-8321
mass.gov/orgs/bureau-of-substance-addict

Nebraska

1813 Department of Public Instruction: Division of Alcoholism and Drug Abuse
301 Centennial Mall South
Lincoln, NE 68509
402-471-3121
866-866-8660
TTY: 800-833-7352
dhhs.ne.gov/Pages/Addiction-Treatment-an

New Jersey

1814 New Jersey Division of Mental Health and Addiction Services
5 Commerce Way
Hamilton, NJ 08691
800-382-6717
www.state.nj.us/humanservices/dmhas/home
Valerie L. Mielke, MSW, Assistant Commissioner

New York

1815 New York Office of Addiction Services and Supports
Substance Abuse Services
1450 Western Avenue
Albany, NY 12203
518-473-3460
877-846-7369
Fax: 518-457-5474
communications@oasas.ny.gov
www.oasas.ny.gov
Chinazo Cunningham, Commissioner
Sean Byrne, Executive Deputy Commissioner

North Carolina

1816 North Carolina Mental Health and Substance Abuse
NC Department of Health and Human Services
2001 Mail Service Center
Raleigh, NC 27699-2000
800-662-7030
www.dhhs.state.nc.us

Oklahoma

1817 Oklahoma Department of Mental Health and Substance Abuse Services
Substance Abuse Program
2000 N. Classen Blvd.
Oklahoma City, OK 73106
405-248-9200
oklahoma.gov/odmhsas.html

553

Substance-Related & Addictive Disorders / Foundations

Rhode Island

1818 **Rhode Island Department of Behavioral Healthcare: Substance Use/Addiction**
14 Harrington Rd.
02920ton, RI 02920
401-462-2339
Fax: 401-462-3204
bhddh.ri.gov/substance-useaddiction

Richard Charest, Director

South Carolina

1819 **South Carolina Department of Alcohol and Drug Abuse Services**
1801 Main Street
Columbia, SC 29201
803-896-5555
www.daodas.org

Tennessee

1820 **Tennessee Department of Mental Health and Substance Abuse Services**
500 Deaderick Street
Nashville, TN 37243
800-560-5767
www.tn.gov/behavioral-health.html

Marie Williams, Commissioner

Texas

1821 **Texas Health And Human Service: Mental Health & Substance Use**
www.hhs.texas.gov

Cecile Erwin Young, Executive Commissioner

Utah

1822 **Utah Department of Health & Human Services : Substance Abuse & Mental Health**
195 North 1950 West
Salt Lake City, UT 84116
dsamh@utah.gov
sumh.utah.gov

Vermont

1823 **Vermont Department of Health: Division of Substance Use Programs (DSU)**
108 Cherry Street
Burlington, VT 05402
802-651-1550
AHS.VDHADAP@vermont.gov
www.healthvermont.gov

Virginia

1824 **Virginia Department of Behavioral Health & Developmental Services**
Substance Use Disorder Services
1220 Bank Street
Richmond, VA 23219
804-786-3921
Fax: 804-371-6638
TTY: 804-371-8977
dbhds.virginia.gov

Nelson Smith, Commissioner

Wyoming

1825 **Wyoming Department of Health: Substance Use and Tobacco Prevention Program**
122 West 25th St.
Cheyenne, WY 82002
307-777-6541
wdh.prevention@wyo.gov
health.wyo.gov

Mica Moeller, Program Manager

Foundations

1826 **AAA Foundation for Traffic Safety**
607 14th Street NW
Washington, DC 20005
202-638-5944
info@aaafoundation.org
www.aaafoundation.org

A non-profit foundation that conducts research with the goal of preventing traffic deaths. Raises awareness on road safety measures and driver education.

C. Y. David Yang, President & Executive Director
William J. Horrey, Technical Director

1827 **ABMRF/The Foundation for Alcohol Research**
1200-C Agora Dr.
Bel Air, MD 21401
800-688-7152
grantinfo@abmrf.org
www.abmrf.org

Founded in 1982 to promote research on testing systems that could diagnose the metabolic aspects of alcoholism. Seeks to educate the public on the validity of the disease concept of alcoholism.

1828 **Brain & Behavior Research Foundation**
747 Third Avenue
New York, NY 10017
646-681-4888
800-829-8289
info@bbrfoundation.org
www.bbrfoundation.org

The Brain and Behavior Research Foundation awards grants aimed at advancing scientific understandings of mental health treatments and mental disorders such as depression and schizophrenia. The Brain and Behavior Research Foundation's mission is to eliminate the suffering caused by mental illness.

Geoffrey A. Simon, Chairman
Miriam E. Katowitz, CPA, Vice President

1829 **Hazelden Betty Ford Foundation**
P.O. Box 11
Center City, MN 55012
844-598-4521
800-257-7810
info@hazeldenbettyford.org
www.hazelden.org

Helps individuals, families, and communities struggling with alcohol abuse, substance abuse, and drug addiction by offering prevention and recovery solutions nationwide.

James A. Blaha, Vice President, CFO & CAO
Alta DeRoo, MD, Chief Medical Officer

Libraries & Resource Centers

1830 **Family-to-Family: National Alliance on Mental Illness**
4301 Wilson Boulevard
Arlington, VA 22203
703-524-7600
888-999-6264
info@nami.org
nami.org

The NAMI Family-to-Family Education Program is a free, 8 session course for family caregivers of individuals with severe mental illnesses. The course is taught by trained family members, all instruction and course materials are free to class participants, and over 300,000 family members have graduated from this national program.

1831 **National Mental Health Consumers' Self-Help Clearinghouse**
selfhelpclearinghouse@gmail.com
mhselfhelp.org

The Clearinghouse is a peer-run national technical assistance center focused on achieving respect and equality of opportunity for those with mental illnesses. The Clearinghouse helps with the growth of the mental health consumer movement by evaluating mental health services, advocating for mental health reform, and providing consumers with news, information, publications, and consultation services.

Joseph Rogers, Founder & Executive Director
Susan Rogers, Director

1832 **Office on Smoking and Health: Centers for Disease Control & Prevention**
1600 Clifton Road
Atlanta, GA 30329
800-232-4636
TTY: 888-232-6348
tobaccoinfo@cdc.gov
www.cdc.gov/tobacco

Offers reference services to researchers through the Technical Information Center. Publishes and distributes a number of titles in the field of smoking and health.

1833 **Parents Resource Institute for Drug Education**
160 Vanderbilt Court
Bowling Green, KY 42103
800-279-6361
Fax: 270-746-9598
info@pridesurveys.com
www.pridesurveys.com

Offers national information and educational materials pertaining to alcohol and drug dependency.

Thomas J. Gleaton, EdD, President
Janie Pitcock, President

Substance-Related & Addictive Disorders / Research Centers

1834 Students Against Destructive Decisions
655 15th Street NW   508-481-3568
Washington, DC 20005   www.sadd.org
Provides students with prevention tools to deal with the issues of underage drinking, drug use, risky and impaired driving, and other destructive decisions.
Rick Birt, President & CEO
Elizabeth Vermette, VP, Public Affairs

Research Centers

1835 Alcohol Research Group Public Health Institute
Public Health Institute
6475 Christie Avenue   510-597-3440
Emeryville, CA 94608   Fax: 510-985-6459
                                                 info@arg.org
                                                 www.arg.org
The Alcohol Research Group (ARG) of the Public Health Institute was established in 1959 to conduct and disseminate high-quality research in epidemiology of alcohol consumption and problems including alcohol use disorders, alcohol-related health services research, and analyses of alcohol policy and its impacts.
Thomas K. Greenfield, Scientific Director

1836 Boston University Laboratory of Neuropsychology
Dept of Behavioral Neuroscience
80 E Concord Street M9   617-638-4803
Boston, MA 02118   Fax: 617-638-4806
                                                 www.bu.edu
Offers research and studies into the effects of Alcoholism pertaining to aphasia, apraxia, dementia, memory disorders and various other neurological malfunctions.

1837 Center for Alcohol & Addiction Studies Brown University
Brown University
121 South Main Street   401-863-6600
Providence, RI 02903   Fax: 401-863-6697
                                                 caas@brown.edu
                                                 www.caas.brown.edu
The Center for Alcohol and Addiction Studies, through its affiliation with the Brown Medical School, occupies a unique position within the University. The Center brings together more that 90 faculty and professional staff members, from 11 University departments and eight affiliated hospitals, to promote the identification, prevention, and effective treatment of alcohol and other substance abuse.
Peter M. Monti, PhD, Center Director
Suzanne Colby, PhD, Associate Director

1838 Centre for Addiction and Mental Health
1001 Queen Street West   416-535-8501
Toronto, ON, M6J-1H4   800-463-2338
                                                 info@camh.ca
                                                 camh.ca
The Centre for Addiction and Mental Health is a mental health and addiction teaching hospital and research centre based in Canada. CAMH seeks to support people affected by mental health and addiction issues through research, education, policy development, clinical care, and the promotion of health.
Sarah Downey, President & CEO

1839 Cornerstone Treatment Facilities Network
Medical Arts Center Hospital
159-05 Union Turnpike   718-906-6700
Fresh Meadows, NY 11366   800-233-9999
                                            Fax: 718-906-6840
                                                 admin@cornerstoneny.com
                                                 www.cornerstoneny.com
Offers a complete integrated program for alcohol assessment alcohol and drug rehabilitation continuing care community education and comprehensive family recovery.
Norine Hurtado, Senior Vice President, Human Resources

1840 Dorothea Dix Hospital Clinical Research Unit
809 Ruggles Drive   919-733-5227
Raleigh, NC 27603   866-349-5627
                                            Fax: 919-733-5351
                                                 www.med.unc.edu
Researches the biological risk factors of alcoholism using young adults without the disease but with history of familial alcoholism.
Terry Spell, Director
William L. Roper, CEO

1841 Ernest Gallo Clinic and Research Center
5858 Horton Street   510-985-3100
Emeryville, CA 94608   Fax: 510-985-3101
                                                 www.galloresearch.org
Alcoholism studies with a special emphasis on genetics.
John A. De Luca, PhD, Chairman of the Board/President
Joseph E. Gallo, President/Chief Executive Officer

1842 Families in Action
National Drug Abuse Center
P.O. Box 3553   252-237-1242
Wilson, NC 27895   Fax: 252-237-6544
                                                 phil@familiesinaction.org
                                                 www.familiesinaction.org
Publish prevention materials and serves as an information clearinghouse for families with a member suffering from a drug or alcohol addiction.
Phillip A. Mooring, Executive Director
Anna Godwin, Coordinator

1843 Friends Medical Science Research Center
1229 West Mount Royal Avenue   410-752-4218
Baltimore, MD 21217   Fax: 310-477-9601
                                                 www.wellness.com
Studies narcotic addictions.
John Valenty, President
Rob Greenstein, President

1844 Hahnemann University Laboratory of Human Pharmacology
Department of Pharmacology
Broad and Vine   215-762-7000
Philadelphia, PA 19102   Fax: 215-762-8109
                                                 www.hahnemannhospital.com
Hahnemann University hospital is committed to providing quality patient care in an academic setting.

1845 Harvard Cocaine Recovery Project
1493 Cambridge Street   617-498-1000
Cambridge, MA 02139   Fax: 617-642-58
Six-year study of relapse and recovery in cocaine addicts.

1846 Interdisciplinary Program in Cell and Molecular Pharmacology
Medical University of South Carolina
173 Ashley Avenue BSB 358   843-792-8975
Charleston, SC 29425   Fax: 843-792-0481
                                                 www.musc.edu/pharm
Research into pharmacology and toxicology.
Kenneth D. Tew, Ph.D., D.Sc., Professor and Chairman
Michelle Shorter, Administrative Coordinator

1847 Johns Hopkins University: Behavioral Pharmacology Research Unit
John Hopkins Bay View Campus
5510 Nathan Shock Drive   410-955-5000
Baltimore, MD 21224   Fax: 410-550-0030
                                                 bigelow@jhmi.edu
                                                 www.hopkinsmedicine.org
An internationally recognized center of excellence in research on psychoactive drugs. As the name implies BPRU's orientation is behavioral and pharmacological, emphasizing a behavioral analysis of drug action.
George E. Bigelow, PhD, Scientific Director
Eric C. Strain, MD, Medical Director

1848 Kettering-Scott Magnetic Resonance Laboratory
Wright State University, School of Medicine
P.O. Box 927   937-775-2934
Dayton, OH 45435   www.med.wright.edu
No information found on the website.
Marjorie Bowman, MD, Dean
Betty Kangas, Assistant to the dean

1849 Marin Institute
24 Belvedere Street   415-456-5692
San Rafael, CA 94901   Fax: 415-456-0491
                                                 www.marinInstitute.org

Substance-Related & Addictive Disorders / Research Centers

The mission of this Institute is to reduce the toll of alcohol and other drug problems on Marin County and society in general. The Institute fulfills this mission by developing, implementing, evaluating and disseminating innovative approaches to prevention locally, nationally and internationally.
Bruce Lee Livingston, MPP, Executive Director

1850 Narcotic and Drug Research
11 Beach Street
New York, NY 10013
212-966-8700
Fax: 212-334-8058
Nonprofit organization that is devoted to drug abuse education treatment and prevention.
Douglas S. Lipton, PhD, Director

1851 National Center on Addiction and Substance Abuse
Columbia University
633 3rd Avenue
New York, NY 10017
212-841-5200
800-622-4357
Fax: 212-956-8020
www.casacolumbia.org
The only nation-wide organization that brings together under one roof all the professional disciplines needed to study and combat abuse of all substances - alcohol nicotine as well as illegal prescription and performance enhancing drugs - in all sectors of society.
Lee C. Bollinger, President
Ursula M. Burns, Chairman & CEO

1852 National Prevention Resource Center CSAP Division of Communications Programs
CSAP Division of Communications Programs
5600 Fishers Lane
Rockville, MD 20857
301-443-9936
Supports an array of prevention program evaluation approaches including individual grantee evaluations program evaluations and a National Evaluation Project. Also offers a National Data Base to provide information on programs for prevention of substance abuse.

1853 National Volunteer Training Center for Substance Abuse Prevention
CSAP Division of Communications Programs
5600 Fishers Lane
Rockville, MD 20857
301-443-9936
Volunteers are always on hand to provide answers, information, referrals and resources pertaining to alcohol, drugs and substance abuse.

1854 Ohio State University Clinical Pharmacology Division
College of Medicine
370 Western 9th Avenue
Columbus, OH 43210
614-292-2220
800-252-3636
Fax: 614-292-4293
www.medicine.osu.edu
Substance abuse and alcohol related research.
Robert Bornstein, PhD, Vice Dean, Academic Affairs
Glen Apsloss, Director

1855 Research Institute on Alcoholism
State University of New York at Buffalo
1021 Main Street
Buffalo, NY 14203
716-887-2566
Fax: 716-872-52
connors@ria.buffalo.edu
www.ria.buffalo.edu
Integral part of the New York State Division of Alcoholism and Alcohol Abuse.
Kenneth E. Leonard, PhD, Director
Kimberly S. Walitzer, PhD, Deputy Director

1856 Research Society on Alcoholism
7801 North Lamar Blvd.
Austin, TX 78752-1038
512-454-0022
debbyrsa@sbcglobal.net
researchsocietyonalcohol.org
The Research Society on Alcoholism, founded in 1976, serves as a forum for scientists and researchers focused on the fields of alcoholism and alcohol-related problems. The Society promotes research with the purpose of advancing treatment of alcoholism and finding potential cures.
Lara Ray, PhD, President
Howard Becker, PhD, Vice President

1857 Rockefeller University Laboratory of Biology
1230 York Avenue
New York, NY 10065
212-327-8000
Fax: 212-327-7974
www.rockefeller.edu

1858 Rutgers University Center of Alcohol Studies
Busch Campus
607 Allison Road
Piscataway, NJ 08854
732-445-2190
Fax: 732-445-3500
alclib@rci.rutgers.edu
alcoholstudies.rutgers.edu
Causes and treatment of alcoholism.

1859 Ruth E. Golding Clinical Pharmacokinetics Laboratory
College of Pharmacy
1703 E Mabel
Tucson, AZ 85721
520-626-1938
www.pharmacy.arizona.edu
Conducts studies of drugs in humans and animals.

1860 Southern California Research Institute
7065 Hayvenhurst Avenue
Van Nuys, CA 90066
310-390-8481
Fax: 310-390-8482
www.scri.org
Effects of alcohol and drugs on behavior studies.
Dary Fiorent, PhD, Executive Director

1861 Stanford Center for Research in Disease Prevention
Stanford University School of Medicine
1070 Arastradero Road
Palo Alto, CA 94304
650-723-6254
Fax: 650-723-6254
prevention.stanford.edu
Prevention and control of alcohol and drug abuse related disorders.
John P.A Loannidis, MD, DSc, Director

1862 State University of New York at Buffalo Toxicology Research Center
3435 Main Street
Buffalo, NY 14214
716-831-2125
Fax: 716-829-2806
www.smbs.buffalo.edu
Toxicology-related research and services, including the development of tests to evaluate toxins, chemicals and drugs.
Michale E. Cain, Director
Dr. James R. Olson, Assistant Director

1863 UAMS Psychiatric Research Institute
4224 Shuffield Drive
Little Rock, AR 72205
501-526-8100
kramerteresal@uams.edu
www.psychiatry.uams.edu
Combining research, education and clinical services into one facility, PRI offers inpatiend and outpatient services, with 40 psychiatric beds, therapy options, and specialized treatment for specific disorders, including: addictive eating, anxiety, deppressive and post-traumatic stress disorders. Research focuses on evidence-based care takes into consideration the education of future medical personnel while relying on research scientists to provide innovative forms of treatment.

1864 University of California: Los Angeles Alcohol Research Center
405 Hilgard Ave
Los Angeles, CA 90095
310-825-4321
Fax: 310-206-7309
www.ucla.edu
Causes of alcoholism, including genetics.
Dr. Ernest Noble, Director

1865 University of Michigan: Alcohol Research Center
400 E Eisenhower Parkway
Ann Arbor, MI 48108
734-764-1817
Fax: 734-998-7994
www.umich.edu
Alcohol abuse studies among the elderly, including the relationship between alcohol and aged disorders.
Robert A. Zucker, PhD, Contact

1866 University of Michigan: Psychiatric Center
4250 Plymouth road
Ann Arbor, MI 48109
734-936-5900
Fax: 734-936-9761
www.umich.edu
Psychiatric disease research pertaining to the effects of alcoholism and drug abuse.

Substance-Related & Addictive Disorders / Support Groups & Hotlines

1867 **University of Minnesota: Program on Alcohol/Drug Control**
Stadium Gate 27 612-624-6861
Minneapolis, MN 55455
Alcohol, tobacco and drug research.
Dr. James Schaefer, Director

1868 **University of Missouri: Kansas City Drug Information Service**
2464 Charlotte 816-235-5490
Kansas City, MO 64108 Fax: 816-235-5491
umkcdruginformation@umkc.edu
dic.umkc.edu
Literature research and evaluation of clinical drug problems and questions.
Pat Bryant, PhD, Director
Heather A. Pace, PhD, Assistant Director

1869 **University of Tennessee Drug Information Center**
875 Monroe Avenue 901-528-5555
Memphis, TN 38163 Fax: 901-448-5419
dop.utmem.edu/dic
Katie Suda, Director
Camille Thornton, Assistant Professor

1870 **University of Texas Health Science Center Neurophysiology Research Center**
Speech & Hearing Institute
7000 Fannin 713-500-4472
Houston, TX 77030 Fax: 713-792-4513
Conducts clinical and animal studies aimed at combating alcohol, drug and tobacco dependence.
Giuseppe N. Colasurdo, Director

1871 **University of Texas at Austin: Drug Synamics Institute**
1 University Station 512-475-9746
Austin, TX 78712 Fax: 512-471-2746
www.utexas.edu
Pharmaceutical and drug research.
Janet C. Walkow, PhD, Director
Carla Van Den Berg, PhD, Associate Professor

1872 **University of Utah: Center for Human Toxicology**
30 South 2000 East 801-581-6731
Salt Lake City, UT 84112 Fax: 801-581-3716
dwilkins@alanine.pharm.utah.edu
www.pharmacy.utah.edu
Clinical, forensic and toxicology research.
Chris M. Ireland, PhD, Dean
Dennis Crouch, Director

1873 **University of Wisconsin Milwaukee Medicinal Chemistry Group**
University of Wisconsin
P.O. Box 413 414-229-1122
Milwaukee, WI 53201 www4.uwm.edu
Research on drugs, including studies of valium receptors.
Michael R. Lovell, Chancellor

Support Groups & Hotlines

1874 **Adult Children of Alcoholics**
P.O. Box 811 310-534-1815
Lakewood, CA 90714 adultchildren.org
An anonymous twelve-step, twelve-tradition program of women and men who grew up in an alcoholic or otherwise dysfunctional homes.

1875 **Al-Anon Alateen Family Group Hotline**
1600 Corporate Landing Parkway 757-563-1600
Virginia Beach, VA 23454 888-425-2666
Fax: 757-563-1655
wso@alanon.org
www.al-anon.alateen.org
A mutual peer-to-peer support program with groups meeting worldwide to provide hope and help to the families of alcoholics. Although a seperate entity from Alcoholics Anonymous, this program is based upon the Twelve Steps.
Ric Buchanan, Executive Director

1876 **Al-Anon Family Group Headquarters**
1600 Corporate Landing Parkway 757-563-1600
Virginia Beach, VA 23454-5617 888-425-2666
Fax: 757-563-1656
wso@al-anon.org
www.al-anon.org
At Al-Anon Family Group meetings, family members and friends of problem drinkers share their experiences and learn how to apply the principles of the Al-Anon program to their individual situations.

1877 **Al-Anon Family Group National Referral Hotline**
1600 Corporate Landing Parkway 757-563-1600
Virginia Beach, VA 23454 wso@al-anon.org
al-anon.alateen.org
Al-Anon is a mutual support group of peers who share their experience in applying the Al-Anon principles to problems related to the effects of a problem drinker in their lives. It is not group therapy and is not led by a counselor or therapist; This support network complements and supports professional treatment.

1878 **Alateen and Al-Anon Family Groups**
1600 Corporate Landing Parkway 757-563-1600
Virginia Beach, VA 23454 888-425-2666
wso@al-anon.org
A fellowship of men, women, children and adult children affected by another persons drinking.
Mary Ann Keller, Director, Members Services

1879 **Alcohol Drug Treatment Referral**
1316 South Coast Highway 800-454-8966
Laguna Beach, CA 92651 Fax: 949-281-1933
National Help and Referral Network, a nonprofit organization available 24 hours a day to assist people troubled by drug or alcohol abuse. Here to provide information on addiction treatment and support services and to help save lives and mend broken dreams.
Mike Cohan, Director

1880 **Alcoholics Anonymous**
475 Riverside Drive at W. 120th St. 212-870-3400
New York, NY 10115 www.aa.org
Alcoholics Anonymous is an international alliance of supportive individuals who have had a drinking problem. Membership is available to anyone wanting to improve their situation.

1881 **Alcoholics Anonymous (AA): World Services**
475 Riverside Drive at W. 120th St. 212-870-3400
New York, NY 10115 www.aa.org
For men and women who share the common problems of alcoholism.

1882 **Chemically Dependent Anonymous**
P.O. Box 423 888-232-4673
Severna Park, MD 21146 www.cdaweb.org
A 12-step fellowship for anyone seeking freedom from drug and alcohol addiction. The basis of the program is abstinence from all mood-changing and mind-altering chemicals, including street-type drugs, alcohol and unnecessary medication.

1883 **Cocaine Anonymous**
21720 S. Wilmington Ave 310-559-5833
Long Beach, CA 90810-1641 cawso@ca.org
ca.org
Fellowship of men and women who share their experience, stength and hope with each other in hope that they may solve their common problem and help others recover from their addiction.

1884 **Common Ground Sanctuary**
1410 S. Telegraph 248-456-8150
Bloomfield Hills, MI 48302 800-231-1127
www.commongroundsanctuary.org
A 24-hour nonprofit agency dedicated to helping youths, adults and families in crisis. Through its crisis line and in person through various programs, Common Ground Sanctuary provides professional and compassionate service to more than 40,000 people a year, with most services provided free of charge. Mission is to provide a lifeline for individuals and families in crisis, victims of crime, persons with mental illness, people trying to cope with critical situations and runaway and homeless youth.
Tony Rothschild, President & CEO
Steve Mitchell, Board Chair

Substance-Related & Addictive Disorders / Support Groups & Hotlines

1885 **Drug Free Workplace Hotline**
Division of Workplace Programs
Samhsa Diagonal CSAP 1 Choke Cherry
Rockville, MD 20857
240-276-2612
877-726-4727
Fax: 240-276-1210
TDD: 800-457-4889
webmaster@samhsa.hhs.gov
www.drugfreeworkplace.gov
A hotline for businesses to obtain information on a wide range of drug abuse related problems, issues and services.
Robert Stephenson II, Director

1886 **Families Anonymous, Inc.**
701 Lee Street
Des Plaines, IL 60016
800-736-9805
847-294-5877
Fax: 847-294-5837
info@familiesanonymous.org
www.familiesanonymous.org
Addresses the needs of families who are concerned about a relative with a drug problem and with related behavioral problems. Offers informational packets, meetings and support networks for these families.

1887 **First Presbyterian Church in the City of New York Support Groups**
First Presbyterian Church in the City of New York
12 West 12th Street
New York, NY 10011
212-675-6150
fpcnyc@fpcnyc.org
www.fpcnyc.org
The First Presbyterian Church in the City of New York provides numerous programs and supports groups for both adults and children including an educational program for children.
Jon M Walton, Senior Pastor
Sarah Segal Mccaslin, Associate Pastor

1888 **Friday Night Live**
California Dept of Drug & Alcohol Programs
1700 K Street
Sacramento, CA 95814
916-445-7456
Fax: 916-230-59
www.communitycounseling.org/fnl
These groups, located in California, are all run by students with a faculty adviser. They arrange local alcohol and drug free events, from dances and movies to visiting hospitalized children. Students not only have fun but they learn to have fun sober.
Jim Kooler, Administrator
Laura Purcellabuzo, Project Coordinator

1889 **Images Within: A Child's View of Parental Alcoholism**
Children of Alcoholics Foundation
P.O. Box 4185
New York, NY 10163
212-595-5810
800-359-2623
www.coaf.org
An innovative program designed to teach all children about family alcoholism. Middle-school-aged children learn how to get help for themselves or give help to their friends.

1890 **Infoline**
United Way of Connecticut
1344 Silas Deane Highway
Rocky Hill, CT 06067
860-571-7500
800-203-1234
TTY: 800-671-0737
ctunitedway.org
Infoline is a free, confidential, help-by-telephone service for information, referral, and crisis intervention. Trained professionals help callers find information, discover options or deal with a crisis by locating hundreds of services in their area on many different issues, from substance abuse to elder needs to suicide to volunteering in your community. Infoline is certified by the American Association of Suicidology. Operates 24 hours a day, everyday. Multilingual caseworkers are available.
Richard Porth, CEO

1891 **MADD-Mothers Against Drunk Drivers**
511 E. John Carpenter Freeway
Irving, TX 75062
877-275-6233
www.madd.org
Mission is to stop drunk driving, support the victims of this violent crime and prevent underage drinking. MADD's work has saved nearly 300,000 lives and counting.
Ellen Willmott, Interim CEO
Andrew Robinson, Chair

1892 **Marijuana Anonymous**
5551 Hollywood Blvd.
Hollywood, CA 90028-6814
800-766-6779
support@marijuana-anonymous.org
marijuana-anonymous.org
A fellowship of men and women who share experience, strength and hope with each other to solve common problem and help others to recover from marijuana addiction.

1893 **Marijuana Anonymous World Services**
5551 Hollywood Blvd.
Hollywood, CA 90028-6814
800-766-6779
support@marijuana-anonymous.org
www.marijuana-anonymous.org
Non-profit fellowship of individuals with marijuana addiction, seeking sobriety and support.

1894 **Nar-Anon Family Groups**
22527 Crenshaw Blvd
Torrance, CA 90505
310-534-8188
800-477-6291
nar-anon.org
Twelve-step program for families and friends of addicts.
Cathy Khaledi, Executive Director

1895 **Narcotics Anonymous**
P.O. Box 9999
Van Nuys, CA 91409
818-773-9999
na.org
Peer support for recovered addicts.

1896 **Narcotics Anonymous World Services**
P.O. Box 9999
Van Nuys, CA 91409
818-773-9999
Fax: 818-700-0700
fsmail@na.org
www.na.org
A fellowship of individuals who meet to help one another with their drug dependency. Support and resources are available.

1897 **National Health Information Center**
Office of Disease Prevention & Health Promotion
1101 Wootton Pkwy
Rockville, MD 20852
Fax: 240-453-8281
odphpinfo@hhs.gov
www.health.gov/nhic
Supports public health education by maintaining a calendar of National Health Observances; helps connect consumers and health professionals to organizations that can best answer questions and provide up-to-date contact information from reliable sources; updates on a yearly basis toll-free numbers for health information, Federal health clearinghouses and info centers.
Don Wright, MD, MPH, Director

1898 **Pathways to Promise**
5400 Arsenal Street
Saint Louis, MO 63139
pathways2promise.org
An interfaith cooperative of many faith groups, providing assistance and a resource center which offers liturgical and educational materials, program models, caring ministry with people experiencing a mental illness and their families.

1899 **Rational Recovery**
P.O. Box 800
Lotus, CA 95651
530-621-2667
rational.org
Exclusive, worldwide source of counseling, guidance and direct instruction on self-recovery from addiction to alcohol and other drugs through planned, permanent abstinence.
Jack Trimpey, President

1900 **SMART Recovery**
7304 Mentor Avenue
Mentor, OH 44060
440-951-5357
866-951-5357
info@smartrecovery.org
smartrecovery.org
The leading self-empowering addiction recovery support group. Participants learn tools for addiction recovery based on the latest scientific research and participate in a world-wide community which includes free, self-empowering, science-based mutual help groups.
Shari Allwood, Executive Director

1901 **Students Against Destructive Decisions (SADD)**
655 15th Street NW
Washington, DC 20005
508-481-3568
www.sadd.org
SADD's mission is to provide students with the best prevention tools possible to deal with the issues of underage drinking, other

drug use, risky and impaired driving, and other destructive decisions.
Rick Birt, President & CEO
Elizabeth Vermette, VP, Public Affairs

1902 ToughLove International
P.O. Box 1069   215-348-7090
Doylestown, PA 18901   800-333-1069
www.toughlove.org
This national self-help group for parents, children and communities emphasizes cooperation, personal initiative and action. Publishes books, brochures and promotional information and holds workshops and seminars across the country.

1903 WFS' New Life Program
Women for Sobriety
P.O. Box 618   215-536-8026
Quakertown, PA 18951   Fax: 215-538-9026
newlife@nni.com
www.womenforsobriety.org
A self-help program for women that can be used independent from AA or with AA. Groups are in many states in the United States. Donations suggested.
Rebecca M. Fenner, Director

Print Resources

1904 ACAP Recap
American Council on Alcohol Problems
3426 Bridgeland Drive   314-739-5944
Bridgeton, MO 63044   Fax: 314-739-0848
www.lifemanagement.com
Offers information on organization activities and events, updates on resources and publications and legislative information for affiliate executives.
Dr. Curt Scarborough, Executive Director

1905 Alcohol Research: Current Reviews (ARCR)
National Institute on Alcohol Abuse and Alcoholism
9000 Rockville Pike   301-443-3860
Bethesda, MD 20892   arcr.niaaa.nih.gov
An open-access, peer-reviewed journal available online with no subscription or pay-per-view fees. Publishes reviews on the field of alcohol research.
Pamela Wernett, PhD, PMP, Editor-in-Chief
Sheri Grabus, PhD, Managing Editor

1906 American Issue
American Council on Alcohol Problems
3426 Bridgeland Drive   314-739-5944
Bridgeton, MO 63044   Fax: 314-739-0848
www.lifemanagement.com
Offered to contributors of the organization.
Dr. Curt Scarborough, Executive Director

1907 American Journal of Psychiatry
American Psychiatric Association Publishing
800 Maine Avenue SW, Suite 900   202-459-9722
Washington, DC 20024   800-368-5777
Fax: 202-403-3094
psychiatryonline@psych.org
ajp.psychiatryonline.org
Official journal of the American Psychiatric Association (APA).
Ned H. Kalin, MD, Editor-in-Chief

1908 American Journal of Psychotherapy
American Psychiatric Association Publishing
800 Maine Avenue SW, Suite 900   202-459-9722
Washington, DC 20024   800-368-5777
Fax: 202-403-3094
psychiatryonline@psych.org
ajp.psychiatryonline.org
Publishes content that aims to advance the theory, science, and clinical practice of psychotherapy.
Holly A. Swartz, MD, Editor-in-Chief

1909 Drug Abuse Update
2296 Henderson Mill Road   770-934-6364
Atlanta, GA 30345
A journal of news and information for persons interested in drug prevention.

1910 Forum Magazine
Al-Anon Alateen Family Group Headquarters
1600 Corp Landing Pkwy.   757-563-1600
Virginia Beach, VA 23454-5617   888-425-2666
Fax: 757-563-1655
wso@al-anon.org
www.al-anon.alateen.org
Contains many personal stories of inspiration, some of which are maade available each month on the Internet by authorization of Al-Anon Family Group Headquarters, Inc.

1911 International Archives of Substance Abuse and Rehabilitation
ClinMed International Library
3511 Silverside Road, Suite 105   302-208-7437
Wilmington, DE 19810   contact@clinmedjournals.org
clinmedjournals.org
Open access, peer-reviewed journal focused on research articles on substance abuse, and development of treatment.
Yury Evgeny Razvodovsky, Editor-in-Chief

1912 International Journal of Addiction Research and Medicine
ClinMed International Library
3511 Silverside Road, Suite 105   302-208-7437
Wilmington, DE 19810   contact@clinmedjournals.org
clinmedjournals.org
Open access, peer-reviewed journal in the field of human addictive behaviors and research medicine.
Raimondo Pavarin, Editor-in-Chief

1913 Lead Line
Grapevine
P.O. Box 1980   212-870-3400
New York, NY 10163   Fax: 212-870-3301
AA members all over the world communicate with each other through the pages of this magazine. It contains: insight into how AAs stay sober; readers' views; old-timers corner, beginners meeting, youth enjoying sobriety, and spotlight on service.

1914 Substance Abuse: Research and Treatment
Sage Publishing
katy.shanahan@sagepub.co.uk
journals.sagepub.com/home/sata
An international, peer-reviewed journal that publishes content on human substance abuse research and treatment.
Gregory L. Stuart, Editor-in-Chief
Susan Ramsey, Deputy Editor-in-Chief

Web Sites

1915 AA-Alcoholics Anonymous
www.aa.org
Group sharing their experience, strength and hope with each other to recover from alcoholism.

1916 AAA Foundation for Traffic Safety
www.aaafoundation.org
The AAA Foundation for Traffic Safety was founded in 1947 by AAA to conduct research to address growing highway safety issues. The organization's mission is to identify traffic safety problems, foster research that seeks solutions and disseminate information and educational materials.

1917 Addiction Resource Guide
www.addictionresourceguide.com
A comprehensive directory of addiction treatment facilities online.

1918 Adult Children of Alcoholics & Dysfunctional Families World Srvc. Org.
www.adultchildren.org
A 12-step and 12-tradition program for adults raised in an environment including alcohol or other dysfunctions.

1919 Al-Anon
www.al-anon.alateen.org
The single purpose of this organization is to help families and friends of alcoholics, whether the alcoholic is still drinking or not.

Substance-Related & Addictive Disorders / Web Sites

1920 Alateen
www.al-anon.org/for-alateen
A part of the Al-Anon program, Alateen is for teenagers who have been affected by someone else's drinking, whether it be a family member or a friend.

1921 Alcoholism Home Page
www.alcoholism.about.com
Information about addictive drug use, behaviors, and alcoholism.

1922 American Council for Drug Education
www.acde.org
This organization provides information on drug use, publishes books and offers films and curriculum materials for prevention.

1923 Association for Addiction Professionals (NAADAC)
www.naadac.org
NAADAC is the premier global organization of addiction focused professionals who enhance the health and recovery of individuals, families and communities. NAADAC's mission is to lead, unify and empower addiction focused professionals to achieve excellence through education, advocacy, knowledge, standards of practice, ethics, professional development and research.

1924 Center for Family Support (CFS)
www.cfsny.org
Devoted to providing support and assistance to individuals with developmental and related disabilities, and to the family members who care for them.

1925 Cocaine Anonymous
www.ca.org
A support group based on the twelve steps of Alcoholics Anonymous that focuses specifically on problems of cocaine addiction.

1926 FASD United
fasdunited.org
Develops and implements innovative prevention and education strategies assessing fetal alcohol syndrome.

1927 Families Anonymous
www.familiesanonymous.org
Addresses the needs of families who are concerned about a relative with a drug problem and with related behavioral problems.

1928 Hazelden
www.hazelden.com
Organization dedicated to providing quality rehabilitation, education and professional services for chemical dependency and related addictive behaviors.

1929 Healing Well
www.healingwell.com
A social network and support community for patients, caregivers, and families coping with the daily struggles of diseases, disorders and chronic illness.

1930 Health Central
www.healthcentral.com
Find clearly explained, medically accurate information regarding conditions, including an overview, symptoms, causes, diagnostic procedures and treatment options. On this site it is possible to ask questions and get information from a neurologist and connect to people who have similar health interests.

1931 Health Finder
www.health.gov
Searchable, carefully developed web site offering information on over 1000 topics. Developed by the US Department of Health and Human Services, thesite can be used in both English and Spanish.

1932 Higher ED Center
www.higheredcenter.org
One-stop resource for information about abuse prevention and addiction treatment.

1933 Indian Health Service
www.ihs.gov
Charged with providing a comprehensive program of alcoholism and substance abuse prevention and treatment for Native Americans and Alaskan natives.

1934 Jewish Alcoholics, Chemically Dependent Persons and Significant Others (JACS)
www.jacsweb.org
Ten articles dealing with denial and ignorance.

1935 Lawyers Concerned for Lawyers
www.mnlcl.org
Lawyers Concerned for Lawyers provides free, confidential peer and professional assistance to Minnesota lawyers, judges, law students, and their immediate family members on any issue that causes stress or distress.

1936 LifeRing Secular Recovery
www.lifering.org
Offers nonreligious approach with links to groups.

1937 Medical News Today
www.medicalnewstody.com
Offers in-depth health information and the latest news in medical research on a wide variety of medical conditions.

1938 MedicineNet
www.medicinenet.com
An online resource for consumers providing easy-to-read, authoritative medical and health information.

1939 MedlinePlus
www.medlineplus.gov
Information regarding a broad range of health,and mental health conditions topics include: Latest news, overview of anatomy and physiology, clinical trials, diagnoses and symptoms, treatment, genetics, plus lots of links to other sites. A service provided by the National Library of Medicine, part of the National Institutes of Health (NIH).

1940 Medscape
www.medscape.com
Medscape offers specialists, primary care physicians, and other health professionals the Web's most robust and integrated medical information and educational tools.

1941 MentalHealth.com
www.mentalhealth.com
Online information and a virtual encyclopedia related to mental disorders, possible causes and treatments. News, articles, on-line diagnostic programs and related links. Designed to improve understanding, diagnosis and treatment of mental illness throughout the world. Awarded the Top Site Award and the NetPsych Cutting Edge Site Award.

1942 Mothers Against Drunk Driving
www.madd.org
A crusade to stop alcohol consumption and underage drinking.

1943 MyHealthfinder
www.healthfinder.gov
Searchable, carefully developed web site offering information on over 1000 topics. Developed by the US Department of Health and Human Services, the site can be used in both English and Spanish.

1944 National Clearinghouse for Alcohol and Drug Information
www.health.org

1945 National Council for Mental Wellbeing
www.thenationalcouncil.org
A network for sharing information and provding assistance among those working in the healthcare management field.

1946 National Council on Alcoholism and Drug Dependence
www.ncadd.org
Provides education, information, help and hope in the fight against addictions. Nationwide network of affiliates, advocates prevention, intervention and treatment, and is committed to ridding the disease of its stigma and its sufferers of their denial and shame.

1947 National Crime Prevention Council
www.ncpc.org
This organization works to prevent crime and drug use in many ways, including developing materials for parents and children.

1948 National Institute on Alcohol Abuse & Alcoholism
www.niaaa.nih.gov

Supports research nationwide on alcohol abuse and alcoholism.

1949 **National Institute on Drug Abuse (NIDA)**
www.drugabuse.gov
NIDA's mission is to lead the Nation in bringing the power of science to bear on drug abuse and addiction.

1950 **National Mental Health Consumers' Self-Help Clearinghouse**
www.mhselfhelp.org
Encourages the development and growth of consumer self-help groups.

1951 **Office on Smoking and Health**
www.cdc.gov/tobacco/
Offers reference services to researchers through the Technical Information Center. Publishes and distributes a number of titles in the field of smoking and health.

1952 **Psych Central**
www.psychcentral.com
Personalized one-stop index for psychology, support, and mental health issues, resources, and people on the Internet.

1953 **SMART Recovery**
www.smartrecovery.org
Four-Point program includes maintaining motivation, coping with urges, managing feelings and behavior, balancing momentary/enduring satisfactions.

1954 **Safe Homes**
www.yescap.org/safehomes/safehomes.htm
This national organization encourages parents to sign a contract stipulating that when parties are held in one another's homes they will adhere to a strict no-alcohol/no-drug-use rule.

1955 **Souls Self Help**
www.soulselfhelp.on.ca/coda.html
Discusses self-help, mental health, issues of co-dependency.

1956 **Students Against Destructive Decisions (SADD)**
www.sadd.org
Peer leadership organization dedicated to preventing destructive decisions.

1957 **Substance Abuse And Mental Health Services Administration**
www.store.samhsa.gov
Resources on mental disorders as well as treatment and recovery.

1958 **Substance Abuse and Mental Health Services Administration (SAMHSA)**
www.samhsa.gov
Provides links to government resources related to substance abuse and mental health.

1959 **WebMD**
www.webmd.com
Provides credible information, supportive communities, and in-depth reference material about health subjects. A source for original and timely health information, as well as material from well-known content providers.

SUICIDE

Suicide is death caused by self-directed behaviors designed to create an intent to die as a result of the individual's actions, or, simply put, attempting to kill oneself. A suicide attempt is a potential behavior with the intent to die that is not successful and might not result in injury. Thinking about, considering, or planning suicide is referred to as suicidal ideation. Suicide is a major public health concern and is among the leading causes of death in the United States. In 2020, suicide was the 12th leading cause of death in the U.S., resulting in almost 50,000 people dying from suicide. Suicide deaths are almost twice that of murders in the U.S. Approximately five percent of individuals 18 and older had serious thoughts about suicide. The financial toll of suicide and non-fatal suicide attempts is significant, with over $500 billion in medical costs, work loss costs and quality of life costs incurred in 2020.

Suicide attempts and suicide create serious physical, emotional and economic impacts, affecting family and friends, co-workers, and the community. If the suicide attempt is successful, surviving family and friends experience long-term grief, anger, and shock, and may even create thoughts of suicide themselves. If a non-fatal attempt occurs, there are often physical, emotional, and mental limitations that result causing a diminished quality of life, including burdens placed on the family, friends, and caregivers.

Clinical depression, also referred to as major depressive disorder, is a common mood disorder that causes severe symptoms and disruptions in daily life. In the individual with depression, thoughts of death or suicide, or suicide attempts may occur. Not everyone who is depressed is considered suicidal, but without intervention, depression can worsen leading to extreme negative thoughts about self leading to suicidal ideation.

Early treatment for depression is more effective, and treatments include medication, psychotherapy, or a combination of the two. Individuals respond differently to depression and treatments should be individualized. Antidepressants, anticonvulsant, or antipsychotic medications may be used. Psychotherapies, also called counseling or talk therapy, can help with depression. Since major depression can lead to suicidal thoughts or actions, it is important to seek care early. A health care provider or mental health professional such as a psychiatrist or psychologist will diagnosis and plan treatments for interventions to control depression and decrease the risk for suicide. Additionally, daily physical activity, regular sleep habits, a healthy diet and social interactions will aid in managing depression.

Thoughts of death or suicide require immediate help! Call the National Suicide Prevention Lifeline toll-free at 1-800-273-TALK (8255), or consider going to a local hospital or calling 911.

Suicide / Agencies & Associations

Agencies & Associations

1960 **American Association of Suicidology**
448 Walton Avenue
Hummelstown, PA 17036
202-237-2280
info@suicidology.org
suicidology.org

The American Association of Suicidology is a nonprofit membership organization for those affected by suicide, as well as those involved in suicide prevention and intervention. AAS aims to foster an environment of understanding and support for all those who have been affected by suicide. AAS works towards the advancement of suicide prevention programs and scientific efforts through research, education, and training, information dissemination, and support services for survivors.
Leeann Sherman, MPS, CAE, Board President & CEO
Jacque Christmas, MPA, BSW, Secretary

1961 **Friends for Survival, Inc.**
PO Box 214463
Sacramento, CA 95821
916-392-0664
800-646-7322
info@friendsforsurvival.org
friendsforsurvival.org

A national nonprofit outreach organization open to those who have lost family or friends by suicide, and also to professionals who work with those who have been touched by a suicide tragedy. Dedicated to providing a variety of peer support services that comfort those in grief, encourage healing and growth, foster the development of skills to cope with a loss and educate the entire community regarding the impact of suicide.

1962 **Help is Here**
North Dakota Behavioral Health Division
600 E Boulevard Avenue
Bismarck, ND 58501
701-328-2310
800-472-2622
dhsbhd@nd.gov
www.helpishere.nd.gov

Promotes the support and treatment of mental illness and emotional disorders. Offers mental health services, addiction servces, and recovery centers.

1963 **Hope for Depression Research Foundation**
40 West 57th Street
New York, NY 10019
212-676-3200
Fax: 212-676-3219
hdrf@hopefordepression.org
www.hopefordepression.org

Promotes, and encourages profits for neuroscience research into the treatments, diagnosis, origins, and prevention of depression, and other mood disorders such as anxiety disorders, post-traumatic stress disorder, postpartum depression, bipolar disorder, and suicide.
Audrey Gruss, Founder & Chairman
Harold W. Koenigsberg, MD, Board Member

1964 **Institute for Contemporary Psychotherapy**
33 W 60th St.
New York, NY 10023
212-333-3444
Fax: 212-333-5444
icpnyc.org

The Institute for Contemporary Psychotherapy is a New York City-based mental health treatment and training facility. Consisting of a group of 150 licensed psychotherapists, the Institute focuses on educating the public about the issues surrounding mental health, providing post-graduate training for therapists, and offering therapy at moderate costs.
Ron Taffel, PhD, Chair
Andrea Green-Lewis, LCSW-R, Director of Operations

1965 **International Academy of Suicide Research**
secretary@suicide-research.org
suicide-research.org

The Academy promotes research and scholarship in the field of suicidal behaviour research. Publishes the Archives of Suicide Research.
Holly Wilcox, President
Anat Klomek, Secretary

1966 **International Association for Suicide Prevention**
6218 Georgia Avenue NW, Suite 1
Washington, DC 20011
www.iasp.info

The International Association for Suicide Prevention (IASP) seeks to prevent suicide and suicidal behaviour, and to alleviate its effects.
Wendy Orchard, Executive Director
Katherine Thomson, Head, Marketing and Campaigns

1967 **Mental Health America**
500 Montgomery Street
Alexandria, VA 22314
703-684-7722
800-969-6642
mhanational.org

Mental Health America is a community-based nonprofit organization committed to enabling the mental wellness of all Americans. MHA advocates for greater access to quality health services and seeks to educate individuals on identifying symptoms, as well as intervention and prevention.
Schroeder Stribling, President & CEO
Sachin Doshi, Sr. Dir., Finance & Operations

1968 **National Alliance on Mental Illness**
4301 Wilson Boulevard
Arlington, VA 22203
703-524-7600
800-950-6264
info@nami.org
nami.org

NAMI is an organization dedicated to raising awareness on mental health and providing support and education for Americans affected by mental illness. NAMI advocates for access to services and treatment and fosters an environment of awareness and understanding for those concerned with mental health.
Shirley J. Holloway, President
Joyce A. Campbell, First Vice President

1969 **National Center for the Prevention of Youth Suicide**
American Association of Suicidology
448 Walton Avenue
Hummelstown, PA 17036
202-237-2280
ajkulp@suicidology.org
suicidology.org/ncpys

The goal of the National Center for the Prevention of Youth Suicide is to reduce the rate of suicide attempts and deaths among youth. The National Center provides information on the warning signs of suicide, works with other organizations to help develop effective suicide prevention practices among youth caregivers, promotes better mental health and forms strategies to address suicide risk factors, and encourages youth to participate in grassroots suicide prevention movements.
Leeann Sherman, MPS, CAE, Board President & CEO
Jacque Christmas, MPA, BSW, Secretary

1970 **National Institute of Mental Health**
6001 Executive Boulevard
Bethesda, MD 20892
866-615-6464
nimhinfo@nih.gov
nimh.nih.gov

The National Institute of Mental Health conducts clinical research on mental disorders and seeks to expand knowledge on mental health treatments.
Joshua Gordon, MD, PhD, Director

1971 **National Organization for People of Color Against Suicide (NOPCAS)**
P.O. Box 75571
Washington, DC 20013
301-529-4699
dhb@dhbwellnessllc.com
www.nopcas.com

NOPCAS is a national organization whose mission is to raise awareness on suicide and to promote suicide education, particularly within communities of color. NOPCAS works with minorities in suicide prevention through the production of education resources and publications for communities of color, the development of culturally appropriate training opportunities for professionals, and the promotion of community-based strategies that mobilize minority communities around suicide prevention efforts.
Donna Barnes, PhD, Co-Founder and President
Doris Smith, Co-Founder, VP and Treasurer

1972 **Suicide Awareness Voices of Education (SAV**
7900 Xerxes Avenue South
Bloomington, MN 55431
952-946-7998
save.org

Suicide Awareness Voices of Education's mission is to prevent suicide through the elimination of stigma and the organization of education programs designed to raise awareness on depression, mental illnesses, the importance of assessment, treatment and interven-

Suicide / Support Groups & Hotlines

tion, the warning signs of suicide, and community resources. SAVE also provides resources for those who have been affected by suicide.
Daniel J. Reidenberg, Psy.D., Executive Director
Linda Mars, National Outreach Network Dir.

1973 **United Brain Association**
202-768-8000
info@unitedbrainassociation.org
unitedbrainassociation.org
Non-profit organization that works to find cures through research for over 600 brain and mental health related issues, and disorders.
J.A. Boulton, Founder
Jay Matey, VP & Treasurer

1974 **Yellow Ribbon Suicide Prevention Program**
Light for Life Foundation International
P.O. Box 644
Westminster, CO 80036
303-429-3530
800-273-8255
ask4help@yellowribbon.org
yellowribbon.org
The Yellow Ribbon Suicide Prevention Program provides support services for survivors; promotes the participation of communities, families, and individuals in suicide prevention efforts; develops community-based programs; partners with local agencies to organize suicide prevention trainings; and gives motivational presentations to schools, youth, and adults.

Foundations

1975 **American Foundation for Suicide Prevention**
120 Wall Street
New York, NY 10005
212-363-3500
888-333-2377
info@afsp.org
afsp.org
AFSP has been at the forefront of a wide range of suicide prevention initiatives, each designed to reduce loss of life from suicide. AFSP is investing in groundbreaking research, new educational campaigns, innovative demonstration projects and critical policy work. Also expanding assistance to people whose lives have been affected by suicide, reaching out to offer support and offering opportunities to become involved in prevention.
Nancy Farrell, M.P.A, Chairman
Yeates Conwell, M.D, President

1976 **Brain & Behavior Research Foundation**
747 Third Avenue
New York, NY 10017
646-681-4888
800-829-8289
info@bbrfoundation.org
www.bbrfoundation.org
The Brain and Behavior Research Foundation awards grants aimed at advancing scientific understandings of mental health treatments and mental disorders such as depression and schizophrenia. The Brain and Behavior Research Foundation's mission is to eliminate the suffering caused by mental illness.
Donald M. Boardman, Treasurer
Jeffrey Borenstein, MD, President and CEO

1977 **Byron Peter Foundation for Hope**
31 Hartfort Pike
North Scituate, RI 02857
401-647-9295
A nonprofit foundation established to honor the life of Byron Peter Harrington II, a young man who took his own life in 2001. The Foundation seeks to inspire troubled young people to attain hope for the future. The Foundation provides opportunities for at risk youth, including those struggling with depression or drug use.

1978 **Jason Foundation, Inc.**
18 Volunteer Drive
Hendersonville, TN 37075
615-264-2323
888-881-2323
contact@jasonfoundation.com
jasonfoundation.com
An educational organization dedicated to the awareness and prevention of youth suicide. Develops educational programs that provide young people, youth workers, educators, and parents with the knowledge and resources needed to help identify and support at-risk youth.
Clark Flatt, President
Michele Ray, Senior Vice President and CEO

1979 **National P.O.L.I.C.E. Suicide Foundation**
6039 Cypress Gardens Boulevard
Winter Haven, FL 33884
863-875-2298
redoug2001@aol.com
psf.org
A nonprofit educational foundation focused on the issue of police suicide. Provides support services and training programs on suicide awareness and prevention for police, emergency responders, and their families. Seeks to address the psychological, emotional, and spiritual needs of officers and law enforcement families affected by suicide.
Robert E. Douglas, Jr., Founder and Executive Director
Orlando Ramos, Board Member

Libraries & Resource Centers

1980 **Suicide Prevention Resource Center**
43 Foundry Avenue
Waltham, MA 2453
877-438-7772
Fax: 617-969-9186
TTY: 617-964-5448
info@sprc.org
www.sprc.org
SPRC is the nation's only federally supported resource center devoted to advancing the National Strategy for Suicide Prevention.
Jerry Reed, PhD, MSW, Director
Chris Miara, MS, Director of Operations & Resources

Support Groups & Hotlines

1981 **Common Ground Sanctuary**
1410 S. Telegraph
Bloomfield Hills, MI 48302
248-456-8150
800-231-1127
www.commongroundsanctuary.org
A 24-hour nonprofit agency dedicated to helping youths, adults and families in crisis. Through its crisis line and in person through various programs, Common Ground Sanctuary provides professional and compassionate service to more than 40,000 people a year, with most services provided free of charge. Mission is to provide a lifeline for individuals and families in crisis, victims of crime, persons with mental illness, people trying to cope with critical situations and runaway and homeless youth.
Tony Rothschild, President & CEO
Steve Mitchell, Board Chair

1982 **Covenant House Nineline**
461 Eighth Avenue
New York, NY 10001
212-613-0300
800-388-3888
nineline.org
Nationwide crisis/suicide hotline.
Andrew P. Bustillo, Board Chair
Kevin Ryan, President and CEO

1983 **Infoline**
United Way of Connecticut
1344 Silas Deane Highway
Rocky Hill, CT 06067
860-571-7500
800-203-1234
TTY: 800-671-0737
ctunitedway.org
Infoline is a free, confidential, help-by-telephone service for information, referral, and crisis intervention. Trained professionals help callers find information, discover options or deal with a crisis by locating hundreds of services in their area on many different issues, from substance abuse to elder needs to suicide to volunteering in your community. Infoline is certified by the American Association of Suicidology. Operates 24 hours a day, everyday. Multilingual caseworkers are available.
Richard Porth, CEO

1984 **Survivors of Loved Ones' Suicides (SOLOS)**
8310 Ewing Halsell Drive
San Antonio, TX 78229
210-885-7069
solossanantonio@gmail.com
solossa.org
Located in San Antonio, Texas, SOLOS organizes ongoing support group meetings for persons affected by the loss of loved ones from suicide.

Suicide / Print Resources

Print Resources

1985 **Archives of Suicide Research**
International Academy of Suicide Research
archives@suicide-research.org
suicide-research.org
International journal devoted to the field of suicide research.
Barbara Stanley, Editor-in-Chief
Rory O'Connor, Co-Editor

1986 **Crisis: The Journal of Crisis Intervention and Suicide Prevention**
Hogrefe Publishing Corp.
44 Merrimac Street, Suite 207   978-255-3700
Newburyport, MA 01950   customersupport@hogrefe.com
www.hogrefe.com/us/journal/crisis
Journal of the International Association for Suicide Prevention (IASP)
Jane Pirkis, Editor-in-Chief

1987 **Suicide and Life-Threatening Behavior**
John Wiley & Sons, Inc.
111 River Street, Suite 300   201-748-6000
Hoboken, NJ 07030-5774   800-567-4797
Fax: 201-748-6088
onlinelibrary.wiley.com/journal/1943278x
Journal of the American Association of Suicidology, focused on the latest research, theories, and intervention approaches for suicide and life-threatening behaviors.
Thomas Joiner, PhD, Editor

Web Sites

1988 **American Association of Suicidology**
www.suicidology.org
AAS is a membership organization for all those involved in suicide prevention and intervention, or touched by suicide. AAS is a leader in the advancement of scientific and programmatic efforts in suicide prevention through research, education and training, the development of standards and resources, and survivor support services.

1989 **American Foundation For Suicide Prevention**
www.afsp.org
AFSP has been at the forefront of a wide range of suicide prevention initiatives, each designed to reduce loss of life from suicide. AFSP is investing in groundbreaking research, new educational campaigns, innovative demonstration projects and critical policy work. Also expanding assistance to people whose lives have been affected by suicide, reaching out to offer support and offering opportunities to become involved in prevention.

1990 **Break The Silence**
www.break-the-silence.org
A non profit organization whose basis and foundation came from first-hand knowledge and experience that inpatient safety is not always provided to those in need of protection, causing a desperate need for a watch-dog organization like Break the Silence.

1991 **Covenant House Nineline**
www.nineline.org
Nationwide crisis/suicide hotline.

1992 **Friends For Survival**
www.friendsforsurvival.org
Assisting anyone who has suffered the loss of a loved one through suicide death.

1993 **Grief Guidance Inc.**
www.griefguidance.com
A company created by Doreen Cammarata to promote intervention services for suicide survivors.

1994 **Healing Well**
www.healingwell.com
An online health resource guide to medical news, chat, information and articles, newsgroups and message boards, books, disease-related web sites, medical directories, and more for patients, friends, and family coping with disabling diseases, disorders, or chronic illnesses.

1995 **Health Central**
www.healthcentral.com
Find clearly explained, medically accurate information regarding conditions, including an overview, symptoms, causes, diagnostic procedures and treatment options. On this site it is possible to ask questions and get information from a neurologist and connect to people who have similar health interests.

1996 **Internet Mental Health**
www.mentalhealth.com
Offers online psychiatric diagnosis in the hope of reaching the two-thirds of individuals with mental illness who do not seek treatment.

1997 **Jason Foundation, Inc.**
www.jasonfoundation.com
An educational organization dedicated to the awareness and prevention of youth suicide. JFI believes that awareness and education are the first steps to prevention.

1998 **Medical News Today**
www.medicalnewstody.com
Offers in-depth health information and the latest news in medical research on a wide variety of medical conditions.

1999 **MedicineNet**
www.medicinenet.com
An online resource for consumers providing easy-to-read, authoritative medical and health information.

2000 **MedlinePlus**
www.medlineplus.gov
Information regarding a broad range of health,and mental health conditions topics include: Latest news, overview of anatomy and physiology, clinical trials, diagnoses and symptoms, treatment, genetics, plus lots of links to other sites. A service provided by the National Library of Medicine, part of the National Institutes of Health (NIH).

2001 **Medscape**
www.medscape.com
Medscape offers specialists, primary care physicians, and other health professionals the Web's most robust and integrated medical information and educational tools.

2002 **National Alliance On Mental Illness**
www.nami.org
Nation's leading self-help organization for all those affected by severe brain disorders. Mission is to bring consumers and families with similar experiences together to share information about services, care providers, and ways to cope with the challenges of schizophrenia, manic depression, and other serious mental illnesses.

2003 **National Organization For People Of Color Against Suicide**
www.nopcas.com
NOPCAS serves as the only national organization of its kind addressing the issue of suicide prevention and intervention, specifically in communities of color. Primary focus and mission is to increase suicide education and awareness. Offering unique opportunities for outreach partnerships and community education efforts directed at communities of color across the nation.

2004 **National P.O.L.I.C.E. Suicide Foundation**
www.psf.org
This foundation provides educational training seminars for emergency responders, primarily associated with law enforcement on the issue of police suicide. Providing police suicide awareness and prevention training programs and support services that will meet the psychological, emotional, and spiritual needs of law enforcement, on every level, and their families.

2005 **Substance Abuse & Mental Health Services Administration**
www.mentalhealth.samhsa.gov
Information about resources, technical assistance, research, training, networks, and other federal clearing houses, and fact sheets and materials. Information specialists refer callers to mental health resources in their communities as well as state, federal and nonprofit contacts.

Suicide / Web Sites

2006 Substance Abuse And Mental Health Services Administration
www.store.samhsa.gov
Resources on mental disorders as well as treatment and recovery.

2007 Suicide Awareness Voices Of Education (SAVE)
www.save.org
One of the nation's first organizations dedicated to the prevention of suicide and was a co-founding member of the National Council for Suicide Prevention. Leading national non profit organization with staff dedicated to prevent suicide. Based on the foundation and belief that suicide should no longer be considered a hidden or taboo topic and that through raising awareness and educating the public, we can SAVE lives.

2008 Support Groups
www.suicide.supportgroups.com
An online support group community bringing people together around life's challenges by providing concise, up-to-date information and a meeting place for individuals, their friends and families, and professionals who offer pathways to help.

2009 Survivors Of Loved Ones' Suicides (Solos)
www.solossa.org
Organization to help provide support for the families and friends who have suffered the suicide loss of a loved one.

2010 Verywell Mind
www.verywellmind.com
Provides up-to-date information on mental health topics. mission is to prioritize mental health and promote balance for day to day living. offers over 5,500 online articles that are researched based, and reviwed by medical professionals.
Kristen Altmeyer, MBA, VP & General Manager
Nick Ingalls, MA, Associate Editorial Director

2011 Yellow Ribbon Suicide Prevention Program
www.yellowribbon.org
Dedicated to preventing suicide and attempts by making suicide prevention accessible to everyone and removing barriers to help by empowering individuals and communities through leadership, awareness and education, and by collaborating and partnering with support networks to reduce stigma and help save lives.

TRAUMA & STRESSOR-RELATED DISORDERS

Trauma and stressor-related disorders (TSRD) are seen when an individual has experienced exposure to a traumatic or stressful event causing psychological distress. Examples of traumatic events can include natural and manmade disasters, violence such as assault and abuse, mass shootings, and car crashes.

Exposure to trauma may cause development of anxiety, sadness, and sleep problems, and cause the individual to replay the event over in the mind. Individuals who experience traumatic events may develop depression, panic disorder, substance use or suicidal thoughts. Previously, TRSD was diagnosed as a type of anxiety disorder. TSRD is like posttraumatic stress disorder (PTSD) but differences in timing differentiate the disorders. TSRD usually occurs immediately after exposure to the trauma and lasts up to one month, while PTSD may be a continuation of TSRD or a separate occurrence happening a month or more after the trauma. Both are considered mental health disorders that may lead to disruptions in physical, emotional, social, or general well-being. Feelings may persist long after the traumatic event has ended.

Acute stress disorder, adjustment disorder, disinhibited social engagement disorder (DSED), and reactive attachment disorder (RAD) are also considered stressor-related disorders. Acute stress disorder develops when an individual is exposed to a perceived or actual threat to life, potential injury, or sexual violence directly or by viewing the event. In adjustment disorders, emotional or behavioral symptoms develop within 3 months of a situation occurring. Depression and anxiety are often symptoms with adjustment disorders. DSED is primarily seen in children as a result of social neglect or frequent changes in caregivers. Children with DSED have no fear of strangers and may depart with a stranger inappropriately. RAD is also seen in children and is characterized by emotionally withdrawn behavior towards caregivers. Unspecified trauma and stressor related disorders may be diagnosed absent sufficient evidence of other disorders.

Treatment must be individualized as trauma elicits different reactions in people and not everyone develops TSRD or PTSD. Even if symptoms develop, they may subside without treatment. It is important for the individual to seek professional help if symptoms do not subside. Mental health professionals will assess the individual, make a diagnosis, and develop the plan of care that may include cognitive behavioral therapy and medications. Group therapy, acupuncture, yoga, and other complementary treatments may also be helpful.

Trauma & Stressor-Related Disorders / Agencies & Associations

Agencies & Associations

2012 Administration for Children and Families
330 C Street SW
Washington, DC 20201
877-696-6775
www.acf.hhs.gov
The Administration for Children & Families (ACF) is a division of the U.S. Department of Health & Human Services (HHS). ACF promotes the economic and social well-being of families, children, individuals and communities.
Jeff Hild, Principal Deputy Assistant Secretary
Larry Handerhan, Chief of Staff

2013 African American Post Traumatic Stress Disorder Association
9129 Veterans Drive SW
Lakewood, WA 98498
253-589-0766
aaptsda.org
Non-profit organization supporting Post-Traumatic Stress Disorder (PTSD) research, and individuals with PTSD. Develops programs that encourage healthy living and provides assistance to individuals with PTSD.

2014 Agency for Healthcare Research and Quality
5600 Fishers Lane
Rockville, MD 20857
301-427-1104
www.ahrq.gov
The Agency for Healthcare Research and Quality's (AHRQ) mission is to produce evidence to make health care safer, higher quality, more accessible, equitable, and affordable, and to work within the U.S. Department of Health and Human Services and with other partners to make sure that the evidence is understood and used.
Robert Otto Valdez, PhD, MHSA, Acting Director
Howard E. Holland, Director, Communications

2015 Agency for Toxic Substances and Disease Registry
1600 Clifton Rd. NE
Atlanta, GA 30329
800-232-4636
www.atsdr.cdc.gov
The Agency for Toxic Substances and Disease Registry (ATSDR), based in Atlanta, Georgia, is a federal public health agency of the U.S. Department of Health and Human Services. ATSDR serves the public by using the best science, taking responsive public health actions, and providing trusted health information to prevent harmful exposures and diseases related to toxic substances.
Robin M. Ikeda, MD, MPH, Acting Director

2016 Agent Orange Registry Department of Veterans Affairs
Department of Veterans Affairs Headquarters
810 Vermont Avenue NW
Washington, DC 20420
877-222-8387
800-827-1000
TTY: 800-829-4833
www.publichealth.va.gov
A resource for veterans who have been exposed to chemical herbicides which might be causing a variety of ill effects. Contains information on exposure locations, available benefits, research studies on Agent Orange, and more. Services available to any eligible veteran who had active military service.

2017 American Academy of Child and Adolescent Psychiatry (AACAP)
3615 Wisconsin Avenue NW
Washington, DC 20016
202-966-7300
Fax: 202-464-0131
clinical@aacap.org
www.aacap.org
Promotes the healthy development of children, adolescents, and families through advocacy, education, and research.
Warren Y.K. Ng, MD, MPH, President
Debra E. Koss, MD, Secretary

2018 American Chronic Pain Association
11936 W. 119th Street
Overland Park, KS 66213
913-991-4740
www.acpanow.com
The ACPA facilitates peer support and education for individuals with chronic pain in its many forms, in order to increase quality of life. Also raises awareness among the healthcare community, and with policy makers.
Penney Cowan, Founder
Trupti Gokani, MD, President

2019 American Medical Association (AMA)
330 N Wabash Ave.
Chicago, IL 60611
312-464-4782
800-262-3211
www.ama-assn.org
Committed to ensuring sustainable physician practices that result in better health outcomes for patients.

2020 American Psychiatric Association
800 Maine Avenue SW
Washington, DC 20024
202-559-3900
apa@psych.org
www.psychiatry.org
A medical specialty society representing a growing membership of psychiatrists. Offers information for psychiatrists, medical students, patients and families.
Saul Levin, MD, MPA, FRCP-E, CEO

2021 American Psychological Association
750 First Street NE
Washington, DC 20002
202-336-5500
800-374-2721
TTY: 202-336-6123
www.apa.org
Advancing the creation, communication and application of psychological knowledge to benefit society and improve people's lives.
Thema S. Bryant, PhD, President
Arthur C. Evans, Jr, PhD, CEO & EVP

2022 American Public Health Association (APHA)
800 I Street NW
Washington, DC 20001
202-777-2742
Fax: 202-777-2534
TTY: 202-777-2500
www.apha.org
Aims to strengthen the public health profession and promote and advocate for public health issues and policies backed by science.
Chris Chanyasulkit, PhD, MPH, President
Georges C. Benjamin, MD, Executive Director

2023 American Trauma Society (ATS)
201 Park Washington Court
Falls Church, VA 22046
703-538-3544
800-556-7890
Fax: 703-241-5603
info@amtrauma.org
www.amtrauma.org
American Trauma Society (ATS) is committed to the elimination of needless death and disability from injury. Advocates for trauma prevention programs.
Krista Brands, CAE, CEO
Suzanne M. Prentiss, Executive Director

2024 Anxiety Disorders Association of America
8701 Georgia Avenue
Silver Spring, MD 20910
240-485-1018
information@adaa.org
www.adaa.org
ADAA is a national non-profit organization dedicated to the prevention, treatment, and cure of anxiety, depression, OCD, PTSD, and related disorders, and to improving the lives of all people who suffer from them through education, practice, and research.
Charles B. Nemeroff, MD, PhD, President
Susan K. Gurley, Executive Director

2025 Association for Behavioral and Cognitive Therapies
305 7th Avenue
New York, NY 10001
212-647-1890
Fax: 212-647-1865
www.abct.org
Multidisciplinary organization committed to the advancement of evidence-based approaches to treating and improving human functioning.
Mary Jane Eimer, CAE, Executive Director
David Teisler, CAE, Director, Publications/Deputy Director

2026 Association for Traumatic Stress Specialists
5052 Old Buncombe Road
Greenville, SC 29617
admin@atss.info
www.atss.info
Professional membership organization of individuals engaged in and committed to excellence in trauma services, response, and treatment.
Jayne Crisp, CTTS, Administrator

2027 Association of Traumatic Stress Specialist
5052 Old Buncombe Road
Greenville, SC 29617
864-294-4337
admin@atss.info
atss.info

Trauma & Stressor-Related Disorders / Agencies & Associations

An international organization that helps those suffering from trauma by offering education, training, and professional development resources.
Jeff Cartwright, CTR, CWT, President
Lisseth London, Ph.D, MSW,, Vice President

2028 **Center for Family Support**
2811 Zulette Avenue 718-518-1500
Bronx, NY 10461 svernikoff@cfsny.org
www.cfsny.org
The Center for Family Support offers assistance to individuals with developmental and related disabilities, as well as their families, and provides support services and programs that are designed to accommodate individual needs. Offers services throughout New York City, Westchester County, Long Island, and New Jersey.
Steven Vernikoff, Executive Director
Barbara Greenwald, Chief Operating Officer

2029 **Center for Mental Health Services (CMHS)**
Substance Abuse and Mental Health Services Adminis
5600 Fishers Lane 240-276-1310
Rockville, MD 20857 samhsa.gov/about-us/who-we-are/offices-c
Promotes the treatment of mental illness and emotional disorders by increasing accessibility to mental health programs; supporting outreach, treatment, rehabilitation, and support programs and networks; and encouraging the use of scientifically-based information when treating mental disorders. CMHS provides information about mental health via a toll-free number and numerous publications. Developed for users of mental health services and their families, the general public, policy makers, provider
Anita Everett, MD, DFAPA, Director

2030 **Centers for Disease Control**
1600 Clifton Road 800-232-4636
Atlanta, GA 30329 TTY: 888-232-6348
cdcinfo@cdc.gov
www.cdc.gov
Offers reprints from the CDC Health Status of Vietnam veterans and the Journal of the American Medical Association. Also offers reports from the Centers for Disease Control Vietnam Experience Study, which was a multidimensional assessment of the health of Vietnam War veterans. Contains survey results of Gulf War veterans, and background information on the health concerns of veterans, symptoms, and related diagnoses, as well as documentation on hospitalizations.
Rochelle P. Walensky, MD, MPH, Director
Nirav D. Shah, MD, JD, Principal Deputy Director

2031 **Centers for Medicare & Medicaid Services**
7500 Security Boulevard
Baltimore, MD 21244 www.cms.gov
U.S. federal agency which administers Medicare, Medicaid, and the State Children's Health Insurance Program.
Chiquita Brooks-Lasure, Acting Administrator
Jonathan Blum, Principal Deputy Administrator & COO

2032 **Disabled American Veterans Organization**
807 Maine Avenue SW 202-554-3501
Washington, DC 20024 www.dav.org
The Disabled American Veterans Organization (DAV) is a non-profit charity that guides veterans as they transition back to civilian life. The DAV helps veterans navigate the VA health care system, and assists veterans in accessing their benefits through legislative work. The DAV is an advocate for veterans, and expands their assistance to veterans through the establishment of voluntary community programs.
Joe Parsetich, National Commander
Barry A. Jesinoski, National Adjutant & CEO

2033 **Freedom From Fear**
308 Seaview Avenue 718-351-1717
Staten Island, NY 10305 help@freedomfromfear.org
www.freedomfromfear.org
Freedom From Fear is a national non-profit mental health advocacy organization providing community support and promoting research and education.
Mary Guardino, Founder & Executive Director

2034 **Goodwill Industries International, Inc.**
15810 Indianola Drive contactus@goodwill.org
Rockville, MD 20855 www.goodwill.org
A nonprofit, community-based organization whose mission is to help people achieve self-sufficiency through the dignity and power of work, serving people who are disadvantaged, disabled or elderly. The mission is accomplished through providing independent living skills, affordable housing, and training and placement in community employment. The GoodWill Network includes 160 independent, local locations across the U.S. and Canada.
Ned Helms, Chair
Steven C. Preston, President & CEO

2035 **Goodwill's Community Employment Services**
Goodwill Industries-Suncoast, Inc.
10596 Gandy Blvd. 727-523-1512
St. Petersburg, FL 33702 888-279-1988
TDD: 727-579-1068
goodwill-suncoast.org
The St. Petersburg headquarters serves ten counties in the state of Florida. Their mission is to help people with disabilities gain employment through training programs, employment services, and affordable housing.
Sandra Young, Chair
Louise Lopez, Sr. Vice Chair

2036 **Help is Here**
North Dakota Behavioral Health Division
600 E Boulevard Avenue 701-328-2310
Bismarck, ND 58501 800-472-2622
dhsbhd@nd.gov
www.helpishere.nd.gov
Promotes the support and treatment of mental illness and emotional disorders. Offers mental health services, addiction servces, and recovery centers.

2037 **Hope for Depression Research Foundation**
40 West 57th Street 212-676-3200
New York, NY 10019 Fax: 212-676-3219
hdrf@hopefordepression.org
www.hopefordepression.org
Promotes, and encourages profits for neuroscience research into the treatments, diagnosis, origins, and prevention of depression, and other mood disorders such as anxiety disorders, post-traumatic stress disorder, postpartum depression, bipolar disorder, and suicide.
Audrey Gruss, Founder & Chairman
Harold W. Koenigsberg, MD, Board Member

2038 **Institute for Contemporary Psychotherapy**
33 W 60th St. 212-333-3444
New York, NY 10023 Fax: 212-333-5444
icpnyc.org
The Institute for Contemporary Psychotherapy is a New York City-based mental health treatment and training facility. Consisting of a group of 150 licensed psychotherapists, the Institute focuses on educating the public about the issues surrounding mental health, providing post-graduate training for therapists, and offering therapy at moderate costs.
Ron Taffel, PhD, Chair
Andrea Green-Lewis, LCSW-R, Director of Operations

2039 **International Society for Traumatic Stress Studies**
111 West Jackson Blvd. 847-686-2234
Chicago, IL 60604 Fax: 847-686-2251
info@istss.org
www.istss.org
The International Society for Traumatic Stress Studies is dedicated to sharing information about the effects of trauma and traumatic stress.
Marit Sijbrandij, PhD, President
Andrea J. Phelps, PhD, Vice President

2040 **International Society for the Study of Trauma and Dissociation**
4201 Wilson Blvd 844-994-7783
Arlington, VA 22203 Fax: 888-966-0310
info@isst-d.org
www.isst-d.org
The International Society for the Study of Trauma and Dissociation is a non-profit, professional association organized to develop

571

Trauma & Stressor-Related Disorders / Agencies & Associations

clinically effective and empirically based resources and responses to trauma and dissociation.

2041 Mental Health America
500 Montgomery Street
Alexandria, VA 22314
703-684-7722
800-969-6642
mhanational.org

Mental Health America is a community-based nonprofit organization committed to enabling the mental wellness of all Americans. MHA advocates for greater access to quality health services and seeks to educate individuals on identifying symptoms, as well as intervention and prevention.
Schroeder Stribling, President & CEO
Sachin Doshi, Sr. Dir., Finance & Operations

2042 National Alliance on Mental Illness
4301 Wilson Boulevard
Arlington, VA 22203
703-524-7600
800-950-6264
info@nami.org
nami.org

NAMI is an organization dedicated to raising awareness on mental health and providing support and education for Americans affected by mental illness. NAMI advocates for access to services and treatment and fosters an environment of awareness and understanding for those concerned with mental health.
Shirley J. Holloway, President
Joyce A. Campbell, First Vice President

2043 National Alliance on Mental Illness (NAMI)
4301 Wilson Blvd.
Arlington, VA 22203
703-524-7600
888-999-6264
www.nami.org

Committed to building better lives for the millions of Americans affected by mental illness by raising awareness and offering community support.
Daniel H. Gillison, Jr., CEO
Ken Duckworth, Chief Medical Officer

2044 National Association for the Dually Diagnosed (NADD)
321 Wall Street
Kingston, NY 12401
845-331-4336
info@thenadd.org
thenadd.org

NADD is a nonprofit organization designed to increase awareness of, and provide services for, individuals with developmental disabilities and mental illness. NADD emphasizes the importance of quality mental healthcare for people with mental health needs and offers conferences, information resources, educational programs, and training materials to professionals, parents, and organizations.
Jeanne M. Farr, MA, Chief Executive Officer
Bruce Davis, President

2045 National Association of Social Workers (NASW)
750 First Street NE
Washington, DC 20002
202-408-8600
800-742-4089
membership@socialworkers.org
www.socialworkers.org

The National Association of Social Workers (NASW) is the largest membership organization of professional social workers in the world, working to enhance and maintain professional standards and advance social policies.
Mildred C. Joyner, DPS, MSW, LCSW, President
Anthony Estreet, PhD, MBA, LCSWC, CEO

2046 National Association of State Directors of Veterans Affairs
700 Summer Street NW
Salem, OR 97301
www.nasdva.us

The National Association of State Directors of Veterans Affairs (NASDVA) is an organization operating in each state of the United States, with its headquarters in Oregon. The State Directors at NASDVA work to ensure that veterans receive their benefits and entitlements regardless of their age, gender, and era of service.
Alfie Alvarado-Ramos, President

2047 National Center for Complementary and Integrative Health
9000 Rockville Pike
Bethesda, MD 20892
888-644-6226
TTY: 866-464-3615
info@nccih.nih.gov
nccih.nih.gov

The National Center for Complementary and Integrative Health (NCCIH) is the Federal Government's lead agency for scientific research on the diverse medical and health care systems, practices, and products that are not generally considered part of conventional medicine.
Helene M. Langevin, MD, Director
David Shurtleff, PhD, Deputy Director

2048 National Human Genome Research Institute
Building 31, Room 4B09
Bethesda, MD 20892
301-402-0911
Fax: 301-402-2218
www.genome.gov

The National Human Genome Research Institute began as the National Center for Human Genome Research (NCHGR), which was established in 1989 to carry out the role of the National Institutes of Health (NIH) in the International Human Genome Project (HGP).
Eric D. Green, MD, PhD, Director
Nicole C. Lockhart, PhD, Program Director

2049 National Institute of Environmental Health Sciences
111 T.W. Alexander Drive
Durham, NC 27709
919-541-3201
Fax: 919-541-5136
webcenter@niehs.nih.gov
www.niehs.nih.gov

The mission of the NIEHS is to discover how the environment affects people in order to promote healthier lives.
Rick Woychik, PhD, Director
Trevor K. Archer, PhD, Deputy Director

2050 National Institute of General Medical Sciences
45 Center Drive
Bethesda, MD 20892
301-496-7301
info@nigms.nih.gov
www.nigms.nih.gov

The National Institute of General Medical Sciences (NIGMS) supports basic research that increases understanding of biological processes and lays the foundation for advances in disease diagnosis, treatment and prevention.
Jon R. Lorsch, PhD, Director
Dorit Zuk, PhD, Acting Deputy Director

2051 National Institute of Mental Health
6001 Executive Boulevard
Rockville, MD 20852
866-615-6464
Fax: 301-443-4279
TTY: 866-415-8051
nimhinfo@nih.gov
www.nimh.nih.gov

The National Institute of Mental Health works to transform the understanding and treatment of mental illnesses through basic and clinical research, paving the way for prevention, recovery, and cure.
Joshua A. Gordon, MD, PhD, Director

2052 Posttraumatic Stress Disorder (PTSD) Alliance
888-436-6306
contact@ptsdalliance.org
www.ptsdalliance.org

Provides educational resources to individuals diagnosed with PTSD and their loved ones; those at risk for developing PTSD; and medical, healthcare and other frontline professionals.

2053 Sidran Institute
370 Linwood Street
New Britain, CT 06052
410-825-8888
Fax: 410-560-0134
help@sidran.org
www.sidran.org

Sidran (SID-run) began in 1986 out of a family tragedy when a beloved family member who had been abused in childhood was subsequently diagnosed with serious, debilitating psychiatric problems and a related life-threatening medical disorder.
Esther Giller, President/ Director
Tracy Howard, Book Sales/ Office Manager

2054 Sidran Traumatic Stress Institute
370 Linwood Street
New Britain, CT 06052
410-825-8888
admin@sidran.org
sidran.org

Sidran Institute provides useful, practical information for child and adult survivors of any type of trauma, for families/friends, and for the clinical and frontline service providers who assist in their recovery. Sidran's philosophy of education through collaboration brings together great minds (providers, survivors, and loved ones)

to develop comprehensive programs to address the practical, emotional, spiritual, and medical needs of trauma survivors.
Esther Giller, President and Director
Ruta Mazelis, Editor, The Cutting Edge/Trainer

2055 Society of Federal Health Professionals (AMSUS)
12154 Darnestown Road 301-897-8800
Gaithersburg, MD 20878 www.amsus.org
The Society of Federal Health Professionals (AMSUS) is a non-profit organization for federal and international health professionals committed to improving the health of all Americans.
John M. Cho, MD, Executive Director & CEO
Ken Canestrini, Deputy Executive Director, COO & CFO

2056 Territorial Apprehensiveness (TERRAP) Anxiety & Stress Program
755 Park Avenue 631-549-8867
Huntington, NY 11743 Fax: 631-423-8446
info@anxietyandpanic.com
anxietyandpanic.com
Helps to treat anxiety and stress disorders through Territorial Apprehensiveness Programs, developed by Dr. Arthur Hardy in the 1960s. The program systematically addresses the behavioral and thought processes of those suffering from stress and anxiety.
Julian Herskowitz, PhD, Director

2057 U.S. Department of Health and Human Services
200 Independence Ave, SW 877-696-6775
Washington, DC 20201 www.hhs.gov
The U.S. Department of Health and Human Services (HHS) is the U.S. government's principal agency for protecting the health of all Americans and providing essential human services, especially for those who are least able to help themselves.
Sylvia M. Burwell, Secretary
Mary K. Wakefield, Acting Deputy Secretary

2058 United Brain Association
202-768-8000
info@unitedbrainassociation.org
unitedbrainassociation.org
Non-profit organization that works to find cures through research for over 600 brain and mental health related issues, and disorders.
J.A. Boulton, Founder
Jay Matey, VP & Treasurer

2059 VA Austin Information Technology Center
U.S. Department of Veterans Affairs
810 Vermont Ave., NW 800-698-2411
Washington, DC 20420 www.oit.va.gov
Helps veterans register after receiving the Agent Orange examination through the Veterans Affairs Department.

2060 Veterans Benefits Clearinghouse
Veterans Benefit Clearinghouse Development Corp.
495 Blue Hill Ave. 617-445-8262
Boston, MA 02186 Fax: 617-445-8266
vbcdc495@gmail.com
www.vbcdevelopmentcorporation.com
Develops affordable housing, provides services to veterans and their family members, and assists low income families.

Foundations

2061 Brain & Behavior Research Foundation
747 Third Avenue 646-681-4888
New York, NY 10017 800-829-8289
info@bbrfoundation.org
www.bbrfoundation.org
The Brain and Behavior Research Foundation awards grants aimed at advancing scientific understandings of mental health treatments and mental disorders such as depression and schizophrenia. The Brain and Behavior Research Foundation's mission is to eliminate the suffering caused by mental illness.
Donald M. Boardman, Treasurer
Jeffrey Borenstein, MD, President and CEO

2062 Dana Foundation
1270 Avenue Of The Americas 212-223-4040
New York, NY 10020 Fax: 212-317-8721
danainfo@dana.org
www.dana.org
The Dana Foundation is a private philanthropic organization that supports brain research through grants, publications, and educational programs.
Caroline. Montojo, PhD, President & CEO
Geraldine Amera, COO & Treasurer

2063 Desert Storm Justice Foundation: Minnesota
PO Box 186 218-258-3685
Buhl, MN 55713
Jeff Zakula

2064 Desert Storm Justice Foundation: Florida
10 Marlow Road 813-635-3261
Frostproof, FL 33843 Fax: 813-635-3261
BillCarpenter@cjewel.com
William Carpenter

2065 Desert Storm Justice Foundation: Illinois
Rural Route 4 618-457-2621
Carbondale, IL 62901
Shan Now

2066 Desert Storm Veterans of Florida, Inc.
PO Box 6081 407-269-3453
Titusville, FL 32782 PersianVet@aol.com
Kevin Knight

2067 HonorBound Foundation
PO Box 2465 800-521-0198
Darien, CT 06820 www.honorboundfoundation.org
Previously known as the National Veterans Services Fund, the HonorBound Foundation has expanded their support to all veterans in need. HonorBound provides support to those who were exposed to the defoliant Agent Orange while serving the US in the conflict in Vietnam by providing medical and financial assistance to veterans. Veterans are assisted by social workers, who ensure that veterans are better able to navigate the VA system.
Pamela Harper Kushner, Executive Director
Susan Tosto, Director, Program Services

2068 International Critical Incident Stress Foundation
3290 Pine Orchard Lane 410-750-9600
Ellicott City, MD 21042 info@icisf.org
icisf.org
A nonprofit, open membership foundation committed to preventing disabling stress by providing education, training, support, and consultation services for emergency service professionals and organizations around the world.
Richard Barton, Chief Executive Officer
Victor Welzant, PsyD, Education & Training Director

2069 National Headache Foundation
820 N. Orleans 312-274-2650
Chicago, IL 60610 888-643-5552
info@headaches.org
www.headaches.org
The mission at the National Headache Foundation has been to further awareness of headache and migraine as legitimate neurobiological diseases.
Arthur H. Elkind, M.D., President
Vincent Martin, M.D., Vice President

2070 National Science Foundation
2415 Eisenhower Avenue 703-292-5111
Alexandria, VA 22314 TDD: 703-292-5090
info@nsf.gov
www.nsf.gov
NSF is the only federal agency whose mission includes support for all fields of fundamental science and engineering, except for medical sciences.
Sethuraman Panchanathan, Director
Karen A. Marrongelle, Chief Operating Officer

Trauma & Stressor-Related Disorders / Libraries & Resource Centers

Libraries & Resource Centers

2071 **Administration for Community Living**
One Massachusetts Avenue
Washington, DC 20001
202-619-0724
800-677-1116
Fax: 202-357-3555
aclinfo@acl.hhs.gov
www.acl.gov

ACL brings together the efforts and achievements of the Administration on Aging, the Administration on Intellectual and Developmental Disabilities, and the HHS Office on Disability to serve as the Federal agency responsible for increasing access to community supports, while focusing attention and resources on the unique needs of older Americans and people with disabilities across the lifespan.
Kathy Greenlee, Administrator
Sharon Lewis, Principal Deputy Administrator

2072 **Anxiety Resource Center**
312 Grandville Ave.
Grand Rapids, MI 49503
616-356-1614
director@anxietyresourcecenter.org
anxietyresourcecenter.org

The Anxiety Resource Center, Inc. of Grand Rapids, Michigan, was founded to educate the public and professional communities about anxiety disorders, including Obsessive-Compulsive Disorder and OCD Spectrum Disorders; to reduce the stigma associated with these illnesses; and to provide a place that offers support, hope and inspiration.

2073 **Brain Injury Resource Center**
P.O.BOX 84151
Seattle, WA 98124
206-621-8558
brain@headinjury.com
www.headinjury.com

Providing wealth of information, creative solutions and leadership on issues related to brain injury since 1985.

2074 **BrainLine.org**
2775 South Quincy Street
Arlington, VA 22206
703-998-2020
info@BrainLine.org
www.brainline.org

BrainLine is a national multimedia project offering information and resources about preventing, treating, and living with TBI.
Noel Gunther, Executive Director
Christian Lindstrom, Director, Learning Media

2075 **Center for the Study of Traumatic Stress**
4301 Jones Bridge Road
Bethesda, MD 20814
cstsinfo@usuhs.mil
www.cstsonline.org

There sustained mission is to advance scientific and academic knowledge, interventions, educational resources and outreach to mitigate the impact of trauma from exposure to war, disasters, terrorism, community violence and public health threats.
Robert J. Ursano, MD, Director

2076 **Family-to-Family: National Alliance on Mental Illness**
4301 Wilson Boulevard
Arlington, VA 22203
703-524-7600
888-999-6264
info@nami.org
nami.org

The NAMI Family-to-Family Education Program is a free, 8 session course for family caregivers of individuals with severe mental illnesses. The course is taught by trained family members, all instruction and course materials are free to class participants, and over 300,000 family members have graduated from this national program.

2077 **Gift From Within**
16 Cobb Hill Rd.
Camden, ME 4843
207-236-8858
Fax: 207-236-2818
JoyceB3955@aol.com
www.giftfromwithin.org

PTSD Resources for Survivors and Caregivers.

2078 **Institute on Violence, Abuse and Trauma**
10065 Old Grove Road
San Diego, CA 92131
858-527-1860
Fax: 858-527-1743
www.ivatcenters.org

The Institute on Violence, Abuse and Trauma (IVAT) is an international resource and training center at Alliant International University.
Robert Geffner, Ph.D., President
Sandi Capuano Morrison, M.A., Executive Director

2079 **International Society for Traumatic Stress Studies**
111 West Jackson Blvd.
Chicago, IL 60604
847-686-2234
info@istss.org
istss.org

An organization that serves as a forum for the sharing of research, clinical strategies, public policy concerns, and other information resources on trauma throughout the world. Dedicated to discovering information and circulating knowledge about policies, programs, and services that focus on reducing traumatic stressors and their consequences.
Ananda Amstadter, PhD, President
Nicole Nugent, PhD, Vice President

2080 **Kennedy-Krieger Institute**
707 N Broadway
Baltimore, MD 21205
443-923-9200
800-873-3377
Fax: 443-923-9405
www.kennedykrieger.org

Kennedy Krieger Institute is an internationally recognized institution dedicated to improving the lives of individuals with disorders of the brain, spinal cord, and musculoskeletal system through Patient Care, Research and Professional Training, Special Education and Community. We at the Kennedy Krieger Institute dedicate ourselves to helping children and adolescents with disorders of the brain, spinal cord and musculoskeletal system achieve their potential and participate as fully as possible i
Jennifer Accardo, M.D., Neurologist
Adrianna Amari, Ph.D., Training and research coordinator

2081 **National Center for PTSD**
802-296-6300
ncptsd@va.gov
www.ptsd.va.gov

The National Center for PTSD is dedicated to research and education on trauma and PTSD.

2082 **National Center for Victims of Crime**
2000 M Street NW
Washington, DC 20036
202-467-8700
Fax: 202-467-8701
www.victimsofcrime.org

The mission of the National Center for Victims of Crime is to forge a national commitment to help victims of crime rebuild their lives. They are dedicated to serving individuals, families, and communities harmed by crime.
Mai Fernandez, Executive Director
Jeffrey R. Dion, Deputy Executive Director

2083 **National Institute of Mental Health**
6001 Executive Boulevard
Bethesda, MD 20892
866-615-6464
nimhinfo@nih.gov
nimh.nih.gov

The National Institute of Mental Health conducts clinical research on mental disorders and seeks to expand knowledge on mental health treatments.
Joshua Gordon, MD, PhD, Director

2084 **National Sexual Violence Resource Center**
123 North Enola Drive
Enola, PA 17025
717-909-0710
877-739-3895
Fax: 717-909-0714
TTY: 717-909-0715
resources@nsvrc.org
www.nsvrc.org

The NSVRC's Mission is to provide leadership in preventing and responding to sexual violence through collaboration, sharing and creating resources, and promoting research.

2085 **Posttraumatic Stress Disorder (PTSD) Alliance**
888-436-6306
contact@ptsdalliance.org
www.ptsdalliance.org

The Posttraumatic Stress Disorder (PTSD) Alliance is a group of professional and advocacy organizations that have joined forces to provide educational resources to individuals diagnosed with

Trauma & Stressor-Related Disorders / Research Centers

PTSD and their loved ones; those at risk for developing PTSD; and medical, healthcare and other frontline professionals.

2086 RNtoBSN.org
1001 McKinney St. 505-221-6056
Houston, TX 77002 www.rntobsn.org
RNtoBSN.org's mission is plain: Further the education of new and established nurses.
Caroline Porter Thomas, BSN, RN, Expert

2087 Shriver Center University Affiliated Program
Eunice Kennedy Shriver Center
200 Trapelo Road 781-642-0001
Waltham, MA 02452 shriver.center@umassmed.edu
www.umassmed.edu/shriver
The Eunice Kennedy Shriver Center has a four-decade history of pioneering research, education, and service for people with intellectual and developmental disabilities (IDD) and their families. Founded in 1970, the Center was one of twelve original Intellectual and Developmental Disabilities Research Centers (IDDRCs) established by US Congress at that time and also one of the earliest-established University Centers of Excellence in Developmental Disabilities (UCEDD). The Center was named after Mr
William McIlvane, Director
Charles Hamad, Associate Director

2088 Suicide Prevention Resource Center
43 Foundry Avenue 877-438-7772
Waltham, MA 2453 Fax: 617-969-9186
  TTY: 617-964-5448
  info@sprc.org
  www.sprc.org
SPRC is the nation's only federally supported resource center devoted to advancing the National Strategy for Suicide Prevention.
Jerry Reed, PhD, MSW, Director
Chris Miara, MS, Director of Operations & Resources

2089 Trauma Center
1269 Beacon Street 617-232-1303
Brookline, MA 2446 Fax: 617-232-1280
  www.traumacenter.org
The Trauma Center is a program of Justice Resource Institute (JRI), a large nonprofit organization dedicated to social justice by offering hope and promise of fulfillment to children, adults, and families who are at risk of not receiving effective services essential to their safety, progress, and/or survival.
Dr. Bessel van der Kolk, Founder
Margaret Blaustein, Ph.D, Director of Training and Education

2090 US Department Of Veterans Affairs
810 Vermont Avenue NW 202-273-5400
Washington, DC 20420 844-698-2311
  TTY: 711
  www.va.gov
Provides a wide range of services for those who have been in the military and their dependents as well as offering information on driver assessment and education programs. Health care and disability records can be created and accessed. The US Department of Veterans Affairs has a complete directory of VA locations listed for veterans.
Robert Wilkie, Secretary of Veterans Affairs
James Byrne, Deputy Secretary

2091 Women's Resource Center
113 W. Wayne Avenue 610-687-6391
Wayne, PA 19087 Fax: 610-687-2967
  info@womensrc.org
  womensresourcecenter.net
Women's Resource Center (WRC) is a registered 501c3 nonprofit that supports women, strengthens families and builds communities through information, referral, counseling, legal, and educational services.
Shelley Potente, MA, President
Virginia Bowden, Vice President

Research Centers

2092 Alaska VA Healthcare System
1201 N Muldoon Road 907-257-4700
Anchorage, AK 99504 888-353-7574
  Fax: 907-257-6774
  www.alaska.va.gov
The Alaska VA Healthcare System provides primary healthcare services to veterans. The facility offers specialty care, as well as mental health outpatient care. The facility has a partnership with the United States Air Force at Elmendorf Base, and provides assistance to homeless veterans, and those undergoing therapy.
Timothy Ballard, MD, MS, Director
Thomas A. Steinbrunner, FACHE, Associate Director

2093 Albany Stratton VA Medical Center
113 Holland Avenue 518-626-5000
Albany, NY 12208 800-223-4810
  www.albany.va.gov
Albany Stratton VA Medical Center in Albany, New York, serves veterans in 22 counties of upstate New York, western Massachusetts and Vermont.
Darlene DeLancey, Director
Mary Ann Witt, Associate Director

2094 Aleda E. Lutz VA Medical Center: Saginaw, Michigan
1500 Weiss Street 989-497-2500
Saginaw, MI 48602 800-406-5143
  www.saginaw.va.gov
Aleda E. Lutz VA Medical Center provides services for veterans living in all 35 counties located in central and northern Michigan's Lower Peninsula.
Barbara Bates, MD, Director
Thomas Campana, Acting Chief of Staff

2095 Alexandria VA Healthcare System
2495 Shreveport Highway 318-466-4000
Pineville, LA 71360 800-375-8387
  www.alexandria.va.gov
Alexandria VA Healthcare System provides health care services to veterans in need. Alexandria offers a number of specialized programs for eligible veterans, some of which include home-based primary care, an adult day care program, and a homeless program.
Peter C. Dancy, Jr., Director
Lisa M. Hamilton, Associate Director

2096 Alvin C. York VA Medical Center Tennessee Valley Healthcare System
3400 Lebanon Pike 615-867-6000
Murfreesboro, TN 37129 800-228-4973
  www.tennesseevalley.va.gov
Alvin C. York VA Medical Center is part of the Tennessee Healthcare System. Tennessee Valley Healthcare System provides primary and secondary care, general medicine, surgery and specialized care to veterans. The Alvin C. York VA Medical Center is a referral center for mental health services, geriatrics, and extended care.
Jennifer Vedral-Baron, MN, FAANP, Director
Suzanne L. Jene, MBA, VHA-CM, Deputy Director

2097 Atlanta VA Medical Center Atlanta VA Health Care System
Atlanta VA Medical Center
1670 Clairmont Road 404-321-6111
Decatur, GA 30033 844-698-2311
  www.atlanta.va.gov
Part of the VA Southeast Network (VISN 7), the Atlanta VA Medical Center fulfills the health care needs of eligible veterans within the area.
Ajay Dhawan, MD, Director
Stephanie Repasky, Deputy Director

2098 Audie L. Murphy Memorial VA Hospital South Texas Veterans Health Care System
7400 Merton Minter 210-617-5300
San Antonio, TX 78229 877-469-5300
  www.southtexas.va.gov
Part of the VA Heart of Texas Veterans Integrated Service Network (VISN 17), the South Texas Veterans Health Care System is comprised of two inpatient campuses: the Audie L. Murphy Memorial

Trauma & Stressor-Related Disorders / Research Centers

VA Hospital in San Antonio and the Kerrville VA Hospital in Kerrville, Texas. Audie L. Murphy is a quaternary care facility.
Christopher R. Sandles, MBA, FACHE, Director
Julianne Flynn, MD, Chief of Staff

2099 Baltimore VA Medical Center VA Maryland Health Care System
10 N Greene Street 410-605-7000
Baltimore, MD 21201 www.maryland.va.gov
The Baltimore VA Medical Center offers health care services to veterans, and is home to the world's first filmless radiology department, allowing medical professionals to view radiology imaging almost instantly.
Adam M. Robinson, Jr., MD, Director
Sandra Marshall, MD, Chief of Staff

2100 Batavia VA Medical Center VA Western New York Healthcare System
222 Richmond Avenue 585-297-1000
Batavia, NY 14020 www.buffalo.va.gov
Batavia houses separate residential post-traumatic stress disorder units for men and women veterans, and is part of the VA Western New York Healthcare System.
Michael J. Swartz, Director
Grace L. Stringfellow, MD, Chief of Staff

2101 Bath VA Medical Center
76 Veterans Avenue 607-664-4000
Bath, NY 14810 877-845-3247
www.bath.va.gov
A medical center serving veterans with a comprehensive range of health care services, including mental health care provided by community-based outpatient clinics located in Coudersport, Elmira, Mansfield, and Wellsville.
Bruce Tucker, Director
Susan Herson, MD, Chief of Staff

2102 Battle Creek VA Medical Center
5500 Armstrong Road 269-966-5600
Battle Creek, MI 49037 888-214-1247
www.battlecreek.va.gov
A medical facility offering both inpatient and outpatient care. Each veteran enrolling for care is assigned their own primary care provider and team, who manage their case and provide consistent and coordinated care.
James Doelling, Director
Edward Dornoff, MPH, FACHE, Associate Director

2103 Bay Pines VA Healthcare System
10000 Bay Pines Boulevard 727-398-6661
Bay Pines, FL 33744 888-820-0230
Fax: 727-398-9442
www.baypines.va.gov
Provides health care services to eligible veterans within ten counties in central southwest Florida. Also offers a telehealth service, so that veterans can access health care at their convenience.
Paul M. Russo, FACHE, RD, Director & CEO
Kristine Brown, MPH, Associate Director

2104 Beckley VA Medical Center
200 Veterans Avenue 304-255-2121
Beckley, WV 25801 877-902-5142
www.beckley.va.gov
Beckley VA Medical Center is a rural access facility, offering nursing care, post-acute rehabilitation care, palliative care, and respite care for veterans. A home based primary care program is also available.
Stacy J. Vasquez, Director
John D. Stout, MBA, Associate Director

2105 Boise VA Medical Center
500 Fort Street 208-422-1000
Boise, ID 83702 866-437-5093
www.boise.va.gov
Boise VA Medical Center serves veterans in Boise, and also operates outpatient clinics in the surrounding areas.
David Wood, Director
Nate Stewart, Associate Director

2106 Brockton Division VA Boston Healthcare System
940 Belmont Street 508-583-4500
Brockton, MA 02301 800-865-3384
www.boston.va.gov
The Brockton Division of the VA Boston Healthcare System is dedicated to providing health care to veterans located in Boston.
Vincent Ng, Director
Michael E. Charness, MD, Chief of Staff

2107 Brooklyn Campus VA NY Harbor Health Care System
800 Poly Place 718-836-6600
Brooklyn, NY 11209 www.nyharbor.va.gov
The NY Harbor Healthcare System delivers health care services to veterans living in the 5 boroughs of New York City at their Brooklyn and Manhattan Campuses, and at the St. Albans Community Living Center.
Martina A. Parauda, Director
Cynthia Caroselli, PhD, RN, Associate Director

2108 Buffalo VA Medical Center VA Western New York Healthcare System
3495 Bailey Avenue 716-834-9200
Buffalo, NY 14215 800-532-8387
www.buffalo.va.gov
The Buffalo VA Medical Center provides a broad range of inpatient and outpatient long term care services for veterans. In addition, it is the main referral center for cardiac surgery, cardiology and comprehensive cancer care in the VA Western New York Healthcare System.
Michael J. Swartz, Director
Grace L. Stringfellow, MD, Chief of Staff

2109 Canandaigua VA Medical Center VA Health Care Upstate New York
400 Fort Hill Avenue 585-394-2000
Canandaigua, NY 14424 800-204-9917
www.canandaigua.va.gov
The Canandaigua VA Medical Center, part of VA Health Care Upstate New York provides inpatient and outpatient care to veterans. Canadaigua VA Medical Center is known for its focus on mental health issues, and conducts research on mental health.
Bruce Tucker, Director
Kenneth Piazza, Associate Director

2110 Captain James A. Lovell Federal Health Care Center
3001 Green Bay Road 847-688-1900
North Chicago, IL 60064 800-393-0865
www.lovell.fhcc.va.gov
The Captain James A. Lovell Federal Health Care Center (FHCC) fulfills the health care needs of active and retired veterans, and their families.
Robert Buckley, Director
CAPT Gregory T. Thier, Deputy Director & Commanding Officer

2111 Carl Vinson VA Medical Center Dublin VA Medical Center
1826 Veterans Boulevard 912-272-1210
Dublin, GA 31021 800-595-5229
TTY: 711
www.dublin.va.gov
The Carl Vinson VA Medical Center provides health care to veterans within the Middle Georgia area. Additionally, six community-based outpatient clinics exist to better serve veterans.
David L. Whitmer, FACHE, Director
Connie Hampton, DNP, RN, Interim Director

2112 Center for Anxiety and Related Disorders at Boston University
648 Beacon St. 617-353-9610
Boston, MA 2215 bonnieb@bu.edu
www.bu.edu/card
The Center for Anxiety and Related Disorders (CARD) is an internationally known clinical and research center dedicated to advancing knowledge and providing care for anxiety, mood, eating, sleep, and related disorders.
David H. Barlow, Ph.D., Founder and Director Emeritus
Timothy A. Brown, Psy.D., Director of Research and Research Admin

Trauma & Stressor-Related Disorders / Research Centers

2113 Center for Anxiety and Traumatic Stress
Guthrie Annex 2 206-685-3617
Seattle, WA faculty.washington.edu/zoellner/
Lori A. Zoellner, PhD, Director
Richard Ries, MD, Medical Director

2114 Center for Culture, Trauma and Mental Health Disparities
760 Westwood Plaza 310-794-9929
Los Angeles, CA 90024 www.semel.ucla.edu/cctmhd
The Center for Culture, Trauma, and Mental Health Disparities is a multi-ethnic and multi-disciplinary group promoting interdisciplinary research examining the prevalence and impact of traumatic experiences on PTSD, depression and concomitant cognitive/emotional, behavioral, psychological and biological processes in ethnic minority populations.
Gail Wyatt, Director

2115 Center for Mental Health Services
Room 6-1057 240-276-1310
Rockville, MD 20857 www.samhsa.gov
The Center for Mental Health Services leads federal efforts to promote the prevention and treatment of mental disorders. Congress created CMHS to bring new hope to adults who have serious mental illness and children with emotional disorders.
Paolo del Vecchio, M.S.W., Director
Elizabeth Lopez, Ph.D., Deputy Director

2116 Center for Mind-Body Medicine
5225 Connecticut Avenue 202-966-7338
Washington, DC 20015 cmbm.org
The Center for Mind-Body Medicine creates communities of hope and healing.
James S. Gordon, MD, President
James S. Gordon, MD, Founder/Director

2117 Center for the Study of Emotion and Attention
University of Florida Fax: 352-392-6047
Gainesville, FL 32611 csea.phhp.ufl.edu
The Center for the Study of Emotion & Attention is a facility for the scientific study of human emotion, highlighting emotion's foundation on survival circuits in the mammalian brain, and its motivational significance for attentional engagement and response mobilization.

2118 Center for the Study of Traumatic Stress
Uniformed Services Uni. cstsinfo@usuhs.mil
Bethesda, MD 20814 www.cstsonline.org
Robert J. Ursano, MD, Director

2119 Central Texas Veterans Health Care System
1901 Veterans Memorial Drive 254-778-4811
Temple, TX 76504 800-423-2111
deborah.meyer@va.gov
www.centraltexas.va.gov
The Central Texas Veterans Health Care System consists of two VA medical centers located in Temple and Waco, one outpatient clinic in Austin, four community-based outpatient clinics in Brownwood, Bryan/College Station, Cedar Park, and Palestine, with a rural outreach clinic in La Grange.
Andrew T. Garcia, MHA, Director
Olawale O. Fashina, MD, MHSA, CPE, Chief of Staff

2120 Chalmers P. Wylie Ambulatory Care Center VA Central Ohio Healthcare System
420 N James Road 614-257-5200
Columbus, OH 43219 888-615-9448
www.columbus.va.gov
Chalmers P. Wylie Ambulatory Care Center provides veterans with medical care, from surgery to rehabilitation. Four community-based clinics focused on outpatient care are located in Grove City, Marion, Newark, and Zanesville.
Vivian T. Hutson, Director
Jamie Kuhne, LISW-S, Associate Director

2121 Charles George VA Medical Center
1100 Tunnel Road 828-298-7911
Asheville, NC 28805 800-932-6408
www.asheville.va.gov
Part of the VA Mid-Atlantic Healthcare Network (VISN 6), Charles George VA Medical Center has been serving veterans since 1922. Outpatient clinics are located in Franklin, Rutherford County, and Hickory.
Stephanie Young, Director
Robert Evans, Associate Director

2122 Charlie Norwood VA Medical Center
950 15th Street Downtown 706-733-0188
Augusta, GA 30904 800-836-5561
Fax: 706-823-3934
TTY: 711
www.augusta.va.gov
Charlie Norwood VA Medical Centre is separated into two divisions to better serve the uptown and the downtown core. The uptown division provides psychiatric care, and rehabilitation, whereas the downtown core provides general medicine and surgical care for veterans.
Robin E. Jackson, Director
Srinivas Ginjupalli, Chief of Staff

2123 Cheyenne VA Medical Center
2360 E Pershing Boulevard 307-778-7550
Cheyenne, WY 82001 888-483-9127
www.cheyenne.va.gov
The Cheyenne VA Medical Center provides health care services to veterans residing in the tri-state area of southeastern Wyoming, northeastern Colorado and southwestern Nebraska.
Paul L. Roberts, Director
Michael Chad Cartwright, Associate Director

2124 ChildTrauma Academy
866-943-9779
Fax: 713-513-5465
cta@childtrauma.org
childtrauma.org
CTA is a not-for-profit organization based in Houston, Texas working to improve the lives of high-risk children through direct service, research and education.
Bruce D. Perry, M.D., Ph.D., Founder/Senior Fellow
Jana Rosenfelt, M.Ed., Executive Director

2125 Chillicothe VA Medical Center
17273 State Route 104 740-773-1141
Chillicothe, OH 45601 800-358-8262
www.chillicothe.va.gov
The Chillicothe VA Medical Center provides acute and chronic mental health services, primary and secondary medical care, among other services. Chillicothe houses a specialized women veterans health clinic and serves as a chronic mental health referral center for other VA Medical Centers in southern Ohio and parts of West Virginia and Kentucky.
Kathy W. Berger, MHA, DNP, Director
James V. Zeigler, MA, CCC-SLP, Acting Associate Director

2126 Cincinnati VA Medical Center
3200 Vine Street 513-861-3100
Cincinnati, OH 45220 www.cincinnati.va.gov
Cincinnati VA Medical Center consists of 2 divisions located in Cincinnati, Ohio and Fort Thomas, Kentucky. Services are provided for 15 counties in Ohio, Kentucky, and Indiana. Cincinnati also acts as a referral center for neurosurgery.
Mark Murdock, MHA, FACHE, Director
Gregory Goins, Associate Director

2127 Cleveland VA Medical Center VA Northeast Ohio Healthcare System
10701 E Boulevard 216-791-3800
Cleveland, OH 44106 877-838-8262
www.cleveland.va.gov
Cleveland VA Medical Center is part of VISN 10, and provides a full range of primary, secondary and tertiary care services offered to an eligible veteran population covering 24 counties in northeast Ohio.
Susan M. Fuehrer, Director
Brian Cmolik, MD, FACS, Chief of Staff

2128 Coatesville VA Medical Center
1400 Blackhorse Hill Road 610-384-7711
Coatesville, PA 19320 800-290-6172
www.coatesville.va.gov

Trauma & Stressor-Related Disorders / Research Centers

Coatesville VA Medical Center provides primary, urgent, and specialty care to veterans in Spring City and Newtown Square, Pennsylvania. In addition, Coatesville offers mental health care and operates a pharmacy.
Carla Sivek, Director
Michael F. Gliatto, MD, Chief of Staff

2129 **Colmery-O'Neil VA Medical Center VA Eastern Kansas Health Care System**
2200 SW Gage Boulevard — 785-350-3111
Topeka, KS 66622 — 800-574-8387
www.leavenworth.va.gov
Part of the Heartland Network (VISN 15), the Colmery-O'Neil VA Medical Center improves the health of veterans living in Topeka, Kansas.
A. Rudy Klopfer, Director
Lisa Curnes, Associate Director

2130 **Columbia VA Health Care System**
6439 Garners Ferry Road — 803-776-4000
Columbia, SC 29209 — 888-651-2683
www.columbiasc.va.gov
Columbia VA Health Care System serves veterans by providing a full range of patient care services, including primary, secondary, and tertiary care. 7 community-based outpatient clinics located throughout South Carolina serve veterans residing in 36 counties.
David L. Omura, Director & CEO
Jeffrey Soots, Associate Director

2131 **Corporal Michael J. Crescenz VA Medical Center**
3900 Woodland Avenue — 215-823-5800
Philadelphia, PA 19104 — 800-949-1001
www.philadelphia.va.gov
Provides medical care for veterans in the city of Philadelphia including six surrounding counties in southeastern Pennsylvania and southern New Jersey.
Patricia O'Kane, MSS, Director
John J. Kelly, MD, Chief of Staff

2132 **Dayton VA Medical Center**
4100 W 3rd Street — 937-268-6511
Dayton, OH 45428 — 800-368-8262
TTY: 800-829-4833
www.dayton.va.gov
A medical facility offering comprehensive health care to veterans in Dayton, Ohio. A variety of specialized programs from an Alzheimer's unit to sleep disorder programs exist to better serve veterans.
Jill Dietrich, JD, MBA, FACHE, Director
Mark E. Butler, RPh, Acting Associate Director

2133 **Durham VA Health Care System**
508 Fulton Street — 919-286-0411
Durham, NC 27705 — 888-878-6890
www.durham.va.gov
Durham Veterans Affairs Medical Center serves the health care needs of eligible veterans living within 27 counties of central and eastern North Carolina.
Paul S. Crews, MPH, CPHQ, FACHE, Director
Kenneth C. Goldberg, MD, Chief of Staff

2134 **Dwight D. Eisenhower VA Medical Center VA Eastern Kansas Health Care System**
4101 4th Street Trafficway — 913-682-2000
Leavenworth, KS 66048 — 800-952-8387
www.leavenworth.va.gov
Located within the VA Heartland Network (VISN 15), the Dwight D. Eisenhower VA Medical Center improves the health of veterans in Leavenworth, Kansas.
A. Rudy Klopfer, Director
Lisa Curnes, Associate Director

2135 **East Orange Campus VA New Jersey Health Care System**
385 Tremont Avenue — 973-676-1000
East Orange, NJ 07018 — www.newjersey.va.gov
Part of the VA New Jersey Health Care System, the East Orange Campus provides primary care to veterans, in addition to a great variety of specialized programs.
Vincent F. Immiti, MBA, FACHE, Director
Mara Davis, Associate Director

2136 **Edith Nourse Rogers Memorial Veterans Hospital: Bedford VA**
200 Springs Road — 781-687-2000
Bedford, MA 01730 — 800-838-6331
www.bedford.va.gov
Bedford VA is a long-term care facility specializing in psychiatric care. Bedford VA provides inpatient and outpatient care.
Joan Clifford, Director
Ed Koetting, Associate Director

2137 **Edward Hines Jr. VA Hospital**
5000 S 5th Avenue — 708-202-8387
Hines, IL 60141 — 888-598-7793
richard.fox@va.gov
www.hines.va.gov
Edward Hines Jr. VA Hospital provides veterans with primary care and specialty care. The hospital also operates as a tertiary care referral center for the VISN 12.
Steven E. Braverman, MD, Director
Elaine Adams, MD, Chief of Staff

2138 **El Paso VA Health Care Center**
5001 N Piedras — 915-564-6100
El Paso, TX 79930 — 800-672-3782
Fax: 915-564-7920
www.elpaso.va.gov
The El Paso VA Health Care System serves Veterans in southwest Texas and Dona Ana County, New Mexico. The El Paso VA Health Care System provides primary and specialized ambulatory care services at its main campus, and operates two outpatient clinics.
Michael L. Amaral, Director
Jamie D. Park, Associate Director

2139 **Erie VA Medical Center**
135 E 38th Street Boulevard — 814-868-8661
Erie, PA 16504 — 800-274-8387
www.erie.va.gov
Medical center serving veterans across 9 counties within northwestern Pennsylvania, eastern Ohio, and southwestern New York.
John A. Gennaro, Director
David M. Lavin, Chief of Staff

2140 **Eugene J. Towbin Healthcare Center Central Arkansas VA Healthcare System**
Eugene J. Towbin Healthcare Center
2200 Fort Roots Drive — 501-257-1000
North Little Rock, AR 72114 — 800-224-8387
TTY: 711
www.littlerock.va.gov
The Eugene J. Towbin Healthcare Center operates within the Central Arkansas VA Healthcare System. Located in North Little Rock and Little Rock (John L. McClellan Memorial Veterans Hospital), the Healthcare Center is able to address a large variety of health concerns for eligible veterans, offering community-based care through eight outpatient clinics.
Margie A. Scott, MD, Director
Cyril O. Ekeh, MHA, VHA-CM, Associate Director

2141 **Fargo VA Health Care System**
2101 N Elm Street — 701-239-3700
Fargo, ND 58102 — 800-410-9723
www.fargo.va.gov
Fargo VA provides health care services to veterans, and operates 10 community-based outpatient clinics to better serve veterans in need.
Lavonne K. Liversage, FACHE, Director
Breton M. Weintraub, MD, FACP, Chief of Staff

2142 **Fayetteville VA Medical Center**
2300 Ramsey Street — 910-488-2120
Fayetteville, NC 28301 — 800-771-6106
TTY: 711
www.fayettevillenc.va.gov
The Fayetteville Veterans Affairs Medical Center provides general medicine, surgery, and mental health care to veterans across nineteen counties located in the Southeastern Northern Carolina area.
Webster C. Bazemore, Interim Director
Gregory A. Antoine, Chief of Staff

Trauma & Stressor-Related Disorders / Research Centers

2143 Fort Meade Campus VA Black Hills Health Care System
113 Comanche Road
Fort Meade, SD 57741
605-347-2511
800-743-1070
www.blackhills.va.gov
VA Black Hills Health Care System is comprised of two campuses: Fort Meade and Hot Springs. Both facilities provide primary and secondary medical and surgical care, residential rehabilitation treatment programs, extended nursing home care and psychiatric inpatient services for veterans living in South Dakota, portions of Nebraska, North Dakota, Wyoming and Montana.
Sandra L. Horsman, MBM, Director
C.B. Alexander, FACHE, Associate Director

2144 Fort Wayne Campus VA Northern Indiana Health Care System
2121 Lake Avenue
Fort Wayne, IN 46805
260-426-5431
800-360-8387
VHANINPublicAffairs@va.gov
www.northernindiana.va.gov
The Fort Wayne Campus provides veterans with primary and seconday cmedical services, as well as surgical care.
Michael E. Hershman, Director
Jay Miller, Associate Director of Operations

2145 G.V. (Sonny) Montgomery VA Medical Center
1500 E Woodrow Wilson Avenue
Jackson, MS 39216
601-362-4471
800-949-1009
TTY: 711
www.jackson.va.gov
A medical center providing veterans with primary, secondary, and tertiary medical care. In addition, G.V. (Sonny) Montgomery offers inpatient mental health care, as well as comprehensive health care for female veterans.
David M. Walker, Director
Kai D. Mentzer, Associate Director

2146 George E. Wahlen Medical Center VA Salt Lake City Health Care System
500 Foothill Drive
Salt Lake City, UT 84148
801-582-1565
800-613-4012
www.saltlakecity.va.gov
The George E. Wahlen Department of Veterans Affairs Medical Center is a tertiary care facility and provides a comprehensive range of patient care services, from general medicine to surgery.
Shella Stovall, MNA, RN, NE-BC, Director
Warren E. Hill, Associate Director

2147 George H. O'Brien, Jr. VA Medical Center West Texas VA Health Care System
300 Veterans Boulevard
Big Spring, TX 79720
432-263-7361
800-472-1365
www.bigspring.va.gov
George H. O'Brien, Jr. VA Medical Center fulfills the health care needs of veterans residing in Big Spring, Texas. This medical center maintains a domiciliary program, and provides mental health and dental care.
Kalautie S. JangDhari, Director
Manuel M. Davila, Associate Director

2148 GoldPoint Clinical Research
8902 North Meridian Strt.
Indianapolis, IN 46260
317-229-6202
Fax: 317-218-3347
goldpointcr.com
GoldPoint Clinical Research of Indianapolis' team has 20 years of experience conducting more than 250 Phase II, III & IV neuroscience clinical trials. As one of the Midwest's leading research study centers, GoldPoint is led by medical director and board-certified addiction psychiatrist, Richard Saini, MD. - See more at: http://goldpointcr.com/about-us/leadership/#sthash.oaNpLa69.dpuf
Mary Newkerk, Director of Operations

2149 Goodwill Industries-Suncoast
10596 Gandy Boulevard
St. Petersburg, FL 33702
727-523-1512
888-279-1988
TTY: 727-579-1068
www.goodwill-suncoast.org
A nonprofit, community-based organization whose mission is to help people achieve self-sufficiency through the dignity and power of work, serving people who are disadvantaged, disabled or elderly. The mission is accomplished through providing independent living skills, affordable housing, and training and placement in community employment.
Heather Ceresoli, CPA, Chair
Deborah A. Passerini, President & CEO

2150 Gulf Coast Veterans Health Care System
400 Veterans Avenue
Biloxi, MS 39531
228-523-5000
800-296-8872
www.biloxi.va.gov
Part of the South Central VA Health Care Network (VISN16), Gulf Coast serves veterans in the region by providing medical care, and readjustment counseling centers.
Bryan C. Matthews, MBA, Director
Adam G. Bearden, MBA, FACHE, Acting Associate Director

2151 H.J. Heinz Campus VA Pittsburgh Healthcare System
1010 Delafield Road
Pittsburgh, PA 15215
412-822-2222
866-482-7488
www.pittsburgh.va.gov
VA Pittsburgh Healthcare System is composed of two main campuses: University Drive and H.J. Heinz. The healthcare system serves veterans living in the tri-state area of Pennsylvania, Ohio, and West Virginia. H.J. Heinz campus is a community living center and an ambulatory care center providing outpatient services, including dental care.
Barbara Forsha, MSN, RN, ET, Director
Ali Sonel, MD, Chief of Staff

2152 Hampton VA Medical Center
100 Emancipation Drive
Hampton, VA 23667
757-722-9961
866-544-9961
www.hampton.va.gov
Hampton VA Medical Center provides comprehensive primary and specialty care at its main facility for veterans in southeastern Virginia and northeastern North Carolina. Two community-based outpatient clinics are located in Elizabeth City, Chesapeake, and Virginia Beach.
Taquisa K. Simmons, PhD, Director
Priscilla Hankins, MD, Chief of Staff

2153 Harry S. Truman Memorial Veterans' Hospital
800 Hospital Drive
Columbia, MO 65201
573-814-6000
800-349-8262
www.columbiamo.va.gov
Part of the Heartland Network (VISN 15), Harry S. Truman Memorial Veterans' Hospital specializes in providing medical care to veterans in 43 counties in Missouri and Pike County, Illinois.
David Isaacks, FACHE, Director
Lana Zerrer, MD, Chief of Staff

2154 Hershel Woody Williams VA Medical Center
1540 Spring Valley Drive
Huntington, WV 25704
304-429-6741
800-827-8244
www.huntington.va.gov
Hershel Woody Williams VA Medical Center provides medical care to veterans in its main facility in Huntington. Two community-based outpatient clinics and two rural health outreach clinics exist to better serve veterans. Services are available to veterans living in southwestern West Virginia, southern Ohio, and eastern Kentucky.
J. Brian Nimmo, Director
Kenneth Mortimer, FACHE, Associate Director

2155 Hot Springs Campus VA Black Hills Health Care System
500 N 5th Street
Hot Springs, SD 57747
605-745-2000
800-764-5370
www.blackhills.va.gov
VA Black Hills Health Care System is comprised of two campuses: Fort Meade and Hot Springs. Both facilities provide primary and secondary medical and surgical care, residential rehabilitation treatment programs, extended nursing home care and psychiatric inpatient services for veterans living in South Dakota, portions of Nebraska, North Dakota, Wyoming and Montana.
Sandra L. Horsman, MBM, Director
C.B. Alexander, FACHE, Associate Director

2156 Hunter Holmes McGuire VA Medical Center
1201 Broad Rock Boulevard
Richmond, VA 23249
804-675-5000
800-784-8381
www.richmond.va.gov

Trauma & Stressor-Related Disorders / Research Centers

With its main facility located in Richmond, Virginia, Hunter Holmes provides medical services available to eligible veterans from 52 cities and counties in central and southern Virginia, and parts of North Carolina.
J. Ronald Johnson, FACHE, Director
James W. Dudley, Associate Director

2157 **Idaho Persian Gulf Veterans**
2055 S Colorado Street   208-344-3028
Boise, ID 83706
Vaughn Kidwell
Teresa Kidwell

2158 **Injury Research Center**
8701 Watertown Plank Rd.   414-955-7670
Milwaukee, WI 53226   Fax: 414-955-6470
                                     irc@mcw.edu
                                     www.mcw.edu
The Injury Research Center (IRCInjury Research Center at the Medical College of Wisconsin) at the Medical College was established as a comprehensive federally funded injury control research center to address the burden of injury in the Great Lakes Region of the Midwest (WI, MN, IL, IN, MI and OH).
Stephen Hargarten, MD, MPH, Director
E. Brook Lerner, PhD, Deputy Director

2159 **International Society for Traumatic Stress Studies**
111 West Jackson Blvd.   847-480-9028
Chicago, IL 60604   Fax: 847-686-2251
                                    info@istss.org
                                    www.istss.org
The International Society for Traumatic Stress Studies is dedicated to sharing information about the effects of trauma and the discovery and dissemination of knowledge about policy, program and service initiatives that seek to reduce traumatic stressors and their immediate and long-term consequences.
Marit Sijbrandij, PhD, President
Andrea J. Phelps, PhD, Vice President

2160 **Iowa City VA Health Care System**
601 Highway 6 W   319-338-0581
Iowa City, IA 52246   800-637-0128
                                     www.iowacity.va.gov
Iowa City VA Health Care System provides a wide range of health care services to veterans within 50 counties in Eastern Iowa, Western Illinois, and Northern Missouri.
Judith Johnson-Mekota, Director
Javed H. Tunio, Chief of Staff

2161 **Jack C. Montgomery VA Medical Center Eastern Oklahoma VA Health Care System**
1011 Honor Heights Drive   918-577-3000
Muskogee, OK 74401   888-397-8387
                                     www.muskogee.va.gov
Medical facility serving veterans in 25 counties in eastern Oklahoma. Comprehensive health care services are offered.
Mark Morgan, MHA, FACHE, Director
Jonathan M. Plasencia, MBA, FACHE, Associate Director

2162 **Jamaica Plain Division VA Boston Healthcare System**
150 S Huntington Avenue   617-232-9500
Boston, MA 02130   800-865-3384
                                     www.boston.va.gov
The Jamaica Plain Division of the VA Boston Healthcare System is dedicated to providing health care to veterans located in Boston.
Vincent Ng, Director
Michael E. Charness, MD, Chief of Staff

2163 **James A. Haley Veterans' Hospital**
13000 Bruce B. Downs Boulevard   813-972-2000
Tampa, FL 33612   888-716-7787
                                     www.tampa.va.gov
A tertiary care facility that offers veterans a wide variety of health care services, from primary care to long-term care. Dentistry and extended care is also made available to eligible veterans.
Joe D. Battle, Director
Melissa Sundin, Acting Deputy Director

2164 **James H. Quillen VA Healthcare System Mountain Home VA Healthcare System**
Corner Of Lamont & Veterans Way   423-926-1171
Mountain Home, TN 37684   877-573-3529
                                     www.mountainhome.va.gov
As part of the VA Midsouth Healthcare Network (VISN 9), James H. Quillen VA Healthcare System provides services available to veterans residing in the 41-county area of Tennessee, Virginia, Kentucky, and North Carolina.
Dean B. Borsos, MHSA, Director
David S. Hecht, MD, MBA, Chief of Staff

2165 **Jesse Brown VA Medical Center**
820 S Damen Avenue   312-569-8387
Chicago, IL 60612   888-569-5282
                                     www.chicago.va.gov
The Jesse Brown VA Medical Center cares for veterans in the city of Chicago, Cook County in Illinois, and four counties in northwestern Indiana. In addition to addressing the health care needs of veterans, the medical center is engaged in an outreach program with the goal of informing veterans of the health benefits they are entitled to.
Marc A. Magill, MS, Director
James Brunner, Acting Chief of Staff

2166 **John D. Dingell VA Medical Center**
4646 John R. Street   313-576-1000
Detroit, MI 48201   800-511-8056
                                     www.detroit.va.gov
Part of the VA Healthcare System serving Ohio, Indiana, and Michigan (VISN 10), John D. Dingell VA Medical Center provides health care services to all veterans located in the Wayne, Oakland, Macomb and St. Clair counties.
Pamela J. Reeves, MD, Director
Michelle S. Werner, Associate Director

2167 **John J. Pershing VA Medical Center**
1500 N Westwood Boulevard   573-686-4151
Poplar Bluff, MO 63901   888-557-8262
                                     www.poplarbluff.va.gov
A medical center providing primary care to veterans across 29 counties of southeast Missouri and northeast Arkansas. Outpatient clinics provide mental health services.
Patricia L. Hall, RN, MSN, PhD, Director
Libby J. Johnson, Associate Director

2168 **Jonathan M. Wainwright Memorial VA MC Walla Walla VA Medical Center**
77 Wainwright Drive   509-525-5200
Walla Walla, WA 99362   888-687-8863
                                     www.wallawalla.va.gov
Jonathan M. Wainwright Memorial VA Medical Center in Walla Walla serves the health care needs of veterans living in eastern Washington, Oregon, and western Idaho.
Christopher R. Bjornberg, Director
Marvin R. Crawford, MBA, Associate Director

2169 **Kansas City VA Medical Center**
4801 Linwood Boulevard   816-861-4700
Kansas City, MO 64128   800-525-1483
                                     www.kansascity.va.gov
Part of the Heartland Network (VISN 15), Kansas City VA Medical Center provides veterans with health care services.
Kathleen Fogarty, Director
Paula Roychaudhuri, FACHE, Associate Director

2170 **Kerrville VA Hospital South Texas Veterans Health Care System**
3600 Memorial Boulevard   830-896-2020
Kerrville, TX 78028   866-487-7653
                                     www.southtexas.va.gov
Part of the VA Heart of Texas Veterans Integrated Service Network (VISN 17), the South Texas Veterans Health Care System is comprised of two inpatient campuses:the Audie L. Murphy Memorial VA Hospital in San Antonio and the Kerrville VA Hospital in Kerrville, Texas. Kerrville provides primary care along with palliative care.
Christopher R. Sandles, MBA, FACHE, Director
Julianne Flynn, MD, Chief of Staff

Trauma & Stressor-Related Disorders / Research Centers

2171 Lake City VA Medical Center North Florida/South Georgia
Lake City VA Medical Center
619 S Marion Avenue   386-755-3016
Lake City, FL 32025   800-308-8387
                                        www.northflorida.va.gov
Operated by the North Florida/South Georgia Veterans Health System, the Lake City VA Medical Center serves eligible veterans within the area, providing them with multiple health services.
Thomas Wisnieski, MPA, FACHE, Director
Wende Dottor, Deputy Director

2172 Lebanon VA Medical Center
1700 S Lincoln Avenue   717-272-6621
Lebanon, PA 17042   800-409-8771
                                        www.lebanon.va.gov
Lebanon VA Medical Center is located at the heart of Pennsylvania Dutch country and provides a comprehensive range of medical care for eligible veterans within the area. Additionally, Lebanon VA offers telehealth services, making health care accessible to veterans from their homes.
Robert W. Callahan Jr., Director
Jeffrey A. Beiler, Associate Director

2173 Lexington VA Health Care System
1101 Veterans Drive   859-233-4511
Lexington, KY 40502   www.lexington.va.gov
The Lexington VA Health Care System is comprised of two main campuses, the Troy Bowling Campus, and the Franklin R. Sousley Campus. The Lexington VA Health Care System offers inpatient care for veterans.
Emma Metcalf, MSN, RN, Director
Patricia Breeden, MD, Chief of Staff

2174 Louis A. Johnson VA Medical Center
1 Medical Center Drive   304-623-3461
Clarksburg, WV 26301   800-733-0512
                                        www.clarksburg.va.gov
A medical facility serving the health care needs of veterans in Clarksburg, West Virginia since 1950.
Glenn R. Snider, Jr., MD, FACP, Director
Terry Massey, Associate Director

2175 Lyons Campus VA New Jersey Health Care System
151 Knollcroft Road   908-647-0180
Lyons, NJ 07939   www.newjersey.va.gov
Part of the VA New Jersey Health Care System, the Lyons Campus provides primary care to veterans, in addition to a great variety of specialized programs.
Vincent F. Immiti, MBA, FACHE, Director
Mara Davis, Associate Director

2176 Maine VA Medical Center VA Maine Healthcare System
1 VA Center   207-623-8411
Augusta, ME 04330   877-421-8263
                                        TTY: 711
                                        TDD: 800-829-4833
                                        www.maine.va.gov
A medical facility offerring general medical, surgical, and mental health services to veterans.
Tracey B. Davis, Director
Russell Armstead, CGFM, Acting Associate Director

2177 Malcom Randall VA Medical Center North Florida/South Georgia
1601 SW Archer Road   352-376-1611
Gainesville, FL 32608   800-324-8387
                                        TTY: 711
                                        www.northflorida.va.gov
Operated by the North Florida/South Georgia Veterans Health System, the Malcom Randall VA Medical Center serves eligible veterans within the area, providing them with multiple health services.
Thomas Wisnieski, MPA, FACHE, Director
Wende Dottor, Deputy Director

2178 Manchester VA Medical Center VAMC Manchester, New Hampshire
718 Smyth Road   603-624-4366
Manchester, NH 03104   800-892-8384
                                        www.manchester.va.gov
Since 1950, Manchester VA Medical Center has been providing veterans with health care services across the VA New England Healthcare System Network (VISN 1).
Alfred A. Montoya, Jr., MHA, FACHE, Director
Paul Zimmerman, DDS, Chief of Staff

2179 Manhattan VA Medical Center VA NY Harbor Health Care System
423 E 23rd Street   212-686-7500
New York, NY 10010   www.nyharbor.va.gov
Medical facility serving veterans in the NY Harbor area. Provides a full range of medical services.
Martina A. Parauda, Director
Cynthia Caroselli, PhD, RN, Associate Director

2180 Marion Campus VA Northern Indiana Health Care System
1700 E 38th Street   765-674-3321
Marion, IN 46953   800-360-8387
                                        VHANINPublicAffairs@va.gov
                                        www.northernindiana.va.gov
The Marion Campus focuses on improving the mental health of veterans, and provides extended care. Marion Campus offers nursing home care as an alternative.
Michael E. Hershman, Director
Jay Miller, Associate Director of Operations

2181 Marion VA Medical Center
Marion VA Medical Center
2401 W Main Street   618-997-5311
Marion, IL 62959   www.marion.va.gov
Marion VA Medical Center provides general and surgical care to eligible veterans within several counties in Illinois, southwestern Indiana, and northwest Kentucky.
Jo-Ann M. Ginsberg, MSN, RN, Director
Seth W. Barlage, Associate Director

2182 Martinsburg VA Medical Center
510 Butler Avenue   304-263-0811
Martinsburg, WV 25405   800-817-3807
                                        www.martinsburg.va.gov
The Martinsburg VA Medical Center offers medical services made available to veterans living in 22 counties in Western Maryland, West Virginia, South Central Pennsylvania, and Northwest Virginia.
Timothy J. Cooke, Director
Kenneth W. Allensworth, FACHE, Associate Director

2183 Mayo Clinic
13400 E. Shea Blvd.   480-301-8000
Scottsdale, AZ 85259   800-446-2279
                                        www.mayoclinic.org
Mayo Clinic is a not-for-profit organization and proceeds from Web advertising help support our mission. Mayo Clinic does not endorse any of the third party products and services advertised.
Sandhya Pruthi, M.D., Medical Director
Kenneth G. Berge, M.D., Senior Medical Editor

2184 Medical Center & Ambulatory Care Clinic Montana VA Health Care System
3687 Veterans Drive   406-442-6410
Fort Harrison, MT 59636   877-468-8387
                                        www.montana.va.gov
The medical center and ambulatory care clinic operated by the Montana VA Health Care System provides care to veterans through an acute medical center, and multiple community-based clinics.
Paul Gregory, Acting Director
Anthony Giljum, Associate Director

2185 Memphis VA Medical Center
1030 Jefferson Avenue   901-523-8990
Memphis, TN 38104   800-636-8262
                                        www.memphis.va.gov
Memphis VA Medical Center improves the health of veterans residing in 53 counties in western Tennessee, northern Mississippi, and northwest Arkansas.
David K. Dunning, MPA, Director & CEO
Frank W. Kehus, Associate Director & COO

Trauma & Stressor-Related Disorders / Research Centers

2186 Miami VA Healthcare System
1201 NW 16th Street 305-575-7000
Miami, FL 33125 888-276-1785
Fax: 305-575-3232
www.miami.va.gov

Serves veterans located in three countries in South Florida: Miami-Dade, Broward, and Monroe. Miami VA Healthcare System provides veterans with general medical care, as well as specialty care, such as open-heart surgery, a specialization that they provide to other VA facilities.
David J. VanMeter, FACHE, Acting Director
Loyman R. Marin, Associate Director

2187 Michael E. DeBakey VA Medical Center
2002 Holcombe Boulevard 713-791-1414
Houston, TX 77030 800-553-2278
www.houston.va.gov

Provides medical services for the veteran population of southeast Texas, and operates a post-traumatic stress disorder clinic.
Francisco Vasquez, MBA, Director
J. Kalavar, MD, Chief of Staff

2188 Miles City VA Clinic & Community Living Center
210 S Winchester Avenue 406-874-5600
Miles City, MT 59301 877-468-8387
Fax: 406-874-5696
www.montana.va.gov

Serving veterans in southeastern Montana in Miles City, the Miles City VA Clinic and Community Living Center also operates a community based outpatient clinic.

2189 Milwaukee VA Medical Center (Zablocki)
5000 W National Avenue 414-384-2000
Milwaukee, WI 53295 888-598-7793
www.milwaukee.va.gov

The medical center in Milwaukee delivers primary, secondary, and tertiary medical care to eligible veterans. In addition, the medical center operates a mobile clinic that serves veterans four days a week.
Daniel Zomchek, PhD, Director
Michael Erdmann, MD, Chief of Staff

2190 Minneapolis VA Health Care System
1 Veterans Drive 612-725-2000
Minneapolis, MN 55417 866-414-5058
www.minneapolis.va.gov

Minneapolis VA Health Care System is a teaching hospital serving veterans with a broad range of medical services.
Patrick J. Kelly, FACHE, Director
Kent Crossley, MD, MHA, Chief of Staff

2191 Montrose Campus: Franklin Delano Roosevelt VA Hudson Valley Health Care System
2094 Albany Post Road 914-737-4400
Montrose, NY 10548 www.hudsonvalley.va.gov

The Montrose Campus of the VA Hudson Valley Health Care System is a provider of urgent health care services to veterans.
Margaret B. O'Shea Caplan, Director
Dawn M. Schaal, Associate Director

2192 Mood and Anxiety Disorders Program of Emory University
12 Executive Park Dr., NE 404-778-6663
Atlanta, GA 30329 studies@emoryclinicaltrials.com
www.psychiatry.emory.edu

The Mood and Anxiety Disorders Program of Emory Univeristy's School of Medicine is a dedicated research program within Emory's Department of Psychiatry and Behavioral Sciences.
Boadie Dunlop, M.D., Assistant Professor
Jeff Rakofsky, M.D., Associate Professor

2193 Nashville VA Medical Center Tennessee Valley Healthcare System
1310 24th Avenue S 615-327-4751
Nashville, TN 37212 800-228-4973
www.tennesseevalley.va.gov

Nashville VA Medical Center is part of the Tennessee Healthcare System. Tennessee Valley Healthcare System provides primary and secondary care, general medicine, surgery and specialized care to veterans. The Nashville VA Medical Center is the only VA facility supporting solid organ transplant programs, including total in-house kidney and bone marrow transplants.
Jennifer Vedral-Baron, MN, FAANP, Director
Suzanne L. Jene, MBA, VHA-CM, Deputy Director

2194 National Center for PTSD
802-296-6300
ncptsd@va.gov
www.ptsd.va.gov

The National Center for PTSD is dedicated to research and education on trauma and PTSD.

2195 National Institute of Mental Health
6001 Executive Boulevard 866-615-6464
Rockville, MD 20852 Fax: 301-443-4279
TTY: 866-415-8051
NIMHinfo@mail.nih.gov
www.nimh.nih.gov

The mission of NIMH is to transform the understanding and treatment of mental illnesses through basic and clinical research, paving the way for prevention, recovery, and cure.

2196 New York/New Jersey VA Health Care Network
130 W Kingsbridge Road 718-741-4134
Bronx, NY 10468 718-741-4134
www.visn2.va.gov

The New York/New Jersey VA Health Care Network, or VISN 2, consists of 10 medical centers, and 59 community-based outpatient clinics to better serve the veteran population in New York and New Jersey.
Joan E. McInerney, MD, MBA, MA, Director

2197 North Las Vegas VA Medical Center VA Southern Nevada Healthcare System
6900 North Pecos Road 702-791-9000
North Las Vegas, NV 89086 888-633-7554
www.lasvegas.va.gov

Medical facility serving veterans in Las Vegas, with community-based outpatient clinics located across Nevada.
Tracy L. Skala, Acting Director
John L. Stelsel, Assistant Director

2198 Northport VA Medical Center
79 Middleville Road 631-261-4400
Northport, NY 11768 www.northport.va.gov

The Northport VA Medical Center specializes in providing health care services to veterans in need.
Cathy Cruise, MD, Acting Director
Colleen Luckner, MBA, Associate Director

2199 Oklahoma City VA Health Care System
921 NE 13th Street 405-456-1000
Oklahoma City, OK 73104 866-835-5273
www.oklahoma.va.gov

The Oklahoma City VA Medical Center is a tertiary care facility and a referral center. The medical center provides a full range of patient care services for veterans.
Kristopher Wade Vlosich, Director
Paul Gregory, Associate Director

2200 Oscar G. Johnson VA Medical Center
325 E H. Street 906-774-3300
Iron Mountain, MI 49801 800-215-8262
www.ironmountain.va.gov

A primary and secondary level care facility providing veterans with acute care and general medicine care. The facility offers rehabilitation, extended care, and emergency services.
James W. Rice, Director
Drew A. DeWitt, FACHE, Associate Director

2201 Overton Brooks VA Medical Center
510 E Stoner Avenue 318-221-8411
Shreveport, LA 71101 800-863-7441
www.shreveport.va.gov

A medical facility serving veterans in the South Central VA Health Care Network (VISN 16). Overton Brooks VA Medical Center is a primary receiving center for military casualties, and accepts referrals from the southeast Lousiana Veterans Healthcare System and the Alexandria VA Health Science Center.
Richard L. Crockett, Director
Zachary Sage, Associate Director

Trauma & Stressor-Related Disorders / Research Centers

2202 **Perry Point VA Medical Center VA Maryland Health Care System**
515 Broad Street   410-642-2411
Perry Point, MD 21902   www.maryland.va.gov
The largest medical facility in the VA Maryland Health Care System, Perry Point provides long-term care, nursing home care, and hospice care for veterans.
Adam M. Robinson, Director
Sandra Marshall, Chief of Staff

2203 **Phoenix VA Health Care System**
Phoenix VA Health Care System
650 E Indian School Road   602-277-5551
Phoenix, AZ 85012   800-554-7174
   TTY: 711
   www.phoenix.va.gov
The Phoenix VA Health Care System serves veterans at its main medical center in central Arizona. In addition, the Phoenix VA Health Care System has nine outpatient clinics for veterans. The Phoenix VA Health Care System offers community-based, patient-focused care with their PACT system, Patient Aligned Care Team; ensuring that communication between patient and health care providers is uncomplicated.
RimaAnn Nelson, Director
Shawn Bransky, Deputy Director

2204 **Portland VA Medical Center VA Portland Health Care System**
3710 SW U.S. Veterans Hospital Road   503-220-8262
Portland, OR 97239   800-949-1004
   www.portland.va.gov
The Portland VA Medical Center serves veterans in Oregon and southwest Washington. In addition to comprehensive medical and mental health services, the medical center supports ongoing research and medical education.
Darwin G. Goodspeed, Director
Cheryl L. Thieschafer, Deputy Director

2205 **Providence VA Medical Center**
830 Chalkstone Avenue   401-273-7100
Providence, RI 02908   866-363-4486
   www.providence.va.gov
The Providence VA Medical Center provides comprehensive outpatient and inpatient health care to veterans in Rhode Island and southeastern Massachusetts. Personalized care is offered to every veteran.
Susan MacKenzie, PhD, Director
Erin Clare Sears, MBA, MSW, Associate Director

2206 **Ralph H. Johnson VA Medical Center**
109 Bee Street   843-577-5011
Charleston, SC 29401   888-878-6884
   www.charleston.va.gov
The Ralph H. Johnson VA Medical Center serves veterans in 22 counties along the South Carolina and Georgia coastline. Six community-based outpatient clinics exist to better serve the veteran population.
Scott R. Isaacks, MBA, FACHE, Director & CEO
Sharon Castle, PharmD, BCPS, Acting Associate Director & COO

2207 **Raymond G. Murphy VA Medical Center New Mexico VA Health Care System**
1501 San Pedro Drive SE   505-265-1711
Albuquerque, NM 87108   800-465-8262
   www.albuquerque.va.gov
Provides medical care to veterans, and specializes in delivering rural health care in New Mexico.
Andrew M. Welch, MHA, FACHE, Director
Sonja Brown, Associate Director

2208 **Roanoke Vet Center**
350 Albemarle Avenue SW   540-342-9726
Roanoke, VA 24016   877-927-8387
   www.va.gov
A medical facility serving the health needs of veterans in Roanoke, Virginia.
Michael Jenkins, Director
John Whitlock, Counselor

2209 **Robert J. Dole VA Medical Center**
5500 E Kellogg Avenue   316-685-2221
Wichita, KS 67218   888-878-6881
   www.wichita.va.gov
Located in the largest city in Kansas, Robert J. Dole VA Medical Center addresses the health of veterans by providing a large range of primary health services. The medical center offers specialty care in the form of rehabilitation programs, and houses a prosthetic laboratory.
Rick A. Ament, FACHE, Director
Dana Foley, PhD, Associate Director

2210 **Robley Rex VA Medical Center Louisville VA Medical Center**
800 Zorn Avenue   502-287-4000
Louisville, KY 40206   800-376-8387
   www.louisville.va.gov
Robley Rex offers health care services to veterans within the 35-county area of Kentuckiana.
Stephen D. Black, Director
Larry D. Roberts, Associate Director

2211 **Roseburg VA Health Care System**
913 NW Garden Valley Boulevard   541-440-1000
Roseburg, OR 97471   800-549-8387
   www.roseburg.va.gov
The Roseburg VA Health Care System consists of one main facility located in Roseburg and four community-based outpatient clinics. Roseburg offers primary care and hospital services in medicine, surgery and mental health for veterans.
Keith M. Allen, Director
Ryan Baker, CDFM, MBA, Associate Director

2212 **Sacramento Veterans Center**
1111 Howe Avenue   916-566-7430
Sacramento, CA 95825   877-927-8387
   Fax: 916-566-7433
   www.va.gov/directory/guide/facility.asp?
Sandra Moreno, Acting Director
Albert Revives, Outreach Specialist

2213 **Salem VA Medical Center**
1970 Roanoke Boulevard   540-982-2463
Salem, VA 24153   888-982-2463
   www.salem.va.gov
Medical facility located in Salem, Virginia, with services available to eligible veterans living in 26 counties in southwestern Virginia.
Rebecca J. Stackhouse, MA, CTRS, Director
Allen R. Moye, MS, Associate Director

2214 **Samueli Institute**
1737 King Street   703-299-4800
Alexandria, VA 22314   Fax: 703-535-6752
   www.samueliinstitute.org
Samueli Institute is advancing the science of healing worldwide by applying academic rigor to research on healing, well-being and resilience; translating evidence into action for the U.S. Military and large-scale health systems; and fostering wellness through self-care to create a flourishing society.
Susan Samueli, PhD, Co-Founder
Wayne B. Jonas, MD, President/ CEO

2215 **San Francisco VA Medical Center**
4150 Clement Street   415-221-4810
San Francisco, CA 94121   877-487-2838
   www.sanfrancisco.va.gov
The San Francisco VA Health Care System provides health care to veterans through the San Francisco VA Medical Center, as well as through six outpatient clinics based in the community. The San Francisco VA Health Care System conducts research, and develops treatment programs aimed at improving the health of eligible veterans.
Bonnie S. Graham, MBA, Director
Jia F. Li, MBA, Associate Director

2216 **Sheridan VA Medical Center**
1898 Fort Road   307-672-3473
Sheridan, WY 82801   866-822-6714
   www.sheridan.va.gov

Trauma & Stressor-Related Disorders / Research Centers

The Sheridan VA Medical Center provides medical care to eligible veterans. Additionally, 8 community-based outpatient clinics exist to better serve veterans across Wyoming.
Pamela S. Crowell, MPA, Director
Donald T. McGraw, Associate Director

2217 Sioux Falls VA Health Care System
2501 W 22nd Street 605-336-3230
Sioux Falls, SD 57105 800-316-8387
www.siouxfalls.va.gov
Sioux Falls VA Health Care System provides inpatient and outpatient care for veterans in eastern South Dakota, southwestern Minnesota, and northwestern Iowa. Services include primary and specialty medical care, mental health care, and rehabilitation.
Barbara Teal, Acting Director
Timothy L. Pendergrass, MD, Chief of Staff

2218 South Central VA Health Care Network
715 S Pear Orchard Road 601-206-6900
Ridgeland, MS 39157 800-639-5137
Fax: 601-206-7018
www.visn16.va.gov
The South Central VA Health Care Network is a Veterans Integrated Service Network (VISN) serving veterans in Arkansas, Louisiana, Mississippi, parts of Texas, Missouri, Alabama, Oklahoma, and Florida.
Skye McDougall, PhD, Director
Shannon C. Novotny, MPA, FACHE, Deputy Director

2219 Southeast Louisiana Veterans Health Care System
2400 Canal Street 800-935-8387
New Orleans, LA 70119 www.neworleans.va.gov
Southeast Louisiana Veterans Health Care System (SLVHCS) improves the health of veterans. SLVHCS offers specialty care in the form of respite care and community adult day care programs. In addition, SLVHCS operates a telehealth system, ensuring any veteran can access health care services from the comfort of their home.
Fernando O. Rivera, Director
Ralph Schapira, MD, Chief of Staff

2220 Southern Arizona VA Health Care System
Southern Arizona VA Health Care System
3601 S 6th Avenue 520-792-1450
Tucson, AZ 85723 800-470-8262
Fax: 520-629-1820
www.tucson.va.gov
The Southern Arizona VA Health Care System located in Tucson, Arizona, serves eligible veterans across seven counties in Southern Arizona, and one county in New Mexico. The Southern Arizona VA Health Care System offers specialized treatment programs to serve veterans.
William J. Caron, FACHE, Director
Katie A. Landwehr, MBA, FACHE, Associate Director

2221 Spark M. Matsunaga VA Medical Center VA Pacific Islands Health Care System
VA Pacific Islands Health Care System
459 Patterson Road 808-433-0600
Honolulu, HI 96819 800-214-1306
www.hawaii.va.gov
Existing within the VA Pacific Islands Health Care System, Spark M. Matsunaga VA Medical Center covers a wide range of health care needs for veterans across Hawaii and the Pacific Islands. In addition, the health care system oversees seven outpatient clinics: West Oahu, Hawaii, Maui, Kauai, American Samoa, and Guam.
Jennifer S. Gutowski, MHA, FACHE, Director
Chandra S. Lake, MPA, ACHE, HCLDP, Associate Director

2222 Spokane VA Medical Center Mann-Grandstaff VA Medical Center
4815 N Assembly Street 509-434-7000
Spokane, WA 99205 800-325-7940
www.spokane.va.gov
The Spokane VA Medical Center serves the health care needs of veterans in Spokane, Washington, providing primary and secondary care, with a focus on preventive health and chronic disease management.
Robert J. Fischer, MD, FACOG, CPE, Director
Richard Rick Richards, MS, MBA, FACHE, Associate Director

2223 Synergy Clinical Research Center
1908 Sweetwater Road 888-539-0282
National City, CA 91950 Fax: 619-327-0163
www.synergyresearchcenters.com
Synergy is dedicated to providing comprehensive and exemplary clinical research services to advance the science of medicine.
Dr. Bari, Medical Director, Principal Investigator
Dr. Ishaque, Medical Director, Principal Investigator

2224 Syracuse VA Medical Center
800 Irving Avenue 315-425-4400
Syracuse, NY 13210 800-792-4334
www.syracuse.va.gov
The Syracuse VA Medical Center provides a full range of patient care services, education and research to serve veterans.
Judy Hayman, PhD, Director
Richard W. Salgueiro, Associate Director

2225 Tacoma Vet Center
4916 Center Street 253-565-7038
Tacoma, WA 98409 Fax: 253-254-0079
www.va.gov
Medical facility serving veterans, and part of the VISN 20 Northwest Network.
William Philadelphia, PhD, LPC, Director
Audrey Dangtwu, Counselor

2226 Thomas E. Creek VA Medical Center Amarillo VA Health Care System
6010 Amarillo Boulevard W 806-355-9703
Amarillo, TX 79106 800-687-8262
www.amarillo.va.gov
The Amarillo VA Health Care System, a division of the Southwest VA Health Care Network (VISN 18), provides primary, specialty, and extended care to veterans throughout the Texas and Oklahoma panhandles, eastern New Mexico, and southern Kansas.
Michael L. Kiefer, MHA, FACHE, Director
Elizabeth Lowery, Associate Director

2227 Tomah VA Medical Center
500 E Veterans Street 608-372-3971
Tomah, WI 54660 800-872-8662
TTY: 888-598-7793
www.tomah.va.gov
As part of the VA Great Lakes Health Care System (VISN 12), Tomah VA Medical Center provides medical care available to veterans living in Western and Central Wisconsin.
Victoria P. Brahm, Director
Staci Williams, Associate Director

2228 Trauma Center
1269 Beacon Street 617-232-1303
Brookline, MA 2446 Fax: 617-232-1280
www.traumacenter.org
The Trauma Center is a program of Justice Resource Institute (JRI), a large nonprofit organization dedicated to social justice by offering hope and promise of fulfillment to children, adults, and families who are at risk of not receiving effective services essential to their safety, progress, and/or survival.
Dr. Bessel van der Kolk, Founder
Margaret Blaustein, Ph.D, Director of Training and Education

2229 UAMS Psychiatric Research Institute
4224 Shuffield Drive 501-526-8100
Little Rock, AR 72205 kramerteresal@uams.edu
www.psychiatry.uams.edu
Combining research, education and clinical services into one facility, PRI offers inpatient and outpatient services, with 40 psychiatric beds, therapy options, and specialized treatment for specific disorders, including: addictive eating, anxiety, deppressive and post-traumatic stress disorders. Research focuses on evidence-based care takes into consideration the education of future medical personnel while relying on research scientists to provide innovative forms of treatment.
Dan Rahn, MD, Chancellor

2230 UCLA Anxiety Disorders Research Center
Department of Psychology 310-825-9312
Los Angeles, CA 90094 rose@psych.ucla.edu
anxiety.psych.ucla.edu

Trauma & Stressor-Related Disorders / Research Centers

The purpose of The ADRC is to further our understanding of the factors that place individuals at risk for developing phobias, anxiety disorders and related conditions, and to develop more effective treatments that have long lasting effects and are cost effective.
Michelle G. Craske, Ph.D., Director
Raphael Rose, Ph.D., Associate Director

2231 University Drive Campus VA Pittsburgh Healthcare System
University Drive C
Pittsburgh, PA 15240
412-822-2222
866-482-7488
www.pittsburgh.va.gov
VA Pittsburgh Healthcare System is composed of two main campuses: University Drive and H.J. Heinz. The healthcare system serves veterans living in the tri-state area of Pennsylvania, Ohio, and West Virginia. University Drive campus serves as an acute care facility.
Barbara Forsha, MSN, RN, ET, Director
Ali Sonel, MD, Chief of Staff

2232 VA Ann Arbor Healthcare System
2215 Fuller Road
Ann Arbor, MI 48105
734-769-7100
800-361-8387
www.annarbor.va.gov
VA Ann Arbor is a medical facility that doubles as a referral center for specialty care for veterans located within the 15-county area of Michigan and northwest Ohio.
Ginny Creasman, Pharm D, FACHE, Director
Chris Cauley, FACHE, Associate Director

2233 VA Austin Outpatient Clinic
7901 Metropolis Drive
Austin, TX 78744
512-823-4000
www.centraltexas.va.gov
VA Austin Outpatient Clinic is the largest clinic in the nation, offering numerous specialty services from chemotherapy to gastroenterology.
Andrew T. Garcia, MHA, Director
Olawale O. Fashina, MD, MHSA, CPE, Chief of Staff

2234 VA Capitol Health Care Network
849 International Drive
Linthicum, MD 21090
410-691-1131
www.va.gov
The VA Capitol Health Care Network (VISN 5) serves veterans from within Maryland, the District of Columbia, select areas of Virginia, West Virginia, and Pennsylvania.
Robert Walton, Director
Raymond Chung, MD, Chief Medical Officer

2235 VA Central California Health Care System
2615 E Clinton Avenue
Fresno, CA 93703
559-225-6100
888-826-2838
www.fresno.va.gov
The VA Central California Health Care System provides general and acute care to its patients. The VA Central California Health Care System serves veterans located in six counties in the San Joaquin Valley, and currently operates three outpatient clinics.
Charles Benninger, Acting Director
Demitric Franklin, Associate Director

2236 VA Central Iowa Health Care System
3600 30th Street
Des Moines, IA 50310
515-699-5999
800-294-8387
www.centraliowa.va.gov
The VA Central Iowa Health Care System provides acute and specialized health care to veterans. The medical facility operates an extensive range of mental health services, including specialized treatments for substance abuse and post-traumatic stress.
Gail Graham, Director
Jerry Blow, MD, Chief of Staff

2237 VA Great Lakes Health Care System
Four Westbrook Corporate Tower
Westchester, IL 60154
708-492-3900
www.visn12.va.gov
The VA Great Lakes Health Care System consists of eight VA medical centers, all focused around the goal of fulfilling the health care needs of veterans.
Renee Oshinski, Director
Lynette J. Taylor, Deputy Director

2238 VA Greater Los Angeles Healthcare System
11301 Wilshire Boulevard
Los Angeles, CA 90073
310-478-3711
877-252-4866
TTY: 711
www.losangeles.va.gov
The VA Greater Los Angeles Healthcare System is comprised of three main centers; the West Los Angeles Medical Center, the Sepulveda Ambulatory Care Center, and the Los Angeles Ambulatory Care Center. The VA Greater Los Angeles Healthcare System is responsible for providing care to veterans located in five counties: Los Angeles, Ventura, Kern, Santa Barbara, and San Luis Obispo.
Ann Brown, FACHE, Director
Robert W. McKenrick, Executive Director

2239 VA Healthcare System of Ohio
11500 Northlake Drive
Cincinnati, OH 45249
513-247-4621
www.visn10.va.gov
The VA Healthcare System (VISN 10) serves Ohio, Indiana, and Michigan. VISN 10 consists of 10 medical centers and 63 community-based outpatient clinics to better serve veterans.
Shella D. Stovall, Acting Director
Ronald Stertzbach, Deputy Director

2240 VA Heart of Texas Health Care Network Dallas VA Medical Center
4500 S Lancaster Road
Dallas, TX 75216
214-742-8387
800-849-3597
www.northtexas.va.gov
The VA Heart of Texas Health Care Network provides health care services to veterans in 38 counties in Texas, and 2 counties in southern Oklahoma.
Stephen R. Holt, Director
Kendrick Brown, Associate Director

2241 VA Heartland Network
1201 Walnut Street
Kansas City, MO 64106
816-701-3002
www.visn15.va.gov
The VA Heartland Network (VISN 15) provides health care services to veterans in Kansas and Missouri, as well as parts of Illinois, Indiana, Kentucky and Arkansas. The Heartland Network is comprised of 7 medical facilities.

2242 VA Illiana Health Care System
1900 E Main Street
Danville, IL 61832
217-554-3000
800-320-8387
www.danville.va.gov
VA Illiana Health Care System is focused on improving the health of veterans throughout 34 counties in Illinois and Indiana.
Kelley A. Sermak, Acting Director
Diana Carranza, FACHE, Associate Director

2243 VA Loma Linda Healthcare System
11201 Benton Street
Loma Linda, CA 92357
909-825-7084
800-741-8387
Fax: 909-422-3106
TTY: 711
www.lomalinda.va.gov
The VA Loma Linda Healthcare System serves veterans within the San Bernardino and Riverside 2-county area. The main medical center is located in Loma Linda, where veterans are cared for.
Karandeep Sraon, MBA, FACHE, Director
Shane M. Elliott, MBA, Associate Director

2244 VA MidSouth Healthcare Network (VISN 9)
1801 W End Avenue
Nashville, TN 37203
615-695-2200
877-291-5311
Fax: 615-321-2721
www.visn9.va.gov
VA MidSouth Healthcare Network (VISN 9) is an integrated healthcare delivery system consisting of 9 medical centers located in Lexington and Louisville in Kentucky; and Memphis, Mountain Home, Murfreesboro and Nashville in Tennessee. In total, VISN 9 provides medical care to veterans in 238 counties within the MidSouth.
Cynthia Breyfogle, FACHE, Director
Todd D. Burnett, PsyD, Deputy Director

Trauma & Stressor-Related Disorders / Research Centers

2245 **VA Northern California Health Care System**
10535 Hospital Way   916-843-7000
Mather, CA 95655   844-698-2311
www.northerncalifornia.va.gov

The VA Northern California Health Care System offers health care services to veterans in the form of general medical care, surgery, rehabilitative care, and mental health care. The VA Northern California Health Care System achives these goals through one medical center in Sacramento, one outpatient clinic in Martinez, and seven other outpatient clinics.
David Stockwell, Director
Timothy Graham, Associate Director

2246 **VA Palo Alto Health Care System**
3801 Miranda Avenue   650-493-5000
Palo Alto, CA 94304   800-455-0057
                              Fax: 925-449-6522
                              TTY: 711
www.palotalto.va.gov

The VA Palo Alto Health Care System provides care to veterans through three inpatient centers located at Palo Alto, Menlo Park, and Livermore, with seven outpatient clinics in San Jose, Fremont, Capitola, Monterey, Stockton, Modesto, and Sonora. The VA Palo Alto Health Care System offers engaged and extensive health care to all eligible veterans.
Thomas J. Fitzgerald III, CHESP, Director
Daniel Kulenich, Deputy Director

2247 **VA Puget Sound Health Care System**
1660 S Columbian Way   206-762-1010
Seattle, WA 98108   800-329-8387
www.pugetsound.va.gov

VA Puget Sound Health Care System provides medical services for veterans residing in 14 counties around the Puget Sound in the Pacific Northwest, in addition to operating two main divisions located at American Lake, and Seattle.
Michael Tadych, FACHE, Director
Kathryn Sherrill, MSW, LCSW, BSN, Deputy Director

2248 **VA Sierra Nevada Health Care System**
975 Kirman Avenue   775-786-7200
Reno, NV 89502   888-838-6256
www.reno.va.gov

The VA Sierra Nevada Health Care System provides primary and secondary care to veterans across 20 counties in northern Nevada and northeastern California.
Lisa Howard, Director
Jack R. Smith, Associate Director

2249 **VA Southeast Network**
3700 Crestwood Parkway   678-924-5700
Duluth, GA 30096   844-698-2311
www.southeast.va.gov

The VA Southeast Network (VISN 7) is the largest integrated health care system in America, and focuses on meeting the health care needs of veterans within the 244-county area.
Leslie Wiggins, Director
Ajay K. Dhawan, MD, FACHE, Chief Medical Officer

2250 **VA St. Louis Health Care System John Cochran & Jefferson Barracks**
915 N Grand Boulevard   314-652-4100
St. Louis, MO 63106   800-228-5459
www.stlouis.va.gov

Part of the Heartland Network (VISN 15), the St. Louis Health Care System offers medical care to veterans in east central Missouri and southwestern Illinois. The John Cochran Division provides surgical care, ambulatory medicine, and houses intensive care units, while the Jefferson Barracks Division provides psychiatric treatment and a nursing home care unit.
Keith D. Repko, Director
Michael D. Crittenden, MD, Chief of Staff

2251 **VA Western Colorado Health Care System**
2121 N Avenue   970-242-0731
Grand Junction, CO 81501   866-206-6415
www.grandjunction.va.gov

The VA Western Colorado Health Care System provides veterans with primary and secondary care, acute care, surgery, and psychiatric care. The main medical center is located in Grand Junction, with one community-based outpatient clinic, and one telehealth outreach clinic.
Michael T. Kilmer, Director
Srinivas Ginjupalli, Chief of Staff

2252 **Veterans Administration Medical Center: Alabama**
3701 Loop Road E   205-554-2000
Tuscaloosa, AL 35404   888-651-2685
                              Fax: 205-554-2034
                              TTY: 711
www.tuscaloosa.va.gov

The Tuscaloosa VA Medical Center (TVAMC) is located in West Alabama. The medical center provides primary and long-term healthcare to eligible veterans in the VA Southeast Network. Mental health services are also provided.
John F. Merkle, FACHE, Director
Amir Farooqi, FACHE, Associate Director

2253 **Veterans Association Medical Center**
700 S 19th Street   205-933-8101
Birmingham, AL 35233   866-487-4243
                              Fax: 205-933-4484
                              TTY: 711
www.birmingham.va.gov

The Birmingham VA Medical Center provides acute tertiary care for eligible veterans in the VA Southeast Network. The medical centre provides a wide range of medical care, and is also a referral center for veterans and their beneficiaries.
Stacy J. Vasquez, Director
Mary Mitchell, Associate Director

2254 **W. G. (Bill) Hefner VA Medical Center**
1601 Brenner Avenue   704-638-9000
Salisbury, NC 28144   800-469-8262
www.salisbury.va.gov

A medical center offering primary and secondary inpatient health care to veterans living in 21 counties of the Central Piedmont Region of North Carolina.
Joseph Vaughn, MBA, FACHE, Director
Subbarao Pemmaraju, MD, Chief of Staff

2255 **Washington DC VA Medical Center**
50 Irving Street NW   202-745-8000
Washington, DC 20422   877-328-2621
                              Fax: 202-754-8530
www.washingtondc.va.gov

Veterans can acquire a great variety of health care services at the Washington DC VA Medical Center, which serves veterans of the national capital area. The Medical Center oversees a Community Resource and Referral Center for homeless and at-risk veterans, which operates 24 hours a day, 7 days a week.
Michael S. Heimall, Director
Christopher J. Irwin, Associate Director

2256 **West Palm Beach VA Medical Center**
7305 N Military Trail   561-422-8262
West Palm Beach, FL 33410   800-972-8262
www.westpalmbeach.va.gov

The West Palm Beach VA Medical Center consists of one major medical facility, and provides general medical care, in addition to psychiatric and surgical care. A Blind Rehabilitation Center is operated by the major medical facility, and serves as a referral center for blind and visually impaired veterans.
Donna Katen-Bahensky, MSPH, Director & CEO
Cynthia O'Connell, MHA, FACHE, Associate Director

2257 **West Roxbury Division VA Boston Healthcare System**
1400 VFW Parkway   617-323-7700
West Roxbury, MA 02132   800-865-3384
www.boston.va.gov

The West Roxbury Division of the VA Boston Healthcare System is dedicated to providing health care to veterans located in Boston.
Vincent Ng, Director
Michael E. Charness, MD, Chief of Staff

2258 **White City VA Rehabilitation Center VA Southern Oregon**
8495 Crater Lake Highway   541-826-2111
White City, OR 97503   800-809-8725
                              Fax: 541-830-3500
www.southernoregon.va.gov

Trauma & Stressor-Related Disorders / Support Groups & Hotlines

White City VA Rehabilitation Center is the only freestanding residential rehabilitation center, and provides veterans with short-term rehabilitative and long-term health care. The center maintains a focus on patient-centered care.
Philip G. Dionne, Director
Sharee Taylor, Associate Director

2259 **White River Junction VA Medical Center**
215 N Main Street 802-295-9363
White River Junction, VT 05009 866-687-8387
www.whiteriver.va.gov
The White River Junction VA Medical Center provides health care services to eligible Veterans in Vermont and the 4 counties in New Hampshire. The medical center is affiliated with the Geisel School of Medicine, formerly known as Dartmouth Medical School.
Brett Rusch, MD, Executive Director
Becky Rhoads, Au.D, Associate Director

2260 **Wilkes-Barre VA Medical Center**
1111 E End Boulevard 570-824-3521
Wilkes-Barre, PA 18711 877-928-2621
www.wilkes-barre.va.gov
Wilkes-Barre VA Medical Center offers comprehensive health care to veterans residing in 18 counties in Pennsylvania and one county in New York.
Russell E. Lloyd, Director
Mirza Z. Ali, MD, Chief of Staff

2261 **William S. Middleton Memorial Veterans Hospital**
2500 Overlook Terrace 608-256-1901
Madison, WI 53705 888-478-8321
TTY: 888-598-7793
www.madison.va.gov
The William S. Middleton Memorial Veterans Hospital provides tertiary medical, surgical, neurological, and psychiatric care. Outpatient services are also available to eligible veterans within 15 counties in south-central Wisconsin and 5 counties in northwestern Illinois.
John J. Rohrer, Director
Christine M. Kleckner, Associate Director

2262 **Wilmington VA Medical Center**
1601 Kirkwood Highway 302-994-2511
Wilmington, DE 19805 800-461-8262
www.wilmington.va.gov
The Wilmington VA Medical Center offers eligible veterans a wide range of health services, from preventative care to long-term care. The Wilmington VA Medical Center overlooks community-based outpatient clinics which operate in Delaware.
Vince Kane, Director
George Tzanis, Chief of Staff

2263 **Yale Child Study Center**
230 South Frontage Rd. 203-785-2540
New Haven, CT 6519 childstudycenter.yale.edu
At our core is the mission to improve the lives of children and families through research, service, and training.
Dr. Linda Mayes, Interim Director

Support Groups & Hotlines

2264 **American Self-Help Group Clearinghouse**
www.selfhelpgroups.org
American Self-Help Group Clearinghouse has a keyword-searchable database of over 1,100 national, international, model and online self-help support groups for addictions, bereavement, health, mental health, disabilities, abuse, parenting, caregiver concerns and many other stressful life situations.

2265 **COPLINE**
501 Iron Bridge Rd. 800-267-5463
Freehold, NJ 7728 Copline@optonline.net
www.copline.org
Copline is the first national law enforcement officers hotline in the country that is manned by retired law enforcement officers. Retired law enforcement officers are trained in active listening and bring the knowledge and understanding of the many psychosocial stressors.
Stephanie Samuels, M.A., MSW, LCSW, President/ Creator/ Founder
Dennis Cronin, Vice President

2266 **Child Help**
4350 E. Camelback Road 480-922-8212
Phoenix, AZ 85018 800-422-4453
www.childhelp.org
Michael Medoro, Child Development Officer
Jon Taylor, Chief Financial Officer

2267 **Common Ground Sanctuary**
1410 S. Telegraph 248-456-8150
Bloomfield Hills, MI 48302 800-231-1127
www.commongroundsanctuary.org
A 24-hour nonprofit agency dedicated to helping youths, adults and families in crisis. Through its crisis line and in person through various programs, Common Ground Sanctuary provides professional and compassionate service to more than 40,000 people a year, with most services provided free of charge. Mission is to provide a lifeline for individuals and families in crisis, victims of crime, persons with mental illness, people trying to cope with critical situations and runaway and homeless youth.
Tony Rothschild, President & CEO
Steve Mitchell, Board Chair

2268 **Crime Survivors**
PO Box 54552 949-872-7895
Irvine, CA 92619 844-853-4673
crimesurvivors@aol.com
www.crimesurvivors.org
Crime Survivors vision is for victims of crime to recover from their experience mentally, physically, emotionally, and financially, by receiving the respect, support, and protection from law enforcement, the judicial system, and the community.
Patricia Wenskunas, Founder / CEO
Janet Wilson Irving, Chairperson

2269 **Heal My PTSD with Michele Rosenthal**
healmyptsd.com
Offers information anyone would need to discover what there is to know about symptoms of PTSD, treatment options and the path to feeling better.
Michele Rosenthal, Founder

2270 **Holliswood Hospital Psychiatric Care, Services and Self-Help/Support Groups**
87-37 Palermo Street 718-776-8181
Holliswood, NY 11423 800-486-3005
Fax: 718-776-8572
HolliswoodInfo@libertymgt.com
www.holliswoodhospital.com/
The Holliswood Hospital, a 110-bed private psychiatric hospital located in a quiet residential Queens community, is a leader in providing quality, acute inpatient mental health care for adult, adolescent, geriatric and dually diagnosed patients. Holliswood Hospital treats patients with a broad range of psychiatric disorders. Additionally, specialized services are available for patients with psychiatric diagnoses compounded by chemical dependency, or a history of physical or sexual abuse.
Susan Clayton, Support Group Coordinator
Angela Hurtado, Support Group Coordinator

2271 **Loch Raven VA Community Living & Rehabilitation Center**
3901 The Alameda 410-605-7000
Baltimore, MD 21218 www.maryland.va.gov
The Loch Raven VA Community Living & Rehabilitation Center works to restore independence for Maryland's veterans by providing a wide variety of physical therapies and rehabilitation programs.
Adam M. Robinson, Jr., MD, Director
Sandra Marshall, MD, Chief of Staff

2272 **Mental Health America**
500 Montgomery Street 703-684-7722
Alexandria, VA 22314 800-969-6642
Fax: 703-684-5968
mhanational.org

Trauma & Stressor-Related Disorders / Print Resources

Mental Health America (MHA) - founded in 1909 - is the nation's leading community-based non-profit dedicated to helping all Americans achieve wellness by living mentally healthier lives.
Schroeder Stribling, President & CEO
Stuart Allen, Chief Marketing & Advancement Officer

2273 National Health Information Center
Office of Disease Prevention & Health Promotion
1101 Wootton Pkwy
Rockville, MD 20852
Fax: 240-453-8281
odphpinfo@hhs.gov
www.health.gov/nhic

Supports public health education by maintaining a calendar of National Health Observances; helps connect consumers and health professionals to organizations that can best answer questions and provide up-to-date contact information from reliable sources; updates on a yearly basis toll-free numbers for health information, Federal health clearinghouses and info centers.
Don Wright, MD, MPH, Director

2274 National Veterans Services Fund
Darien, CT 06820
203-656-0003
800-521-0198
Fax: 203-656-1957
NatVetSvc@aol.com
www.nvsf.org

NVSF, Inc. provides an integrated program of services managed by veterans that include the following: a national hotline for veterans and their families that responds to hundreds of inquiries each month from throughout the country; an extensive repository of free information on topics ranging from the history of the Agent Orange lawsuit to the most recent Gulf War legislation; a special fund that offers limited emergency economic assistance and relief for families in crisis; business partnership
Phil Kraft, President

2275 Out of the Storm
cptsd.org

Out of the Storm is a discussion group and resource site for those whose lives have been affected by Complex Post Traumatic Disorder (CPTSD).

2276 PTSD Family Support Group
2133 Upton Drive
Virginia Beach, VA 23454
757-222-2247
love4vets.org

Love4Vets will ambitiously, humbly, and respectfully aim to become a proactive organization throughout the nation that military veterans will have as a first choice for empowerment and support.
April Krowel, Chairman
Ela Kelly, Founder/ CEO

2277 PTSD Hotline
800-273-8255
www.ptsdhotline.com/index.html

This Website deals primarily with PTSD as it relates to Veterans.

2278 PTSDanonymous.org
ptsda@comcast.net
www.ptsdanonymous.org

A nationwide network of community based, non-clinical, veteran lead support group meetings for those suffering from military trauma and seeking the fellowship of their peers.

2279 Pandora's Aquarium
www.pandys.org

A rape, sexual assault, and sexual abuse survivor message board and chat room.

2280 Panic Survivor
www.panicsurvivor.com

A community to sove anxiety disorder problem.

2281 Rape, Abuse & Incest National Network
1220 L Street, NW
Washington, DC 20005
202-544-3064
Fax: 202-544-3556
info@rainn.org
rainn.org

RAINN (Rape, Abuse & Incest National Network) is the nation's largest anti-sexual violence organization and was named one of America's 100 Best Charities by Worth magazine.
Scott Berkowitz, President/ Founder
Regan Burke, Chairperson

2282 Recovery International
105 W. Adams St.
Chicago, IL 60603
312-337-5661
866-221-0302
Fax: 312-726-4446
Christine@recoveryinternational.org
www.recoveryinternational.org

Recovery International offers meetings to men and women of all ages that ease the suffering from mental health issues by gaining skills to lead more peaceful and productive lives. In the last 76 years RI has equipped over 1 million people with tools to control behavior and change attitudes.
Christine Lewis, Executive Director
Caitlin Fahey, Project Coordinator

2283 Suicide.org
800-784-2433
Kevin@Suicide.org
www.suicide.org

If you are suicidal, have attempted suicide, or are a suicide survivor, you will find help, hope, comfort, understanding, support, love, and extensive resources here.
Kevin Caruso, Founder
Adam Sutherland, Vice President

2284 Support4Hope
PO Box 184
Deer Lodge, TN 37726
Admin@Support4hope.com
www.support4hope.com

Support4Hope is dedicated to support of various mental health issues such as Bipolar Disorder, Depression, Anxiety Disorders, Schizophrenia, Post Traumatic Stress Disorder (PTSD) and the problems that arise from them along with other problems such as Domestic Abuse.

2285 United States 211 Information and Referral Systems
www.211.org

Helps connect to a community resource specialist in an area to get in touch with local organizations that provide critical services.

2286 Veterans Crisis Line
800-273-8255
www.veteranscrisisline.net

The Veterans Crisis Line connects Veterans in crisis and their families and friends with qualified, caring Department of Veterans Affairs responders through a confidential toll-free hotline, online chat, or text.

2287 Vetwives Living With PTSD
livingwithptsd.yuku.com

Forum for people suffering with PTSD.

Print Resources

2288 American Journal of Psychiatry
American Psychiatric Association Publishing
800 Maine Avenue SW, Suite 900
Washington, DC 20024
202-459-9722
800-368-5777
Fax: 202-403-3094
psychiatryonline@psych.org
ajp.psychiatryonline.org

Official journal of the American Psychiatric Association (APA).
Ned H. Kalin, MD, Editor-in-Chief

2289 American Journal of Psychotherapy
American Psychiatric Association Publishing
800 Maine Avenue SW, Suite 900
Washington, DC 20024
202-459-9722
800-368-5777
Fax: 202-403-3094
psychiatryonline@psych.org
ajp.psychiatryonline.org

Publishes content that aims to advance the theory, science, and clinical practice of psychotherapy.
Holly A. Swartz, MD, Editor-in-Chief

2290 Journal of Psychiatry, Depression & Anxiety
Herald Scholarly Open Access
2561 Cornelia Road, Suite 205
Herndon, VA 20171
202-499-9679
Fax: 202-217-4195
contact@heraldsopenaccess.us
www.heraldopenaccess.us

Online, international, open access, peer-reviewed journal focused primarily on depression and anxiety, but also on other related areas of psychiatry as well.
Sam Vaknin, Editor-in-Chief

2291 Journal of Traumatic Stress
John Wiley & Sons, Inc.
111 River Street, Suite 300
Hoboken, NJ 07030-5774
201-748-6000
800-567-4797
Fax: 201-748-6088
onlinelibrary.wiley.com/journal/15736598
Publishes peer-reviewed content on the biopsychosocial aspects of trauma. It is the official publication of the International Society for Traumatic Stress Studies (ISTSS).
Denise Sloan, PhD, Editor

Web Sites

2292 Aces Too High
acestoohigh.com
ACESTooHigh is a news site that reports on research about adverse childhood experiences, including developments in epidemiology, neurobiology, and the biomedical and epigenetic consequences of toxic stress.

2293 AdvocateWeb
www.advocateweb.org
AdvocateWeb is a nonprofit organization providing information and resources to promote awareness and understanding of the issues involved in the exploitation of persons by trusted helping professionals.

2294 AfterTheInjury
www.aftertheinjury.org
This website was developed by an interdisciplinary team of researchers and practitioners with expertise in pediatric injury, child health care, and traumatic stress.

2295 American Psychological Association
www.apa.org/practice/traumaticstress.htm
Provides tips for recovering from disasters and other traumatic events.

2296 Athealth.com
athealth.com
Athealth.com was founded in 1997 by a psychiatrist to provide mental health information and services for mental health professionals and those they serve.

2297 Bright Side, The
www.the-bright-side.org
The Bright Side was created as a means of support - whether you are dealing with depression, grief, suicide, mental illness, emotional crisis, or are just feeling overwhelmed with life, you are not alone!

2298 Caregivers Series
www.bcm.tmc.edu/civitas/caregivers.html
Sophisticated articles describing the effects of childhood trauma on brain development and relationships.

2299 CyberPsych
www.cyberpsych.org
CyberPsych presents information about psychoanalysis, psychotherapy and topics like anxiety disorders, substance abuse, homophobia, and traumas. It hosts mental health organizations and individuals with content of interest to the public and professional communities. There is also a free therapist finder service.

2300 David Baldwin's Trauma Information Pages
www.trauma-pages.com
These Trauma Pages focus primarily on emotional trauma and traumatic stress, including PTSD (Post-traumatic Stress Disorder) and dissociation, whether following individual traumatic experience(s) or a large-scale disaster.

2301 Family Of a Vet
www.familyofavet.com
Family Of a Vet was started by the proud wife of an OIF Veteran who suffers from PTSD (Post Traumatic Stress Disorder) and TBI (Traumatic Brain Injury).

2302 Gift From Within
www.giftfromwithin.org
PTSD Resources for Survivors and Caregivers.

2303 Gulf War Syndrome Database
www.louisville.edu/library/ekstrom
This is a substantial database of relevant documents and studies kept by University of Louisville, Ekstrom Library.

2304 Gulf War Veteran Resource Pages
www.gulfweb.org
This page is administered by Gulf War veterans and provides a great range of information on a variety of Gulf War-related items, including GWS. The site includes many links to other groups interested in GWS and to GWS studies.

2305 Healing From Complex Trauma & PTSD/CPTSD
www.healingfromcomplextraumaandptsd.com
Assists people in their healing from complex trauma journey.
Lilly Hope Lucario, Survivor/Author/Writer/Blogger

2306 Healing Well
www.healingwell.com
An online health resource guide to medical news, chat, information and articles, newsgroups and message boards, books, disease-related web sites, medical directories, and more for patients, friends, and family coping with disabling diseases, disorders, or chronic illnesses.

2307 Health Central
www.healthcentral.com
Find clearly explained, medically accurate information regarding conditions, including an overview, symptoms, causes, diagnostic procedures and treatment options. On this site it is possible to ask questions and get information from a neurologist and connect to people who have similar health interests.

2308 Health Finder
www.health.gov
Searchable, carefully developed web site offering information on over 1000 topics. Developed by the US Department of Health and Human Services, the site can be used in both English and Spanish.

2309 HealthCentral.com
www.healthcentral.com
The HealthCentral Network has a collection of owned and operated web sites and multimedia affiliate properties providing timely, in-depth, trusted medical information, personalized tools and resources for people seeking to manage and improve their health.

2310 Hope for Healing.Org
hopeforhealing.org

2311 InteliHealth
www.intelihealth.com
InteliHealth's mission is to empower people with trusted solutions for healthier lives. They accomplish this by providing credible information fromt he most trusted sources.
Brian Berkenstock, Writer/Editor

2312 International Critical Incident Stress Foundation
www.icisf.org
A nonprofit, open membership foundation dedicated to the prevention and mitigation of disabling stress by education, training and support services for all emergency service professionals. Continuing education and training in emergency mental health services for psychologists, psychiatrists, social workers and licensed professional counselors.

2313 Internet Mental Health
www.mentalhealth.com
On-line information and a virtual encyclopedia related to mental disorders, possible causes and treatments. News, articles, on-line diagnostic programs and related links. Designed to improve understanding, diagnosis and treatment of mental illness throughout the world. Awarded the Top Site Award and the NetPsych Cutting Edge Site Award.

Trauma & Stressor-Related Disorders / Web Sites

2314 **Make the Connection**
maketheconnection.net
Make the Connection is a public awareness campaign by the U.S. Department of Veterans Affairs (VA) that provides personal testimonials and resources to help Veterans discover ways to improve their lives.

2315 **Medical News Today**
www.medicalnewstody.com
Offers in-depth health information and the latest news in medical research on a wide variety of medical conditions.

2316 **MedicineNet**
www.medicinenet.com
Medicine Net is an online healthcare media publishing company. It provides easy-to-read, in-depth, authoritative medical information for consumers via its robust, user-friendly, interactive web site.

2317 **MedlinePlus**
www.medlineplus.gov
Information regarding a broad range of health,and mental health conditions topics include: Latest news, overview of anatomy and physiology, clinical trials, diagnoses and symptoms, treatment, genetics, plus lots of links to other sites. A service provided by the National Library of Medicine, part of the National Institutes of Health (NIH).

2318 **Medscape**
www.medscape.com
Medscape offers specialists, primary care physicians, and other health professionals the Web's most robust and integrated medical information and educational tools.

2319 **Mental Health Matters**
mental-health-matters.com
MHMatters was founded to supply information and resources to mental health consumers, professionals, students and supporters.

2320 **Mental Health Today**
mental-health-today.com
The purpose of Mental Health Today is to help stop the pain caused by mental health disorders.
Patty Fleener M.S.W., Owner/ Operator

2321 **MentalHelp.net**
www.mentalhelp.net
They provide online mental health and wellness education.

2322 **MyPTSD**
www.myptsd.com
PTSD Forum launched on the 06th Sep, 2005, with one simple aim, to provide quality PTSD information and support to all concerned.

2323 **National Center For PTSD**
www.ncptsd.org
Aims to advance the clinical care and social welfare of U.S. Veterans through research, education and training on PTSD and stress-related disorders

2324 **National Veterans Services Fund**
www.nvsf.org
Supports and informs those who were exposed to the defoliant Agent Orange, or dioxin, while serving the US in the conflict in Vietnam.

2325 **Office of the Special Assistant for Gulf War Illnesses**
www.gulflink.osd.mil
This is a page sponsored by the Defense Department's Special Assistant for Gulf War Illnesses. It provides information on and links to Federal and State-funded studies of Gulf War Illnesses.

2326 **PTSD Support Services**
888-335-8699
www.ptsdsupport.net

2327 **PTSDinfo.org**
www.ptsdinfo.org

2328 **PlanetPsych**
www.planetpsych.com
Learn about disorders, their treatments and other topics in psychology. Articles are listed under the related topic areas. Ask a therapist a question for free, or view the directory of professionals in your area. If you are a therapist sign up for the directory. Current features, self-help, interactive, and newsletter archives.

2329 **Post Traumatic Stress Disorder Alliance**
www.ptsdalliance.org
Website of the Post Traumatic Stress Disorder Alliance.

2330 **Psych Central**
www.psychcentral.com
Personalized one-stop index for psychology, support, and mental health issues, resources, and people on the Internet.

2331 **Psychguides.com**
855-900-6733
www.psychguides.com
There goal is to shed light on psychological disorders, allowing you to recognize, understand and cope with these challenging diagnoses in yourself, friends and family members.

2332 **Sidran Institute, Traumatic Stress Education Administration**
www.sidran.org
Helps people understand, recover from, and treat traumatic stress (including PTSD), dissociative disorders, and co-occuring issues, such as addictions, self injury, and suicidality.

2333 **Substance Abuse And Mental Health Services Administration**
www.store.samhsa.gov
Resources on mental disorders as well as treatment and recovery.

2334 **Trauma Resource Area**
www.sidran.org/trauma.html
Resources and Articles on Dissociative Experiences Scale and Dissociative Identity Disorder, PsychTrauma Glossary and Traumatic Memories.

2335 **VA Caregiver Support**
www.caregiver.va.gov
Tips, tools, and other resources for caregivers of veterans.

2336 **Verywell Mind**
www.verywellmind.com
Provides up-to-date information on mental health topics. mission is to prioritize mental health and promote balance for day to day living. offers over 5,500 online articles that are researched based, and reviwed by medical professionals.
Kristen Altmeyer, MBA, VP & General Manager
Nick Ingalls, MA, Associate Editorial Director

2337 **WebMD**
www.webmd.com
Provides credible information, supportive communities, and in-depth reference material about health subjects. A source for original and timely health information as well as material from well known content providers.

SECTION FOUR:
APPENDIXES & INDEXES

GLOSSARY OF TERMS

Accommodation: A pattern of behavior that involves family members altering their lives and/or reinforcing the avoidance of anxiety-provoking situations to assist a family member who suffers from anxiety disorder.

Anticipatory fears/anxiety: A fear of what lies ahead, almost always involving a fear of failure, rejection, or uncertainty.

Antidepressant: A drug used to treat depression. Selective serotonin reuptake inhibitors (SSRIs) are a class of antidepressants that includes drugs like citalopram (*Celexa*), escitalopram (*Lexapro*), fluoxetine (*Prozac*), paroxetine (*Paxil*), and sertraline (*Zoloft*).

Anxiety disorder: A chronic condition that causes anxiety so severe it interferes with one's life. Some people with depression also have overlapping anxiety disorders.

Attentional bias: Vigilance for potential threats; particularly focusing on perceived threats (failure, rejection, negative things), often at the expense of seeing positives.

Avoidance: A behavior of avoiding anxiety-inducing activities. Avoidance occurs on both an internal (thoughts/feelings) and external (going places/doing things) basis. While it is easy to measure external avoidance (i.e. school attendance, homework, social interaction), it is more difficult to measure/monitor internal avoidance.

Bipolar disorder: A type of depression that cause extreme mood swings between depression and mania (or hypomania.) This condition used to be called manic depression.

Cognitive Behavioral Therapy (CBT): A form of therapy focusing on the relationship between thoughts, behaviors, and emotions (i.e. what we think affects how we act and feel, what we do affects what we think and feel, what we feel affects what we think and do). This form of therapy encourages people to examine and challenge distortive or irrational thoughts, and change problematic behaviors.

Cognition/Cognitive: Thoughts, or relating to thoughts.

Cognitive dissonance: The distress one experiences when thinking of or engaging in some form of behavior that contradicts personal beliefs, values, or ideals.

Cognitive distortions: Distorted or irrational thoughts that contribute to negative emotions or behaviors. Common cognitive distortions of those who struggle with anxiety include overvaluing thoughts, over-predicting the likelihood of negative outcomes, and catastrophizing.

Comorbidity: The co-occurrence of two or more disorders, such as depressive disorder with substance abuse disorder.

Comprehensive suicide prevention plans: Plans that use a multi-faceted approach to addressing the problem; for example, including interventions targeting biopsychosocial, social, and environmental factors.

Glossary of Terms

Connectedness: Closeness to an individual, group, or people within a specific organization; perceived caring by others; satisfaction with one's relationship to others, or feeling loved and wanted by others.

Contagion: A phenomenon whereby susceptible persons are influenced towards suicidal behavior through knowledge of another person's suicidal acts.

Core fear: Fears embedded deep within ones' psyche. Experiencing core fears is a part of the human experience. Often, the struggle to work through these fears allows a person to ascend to higher levels of personal awareness and confidence. Common core fears include fear of inadequacy, a fear of letting others down, rejection, failure, abandonment, and loss of control.

Depression: An illness that involves the body, mood, and thoughts that affect the way a person eats and sleeps, the way one feels about oneself, and the way one thinks about things.

Dialectical Behavioral Therapy (DBT): A form of Cognitive Behavioral Therapy (CBT) that focuses on skill development to help people achieve personal goals that will allow them to live a life they find meaning in. These DBT skills include mindfulness, emotional regulation, distress tolerance, and interpersonal effectiveness.

Distress tolerance: The ability to tolerate the distress one experiences from anxiety-inducing situations.

Dysphoric mood: A low mood that may include dissatisfaction, restlessness, or depression.

Dysthymia: A type of chronic, low-grade depression that is less severe than major depression. It can also last for years. Dysthymia may not disable a person, but it prevents one from functioning normally or feeling well. Modern diagnostic systems include "dysthymia" with "chronic major depression" (that is, a major depressive episode lasting two years or more in an adult or one year or more in children and adolescents) under the general term "persistent depressive disorder."

Electroconvulsive Therapy (ECT): A treatment for depression performed under general anesthesia that uses an electric current to create a brief, controlled seizure. It is safe and often effective for depression that hasn't responded to drugs or therapy, or when symptoms are so severe that a rapid response is especially important.

Environmental approach: An approach to suicide prevention that attempts to influence either the physical environment (such as reducing access to lethal means) or the social environment (such as providing work or academic opportunities).

Executive function: Cognitive functions relating to a person's ability to plan ahead, make good judgments, learn from experience, and adopt appropriate socio-emotional, internally guided behavior.

Glossary of Terms

Exposure Response Prevention (ERP): A form of Cognitive Behavioral Therapy (CBT) that purposefully and deliberately confronts a fear, while not engaging in avoidant behaviors. The more one does this, the more distress tolerance one develops. There are three different types of exposure: imaginal (cognitive), virtual (electronic presentation of visual and/or auditory stimuli), and in-vivo (in real life) situations.

Fear appraisal: A person's ability to accurately and objectively evaluate the world around oneself for potential threats. People suffering from significant anxiety often struggle to make objective evaluations. While they are typically better at distinguishing the difference between overtly hostile or friendly interaction, they struggle in recognizing and interpreting neutral situations. The net result of a person with poor fear-appraisal skills is that they frequently assign a strong likelihood for a negative outcome to a neutral event, or assign high probability of a negative outcome to a low-probability event.

Feared outcome: What one is afraid might happen. Individuals who have avoided (both on an internal and external level) for a long time, are often unaware of what the feared outcome even is. The result is typically an over-estimation of the cost associated with a social mishap, or low-probability events are viewed from a high-probability likelihood of occurring. Identifying the feared outcome helps to combat internal avoidance and puts a face on what the fear is all about.

Fear hierarchy: A list of feared situations ranked in descending order, with the most powerful fears at the top of the list, known as a fear ladder. Situations that create tremendous distress are rated at the top with each successive rung decreasing in intensity of distress experienced in the associated situation.

Habituation: Developing increased distress tolerance towards the effects of a stressful situation. This is achieved through systematic and repeated exposure to the stressful situation.

Hypomania: A milder form of mania.

Hypothyroidism: A condition when the thyroid doesn't produce enough thyroid hormone. This can lead to symptoms of depression, fatigue, weight gain, and other health problems.

Intervention: A strategy or approach that is intended to prevent an outcome, or to alter the course of an existing condition.

Intrusive thoughts: Unwelcome involuntary thoughts, images, or unpleasant ideas that may become an obsession, are upsetting or distressing, and can feel difficult to manage or eliminate. Intrusive thoughts can become extremely disturbing and may induce panic as the thought becomes "stuck," and the individual is unable to let the thought go.

Life-interfering Behaviors (LIBs): Behaviors that prevent one from effectively and meaningfully living one's life. LIBs typically occur due to skill deficits, executive deficits, and/or avoidance.

Glossary of Terms

Light therapy (also called phototherapy): Therapy consisting of exposure to light that is brighter than indoor light and mimics sunlight. It may help treat some forms of depression.

Major depression: The medical diagnosis for an episode of clinical depression that lasts for at least two weeks and interferes with daily life. It causes symptoms like low energy, fatigue, and feelings of hopelessness.

Mania: A phase of bipolar disorder, mania is a period of intense energy, euphoria or irritability, sleeplessness, or recklessness. It is so extreme that it interferes with a person's life and can involve false beliefs (delusions) or perceptions (hallucinations).

Manic depression: An old term for bipolar disorder.

Means: The instrument or object whereby a self-destructive act is carried out (i.e., firearm, poison, medication).

Means-restriction: Techniques, policies, and procedures designed to reduce access or availability to means and methods of deliberate self-harm.

Mindful completion: Purposeful and deliberate act of completing tasks, goals, and responsibilities. Completion is the antithesis of avoidance. Many people who struggle with severe anxiety become chronic "avoiders." As time passes, avoidance results in a lack of skill development, low self-esteem and eventually lack of identify formation.

Monoamine Oxidase Inhibitors (MAOIs): A group of medicines sometime prescribed to treat severe depression. MAOIs increase the concentration of chemicals responsible for sending information between nerves in particular regions of the brain, which may lead to better mental functioning.

Mood disorders: A term used to describe all mental disorders that are characterized by a prominent or persistent mood disturbance; disturbances can be in the direction of elevated expansive emotional states, or, if in the opposite direction, depressed emotional states. Included are depressive disorders, bipolar disorders, mood disorders due to a medical condition, and substance-induced mood disorders.

Mood stabilizers: A class of drugs used to treat some types of depression, like bipolar disorder. They include lithium and some drugs originally used for seizures called anticonvulsants. These include carbamazepine (*Tegretol*), divalproex (*Depakote*), and lamotrigine (*Lamictal*).

Morbidity: The relative frequency of illness or injury, or the illness or injury rate, in a community or population.

Mortality: The relative frequency of death, or the death rate, in a community or population.

Neurotransmitter: A chemical in the brain, like serotonin or norepinephrine, that sends messages between brain cells. Medicines that treat depression often alter the levels or functioning of these chemicals.

Glossary of Terms

Nonsuicidal self-directed violence: Behavior that is self-directed and deliberately results in injury, or the potential for injury, to oneself. There is no evidence, whether implicit or explicit, of suicidal intent.

Other suicidal behavior including preparatory acts: Acts or preparation toward making a suicide attempt, but before potential for harm has begun. This can include anything beyond a verbalization or thought, such as assembling a method (such as collecting pills) or preparing for one's death by suicide (such as writing a suicide note or giving things away).

Outcome: A measurable change in the health of an individual or group of people that is attributable to an intervention.

Panic attack: A sudden feeling of intense fear or anxiety, accompanied by physical symptoms, that isn't triggered by real danger. Panic attacks are common in many anxiety disorders.

Perfectionism: Striving for flawlessness and holding unrealistic expectations regarding performance. For example, individuals struggling with perfectionism will avoid handing in assignments even when completed, or are unable to finish assignments due to the amount of time spent trying to make it perfect. Often at the core of these issues is an inability to tolerate the uncertainty of how others will perceive their work.

Persistent depressive disorder: When a low mood lasts for two or more years in adults, and at least one year in children and adolescents. A person with this disorder may experience episodes of major depressive disorder along with periods of less severe symptoms where they are typically able to function day-to-day.

Personality disorders: A class of mental disorders characterized by deeply ingrained, often inflexible, maladaptive patterns of relating, perceiving, and thinking of sufficient severity to cause either impairment in functioning or distress.

Postpartum depression: Depression that affects women who have recently given birth. Many new mothers experience a brief episode of mild mood changes known as the "baby blues," but some will have postpartum depression, a much more serious condition that requires active treatment and emotional support for the new mother.

Postvention: A strategy or approach that is implemented after a crisis or traumatic event has occurred.

Prevention: A strategy or approach that reduces the likelihood of risk of onset, or delays the onset of adverse health problems, or reduces the harm resulting from conditions or behaviors.

Processing speed: The speed in which an individual recognizes and processes visual or auditory data. Anxiety can negatively affect processing speed. Conversely, slow processing speeds can be a contributor to anxiety. Perfectionism, ruminating, and intrusive thoughts can also negatively impact processing speed. Slow processing speed is one of the most common occurrences with individuals who suffer from moderate and severe anxiety.

Glossary of Terms

Proportionate response: Responding in a manner that is commensurate of the situation — neither under- nor over-reacting.

Protective factors: Factors that make it less likely that individuals will develop a disorder; protective factors may encompass biological, psychological or social factors in the individual, family and environment.

Psychiatrist: A medical doctor (MD or DO) who specializes in treating mental health disorders. Because psychiatrists are doctors, they can prescribe drugs like antidepressants. Some also use psychotherapy.

Psychologist: A non-MD professional (PhD or PsyD) who specializes in the treatment of mental or emotional disorders. Psychologists typically use psychotherapy to treat people with depression and other conditions. They are also trained to give psychological tests such as IQ tests, cognitive function tests, or personality measures.

Psychotherapy: A way of treating a mental or emotional disorder by talking with a therapist. It may also be called "talking therapy" or "talk therapy."

Psychotic depression: A form of depression with psychosis that comes when people get very depressed, such as delusions (false beliefs) and/or hallucinations (hearing or seeing things that are not there).

Reassurance-seeking: A form of compulsive behavior (like hand washing, or checking/re-checking) that is manifest in virtually all individuals affected with OCD, social anxiety, and/or body dysmorphia. Reassurance-seeking is a way to seek stress relief by turning to friends, family, or the internet. Unfortunately, seeking reassurance does not provide an environment that teaches or demands increased distress tolerance. It is a short-term symptom relief approach which ultimately perpetuates the problem, as the individual repetitively utilizes this approach. Over time, this process results in skill deficits, poor self-esteem, lack of healthy identity formation, and dependency upon others for basic functioning.

Residential Treatment Center (RTC): A live-in health care facility that provides therapy.

Resilience: Capacities within a person that promote positive outcomes, such as mental health and well-being, and provide protection from factors that might otherwise place that person at risk for adverse health outcomes.

Risk factors: Those factors that make it more likely that individuals will develop a disorder; risk factors may encompass biological, psychological or social factors in the individual, family and environment.

Safety-seeking behaviors: Behaviors that are used to relieve stress and fear (often during exposure exercises) when feeling threatened or unable to cope with rising levels of distress. The most common forms of safety-seeking behaviors are avoidance, reassurance seeking, and distraction. Like reassurance-seeking, safety-seeking behaviors provide temporary benefit at the cost of long-term relief — a "Band-Aid" approach to anxiety management. Engaging in these behaviors reinforces cognitive distortions and the faulty belief that the perceived danger is more than one could possibly tolerate or overcome.

Glossary of Terms

Seasonal affective disorder: A mood disorder associated with changes in seasons. This form of depression usually occurs during the fall and winter months when there is less sunlight.

Secondary gain: Attempting to gain something that occurs secondary from the self-reported illness or difficulty (i.e. using illness or emotional difficulties as a way of avoiding work, responsibilities, chores, or to gain attention).

Self-directed violence: Behavior that is self-directed and deliberately results in injury or the potential for injury to oneself.

Self-harm: The various methods by which individuals injure themselves, such as self-laceration, self-battering, taking overdoses, or exhibiting deliberate recklessness.

Social anxiety: The fear of social situations that involve interaction with other people. Virtually all individuals suffering from social anxiety have a fear of being negatively judged and evaluated by other people. It is a pervasive disorder and causes anxiety and fear in nearly all areas of a person's life.

Sociocultural approach: An approach to suicide prevention that attempts to affect the society at large, or particular subcultures within it, to reduce the likelihood of suicide (such as adult-youth mentoring programs designed to improve the well-being of youth).

Social support: Assistance that may include companionship, emotional backing, cognitive guidance, material aid, and special services.

Specialty treatment centers: Health facilities where the personnel and resources focus on specific aspects of psychological or behavioral well-being.

Stigma: An object, idea, or label associated with disgrace or reproach.

Subjective Units of Distress (SUD): A way of measuring the intensity of a distressful experience, rated on a scale of 0-100. SUD measures how intense the distressful experience is and where the event is ranked on the Hierarchy of Fear. The higher the SUDs score, the more distressful the exposure will be. The lower the SUD score, the less distress the exposure will create.

Sub-clinical presentation: Symptoms or characteristics of a particular disorder displayed by an individual that do not reach the frequency or depth to qualify for the full, clinical criteria of a particular diagnosis. Example: a certain diagnosis may require six of the eight established diagnostic markers to qualify for a formal diagnosis, however, the individual may only display five characteristics — one short of what is required for the formal diagnosis. One would conclude that something is trending, yet the individual still lacks enough of the symptoms to meet the threshold required for the diagnosis.

Suicidal ideation: Thoughts of engaging in suicide-related behavior.

Glossary of Terms

Suicidal intent: There is evidence (explicit and/or implicit) that at the time of injury the individual intended to kill his or her self or wished to die, and that the individual understood the probable consequences of his or her actions.

Suicidal plan: A thought regarding a self-initiated action that facilitates self-harm behavior, or a suicide attempt. This will often include an organized manner of engaging in suicidal behavior such as a description of a time frame and method.

Suicidal self-directed violence: Behavior that is self-directed and deliberately results in injury or the potential for injury to oneself. There is evidence, whether implicit or explicit, of suicidal intent.

Suicide: Death caused by self-directed injurious behavior with any intent to die as a result of the behavior.

Suicide attempt: A nonfatal, self-directed, potentially injurious behavior with any intent to die as a result of the behavior. A suicide attempt may or may not result in injury.

Treatment Interfering Behaviors (TIBs): Volitional, repetitive behavior(s) that are not compatible with the effective participation in treatment. Examples: Refusing to talk with therapist, refusal to complete therapeutic assignments, manipulation, lying, denying/justifying problem behavior, etc. TIBs not isolated incidents.

Uncertainty: The unknown. The feeling one experiences when in a position where it is impossible to know or predict the outcome or series of outcomes.

Working Memory: The ability to store, manipulate, and retrieve information over short periods of time. Memory required to function moment-to-moment. There are two forms of working memory: auditory memory, and visual-spatial memory. Auditory memory records what one hears, while visual-spatial records what one sees. Lack of working memory may include forgetting directions, leaving homework at home, difficulty doing mental arithmetic, etc.

Entry Name Index

A

A.I.M. Agoraphobics in Motion, 1, 47, 505
AA-Alcoholics Anonymous, 1915
AAA Foundation for Traffic Safety, 1826, 1916
AABA Support Group, 1144
AARP Alabama, 199
AARP Alaska, 200
AARP Arizona, 201
AARP Arkansas, 202
AARP California: Pasadena, 203
AARP California: Sacramento, 204
AARP Colorado, 205
AARP Connecticut, 206
AARP D.C., 257
AARP Delaware, 207
AARP Florida: Doral, 208
AARP Florida: St. Petersburg, 209
AARP Florida: Tallahassee, 210
AARP Foundation, 262
AARP Georgia, 211
AARP Hawaii, 212
AARP Idaho, 213
AARP Illinois: Chicago, 214
AARP Illinois: Springfield, 215
AARP Indiana, 216
AARP Iowa, 217
AARP Kansas, 218
AARP Kentucky, 219
AARP Louisiana: Baton Rouge, 220
AARP Louisiana: New Orleans, 221
AARP Maine, 222
AARP Maryland, 223
AARP Massachusetts, 224
AARP Michigan, 225
AARP Minnesota, 226
AARP Mississippi, 227
AARP Missouri, 228
AARP Montana, 229
AARP Nebraska: Lincoln, 230
AARP Nebraska: Omaha, 231
AARP Nevada, 232
AARP New Hampshire, 233
AARP New Jersey, 234
AARP New Mexico, 235
AARP New York: Albany, 236
AARP New York: New York City, 237
AARP New York: Rochester, 238
AARP North Carolina, 239
AARP North Dakota, 240
AARP Ohio, 241
AARP Oklahoma, 242
AARP Oregon, 243
AARP Pennsylvania: Harrisburg, 244
AARP Pennsylvania: Philadelphia, 245
AARP Rhode Island, 246
AARP South Carolina, 247
AARP South Dakota, 248
AARP Tennessee, 249
AARP Texas: Austin, 250
AARP Texas: Dallas, 251
AARP Texas: Houston, 252
AARP Texas: San Antonio, 253
AARP Utah, 254
AARP Vermont, 255
AARP Virginia, 256
AARP Washington, 258
AARP West Virginia, 259
AARP Wisconsin, 260
AARP Wyoming, 261
AARP: The Magazine, 305
ABA Commission on Law and Aging, 173
ABMRF/The Foundation for Alcohol Research, 1827
About Kids GI Disorders, 1145
Abstracts in Social Gerontology, 306
Academy for Eating Disorders, 1086, 1136
Academy for Gerontology in Higher Education, 174, 267
Academy of Nutrition & Dietetics, 1087, 1166
Academy of Psychosomatic Medicine, 2, 506, 746, 1049, 1696, 1759
ACAP Recap, 1904
Aces Too High, 2292
Addiction Resource Guide, 1917
ADDitude Magazine, 710

Administration for Children and Families, 3, 623, 1088, 2012
Administration for Community Living, 2071
Adopt-A-Special-Kid America, 1360
Adult Children of Alcoholics, 1874
Adult Children of Alcoholics & Dysfunctional Families World Srvc. Org., 1918
Adult Children of Alcoholics World Service Organization, Inc., 1760
Adventure Camp, 507
AdvocateWeb, 2293
Advocating For Your Child, 717
Affiliated Children's Arthritis Centers of New England, 591
African American Family Services (AAFS), 1761
African American Post Traumatic Stress Disorder Association, 2013
AfterTheInjury, 2294
Agency for Healthcare Research and Quality, 624, 1089, 2014
Agency for Toxic Substances and Disease Registry, 625, 2015
Agent Orange Registry Department of Veterans Affairs, 2016
Aging and Alzheimer's Disease Center Oregon Health Sciences University, 446
Aging and Health Research, 307
Aging In America, 263
Aging.com, 312
Agoraphobia: For Friends/Family, 556
Agoraphobics Building Independent Lives, 508, 540
Al-Anon, 1919
Al-Anon Alateen Family Group Hotline, 1875
Al-Anon Family Group Headquarters, 1876
Al-Anon Family Group National Referral Hotline, 1877
Alabama Department of Mental Health: Div. of Mental Health & Substance Abuse, 1802
Alaska Department of Health: Office of Substance Abuse and Addiction Prevention, 1803
Alaska VA Healthcare System, 2092
Alateen, 1920
Alateen and Al-Anon Family Groups, 1878
Albany Stratton VA Medical Center, 2093
Alcohol and Drug Abuse Council of South Louisiana, 1811
Alcohol and Drug Abuse Division, 1807
Alcohol and Drug Abuse Program, 1805
Alcohol and Drug Services, 1806
Alcohol Drug Treatment Referral, 1879
Alcohol Research Group Public Health Institute, 1835
Alcohol Research: Current Reviews (ARCR), 1905
Alcoholics Anonymous, 1880
Alcoholics Anonymous (AA): World Services, 1881
Alcoholism Home Page, 1921
Aleda E. Lutz VA Medical Center: Saginaw, Michigan, 2094
Alexandria VA Healthcare System, 2095
Alive Alone, 102, 129
Allergy & Asthma Network, 626, 663
Allergy & Asthma Today, 661
Alliance for Aging Research, 313
Alvin C. York VA Medical Center Tennessee Valley Healthcare System, 2096
Alzheimer Disease and Associated Disorders: An International Journal, 485
Alzheimer Research Forum, 489
Alzheimer Society of Alberta and Northwest Territories, 338
Alzheimer Society of British Columbia, 339
Alzheimer Society of Canada, 340
Alzheimer Society of Manitoba, 341
Alzheimer Society of New Brunswick, 342
Alzheimer Society of Newfoundland & Labrador, 343
Alzheimer Society of Nova Scotia, 344
Alzheimer Society of Ontario, 345
Alzheimer Society of Prince Edward Island, 346
Alzheimer Society of Saskatchewan, 347
Alzheimer Society of Toronto, 348
Alzheimer Support, 490
Alzheimer's & Dementia: The Journal of the Alzheimer's Association, 486
Alzheimer's Alliance: Dallas and Northeast Texas, 426
Alzheimer's and Memory Disorders Clinic, 458

Alzheimer's Association, 349, 491
Alzheimer's Association Autopsy Assistance Network, 481
Alzheimer's Association: Alabama, 356
Alzheimer's Association: Alaska, 357
Alzheimer's Association: Arkansas, 361
Alzheimer's Association: Boulder and Mountain Region, 367
Alzheimer's Association: Cali. - Southland, 362
Alzheimer's Association: California - Central Coast, 363
Alzheimer's Association: Capital of Texas, 427
Alzheimer's Association: Central and North Florida, 376
Alzheimer's Association: Central and Western Kansas, 385
Alzheimer's Association: Central and Western Virginia, 434
Alzheimer's Association: Central New York, 402
Alzheimer's Association: Central Ohio, 410
Alzheimer's Association: Cleveland Area, 411
Alzheimer's Association: Connecticut, 373
Alzheimer's Association: Delaware, 374
Alzheimer's Association: Delaware Valley, 417
Alzheimer's Association: Desert Southwest, 358
Alzheimer's Association: East Tennessee, 422
Alzheimer's Association: Eastern North Carolina, 408
Alzheimer's Association: Florida Gulf Coast, 377
Alzheimer's Association: Georgia, 379
Alzheimer's Association: Great Denver Region, 368
Alzheimer's Association: Greater Cincinnati, 409
Alzheimer's Association: Greater East Ohio, 412
Alzheimer's Association: Greater Idaho, 381
Alzheimer's Association: Greater Indiana, 383
Alzheimer's Association: Greater Kentucky and Soutern Indiana, 387
Alzheimer's Association: Greater Maryland, 389
Alzheimer's Association: Greater Michigan, 391
Alzheimer's Association: Greater Missouri, 394
Alzheimer's Association: Greater New Jersey, 399
Alzheimer's Association: Greater Pennsylvania, 418
Alzheimer's Association: Greater Richmond, 435
Alzheimer's Association: Hawaii, 380
Alzheimer's Association: Heart of America, 386
Alzheimer's Association: Houston and Southeast Texas, 428
Alzheimer's Association: Hudson Valley, 401
Alzheimer's Association: Illinois, 382
Alzheimer's Association: Iowa, 384
Alzheimer's Association: Long Island, 403
Alzheimer's Association: Maine, 388
Alzheimer's Association: Massachusetts and New Hampshire, 390
Alzheimer's Association: Miami Valley, 413
Alzheimer's Association: Middle Tennessee, 423
Alzheimer's Association: Minnesota and North Dakota, 392
Alzheimer's Association: Mississippi, 393
Alzheimer's Association: Montana, 395
Alzheimer's Association: National Capital Area, 375
Alzheimer's Association: Nebraska, 396
Alzheimer's Association: New Mexico, 400
Alzheimer's Association: New York City, 404
Alzheimer's Association: North Central Texas, 429
Alzheimer's Association: Northeast Tennessee, 424
Alzheimer's Association: Northeastern Colorado Region, 369
Alzheimer's Association: Northeastern New York, 405
Alzheimer's Association: Northern Arizona, 359
Alzheimer's Association: Northern California, 364
Alzheimer's Association: Northern Colorado Region, 370
Alzheimer's Association: Northern Nevada, 397
Alzheimer's Association: Northwest Ohio, 414
Alzheimer's Association: Oklahoma, 415
Alzheimer's Association: Orange County, 365
Alzheimer's Association: Oregon and SW Washington, 416
Alzheimer's Association: Rhode Island, 419
Alzheimer's Association: Rochester and Finger Lakes Region, 406
Alzheimer's Association: San Antonio and South Texas, 430
Alzheimer's Association: San Diego, 366

601

Entry Name Index

Alzheimer's Association: South Carolina, 420
Alzheimer's Association: South Dakota, 421
Alzheimer's Association: Southeast Florida, 378
Alzheimer's Association: Southeast Tennessee, 425
Alzheimer's Association: Southeastern Virginia, 436
Alzheimer's Association: Southern and Central Colorado Region, 371
Alzheimer's Association: Southern Arizona, 360
Alzheimer's Association: Southern Nevada, 398
Alzheimer's Association: Utah, 432
Alzheimer's Association: Vermont, 433
Alzheimer's Association: Washington State, 438
Alzheimer's Association: West Texas, 431
Alzheimer's Association: West Virginia, 437, 439
Alzheimer's Association: Western Colorado Region, 372
Alzheimer's Association: Western New York, 407
Alzheimer's Association: Wisconsin, 440
Alzheimer's Association: Wyoming, 441
Alzheimer's Disease & Memory Disorders Center, 447
Alzheimer's Disease & Related Dementias, 444
Alzheimer's Disease Center Kentucky University, 449
Alzheimer's Disease Center Mayo Clinic Mayo Medical School, 450
Alzheimer's Disease Center University of Alabama at Birmingham, 448
Alzheimer's Disease Center: Boston University, 451
Alzheimer's Disease Center: Johns Hopkins University School of Medicine, 452
Alzheimer's Disease Center: University of Alabama at Birmingham, 454
Alzheimer's Disease Center: University of California, Davis, 453
Alzheimer's Disease Center: Washington University, 455
Alzheimer's Disease International, 492
Alzheimer's Disease Research Center Duke University, 457
Alzheimer's Disease Research Center Washington University School of Medicine, 456
Alzheimer's Foundation of America, 442
Alzheimer's Support Group, 482
American Academy of Addiction Psychiatry (AAAP), 1762
American Academy of Allergy, Asthma & Immunology, 627, 640, 664
American Academy of Child and Adolescent Psychiatry (AACAP), 2017
American Academy Of Pediatrics Practice Guidelines, 718
American Association of Caregiving Youth, 175
American Association of Children's Residential Centers, 4, 1002
American Association of Clinical Endocrinologists, 1498
American Association of Diabetes Care & Education Specialists, 803, 988
American Association of Retired Persons, 176, 314
American Association of Sexuality Educators, Counselors And Therapists, 1577
American Association of Suicidology, 1960, 1988
American Autoimmune Related Diseases Association, 1197
American Chronic Pain Association, 585, 1380, 1499, 1613, 1763, 2018
American College of Allergy, Asthma & Immunology, 641, 645, 665
American Council for Drug Education, 1922
American Diabetes Association, 804, 978, 989
American Diabetes Association: Alabama, 816
American Diabetes Association: Alaska, 817
American Diabetes Association: Delaware, 821
American Diabetes Association: District of Columbia, 823
American Diabetes Association: Eastern Pennsylvania & Delaware, 822, 845
American Diabetes Association: Florida, 824
American Diabetes Association: Hawaii, 825
American Diabetes Association: Illinois, 826
American Diabetes Association: Kansas, 828
American Diabetes Association: Maryland, 830
American Diabetes Association: Michigan, 831
American Diabetes Association: Minnesota & North Dakota, 832, 840

American Diabetes Association: Mississippi & Louisiana, 829, 834
American Diabetes Association: Missouri, 835
American Diabetes Association: Nebraska, Iowa & South Dakota, 827, 836, 848
American Diabetes Association: Nevada & California (Southern), 819, 837
American Diabetes Association: New England, 805
American Diabetes Association: New Mexico & Arizona, 818, 838
American Diabetes Association: New York (Greater NYC and New Jersey), 839
American Diabetes Association: North Dakota & Minnesota, 833
American Diabetes Association: Northeast Ohio, 841
American Diabetes Association: Northern California, 820
American Diabetes Association: Ohio, 842
American Diabetes Association: Oklahoma, 843
American Diabetes Association: Oregon, 844
American Diabetes Association: Rhode Island, 847
American Diabetes Association: Tennessee, 849
American Diabetes Association: Texas, 850
American Diabetes Association: Virginia/West Virginia, 851, 853
American Diabetes Association: Washington, 852
American Diabetes Association: Western Pennsylvania, 846
American Federation for Aging Research, 264
American Foundation For Suicide Prevention, 1989
American Foundation for Suicide Prevention, 1975
American Heart Association, 1198, 1262, 1725, 1745
American Institutes for Research Center on Aging, 268
American Issue, 1906
American Journal of Hypertension, 1287
American Journal of Psychiatry, 60, 125, 546, 711, 776, 1023, 1065, 1160, 1474, 1549, 1594, 1676, 1706, 1907, 2288
American Journal of Psychotherapy, 61, 126, 547, 712, 777, 1024, 1066, 1161, 1475, 1550, 1595, 1707, 1908, 2289
American Juvenile Arthritis Organization, 586, 612
American Lung Association, 628, 666
American Medical Association (AMA), 2019
American Neuropsychiatric Association, 350
American Obesity Treatment Association, 1416
American Physical Therapy Association, 1500
American Pregnancy Association, 1329
American Psychiatric Association, 5, 103, 509, 678, 747, 1003, 1050, 1090, 1450, 1523, 1578, 1697, 1764, 2020
American Psychological Association, 2021, 2295
American Public Health Association (APHA), 2022
American Public Human Services Association, 1765
American Self-Help Group Clearinghouse, 2264
American Sexual Health Association (ASHA), 1579
American Sleep Apnea Association, 1614, 1680
American Sleep Disorders Association, 1681
American Society for Reproductive Medicine, 1580
American Society for Reproductive Medicine, 1330, 1361
American Society of Addiction Medicine, 1766
American Society of Hypertension, 1292
American Society on Aging, 315
American Stroke Association, 1726
American Stroke Foundation, 1730
American Trauma Society (ATS), 2023
American Urological Association, 1331, 1581
American Urological Association (AUA), 1306
AMERSA, 1758
Anger And Aggressions, 1026
Anorexia Nervosa & Related Eating Disorders, 1167
Anorexia Nervosa And Related Eating Disorders, 1168
Anorexia Nervosa General Information, 1169
Answers To Your Questions About ADD, 719
Anxiety and Depression Association of America, 6, 510, 1451
Anxiety And Phobia Treatment Center, 557
Anxiety and Phobia Treatment Center, 534
Anxiety Disorders, 558
Anxiety Disorders Association of America, 2024
Anxiety Panic Hub, 559
Anxiety Resource Center, 2072

Archives of Suicide Research, 1985
Archstone Foundation, 265
Arizona Heart Institute, 1204
Arthritis and Musculoskeletal Center: UAB Heersink School of Medicine, 592
Arthritis Foundation, 590, 613
Arthritis Foundation Information Helpline, 608
Arthritis Society Canada, 587
Arthritis Today, 611
Association for Addiction Professionals (NAADAC), 1923
Association for Behavioral and Cognitive Therapies, 7, 1004, 2025
Association for Traumatic Stress Specialists, 2026
Association of Gastrointestinal Motility Disorders, 1091
Association of Traumatic Stress Specialist, 2027
Asthma and Allergy Foundation of America, 642, 667
Asthma and Allergy Foundation of America: St. Louis Chapter, 643
Asthma Canada, 629
At Health, 130
Athealth.com, 2296
Atlanta VA Medical Center Atlanta VA Health Care System, 2097
Attention, 713
Attention Deficit Disorder And Parenting Site, 720
Attention Deficit Disorder Association, 679, 721
Attention Deficit Hyperactivity Disorder, 722
Attention Deficit Information Network, 706
Attention Magazine, 714
Audie L. Murphy Memorial VA Hospital South Texas Veterans Health Care System, 2098

B

Babycenter, 723
Balanced Mind Parent Network, 8, 48, 769, 1005
Baltimore VA Medical Center VA Maryland Health Care System, 2099
Barbara Davis Center for Childhood Diabetes, 948
BASH Magazine, 1162
Batavia VA Medical Center VA Western New York Healthcare System, 2100
Bath VA Medical Center, 2101
Battle Creek VA Medical Center, 2102
Bay Pines VA Healthcare System, 2103
Baylor College of Medicine: Children's General Clinical Research Center, 949
Baylor College of Medicine: Debakey Heart Center, 1205
Baylor College of Medicine: Sleep Disorder and Research Center, 1623
Beckley VA Medical Center, 2104
Bees-Stealy Research Foundation, 1206
Befrienders Worldwide, 68
Benaroya Research Institute Virginia Mason Medical Center, 950
Bereaved Parents of the USA, 104
Bereaved Parents Of The Usa (Bp/Usa), 131
Bill Ferguson's How To Divorce As Friends, 132
Biology of Reproduction, 1353
Bipolar Clinic and Research Program, 761
Bipolar Disorders Clinic, 762
Bipolar Disorders Treatment Information Center, 780
Bipolar Research Program at University of Pennsylvania, 763
Birth Defect Research for Children, Inc., 630
Bockus Research Institute Graduate Hospital, 1207
Boise VA Medical Center, 2105
Bone Health & Osteoporosis Foundation, 1505, 1511, 1513
Boston Obesity Nutrition Research Center (BONRC), 1433
Boston University Arthritis Center, 593
Boston University Clinical & Translational Science Institute, 594
Boston University Laboratory of Neuropsychology, 1836
Boston University, Whitaker Cardiovascular Institute, 1208
Bpso-Bipolar Significant Others, 781

Entry Name Index

Brain & Behavior Research Foundation, 35, 532, 703, 758, 1129, 1468, 1524, 1536, 1538, 1556, 1828, 1976, 2061
Brain Health and Memory Center Research, 459
Brain Injury Resource Center, 2073
BrainLine.org, 2074
Break The Silence, 1990
Brigham and Women's Hospital: Center for Neurologic Diseases, 1395
Brigham and Women's Hospital: Rheumatology Immunology, and Allergy Division, 646
Brigham and Women's Orthopedica and Arthritis Center, 595
Bright Side, The, 2297
Brockton Division VA Boston Healthcare System, 2106
Brooklyn Campus VA NY Harbor Health Care System, 2107
Buffalo VA Medical Center VA Western New York Healthcare System, 2108
Bulimia Anorexia Nervosa Association, 1092
Bulimia: News & Discussion Forum, 1170
Bureau of Substance Addiction Services, 1812
Byron Peter Foundation for Hope, 1977

C

Canadian ADHD Resource Alliance, 680
Canadian Adult Congenital Heart Network, 1199
Canadian Diabetes Educator Certification Board, 806
Canadian Men's Health Foundation, 1312
Canadian National Seniors Council, 177, 316
Canadian Sleep Society, 1615
Canadian Society of Allergy and Clinical Immunology, 631
Canadian Society of Nephrology, 1332
Canadian Urological Association (CUA), 1307
Canandaigua VA Medical Center VA Health Care Upstate New York, 2109
Capital Regional Sleep-Wake Disorders Center, 1624
Captain James A. Lovell Federal Health Care Center, 2110
Cardiovascular Research and Training Center University of Alabama, 1209
Career Assessment & Planning Services, 560
Caregiver Action Network, 300
Caregiver Support Services, 301
Caregivers Series, 561, 2298
Caring.com, 317
Carl Vinson VA Medical Center Dublin VA Medical Center, 2111
Case Western Reserve University: Center on Aging and Health, 269
Center for Aging Research and Education at the UW-Madison School of Nursing, 270
Center for Alcohol & Addiction Studies Brown University, 1837
Center for Anxiety and Related Disorders at Boston University, 2112
Center for Anxiety and Traumatic Stress, 2113
Center for Cognitive Neuroscience and Aging, 460
Center for Culture, Trauma and Mental Health Disparities, 2114
Center for Disease Control, 1362
Center for Family Support, 49, 105, 122, 541, 681, 770, 1006, 1051, 1093, 1452, 1525, 1582, 1698, 2028
Center For Family Support (CFS), 69, 724, 1027
Center For Family Support (Cfs), 133
Center for Family Support (CFS), 9, 72, 1767, 1924
Center for Healthy Sex, 1308, 1583
Center for Human Nutrition, 1434
Center For Loss In Multiple Birth (Climb), Inc., 134
Center for Mental Health Services, 2115
Center for Mental Health Services (CMHS), 10, 106, 351, 511, 682, 748, 1007, 1052, 1094, 1453, 1526, 1584, 1699, 1768, 2029
Center For Mental Health Services Knowledg Knowledge Exchange, 71, 782
Center For Mental Health Services Knowledge, 1479
Center For Mental Health Services Knowledge Exchange, 70, 562, 1028
Center for Mind-Body Medicine, 2116

Center for Narcolepsy Research at the University of Illinois at Chicago, 1625
Center for Neuroimmunology: University of Alabama at Birmingham, 1396
Center for Parent Information & Resources, 683
Center for Reconstructive Urology, 1309
Center for Research in Sleep Disorders Affiliated with Mercy Hospital, 1626
Center for Sleep & Wake Disorders: Miami Valley Hospital, 1627
Center for Sleep Medicine of the Mount Sinai Medical Center, 1628
Center for Substance Abuse Prevention: Substance Abuse & Mental Health Services, 1769
Center for the Study of Anorexia and Bulimia, 1095, 1137
Center for the Study of Emotion and Attention, 2117
Center for the Study of Traumatic Stress, 2075, 2118
Center for Women's Health, 1585
Center on Aging and Work at Boston College, 271
Centers for Disease Control, 2030
Centers for Disease Control & Prevention: Division of Adolescent & School Health, 632, 1096
Centers for Medicare & Medicaid Services, 633, 1097, 2031
Central Missouri Regional Arthritis Center Stephen's College Campus, 596
Central Texas Veterans Health Care System, 2119
Centre for Addiction and Mental Health, 1838
Centre for Addiction and Mental Health Foundation, 36
Cerebral Blood Flow Laboratories Veterans Administration Medical Center, 1732
Chalmers P. Wylie Ambulatory Care Center VA Central Ohio Healthcare System, 2120
Charles George VA Medical Center, 2121
Charlie Norwood VA Medical Center, 2122
CheckUp, 1429
Chemically Dependent Anonymous, 1882
Cheyenne VA Medical Center, 2123
Child & Family Center, 1008
Child Help, 2266
Children & Adults with Attention Deficit /Hyperactivity Disorder, 684
Children and Adults with AD/HD (CHADD), 685, 707
Children of Aging Parents, 178
Children's and Adult Center for OCD an Anxiety, 513
Children's and Adult Center for OCD and Anxiety, 512, 1454
Children's Heart Institute of Texas, 1210
Children's Heart Society, 1200
Children/Adults With Attention Deficit/ Hyperactivity, 725
Childrens Hospital Immunology Division Children's Hospital, 647
ChildTrauma Academy, 2124
Chillicothe VA Medical Center, 2125
Cincinnati VA Medical Center, 2126
Cleveland Clinic Lerner Research Institute, 1211
Cleveland VA Medical Center VA Northeast Ohio Healthcare System, 2127
Clinical Immunology, Allergy, and Rheumatology, 648
Clinical Nutrition Research Unit (CNRU), 1435
Close To You, 1171
Coatesville VA Medical Center, 2128
Cocaine Anonymous, 1883, 1925
Cocaine Anonymous World Services, 1770
Coconut Creek Eating Disorders Support Group, 1146
Cognitive Neurology and Alzheimer's Disease Center, 461
Colmery-O'Neil VA Medical Center VA Eastern Kansas Health Care System, 2129
Columbia University Irving Center for Clinical Research Adult Unit, 1212
Columbia University Pediatric Anxiety and Mood Research Clinic, 41, 535
Columbia University Robert N. Butler Aging Center, 272
Columbia VA Health Care System, 2130
Commission on Accreditation of Rehabilitation Facilities, 179
Common Ground Sanctuary, 1018, 1147, 1545, 1884, 1981, 2267

Community Anti-Drug Coalitions of America (CADCA), 1771
Compassionate Friends, 135
Compassionate Friends, Inc, 107
Comprehensive Stroke Center of Oregon, 1733
Controlling Anger-Before It Controls You, 1029
Controlling Asthma, 662
COPLINE, 2265
Cornell University: Winifred Masterson Burke Medical Research-Dementia, 462
Cornerstone Treatment Facilities Network, 1839
Corporal Michael J. Crescenz VA Medical Center, 2131
Council for Exceptional Children, 686
Council on Size and Weight Discrimination (CSWD), 1098
Counseling For Loss And Life Changes, Inc., 136
Countdown, 980
Covenant House Nineline, 1982, 1991
Creighton University Cardiac Center, 1213
Creighton University Midwest Hypertension Research Center, 1276
Crime Survivors, 2268
Crisis: The Journal of Crisis Intervention and Suicide Prevention, 1986
CyberPsych, 73, 137, 563, 726, 1030, 1068, 1172, 1480, 1557, 2299

D

Dana Foundation, 2062
David Baldwin's Trauma Information Pages, 2300
Dayton VA Medical Center, 2132
DBSA Support Groups: An Important Step on the Road to Wellness, 50, 771
De Tornyay Center For Healthy Aging at University of Washington, 273
Death And Dying Grief Support, 138
Delaware Division of Substance Abuse and Mental Health (DSAMH), 1804
Department of Pediatrics, Division of Rheumatology, 597
Department of Psychology, 463
Department of Public Health: Division of Substance Abuse, 1810
Department of Public Instruction: Division of Alcoholism and Drug Abuse, 1813
Departments of Neurology & Neurosurgery: University of California, San Francisco, 1734
Depressed Anonymous, 51
Depression & Anxiety, 62, 548
Depression & Bi-Polar Support Alliance, 783
Depression & Bipolar Support Alliance, 11, 514, 749
Depression and Bipolar Support Alliance, 74
Desert Storm Justice Foundation: Florida, 2064
Desert Storm Justice Foundation: Illinois, 2065
Desert Storm Justice Foundation: Minnesota, 2063
Desert Storm Veterans of Florida, Inc., 2066
Diabetes, 981
Diabetes Action Network for the Blind, 807
Diabetes Care, 982
Diabetes Control Program, 808
Diabetes Dictionary, 990
Diabetes Education and Research Center The Franklin House, 951
Diabetes Exercise, 991
Diabetes Forecast, 983
Diabetes Research and Training Center: University of Alabama at Birmingham, 952
Diabetes Spectrum: From Research to Practice, 984
Diabetes Youth Foundation of Indiana, 854
Disabled American Veterans Organization, 2032
Dissociation, 1551
Division of Diabetes Translation, 809
Division of Digestive & Liver Diseases of Cloumbia University, 1138
Division on Endocrinology Northwestern University Feinberg School, 953
Divorce Central, 139
Divorce Information, 140
Divorce Magazine, 141
Divorce Support, 142
Dorothea Dix Hospital Clinical Research Unit, 1840
Drug Abuse Resistance Education of America, 1772

603

Entry Name Index

Drug Abuse Update, 1909
Drug Free Workplace Hotline, 1885
Duke Asthma, Allergy and Airway Center, 649
Duke University Center for the Study of Aging and Human Development, 274, 464
Duke University Clinical Research Institute, 465
Duke University Pediatric Cardiac Catheterization Laboratory, 1214
Durham VA Health Care System, 2133
Dwight D. Eisenhower VA Medical Center VA Eastern Kansas Health Care System, 2134

E

East Orange Campus VA New Jersey Health Care System, 2135
Eating Disorder Resource Center, 1148
Eating Disorders Anonymous, 1149
Eating Disorders Association of New Jersey, 1150
Eating Disorders Awareness And Prevention, 1173
Eating Disorders Coalition for Research, Policy and Action, 1099
Edith Nourse Rogers Memorial Veterans Hospital: Bedford VA, 2136
Edward Hines Jr. VA Hospital, 2137
El Paso VA Health Care Center, 2138
Eldercare Locator, 318
EMDR Institute, 75
Emotions Anonymous International Service Center, 52, 542
Empty Cradle, 53, 108, 143
Endocrinology Research Laboratory Cabrini Medical Center, 954
Epidemiology-Genetics Program in Psychiatr, 764
Epidemology-Genetics Program In Psychiatry, 1558
Erie VA Medical Center, 2139
Ernest Gallo Clinic and Research Center, 1841
Ethnicity & Disease, 1288
Ethnicity Disease, 1289
Eugene J. Towbin Healthcare Center Central Arkansas VA Healthcare System, 2140

F

False Memory Syndrome Facts, 1069
Families Anonymous, 1927
Families Anonymous, Inc., 1886
Families in Action, 1842
Family Building Magazine, 1354
Family Caregiver Alliance/National Center on Caregiving, 180
Family Of a Vet, 2301
Family-to-Family: National Alliance on Mental Illness, 39, 533, 760, 1016, 1062, 1132, 1470, 1537, 1830, 2076
Fargo VA Health Care System, 2141
FASD United, 1773, 1926
Fayetteville VA Medical Center, 2142
Federation of Quebec Alzheimer Societies, 352
Feingold Association of the US, 687
Fertility and Sterility, 1355
Fertility and Sterility Journal, 1356
Fertility and Women's Health Care Center, 1345
Fertility Clinic at the Shepherd Spinal Center, 1344
Fertility Friends Foundation, 1340
Fertility Matters Canada (FMC), 1341
First Candle, 109, 144
First Presbyterian Church in the City of New York Support Groups, 1151, 1887
Florida Heart Research Institute, 1215
Food & Nutrition, 1163
Food Addicts Anonymous, 1152
Fort Meade Campus VA Black Hills Health Care System, 2143
Fort Wayne Campus VA Northern Indiana Health Care System, 2144
Forum Magazine, 1910
Framingham Heart Study, 1216
Freedom From Fear, 12, 515, 543, 2033
Friday Night Live, 1888
Friends For Survival, 1992
Friends for Survival, 145
Friends for Survival, Inc., 110, 1961
Friends Medical Science Research Center, 1843

G

G.V. (Sonny) Montgomery VA Medical Center, 2145
Gam-Anon Family Groups International Servi Office, Inc., 1019
Gamblers Anonymous, 1020
Gastroenterology Therapy Online, 1175
Gazoontite, 668
Geisinger Wyoming Valley Medical Center: Sleep Disorders Center, 1629
General Clinical Research Center at Beth Israel Hospital, 1217
General Clinical Research Center: University of California at LA, 1218
George E. Wahlen Medical Center VA Salt Lake City Health Care System, 2146
George H. O'Brien, Jr. VA Medical Center West Texas VA Health Care System, 2147
George Washington University Center for Aging, Health and Humanities, 275
GERD Information Resource Center, 1174
Gerontological Society of America, 181, 319
Get Your Angries Out, 1031
Gift From Within, 2077, 2302
Goizueta Alzheimer's Disease Research Center, 466
GoldPoint Clinical Research, 2148
Good Shepherd Homecare & Hospice, 182
Goodwill Industries International, Inc., 183, 688, 2034
Goodwill Industries-Suncoast, 184, 2149
Goodwill Industries-Suncoast, Inc., 1774
Goodwill's Community Employment Services, 516, 1009, 1455, 1527, 1700, 2035
Goodwill-Suncoast, 76
Greater New York Metro Intergroup of Overeaters Anonymous, 1426
Green-Field Library-Alzheimer's Association, 445
Grief And Bereavement, 146
Grief Guidance Inc., 1993
Grief Recovery After A Substance Passing, 147
Grief Recovery After a Substance Passing (GRASP), 111, 123, 1775
GriefNet, 148
A Guide To Psychology & Its Practice, 555, 1478
Guidelines For Families Coping With OCD, 1481
Gulf Coast Veterans Health Care System, 2150
Gulf War Syndrome Database, 2303
Gulf War Veteran Resource Pages, 2304
Gurze Bookstore, 1176

H

H.J. Heinz Campus VA Pittsburgh Healthcare System, 2151
Hahnemann University Hospital, Orthopedic Wellness Center, 598
Hahnemann University Laboratory of Human Pharmacology, 1844
Hahnemann University Likoff Cardiovascular Institute, 1219
Hahnemann University: Division of Surgical Research, 1277
Hampton VA Medical Center, 2152
Happy Healthy Lifestyle Magazine For People with Attention Deficit Disorder, 727
Harris Center for Education and Advocacy in Eating Disorders, 1139
Harry S. Truman Memorial Veterans' Hospital, 2153
Harvard Clinical Nutrition Research Center, 1422
Harvard Cocaine Recovery Project, 1845
Harvard Throndike Laboratory Harvard Medical Center, 1220
Harvey A Friedman Center for Aging Washington University, 276
Hazelden, 1928
Hazelden Betty Ford Foundation, 1829
Heal My PTSD with Michele Rosenthal, 2269
Healing From Complex Trauma & PTSD/CPTSD, 2305

Healing Well, 77, 149, 320, 493, 564, 614, 669, 728, 784, 992, 1032, 1070, 1177, 1263, 1293, 1320, 1363, 1406, 1436, 1482, 1514
Healingwell, 670
Health Central, 78, 150, 321, 494, 565, 615, 671, 729, 785, 993, 1033, 1071, 1178, 1264, 1294, 1321, 1364, 1407, 1437, 1483, 1515
Health Finder, 79, 151, 322, 495, 566, 616, 672, 730, 786, 994, 1034, 1072, 1179, 1265, 1295, 1322, 1365, 1408, 1438, 1484, 1516
Health Science Library, 947
HealthCentral.com, 2309
Healthy Weight Network, 1100
HealthyWomen, 1333, 1366
Heart and Stroke Foundation of Canada, 1731
Heart Disease Research Foundation, 1221
Heart Research Foundation of Sacramento, 1222
Heart Touch Project, 185
HEATH Resource Center, 704
Help is Here, 13, 517, 689, 1010, 1053, 1101, 1456, 1776, 1962, 2036
Henry Ford Hospital: Hypertension and Vascular Research Division, 1278
Hershel Woody Williams VA Medical Center, 2154
Higher ED Center, 1932
Holliswood Hospital Psychiatric Care, Services and Self-Help/Support Groups, 54, 483, 544, 772, 1153, 1546, 1593, 2270
Home Instead Center for Successful Aging University of Nebraska Medical Center, 277
HonorBound Foundation, 2067
Hope for Depression Research Foundation, 14, 518, 750, 1054, 1963, 2037
Hope for Fertility Foundation, 1342
Hope for Healing.Org, 2310
Hope Heart Institute, 1223
Hospital of the University of Pennsylvania, 1735
Hot Springs Campus VA Black Hills Health Care System, 2155
Hunter Holmes McGuire VA Medical Center, 2156
Huxley Insititute-American Schizophrenic Association, 1539
Hypertension: Journal of the American Heart Association, 1296
Hysterectomy Educational Resources & Services (HERS) Foundation, 1343

I

Icahn School of Medicine at Mount Sinai, 467
Idaho Persian Gulf Veterans, 2157
Illinois Department of Alcoholism and Susbstance Abuse, 1808
Images Within: A Child's View of Parental Alcoholism, 1889
Impotents Anonymous, 1316
Impulse Control Disorders Clinic, 1017
Indian Health Service, 1777, 1933
Indiana Division of Addiction Services, 1809
Indiana University Center for Aging Research, 468
Indiana University School of Medicine Center for Aging Research, 278
Indiana University: Area Health Education Center, 955
Indiana University: Center for Diabetes Research, 956
Indiana University: Human Genetics Center of Medical & Molecular Genetics, 469
Indiana University: Hypertension Research Center, 1279
Indiana University: Pharmacology Research Laboratory, 957
Infertility and Adoption, 1357
Infertility Books, 1367
Infoline, 1890, 1983
Injury Research Center, 2158
Innovations, 311
Inside MS, 1405
Institute for Basic Research in Developmental Disabilities, 470
Institute for Contemporary Psychotherapy, 15, 112, 519, 690, 751, 1055, 1102, 1457, 1528, 1586, 1701, 1778, 1964, 2038
Institute for Life Course and Aging, 186
Institute on Violence, Abuse and Trauma, 2078

Entry Name Index

IntelliHealth, 2311
Inter-American Society of Hypertension, 1297
Interdisciplinary Program in Cell and Molecular Pharmacology, 1846
International Academy of Suicide Research, 1965
International Archives of Cardiovascular Diseases, 1261
International Archives of Substance Abuse and Rehabilitation, 1911
International Archives of Urology and Complications, 1318, 1358
International Association for Suicide Prevention, 1966
International Association of Eating Disorders Professionals Foundation, 1103, 1130
International Bipolar Foundation, 759
International Council on Infertility Information Dissemination, 1334, 1368
International Critical Incident Stress Foundation, 2068, 2312
International Diabetes Center at Nicollet, 958
International Federation on Ageing, 187
International Foundation for Research and Education on Depression (iFred), 37
International Journal of Addiction Research and Medicine, 1912
International Journal of Depression and Anxiety, 63, 549
International Journal of Diabetes and Clinical Research, 985
International Journal of Psychology and Psychoanalysis, 64, 127, 550, 778, 1025, 1067, 1476, 1552
International Journal of Technology and Aging, 308
International OCD Foundation, 1458
International OCD Foundation, Inc., 1469
International Society For The Study Of Dissociation, 1073
International Society for the Study of Dissociation, 1074, 1562
International Society for the Study of Trauma and Dissociation, 1056, 1529, 2040
International Society for the Study of Women's Sexual Health (ISSWSH), 1587
International Society for Traumatic Stress Studies, 2039, 2079, 2159
Internet Health Resources, 1369
Internet Mental Health, 80, 152, 567, 731, 787, 1035, 1075, 1485, 1563, 1600, 1712, 1996, 2313
Iowa City VA Health Care System, 2160

J

Jack C. Montgomery VA Medical Center Eastern Oklahoma VA Health Care System, 2161
Jamaica Plain Division VA Boston Healthcare System, 2162
James A. Haley Veterans' Hospital, 2163
James H. Quillen VA Healthcare System Mountain Home VA Healthcare System, 2164
Jason Foundation, Inc., 1978, 1997
JDRF: Akron/Canton Chapter, 916
JDRF: Albuquerque Chapter, 905
JDRF: Bakersfield Chapter, 861
JDRF: Baton Rouge Chapter, 886
JDRF: Berks County Chapter, 923
JDRF: Birmingham, 858
JDRF: Buffalo/Western New York Chapter, 906
JDRF: Capitol Chapter, 939
JDRF: Central Florida Chapter, 873
JDRF: Central Jersey Chapter, 901
JDRF: Central Oklahoma Chapter, 920
JDRF: Central Pennsylvania Chapter, 924
JDRF: Charlotte Chapter, 913
JDRF: Colorado Springs Chapter, 867
JDRF: Dallas Chapter, 933
JDRF: Delaware Chapter, 872
JDRF: East Tennessee Chapter, 931
JDRF: Eastern Iowa Chapter, 883
JDRF: Fairfield County Chapter, 869
JDRF: Florida Sun Coast Chapter, 874
JDRF: Georgia Chapter, 878
JDRF: Greater Blue Ridge Chapter, 938
JDRF: Greater Chicago Chapter, 880
JDRF: Greater Cincinnati Chapter, 917
JDRF: Greater Fort Worth/Arlington Chapter, 934
JDRF: Greater Iowa Chapter, 884
JDRF: Greater Madison Chapter, 944
JDRF: Greater New Haven Chapter, 870
JDRF: Greater Palm Beach County Chapter, 855
JDRF: Hawaii Chapter, 879
JDRF: Houston/Gulf Coast Chapter, 935
JDRF: Hudson Valley Chapter, 907
JDRF: Huntington Chapter, 943
JDRF: Indiana State Chapter, 881
JDRF: Inland Empire Chapter, 862
JDRF: Kentuckiana Chapter, 885
JDRF: Lincoln Chapter, 896
JDRF: Long Island/South Shore Chapter, 908
JDRF: Los Angeles Chapter, 863
JDRF: Louisiana Chapter, 887
JDRF: Low Country Chapter, 928
JDRF: Maryland Chapter, 889
JDRF: Metropolitan Detroit/SE Michigan, 892
JDRF: Mid-Jersey Chapter, 902
JDRF: Mid-Ohio Chapter, 918
JDRF: Middle Tennessee Chapter, 932
JDRF: Minnesota Chapter, 894
JDRF: Nevada Chapter, 898
JDRF: New England/Bay State Chapter, 890
JDRF: New England/Maine Chapter, 891
JDRF: New England/New Hampshire Chapter, 900
JDRF: New York Chapter, 909
JDRF: North Central CT & Western MA, 871
JDRF: North Florida Chapter, 875
JDRF: Northeast Wisconsin Chapter, 945
JDRF: Northeastern New York Chapter, 910
JDRF: Northern California Inland Chapter, 864
JDRF: Northern Indiana Chapter, 882
JDRF: Northern Nevada Branch, 899
JDRF: Northwest Arkansas Branch, 860
JDRF: Northwestern Pennsylvania Chapter, 925
JDRF: Omaha Council Bluffs Chapter, 897
JDRF: Orange County Chapter, 865
JDRF: Oregon/SW Washington Chapter, 922
JDRF: Palmetto Chapter, 929
JDRF: Philadelphia Chapter, 926
JDRF: Phoenix Chapter, 859
JDRF: Piedmont Triad Chapter, 914
JDRF: Rochester Branch/Western New York Chapter, 911
JDRF: Rockland County/Northern New Jersey Chapter, 903
JDRF: Rocky Mountain Chapter, 868
JDRF: San Diego Chapter, 866
JDRF: Seattle Chapter, 940
JDRF: Seattle Guild, 941
JDRF: Shreveport Chapter, 888
JDRF: Sioux Falls Chapter, 930
JDRF: South Central Texas Chapter, 936
JDRF: South Florida Chapter, 876
JDRF: South Jersey Chapter, 904
JDRF: Southeastern Chapter, 946
JDRF: Spokane County Area Chapter, 942
JDRF: St. Louis Chapter, 895
JDRF: Tampa Bay Chapter, 877
JDRF: Toledo/Northwest Ohio Chapter, 919
JDRF: Triangle/Eastern North Carolina Chapter, 915
JDRF: Tulsa Green County Chapter, 921
JDRF: West Michigan Chapter, 893
JDRF: West Texas Chapter, 937
JDRF: Westchester County Chapter, 912
JDRF: Western Pennsylvania, 927
Jean Mayer USDA Human Nutrition Research Center on Aging at Tufts University, 279
Jed Foundation, 38
Jesse Brown VA Medical Center, 2165
Jessie's Legacy, 1104
Jewish Alcoholics, Chemically Dependent Persons and Significant Others (JACS), 1934
Jimmie Heuga Center, 1397
John A. Hartford Foundation, 266
John D. Dingell VA Medical Center, 2166
John Douglas French Alzheimer's Foundation, 443
John J. Pershing VA Medical Center, 2167
John L McClellan Memorial Veterans' Hospital Research Office, 1224
Johns Hopkins Center on Aging and Health, 280
Johns Hopkins University: Asthma and Allergy Center, 650
Johns Hopkins University: Behavioral Pharmacology Research Unit, 1847
Johns Hopkins University: Sleep Disorders Francis Scott Key Medical Center, 1630
Jonathan M. Wainwright Memorial VA MC Walla Walla VA Medical Center, 2168
Joslin Center at University of Maryland Medicine, 810
Joslin Diabetes Center, 959
Joslin Magazine, 986
Journal of Aging and Health, 309
Journal of Alzheimer's Disease (JAD), 487
Journal of Anxiety Disorders, 65, 551
Journal of Geriatric Medicine and Gerontology, 310
Journal of Hypertension and Management, 1290
Journal of Mental Health Research in Intellectual Disabilities (JMHRID), 128
Journal of Mood & Anxiety Disorders, 66, 552
Journal of Neuropsychiatry and Clinical Neurosciences, 488
Journal of Obesity and Weight-loss Medication, 1430
Journal of Psychiatry, Depression & Anxiety, 67, 553, 779, 1164, 1477, 1553, 1677, 1708, 2290
Journal of Sexual Medicine, 1596
Journal of Sleep Disorders and Management, 1678
Journal of the Academy of Nutrition and Dietetics, 1165
Journal of Traumatic Stress, 2291
Journal of Urology, 1319, 1359
Juvenile Diabetes Research Foundation Canada, 856
Juvenile Diabetes Research Foundation International, 857

K

Kansas City VA Medical Center, 2169
Kansas State University Center on Aging, 281
Kennedy-Krieger Institute, 2080
Kerrville VA Hospital South Texas Veterans Health Care System, 2170
Kettering-Scott Magnetic Resonance Laboratory, 1848
Kids on the Block Arthritis Programs, 609
Kleptomaniacs Anonymous, 1021
Knollwoodpark Hospital Sleep Disorders Center, 1631
Krannert Institute of Cardiology, 1225

L

Lake City VA Medical Center North Florida/South Georgia, 2171
Landon Center on Aging University of Kansas Medical Center, 282
Lawyers Concerned for Lawyers, 1779, 1935
Lead Line, 1913
Leading Age, 188
Learning Disabilities Association of America, 691
Learning Disabilities: A Multidisciplinary Journal, 715
Lebanon VA Medical Center, 2172
Legal Council for Health Justice, 189
Lexington VA Health Care System, 2173
Lifeclinic.Com, 995, 1266, 1298
LifeRing Secular Recovery, 1936
Loch Raven VA Community Living & Rehabilitation Center, 2271
Loma Linda University Sleep Disorders Clinic, 1632
Long Island Alzheimers & Dementia Center, 471
LongTermCare.gov, 323
Lotsa Helping Hands, 324
Louis A. Johnson VA Medical Center, 2174
Loyola University of Chicago Cardiac Transplant Program, 1226
Lyons Campus VA New Jersey Health Care System, 2175

M

M.I.S.S. Foundation/Center for Loss & Trauma, 121

605

Entry Name Index

MADD-Mothers Against Drunk Drivers, 1891
Magazine of the National Institute of Hypertension Studies, 1291
Maine VA Medical Center VA Maine Healthcare System, 2176
Make the Connection, 2314
Malcom Randall VA Medical Center North Florida/South Georgia, 2177
Male Sexual Dysfunction Clinic, 1314
Manchester VA Medical Center VAMC Manchester, New Hampshire, 2178
Manhattan VA Medical Center VA NY Harbor Health Care System, 2179
March of Dimes Canada, 1727
Marijuana Anonymous, 1892
Marijuana Anonymous World Services, 1893
Marin Institute, 1849
Marion Campus VA Northern Indiana Health Care System, 2180
Marion VA Medical Center, 2181
Martinsburg VA Medical Center, 2182
Maryland Psychiatric Research Center, 1540
Massachusetts Alzheimers Disease Research Center, 472
Massachusetts Eating Disorder Association, 1127
Massachusetts General Departments of Neurology and Neurosurgery, 1736
Mayo Clinic, 568, 1486, 2183
Mayo Clinic Health Oasis, 1299
Mbp Expert Services, 1713
Medical Center & Ambulatory Care Clinic Montana VA Health Care System, 2184
Medical College of Pennsylvania Center for the Mature Woman, 1507
Medical News Today, 81, 153, 325, 497, 569, 617, 673, 732, 788, 996, 1036, 1076, 1180, 1267, 1300, 1323, 1370, 1409, 1439, 1487, 1517
Medical University of South Carolina, 599
Medical University of South Carolina Center on Aging, 283
Medical University of South Carolina: Division of Rheumatology & Immunology, 600
MedicineNet, 82, 154, 326, 498, 570, 618, 674, 733, 789, 997, 1037, 1077, 1181, 1268, 1301, 1324, 1371, 1410, 1440, 1488, 1518
Meditation, Guided Fantasies, And Other Stress Remedies, 83, 571
MedlinePlus, 84, 155, 327, 499, 572, 619, 675, 734, 790, 998, 1038, 1078, 1182, 1269, 1302, 1325, 1372, 1411, 1441, 1489, 1519
MEDLINEplus Health Information, 496
Medscape, 85, 156, 328, 500, 573, 620, 676, 735, 791, 999, 1039, 1079, 1183, 1270, 1303, 1326, 1373, 1412, 1442, 1490, 1520
Medstar Georgetown University Hospital Facility, 1227
Melpomene Institute for Women's Health Research, 1346
Memphis VA Medical Center, 2185
Mended Hearts, 1256
Mental Health America, 16, 113, 190, 353, 520, 692, 752, 1011, 1057, 1105, 1459, 1530, 1588, 1616, 1702, 1780, 1967, 2041, 2272
Mental Health Matters, 1040, 2319
Mental Health Today, 2320
MentalHealth.com, 1941
MentalHelp.net, 2321
Metabolic Research Institute, 960
Methodist Hospital Sleep Center Winona Memorial Hospital, 1633
MGH Neurology WebForums, 1685
Miami VA Healthcare System, 2186
Michael E. DeBakey VA Medical Center, 2187
Michigan Alzheimer's Disease Research Center, 473
MidWest Medical Center: Sleep Disorders Center, 1634
Miles City VA Clinic & Community Living Center, 2188
Milwaukee VA Medical Center (Zablocki), 2189
MindWise Innovations, 17, 1106, 1781
Minneapolis VA Health Care System, 2190
Minnesota Obesity Center, 1423
Mirror, Mirror, 1184
Mitral Valve Prolapse Program of Cincinnati Support Group, 1257

Montrose Campus: Franklin Delano Roosevelt VA Hudson Valley Health Care System, 2191
Mood and Anxiety Disorders Program of Emory University, 2192
Mood Disorders Center, 18, 753
Mothers Against Drunk Driving, 1942
Mothers Against Drunk Driving (MADD), 1782
Mothers Against Munchausen Syndrome By Proxy Allegations, 1718
Mothers In Sympathy And Support (Miss) Foundation, 157
Mount Sinai Medical Center, 1228
MS Toll-Free Information Line, 1400
MSWorld, 1401
Multiple Sclerosis Action Group, 1402
Multiple Sclerosis Association of America, 1381
Multiple Sclerosis Foundation, 1393, 1413
Multipurpose Arthritis and Musculoskeletal Disease Center, 601
Multiservice Eating Disorders Association, 1107, 1133
Munchause Syndrome, 1719
MyHealthfinder, 501, 1327, 1374, 1690, 1753, 1943
Myositis Association of America, 588
MyPTSD, 2322

N

Naomi Berrie Diabetes Center at Columbia University Medical Center, 811
Nar-Anon Family Groups, 1894
Narcolepsy Institute/Montefiore Medical Center, 1673
Narcolepsy Network, 1617, 1674
Narcotic and Drug Research, 1850
Narcotics Anonymous, 1895
Narcotics Anonymous World Services, 1896
Nashville VA Medical Center Tennessee Valley Healthcare System, 2193
National Academy on an Aging Society, 284
National Adult Day Services Association, 191
National Alliance for Caregiving, 192, 302
National Alliance for Eating Disorders, 1108
National Alliance for the Mentally Ill, 1569
National Alliance On Mental Illness, 86, 574, 736, 792, 1491, 1568, 2002
National Alliance on Mental Illness, 19, 521, 693, 754, 1109, 1460, 1531, 1968, 2042
National Alliance on Mental Illness (NAMI), 20, 87, 1784, 2043
National Arthritis & Musculoskeletal & Skin Diseases Information Clearinghouse, 621
National Association for Anorexia Nervosa and Associated Disorders, 1185
National Association for Children of Alcoholics (NACOA), 1785
National Association For The Dually Diagno Diagnosed (NADD), 88, 737, 1492
National Association For The Dually Diagnosed (NADD), 158, 575, 793, 1041
National Association for the Dually Diagnosed (NADD), 21, 89, 114, 522, 694, 755, 1012, 1058, 1110, 1462, 1532, 1589, 1703, 2044
National Association of Addiction Treatment Providers (NAATP), 1786
National Association of Alcoholism and Drug Abuse Counselors (NAADAC), 1787
National Association of Anorexia Nervosa a Associated Disorders (ANAD), 1112
National Association of Anorexia Nervosa and Associated Disorders, 1111, 1154, 1186
National Association of Chronic Disease Directors, 1501
National Association of Parents with Childen in Special Education, 695
National Association Of Parents With Children in Special Education, 1461
National Association of Parents with Children in Special Education, 523
National Association of Social Workers (NASW), 2045
National Association of State Alcohol/Drug Abuse Directors, 1788
National Association of State Directors of Veterans Affairs, 2046

National Association on Drug Abuse Problems, 1789
National Association to Advance Fat Acceptance (NAAFA), 1113, 1417
National Center for Complementary and Integrative Health, 22, 651, 1114, 2047
National Center for Learning Disabilities, 55, 696, 708
National Center For PTSD, 2323
National Center for PTSD, 2081, 2194
National Center for the Prevention of Youth Suicide, 1969
National Center for Victims of Crime, 2082
National Center on Addiction and Substance Abuse, 1851
National Clearinghouse for Alcohol and Drug Information, 1944
National Coalition for the Homeless, 1790
National Council for Behavioral Health, 23, 524, 1463, 1791
National Council for Mental Wellbeing, 1945
National Council on Aging, 193, 329
National Council on Alcoholism and Drug Dependence, 1946
National Crime Prevention Council, 1792, 1947
National Diabetes Information Clearinghouse, 812, 1000
National Eating Disorder Information Centre, 1115
National Eating Disorder Information Centre Helpline, 1155
National Eating Disorders Association, 1116, 1134, 1187
National Eating Disorders Association Helpline, 1156
National Eating Disorders Organization, 1188
National Families in Action (NFIA), 1793
National Federation of Families for Children's Mental Health, 24, 56, 697
National Headache Foundation, 2069
National Health Information Center, 57, 303, 484, 610, 658, 709, 979, 1157, 1258, 1286, 1317, 1351, 1403, 1427, 1512, 1547, 1675, 1743, 1897, 2273
National Heart, Lung & Blood Institute, 1201, 1273, 1304, 1728, 1754
National Heart, Lung and Blood Institute, 1271
National Hospice & Palliative Care Organization (NHPCO), 194, 330
National Human Genome Research Institute, 634, 1117, 2048
National Infertility Network Exchange, 1352
National Information Center For Children and Youth, 738
National Institute for Occupational Safety and Health, 635, 1118
National Institute of Allergy and Infectious Diseases, 636
National Institute of Arthritis & Musculoskeletal & Skin Diseases, 589, 602
National Institute of Biomedical Imaging and Bioengineering, 637
National Institute of Diabetes & Digestive & Kidney Diseases, 813, 1310
National Institute of Environmental Health Sciences, 25, 652, 1119, 2049
National Institute of General Medical Sciences, 653, 2050
National Institute Of Health, 576, 1493
National Institute of Mental Health, 26, 42, 90, 536, 698, 765, 1464, 1533, 1970, 2051, 2083, 2195
National Institute of Mental Health Eating Disorders Research Program, 1120
National Institute of Neurological Disorders and Stroke, 1382, 1618, 1729
National Institute of Nursing Research, 638
National Institute on Aging, 195, 331, 354
National Institute on Alcohol Abuse & Alcoholism, 1948
National Institute on Alcohol Abuse and Alcoholism (NIAAA), 1794
National Institute on Drug Abuse (NIDA), 1795, 1949
National Institutes of Health, 1375
National Jewish Division of Immunology, 654
National Mental Health Consumers' Self-Help Clearinghouse, 40, 159, 554, 699, 756, 794, 1013, 1042, 1059, 1121, 1534, 1590, 1704, 1831, 1950
National Multiple Sclerosis Society, 1385, 1414

Entry Name Index

National Multiple Sclerosis Society: Idaho Chapter, 1387
National Multiple Sclerosis Society: New Jersey Metro Chapter, 1388
National Multiple Sclerosis Society: North Florida Chapter, 1389
National Multiple Sclerosis Society: Ohio Chapter, 1390
National Multiple Sclerosis Society: Pacific South Coast, 1383
National Multiple Sclerosis Society: Pennsylvania Keystone Chapter, 1384
National Multiple Sclerosis Society: Texas Chapter, 1391
National Multiple Sclerosis Society: Utah Chapter, 1392
National Multiple Sclerosis Society: Wyoming Chapter, 1386
National Organization For People Of Color Against Suicide, 2003
National Organization for People of Color Against Suicide (NOPCAS), 1971
National Organization of Parents of Murdered Children, 115, 160
National P.O.L.I.C.E. Suicide Foundation, 1979, 2004
National Panic/Anxiety Disorder Newsletter, 577
National Prevention Resource Center CSAP Division of Communications Programs, 1852
National Resource Center on ADHD, 716
National Science Foundation, 644, 2070
National Seniors Council, 196
National Sexual Violence Resource Center, 2084
National SHARE Office, 161
National Share Office, 116
National Sleep Foundation, 1620
National Society for MVP and Dysautonomia, 1259
National Stroke Association, 1274, 1755
National Veterans Services Fund, 2274, 2324
National Volunteer Training Center for Substance Abuse Prevention, 1853
National Women's Health Network, 1335
NCADD, 1783
Neurology Channel, 502, 1691, 1756
Neuromuscular Treatment Center: Univ. of Texas Southwestern Medical Center, 1398
New Jersey Division of Mental Health and Addiction Services, 1814
New York Male Reproductive Center: Sexual Dysfunction Unit, 1315
New York Obesity/Nutrition Research Center, 1424
New York Obesity/Nutrition Research Center (ONRC), 1443
New York Office of Addiction Services and Supports, 1815
New York University General Clinical Research Center, 1280
New York/New Jersey VA Health Care Network, 2196
Next Step in Care, 332
NIH Osteoporosis and Related Bone Disease, 1521
NIH Osteoporosis and Related Bone Diseases - National Resource Center, 1506
North American Association for the Study of Obesity, 1444
North Carolina Mental Health and Substance Abuse, 1816
North Las Vegas VA Medical Center VA Southern Nevada Healthcare System, 2197
Northport VA Medical Center, 2198
Northwest Ohio Sleep Disorders Center Toledo Hospital, 1635
Northwestern University: Division of Allergy and Immunology, 655
Nurse Practitioners in Women's Health, 1502

O

Obesity Canada, 1418
Obesity Research Center, 1140
Obesity Research Center St. Luke's-Roosevelt Hospital, 1425
Obsessive-Compulsive Anonymous, 1472
Obsessive-Compulsive Disorder, 1494
Obsessive-Compulsive Foundation, 1495

Office of the Special Assistant for Gulf War Illnesses, 2325
Office of Women's Health, 27, 1122
Office of Women's Services: Substance Abuse & Mental Health Services, 1796
Office on Smoking and Health, 1951
Office on Smoking and Health: Centers for Disease Control & Prevention, 1832
Official Journal of NAASO, 1431
Ohio Sleep Medicine Institute, 1636
Ohio State University Clinical Pharmacology Division, 1854
Oklahoma City VA Health Care System, 2199
Oklahoma Department of Mental Health and Substance Abuse Services, 1817
Oklahoma Medical Research Foundation, 603
Oklahoma Medical Research Foundation: Cardiovascular Research Program, 1229
One ADD Place, 739
Oscar G. Johnson VA Medical Center, 2200
Osteoporosis Canada, 1503
Osteoporosis Center Memorial Hospital/Advanced Medical Diagn, 1508
Out of the Storm, 2275
Overeaters Anonymous, 1428
Overeaters Anonymous General Service Offic, 1158
Overton Brooks VA Medical Center, 2201

P

PACER Center, 28, 700
Pandora's Aquarium, 2279
Panic Disorder, 578
Panic Survivor, 2280
Parents Resource Institute for Drug Education, 1833
Partnership to End Addiction, 1797
Pathways to Promise, 1898
Peace, Love, And Hope, 1189
Penn Center for Sleep Disorders: Hospital of the University of Pennsylvania, 1637
Penn Memory Center, 474
Pennsylvania Educational Network for Eating Disorders, 1128
Pennsylvania State University Artificial Heart Research Project, 1230
Perry Point VA Medical Center VA Maryland Health Care System, 2202
Phoenix VA Health Care System, 2203
Physician Referral and Information Line, 659
PlanetPsych, 162, 1570, 2328
PlanetPsych.com, 1190, 1605
Planetpsych.com, 91, 579, 740, 795, 1043, 1080, 1720
Portland VA Medical Center VA Portland Health Care System, 2204
Post Traumatic Stress Disorder Alliance, 2329
Postpartum Support International, 29
Posttraumatic Stress Disorder (PTSD) Alliance, 2052, 2085
Presbyterian-University Hospital: Pulmonary Sleep Evaluation Center, 1638
Preventive Medicine Research Institute, 1231
Progress Notes, 1432
Progyny, 1376
Providence VA Medical Center, 2205
Psych Central, 92, 163, 580, 741, 796, 1044, 1081, 1191, 1571, 1606, 1721, 1952, 2330
Psychguides.com, 2331
Psychology Information On-Line: Depression, 93
Psycom, 94
PTSD Family Support Group, 2276
PTSD Hotline, 2277
PTSD Support Services, 2326
PTSDanonymous.org, 2278
PTSDinfo.org, 2327
Pulmonary Hypertension Association, 1202
Pulmonary Hypertension Association (PHA), 1203, 1275
Purdue University William A Hillenbrand Biomedical Engineering Center, 1232
Purdue University: Center for Research on Aging and the Life Course, 285

R

Rainbows, 117, 124, 164
Ralph H. Johnson VA Medical Center, 2206
Rape, Abuse & Incest National Network, 2281
Rational Recovery, 1899
Raymond G. Murphy VA Medical Center New Mexico VA Health Care System, 2207
Recovered, 1798
Recovery International, 58, 525, 773, 2282
Regional Bone Center Helen Hayes Hospital, 1509
Relationship Learning Center, 165
Remove Intoxicated Drivers (RID-USA), 1799
Research Center, 333
Research Chair in Obesity Universit, Laval, 1419
Research Chair on Obesity, 1445
Research Institute on Alcoholism, 1855
Research Society on Alcoholism, 1856
RESOLVE, 1377
RESOLVE: New England, 1336
RESOLVE: The National Infertility Association, 1337
Rhode Island Department of Behavioral Healthcare: Substance Use/Addiction, 1818
Richmond Support Group, 1159
RNtoBSN.org, 2086
Roanoke Vet Center, 2208
Robert J. Dole VA Medical Center, 2209
Robley Rex VA Medical Center Louisville VA Medical Center, 2210
Rockefeller University Laboratory of Biology, 1857
Rockefeller University Laboratory of Cardiac Physiology, 1233
Rosalind Russell Medical Research Center for Arthritis at UCSF, 604
Roseburg VA Health Care System, 2211
Roy M and Phyllis Gough Huffington Center on Aging, 286
Rush University Multiple Sclerosis Center, 1399
Rutgers University Center of Alcohol Studies, 1858
Ruth E. Golding Clinical Pharmacokinetics Laboratory, 1859

S

Sacramento Veterans Center, 2212
Safe Crossings Foundation, 166
Safe Homes, 1954
Salem VA Medical Center, 2213
SAMHSA - Center for Mental Health Services, 95
Samueli Institute, 2214
San Francisco Heart & Vascular Institute, 1234
San Francisco VA Medical Center, 2215
Sanders-Brown Center on Aging University of Kentucky, 287
Sanford Center for Aging University Of Nevada, Reno, 288
Sansum Diabetes Research Institute, 961
Schizophrenia, 1572
Schizophrenia Bulletin, 1554
Schizophrenia Research, 1555
Schizophrenia Research Branch: Division of Clinical and Treatment Research, 1541
Schizophrenia Therapy Online Resource Center, 1573
Schulze Diabetes Institute, 814
Scripps Clinic Sleep Disorders Center Scripps Clinic, 1639
Section for Psychiatric and Substance Abuse Services (SPSPAS), 1800
Selective Mutism Association (SMA), 527
Selective Mutism Foundation, 581
Selective Mutism Research Institute, 537
Self Help Magazine, 797
Senior Resource LLC, 197
Seniorresource.com, 334
Sexual Disorders, 1607
Sexual Medicine Society of North America, 1311, 1591
Shared Parenting Information Group (SPIG), 167
Sheridan VA Medical Center, 2216
Shirley Ryan AbilityLab, 605
Shrinktank, 1608
Shriver Center University Affiliated Program, 2087

Entry Name Index

Shulman Center for Compulsive Theft, Spending & Hoarding, 1014
Sidran Institute, 2053
Sidran Institute, Traumatic Stress Education Administration, 2332
Sidran Traumatic Stress Institute, 1060, 2054
Sioux Falls VA Health Care System, 2217
Sleep Alertness Center: Lafayette Home Hospital, 1640
Sleep and Chronobiology Center: Western Psychiatric Institute and Clinic, 1666
Sleep Center: Community General Hospital, 1641
Sleep Disorders Center at California: Pacific Medical Center, 1647
Sleep Disorders Center Bethesda Oak Hospital, 1642
Sleep Disorders Center Columbia Presbyterian Medical Center, 1643
Sleep Disorders Center Dartmouth Hitchcock Medical Center, 1644
Sleep Disorders Center Lankenau Hospital, 1645
Sleep Disorders Center of Metropolitan Toronto, 1648
Sleep Disorders Center of Rochester: St. Mary's Hospital, 1649
Sleep Disorders Center of Western New York Millard Fillmore Hospital, 1650
Sleep Disorders Center Ohio State University Medical Center, 1646
Sleep Disorders Center: Cleveland Clinic Foundation, 1651
Sleep Disorders Center: Community Medical Center, 1652
Sleep Disorders Center: Crozer-Chester Medical Center, 1653
Sleep Disorders Center: Good Samaritan Medical Center, 1654
Sleep Disorders Center: Kettering Medical Center, 1655
Sleep Disorders Center: Medical College of Pennsylvania, 1656
Sleep Disorders Center: Newark Beth Israel Medical Center, 1657
Sleep Disorders Center: Rhode Island Hospital, 1658
Sleep Disorders Center: St. Vincent Medical Center, 1659
Sleep Disorders Center: University Hospital, SUNY at Stony Brook, 1660
Sleep Disorders Center: Winthrop, University Hospital, 1661
Sleep Disorders Unit Beth Israel Deaconess Medical Center, 1662
Sleep Health: Journal of the National Sleep Foundation, 1679
Sleep Laboratory, 1663
Sleep Laboratory, Maine Medical Center, 1664
Sleep Medicine Associates of Texas, 1665
Sleep Research Society (SRS), 1619, 1692
Sleep Research Society Foundation, 1621
Sleep/Wake Disorders Center Montefiore Sleep Disorders Center, 1667
Sleep/Wake Disorders Center: Community Hospitals of Indianapolis, 1668
Sleep/Wake Disorders Center: Hampstead Hospital, 1669
Sleep/Wake Disorders Center: New York Hospital-Cornell Medical Center, 1670
SleepFoundation.org, 1622, 1693
SMart Center: Selective Mutism, Anxiet & Related Disorders Treatment Center, 526
SMART Recovery, 1900, 1953
Society For Post-Acute and Long-Term Care Medicine, 1504
Society for the Study of Reproduction, 1338
Society of Federal Health Professionals (AMSUS), 2055
Society of Mitral Valve Prolapse Syndrome, 1260
Something Fishy Music And Publishing, 1192
Souls Self Help, 1955
South Carolina Department of Alcohol and Drug Abuse Services, 1819
South Central VA Health Care Network, 2218
Southeast Louisiana Veterans Health Care System, 2219
Southern Arizona VA Health Care System, 2220
Southern California Research Institute, 1860

Spark M. Matsunaga VA Medical Center VA Pacific Islands Health Care System, 2221
Special Education Rights and Respnsibilities, 742
Specialized Center of Research in Ischemic Heart Disease, 1235
Spokane VA Medical Center Mann-Grandstaff VA Medical Center, 2222
St. Agnes Hospital Medical: Health Science Library, 1394
St. Joseph's Medical Center, 1141
Stanford Center for Research in Disease Prevention, 1861
Stanford Center on Longevity, 289
Stanford University Center for Narcolepsy, 1671
State University of New York at Buffalo Toxicology Research Center, 1862
Stein Institute for Research on Aging UC San Diego School of Medicine, 290
Stop Biting Nails, 1045
Stroke Connection, 1744
Stroke Research and Treatment Center UAB Medical Center, 1737
Students Against Destructive Decisions, 1834
Students Against Destructive Decisions (SADD), 1901, 1956
Substance Abuse & Mental Health Services Administration, 2005
Substance Abuse And Mental Health Services Administration, 168, 743, 798, 1046, 1082, 1193, 1574, 1609, 1722, 1957, 2006, 2333
Substance Abuse and Mental Health Services Administration (SAMHSA), 1801, 1958
Substance Abuse: Research and Treatment, 1914
Suicide and Life-Threatening Behavior, 1987
Suicide Awareness Voices of Education (SAV, 1972
Suicide Awareness Voices Of Education (SAVE), 2007
Suicide Prevention Resource Center, 1980, 2088
Suicide.org, 2283
Suncoast Residential Training Center, 799
Support for Asthmatic Youth, 660
Support Groups, 2008
Support4Hope, 59, 545, 774, 1064, 1473, 1548, 2284
Survivors Of Loved Ones' Suicides (Solos), 2009
Survivors of Loved Ones' Suicides (SOLOS), 1984
Sutcliffe Clinic, 30, 528, 701, 1465
Synergy Clinical Research Center, 2223
Syracuse VA Medical Center, 2224

T

Tacoma Vet Center, 2225
Tallahassee Memorial Diabetes Center, 815
Taub Institute for Research on Alzheimers Disease and the Aging Brain, 475
Tennessee Department of Mental Health and Substance Abuse Services, 1820
Tennessee Neuropsychiatric Institute Middle Tennessee Mental Health Institute, 1542
Territorial Apprehensiveness (TERRAP) Anxiety & Stress Program, 31, 529, 1466, 2056
Territorial Apprehensiveness Programs (TERRAP), 582
Texas Health And Human Service: Mental Health & Substance Use, 1281
Texas Heart Institute St Lukes Episcopal Hospital, 1236
Thomas E. Creek VA Medical Center Amarillo VA Health Care System, 2226
Thomas Jefferson University: Sleep Disorders Center, 1672
Thriving Minds, 32, 530
TLC Foundation for Body-Focused Repetitive Behaviors, 1015, 1022
Tomah VA Medical Center, 2227
TOPS Take Off Pounds Sensibly, 1123
ToughLove International, 1902
Traditional Tibetan Healing, 1404
Trauma Center, 2089, 2228
Trauma Resource Area, 1083, 2334
Tulane University Center For Aging, 291

U

U.S. Department of Health and Human Services, 2057
U.S. Food and Drug Administration, 639, 1124
UAMS Psychiatric Research Institute, 43, 538, 766, 1142, 1471, 1863, 2229
UC San Diego Center for Healthy Aging, 476
UCLA Anxiety Disorders Research Center, 44, 539, 705, 767, 1063, 1543, 2230
UI Health, 477
UNITE, Inc., 118
Unite, Inc., 169
United Brain Association, 33, 119, 355, 531, 702, 757, 1061, 1467, 1535, 1705, 1973, 2058
United States 211 Information and Referral Systems, 2285
University Drive Campus VA Pittsburgh Healthcare System, 2231
University of Alabama at Birmingham: Congenital Heart Disease Center, 1237
University of California San Diego General Clinical Research Center, 1238
University of California: Cardiovascular Research Laboratory, 1239
University of California: Los Angeles Alcohol Research Center, 1864
University of California: UCLA Population Research Center, 1347
University of Chicago Dept of Neurology, 478
University of Chicago: Comprehensive Diabetes Center, 962
University of Cincinnati Department of Pathology & Laboratory Medicine, 1240
University of Colorado: General Clinical Research Center, Pediatric, 963
University of Connecticut Center on Aging, 294
University of Connecticut Osteoporosis Center, 1510
University of Florida Institute on Aging, 295
University of Iowa College of Medicine, 1738
University of Iowa Mental Health Clinical Research Center, 1544
University of Iowa: Diabetes Research Center, 964
University of Iowa: Iowa Cardiovascular Center, 1241
University of Kansas Cray Diabetes Center, 965
University of Maryland Center for Studies of Cerebrovascular Disease & Stroke, 1739
University of Maryland School of Public Health Center on Aging, 296
University of Maryland: Division of Infectious Diseases, 479
University of Massachusetts: Diabetes and Endocrinology Research Center, 966
University of Miami School of Medicine Department of Neurology, 1740
University of Miami: Diabetes Research Institute, 967
University of Michigan Pulmonary and Critical Care Division, 1242
University of Michigan Reproductive Sciences Program, 1348
University of Michigan: Alcohol Research Center, 1865
University of Michigan: Cardiovascular Medicine, 1243
University of Michigan: Division of Hypertension, 1281
University of Michigan: Orthopaedic Research Laboratories, 606
University of Michigan: Psychiatric Center, 1866
University of Minnesota: Hypertensive Research Group, 1282
University of Minnesota: Program on Alcohol/Drug Control, 1867
University of Missouri Columbia Division of Cardiothoracic Surgery, 1244
University of Missouri: Kansas City Drug Information Service, 1868
University of New Mexico General Clinical Research Center, 968
University of North Carolina School of Medicine Center for Aging and Health, 292
University of Pennsylvania Diabetes and Endocrinology Research Center, 969
University of Pennsylvania Institute on Aging, 297
University of Pennsylvania Muscle Institute, 1245

608

Entry Name Index

University of Pennsylvania Weight and Eating Disorders Program, 1143
University of Pittsburgh Obesity/Nutrition Research Center, 1446
University of Pittsburgh: Department of Molecular Genetics and Biochemistry, 970
University of Pittsburgh: Human Energy Research Laboratory, 1246
University of Rochester: Clinical Research Center, 1247
University of Southern California: Coronary Care Research, 1248
University of Southern California: Division of Nephrology, 1283
University of Tennessee Drug Information Center, 1869
University of Tennessee: Division of Cardiovascular Diseases, 1249
University of Tennessee: General Clinical Research Center, 971
University of Texas at Austin: Drug Synamics Institute, 1871
University of Texas General Clinical Research Center, 972
University of Texas Health Science Center Neurophysiology Research Center, 1870
University of Texas Southwestern Medical Center at Dallas, 1250
University of Texas: Mental Health Clinical Research Center, 45
University of Utah: Artificial Heart Research Laboratory, 1251
University of Utah: Cardiovascular Genetic Research Clinic, 1252
University of Utah: Center for Human Toxicology, 1872
University of Vermont Larner College of Medicine Center on Aging, 298
University of Virginia: General Clinical Research Center, 656
University of Virginia: Hypertension and Atherosclerosis Unit, 1284
University of Washington Diabetes: Endocrinology Research Center, 973
University of Wisconsin Milwaukee Medicinal Chemistry Group, 1873
University of Wisconsin: Asthma, Allergy and Pulmonary Research Center, 657
University Of Wyoming Center on Aging, 293
Up Against Eating Disorders, 1125
Urban Cardiology Research Center, 1253
Urology Care Foundation, 1313, 1592
US Administration on Aging, 198, 335
US Department Of Veterans Affairs, 2090
UT Southwestern Medical Center, 96
Utah Department of Health & Human Services : Substance Abuse & Mental Health, 1822
Uterine Artery Embolization, 1378

V

VA Ann Arbor Healthcare System, 2232
VA Austin Information Technology Center, 2059
VA Austin Outpatient Clinic, 2233
VA Capitol Health Care Network, 2234
VA Caregiver Support, 2335
VA Central California Health Care System, 2235
VA Central Iowa Health Care System, 2236
VA Great Lakes Health Care System, 2237
VA Greater Los Angeles Healthcare System, 2238
VA Healthcare System of Ohio, 2239
VA Heart of Texas Health Care Network Dallas VA Medical Center, 2240
VA Heartland Network, 2241
VA Illiana Health Care System, 2242
VA Loma Linda Healthcare System, 2243
VA MidSouth Healthcare Network (VISN 9), 2244
VA Northern California Health Care System, 2245
VA Palo Alto Health Care System, 2246
VA Puget Sound Health Care System, 2247
VA Sierra Nevada Health Care System, 2248
VA Southeast Network, 2249
VA St. Louis Health Care System John Cochran & Jefferson Barracks, 2250
VA Western Colorado Health Care System, 2251
Vaginismus.Com, 1610
Vanderbilt Clinical Nutrition Research Unit (CNRU), 1447
Vanderbilt University Diabetes Center, 974
Vanderbilt University: Center for Fertility and Reproductive Research, 1349
Vermont Department of Health: Division of Substance Use Programs (DSU), 1823
Verywell Mind, 97, 170, 336, 503, 583, 744, 800, 1047, 1084, 1194, 1496, 1575, 1611, 1694, 1723, 2010, 2336
Veterans Administration Medical Center: Alabama, 2252
Veterans Affairs Medical Center: Research Service, 975
Veterans Association Medical Center, 2253
Veterans Benefits Clearinghouse, 2060
Veterans Crisis Line, 2286
Vetwives Living With PTSD, 2287
Virginia Commonwealth University Virginia Center on Aging, 299
Virginia Department of Behavioral Health & Developmental Services, 1824
Voice of the Diabetic, 987

W

W. G. (Bill) Hefner VA Medical Center, 2254
Wake Forest University: Arteriosclerosis Research Center, 1285
Wake Forest University: Cerebrovascular Research Center, 1741
Warren Grant Magnuson Clinical Center, 607, 976, 1254
Washington DC VA Medical Center, 2255
Washington University School of Medicine, 1742
Washington University: Diabetes Research and Training Center, 977
Wayfinder Family Services, 1339
Wayne State University: University Women's Care, 1350
WebMD, 98, 171, 337, 504, 584, 622, 677, 745, 801, 1001, 1048, 1085, 1195, 1272, 1305, 1328, 1379, 1415, 1448, 1497, 1522
Weight-Control Information Network, 1126, 1135, 1196, 1420, 1421, 1449
Well Spouse Association, 304
West Palm Beach VA Medical Center, 2256
West Roxbury Division VA Boston Healthcare System, 2257
WFS' New Life Program, 1903
White City VA Rehabilitation Center VA Southern Oregon, 2258
White River Junction VA Medical Center, 2259
Widownet, 172
Wilkes-Barre VA Medical Center, 2260
William S. Middleton Memorial Veterans Hospital, 2261
Wilmington VA Medical Center, 2262
Wing of Madness: A Depression Guide, 99
WithAll, 1131
Women's Resource Center, 2091
www.befrienders.org, 775
Wyoming Department of Health: Substance Use and Tobacco Prevention Program, 1825

Y

Yale Child Study Center, 2263
Yale Mood Disorders Research Program, 46, 768
Yale School of Medicine, 100
Yale University School Of Medicine, 101, 802
Yellow Ribbon Suicide Prevention Program, 1974, 2011
Yeshiva University General Clinical Research Center, 1255
Yeshiva University: Resnick Gerontology Center, 480

Z

Zur Institute, 34, 120

Geographic Index / Alabama

Alabama

AARP Alabama, 199
Alabama Department of Mental Health: Div. of Mental Health & Substance Abuse, 1802
Alzheimer's Association: Alabama, 356
Alzheimer's Disease Center University of Alabama at Birmingham, 448
Alzheimer's Disease Center: University of Alabama at Birmingham, 454
American Diabetes Association: Alabama, 816
American Obesity Treatment Association, 1416
American Society for Reproductive Medicine, 1580
Arthritis and Musculoskeletal Center: UAB Heersink School of Medicine, 592
Cardiovascular Research and Training Center University of Alabama, 1209
Center for Neuroimmunology: University of Alabama at Birmingham, 1396
Diabetes Research and Training Center: University of Alabama at Birmingham, 952
JDRF: Birmingham, 858
Knollwoodpark Hospital Sleep Disorders Center, 1631
National Society for MVP and Dysautonomia, 1259
Specialized Center of Research in Ischemic Heart Disease, 1235
Stroke Research and Treatment Center UAB Medical Center, 1737
University of Alabama at Birmingham: Congenital Heart Disease Center, 1237
Veterans Administration Medical Center: Alabama, 2252
Veterans Association Medical Center, 2253

Alaska

AARP Alaska, 200
Alaska Department of Health: Office of Substance Abuse and Addiction Prevention, 1803
Alaska VA Healthcare System, 2092
American Diabetes Association: Alaska, 817

Arizona

AARP Arizona, 201
Alzheimer's Association: Desert Southwest, 358
Alzheimer's Association: Northern Arizona, 359
Alzheimer's Association: Southern Arizona, 360
Arizona Heart Institute, 1204
Child Help, 2266
Commission on Accreditation of Rehabilitation Facilities, 179
JDRF: Phoenix Chapter, 859
Mayo Clinic, 2183
National Association Of Parents With Children in Special Education, 1461
National Association of Parents with Childen in Special Education, 695
National Association of Parents with Children in Special Education, 523
Phoenix VA Health System, 2203
Ruth E. Golding Clinical Pharmacokinetics Laboratory, 1859
Southern Arizona VA Health Care System, 2220

Arkansas

AARP Arkansas, 202
Alzheimer's Association: Arkansas, 361
Eugene J. Towbin Healthcare Center Central Arkansas VA Healthcare System, 2140
JDRF: Northwest Arkansas Branch, 860
John L McClellan Memorial Veterans' Hospital Research Office, 1224
UAMS Psychiatric Research Institute, 43
UAMS Psychiatric Research Institute, 538
UAMS Psychiatric Research Institute, 766
UAMS Psychiatric Research Institute, 1142
UAMS Psychiatric Research Institute, 1471
UAMS Psychiatric Research Institute, 1863
UAMS Psychiatric Research Institute, 2229

California

AARP California: Pasadena, 203
AARP California: Sacramento, 204
Adult Children of Alcoholics, 1874
Adult Children of Alcoholics World Service Organization, Inc., 1760
Alcohol Drug Treatment Referral, 1879
Alcohol Research Group Public Health Institute, 1835
Alzheimer's Association: Cali. - Southland, 362
Alzheimer's Association: California - Central Coast, 363
Alzheimer's Association: Northern California, 364
Alzheimer's Association: Orange County, 365
Alzheimer's Association: San Diego, 366
Alzheimer's Disease Center: University of California, Davis, 453
Archstone Foundation, 265
Bees-Stealy Research Foundation, 1206
Bipolar Disorders Clinic, 762
Center for Culture, Trauma and Mental Health Disparities, 2114
Center for Healthy Sex, 1308
Center for Healthy Sex, 1583
Center for Reconstructive Urology, 1309
Child & Family Center, 1008
Cocaine Anonymous, 1883
Cocaine Anonymous World Services, 1770
Crime Survivors, 2268
Departments of Neurology & Neurosurgery: University of California, San Francisco, 1734
Diabetes Control Program, 808
Drug Abuse Resistance Education of America, 1772
Eating Disorders Anonymous, 1149
Empty Cradle, 53
Empty Cradle, 108
Ernest Gallo Clinic and Research Center, 1841
Family Caregiver Alliance/National Center on Caregiving, 180
Friday Night Live, 1888
Friends for Survival, Inc., 110
Friends for Survival, Inc., 1961
Gamblers Anonymous, 1020
General Clinical Research Center: University of California at LA, 1218
Heart Research Foundation of Sacramento, 1222
Heart Touch Project, 185
Institute on Violence, Abuse and Trauma, 2078
International Bipolar Foundation, 759
JDRF: Bakersfield Chapter, 861
JDRF: Inland Empire Chapter, 862
JDRF: Los Angeles Chapter, 863
JDRF: Northern California Inland Chapter, 864
JDRF: Orange County Chapter, 865
JDRF: San Diego Chapter, 866
John Douglas French Alzheimer's Foundation, 443
Loma Linda University Sleep Disorders Clinic, 1632
Marijuana Anonymous, 1892
Marijuana Anonymous World Services, 1893
Marin Institute, 1849
Nar-Anon Family Groups, 1894
Narcotics Anonymous, 1895
Narcotics Anonymous World Services, 1896
National Families in Action (NFIA), 1793
National Multiple Sclerosis Society: Idaho Chapter, 1387
National Multiple Sclerosis Society: Pacific South Coast, 1383
National Multiple Sclerosis Society: Utah Chapter, 1392
Osteoporosis Center Memorial Hospital/Advanced Medical Diagn, 1508
Preventive Medicine Research Institute, 1231
Rational Recovery, 1899
Rosalind Russell Medical Research Center for Arthritis at UCSF, 604
Sacramento Veterans Center, 2212
San Francisco Heart & Vascular Institute, 1234
San Francisco VA Medical Center, 2215
Sansum Diabetes Research Institute, 961
Scripps Clinic Sleep Disorders Center Scripps Clinic, 1639
Sleep Disorders Center at California: Pacific Medical Center, 1647
Sleep Disorders Center of Metropolitan Toronto, 1648
Southern California Research Institute, 1860
Stanford Center for Research in Disease Prevention, 1861
Stanford Center on Longevity, 289
Stanford University Center for Narcolepsy, 1671
Stein Institute for Research on Aging UC San Diego School of Medicine, 290
Sutcliffe Clinic, 30
Sutcliffe Clinic, 528
Sutcliffe Clinic, 701
Sutcliffe Clinic, 1465
Synergy Clinical Research Center, 2223
TLC Foundation for Body-Focused Repetitive Behaviors, 1015
TLC Foundation for Body-Focused Repetitive Behaviors, 1022
UC San Diego Center for Healthy Aging, 476
UCLA Anxiety Disorders Research Center, 44
UCLA Anxiety Disorders Research Center, 539
UCLA Anxiety Disorders Research Center, 705
UCLA Anxiety Disorders Research Center, 767
UCLA Anxiety Disorders Research Center, 1063
UCLA Anxiety Disorders Research Center, 1543
UCLA Anxiety Disorders Research Center, 2230
University of California San Diego General Clinical Research Center, 1238
University of California: Cardiovascular Research Laboratory, 1239
University of California: Los Angeles Alcohol Research Center, 1864
University of California: UCLA Population Research Center, 1347
University of Southern California: Coronary Care Research, 1248
University of Southern California: Division of Nephrology, 1283
VA Central California Health Care System, 2235
VA Greater Los Angeles Healthcare System, 2238
VA Loma Linda Healthcare System, 2243
VA Northern California Health Care System, 2245
VA Palo Alto Health Care System, 2246
Wayfinder Family Services, 1339
Zur Institute, 34
Zur Institute, 120

Canada

Alzheimer Society of Alberta and Northwest Territories, 338
Alzheimer Society of British Columbia, 339
Alzheimer Society of Canada, 340
Alzheimer Society of Manitoba, 341
Alzheimer Society of New Brunswick, 342
Alzheimer Society of Newfoundland & Labrador, 343
Alzheimer Society of Nova Scotia, 344
Alzheimer Society of Ontario, 345
Alzheimer Society of Prince Edward Island, 346
Alzheimer Society of Saskatchewan, 347
Alzheimer Society of Toronto, 348
Asthma Canada, 629
Bulimia Anorexia Nervosa Association, 1092
Canadian ADHD Resource Alliance, 680
Canadian Adult Congenital Heart Network, 1199
Canadian Diabetes Educator Certification Board, 806
Canadian Men's Health Foundation, 1312
Canadian National Seniors Council, 177
Canadian Society of Allergy and Clinical Immunology, 631
Canadian Society of Nephrology, 1332
Canadian Urological Association (CUA), 1307
Centre for Addiction and Mental Health, 1838
Centre for Addiction and Mental Health Foundation, 36
Children's Heart Society, 1200
Federation of Quebec Alzheimer Societies, 352
Fertility Friends Foundation, 1340
Fertility Matters Canada (FMC), 1341
Heart and Stroke Foundation of Canada, 1731
Institute for Life Course and Aging, 186
International Federation on Ageing, 187
Jessie's Legacy, 1104

611

Geographic Index / Colorado

Juvenile Diabetes Research Foundation Canada, 856
March of Dimes Canada, 1727
National Eating Disorder Information Centre, 1115
National Eating Disorder Information Centre Helpline, 1155
Obesity Canada, 1418
Osteoporosis Canada, 1503
Urology Care Foundation, 1592

Colorado

AARP Colorado, 205
Alzheimer's Association: Boulder and Mountain Region, 367
Alzheimer's Association: Great Denver Region, 368
Alzheimer's Association: Northeastern Colorado Region, 369
Alzheimer's Association: Northern Colorado Region, 370
Alzheimer's Association: Southern and Central Colorado Region, 371
Alzheimer's Association: Western Colorado Region, 372
Barbara Davis Center for Childhood Diabetes, 948
JDRF: Colorado Springs Chapter, 867
JDRF: Rocky Mountain Chapter, 868
Jimmie Heuga Center, 1397
National Association of Addiction Treatment Providers (NAATP), 1786
National Jewish Division of Immunology, 654
National Multiple Sclerosis Society: Wyoming Chapter, 1386
University of Colorado: General Clinical Research Center, Pediatric, 963
VA Western Colorado Health Care System, 2251
Yellow Ribbon Suicide Prevention Program, 1974

Connecticut

AARP Connecticut, 206
Alzheimer's Association: Connecticut, 373
First Candle, 109
HonorBound Foundation, 2067
Infoline, 1890
Infoline, 1983
JDRF: Fairfield County Chapter, 869
JDRF: Greater New Haven Chapter, 870
JDRF: North Central CT & Western MA, 871
National Veterans Services Fund, 2274
Sidran Institute, 2053
Sidran Traumatic Stress Institute, 1060
Sidran Traumatic Stress Institute, 2054
University of Connecticut Center on Aging, 294
University of Connecticut Osteoporosis Center, 1510
Yale Child Study Center, 2263
Yale Mood Disorders Research Program, 46
Yale Mood Disorders Research Program, 768

Delaware

AARP Delaware, 207
Attention Deficit Disorder Association, 679
Delaware Division of Substance Abuse and Mental Health (DSAMH), 1804
JDRF: Delaware Chapter, 872
Wilmington VA Medical Center, 2262

District of Columbia

AAA Foundation for Traffic Safety, 1826
AARP D.C., 257
AARP Foundation, 262
ABA Commission on Law and Aging, 173
Academy for Gerontology in Higher Education, 174
Academy for Gerontology in Higher Education, 267
Administration for Children and Families, 3
Administration for Children and Families, 623
Administration for Children and Families, 1088
Administration for Children and Families, 2012
Administration for Community Living, 2071
Agent Orange Registry Department of Veterans Affairs, 2016
American Academy of Child and Adolescent Psychiatry (AACAP), 2017
American Association of Retired Persons, 176
American Psychiatric Association, 5
American Psychiatric Association, 103
American Psychiatric Association, 509
American Psychiatric Association, 678
American Psychiatric Association, 747
American Psychiatric Association, 1003
American Psychiatric Association, 1050
American Psychiatric Association, 1090
American Psychiatric Association, 1450
American Psychiatric Association, 1523
American Psychiatric Association, 1578
American Psychiatric Association, 1697
American Psychiatric Association, 1764
American Psychiatric Association, 2020
American Psychological Association, 2021
American Public Health Association (APHA), 2022
American Society for Reproductive Medicine, 1330
Caregiver Action Network, 300
Center for Mind-Body Medicine, 2116
Disabled American Veterans Organization, 2032
Eating Disorders Coalition for Research, Policy and Action, 1099
George Washington University Center for Aging, Health and Humanities, 275
Gerontological Society of America, 181
HEATH Resource Center, 704
International Association for Suicide Prevention, 1966
JDRF: Capitol Chapter, 939
Leading Age, 188
Medstar Georgetown University Hospital Facility, 1227
National Academy on an Aging Society, 284
National Alliance for Caregiving, 192
National Alliance for Caregiving, 302
National Association of Social Workers (NASW), 2045
National Association of State Alcohol/Drug Abuse Directors, 1788
National Center for Learning Disabilities, 55
National Center for Learning Disabilities, 696
National Center for Learning Disabilities, 708
National Center for Victims of Crime, 2082
National Coalition for the Homeless, 1790
National Council for Behavioral Health, 23
National Council for Behavioral Health, 524
National Council for Behavioral Health, 1463
National Council for Behavioral Health, 1791
National Crime Prevention Council, 1792
National Institute for Occupational Safety and Health, 635
National Institute for Occupational Safety and Health, 1118
National Organization for People of Color Against Suicide (NOPCAS), 1971
National Sleep Foundation, 1620
National Women's Health Network, 1335
Nurse Practitioners in Women's Health, 1502
Office of Women's Health, 27
Office of Women's Health, 1122
Rape, Abuse & Incest National Network, 2281
Senior Resource LLC, 197
Students Against Destructive Decisions, 1834
Students Against Destructive Decisions (SADD), 1901
U.S. Department of Health and Human Services, 2057
US Administration on Aging, 198
US Department Of Veterans Affairs, 2090
VA Austin Information Technology Center, 2059
Washington DC VA Medical Center, 2255

Florida

AARP Florida: Doral, 208
AARP Florida: St. Petersburg, 209
AARP Florida: Tallahassee, 210
Alcohol and Drug Abuse Program, 1805
Alzheimer's Association: Central and North Florida, 376
Alzheimer's Association: Florida Gulf Coast, 377
Alzheimer's Association: Southeast Florida, 378
American Association of Caregiving Youth, 175
Bay Pines VA Healthcare System, 2103
Birth Defect Research for Children, Inc., 630
Center for Cognitive Neuroscience and Aging, 460
Center for the Study of Emotion and Attention, 2117
Coconut Creek Eating Disorders Support Group, 1146
Desert Storm Justice Foundation: Florida, 2064
Desert Storm Veterans of Florida, Inc., 2066
Florida Heart Research Institute, 1215
Food Addicts Anonymous, 1152
Goodwill Industries-Suncoast, 184
Goodwill Industries-Suncoast, 2149
Goodwill's Community Employment Services, 516
Goodwill's Community Employment Services, 1009
Goodwill's Community Employment Services, 1455
Goodwill's Community Employment Services, 1527
Goodwill's Community Employment Services, 1700
Goodwill's Community Employment Services, 2035
JDRF: Central Florida Chapter, 873
JDRF: Florida Sun Coast Chapter, 874
JDRF: Greater Palm Beach County Chapter, 855
JDRF: North Florida Chapter, 875
JDRF: South Florida Chapter, 876
JDRF: Tampa Bay Chapter, 877
James A. Haley Veterans' Hospital, 2163
Lake City VA Medical Center North Florida/South Georgia, 2171
MSWorld, 1401
Malcom Randall VA Medical Center North Florida/South Georgia, 2177
Metabolic Research Institute, 960
Miami VA Healthcare System, 2186
Mount Sinai Medical Center, 1228
Multiple Sclerosis Foundation, 1393
National Alliance for Eating Disorders, 1108
National Multiple Sclerosis Society: North Florida Chapter, 1389
National P.O.L.I.C.E. Suicide Foundation, 1979
Tallahassee Memorial Diabetes Center, 815
University of Florida Institute on Aging, 295
University of Miami School of Medicine Department of Neurology, 1740
University of Miami: Diabetes Research Institute, 967
West Palm Beach VA Medical Center, 2256

Georgia

AARP Georgia, 211
Agency for Toxic Substances and Disease Registry, 625
Agency for Toxic Substances and Disease Registry, 2015
Alcohol and Drug Services, 1806
Alzheimer's Association: Georgia, 379
Alzheimer's and Memory Disorders Clinic, 458
American Juvenile Arthritis Organization, 586
Arthritis Foundation, 590
Arthritis Foundation Information Helpline, 608
Atlanta VA Medical Center Atlanta VA Health Care System, 2097
Carl Vinson VA Medical Center Dublin VA Medical Center, 2111
Centers for Disease Control, 2030
Centers for Disease Control & Prevention: Division of Adolescent & School Health, 632
Centers for Disease Control & Prevention: Division of Adolescent & School Health, 1096
Charlie Norwood VA Medical Center, 2122
Division of Diabetes Translation, 809
Fertility Clinic at the Shepherd Spinal Center, 1344
Goizueta Alzheimer's Disease Research Center, 466
JDRF: Georgia Chapter, 878
Kids on the Block Arthritis Programs, 609
Mood and Anxiety Disorders Program of Emory University, 2192
National Association of Chronic Disease Directors, 1501
Office on Smoking and Health: Centers for Disease Control & Prevention, 1832
VA Southeast Network, 2249

Geographic Index / Hawaii

Hawaii

AARP Hawaii, 212
Alcohol and Drug Abuse Division, 1807
Alzheimer's Association: Hawaii, 380
JDRF: Hawaii Chapter, 879
Spark M. Matsunaga VA Medical Center VA Pacific Islands Health Care System, 2221

Idaho

AARP Idaho, 213
Alzheimer's Association: Greater Idaho, 381
Boise VA Medical Center, 2105
Idaho Persian Gulf Veterans, 2157

Illinois

AARP Illinois: Chicago, 214
AARP Illinois: Springfield, 215
Academy of Nutrition & Dietetics, 1087
Adventure Camp, 507
Alzheimer's Association, 349
Alzheimer's Association: Illinois, 382
American Association of Diabetes Care & Education Specialists, 803
American Association of Sexuality Educators, Counselors And Therapists, 1577
American College of Allergy, Asthma & Immunology, 645
American College of Allergy, Asthma & Immunology Foundation, 641
American Lung Association, 628
American Medical Association (AMA), 2019
Balanced Mind Parent Network, 8
Balanced Mind Parent Network, 48
Balanced Mind Parent Network, 769
Balanced Mind Parent Network, 1005
Captain James A. Lovell Federal Health Care Center, 2110
Center for Narcolepsy Research at the University of Illinois at Chicago, 1625
Cognitive Neurology and Alzheimer's Disease Center, 461
Compassionate Friends, Inc, 107
DBSA Support Groups: An Important Step on the Road to Wellness, 50
DBSA Support Groups: An Important Step on the Road to Wellness, 771
Depression & Bipolar Support Alliance, 11
Depression & Bipolar Support Alliance, 514
Depression & Bipolar Support Alliance, 749
Desert Storm Justice Foundation: Illinois, 2065
Division on Endocrinology Northwestern University Feinberg School, 953
Edward Hines Jr. VA Hospital, 2137
Families Anonymous, Inc., 1886
Green-Field Library-Alzheimer's Association, 445
Grief Recovery After a Substance Passing (GRASP), 111
Grief Recovery After a Substance Passing (GRASP), 123
Grief Recovery After a Substance Passing (GRASP), 1775
Illinois Department of Alcoholism and Susbstance Abuse, 1808
International Association of Eating Disorders Professionals Foundation, 1103
International Association of Eating Disorders Professionals Foundation, 1130
International Society for Traumatic Stress Studies, 2039
International Society for Traumatic Stress Studies, 2079
International Society for Traumatic Stress Studies, 2159
JDRF: Greater Chicago Chapter, 880
Jesse Brown VA Medical Center, 2165
Legal Council for Health Justice, 189
Loyola University of Chicago Cardiac Transplant Program, 1226
Male Sexual Dysfunction Clinic, 1314
Marion VA Medical Center, 2181
National Association of Anorexia Nervosa a Associated Disorders (ANAD), 1112
National Association of Anorexia Nervosa and Associated Disorders, 1111
National Association of Anorexia Nervosa and Associated Disorders Helpline, 1154
National Headache Foundation, 2069
Northwestern University: Division of Allergy and Immunology, 655
Rainbows, 117
Rainbows, 124
Recovery International, 58
Recovery International, 525
Recovery International, 773
Recovery International, 2282
Rush University Multiple Sclerosis Center, 1399
Section for Psychiatric and Substance Abuse Services (SPSPAS), 1800
Shirley Ryan AbilityLab, 605
Sleep Research Society (SRS), 1619
Sleep Research Society Foundation, 1621
Society of Mitral Valve Prolapse Syndrome, 1260
UI Health, 477
University of Chicago Dept of Neurology, 478
University of Chicago: Comprehensive Diabetes Center, 962
VA Great Lakes Health Care System, 2237
VA Illiana Health Care System, 2242

Indiana

AARP Indiana, 216
Alzheimer's Association: Greater Indiana, 383
Alzheimer's Support Group, 482
Diabetes Youth Foundation of Indiana, 854
Feingold Association of the US, 687
Fort Wayne Campus VA Northern Indiana Health Care System, 2144
GoldPoint Clinical Research, 2148
Indiana University Center for Aging Research, 468
Indiana University School of Medicine Center for Aging Research, 278
Indiana University: Area Health Education Center, 955
Indiana University: Center for Diabetes Research, 956
Indiana University: Human Genetics Center of Medical & Molecular Genetics, 469
Indiana University: Hypertension Research Center, 1279
Indiana University: Pharmacology Research Laboratory, 957
JDRF: Indiana State Chapter, 881
JDRF: Northern Indiana Chapter, 882
Krannert Institute of Cardiology, 1225
Marion Campus VA Northern Indiana Health Care System, 2180
MidWest Medical Center: Sleep Disorders Center, 1634
Multipurpose Arthritis and Musculoskeletal Disease Center, 601
Purdue University William A Hillenbrand Biomedical Engineering Center, 1232
Purdue University: Center for Research on Aging and the Life Course, 285
Sleep Alertness Center: Lafayette Home Hospital, 1640
Sleep/Wake Disorders Center: Community Hospitals of Indianapolis, 1668

Iowa

AARP Iowa, 217
Alzheimer's Association: Iowa, 384
Department of Public Health: Division of Substance Abuse, 1810
Iowa City VA Health Care System, 2160
JDRF: Eastern Iowa Chapter, 883
JDRF: Greater Iowa Chapter, 884
University of Iowa College of Medicine, 1738
University of Iowa Mental Health Clinical Research Center, 1544
University of Iowa: Diabetes Research Center, 964
University of Iowa: Iowa Cardiovascular Center, 1241
VA Central Iowa Health Care System, 2236

Kansas

AARP Kansas, 218
Alzheimer's Association: Central and Western Kansas, 385
Alzheimer's Association: Heart of America, 386
American Chronic Pain Association, 585
American Chronic Pain Association, 1380
American Chronic Pain Association, 1499
American Chronic Pain Association, 1613
American Chronic Pain Association, 1763
American Chronic Pain Association, 2018
American Stroke Foundation, 1730
Colmery-O'Neil VA Medical Center VA Eastern Kansas Health Care System, 2129
Dwight D. Eisenhower VA Medical Center VA Eastern Kansas Health Care System, 2134
Good Shepherd Homecare & Hospice, 182
Kansas State University Center on Aging, 281
Landon Center on Aging University of Kansas Medical Center, 282
Robert J. Dole VA Medical Center, 2209
University of Kansas Cray Diabetes Center, 965

Kentucky

AARP Kentucky, 219
Alzheimer's Association: Greater Kentucky and Soutern Indiana, 387
Alzheimer's Disease Center Kentucky University, 449
Depressed Anonymous, 51
JDRF: Kentuckiana Chapter, 885
Lexington VA Health Care System, 2173
Parents Resource Institute for Drug Education, 1833
Robley Rex VA Medical Center Louisville VA Medical Center, 2210
Sanders-Brown Center on Aging University of Kentucky, 287

Louisiana

AARP Louisiana: Baton Rouge, 220
AARP Louisiana: New Orleans, 221
Alcohol and Drug Abuse Council of South Louisiana, 1811
Alexandria VA Healthcare System, 2095
Clinical Immunology, Allergy, and Rheumatology, 648
JDRF: Baton Rouge Chapter, 886
JDRF: Louisiana Chapter, 887
JDRF: Shreveport Chapter, 888
Overton Brooks VA Medical Center, 2201
Southeast Louisiana Veterans Health Care System, 2219
Tulane University Center For Aging, 291

Maine

AARP Maine, 222
Alzheimer's Association: Maine, 388
Gift From Within, 2077
JDRF: New England/Maine Chapter, 891
Maine VA Medical Center VA Maine Healthcare System, 2176
Sleep Laboratory, Maine Medical Center, 1664

Maryland

AARP Maryland, 223
ABMRF/The Foundation for Alcohol Research, 1827
Academy of Psychosomatic Medicine, 2
Academy of Psychosomatic Medicine, 506
Academy of Psychosomatic Medicine, 746
Academy of Psychosomatic Medicine, 1049
Academy of Psychosomatic Medicine, 1696
Academy of Psychosomatic Medicine, 1759

613

Geographic Index / Massachusetts

Agency for Healthcare Research and Quality, 624
Agency for Healthcare Research and Quality, 1089
Agency for Healthcare Research and Quality, 2014
Alzheimer's Association: Greater Maryland, 389
Alzheimer's Disease & Related Dementias, 444
Alzheimer's Disease Center: Johns Hopkins University School of Medicine, 452
American Society of Addiction Medicine, 1766
American Urological Association, 1331
American Urological Association, 1581
American Urological Association (AUA), 1306
Anxiety Disorders Association of America, 2024
Anxiety and Depression Association of America, 6
Anxiety and Depression Association of America, 510
Anxiety and Depression Association of America, 1451
Baltimore VA Medical Center VA Maryland Health Care System, 2099
Center for Mental Health Services, 2115
Center for Mental Health Services (CMHS), 10
Center for Mental Health Services (CMHS), 106
Center for Mental Health Services (CMHS), 351
Center for Mental Health Services (CMHS), 511
Center for Mental Health Services (CMHS), 682
Center for Mental Health Services (CMHS), 748
Center for Mental Health Services (CMHS), 1007
Center for Mental Health Services (CMHS), 1052
Center for Mental Health Services (CMHS), 1094
Center for Mental Health Services (CMHS), 1453
Center for Mental Health Services (CMHS), 1526
Center for Mental Health Services (CMHS), 1584
Center for Mental Health Services (CMHS), 1699
Center for Mental Health Services (CMHS), 1768
Center for Mental Health Services (CMHS), 2029
Center for Substance Abuse Prevention: Substance Abuse & Mental Health Services, 1769
Center for the Study of Traumatic Stress, 2075
Center for the Study of Traumatic Stress, 2118
Centers for Medicare & Medicaid Services, 633
Centers for Medicare & Medicaid Services, 1097
Centers for Medicare & Medicaid Services, 2031
Chemically Dependent Anonymous, 1882
Children & Adults with Attention Deficit /Hyperactivity Disorder, 684
Children and Adults with AD/HD (CHADD), 685
Children and Adults with AD/HD (CHADD), 707
Diabetes Action Network for the Blind, 807
Drug Free Workplace Hotline, 1885
Epidemiology-Genetics Program in Psychiatr, 764
Friends Medical Science Research Center, 1843
Goodwill Industries International, Inc., 183
Goodwill Industries International, Inc., 688
Goodwill Industries International, Inc., 2034
Impotents Anonymous, 1316
Indian Health Service, 1777
International Critical Incident Stress Foundation, 2068
International Foundation for Research and Education on Depression (iFred), 37
JDRF: Maryland Chapter, 889
Johns Hopkins Center on Aging and Health, 280
Johns Hopkins University: Asthma and Allergy Center, 650
Johns Hopkins University: Behavioral Pharmacology Research Unit, 1847
Johns Hopkins University: Sleep Disorders Francis Scott Key Medical Center, 1630
Joslin Center at University of Maryland Medicine, 810
Kennedy-Krieger Institute, 2080
Loch Raven VA Community Living & Rehabilitation Center, 2271
Maryland Psychiatric Research Center, 1540
Mood Disorders Center, 18
Mood Disorders Center, 753
Myositis Association of America, 588
NCADD, 1783
NIH Osteoporosis and Related Bone Diseases - National Resource Center, 1506
National Association for Children of Alcoholics (NACOA), 1785
National Center for Complementary and Integrative Health, 22
National Center for Complementary and Integrative Health, 651

National Center for Complementary and Integrative Health, 1114
National Center for Complementary and Integrative Health, 2047
National Diabetes Information Clearinghouse, 812
National Federation of Families for Children's Mental Health, 24
National Federation of Families for Children's Mental Health, 56
National Federation of Families for Children's Mental Health, 697
National Health Information Center, 57
National Health Information Center, 303
National Health Information Center, 484
National Health Information Center, 610
National Health Information Center, 658
National Health Information Center, 709
National Health Information Center, 979
National Health Information Center, 1157
National Health Information Center, 1258
National Health Information Center, 1286
National Health Information Center, 1317
National Health Information Center, 1351
National Health Information Center, 1403
National Health Information Center, 1427
National Health Information Center, 1512
National Health Information Center, 1547
National Health Information Center, 1675
National Health Information Center, 1743
National Health Information Center, 1897
National Health Information Center, 2273
National Heart, Lung & Blood Institute, 1201
National Heart, Lung & Blood Institute, 1273
National Heart, Lung & Blood Institute, 1728
National Human Genome Research Institute, 634
National Human Genome Research Institute, 1117
National Human Genome Research Institute, 2048
National Institute of Allergy and Infectious Diseases, 636
National Institute of Arthritis & Musculoskeletal & Skin Diseases, 589
National Institute of Arthritis & Musculoskeletal & Skin Diseases, 602
National Institute of Biomedical Imaging and Bioengineering, 637
National Institute of Diabetes & Digestive & Kidney Diseases, 813
National Institute of Diabetes & Digestive & Kidney Diseases, 1310
National Institute of General Medical Sciences, 653
National Institute of General Medical Sciences, 2050
National Institute of Mental Health, 26
National Institute of Mental Health, 42
National Institute of Mental Health, 536
National Institute of Mental Health, 698
National Institute of Mental Health, 765
National Institute of Mental Health, 1464
National Institute of Mental Health, 1533
National Institute of Mental Health, 1970
National Institute of Mental Health, 2051
National Institute of Mental Health, 2083
National Institute of Mental Health, 2195
National Institute of Mental Health Eating Disorders Research Program, 1120
National Institute of Neurological Disorders and Stroke, 1382
National Institute of Neurological Disorders and Stroke, 1618
National Institute of Neurological Disorders and Stroke, 1729
National Institute of Nursing Research, 638
National Institute on Aging, 195
National Institute on Aging, 354
National Institute on Alcohol Abuse and Alcoholism (NIAAA), 1794
National Institute on Drug Abuse (NIDA), 1795
National Prevention Resource Center CSAP Division of Communications Programs, 1852
National Volunteer Training Center for Substance Abuse Prevention, 1853
New York Obesity/Nutrition Research Center, 1424
Office of Women's Services: Substance Abuse & Mental Health Services, 1796
Perry Point VA Medical Center VA Maryland Health Care System, 2202

Pulmonary Hypertension Association, 1202
Pulmonary Hypertension Association (PHA), 1203
Pulmonary Hypertension Association (PHA), 1275
Schizophrenia Research Branch: Division of Clinical and Treatment Research, 1541
Society For Post-Acute and Long-Term Care Medicine, 1504
Society of Federal Health Professionals (AMSUS), 2055
St. Joseph's Medical Center, 1141
Substance Abuse and Mental Health Services Administration (SAMHSA), 1801
U.S. Food and Drug Administration, 639
U.S. Food and Drug Administration, 1124
University of Maryland Center for Studies of Cerebrovascular Disease & Stroke, 1739
University of Maryland School of Public Health Center on Aging, 296
University of Maryland: Division of Infectious Diseases, 479
Urban Cardiology Research Center, 1253
Urology Care Foundation, 1313
VA Capitol Health Care Network, 2234
Warren Grant Magnuson Clinical Center, 607
Warren Grant Magnuson Clinical Center, 976
Warren Grant Magnuson Clinical Center, 1254
Weight-Control Information Network, 1126
Weight-Control Information Network, 1135
Weight-Control Information Network, 1420
Weight-Control Information Network, 1421

Massachusetts

AARP Massachusetts, 224
Affiliated Children's Arthritis Centers of New England, 591
Alzheimer's Association: Massachusetts and New Hampshire, 390
Alzheimer's Disease Center: Boston University, 451
Association of Gastrointestinal Motility Disorders, 1091
Attention Deficit Information Network, 706
Bipolar Clinic and Research Program, 761
Boston University Arthritis Center, 593
Boston University Clinical & Translational Science Institute, 594
Boston University Laboratory of Neuropsychology, 1836
Boston University, Whitaker Cardiovascular Institute, 1208
Brigham and Women's Hospital: Center for Neurologic Diseases, 1395
Brigham and Women's Hospital: Rheumatology Immunology, and Allergy Division, 646
Brigham and Women's Orthopedica and Arthritis Center, 595
Brockton Division VA Boston Healthcare System, 2106
Bureau of Substance Addiction Services, 1812
Center for Anxiety and Related Disorders at Boston University, 2112
Center on Aging and Work at Boston College, 271
Childrens Hospital Immunology Division Children's Hospital, 647
Edith Nourse Rogers Memorial Veterans Hospital: Bedford VA, 2136
Fertility and Women's Health Care Center, 1345
Framingham Heart Study, 1216
General Clinical Research Center at Beth Israel Hospital, 1217
Harris Center for Education and Advocacy in Eating Disorders, 1139
Harvard Clinical Nutrition Research Center, 1422
Harvard Cocaine Recovery Project, 1845
Harvard Throndike Laboratory Harvard Medical Center, 1220
International OCD Foundation, 1458
International OCD Foundation, Inc., 1469
JDRF: New England/Bay State Chapter, 890
Jamaica Plain Division VA Boston Healthcare System, 2162
Jean Mayer USDA Human Nutrition Research Center on Aging at Tufts University, 279
Joslin Diabetes Center, 959

Geographic Index / Michigan

Massachusetts Alzheimers Disease Research Center, 472
Massachusetts Eating Disorder Association, 1127
Massachusetts General Departments of Neurology and Neurosurgery, 1736
MindWise Innovations, 17
MindWise Innovations, 1106
MindWise Innovations, 1781
Multiservice Eating Disorders Association, 1107
Multiservice Eating Disorders Association, 1133
RESOLVE: New England, 1336
Shriver Center University Affiliated Program, 2087
Sleep Disorders Unit Beth Israel Deaconess Medical Center, 1662
Suicide Prevention Resource Center, 1980
Suicide Prevention Resource Center, 2088
Traditional Tibetan Healing, 1404
Trauma Center, 2089
Trauma Center, 2228
University of Massachusetts: Diabetes and Endocrinology Research Center, 966
Veterans Benefits Clearinghouse, 2060
West Roxbury Division VA Boston Healthcare System, 2257

Michigan

A.I.M. Agoraphobics in Motion, 1
A.I.M. Agoraphobics in Motion, 47
A.I.M. Agoraphobics in Motion, 505
AARP Michigan, 225
Aleda E. Lutz VA Medical Center: Saginaw, Michigan, 2094
Alzheimer's Association: Greater Michigan, 391
American Autoimmune Related Diseases Association, 1197
Anxiety Resource Center, 2072
Battle Creek VA Medical Center, 2102
Common Ground Sanctuary, 1018
Common Ground Sanctuary, 1147
Common Ground Sanctuary, 1545
Common Ground Sanctuary, 1884
Common Ground Sanctuary, 1981
Common Ground Sanctuary, 2267
Henry Ford Hospital: Hypertension and Vascular Research Division, 1278
JDRF: Metropolitan Detroit/SE Michigan, 892
JDRF: West Michigan Chapter, 893
John D. Dingell VA Medical Center, 2166
Kleptomaniacs Anonymous, 1021
Michigan Alzheimer's Disease Research Center, 473
Oscar G. Johnson VA Medical Center, 2200
Shulman Center for Compulsive Theft, Spending & Hoarding, 1014
Thriving Minds, 32
Thriving Minds, 530
University of Michigan Pulmonary and Critical Care Division, 1242
University of Michigan Reproductive Sciences Program, 1348
University of Michigan: Alcohol Research Center, 1865
University of Michigan: Cardiovascular Medicine, 1243
University of Michigan: Division of Hypertension, 1281
University of Michigan: Orthopaedic Research Laboratories, 606
University of Michigan: Psychiatric Center, 1866
VA Ann Arbor Healthcare System, 2232
Wayne State University: University Women's Care, 1350

Minnesota

AARP Minnesota, 226
African American Family Services (AAFS), 1761
Alzheimer's Association: Minnesota and North Dakota, 392
Alzheimer's Disease Center Mayo Clinic Mayo Medical School, 450
Desert Storm Justice Foundation: Minnesota, 2063
Emotions Anonymous International Service Center, 52
Emotions Anonymous International Service Center, 542
Hazelden Betty Ford Foundation, 1829
Impulse Control Disorders Clinic, 1017
International Diabetes Center at Nicollet, 958
International Society for the Study of Women's Sexual Health (ISSWSH), 1587
JDRF: Minnesota Chapter, 894
Lawyers Concerned for Lawyers, 1779
Melpomene Institute for Women's Health Research, 1346
Minneapolis VA Health Care System, 2190
Minnesota Obesity Center, 1423
PACER Center, 28
PACER Center, 700
Schulze Diabetes Institute, 814
Sexual Medicine Society of North America, 1311
Sexual Medicine Society of North America, 1591
Suicide Awareness Voices of Education (SAV), 1972
University of Minnesota: Hypertensive Research Group, 1282
University of Minnesota: Program on Alcohol/Drug Control, 1867
WithAll, 1131

Mississippi

AARP Mississippi, 227
G.V. (Sonny) Montgomery VA Medical Center, 2145
Gulf Coast Veterans Health Care System, 2150
South Central VA Health Care Network, 2218

Missouri

AARP Missouri, 228
Alzheimer's Association: Greater Missouri, 394
Alzheimer's Disease Research Center Washington University School of Medicine, 456
American Diabetes Association: Missouri, 835
Asthma and Allergy Foundation of America: St. Louis Chapter, 643
Central Missouri Regional Arthritis Center Stephen's College Campus, 596
Harry S. Truman Memorial Veterans' Hospital, 2153
Harvey A Friedman Center for Aging Washington University, 276
JDRF: St. Louis Chapter, 895
John J. Pershing VA Medical Center, 2167
Kansas City VA Medical Center, 2169
National Share Office, 116
Pathways to Promise, 1898
University of Missouri Columbia Division of Cardiothoracic Surgery, 1244
University of Missouri: Kansas City Drug Information Service, 1868
VA Heartland Network, 2241
VA St. Louis Health Care System John Cochran & Jefferson Barracks, 2250
Washington University School of Medicine, 1742
Washington University: Diabetes Research and Training Center, 977

Montana

AARP Montana, 229
Alzheimer's Association: Montana, 395
Medical Center & Ambulatory Care Clinic Montana VA Health Care System, 2184
Miles City VA Clinic & Community Living Center, 2188

Nebraska

AARP Nebraska: Lincoln, 230
AARP Nebraska: Omaha, 231
Caregiver Support Services, 301
Creighton University Cardiac Center, 1213
Creighton University Midwest Hypertension Research Center, 1276
Department of Public Instruction: Division of Alcoholism and Drug Abuse, 1813
Home Instead Center for Successful Aging University of Nebraska Medical Center, 277
JDRF: Lincoln Chapter, 896
JDRF: Omaha Council Bluffs Chapter, 897

Nevada

AARP Nevada, 232
Alzheimer's Association: Northern Nevada, 397
Alzheimer's Association: Southern Nevada, 398
JDRF: Nevada Chapter, 898
JDRF: Northern Nevada Branch, 899
National Association to Advance Fat Acceptance (NAAFA), 1113
National Association to Advance Fat Acceptance (NAAFA), 1417
North Las Vegas VA Medical Center VA Southern Nevada Healthcare System, 2197
Sanford Center for Aging University Of Nevada, Reno, 288
VA Sierra Nevada Health Care System, 2248

New Hampshire

AARP New Hampshire, 233
JDRF: New England/New Hampshire Chapter, 900
Manchester VA Medical Center VAMC Manchester, New Hampshire, 2178
Sleep Disorders Center Dartmouth Hitchcock Medical Center, 1644
Sleep/Wake Disorders Center: Hampstead Hospital, 1669

New Jersey

AARP New Jersey, 234
Alzheimer's Association: Greater New Jersey, 399
COPLINE, 2265
Center for Parent Information & Resources, 683
East Orange Campus VA New Jersey Health Care System, 2135
Eating Disorders Association of New Jersey, 1150
HealthyWomen, 1333
Huxley Insititute-American Schizophrenic Association, 1539
JDRF: Central Jersey Chapter, 901
JDRF: Mid-Jersey Chapter, 902
JDRF: Rockland County/Northern New Jersey Chapter, 903
JDRF: South Jersey Chapter, 904
Lyons Campus VA New Jersey Health Care System, 2175
Multiple Sclerosis Association of America, 1381
National Multiple Sclerosis Society: New Jersey Metro Chapter, 1388
New Jersey Division of Mental Health and Addiction Services, 1814
Rutgers University Center of Alcohol Studies, 1858
Sleep Disorders Center: Newark Beth Israel Medical Center, 1657
Well Spouse Association, 304

New Mexico

AARP New Mexico, 235
Alzheimer's Association: New Mexico, 400
JDRF: Albuquerque Chapter, 905
Overeaters Anonymous, 1428
Overeaters Anonymous General Service Offic, 1158
Raymond G. Murphy VA Medical Center New Mexico VA Health Care System, 2207
University of New Mexico General Clinical Research Center, 968

New York

AARP New York: Albany, 236

615

Geographic Index / New York

AARP New York: New York City, 237
AARP New York: Rochester, 238
Aging In America, 263
Albany Stratton VA Medical Center, 2093
Alcoholics Anonymous, 1880
Alcoholics Anonymous (AA): World Services, 1881
Alzheimer's Association: Central New York, 402
Alzheimer's Association: Hudson Valley, 401
Alzheimer's Association: Long Island, 403
Alzheimer's Association: New York City, 404
Alzheimer's Association: Northeastern New York, 405
Alzheimer's Association: Rochester and Finger Lakes Region, 406
Alzheimer's Association: Western New York, 407
Alzheimer's Foundation of America, 442
American Federation for Aging Research, 264
American Foundation for Suicide Prevention, 1975
Anxiety and Phobia Treatment Center, 534
Association for Behavioral and Cognitive Therapies, 7
Association for Behavioral and Cognitive Therapies, 1004
Association for Behavioral and Cognitive Therapies, 2025
Batavia VA Medical Center VA Western New York Healthcare System, 2100
Bath VA Medical Center, 2101
Bereaved Parents of the USA, 104
Brain & Behavior Research Foundation, 35
Brain & Behavior Research Foundation, 532
Brain & Behavior Research Foundation, 703
Brain & Behavior Research Foundation, 758
Brain & Behavior Research Foundation, 1129
Brain & Behavior Research Foundation, 1468
Brain & Behavior Research Foundation, 1524
Brain & Behavior Research Foundation, 1536
Brain & Behavior Research Foundation, 1538
Brain & Behavior Research Foundation, 1828
Brain & Behavior Research Foundation, 1976
Brain & Behavior Research Foundation, 2061
Brooklyn Campus VA NY Harbor Health Care System, 2107
Buffalo VA Medical Center VA Western New York Healthcare System, 2108
Canandaigua VA Medical Center VA Health Care Upstate New York, 2109
Capital Regional Sleep-Wake Disorders Center, 1624
Center for Family Support, 49
Center for Family Support, 105
Center for Family Support, 122
Center for Family Support, 541
Center for Family Support, 681
Center for Family Support, 770
Center for Family Support, 1006
Center for Family Support, 1051
Center for Family Support, 1093
Center for Family Support, 1452
Center for Family Support, 1525
Center for Family Support, 1582
Center for Family Support, 1698
Center for Family Support, 2028
Center for Family Support (CFS), 9
Center for Family Support (CFS), 1767
Center for Sleep Medicine of the Mount Sinai Medical Center, 1628
Center for the Study of Anorexia and Bulimia, 1095
Center for the Study of Anorexia and Bulimia, 1137
Columbia University Irving Center for Clinical Research Adult Unit, 1212
Columbia University Pediatric Anxiety and Mood Research Clinic, 41
Columbia University Pediatric Anxiety and Mood Research Clinic, 535
Columbia University Robert N. Butler Aging Center, 272
Cornell University: Winifred Masterson Burke Medical Research-Dementia, 462
Cornerstone Treatment Facilities Network, 1839
Council on Size and Weight Discrimination (CSWD), 1098
Covenant House Nineline, 1982
Dana Foundation, 2062
Division of Digestive & Liver Diseases of Cloumbia University, 1138

Eating Disorder Resource Center, 1148
Endocrinology Research Laboratory Cabrini Medical Center, 954
First Presbyterian Church in the City of New York Support Groups, 1151
First Presbyterian Church in the City of New York Support Groups, 1887
Freedom From Fear, 12
Freedom From Fear, 515
Freedom From Fear, 543
Freedom From Fear, 2033
Gam-Anon Family Groups International Servi Office, Inc., 1019
Greater New York Metro Intergroup of Overeaters Anonymous, 1426
Heart Disease Research Foundation, 1221
Holliswood Hospital Psychiatric Care, Services and Self-Help/Support Groups, 54
Holliswood Hospital Psychiatric Care, Services and Self-Help/Support Groups, 483
Holliswood Hospital Psychiatric Care, Services and Self-Help/Support Groups, 544
Holliswood Hospital Psychiatric Care, Services and Self-Help/Support Groups, 772
Holliswood Hospital Psychiatric Care, Services and Self-Help/Support Groups, 1153
Holliswood Hospital Psychiatric Care, Services and Self-Help/Support Groups, 1546
Holliswood Hospital Psychiatric Care, Services and Self-Help/Support Groups, 1593
Holliswood Hospital Psychiatric Care, Services and Self-Help/Support Groups, 2270
Hope for Depression Research Foundation, 14
Hope for Depression Research Foundation, 518
Hope for Depression Research Foundation, 750
Hope for Depression Research Foundation, 1054
Hope for Depression Research Foundation, 1963
Hope for Depression Research Foundation, 2037
Icahn School of Medicine at Mount Sinai, 467
Images Within: A Child's View of Parental Alcoholism, 1889
Institute for Basic Research in Developmental Disabilities, 470
Institute for Contemporary Psychotherapy, 15
Institute for Contemporary Psychotherapy, 112
Institute for Contemporary Psychotherapy, 519
Institute for Contemporary Psychotherapy, 690
Institute for Contemporary Psychotherapy, 751
Institute for Contemporary Psychotherapy, 1055
Institute for Contemporary Psychotherapy, 1102
Institute for Contemporary Psychotherapy, 1457
Institute for Contemporary Psychotherapy, 1528
Institute for Contemporary Psychotherapy, 1586
Institute for Contemporary Psychotherapy, 1701
Institute for Contemporary Psychotherapy, 1778
Institute for Contemporary Psychotherapy, 1964
Institute for Contemporary Psychotherapy, 2038
JDRF: Buffalo/Western New York Chapter, 906
JDRF: Hudson Valley Chapter, 907
JDRF: Long Island/South Shore Chapter, 908
JDRF: New York Chapter, 909
JDRF: Northeastern New York Chapter, 910
JDRF: Rochester Branch/Western New York Chapter, 911
JDRF: Westchester County Chapter, 912
Jed Foundation, 38
John A. Hartford Foundation, 266
Juvenile Diabetes Research Foundation International, 857
Long Island Alzheimers & Dementia Center, 471
MS Toll-Free Information Line, 1400
Manhattan VA Medical Center VA NY Harbor Health Care System, 2179
Montrose Campus: Franklin Delano Roosevelt VA Hudson Valley Health Care System, 2191
Multiple Sclerosis Action Group, 1402
Naomi Berrie Diabetes Center at Columbia University Medical Center, 811
Narcolepsy Institute/Montefiore Medical Center, 1673
Narcotic and Drug Research, 1850
National Association for the Dually Diagnosed (NADD), 21
National Association for the Dually Diagnosed (NADD), 114

National Association for the Dually Diagnosed (NADD), 522
National Association for the Dually Diagnosed (NADD), 694
National Association for the Dually Diagnosed (NADD), 755
National Association for the Dually Diagnosed (NADD), 1012
National Association for the Dually Diagnosed (NADD), 1058
National Association for the Dually Diagnosed (NADD), 1110
National Association for the Dually Diagnosed (NADD), 1462
National Association for the Dually Diagnosed (NADD), 1532
National Association for the Dually Diagnosed (NADD), 1589
National Association for the Dually Diagnosed (NADD), 1703
National Association for the Dually Diagnosed (NADD), 2044
National Association on Drug Abuse Problems, 1789
National Center on Addiction and Substance Abuse, 1851
National Eating Disorders Association, 1116
National Eating Disorders Association Helpline, 1156
National Infertility Network Exchange, 1352
National Multiple Sclerosis Society, 1385
New York Male Reproductive Center: Sexual Dysfunction Unit, 1315
New York Office of Addiction Services and Supports, 1815
New York University General Clinical Research Center, 1280
New York/New Jersey VA Health Care Network, 2196
Northport VA Medical Center, 2198
Obesity Research Center, 1140
Obesity Research Center St. Luke's-Roosevelt Hospital, 1425
Obsessive-Compulsive Anonymous, 1472
Partnership to End Addiction, 1797
Recovered, 1798
Regional Bone Center Helen Hayes Hospital, 1509
Remove Intoxicated Drivers (RID-USA), 1799
Research Institute on Alcoholism, 1855
Rockefeller University Laboratory of Biology, 1857
Rockefeller University Laboratory of Cardiac Physiology, 1233
Sleep Center: Community General Hospital, 1641
Sleep Disorders Center Columbia Presbyterian Medical Center, 1643
Sleep Disorders Center of Rochester: St. Mary's Hospital, 1649
Sleep Disorders Center of Western New York Millard Fillmore Hospital, 1650
Sleep Disorders Center: University Hospital, SUNY at Stony Brook, 1660
Sleep Disorders Center: Winthrop, University Hospital, 1661
Sleep Laboratory, 1663
Sleep/Wake Disorders Center Montefiore Sleep Disorders Center, 1667
Sleep/Wake Disorders Center: New York Hospital-Cornell Medical Center, 1670
St. Agnes Hospital Medical: Health Science Library, 1394
State University of New York at Buffalo Toxicology Research Center, 1862
Support for Asthmatic Youth, 660
Syracuse VA Medical Center, 2224
Taub Institute for Research on Alzheimers Disease and the Aging Brain, 475
Territorial Apprehensiveness (TERRAP) Anxiety & Stress Program, 31
Territorial Apprehensiveness (TERRAP) Anxiety & Stress Program, 529
Territorial Apprehensiveness (TERRAP) Anxiety & Stress Program, 1466
Territorial Apprehensiveness (TERRAP) Anxiety & Stress Program, 2056
University of Rochester: Clinical Research Center, 1247

Geographic Index / North Carolina

Yeshiva University General Clinical Research Center, 1255
Yeshiva University: Resnick Gerontology Center, 480

North Carolina

AARP North Carolina, 239
Alzheimer's Association: Eastern North Carolina, 408
Alzheimer's Disease Research Center Duke University, 457
American Sexual Health Association (ASHA), 1579
Charles George VA Medical Center, 2121
Department of Pediatrics, Division of Rheumatology, 597
Dorothea Dix Hospital Clinical Research Unit, 1840
Duke Asthma, Allergy and Airway Center, 649
Duke University Center for the Study of Aging and Human Development, 274
Duke University Center for the Study of Aging and Human Development, 464
Duke University Clinical Research Institute, 465
Duke University Pediatric Cardiac Catheterization Laboratory, 1214
Durham VA Health Care System, 2133
Families in Action, 1842
Fayetteville VA Medical Center, 2142
JDRF: Charlotte Chapter, 913
JDRF: Piedmont Triad Chapter, 914
JDRF: Triangle/Eastern North Carolina Chapter, 915
National Institute of Environmental Health Sciences, 25
National Institute of Environmental Health Sciences, 652
National Institute of Environmental Health Sciences, 1119
National Institute of Environmental Health Sciences, 2049
North Carolina Mental Health and Substance Abuse, 1816
University Of North Carolina School of Medicine Center for Aging and Health, 292
W. G. (Bill) Hefner VA Medical Center, 2254
Wake Forest University: Arteriosclerosis Research Center, 1285
Wake Forest University: Cerebrovascular Research Center, 1741

North Dakota

AARP North Dakota, 240
Fargo VA Health Care System, 2141
Healthy Weight Network, 1100
Help is Here, 13
Help is Here, 517
Help is Here, 689
Help is Here, 1010
Help is Here, 1053
Help is Here, 1101
Help is Here, 1456
Help is Here, 1776
Help is Here, 1962
Help is Here, 2036

Ohio

AARP Ohio, 241
Alive Alone, 102
Alzheimer's Association: Central Ohio, 410
Alzheimer's Association: Cleveland Area, 411
Alzheimer's Association: Greater East Ohio, 412
Alzheimer's Association: Miami Valley, 413
Alzheimer's Association: Northwest Ohio, 414
Brain Health and Memory Center Research, 459
Case Western Reserve University: Center on Aging and Health, 269
Center for Research in Sleep Disorders Affiliated with Mercy Hospital, 1626
Center for Sleep & Wake Disorders: Miami Valley Hospital, 1627
Chalmers P. Wylie Ambulatory Care Center VA Central Ohio Healthcare System, 2120
Chillicothe VA Medical Center, 2125
Cincinnati VA Medical Center, 2126
Cleveland Clinic Lerner Research Institute, 1211
Cleveland VA Medical Center VA Northeast Ohio Healthcare System, 2127
Dayton VA Medical Center, 2132
Department of Psychology, 463
JDRF: Akron/Canton Chapter, 916
JDRF: Greater Cincinnati Chapter, 917
JDRF: Mid-Ohio Chapter, 918
JDRF: Toledo/Northwest Ohio Chapter, 919
Kettering-Scott Magnetic Resonance Laboratory, 1848
Mitral Valve Prolapse Program of Cincinnati Support Group, 1257
National Multiple Sclerosis Society: Ohio Chapter, 1390
National Organization of Parents of Murdered Children, 115
Northwest Ohio Sleep Disorders Center Toledo Hospital, 1635
Ohio Sleep Medicine Institute, 1636
Ohio State University Clinical Pharmacology Division, 1854
SMART Recovery, 1900
Sleep Disorders Center Bethesda Oak Hospital, 1642
Sleep Disorders Center Ohio State University Medical Center, 1646
Sleep Disorders Center: Cleveland Clinic Foundation, 1651
Sleep Disorders Center: Kettering Medical Center, 1655
Sleep Disorders Center: St. Vincent Medical Center, 1659
University of Cincinnati Department of Pathology & Laboratory Medicine, 1240
VA Healthcare System of Ohio, 2239

Oklahoma

AARP Oklahoma, 242
Alzheimer's Association: Oklahoma, 415
JDRF: Central Oklahoma Chapter, 920
JDRF: Tulsa Green County Chapter, 921
Jack C. Montgomery VA Medical Center Eastern Oklahoma VA Health Care System, 2161
Oklahoma City VA Health Care System, 2199
Oklahoma Department of Mental Health and Substance Abuse Services, 1817
Oklahoma Medical Research Foundation, 603
Oklahoma Medical Research Foundation: Cardiovascular Research Program, 1229

Oregon

AARP Oregon, 243
Aging and Alzheimer's Disease Center Oregon Health Sciences University, 446
Alzheimer's Association: Oregon and SW Washington, 416
Center for Women's Health, 1585
Comprehensive Stroke Center of Oregon, 1733
JDRF: Oregon/SW Washington Chapter, 922
National Association of State Directors of Veterans Affairs, 2046
Portland VA Medical Center VA Portland Health Care System, 2204
Postpartum Support International, 29
Roseburg VA Health Care System, 2211
White City VA Rehabilitation Center VA Southern Oregon, 2258

Pennsylvania

AARP Pennsylvania: Harrisburg, 244
AARP Pennsylvania: Philadelphia, 245
Alzheimer's Association: Delaware, 374
Alzheimer's Association: Delaware Valley, 417
Alzheimer's Association: Greater Pennsylvania, 418
American Association of Suicidology, 1960
Bipolar Research Program at University of Pennsylvania, 763
Bockus Research Institute Graduate Hospital, 1207
Children of Aging Parents, 178
Children's and Adult Center for OCD an Anxiety, 513
Children's and Adult Center for OCD and Anxiety, 512
Children's and Adult Center for OCD and Anxiety, 1454
Coatesville VA Medical Center, 2128
Corporal Michael J. Crescenz VA Medical Center, 2131
Diabetes Education and Research Center The Franklin House, 951
Erie VA Medical Center, 2139
Geisinger Wyoming Valley Medical Center: Sleep Disorders Center, 1629
H.J. Heinz Campus VA Pittsburgh Healthcare System, 2151
Hahnemann University Hospital, Orthopedic Wellness Center, 598
Hahnemann University Laboratory of Human Pharmacology, 1844
Hahnemann University Likoff Cardiovascular Institute, 1219
Hahnemann University: Division of Surgical Research, 1277
Hospital of the University of Pennsylvania, 1735
JDRF: Berks County Chapter, 923
JDRF: Central Pennsylvania Chapter, 924
JDRF: Northwestern Pennsylvania Chapter, 925
JDRF: Philadelphia Chapter, 926
JDRF: Western Pennsylvania, 927
Learning Disabilities Association of America, 691
Lebanon VA Medical Center, 2172
Medical College of Pennsylvania Center for the Mature Woman, 1507
National Center for the Prevention of Youth Suicide, 1969
National Multiple Sclerosis Society: Pennsylvania Keystone Chapter, 1384
National Sexual Violence Resource Center, 2084
Penn Center for Sleep Disorders: Hospital of the University of Pennsylvania, 1637
Penn Memory Center, 474
Pennsylvania Educational Network for Eating Disorders, 1128
Pennsylvania State University Artificial Heart Research Project, 1230
Presbyterian-University Hospital: Pulmonary Sleep Evaluation Center, 1638
SMart Center: Selective Mutism, Anxiet & Related Disorders Treatment Center, 526
Selective Mutism Research Institute, 537
Sleep Disorders Center Lankenau Hospital, 1645
Sleep Disorders Center: Community Medical Center, 1652
Sleep Disorders Center: Crozer-Chester Medical Center, 1653
Sleep Disorders Center: Good Samaritan Medical Center, 1654
Sleep Disorders Center: Medical College of Pennsylvania, 1656
Sleep and Chronobiology Center: Western Psychiatric Institute and Clinic, 1666
Thomas Jefferson University: Sleep Disorders Center, 1672
ToughLove International, 1902
UNITE, Inc., 118
University Drive Campus VA Pittsburgh Healthcare System, 2231
University of Pennsylvania Diabetes and Endocrinology Research Center, 969
University of Pennsylvania Institute on Aging, 297
University of Pennsylvania Muscle Institute, 1245
University of Pennsylvania Weight and Eating Disorders Program, 1143
University of Pittsburgh: Department of Molecular Genetics and Biochemistry, 970
University of Pittsburgh: Human Energy Research Laboratory, 1246
WFS' New Life Program, 1903
Wilkes-Barre VA Medical Center, 2260
Women's Resource Center, 2091

Geographic Index / Rhode Island

Rhode Island

AARP Rhode Island, 246
AMERSA, 1758
Alzheimer's Association: Rhode Island, 419
American Academy of Addiction Psychiatry (AAAP), 1762
American Diabetes Association: Rhode Island, 847
Byron Peter Foundation for Hope, 1977
Center for Alcohol & Addiction Studies Brown University, 1837
Providence VA Medical Center, 2205
Rhode Island Department of Behavioral Healthcare: Substance Use/Addiction, 1818
Sleep Disorders Center: Rhode Island Hospital, 1658

South Carolina

AARP South Carolina, 247
Alzheimer's Association: South Carolina, 420
Association for Traumatic Stress Specialists, 2026
Association of Traumatic Stress Specialist, 2027
Columbia VA Health Care System, 2130
Interdisciplinary Program in Cell and Molecular Pharmacology, 1846
JDRF: Low Country Chapter, 928
JDRF: Palmetto Chapter, 929
Medical University of South Carolina, 599
Medical University of South Carolina Center on Aging, 283
Medical University of South Carolina: Division of Rheumatology & Immunology, 600
Ralph H. Johnson VA Medical Center, 2206
South Carolina Department of Alcohol and Drug Abuse Services, 1819

South Dakota

AARP South Dakota, 248
Alzheimer's Association: South Dakota, 421
Fort Meade Campus VA Black Hills Health Care System, 2143
Hot Springs Campus VA Black Hills Health Care System, 2155
JDRF: Sioux Falls Chapter, 930
Sioux Falls VA Health Care System, 2217

Tennessee

AARP Tennessee, 249
Alvin C. York VA Medical Center Tennessee Valley Healthcare System, 2096
Alzheimer's Association: East Tennessee, 422
Alzheimer's Association: Middle Tennessee, 423
Alzheimer's Association: Northeast Tennessee, 424
Alzheimer's Association: Southeast Tennessee, 425
JDRF: East Tennessee Chapter, 931
JDRF: Middle Tennessee Chapter, 932
James H. Quillen VA Healthcare System Mountain Home VA Healthcare System, 2164
Jason Foundation, Inc., 1978
Memphis VA Medical Center, 2185
Nashville VA Medical Center Tennessee Valley Healthcare System, 2193
Support4Hope, 59
Support4Hope, 545
Support4Hope, 774
Support4Hope, 1064
Support4Hope, 1473
Support4Hope, 1548
Support4Hope, 2284
Tennessee Department of Mental Health and Substance Abuse Services, 1820
Tennessee Neuropsychiatric Institute Middle Tennessee Mental Health Institute, 1542
University of Tennessee Drug Information Center, 1869
University of Tennessee: Division of Cardiovascular Diseases, 1249
University of Tennessee: General Clinical Research Center, 971
VA MidSouth Healthcare Network (VISN 9), 2244
Vanderbilt University Diabetes Center, 974
Vanderbilt University: Center for Fertility and Reproductive Research, 1349

Texas

AARP Texas: Austin, 250
AARP Texas: Dallas, 251
AARP Texas: Houston, 252
AARP Texas: San Antonio, 253
Alzheimer's Alliance: Dallas and Northeast Texas, 426
Alzheimer's Association: Capital of Texas, 427
Alzheimer's Association: Houston and Southeast Texas, 428
Alzheimer's Association: North Central Texas, 429
Alzheimer's Association: San Antonio and South Texas, 430
Alzheimer's Association: West Texas, 431
Alzheimer's Disease & Memory Disorders Center, 447
American Heart Association, 1198
American Heart Association, 1725
American Stroke Association, 1726
Audie L. Murphy Memorial VA Hospital South Texas Veterans Health Care System, 2098
Baylor College of Medicine: Children's General Clinical Research Center, 949
Baylor College of Medicine: Debakey Heart Center, 1205
Baylor College of Medicine: Sleep Disorder and Research Center, 1623
Central Texas Veterans Health Care System, 2119
Cerebral Blood Flow Laboratories Veterans Administration Medical Center, 1732
Children's Heart Institute of Texas, 1210
El Paso VA Health Care Center, 2138
George H. O'Brien, Jr. VA Medical Center West Texas VA Health Care System, 2147
JDRF: Dallas Chapter, 933
JDRF: Greater Fort Worth/Arlington Chapter, 934
JDRF: Houston/Gulf Coast Chapter, 935
JDRF: South Central Texas Chapter, 936
JDRF: West Texas Chapter, 937
Kerrville VA Hospital South Texas Veterans Health Care System, 2170
M.I.S.S. Foundation/Center for Loss & Trauma, 121
MADD-Mothers Against Drunk Drivers, 1891
Mended Hearts, 1256
Methodist Hospital Sleep Center Winona Memorial Hospital, 1633
Michael E. DeBakey VA Medical Center, 2187
Mothers Against Drunk Driving (MADD), 1782
National Eating Disorders Association, 1134
National Multiple Sclerosis Society: Texas Chapter, 1391
National Stroke Association, 1274
Neuromuscular Treatment Center: Univ. of Texas Southwestern Medical Center, 1398
RNtoBSN.org, 2086
Research Society on Alcoholism, 1856
Roy M and Phyllis Gough Huffington Center on Aging, 286
Sleep Medicine Associates of Texas, 1665
Survivors of Loved Ones' Suicides (SOLOS), 1984
Texas Heart Institute St Lukes Episcopal Hospital, 1236
Thomas E. Creek VA Medical Center Amarillo VA Health Care System, 2226
University of Texas General Clinical Research Center, 972
University of Texas Health Science Center Neurophysiology Research Center, 1870
University of Texas Southwestern Medical Center at Dallas, 1250
University of Texas at Austin: Drug Synamics Institute, 1871
University of Texas: Mental Health Clinical Research Center, 45
VA Austin Outpatient Clinic, 2233
VA Heart of Texas Health Care Network Dallas VA Medical Center, 2240

Utah

AARP Utah, 254
Alzheimer's Association: Utah, 432
George E. Wahlen Medical Center VA Salt Lake City Health Care System, 2146
University of Utah: Artificial Heart Research Laboratory, 1251
University of Utah: Cardiovascular Genetic Research Clinic, 1252
University of Utah: Center for Human Toxicology, 1872
Utah Department of Health & Human Services : Substance Abuse & Mental Health, 1822
Veterans Affairs Medical Center: Research Service, 975

Vermont

AARP Vermont, 255
Alzheimer's Association: Vermont, 433
University of Vermont Larner College of Medicine Center on Aging, 298
Vermont Department of Health: Division of Substance Use Programs (DSU), 1823
White River Junction VA Medical Center, 2259

Virginia

AABA Support Group, 1144
AARP Virginia, 256
Academy for Eating Disorders, 1086
Academy for Eating Disorders, 1136
Agoraphobics Building Independent Lives, 508
Agoraphobics Building Independent Lives, 540
Al-Anon Alateen Family Group Hotline, 1875
Al-Anon Family Group Headquarters, 1876
Al-Anon Family Group National Referral Hotline, 1877
Alateen and Al-Anon Family Groups, 1878
Allergy & Asthma Network, 626
Alzheimer's Association: Central and Western Virginia, 434
Alzheimer's Association: Greater Richmond, 435
Alzheimer's Association: National Capital Area, 375
Alzheimer's Association: Southeastern Virginia, 436
American Diabetes Association, 804
American Diabetes Association, 978
American Institutes for Research Center on Aging, 268
American Neuropsychiatric Association, 350
American Physical Therapy Association, 1500
American Public Human Services Association, 1765
American Trauma Society (ATS), 2023
Asthma and Allergy Foundation of America, 642
Bone Health & Osteoporosis Foundation, 1505
Bone Health & Osteoporosis Foundation, 1511
BrainLine.org, 2074
Community Anti-Drug Coalitions of America (CADCA), 1771
Council for Exceptional Children, 686
FASD United, 1773
Family-to-Family: National Alliance on Mental Illness, 39
Family-to-Family: National Alliance on Mental Illness, 533
Family-to-Family: National Alliance on Mental Illness, 760
Family-to-Family: National Alliance on Mental Illness, 1016
Family-to-Family: National Alliance on Mental Illness, 1062
Family-to-Family: National Alliance on Mental Illness, 1132
Family-to-Family: National Alliance on Mental Illness, 1470
Family-to-Family: National Alliance on Mental Illness, 1537
Family-to-Family: National Alliance on Mental Illness, 1830
Family-to-Family: National Alliance on Mental Illness, 2076

Hampton VA Medical Center, 2152
Hunter Holmes McGuire VA Medical Center, 2156
International Council on Infertility Information Dissemination, 1334
International Society for the Study of Trauma and Dissociation, 1056
International Society for the Study of Trauma and Dissociation, 1529
International Society for the Study of Trauma and Dissociation, 2040
JDRF: Greater Blue Ridge Chapter, 938
Mental Health America, 16
Mental Health America, 113
Mental Health America, 190
Mental Health America, 353
Mental Health America, 520
Mental Health America, 692
Mental Health America, 752
Mental Health America, 1011
Mental Health America, 1057
Mental Health America, 1105
Mental Health America, 1459
Mental Health America, 1530
Mental Health America, 1588
Mental Health America, 1616
Mental Health America, 1702
Mental Health America, 1780
Mental Health America, 1967
Mental Health America, 2041
Mental Health America, 2272
National Adult Day Services Association, 191
National Alliance on Mental Illness, 19
National Alliance on Mental Illness, 693
National Alliance on Mental Illness, 754
National Alliance on Mental Illness, 1109
National Alliance on Mental Illness, 1460
National Alliance on Mental Illness, 1531
National Alliance on Mental Illness, 1968
National Alliance on Mental Illness, 2042
National Alliance on Mental Illness (NAMI), 20
National Alliance on Mental Illness (NAMI), 1784
National Alliance on Mental Illness (NAMI), 2043
National Association of Alcoholism and Drug Abuse Counselors (NAADAC), 1787
National Council on Aging, 193
National Hospice & Palliative Care Organization (NHPCO), 194
National Science Foundation, 644
National Science Foundation, 2070
National Seniors Council, 196
PTSD Family Support Group, 2276
RESOLVE: The National Infertility Association, 1337

Richmond Support Group, 1159
Roanoke Vet Center, 2208
Salem VA Medical Center, 2213
Samueli Institute, 2214
Society for the Study of Reproduction, 1338
University of Virginia: General Clinical Research Center, 656
University of Virginia: Hypertension and Atherosclerosis Unit, 1284
Virginia Commonwealth University Virginia Center on Aging, 299
Virginia Department of Behavioral Health & Developmental Services, 1824

Washington

AARP Washington, 258
African American Post Traumatic Stress Disorder Association, 2013
Alzheimer's Association Autopsy Assistance Network, 481
Alzheimer's Association: Washington State, 438
Alzheimer's Disease Center: Washington University, 455
American Sleep Apnea Association, 1614
Benaroya Research Institute Virginia Mason Medical Center, 950
Brain Injury Resource Center, 2073
Center for Anxiety and Traumatic Stress, 2113
De Tornyay Center For Healthy Aging at University of Washington, 273
Hope Heart Institute, 1223
JDRF: Seattle Chapter, 940
JDRF: Seattle Guild, 941
JDRF: Spokane County Area Chapter, 942
Jonathan M. Wainwright Memorial VA MC Walla Walla VA Medical Center, 2168
Narcolepsy Network, 1617
Narcolepsy Network, 1674
SleepFoundation.org, 1622
Spokane VA Medical Center Mann-Grandstaff VA Medical Center, 2222
Tacoma Vet Center, 2225
University of Washington Diabetes: Endocrinology Research Center, 973
VA Puget Sound Health Care System, 2247

West Virginia

AARP West Virginia, 259
Alzheimer's Association: West Virginia, 437

Alzheimer's Association: West Virginia, 439
Beckley VA Medical Center, 2104
Health Science Library, 947
Hershel Woody Williams VA Medical Center, 2154
JDRF: Huntington Chapter, 943
Louis A. Johnson VA Medical Center, 2174
Martinsburg VA Medical Center, 2182

Wisconsin

AARP Wisconsin, 260
About Kids GI Disorders, 1145
Alzheimer's Association: Wisconsin, 440
American Academy of Allergy, Asthma & Immunology, 627
American Academy of Allergy, Asthma & Immunology Foundation, 640
American Association of Children's Residential Centers, 4
American Association of Children's Residential Centers, 1002
Center for Aging Research and Education at the UW-Madison School of Nursing, 270
Injury Research Center, 2158
JDRF: Greater Madison Chapter, 944
JDRF: Northeast Wisconsin Chapter, 945
JDRF: Southeastern Chapter, 946
Milwaukee VA Medical Center (Zablocki), 2189
Physician Referral and Information Line, 659
TOPS Take Off Pounds Sensibly, 1123
Tomah VA Medical Center, 2227
University of Wisconsin Milwaukee Medicinal Chemistry Group, 1873
University of Wisconsin: Asthma, Allergy and Pulmonary Research Center, 657
William S. Middleton Memorial Veterans Hospital, 2261

Wyoming

AARP Wyoming, 261
Alzheimer's Association: Wyoming, 441
Cheyenne VA Medical Center, 2123
Sheridan VA Medical Center, 2216
University Of Wyoming Center on Aging, 293
Wyoming Department of Health: Substance Use and Tobacco Prevention Program, 1825

Titles from Grey House

Visit www.GreyHouse.com for Product Information, Table of Contents, and Sample Pages.

Opinions Throughout History
Opinions Throughout History: Church & State
Opinions Throughout History: Conspiracy Theories
Opinions Throughout History: The Death Penalty
Opinions Throughout History: Diseases & Epidemics
Opinions Throughout History: Drug Use & Abuse
Opinions Throughout History: The Environment
Opinions Throughout History: Free Speech & Censorship
Opinions Throughout History: Gender: Roles & Rights
Opinions Throughout History: Globalization
Opinions Throughout History: Guns in America
Opinions Throughout History: Immigration
Opinions Throughout History: Law Enforcement in America
Opinions Throughout History: Mental Health
Opinions Throughout History: Nat'l Security vs. Civil & Privacy Rights
Opinions Throughout History: Presidential Authority
Opinions Throughout History: Robotics & Artificial Intelligence
Opinions Throughout History: Social Media Issues
Opinions Throughout History: The Supreme Court
Opinions Throughout History: Voters' Rights
Opinions Throughout History: War & the Military
Opinions Throughout History: Workers Rights & Wages

This is Who We Were
This is Who We Were: Colonial America (1492-1775)
This is Who We Were: 1880-1899
This is Who We Were: In the 1900s
This is Who We Were: In the 1910s
This is Who We Were: In the 1920s
This is Who We Were: A Companion to the 1940 Census
This is Who We Were: In the 1940s (1940-1949)
This is Who We Were: In the 1950s
This is Who We Were: In the 1960s
This is Who We Were: In the 1970s
This is Who We Were: In the 1980s
This is Who We Were: In the 1990s
This is Who We Were: In the 2000s
This is Who We Were: In the 2010s

Working Americans
Working Americans—Vol. 1: The Working Class
Working Americans—Vol. 2: The Middle Class
Working Americans—Vol. 3: The Upper Class
Working Americans—Vol. 4: Children
Working Americans—Vol. 5: At War
Working Americans—Vol. 6: Working Women
Working Americans—Vol. 7: Social Movements
Working Americans—Vol. 8: Immigrants
Working Americans—Vol. 9: Revolutionary War to the Civil War
Working Americans—Vol. 10: Sports & Recreation
Working Americans—Vol. 11: Inventors & Entrepreneurs
Working Americans—Vol. 12: Our History through Music
Working Americans—Vol. 13: Education & Educators
Working Americans—Vol. 14: African Americans
Working Americans—Vol. 15: Politics & Politicians
Working Americans—Vol. 16: Farming & Ranching
Working Americans—Vol. 17: Teens in America
Working Americans—Vol. 18: Health Care Workers
Working Americans—Vol. 19: The Performing Arts

Grey House Health & Wellness Guides
Addiction Handbook & Resource Guide
The Autism Spectrum Handbook & Resource Guide
Autoimmune Disorders Handbook & Resource Guide
Cardiovascular Disease Handbook & Resource Guide
Dementia Handbook & Resource Guide
Depression Handbook & Resource Guide
Diabetes Handbook & Resource Guide
Nutrition, Obesity & Eating Disorders Handbook & Resource Guide

Consumer Health
Complete Mental Health Resource Guide
Complete Resource Guide for Pediatric Disorders
Complete Resource Guide for People with Chronic Illness
Complete Resource Guide for People with Disabilities
Older Americans Information Resource
Parenting: Styles & Strategies
Teens: Growing Up, Skills & Strategies

General Reference
American Environmental Leaders
Constitutional Amendments
Encyclopedia of African-American Writing
Encyclopedia of Invasions & Conquests
Encyclopedia of Prisoners of War & Internment
Encyclopedia of the Continental Congresses
Encyclopedia of the United States Cabinet
Encyclopedia of War Journalism
The Environmental Debate
Financial Literacy Starter Kit
From Suffrage to the Senate
The Gun Debate: Gun Rights & Gun Control in the U.S.
Historical Warrior Peoples & Modern Fighting Groups
Human Rights and the United States
Political Corruption in America
Privacy Rights in the Digital Age
The Religious Right and American Politics
Speakers of the House of Representatives, 1789-2021
US Land & Natural Resources Policy
The Value of a Dollar 1600-1865 Colonial to Civil War
The Value of a Dollar 1860-2019

Business Information
Business Information Resources
Complete Broadcasting Industry Guide: TV, Radio, Cable & Streaming
Directory of Mail Order Catalogs
Environmental Resource Handbook
Food & Beverage Market Place
The Grey House Guide to Homeland Security Resources
The Grey House Performing Arts Industry Guide
Guide to Healthcare Group Purchasing Organizations
Guide to U.S. HMOs and PPOs
Guide to Venture Capital & Private Equity Firms
Hudson's Washington News Media Contacts Guide
New York State Directory
Sports Market Place

Grey House Publishing | Salem Press | H.W. Wilson | 4919 Route 22, PO Box 56, Amenia NY 12501-0056

Grey House Imprints

Visit www.GreyHouse.com for Product Information, Table of Contents, and Sample Pages.

Grey House Titles, continued

Education
Complete Learning Disabilities Resource Guide
Digital Literacy: Skills & Strategies
Educators Resource Guide
The Comparative Guide to Elem. & Secondary Schools
Special Education: Policy & Curriculum Development

Statistics & Demographics
America's Top-Rated Cities
America's Top-Rated Smaller Cities
The Comparative Guide to American Suburbs
Profiles of America
Profiles of California
Profiles of Florida
Profiles of Illinois
Profiles of Indiana
Profiles of Massachusetts
Profiles of Michigan
Profiles of New Jersey
Profiles of New York
Profiles of North Carolina & South Carolina
Profiles of Ohio
Profiles of Pennsylvania
Profiles of Texas
Profiles of Virginia
Profiles of Wisconsin

Canadian Resources
Associations Canada
Canadian Almanac & Directory
Canadian Environmental Resource Guide
Canadian Parliamentary Guide
Canadian Venture Capital & Private Equity Firms
Canadian Who's Who
Cannabis Canada
Careers & Employment Canada
Financial Post: Directory of Directors
Financial Services Canada
FP Bonds: Corporate
FP Bonds: Government
FP Equities: Preferreds & Derivatives
FP Survey: Industrials
FP Survey: Mines & Energy
FP Survey: Predecessor & Defunct
Health Guide Canada
Libraries Canada

Weiss Financial Ratings
Financial Literacy Basics
Financial Literacy: How to Become an Investor
Financial Literacy: Planning for the Future
Weiss Ratings Consumer Guides
Weiss Ratings Guide to Banks
Weiss Ratings Guide to Credit Unions
Weiss Ratings Guide to Health Insurers
Weiss Ratings Guide to Life & Annuity Insurers
Weiss Ratings Guide to Property & Casualty Insurers
Weiss Ratings Investment Research Guide to Bond & Money Market Mutual Funds
Weiss Ratings Investment Research Guide to Exchange-Traded Funds
Weiss Ratings Investment Research Guide to Stock Mutual Funds
Weiss Ratings Investment Research Guide to Stocks

Books in Print Series
American Book Publishing Record® Annual
American Book Publishing Record® Monthly
Books In Print®
Books In Print® Supplement
Books Out Loud™
Bowker's Complete Video Directory™
Children's Books In Print®
El-Hi Textbooks & Serials In Print®
Forthcoming Books®
Law Books & Serials In Print™
Medical & Health Care Books In Print™
Publishers, Distributors & Wholesalers of the US™
Subject Guide to Books In Print®
Subject Guide to Children's Books In Print®

Grey House Publishing | Salem Press | H.W. Wilson | 4919 Route 22, PO Box 56, Amenia NY 12501-0056

Titles from Salem Press

SALEM PRESS | **SALEM PRESS**

Westfield Memorial Library, Westfield, New Jersey

Visit www.SalemPress.com for Product Information, Table of Contents, and Sample Pages.

LITERATURE

Critical Insights: Authors

- Louisa May Alcott
- Sherman Alexie
- Isabel Allende
- Maya Angelou
- Isaac Asimov
- Margaret Atwood
- Jane Austen
- James Baldwin
- Saul Bellow
- Roberto Bolano
- Ray Bradbury
- The Brontë Sisters
- Gwendolyn Brooks
- Albert Camus
- Raymond Carver
- Willa Cather
- Geoffrey Chaucer
- John Cheever
- Joseph Conrad
- Charles Dickens
- Emily Dickinson
- Frederick Douglass
- T. S. Eliot
- George Eliot
- Harlan Ellison
- Ralph Waldo Emerson
- Louise Erdrich
- William Faulkner
- F. Scott Fitzgerald
- Gustave Flaubert
- Horton Foote
- Benjamin Franklin
- Robert Frost
- Neil Gaiman
- Gabriel Garcia Marquez
- Thomas Hardy
- Nathaniel Hawthorne
- Robert A. Heinlein
- Lillian Hellman
- Ernest Hemingway
- Langston Hughes
- Zora Neale Hurston
- Henry James
- Thomas Jefferson
- James Joyce
- Jamaica Kincaid
- Stephen King
- Martin Luther King, Jr.
- Barbara Kingsolver
- Abraham Lincoln
- C.S. Lewis
- Mario Vargas Llosa
- Jack London
- James McBride
- Cormac McCarthy
- Herman Melville
- Arthur Miller
- Toni Morrison
- Alice Munro
- Tim O'Brien
- Flannery O'Connor
- Eugene O'Neill
- George Orwell
- Sylvia Plath
- Edgar Allan Poe
- Philip Roth
- Salman Rushdie
- J.D. Salinger
- Mary Shelley
- John Steinbeck
- Amy Tan
- Leo Tolstoy
- Mark Twain
- John Updike
- Kurt Vonnegut
- Alice Walker
- David Foster Wallace
- Edith Wharton
- Walt Whitman
- Oscar Wilde
- Tennessee Williams
- Virginia Woolf
- Richard Wright
- Malcolm X

Critical Insights: Works

- Absalom, Absalom!
- Adventures of Huckleberry Finn
- The Adventures of Tom Sawyer
- Aeneid
- All Quiet on the Western Front
- All the Pretty Horses
- Animal Farm
- Anna Karenina
- The Awakening
- The Bell Jar
- Beloved
- Billy Budd, Sailor
- The Book Thief
- Brave New World
- The Canterbury Tales
- Catch-22
- The Catcher in the Rye
- The Color Purple
- The Crucible
- Death of a Salesman
- The Diary of a Young Girl
- Dracula
- Fahrenheit 451
- The Grapes of Wrath
- Great Expectations
- The Great Gatsby
- Hamlet
- The Handmaid's Tale
- Harry Potter Series
- Heart of Darkness
- The Hobbit
- The House on Mango Street
- How the Garcia Girls Lost Their Accents
- The Hunger Games Trilogy
- I Know Why the Caged Bird Sings
- In Cold Blood
- The Inferno
- Invisible Man
- Jane Eyre
- The Joy Luck Club
- Julius Caesar
- King Lear
- The Kite Runner
- Life of Pi
- Little Women
- Lolita
- Lord of the Flies
- The Lord of the Rings
- Macbeth
- The Merchant of Venice
- The Metamorphosis
- Midnight's Children
- A Midsummer Night's Dream
- Moby-Dick
- Mrs. Dalloway
- Nineteen Eighty-Four
- The Odyssey
- Of Mice and Men
- The Old Man and the Sea
- On the Road
- One Flew Over the Cuckoo's Nest
- One Hundred Years of Solitude
- Othello
- The Outsiders
- Paradise Lost
- The Pearl
- The Plague
- The Poetry of Baudelaire
- The Poetry of Edgar Allan Poe
- A Portrait of the Artist as a Young Man
- Pride and Prejudice
- A Raisin in the Sun
- The Red Badge of Courage
- Romeo and Juliet
- The Scarlet Letter
- Sense and Sensibility
- Short Fiction of Flannery O'Connor
- Slaughterhouse-Five
- The Sound and the Fury
- A Streetcar Named Desire
- The Sun Also Rises
- A Tale of Two Cities
- The Tales of Edgar Allan Poe
- Their Eyes Were Watching God
- Things Fall Apart
- To Kill a Mockingbird
- War and Peace
- The Woman Warrior

Critical Insights: Themes

- The American Comic Book
- American Creative Non-Fiction
- The American Dream
- American Multicultural Identity
- American Road Literature
- American Short Story
- American Sports Fiction
- The American Thriller
- American Writers in Exile
- Censored & Banned Literature
- Civil Rights Literature, Past & Present
- Coming of Age
- Conspiracies
- Contemporary Canadian Fiction
- Contemporary Immigrant Short Fiction
- Contemporary Latin American Fiction
- Contemporary Speculative Fiction

Grey House Publishing | Salem Press | H.W. Wilson | 4919 Route 22, PO Box 56, Amenia NY 12501-0056

Titles from Salem Press

Visit www.SalemPress.com for Product Information, Table of Contents, and Sample Pages.

Crime and Detective Fiction
Crisis of Faith
Cultural Encounters
Dystopia
Family
The Fantastic
Feminism Flash Fiction
Gender, Sex and Sexuality
Good & Evil
The Graphic Novel
Greed
Harlem Renaissance
The Hero's Quest
Historical Fiction
Holocaust Literature
The Immigrant Experience
Inequality
LGBTQ Literature
Literature in Times of Crisis
Literature of Protest
Love
Magical Realism
Midwestern Literature
Modern Japanese Literature
Nature & the Environment
Paranoia, Fear & Alienation
Patriotism
Political Fiction
Postcolonial Literature
Power & Corruption
Pulp Fiction of the '20s and '30s
Rebellion
Russia's Golden Age
Satire
The Slave Narrative
Social Justice and American Literature
Southern Gothic Literature
Southwestern Literature
Survival
Technology & Humanity
Truth & Lies
Violence in Literature
Virginia Woolf & 20th Century Women Writers
War

Critical Insights: Film
Bonnie & Clyde
Casablanca
Alfred Hitchcock
Stanley Kubrick

Critical Approaches to Literature
Critical Approaches to Literature: Feminist
Critical Approaches to Literature: Moral
Critical Approaches to Literature: Multicultural
Critical Approaches to Literature: Psychological

Literary Classics
Recommended Reading: 600 Classics Reviewed

Novels into Film
Novels into Film: Adaptations & Interpretation
Novels into Film: Adaptations & Interpretation, Volume 2

Critical Surveys of Literature
Critical Survey of American Literature
Critical Survey of Drama
Critical Survey of Long Fiction
Critical Survey of Mystery and Detective Fiction
Critical Survey of Poetry
Critical Survey of Poetry: Contemporary Poets
Critical Survey of Science Fiction & Fantasy Literature
Critical Survey of Shakespeare's Plays
Critical Survey of Shakespeare's Sonnets
Critical Survey of Short Fiction
Critical Survey of World Literature
Critical Survey of Young Adult Literature

Critical Surveys of Graphic Novels
Heroes & Superheroes
History, Theme, and Technique
Independents & Underground Classics
Manga

Critical Surveys of Mythology & Folklore
Creation Myths
Deadly Battles & Warring Enemies
Gods & Goddesses
Heroes and Heroines
Love, Sexuality, and Desire
World Mythology

Cyclopedia of Literary Characters & Places
Cyclopedia of Literary Characters
Cyclopedia of Literary Places

Introduction to Literary Context
American Poetry of the 20th Century
American Post-Modernist Novels
American Short Fiction
English Literature
Plays
World Literature

Magill's Literary Annual
Magill's Literary Annual, 2023
Magill's Literary Annual, 2022
Magill's Literary Annual, 2021
Magill's Literary Annual (Backlist Issues 2020-1977)

Masterplots
Masterplots, Fourth Edition
Masterplots, 2010-2018 Supplement

Notable Writers
Notable African American Writers
Notable American Women Writers
Notable Mystery & Detective Fiction Writers
Notable Writers of the American West & the Native American Experience
Notable Writers of LGBTQ+ Literature

Titles from Salem Press

Visit www.SalemPress.com for Product Information, Table of Contents, and Sample Pages.

HISTORY

The Decades
The 1910s in America
The Twenties in America
The Thirties in America
The Forties in America
The Fifties in America
The Sixties in America
The Seventies in America
The Eighties in America
The Nineties in America
The 2000s in America
The 2010s in America

Defining Documents in American History
Defining Documents: The 1900s
Defining Documents: The 1910s
Defining Documents: The 1920s
Defining Documents: The 1930s
Defining Documents: The 1950s
Defining Documents: The 1960s
Defining Documents: The 1970s
Defining Documents: The 1980s
Defining Documents: American Citizenship
Defining Documents: The American Economy
Defining Documents: The American Revolution
Defining Documents: The American West
Defining Documents: Business Ethics
Defining Documents: Capital Punishment
Defining Documents: Civil Rights
Defining Documents: Civil War
Defining Documents: The Constitution
Defining Documents: The Cold War
Defining Documents: Dissent & Protest
Defining Documents: Domestic Terrorism & Extremism
Defining Documents: Drug Policy
Defining Documents: The Emergence of Modern America
Defining Documents: Environment & Conservation
Defining Documents: Espionage & Intrigue
Defining Documents: Exploration and Colonial America
Defining Documents: The First Amendment
Defining Documents: The Free Press
Defining Documents: The Great Depression
Defining Documents: The Great Migration
Defining Documents: The Gun Debate
Defining Documents: Immigration & Immigrant Communities
Defining Documents: The Legacy of 9/11
Defining Documents: LGBTQ+
Defining Documents: Manifest Destiny and the New Nation
Defining Documents: Native Americans
Defining Documents: Political Campaigns, Candidates & Discourse
Defining Documents: Postwar 1940s
Defining Documents: Prison Reform
Defining Documents: Secrets, Leaks & Scandals
Defining Documents: Slavery
Defining Documents: Supreme Court Decisions
Defining Documents: Reconstruction Era
Defining Documents: The Vietnam War
Defining Documents: U.S. Involvement in the Middle East
Defining Documents: Workers' Rights
Defining Documents: World War I
Defining Documents: World War II

Defining Documents in World History
Defining Documents: The 17th Century
Defining Documents: The 18th Century
Defining Documents: The 19th Century
Defining Documents: The 20th Century (1900-1950)
Defining Documents: The Ancient World
Defining Documents: Asia
Defining Documents: Genocide & the Holocaust
Defining Documents: Human Rights
Defining Documents: The Middle Ages
Defining Documents: The Middle East
Defining Documents: Nationalism & Populism
Defining Documents: The Nuclear Age
Defining Documents: Pandemics, Plagues & Public Health
Defining Documents: Renaissance & Early Modern Era
Defining Documents: Revolutions
Defining Documents: Women's Rights

Great Events from History
Great Events from History: American History, Exploration to the Colonial Era, 1492-1775
Great Events from History: The Ancient World
Great Events from History: The Middle Ages
Great Events from History: The Renaissance & Early Modern Era
Great Events from History: The 17th Century
Great Events from History: The 18th Century
Great Events from History: The 19th Century
Great Events from History: The 20th Century, 1901-1940
Great Events from History: The 20th Century, 1941-1970
Great Events from History: The 20th Century, 1971-2000
Great Events from History: Modern Scandals
Great Events from History: African American History
Great Events from History: The 21st Century, 2000-2016
Great Events from History: LGBTQ Events
Great Events from History: Human Rights
Great Events from History: Women's History

Great Lives from History
Great Athletes
Great Athletes of the Twenty-First Century
Great Lives from History: The 17th Century
Great Lives from History: The 18th Century
Great Lives from History: The 19th Century
Great Lives from History: The 20th Century
Great Lives from History: The 21st Century, 2000-2017
Great Lives from History: African Americans
Great Lives from History: The Ancient World
Great Lives from History: American Heroes
Great Lives from History: American Women
Great Lives from History: Asian and Pacific Islander Americans
Great Lives from History: Autocrats & Dictators
Great Lives from History: The Incredibly Wealthy
Great Lives from History: Inventors & Inventions
Great Lives from History: Jewish Americans
Great Lives from History: Latinos
Great Lives from History: The Middle Ages
Great Lives from History: The Renaissance & Early Modern Era
Great Lives from History: Scientists and Science

Titles from Salem Press

Visit www.SalemPress.com for Product Information, Table of Contents, and Sample Pages.

History & Government
American First Ladies
American Presidents
The 50 States
The Ancient World: Extraordinary People in Extraordinary Societies
The Bill of Rights
The Criminal Justice System
The U.S. Supreme Court

Innovators
Computer Technology Innovators
Fashion Innovators
Human Rights Innovators
Internet Innovators
Music Innovators
Musicians and Composers of the 20th Century
World Political Innovators

SOCIAL SCIENCES
Civil Rights Movements: Past & Present
Countries, Peoples and Cultures
Countries: Their Wars & Conflicts: A World Survey
Education Today: Issues, Policies & Practices
Encyclopedia of American Immigration
Ethics: Questions & Morality of Human Actions
Issues in U.S. Immigration
Principles of Sociology: Group Relationships & Behavior
Principles of Sociology: Personal Relationships & Behavior
Principles of Sociology: Societal Issues & Behavior
Racial & Ethnic Relations in America
Weapons, Warfare & Military Technology
World Geography

HEALTH
Addictions, Substance Abuse & Alcoholism
Adolescent Health & Wellness
Aging
Cancer
Community & Family Health Issues
Integrative, Alternative & Complementary Medicine
Genetics and Inherited Conditions
Infectious Diseases and Conditions
Magill's Medical Guide
Nutrition
Parenting: Styles & Strategies
Psychology & Behavioral Health
Teens: Growing Up, Skills & Strategies
Women's Health

Principles of Health
Principles of Health: Allergies & Immune Disorders
Principles of Health: Anxiety & Stress
Principles of Health: Depression
Principles of Health: Diabetes
Principles of Health: Nursing
Principles of Health: Obesity
Principles of Health: Occupational Therapy & Physical Therapy
Principles of Health: Pain Management
Principles of Health: Prescription Drug Abuse

SCIENCE
Ancient Creatures
Applied Science
Applied Science: Engineering & Mathematics
Applied Science: Science & Medicine
Applied Science: Technology
Biomes and Ecosystems
Digital Literacy: Skills & Strategies
Earth Science: Earth Materials and Resources
Earth Science: Earth's Surface and History
Earth Science: Earth's Weather, Water and Atmosphere
Earth Science: Physics and Chemistry of the Earth
Encyclopedia of Climate Change
Encyclopedia of Energy
Encyclopedia of Environmental Issues
Encyclopedia of Global Resources
Encyclopedia of Mathematics and Society
Forensic Science
Notable Natural Disasters
The Solar System
USA in Space

Principles of Science
Principles of Aeronautics
Principles of Anatomy
Principles of Astronomy
Principles of Behavioral Science
Principles of Biology
Principles of Biotechnology
Principles of Botany
Principles of Chemistry
Principles of Climatology
Principles of Computer-aided Design
Principles of Computer Science
Principles of Digital Arts & Multimedia
Principles of Ecology
Principles of Energy
Principles of Fire Science
Principles of Forestry & Conservation
Principles of Geology
Principles of Information Technology
Principles of Marine Science
Principles of Mathematics
Principles of Mechanics
Principles of Microbiology
Principles of Modern Agriculture
Principles of Pharmacology
Principles of Physical Science
Principles of Physics
Principles of Programming & Coding
Principles of Robotics & Artificial Intelligence
Principles of Scientific Research
Principles of Sports Medicine & Exercise Science
Principles of Sustainability
Principles of Zoology

Titles from Salem Press

Visit www.SalemPress.com for Product Information, Table of Contents, and Sample Pages.

CAREERS

Careers: Paths to Entrepreneurship
Careers in Archaeology & Museum Services
Careers in Artificial Intelligence
Careers in the Arts: Fine, Performing & Visual
Careers in the Automotive Industry
Careers in Biology
Careers in Biotechnology
Careers in Building Construction
Careers in Business
Careers in Chemistry
Careers in Communications & Media
Careers in Cybersecurity
Careers in Education & Training
Careers in Engineering
Careers in Environment & Conservation
Careers in Financial Services
Careers in Fish & Wildlife
Careers in Forensic Science
Careers in Gaming
Careers in Green Energy
Careers in Healthcare
Careers in Hospitality & Tourism
Careers in Human Services
Careers in Information Technology
Careers in Law, Criminal Justice & Emergency Services
Careers in the Music Industry
Careers in Manufacturing & Production
Careers in Nursing
Careers in Physics
Careers in Protective Services
Careers in Psychology & Behavioral Health
Careers in Public Administration
Careers in Sales, Insurance & Real Estate
Careers in Science & Engineering
Careers in Social Media
Careers in Sports & Fitness
Careers in Sports Medicine & Training
Careers in Technical Services & Equipment Repair
Careers in Transportation
Careers in Writing & Editing
Careers Outdoors
Careers Overseas
Careers Working with Infants & Children
Careers Working with Animals

BUSINESS

Principles of Business: Accounting
Principles of Business: Economics
Principles of Business: Entrepreneurship
Principles of Business: Finance
Principles of Business: Globalization
Principles of Business: Leadership
Principles of Business: Management
Principles of Business: Marketing

Grey House Publishing | Salem Press | H.W. Wilson | 4919 Route 22, PO Box 56, Amenia NY 12501-0056

Westfield Memorial Library
Westfield, New Jersey

Titles from H.W. Wilson

Visit www.HWWilsonInPrint.com for Product Information, Table of Contents, and Sample Pages.

The Reference Shelf
Affordable Housing
Aging in America
Alternative Facts, Post-Truth and the Information War
The American Dream
Artificial Intelligence
The Business of Food
Campaign Trends & Election Law
College Sports
Democracy Evolving
The Digital Age
Embracing New Paradigms in Education
Food Insecurity & Hunger in the United States
Future of U.S. Economic Relations: Mexico, Cuba, & Venezuela
Gene Editing & Genetic Engineering
Global Climate Change
Guns in America
Hacktivism
Hate Crimes
Immigration
Income Inequality
Internet Abuses & Privacy Rights
Internet Law
LGBTQ in the 21st Century
Marijuana Reform
Mental Health Awareness
Money in Politics
National Debate Topic 2014/2015: The Ocean
National Debate Topic 2015/2016: Surveillance
National Debate Topic 2016/2017: US/China Relations
National Debate Topic 2017/2018: Education Reform
National Debate Topic 2018/2019: Immigration
National Debate Topic 2019/2021: Arms Sales
National Debate Topic 2020/2021: Criminal Justice Reform
National Debate Topic 2021/2022: Water Resources
National Debate Topic 2022/2023: Emerging Technologies & International Security
National Debate Topic 2023/2024: Economic Inequality
New Frontiers in Space
Policing in 2020
Pollution
Prescription Drug Abuse
Propaganda and Misinformation
Racial Tension in a Postracial Age
Reality Television
Renewable Energy
Representative American Speeches, Annual Editions
Rethinking Work
Revisiting Gender
The South China Sea Conflict
Sports in America
The Supreme Court
The Transformation of American Cities
The Two Koreas
UFOs
Vaccinations
Voting Rights
Whistleblowers

Core Collections
Children's Core Collection
Fiction Core Collection
Graphic Novels Core Collection
Middle & Junior High School Core
Public Library Core Collection: Nonfiction
Senior High Core Collection
Young Adult Fiction Core Collection

Current Biography
Current Biography Cumulative Index 1946-2021
Current Biography Monthly Magazine
Current Biography Yearbook

Readers' Guide to Periodical Literature
Abridged Readers' Guide to Periodical Literature
Readers' Guide to Periodical Literature

Indexes
Index to Legal Periodicals & Books
Short Story Index
Book Review Digest

Sears List
Sears List of Subject Headings
Sears List of Subject Headings, Online Database
Sears: Lista de Encabezamientos de Materia

History
American Game Changers: Invention, Innovation & Transformation
American Reformers
Speeches of the American Presidents

Facts About Series
Facts About the 20th Century
Facts About American Immigration
Facts About China
Facts About the Presidents
Facts About the World's Languages

Nobel Prize Winners
Nobel Prize Winners: 1901-1986
Nobel Prize Winners: 1987-1991
Nobel Prize Winners: 1992-1996
Nobel Prize Winners: 1997-2001
Nobel Prize Winners: 2002-2018

Famous First Facts
Famous First Facts
Famous First Facts About American Politics
Famous First Facts About Sports
Famous First Facts About the Environment
Famous First Facts: International Edition

American Book of Days
The American Book of Days
The International Book of Days

Grey House Publishing | Salem Press | H.W. Wilson | 4919 Route 22, PO Box 56, Amenia NY 12501 0056